Harold Schwertfeger 8/27/36

No. 4.

ASSYRIA

& OTHER COUNTRIES ADJOINING CANAAN

ILLUSTRATING THE CAPTIVITIES OF THE JEWS

Popular Commentary of the Bible

THE OLD TESTAMENT

Volume II

The Poetical and the Prophetical Books

By

PAUL E. KRETZMANN, Ph. D., D. D.

ST. LOUIS, MO.
CONCORDIA PUBLISHING HOUSE
1924

TABLE OF CONTENTS.

THE BOOK OF JOB.

INTRODUCTION.

The Book of Job bears the name of the patient sufferer whose history is rightly regarded as the great example of ready submission to the will of God. The purpose of the book is to discuss the question, the great and perplexing problem, why the righteous God inflicts suffering on a good man while many a godless person seems to be enjoying nothing but the greatest good fortune. The question is answered in such a manner as to show that Job is a righteous man, that his faith and patience are exemplary, that his sufferings were sent upon him not as a punishment, but as a wholesome chastisement, to prove, test, and purify his faith, and that they, in the last analysis, served for the glorification of God. It was not because Job had committed some extraordinary sin that he was afflicted with such extraordinary suffering, but because the Lord, in His sovereign majesty, chose to apply such measures for the highest spiritual welfare of His servant.

Although the Book of Job, with the exception of the introduction, is a poem, one of the grandest productions, not only of Hebrew poetry, but of the literature of all ages and all nations, it is nevertheless founded on historical fact and contains actual historical material. The prophet Ezekiel, chap. 14, 14. 20, as well as James, the brother of the Lord, chap. 5, 11, refer to Job as a historical person. The land of Uz, in which Job lived, was probably a district of Northern Arabia. He himself seems to have lived in the age of the patriarchs, to whom he may have been remotely related. His story, however, occurred just before the children of Israel were delivered from the bondage of Egypt.

The Book of Job is obviously divided into three parts. After the prolog, which tells of Job's piety and good fortune, of his subsequent misfortune, and how he bore up under it, there follows the main part of the narrative, altogether in poetical form. We have here the dispute between Job and his friends concerning the cause of his calamities, followed by the vindication of God's righteousness in His government of the world, and finally by the intervention of God Himself, who reproves Job and gives the solution of the problem which was challenging the faith of Job.

The author and the date of the book cannot be fixed with certainty. It has been ascribed to Moses, to Job himself, to Solomon, and to some prophet at the time of Israel's greatest glory. It cannot be dated before Moses nor later than about the eighth century before Christ. The Book of Job is so obviously a unit, as the entire outline and form indicate, that its integrity cannot be questioned with any degree of plausibility.1)

1) Cp. Fuerbringer, *Einleitung in das Alte Testament*, 45—49; *Concordia Bible Class*, April, 1919, 54—57; *Theol. Monthly*, 1921, 161 ff.

CHAPTER 1.

Job Loses His Great Good Fortune.

JOB'S WEALTH AND PIETY. — V. 1. **There was a man in the land of Uz,** in Northern Arabia, toward the Euphrates, **whose name was Job,** generally considered a descendant of Aram, Gen. 22, 21, and therefore related to the patriarchs, although very distantly; **and that man was perfect and upright,** his moral integrity and blamelessness resulting in the true righteousness of life, **and one that feared God and eschewed evil,** his heart being disposed in the right manner toward God and everything good, and therefore also filled with loving regard for all men. Job seems to have been an emir, or chief, of the country, both on account of his wealth and on account of his ability as leader. V. 2. **And there were born unto him seven sons and three daughters,** a great blessing of God; for children, according to Scriptures, are special gifts of His kindness, Ps. 127 and 128. V. 3. **His substance also,** that is, his possessions, his wealth, **was seven thousand sheep, and three thousand camels, and five hundred yoke of oxen, and five hundred she-asses, and a very great household,** very many servants, these being needed to maintain an establishment of such princely magnitude, **so that this man was the greatest of all the men of the East,** he outranked in wealth and power all the inhabitants of this section of Arabia. V. 4. **And his sons went and feasted in their**

houses, every one his day, they observed the custom of celebrating the several birthdays in the family, or some other special holidays, with banquets connected with wine-drinking; **and sent and called for their three sisters to eat and to drink with them,** for the sons had establishments of their own, while the unmarried sisters lived at home with their mother. These invitations were regularly issued and as regularly accepted. V. 5. **And it was so, when the days of their feasting were gone about,** when the annual period of these festivals had come to a close, when every one of the brothers had arranged and celebrated his feast, **that Job sent and sanctified them,** to atone for probable transgressions by sacrifices of purification, **and rose up early in the morning and offered burnt offerings according to the number of them all,** Job himself officiating as priest of the congregation of his family and making his offering at a time when the hearts would be most inclined to quiet contemplation; **for Job said, It may be that my sons have sinned,** forgetting the careful watch over every single word and act which quiet sobriety demands, **and cursed God in their hearts,** renouncing or forgetting Him and His fear, as they abandoned themselves to their pleasure. **Thus did Job continually,** he was wont to do that as often as occasion demanded, every year. Job is an example of a pious father, who fears God and brings up his children in the nurture and admonition of the Lord, who also patiently corrects their faults and guides them in the paths of righteousness.

SATAN GIVEN PERMISSION TO AFFLICT JOB. — V. 6. **Now, there was a day when the sons of God,** God's own holy spirits, the angels ministering unto Him, **came to present themselves before the Lord,** the picture being that of a great monarch who daily assembles his ministers and servants about him, **and Satan,** the great adversary of God and men, **came also among them.** Although condemned to the chains of hell, the devil, as the prince of this world, has as much freedom as the Lord permits him to have, not only in governing his own subjects, but also in afflicting the children of God and in leading them into temptation, 1 Cor. 10, 13. V. 7. **And the Lord said unto Satan, Whence comest thou?** The object of the question was to find out whence the devil was just then coming, what he had most recently been trying to accomplish. **Then Satan,** who is bound in obedience to the almighty Ruler of the universe, although most unwillingly, **answered the Lord and said, From going to and fro in the earth and from walking up and down in it.** The words refer to the peculiar characteristic of Satan, for it is his custom to roam about, seeking whom he might devour, 1 Pet. 5, 8; he is a being without stability, malicious, intent upon evil. V. 8. **And the Lord said unto Satan,** in His omniscience familiar with the evil intent of Satan, **Hast thou considered My servant Job,** literally, "set thy heart upon him," **that there is none like him in the earth, a perfect and an upright man,** standing out among men both for the piety of his heart and for the righteousness of his life, **one that feareth God and escheweth evil?** V. 9. **Then Satan answered the Lord and said, Doth Job fear God for naught?** That is, Dost Thou suppose he is pious and God-fearing without good reason, without reward or profit? Satan's sneering implication was, of course, that Job feared God only because he had been so abundantly blessed with wealth and honor, that it was only this fact which caused him to feign a piety which he did not really feel. V. 10. **Hast not Thou made an hedge about him and about his house and about all that he hath on every side?** Under such conditions, Satan implies, it would be an easy matter for any person to make a show of piety. **Thou hast blessed the work of his hands, and his substance,** his wealth, especially that in cattle, **is increased in the land;** it has become so numerous that it can no longer be confined to a small area. Genuine piety loves God for His own sake, regardless of special earthly blessings, without specific stipulation and claim. Satan denied that Job's piety was of this kind. V. 11. **But put forth Thine hand now and touch all that he hath,** namely, to smite, to injure, and destroy it, **and he will curse Thee to Thy face,** the form of the Hebrew sentence showing that Satan affirmed his statement as in the case of an oath: Verily, most surely. V. 12. **And the Lord said unto Satan,** accepting the challenge contained in his words, **Behold, all that he hath is in thy power; only upon himself put not forth thine hand.** Satan thereby received permission to deprive Job of all his property, of all his immense wealth; but he was not allowed to touch the person of Job. The obvious intention of the Lord, in granting this permission to Satan, was to test the integrity and the piety of Job, to prove his sincerity over against the devil's sneering insinuations. It was a phase of the battle of light with darkness. **So Satan went forth from the presence of the Lord,** ready to begin his work of destruction, for he is a murderer from the beginning; plunder and destruction are his delight. The thought that the Lord, in permitting misfortune to come upon His children in this world through the hatred of Satan, has the purpose of proving the sincerity of the believers should stimulate the latter to meet the attacks of the devil with the spirit of true loyalty to their Father in heaven.

JOB'S GREAT AFFLICTION. — V. 13. **And there was a day when his sons and his daughters were eating and drinking wine in** their eldest brother's house, at one of their customary banquets; v. 14. and there came a messenger unto Job and said, The oxen were plowing and the asses feeding beside them, grazing in the meadows near by, v. 15. and the Sabeans, a nomadic tribe of Northeastern Arabia, fell upon them, and took them away, took everything along as welcome plunder; yea, they have slain the servants, those in charge of the work, with the edge of the sword, sparing none whom they could find; and I only am escaped alone to tell thee, the only survivor of the massacre. V. 16. While he was yet speaking, before he had even finished his message of misfortune, there came also another and said, The fire of God, evidently a shower of fire and brimstone, is fallen from heaven and hath burned up the sheep and the servants and consumed them, completely destroying also this part of Job's possessions; and I only am escaped alone to tell thee. V. 17. While he was yet speaking, there came also another and said, The Chaldeans, at that time a nomadic tribe living near the Euphrates, made out three bands, attacking in three divisions, and fell upon the camels, and have carried them away, yea, and slain the servants with the edge of the sword, sparing none; and I only am escaped alone to tell thee. V. 18. While he was yet speaking, there came also another, a fourth messenger of evil, and said, Thy sons and thy daughters were eating and drinking wine in their eldest brother's house; v. 19. and, behold, there came a great wind from the wilderness, a violent tornado from the east or northeast, and smote the four corners of the house, taking hold upon the whole house or tent at one time, and it fell upon the young men, upon all the young people there assembled, and they are dead; and I only am escaped alone to tell thee. In each case the messenger implies that his escape was effected only with the greatest difficulty, and each message increases the sense of the greatness of the calamity. V. 20. Then Job, who was more deeply affected by the information of the death of his children than by the loss of his entire property, arose and rent his mantle, showing the violence of his grief, and shaved his head, another sign of deep mourning among certain ancient nations, and fell down upon the ground, and worshiped, in the attitude of the most humble and submissive adoration, v. 21. and said, Naked came I out of my mother's womb, and naked shall I return thither, that is, into the bosom of the earth, from which man was originally made, departing as poor and as helpless as when he came. The Lord, the great Jehovah, gave, from Him had all the blessings come which Job had enjoyed, and the Lord hath taken away; blessed be the name of the Lord! This is an example of most patient submission, of bowing to the will of the Lord in childlike trust and in firm confidence. It is in this sense that all believers must learn to think of God as praiseworthy at all times, whether His wisdom sees fit to give or to take away. V. 22. In all this Job sinned not, not even in questioning God's decrees, nor charged God foolishly, attributing senseless or foolish acting to God. It is this phase of Job's character, a patient submission to the will of God at all times, which believers should be zealous to copy.

CHAPTER 2.

The Severer Trial and the Visit of Job's Friends.

JOB STRICKEN WITH A SEVERE DISEASE. — V. 1. Again there was a day, some time after Satan had exhausted his efforts to shake the piety of Job by the destruction of his property and the slaughter of his children, when the sons of God, the angels, as ministers of Jehovah, came to present themselves before the Lord, and Satan came also among them to present himself before the Lord, as on the previous occasion, chap. 1, 13. V. 2. And the Lord said unto Satan, From whence comest thou? And Satan answered the Lord and said, just as he had done before, From going to and fro in the earth and from walking up and down in it, in his restless, ceaseless endeavor to harm the works of the Lord and to lead men into sin. V. 3. And the Lord said unto Satan, Hast thou considered My servant Job, namely, by concentrating his attention upon him, that there is none like him in the earth, a perfect and an upright man, one that feareth God and escheweth evil? Cp. chap. 1, 1. And still, in spite of the severe affliction which had come upon him, he holdeth fast his integrity, to his piety and to the perfection of his righteousness before men, although thou movedst Me against him to destroy him without cause, namely, by giving Satan permission to send such great misfortunes upon him, part of which included the use of the forces of nature, which God, in a manner of speaking, placed at his disposal. Note the divine irony in the language of Jehovah, especially as contrasted with the baffled sneering of Satan. V. 4. And Satan answered the Lord and said, in the rage due to his failure, Skin for skin; yea, all that a man hath will he give for his life. The meaning of this proverbial saying is that nothing outward is so dear to a man but that he will gladly give it for something similar; the life of a man, however, cannot be replaced, and therefore a man will sacrifice everything else for the sake of his life. V. 5. **But put forth Thine hand now and touch his bone and his flesh,** striking at him even from a distance in making a pass for his life, **and he will curse,** renounce and reject, **Thee to Thy face.** V. 6. **And the Lord,** willing to permit even this test of Job's integrity, of the sincerity of his righteousness and piety, **said unto Satan, Behold, he is in thine hand,** namely, to afflict with severe diseases; **but save his life,** the latter could be imperiled in the proposed test, but he must not be deprived of it. V. 7. **So went Satan forth from the presence of the Lord and smote Job with sore boils from the sole of his foot unto his crown,** the disease being the worst form of leprosy, with horrible ulcers or boils and a swollen condition of the joints, which rendered the afflicted person almost helpless. V. 8. **And he took him a potsherd to scrape himself withal,** evidently to relieve the intolerable itching of the festering sores; **and he sat down among the ashes,** to indicate that he was submerged in grief and mourning. The few words paint a picture of such utter degradation and misery after the great happiness which Job had enjoyed, that the contrast is extremely shocking. It is but seldom that a believer is so severely tried as was Job, and therefore his example serves to encourage and inspire the children of God for all times.

JOB REBUKES HIS WIFE. — V. 9. **Then said his wife,** whose trust in God was evidently not as strongly founded as that of the sufferer, **unto him, Dost thou still retain thine integrity?** He was clinging to a virtue which, as she supposed, availed him nothing at this time. The astonishment shown by Job's wife is that found in all unbelievers and false Christians when they cannot explain to their own satisfaction every act of God and every misfortune which befalls them. **Curse God and die.** She wanted him to renounce God, all his trust in Jehovah, and then give up the struggle for life or suffer the penalty of blasphemy. V. 10. **But he,** sharply reproving her for her lack of trust in the goodness of Jehovah, **said unto her, Thou speakest as one of the foolish women speaketh,** in a godless and impious manner, which he, as his words imply, would not have expected from her. **What? Shall we receive good at the hand of God, and shall we not receive,** accept and willingly bear, **evil? In all this did not Job sin with his lips.** If there was a temptation to murmur in the heart of Job, he had so far fought it down. V. 11. **Now, when Job's three friends heard of all this evil that was come upon him, they came every one from his own place: Eliphaz, the Temanite,** probably from Idumea, and **Bildad, the Shuhite,** in the desert east of the Dead Sea, and **Zophar, the Naamathite,** that is, from a region in Lower Arabia; **for they had made an appointment together to come to mourn with him and to comfort him,** they met together by appointment and traveled to Job's home to bring him some form of consolation, if that were possible. V. 12. **And when they lifted up their eyes afar off and knew him not,** did not recognize their friend in this formless mass of diseased flesh, **they lifted up their voice and wept,** in sympathy over their friend's suffering; **and they rent every one his mantle and sprinkled dust upon their heads toward heaven,** that is, they threw up handfuls of dust as high as possible to signify that the misery of Job cried to heaven, and then let it fall back on their heads to show the depth of their grief. V. 13. **So they sat down with him upon the ground seven days and seven nights, and none spake a word unto him,** their sympathetic sorrow being too great for utterance; **for they saw that his grief was very great,** that the affliction of his pain was unbearable. It is altogether commendable for friends to sympathize with a sufferer, mingling their own tears with his and showing that they truly feel for him, Rom. 12, 15.

CHAPTER 3.

Job's Impatient Outburst.

JOB CURSES THE DAY OF HIS BIRTH. — Up till now Job had suppressed all thoughts of rebellion against God, every notion of dissatisfaction and impatience with the ways of Jehovah. But now he gives evidence of weakness. V. 1. **After this opened Job his mouth,** in the formal manner, with deliberation and gravity, after the custom of the ancient sages, **and cursed his day,** namely, the day of his birth. V. 2. **And Job spake and said,** in a wild and bold outburst, which showed that he was impatient with the afflictions laid upon him by God, cp. Jer. 20, 14, v. 3. **Let the day perish wherein I was born, and the night in which it was said, There is a man-child conceived,** rather, "the night which said," for that night is personified as the witness and messenger of evil. V. 4. **Let that day be darkness,** be covered with the everlasting shadows of death; **let not God regard it from above,** in any way inquire after it, as though interested in such an execrable time, **neither let the light shine upon it,** it should be shut out forever from the light of God's presence. V. 5. **Let darkness and the shadow** of **death stain it,** the thickest darkness, the deepest death-gloom reclaiming and covering it as an unclean thing; **let a cloud dwell upon it,** encamping over it, obscuring and hiding it forever; **let the blackness of the day terrify it,** the thought being that, just as a day seems all the gloomier and more dismal after it has once been lit up by a flash of light, so the dismal bitterness of darkness should settle upon the day of his birth as a form of retribution for permitting his being born. V. 6. **As for that night, let darkness seize upon it,** everlasting darkness holding it in its possession; **let it not be joined unto the days of the year,** rather, "let it not be glad of its existence among the days of the year," as one of a joyful troop of nights which march by in glittering procession; **let it not come into the number of the months,** it should be omitted and forgotten, as utterly detestable. V. 7. **Lo, let that night be solitary,** or, more forceful, "See, that night!" Let it be barren, and therefore utterly desolate, without a cheering voice; **let no joyful voice come therein,** not a single jubilant shout, as over the happy birth of a welcome child. V. 8. **Let them curse it that curse the day,** the sorcerers of old, whose ban was thought to bewitch a day so as to make it a day of misfortune, **who are ready to raise up their mourning,** literally, "those who are skilful in rousing up leviathan," the great dragon of whom the ancients believed that he devoured the sun and the moon at the time of eclipses, whom the heathen sorcerers tried to drive away with their incantations. All the men who had influence over the powers of evil should join in cursing the night of Job's conception. V. 9. **Let the stars of the twilight thereof be dark,** refusing to be the heralds of the dawn and thereby continuing the darkness; **let it look for light, but have none,** condemned to the everlasting curse of darkness; **neither let it see the dawning of the day,** literally, "the eyelashes of the dawn," by which it might be refreshed and filled with pleasure; v. 10. **because it shut not up the doors of my mother's womb,** thus hindering his being conceived and born, **nor hid sorrow from mine eyes,** for if he had never been born, he would not now have been afflicted with this suffering. It was an impatient outburst which, although not directed at God outright, yet had the effect of a challenge of His providence and government of the world, and therefore was just as objectionable as similar outbursts on the part of believers to-day.

JOB LONGS FOR DEATH. — V. 11. **Why died I not from the womb,** immediately after birth? **Why did I not give up the ghost when I came out of the belly?** V. 12. **Why did the knees prevent me?** "Prevent" is here used in the old sense of anticipate, be ready for, said of the father, who took the new-born child on his lap, joyfully acknowledging his son. **Or why the breasts that I should suck?** Said of the readiness, of the anxious longing, of the mother to nurse her child, to give him the food needed in order to sustain life. V. 13. **For now should I have lain still and been quiet,** not bothered with any of the misery which he was now suffering; **I should have slept,** in the untroubled sleep of the grave; **then had I been at rest,** v. 14. **with kings and counselors of the earth,** the highest officers of the state, the royal advisers and ministers, **which built desolate places for themselves,** who erected for themselves what proved to be, not palaces, but ruins; ("The paths of glory lead but to the grave";) v. 15. **or with princes that had gold, who filled their houses with silver,** those who heaped up countless treasures for themselves; v. 16. **or as an hidden, untimely birth I had not been,** he would not exist at all, as **infants which never saw light.** All of them, the builders of great palaces, the rich millionaires, together with the still-born babes, they all enter into the rest of the grave, whether this be decorated with a structure upon whose ruins men gaze with wondering surprise, or whether it be a hole in the ground whose very location is afterward forgotten. V. 17. **There the wicked cease from troubling,** no longer being engaged in raging; **and there the weary,** those who suffered misery and trouble in this life, **be at rest,** removed from everything that wearied out their strength. V. 18. **There the prisoners rest together,** as many as there may be; **they hear not the voice of the oppressor,** no taskmaster, or overseer, threatens them any longer. V. 19. **The small and great are there,** for death makes all men equal; **and the servant is free from his master.** The very thought of the rest and quiet of the grave, with its surcease from sorrow and misery, is fascinating to Job; he lingers over the thought before continuing his complaint in which he desires death for himself. V. 20. **Wherefore is light,** namely, the light of life, **given to him that is in misery and life unto the bitter in soul,** why should God continue them in this miserable life, v. 21. **which long for death, but it cometh not, and dig for it,** with frantic desire, **more than for hid treasures,** v. 22. **which rejoice exceedingly,** in an excess of jubilation, **and are glad when they can find the grave?** It is a cry of extreme anguish which longs for deliverance by death and is unable to explain why this coveted deliverance is denied. V. 23. **Why is light given to a man whose way is hid,** the light of life continued to a man as helpless and forsaken as Job, **and whom God hath hedged in,** so that he is unable to find deliverance? V. 24. **For my sighing cometh before I eat,** instead of eating and enjoying his food he is constrained to groan in his misery, **and my roarings are poured out like the waters,** in a steady, unremittent flow, without relief. V. 25. **For the thing which I greatly feared is come upon me,** if he but thought of a terrible thing, he was immediately struck by it, **and that which I was afraid of is come unto me,** if he dreaded a thing, he was immediately overtaken by it, he was obliged to endure all that he had ever considered frightful. V. 26. **I was not in safety, neither had I rest, neither was I quiet,** he was so troubled then that he had neither respite nor repose; **yet trouble came,** it was coming upon him in an endless stream. Thus even believers are sometimes overwhelmed by impatience, giving way to expressions which are full of accusations against God. A Christian should always be prepared to die, but he should not impatiently desire death at any time. He is ill prepared for death who is unwilling to live.

CHAPTER 4.

The First Rejoinder of Eliphaz.

Job having thus given way to his impatience, his friends thought it their duty to correct him. But instead of showing him in what respect his position was wrong, they proceed according to the assumption that Job must be guilty of some special fault or sin, and chide him accordingly. V. 1. **Then Eliphaz, the Temanite, answered and said,** v. 2. **If we essay to commune with thee, wilt thou be grieved?** Eliphaz wanted to be sure from the outset that Job would not misunderstand his friends if they ventured some suggestions, that he would not be insulted or offended if they spoke a word in his behalf. **But who can withhold himself from speaking?** He felt that he must express his opinion at this time. V. 3. **Behold, thou hast instructed many,** namely, with words of loving reproof and admonition, **and thou hast strengthened the weak hands,** causing the slack hands to take up their tasks with new vigor. V. 4. **Thy words have upholden him that was falling, and thou hast strengthened the feeble knees,** by holding men upright who were about to sink down, figuratively speaking, by his moral support, by his encouragement. V. 5. **But now it is come upon thee and thou faintest;** now that misfortune, in turn, had struck Job, all his fine admonitions to others were forgotten, and he was faint and impatient. **It toucheth thee and thou art troubled,** confounded, seized with terror, filled with feebleness and despondency when suffering came to his own door. V. 6. **Is not this thy fear, thy confidence, thy hope, and the uprightness of thy ways?** or, "Is not thy piety, thy confidence, and thy hope the righteousness of thy ways?" Eliphaz implied that Job surely did not have an evil conscience, that he certainly could and should remember the uprightness of his life, which his friend was not prepared to question. V. 7. **Remember, I pray thee, who ever perished being innocent? Or where were the righteous cut off?** This overemphasis on the safety of the upright shows that Eliphaz intended to voice his doubts concerning the unvarying piety of Job, trying to convey the idea that there must have been, after all, something that merited an extraordinary punishment at the hand of God. This thought is now elaborated in detail. V. 8. **Even as I have seen, they that plow iniquity,** sowing mischief in their fields, **and sow wickedness,** misery and ruin for others, **reap the same.** "Whatsoever a man soweth, that shall he also reap," Gal. 6, 7. 8. V. 9. **By the blast of God they perish,** as God breathes upon them in anger, **and by the breath of His nostrils are they consumed,** like plants which a burning wind scorches, so that they shrivel up and wither away. V. 10. **The roaring of the lion,** as he goes forth to seize and tear his prey, **and the voice of the fierce lion,** of the roarer who shows his angry temper, **and the teeth of the young lions are broken.** V. 11. **The old lion,** he who enjoys the fulness of adult strength, **perisheth,** wanders about helplessly, **for lack of prey, and the stout lion's whelps are scattered abroad,** rather, the whelps of the lioness. Lions of every age and of every condition of strength are mentioned in order to picture the destruction of the haughty sinner with all his household. Eliphaz now draws a conclusion which he expresses very carefully. V. 12. **Now, a thing was secretly brought to me,** it came to him in a stealthy, mysterious manner, **and mine ear received a little thereof,** a faint whisper or lisp, as from an oracle, which he hardly dared utter. V. 13. **In thoughts from the visions of the night,** in pictures such as the thoughts paint in dreams, **when deep sleep falleth on men,** when the spirit of man seems to penetrate into superhuman realms, v. 14. **fear came upon me and trembling,** meeting him in such a way as to cause a shudder to pass over him, **which made all my bones to shake,** in a deep and fearful agitation. V. 15. **Then a spirit passed before my face,** gliding or flitting before him like the apparition of an angel; **the hair of my flesh stood up,** as in sudden, extreme terror; v. 16. **it stood still, but I could not discern the form thereof,** it had the shadowy indistinctness which creates such an impression of awe; **an image was before mine eyes, there was silence, and I heard a voice,** rather, a lisping murmur and a voice, a lisping or murmuring voice, saying, v. 17. **Shall mortal man be more just than God? Shall a man be more pure than his Maker?** The thought contained here is this, that whoever censures the government of God, as Job had done in his complaint, thereby claims to be more just than God and thus becomes guilty. V. 18. **Behold, He put no trust in His servants,** the ministering angels; **and His angels he charged with folly,** to the very spirits of light He imputes error, they cannot compare with Him in holiness and purity; v. 19. **how much less in them that dwell in houses of clay,** frail men with material, earthly bodies, **whose foundation is in the dust,** out of which their bodies were originally framed, **which are crushed before the moth,** utterly consumed as though they were nothing but moths! V. 20. **They are destroyed,** beaten into small pieces and thus returned to dust, **from morning to evening,** their life being but an extremely short span of time; **they perish forever without any regarding it,** soon dead and rapidly forgotten. V. 21. **Doth not their excellency which is in them go away? They die, even without wisdom,** literally, "Is it not: torn away is their cord?" the picture being taken from the quick striking of a tent. Without having found true wisdom in their lives, having lived in short-sightedness and folly all their days, men die, they are cut off and taken away, Ps. 90, 9. 10. Remembering this, the Christian will at all times be constrained to pray: "So teach us to number our days that we may apply our hearts unto wisdom."

CHAPTER 5.

The Conclusion of the First Speech of Eliphaz.

Answering a Possible Objection on Job's Part. — V. 1. **Call now, if there be any that will answer thee,** rather, "will any one reply?" Having complained against God as though he were just and God unjust, will Job find any one to intercede for him or to help him in his trouble? **And to which of the saints wilt thou turn?** Would he find so much as a single angel to take his part? He whom God will not help no creature can help, and an impatient murmuring against misfortune would only challenge the anger of God. V. 2. **For wrath killeth the foolish man,** grief slays the complaining fool, **and envy slayeth the silly one,** his own impatient repining brings destruction upon himself. V. 3. **I have seen the foolish taking root,** like a luscious plant in rich soil, as though his prosperity would endure forever; **but suddenly I cursed his habitation,** that is, a sudden destruction at the hand of God occurred, which showed that his apparently prosperous dwelling was, after all, under God's curse, Ps. 73, 18. 19. V. 4. **His children are far from safety,** they were without help, when the curse of God descended upon him, **and they are crushed in the gate, neither is there any to deliver them,** the reference being to the gate as the place of judgment in the Oriental cities. V. 5. **Whose harvest the hungry eateth up,** namely, that of the man whom the Lord cast down from the height of his prosperity, **and taketh it even out of the thorns,** the very last gleanings of the harvest of the wicked being swept away in the calamity which befalls him, **and the robber swalloweth up their substance,** literally, "the thirsty," or, "those who lay snares, swallow his wealth"; he is deprived of all he has, which was obtained either by deceit or by outright robbery, as a punishment of the Lord. V. 6. **Although affliction,** every kind of misery and evil, **cometh not forth of the dust, neither doth trouble spring out of the ground,** that is, the misfortunes of men are not like accidental weedy growths; v. 7. **yet man is born unto trouble,** man, being enticed by his own lust, inherited since the time of Adam, commits sin and as a consequence brings misery upon himself, **as the sparks fly upward,** carried up on high by the heat engendered in the flame. So much for man's natural condition. V. 8. **I,** that is, Eliphaz on his part, **would seek unto God, and unto God would I commit my cause,** leaving everything in the hands of the most high God, and not in any way impatient of His government, v. 9. **which doeth great things and unsearchable,** whose ways are beyond finding out and therefore beyond question on the part of men; **marvelous things without number,** all of which are beyond the grasp of the human mind; v. 10. **who giveth rain upon the earth and sendeth waters upon the fields,** the open land outside the cities, as the water of springs and brooks irrigates the land, v. 11. **to set up on high those that be low,** namely, by pouring out His blessings upon them, **that those which mourn may be exalted to safety,** raised up to prosperity, enjoy the rich benefits showered upon them. V. 12. **He disappointeth the devices of the crafty,** bringing all their schemes to naught, **so that their hands cannot perform their enterprise,** cannot realize what they wanted to accomplish, not bring about anything solid or lasting, no matter how great their success may seem for a while. V. 13. **He taketh the wise in their own craftiness,** so that they are shown to be fools before Him and their plans result in ruin to themselves, **and the counsel of the froward,** those who try to be cunning in setting aside His will, **is carried** headlong, is overthrown. V. 14. **They meet with darkness in the daytime and grope in the noonday as in the night,** afflicted with blindness by God, being punished for their impertinent behavior in vaunting their own wisdom. V. 15. **But He saveth the poor from the sword, from their mouth,** that is, from the sword which proceeds out of their mouth in the form of wicked slander, **and from the hand of the mighty,** the strong who delight in violence and bloodshed. V. 16. **So the poor hath hope, and iniquity stoppeth her mouth.** Believers may at all times and in all circumstances place their full confidence in Jehovah, knowing that He will always work deliverance from every evil work, no matter how hopeless the outlook.

Eliphaz Admonishes Job to Bear His Trial Patiently. — V. 17. **Behold, happy is the man,** the mortal, in all his feebleness, **whom God correcteth,** since such an action on the part of God shows His fatherly interest. **Therefore despise not thou the chastening of the Almighty,** by a want of submission, by a rebellious attitude; v. 18. **for He maketh sore and bindeth up,** in order to heal the wound which He has inflicted, Hos. 6, 1; Deut. 32, 39; **He woundeth, and His hands make whole.** Cp. Prov. 3, 11—13; Ps. 94, 12. V. 19. **He shall deliver thee in six troubles,** in a great number of afflictions; **yea, in seven there shall no evil touch thee,** Ps. 91, 10. The believer, trusting in the goodness and mercy of Jehovah, is safe at all times. V. 20. **In famine He shall redeem thee from death,** Ps. 33, 19, **and in war from the power of the sword,** so that it cannot strike and kill. V. 21. **Thou shalt be hid from the scourge of the tongue,** from all slander and reviling, which would not be able to detract from his good name, Ps. 31, 20; Jer. 18, 18; **neither shalt thou be afraid of destruction when it cometh,** no matter what catastrophe threatens, Ps. 32, 6. V. 22. **At destruction and famine thou shalt laugh,** knowing that they are powerless to harm him; **neither shalt thou be afraid of the beasts of the earth,** who in ancient times were often a severe scourge. V. 23. **For thou shalt be in league with the stones of the field,** who would not harm the fertility of the soil nor interfere with its tilling; **and the beasts of the field shall be at peace with thee,** harming neither him nor his flocks and herds. V. 24. **And thou shalt know that thy tabernacle,** the tent where he dwelled and all his possessions, **shall be in peace,** altogether safe and uninjured; **and thou shalt visit thy habitation and shalt not sin,** rather, in reviewing thy household, thou findest no gap, nothing would be missing of all his property. V. 25. **Thou shalt know also that thy seed shall be great,** plentiful in numbers, **and thine offspring as the grass of the earth,** this being considered a very great blessing throughout the Bible, just as childlessness was regarded as a lack of blessing and even as a curse. V. 26. **Thou shalt come to thy grave in a full age,** in a ripe old age, in unbroken vigor, **like as a shock of corn cometh in in his season,** dead ripe, and carried up to the threshing-floor, yielding up its riches of grain. V. 27. **Lo this, we have searched it,** found out by careful investigating; **hear it and know thou it for thy good,** the warning being again addressed to Job, lest he once more murmur and complain. Note that Eliphaz speaks the truth, but not all the truth, for the application of his statements to the case of Job did not follow. It is a dangerous conclusion to infer that a fellow-Christian is under God's wrath just because he is suffering misfortunes.

CHAPTER 6.

Job's Reply to Eliphaz.

Job Defends His Desire for Death. — V. 1. **But Job answered and said,** v. 2. **Oh, that my grief were throughly weighed,** namely, the suffering which he was enduring, **and my calamity,** the bitter and unexplainable affliction, **laid in the balances together!** Both pans being thus adjusted, his misfortunes would be found to outweigh his sorrows, his complaint. V. 3. **For now it would be heavier than the sand of the sea,** his woe was heavy beyond measure; **therefore my words are swallowed up,** rather, "they raved," they were spoken rashly. Although the greatness of his misery explained his complaining, yet he himself confessed that this fact did not really justify his untamed sorrow, his foolish raving. His better knowledge told him that he should not indulge his grief, but the unequaled greatness of his misery drove his tongue to the complaint which he made. V. 4. **For the arrows of the Almighty are within me,** the sickness, pains, and plagues which God inflicted upon him, **the poison whereof drinketh up my spirit,** like a venom whose burning heat dried up his soul; **the terrors of God do set themselves in array against me,** like an attacking army storming a citadel, Is. 42, 13. Job now argues that the demand which wanted him to submit without a murmur is unnatural. V. 5. **Doth the wild ass bray when he hath grass,** literally, "by the fresh grass"? **Or loweth the ox over his fodder?** That is, even an irrational beast will not groan or utter discontented cries if it is fully provided with food; much less would Job lament without sufficient cause. V. 6. **Can that which is unsavory,** tasteless, **be eaten without** salt? **Or is there any taste in the white of an egg?** In either case the lack of flavor, the insipid taste, tends to make the food nauseating; even so Job cannot relish his present sufferings, which to him are like a loathsome food. V. 7. **The things that my soul refused to touch are as my sorrowful meat,** or, What my soul abhorred to touch, that is to me as my loathsome food; he had to smell and touch the putrid matter of leprosy day after day. V. 8. **Oh, that I might have my request,** literally, "that it might come," be fulfilled; **and that God would grant me the thing that I long for!** He was crying and longing for release from his misery. V. 9. **Even that it would please God to destroy me,** snuffing out his life by an early death; **that He would let loose His hand and cut me off!** The picture is that of the cutting of a cord or string, which was synonymous with death. It was an intense, an impatient desire for death. V. 10. **Then should I yet have comfort,** he would find consolation in this fact; **yea, I would harden myself in sorrow. Let Him not spare,** rather, "I would leap up in unsparing pain," due to its excessive force which promised him no respite; **for I have not concealed the words of the Holy One.** The fact that he had not denied the Lord was Job's confidence in the midst of all distress and misery, even if the pain it caused him should be practically unbearable. V. 11. **What is my strength that I should hope,** continue to wait, persevere as heretofore? **And what is mine end that I should prolong my life,** literally, "lengthen my soul," be patient? His strength was completely gone, and therefore he looked forward to death with eager impatience. V. 12. **Is my strength the strength of stones? Or is my flesh of brass?** He certainly did not have the power of endurance which inorganic matter possesses. V. 13. **Is not my help in me,** rather, "Is not the nothingness of my help with me," that is, Am I not utterly helpless? **And is wisdom driven quite from me?** His well-being, his prospect of strength in the future, of an eventual recovery, had been driven away from him and thus utterly lost. An early death was the only hope he cherished, and that he desired with an intense longing. A Christian will always be ready for death, but it would be wrong for him to demand death at the hands of God. We must at all times submit our will to that of our heavenly Father.

JOB CRITICIZES ELIPHAZ FOR HIS CONDUCT. V. 14. **To him that is afflicted pity should be showed from his friend,** or, to him who is melting on account of the fierceness of his misery, and therefore in despair, gentleness should be shown by his friends; **but he forsaketh the fear of the Almighty,** rather, even if he should, or, lest he should, forsake the fear of the Almighty. Friends worthy of the name should stand by one who is in misery and distress, lest he give way entirely to despair and forsake the Lord. V. 15. **My brethren have dealt deceitfully as a brook,** false and treacherous as a torrent, as an arroyo in the wilderness, which presents a dry bed at just the time when water is most needed, **and as the stream of brooks they pass away,** torrents which overflow one day and disappear on the next, absolutely unreliable; v. 16. **which are blackish,** turbid, dark, foul, **by reason of the ice,** as the melting ice is carried down by the spring floods, **and wherein the snow is hid,** seeming to offer a solid surface to stand on, but in reality altogether treacherous; v. 17. **what time they wax warm, they vanish,** after the short spring flow, which seemed to carry so much promise, their bed is soon parched; **when it is hot, they are consumed out of their place,** altogether extinguished. To this characterization of unreliable friends Job adds a description of the disappointment which filled his heart on account of the attitude of his visitors. V. 18. **The paths of their way are turned aside,** their course winds hither and thither, just like that of the arroyos in the wilderness; **they go to nothing, and perish,** vanishing out in the desert wastes, sinking from sight, failing men when they are most in need of water. V. 19. **The troops of Tema looked,** the caravans of a nomadic tribe in Northern Arabia, **the companies of Sheba waited for them,** hoping to obtain water for their parched lips. In Job's picture his friends are the unreliable arroyos, while he is the thirsty traveler searching for a drink of cooling water. V. 20. **They were confounded because they had hoped,** put to shame on account of their confident hope, just as Job was in this instance; **they came thither, and were ashamed,** red with shame on account of the deceit which they finally perceived, betrayed by a lying brook. V. 21. **For now ye are no thing,** they had shown that they did not exist as real friends; **ye see my casting down, and are afraid,** full of terror and dismay, fearing to identify themselves with one whom they believed struck down by the wrath of God. V. 22. **Did I say, Bring unto me? or, Give a reward for me of your substance?** He had not asked any sacrifice from them, had not even desired a gift from them; he had expected only the sympathy of true friends. V. 23. **Or, Deliver me from the enemy's hand? or, Redeem me from the hand of the mighty,** of the oppressor? He had never yet asked for such a proof of their friendship; therefore he was all the more sorely disappointed at their failing to show even the least friendly interest in him and compassion for him. V. 24. **Teach me, and I will hold my tongue;** he was willing to be set right and to cease his complaint; **and cause me to understand wherein I have erred,** this being preferable to any silent or open accusation on their part. V. 25. **How forcible are right words,** such as are based upon sound knowledge! **But what doth your arguing reprove?** What Job missed so sorely in the case of his friends was this, that they did not substantiate their accusations, that they judged merely according to their feelings. V. 26. **Do ye imagine to reprove words,** were they trying to fasten only upon the words which his misery pressed out of his mouth, **and the speeches of one that is desperate, which are as wind?** They had his blameless conduct to judge him by and should draw no conclusions from his present complaints. V. 27. **Yea, ye overwhelm the fatherless,** like unrelenting creditors they would cast lots for the orphans left by a debtor to make them bond-servants, **and ye dig a pit for your friend,** trafficking or bargaining for him, to sell him as a slave; they were traitors to the cause of true friendship. V. 28. **Now, therefore, be content, look upon me,** they should be pleased to scrutinize his face closely; **for it is evident unto you if I lie,** they would be able to read in his face whether he were really the hypocrite they supposed him to be. V. 29. **Return, I pray you, let it not be iniquity; yea, return again, my righteousness is in it.** They should turn from their present position of unfriendly suspicion and make a careful examination of his case, so that they would do no wrong, but find the evidence of his righteousness. V. 30. **Is there iniquity in my tongue?** Had he actually, thus far in his complaint, spoken wrong? **Cannot my taste discern perverse things?** Was his palate, figuratively speaking, in such a poor condition that they believed him to have lost all consciousness of guilt, or that he could no longer understand the meaning of his misfortunes? True friends are a blessing, but false friends destroy a person's faith in humanity.

CHAPTER 7.

Job Renews His Lamentation.

The General Misery of Human Life. — V. 1. **Is there not an appointed time,** warfare, a fixed and wearing service, **to man upon earth? Are not his days also like the days of an hireling,** one who works for wages? The figure is that of a man drafted for military service, and then of a man who has hired out to perform a certain task, the idea being that in either case man longs for the end of the labor appointed to him. V. 2. **As a servant earnestly desireth the shadow,** as the slave eagerly looks forward to the rest after the completion of his work, **and as an hireling looketh for the reward of his work,** for he also, after receiving his wages, may rest, v. 3. **so am I,** instead of enjoying the expected rest, spoken in irony, **made to possess months of vanity,** this time of wretchedness was allotted to him, **and wearisome nights are appointed to me,** they have been dealt out to him without his desire, although he has not done anything to merit them to this degree. V. 4. **When I lie down, I say, When shall I arise and the night be gone?** The sleeplessness caused by his terrible illness made him wish that the night would soon fly away. **And I am full of tossings to and fro unto the dawning of the day,** weary with his restless rolling about in the endeavor to find rest. V. 5. **My flesh is clothed with worms,** maggots breeding in the ulcers, **and clods of dust,** the crust of dried filth covering his entire body; **my skin is broken and become loathsome,** whenever the skin made an attempt to heal, to come together, to become hard and stiff, the festering sores broke open again. V. 6. **My days are swifter than a weaver's shuttle and are spent without hope,** vanish without hope of deliverance, just as the web on the loom of the weaver is cut off. V. 7. **O remember that my life is wind,** his days are like a breath of air, which is soon wafted away, Ps. 78, 39; **mine eye shall no more see good,** will not return to see good fortune or prosperity; an early death would put an end to his chances of happiness in this life. V. 8. **The eye of him that hath seen me shall see me no more,** he would soon pass from the circle of those whom he had formerly considered his friends; **Thine eyes are upon me,** namely, those of the Lord, **and I am not;** even if He should turn to Job in sympathy in order to help him, it would be too late, since he knew he would soon be removed from the land of the living. Such bitterness of soul as here shown by Job is not compatible with true trust in the Lord.

Job Arraigns God. — V. 9. **As the cloud is consumed and vanisheth away,** the vapor disappearing in the dry air of the wilderness, **so he that goeth down to the grave shall come up no more,** if he is once in the realm of the dead, he cannot return to the former life on earth. V. 10. **He shall return no more to his house, neither shall his place,** his home, **know him any more,** this earthly life is past forever, so far as he is concerned. V. 11. **Therefore,** since God had practically abandoned him to dwell in the realm of the dead, **I will not refrain my mouth,** put no restraint on his speech; **I will speak in the anguish of my spirit,** in the bitterness and pain which possessed his soul; **I will complain in the bitterness of my soul,** because his soul was so disturbed and troubled; he threw aside, for once, the awe which he ordinarily showed in the presence of God. V. 12. **Am I a sea or a whale,** some monster of the deep, that Thou settest a watch over me? He felt himself watched, shut in, by God, like a dangerous creature which might threaten to overwhelm the world. V. 13. **When I say, My bed shall comfort me, my couch shall ease,** help bear, **my complaint,** a fact which is usually the case, v. 14. **then Thou scarest me with dreams,** shaking him thereby to prevent his resting in comfort, **and terrifiest me through visions,** in consequence of them, v. 15. **so that my soul chooseth strangling,** in wishing that the asthma which accompanied his illness might choke him, **and death rather than my life,** literally, "than these bones," that is, in preference to having his body reduced to a skeleton. V. 16. **I loathe it,** he was disgusted with this life; **I would not live alway,** on account of the unendurable pain which he suffered. **Let me alone,** he asked God to withdraw His chastening hand from him; **for my days are vanity,** a puff of breath which vanishes away. V. 17. **What is man that Thou shouldest magnify him, and that Thou shouldest set Thine heart upon him,** — the bitter irony of this passage consists in Job's asking why the great and majestic God should single out him, insignificant as he was, for the object of ever new and unceasing sufferings, — v. 18. **and that Thou shouldest visit him every morning and try him every moment,** putting his patience and power to a continuous test? V. 19. **How long wilt Thou not depart from me,** looking away from him, turning His attention to some other object upon which He might vent His wrath, **nor let me alone till I swallow down my spittle,** at least for a little instant, for one moment of time? V. 20. **I have sinned; what shall I do unto Thee, O thou Preserver of men?** The thought is really conditional: If I have sinned, what harm could thereby strike Thee; what detriment would be caused to Thy great glory and majesty? **Why hast Thou set me as a mark against Thee,** a target, or mark, for every blow, **so that I am a burden to myself,** which the Lord Himself would try to shake off? V. 21. **And why dost Thou not pardon my transgression and take away mine iniquity,** pardon his guilt, since the end was now so near? **For now shall I sleep in the dust; and Thou shalt seek me in the morning, but I shall not be.** He requests God's immediate help, fearing that else he must die. The thought in the speech of Job is that of an accusation of cruelty on the part of God, an idea which may readily become blasphemous, if not driven away by a proper regard for tho righteousness of God at all times.

CHAPTER 8.

The Speech of Bildad.

An Admonition to Job to Repent of His Sin. — V. 1. **Then answered Bildad, the Shuhite,** chap. 2, 11, **and said,** v. 2. **How long wilt thou speak these things?** An exclamation of impatience over the blasphemous impertinence which he read in Job's words. **And how long shall the words of thy mouth be like a strong wind?** He made this comparison both on account of the emptiness and bluster of the wind and on account of its destructive tendency. V. 3. **Doth God pervert judgment? Or doth the Almighty pervert justice?** Would Job in his sober mind accuse God of injustice, either in principle or in act? V. 4. **If thy children have sinned against him,** namely, in celebrating their feasts and banquets, chap. 1, 5. 18, **and he have cast them away for their transgression,** abandoning them to the destructive hand of their own guilt, for sin will invariably punish the transgressor; v. 5. **if thou wouldest seek unto God betimes,** turning to Him with earnest, humble entreaty, **and make thy supplication to the Almighty,** with the object of rendering God gracious to himself; v. 6. **if thou wert pure and upright,** Bildad's inference being that this could not be the case in the circumstances, **surely now He would awake for thee,** arousing Himself for Job's protection and deliverance, **and make the habitation of thy righteousness prosperous,** He would restore to Job the home and the possession which he had had as a righteous man, He would let him once more enjoy the fruits of his righteousness in peace. V. 7. **Though thy beginning was small, yet thy latter end should greatly increase,** his prosperity would certainly be very great, he would once more flourish greatly. All this God would surely send upon Job if he were the righteous, pure, and upright man which he represented himself to be. Bildad's statement was an unconscious prophecy of that which afterwards really came to pass, chap. 42, 12.

An Accusation of Wickedness against Job. — Bildad was convinced that Job was, in some way, guilty of some special great transgression against the Lord, that his present affliction was the punishment for some specific wrong committed by him. Therefore he continued his harangue in this strain. V. 8. **For enquire, I pray thee, of the former age,** generations of men which have gone before, **and prepare thyself to the search of their fathers,** searching through the annals of history, finding out what the fathers had investigated and learned; v. 9. **(for we are but of yesterday and know nothing,** our own experience alone counts for nothing, **because our days upon earth are a shadow,** the term of a single human life is insufficient to fathom the eternal laws which govern the universe and determine its history;) v. 10. **shall not they teach thee and tell thee,** uttering their thoughts and experiences plainly, **and utter words out of their heart?** Note that the heart, as the seat of understanding, is here mentioned over against the words of Job as mere products of the lips. Bildad now introduces some of the sayings of the ancients. V. 11. **Can the rush,** the papyrus reed, **grow up without mire,** outside of the rich, moist marsh soil? **Can the flag grow without water?** V. 12. **Whilst it is yet in his greenness and not cut down,** namely, if growing in soil which is not continually moist, though rich enough otherwise, **it withereth before any other herb.** Swamp-plants may thrive for a while on dry ground, if there is enough water to start their growth, but as soon as moisture fails them, they immediately wither to the ground, even if all other plants are still in rich verdure. V. 13. **So are the paths of all that forget God,** in the midst of their apparent prosperity they suddenly fail; **and the hypocrite's hope shall perish,** the expectation of the ungodly, of him who has fallen away from the paths of righteousness, shall fail; v. 14. **whose hope shall be cut off, and whose trust shall be a spider's web,** that in which the godless trust, on which they place their confidence, is like a spider's web, which is broken at the slightest touch. V. 15. **He shall lean upon his house,** thinking that his possessions, the object of his trust, are secure, **but it shall not stand; he shall hold it fast,** as he feels it collapsing beneath his weight, **but it shall not endure,** it will tumble into ruins with all his hopes. There follows another picture of the uncertainty of the godless person's trust. V. 16. **He is green before the sun,** like a succulent creeper in the sunshine, **and his branch shooteth forth in his garden,** the whole garden being overrun with his root-sprouts. V. 17. **His roots are wrapped about the heap,** taking hold in piles of stones, **and seeth the place of stones,** having entwined himself between the stones by means of all his shoots, so that he embraces the entire house. So the godless person believes that nothing will cause him to lose the house of his good fortune. V. 18. **If he destroy him from his place,** namely, if the Lord takes his prosperity from him, **then it,** the former place of his happiness, **shall deny him, saying, I have not seen thee,** his very native ground denying him and refusing to have anything more to do with him. V. 19. **Behold, this is the joy of his way,** thus his pretended joyful way of living comes to a sudden, disastrous end, **and out of the earth shall others grow,** out of the dust other men blessed with external prosperity will sprout, who, in turn, will crumble away as the first ones did. Bildad now again presents a contrast. V. 20. **Behold, God will not cast away a perfect man,** He will not despise the pious man, the inference once more being that Job could not have been really pious, **neither will He help the evil-doers,** He will not grasp their hand to support them, v. 21. **till He,** or, while He will, **fill thy mouth with laughing and thy lips with rejoicing.** That, Bildad intimates, would have been the lot of Job always if he had not become guilty in some unusually bad way. V. 22. **They that hate thee shall be clothed with shame,** Jer. 3, 25; Ps. 35, 26; 109, 29; **and the dwelling-place of the wicked shall come to naught,** literally, "and the tent of the wicked, it is no more." Bildad here acts as though he were ready to give Job the benefit of the doubt and to take his part against the wicked, but the entire purpose of his reproof is evidently that of accusing Job of some heinous act, which he wanted him to confess. He also, like many others since his time, had not grasped the purpose of God's chastisement, but accused Job wrongfully.

CHAPTER 9.

Job's Reply to Bildad.

JOB'S DEFENSE AGAINST SUSPICION. — Both Eliphaz and Bildad had attempted to fasten upon Job some specific wrong, seeking from him a confession to that effect. He therefore defends himself against this manner of drawing conclusions in his case. V. 1. **Then Job answered and said,** v. 2. **I know it is so of a truth,** namely, that God is righteous in all His doing, that He never perverts justice; **but how should man,** a mortal being, man in his mortality and weakness, **be just with God?** Even if mortal man should, in his own opinion, be in the right over against God, his own judgment is without value; for no man, as God plainly states, can be just in His sight. V. 3. **If he will contend with Him,** if mortal man should dare to enter into litigation with the great God, **he cannot answer Him one of a thousand;** if man's case were brought to trial, God could and would so quickly embarrass and overwhelm him with questions that he would quickly stand there in mute shame, unable to justify himself in one item. V. 4. **He is wise in heart and mighty in strength;** those are two outstanding attributes of God. **Who hath hardened himself against Him,** stiffening his neck in foolish opposition, bidding Him defiance, **and hath prospered?** With His wisdom the Lord can confuse man, and with His strength He can overcome him; so no mortal can maintain his cause before God. V. 5.

Which removeth the mountains and they know not, without their being aware of the fact; **which overturneth them in His anger**; His wrath strikes them with such sudden fury that they are not even conscious of the change effected by His power until all has been done. V. 6. **Which shaketh the earth out of her place**, causing not only the mountains, but the entire earth to tremble in mighty earthquakes, **and the pillars thereof tremble**, its very foundations are rocked and shaken, Ps. 75, 3; Is. 24, 20. V. 7. **Which commandeth the sun, and it riseth not**, withholding his golden rays from the earth; **and sealeth up the stars**, setting a seal round about them, veiling them by thick clouds and darkening the night as well as the day, as He chooses. V. 8. **Which alone spreadeth out the heavens**, like an immense tent, Is. 40, 22, **and treadeth upon the waves of the sea**, He is their Master; though they rise up in threatening heights, Ps. 107, 26, at His almighty command they must serve Him with meekness. V. 9. **Which maketh Arcturus**, the constellation of the Great Bear, in the northern part of the sky, **Orion**, a constellation of the southern sky, **and Pleiades**, a constellation of the eastern sky, **and the chambers of the south**, the secret places of the Antarctic sky, for in that direction the endless spaces of the heavens were hidden from the sight of the Arabian astronomers. V. 10. **Which doeth great things past finding out, yea, and wonders without number.** Job cheerfully agreed with his friend, chap. 5, 9, on the absolute power and the inexpressible majesty of God. The Lord's great power is put forth not only in the kingdom of nature, but also in His government of man. V. 11. **Lo, He goeth by me, and I see Him not; He passeth on also, but I perceive Him not.** Though his eyes cannot see the great and mighty God, his spirit perceives His nearness, as He sweeps by like a destructive wind before which no man can stand. V. 12. **Behold, He taketh away**, snatching away His victim and all the spoil He chooses to take; **who can hinder Him**, holding Him back from His course, placing hindrances in His way? **Who will say unto Him, What doest Thou?** This thought of God's overwhelming and often apparently arbitrary power now prompts Job to speak in an almost defiant manner. V. 13. **If God will not withdraw His anger**, rather, affirmatively, "He will not cause it to return," He will not recall it, **the proud helpers do stoop under Him**, literally, "the helpers of Rahab cringe before Him," the reference being to a historical or a legendary defeat of some mighty enemies of Jehovah. V. 14. **How much less shall I answer Him**, namely, than such great and mighty adversaries, **and choose out my words to reason with Him?** No matter how carefully he might choose his words, attempting to get just the right expression, he could not escape rebuke on the part of God. V. 15. **Whom, though I were righteous**, even if Job were in the right, free from blame according to standards of right as commonly accepted, **yet would I not answer**, that is, Job could not answer, **but I would make supplication to my Judge**, being brought to the humiliating position of beseeching the Judge, who was his adversary, accuser, and judge in one person. V. 16. **If I had called, and He had answered me**, if Job's pleading would apparently find favor, **yet would I not believe that He had hearkened unto my voice**; he feared that God's infinite exaltation would keep Him from showing such kindness. V. 17. **For He breaketh me with a tempest**, that is, He would overwhelm Job with a storm, should he attempt such a course, **and multiplieth my wounds without cause**, in spite of Job's innocence He would pursue him with calamities. V. 18. **He will not suffer me to take my breath, but filleth me with bitterness**, this being considered the food with which Job should satisfy his soul. V. 19. **If I speak of strength, lo, He is strong**, in a trial of strength Job would, of course, not stand a show; **and if of judgment, who shall set me a time to plead?** If it were a question of right and judgment, the mighty word of God would be thundered at him: Who will cite Me? In either case, there was no hope for weak and mortal man. V. 20. **If I justify myself, mine own mouth shall condemn me**; even if he were right, the confusion of his speech would condemn him; **if I say, I am perfect**, innocent, without guilt, **it shall also prove me perverse**, set him forth as guilty. V. 21. **Though I were perfect, yet would I not know my soul**, he had reached the point where he no longer knew himself; **I would despise my life**, it had become a burden to him. He felt so unspeakably wretched that he wished to die. In all this Job forgot that even the breath of an accusation against God as though He were not just and righteous in all His works is an insult to His glorious majesty.

Job Insists that God Visits also the Righteous with Affliction. — V. 22. **This is one thing**, it is all one, or, it makes no difference whether a person is innnocent or guilty; **therefore I said it, He destroyeth the perfect and the wicked**; this statement Job feels constrained to make against God. V. 23. **If the scourge slay suddenly**, namely, by means of any calamity, **he will laugh at the trial of the innocent**, God will mock at the despair of the guiltless, not permitting Himself to be disturbed in the enjoyment of His heavenly bliss. V. 24. **The earth is given into the hand of the wicked**, this God readily permits; **He covereth the faces of the judges thereof**, veiling their eyes and permitting them to render wicked decisions, to practise unrighteousness; **if not, where and who is He?** Who but God could it be that does this? V. 25. **Now, my days are swifter than a post,** flying away more swiftly than the motion of a courier, or runner; **they flee away, they see no good;** Job despairs of ever being released of his affliction, he has entirely forgotten his former state of prosperity. V. 26. **They are passed away as the swift ships,** sweeping past like vessels of bulrush, known for their lightness and swiftness; **as the eagle that hasteth to the prey,** swooping down upon it with almost incredible speed. Thus Job illustrates the hasty flight of his life. V. 27. **If I say, I will forget my complaint,** making an attempt to rouse himself from his stupor, **I will leave off my heaviness,** literally, "my countenance," that is, his gloomy and downcast look, **and comfort myself,** looking cheerful once more. V. 28. **I am afraid of all my sorrows,** he is once more forced to shudder with pain; **I know that Thou wilt not hold me innocent,** that God would not declare him guiltless. V. 29. **If I be wicked,** rather, "I am to be guilty," declared to be wicked by the decree of God, **why, then, labor I in vain?** It was a useless endeavor on his part trying to appear innocent; he felt that he was tiring himself out without result. V. 30. **If I wash myself with snow-water,** which was considered as containing greater cleansing power than ordinary water, **and make my hands never so clean,** literally, "cleansing my hands with lye," in an effort to purge away all impurities, v. 31. **yet shalt Thou plunge me in the ditch,** into a sink or sewer, **and mine own clothes shall abhor me.** This would happen while he was still naked after his washing and would cause him to become so filthy as to make his own clothes ashamed of him. That is: "Not even the best-grounded self-justification can avail him; for God would still bring it to pass that his clearly proved innocence should change to the most horrible impurity." (Delitzsch.) V. 32. **For He is not a man, as I am, that I should answer Him,** standing on the same level with Him before a court of justice, **and we should come together in judgment.** V. 33. **Neither is there any daysman,** arbitrator or mediator, **betwixt us that might lay his hand upon us both,** acting as umpire between God and Job to settle his case; for God was both accuser and judge. V. 34. **Let Him take His rod away from me,** the scourge and calamity wherewith He was smiting Job, **and let not His fear terrify me,** stupefying him by His majestic presence; v. 35. **then would I speak and not fear Him,** namely, with this handicap of overpowering majesty removed; **but it is not so with me,** in his own person he was not conscious of any reason why he should fear Him. Job's defense of himself becomes so emphatic that it verges on self-righteous boasting, an act against which every believer must guard with the greatest care.

CHAPTER 10.

Job's Direct Address to God.

JOB'S PRAYER FOR ENLIGHTENMENT. — Job now launches forth into a pitiful complaint, addressing God Himself on the great severity with which He was treating him, although He knew that he was innocent of any specific guilt. V. 1. **My soul is weary of my life,** filled with disgust and loathing; **I will leave my complaint upon myself,** giving free course to his sorrowful statement; **I will speak in the bitterness of my soul.** V. 2. **I will say unto God, Do not condemn me,** letting him die the death of a guilty person against the testimony of his conscience. **Show me wherefore Thou contendest with me,** letting him know the definite charge which He preferred against him. V. 3. **Is it good unto Thee that Thou shouldest oppress, that Thou shouldest despise the work of Thine hands and shine upon the counsel of the wicked?** Surely God would not take pleasure, find joy, in cruelly abusing a creature of His own hands, in treating Job as possessing no value, while favoring, at the same time, the success of the wicked and giving prosperity to their endeavors. V. 4. **Hast Thou eyes of flesh?** Would God judge like a man, perceiving the objects only from the outside, judging only by the outward look of things? **Or seest Thou as man seeth?** V. 5. **Are Thy days as the days of man,** of a mortal, changeable creature? **Are Thy years as man's days,** v. 6. **that Thou enquirest,** seekest, **after mine iniquity and searchest after my sin?** Surely God's life was not so short that He was obliged to resort to tortures of this kind, in order to force an unwilling confession of guilt from the mouth of Job. Such a way of dealing could be expected in an earthly ruler, but not in the great King of heaven. V. 7. **Thou knowest that I am not wicked,** rather, "although Thou knowest that I am not guilty"; **and there is none that can deliver out of Thine hand;** although He had all men absolutely in His power, He surely would not act like a tyrant, for they could not escape His justice in any event. Job argued that all three possibilities: gratification of a whim, judgment according to appearances only, and the necessity of deciding quickly, were out of the question in the case of God. V. 8. **Thine hands have made me and fashioned me together round about,** having carefully and elaborately formed and fashioned his intricate organism; **yet Thou dost destroy me!** An exclamation of reproachful amazement. V. 9. **Remember, I beseech thee, that Thou hast made me as the clay,** as a potter fashions a vessel out of clay; **and wilt Thou bring me into dust again?** Out of dust was man originally formed, and to dust he must return. V. 10. **Hast Thou not poured me out as milk and curdled me like cheese?** This describes the entire molding of the body before birth, one of God's great mysteries. V. 11. **Thou hast clothed me with skin and flesh and hast fenced me with bones and sinews,** interweaving them into the pattern of the body in that wonderful process of creation. V. 12. **Thou hast granted me life and favor,** his life having been preserved by reason of the divine kindness, **and Thy visitation hath preserved my spirit;** by the providence of God his life had been spared and the breath kept in his body. Should all these miraculous acts be in vain? All believers should appreciate the wonderful kindness of God; for to all men He gives body and soul, eyes, ears, and all their members, their reason, and all their senses, and still preserves them.

JOB RENEWS HIS COMPLAINT OF HIS AFFLICTION. — V. 13. **And these things hast Thou hid in Thine heart; I know that this is with Thee,** that is: In spite of all God's care in the creation and preservation of Job, in spite of all His apparent kindness in the past, His hidden purpose had planned Job's destruction. V. 14. **If I sin, then Thou markest me,** that is, If Job should sin, God had intended to watch very carefully and immediately charge it against him, **and Thou wilt not acquit me from mine iniquity;** He carefully notes down every evidence of wickedness. V. 15. **If I be wicked, woe unto me!** He must expect a sudden and violent punishment. **And if I be righteous, yet will I not lift up my head,** even if he were right, he would not dare to look up with freedom and confidence, for this would not be acknowledged. **I am full of confusion,** filled with shame; **therefore see Thou mine affliction.** He always had his misery in sight and must hang his head in shame, like a wicked sinner who was getting his just deserts. V. 16. **For it increaseth,** rather, "and should my head lift itself up," should Job dare to show a cheerful courage, **Thou huntest me as a fierce lion; and again Thou showest Thyself marvelous upon me,** God would show His wonderful power in destroying him. V. 17. **Thou renewest Thy witnesses against me,** God would cause ever new witnesses to appear against Job, **and increasest Thine indignation upon me,** with an ever new amount of displeasure. **Changes and war are against me;** Job would have to consider ever new troops and a whole army opposed to him. He alone is the mark of God's displeasure. V. 18. **Wherefore, then, hast Thou brought me forth out of the womb?** He renews his complaint, bewailing the fact that he was ever born. **Oh, that I had given up the ghost, and no eye had seen me!** He would have died, never have seen the light of day, if God had not called him into being. V. 19. **I should have been as though I had not been; I should have been carried from the womb to the grave,** still-born, a corpse, and out of misery. V. 20. **Are not my days few?** Was not the time of his life short enough? Could not God take from him some of the burden which was weighting him down? **Cease, then, and let me alone,** turning His attention elsewhere, **that I may take comfort a little,** enjoy just a little brightness and cheerfulness, v. 21. **before I go whence I shall not return,** or, "go hence and return not," **even to the land of darkness and the shadow of death;** v. 22. **a land of darkness, as darkness itself,** black as the shades of midnight; **and of the shadow of death, without any order,** filled with chaotic confusion, **and where the light is as darkness,** literally, "where it is light as midnight," said of the most intense darkness, an utterly sunless gloom. Job here, in the bitterness of his soul, gave way to a hopelessness which should never be found in a believer, but which sometimes threatens to overwhelm him. It is only the remembrance of God's unwavering kindness, as a characteristic of faith, that will keep us from such depths of despair.

CHAPTER 11.

Zophar Reproves Job.

ZOPHAR TRIES TO REPROVE JOB. — V. 1. **Then answered Zophar, the Naamathite,** chap. 2, 11, **and said,** v. 2. **Should not the multitude of words,** as just brought out in the speech of Job, **be answered? And should a man full of talk,** literally, "a man of lips," that is, of many words, a vain and foolish babbler, **be justified,** be right? Zophar was a man of zealous and violent spirit, and he was very emphatic in his statement that Job must not be allowed the last word in this matter. V. 3. **Should thy lies,** rather, "chatter, vain babbling," **make men hold their peace?** "Men" is emphatic; no one who calls himself a man will remain silent with such talk going on. **And when thou mockest,** both men and God, in Zophar's opinion, being included in Job's upbraiding, **shall no man make thee ashamed?** It was necessary that his statements be refuted, lest he consider himself justified. V. 4. **For thou hast said, My doctrine,** the moral teaching, the tenets which Job had expounded, **is pure, and I am clean in Thine eyes,** Job maintained his purity even over against God. V. 5. **But oh, that God would speak and open His lips against thee,** since such an action would put an immediate end to Job's boasting, as Zophar confidently believed; v. 6. **and that He would show thee the secrets of wisdom,** making known the true, divine wisdom over against Job's doctrine, **that they are double to that which is,** that God's wisdom immeasurably surpasses everything that men consider wisdom! **Know, therefore, that God exacteth of thee less than thine iniquity deserveth,** literally, "that God consigns to oblivion [a large part of] thy guilt," leaving it out of account against Job, who would otherwise long have been overwhelmed by God's punishment. V. 7. **Canst thou by searching find out God,** reaching the bottom of the mystery of God's wonderful essence? **Canst thou find out the Almighty unto perfection,** penetrating to the uttermost parts of the divine nature? "The nature of God may be sought after, but cannot be found out; and the end of God is unattainable, for He is both: the perfect or absolute God and the endless or infinite God." (Delitzsch.) V. 8. **It is as high as heaven,** literally, "heights of heaven," namely, those are the distances which extend between man's understanding and God's infinity; **what canst thou do? Deeper than hell,** far below the realm of the dead the hidden depths of the divine wisdom extend; **what canst thou know?** Man's utter powerlessness in the face of God's immeasurable essence is here brought out with a force rarely equaled. V. 9. **The measure thereof is longer than the earth and broader than the sea,** the length of God's wisdom is unbounded, and its breadth extends far beyond human understanding. V. 10. **If He cut off,** passing over, or rushing upon, in anger, **and shut up, or gather together,** that is, if God arrests a man and calls him to judgment, holds a public trial, **then who can hinder Him?** Who can turn Him aside, who will oppose Him? God will render judgment, God will pass sentence upon every prisoner whom He summons, in spite of all opposition. V. 11. **For He knoweth vain men,** such evil men as try to disguise their godlessness; **He seeth wickedness also; will He not, then, consider it?** The statement is rather affirmative: God sees wickedness without considering it, although it is open before His eyes; He does not immediately punish the transgressors. V. 12. **For vain man would be wise, though man be born like a wild ass's colt,** literally, "And a hollow-headed, witless man will gain wisdom, and the foal of a wild ass a man will be born," which means, either: Before an empty head gains understanding, a wild ass's foal will be born a man, or: A witless fool should be filled with understanding, he should be regenerated and made over into a man, though by nature as untamed as the colt of a wild ass. Zophar wanted to make his rebuke as emphatic as possible, even by means of biting comparisons, in order to overcome Job's calm arguments.

ZOPHAR ADMONISHES JOB TO REPENT. — V. 13. **If thou prepare thine heart,** bringing it into the proper condition over against God, **and stretch out thine hands toward Him,** in a gesture of pleading, of asking for mercy; v. 14. **if iniquity be in thine hand, put it far away, and let not wickedness dwell in thy tabernacles,** for without this evidence of a repentant heart the Lord would not heed his prayer. V. 15. **For then shalt thou lift up thy face without spot;** having received the assurance of the forgiveness of his sins, his face would show no consciousness of guilt; **yea, thou shalt be steadfast and shalt not fear,** without wavering, like metals which have hardened in the mold, v. 16. **because thou shalt forget thy misery,** all the trouble which was now besetting him, **and remember it as waters that pass away,** that flow by in a stream and make no lasting impression upon the memory, v. 17. **and thine age shall be clearer than the noonday,** literally, "brighter than noon shall be the duration or way of thy life," his entire future life would be lifted out of the darkness of the present misery; **thou shalt shine forth, thou shalt be as the morning,** that is, if any darkness should come, if any new adversity should befall him, it would nevertheless resolve itself into the brightness of a clear morning. V. 18. **And thou shalt be secure,** have the firm confidence, **because there is hope,** the text emphasizing the real and lasting existence of this hope; **yea, thou shalt dig about thee,** looking about through his household to find whether everything was safe and sound; **and thou shalt take thy rest in safety,** able to lie down and sleep without the slightest worry. V. 19. **Also thou shalt lie down, and none shall make thee afraid,** in full peace and security; **yea, many shall make suit unto thee,** literally, "stroke thy face," flattering him and begging a special favor from him. V. 20. **But the eyes of the wicked shall fail,** wasting away in a vain search for help, **and they shall not escape,** every refuge being taken away from them, **and their hope shall be as the giving up of the ghost,** death remaining as their last hope, as bringing them deliverance from the evils which were laid upon them. This picture of a hopeful future, as painted by Zophar, was also an unconscious prophecy concerning the deliverance which finally came upon Job.

CHAPTER 12.

Job's Reply to Zophar.

THE STRANGE GOOD FORTUNE OF THE GODLESS. — If Zophar's arguments had been valid and Job's suffering was to be regarded as the direct punishment for a specific sin, then his faith in the justice of God would have been severely shaken. For that reason Job answers in a tone of great severity. V. 1. **And Job answered and said,** in a tone and with words of bitter sarcasm, v. 2. **No doubt but ye are the people,** that is, the right kind, the representative men, **and wisdom shall die with you,** since, by their own statements, they possessed it all, and no one dared to differ with them. V. 3. **But I have understanding as well as you,** he was in no wise lacking in the understanding of which they thought they had the monopoly; **I am not inferior to you,** he was not meaner in wisdom than they and therefore did not have to give way one inch; **yea, who knoweth not such things as these?** What they had brought forward was a matter of common knowledge, by no means unusual; they had no reason to take special pride in their remarks. V. 4. **I am as one mocked of his neighbor,** he had become a laughing-stock to his own friends, **who calleth upon God, and He answereth him,** that is, I who called to God and found a hearing, who had made the worship of God the rule of my life. **The just, upright man is laughed to scorn,** a target for the mockery of those who called themselves his friends. V. 5. **He that is ready to slip with his feet is as a lamp despised in the thought of him that is at ease,** literally, "For misfortune scorn, according to the opinion of the prosperous, ready for those whose foot wavers," that is, fortunate and successful people ordinarily have nothing but scorn and contempt for the unfortunate, for such as are overtaken with misfortune. V. 6. **The tabernacles of robbers prosper,** powerful tyrants, men who make it a practise to spoil others, live in safety, **and they that provoke God are secure,** Ps. 73, 12; **into whose hand God bringeth abundantly,** rather, "he who has God enter into his hand," trusting in the weapon which he wields with his right hand. The strange good fortune of the godless has often puzzled believing children of God, but the solution of the question is found Ps. 73.

GOD'S GOVERNMENT OF THE WORLD. — V. 7. **But ask now the beasts, and they shall teach thee,** every man can learn from them what Job very well knew, the majesty of God in the government of the world; **and the fowls of the air, and they shall tell thee;** v. 8. **or speak to the earth,** addressing it for information, **and it shall teach thee, and the fishes of the sea shall declare unto thee.** All nature unites in declaring the greatness of God. V. 9. **Who knoweth not in all these,** gaining his understanding from observing them, **that the hand of the Lord hath wrought this?** The entire visible universe proclaims the creation of Jehovah. V. 10. **In whose hand is the soul of every living thing,** the life which He has given to all creatures, **and the breath of all mankind,** literally, "the spirit of all flesh of man." All this must be acknowledged by all observers of nature. V. 11. **Doth not the ear try words,** prove sayings or proverbs, testing their inner worth, **and the mouth taste his meat?** Even as the palate discriminates between the foods which are taken into the mouth, so the spirit of man should distinguish between matters brought to its attention. V. 12. **With the ancient is wisdom;** aged men, in the course of their long life, acquire a true insight into the nature of things; **and in length of days understanding;** when a person has lived many years and always carefully observed things, his judgment is usually reliable. But now, by way of contrast and in bringing out a climax, Job refers to God. V. 13. **With Him is wisdom and strength,** He possesses them as His personal qualities, as His essential attributes; **He hath counsel and understanding,** the ability to discern what is right and wrong, sound and corrupt. V. 14. **Behold, He breaketh down,** in the irresistible exercise of His almighty power, **and it cannot be built again,** man being powerless before His might; **He shutteth up a man,** imprisoning him in troubles as in a cistern or dungeon, **and there can be no opening,** there is no escape from His power. V. 15. **Behold, He withholdeth the waters,** restraining all calamity at His will, **and they dry up; also He sendeth them out,** releasing their devastating power, **and they overturn the earth.** V. 16. **With Him is strength and wisdom,** true, essential knowledge; **the deceived and the deceiver are His,** both he who errs and he who causes others to err. God's wisdom is far above that of all men, whether they use their knowledge for the good of their fellow-men or abuse it in leading others astray. V. 17. **He leadeth counselors away spoiled,** stripped of everything they valued, especially the badges of their rank, **and maketh the judges fools,** depriving them of both their power and prestige. V. 18. **He looseth the bond of kings,** breaking the fetters, the yoke, with which they kept their subjects in obedience, **and girdeth their loins with a girdle,** placing them in bonds, in turn. V. 19. **He leadeth princes,** priests who were at the same time rulers, **away spoiled,** all their authority being taken from them, **and overthroweth the mighty,** those who considered themselves firmly established, mighty and influential persons. V. 20.

He removeth away the speech of the trusty, taking away the eloquence of the people's orators and counselors, **and taketh away the understanding of the aged,** so that they no longer have the right judgment. V. 21. **He poureth contempt upon princes,** upon the nobility of the land, **and weakeneth the strength of the mighty,** literally, either, "He causes the dam of the canals to sink down," or, "He lets down that which holds together the containing of great capacity"; that is, He disables the mighty for the contest by causing their undergarments to hang down loosely, a fact which hinders them in fighting. V. 22. **He discovereth deep things out of darkness and bringeth out to light the shadow of death;** that is, all the dark plans and the wickedness of men which they believe hidden from the eyes of men He brings forth into the light. Cp. 1 Cor. 4, 5. V. 23. **He increaseth the nations,** making them great, giving them prosperity, **and destroyeth them; He enlargeth the nations,** spreading them abroad, increasing their territory, **and straiteneth them again,** causes them to be carried away into captivity and to lose all they gained. V. 24. **He taketh away the heart of the chief of the people of the earth,** the understanding of those who are held together by the ties of a common origin, language, and country, **and causeth them to wander in a wilderness where there is no way,** in pathless wastes, following leads which are utterly foolish. V. 25. **They grope in the dark without light, and He maketh them to stagger like a drunken man.** Cp. Is. 19, 14. The entire passage reminds one of the great hymn of Mary with its praise of the strength and mercy of God, Luke 1, 46—55. Job certainly proved that he was in no wise inferior to Eliphaz in His knowledge of the wisdom and strength of Jehovah.

CHAPTER 13.

Job's Further Defense against Zophar.

JOB DEFENDS GOD AGAINST THE SUSPICION OF ARBITRARINESS. — V. 1. **Lo, mine eye hath seen all this, mine ear hath heard and understood it,** gotten the knowledge for itself, namely, concerning all that had been set forth in the last chapter regarding the wisdom and omnipotence of God. V. 2. **What ye know, the same do I know also; I am not inferior unto you;** Job in no way stood behind or beneath his friends in the proper understanding of the Lord's attributes, chap. 12, 3. V. 3. **Surely I would speak to the Almighty,** that is, in spite of the fact that Job had this knowledge and in view of the fact that it seemed folly to speak to his friends in their present attitude of antagonism, while they paraded their knowledge of God in order to confound Job, **and I desire to reason with God,** pleading with Him in defense of himself, confidently hoping for a vindication. V. 4. **But ye are forgers of lies,** literally, "daubers, smearers, of lies," such as invented falsehoods to gain their ends. **Ye are all physicians of no value,** miserable quacks, who were entirely unfit and incapable of applying the proper remedy to the wounds of Job. V. 5. **Oh, that ye would altogether hold your peace!** He would much prefer their saying nothing at all than to have them make matters worse by their bungling talk. **And it should be your wisdom;** they would then not only have had a higher reputation for wisdom, but would also have come nearer to the solution of Job's difficulty. V. 6. **Hear now my reasoning,** his apology or defense of himself, **and hearken to the pleadings of my lips;** as he, in vindicating himself, brought charges against them. V. 7. **Will ye speak wickedly for God and talk deceitfully for Him?** Were they really of the opinion that they must act in favor of God by telling lies and by using deceit? V. 8. **Will ye accept His person?** That is, would they show preference for His countenance, partiality for His person? **Will ye contend for God,** acting the part of God's advocates or lawyers? Their actions seemed to indicate that such was their intention. V. 9. **Is it good that He should search you out?** Did they honestly believe that it would be well with them, that they would be safe, if He would really go to the bottom of things and search out their motives? **Or as one man mocketh another, do ye so mock Him?** Were they under the delusion that they could deceive God, hide from Him the real disposition and sentiment of their hearts? V. 10. **He will surely reprove you,** most emphatically denouncing them, **if ye do secretly accept persons,** showing partiality, the motive driving them being not honest conviction, but selfish interest. V. 11. **Shall not His excellency,** the display of God's exalted majesty, **make you afraid and His dread fall upon you?** The dread of God as the great Judge should have deterred them from their course of action in employing dishonest means against Him. V. 12. **Your remembrances are like unto ashes,** literally, "your axioms, proverbs, or maxims are proverbs of ashes," for such they would become when God would set out to judge and punish them, **your bodies to bodies of clay,** their bulwarks, their breastworks, of reasoning upon which they relied would prove frail mud, altogether unreliable, incapable of resistance. Note that there is an occasional hint of the final outcome of the matter and the rebuke of Job's friends.

Job's Comfort and Prayer. — V. 13. **Hold your peace, let me alone,** they should desist from their undeserved attacks, **that I may speak, and let come on me what will,** he was ready to take the consequences of his open speaking. V. 14. **Wherefore do I take my flesh in my teeth,** anxious to save his body and life at any price, **and put my life in mine hand,** seeking to save his soul or life by one final desperate exertion of all his strength? He had no intention of making such efforts because he did not feel himself guilty of the accusations brought against him. He still trusted in the Lord. V. 15. **Though He slay me,** namely, through the disease which was now racking him, **yet will I trust in Him,** he would not give way to dread for the future, hopeless as it seemed; **but I will maintain mine own ways before Him,** namely, in proving to God the blamelessness of his life. V. 16. **He also shall be my salvation; for an hypocrite shall not come before Him;** that was Job's trust, his pledge of salvation, of final victory in the trial which he was now undergoing, that an unholy person could not come before the Lord. It is the consciousness of his blamelessness which gives him the confidence to appear before God. V. 17. **Hear diligently my speech,** they should listen most attentively to his declaration, **and my declaration with your ears,** his utterance sounding in their ears and demanding the closest application. V. 18. **Behold now, I have ordered my cause,** he had prepared all the arguments for his side of the case. **I know that I shall be justified,** finally be given right in this long trial. V. 19. **Who is he that will plead with me,** contending with him, successfully attempting to prove him to be wrong? **For now, if I hold my tongue, I shall give up the ghost,** if any one should succeed in fastening guilt upon him, he would be silent and let death come as a merited punishment. V. 20. **Only do not two things unto me,** those mentioned in the next verse, calamities and terror; **then will I not hide myself from Thee,** rather standing forth boldly to maintain his cause. V. 21. **Withdraw Thine hand far from me,** keeping from Job the heavy chastisements under whose burden he was groaning; **and let not Thy dread make me afraid,** namely, the dread produced by the revelation of His majesty; for these two factors would take the heart from him. V. 22. **Then call Thou, and I will answer;** with these two factors removed, he would gladly obey the summons to stand trial; **or let me speak, and answer Thou me,** for Job intended to maintain the justice of his cause. V. 23. **How many are mine iniquities and sins? Make me to know my transgression and my sin!** He was ready to have not only his general transgressions, but especially his graver offenses, any flagrant wickedness, any open apostasy, set forth. He does not mention ordinary, small, and slight offenses, the sins of weakness to which all believers are subject. He is speaking of specific trespasses of a grave nature, such as take away faith out of the heart and are often punished directly. V. 24. **Wherefore hidest Thou Thy face,** in apparent displeasure and anger, **and holdest me for Thine enemy?** Such God seemed to him to be, judging from His treatment of Job at that time. V. 25. **Wilt Thou break a leaf driven to and fro,** shaking him, who was already broken with misery, with further terrors? **And wilt Thou pursue the dry stubble?** On account of the fearful visitation which had struck him, Job was like dry chaff. V. 26. **For Thou writest bitter things against me,** in written decrees announcing the sentence of punishment, **and makest me to possess the iniquities of my youth,** his old age, as it were, inheriting the accumulated usury and consequence of youthful sins, a treatment which seemed unduly cruel to Job. V. 27. **Thou puttest my feet also in the stocks,** treating him like a prisoner who was tortured by having his feet fastened to a block, **and lookest narrowly unto all my paths,** watching him so closely as not to permit the slightest freedom of action. **Thou settest a print upon the heels of my feet,** literally, "around the soles of my feet Thou makest marks, or incisions," setting the boundary over which he dared not pass so close that he was really rooted to the ground, so that he was cruelly and narrowly imprisoned. V. 28. **And he,** namely, Job, the persecuted one, **as a rotten thing, consumeth,** wasting away, falling into nothingness from rottenness, **as a garment that is moth-eaten.** The defiant mood of Job once more changes to despair, since God did not answer him, the same feeling which takes hold of believers in our days when they think their prayers for relief are not heeded by the Lord.

CHAPTER 14.

Job Deplores Mankind's Common Misery.

A Complaint over Life's Troubles. — V. 1. **Man that is born of a woman,** feeble, frail mortal that he is, **is of few days and full of trouble,** Ps. 90, 10. V. 2. **He cometh forth like a flower and is cut down,** coming up quickly, maturing rapidly, and withering as soon; **he fleeth also as a shadow and continueth not,** as the shadow of a cloud hastens over the landscape in a moment of time. The entire first verse is really the subject of the second, the clauses showing man's frailty, his mortality, and his natural affliction modifying the subject "man." V. 3. **And dost Thou open Thine eyes upon such an one,** watching him only for the sake of punishing him, feeble and frail as he is, **and bringest me into judgment with Thee?** Job, who considered himself a particularly wretched example of the human race, was placed before the tribunal of God's justice, where he knew that it was impossible for him to maintain his cause. V. 4. **Who can bring a clean thing out of an unclean? Not one.** It is a deep cry of misery over the universal sinfulness of the human race, which caused the unpitying severity of God to strike them all, and Job in particular. The human race having once been contaminated by sin, not one pure person will ever come forth in the natural line of development; the wrath and punishment of God rests on all mortals. V. 5. **Seeing his days are determined,** cut off, sharply bounded, **the number of his months are with Thee,** also established beforehand by God; **Thou hast appointed his bounds that he cannot pass,** the term of his earthly life is set, and he cannot change it; this being so, then v. 6 **turn from him that he may rest,** have surcease from sorrow and misery, **till he shall accomplish, as an hireling, his day,** that he at least, while this life lasts, may enjoy it, as a day-laborer finds pleasure in his day, namely, in the rest which the shadow of evening brings after the day's task is finished. V. 7. **For there is hope of a tree, if it be cut down, that it will sprout again,** the stump sending up a new shoot, **and that the tender branch thereof,** the suckling which is thus growing up, **will not cease.** The date-palm of the Orient is especially noted for its great vitality in this respect. V. 8. **Though the root thereof wax old in the earth,** apparently yielding to decay, **and the stock thereof die in the ground,** the trunk decaying down to the roots, v. 9. **yet through the scent of water it will bud,** it will sprout with new life as soon as the rainy season brings the vigor of water, **and bring forth boughs like a plant,** just like a sapling but recently planted. V. 10. **But man dieth and wasteth away,** lying there prostrate; **yea, man giveth up the ghost,** expiring miserably, without the hope of rejuvenation, **and where is he?** What becomes of him, of his proud body? Cp. Eccl. 3, 21. V. 11. **As the waters fail from the sea,** literally, "the waters roll off," disappear, out of the sea, **and the flood,** a stream, **decayeth and drieth up,** the evaporating of even large bodies of water during the dry season being no uncommon phenomenon in the torrid regions of the Orient, v. 12. **so man lieth down and riseth not,** there will be no return for him to this earthly life, **till the heavens be no more; they shall not awake nor be raised out of their sleep,** they sleep the long sleep of death, which will be terminated only by the great catastrophe at the end of the world. For the ordinary person there is only the dark night of the grave ahead, a poor improvement upon the miserable present. Only the believer has something more and better to hope for.

A PRAYER TO BE DELIVERED FROM HIS AFFLICTION. — V. 13. **Oh, that Thou wouldest hide me in the grave,** secure in the realm of the dead, **that Thou wouldest keep me secret,** safely hidden, **until Thy wrath be past,** change once more into kindness, **that Thou wouldest appoint me a set time and remember me!** Job pleaded to be remembered in mercy, to be reestablished in God's grace. But for him, the reality differs much from this wish. V. 14. **If a man die, shall he live again?** It is the voice of suspicion, of skepticism, which desires to banish all hope for the future, the doubt which endeavors to enter the heart of believers from time to time. **All the days of my appointed time will I wait till my change come.** The figure is taken from the life of the soldier, who will not abandon his post until he is relieved, discharged, or exchanged. The idea of an eventual deliverance from the realm of death is brought out pretty strongly at this point. V. 15. **Thou shalt call,** that is, God would call to him, in granting him the discharge which he hoped for, **and I will answer Thee; Thou wilt have a desire to the work of Thine hands,** God would feel an affectionate yearning for Job, the poor, miserable creature, who was now groaning under such great afflictions. V. 16. **For now Thou numberest my steps,** at this time God was still watching his every move as that of a transgressor; **dost Thou not watch over my sin?** So deep was Job's despair that he believed God was still holding back, that He was still keeping anger, that His full manifestation of it had not yet taken place. V. 17. **My transgression is sealed up in a bag,** his guilt, or wickedness, was kept in remembrance, **and Thou sewest up mine iniquity,** literally, "Thou hast stitched on to my transgressions," that is, made Job's iniquity greater than it was in truth, and then punished him accordingly. V. 18. **And surely the mountain falling cometh to naught,** it crumbles to pieces under the destroying influence of the elements, **and the rock is removed out of his place,** growing old and decaying in the same manner. V. 19. **The waters wear the stones,** hollowing them out by continual dripping; **Thou washest away the things which grow out of the dust of the earth,** the floods of water carry away the fruitful soil very quickly; **and Thou destroyest the hope of man,** for mortal man also perishes without the slightest hope of being brought back to this life again. The strongest and most substantial things in nature are unable to withstand the destructive power of the elements in the hand of God; how much less will mortal man escape this destruction? V. 20. **Thou prevailest forever against him,** overpowering him with His might, **and he passeth; Thou changest his countenance,** disfiguring him, distorting his features in the agony of death, **and sendest him away,** forth out of this earthly life. V. 21. **His sons come to honor,** or, "should his children be in honor?" **and he knoweth it not; and they are brought low,** abased and disgraced; **but he perceiveth it not of them.** Man in the realm of death is utterly ignorant of that which takes place on this earth, being affected neither by the good nor by the ill fortune of his surviving relatives. V. 22. **But his flesh upon him shall have pain,** feeling pain in the thought of his own misery, **and his soul within him shall mourn.** Pain is here, by personification, from our feelings while alive, attributed to the flesh and the soul, as if man could feel it in his body when dead. Note that the restoration of the body together with the soul is assumed in this passage, in a final awakening of the dead.

CHAPTER 15.

The Second Speech of Eliphaz.

ELIPHAZ ATTEMPTS TO REBUKE JOB. — V. 1. **Then answered Eliphaz, the Temanite,** feeling constrained to reply to Job the second time, v. 2. **Should a wise man utter vain knowledge and fill his belly,** literally, "his inward parts," his breast, **with the east wind?** The east wind was noted for its stormy bluster. His point was that Job's own speeches were empty roarings and disproved his claim of being a wise man. V. 3. **Should he reason with unprofitable talk,** contending with arguments that have no point, **or with speeches wherewith he can do no good?** It is not only that empty words convince no one, but also that such efforts at self-justification are useless, being opposed by the facts. V. 4. **Yea, thou castest off fear,** bringing to naught, making void, breaking down true piety, **and restrainest prayer before God,** injuring and removing the proper devotional attitude, both of which are necessary for the observation of proper worship of the Lord. V. 5. **For thy mouth uttereth thine iniquity,** his statements showed that he was wholly influenced, utterly ruled, by his wickedness, **and thou choosest the tongue of the crafty,** of clever sophists, who are adept in the art of covering their guilt with a show of innocence. V. 6. **Thine own mouth condemneth thee, and not I,** like a judge pronouncing a sentence upon one who has been found to be guilty; **yea, thine own lips testify against thee.** Cp. Matt. 12, 37. The position of Eliphaz was this, that Job's empty protestations of innocence were in themselves proofs of sinful actions committed by him, on account of which God had laid such sufferings upon him. V. 7. **Art thou the first man that was born?** Did Job believe that he had the deepest insight into the process of creation and all the works of God? **Or wast thou made before the hills,** brought forth before God created the world, and therefore included in the councils of God from eternity? V. 8. **Hast thou heard the secret of God,** attending the divine councils and getting his information at first hand? **And dost thou restrain wisdom to thyself,** reserving it, keeping it secret, as a confidant of God who refrains from divulging His counsels? V. 9. **What knowest thou that we know not? What understandest thou which is not in us?** Cp. chaps. 12, 3; 13, 2, Eliphaz replying to Job's pertinent questions in this manner. V. 10. **With us are both the gray-headed and very aged men,** or, "Also among us are the gray-haired, the aged," **much elder than thy father,** these old men of the various tribes which they represented ranking with Job in wisdom, for which reason he should not presume to arrogate all wisdom to himself. V. 11. **Are the consolations of God small with thee?** literally, "Too little for thee are the consolations of God?" Eliphaz, who was not suffering with overmuch modesty, meant to say that Job surely should have been satisfied with such words of comfort as he and his friends had brought. **Is there any secret thing with thee?** literally, "a word so gentle with thee?" for Job should realize that his friends were dealing with him in great tenderness. V. 12. **Why doth thine heart carry thee away?** Why should Job's inner excitement, his wounded pride, cause him to meet their efforts with such bitter passion? **And what do thy eyes wink at,** with an excited, angry snapping and rolling, v. 13. **that thou turnest thy spirit against God,** snorting against Him in anger, **and lettest such words go out of thy mouth,** letting his anger break forth in vehement speeches? Altogether, Eliphaz insisted that Job's statements disproved his wisdom, injured the proper reverent attitude toward God, and were utterly wrong. The point of his rebuke is that Job should look for the reason for his sufferings solely in himself.

ELIPHAZ ACCUSES JOB OF IMPIETY. — V. 14. **What is man that he should be clean, and he which is born of a woman that he should be righteous?** Eliphaz here takes up a point which he had broached in his first discourse, chap. 4, 17—20, and which Job himself had conceded, chap. 14, 1—4. If Job admitted man's mortality and frailty in general, he should also concede his own particular wickedness. V. 15. **Behold, He putteth no trust in His saints,** not even in His holy angels, because they are finite and beneath Him in dignity; **yea, the heavens,** the very home of bliss, **are not clean in His sight,** they do not measure up to the essential purity of God's nature. V. 16. **How much more abominable and filthy is man,** or, "much less, then, is the utterly corrupt man," **which drinketh iniquity like water?** The characteristic of natural man is that he is so desirous for wickedness in one form or other that he pants for it like a thirsty person. — After this sharp arraignment of Job, Eliphaz attempts a more objective form of rebuke. V. 17. **I will show thee, hear me,** giving Job the information which he needed; **and that which I have seen,** what he has gained by experience, **I will declare,** v. 18. **which wise men have told from their fathers and have not hid it,** setting it forth without concealment, without deception, without hypocrisy or hidden meanness; v. 19. **unto whom alone the earth was given,** their tribe alone inhabited the land where they first settled, **and no stranger passed among them,** the purity of their race had been maintained from the earliest times, a fact which was considered the sign of the highest nobility. Eliphaz now sets forth this doctrine of the moral order of the world, in order to convince Job of the justice of his sufferings. V. 20. **The wicked man travaileth with pain all his days,** writhing, twisting, and trembling in torments of one form or other, **and the number of years is hidden to the oppressor,** rather, a definite number of years is set aside for the tyrant, the one who commits violence in any manner. V. 21. **A dreadful sound is in his ears,** noises that fill him with terror; **in prosperity the destroyer shall come upon him,** falling upon him in the midst of peace, when he is expecting no such evil. V. 22. **He believeth not that he shall return out of darkness,** he despairs of ever being relieved of his misfortune, **and he is waited for of the sword,** marked out, destined for its attack and for destruction by it. V. 23. **He wandereth abroad for bread, saying, Where is it?** In the midst of plenty the miser is tortured by anxiety concerning his food. **He knoweth that the day of darkness is ready at his hand,** namely, to seize him and to thrust him into punishment of the most severe kind. V. 24. **Trouble and anguish shall make him afraid,** fill him with terror, anguish, and alarm; **they shall prevail against him,** overpower, overthrow him, **as a king ready to the battle,** the rush of the sudden attack sweeping over him and leaving him prostrate and beaten. V. 25. **For he,** the wicked one, **stretcheth out his hand against God,** in a bold show of rebellion, **and strengtheneth himself against the Almighty,** boasting himself in proud insolence. V. 26. **He runneth upon him, even on his neck,** that is, with his neck rigid, with all the muscles of his body taut for the attack, **upon the thick bosses of his bucklers,** as the leader of a whole army of rebels he rushes forward with his weapons of offense and of defense, v. 27. **because he covereth his face with his fatness,** a mark of his unbounded greed, **and maketh collops of fat on his flanks,** having gathered lumps of fat upon his loins as a result of his immoderate indulgence. V. 28. **And he dwelleth in desolate cities, and in houses which no man inhabiteth, which are ready to become heaps,** about to fall into ruins. The description is that of a tyrant who sets aside all regard for the opinion of men, living even among the ruins of an accursed city. The result of such unparalleled insolence is now shown. V. 29. **He shall not be rich, neither shall his substance continue,** his wealth would have no stability, **neither shall he prolong the perfection thereof upon the earth,** literally, "not bow down to the earth the gains of such"; that is, even if the wicked succeed in having the finest stand of grain, the ears do not fill out; they may have a show of opulence, but it is not substantial. V. 30. **He shall not depart,** not escape, **out of darkness; the flame shall dry up his branches,** a parching heat withering his shoots, destroying his hopes for new gains, **and by the breath of his mouth shall he go away,** the Lord Himself sending the last great catastrophe upon him. V. 31. **Let not him that is deceived trust in vanity,** rather, let him not trust in vanity, he deceives himself; **for vanity shall be his recompense,** every one who trusts in the vain possessions of this world will find himself rewarded with their hollow emptiness. V. 32. **It shall be accomplished before his time,** before his appointed time has run its course, the fulfilment of the evil will strike him, **and his branch shall not be green,** the picture of a decaying palm-tree being applied to the wicked person. V. 33. **He shall shake off his unripe grape as the vine,** losing his gains before he has had any enjoyment of them, **and shall cast off his flower as the olive.** As the olive-tree, every other year, casts its blossoms without bearing fruit, so the godless will not realize their hopes, which are directed entirely upon vanity. V. 34. **For the congregation of hypocrites,** the company of the wicked and profligate, **shall be desolate,** barren, having no lasting good fortune, **and fire shall consume the tabernacles of bribery,** the fire of God's judgment devours the dwellings of those who build up their substance on bribery and wickedness. V. 35. **They conceive mischief,** pregnant with misery, **and bring**

forth vanity, and their belly prepareth deceit, bearing it, bringing it forth, as a child of their wickedness. The point of this speech of Eliphaz is, of course, directed against Job, whom he wants to include in the category of such wicked and godless people as he has here described. The same bad habit of drawing unwarranted conclusions and placing innocent men under suspicion is employed to this day, and believers must guard most carefully against the practise of judging and condemning others.

CHAPTER 16.

Job Replies to Eliphaz.

Job Complains of the Unmerciful Attitude of His Friends. — V. 1. **Then Job answered and said,** in repudiating also this speech and its insinuations, v. 2. **I have heard many such things,** he had now heard arguments of this kind in a greater amount than he cared for. **Miserable comforters,** literally, "consolers of distress," **are ye all,** men whose words, instead of comforting and lifting up, only intensified the burden of Job's distress. V. 3. **Shall vain,** windy, empty, **words have an end?** It was about time that they brought something more substantial if they intended to comfort him. **Or what emboldeneth thee that thou answerest?** What particular thing had vexed, goaded, incited Eliphaz so as to feel called upon to bring this new insult? V. 4. **I also could speak as ye do,** he might serve them in the same manner, pay them in like coin; **if your soul were in my soul's stead,** if they were in his place, **I could heap up words against you,** weaving a web of them, stringing them together, in the same form of unnatural statements which came from them, **and shake mine head at you,** in a gesture of questioning scorn, of malicious doubt, just as they had been doing in making him smart under their suspicions. V. 5. **But I would strengthen you with my mouth,** mere words taking the place of real deeds of love, **and the moving of my lips should assuage your grief,** a bitter reference to the hollow consolations which Eliphaz had spoken of, chap. 15, 11. Such sympathy, Job insists, is easily given, since it is so cheap. V. 6. **Though I speak, my grief is not assuaged,** if he gives vent to his misery, it does him no good, namely, with such poor comforters at hand; **and though I forbear, what am I eased?** If he desists from speaking, his pain does not leave, and his friends have no more true sympathy for him than before. Their unmerciful attitude is that of many others of their kind, whose very sympathy for those in misery has a cutting quality, which hurts more than it comforts.

Job Shows the Pitifulness of His Case and Maintains His Innocence. — V. 7. **But now He hath made me weary,** God had brought him to the point of utter exhaustion; **Thou hast made desolate all my company,** his whole family, the loss of which, together with the estrangement of his wife, was doubly hard to bear, now that his friends had become hostile to him. V. 8. **And Thou hast filled me with wrinkles, which is a witness against me,** the fact that God had seized him and placed him in a shriveled and wrinkled condition seemed a witness of his guilt; **and my leanness rising up in me beareth witness to my face,** his wasted condition appeared against him, accusing him to his face, this also being construed as a proof of his guilt. V. 9. **He teareth me in His wrath, who hateth me,** God's anger had apparently made war upon him, torn him, was pursuing him hard; **He gnasheth upon me with His teeth,** as though He were truly enraged against Job; **mine Enemy,** which God now seemed to have become, **sharpeneth His eyes upon me,** whetting them as though He intended to use them for piercing Job through as with swords. V. 10. **They,** the enemies of Job among men, **have gaped upon me with their mouth,** in a gesture of insolent mockery; **they have smitten me upon the cheek reproachfully,** to show their contempt of him; **they have gathered themselves together against me,** coming in ranks and heaps and strengthening one another for the attack. V. 11. **God hath delivered me to the ungodly,** exposing him to the attacks of the unrighteous, **and turned me over into the hands of the wicked,** casting him headlong into the power of knaves and rascals, these harsh expressions being directed also against his professed friends. V. 12. **I was at ease, but He hath broken me asunder,** shattering him, dashing him to pieces; **He hath also taken me by my neck and shaken me to pieces,** like a man who is seized by his head and thrown down over a precipice, where all his limbs are broken, **and set me up for His mark,** the target at which He directed His shafts. V. 13. **His archers compass me round about,** rather, whirred about me His arrows or darts; **He cleaveth my reins asunder and doth not spare,** cutting open vital organs of his body; **He poureth out my gall upon the ground,** spoken figuratively of the violent pain which affected his entire being. The picture is now changed to that of a besieged city or fortress. V. 14. **He breaketh me with breach upon breach,** like a wall which is being battered down by heavy projectiles; **He runneth upon me like a giant,** like a mighty warrior striking down everything in his path. V. 15. **I have sewed sackcloth upon my skin,** stitching it about his loins as a garment of mourning, **and defiled my horn in the dust,** all his power and dignity had been covered with the deepest humiliation. V. 16. **My face is foul with weeping,** burning, glowing red, almost inflamed with the sharp pain caused by the tears, **and on my eyelids is the shadow of death,** he had wept himself almost to blindness or out of life. V. 17. **Not for any injustice in mine hands,** all this had come upon him although no violence clung to his hands, he was not guilty of gross wickedness; **also my prayer is pure,** it was made without hypocrisy, in all sincerity of his heart. V. 18. **O earth, cover not thou my blood,** so that it might cry to heaven in witness of his innocence, **and let my cry have no place,** his call for vengeance should not be quieted until an avenger had arisen for his blood; for Job still believed that God would finally avenge the blood which His wrath had shed, as blood which had been innocently poured out. V. 19. **Also now, behold, my Witness is in heaven, and my Record,** He who attested to his innocence, is **on high,** even though all appearances are now against him. V. 20. **My friends scorn me,** literally, "although mockers of me my friends"; **but mine eye poureth out tears unto God,** directing his tearful entreaty to the Lord for justice and help. V. 21. **Oh, that one might plead for a man with God,** that God would decide before His own tribunal in favor of Job, that He would pronounce him not guilty, **as a man pleadeth for his neighbor,** that God would also decide in favor of Job over against his friends, setting him forth as innocent. V. 22. **When a few years are come,** the years which are numbered very carefully, the last ones which remain before death, **then I shall go the way whence I shall not return,** for Job knew that the course of the illness with which he was suffering was rapid and invariably fatal. Some commentators find a reference to the intercessory work of Christ in the words: The Son of Man for His neighbor. The words may surely be taken as typical of the work of the Savior as our Advocate with the Father.

CHAPTER 17.

Job's Reply Continued.

JOB COMPLAINS OF HIS WEAKNESS. — V. 1. **My breath is corrupt,** or, "my spirit is violently disturbed"; his power of life was fast waning as his bodily organism was succumbing to the illness racking him. **My days are extinct, the graves are ready for me;** his life was like a lamp whose oil was about consumed, and so he saw nothing but the tomb before him. V. 2. **Are there not mockers with me?** or, "truly, mockery surrounds me," namely, in the persons of these false friends. **And doth not mine eye continue in their provocation?** The eyes of Job were obliged to rest, to dwell, on their quarreling, on their contentions, a fact which increased his misery. V. 3. **Lay down now,** Job pleads with God to furnish him a pledge, or security, to bind Himself as surety; **put me in a surety with Thee,** He Himself being bondsman for Job before the tribunal of divine justice. **Who is he that will strike hands with me?** or, "who else would guarantee or furnish me surety?" Both parties in a trial were obliged to pledge a sum or guarantee before court was opened, and it is with reference to this custom that Job asks God to go on his bond. V. 4. **For Thou hast hid their heart from understanding,** his friends were so short-sighted and narrow-minded that they were prevented from seeing and acknowledging Job's innocence; **therefore shalt Thou not exalt them,** not let them prevail against Job, whom they were unjustly accusing. And the attitude of his friends forces another exclamation from his lips. V. 5. **He that speaketh flattery to his friends, even the eyes of his children shall fail,** literally, "he who offers his friends for a prey," exposing them to unjust accusations, as did the three friends of Job, the eyes of his children will languish. The thought is that God certainly could not favor these false friends, since they had betrayed Job's friendship and thus had incurred judgment in which their children were bound to share. V. 6. **He hath made me also a byword of the people,** God had set him as a proverb before the whole world, the name of Job suggested to the minds of men everywhere a great misery inflicted by the Lord; **and aforetime I was as a tabret,** one into whose face the passers-by could freely spit, the object of the most unqualified contempt. V. 7. **Mine eye also is dim by reason of sorrow,** the light of his eyes was expiring from weeping and grief, **and all my members are as a shadow,** wasted away like phantoms. V. 8. **Upright men shall be astonied at this,** they are astonished and horrified that such a fate can strike the righteous, **and the innocent shall stir up himself against the hypocrite,** roused up in anger against the ungodly, his sense of justice being outraged by the prosperity of the wicked. V. 9. **The righteous also shall hold on his way,** that is, in spite of such happenings the truly pious person will cling to his righteousness, **and he that hath clean hands shall be stronger and stronger,** increase in inward, spiritual strength. This is one of the passages which show the purpose of the book, lighting up its darkness like a flash of encouraging brightness.

V. 10. **But as for you all,** Job here addressing himself once more to his false friends, **do ye return and come now,** he challenged them to come forward with some real wisdom; **for I cannot find one wise man among you,** their hearts remained closed to the right understanding of Job's condition, they were still deceiving themselves concerning the actual state of the case before them. Thus false friends everywhere, if once they have rendered judgment, are most unwilling to retract their false statements, preferring, rather, to have their victim suffer unjustly.

JOB'S HOPELESSNESS IN HIS AFFLICTION. — V. 11. **My days are past,** he felt that he was near the end, and he sank back into his former hopeless complaint, **my purposes are broken off,** the plans which he had made for his life were cut off, destroyed, **even the thoughts of my heart,** the projects which he had secretly nursed and affectionately cherished. V. 12. **They change the night into day,** namely, such joyous plans for life as his friends held before him; **the light is short because of darkness,** in the presence of darkness, for, according to the consolations of his friends, his present trouble was just like the darkest hour which just precedes the dawn, if he would but admit the guilt which they ascribed to him. All this was being alleged while Job saw before him only the dark night of death. V. 13. **If I wait, the grave is mine house,** if he hopes for the realm of death as his dwelling-place; **I have made my bed in the darkness,** having spread his couch in the darkness of death. V. 14. **I have said to corruption, Thou art my father,** if he has so cried out to the pit or grave; **to the worm, Thou art my mother and my sister;** v. 15. **and where,** or, "where, then," **is now my hope? As for my hope, who shall see it?** Who would disclose and prove to him that he had any hope of being restored to health and strength? V. 16. **They shall go down to the bars of the pit,** that is, his hope sinks down to the bars of the underworld, to the realm of death, **when our rest together is in the dust,** that is, while his body rests in the dust of the earth, in the grave, his soul would descend into the realm of the dead, the place where the souls are kept till the great day of resurrection. When his hope of death would become a certainty, then the misery of his suffering would become the rest of the grave. Similar sighs are voiced to this day, even by true believers, who are tired of the misery of this world; but they must never turn into impatient demands addressed to God.

CHAPTER 18.

Bildad Undertakes to Reprove Job.

BILDAD ATTACKS JOB. — V. 1. **Then answered Bildad, the Shuhite,** in a reprimand which was more severe even than his first, chap. 8, **and said,** v. 2. **How long will it be ere ye make an end of words?** He accuses Job of hunting for words, of offering long-winded, endless discourses, useless arguments. **Mark, and afterwards we will speak.** Job should first make use of sense, get the proper understanding, then there would be some chance to reach an agreement. V. 3. **Wherefore are we counted as beasts,** as the brute, a harsh allusion to chap. 17, 4. 10, **and reputed vile in your sight,** regarded as stubborn blockheads by Job? V. 4. **He teareth himself in his anger,** an exclamation referring to Job and accusing him of a furious temper, which causes him to tear around in his rage. **Shall the earth be forsaken for thee?** Did Job think that on his account the earth would be depopulated? **And shall the rock be removed out of his place?** Just as little as Job could change the fact that men lived on the earth and that rocks were given their place for resting, so little could he change the fact that suffering was sent as a punishment for crimes of every kind. Just as little as he could expect everything to be plunged into desolation and chaos, so little could he expect the divine order to be overthrown for his sake. Bildad was firmly convinced that his opinion concerning the guilt of Job was right.

BILDAD RECKONS JOB WITH THE HARDENED SINNERS. — V. 5. **Yea,** that is, in spite of all Job's ranting, **the light of the wicked shall be put out,** his prosperity utterly destroyed, **and the spark of his fire shall not shine,** the flames of his snug and safe hearth-fire would be extinguished. V. 6. **The light shall be dark in his tabernacle, and his candle,** the lamp suspended from the crosspiece above his head, **shall be put out with him,** this being a picture of utter desolation to the Oriental mind. V. 7. **The steps of his strength,** the firm and mighty steps which he took in his self-conscious pride, **shall be straitened,** his movements hampered, his power shut in, **and his own counsel shall cast him down,** he is felled by his own wicked designs. V. 8. **For he is cast into a net by his own feet,** driven by his own foolishness, he rushes to his ruin, **and he walketh upon a snare,** over pitfalls. He foolishly thinks that he is walking upon solid ground, whereas it is a network through which he is destined to plunge into a bottomless pit, to his everlasting destruction. V. 9. **The gin shall take him by the heel,** literally, "shall take hold of his heel the trap-net," **and the robber shall prevail against him,** the snare shall fasten upon him, the noose holding him a prisoner. V. 10. **The** snare is laid for him in the ground, the cord of the fowler, and a trap for him in the way, into which he steps unawares. Note the heaping of the expressions emphasizing the fate of the godless person. V. 11. **Terrors shall make him afraid on every side,** fearful thoughts, as sent upon the wicked by God, to disturb him, **and shall drive him to his feet,** pursuing and scaring him with every step that he takes, like specters of horror. V. 12. **His strength shall be hunger-bitten,** or, "his calamity presents itself hungry," it seems hungry, greedy to devour him, **and destruction shall be ready at his side,** waiting for his fall, ready to pounce upon him. V. 13. **It shall devour the strength of his skin,** literally, "the branches of his skin," the members of his body; **even the first-born of death shall devour his strength,** a picture emphasizing its destructive power and pointing out the terrible doom of death. V. 14. **His confidence shall be rooted out of his tabernacle,** he is torn from his tent, his dwelling, in which he trusted, away from everything that made him happy, so that he is deprived of all hopes of the future, **and it shall bring him to the king of terrors,** making him march down to his execution at the hand of death. V. 15. **It shall dwell in his tabernacle, because it is none of his,** literally, "There lives in his tent what is none of his," strange beings making their dwelling there, wild beasts or specters of horror; **brimstone shall be scattered upon his habitation,** being thrown down from heaven like the fire of God, chap. 1, 16, in order to make his dwelling a solitude, the monument of an everlasting curse. V. 16. **His roots shall be dried up beneath,** as in a tree which is dead, **and above shall his branch be cut off,** withering and decaying with the trunk, both the wicked person and his children being struck by God's punishment. V. 17. **His remembrance shall perish from the earth, and he shall have no name in the street,** both in the inhabited part of the land and out on the plains, on the open steppes, the memory of his name would be forgotten. V. 18. **He shall be driven from light into darkness,** out of the happiness of life into the misery of death, **and chased out of the world,** excluded forever from the habitations of men. V. 19. **He shall neither have son nor nephew,** literally, "no sprout, no shoot," neither descendants nor progeny, **among his people, nor any remaining in his dwellings,** not a single one of his relationship escaping the terrible doom of extermination. V. 20. **They that come after him,** the people of the West, **shall be astonied at his day,** horrified at the doom of destruction which came upon him, **as they that went before,** the people of the East, **were affrighted,** seized with terror, the neighbors on both sides feeling the horror which takes hold on men beholding such a judgment of extermination. V. 21. **Surely such are the dwellings of the wicked,** thus it happens to the habitations of the unrighteous, **and this is the place of him that knoweth not God,** does not recognize and honor Him in the proper manner. The point of Bildad's speech and comparison is, of course, this, that the misfortunes which had befallen Job showed that he belonged to this class of enemies of God.

CHAPTER 19.

Job's Reply to Bildad.

JOB REPROACHES HIS FRIENDS FOR THEIR SUSPICIONS. — V. 1. **Then Job answered and said,** v. 2. **How long will ye vex my soul,** torturing his mind with their accusations and insinuations, **and break me in pieces,** crushing him to the point of annihilation, **with words?** V. 3. **These ten times,** that is, very often, again and again, **have ye reproached me,** in attacking his innocence; **ye are not ashamed that ye make yourselves strange to me,** stunning him without shame, trying to overwhelm him and render him stupid with their repeated charges. V. 4. **And be it indeed that I have erred,** for Job had no intention of denying his sinfulness in general, **mine error remaineth with myself,** he alone was conscious of it, he was not trying to lead others astray nor causing them to become partakers of his guilt. V. 5. **If indeed ye will magnify yourselves against me,** or, "Will ye indeed boast yourselves against me?" **and plead against me my reproach.** If they were assuming his guilt without further proof, Job considered their procedure wrong; they should at least try to convict him with sound arguments. It is the way of meddling friends at all times to give themselves grave concern over a supposed transgression on the part of some one they **know.**

JOB COMPLAINS OF THE NEGLECT HE SUFFERS. — V. 6. **Know now that God hath overthrown me,** wresting him, treating him without proper regard for the justness of the case, **and hath compassed me with His net,** like a wild beast which is so wound up in the meshes of the hunter's net that it cannot move. V. 7. **Behold, I cry out of wrong,** crying out in complaint over the violence which he was experiencing, **but I am not heard; I cry aloud, but there is no judgment,** God will not vindicate his just cause, nor will his friends impartially examine and decide his case. V. 8. **He hath fenced up my way,** hedging it up so closely that there is no passage, **that I cannot pass, and He hath**

set darkness in my paths, making it impossible for Job to continue his way. V. 9. **He hath stripped me of my glory,** the honor which his righteousness had formerly given him before men, **and taken the crown,** namely, that of his good name, **from my head.** Cp. Is. 41, 10; 42, 3. V. 10. **He hath destroyed me on every side,** like a building doomed for destruction, which is razed to the ground, **and I am gone,** both his prosperity and his health having been taken from him; **and mine hope hath He removed like a tree,** tearing it out, uprooting it entirely. V. 11. **He hath also kindled His wrath against me,** like a forest-fire, which devours everything in its path; **and He counteth me unto Him as one of His enemies,** regarding and treating him as the representative of all His foes and therefore concentrating all His hostility upon him. V. 12. **His troops come together,** the armies of God, the calamities and sufferings advance, **and raise up their way against me,** erecting bulwarks as they proceed to their attack, **and encamp round about my tabernacle,** besieging him on every side. V. 13. **He hath put my brethren far from me,** driving his nearest kinsmen away from him, **and mine acquaintance,** his very bosom friends, **are verily estranged from me.** V. 14. **My kinsfolk,** his house associates, those who lived with him under the same roof, **have failed,** remained away from him in his present misery, **and my familiar friends have forgotten me,** those whose confidence and respect he had formerly enjoyed. V. 15. **They that dwell in mine house,** the sojourners who partook of Job's hospitality, **and my maids,** all his hired servants, **count me for a stranger; I am an alien in their sight,** an outsider, a man hailing from a strange country. V. 16. **I called my servant, and he gave me no answer,** treating his master with such contempt that he calmly ignored his call; **I intreated him with my mouth,** where formerly a beckoning nod was sufficient, Job was now obliged to beg for any service which he wished to have performed. V. 17. **My breath is strange to my wife,** the evil odor of his festering ulcers had caused his wife to turn from him with loathing, **though I intreated for the children's sake of mine own body,** that is, the stench of his wounds had driven away also other relatives, probably grandsons, Job speaking of his great wretchedness in general terms. V. 18. **Yea, young children,** wicked youngsters, rude and impudent mockers, **despised me,** he had become a target of mockery on every side; **I arose, and they spake against me,** if he did arise to assert his former influence and authority, they made him the butt for their coarse jokes. V. 19. **All my inward friends,** his bosom friends, who enjoyed his confidence, **abhorred me; and they whom I loved are turned against me,** the reference being undoubtedly to the friends who had so openly spurned and attacked him. V. 20. **My bone cleaveth to my skin and to my flesh,** he was wasted away to such a degree that his bones showed through his skin and his flesh, **and I am escaped with the skin of my teeth,** his gums at least not yet having been attacked by the fearful malady, so that he could still speak. V. 21. **Have pity upon me, have pity upon me, O ye my friends; for the hand of God hath touched me,** namely, in this terrible plague with which he was afflicted. He begs for a show of pity, since he is already suffering with the fearful disease, apparently the punishment of an angry God. V. 22. **Why do ye persecute me as God,** why should they assume divine authority in adding their persecution to that which the Lord had laid upon him, **and are not satisfied with my flesh?** Though they were gnawing at his very life with the tooth of suspicion and slander and thus devouring his very flesh, they did not yet seem to be satisfied, but were continuing their persecutions and increasing Job's agony. It is the way of officious meddlers to continue their boring with bland and torturing persistence, thus adding to the misery of the afflicted.

JOB STATES HIS BELIEF IN FINAL VINDICATION. — V. 23. **Oh, that my words were now written!** those with which he protested his innocence. **Oh, that they were printed in a book!** inscribed in a writing-roll, to be kept for later generations as a record of his protest. V. 24. **That they were graven with an iron pen and lead in the rock forever!** chiseled in the rock and the letters then filled with lead, as a witness to future generations. This hope, as Job knew, would not be fulfilled; he could not hope for a vindication of his righteousness before men. But he trusted in another fact, his faith was based upon another wonderful truth. V. 25. **For I know that my Redeemer liveth,** he had that conviction of faith which he, for his own person, held, that his Avenger, his Vindicator, his Redeemer, was even then living, not only as the Possessor, but as the very Source, of all true life, **and that He shall stand at the latter day upon the earth,** literally, "for as the last He will arise on earth." The time will come when the Redeemer will appear as the Advocate and Vindicator of those who put their trust in Him, as the Savior who leads to the beholding of God. When He, on the Last Day, will step on this earth, the many millions of bodies that have returned to the dust will feel the influence of His almighty power, arise from their graves, and join the Redeemer, to be led by Him into everlasting glory. V. 26. **And though after my skin worms destroy this body,** literally, "and afterward will with my skin be surrounded this" (body). He is sure that there will be a glorious resurrection of the body on the Last Day, that the very skin which clothed him during his mortal life here on earth will again cover the flesh which has become subject to decay and corruption. **Yet in my flesh shall I see God,** literally, "Out of my flesh shall I behold God." The body which, in the corruption of death, was stripped of its skin will once more be clothed with that covering, and then, from out of that same body, Job would see God. Job is so sure of this fact that he pictures the scene in concrete terms. V. 27. **Whom I shall see for myself,** literally, "behold unto me," for my benefit, **and mine eyes shall behold, and not another,** not a stranger. It is a beholding, a seeing, in the supernatural manner which is often connected with visions. It is a beholding of God in the bliss of eternal salvation. So great is Job's longing for the wonderful revelation to which he is looking forward that he cries out: **Though my reins be consumed within me,** literally, "are consumed my reins in my abdomen," it is a consuming anxiousness which filled Job in the midst of his great tribulation; he was eating out his heart in longing for the last great day of salvation. V. 28. **But ye should say, Why persecute we him,** if they should still insist upon pursuing him, **seeing the root of the matter is found in me?** If they still persisted in charging him with guilt, with harboring in his own heart the root of the calamities which had befallen him, they should beware. V. 29. **Be ye afraid of the sword,** which the vengeance of God would bring upon them; **for wrath bringeth the punishments of the sword,** the crimes, the transgressions, of the sword are invariably overtaken by wrath, **that ye may know there is a judgment,** the slanderers and blasphemers will finally be laid low by the justice of the Lord, a statement which is full of consolation also in these last days of the world.

CHAPTER 20.

Zophar's Second Speech.

ZOPHAR STATES WHY HE MUST SPEAK. — V. 1. **Then answered Zophar, the Naamathite,** speaking for the second time, cp. chap. 11, **and said,** v. 2. **Therefore do my thoughts cause me to answer,** because the statements of Job filled him with excitement, for that very reason he felt that his reply should be tempered by calm consideration, **and for this I make haste,** he was storming inwardly, he was deeply perturbed, his inward impulse gave him no rest, he felt constrained to furnish an answer because of the surging excitement in his mind, which, however, should be governed by calm thoughts. V. 3. **I have heard the check of my reproach,** he was obliged to hear Job's chiding, to his disgrace, as he regarded it, **and the spirit of my understanding causeth me to answer,** the knowledge which his mind had gained in the course of the dispute furnished him with information concerning the proper way of judging Job, with the latter's insulting attacks. He was eagerly impetuous to give Job back blow for blow. V. 4. **Knowest thou not this of old, since man was placed upon earth,** since earth was inhabited, as far as the accounts of men go back, v. 5. **that the triumphing of the wicked is short,** that it never extends over a long period of time, **and the joy of the hypocrite but for a moment,** that the joyful confidence of the ungodly cannot last? This was probably directed at Job's certainty of eventual vindication, as he had expressed it at the end of his last speech, chap. 19, 25—27. Zophar was a representative of the class of people who feel obliged to parade their own judgment in every case that comes to their notice.

ZOPHAR PICTURES THE END OF THE UNGODLY. V. 6. **Though his excellency mount up to the heavens,** that is, his ambitious plans, his exaltation in rank and power, **and his head reach unto the clouds,** the ungodly apparently gaining all that his heart desires; v. 7. **yet he shall perish forever like his own dung,** spurned, falling into decay, and forgotten; **they which have seen him shall say, Where is he?** He will have disappeared so utterly and quickly that his vanishing will occasion surprise. V. 8. **He shall fly away as a dream and shall not be found,** just as fleeting, just as perishable; **yea, he shall be chased away as a vision of the night,** scared away like a phantom before God's mighty intervention. V. 9. **The eye also which saw him shall see him no more,** even a careful scanning would yield no results, since God's removal of the wicked would not leave a trace behind; **neither shall his place any more behold him.** V. 10. **His children shall seek to please the poor,** that is, they will be obliged to do that by God's judgment, God will compel them to pay out to them, **and his hands shall restore their goods,** through his children, who would be under compulsion to give back the wealth, the money, which he had taken from the poor by his wicked exactions. V. 11. **His bones are full of the sin of his youth,** they were indeed full of the vigor of youth, **which shall lie down with him in the dust,** all the strength and vigor of his body will be laid in the grave. V. 12. **Though wickedness be sweet in his mouth, though he hide it under his tongue,** holding evil in his mouth like a sweet-tasting morsel, v. 13. **though he spare it and forsake it not,** sparing it to prolong his enjoyment of it, **but keep it still within his mouth,** retaining it against his palate, persisting in the lustful enjoyment of his wickedness, v. 14. **yet his meat in his**

bowels is turned, the food of wickedness which he finally swallows, **it is the gall of asps within him,** the venom of serpents in his intestines. V. 15. **He hath swallowed down riches,** all the possessions which he gained by his wicked grasping, **and he shall vomit them up again,** unable to retain what he had so eagerly appropriated; **God shall cast them out of his belly,** administering an emetic to him, forcing him to disgorge his ill-gotten wealth. V. 16. **He shall suck the poison of asps,** this will turn out to be the effect upon him; **the viper's tongue shall slay him,** his punishment will come upon him as quickly as the striking of one of the very venomous serpents of the Arabian desert, whose sting is almost immediately fatal. V. 17. **He shall not see the rivers, the floods, the brooks of honey and butter,** the wicked would get no opportunity to delight in, to enjoy, brooks, creeks, rivers of honey and cream, he would be given no opportunity to enjoy his prosperity. V. 18. **That which he labored for shall he restore,** being obliged to give it back to those from whom he has wrested it, **and shall not swallow it down,** not enjoy it; **according to his substance shall the restitution be, and he shall not rejoice therein,** that is, in the same ratio as he heaped up his property by forbidden means his enjoyment in it would be diminished, he must lack the enjoyment which he had promised himself in them. V. 19. **Because he hath oppressed and hath forsaken the poor,** first crushed and then abandoned the defenseless, **because he hath violently taken away an house which he builded not,** not being able to fit out and to arrange the houses which he gained by unjust means, v. 20. **surely he shall not feel quietness in his belly,** rest in the seat of his gluttony and avarice, **he shall not save of that which he desired,** literally, "with his most valued treasure he shall not escape." The allusion is probably to the fact that Job had been stripped of all he had. V. 21. **There shall none of his meat be left,** literally, "there is nothing remaining to his food," that is, nothing escaped his greediness; **therefore shall no man look for his goods,** his ill-gotten prosperity will not endure. V. 22. **In the fulness of his sufficiency,** while he has more than he needs for his actual wants, while he is surfeited with good things, **he shall be in straits,** poverty and distress will take hold on him; **every hand of the wicked shall come upon him,** the wretched people who were abused by him will inflict vengeance on him for the violence which they had suffered. V. 23. **When he is about to fill his belly,** or, "That it may serve for the filling of his belly," that for once the wicked may have enough and more than enough, **God shall cast the fury of His wrath upon him,** as it glows with a white heat, **and shall rain it upon him while he is eating,** with his food, so that he consumes the fire of God's wrath with every meal. V. 24. **He shall flee from the iron weapon,** while the wicked flees from the iron armor, **and the bow of steel shall strike him through,** the arrow from a brass bow will pierce him. V. 25. **It is drawn and cometh out of the body,** the wicked himself drawing the arrow of God out of his body, in order to save his life, if possible; **yea, the glittering sword cometh out of his gall,** for he himself removes the gleaming steel; **terrors are upon him,** as he realizes that his doom is upon him. V. 26. **All darkness shall be hid in his secret places,** is saved up to strike that which he has hoarded, that is, every kind of calamity will descend upon the precious things which he fondly believed to be safe; **a fire not blown shall consume him,** that is, such a fire as requires no human agency to keep it alive, a supernatural fire; **it shall go ill with him that is left in his tabernacle,** the fire of God devouring that which still remains after former calamities have passed by. V. 27. **The heaven shall reveal his iniquity,** they do so at all times, God Himself witnessing against him; **and the earth shall rise up against him,** all creation testifying the fact that he merits destruction. V. 28. **The increase of his house shall depart,** all that he has garnered, **and his goods shall flow away in the day of his wrath,** when the divine wrath will descend upon him. V. 29. **This is the portion of a wicked man from God,** that which is assigned to him, what he must finally expect, **and the heritage appointed unto him by God.** In the end the wicked has nothing but misery and wretchedness for his portion. In the entire discourse it is evident that Zophar has Job in mind and wants him to apply the statements to himself. The sneering insinuations in similar cases are intended to cut the victim to the quick.

CHAPTER 21.

Job's Reply to Zophar's Speech.

JOB APPEALS FOR CONSIDERATION.—V. 1. **But Job answered and said,** in setting aside the insinuations of Zophar, v. 2. **Hear diligently my speech and let this be your consolations.** What Job was about to state was to take the place of the bungling attempts of his friends to set matters right. At the same time attentive silence would provide more real comfort than all their empty talk. V. 3. **Suffer me that I may speak,** they should consent to his speaking, enduring it once more; **and after that I have spoken, mock on,** this last being addressed to Zophar on account of his cutting statements. V. 4. **As for me, is my complaint to man,** that is, was it in regard to man, did it concern men, being directed against them? **And if it were so, why should not my spirit be troubled?** It was an extraordinary, superhuman burden under which Job was groaning, bearing which he might well have become impatient. V. 5. **Mark me and be astonished and lay your hand upon your mouth,** being awed into silence by the intensity of Job's suffering. V. 6. **Even when I remember, I am afraid,** his own thinking of it made him stand confused and aghast with astonishment, **and trembling taketh hold on my flesh,** his body shaking with terror. "It is to be noted how by these strong expressions the friends are prepared to hear something grave, fearful, astounding, to wit, a proposition, founded on experience which seems to call in question the divine justice, and to the affirmation of which Job accordingly proceeds hesitatingly and with visible reluctance." (Lange.)

JOB POINTS OUT THE DIFFERENCE IN CALAMITIES BEFALLING MEN. — V. 7. **Wherefore do the wicked live, become old, yea, are mighty in power?** Whereas Zophar had maintained that they die early, chap. 20, 5, Job here states that they live on, that they reach a ripe old age, that they are mighty in possessions. V. 8. **Their seed is established in their sight with them;** their posterity, their children, endure, they remain, they surround the wicked, so that the latter have the benefit and the enjoyment of their companionship, **and their offspring before their eyes,** all this in contrast with Job's having been bereaved of all his children. V. 9. **Their houses are safe from fear,** literally, "peace from fear," peace lives in them, and they are far removed from fear, **neither is the rod of God upon them,** namely, for the purpose of punishing them. They suffer neither such terrors nor such scourges as had brought ruin upon Job. V. 10. **Their bull gendereth and faileth not; their cow calveth and casteth not her calf,** neither miscarriage nor any other accident hinders the increase of their herds. V. 11. **They send forth their little ones like a flock,** their large number in itself being a sign of blessing, **and their children dance,** skipping in joyous and healthful play, the possession of a flourishing troop of children being regarded as a piece of good fortune throughout the Bible. V. 12. **They take the timbrel and harp,** singing aloud in their festivities, **and rejoice at the sound of the organ,** a pipe or a set of pipes, the three instruments mentioned being the simplest and the most ancient species, the first representatives of instruments of percussion (tambourines), of string instruments (a small lute or lyre), and wind instruments. V. 13. **They spend their days in wealth,** in the full enjoyment of prosperity, **and in a moment go down to the grave;** having had a care-free life, they enjoy also a quick death, without prolonged suffering. V. 14. **Therefore,** or "yet," **they say unto God, Depart from us; for we desire not the knowledge of Thy ways.** Their prosperity, which should have constrained them to turn to God in appreciation and gratitude, rather makes them proud and conceited. V. 15. **What is the Almighty that we should serve Him? And what profit should we have if we pray unto Him?** Filled with haughty self-assurance, they account the service of God and prayer to Him as useless. V. 16. **Lo, their god is not in their hand!** Their prosperity, as Job contends, surely cannot be a matter of their own power; God must in some way be connected with it, a fact which makes the solution of the problem so difficult. **The counsel of the wicked is far from me.** Job refuses in any manner to take the part of the ungodly or to renounce God, even if he cannot understand this part of the Lord's government. V. 17. **How oft is the candle of the wicked put out!** that is, How rarely is their lamp, the light of their prosperity, extinguished! **And how oft cometh their destruction upon them?** The answer implied is: Seldom enough. **God distributeth sorrows in His anger,** rather, "How often does He distribute sorrows in His anger?" The answer is again implied: It happens only rarely that they suffer calamities; usually they are perfectly happy all their lives. V. 18. **They are as stubble before the wind and as chaff that the storm carrieth away.** Here again a question is intended: How often does this well-deserved punishment strike them? Cp. Ps. 73, 3—8. V. 19. **God layeth up his iniquity for his children,** that is, for the children of the wicked, this exclamation showing what hopes Job still held. **He rewardeth him, and he shall know it,** or, Let God recompense, repay it to the ungodly, that he may feel it. That is what Job expects from the justice of God. V. 20. **His eyes,** those of the wicked person, **shall see his destruction,** feeling the blow of the divine punishment, **and he shall drink of the wrath of the Almighty,** quaffing it like a bitter draught. V. 21. **For what pleasure hath he in his house after him,** what does the wicked care about those whom he leaves behind, what interest has he in their welfare, **when the number of his months is cut off in the midst?** As long as he can enjoy the full term of his life and have the full benefit of its pleasures, the selfish evildoer is satisfied. What comes after him does not bother him. Job implies, of course, that the wicked should therefore be punished during his life, for this very reason, but that events seldom take this just turn. Not only is it impossible, however, to judge God correctly in this respect; His present dealings with men are, in general, beyond the knowledge and teaching of men. V. 22. **Shall any teach God knowledge? seeing He judgeth those that are high,** the heavenly dignitaries, the angels themselves. How, then, can a mere mortal presume to be the teacher of God? V. 23. **One dieth in his full strength,** in the full possession of the highest prosperity, **being wholly at ease and quiet,** lacking nothing in human happiness. V. 24. **His breasts,** rather, his troughs, milk-pails, skins for carrying liquids, **are full of milk, and his bones are moistened with marrow,** literally, "the marrow of his bones is well watered," like rich, irrigated meadow-land. V. 25. **And another,** in contrast with this person, **dieth in the bitterness of his soul and never eateth with pleasure,** not even having tasted of prosperity. V. 26. **They,** the fortunate with the unfortunate, **shall lie down alike in the dust,** in the grave, **and the worms shall cover them.** In death all men are equal, becoming a prey to the worms. No mere man, then, has the right to draw conclusions or to judge the righteousness of God from the evidence of his eyes alone.

Job Rebukes His Friends for Their One-sidedness. — V. 27. **Behold, I know your thoughts,** Job knows the plans of their hearts, **and the devices,** the careful reasonings, the schemes, **which ye wrongfully imagine against me,** doing violence to him by trying to force him into a confession of guilt. V. 28. **For ye say, Where is the house of the prince,** of the mighty and influential nobleman? **And where are the dwelling-places of the wicked,** literally, "the tent of the dwellings of the wicked"? The text emphasizes the splendor and the spaciousness of the wicked person's dwelling. Such taunts as this were directed at Job in fastening the blame of wickedness upon him. Upon this sneering question Job answers. V. 29. **Have ye not asked them that go by the way,** inquiring of travelers well acquainted with history and human destinies? **And do ye not know their tokens,** they should not fail to note and to know what such experienced people would be able to tell them of the different fate of men, v. 30. **that the wicked is reserved to the day of destruction,** held back, spared in the day of ruin? **They shall be brought forth to the day of wrath,** led away from the overflowing wrath, taken beyond its reach. Job's argument is that the wicked must indeed die like every other person, but that he is spared all the misfortune of life, that he is happy to the day of his death. V. 31. **Who shall declare his way to His face?** namely, that of God, in questioning His judgments. **And who shall repay Him what He hath done?** No man will successfully challenge the divine conduct, for God renders to no man an account of His actions. V. 32. **Yet shall he be brought to the grave,** Job here brings out the opinion and experience of travelers, **and shall remain in the tomb,** even after the burial of the wicked his monument or burial mound keeps watch at his tomb and keeps his memory alive. V. 33. **The clods of the valley shall be sweet unto him,** the very earth under which he rests being like a soft couch to him, **and every man shall draw after him,** imitating his example of a happy life and an easy death, **as there are innumerable before him.** V. 34. **How, then, comfort ye me in vain, seeing in your answers there remaineth falsehood,** and nothing else? Since they cast unfounded suspicions upon the character of Job, they were guilty of a perfidious transgression against God, namely, on account of the lack of charity and by reason of the injustice which they exhibited. Note the warning contained in this verse, which bids all men desist from judging and condemning.

CHAPTER 22.

The Third Speech of Eliphaz.

Eliphaz Charges Job with Wickedness. — V. 1. **Then Eliphaz, the Temanite, answered and said,** ignoring Job's argument concerning the prosperity of the ungodly, v. 2. **Can a man be profitable unto God,** no matter how good or how great he may be in this world, **as he that is wise may be profitable unto himself?** This is really the answer to the first part of the verse: God, being absolutely wise, is not influenced by the wisdom of any man. V. 3. **Is it any pleasure to the Almighty,** a gain or advantage to Him, who Himself is perfection, **that thou art righteous?** The most blameless life of men cannot add to His bliss; He is never actuated by selfish motives. **Or is it gain to Him that thou makest thy ways perfect,** striving to be absolutely righteous in his manner of living? God does not reward the pious because they bring Him any benefit by their piety, nor does He punish sinners because their transgressions diminish His blessedness. V. 4. **Will He reprove thee for fear of thee? Will He enter with thee into judgment?** It must not enter one's mind that God was sending this punishment upon Job on account of his godliness, since God never acts from selfish motives, and because the cause of Job's calamity must lie in himself, as Eliphaz supposed. V. 5. **Is not thy wickedness great and thine iniquities infinite?** Eliphaz here boldly draws the conclusion to which his first statements entitled him, as he thought: Because

God sends such afflictions only as punishment for transgressions, and because He is never influenced and guided by any selfish motives and arbitrary notions, therefore it follows that Job is guilty. This accusation he now tries to back up by an enumeration of sins of which he supposed Job had become guilty. V. 6. **For thou hast taken a pledge from thy brother for naught,** there being no need for Job, who had been wealthy, to be so exacting in collecting moneys due him from his relatives, **and stripped the naked of their clothing,** taking even the last piece of garment which they possessed, Ex. 22, 25. 26; Deut. 24, 6. 10. 11, against every sentiment of humanity. V. 7. **Thou hast not given water to the weary to drink,** as they fainted in their thirst, **and thou hast withholden bread from the hungry,** thus setting aside the fundamental demands of charity. V. 8. **But as for the mighty man,** literally, "the man of the arm or fist," **he had the earth, and the honorable man dwelt in it,** that is, the honored, influential one. Thus Eliphaz accused Job of selfishness and greed, of taking the whole land for himself and letting the poor suffer. V. 9. **Thou hast sent widows away empty,** when they appealed to him for help, **and the arms of the fatherless have been broken,** they were treated with the most inhuman cruelty, deprived of all their rights and powers. V. 10. **Therefore,** as a punishment of such sins, **snares are round about thee,** various forms of destruction besieged him, **and sudden fear troubleth thee,** a sudden deadly anguish overpowered him time and again, v. 11. **or darkness, that thou canst not see,** the night of suffering admitting no ray of consoling light; **and abundance of waters cover thee,** bursting upon him with overwhelming misery. It was a bitter and unjust accusation which Eliphaz heaped upon Job.

Warning to Avoid Further Punishments. V. 12. **Is not God in the height of heaven,** the infinitely Exalted One, ruling the world and punishing evil? **And behold the height of the stars, how high they are!** God is immensely exalted over puny man with his feeble criticism of divine justice and every suspicion of God's wisdom. V. 13. **And thou sayest, How doth God know?** His wisdom cannot extend to the every-day affairs of men. **Can He judge through the dark cloud?** The idea is that God is wholly separated and shut off from the business of men, so that He does not concern Himself about them. V. 14. **Thick clouds are a covering to Him that He seeth not; and He walketh in the circuit of heaven,** on its immense vault, so engrossed in His own exaltation that He overlooks and neglects the affairs of the insignificant world of men. V. 15. **Hast thou marked the old way which wicked men have trodden?** Did Job intend to observe and follow the way of the wicked children of the world? V. 16. **Which were cut down out of time,** being swept away by a calamity before they had reached the normal span of life, **whose foundation was overflown with a flood,** the place where they and their dwellings stood became fluid as quicksand, causing them to sink down; v. 17. **which said unto God, Depart from us! and what could the Almighty do for them?** Both speeches are attributed to the ungodly, with whom Eliphaz here classes Job, in allusion to chap. 21, 14. 15. V. 18. **Yet He filled their houses with good things,** it was God who had granted to these very scoffers the prosperity which they enjoyed; **but the counsel of the wicked is far from me!** Eliphaz here echoes the declaration of Job, chap. 21, 16, but includes Job in the number of the wicked. V. 19. **The righteous see it and are glad,** namely, over the destruction which would surely come upon the wicked; **and the innocent laugh them to scorn,** mocking at those whose insolence has such a shameful end. V. 20. **Whereas our substance is not cut down, but the remnant of them the fire consumeth.** That is the sum of the mocking speeches which the righteous heap upon the ungodly: Verily, destroyed is our adversary, and what is left of their prosperity the fire has devoured! In this sneering manner Eliphaz attempted to apply the doctrine of divine retribution to the case of Job.

An Admonition to Repent. — V. 21. **Acquaint now thyself with Him,** make friends with the Lord while there is yet time, **and be at peace; thereby good shall come unto thee,** Job would again receive the blessing of the Lord if he would but repent of his wickedness. V. 22. **Receive, I pray thee, the law from His mouth,** the instruction from the mouth of God should guide him on the right way, **and lay up His words in thy heart,** he should keep them like a precious treasure from which he might draw at all times. V. 23. **If thou return to the Almighty,** coming close to Him once more by real sorrow and penitence, **thou shalt be built up, thou shalt put away iniquity far from thy tabernacles,** for that must ever be the result of the true godly sorrow over sins. V. 24. **Then shalt thou lay up gold as dust,** casting down the gold ore as it comes from the mines as so much worthless trash, **and the gold of Ophir as the stones of the brooks,** dropping it among the pebbles of the streams as possessing no lasting value. V. 25. **Yea, the Almighty shall be thy defense,** literally, "and shall become the Almighty thy pieces of gold," Job's one rich treasure, **and thou shalt have plenty of silver,** silver in bars or heaps, the greatest riches in the possession of God's mercy. V. 26. **For then shalt thou have thy delight in the Almighty,** since in Him is the greatest joy of the righteous, **and shalt lift up thy face unto God,** with the confidence of a favorite son. V. 27. **Thou shalt make thy prayer unto Him,** with a firm trust in God's willingness to hear, **and He shall hear thee, and thou shalt pay thy vows,** fulfilling the pledges which he had made in the event of his prayer's being heard. V. 28. **Thou shalt also decree a thing,** planning the doing of it, **and it shall be established unto thee,** it will surely come to pass; **and the light shall shine upon thy ways,** his labors would surely be crowned with success. V. 29. **When men are cast down,** or "when his ways led downwards," into trouble of any kind, **then thou shalt say, There is lifting up,** that is, Upward, arise! a call of encouragement; **and he shall save the humble person,** bringing salvation or deliverance to the man of downcast eyes. Job would, in turn, be able to comfort and inspire all men who might find themselves in trouble. V. 30. **He shall deliver the island of the innocent,** rather, "God will rescue him that is not guiltless"; **and it is delivered by the pureness of thine hands,** God, on account of His high regard for Job, would be gracious even to others who were in need of atonement for their sins. In his zeal Eliphaz overshoots the mark, attributing to Job's conversion a power which it could never possess. It is the way of professional exhorters to make extravagant statements and to ascribe to men what God alone can perform, and that out of pure grace.

CHAPTER 23.

Job's Answer to Eliphaz.

Job Desires a Judicial Decision of God. V. 1. **Then Job answered and said,** v. 2. **Even to-day is my complaint bitter,** full of defiance, maintaining its attitude of opposition against the admonitions of Eliphaz; **my stroke is heavier than my groaning,** his hand was weighing down heavily upon his groaning, he was constrained once more to break forth in moaning. V. 3. **Oh, that I knew where I might find Him! that I might come even to His seat,** come before God's judgment-seat and present his plea, make his defense. V. 4. **I would order my cause before Him,** stating in order the reasons for his plea, **and fill my mouth with arguments,** with objections, with proofs for the justice of his cause. V. 5. **I would know the words which He would answer me, and understand what He would say unto me,** this knowledge enabling him to make his defense successfully. V. 6. **Will He plead against me with His great power,** making use of His omnipotence to overthrow the contention of Job? **No; but He would put strength in me,** regard Job favorably. He feels confident that, if he could only find God and cause Him to take up his case, He would give him a hearing, not letting His omnipotent majesty stand in the way. V. 7. **There the righteous might dispute with Him,** he who pleads would be shown to be a righteous man; **so should I be delivered forever from my Judge,** he would escape condemnation on the part of the Judge by virtue of his uprightness. With all evidences of weakness Job still clung to his trust in the Lord — a type for all those in affliction.

Job Despairs of Finding Vindication in This Life. — V. 8. **Behold, I go forward, but He is not there; and backward, but I cannot perceive Him;** whether he goes to the east or to the west, he cannot find the judgment-seat of God, and so the joyful prospect which just opened hopefully before him is again swept away; v. 9. **on the left hand,** that is, to the North, **where He doth work,** where His activity is evident, **but I cannot behold Him; He hideth Himself on the right hand,** turning to the south, **that I cannot see Him.** No matter in which quarter of the world he seeks the omnipresent God, he is disappointed in his hope of finding God's visible presence, the throne of His judgment. V. 10. **But He,** while concealing Himself and thus escaping the necessity of acknowledging the innocence of the sufferer, **knoweth the way that I take,** He knows Job's accustomed way, that which he always took, that which his conscience approved. **When He hath tried me, I shall come forth as gold,** like the purest precious metal out of the crucible of the assayer, innocent of any specific great crime. V. 11. **My foot hath held His steps,** clinging firmly and unwaveringly to the path pointed out by God; **His way have I kept,** observing it most carefully, **and not declined.** V. 12. **Neither have I gone back from the commandment of His lips,** he has in no way departed from the Law of God; **I have esteemed the words of His mouth more than my necessary food,** literally, "more than that appointed to me have I kept the sayings of His mouth"; Job regarded them more highly than anything which he may have considered his due portion. V. 13. **But He is in one mind,** He is unchangeable, constant in all His work, **and who can turn Him,** causing Him to swerve from His fixed purpose? **And what His soul desireth, even that He doeth,** the reference being to the determination of God, as Job sees it, to cause him suffering. V. 14. **For He performeth the thing that is appointed for me,** accomplishing the destiny which He had ordained for Job; **and many such things are with Him,** this including all similar decrees affecting mankind in general. V. 15. **Therefore am I troubled at His presence,** trembling before the face of

God; **when I consider, I am afraid of Him,** aghast at His unfathomable decree, which laid such suffering upon him. V. 16. **For God maketh my heart soft,** causing it to be faint, to lose all courage, **and the Almighty troubleth me,** plunging him into confusion, anguish, and terror, v. 17. **because I was not cut off before the darkness,** his calamity alone did not strike him with dumb terror, **neither hath He covered the darkness from my face,** he did not shrink back from his own face, though it showed the evidence of the deepest misery. Job indeed realized the depth of his suffering, but that was not the real reason for his destruction. This was due rather to the condemning attitude of God which took all hope and comfort from him and plunged him into the deepest despair.

CHAPTER 24.

Job's Complaint Continued.

THE HIDDEN WAYS OF GOD WITH REGARD TO THE WICKED. — V. 1. **Why, seeing times are not hidden from the Almighty,** judicial terms, at which He might condemn the wicked as they deserve, do **they that know Him not see His days?** Why do His friends not see such days of judgment, have evidence that God does punish the ungodly? The underlying thought is that there is no just retribution for the wicked, that God does not seem to care how men sin or suffer. Job now mentions some such hideous transgressions which apparently go unpunished. V. 2. **Some remove the landmarks,** change the boundaries in their own favor; **they violently take away flocks and feed thereof,** becoming guilty of plunder and robbery, brazenly pasturing the stolen flocks. V. 3. **They drive away the ass of the fatherless, they take the widow's ox for a pledge,** in either case taking the most valued possession of the defenseless, the animal upon which their livelihood depended. V. 4. **They turn the needy out of the way,** disdainfully thrusting them out of the way into roadless regions; **the poor of the earth hide themselves together,** being obliged to hide before the insolence of their oppressors. V. 5. **Behold, as wild asses in the desert,** in untamed fierceness and absolute disregard of other people's rights, **go they forth to their work; rising betimes for a prey,** eager for plunder; **the wilderness yieldeth food for them and for their children,** "the steppe, with its scant supply of roots and herbs, is to him food for the children" (Delitzsch), and what the desert does not furnish him he obtains by a life of robbery and plunder. The wild asses of the waste regions, untractable in their love of freedom, are represented as a type of gregarious vagrants, of freebooters, who live by plunder. V. 6. **They reap every one his corn in the field,** they are always lucky in getting enough fodder for their cattle; **and they gather the vintage of the wicked,** gleaning the late-ripe fruit, boldly stealing it whenever it suits their purpose. V. 7. **They cause the naked to lodge without clothing,** the poor, oppressed by the wicked robbers, are deprived even of their one garment which served for their covering by night, **that they have no covering in the cold.** V. 8. **They are wet with the showers of the mountains,** where the poor try to find refuge, **and embrace the rock for want of a shelter,** clinging closely to it, crouching beneath it in the vain attempt to find a covering. The description of the tyrants themselves is now resumed. V. 9. **They pluck the fatherless from the breast,** snatching orphans from the arms of their mothers in order to bring them up as slaves, **and take a pledge of the poor,** what little is left to the miserable one they appropriate with a show of right. V. 10. **They cause him to go naked without clothing,** literally, "Naked they [the poor] slink about, without clothing," **and they take away the sheaf from the hungry,** rather, "and hungry they [the poor] bear the sheaves," namely, for the rich, who press them into their service without even giving them sufficient food for their needs, v. 11. **which make oil within their walls,** under strict supervision they are obliged to press out the oil from the olives, **and tread their wine-presses,** stamping out the grapes in the wine-vats, **and suffer thirst,** not even permitted to quench their thirst while engaged in working for the rich oppressors. V. 12. **Men groan from out of the city,** strong men moan with the torture to which they are put, which threatens their very lives, **and the soul of the wounded crieth out,** as the wicked attack them with weapons of blood; **yet God layeth not folly to them,** He does not seem to regard the violence of the godless while they are engaged in this manner. It is a source of great surprise to Job, he cannot understand it, that God should not heed this mockery of the divine order. V. 13. **They are of those that rebel against the light,** enemies of the light, of that which is good and noble, children of darkness and night, Rom. 13, 12; 1 Thess. 5, 8; **they know not the ways thereof nor abide in the paths thereof,** they will not know the ways of the light, where their deeds may be seen by all men, John 3, 20. 21. V. 14. **The murderer rising with the light,** at the dawn, before it is yet broad daylight, **killeth the poor and needy,** slaying the defenseless to satisfy his bloodthirstiness, **and in the night is as a thief,** when there are no unsuspecting wanderers to strike down, he plies his trade as burglar. V. 15. **The eye also of the adulterer waiteth for the twilight,** the approach of the evening when he can follow his unclean craft, saying, **No eye shall see me; and disguiseth his face,** putting on not only a heavy veil, but apparently assuming the garments of a woman, in order to remain unknown. V. 16. **In the dark they dig through houses,** the walls of the poorer houses being constructed of dried mud, through which the thief could force his way, **which they had marked for themselves in the daytime; they know not the light,** literally, "they shut up themselves during the day and want to know nothing of its light." A fine description of criminals. V. 17. **For the morning is to them even as the shadow of death;** the darkest night is like morning to them, for then they start out on their nefarious pursuits. **If one know them, they are in the terrors of the shadow of death;** they are as familiar with the terrors of the darkest night as honest men are with the open day and therefore do not shun them. The description tallies exactly with that of criminals of all times.

OTHER CASES SEEM TO SUPPORT JOB'S IDEA. V. 18. **He is swift as the waters,** he is swept away irresistibly, as by a flood; **their portion is cursed in the earth,** whatever they have called their own; **he beholdeth not the way of the vineyards,** that is, he does not enter there any more, the wealthy evil-doer is kept from enjoying his ill-gotten possessions. V. 19. **Drought and heat consume the snow-waters,** bearing them away, lapping them up, consuming them quickly; **so doth the grave those which have sinned,** they are swallowed, consumed, by the realm of the dead. V. 20. **The womb,** the mother who bore him, **shall forget him; the worm shall feed sweetly on him,** enjoying the pleasant meal which his dead body offers; **he shall be no more remembered; and wickedness shall be broken as a tree,** iniquity is like a felled tree, suddenly chopped down. V. 21. **He evil entreateth the barren that beareth not,** plundering her who has no children to protect her, **and doeth not good to the widow,** showing himself unmerciful to all the defenseless. V. 22. **He draweth also the mighty with His power,** God preserves the men of might by His strength, prolonging the life of such mighty evil-doers. **He riseth up, and no man is sure of life,** literally, "such a one rises up again although not sure of his life," even when he has despaired of his life. V. 23. **Though it be given him to be in safety whereon he resteth,** that is, God grants him a quiet existence so that he is sustained in life, **yet His eyes are upon their ways,** God watches over the paths of the prosperous wicked, blesses and protects them. V. 24. **They are exalted for a little while, but are gone and brought low; they are taken out of the way as all other,** they perish like the rest, **and cut off as the tops of the ears of corn,** the spikes of the wheat-stalks, the harvesting at that time being largely done by the process of heading. V. 25. **And if it be not so now, who will make me a liar,** convicting him of falsehood, **and make my speech nothing worth?** Job very emphatically expresses his conviction that he now had the advantage of his opponents, by virtue of the arguments which he last advanced. He felt that they could offer no solution to the riddle which confronted them in the fact of his affliction.

CHAPTER 25.

Bildad Rebukes Job Again.

Since Job had asserted his innocence in such emphatic terms, Bildad believed it incumbent upon him to reprove him, chiefly in two propositions, namely, that man cannot argue with God, and that no man is pure before God. He thereby changed the issue; for the original point of the friends had been that Job's affliction proved him guilty of some special transgression in the sight of God. V. 1. **Then answered Bildad, the Shuhite, and said,** speaking for the last time, v. 2. **Dominion and fear are with Him,** the awe through which God exercises His sovereign power; **He maketh peace in His high places,** even the heavens and all their host being subject to Him and bowing to His decrees without argument. V. 3. **Is there any number of His armies,** of whatever forces of angels and of heavenly powers He chooses to carry out His will? **And upon whom doth His light arise?** The great light of God's majesty surpasses all understanding of creatures, it cannot be grasped by their finite minds, 1 Tim. 6, 16. It shuts off in advance all criticism on the part of men. V. 4. **How, then, can man be justified with God?** How could any mortal hope to vindicate himself in God's sight? **Or how can he be clean that is born of a woman?** It is impossible for any man to contend with the Almighty in the hope of establishing his moral purity. V. 5. **Behold even to the moon, and it shineth not,** the moon itself pales beside the absolute glory of God's light; **yea, the stars are not pure in His sight,** their scintillating brilliancy also fades into darkness beside God's majesty. V. 6. **How much less man, that is a worm,** mortal man being like a maggot given to corruption in God's sight, **and the son of man, which is a worm,** weak and groveling in the dust before the Lord's almighty power! So Bildad emphasized the general sinfulness of man, his statements implying the admonition that Job should now confess with proper humility. It is so much easier to reprove others than to take a proper inventory of one's own weaknesses and sins.

CHAPTER 26.

Job's Reply to Bildad.

A SHARP IRONICAL REPROOF. — V. 1. **But Job answered and said,** v. 2. **How hast thou helped him that is without power?** How fine, indeed, how excellently well had Bildad shown himself a friend to Job, enfeebled as the latter was with illness! **How savest thou the arm that hath no strength?** coming to the rescue of him whose physical stamina had been taken from him. V. 3. **How hast thou counseled him that hath no wisdom?** For the friends had declared Job to be an ignorant fool. Their intention may have been good enough, Job bitterly declares, but they certainly had a strange way of showing their friendly interest. **And how hast thou plentifully declared the thing as it is,** sufficiently and abundantly exhibited proper and thorough knowledge, a real understanding of matters? V. 4. **To whom hast thou uttered words?** Did Bildad really hope to strike Job with his empty talk? Did he realize that it would not make the slightest impression on him? **And whose spirit came from thee?** From whom had he gotten his inspiration for the wisdom which he promulgated? Surely not from God; probably from Eliphaz? Much of the cruel and biting criticism practised among men is a mere repetition of statements which have been made by others.

A DESCRIPTION OF GOD'S SURPASSING GLORY. Job now, in order to refute Bildad more thoroughly, shows his understanding of the almighty power of God both in the creation and in the government of the world. V. 5. **Dead things are formed from under the waters and the inhabitants thereof,** the giant shades or phantoms of the dead whirl and writhe in the underworld, shaking with every manifestation of the divine majesty. V. 6. **Hell is naked before Him,** the very abode of darkness cannot hide before His omniscient eye, **and destruction,** the abyss of hell, **hath no covering,** all its wasting horrors are open before the eyes of God. V. 7. **He stretcheth out the north over the empty place,** the northern half of the vault of heaven being compared to a great canopy which the Creator spread out, **and hangeth the earth upon nothing,** it is suspended in space, held there by His almighty power. V. 8. **He bindeth up the waters in His thick clouds,** shutting them in, holding them suspended as in immense containers; **and the cloud is not rent under them,** it does not burst under the enormous pressure of the water, the laws of rain being entirely of God's appointment. V. 9. **He holdeth back the face of His throne,** enshrouding the throne of heaven by causing clouds to come between it and the earth, **and spreadeth His cloud upon it,** to screen the majesty of His power from profane eyes. V. 10. **He hath compassed the waters with bounds,** literally, "He has rounded off a circular boundary on the face of the waters," the horizon appearing as a bounding circle, **until the day and night come to an end,** where the light merges into darkness. V. 11. **The pillars of heaven,** the great mountains which seem to bear on their summits the great vault of heaven, **tremble and are astonished at His reproof,** both by reason of earthquakes and by the awe-inspiring peals of His thunderstorms. V. 12. **He divideth the sea with His power,** frightening up, arousing, its billows in frightful storms, **and by His understanding He smiteth through the proud,** literally, "Rahab," a great monster of the deep. As the sea is aroused to the greatest pitch of fury at His command, so it subsides into stillness at His word. V. 13. **By His spirit He hath garnished the heavens,** His breath scatters the clouds and brightens the face of the sky; **His hand hath formed the crooked serpent,** pierces or strangles the constellation of the Dragon, which popular belief brought into connection with eclipses. V. 14. **Lo, these are parts of His ways,** just a few instances, accessible to our understanding, of His almighty power in the government of the world; **but how little a portion is heard of Him!** What evidences of God's great majesty we hear in all these natural phenomena are but the faintest whisperings of His real essence. **But the thunder of His power, who can understand?** It would be impossible for frail mortal beings to comprehend a full revelation of His omnipotence. The divine glory surpasses all human knowledge to an infinite degree; even the works of God's creation and providence are past finding out.

CHAPTER 27.

Job's Final Address to His Friends.

JOB AGAIN PROTESTS HIS INNOCENCE. — V. 1. **Moreover, Job continued his parable,** his proverbial discourse, **and said,** v. 2. **As God liveth,** a solemn oath intended to impress his hearers with the importance of his statements, **who hath taken away my judgment,** who refused to give Job right in this case, who would not declare him innocent, **and the Almighty, who hath vexed my soul,** filling it with bitter anxiety and sorrow, v. 3. **all the while my breath is in me, and the spirit of God is in my nostrils,** Job still possessed life and breath, he could still give a valid testimony concerning his innocence: v. 4. **my lips shall not speak wickedness**, falseness, lies, **nor my tongue utter deceit!** Such were the contents of Job's solemn oath that he would speak the full truth without fear or favor. V. 5. **God forbid that I should justify you**, that is, Far be it from me to declare you to be right; **till I die I will not remove mine integrity from me**, he would not cease to assert his innocence. V. 6. **My righteousness I hold fast and will not let it go**, in spite also of the sneering remark of his wife, chap. 2, 9; **my heart shall not reproach me so long as I live**, not blaming him for one deliberate wickedness during his whole life. V. 7. **Let mine enemy be as the wicked and he that riseth up against me**, the adversary of Job, **as the unrighteous**, that being the just reward of Job's enemies for doubting and disputing his innocence. V. 8. **For what is the hope of the hypocrite**, of an ungodly person, **though he hath gained, when God taketh away his soul**, when God cuts off, when God draws forth his soul? The evildoer has nothing to hope for any more when God once severs the thread of his life and takes his soul from him. V. 9. **Will God hear his cry when trouble cometh upon him?** Cp. Ps. 66, 18. The answer evidently is that the Lord would pay no attention to him, but would let him be submerged in his misery. V. 10. **Will he delight himself in the Almighty? Will he always call upon God?** There is no possibility of a trusting, joyful, loving fellowship between the ungodly person and God. Even when the heart of the believer is filled with dread and apprehension, his trust in God is unwavering, even though it be necessary for the Spirit to make intercession for him with groanings which cannot be uttered.

Belief in the Final Destruction of the Ungodly. — V. 11. **I will teach you by the hand of God**, concerning the way, the manner, in which His hand works; **that which is with the Almighty will I not conceal**, he would declare to his friends the very counsels and thoughts of God which govern His dealings with men. V. 12. **Behold, all ye yourselves have seen it**, he concedes that the final lot of the wicked is often one of extreme affliction, he agrees to accept this observation; **why, then, are ye thus altogether vain**, guided so completely by empty and foolish delusions? V. 13. **This is the portion of the wicked man with God**, the lot which is bound to strike him, **and the heritage of oppressors which they shall receive of the Almighty**, the judgment of God being carried out chiefly in three forms of punishment, as Job now shows. V. 14. **If his children be multiplied**, their great number being considered a proof of the divine blessing, **it is for the sword**, that being the first great scourge in the hand of God; **and his offspring shall not be satisfied with bread**, famine being a second scourge of nations. V. 15. **Those that remain of him shall be buried in death**, those who escaped the first punishments would become victims of the pestilence; **and his widows shall not weep**, being hindered even from observing the usual ceremonies of mourning by the severity of the plague. V. 16. **Though he heap up silver as the dust**, in immeasurable quantities, **and prepare raiment**, fine garments, **as the clay**, that they are as numerous, as common, as the mud of the streets; v. 17. **he may prepare it, but the just shall put it on**, for he will enter into the heritage of the godless, **and the innocent shall divide the silver**, Cp. Ps. 37, 29. 34; Eccl. 2, 16. V. 18. **He buildeth his house as a moth**, a frail and temporary dwelling, **and as a booth that the keeper maketh**, a shed which a watchman puts up for a few days. V. 19. **The rich man shall lie down, but he shall not be gathered**, he lies down once and not again, that is, he never arises; **he openeth his eyes, and he is not**, at the time of awakening he is gone, snatched away suddenly by the hand of death. V. 20. **Terrors take hold on him as waters**, the fear of death comes upon him like the torrents of an overflowing stream; **a tempest stealeth him away in the night**, a sudden gust of the violent east wind carries him off. V. 21. **The east wind carrieth him away, and he departeth**, going off without returning; **and as a storm hurleth him out of his place**, he being helpless in its power. V. 22. **For God shall cast upon him and not spare**, hurling the arrows of His wrath and vengeance upon him; **he would fain flee out of his hand**, all his attempts to escape the doom at the hand of God are futile. V. 23. **Men shall clap their hands at him**, in mockery and derision, **and shall hiss him out of his place**, forcing him to leave his dwelling under their scornful jeering. Job thus pictured the final misfortune of the wicked in terms which even went beyond those employed by his friends.

CHAPTER 28.

Job's Discourse on True Wisdom.

Man's Foolish Search for Riches. — V. 1. **Surely there is a vein for the silver**, a place prepared by the Creator where it is found, **and a place for gold where they fine it**, where men refine gold, after the ore has been taken out of the ground. The connection of thought between the statements in this paragraph and that of the previous chapter is this, that true wisdom cannot be dug out of the earth or acquired by the wicked rich like minerals. V. 2. **Iron is taken out of the** earth, brought out by means of deep shafts, **and brass is molten out of the stone,** that is, the stone of the ore is smelted into copper, this metal being comparatively easily gained. V. 3. **He setteth an end to darkness,** men have found ways of lighting up even the dark shafts of the mines beneath the earth, **and searcheth out all perfection: the stones of darkness and the shadow of death,** that is, the enterprise of men has enabled them to penetrate into the earth in every direction, building their shafts in the subterranean darkness and following the lead of the veins of ore to their very end. V. 4. **The flood,** the place of cutting through, **breaketh out from the inhabitant,** that is, man opens or cuts through a shaft, away from those sojourning above, straight down into the earth; **even the waters forgotten of the foot; they are dried up, they are gone away from men,** literally, "where forgotten by every one's foot they dangle, far from mortals, they swing," that is, men dig their shafts down so deeply that they are entirely out of sight and ken of men walking above; they are suspended by ropes far from the surface where other men are living and going about their business. All this is done in order to bring metals up to the surface. But true wisdom cannot be so acquired. V. 5. **As for the earth, out of it cometh bread,** on its surface the cultivated fields yield grain for man's food; **and under it,** by contrast, **it is turned up as it were fire,** cut up into shafts and galleries, as though fire had eaten through. Man is not satisfied with the products which grow out of the earth, but digs for treasures in its deepest recesses. V. 6. **The stones of it are the place of sapphires,** for this precious stone is found in the earth; **and it hath dust of gold,** the nuggets and grains of gold which settle in pockets of mountain streams become the property of the miner. V. 7. **There is a path which no fowl knoweth,** no eagle knows the path to the hidden treasures, **and which the vulture's eye,** as sharp as it is, **hath not seen,** not even he has gazed upon them: v. 8. **the lion's whelps have not trodden it,** the proud beasts of prey, **nor the fierce lion passed by it.** None of them knew the places where all these riches were hidden. V. 9. **He,** that is, man in his restless search for wealth, **putteth forth his hand upon the rock,** laying his hand even upon flint, the hardest of rocks; **he overturneth the mountains by the roots,** by digging and blasting for the treasures contained in the ground. V. 10. **He cutteth out rivers among the rocks,** cutting passages through solid granite; **and his eye seeth every precious thing,** for by such digging and blasting the hidden treasures are revealed to the eyes of men. V. 11. **He bindeth the floods from overflowing,** stopping the dripping or the seams of water which threaten to fill up the pits and galleries of the mines; **and the thing that is hid bringeth he forth to light,** by such strenuous mining operations men succeed in bringing up the precious metals and stones hidden in the bosom of the earth. They spare themselves no trouble to gain the vain treasures of this world.

GOD ALONE THE POSSESSOR OF TRUE WISDOM. Over against man's foolish quest for vain and unstable riches Job places the wisdom of God, unattainable by the outward seeking and searching of men. V. 12. **But where shall wisdom be found? And where is the place of understanding?** True wisdom, the understanding of God, the knowledge of the revelation of God, is the highest good of man. V. 13. **Man knoweth not the price thereof,** no mortal realizes its value for purchase or exchange; **neither is it found in the land of the living,** on the earth as inhabited by men, as a product of their labor. V. 14. **The depth,** the abyss of waters beneath the earth, **saith, It is not in me; and the sea,** the great and mighty ocean, **saith, It is not with me.** V. 15. **It cannot be gotten for gold,** the purest gold cannot be given in exchange for it, **neither shall silver be weighed for the price thereof.** V. 16. **It cannot be valued with the gold of Ophir,** with the finest gold known to the ancients, **with the precious onyx or the sapphire,** both of which were valued very highly in the Orient. V. 17. **The gold and the crystal,** glass, upon which at that time a very high valuation was placed, whether it was natural or artificial, **cannot equal it, and the exchange of it shall not be for jewels of fine gold,** they simply could not be considered as equivalent to it. V. 18. **No mention shall be made of coral or of pearls,** that is, corals and quartz-crystal could not even be named in comparison with it; **for the price of wisdom is above rubies,** it is immeasurably exalted in value over the most precious treasures of men. V. 19. **The topaz of Ethiopia shall not equal it, neither shall it be valued with pure gold,** that which has gone through the most careful process of refining. Job exhausts all comparisons which men would suggest in trying to obtain a fair valuation of the rich treasure of which he speaks. V. 20. **Whence, then, cometh wisdom, and where is the place of understanding?** The same question is propounded again in order to drive home the truth about to be stated. V. 21. **Seeing it is hid from the eyes of all living,** the creatures of the earth endowed with senses, **and kept close from the fowls of the air,** even from the sharp-sighted winged tribe. V. 22. **Destruction and death,** the realm of the dead and the place reserved for the wicked, **say, We have heard the fame thereof with our ears,** they knew of it only by hearsay, they had no personal acquaintance with it. V. 23. **God understandeth the way thereof,** He alone is familiar with true wisdom, **and He knoweth the place thereof,** He knows exactly where it may be found. V. 24. **For He looketh to the ends of the earth and seeth under the whole heaven,** nothing is hidden from His wisdom and omniscience, v. 25. **to make the weight for the winds; and He weigheth the waters by measure,** they are entirely under His direction and government. V. 26. **When He made a decree for the rain,** appointing to it when and how often it should fall, **and a way for the lightning of the thunder,** a path for the thunder-flash through the clouds, all these phenomena being regulated by Him, v. 27. **then,** when He exercised His creative and providential power, **did He see it and declare it,** He unfolded and set forth before men some of the evidences of eternal wisdom; **He prepared it, yea, and searched it out,** establishing its foundation throughout nature, making everything subject to the laws of His wisdom. V. 28. **And unto man He said,** singling him out for this revelation, as the highest creature of His almighty power, **Behold, the fear of the Lord, that is wisdom,** to know Him and to reverence Him as the one true God is the sum of all wisdom; **and to depart from evil is understanding.** To forsake the evil, as being utterly contrary to God, His essence and His will, and to live in accordance with the demands of His holiness, that is the highest form of wisdom. This wisdom can be attained to through the knowledge of Jesus Christ as the Savior of mankind, for by faith in Him all believers are brought into that communion with God which will reveal to them the fulness of His wisdom and give them the strength to do His will.

CHAPTER 29.

Job Reviews His Former Life.

JOB DESCRIBES HIS FORMER PROSPERITY. — V. 1. **Moreover, Job continued his parable,** his proverbial sayings, **and said,** v. 2. **Oh, that I were as in months past, as in the days when God preserved me,** sighing for the happy condition of that period of his life which now seems to belong to the remote past; v. 3. **when His candle shined upon my head,** when the lamp of God's favor illuminated Job's pathway, **and when by His light I walked through darkness,** secure in the midst of the greatest dangers, v. 4. **as I was in the days of my youth,** literally, "of my autumn or harvest," the days of his prime, of his ripe manhood, **when the secret of God was upon my tabernacle,** when His friendship, His companionship hovered over Job's tent, when he was in confidential, blessed intercourse with the Lord; v. 5. **when the Almighty was yet with me,** giving Job His protection and blessing, **when my children were about me,** as a most highly valued blessing, Ps. 127 and 128; v. 6. **when I washed my steps with butter,** with the richest cream, **and the rock poured me out rivers of oil,** both pictures pointing to the riches of God's kindness which were granted to Job, when he was prosperous in all his work; v. 7. **when I went out to the gate through the city,** up to the city from the place of his residence in the country, **when I prepared my seat in the street,** when he took his place in the market, in the open space near the city gate, where the men of influence and honor, the most respected men of the community, were wont to assemble! V. 8. **The young men saw me and hid themselves,** out of great reverence for Job's wisdom and influence, **and the aged arose and stood up,** the very gray-headed men showing him deference in the most marked manner. V. 9. **The princes refrained talking,** stopped in the middle of their speech, **and laid their hand on their mouth,** in reverential silence, yielding him the floor whenever he indicated that he had something to say. V. 10. **The nobles held their peace,** literally, "the voice of nobles hid itself," or, "themselves," it was no longer heard, **and their tongue cleaved to the roof of their mouth,** awed by the presence of the wise and holy man in their midst. V. 11. **When the ear heard me,** as he gave his counsel in the assembly of the people, **then it blessed me,** calling him happy in the possession of so much wisdom; **and when the eye saw me, it gave witness to me,** praising him for the good fortune which attended him at all times. Altogether, Job had enjoyed the greatest prosperity, honor, and dignity in the land.

JOB SPEAKS OF HIS BENEVOLENCE AND THE HONOR ACCORDED HIM. — V. 12. **Because I delivered the poor that cried,** making a plea for assistance, **and the fatherless, and him that had none to help him,** the orphan who had no helper, Job practised true benevolence, dispensed real charity. V. 13. **The blessing of him that was ready to perish came upon me,** the forsaken and miserable ones blessed him with grateful wishes for the help he gave them; **and I caused the widow's heart to sing for joy,** by the willing charity which he dispensed, relieving her of all her cares of this life. V. 14. **I put on righteousness, and it clothed me,** putting it on as a robe, wearing it always, so that the proper holy conduct at all times was identified with him; **my judgment was as a robe and a diadem,** justice and fairness in all his dealings were his mantle and his turban, characterizing him before all men. V. 15. **I was eyes to the blind, and feet was I to the lame,** his charity and largess was so great as to make men forget their misfortunes, no matter whether these consisted even in lameness or blindness. V. 16. **I was a father to the poor,** attending to the wants of the needy like a natural father; **and the cause which I knew not I searched out,** he made it his business to find out about the friendless in the community, in order to come to their assistance in anything they needed. V. 17. **And I brake the jaws of the wicked,** of all the hard-hearted, who oppressed the poor, especially of unrighteous judges, **and plucked the spoil out of his teeth,** rescuing them from the power of the wicked, as out of the claws of beasts of prey. In this way had Job spent his days, dispensing benevolence on all sides. V. 18. **Then I said, I shall die in my nest,** safe in the bosom of his family, **and I shall multiply my days as the sand,** dying in a ripe old age, after the grains of sand in the hour-glass of his life had fully run their course. V. 19. **My root was spread out by the waters,** he had hoped that he would flourish like a tree plentifully watered, **and the dew lay all night upon my branch,** like the moisture which sustains the life of the desert plant. V. 20. **My glory was fresh in me,** he thought he would always be given the honor which he then enjoyed, **and my bow was renewed in my hand,** the bow being a symbol of manliness and strength, which, he trusted, would always grow young again. V. 21. **Unto me men gave ear and waited,** they paused for Job to speak first, his counsel being decisive, **and kept silence at my counsel,** not presuming to contradict him. V. 22. **After my words they spake not again,** his solution of the matter under consideration being final; **and my speech dropped upon them,** as the refreshing rain does upon the dry soil eager for its fructifying power. V. 23. **And they waited for me as for the rain,** to have his counsel come to them as such a gentle shower; **and they opened their mouth wide as for the latter rain,** the rain of early spring, which determines the richness of the harvest. V. 24. **If I laughed on them, they believed it not,** literally, "when they had no confidence," when they were despondent about something, his cheering smile gave them new courage; **and the light of my countenance they cast not down,** could not darken; no matter how cheerless the prospect, they could not take the hopefulness out of Job's heart nor the encouraging smile from his face. V. 25. **I chose out their way and sat chief,** he took pleasure in attending their assemblies and in taking part in their affairs, **and dwelt as a king in the army,** assuming the leadership altogether naturally, **as one that comforteth the mourners,** with the encouragement which a true leader will give to those depending on him. Such was Job's happiness and prosperity, and such were his hopes for the future in the days when he was an honored man in the community.

CHAPTER 30.

Job's Sorrowful Description of His Present State.

JOB COMPLAINS OF THE CONTEMPT HE RECEIVES FROM MEN. — V. 1. **But now they that are younger than I have me in derision,** foolish and immature youngsters, **whose fathers I would have disdained to have set with the dogs of my flock,** to put on a level with the lowest shepherds in his employ, mainly on account of their general untrustworthiness and improvidence. V. 2. **Yea, whereto might the strength of their hands profit me,** what use could he possibly make of it, **in whom old age was perished,** whose mode of living kept them from reaching full manly vigor? V. 3. **For want and famine they were solitary,** through want and hunger they were starved, their energy and strength were exhausted; **fleeing into the wilderness in former time desolate and waste,** they gnaw at the desert, which has long been a waste and a wilderness, affording them only the scantiest living; v. 4. **who cut up mallows,** the saltwort of the desert, **by the bushes,** where it led a precarious existence in the shadow of larger bushes, **and juniper roots for their meat,** a kind of broom-root or furze being their food. V. 5. **They were driven forth from among men,** excluded from human society, (**they cried after them as after a thief,** such a hue and cry is raised by the Arab inhabitants of the villages when the vagabonds appear,) v. 6. **to dwell in the cliffs of the valleys, in caves of the earth, and in the rocks,** those were the dwelling-places of this low class of people, whose youngsters now dared to insult Job as he sat there in great misery. V. 7. **Among the bushes they brayed,** crying out like the wild ass of the steppes; **under the nettles,** the brambles of the desert, **they were gathered together,** like herds of beasts of the wilderness. V. 8. **They were children of fools, yea, children of base men,** really, no-account men; **they were viler than the earth,** literally, "who are whipped out of the country," as useless and dangerous rabble, on the order of vagabonds and gypsies. V. 9. **And now am I their song,** their shout of mockery and derision, **yea, I am their byword,** they refer to Job only in a malicious, contemptuous manner. V. 10. **They abhor me, they flee far from me,** shunning him with a most abject abhorrence, **and spare not to spit in my face,** as an expression of their unbounded contempt. So greatly had Job been degraded by God. V. 11. **Because He hath loosed my cord,** God had let loose upon Job the horde of His calamities, **and afflicted me, they have also let loose the bridle before me,** men were giving free rein to their violent and hateful attacks upon him. God and men had united in making Job the target of their scorn. V. 12. **Upon my right hand rise the youth,** a brood of diseases and sufferings, or, the brood of young rascals who were now mocking him; **they push away my feet,** leaving him no foothold, no place to stand on, **and they raise up against me the ways of their destruction,** besieging him on all sides, making him the object of their assaults. V. 13. **They mar my path,** tearing it down, making it impassable; **they set forward my calamity,** promoting it, helping it along as it speeds to Job's destruction; **they have no helper,** there is no helper against them, they come on without hindrance. V. 14. **They came upon me as a wide breaking in of waters,** like a wide breach made in a dam or levee; **in the desolation,** in the midst of the falling ruins, **they rolled themselves upon me,** like an inrushing army which lays everything low by the force of its impact and assault. V. 15. **Terrors are turned upon me,** the sudden fear of death; **they pursue my soul as the wind,** his dignity, his respect, and his influence like a storm; **and my welfare passeth away as a cloud,** his prosperity has vanished without leaving a trace. Thus Job brings out the great contrast between his former happy state and that of his present deep dishonor.

THE UNSPEAKABLE MISERY AND DISAPPOINTMENT WITH WHICH JOB BATTLED. — V. 16. **And now my soul is poured out upon me,** dissolved in suffering and anguish; **the days of affliction have taken hold upon me,** he was in the strong clutches of suffering and found himself unable to shake them off. V. 17. **My bones are pierced in me in the night season,** the restless night itself, which increases the pains of every affliction, pierces his bones from his body; **and my sinews take no rest,** literally, "my gnawers, not do they sleep," a reference either to the gnawing pains throughout his body or to the maggots in his ulcers. V. 18. **By the great force of my disease is my garment changed,** by God's fearful power his clothes lost all their semblance, hanging about his shrunken form loose and flapping, more like a sack than a dress; **it bindeth me about as the collar of my coat,** it no longer stands off properly, but clings to him like a tight-fitting shirt-collar. V. 19. **He hath cast me into the mire,** as an evidence of His great contempt, **and I am become like dust and ashes,** both on account of the appearance of his skin and the dirt which he had strewn upon himself. V. 20. **I cry unto Thee, and Thou dost not hear me,** God acted as though He paid no attention to Job's pleading; **I stand up, and Thou regardest me not,** looking at him fixedly, indeed, but in the absent-minded manner which made Him lose the import of Job's complaint. V. 21. **Thou art become cruel to me,** the Lord changing His nature into that of a cruel tormentor; **with Thy strong hand Thou opposest Thyself against me,** making war upon him. V. 22. **Thou liftest me up to the wind,** making him a plaything of the storm; **Thou causest me to ride upon it and dissolvest my substance,** rending him apart by the fierceness of the tempest. V. 23. **For I know that Thou wilt bring me to death,** or, "back from the dust of death," **and to the house appointed for all living,** where the living assemble, a confident cry in the midst of hopelessness, looking forward to the resurrection of the dead. V. 24. **Howbeit, he will not stretch out his hand to the grave, though they cry in his destruction,** literally, "But is it not in falling one stretches out his hand, in destruction raises a call for help?" Such actions are the expression of man's natural, instinctive impulse to save his life if threatened by death, and therefore no one should blame Job for his cry for help. V. 25. **Did not I weep for him that was in trouble? Was not my soul grieved for the poor?** He who showed true sympathy with the poor and miserable in their afflictions would surely not be denied this show of the instinct of self-preservation, this plea for help! V. 26. **When I looked for good, then evil came unto me,** this being another reason why his craving for help should go unchallenged; **and when I waited for light, there came darkness,** he had nothing but misfortune to contend with. V. 27. **My bowels boiled and rested not,** on account of the intense heat of the fever which was devouring him and the torments of his anxiety; **the days of affliction prevented me,** flinging themselves in his way, encountering him with all fierceness. V. 28. **I went mourning without the sun,** blackened, not by the heat of the sun, but as a consequence of his illness; **I stood up, and I cried in the congregation,** complaining aloud on account of the pain of his sufferings. V. 29. **I am a brother to dragons,** to the jackals of the desert in appearance, **and a companion to owls,** to the ostriches of the wilderness. V. 30. **My skin is black upon me,** having become blackened with his sickness, it peeled off his flesh, **and my bones are burned with heat,** drying up with the heat of his disease. V. 31. **My harp also,** the lyre, or zither, or lute, as an instrument used upon joyful occasions, **is turned to mourning and my organ,** the pipe also being an instrument of joy, **into the voice of them that weep.** All the festive and joyous music, so expressive of Job's former prosperity, was hushed, and only the tones of sadness and deepest lamentation remained. He had reached a point of degradation and suffering unequaled in the history of the human race.

CHAPTER 31.

Job's Last Protestation of Innocence.

JOB RECOUNTS HIS BLAMELESS CONDUCT. — V. 1. **I made a covenant with mine eyes,** prescribing to his organs of vision their conduct; **why, then, should I think upon a maid,** casting lustful, adulterous looks upon a person of the opposite sex? V. 2. **For what portion of God is there from above?** What dispensation would come from Him, namely, in the form of punishment for such a sinful thought? **And what inheritance of the Almighty from on high?** What would His portion have been in punishing him for such a transgression, God surely would not let such sins go without just retribution. V. 3. **Is not destruction to the wicked and a strange punishment to the workers of iniquity?** Misfortune and calamity are the consequence of sins against the Sixth Commandment. V. 4. **Doth not He see my ways and count all my steps?** It was the consciousness of God's omniscience and righteousness which caused Job to avoid even lustful glances and sinful desires. V. 5. **If I have walked with vanity,** making falsehood and duplicity his companions, **or if my foot hath hasted to deceit,** eager to make use of its cheating appearance, v. 6. **let me be weighed in an even balance,** in a balance of justice, cp. Dan. 5, 25, **that God may know mine integrity,** for a careful weighing of the evidence against him would establish the truth of his utterances. V. 7. **If my step hath turned out of the way,** namely, from the right way as prescribed by God, **and mine heart walked after mine eyes,** yielding to the lust which often takes hold of the eyes, **and if any blot hath cleaved to mine hands,** any spot of unchaste, immoral actions, v. 8. **then let me sow and let another eat,** enjoying the fruit of his hard labors; **yea, let my offspring be rooted out,** the products of the soil as planted by him be destroyed. Cp. Lev. 26, 16; Amos 9, 14; Ps. 128, 2. Thus Job protested that he had always avoided all sinful lust. V. 9. **If mine heart have been deceived by a woman,** enticed into adulterous relations with another man's wife, **or if I have laid wait at my neighbor's door,** cp. Prov. 7, 7. 8, v. 10. **then let my wife grind unto another,** in the position of the lowest secondary wife, who had to attend to the grinding of the household flour on the hand-mill, **and let others bow down upon her,** in lustful, forbidden intercourse. V. 11. **For this is an heinous crime,** his yielding to adultery would be an infamous act; **yea, it is an iniquity to be punished by the judges,** worthy of the severest punishment. Cp. Matt. 5, 21. V. 12. **For it is a fire that consumeth to destruction,** such an adulterous passion on Job's part would merit for him the devouring punishment of the abyss of hell, **and would root out all mine increase,** destroying all the fruit of his labor, all his prosperity, Job thus rejecting also this possible accusation against his life. He next touches upon his conduct toward his house-slaves. V. 13. **If I did despise the cause of my man-servant or of my maid-servant,** treating them as though they had no rights, **when they contended with me,** ruthlessly trampling on that which they had a right to expect, v. 14. **what, then, shall I do when God riseth up,** if He arose in judgment upon such behavior? **And when He visiteth, what shall I answer Him?** If Job had been guilty as here outlined, then, indeed, would the Lord have had the right to lay the heaviest judgments upon him. V. 15. **Did not He that made me in the womb make him? And did not One,** that is, one and the same God, **fashion us in the womb?** God is the Creator of the slave as well as of the master, and there is for that reason no respect of persons with Him, Eph. 6, 9. From the case of his servants Job now turns to that of all the poor and neglected everywhere. V. 16. **If I have withheld the poor from their desire,** refusing them what they needed to sustain their lives, **or have caused the eyes of the widow to fail,** since they became weak and lost their power to see on account of their unfulfilled yearning for help, v. 17. **or have eaten my morsel myself alone and the fatherless hath not eaten thereof,** if selfishness had caused him to withhold food or assistance from the needy; v. 18. (**for,** or, nay, rather, **from my youth he was brought up with me, as with a father,** such consideration the orphan received from him, **and I have guided her,** namely, the widow, **from my mother's womb,** the strong expression being intended to show that Job's humane and friendly treatment of widows and orphans had been his practise from his earliest youth;) v. 19. **if I have seen any perish for want of clothing,** some poor, forsaken soul without so much as a garment to cover his nakedness, **or any poor without covering,** in the condition of the greatest extremity; v. 20. **if his loins,** covered by the bounty of Job, **have not blessed me, and if he were not warmed with the fleece of my sheep,** namely, in the form of substantial, warm clothing; v. 21. **if I have lifted up my hand against the fatherless,** shaking his fist at the orphan in a violent and threatening manner, **when I saw my help in the gate,** believing that he could readily bribe the judges who might try a case of such violence: v. 22. **then let mine arm fall from my shoulder-blade,** being severed from the joint which held it, **and mine arm be broken from the bone,** literally, "the pipe," from the hollow, pipelike bones to which it was attached. V. 23. **For destruction from God was a terror to me,** Job's fear of God's vengeance had always kept him from wicked acts of this kind, **and by reason of His highness I could not en-**

dure, being powerless before the majesty of God, a fact which made it morally impossible for him to become guilty of merciless conduct. V. 24. **If I have made gold my hope,** putting his trust in it, **or have said to the fine gold, Thou art my confidence;** v. 25. **if I rejoiced because my wealth was great, and because mine hand had gotten much,** had accumulated large amounts, great riches, all this being equal to his making money his god; v. 26. **if I beheld the sun when it shined,** his light being worshiped by the Chaldeans as an emanation from God, **or the moon walking in brightness,** wandering her course in solemn majesty, v. 27. **and my heart hath been secretly enticed,** namely, away from the true God to the foolishness of idolatry, **or my mouth hath kissed my hand,** literally, "so that I touched my hand to my mouth," in throwing to the sun and the moon, as heathen divinities, a kiss, as a sign of adoration: v. 28. **this also,** as a form of gross idolatry, **were an iniquity to be punished by the judge; for I should have denied the God that is above,** acting falsely, becoming guilty of denial. V. 29. **If I rejoiced at the destruction of him that hated me,** in vindictive hate and malice, **or lifted up myself when evil found him,** in joyful excitement over any misfortune which might strike him, for the love of enemies was required even in the Old Testament; v. 30. **neither have I suffered my mouth to sin by wishing a curse to his soul,** his palate, as an instrument of speech, he did not wish for the death of his enemy, he had not been guilty of such vindictive hatred. V. 31. **If the men of my tabernacle said not, Oh, that we had of his flesh! We cannot be satisfied,** literally, "If the people of my tent," that is, his household associates and servants, "had not been obliged to say, Where could one be found who had not been satisfied with his flesh?" Job had freely distributed of the flesh of his slaughtered cattle to such as were in need, as his servants would readily testify. V. 32. **The stranger did not lodge in the street,** for want of hospitality on Job's part, **but I opened my doors to the traveler,** so that every one who passed by was made welcome, according to Oriental custom. V. 33. **If I covered my transgressions as Adam,** covering his wickedness after the manner of men, after the ways of the world in general, **by hiding mine iniquity in my bosom,** trying to conceal it from men and God: v. 34. **did I fear a great multitude,** because he feared the contempt of the multitude, the nobler families, from the intercourse with which he might have been excluded, **or did the contempt of families terrify me that I kept silence and went not out of the door,** lest his iniquity become evident to all? Thus Job protested that he practised what was right and good in all his relations toward God and men and abstained from that which was wrong in God's sight.

Job's Appeal to be Heard. — V. 35. **Oh, that one would hear me!** namely, as he here asserted his innocence, for his complaint had been all along that God paid no attention to his crying. **Behold, my desire is that the Almighty would answer me,** or, "Behold my signature: let the Almighty answer me!" Job had, as it were, set forth his vindication in writing; he was now ready to hear the verdict of God. **And that mine adversary had written a book!** That God would write down and fix against him the definite charge on account of which He laid this suffering upon him, was Job's great wish. V. 36. **Surely I would take it upon my shoulder,** as a trophy, as a badge of honor and dignity, **and bind it as a crown to me,** as a diadem, since he is confident of victory in advance, sure of his vindication. V. 37. **I would declare unto Him the number of my steps,** concealing none of his actions before the divine Judge; **as a prince would I go near unto Him,** with a stately dignity, proud of his innocence, not like an accused person, trembling in the consciousness of his guilt. V. 38. **If my land cry against me,** if his field should cry out for vengeance against its owner, **or that the furrows likewise thereof complain,** weeping in impotent pleading against Job's abuse; v. 39. **if I have eaten the fruits thereof without money,** having taken some one's land in injustice, without payment, **or have caused the owners thereof to lose their life,** either directly or indirectly: v. 40. **let thistles grow instead of wheat,** briars, which would spoil the productiveness of the soil, **and cockle,** noxious, stinking weeds, **instead of barley.** Thus boldly did Job assert his innocence of any specific wickedness over against the friends who were casting the suspicion of evil upon him. **The words of Job,** namely, those in which he vindicated his innocence over against his former friends, **are ended.**

CHAPTER 32.

Elihu Opens His Discourses.

The Pause after Job's Speech. — V. 1. **So these three men ceased to answer Job because he was righteous in his own eyes,** because they could not get him to admit that his sufferings were in any way the result of some particular iniquity, because his protestations of his innocence silenced them. V. 2. **Then was kindled the wrath of Elihu, the son of Barachel, the Buzite,** a descendant of Nahor, whose tribe also lived a nomadic life in the Arabian Desert, **of the kindred of Ram,** that being the name of his immediate family; **against Job was his wrath kindled**

because he justified himself rather than God, declaring himself to be righteous before God and insisting that he had not merited the sufferings which had come upon him. V. 3. **Also against his three friends was his wrath kindled because they had found no answer and yet had condemned Job.** They had not been able to refute his statements, they had not hit upon the right answer to his arguments; their condemnation of Job in those circumstances was a poor substitute for a conviction, a cowardly expedient. V. 4. **Now, Elihu,** who may have been present from the beginning of the debate or had heard at least a large part of it, **had waited till Job had spoken,** until he had finished his entire argument, all that he had to say in his own defense, **because they were elder than he,** he was younger than any of those who had joined in the debate till now. V. 5. **When Elihu saw that there was no answer in the mouth of these three men,** they were unable to present a solution of the problem, **then his wrath was kindled,** he felt that he could now no longer be quiet. The respect shown by Elihu in waiting till the older men had finished their discussion is very commendable and may well serve as an example to many forward young people of our day.

ELIHU GIVES THE REASON FOR HIS SPEAKING. — V. 6. **And Elihu, the son of Barachel, the Buzite, answered and said,** opening his discourse with statements calculated to win the good will of all former speakers, **I am young, and ye are very old,** hoary with age; **wherefore I was afraid,** held back by diffidence and awe, **and durst not show you mine opinion,** make known the knowledge which he possessed concerning this matter. V. 7. **I said, Days should speak,** figuratively for, those full of days, the aged, **and multitude of years should teach wisdom.** It was the normal thing, the natural state of affairs, that older people should find the solution of difficulties, by virtue of their accumulated knowledge. V. 8. **But there is a spirit in man,** or, "for all that the spirit is in mortal man"; **and the inspiration of the Almighty giveth them understanding,** the divine creative breath has given all men reason, and all, whether young or old, should use it in the proper manner. V. 9. **Great men are not always wise,** that is, the great in years, the aged, have no monopoly of wisdom; **neither do the aged understand judgment,** being the only ones who know what is right and good. V. 10. **Therefore I said, Hearken to me,** each one of his hearers being summoned to hear; **I also will show mine opinion.** V. 11. **Behold, I waited for your words,** for real words, sound arguments on their part; **I gave ear to your reasons,** always waiting for some striking point that would refute Job, **whilst ye searched out what to say,** counter-arguments to the claims of Job. V. 12. **Yea, I attended unto you,** he gave heed most eagerly, **and, behold, there was none of you that convinced Job,** who refuted his claims and convicted him of error, **or that answered his words;** v. 13. **lest ye should say,** in trying to excuse their failure, **We have found out wisdom; God thrusteth him down, not man,** they had found such superior wisdom in Job that they were convinced of their own inability to cope with him; only God would be able to drive him off the field. V. 14. **Now, he hath not directed his words against me,** Job had not arrayed arguments against Elihu, he had brought no facts which convinced Elihu of his innocence; **neither will I answer him with your speeches,** he would not use their line of argument at all, believing it to be the wrong form of attack. V. 15. **They were amazed, they answered no more; they left off speaking,** words had fled away from them, had deserted them. This sentence has the force of an exclamation, caused by the surprise which Elihu felt because Job's friends had been so easily confounded. V. 16. **When I had waited, (for they spake not, but stood still and answered no more;** the sentence has the force of a question, Should I still wait, because they are unable to find the right arguments to refute Job?) v. 17. **I said, I will answer also my part,** for his own person, **I also will show mine opinion,** throwing the weight of his opinion in the scales against Job. V. 18. **For I am full of matter,** full of statements and arguments which he believes he can use, **the spirit within me constraineth me,** urging and impelling him to speak. V. 19. **Behold, my belly is as wine which hath no vent,** the extracted juice of grapes in the process of fermentation, which threatens to burst its vessel; **it is ready to burst like new bottles,** skins but recently filled, where the wine is not yet settled. V. 20. **I will speak that I may be refreshed,** that he might catch his breath once more, that he might have air again, that he might relieve the pressure of his speech by saying a few things which he had on his mind; **I will open my lips and answer.** V. 21. **Let me not, I pray you, accept any man's person,** he intended to show no partiality, **neither let me give flattering titles unto man,** he was unacquainted with the arts of complimentary speech. V. 22. **For I know not to give flattering titles; in so doing my Maker would soon take me away,** for having become guilty of insincerity and hypocrisy. If men are sincere in seeking the glory of God, they may readily express their views, without fear or flattery.

CHAPTER 33.

Elihu Declares the Guilt of Man before God.

ELIHU CHALLENGES JOB AND QUESTIONS HIS INNOCENCE. — V. 1. **Wherefore, Job, I pray thee, hear my speeches,** the special summons being directed to Job as the one in need of correction, **and hearken to all my words.** V. 2. **Behold, now I have opened my mouth, my tongue hath spoken in my mouth.** Elihu announces the beginning of his discourse in a circumstantial and pompous manner agreeing with his entire form of discourse. V. 3. **My words shall be of the uprightness of my heart,** the honest and open expression of his frank opinion, **and my lips shall utter knowledge clearly,** literally, "and the knowledge of my lips, purely they speak out," without hypocrisy. V. 4. **The Spirit of God hath made me,** He is his Creator, who gave him not only his body, but also his soul, his mind and reason, **and the breath of the Almighty hath given me life,** he is endowed with understanding given to him from above and is willing to use this in defense of God. Note that not only creative power, but also the creative act is here ascribed to the Holy Spirit, the third person of the Godhead, that He is placed on a level with the Almighty. V. 5. **If thou canst answer me,** endowed as Elihu was by the act of his creation, **set thy words in order before me, stand up,** drawing up in the attitude of defense, taking his stand for the combat of wits, the entire statement being a haughty challenge. V. 6. **Behold, I am according to thy wish in God's stead,** like Job, Elihu was God's creature, dependent upon God, in the same relation to God; **I also am formed out of the clay,** literally, "out of clay was I nipped off," as when a potter takes a piece of clay to form a vessel, a reference both to the original creation of man and to God's freedom in creating all men alike. For that reason no special horror of his appearance would overawe Job and therefore cause him to bow down to Elihu. V. 7. **Behold, my terror shall not make thee afraid,** since he was a genuinely human and earthly being, **neither shall my hand be heavy upon thee,** in pressing Job down unduly, in taking a mean advantage of him. V. 8. **Surely thou hast spoken in mine hearing,** loudly and distinctly, so that there could be no mistake about it, **and I have heard the voice of thy words, saying,** v. 9. **I am clean without transgression,** pure in character and life and altogether without wickedness; **I am innocent,** not a single blame attaching to him; **neither is there iniquity in me,** Elihu understanding this statement of Job as insisting upon his absolute sinlessness. V. 10. **Behold, He findeth occasions,** oppositions, hostilities, **against me; He counteth me for His enemy.** V. 11. **He putteth my feet in the stocks; He marketh all my paths,** penning him in like a prisoner. Elihu summarized some of the statements of Job, especially that criticism which was directed against the justice of God, chap. 13, 27, at which he had taken particular offense. Elihu purposely made his introduction long, wishing to add to the impressiveness of the arguments which he intended to bring against Job.

OF THE TRUE RELATION OF SINFUL MAN TOWARD GOD. — V. 12. **Behold, in this thou art not just,** Job was not right in making such statements. **I will answer thee that God is greater than man,** God, being highly exalted over mortal man, deems it below His dignity to defend Himself against attacks combined with self-glorification. V. 13. **Why dost thou strive against Him,** with such murmurings and contentions as Elihu had heard? **For He giveth not account of any of His matters,** He is not compelled to give an account of His judgments and actions to His creatures, and He also refuses to do so. V. 14. **For God speaketh once, yea, twice,** God, on His part, is obliged to repeat His words time and again; **yet man perceiveth it not.** In many ways and by many means God tries to make His will known to mortals, but they pay no attention to Him. Some of these means are now enumerated. V. 15. **In a dream, in a vision of the night, when deep sleep falleth upon men, in slumberings upon the bed,** through all of which the Lord tries to communicate with men, v. 16. **then He openeth the ears of men,** uncovering, unlocking them that His Word might find entrance, **and sealeth their instruction,** literally, "and upon warnings to them He presses the seal," impressing it upon their mind that they should heed the various experiences of life through which He admonishes them for their own good, v. 17. **that He may withdraw man from his purpose,** from transgression and evil-doing, **and hide pride from man,** so that he does not see it and therefore has no desire to indulge in self-glorification. V. 18. **He keepeth back his soul from the pit,** preserving men from death in their sins, **and his life from perishing by the sword,** by any weapon which brings destruction. That is one way in which God warns men for their own benefit. V. 19. **He is chastened also with pain upon his bed,** which is also a form of warning on the part of God, **and the multitude of his bones with strong pain,** literally, "with strife in his bones continually," the disease with which he suffers being of a kind to affect all his strength and powers, v. 20. **so that his life abhorreth bread,** the very thought of food excites loathing in him, **and his soul dainty meat,** the most appetizing dishes only fill him with disgust. V. 21. **His flesh is con-**

sumed away that it cannot be seen, shrinking into nothingness on his bones; **and his bones that were not seen stick out,** he becomes a mere shadow of his former self. V. 22. **Yea, his soul draweth near unto the grave and his life to the destroyers,** the angels of death, who lead men to the realms of death. V. 23. **If there be a messenger,** an angel, **with him, an interpreter,** a mediator in his behalf, **one among a thousand,** belonging to the innumerable host of angels, the ministers of men by God's command, **to show unto man his uprightness,** to point out his duty to him: v. 24. **then He is gracious unto him,** God Himself has mercy on the poor mortal, **and saith,** namely, to the angel fulfilling His will, **Deliver him from going down to the pit; I have found a ransom,** an atonement, a price paid for deliverance. Note that the application may well be made at this point to the atonement of Jesus Christ, by which man has been delivered from death and everlasting destruction. V. 25. **His flesh shall be fresher than a child's,** in consequence of his being delivered from his disease after his conversion; **he shall return to the days of his youth,** his flesh swelling, filling out, with the vigor of youth; v. 26. **he shall pray unto God, and He will be favorable unto him,** accepting the repentant sinner graciously; **and he shall see His face with joy,** beholding the face of God with rejoicing; **for He will render unto man his righteousness,** this being restored to him as a free gift by God. V. 27. **He looketh upon men,** the redeemed and justified sinner chants a psalm of thanksgiving to his fellow-mortals; **and if any say, I have sinned and perverted that which was right, and it profited me not,** rather, as the words of the repentant sinner, I had sinned and perverted the right, yet it was not recompensed to me, v. 28. **He will deliver his soul from going into the pit,** rather, He, God, has delivered my soul, **and his life shall see the light,** literally, my life shall enjoy seeing the light of the world of men, in contrast to the darkness of the grave. V. 29. **Lo, all these things worketh God oftentimes with man,** dealing with him repeatedly and in such a manner, in order to impress His warnings upon the mind of man, v. 30. **to bring back his soul from the pit, to be enlightened with the light of the living,** instead of being overshadowed with the darkness of death. V. 31. **Mark well, O Job, hearken unto me,** for the point of this entire discussion was, of course, directed against Job; **hold thy peace, and I will speak.** V. 32. **If thou hast anything to say, answer me,** if he were able to find a reply to these facts as now presented; **speak, for I desire to justify thee,** that Job might stand vindicated, if possible. V. 33. **If not, hearken unto me,** Job on his part should attend most carefully; **hold thy peace, and I shall teach thee wisdom,** for Elihu now made ready to launch forth in a more stinging tirade. Note that chastisements are sent to men by God in order to lead them to repentance and to reinstate them in the right relation toward their Creator.

CHAPTER 34.

Elihu's Censure of Job.

JOB ACCUSED OF FALSEHOOD AND BLASPHEMY. V. 1. **Furthermore Elihu answered and said,** in further refuting Job's charge that God was acting in a cruel and unjust manner, v. 2. **Hear my words, O ye wise men,** the presence of an audience listening to the debate being assumed; **and give ear unto me, ye that have knowledge,** impartial men, with a calm and judicious mind. V. 3. **For the ear trieth words,** proving, testing, sifting the true from the false, the good from the bad, **as the mouth,** the palate, **tasteth meat,** making a careful distinction between various foods taken into the mouth. V. 4. **Let us choose to us judgment,** proving, testing, what was right in the controversy between God and Job; **let us know among ourselves what is good,** reaching a common conclusion concerning their verdict in the case. V. 5. **For Job hath said, I am righteous,** I am right, innocent; **and God hath taken away my judgment,** depriving him of his right; for so Job had insisted, chap. 27, 2. V. 6. **Should I lie against my right,** or, in spite of the fact that right is on my side I shall still be counted a liar, this being the sense of Job's remarks in chap. 9, 20. **My wound is incurable without transgression,** literally, "mine arrow," for the arrow of God's punishment piercing him was inflicting an incurable wound without Job's having deserved it, as he thought. These statements excited Elihu to the deepest resentment. V. 7. **What man is like Job, who drinketh up scorning like water?** For in his suspecting the divine justice Job was filling himself with scornful speeches and then uttering them in a blasphemous manner. V. 8. **Which goeth in company with the workers of iniquity, and walketh with wicked men,** making it a habit to consort with men of wickedness; for by uttering his blasphemous speeches, Job had lowered himself to the level of evil-doers, of the blaspheming rabble. V. 9. **For he hath said, It profiteth a man nothing that he should delight himself with God,** by living in friendship and fellowship with God, this sentiment having frequently been uttered by Job as his impatience carried him away in his complaint. It is such an easy matter to go too far in making complaints, to use expressions which, if not actually accusing God of injustice, at least sound very much like an attempt at it.

Proof of the Divine Righteousness. — V. 10. **Therefore hearken unto me, ye men of understanding,** the same men being appealed to for a verdict to whom Elihu had first addressed himself. **Far be it from God that He should do wickedness,** to deal in a mean, unjust, and cruel manner, **and from the Almighty that He should commit iniquity,** actually commit a crime. V. 11. **For the work of a man shall He render unto him,** recompensing to every man according to his deeds, **and cause every man to find according to his ways,** each one receiving what his works are worth, what his conduct deserves. V. 12. **Yea, surely God will not do wickedly, neither will the Almighty pervert judgment,** this thought being repeated for the sake of emphasis. V. 13. **Who hath given Him a charge over the earth,** delivering the earth to his power, placing it under His direction? **Or who hath disposed the whole world,** establishing and governing the whole circle of the universe? The answer evidently is: No one but God Himself; He is the absolute Creator and Ruler, this thought excluding every selfish motive on the part of God. V. 14. **If He set his heart upon man,** rather, upon Himself, **if He gather unto Himself His spirit and His breath,** that by which the existence of all creatures is maintained, v. 15. **all flesh shall perish together,** with the withdrawal of the divine power and sustaining strength, **and man shall turn again unto dust.** Man is completely dependent upon the providence of God, and yet God does not use His majestic power in an arbitrary manner, making use of cruelty toward His creatures. V. 16. **If, now, thou hast understanding, hear this,** Job should use his powers of observation in a proper way; **hearken to the voice of my words.** Elihu wanted to impress upon Job the importance of his argument. V. 17. **Shall even he that hateth right govern?** The love of righteousness and justice is a condition of proper government. **And wilt thou condemn Him that is most just,** the mighty Just One, that is, God Himself? Surely Job would not presume upon such a course. V. 18. **Is it fit to say to a king, Thou art wicked?** calling him worthless and a scoundrel, **and to princes, Ye are ungodly?** Even to human rulers and governors one would not dare to speak thus, how much less to the almighty and all-just God on high, as Job had done! V. 19. **How much less to Him that accepteth not the persons of princes nor regardeth the rich more than the poor;** for with God there is no distinction of persons or rank. **For they all are the work of His hands,** and therefore all are held in the same regard by Him. V. 20. **In a moment shall they die,** perish with the greatest suddenness, **and the people shall be troubled at midnight and pass away,** entire nations passing away, as a sleeper who is awakened at midnight only to meet a violent death; **and the mighty shall be taken away without hand,** without having the hand of men touching them, being destroyed by a higher invisible power, by the command of God. V. 21. **For His eyes are upon the ways of man, and He seeth all his goings,** watching most carefully over every person's conduct in life. V. 22. **There is no darkness nor shadow of death where the workers of iniquity may hide themselves,** since the omniscient eye of God will penetrate to every hiding-place which men may devise or discover, Ps. 139, 11. 12. V. 23. **For He will not lay upon man more than right,** that is, God does not need to wait long for any examination which He desires to make, for He has all men before His eyes continually, **that he should enter into judgment with God.** Job had pleaded that God would enter into judgment with him, since he was anxious to demonstrate his innocence. Elihu replies that God, by virtue of His omniscience, finds out men in a moment and summons them before His judgment; God was acquainted with all his ways long before any formal examination had taken place. V. 24. **He shall break in pieces mighty men without number,** without a long inquiry into their past records, since He is familiar with their whole lives, **and set others in their stead,** Luke 1, 52. V. 25. **Therefore He knoweth their works,** looking through even their intentions, **and He overturneth them in the night,** with a sudden overthrow, **so that they are destroyed,** crushed out of existence. V. 26. **He striketh them as wicked men,** as evil-doers are scorned and smitten, **in the open sight of others,** as a public example and a warning to all men, v. 27. **because they turned back from Him,** or, "for that reason they turn away from Him," **and would not consider any of His ways,** v. 28. **so that they cause the cry of the poor to come unto Him,** in consequence of the oppression exerted upon them; **and He heareth the cry of the afflicted,** which is brought to His notice because the persistent wicked conduct of the godless causes the complaint of the downtrodden to penetrate to the notice of God. Thus the justice of God strikes the unrighteous. V. 29. **When He giveth quietness,** giving rest and relief to the poor and oppressed, **who then can make trouble,** who will condemn the course of God in so acting? **And when He hideth His face, who then can behold Him?** If God chooses not to be graciously disposed, who will compel Him to feel that way? **Whether it be done against a nation or against a man only,** individuals and peoples are alike under God's government, v. 30. **that the hypocrite reign not,** the ungodly person assuming control of affairs, **lest the people be ensnared,** their wicked rulers plunging them into ruin. All this Elihu maintained in defense of God's righteousness and justice at all times.

JOB CHARGED WITH INCONSISTENCY. — V. 31. **Surely it is meet to be said unto God,** or, "Is it that one indeed says to God?" **I have borne chastisement, I will not offend any more,** expiating, bearing punishment without having done evil. V. 32. **That which I see not,** not being aware of having done wrong, **teach Thou me; if I have done iniquity, I will do no more,** if convinced and convicted, he would be truly penitent. V. 33. **Should it be according to thy mind? He will recompense it, whether thou refuse or whether thou choose, and not I; therefore speak what thou knowest.** These words are addressed to Job, sneeringly asking, Shall God recompense as thou wilt, following Job's claims and demands? Should God change the rules of His righteous government to please him? Job having so criticized God, the Lord, in turn, challenges his knowledge of the right form of retribution, which is equivalent to accusing Job of downright ignorance of the worst type. V. 34. **Let men of understanding tell me,** to whom Elihu had twice appealed in this chapter, **and let a wise man hearken unto me,** that is, he who as a wise man hearkens to him. V. 35. **Job hath spoken without knowledge, and his words were without wisdom.** That, Elihu thinks, must be the verdict of all men of true wisdom. V. 36. **My desire is that Job may be tried unto the end because of his answers for wicked men,** or, "Oh, that Job were but tested to the utmost on account of his objections after the manner of wicked men!" V. 37. **For he addeth rebellion unto his sin,** namely, by his bold and accusing speeches against God, **he clappeth his hands among us,** in mockery and derision, **and multiplieth his words against God.** Such a behavior, Elihu infers, is altogether inconsistent with the claims of true piety, as constantly made by Job. True consciousness of sinfulness would not permit a believer to address the Lord in the manner assumed by Job.

CHAPTER 35.

Elihu's Further Refutation of Job.

JOB'S STANDPOINT OF THE FUTILITY OF PIETY FALSE. — V. 1. **Elihu spake moreover,** since Job made no move to answer him, **and said,** v. 2. **Thinkest thou this to be right, that thou saidst, My righteousness is more than God's?** Did Job believe he was right in making such assertions? V. 3. **For,** or that, **thou saidst, What advantage will it be unto thee,** namely, to Job? **and, What profit shall I have if I be cleansed from my sin,** literally, "more than by my sin"? Job had charged God with being indifferent to moral character in dealing with men and stated that in the present controversy his cause was more just than that of God Himself. In other words, it made no difference how pious or how sinful a person was, God acted simply according to whim in sending afflictions. V. 4. **I will answer thee, and thy companions with thee,** all those to whose level of wickedness Job had lowered himself. V. 5. **Look unto the heavens and see,** trying to comprehend, to some extent, God's majesty by contemplating the throne of His power; **and behold the clouds which are higher than thou,** their lofty heights illustrating God's immeasurable exaltation over the world. V. 6. **If thou sinnest, what doest thou against Him?** How will any sin affect his relation to the great and exalted God? **Or if thy transgressions be multiplied, what doest thou unto Him?** Had he ever thought about the effect such conduct would have on his status with God? V. 7. **If thou be righteous, what givest thou Him, or what receiveth He of thine hand?** Neither the sins of men nor their good deeds have any effect upon the blessedness of the great God; in either case only their own condition is affected. Cp. Ps. 16, 2; Prov. 9, 12; Luke 17, 10. V. 8. **Thy wickedness may hurt a man as thou art,** producing its harmful effects; **and thy righteousness may profit the son of man,** it might avail him for his own person, but serve no further ends. The entire section sets forth the frailty of men in comparison with the absolute blessedness of God.

THE REASONS FOR GOD'S DELAY IN HELPING SUFFERING. — V. 9. **By reason of the multitude of oppressions they make the oppressed to cry,** that is the way of men, to make an outcry over cruelty thus shown; **they cry out by reason of the arm of the mighty,** wailing on account of the violence shown by those in power, v. 10. **but none saith, Where is God, my Maker, who giveth songs in the night,** His speedy and mighty deliverance causing men to rejoice and sing while the darkness of their affliction is still about them; v. 11. **who teacheth us more than the beasts of the earth,** setting men high above the brutes in wisdom, honor, and blessing, **and maketh us wiser than the fowls of heaven?** Man's relation toward God should be that of a creature endowed with reason and understanding, and his prayer should not be the involuntary cry of distress, but the outpouring of the heart which sees in God the kind heavenly Father. V. 12. **There**

they cry, but none giveth answer, God pays no attention to such prayers, **because of the pride of evil men,** He will not hear so as to deliver them from the oppression of wicked men. V. 13. **Surely God will not hear vanity,** what is only empty sound, **neither will the Almighty regard it,** namely, all such crying and praying which is not done in sincerity, whereas, on the other hand, as is here implied, the earnest prayer of the righteous avails much in His sight. V. 14. **Although thou sayest thou shalt not see Him,** in such a case when, as Job insisted, the Lord would not show His face at all, He would most assuredly withdraw His kind presence entirely, **yet judgment is before Him,** namely, the cause of Job which he was trying to defend; **therefore trust thou in Him.** As long as Job felt that way about his case, as up for trial at the hand of God, namely, that he believed God had no intention to let justice prevail, so long he would wait and trust in vain for a vindication. V. 15. **But now, because it is not so, He hath visited in His anger,** because the wrath of God had not yet interposed to punish, **yet He knoweth it not in great extremity,** rather, should He not nevertheless be well acquainted with presumption? Elihu contended that God knew the arrogance of Job and would treat it accordingly. V. 16. **Therefore doth Job open his mouth in vain,** to no purpose, without object; **he multiplieth words without knowledge,** in an altogether unintelligent and foolish manner. For this reason sufferers remain unheard for a long time, both because they have no genuine reverence for God and because they are presumptuous in their speeches against Him.

CHAPTER 36.

Elihu's Further Defense of God.

THE BENEVOLENT PURPOSES OF DIVINE JUSTICE. — V. 1. **Elihu also proceeded,** since Job continued to hold his peace, **and said,** v. 2. **Suffer me a little,** hearing his instructions only a little while longer, **and I will show thee that I have yet to speak on God's behalf,** there was still something to say on the Lord's side of the question, something that had greater weight even than the arguments advanced up till now. V. 3. **I will fetch my knowledge from afar,** not in far-fetched arguments, but from the wide expanse of history and the realm of nature, **and will ascribe righteousness to my Maker,** his topic being so great and wonderful that it inspired Elihu with an impressive array of arguments, especially in setting forth the unchanging justice of God, Ps. 51, 4. V. 4. **For truly my words shall not be false,** not even tinged with falsehood and deceit; **he that is perfect in knowledge is with thee,** Elihu, as one faultless in the knowledge of God's attributes and works, stood before Job, in order to instruct him in the truth, defending, first of all, His justice in fixing the destinies of men. V. 5. **Behold, God is mighty, and despiseth not any,** in spite of His greatness and exaltation He does not disdain to take the proper interest in even the lowliest of His creatures; **He is mighty in strength and wisdom,** in the vigor of His understanding, which enables Him to find the motives of all men's hearts and causes Him to rule everything with the highest wisdom. V. 6. **He preserveth not the life of the wicked,** this statement being made in opposition to the declaration of Job, chap. 21, 7—14; **but giveth right to the poor,** espousing the cause of the afflicted. V. 7. **He withdraweth not His eyes from the righteous,** watching over them, rather, with tender solicitude; **but with kings are they on the throne; yea, he doth establish them forever, and they are exalted,** Luke 1, 52b. V. 8. **And if they be bound in fetters,** held so firmly in their affliction that they cannot move, **and be holden in cords of affliction,** in every form of distress, v. 9. **then He showeth them their work,** namely, their evildoing, **and their transgressions that they have exceeded,** having been presumptuous and proud in opposing God. V. 10. **He openeth also their ear to discipline,** in admonishing them to lay aside their pride, **and commandeth that they return from iniquity,** from the vanity of the various forms of transgression into which they might have fallen. V. 11. **If they obey and serve Him,** yielding to His entreaties, **they shall spend their days in prosperity and their years in pleasures,** as the result of God's blessings upon them. V. 12. **But if they obey not, they shall perish by the sword,** falling into the dart or some other sharp weapon which takes away their life, **and they shall die without knowledge,** breathing out their soul in ignorance of the bliss of being united with God in true fellowship. V. 13. **But the hypocrites in heart heap up wrath,** the ungodly cherish wrath against God, they wage continual warfare against Him; **they cry not when He bindeth them,** they stubbornly refuse to make an outcry or to pray when He lays them in chains. V. 14. **They die in youth,** they must perish in consequence of their attitude, **and their life is among the unclean,** among the polluted and effeminate slaves of vice, as they were found in the heathen temples of that day, the reference being to the shamefulness of their early death. V. 15. **He delivereth the poor in his affliction,** in the case of such suffering God makes the endurance itself serve as a means of deliverance, He rewards such patience in misery, **and openeth their ears in oppression,** by means of such trials God brings blessings to them, their very afflictions standing them in good stead, Rom. 8, 18—28. V. 16. **Even so would He have removed thee,** Elihu here making the application to the case of Job, **out of the strait into a broad place, where there is no straitness,** God would have lured and coaxed him out of the very jaws of distress into a wide place, where he would no longer have felt the cramping effect of his troubles; **and that which should be set on thy table should be full of fatness,** literally, "the setting of thy table fulness of fatness," signifying the highest form of rich prosperity. V. 17. **But thou hast fulfilled the judgment of the wicked,** rather, thou art filled with this judgment, Job was experiencing its misery; **judgment and justice take hold on thee,** not departing from his person and home. V. 18. **Because there is wrath, beware lest He take thee away with His stroke,** Job should not let the heat of his afflictions mislead him by its greatness and thus become guilty of presumptuous mocking; **then a great ransom cannot deliver thee,** that is, he should not let the size of the ransom which, by his sufferings, he seemed to be paying for his sins, ensnare him into a false idea of the goodness and justice of God. V. 19. **Will He esteem thy riches? No, not gold nor all the forces of strength,** literally, "Shall thy outcry for assistance place thee outside of distress, likewise the exertions of thy strength?" All Job's violent insisting upon his rights over against God was futile. V. 20. **Desire not the night, when people are cut off in their place,** the picture being that of chaff being carried away by a sudden gust of the tempest coming up at night. Job should not foolishly long for the night of the judgment; for then entire nations would be swept away, and he might share their lot. V. 21. **Take heed, regard not iniquity,** not turning to vanity and wickedness in the manner shown; **for this hast thou chosen rather than affliction,** that is, in Elihu's opinion Job was too much inclined to arrogant vanity, to rebellion against God, and objected to the affliction which had come upon him in a spirit which was anything but meek. True humility in suffering is the believer's finest ornament.

THE DIVINE JUSTICE AS SUPREME POWER AND WISDOM. — V. 22. **Behold, God exalteth by His power,** He works loftily in His might, in all the acts of His creative power; **who teacheth like Him,** since He is the great Master of the universe? V. 23. **Who hath enjoined Him His way,** charging Him or prescribing to Him what way He should go? **Or who can say, Thou hast wrought iniquity?** Man can but stand by in humble awe when God acts, not daring to question Him on account of any work which He does nor any judgment which He performs. V. 24. **Remember that thou magnify His work, which men behold,** exalting the doing of the great Creator, about which men have always sung hymns of praise. V. 25. **Every man may see it,** all people gazing on it with delight, with wondering admiration; **man may behold it afar off,** mortals stand in reverent contemplation of God's unparalleled majesty. V. 26. **Behold, God is great,** exalted far above all human contemplation, **and we know Him not,** cannot grasp His majesty, even in the works of His creation, **neither can the number of His years be searched out,** the eternity of God is incomprehensible to mortal man, and therefore also His greatness and wisdom. V. 27. **For He maketh small the drops of water,** drawing them up from the earth in the form of vapor; **they pour down rain according to the vapor thereof,** the mist which He spreads out in the form of clouds furnishing the rain, which again descends in drops; v. 28. **which the clouds do drop,** namely, those coming up in a thick mass, as in the case of a thunder-shower, **and distil upon man abundantly.** V. 29. **Also, can any understand the spreadings of the clouds,** how they expand over the vault of heaven, **or the noise of His tabernacle,** the loud crashing of the great tent of the sky, when the thunderbolts shoot forth and its echoes roll between the clouds and the earth? V. 30. **Behold, He spreadeth his light upon it,** He surrounds Himself with the heavenly veil of light in which He continually lives, **and covereth the bottom of the sea,** the roots of the sea, which are drawn up into the atmosphere in the form of clouds and thus form a veil, or covering, for the brightness of the sky and the throne of God. V. 31. **For by them judgeth He the people,** by means of His lightnings and the action of His clouds the Lord gives evidence also of His power as the Judge of the world; **He giveth meat in abundance,** for the same agencies that show Him as the almighty Judge also yield the moisture which causes the grain to grow and furnishes food to men. V. 32. **With clouds He covereth the light,** literally, "Upon both hands He covers light," namely, with the lightnings which He casts forth over the earth; **and commandeth it not to shine by the cloud that cometh betwixt,** He sends out His lightnings against His adversaries, striking down all the hostile forces which presume to battle against Him. V. 33. **The noise thereof showeth concerning it,** His alarm-cry, the noise of His thunder, announces Him, as He goes forward in His strength, **the cattle also concerning the vapor,** even the dumb beasts announce and indicate in their actions that He is on the march, for they instinctively feel the power of the elements as these are unloosed in a great storm. Thus is the supreme power and wisdom of the Creator made manifest and God Himself vindicated in all His actions.

CHAPTER 37.

The End of Elihu's Speech.

THE LAST WORD ON THE MIRACLES IN NATURE. — V. 1. **At this,** namely, the powerful exhibition of God's majesty, as just described, **also my heart trembleth and is moved out of his place,** springing up, giving a bound, as the awe of the spectacle took hold upon it. It seems also that the storm of which the next chapter speaks had gathered and was about to break at this point. V. 2. **Hear attentively the noise of His voice,** the roar of the Lord's voice in the thunder which was now to be heard plainly, **and the sound that goeth out of His mouth,** the great rumbling as the distant storm rolled forward. V. 3. **He directeth it under the whole heaven,** sending forth the roaring and rumbling, **and His lightning unto the ends of the earth,** for the entire earth is lit up by each flash. V. 4. **After it a voice roareth,** the thunder-clap following after the flash; **He thundereth with the voice of His excellency,** in token of His great majesty; **and He will not stay them,** not restrain the lightnings, **when His voice is heard,** for as the storm approaches, the flash of the lightning and the roar of thunder follow in quick succession, there being an almost uninterrupted crashing. V. 5. **God thundereth marvelously with His voice,** this remark closing the description of the coming storm; **great things doeth He, which we cannot comprehend,** this statement leading the way to a description of other wonderful phenomena in nature. V. 6. **For He saith to the snow, Be thou on the earth,** His command being, Fall to the earth, and the snow doing His behest; **likewise to the small rain,** the showers of rain, **and to the great rain of His strength,** torrents, which fall at His command. V. 7. **He sealeth up the hand of every man,** keeping him from doing his ordinary work at the time of such rains, **that all men may know His work,** come to the knowledge of His almighty power and realize their absolute dependence upon Him. V. 8. **Then the beasts go into dens,** creeping into their coverts at the approach of winter or of the rainy season, **and remain in their places,** hibernating in their lairs while the fields are desolate. V. 9. **Out of the south cometh the whirlwind,** rushing forth as from an enclosure in which it had been confined, **and cold out of the north,** literally, "from the cloud-scatterers," for frost usually follows clearing skies. V. 10. **By the breath of God frost is given,** the cold blast, sent from God, sweeps over the face of the water and forms ice; **and the breadth of the waters is straitened,** arrested, bound in the icy fetters of winter. V. 11. **Also by watering He wearieth the thick cloud,** loading it, weighting it down with a burden of moisture; **He scattereth His bright cloud,** spreading out far and wide the clouds of His light, those which contain His lightning; v. 12. **and it is turned round about by His counsels,** that is, the cloud twists and turns and revolves as the storm approaches, piloted by the will of God, **that they may do whatever He commandeth them upon the face of the world in the earth,** that is, over the wide expanse, the habitable land of the earth. Cp. Ps. 148, 7. 8. V. 13. **He causeth it to come,** steering the storm, causing the clouds to unload their burdens, **whether for correction,** namely, when a devastating storm proves a scourge, **or for His land, or for mercy,** when He knows it to be necessary for the earth, when He wants to dispense His blessings in a gentle rain. Thus the majesty of God, as apparent in nature, vindicates all His actions, showing that it is His privilege, His right, to deal with men as He sees fit.

FINAL ADMONITION ADDRESSED TO JOB. — V. 14. **Hearken unto this, O Job! Stand still,** spending some time in contemplation of the miracles just set forth by Elihu, **and consider the wondrous works of God.** V. 15. **Dost thou know when God disposed them,** when He thinks about these miracles, when He plans to have them performed, **and caused the light of His cloud to shine?** Could Job explain the phenomenon of lightning as it flashes forth from the dark mass of clouds? V. 16. **Dost thou know the balancings of the clouds,** by what power they are poised and gently float along in the atmosphere, **the wondrous works of Him which is perfect in knowledge?** Elihu here digresses to set forth another phenomenon, which likewise teaches the wisdom of the Creator. V. 17. **How thy garments are warm when He quieteth the earth by the south wind!** It is a direct challenge to Job: Thou, whose clothes become hot when the land becomes sultry from the south, as the torrid heat of summer gradually travels northward! V. 18. **Hast thou with Him spread out the sky,** the vault, or firmament, of the clouds and the arch of the sky, **which is strong and as a molten looking-glass?** the reference being to the polished metal mirrors then in use. The description exactly fits the dazzling brilliance of the Oriental sky in summer. V. 19. **Teach us what we shall say unto Him,** how mortal man may argue with the almighty Creator and Preserver of the world; **for we cannot order our speech by reason of darkness,** man's understanding being incapable of grasping and explaining the miracles of nature. V. 20. **Shall it be told Him that I speak?** Elihu here realizes, as it were, in a flash that even his speech is almost presumption in God's sight. **If a man speak, surely he shall be swal-**

lowed up. The thought underlying this statement or question is that man courts destruction even in trying to explain adequately the miracles of God. V. 21. **And now men see not the bright light which is in the clouds,** the brightness which shines behind the clouds being veiled from the eyes; **but the wind passeth and cleanseth them,** clearing the sky, dispelling the clouds, so that the brilliance of the heavens is again seen. V. 22. **Fair weather cometh out of the north,** literally, "golden brightness," for when the north wind scatters the clouds after a storm, light shines forth in wonderful splendor; **with God is terrible majesty,** shining from the garment of His glory, which, in the poet's mind, fills the whole sky. V. 23. **Touching the Almighty, we cannot find Him out,** man can understand and fathom His essence neither with his senses nor with his mind; **He is excellent in power and in judgment and in plenty of justice; He will not afflict,** in spite of His incomparable excellence and majesty He is not like a cruel and arbitrary tyrant, He in no wise perverts the ends of justice. V. 24. **Men do therefore fear Him,** namely, such as follow true wisdom; **He respecteth not any that are wise of heart,** He does not deem those worthy of notice who are proud of their own knowledge, wise in their own conceit. All the knowledge which men now have of God is but imperfect. Only when that which is perfect is come, that which is in part shall be done away.

CHAPTER 38.

God's Answer to Job.

THE MANIFESTATION OF GOD'S MAJESTY IN CREATION. — V. 1. **Then the Lord answered Job,** who had repeatedly challenged Him to explain His manner of acting, cp. chap. 31, 35, **out of the whirlwind,** the tempest itself being a manifestation of the almighty power of God, **and said,** v. 2. **Who is this that darkeneth counsel by words without knowledge?** In permitting Job to suffer, the Lord was not acting in a capricious, arbitrary way, but according to a plan which He considered good, which Job, however, without a proper understanding of God's motives, was distorting and questioning; hence the challenge of God. V. 3. **Gird up now thy loins like a man,** like a hero ready for battle; **for I will demand of thee, and answer thou Me.** Job should show his wisdom and therefore his right to criticize by the proper explanation of the phenomena which the Lord intended to discuss. V. 4. **Where wast thou when I laid the foundations of the earth? Declare if thou hast understanding.** No human being having been present at the creation of the world, no human being can presume to tell God's secrets concerning its making; the finite mind cannot grasp the infinite wisdom of the Creator. V. 5. **Who hath laid the measures thereof if thou knowest?** so that Job should know the proportions and plans; for the figure is taken from an architects' plans and sketches. **Or who hath stretched the line upon it?** The thought implied is this, that the Architect of the universe, who planned and executed such a magnificent building, must be far beyond human comprehension and criticism. V. 6. **Whereupon are the foundations thereof fastened?** That is, on what kind of foundation are its pillars sunken? What makes it stand so firm and safe? **Or who laid the corner-stone thereof,** with the certainty of a trained builder, v. 7. **when the morning-stars,** all the heavenly host, creatures of the highest brilliance, **sang together and all the sons of God shouted for joy,** in celebrating the festal occasion? Light and beauty and song attended the creation of the world; the highest and most splendid creatures raised their voices in songs of praise. V. 8. **Or who shut up the sea with doors,** penning it up in the bed of the ocean, **when it brake forth as if it had issued out of the womb,** when order was established out of chaos and the raging and swelling waters were separated from the dry land, Gen. 1, 9? V. 9. **When I made the cloud the garment thereof,** wrapping the mighty ocean in swaddling-clothes, like a helpless infant, **and thick darkness,** that of the heaviest cloud-covering, **a swaddling-band for it,** v. 10. **and brake up for it My decreed place,** setting its bounds in the abysses of the deep, **and set bars and doors,** as for a wild and unruly creature, v. 11. **and said, Hitherto shalt thou come, but no further, and here shall thy proud waves be stayed?** God Himself has placed the boundary and the dam for the ocean's pride, and without His permission not one billow can overstep the bounds. V. 12. **Hast thou commanded the morning since thy days,** with power to make its light rise in the east ever since he was born, **and caused the dayspring,** the dawn of the morning, **to know his place,** so that it knows just where to appear on the horizon in the various seasons of the year, v. 13. **that it might take hold of the ends of the earth,** taking hold of them as of the fringes of an outspread carpet, **that the wicked might be shaken out of it,** as dirt is shaken out of a rug? The allusion is to the fact that the evil-doers of the night season cease to ply their trade with the coming of the morning. V. 14. **It is turned as clay to the seal,** the earth's surface changing with the coming of morning like signet-clay, all its contours and forms standing out sharply; **and they stand as a garment,** all the prairies, hills, valleys, trees, and all other objects being set forth in all the various forms and colors of a beautiful garment. V. 15. **And from the wicked their light is withholden,** the darkness which they love and which they need for their sinful pursuits, **and the high arm shall be broken,** the uplifted arm of violence sinking down as the light of day comes. These are some of the facts of creation which set forth the almighty majesty of God, which no man is able adequately to explain.

God's Majesty in the Forces of Nature. V. 16. **Hast thou entered into the springs of the sea,** the great fountains of the deep, Gen. 7, 11? **Or hast thou walked in the search of the depth,** to examine the ocean's bottom and discover its secrets? V. 17. **Have the gates of death been opened unto thee,** so that Job was familiar with the realm of the dead? **Or hast thou seen the doors of the shadow of death,** so that he could examine them and bring back the knowledge which is beyond death? V. 18. **Hast thou perceived the breadth of the earth,** observing and examining it to its very limits? **Declare if thou knowest it all;** for God knows all this, and he who would criticize God should have the same understanding. V. 19. **Where is the way where light dwelleth?** Could Job explain the phenomenon of light and tell where it originally came from? **And as for darkness, where is the place thereof,** v. 20. **that thou shouldest take it to the bound thereof,** tracing both light and darkness to the place where they originated, **and that thou shouldest know the paths to the house thereof?** In spite of the most careful investigations the secrets connected with light and darkness have not been revealed. V. 21. **Knowest thou it because thou wast then born?** Was Job present at the creation of light, so that he understood all its secrets, **or because the number of thy days is great?** In a sharply ironical veil the Lord reminds Job of the fact that he is not eternal and therefore could not possess the information to which reference is here made. V. 22. **Hast thou entered into the treasures of the snow?** Did Job have access to the immense storehouses from which it came in such immeasurable quantities? **Or hast thou seen the treasures of the hail,** v. 23. **which I have reserved against the time of trouble,** for seasons of distress upon mankind, **against the day of battle and war?** For both snow and hail sometimes serve the purposes of the divine government in the world. V. 24. **By what way is the light parted,** that is, what road leads there, **which scattereth the east wind upon the earth?** Both the light and the east wind defy the calculation of men in the swiftness of their changes and in many other points connected with their phenomena. V. 25. **Who hath divided a watercourse for the overflowing of waters,** conducting the rain-torrents through the thick masses of cloud to such portions of the earth as the Lord intended to moisten, **or a way for the lightning of thunder,** v. 26. **to cause it to rain on the earth where no man is,** in uninhabited regions, where human beings have no interests; **on the wilderness, wherein there is no man,** none to be personally interested, God's providence alone having such a wide range of vision; v. 27. **to satisfy the desolate and waste ground,** the wilderness being thought of as a parched wanderer, **and to cause the bud of the tender herb to spring forth?** Not only in inhabited districts of the world does God exhibit His providential care, but also in such about which the average person never or rarely thinks: so much greater is He than mere man.

God's Majesty in the Wonders above the Earth. — V. 28. **Hath the rain a father,** as it drops down from the clouds of the sky? **Or who hath begotten the drops of dew,** which assemble from the vapor of the atmosphere above, and are therefore also brought into direct relation to God? V. 29. **Out of whose womb came the ice?** A mother is assumed here because ice is associated with the earth. **And the hoary frost of heaven, who hath gendered it?** V. 30. **The waters are hid as with a stone,** drawing themselves together in a rigid mass as the frost takes hold of them, **and the face of the deep is frozen,** hanging together in a solid mass. V. 31. **Canst thou bind the sweet influences of Pleiades,** the band of that constellation of springtime, in the larger constellation of Taurus, **or loose the bands of Orion,** the cords which hold this constellation to its place in the heavens, causing the stars to fall to the ground? V. 32. **Canst thou bring forth Mazzaroth,** a very bright constellation, **in his season? Or canst thou guide Arcturus,** the Great Bear of the northern sky, **with his sons?** V. 33. **Knowest thou the ordinances of heaven,** the laws which guide the stars in their courses? **Canst thou set the dominion thereof in the earth?** Did Job possess the authority and power to regulate the influence of the heavens and their stars upon earthly destinies? V. 34. **Canst thou lift up thy voice to the clouds,** in commanding them to yield their moisture, **that abundance of waters may cover thee?** V. 35. **Canst thou send lightnings that they may go,** at the command of Job, **and say unto thee, Here we are,** namely, at his disposal, ready to do his bidding? V. 36. **Who hath put wisdom in the inward parts,** teaching the dark clouds how to perform their work in the world? **Or who hath given understanding to the heart,** to the creatures of the atmosphere, so that the clouds know their arrangement in the various circumstances? V. 37. **Who can number the clouds in wisdom,** appointing to them their number and extent? **Or who can stay the bottles of heaven,** who tilts them, who pours out their liquid contents, v. 38. **when the dust groweth into hardness,** becoming a firm mass as the rain-water molds its particles together, **and the clods cleave fast together,** caking into a hard mass? In all these things God is supreme, all the forces of the atmosphere and of the sky being subject to Him, by whose laws they are guided. The insignificance of man stands out all the more strongly by contrast.

CHAPTER 39.

(Chapter 38, 39—39, 30.)

Continuation of God's Discourse.

GOD'S POWER IN THE ANIMAL KINGDOM.—V. 39. **Wilt thou hunt the prey for the lion,** or the lioness, **or fill the appetite of the young lions,** appeasing their constant craving for food, v. 40. **when they crouch in their dens,** in the thickets where they have their lairs, **and abide in the covert to lie in wait,** always on the lookout for possible prey? V. 41. **Who provideth for the raven his food when his young ones cry unto God? They wander for lack of meat,** their voracious appetite never being satisfied. Cp. Ps. 147, 9; 146, 15. 16. God performs as a matter of course what all men could never hope and undertake to do, this providential care placing Him far above all creatures. V. 1. **Knowest thou the time when the wild goats of the rock bring forth,** their homes being on the rocks near the summits of the mountains? **Or canst thou mark when the hinds do calve,** noting the travail of the many countless animals scattered in the wilderness? V. 2. **Canst thou number the months that they fulfil,** namely, in bearing their young? **Or knowest thou the time when they bring forth?** The external knowledge concerning these facts Job may have possessed, but he had no idea of the providential care which was needed in bringing these animals safely through the dangerous period until the young were born. V. 3. **They bow themselves,** cp. 1 Sam. 4, 19, **they bring forth their young ones, they cast out their sorrows,** shaking off the pains of birth with its fruit, all under the influence of God's providential care. V. 4. **Their young ones are in good liking,** in fine condition from the start, **they grow up with corn,** out in the desert; **they go forth,** reaching maturity and independence in just a short while, **and return not unto them,** they are soon able to dispense with the care of their parents, all this under the direction of God. V. 5. **Who hath sent out the wild ass free?** whose wildness is proverbial. **Or who hath loosed the bands of the wild ass,** literally, "of the fleeing one," of the fugitive? The very fact that the wild ass scorns all human control and nurture makes him a good example in this connection, where the power and wisdom of God is emphasized. V. 6. **Whose house I have made the wilderness, and the barren land,** the desert, the salt-steppe, **his dwellings;** for it was there that he preferred to live, satisfied with the food offered by the saline plants of the alkali wastes. V. 7. **He scorneth the multitude of the city,** mocking at the clamor of the city, **neither regardeth he the crying of the driver,** paying no attention to the shouts which the domesticated ass and the mule must obey. V. 8. **The range of the mountains is his pasture,** whatever food his search brings to his attention, **and he searcheth after every green thing,** all his wants being provided for in this manner by the Creator. V. 9. **Will the unicorn,** probably the oryx, a wild and powerful species of antelope found in the desert at that time, **be willing to serve thee or abide by thy crib,** readily domesticated? V. 10. **Canst thou bind the unicorn with his band in the furrow,** compelling him to draw a furrow with the plow while being led or guided with a cord? **Or will he harrow the valleys after thee,** in the regular labor of preparing the soil for sowing? V. 11. **Wilt thou trust him,** readily depending upon him, **because his strength is great?** That very fact would cause men to mistrust the untamed animal. **Or wilt thou leave thy labor to him,** trusting him to bring home the product of the soil, as a tame ox would? V. 12. **Wilt thou believe him,** again depending upon him, **that he will bring home thy seed,** the harvested grain, **and gather it into thy barn?** All this, again, is beyond the control of man, but a small matter in the hand of God. V. 13. **Gavest thou the goodly wings unto the peacocks?** literally, "The wing of the female ostrich claps joyously," in time with her piercing cries, **or wings and feathers unto the ostrich,** literally, "Is it the pinion and feather of the stork," a quiet and tame bird? The ostrich is as a representative of all that is wild and untamable among the birds. V. 14. **Which,** or, No, on the contrary, far from being good and quiet, she **leaveth her eggs in the earth,** the reference being to the habit of the wild ostrich of abandoning her nest at the approach of danger and remaining away for a long time, **and warmeth them in dust,** trusting to the warm sand to keep the eggs from chilling; v. 15. **and forgetteth that the foot**

may crush them, or that the wild beast may break them, stamping them to pieces by walking over the nest. V. 16. **She is hardened against her young ones,** apparently dealing harshly with them, **as though they were not hers; her labor is in vain without fear,** it does not seem to bother the ostrich that her labor in laying the eggs is vain when they are crushed in this manner, v. 17. **because God hath deprived her of wisdom, neither hath He imparted to her understanding,** the stupidity of the ostrich being proverbial in Arabia. V. 18. **What time she lifteth up herself on high,** lifting herself to her full height with a lashing movement, **she scorneth the horse and his rider,** mocking them by the swiftness of her flight. The Lord now turns to the description of the war-horse, highly prized and praised in Arabia since ancient times. V. 19. **Hast thou given the horse strength,** namely, his warlike strength? **Hast thou clothed his neck with thunder,** literally, "with fluttering hair," with a waving mane? V. 20. **Canst thou make him afraid as a grasshopper,** rather, make him leap or gallop like the locust? **The glory of his nostrils is terrible;** when he snorts, it strikes terror to the heart. V. 21. **He paweth in the valley,** while the soldiers are scouting and making preparations for a battle, he is impatient for the fray, **and rejoiceth in his strength; he goeth on to meet the armed men,** ready to meet even a host in armor. V. 22. **He mocketh at fear and is not affrighted,** the excitement of the battle rather taking hold of him, **neither turneth he back from the sword.** V. 23. **The quiver,** namely, that of the horseman seated upon him, **rattleth against him, the glittering spear and the shield,** all sounds which would terrorize a timid animal. V. 24. **He swalloweth the ground with fierceness and rage,** as he rushes over it in full gallop; **neither believeth he that it is the sound of the trumpet,** he does not stand still, he cannot contain himself when the trumpet sounds, he must get into the fray. V. 25. **He saith among the trumpets, Ha, ha!** neighing with joyful eagerness for the battle; **and he smelleth the battle afar off, the thunder of the captains, and the shouting,** the battle-cries of the soldiers engaged in battle. Of all the poetic descriptions of the war-horse in the entire ancient literature, this, aside from the fact of its divine inspiration, is the oldest and most beautiful. V. 26. **Doth the hawk fly by thy wisdom,** flying up to great heights as a result of Job's understanding, **and stretch her wings toward the south,** in the annual migration, to this day one of the secrets of bird-life? V. 27. **Doth the eagle mount up,** soaring in stately flight, **at thy command and make her nest on high?** Was all this a result of Job's power and authority? V. 28. **She dwelleth and abideth on the rock,** that being the place where she locates her aerie, from which she has a wide outlook over the country, **upon the crag of the rock, and the strong place,** a mighty castle and watch-tower. V. 29. **From thence she seeketh her prey,** piercing the atmosphere far and wide with her sharp vision, **and her eyes behold afar off.** V. 30. **Her young ones also,** as true birds of prey, **suck up blood; and where the slain are, there is she,** the vulture being here included in the genus eagle. All these considerations, the mere recital of which had the effect of rendering Job speechless with awe, showed that God's majesty is infinitely exalted above man's criticism, that man simply cannot undertake to measure God according to the rules and ideas of mortal men.

CHAPTER 40.

Job's Confession and God's Second Address.

JOB RETRACTS HIS CHARGES. — V. 1. **Moreover,** since Job was still silent, **the Lord answered Job and said,** v. 2. **Shall he that contendeth with the Almighty instruct Him,** continue his critical attitude after all that had now been laid before him? **He that reproveth God, let him answer it,** giving the proper replies and explanations of all the marvels set forth. Job had censured: let him now make good his charges. V. 3. **Then Job answered the Lord and said,** v. 4. **Behold, I am vile,** too base to offer a solution of the problems presented; **what shall I answer Thee?** He was unable to present so much as another argument. **I will lay mine hand upon my mouth,** closing it tightly, imposing absolute silence upon himself. V. 5. **Once have I spoken,** in making his challenge against God; **but I will not answer,** not making another attempt to censure the Lord; **yea, twice,** referring to his repeated charges; **but I will proceed no further.** He retracted his former statements, he no longer dared to criticize God, since the Lord's miraculous wisdom and providential care was too evident to permit of his further opposition.

THE LORD REBUKES JOB'S PRESUMPTION. — V. 6. **Then answered the Lord unto Job out of the whirlwind,** in order to lead him to a still higher stage of humiliation, so that he would willingly bow under the chastening hand of God, **and said,** v. 7. **Gird up thy loins now like a man,** again making ready for a sharp encounter; **I will demand of thee,** asking some further explanations, **and declare thou unto Me.** Cp. chap. 38, 3. V. 8. **Wilt thou also disannul My judgment,** altogether abolishing and setting aside God's right? **Wilt thou condemn Me,** boldly stating that God was unjust, **that thou mayest be righteous?** For that is what Job's contentions really had been equivalent to. V. 9. **Hast thou an arm like God,** possessing almighty power? **Or canst thou thunder with a voice like Him?** this being an evidence of divine omnipotence and government in nature. V. 10. **Deck thyself now with majesty and excellency,** Job should put on these attributes of divine greatness and authority, if he made such claims; **and array thyself with glory and beauty,** with all the proofs of the Creator's majesty. V. 11. **Cast abroad the rage of thy wrath,** letting it break forth and overflow in a flood, as the almighty Lord is able to do; **and behold every one that is proud, and abase him,** displaying such authority to punish as God exercises continually. V. 12. **Look on every one that is proud and bring him low,** as God can by a mere angry glance destroy the wicked; **and tread down the wicked in their place,** overthrowing them and annihilating their power. V. 13. **Hide them in the dust together,** so that the earth covers their graves; **and bind their faces in secret,** in the darkness and secrecy of death's realm, with the voice of their presumption and pride forever stilled. V. 14. **Then will I also confess unto thee,** joining in Job's praise of himself, **that thine own right hand can save thee,** bringing him help and salvation, this idea being implied in Job's charges, together with this, that he would vigorously administer true justice. The Lord's questions are full of majestic irony, in order to bring Job to the full realization of his untenable position.

JOB'S WEAKNESS CONTRASTED WITH THE STRENGTH EVEN OF THE HIPPOPOTAMUS.—V. 15. **Behold now behemoth,** a monster beast, the water-ox, or hippopotamus, **which is made with thee,** created by the hand of God like the human beings and living with them on the earth; **he eateth grass as an ox,** the tender plants, the reeds of the Nile, after the manner of domesticated cattle. V. 16. **Lo, now, his strength is in his loins, and his force is in the navel of his belly,** in the sinews and muscles of his abdomen. V. 17. **He moveth his tail like a cedar,** bending it like a cedar-bough, with great firmness and elasticity; **the sinews of his stones,** rather, of his thighs, **are wrapped together,** firmly knit or twisted, like the tendrils of the vine or like a strong rope. V. 18. **His bones are as strong pieces of brass,** tubes or channels of strength; **his bones are like bars of iron,** tenacious as wrought iron. V. 19. **He is the chief of the ways of God,** the firstling of God's almighty power, among the mightiest of His creatures; **He that made him can make his sword to approach unto him,** literally, his Maker furnished to him his sword, the sharp teeth with which he cuts down his food and which he uses in his own defense. V. 20. **Surely the mountains bring him forth food,** being obliged to provide food for him, if need be, **where all the beasts of the field play,** unhurt by him, since he is not a beast of prey, but a herbivorous animal. V. 21. **He lieth under the shady trees,** the lotus-bushes of the lowlands of Egypt and the eastern Mediterranean countries, **in the covert of the reed and fens;** for the lowlands near the river are his habitat. V. 22. **The shady trees,** the lotus-bushes, **cover him with their shadow; the willows of the brook compass him about,** there are his favorite haunting-places. V. 23. **Behold, he drinketh up a river and hasteth not,** rather, the river becomes violent, turbulent with a quick rise, but he is not startled; **he trusteth that he can draw up Jordan into his mouth,** he is unconcerned even if a river with the swiftly rushing course of Jordan overflows its banks, swelling up to its mouth during the spring freshets. V. 24. **He taketh it with his eyes; his nose pierceth through snares.** The Hebrew rather seems a challenging question: Will any one take him before his eyes, with open force, or pierce through his nose with cords? The answer is implied: No man will dare to undertake such a dangerous attack; the only way of taking the hippopotamus being by guile, in pitfalls. This picture was painted before Job's eyes in order to make him realize his own insignificance, because one of his own fellow-creatures, entirely in the power of God's providence, was mightier than he himself. What little cause, then, did he have for arrogance and conceit!

CHAPTER 41.

Further Reproof of Job.

JOB'S WEAKNESS WHEN COMPARED WITH THE STRENGTH OF THE CROCODILE.—V. 1. **Canst thou draw out leviathan,** the great and fierce crocodile of Egypt and other Mediterranean countries, **with an hook,** or purse-net, **or his tongue with a cord which thou lettest down?** Rather, "Into the line dost thou press down his tongue," namely, when he has taken the bait and the drawing of the line pushes aside his tongue. V. 2. **Canst thou put an hook,** a ring made of plaited rushes, such as were drawn through the gills of captured fishes to prevent their escaping, **into his nose, or bore his jaw through with a thorn,** with an iron hook or ring, in order to tame him? V. 3. **Will he,** in order to regain his freedom, **make many supplications unto thee? Will**

he speak soft words unto thee, pleading for the master's favor with flatteries, as a domesticated animal might? V. 4. **Will he make a covenant with thee,** an agreement to submit himself? **Wilt thou take him for a servant forever,** making him a slave? V. 5. **Wilt thou play with him as with a bird,** as one coddles and teases a pet canary? **Or wilt thou bind him for thy maidens,** making him a pet of the female house-slaves? The answer is implied in every case: No; for he is utterly untamable. V. 6. **Shall the companions make a banquet of him?** That is, Do the members of the fishermen's guild make him an object of trade and barter? **Shall they part him among the merchants?** Can they divide him among the Canaanites? Can they handle him that easily? V. 7. **Canst thou fill his skin with barbed irons,** in trying to kill him with a spear or dart? **or his head with fish-spears,** in hunting him with a harpoon? V. 8. **Lay thine hand upon him; remember the battle, do no more,** that is, if one should have the foolhardiness to attempt a fight with a fierce crocodile, he would never try it again, the remembrance of that one attempt would last forever. V. 9. **Behold, the hope of him is in vain,** namely, the hope of the man who would risk an encounter with such a monster. **Shall not one be cast down even at the sight of him?** The very sight of the fierce amphibian fills the heart of the beholder with terror. V. 10. **None is so fierce,** rash or foolhardy, **that dare stir him up,** although, after all, he is a mere animal. **Who, then, is able to stand before Me?** Who will dare to appear before the Lord as His adversary? V. 11. **Who hath prevented Me,** having given something to God in the first place, having become His creditor, **that I should repay him?** Who among all men has the right to claim anything at the hand of God? **Whatsoever is under the whole heaven is Mine;** therefore He owes nothing to any creature. To these facts the Lord adds an impressive description of the crocodile's structure and mode of living. V. 12. **I will not conceal his parts,** He feels constrained to mention also his members, **nor his power, nor his comely proportion,** his gracefulness in spite of his great size. V. 13. **Who can discover the face of his garment,** the scaly coat of mail on his back? This is so firmly connected with his body that no man can take it off. **Or who can come to him with his double bridle?** Who would venture to enter into the open jaws of the crocodile, as he stretches his mouth with its double row of sharp teeth? V. 14. **Who can open the doors of his face,** the mighty, slashing jaws? **His teeth are terrible round about,** their terror being all the greater since his sixty-six teeth are not covered by the lips. V. 15. **His scales are his pride,** the bony shields of his back, divided by furrows, **shut up together as with a close seal,** fitted together with the exactness of a seal pressed down on paper or parchment. V. 16. **One is so near to another that no air can come between them.** V. 17. **They are joined one to another, they stick together that they cannot be sundered,** they form a perfect and impenetrable shield. V. 18. **By his neesings,** when he blows out his breath, together with water and slime, through his nostrils, **a light doth shine,** it seems like a flash of light, **and his eyes are like the eyelids of the morning,** of the dawn, when the first red glow appears in the east. V. 19. **Out of his mouth go burning lamps,** streams of water shining like torches, **and sparks of fire leap out.** V. 20. **Out of his nostrils goeth smoke, as out of a seething pot or cauldron,** as when a kettle is heated over a strongly smoking fire of reeds, all this describing the snorting and fretting of the crocodile when angry. V. 21. **His breath kindleth coals, and a flame goeth out of his mouth,** this being a highly poetic description of the crocodile's fiery breath, of the steaming of his nostrils. V. 22. **In his neck remaineth strength,** dwelling there, making its permanent home there, **and sorrow is turned into joy before him,** before his advance terror and despair leap with fearful strides, this showing the effect of his appearance upon men and beasts. V. 23. **The flakes of his flesh are joined together,** his very flanks and dewlaps make no impression of looseness or flabbiness; **they are firm in themselves; they cannot be moved,** being fixed upon him in rows of smaller scales, solid as a shield. V. 24. **His heart is as firm as a stone,** molded into a solid piece, yea, **as hard as a piece of the nether millstone,** which was always particularly hard, in order to bear the movement of the grinding. V. 25. **When he raiseth up himself,** with all this fierceness of his heart, **the mighty are afraid; by reason of breakings they purify themselves,** that is, they are so overcome with astonishment and terror that they miss their aim. V. 26. **The sword of him that layeth at him,** in an effort to wound or kill him, **cannot hold,** it glances off without effect; **the spear, the dart, nor the habergeon,** no matter what weapon or missile is used. V. 27. **He esteemeth iron as straw,** for it has no effect on his mailed hide, **and brass as rotten wood,** since it bends and breaks on the shield of his back. V. 28. **The arrow,** literally, "the son of the quiver," **cannot make him flee; slingstones are turned with him into stubble,** utterly powerless to harm him. V. 29. **Darts are counted as stubble,** large clubs considered as so much chaff; **he laugheth at the shaking of a spear,** mocking at all human weapons. V. 30. **Sharp stones are under him,**

the ventral part, or plastron, of his skin consists of pointed shards, sharp scales; **he spreadeth sharp pointed things upon the mire,** the pointed scales of his plastron leaving marks on the soft ground like those made by the iron spikes of the ancient threshing-sledge. V. 31. **He maketh the deep to boil like a pot,** namely, by his threshings and slashings of the water; **he maketh the sea like a pot of ointment,** all frothy and foamy as a result of his tumbling and rushing in the water. V. 32. **He maketh a path to shine after him,** his trail, or wake, on the surface of the water is shiny; **one would think the deep to be hoary,** the foam looking like gray hair scattered on the water. V. 33. **Upon earth there is not his like,** or, "one who has dominion over him," **who is made without fear,** he is altogether fearless. V. 34. **He beholdeth all high things,** looking them boldly in the face, without the slightest flinching; **he is a king over all the children of pride,** a tyrant and ruler even in the midst of animals who are fearless. This being true, and man being powerless to control this creature, how dare he criticize the great Creator?

CHAPTER 42.

Job Reinstated by God.

JOB'S HUMBLE CONFESSION. — V. 1. **Then Job,** now fully overcome by the Lord's arguments, **answered the Lord and said,** v. 2. **I know that Thou canst do everything,** the omnipotence, the creative power of God, had been set before him in the most convincing manner, **and that no thought can be withholden from Thee,** no undertaking, no venture, is forbidden to Him; no matter what He does, His justice cannot be questioned. No matter how hard it is for men to understand, God's ways are always right. V. 3. **Who is he that hideth counsel without knowledge?** That was the question which the Lord had addressed to Job at the beginning of His discourse, chap. 38, 2, and Job now acknowledges the truth of this verdict. **Therefore have I uttered that I understood not,** making statements concerning things beyond his comprehension; **things too wonderful for me, which I knew not,** passing judgment on God's government of human affairs which cannot be fathomed by man's finite mind as long as he is in this world. V. 4. **Hear, I beseech Thee, and I will speak,** for Job was ready now to make the right answer; **I will demand of Thee, and declare Thou unto me,** he was ready humbly to ask and to receive instruction. V. 5. **I have heard of Thee by the hearing of the ear,** he had drawn his conclusions from outward and incomplete observation only, which, as he now realizes, was faulty; **but now mine eye seeth Thee,** he had had his spiritual vision opened to the real essence of God, to an understanding of His attributes. V. 6. **Wherefore I abhor myself,** Job utterly repudiated and rejected all his rash statements, which had cast slurs upon God's justice, **and repent in dust and ashes,** in the deepest humiliation and mourning. That is the proper attitude to take if one is convinced of any wrong in his past life; not to slur over the matter, but to make a full confession, to come to the Lord with meekness and repentance, asking His forgiveness.

JOB VINDICATED AND RESTORED TO PROSPERITY. — V. 7. **And it was so that after the Lord had spoken these words unto Job,** after Job had made his penitent reply, **the Lord said unto Eliphaz, the Temanite,** as the spokesman and leader of the three friends, **My wrath is kindled against thee and against thy two friends,** Bildad and Zophar; **for ye have not spoken of Me the thing that is right as My servant Job hath,** they had persisted in their endeavor to brand Job as an enormous sinner, guilty of gross trespasses, their conclusion therefore having been that calamities always prove guilt, this being a false representation of God's manner of dealing with Job. V. 8. **Therefore take unto you now seven bullocks and seven rams,** cp. Num. 23, 1, **and go to My servant Job,** who was to act in the capacity of priest, **and offer up for yourselves a burnt offering,** to make an atonement for themselves; **and My servant Job shall pray for you,** acting as mediator in their behalf, interceding for them; **for him will I accept,** regarding him favorably, **lest I deal with you after your folly,** visiting the penalty of their foolishness upon them, **in that ye have not spoken of Me the thing which is right like My servant Job.** V. 9. **So Eliphaz, the Temanite, and Bildad, the Shuhite, and Zophar, the Naamathite, went and did according as the Lord commanded them. The Lord also accepted Job,** regarding him favorably in his intercession for his friends. V. 10. **And the Lord turned the captivity of Job,** restored him, vindicated him, amply indemnified him for the losses which he had sustained, **when he prayed for his friends,** thus showing the proper forgiving spirit; also **the Lord gave Job twice as much as he had before.** V. 11. **Then came there unto him all his brethren and all his sisters,** all the relatives who had so heartlessly withdrawn from him during his misery, **and all they that had been of his acquaintance before,** cp. chap. 19, 13—19, **and did eat bread with him in his house,** once more glad to enjoy his hospitality; **and they bemoaned him,** after the fashion of friends of this type, **and comforted him over all the evil that the Lord had brought upon him. Every man also gave him a piece of money,** a piece of gold believed to have been stamped with the figure of a lamb, worth about four times as much as a shekel, Gen. 33, 19, **and every one an earring of gold,** for nose-rings and earrings were worn by both men and women at that time. V. 12. **So the Lord blessed the latter end of Job more than his beginning,** by doubling his former substance; **for he had fourteen thousand sheep, and six thousand camels, and a thousand yoke of oxen, and a thousand she-asses,** cp. chap. 1, 3. V. 13. **He had also seven sons and three daughters,** a large family being a special sign of God's blessing upon a household. V. 14. **And he called the name of the first, Jemima; and the name of the second, Kezia; and the name of the third, Keren-happuch,** all three names being descriptive of the beauty, charm, and grace of the young women and of the happy change in Job's fortunes. V. 15. **And in all the land were no women found so fair as the daughters of Job,** distinguished for extraordinary beauty; **and their father gave them inheritance among their brethren,** this being an indication of the fine harmony which prevailed in this family. V. 16. **After this lived Job an hundred and forty years and saw his sons and his son's sons, even four generations,** a special proof of divine favor, Ps. 128, 6; Prov. 17, 6. V. 17. **So Job died, being old and full of days,** a long and happy life also being a blessing of Jehovah, Gen, 25, 8; 35, 29. Note: Many a Christian who is bearing heavy crosses has received comfort from the lesson of Job. It may not always happen so that sufferers among the believers are returned to health and prosperity as was Job, but the time will come when they will know and understand the ways of God, realizing fully that He always has thoughts of peace toward us and never thoughts of evil, that He always desires our welfare.

THE BOOK OF PSALMS.

INTRODUCTION.

The Book of Psalms, or the Psalter, is the great prayer-book of the Church of all times, the collection of divinely inspired odes or songs whose singing was of old accompanied by instruments of music. Under the guidance of God the Psalms as we now know them were at various times collected, five sections, or books, being distinguished (Ps. 41, 13; 72, 18. 19; 89, 52; 106, 48; 150), the final arrangement being made after the Babylonian Captivity by Ezra, as the tradition of the Jews has it.

To more than one hundred psalms are prefixed inscriptions which give one or more particulars and directions for the public rendering of the sacred song, such as the name of the author, of the instrument on which the accompaniment was to be played, of the style of the music or of the poetry, of the melody which the choirmaster was to choose, of the subject or occasion for which it was written. The "chief musician" was the superintendent of the Temple music, who was probably at the same time the leader of the Temple orchestra and the director of the Temple chorus of priests and Levites.

The Psalter is usually called "The Psalms of David," since he is the only author mentioned in the New Testament, Luke 20, 42, and because his name appears in more titles than that of any other writer. The name of David appears in the heading of about one half of the psalms; besides, the authorship of Ps. 2 and Ps. 95 is ascribed to him, Acts 4, 25; Heb. 4, 7. He may have written others which are not credited to him. To Asaph, a Levite and one of the three heads of David's choir at Jerusalem, are ascribed twelve psalms; to the sons of Korah, a celebrated family of singers and poets in the time of David, eleven, including Ps. 88, whose author, Heman, belonged to the sons of Korah; to Solomon, two; to Moses, one; and to Ethan, one of the three masters of the Temple music, one.

Of special interest to us are the Messianic psalms, including Ps. 2, 8, 16, 22, 24, 40, 45, 47, 68, 69, 72, 89, 93, 97, 110, 118; they refer to the Messiah, the promised Redeemer of the world, portraying more or less vividly and completely His person and work, His birth, betrayal, agony, and death, His triumph over death, His ascension into heaven and enthronement at the right hand of God the Father Almighty.[1]

Of the general contents of the psalter, Luther writes: "It should be noted that the entire Psalter deals with five subjects; therefore we divide it into five parts. In the first place, some psalms prophesy of Christ and of the

1) Cp. *Concordia Bible Class*, April, 1919, 57 to 60; Fuerbringer, ***Einleitung in das Alte Testament***, 49—53.

Church, or the saints, what would happen to them, etc.; and to this class belong all the psalms in which there are promises given to the pious and threats to the ungodly. In the second place, there is a number of doctrinal psalms, which teach us what we should do and what omit according to the Law of God; and to this class belong all the psalms which condemn the doctrine of men and extol the Word of God. In the third place, there are several psalms of consolation, which comfort the sorrowing and suffering saints and, on the other hand, condemn and terrify the tyrants. . . . In the fourth place, there are a few psalms of prayer, in which we pray to God and cry in all distress; and to this class belong all psalms which lament and mourn and cry over the enemies. In the fifth place, we have psalms of thanksgiving, in which we laud and praise God for His various benefits and His assistance; and to this class belong all psalms which praise God in His works, these being the finest and principal psalms. . . . But we must know that the psalms cannot be just exactly and evenly divided into such parts and verses, for sometimes two, three, and even all five divisions, as noted above, are found in one psalm, so that prophecy, doctrine, consolation, prayer, and thanksgiving are found together. But this division serves for the better understanding of the psalms and that we may the more easily learn and remember them."

PSALM 1.

The Difference Between the Righteous and the Ungodly.

All men are sinners: all have sinned and come short of the glory of God, Rom. 3, 23. No man is able to stand before God by virtue of his own righteousness, Is. 64, 6; Dan. 9, 7. But all believers have the righteousness of God in Jesus Christ, appropriated to them by faith, Phil. 3, 9. And so all true believers are righteous in the eyes of God, while all unbelievers are unrighteous and ungodly in His sight. V. 1. **Blessed is the man,** literally, "blessednesses, or happinesses, of the man," **that walketh not in the counsel of the ungodly,** making the plans of the wicked his concern, making it his business to follow out their godless undertakings, **nor standeth in the way of sinners,** making it a point to linger in the company of those whom he should shun, **nor sitteth in the seat of the scornful,** those who scorn the belief in God in the sense of mocking and sneering at true religion. Note the climax in the verse: first comes the meditating of evil, then a wilful performance of that which is sinful, then the suppressing of a good conscience and the mockery of everything sacred; and, on the other hand, first the seeking of the society of the godless, then a somewhat uncertain standing at the outside of their circle, then a deliberate participation in their mockery. V. 2. **But his delight is in the Law of the Lord,** in the meditation and study of the Law, of the Word of Jehovah, he finds full inner satisfaction and happiness; **and in His Law doth he meditate day and night,** reflecting upon its injunctions, applying its instructions always and in all circumstances. Just how the blessings of Jehovah come upon such a person is now described. V. 3. **And he shall be like a tree planted by the rivers of water,** where his roots reach deep down to the hidden reservoirs of moisture, where he has a never-ending supply of vitality and power, **that bringeth forth his fruit in his season,** as the result of a faith grounded deep in the power of Jehovah, which never disappoints the hopes of the great Gardener above, Luke 13, 7; **his leaf also shall not wither,** not be affected by the drought of hostility or adversity; **and whatsoever he doeth shall prosper,** with a prosperity at least in the sight of God, no matter how little the world thinks of his success. Not an outward good fortune in amassing the riches of this earth counts in the sight of Jehovah, but the possession of a trusting faith abounding in real good works. V. 4. **The ungodly are not so,** either in conduct or happiness, and therefore both their condition and their destiny in the sight of God differ widely and radically from that of the believers; **but are like the chaff which the wind driveth away,** they have been weighed and found wanting, and therefore utter destruction comes upon them in consequence of their emptiness and vanity, just as the chaff on the open threshing-floors of the Orient is scattered to the four winds, while the heavier grain remains. V. 5. **Therefore the ungodly,** the wicked unbelievers, **shall not stand in the Judgment,** will not be acquitted before the tribunal of God, will not be able to stand up and hold their own in the last great investigation, **nor sinners in the congregation of the righteous,** they will not be placed with the blessed of the Father at the right hand of the Judge, Matt. 3, 12; Ps. 35, 5; Zeph. 2, 1. 2. V. 6. **For the Lord knoweth the way of the righteous,** He knows them and is known of them, He is united with them by the closest band of union, in the most intimate fellowship, John 10, 14. 15, and therefore their path through life is sure to lead to God, certain to reach the goal of everlasting bliss in Him; **but the way of the ungodly shall perish,** it leads into the abyss of everlasting destruction and damnation. Thus is the foolishness of the wicked punished and the hope of the believers rewarded.

PSALM 2.

Of the Eternal Sonship of the Messiah.

THE FUTILE RAGE OF THE NATIONS. — That the entire psalm is Messianic is clearly shown by the quotation Acts 4, 25. 26, together with the explanation there added: "For of a truth against Thy holy Child Jesus, whom Thou hast anointed, . . . the people . . . were gathered together," v. 27. Cp. Acts 13, 33; Heb. 1, 5. V. 1. **Why do the heathen rage,** the nations seething, surging, with resentful murmurings, **and the people imagine a vain thing?** The inspired poet's indignation and contempt is immediately expressed in the rhetorical question: What madness for them to act thus! V. 2. **The kings of the earth set themselves,** sitting together in conspiracy, **and the rulers take counsel together,** all the earth's greatest dignitaries consulting with one another in sullen rebellious activity, **against the Lord,** Jehovah, the great Ruler of the earth, **and against His Anointed,** the singular High Priest and Prophet of Jehovah, the Messiah, anointed with the Holy Ghost and with power above all His fellows, Ps. 45, 7; Acts 10, 38, saying, v. 3. **Let us break their bands asunder and cast away their cords from us.** The wicked of all times resent the kingly dignity and power, the government, of Jesus Christ; they consider the bearing of His gentle burden, Matt. 11, 30, as a tying with bands, as an imprisoning with cords. They want to live in the unbridled licentiousness of their hearts. But how does the Lord regard this rebellion of the nations and of their rulers? V. 4. **He that sitteth in the heavens shall laugh; the Lord shall have them in derision,** mocking at them, deriding them, for their futile attempts to put Him from the throne of His majesty in the heavens. His mocking is a sign of the unshakable safety of His dominion and of His contempt for the puny creatures who desire to dethrone Him. At the same time His patience will come to an end at the period determined by Him. V. 5. **Then,** on the great day of wrath and Judgment, **shall He speak unto them in His wrath,** in the white heat of His just anger, **and vex them in His sore displeasure,** trouble, terrify, and utterly overthrow them in the greatest destruction of all. So much the Lord says for the consolation of His children, who suffer much on account of the enmity of the unbelievers. In addition to this the Lord opposes one word of majesty to the puny endeavors of the enemies. V. 6. **Yet have I set My King,** Messiah, Christ, the Anointed of the Lord, the King with everlasting sovereignty and power, **upon My holy hill of Zion.** Originally denoting the hill where the Temple stood, this word came to signify the place of God's merciful presence and especially His holy Christian Church, the communion of saints. Christ, firmly established, enthroned in the heavens, of equal power and majesty with the Father from eternity, is at the same time in the midst of His Church, Ps. 46, 5, which He endows with the blessings of His salvation, which He governs with His Word and Spirit.

THE DIVINE ANNOUNCEMENT. — It is the Anointed of Jehovah, Jesus Christ Himself, who now speaks in person. V. 7. **I will declare the decree,** make known, express for a statute, publish as a resolution: **The Lord,** the great Jehovah, the almighty God of the heavens, **hath said unto Me, Thou art My Son,** standing in the relation of essential Sonship to God; **this day,** in the great, eternal to-day, in the timeless period of eternity, **have I begotten Thee,** Christ being generated out of the essence of God. The Son of God was from eternity brought forth by the eternal Father as His essential image, by the transmission of the divine essence, in an incomprehensible, supernatural manner. Cp. Matt. 3, 17; 17, 5. Messiah now states what the Father, in His great commission, had spoken to Him. V. 8. **Ask of Me,** the Son should freely demand of the Father, for the Father's love would withhold nothing from the Son of His eternal begetting, **and I shall give Thee the heathen for Thine inheritance and the uttermost parts of the earth for Thy possession.** Nations, dominions, the very ends of the world are placed in the hands of Messiah; men from all nations, people from the very ends of the inhabited earth, would acknowledge Christ as their gracious Lord, their merciful Sovereign. V. 9. **Thou shalt break them with a rod of iron; Thou shalt dash them in pieces like a potter's vessel.** This is the judgment upon the rebels, upon the scoffers, the manifestation of Christ's consuming anger on the great Day of Judgment. The breaking, the dashing to pieces, is a picture of eternal damnation, Rev. 2, 27; 12, 5; 19, 15. Since, however, the mercy of God turns to thoughts of peace rather than to anger, His warning, coaxing cry goes forth in the closing words of the psalmist. V. 10. **Be wise now therefore, O ye kings; be instructed, ye judges of the earth!** The rulers of the earth should show sense, the men whose business it is to dispense judgment, all those occupying positions of honor and influence, should make use of the proper wisdom, learn the true understanding which leads to eternal peace and happiness. V. 11. **Serve the Lord with fear, and rejoice with trembling;** they should place themselves fully and unreservedly in His service, although this joyful service would be attended with sacred awe, fear, and trembling, Phil. 2, 12, lest His mercy be abused and His love forgotten. V. 12. **Kiss the Son,** hailing Him with the true kiss of homage, lest **He be angry and ye perish from the way when His wrath is kindled but a little.** The day of wrath is near; but a little while and the anger of the great Judge of the world will strike the proud scorners of His grace. It is time for all men seriously to think about the salvation of their souls. **Blessed are all they,** the thousandfold blessings are upon them, **that put their trust in Him,** taking refuge in His mercy; for eternal salvation is theirs. All those who put their faith and trust in Jesus Christ as their one Redeemer will not be put to shame, but will be safe in His love throughout eternity.

PSALM 3.

Morning Prayer of a Christian in Danger and Affliction.

A Psalm of David, when he fled from Absalom, his son, 2 Sam. 15, 14, probably written on the morning after the day of the flight, when David saw nothing but danger and destruction on every side, when his heart expressed the thoughts which arise in the hearts of all children of God as they battle with affliction. V. 1. **Lord, how are they increased that trouble me,** the idea of their increasing number being brought home to David by the fact that his own son had joined their ranks. **Many are they that rise up against me,** as his adversaries along every line, but particularly in the rebellion of Absalom. V. 2. **Many there be which say of my soul, There is no help for him in God. Selah.** David's condition at that time, as history shows, 2 Sam. 15, 23. 30, was such as to make all men doubt the possibility of his deliverance, while his enemies openly stated that he could no longer expect any help from the Lord. The word Selah was a term used in music which, according to its etymology, denoted some sort of augmentation or elevation; either the orchestra at this point played in full strength, or the accompaniment was increased in loudness, or both voices and instruments were raised in loud tones. In this way David set forth the greatness of the distress under which he was laboring. He does not, however, give way to despair, but turns to the Lord in a fervent prayer for deliverance. V. 3. **But Thou, O Lord, art a Shield for me,** protecting him against all the attacks of the enemies; **my Glory,** the source of all David's dignity and authority as king, **and the Lifter-up of mine head,** sure to raise him out of the deep depression with which he was then battling, which beset him on all sides. It is the lot of the children of God in this world which they must suffer that they are always in deep tribulation; but out of the very depths of their misery and woe they can and shall look up to the God of their salvation. V. 4. **I cried unto the Lord with my voice,** in loud and fervent supplication, **and He heard me out of His holy hill,** the mountain of His presence, Mount Zion, where the Tabernacle had now been erected and where the Temple was afterwards built. **Selah.** Again a pause in the psalm, in order to bring home the great truth of the Lord's answering prayer. V. 5. **I laid me down and slept,** instead of spending the night in useless lamentation; **I awaked,** still safe and secure, not yet delivered into the power of his enemies; **for the Lord sustained me,** it was David's confidence that the hand of Almighty God was upholding him, and this fact gave him his calm assurance in the midst of dangers. V. 6. **I will not be afraid of ten thousands of people,** no matter how great a multitude Absalom might gather to crush him, **that have set themselves against me round about.** This was not spoken in boastfulness, but with the quiet assurance of faith in the almighty protection of Jehovah. V. 7. **Arise, O Lord; save me, O my God!** a confident cry to Jehovah to interfere now in the happenings of the world; **for Thou hast smitten all mine enemies upon the cheekbone; Thou hast broken the teeth of the ungodly,** like the jaws of ravenous beasts or tearing monsters, the crushing of whose jaws and teeth not only renders them harmless, but is equivalent to their complete overthrow. V. 8. **Salvation belongeth unto the Lord,** He can and will help in every trouble, for there is no limit to the power at His disposal. **Thy blessing is upon Thy people.** David prays not only for his own deliverance, but for the welfare of his whole nation, a large part of which had been led astray in the rebellion then incited by Absalom. **Selah.** Thus David prayed even for his enemies, just as all Christians, sure of their own deliverance, make intercession for all men, also in the petition: "Thy kingdom come!"

PSALM 4.

Evening Prayer of a Christian in Every Kind of Trouble.

David, in his flight before Absalom, had come to Mahanaim, on the east side of Jordan, 2 Sam. 17, 24—26. He had a number of faithful men with him, but the army of Absalom, recruited from all Israel, was much larger. In order, therefore, to stimulate his own courage and to revive the drooping spirits of his men, David wrote this hymn, which, on account of its divine inspiration, has become a song of consolation for all those who are in trouble. **To the chief musician**, the man in charge of the liturgical music in the Temple-services, **on Neginoth**, the stringed instruments of the Temple-orchestra, **a psalm of David.** V. 1. **Hear me when I call**, offering ears favorable to his cause, **O God of my righteousness**, literally, "my God of righteousness," since Jehovah is the Vindicator of righteousness when it is falsely represented and persecuted. **Thou hast enlarged me when I was in distress**, making room, space, for his anxious heart when he was in straits. **Have mercy upon me**, the idea of unmerited favor coming to the front here, **and hear my prayer.** David urges his fellowship with Jehovah and the fact of his recent deliverance as reasons why God should show him further favors. He now, in a rhetorical manner, turns to the followers of Absalom, the proud and rebellious company. V. 2. **O ye sons of men**, men of prominence as many of them were, **how long will ye turn my glory**, the kingly dignity and authority given to him by God, **into shame? How long will ye love vanity**, the deceitful character of their rebellious plans, **and seek after leasing**, the lying and falsehood with which they tried to bolster up their schemes to dethrone David? **Selah.** V. 3. **But know that the Lord hath set apart him that is godly for himself**; He had, in a wonderful manner, selected David, and elevated him to the royal dignity. **The Lord will hear when I call unto Him**; this was the confidence of his pious heart. V. 4. **Stand in awe**, trembling before the wrath of God, **and sin not**, considering carefully lest they definitely endanger their own salvation; **commune with your own heart upon your bed**, deliberating when the silence of night was suited for such reflections, **and be still**, ceasing from their rebellious activities. **Selah.** V. 5. **Offer the sacrifices of righteousness**, showing the soundness of their penitence, the real character of their conversion, by sacrifices of atonement, **and put your trust in the Lord**, who would abundantly pardon after such an evidence of true godly sorrow. V. 6. **There be many that say**, even in the little band of his faithful followers, **Who will show us any good?** Would it be possible for them to experience deliverance in this time of great trouble? It is the cry which is apt to come to the lips of the truest children of God when all hope seems to be cut off. Therefore David's urgent prayer now rises to the throne of Jehovah. **Lord, lift Thou up the light of Thy countenance upon us**, in the blessing of God's kindness and mercy which He Himself had laid upon His children in the Aaronic benediction, Num. 6, 26. And so the pleading of David changes into a confident assertion. V. 7. **Thou hast put gladness in my heart**, causing him to rejoice in the midst of his outward affliction and to await the deliverance of Jehovah with calm trust, **more than in the time that their corn and their wine increased.** In spite of the fact that the party of Absalom had rich provisions at their disposal, the joyful confidence of David was a richer treasure than all the abundance of their barns and cellars. The conclusion of the prayer, therefore, is in line with David's trust in Jehovah and in the certainty of his salvation. V. 8. **I will both lay me down in peace**, without further thought of worry, **and sleep**, immediately drop off into a refreshing sleep, undisturbed by anxious thoughts; **for Thou, Lord, only makest me dwell in safety**, under the shelter of God's protecting hand the believer is always safe. For a Christian to spend the night in restless worry and forego the pleasure of a refreshing sleep is not only foolish, but may also verge on the sinful, namely, if it is equivalent to forsaking his trust in Jehovah.

PSALM 5.

Morning Prayer before Worship.

To the chief musician, for use in the liturgical service, **upon Nehiloth**, flutes or wind instruments of the Temple-orchestra, **a psalm of David.** David was at this time in Jerusalem and composed the hymn before attending divine worship. V. 1. **Give ear to my words, O Lord**, for the purpose of answering his prayer speedily; **consider my meditation**, hearing his sighs, his gentle complaints. V. 2. **Hearken unto the voice of my cry**, his loud and insistent clamoring for help, **my King**, the special Ruler of Israel, **and my God**, for whose protection David pleads, expecting it with all confidence; **for unto Thee will I pray**, that being the proper attitude of the Christian at all times, and especially when he draws near to the Lord in worship. V. 3. **My voice shalt Thou hear in the morning, O Lord; in the morning**, at the time of the morning sacrifice, **will I direct my prayer unto Thee**, laying it on the altar as a sacrifice to God, for without true prayer neither the wood nor the burnt offering has any value, **and will look up**, carefully watching for every token of divine favor. David now gives the reason for his confident approach to the Lord. V. 4. **For Thou art not a God that hath pleasure in wickedness**, God's holiness cannot abide godless meanness; **neither shall evil dwell with Thee**, not being accepted as a guest of God, not abiding in His presence. V. 5. **The foolish**, the boasters, the vain mockers, **shall not stand in Thy sight**, be in any way regarded with favor, regard, and affection; **Thou hatest all workers of iniquity**, those who make wrong-doing a practise. V. 6. **Thou shalt destroy them that speak leasing**, engaging in falsehood and lying; **the Lord will abhor the bloody and deceitful man.** All the ungodly people, as here described, are an abomination before the Lord, and all their service is blasphemy before Him, Rev. 21, 8. 27. In opposition to them stands David, who knows himself to be sincere in his relation toward Jehovah. V. 7. **But as for me, I will come into Thy house**, the Tabernacle, whose place was to be taken by a fine permanent structure, **in the multitude of Thy mercy**, the riches of the grace of God in the Messiah; **and in Thy fear**, in the proper childlike awe and reverence, **will I worship toward Thy holy Temple**, the place of Jehovah's throne, for the lowly Tabernacle was soon to be replaced with a magnificent palace dedicated to God. It is in the spirit of true worship that David now makes his plea. V. 8. **Lead me, O Lord, in Thy righteousness**, in the virtue of true piety, which is a gift of God, **because of mine enemies**, the adversaries who were carefully watching, who would have been more than pleased with any misfortune which might have befallen David; **make Thy way**, the path which accorded with the will of God, **straight before my face**, so that he might walk without hindrance and without the danger of losing his way. This is so very necessary for all believers because of the occasions of temptation and the ambushes which beset their path. V. 9. **For there is no faithfulness in their mouth**, they are not steadfast and of one mind in their speech, they cannot be depended upon in what they say; **their inward part**, their entire heart and mind, **is very wickedness**, an abyss of destruction; **their throat is an open sepulcher**, held wide apart, in order to grab and to devour; **they flatter with their tongue**, they hide their real intentions under the guise of flattery. This description is used also by Paul in his description of the godless, Rom. 3, 13. David now calls down upon all such the anger of Jehovah. V. 10. **Destroy Thou them, O God**, letting them expiate their guilt by a well-merited destruction; **let them fall by their own counsels**, the foolishness of their own planning being the cause of their overthrow; **cast them out in the multitude of their transgressions**, thrusting them aside from the midst of the congregation of believers, to whom they do not rightfully belong; **for they have rebelled against Thee**, this rebellion showing also in their refusal to turn to the Lord in true penitence. V. 11. **But let all those that put their trust in Thee rejoice**, this sentence being the statement of a definite fact, for all believers rejoice in the Lord of their salvation; **let them ever shout for joy**, in an ecstasy of pleasure, **because Thou defendest them**, the protection of Jehovah being their safeguard against all attacks of the enemies; **let them also that love Thy name be joyful in Thee**, Phil. 4, 4. V. 12. **For Thou, Lord, wilt bless the righteous**, with such spiritual blessings as make for eternal happiness; **with favor wilt Thou compass him**, surround him on all sides, **as with a shield**, the large buckler which covered the whole body being meant. That is the blessed assurance of the believers of all times, the certain protection of God against all wicked designs of all opponents, no matter how numerous and how mighty they may be. The believer trusts in Jehovah, the God of his salvation, and worships Him in holy fear, knowing that he is safe in His care.

PSALM 6.

A Prayer in Anxiety over Sin.

To the chief musician on Neginoth, the stringed instruments of the Temple-orchestra, **upon Sheminith**, that is, on the octave, probably in bass, the voice suited to the nature of its complaint, **a psalm of David.** The entire psalm is the cry of a soul beset with the deepest distress on account of the consciousness of sin and guilt, his prayer being that God would change the punishment of wrath into the gentle chastisement of love. V. 1. **O Lord, rebuke me not in Thine anger**, as just as this wrath is on account of the great transgressions whose weight the sinner feels, **neither chasten me in Thy hot displeasure**, which threatened to consume him altogether and pressed this cry for mercy from his anxious heart. V. 2. **Have mercy upon me, O Lord**, the free grace and favor of Jehovah being his only hope; **for I am weak**, so terrified as to make him languish and droop like a withered flower. **O Lord, heal me**, He being the only Physician whose skill could avail anything at all in this emergency; **for my bones are vexed**, his entire body threatening to come apart under the severe stress of the affliction besetting him. V. 3. **My soul is also sore vexed**, troubled, filled with the greatest terror; **but Thou, O Lord, how long?** When could he expect the relief for which he was so eagerly longing? He now follows up his question with a pleading cry. V. 4. **Return, O Lord**, for it seemed to the sufferer that Jehovah must have been absent during the severity of his trouble, **deliver my soul**, redeeming it from its depth of suffering. **O save me for Thy mercies' sake**, Jehovah's loving-kindness being the only hope of the sinner.

V. 5. **For in death there is no remembrance of Thee; in the grave, who shall give Thee thanks?** David wants God to consider that a condemnation of the sinner to the realm of death at that time, a definite rejection of him into the abyss of hell, would deprive Him of a willing worshiper, for which reason he asks relief before this extreme stage is reached. V. 6. **I am weary with my groaning,** utterly fatigued and worn out with the severity of his suffering; **all the night make I my bed to swim,** with streams of penitent tears; **I water my couch with my tears,** so that it is almost dissolved in consequence of their multitude. V. 7. **Mine eye,** as the mirror of man's entire being, **is consumed because of grief,** dissolved with mourning; **it waxeth old because of all mine enemies,** the power of vision and all the strength of the soul being blunted as with old age. However, in the midst of the sinner's sorrow and cry, while he utters his prayer for relief, his courage and strength grow. V. 8. **Depart from me, all ye workers of iniquity;** the sinner being sure of God's favorable answer to his prayer, his complaint changes to a joyful confidence; **for the Lord hath heard the voice of my weeping,** and so the voice of God's free Spirit takes hold of him and causes him to rejoice. V. 9. **The Lord hath heard my supplication,** as it was pressed from his overburdened heart; **the Lord will receive my prayer,** wherefore he no longer fears his enemies, the ungodly, the hypocrites, but can defy them with holy courage. V. 10. **Let all mine enemies be ashamed and sore vexed,** rather, in a definite statement, "they will be brought to shame," they will be terrified; **let them return and be ashamed suddenly,** their sneering mockery being changed to the most abject shame in one terrible moment, when the punishment of God strikes them. Thus every poor sinner, in the very midst of his anxiety, may look up to the Savior in the simple confidence of faith and rejoice in his salvation, no matter what attitude the enemies take.

PSALM 7.

Supplication of a Believer against Slander.

THE PETITION. — **Shiggaion of David,** a plaintive song, or elegy, full of emotion, which is apparent both in the structure and in the accompanying music, **which he sang unto the Lord concerning the words of Cush, the Benjamite,** one of his detractors at the court of Saul. David prays for the establishment of his innocence, because he knows himself to be guiltless and because Jehovah will be glorified in his vindication. V. 1. **O Lord, my God,** his Creator and the Guide of his pathway, **in Thee do I put my trust,** this word of faith, love, and hope stating the motive for his confident approach to the Throne of Grace; **save me from all them that persecute me,** during the time when he was never sure of his life, 1 Sam. 24 to 26, **and deliver me,** v. 2. **lest he tear my soul like a lion,** a ravenous beast, **rending it in pieces, while there is none to deliver.** So eager are his enemies to take his life, and so hopeless seems his case. But David makes his appeal for help in the consciousness of his innocence of any deliberate wrong-doing. V. 3. **O Lord, my God,** here the mighty Ruler and Judge of the universe, **if I have done this; if there be iniquity in my hands,** namely, the crime charged to him by Cush; v. 4. **if I have rewarded evil unto him that was at peace with me,** becoming guilty of treachery toward those who trusted him; **(yea, I have delivered him that without cause is mine enemy,** rather, plundered without reason, in pure wantonness, my adversary;) v. 5. **let the enemy persecute my soul,** in just retribution, **and take it; yea, let him tread down my life upon the earth,** trampling it into extinction, **and lay mine honor,** his personal and official dignity, **in the dust,** bringing it to the deepest humiliation. **Selah.** It is only the sense of his innocence which can give David the assurance expressed in this offer, which is now followed by a call to revenge his wrongs. V. 6. **Arise, O Lord, in Thine anger,** the appeal being all the more importunate since it seemed that God had hitherto been careless of him, **lift up Thyself,** towering up on high, **because of the rage of mine enemies,** His great power alone being able to crush them in spite of their threatening attitude, **and awake for me to the judgment that Thou hast commanded,** the decision which, as David confidently believed, the Lord had ordained in this case. V. 7. **So shall the congregation of the people compass Thee about,** the scene being that of the last great Judgment, when God will gather the nations before Him; **for their sakes, therefore, return Thou on high,** assuming the judgment-seat as the great Ruler and Judge of all men. David's single case is merged with the judgment of all men; he is willing to put his matter to the supreme test. Every believer, in spite of all his sinful weakness, must be ready always to have the record of his daily life examined, for he must ever abstain from all crimes and wicked deeds.

DAVID'S CONFIDENT TRUST.—V. 8. **The Lord,** the great Judge of all men, **shall judge the people,** David at that time confidently expecting a decision in his favor. **Judge me, O Lord, according to my righteousness;** for he was sure of being acquitted of deliberate wrong-doing if the record of his life were tested, **and according to mine integrity that is in me,** according to which David always led his life. V. 9. **Oh, let the wickedness of the wicked come to an end,** putting a stop to their torturing of the believers; **but establish the just,** protecting them in their righteous cause; **for the righteous God trieth the hearts and the reins,** the affections and motives of man named after their supposed seat. With this certainty, David's prayer gains in confidence. V. 10. **My defense is of God,** He Himself having undertaken his protection and vindication, **which saveth the upright in heart,** those who are believers in truth, without a show of hypocrisy. V. 11. **God judgeth the righteous,** being just in all His judgments, **and God is angry with the wicked every day,** always abhorring their evil ways and preparing for their punishment. V. 12. **If he,** namely, the wicked person, **turn not, He will whet His sword,** for a just and severe retribution; **He hath bent His bow and made it ready,** for the sudden destruction of the ungodly. V. 13. **He hath also prepared for him the instruments of death; He ordaineth His arrows against the persecutors,** the burning arrows and darts of His lightnings being the messengers of His punishment. V. 14. **Behold, he,** the wicked man, **travaileth with iniquity,** laboring and struggling, as in the throes of childbirth, in bringing forth transgression, **and hath conceived mischief, and brought forth falsehood,** his intention is to do harm to others, but in the end the deception will strike himself. V. 15. **He made a pit and digged it,** with the intention of destroying the righteous, **and is fallen into the ditch which he made.** V. 16. **His mischief shall return upon his own head,** slaying him with his own weapons, **and his violent dealing shall come down upon his own pate,** the wrath of God thereby being made manifest upon the oppressors. V. 17. **I will praise the Lord according to His righteousness,** giving Him thanks even now because of the certainty of deliverance from the present distress; **and I will sing praise to the name of the Lord most high.** Beginning in a tone almost of despair, the believer ends his prayer with a confident, a triumphant shout; for such is the effect of faith.

PSALM 8.

The Glory of Messiah's Name.

To the chief musician, for liturgical performance, **upon Gittith,** a form of zither, named from the Philistine city of Gath, where the author had lived for some time, **a psalm of David.** V. 1. **O Lord, our Lord,** Jehovah, our Ruler, **how excellent is Thy name in all the earth!** The congregation here praises the imprint and evidence of God's being, both in the works of creation and in the miracles of redemption. **Who hast set Thy glory above the heavens,** on the entire heavens; for they are fitted out and adorned with His glory. This Lord, the infinite excellence and majesty of whose essence is reflected in the heavens, is glorified also here on earth, in the midst of His congregation. V. 2. **Out of the mouth of babes and sucklings hast Thou ordained strength,** the praise of the very infants in arms proving a victorious power, a rampart and bulwark of might, **because of Thine enemies,** on account of the adversaries, whose attack would be foiled by the almighty power of God in the praise out of the mouth of children, **that Thou mightest still the enemy and the avenger,** causing Satan and all his allies to be quiet, fully silenced in their opposition to the works of God. After this stately introduction, to which Jesus Himself refers as finding its fulfilment on the Sunday before His death, Matt. 21, 15—17, David describes the mystery of the exaltation of the human nature in the person of Christ. V. 3. **When I consider Thy heavens, the work of Thy fingers,** productions of Jehovah's almighty power, **the moon and the stars, which Thou hast ordained,** all of them examples and proofs of the infinite greatness and immeasurable power of God, v. 4. **what is man that Thou art mindful of him,** that the great God should spend any thoughts upon human nature, so far below Him that a comparison is not possible, **and the Son of Man, that Thou visitest Him?** The reference, as Heb. 2, 6—10 shows, is to Christ, who assumed human nature, with all its weakness and lowliness, who was made in the likeness of men and was found in fashion as a man, Phil. 2, 7. 8. It is to this singular man alone that the next words can apply. V. 5. **For Thou hast made Him a little lower than the angels,** literally, "Thou hast caused Him to lack a little of God," this being fulfilled when the Son of Man, in the depths of His sufferings for mankind, was forsaken by His heavenly Father, as He Himself cries out, **and hast crowned Him with glory and honor,** with the majesty and glory peculiar to the essence of God, this taking place when Jesus Christ, the Son of Man, entered upon His state of exaltation, when the Savior, who had deliberately waived the right to use the divine power and majesty communicated to His human nature, assumed and practised this right, also according to His humanity. V. 6. **Thou madest Him to have dominion over the works of Thy hands,** as the Ruler of the entire universe, with boundless power and majesty, and that according to His human nature; **Thou hast put all things under His feet,** Eph. 1, 22: v. 7. **all sheep and oxen,**

yea, and the beasts of the field, v. 8. **the fowls of the air, and the fish of the sea, and whatsoever passeth through the paths of the seas,** these creatures being mentioned as the representatives of all creation. Into the heritage of mankind, lost by the Fall, the singular Son of Man, the Restorer of the human race, has entered. In this one Man, the Messiah, Jesus Christ, mankind has regained the lost happiness and dominion, the lost honor and dignity. In this Man the name of Jehovah has been revealed in its full glory. V. 9. **O Lord, our Lord, how excellent is Thy name in all the earth,** and not only in the Kingdom of Grace, whose representatives are here praising His great name, but in the Kingdom of Power! Jehovah, Jesus Christ, Messiah, Son of Man, our almighty King: that is the Church's consolation, that is the sum of its message.

PSALM 9.

A Song of Praise for Victory over the Enemies.

THANKSGIVING FOR THE VICTORY GAINED. — **To the chief musician,** for use in liturgical services, **upon Muth-labben,** that is, to be sung after the melody known as "Death to the Son," probably that of a folk-song, **a psalm of David.** V. 1. **I will praise Thee, O Lord,** in a song of thanksgiving, **with my whole heart,** with all the powers of the soul; **I will show forth all Thy marvelous works,** declaring their greatness before all men. V. 2. **I will be glad and rejoice in Thee,** exulting in the favor shown him by Jehovah; **I will sing praise to Thy name, O Thou Most High,** giving Him the credit for the victories gained by singing psalms extolling His honor, the greatness of His attributes. V. 3. **When mine enemies are turned back,** overthrown in battle, **they shall fall and perish at Thy presence,** when God sets His face against them. V. 4. **For Thou hast maintained my right and my cause,** upholding him and vindicating him by granting him the victory; **Thou satest in the throne judging right,** dispensing justice. V. 5. **Thou hast rebuked the heathen,** in granting the victory to the arms of David; **Thou hast destroyed the wicked, Thou hast put out their name forever and ever,** blotting it out of history, destroying its remembrance. V. 6. **O thou enemy, destructions are come to a perpetual end,** desolation and ruin is found where the enemy formerly flourished; **and Thou,** Jehovah as the Leader of Israel's armies, **hast destroyed cities,** plucking them up, rooting them out; **their memorial is perished with them,** God had caused their complete annihilation. Note: The way of unbelief is to praise human power and valor, but believers give thanks to God alone for His almighty assistance in all troubles.

A PROPHETIC VIEW OF THE VICTORY OF FAITH. V. 7. **But the Lord shall endure forever,** sitting secure on the throne of His majesty; **He hath prepared His throne for judgment,** and the last Great Day is foreshadowed by every individual punishment upon nations. V. 8. **And He shall judge the world in righteousness,** dispensing justice by virtue of His righteousness; **He shall minister judgment to the people in uprightness,** as the highest principles of divine right demand it. V. 9. **The Lord also will be a Refuge,** a height, or stronghold, **for the oppressed,** where they may be safe from the attacks of their enemies, **a Refuge in times of trouble,** when all hope seems to be cut off. V. 10. **And they that know Thy name will put their trust in Thee,** sure of a safe refuge under the shadow of His wings; **for Thou, Lord, hast not forsaken them that seek Thee.** Cp. Luke 21, 16—19; 22, 30. V. 11. **Sing praises to the Lord, which dwelleth in Zion,** intoning psalms to Jehovah, as He dwells in the midst of His people, His Church; **declare among the people His doings,** every believer feeling constrained to publish the facts pertaining to his salvation. V. 12. **When He maketh inquisition for blood, He remembereth them,** rather, "For the Avenger of blood, He who avenges bloodshed by punishing the murderers, remembers them"; **He forgetteth not the cry of the humble,** those who are subject to violence at the hands of the wicked. V. 13. **Have mercy upon me, O Lord,** showing him His divine favor or grace; **consider my trouble which I suffer of them that hate me,** being afflicted by them on all sides, **Thou that liftest me up from the gates of death,** where he was almost ready to be imprisoned, as the enemies sought his life, v. 14. **that I may show forth all Thy praise in the gates of the daughter of Zion,** proclaiming it in public, making it known to numbers of people everywhere. **I will rejoice in Thy salvation,** happy over his deliverance from the hands of all enemies, whether physical or spiritual. V. 15. **The heathen,** the enemy nations who hoped to gain a victory over Israel, **are sunk down in the pit that they made,** being plunged down suddenly; **in the net which they hid,** hoping to snare the members of the Lord's people, **is their own foot taken.** V. 16. **The Lord is known by the judgment which He executeth,** in overthrowing the plans of the wicked; **the wicked is snared in the work of his own hands,** his plans resulting in his own detriment. **Higgaion,** that is, meditation, a long pause being made here in order to impress the truth of the last statements upon the hearers.

Selah. V. 17. **The wicked shall be turned into hell,** to suffer everlasting punishment, **and all the nations that forget God.** V. 18. **For the needy shall not alway be forgotten,** though it may often seem that his misery will never be ended; **the expectation of the poor shall not perish forever,** those humbled by strokes of affliction will finally see their deliverance. V. 19. **Arise, O Lord,** David's usual powerful appeal; **let not man prevail,** grow strong to carry out his evil designs; **let the heathen be judged in Thy sight,** the condemnation striking them and preventing their wicked designs. V. 20. **Put them in fear, O Lord,** constant terror keeping them in subjection, **that the nations may know themselves to be but men,** a fact which ought to keep them from every form and show of conceit and arrogance, ever humble in the sight of Jehovah. **Selah.** The prayer of all afflicted believers is this, that God would make the enemies realize their puny strength and keep them from harming the Church of God.

PSALM 10.

Prayer against the Enemy of the Church.

Luther writes in his summary of this psalm: "This is a psalm of prayer which complains about the arch-enemy of the kingdom of Christ, that is, Antichrist, who for the sake of his covetousness and pomp troubles Christendom with both might and guile; he wields both the sword of worldly tyranny over the body and the net of false doctrine over the souls."

David Complains of the Outrage of the Wicked.—V. 1. **Why standest Thou afar off, O Lord?** apparently indifferent to the oppression of His people. **Why hidest Thou Thyself in times of trouble?** both His eyes and His ears being covered, so that He seems to be altogether unconcerned about the misery which comes upon His believers. V. 2. **The wicked in his pride doth persecute the poor,** rather, "Through the pride of the wicked the afflicted is burning," consumed with the heat of anxiety. **Let them be taken in the devices that they have imagined,** that is, the believers are taken and harmed by reason of the plots devised by the wicked. There is oppression on every hand and apparently no deliverance for the godly. V. 3. **For the wicked boasteth of his heart's desire,** of the fact that he succeeds in his evil plans, **and blesseth the covetous, whom the Lord abhorreth,** that is, he renounces and despises Jehovah, while he praises the defrauder, who makes his gains by craft or force. V. 4. **The wicked, through the pride of his countenance,** the fact that he literally carries his nose high, in haughty disdain and contempt of God, **will not seek after God; God is not in all his thoughts.** Those are his thoughts, that is the way he has figured it out for himself: God does not punish; there is no God! He believes that he can go right ahead with his pride and his trespasses; he tries to make himself believe that there will be no day of reckoning. V. 5. **His ways are always grievous,** the manner in which he acts seems to be safe against punishment at all times; **Thy judgments are far above out of his sight,** out of the range of his vision; wherefore, in the opinion of the wicked, they do not exist. **As for all his enemies, he puffeth at them,** in an act of sneering contempt, his arrogance causing him to despise both God and men. V. 6. **He hath said in his heart, I shall not be moved,** he is filled with unlimited pride and security; **for I shall never be in adversity,** one generation after the other in his family being safe against misfortune, in his opinion, his prosperity, his wealth and honor, safe to far distant times. V. 7. **His mouth is full of cursing,** blasphemous reviling and execration, **and deceit and fraud,** by which he oppresses the godly; **under his tongue is mischief and vanity,** violence for others and the essence of meanness for himself. V. 8. **He sitteth in the lurking places of the villages,** in his nomad encampment, where he could easily waylay unsuspecting travelers; **in the secret places,** where he believes himself safe from observation, **doth he murder the innocent,** him who has in no way provoked him, out of mere lust for killing; **his eyes are privily set against the poor,** watching and planning to bring harm upon the godly sufferer. V. 9. **He lieth in wait secretly,** hidden in ambush, **as a lion in his den,** in the thicket where he has his lair; **he lieth in wait to catch the poor,** like a hunter taking wild animals in his net; **he doth catch the poor,** the righteous sufferer, **when he draweth him into his net.** V. 10. **He croucheth,** the description again being that of a beast of prey, **and humbleth himself,** ducking low, getting ready for the sudden spring, **that the poor may fall by his strong ones,** his wicked helpers, who also rejoice in iniquity. V. 11. **He hath said in his heart, God hath forgotten; He hideth His face; He will never see it.** This blasphemous thought is the consolation of the wicked; by it they lull themselves into a false security, stifling the voice of their conscience in order to ply their wicked trade without hindrance.

David Makes a Plea for Speedy Deliverance. — V. 12. **Arise, O Lord,** David's usual powerful and importunate appeal to Jehovah, the true God; **O God, lift up Thine hand,** namely, for the purpose of punishing the wicked; **forget not the humble,** forsaking them, giving them up to the cruelty of the wicked. V. 13. **Wherefore doth the wicked contemn God?** How is it possible that God should permit such a blasphemous challenge of His government? **He hath said in his heart, Thou wilt not require it,** not call the wicked to account for his every misdeed. V. 14. **Thou hast seen it,** this being set against the false security of the wicked; **for Thou beholdest mischief and spite,** all the grief which the ungodly lays upon the righteous, **to requite it with Thy hand,** with the full punishment which it deserves. **The poor committeth himself unto Thee,** trusting in God's righteous judgment; **Thou art the Helper of the fatherless,** those without natural protectors to defend them. V. 15. **Break Thou the arm of the wicked,** definitely putting a stop to his wicked acts, **and the evil man; seek out his wickedness till Thou find none,** the result being such a reverent awe of God that all meanness would be removed and disappear without leaving a trace. V. 16. **The Lord is King forever and ever,** He is not dethroned despite all the attacks of the enemies; **the heathen are perished out of His land,** cut off entirely, annihilated, no remnant remaining. This being the poet's assurance, he adds his last plea. V. 17. **Lord, Thou hast heard the desire of the humble,** their longing for help; **Thou wilt prepare their heart,** establishing it by firm confidence in Him; **Thou wilt cause Thine ear to hear,** to attend closely to their cry, v. 18. **to judge the fatherless and the oppressed,** executing judgment upon their oppressors, **that the man of the earth,** the haughty wicked adversary, **may no more oppress,** by terrifying the believers. That is the consolation of the children of God at all times, that He will finally vindicate His might and execute judgment upon all enemies of His people.

PSALM 11.

David's Refusal to Flee When in Danger of Life.

There was a time when David's throne was in danger, when Absalom was scheming to usurp the royal power in Israel, when David's very life was no longer secure. It was when the situation finally became acute that some of David's faithful counselors seem to have urged him to flee from Jerusalem, in order to save his life and to let the danger blow over. But David, far from heeding their urging, composed this psalm of faith. **To the chief musician,** for use in the liturgical services of the Tabernacle, **a psalm of David.** V. 1. **In the Lord put I my trust,** with Jehovah he had found refuge, wherefore he surely needed no other; **how say ye to my soul, Flee as a bird to your mountain?** As a bird, when in danger, seeks the refuge of the wooded mountains, so the friends of David urged him to flee to the rocky caves of the mountainous section of Palestine, there to remain secure until conditions proved more favorable. V. 2. **For, lo,** so the counselors of David told him, **the wicked bend their bow, they make ready their arrow upon the string,** adjusting it for a sudden shot, **that they may privily shoot at the upright in heart,** in a treacherous attempt at assassination. V. 3. **If the foundations be destroyed,** the laws and ordinances of public justice were rudely overthrown, **what can the righteous do?** In such an event the outlook evidently is hopeless for those who loved law and order, and therefore David should seek safety in flight. But he felt differently about it. V. 4. **The Lord is in His holy Temple,** on the throne of His palace, His heavenly Temple; **the Lord's throne is in heaven,** all the earth is absolutely under His government. **His eyes behold, His eyelids try,** with a penetrating, all-seeing glance, **the children of men.** Jehovah was fully conscious of everything that was going on in the world, and David felt that he could safely trust in His powerful and just rule, that nothing could harm him without the permission of the heavenly King. V. 5. **The Lord trieth the righteous,** proving or testing them for evidences of their sincerity and then giving them the full measure of His protection; **but the wicked and him that loveth violence His soul hateth,** upon them His judgment will finally descend. V. 6. **Upon the wicked He shall rain,** sending down in great abundance, **snares,** to prevent the escape of the ungodly, **fire and brimstone,** usually associated with the pains of hell, **and an horrible tempest,** the word really signifying the fiery, poisonous wind of the desert, the *samum,* to indicate the terrible form of punishment sent upon the wicked by God; **this shall be the portion of their cup,** that which was measured out to them to drink, what was included in the punishment which they must suffer. V. 7. **For the righteous Lord loveth righteousness,** such acts of righteousness as His children on earth delight in; **His countenance doth behold the upright,** they alone behold His face, they alone are worthy of standing in His sight. Thus the Christians place their trust in their heavenly Father and proudly confess His name, for they know that God looks upon them in love for the sake of their Savior, Jesus Christ, His Son, and that they will finally be delivered from every evil work, to be taken up to the realms of glory.

PSALM 12.

Prayer for God's Protection of His Church.

This psalm again shows a prophetical strain; it is applicable throughout to the little flock, the poor, small crew of the Christian Church, in its many vicissitudes. Cp. Acts 2, 30. **To the chief musician upon Sheminith,** upon the octave, to be sung or played with bass voices, or, on an eight-stringed instrument, **a psalm of David.** V. 1. **Help, Lord, for the godly man ceaseth,** it was a time when true piety was decreasing both in amount and in influence; **for the faithful fail from among the children of men,** true loyalty and faithfulness having become exceedingly rare in the world, vanished, to all intents and purposes. V. 2. **They,** namely, men in general, the rank and file of people on earth, **speak vanity every one with his neighbor,** falsehood, lies, being the order of the day; **with flattering lips,** without a shred of sincerity, **and with a double heart,** both hypocritical and inconsistent, **do they speak.** Cp. Hos. 4, 1—6. V. 3. **The Lord shall cut off all flattering lips, and the tongue that speaketh proud things,** great and swelling words of boastfulness, utterly uprooting the whole kingdom of lies; v. 4. **who have said, With our tongues will we prevail,** showing strength with them, believing themselves to be absolute masters of their words; **our lips are our own,** to formulate all the flattering speeches which they might choose to make; **who is lord over us?** Who would dare to interfere with their haughtiness; who would prevent their doing as they pleased? This being the situation, the psalmist now sets forth the views of the Lord. V. 5. **For the oppression of the poor,** those in misery and distress, **for the sighing of the needy, now will I arise, saith the Lord,** as the almighty Avenger of wrong; **I will set him,** the poor and downtrodden, **in safety from him that puffeth at him,** with a gesture of proud disdain, or, "I will place him in safety who panteth after it," being filled with eager longing to escape the continual oppression of the mighty. This being the attitude of the Lord, the psalmist praises Him. V. 6. **The words of the Lord are pure words; as silver tried in a furnace of earth,** a workshop with its crucible surrounded with earth being in the poet's mind, **purified seven times,** to insure the highest possible degree of purity. V. 7. **Thou shalt keep them, O Lord,** namely, the believers, the faithful; **Thou shalt preserve them from this generation,** from those pervaded with the wicked spirit of the age, **forever.** V. 8. **The wicked walk on every side,** their entire bearing showing the pride of their hearts, **when the vilest men are exalted,** in accordance with the increase of vileness among the sons of men, that is, the more the Christians neglect to act as the salt of the earth, as the leaven in the perverse generation of these latter days, and the more their own behavior is subject to just criticism as not in accordance with the Word of God, the more will the enemies of the Lord take occasion to lift up their heads in proud blasphemy and increase their hatred of the Lord's work.

PSALM 13.

A Prayer for Relief in the Midst of Trouble.

David may well apply as a type, so far as his experience during the persecution by Saul is concerned, to the believing sufferer and Christian martyr of every age. **To the chief musician,** to be used in the Temple services, **a psalm of David.** V. 1. **How long wilt Thou forget me, O Lord? Forever?** It seemed to David, in the anguish of his spirit during the long period when he was hunted almost like a wild beast, that the Lord had entirely forsaken him. **How long wilt Thou hide Thy face from me?** as though He abandoned him to the fate which was staring him in the face. V. 2. **How long shall I take counsel in my soul,** being filled with worry and distress over the apparent neglect of Jehovah, **having sorrow in my heart daily?** There was no intermission in his troubles; all the counsels which his heart thought of brought no relief. **How long shall mine enemy be exalted over me?** having the upper hand, continuing his tactics of oppression. V. 3. **Consider and hear me, O Lord,** my **God,** paying attention to his plight, giving him an answer upon his appeal; **lighten mine eyes,** making them clear, giving them new vitality and cheerfulness in view of the coming deliverance, **lest I sleep the sleep of death,** falling asleep, never to awake again, v. 4. **lest mine enemy say, I have prevailed against him,** and therefore also against the Lord in whom David trusted; **and those that trouble me rejoice when I am moved,** having lost the firmness of his faith, deceived in his trust, overcome by their wicked schemes. During his prayer the faith of David has grown and has been invested with new strength, causing his humble cry to be changed into a song of praise. V. 5. **But I have trusted in Thy mercy,** with the firm confidence in his final salvation; **my**

heart shall rejoice in Thy salvation, by which he would be delivered both physically and spiritually. V. 6. **I will sing unto the Lord because He hath dealt bountifully with me,** rewarding him richly in compensation for his season of trouble. That is David's firm confidence. Thus the heart of every believer, in the midst of the storms of life, experiences the wonderful peace of God which passes all understanding, which causes him to trust in his heavenly Father's mercy, no matter what may befall him.

PSALM 14.

Of the Corruption of Natural Man and the Lord's Salvation.

This psalm may well have been composed at the time when David was specially impressed with the wickedness of men, when he felt the oppression of persecution, or experienced the dangers of rebellion. He saw the great and apparently universal depravity of men, against which there is only one remedy, namely, the salvation of the Lord, whose delivering power is able to lift even the most besotted sinner to the plane of redemption. **To the chief musician, a psalm of David.** V. 1. **The fool,** the spiritually worthless, the madman in things pertaining to his soul's salvation, **hath said in his heart,** it is his steady secret thought and delusion, **There is no God.** A person who denies the existence of God is truly foolish, filled with madness; he denies the evidences of his own senses, he deliberately silences the voice of his own conscience. **They,** all those who give way to foolishness in this manner, **are corrupt, they have done abominable works,** the idea of badness being emphasized by the whole structure of the text. **There is none that doeth good,** the inherited wickedness of the human heart is intensified in the case of those who deliberately give way to godlessness. V. 2. **The Lord looked down from heaven,** bowing forward for the purpose of examining very closely, **upon the children of men, to see if there were any that did understand,** if any of the sons of Adam, any member of the human race, had an insight into divine things, **and seek God,** acknowledging Him and His fellowship as the highest good. The result of this careful examination is now stated. V. 3. **They are all gone aside,** turning away from the path of righteousness and holiness which the divine will has set forth for them to walk, **they are all together become filthy,** tainted, filled with corruption, so that their stench rises to the nostrils of God; **there is none that doeth good, no, not one,** the universality of human depravity being stated in the most emphatic terms. But this corruption shows itself most strongly in the children of wickedness, as the question of the psalmist shows. V. 4. **Have all the workers of iniquity no knowledge?** Are they so utterly stupid, devoid of all sense? Has the judgment upon them so stultified their minds that they believe their hypocrisy undiscovered by God? **Who eat up my people as they eat bread,** not only supporting themselves by devouring the substance of the godly, but also considering their oppression of the righteous altogether self-evident and justified, **and call not upon the Lord.** They are not in prayerful communion with Jehovah, hence they act like beasts of prey. V. 5. **There were they in great fear,** namely, at the time when the thunder of Jehovah's wrath hurls them down, they cringe and cower in terror when His judgment approaches; **for God is in the generation of the righteous,** He protects and governs His children and brings about their complete victory over their enemies. The attitude of the unbelievers at such a time is the same as that of the Egyptians when the Lord troubled them, Ex. 14, 24. 25. V. 6. **Ye have shamed the counsel of the poor,** the wicked may do so, but in vain, the Lord cries out to them through the poet, **because the Lord is his Refuge,** Jehovah is his Stronghold, his Defense and Protection. But in view of these conditions the psalmist is constrained to call to the Lord for deliverance. V. 7. **Oh, that the salvation of Israel were come out of Zion!** Mount Zion, the place where the Ark of the Covenant had found its resting-place, was the place of the presence of God in the midst of His people. It was here that David looked for deliverance upon his poor people, the true believers, suffering under the oppression of the wicked. **When the Lord bringeth back the captivity of His people,** delivering them from the oppression of this great evil which was now besetting them, **Jacob shall rejoice and Israel shall be glad,** these two names, Jacob and Israel, being designations of the Church of God, not only in the Old Testament, but at all times. It is, in reality, a Messianic call: Oh, that Jehovah, from His throne in Zion, would grant salvation to His people by revisiting them in their captive, forsaken state, by sending the Messiah to bring them deliverance, thus giving occasion of the greatest rejoicing to the Church of all times! This was fulfilled when the Son of God became man and delivered all mankind from the oppression of all enemies; then it was that salvation of the right kind came upon Israel.

PSALM 15.

The Conditions of Access to God.

Every true believer who places his trust in the atonement of Jesus will, by virtue of this faith of his heart, repudiate sin and walk in the way of God's will. He is thereby distinguished from the hypocrite, the confession of whose lips does not agree with the condition of his heart, as this sacred poem shows. **A psalm of David.** V. 1. **Lord, who shall abide in Thy Tabernacle?** making the dwelling of God his everlasting habitation, being in constant communion with Jehovah. **Who shall dwell in Thy holy hill?** being at home in the glory of Jehovah's presence, having the right of access to Him at all times, not only in the outward communion of the visible Church, but in spirit and in truth. V. 2. **He that walketh uprightly,** without blame, so that his entire conduct agrees with the will of Jehovah, **and worketh righteousness,** exercising himself in a righteous manner always, **and speaketh the truth in his heart,** with all sincerity. V. 3. **He that backbiteth not with his tongue,** either by defaming his neighbor or by spreading slander, **nor doeth evil to his neighbor,** by performing any kind of wickedness against him, **nor taketh up a reproach against his neighbor,** bringing disgrace upon him in any form whatsoever; v. 4. **in whose eyes a vile person is contemned,** who despises and rejects those who are reprobate in the eyes of Jehovah, shunning their company at all times; **but he honoreth them that fear the Lord,** in every way anxious to please them, to show his appreciation of their fellowship. **He that sweareth to his own hurt,** standing by the oaths or vows made by him even if it meant a loss to him, Lev. 5, 4; 27, 10. 33, **and changeth not,** letting true piety govern his whole life and all his actions. V. 5. **He that putteth not out his money to usury,** thereby oppressing his poorer neighbor, Lev. 25, 37; Deut. 16, 19, **nor taketh reward against the innocent,** setting aside right and justice for the sake of a bribe, Deut. 27, 25. **He that doeth these things,** thereby proving the stainlessness of his honor and the piety of his character, as evidences of the faith of his heart, **shall never be moved,** being secure in the fellowship of Jehovah forever. True faith is always active in love; a Christian can no more desist from showing the faith of his heart in acts of love than the sun can desist from shining. The facts here brought out will also tend to keep the believer meek and humble, since God's ideal of a Christian is set so high.

PSALM 16.

Prophecy of Christ's Suffering and Resurrection.

According to Peter, Acts 2, 25—31, and Paul, Acts 13, 35, this psalm relates to Christ, expressing the feelings of His human nature in view of His sufferings and His victory over death and the grave, including His exaltation to the right hand of God. The words of Paul, Phil. 2, 6—11, are a fine commentary to this psalm. **Michtam,** a hymn, or anthem, distinguished by the use of epigrams, **of David.** V. 1. **Preserve Me, O God,** protecting the Petitioner who speaks through David from harm and danger; **for in Thee do I put My trust,** seeking refuge in Jehovah alone. V. 2. **O My soul, thou hast said unto the Lord, Thou art My Lord;** rather, "I say to Jehovah, My Lord art Thou," His Ruler, His all-powerful Stay and Defense; **My goodness extendeth not to Thee,** rather, "is not beyond Thee"; for He knows nothing that He can consider truly good beyond God; the Lord is His highest and most precious possession; v. 3. **but to the saints that are in the earth and to the excellent, in whom is all My delight,** that is, God is the Speaker's Lord for the holy ones who are on the earth and the excellent in the sight of God. He is in close relationship with these saints, with those who place their trust in the God of their salvation; He has all His delight in such truly excellent people, and He is therefore anxious to have them all become partakers of this delight. V. 4. **Their sorrows shall be multiplied that hasten after another god,** trying to place anything else beside, or in the place of, the true God, whether it be mammon, honor, pride, lustful indulgence, or any other evil, the result of this foolish exchange being that the sorrows of the offenders are increased. **Their drink-offerings of blood will I not offer,** He will not sacrifice in their name, because their hands are steeped in blood, because their consciences are burdened with deeds of blood, **nor take up their names into My lips,** so much as mention them favorably in the hearing of God. He renounces all connection with the wicked world, everything that even savors of friendship with such blasphemers. Instead, He turns to Jehovah alone. V. 5. **The Lord is the Portion of Mine inheritance,** the allotment of His portion, **and of My cup; Thou maintainest My lot.** His lot is the enjoyment of Jehovah's mercy, who continues to shed upon Him the fulness of His kindness. V. 6. **The lines,** the fortune allotted to Him by God, **are fallen unto Me in pleasant places,** in joyful regions, where it is a pleasure and a delight to be; **yea, I have a goodly heritage,** an inheritance of joy given to Him by Jehovah; all the glories of eternal bliss in heaven are His. For this kindness of Jehovah the praises of the Speaker arise. V. 7. **I will bless the Lord, who hath given Me counsel,** praising Jehovah for the counsel and assistance afforded Him in every emergency of His life; **My reins also instruct Me in the night seasons,** the inmost feelings of His heart and mind bring all these facts to His remembrance. V. 8. **I have set the Lord always before Me,** over against His eyes, as the one object which He must never forget, upon which He must concentrate His grateful thoughts. **Because He is at My right hand, I shall not be moved,** with Jehovah at His side to uphold and sustain Him, He will never sink down, never be overcome. V. 9. **Therefore My heart is glad, and My glory rejoiceth,** the dignity of His soul is lifted up in exultation; **My flesh also shall rest in hope,** dwelling in security, His body resting in safety. The contrast shows that the body of the Messiah is thought of as separate from the soul in the rest of the grave. Even when His mortal body is placed in the grave, will it be secure under God's protecting hand. V. 10. **For Thou wilt not leave My soul in hell,** letting it be forgotten in the realms of the dead; **neither wilt Thou suffer Thine Holy One to see corruption,** the decay of the grave, Job 17, 14. The Messiah's human body, though placed in the grave, was not to be subject to decay, the process of corruption was not to start in His case. V. 11. **Thou wilt show Me,** true human being though He was, **the path of life,** the way which leads to the full and unlimited enjoyment of eternal life; **in Thy presence is fulness of joy,** before the face of Jehovah, in the gracious light of His countenance; **at Thy right hand there are pleasures forevermore,** such as last throughout eternity. Jesus Christ, though laid in the grave, held by the power of death apparently like all human beings, His soul being separated from His body, yet was not subject to corruption and decay, but arose on the third day, His human nature now having entered upon the full use of the divine glory and majesty communicated to it in the incarnation. All believers, moreover, who are joined to Him in true fellowship, will with Christ be partakers of the eternal pleasures of heaven.

PSALM 17.

The Believer Takes His Refuge in God.

Every true believer is a poor sinner in the sight of God, knowing that his natural sinfulness will not permit justifying himself before the tribunal of divine justice. At the same time every believer can and does cheerfully approach God, not on the strength of his own merits, but by virtue of his trust in the righteousness of Christ imputed to him. Moreover, he may, at such a time, urge the sincerity of his conduct, the righteousness of his life, for the good works which he performs are the work of God in him and will therefore well merit the Lord's attention. **A prayer of David.**

MAKING A PLEA ON THE STRENGTH OF HIS RIGHTEOUSNESS OF LIFE. — V. 1. **Hear the right, O Lord,** listening as the believer presents the argument of his righteousness, **attend unto my cry,** his loud and importunate call; **give ear unto my prayer, that goeth not out of feigned lips,** out of lips that have nothing to do with hypocrisy and deceit; for if he were defiled with guilt, he would not dare to approach the Lord, praying lips, in that case, being filled with falsehood. V. 2. **Let my sentence come forth from Thy presence,** that acquitting him of wrong-doing, God Himself stating that David was not guilty before Him; **let Thine eyes behold the things that are equal,** God sees and judges aright, He reads the hearts and minds and knows true uprightness. V. 3. **Thou hast proved mine heart,** testing it for its sincerity; **Thou hast visited me in the night,** an investigation at that time being especially searching since the soul is then undisturbed by the happenings and noises of the outside world; **Thou hast tried me,** making a very careful examination, **and shalt find nothing,** no wicked thoughts; **I am purposed that my mouth shall not transgress,** he would not permit a sinful thought to pass the door of his mouth. V. 4. **Concerning the works of men,** as David noted in what manner men in general behaved, **by the word of Thy lips,** in accordance with God's command, **I have kept me from the paths of the destroyer,** he had not followed the example of the wicked in becoming guilty of oppression, of robbery and violence. V. 5. **Hold up my goings in Thy paths,** his steps follow the ways outlined by God, **that my footsteps slip not,** he has not left the way of God's command on either side, he can in all sincerity urge his righteousness before the tribunal of God. This is an example to all believers and at the same time a warning against hypocrisy; for only he who has a good conscience is able to pray in this manner.

DAVID CALLS UPON GOD FOR HELP. — V. 6. **I have called upon Thee,** namely, in the capacity in which he described himself, as a child of God who could rightfully point to the righteousness of his life, **for Thou wilt hear me, O God,** of this David was sure. **Incline Thine ear unto me,** in the attitude of most careful attention, **and hear my speech.** V. 7. **Show Thy marvelous loving-kindness,** giving him a proof, an exhibition, of His grace, **O Thou that savest by Thy right hand them which put their trust in Thee from those that rise up against them,** this being the reason why David puts his trust in the Lord with such firm confidence. V. 8. **Keep me as the apple of the eye,** this being named as a possession most dear to men; **hide me under the shadow of Thy wings,** as the mother-bird shelters her young in tender protection, cp. Deut. 32, 10. 11; Ps. 36, 7; Matt. 23, 37, v. 9. **from the wicked that oppress me,** greedily surrounding him for the purpose of wasting and devouring him, **from my deadly enemies, who compass me about,** ready to attack him from all sides. V. 10. **They are enclosed in their own fat,** they are dead to all human feeling; **with their mouth they speak proudly,** they are insolent in their behavior, as though certain victory were near. V. 11. **They have now compassed us in our steps,** so that the believers cannot make a move without their knowledge; **they have set their eyes bowing down to the earth,** they were eagerly watching in order to take their chance and throw down the believers to the ground, thereby completely overwhelming them; v. 12. **like as a lion that is greedy of his prey,** eagerly lurking on its path, **and as it were a young lion lurking in secret places,** cowering in his hiding-places, ready to spring upon an unsuspecting victim. V. 13. **Arise, O Lord,** again David's ringing appeal, **disappoint him,** going forth to meet the adversary and to anticipate his wicked move, **cast him down; deliver my soul from the wicked,** from all the unrighteous under the leadership of Satan, **which is Thy sword,** by His almighty sword the Lord can quickly bring deliverance, v. 14. **from men which are Thy hand,** rather, delivering from the wicked projects of these people with His hand, **O Lord, from men of the world,** whose entire interest is in this life, **which have their portion,** the measure of all they desire, **in this life, and whose belly Thou fillest with Thy hid treasure,** giving them of the rich store of temporal goods which are under His control. **They are full of children,** being blessed also in this respect, **and leave the rest of their substance to their babes,** their children inheriting this world's goods from them in great plenty. Thus the good fortune of the ungodly is shown to consist only in this world's treasures, the height of their ambition being reached when money, honor, and pleasures are theirs. But the psalmist, in conclusion, places himself in direct contrast to all this earthly happiness with its attendant sins. V. 15. **As for me, I will behold Thy face in righteousness,** as the happy possessor of the righteousness of God in Christ Jesus, the most glorious treasure of the Christian; **I shall be satisfied,** with an everlasting satisfaction, unlike any transient enjoyment in this world, **when I awake, with Thy likeness,** the original image of God restored in the risen believers in the form of a perfect knowledge of God and in true righteousness and holiness, Eph. 4, 24; Col. 3, 10. That, in a word, will be the happiness of the great resurrection at the end of time, to see God face to face and to be with Him in everlasting righteousness and holiness, world without end.

PSALM 18.

A Psalm of Thanksgiving for Deliverance and Victory.

To the chief musician, for performance in the liturgical service of the Tabernacle and the Temple, **a psalm of David, the servant of the Lord,** His prophet and minister in making known the Word of the Lord and in doing His will, **who spake unto the Lord the words of this song in the day that the Lord delivered him from the hand of all his enemies and from the hand of Saul,** in the last part of Saul's reign, 2 Sam. 7, 1; **and he said,** cp. 2 Sam. 22: —

A RECITAL OF GOD'S BLESSINGS.—V. 1. **I will love Thee,** with the most tender affection, **O Lord, my Strength,** in protecting and defending him. V. 2. **The Lord is my Rock,** his safe place of concealment, **and my Fortress,** his Stronghold, affording refuge and safety, **and my Deliverer; my God, my Strength,** his Rock of Ages, firm, immovable, **in whom I will trust; my Buckler,** the large shield which protected the whole body against injury, **and the Horn of my salvation,** the horn of the altar being the figure of protective strength and victorious deliverance, **and my high Tower,** inaccessible to the enemies. Having thus given the reason for his firm trust, the psalmist gives a recital of some of the occasions when his confidence was justified. V. 3. **I will call upon the Lord, who is worthy to be praised,** for all the favors shown in the past; **so shall I be saved from mine enemies;** that had been his constant experience. V. 4. **The sorrows of death,** the bands of death, **compassed me, and the floods of ungodly men made me afraid,** the brooks of abysmal evil and perdition terrifying him. V. 5. **The sorrows of hell,** the bands of the realm of death, **compassed me about; the snares of death prevented me,** going ahead, anticipating his every move, seizing upon him suddenly. V. 6. **In my distress I called upon the Lord,** when the persecution of Saul and other troubles came upon him, **and cried unto my God. He heard my**

voice out of His temple, out of the palace of heaven, the throne of His glory, **and my cry came before Him,** being hindered by nothing on its way, **even into His ears,** so that God certainly heard it. David now describes, in a highly poetic form, how the Lord worked His deliverance. V. 7. **Then the earth shook and trembled,** with violent earthquakes; **the foundations also of the hills moved and were shaken, because He was wroth.** V. 8. **There went up a smoke out of His nostrils,** from His angry snorting, **and fire out of His mouth devoured,** with a consuming power; **coals were kindled by it,** glowing coals blazing out from Him, the description being that of a violent thunderstorm. V. 9. **He bowed the heavens also,** as the dark masses of clouds roll and descend, **and came down; and darkness was under His feet,** the dark storm-clouds being His footstool. V. 10. **And He rode upon a cherub,** an angelic minister who represented the entire creation as serving Jehovah, **and did fly; yea, He did fly upon the wings of the wind,** whose rushing might fitly represent His dignity. V. 11. **He made darkness His secret place,** to veil and to hide Him; **His pavilion round about Him,** the tent of His dwelling, **were dark waters and thick clouds of the skies,** heavy with vapor, ready to shed the rain in streams. V. 12. **At the brightness that was before Him,** out from the brightness which surrounded His throne, **His thick clouds passed hailstones and coals of fire,** for Jehovah discharged through the clouds that veiled His brightness the weapons of His wrath, hail and bolts of lightning. V. 13. **The Lord also thundered in the heavens,** the roll of thunder following the strokes of lightning, **and the Highest gave His voice, hailstones and coals of fire.** V. 14. **Yea, He sent out His arrows,** the sharp points of His lightning, **and scattered them,** the enemies being obliged to flee in all directions; **and He shot out lightnings and discomfited them,** so that they were utterly at a loss, helpless in their confusion. So great was the force of the storm, moreover, that the very beds of the waters were laid bare. V. 15. **Then the channels of waters were seen,** the water being forced away by the mighty wind, **and the foundations of the world,** the very depths of the earth, **were discovered at Thy rebuke, O Lord, at the blast of the breath of Thy nostrils,** the storm which denoted His anger. V. 16. **He sent from above,** stretching out His hand, reaching down; **He took me, He drew me out of many waters,** so that David was not carried away in the great catastrophe which struck the earth. V. 17. **He delivered me from my strong enemy,** Saul chiefly being meant, **and from them which hated me,** all those who sought to harm him; **for they were too strong for me.** V. 18. **They prevented me,** falling upon him suddenly, **in the day of my calamity; but the Lord was my Stay,** supporting him so that all their wickedness came to naught. V. 19. **He brought me forth also,** from all his straits of trouble, **into a large place,** to full safety and relief; **He delivered me because He delighted in me,** His regard for David being His motive for acting as He did. V. 20. **The Lord rewarded me according to my righteousness,** the evidence of which came out in his entire conduct and life; **according to the cleanness of my hands,** in the management of his personal and official affairs, **hath He recompensed me.** V. 21. **For I have kept the ways of the Lord,** closely followed the paths pointed out to him by Jehovah, **and have not wickedly departed from my God.** V. 22. **For all His judgments were before me,** the obligations which His commandments laid upon all men, **and I did not put away His statutes from me,** namely, all the precepts of His covenant. V. 23. **I was also upright before Him,** in the outward observance of the Law, **and I kept myself from mine iniquity,** from bold transgression and wickedness. V. 24. **Therefore hath the Lord recompensed me according to my righteousness, according to the cleanness of my hands in His eyesight.** It was not arrogant boastfulness which caused David to make these statements, but the simplicity and trust of his heart. V. 25. **With the merciful Thou wilt show thyself merciful,** showing kindness to him who practised kindness; **with an upright man Thou wilt show Thyself upright;** v. 26. **with the pure Thou wilt show Thyself pure; and with the froward Thou wilt show Thyself froward,** God's dealing with men being the mirror of the relation in which God puts Himself to him, rewarding every man according to his deserts. V. 27. **For Thou wilt save the afflicted people,** delivering them from the trouble which oppresses them, **but wilt bring down high looks,** humbling those who exalt themselves. V. 28. **For Thou wilt light my candle,** making the lamp of his happiness and its light very bright; **the Lord will enlighten my darkness,** bringing him relief after the misfortunes which he endured. V. 29. **For by Thee I have run through a troop,** rushing upon hostile bands and overthrowing them; **and by my God have I leaped over a wall,** capturing the fortified towns of the enemies with ease. In the same manner all Christians will experience the gracious help of Jehovah against all the enemies of their souls if they but cling to their trust in the Lord.

GIVING ALL GLORY TO GOD ALONE. — V. 30. **As for God, His way is perfect,** always faultless and unblamable; **the Word of the Lord is tried,** refined and found, not drossy ore, but pure gold. **He is a Buckler,** a reliable Protection, **to all those that trust in Him.** V. 31. **For who is God save the Lord? Or who is a rock,** a certain refuge and concealment, **save our God?** Jehovah alone is the true God, who can and will help. V. 32. **It is God that girdeth me with strength,** enabling him to meet all dangers and all enemies successfully, **and maketh my way perfect,** giving him success in his rightful undertakings. V. 33. **He maketh my feet like hinds' feet,** gifted with fleetness to pursue the enemy, **and setteth me upon my high places,** as the master of the whole country. V. 34. **He teacheth my hands to war,** his skill in battle being a gift of the Lord, **so that a bow of steel is broken by mine arms,** rather, his arms bending the bow of brass or tempered bronze, a feat which took considerable strength. V. 35. **Thou hast also given me the shield of Thy salvation,** the protection of Jehovah proving his deliverance; **and Thy right hand hath holden me up, and Thy gentleness,** as the great God of heaven condescended to come to his assistance, **hath made me great.** V. 36. **Thou hast enlarged my steps under me,** giving him plenty of room for his feet, **that my feet did not slip,** being able to walk with a firm step, without limping. V. 37. **I have pursued mine enemies and overtaken them,** by virtue of the strength of the Lord which he had received; **neither did I turn again till they were consumed,** utterly overthrown. V. 38. **I have wounded them that they were not able to rise,** in all internal strife and in all foreign wars; **they are fallen under my feet.** V. 39. **For Thou hast girded me with strength unto the battle; Thou hast subdued under me those that rose up against me.** V. 40. **Thou hast also given me the necks of mine enemies,** so that they turned their backs to David in precipitate flight, **that I might destroy them that hate me.** V. 41. **They cried,** calling upon their idols to help them, **but there was none to save them; even unto the Lord,** turning to the true God in the last emergency, **but He answered them not;** it was too late, and their motive in seeking His assistance was not the proper one. V. 42. **Then did I beat them small as the dust before the wind,** driven in hopeless confusion; **I did cast them out as the dirt in the streets,** the dust that is trodden under foot. V. 43. **Thou hast delivered me from the strivings of the people,** preserving him in the midst of all internal conflicts; **and Thou hast made me the head of the heathen,** the ruler over all the nations round about; **a people whom I have not known shall serve me,** strangers bowing to his sovereignty. V. 44. **As soon as they hear of me, they shall obey me; the strangers shall submit themselves unto me.** V. 45. **The strangers shall fade away,** like flowers or grasses withering away before a fiery wind, **and be afraid out of their close places,** coming out with trembling from their strongholds. The song of David, therefore, ends in a mighty burst of triumphant praise. V. 46. **The Lord liveth,** in contrast to the dead idols of the heathen; **and blessed be my Rock,** in whom David trusted; **and let the God of my salvation,** who has granted him deliverance, **be exalted.** V. 47. **It is God that avengeth me,** He had taken David's cause in hand as His own, **and subdueth the people under me,** reducing them to the position of slaves. V. 48. **He delivereth me from mine enemies; yea, Thou liftest me up above those that rise up against me,** to a position of authority and influence; **Thou hast delivered me from the violent man,** this being said collectively of all David's enemies. V. 49. **Therefore will I give thanks unto Thee, O Lord, among the heathen,** for the praise of Jehovah would finally be general also among the Gentiles, as the fame of His great deeds would be made known, Rom. 15, 9, **and sing praises unto Thy name.** V. 50. **Great deliverance giveth He to His king,** making him a partaker of the fulness of His salvation; **and showeth mercy to His anointed, to David, and to his Seed forever.** The last words connect this psalm with the Messianic promise, 2 Sam. 7, 12—16; for in Christ, the Son of David, the fulness of God's grace and mercy, not only upon individuals, not only upon the children of Israel, but upon the Gentiles as well, was revealed. He who clings to this assurance in faith may safely trust in God as His Rock and the God of his salvation.

PSALM 19.

A Prophecy of the Gospel.

Luther says of this psalm that it is a prophecy of the Gospel as it was intended to go forth into all the world, as wide as the heavens extend, and to be proclaimed and taught both day and night, and not only in the language of the Jews, but in all tongues. **To the chief musician, a psalm of David.** V. 1. **The heavens declare the glory of God, and the firmament showeth,** is announcing or extolling, **His handiwork.** The entire universe reflects the majesty of God's creative power, and therefore all nature is here personified as a preacher of His omnipotence and providence. V. 2. **Day unto day uttereth speech, and night unto night showeth knowledge,** all nature being engaged in one mighty and uninterrupted sermon and anthem of praise, which will last as long as the change of day and night will continue, all creation being a witness to the majesty of the Creator. V. 3. **There is no speech nor language,** literally, "Not is there speech, and not are there words," **where their voice is not heard.** The message proclaimed by the inanimate creatures everywhere and at all times is of a nature to be clearly discernible to all ears which are not deliberately stopped up. God has always manifested Himself, made Himself known in such a way as to be seen and recognized by all who had their eyes and ears open. There is no excuse if men have not understood God's eternal power and Godhead, Rom. 1, 20. V. 4. **Their line,** the territory belonging to the sphere of the heavens, as they proclaim the glory of God, **is gone out through all the earth,** has encompassed the earth, has reached as far as creation extends, **and their words to the end of the world.** All the inhabitants of the earth are able to hear the announcement and to give glory and honor to the Lord of creation. St. Paul applies these words to the Gospel message which now has gone out "into all the earth" and its words "unto the ends of the world," Rom. 10, 18. **In them hath He set a tabernacle for the sun,** namely, in the regions of the heavens, v. 5. **which is as a bridegroom coming out of his chamber,** happy in the possession of the bride whose love gives him strength to cope with the problems of life, **and rejoiceth as a strong man,** like a valiant hero, **to run a race.** V. 6. **His going forth is from the end of the heaven, and his circuit unto the ends of it,** as he completes his course to the western horizon; **and there is nothing hid from the heat thereof,** the beneficial effects of its light and warmth are felt by all creatures. But in addition to this revelation of God in nature He has made Himself known to men in a much more wonderful manner, namely, in the message of the grace of God in Christ Jesus, in the Gospel. V. 7. **The Law of the Lord,** Holy Writ, the Word of the Lord, **is perfect, converting the soul,** restoring it to its fulness, to the strength it ought to have; **the testimony of the Lord is sure,** trustworthy, dependable, **making wise the simple.** V. 8. **The statutes of the Lord are right,** straight, without devious bypaths, **rejoicing the heart; the commandment of the Lord is pure, enlightening the eyes;** in short, the Word of God, the glorious message of the Gospel, contains in itself the power to sanctify men, for it is the truth, John 17, 17. V. 9. **The fear of the Lord is clean, enduring forever; the judgments of the Lord are true and righteous altogether.** The childlike fear and reverence of God is purity, holiness, truth, because it flows out of the Gospel. V. 10. **More to be desired are they,** the contents of the Word, **than gold, yea, than much fine gold, sweeter also than honey and the honeycomb,** the droppings of honeycombs, on account of the incomparably beautiful facts stated in the Gospel. V. 11. **Moreover, by them,** by these same glorious truths as contained in Scripture, **is Thy servant warned,** lest he forget their beauties, **and in keeping of them there is great reward,** namely, the reward of God's mercy, of the indwelling of the Triune God, John 14, 23. What application will the believer, then, make of the wonderful truths thus presented? V. 12. **Who can understand,** who can notice, who can keep track of, **his errors?** How far is the ideal which the Christian holds before him from the reality in which he finds himself! Even the believer still has so many weaknesses that he is hardly conscious of them. Therefore he adds the plea: **Cleanse Thou me from secret faults.** The reference is to all the transgressions which remain unnoticed, particularly also the guilt of inherited sin. V. 13. **Keep back Thy servant also from presumptuous sins,** from proud wickedness; **let them not have dominion over me,** for open transgression will surely drive faith out of the heart; **then shall I be upright,** perfect, making progress in true sanctification, **and I shall be innocent from the great transgression,** of the great crime of faithlessness, of apostasy, which to all believers is a horror. It is a work of God's mercy to keep His servants in true faith and obedience to the end. And therefore the believer prays in conclusion: v. 14. **Let the words of my mouth,** his sincere prayer, **and the meditation of my heart,** which dictates the prayer, **be acceptable in Thy sight, O Lord, my Strength,** the Rock of his refuge, **and my Redeemer,** by whose deliverance he has been kept time and again. Thus every child of God will pray and sing with mouth and heart, in true faith in the Gospel, in firm trust in the redemption earned by Christ, in whom we have both forgiveness and strength for a life of true sanctification.

PSALM 20.

Prayer in Time of War.

To the chief musician, a psalm of David, evidently composed to be sung by the Tabernacle chorus while the king and his army were in the field, the purpose being to implore Jehovah to grant victory to the arms of Israel. The chorus as such opens the hymn. V. 1. **The Lord hear thee in the day of trouble,** graciously and attentively listening to the king's call when he would find himself in a difficult and dangerous position; **the name of the God of Jacob,** the mighty God of Jacob, the great Protector of Israel Himself, **defend thee,** setting him up on high, on a stronghold where no enemy could harm him; v. 2. **send thee help,** that for which he called, **from the Sanctuary,** from His dwelling-place on Zion, where this prayer was made, **and strengthen,** support and assist, **thee out of Zion,** the place of His habitation among men; v. 3. **remember all thy offerings,** such as were always made before opening a battle, **and accept thy burnt sacrifice,** finding it fat and therefore acceptable; **Selah.** Cp. Ps. 3, 2. V. 4. **Grant thee according to thine own heart,** exactly as the king desired it, **and fulfil all thy counsel,** permitting all his plans and measures in the war to be successful. V. 5. **We will rejoice in thy salvation,** over the victory which would be sure to come to the king's arms, **and in the name of our God we will set up our banners,** letting them wave in token of the victory gained; **the Lord fulfil all thy petitions,** granting the king all that he desired to bring the campaign to a successful conclusion. This section of the psalm was probably sung while the offerings of the day were lighted. A solo voice now continues: V. 6. **Now know I that the Lord saveth His anointed,** letting him experience His gracious assistance, as the singer states in the confidence of faith; **He will hear him from His holy heaven,** the throne of His majesty, **with the saving strength of His right hand,** with the wonderful deeds of His almighty power. This confidence is based on the means of grace, on the sacrifice and the Word which accompanied it. V. 7. **Some trust in chariots and some in horses,** making flesh their arm, depending upon their own strength and resources; **but we will remember the name of the Lord, our God,** making mention of Jehovah, their confidence being founded in Him alone. V. 8. **They,** the enemies who so foolishly trust in their own power, **are brought down and fallen,** first bowing down, sinking to the knees, and then lying prostrate; **but we are risen and stand upright,** firm and secure, holding the field with ease, without the slightest distress and fear. The Levitical soloist having finished his air, the entire chorus takes up the theme in a triumphant conclusion. V. 9. **Save, Lord! Let the King hear us when we call,** or, "Save the king, O Jehovah, hear us in the day of our calling"; just the right proportion of humble pleading and confident requesting, as it behooves believers in stepping before the throne of God. The sentiments here expressed have a permanent value, for, as one commentator has it, the prosperity of the kingdom of Christ is not merely typified, but also involved, in that of Israel and its king.

PSALM 21.

A Prayer of Thanksgiving for Victory.

THANKSGIVING FOR THE GREAT VICTORY. — **To the chief musician, a psalm of David,** probably composed after his return from a victorious campaign, but certainly typifying and prophesying the great victory of Christ over all the enemies of mankind. V. 1. **The king shall joy in Thy strength, O Lord,** rejoicing in the fact that God gave him the strength to subdue the enemies; **and in Thy salvation how greatly shall he rejoice!** exulting over the deliverance which was granted him by Jehovah. V. 2. **Thou hast given him his heart's desire,** the victory which he so earnestly longed for, **and hast not withholden the request of his lips,** for the longing of his heart was brought out in a spoken prayer. **Selah.** V. 3. **For Thou preventest him,** the Lord anticipated him, made ready the blessing even before the request was uttered, **with the blessings of goodness; Thou settest a crown of pure gold on his head,** as a token of triumph. V. 4. **He asked life of Thee,** to be preserved in the midst of all the dangers which threatened his life, **and Thou gavest it him, even length of days forever and ever,** not merely preserving his life at his prayer, but granting him a long life, in the case of Christ a life of endless glory, His human nature entering upon the unlimited use of the divine attributes communicated to it in the incarnation. V. 5. **His glory is great in Thy salvation,** the saving help of God in granting him the victory making his glory great, his name exalted; **honor and majesty hast Thou laid upon him,** his kingdom being maintained and strengthened in the eyes of all that heard of his great victory, before all the world. V. 6. **For Thou hast made him most blessed forever,** setting him as a blessing to mankind or to the world, a source of everlasting blessing, this fact again finding its highest fulfilment in Jesus Christ, the promised Messiah; **Thou hast made him exceeding glad with Thy countenance,** gladdening him with joy in the presence of Jehovah, for to behold His face is the essence of eternal bliss in heaven. V. 7. **For the king trusteth in the Lord,** this being the reason why the blessings of Jehovah were laid upon him, **and through the mercy of the Most High he shall not be moved,** not be shaken from the firm rock of his confidence in the God of his salvation. It is the mercy of God which keeps all believers in faith and sets before them the certainty of everlasting bliss in heaven.

THE CONFIDENCE OF FINAL TRIUMPH. — V. 8. **Thine hand shall find out all Thine enemies,** the psalmist's hopeful statement now becoming a definite prophecy concerning the final revenge of Jehovah; **Thy right hand shall find out those that hate Thee,** reaching out for them to inflict a certain punishment upon them. V. 9. **Thou shalt make them as a fiery oven,** a very strong expression to show how utterly the Lord's vengeance would consume them, **in the time of Thine anger; the Lord shall swallow them up in His wrath, and the fire shall devour them,** this being an unmistakable reference to the punishment following the final Judgment, 2 Pet. 3, 10. V. 10. **Their fruit,** that is, their children, their posterity, **shalt Thou destroy from the earth and their seed,** all those descending from them, **from among the children of men,** because they followed their parents in their wickedness. V. 11. **For they intended evil against Thee,** the figure being taken from the laying or stretching out of snares for the purpose of catching wild beasts; **they imagined a mischievous device,** plans for bringing harm upon the king, **which they are not able to perform,** due to the interference of the Lord they shall not prevail with their wickedness. V. 12. **Therefore shalt Thou make them turn their back,** make them turn their shoulder, force them to retreat and flee, **when Thou shalt make ready Thine arrows upon Thy strings against the face of them,** that is, when their troubles would cause them to flee, the Lord would overtake them and set His bow to aim at their face, thereby harassing them on both sides, placing them between two fires, and thus annihilating them. V. 13. **Be Thou exalted, Lord, in Thine own strength,** with the glory which rightly belonged to Him for this mighty deliverance; **so will we sing and praise Thy power.** Thus the believers ever acknowledge and praise the mercy of God and the wonderful manifestation of His might, who in Jesus Christ has given them a perfect, eternal deliverance.

PSALM 22.

The Messiah in His Great Passion.

A PROPHECY OF THE MESSIAH'S SUFFERING. **To the chief musician upon Aijeleth Shahar,** that is, "Of the hind of the dawn," **a psalm of David.** The words "Of the hind of the dawn" refer either to the melody or chant according to which this psalm was to be rendered, or they summarize the contents. As the hind is the emblem of the hunted soul panting for deliverance, so the dawn pictures the deliverance which follows the dark night of misery and wretchedness. In the humiliation of His great Passion, Christ was like the hind; in the exaltation following His overthrow of the enemies of mankind the rich beauty of the eternal morning dawned over Him. V. 1. **My God, My God, why hast Thou forsaken Me?** Here the speaker, the Messiah, speaking through the prophecy of His servant David, plunges immediately into the midst of His bitter cry of anguish which marked the climax of His suffering on the cross. Prophecy and fulfilment come together here; we are taken fully a thousand years into the future to Calvary, the Mount of Suffering. There it was that Christ cried out these words, as He felt the damnation of hell closing in upon Him, Matt. 27, 45. 46. It was not only the fatherly love of God, His heavenly Father and King, which had been withdrawn from Christ in those terrible hours of unspeakable suffering, but His very goodness had likewise forsaken Him. Without the slightest comfort and consolation He endured the tortures of the damned. So unfathomably deep was that suffering that the Messiah Himself felt constrained to ask, Why? The counsel of God, with which He had from eternity declared Himself in complete harmony, was, for the time being, hidden from His consciousness. And yet He clings to God as to His God and Father, His cry of excruciating misery thereby proving the almighty call of victory wherewith the Messiah conquered hell and all its hosts. **Why art Thou so far from helping Me, and from the words of My roaring?** Rather, Far from My help are the words of My roaring. The Messiah's heartrending cry over His being forsaken by God is here explained and further extended. The cry of His pain and torture assumed the nature of a roaring; it rose up on high, during an eternity of agony, without, however, bringing Him help. V. 2. **O My God, I cry in the daytime, but Thou hearest not; and in the night season, and am not silent.** There was no rest, no easement, no repose, for the suffering Messiah; He must drink the cup of God's anger to its very dregs. V. 3. **But Thou art holy,** and His holiness is acknowledged by the Messiah even in the depths of His suffering, **O Thou that inhabitest the praises of Israel,** praised in all of Israel's hymns of thanksgiving, magnified by all true believers. V. 4. **Our fathers trusted in Thee; they trusted, and Thou didst deliver them,** showing His mighty deliverance time and again. V. 5. **They cried unto Thee and were delivered,** they escaped the threatened danger, the attacks of the enemies; **they trusted in Thee and were not confounded,** they did not harbor vain hopes when they placed their trust in Jehovah. But the Messiah is constrained to cry out, by way of contrast, v. 6. **But I am a worm and no man,** He is like a worm which has been stepped on and winds back and forth in pain;

He no longer resembles a man, a human being, His sufferings being more than human nature could endure; **a reproach of men and despised of the people,** heaped with shame and contempt during the entire period of His suffering. V. 7. **All they that see Me laugh Me to scorn,** making Him a target of their blasphemous mockery, cp. Luke 23, 35; **they shoot out the lip,** in a grimace conveying their contempt; **they shake the head,** wagging it in a gesture denoting their doubt as to His being in His right mind, **saying,** v. 8. **He trusted on the Lord that He would deliver Him,** literally, "Roll it upon Jehovah," jeeringly urging Christ to cast His troubles upon the Lord; **let Him deliver Him, seeing He delighted in Him.** That was the bitter, blasphemous irony and mockery which the Jews flung at Christ there on Calvary's mount, taunting Him with being a cursed criminal, forsaken of God. V. 9. **But Thou art He that took Me out of the womb,** the unshaken trust of the Messiah in the God of His salvation appearing here; **Thou didst make Me hope,** causing Him to trust with full confidence, **when I was upon My mother's breasts,** in earliest infancy. V. 10. **I was cast upon Thee from the womb,** from His birth; **Thou art My God from My mother's belly,** His heavenly Father's care having enveloped and kept Him during His entire life, thus giving Him evidence that He was His God, His highest and most precious Treasure. Note that the human mother of Christ is referred to four times in this passage, and it is remarkable that in the entire Old Testament a human father is never mentioned or suggested, only a mother, Is. 7, 14; Gen. 3, 15. The fact that God is still His God causes the Messiah once more to turn to Him with an imploring cry. V. 11. **Be not far from Me, for trouble is near,** a most terrible distress was threatening; **for there is none to help,** no human being, no creature, to bring Him relief. Instead of finding helpers among men in the world, the very opposite holds true. V. 12. **Many bulls,** numerous and dangerous enemies, **have compassed Me; strong bulls of Bashan,** the rich meadow country northeast of Gilead, **have beset Me round,** threatening Him from all sides. V. 13. **They gaped upon Me with their mouths,** stretching them wide open, in order to tear Him to pieces, **as a ravening and a roaring lion.** Both the Jews and the arch-enemy of Christ are here included in this description. V. 14. **I am poured out like water,** His life is in the process of dissolution as the result of all these sufferings, **and all My bones are out of joint,** due to the torture of the cross; **My heart is like wax,** from the agony and terror of His soul; **it is melted in the midst of My bowels.** V. 15. **My strength is dried up like a potsherd,** all His vitality having left Him; **and My tongue cleaveth to My jaws,** in the agony of burning thirst from which He suffered on the cross; **and Thou hast brought Me into the dust of death,** laid there by God, in accordance with the eternal counsel concerning man's salvation. Both the Jews and the heathen would have had no power over Christ if it had not been given them from above; the death of Christ took place by the will of God. V. 16. **For dogs have compassed Me,** as the Messiah, in resuming His complaint, cries out; **the assembly of the wicked have enclosed Me; they pierced My hands and My feet,** digging through them with the nails which fastened Jesus to the cross. V. 17. **I may tell all My bones,** for He was so wasted away with suffering that every bone was to be seen; **they look and stare upon Me,** partly in indifference and partly in hatred. V. 18. **They part My garments among them and cast lots upon My vesture,** Luke 23, 34; John 19, 23. 24. Such were the indignities that were heaped upon the Lord. Therefore He cries out once more: v. 19. **But be not Thou far from Me, O Lord,** remaining at a distance; **O My Strength, haste Thee to help Me,** speedily coming to His assistance. V. 20. **Deliver My soul from the sword,** from the murderous weapons, from the instruments of torture; **My darling,** His precious life, **from the power of the dog,** the low and mean tormentors. V. 21. **Save Me from the lion's mouth,** Satan himself being referred to here; **for Thou hast heard me from the horns of the unicorns,** the wild oxen representing all His fierce enemies. The Messiah is so confident that God will hear Him that He states, Thou hast heard, Thou hast answered Me. All the forces of evil, the very powers of death, could not keep Him in subjection. It is the Christian's great comfort that Christ suffered willingly, that He endured all the sufferings laid upon Him to the end, to the time when He knew that redemption had been gained, that all was finished.

A PROPHECY OF THE MESSIAH'S GLORY. — V. 22. **I will declare Thy name unto My brethren,** proclaiming it aloud; **in the midst of the congregation will I praise Thee.** It is the delivered, the victorious Messiah who speaks in the last part of the psalm. The dawn of salvation has arisen upon the hind that was pursued. Christ, the Messiah, risen from the dead, is now enthroned at the right hand of God, while He is at the same time in the midst of His brethren, in the glorious Word of the Gospel. Those who believe in Him are the congregation of Jehovah, and their songs of praise rise in honor of His redemption. V. 23. **Ye that fear the Lord,** in humble reverence flowing from true faith, **praise Him; all ye, the seed of Jacob,** His spiritual children, **glorify Him; and fear Him, all ye, the seed of Israel,** all these terms being descriptive of the congregation of believers, of the Church of Christ. V. 24. **For He hath not despised nor abhorred the affliction of the**

afflicted, the poverty of the poor, the natural, miserable state of all men; **neither hath He hid His face from Him**, in indifference and anger; **but when He cried unto Him, He heard**, the Lord delivered all men, who were in spiritual misery and poverty, from sin, death, and the power of the devil. V. 25. **My praise shall be of Thee in the great congregation**, the believers of the Old and of the New Testament forming one great body, the same people of God, the one in hope and anticipation, the other in possession and realization; **I will pay my vows before them that fear Him**, the great sacrifice by which He atoned for our sins. And now that the great deed is accomplished, Christ distributes the fruit and blessing of His atoning work. V. 26. **The meek**, the poor sinners who realize their own unworthiness and desire only the grace and mercy of Jehovah, **shall eat and be satisfied**, partaking of the fulness of Christ's redemption; **they shall praise the Lord that seek Him**, full of the deepest gratitude for the benefits given by Him; **your heart shall live forever**, kept by the strength of the Redeemer in the Gospel. V. 27. **All the ends of the world shall remember and turn unto the Lord**, even the heathen from the extreme borders of the world, from distant lands, for His salvation is not only for the Jews, but also for the Gentiles; **and all the kindreds of the nations shall worship before Thee**, men from all tongues and peoples. V. 28. **For the kingdom**, namely, that of grace and glory, **is the Lord's**, Jehovah is its Ruler; **and He is the Governor among the nations.** Not that all nations, in all their individual component elements and members, will bow under the reign of the Messiah; but He has representatives from all parts of the earth who will finally be received into His kingdom by faith. V. 29. **All they that be fat upon earth shall eat**, of the blessings of His grace, **and worship**, some of the powerful and influential people of the earth would bow under the Messiah's reign; **all they that go down to the dust**, the most miserable among human beings, who hardly manage to keep their life from being snuffed out by the adversities of this world, **shall bow before Him**, the rich and the poor, the mighty and the lowly, being on the same level before Him; **and none can keep alive his own soul**, this being done by the power of the Redeemer through the means of grace. V. 30. **A seed**, a holy, chosen seed, consecrated to Him, **shall serve Him**, pledged to His ministry; **it shall be accounted to the Lord for a generation.** As generation succeeds generation, there will always be spiritual children born to Him pertaining to His household. V. 31. **They shall come and shall declare His righteousness**, the faithfulness of Jehovah in keeping His promises concerning the salvation of men, **unto a people that shall be born, that He hath done this.** As long as men live on the earth, till the last mortal has been born into this world of sin, shall the glorious victory of Christ be proclaimed in His great cry: "It is finished!" Thus mightily did the Messiah, through the mouth of His prophet, preach of the coming salvation through the sufferings, the death, and the resurrection of Jesus Christ. His victory is ours by faith.

PSALM 23.

Jehovah the Good Shepherd.

A psalm of David, a hymn written by David by the inspiration of the Holy Ghost, an expression not only of David's personal faith and trust, but of the confidence which all believers have in the goodness, love, and grace of God and of their Savior Jesus Christ, brought out all the more strongly since it is spoken in the name of each individual Christian. V. 1. **The Lord**, Jehovah, the God of grace and faithfulness, the Redeemer of mankind, not only God the Father, Gen. 48, 15; 49, 24, but also God the Son, Jesus Christ in particular, **is my Shepherd**, to whom every believer stands in the relation of the most intimate fellowship, by whom and in whom he lives, through whose mighty power the life of his soul is sustained; **I shall not want**, being supplied with all gifts and blessings for this world and for the world to come. V. 2. **He maketh me to lie down in green pastures**, where the meadows are lush with young, vigorous grass, where the best spiritual food is found in rich abundance; **He leadeth me beside the still waters**, where the refreshing streams of His grace flow softly and gently, not with the boisterous threats of the Law, but with the coaxing beauty of the Gospel. The Good Shepherd gives food and drink, rest and peace, the fulness of His gifts of love, both for this world and for the world to come. V. 3. **He restoreth my soul**, reviving, quickening, relieving it, when the spirits droop with weariness on account of the misery of sin and the afflictions of this world; **He leadeth me in the paths of righteousness**, walking ahead after the manner of Oriental shepherds and choosing such roads as are straight and even, where there is no danger of stumbling and falling, even if they often seem strange to the sheep themselves, **for His name's sake**, to reveal and make known His faithfulness and mercy, not because of any merit or worthiness in us. These wonderful blessings of the Lord awaken and nourish the true confidence of faith in the hearts of the believers, as the next words show. V. 4. **Yea,** even when conditions are not so favorable, **though I walk through the valley of the shadow of death,** where darkness and terror surround the believer, where the cry of wild beasts from the mountain caverns tends to take the confidence out of the heart of the sheep, when misfortune and trouble harass them, **I will fear no evil,** said in the proper defiance of faith, the believer trusting not in his own power, but in that of the upholding might of Jehovah's strength. **For Thou art with me,** even in the darkest night of tribulation, even in the peril of death; **Thy rod and Thy staff,** the protecting and sustaining power of Jehovah's mercy in the means of grace, **they comfort me,** offering the right consolation in every trouble affecting both body and soul. That is the second great fact upon which the believer places his trust. V. 5. **Thou preparest a table before me,** a joyful and rich festival meal, **in the presence of mine enemies,** not a bulwark or fort, for they were helpless in the presence of the almighty Shepherd, and the full power of Jehovah is assured in the protection of His believers, the idea of full security in spite of all adversaries, of refreshing and satisfying joys after all afflictions. **Thou anointest my head with oil,** this act preceding the festival meal of old and assuring the guest of the most cordial welcome on the part of the host; **my cup runneth over,** with more than a full measure of spiritual blessings and joys. V. 6. **Surely goodness and mercy,** the greatest good fortune in the possession of the grace of Jehovah, **shall follow me all the days of my life,** in everything pertaining to both body and soul the way of the Lord is always gracious and merciful, is always the best; **and I will dwell in the house of the Lord,** in the midst of the church of Jehovah, as a member of the congregation of saints, **forever,** here in time, in the Kingdom of Grace, and hereafter in eternity, in the Kingdom of Glory; for the home of everlasting glory awaits all true believers above, John 14, 2; Rev. 21, 1—5. It is theirs even now, by faith.

PSALM 24.

The Coming of the King of Glory.

THE MESSIANIC KINGDOM. — **A psalm of David,** another hymn of the Messiah and His kingdom, to prepare the believers of the Old Testament for His coming and to inspire the believers of the New Testament with the proper regard for their King. V. 1. **The earth is the Lord's,** the entire visible creation belongs to Jehovah, as the product of His almighty power, **and the fulness thereof,** what fills up its contents, everything it contains, is in His power; **the world and they that dwell therein,** not only the inanimate creatures, but all the living creatures which inhabit the world. All this is in His absolute, unlimited power, it belongs to His Kingdom of Power. V. 2. **For He hath founded it upon the seas,** He set the foundation of the earth in the midst of the mighty ocean, **and established it upon the floods,** giving it a firm base when He separated the water from the dry land and called the latter earth. This is the largest and most extensive kingdom of Jehovah, that which includes all created beings. But the description now narrows down to a smaller kingdom. V. 3. **Who shall ascend into the hill of the Lord,** the mountain of Jehovah, or Zion, the place of His presence in the midst of His people and type of His holy congregation? **Or who shall stand in His Holy Place?** the place of His holiness, where He revealed Himself to the members of His Church; for at that time only such persons were permitted to enter the inner courts as were members of the Jewish Church. V. 4. **He that hath clean hands,** which were Levitically pure and unstained with crimes, **and a pure heart,** whose love to Jehovah is without hypocrisy; **who hath not lifted up his soul unto vanity,** in any form of idolatrous behavior, **nor sworn deceitfully,** in false oaths. The true members of the Jewish Church are a type of the Church of the New Testament, to which all men belong whose hearts have been purified by faith in the Redeemer, whose hands are kept clean from sin and every form of vileness for love of Him, whose souls are in no way concerned with the idolatrous vanities of the present world. Men to whom this description applies are welcome on the mount of Jehovah, they are eagerly sought by Him in the place of His holiness. V. 5. **He shall receive the blessing from the Lord,** namely, the righteousness of God in Jesus Christ, imputed to all believers and assuring them of their salvation, **and righteousness from the God of his salvation.** It is by this process of granting righteousness to one hearer of the Word after another that a generation, a people, is gathered whose chief aim in life is to learn more of Jehovah, their God. V. 6. **This is the generation of them that seek Him, that seek thy face, O Jacob,** desiring to follow the God of Jacob, to do His bidding, to enter into an ever more perfect communion with Him, for in inquiring for Jacob, patriarch of the true religion, they inquire for Him who inspired it, the eternal God of their salvation. **Selah.** Thus the Kingdom of Grace, the Church of Jesus Christ, is briefly, but fittingly described.

THE WELCOME OF THE KING. — V. 7. **Lift up your heads, O ye gates; and be ye lift up,**

ye everlasting doors; and the King of Glory shall come in. The picture is that of a mighty host moving forward to take possession of Mount Zion, with a great King, who wants to enter the city, the congregation of the saints, at its head. The challenging cry rings out that the gates of Zion, of the spiritual Temple of the Lord, should lift up their heads, their lintels, widen out, make room for the entering of this great King. Doors of eternity they are called, because they were in existence since the first man accepted the promise of the Messiah, and will remain throughout eternity, in spite of all attempts on the part of the portals of hell to overthrow them. A solo voice now asks, v. 8. **Who is this King of Glory?** And the chorus joyfully answers: **The Lord strong and mighty, the Lord mighty in battle.** The Messiah is the almighty God, mighty, invincible in war, clothed with everlasting glory and majesty. He is here represented as coming to His people as One to whom the victory over all enemies is assured from the outset, who will overwhelm all His foes. Once more the challenge rings out, v. 9. **Lift up your heads, O ye gates; even lift them up, ye everlasting doors; and the King of Glory shall come in.** The Messiah is eager to enter into the hearts of all those who will accept His love and mercy. A single voice: v. 10. **Who is this King of Glory?** And the chorus answers, in joyful exultation: **The Lord of hosts,** the great Jehovah Sabaoth, **He is the King of Glory. Selah.** May every heart be opened to Him in joyful welcome in order that He may enter in and abide throughout eternity, in the majesty of His greatness and in the beauty of His love.

PSALM 25.

A Prayer for Merciful Protection and Guidance.

A psalm of David. V. 1. **Unto thee, O Lord,** in an emphatic singling out of Jehovah as the one true God, **do I lift up my soul,** withdrawn from all earthly desires, with a fervent longing for Jehovah's salvation. V. 2. **O my God, I trust in Thee,** abiding firmly in this confidence; **let me not be ashamed,** become an object of mockery; **let not mine enemies triumph over me,** with exulting jeers over the foolishness of his trust. V. 3. **Yea, let none that wait on Thee be ashamed,** their hope coming to naught; **let them be ashamed,** all their vain hopes being dashed to the ground, **which transgress without cause,** becoming traitors, perfidious, to the cause of the Lord and of righteousness without provocation, out of pure wickedness. V. 4. **Show me Thy ways, O Lord,** so that he might know and understand them properly; **teach me Thy paths,** God's gracious ways of dealing with His children on earth. V. 5. **Lead me in Thy truth,** that of His eternal Word, **and teach me,** that being the only true source of knowledge; **for Thou art the God of my salvation,** the true and only Deliverer from every form of danger, sin, and death; **on Thee do I wait all the day,** looking to Him alone for guidance. V. 6. **Remember, O Lord, Thy tender mercies and Thy loving-kindnesses,** the many instances in which He had shown His kindness and mercy; **for they have been ever of old,** they are the attributes of the eternal God and heavenly Father. V. 7. **Remember not the sins of my youth nor my transgressions,** those committed in youthful folly often resting heavily upon the conscience throughout all the years of maturity, and the assurance of their being forgiven yielding great comfort to a harassed heart; **according to Thy mercy,** His unmerited favor in Christ Jesus, the Messiah, **remember Thou me for Thy goodness' sake, O Lord,** that being the only hope of a poor sinner. And this hope has the soundest basis. V. 8. **Good and upright is the Lord,** faithful, acting in accordance with His promises; **therefore will He teach sinners in the way,** instructing them which is the right way to go. V. 9. **The meek,** the humble in heart, **will He guide in judgment,** guiding them in the knowledge of what is right; **and the meek,** the real poor sinners, **will He teach His way,** which is the only right way. V. 10. **All the paths of the Lord,** His modes of dealing with His children, **are mercy and truth,** grace in promising and faithfulness in performing, **unto such as keep His covenant and His testimonies,** letting the Word of God be their only guide in all the vicissitudes of their lives. All this being true with regard to Jehovah, the petition of the poor sinner will surely be heard. V. 11. **For Thy name's sake, O Lord,** in order to bring honor and glory upon Himself, **pardon mine iniquity,** the guilt which he had loaded upon himself by his transgressions; **for it is great,** a confession to which all true children of God will agree as they realize their sinfulness more and more. V. 12. **What man is he that feareth the Lord,** after having seen such manifestations of God's pardoning love as here set forth? **Him shall He teach in the way that he shall choose,** so that the sinner, assured of the pardon of the Lord, will be eager to choose the right, the best way. V. 13. **His soul shall dwell at ease,** enjoying good fortune and prosperity under the blessing of God; **and his seed shall inherit the earth,** the promise of the possession of Canaan having been given to Israel and that of a happy life on earth being held out to all believers. V. 14. **The secret of the Lord,** the intimate association of His friendship, **is with them that fear Him,** so that He makes known to them things which are hidden to others; **and He will show them His covenant,** making known to them the gracious terms of His pardon in the Gospel-message. V. 15. **Mine eyes are ever toward the Lord,** fixed upon Him in hope and trust; **for He shall pluck my feet out of the net,** delivering him from all the dangers arising from the craft and guile of the enemies. V. 16. **Turn Thee unto me,** in compassionate attention, **and have mercy upon me; for I am desolate and afflicted,** it being the lot of the true believers to be isolated and ostracized by the children of the world. V. 17. **The troubles of my heart are enlarged,** distresses had extended themselves and spread out over his heart, engulfing it beneath their flood. **O bring Thou me out of my distresses!** leading him out of all narrow and oppressive circumstances. V. 18. **Look upon mine affliction and my pain,** his dejection due to his misery and hardship, **and forgive all my sins,** this pardon being the greatest spiritual gift. V. 19. **Consider mine enemies,** looking upon them; **for they are many,** that being the experience of all believers; **and they hate me with cruel hatred,** their hatred being unreasonable and contemplating injury and violence. V. 20. **O keep my soul and deliver me,** this being an easy matter for the almighty power of Jehovah; **let me not be ashamed, for I put my trust in Thee,** and therefore any mockery on the part of the enemies would reflect dishonor on the Lord as well. V. 21. **Let integrity and uprightness,** true piety and honesty, which despises hypocrisy and every form of crookedness, **preserve me,** being his companions on the way of righteousness; **for I wait on Thee,** Jehovah being the foundation of his hope. V. 22. **Redeem Israel, O God,** not only David, but the entire congregation of believers of all times and in all circumstances, **out of all his troubles.** May God deliver the entire Christian Church from all evils of body and soul, property and honor, and finally take all His children from this vale of tears to Himself in heaven!

PSALM 26.

Prayer of One Persecuted without Cause.

A psalm of David, who probably composed this hymn when he himself was suffering persecution, being obliged to flee before Absalom. The contents of this psalm, however, apply to many situations in the lives of all children of God. V. 1. **Judge me, O God,** declaring him righteous by a judicial sentence, deciding in his favor, and thereby setting aside the false accusations of the enemies; **for I have walked in mine integrity,** in purity of heart, free from wickedness. **I have trusted also in the Lord; therefore I shall not slide,** rather, without wavering had he placed his trust in Jehovah, hence he confidently expected the Lord to take his part in his present misfortune. V. 2. **Examine me, O Lord, and prove me,** making a careful investigation; **try my reins and my heart,** as an assayer tests ore for gold. He is ready to submit himself to the most searching examination, both to prove his innocence and to have the dross of any self-deception purged away, whether this would be found in the lower passions or in the higher affections. V. 3. **For Thy loving-kindness is before mine eyes,** the remembrance of former favors encouraging David in his prayer; **and I have walked in Thy truth,** the grace which God shows to sinners was his aim, his model, and the faithfulness with which He kept His promises was the rule and criterion of His conduct. V. 4. **I have not sat with vain persons,** with men of falsehood, with liars and deceivers, **neither will I go in with dissemblers,** those who disguise their real intentions under the mask of hypocrisy. V. 5. **I have hated the congregation of evil-doers,** those openly guilty of wickedness, **and will not sit with the wicked,** not joining their assembly and taking part in their discussions. V. 6. **I will wash mine hands in innocency,** the words referring to a symbolical act, declaring a person to be clean of vile and godless conduct, also to the act of priests who were obliged to wash themselves before bringing the offerings in public worship; **so will I compass Thine altar, O Lord,** being privileged, as pure and pious in heart, to perform the service of the priests of Jehovah, this being the condition in which God expects the heart of every believer to be; v. 7. **that I may publish with the voice of thanksgiving,** joining with the Temple chorus in psalms of praise, **and tell of all Thy wondrous works,** the miracles of mercy which God performed in the Old Testament as well as now, and which all true believers celebrate by faithfully using the means of grace. V. 8. **Lord, I have loved the habitation of Thy house,** the place where Jehovah revealed His presence in the midst of His people, **and the place where Thine honor dwelleth,** the glorious dwelling-place of Jehovah, where He was pleased to manifest Himself. In the same way all true Christians love the house of worship, whether a log hut in the wilderness or a granite palace in the city, where the glory of Jehovah is revealed in the preaching of the pure Gospel and in the administration of the Sacraments in accordance with God's own institution. It is with this longing that David addresses his last petition to the Lord. V. 9. **Gather not my soul with sinners,** binding it up in the same bundle with them, like wheat bound together with tares, **nor my life with bloody men,** murderers and sinners of the worst class, v. 10. **in whose hands is mischief,** crime, their whole conduct violence and fraud, **and their right hand is full of bribes,** full of trickery and deceit, as that of wicked men in public office. V. 11. **But as for me,** in contrast to these ungodly people, **I will walk in mine integrity,** continuing his course in the purity of his conduct. **Redeem me and be merciful unto me,** the deliverance which he longs for being a proof of God's mercy. V. 12. **My foot standeth in an even place,** in a wide and safe space, where his enemies can no longer hinder him or bring destruction upon him. **In the congregations will I bless the Lord,** publicly pouring out his thanksgiving to God for his salvation. All true believers count it a glorious privilege to be able to visit their house of worship and to join with the entire congregation in hymns of praise to His glory.

PSALM 27.

The Believer's Trust in God and His Word.

A psalm of David, written probably about the same time as the preceding one, picturing the state of mind of one who is persecuted without cause and longs for the blessings of the worship in the midst of the congregation. V. 1. **The Lord is my Light,** the only Source of all spiritual light, **and my Salvation,** He who saves him from the darkness of oppression and persecution; **whom shall I fear? The Lord is the Strength of my life,** his Stronghold, his Bulwark, his sure Defense, keeping his life from destruction; **of whom shall I be afraid?** The entire song has the ring of Paul's mighty hymn of triumph, Rom. 8, 31—39. V. 2. **When the wicked,** the doers of evil and mischief, **even mine enemies and my foes,** those who oppose and oppress him on all sides, **came upon me,** approaching him with marked hostility, **to eat up my flesh,** as wild beasts eager to tear and devour their prey, **they stumbled and fell,** unable to carry out their object because of the protection afforded David by Jehovah. V. 3. **Though an host,** a whole army or camp of adversaries, **should encamp against me,** besieging him on all sides, **my heart shall not fear; though war should rise against me, in this,** even in such a great extremity, **will I be confident,** in spite of all that he would calmly trust in Jehovah, his Stronghold. Both the words and the tone of the psalm denote the holy and calm defiance with which all believers may await the attack of the enemies. V. 4. **One thing have I desired of the Lord,** in the midst of all these threatening dangers, **that will I seek after,** with a great desire: **that I may dwell in the house of the Lord,** the Tabernacle of His presence, **all the days of my life,** in the delight of intimate fellowship with Jehovah, **to behold the beauty of the Lord,** His favor and kindness as revealed in the Word of His grace, **and to enquire in His Temple,** meditating upon the wonderful blessings of His mercy in the message of the Gospel. V. 5. **For,** because of the believer's close communion with God, **in the time of trouble He shall hide me in His pavilion,** in the Tabernacle, where His almighty hand protects; **in the secret of His Tabernacle shall He hide me,** sheltering the believer in the safety of His tent; **He shall set me upon a rock,** the house of Jehovah being a refuge and stronghold beyond the reach of puny men. V. 6. **And now shall mine head be lifted up,** in the triumph of a certain victory, **above mine enemies round about me,** the fact of whose defeat places the believer beyond their reach; **therefore will I offer in His Tabernacle sacrifices of joy,** thank-offerings always being occasions of great rejoicing. **I will sing, yea, I will sing praises unto the Lord,** which the faithful Israelites were wont to do at the festival meal connected with their thank-offerings. At the same time David does not, even in the remotest way, rely upon his own strength, and for this reason the triumphant strain of confidence now gives way to an earnest appeal. V. 7. **Hear, O Lord, when I cry with my voice,** calling loudly and emphatically; **have mercy also upon me,** that being the one safe reliance of the believer, **and answer me,** with a favorable reply. V. 8. **When Thou saidst, Seek ye My face,** at Jehovah's call to seek His face, **my heart said unto Thee, Thy face, Lord, will I seek;** the heart of the believer being attuned to the fellowship with Jehovah, it gladly answers His call, assenting thereto as an echo of it, happy in the knowledge that it pleases Jehovah if His children enter into the presence of God, in order to gain comfort, assistance, and blessings of every kind. V. 9. **Hide not thy face (far) from me,** veiling it from the prayer of the believer; **put not Thy servant away in anger,** thrusting him aside as unworthy; **Thou hast been my Help,** and the former mercy and love emboldens David to plead against rejection. **Leave me not, neither forsake me, O God of my salvation.** It is the cry of Jacob: "I will not let Thee go except Thou bless me," Gen. 32, 26, a call which holds the Lord to the promise of His salvation. V. 10. **When my father and my mother forsake me,** the very nearest earthly relatives abandoning him who seems doomed to destruction, Matt. 10, 35. 36, **then the Lord will take me up**, receiving the believer into His care and protection, adopting him as His own child. V. 11. **Teach me Thy way**, the road according with Jehovah's will, **O Lord, and lead me in a plain path**, even, level, without pitfalls, **because of mine enemies**, since they dog his every footstep and are trying to lead him into sin, his fall at the same time heaping dishonor upon God. V. 12. **Deliver me not over unto the will of mine enemies**, to the destruction which they had planned against him; **for false witnesses are risen up against me**, such being the methods employed by the enemies in their persecution of the believer, **and such as breathe out cruelty**, their every breath being charged with violence. V. 13. **I had fainted unless I had believed to see the goodness of the Lord in the land of the living**, literally, "If I did not trust to behold the excellence of Jehovah —!" He leaves the sentence unfinished, for it is too hard to picture and imagine life without the sustaining mercy of Jehovah. And so David encourages himself and all believers in conclusion, v. 14. **Wait on the Lord**, firmly trusting in the revelation of His mercy; **be of good courage**, strong of heart, **and He shall strengthen thine heart**, rather, let thy heart show itself mighty. **Wait, I say, on the Lord.** With this confident expectation the prayer of every believer must be concluded; for the Lord will, at His own time, bring salvation in rich measure upon His children, here in time and hereafter in eternity.

PSALM 28.

Prayer and Comfort in Times of Rebellion.

A psalm of David, written in similar circumstances as the two foregoing ones, his heart apparently being so full that his mouth was bound to speak, David in this case including himself with the people of God in praying against the oppression of the wicked and the unbelievers. V. 1. **Unto Thee will I cry**, once more with importunate earnestness, **O Lord, my Rock**, his impregnable Stronghold, Ps. 18, 2. **Be not silent to me**, being deaf to his prayer and so refusing to answer, **lest, if Thou be silent to me, I become like them that go down into the pit**, sinking down into the grave in utter hopelessness. V. 2. **Hear the voice of my supplications**, of his loud and earnest entreaty, **when I cry unto Thee, when I lift up my hands**, in a gesture of urgent pleading, **toward Thy holy oracle**, literally, "throne-hall," this word here being used to designate the Most Holy Place, for the lid of the Ark of the Covenant was the place of the Lord's presence in the midst of His people, Ex. 25, 22. V. 3. **Draw me not away**, to destruction, to punishment in time and eternity, **with the wicked and with the workers of iniquity, which speak peace to their neighbors**, with an outward profession of friendliness, **but mischief is in their hearts**, their outward show of kindness being assumed in order to mislead the trusting believers and thus to bring destruction upon them all the more quickly. V. 4. **Give them according to their deeds**, all that their wickedness deserved, **and according to the wickedness**, the evil and hypocrisy, **of their endeavors; give them after the work of their hands**, paying them back in kind; **render to them their desert.** Note that a true believer places his case into the hands of the Lord, to whom revenge belongs. V. 5. **Because they regard not the works of the Lord**, they are blind to the righteous and gracious government of Jehovah, **nor the operation of His hands**, in everything that He does for mankind, **He shall destroy them and not build them up**, the picture being that of a building which is torn down instead of having its construction finished. V. 6. **Blessed be the Lord because He hath heard the voice of my supplications**, his cries for mercy, the believer being sure even in advance of being heard. V. 7. **The Lord is my Strength**, which serves to protect him, **and my Shield**, safe-guarding him against every attack. **My heart trusted in Him, and I am helped**, the fulfilment of his prayer being represented as already present; **therefore my heart greatly rejoiceth, and with my song will I praise Him**, giving all glory to Him alone for His merciful salvation. V. 8. **The Lord is their Strength**, a protection to all those who believe and trust in Him, **and He is the saving Strength of His anointed**, mightily preserving all those consecrated to Him from every form of destruction by placing them in such places of refuge where the wiles of the enemies cannot reach them. It is in this joyful and certain confidence that the concluding prayer is made for the Christian Church of all times, v. 9. **Save Thy people**, with an everlasting redemption, **and bless Thine inheritance**, the people whom Jehovah Himself had chosen for His portion; **feed them also**, as a true Shepherd, **and lift them up forever**, bearing them up, carrying them in His arms. Cp. Deut. 32, 11. That is the proper prayer of the Church at all times, especially when the forces of darkness are unusually active in assailing the work of the Lord as effected through the means of grace.

PSALM 29.

The Almighty Power of God's Voice in His Word.

A psalm of David, the writing of which may have been occasioned by a terrible thunderstorm, but the description of which goes beyond the natural plane to show the power of the voice of God in overcoming even the mightiest forces and people of the world and making them serve His purposes. V. 1. **Give unto the Lord, O ye mighty,** literally, "sons of gods," that is, the rulers, the governments of the world, **give unto the Lord glory and strength,** offering Him this tribute as the King of kings and Lord of lords. V. 2. **Give unto the Lord the glory due unto His name,** to the revelation of His divine majesty and power; **worship the Lord in the beauty of holiness,** in holy attire, as priests clothed for the ministry and worship of Jehovah, ready to give Him homage and to exalt Him. And now David shows how the Word of God, His mighty voice, works such a feeling of homage and devotion in the hearts of men. V. 3. **The voice of the Lord is upon the waters,** the voice of Jehovah, thundering mightily, over the vapors of the clouds, with their heavy load of water; **the God of glory thundereth; the Lord is upon many waters,** the heavy, lowering clouds of the advancing storm being indicated. But David, in the voice of the thunder, always has the Word of the Lord in mind. V. 4. **The voice of the Lord is powerful; the voice of the Lord is full of majesty,** going forth invested with these qualities, Heb. 4, 12. V. 5. **The voice of the Lord breaketh the cedars; yea, the Lord breaketh the cedars of Lebanon,** the mighty giants of the forests being laid low before the stormwind, just as many a wise and mighty person in this world has been overcome by the Word of Jehovah. V. 6. **He maketh them also to skip like a calf,** the mighty forests waving and bowing in the wind; **Lebanon and Sirion like a young unicorn,** like the young of the wild oxen or buffaloes, Sirion being Mount Hermon, the loftiest peak in the eastern range of Lebanon. V. 7. **The voice of the Lord divideth the flames of fire,** the lightning preceding the thunder cutting through the air like immense sparks of fire; even so does the Word of the Lord burn in the hearts of men with a mighty, devouring, and sustaining flame. V. 8. **The voice of the Lord shaketh the wilderness,** the mighty thunder making the mighty wilderness tremble as in an earthquake; **the Lord shaketh the wilderness of Kadesh,** that of the Arabian Desert west of Edom, in whose desolate regions such a storm makes an unusual impression of grandeur. Thus the Word of Jehovah arouses men everywhere, especially when they behold the Desire of the Nations in the Gospel, Hag. 2, 6. V. 9. **The voice of the Lord maketh the hinds to calve,** in a premature delivery, brought on by the terror of the storm, **and discovereth the forests,** stripping them bare, the very peelings of the bark being taken off by the lightning. **And in His Temple,** in the great palace of His might, both on earth and in heaven, **doth every one speak of His glory,** crying out, Glory and majesty to God alone for the revelation of His almighty power and mercy! V. 10. **The Lord sitteth upon the flood,** He sat upon the throne of His judgment when He condemned the godless world and punished the wicked through the catastrophe of the Flood; **yea, the Lord sitteth King forever,** and all those who haughtily reject His Word will feel the power of His anger. V. 11. **The Lord will give strength unto His people,** sustaining His own children, those united with Him in true fellowship, Is. 45, 24; **the Lord will bless His people with peace,** with the peace of God, which passes all understanding, as given through the glorious Gospel of God's mercy in Christ Jesus, Phil. 4, 7. "How impressive the closing words of this psalm! They are arched as a rainbow above it. The beginning of the psalm shows us the heavens open and the throne of God in the midst of angelic songs of praise, and the close of the psalm shows us on earth, in the midst of the angry voices of Jehovah shaking all things, His people victorious and blessed with peace. 'Glory in the highest' is the beginning, and 'Peace on earth' is the end." (Delitzsch.)

PSALM 30.

A Prayer of Thanksgiving for Deliverance from Death.

A psalm and song, literally, "a psalm-song," a composition to be sung with musical accompaniment, **at the dedication of the house of David,** of his palace on the hill of Zion, this festivity taking place shortly after he had recovered from a severe illness. V. 1. **I will extol Thee, O Lord,** lifting up high the praises of Jehovah, exalting Him greatly; **for Thou hast lifted me up,** drawing him out of the deep well or pit of his illness and distress, **and hast not made my foes to rejoice over me,** as they would have had occasion to do if he had succumbed to the disease and its attending troubles. V. 2. **O Lord, my God, I cried unto Thee,** with a loud and earnest call, **and Thou hast healed me,** given him back his health after he had been in peril of death. V. 3. **O Lord, Thou hast brought up my soul from the grave,** restoring him when his soul had almost reached the realms of the dead; **Thou hast kept me alive that I should not go down to the pit,** quickening him from among those who go down to the grave, so that it was his good fortune to be saved while many others had to die. V. 4. **Sing unto the Lord, O ye saints of His,** in psalms of joy, **and give thanks at the remembrance of His holiness,** praising His holy memory by keeping His name before their hearts and minds always. V. 5. **For His anger endureth but a moment,** passing by very rapidly on account of the urging of His mercy; **in His favor is life,** His loving-kindness lasts a lifetime. **Weeping may endure for a night,** that is, the night may be passed in weeping, **but joy cometh in the morning,** for His mercies are new every morning, and His compassions fail not. David, indeed, has a confession to make, v. 6. **And in my prosperity I said, I shall never be moved,** he had begun to trust in himself, as even believers will be in danger of doing if all things are in their favor. He even tried to explain his self-assurance to himself, v. 7. **Lord, by Thy favor Thou hast made my mountain to stand strong,** given him a safe and impregnable place. Being specially favored by the Lord, David had begun to feel fleshly security. However, he was soon brought back to his senses. **Thou didst hide Thy face, and I was troubled;** when it seemed that God had withdrawn His favor from him, David became frightened; he realized once more that it is necessary at all times to work out one's own salvation with fear and trembling. He did not despair, however. V. 8. **I cried to Thee, O Lord,** as all believers should do in a similar position; **and unto the Lord I made supplication,** appealing to Him for mercy. Cp. Ps. 6, 5; 88, 10; Is. 38, 18. V. 9. **What profit is there in my blood when I go down to the pit?** Of what use would he be to Jehovah in the grave? **Shall the dust praise Thee?** namely, himself, when turned to dust. **Shall it declare Thy truth?** This he considered the main purpose of his life, to sing praises to God, to make known His faithfulness. Of this praise God would deprive Himself if He would cut off his life at this time. V. 10. **Hear, O Lord, and have mercy upon me,** extending His grace to him: **Lord, be Thou my Helper.** That had been David's prayer in his great trouble, and the Lord had heard him. V. 11. **Thou hast turned for me my mourning into dancing,** the reference being to the exultant joy of the lute-playing accompanying such leaping for happiness as done by the women celebrating a victory, Ex. 15, 20; Judg. 11, 34; 1 Sam. 18, 6; **Thou hast put off my sackcloth,** the garment of sorrow and penitence, **and girded me with gladness,** signifying both strength and rejoicing; v. 12. **to the end that my glory,** David's ransomed soul expressing its thanks through his tongue, as the organ of praise, **may sing praise to Thee, and not be silent. O Lord, my God, I will give thanks unto Thee forever.** Such is the joyful prayer of every believer, in grateful remembrance of the Lord's many mercies upon him during his whole life.

PSALM 31.

The Believer's Humble and Confident Submission to the Hand of God.

To the chief musician, for performance in the liturgical part of the Tabernacle worship, **a psalm of David,** written at some time when he was in very great trouble. Luther rightly makes the application when he writes that the psalm is spoken in the person of Christ and His saints, who are plagued during their whole life, internally by trembling and alarm, externally by persecution, slander, and contempt, for the sake of the Word of God, and yet are delivered by God from them all and receive the fulness of divine comfort.

A CONFIDENT ENTREATY. — V. 1. **In Thee, O Lord, do I put my trust,** having taken refuge with Jehovah, sheltered by His almighty power; **let me never be ashamed,** such shame bringing disgrace also upon Him to whom he entrusted himself; **deliver me in Thy righteousness,** by a manifestation of His essence which would prove Him to be the righteous God. V. 2. **Bow down Thine ear to me,** in the attitude of most careful attention; **deliver me speedily,** since the need was so urgent. **Be Thou my strong Rock,** a pinnacle of defense, **for an house of defense,** a fortress, or stronghold, **to save me.** This is the humble, but bold and courageous manner in which a believer may at all times approach his heavenly Father. V. 3. **For Thou art my Rock and my Fortress,** it was because David knew this that he prayed so confidently; **therefore for Thy name's sake lead me and guide me,** rather, "Thou wilt lead me and guide me," for it expresses the strong hope and confidence that it will be done according to the believer's faith and prayer. V. 4. **Pull me out of the net,** again a definite statement, "Thou wilt bring me out of the net," **that they have laid privily for me,** Ps. 9, 15; 25, 15; **for Thou art my Strength,** his Defense and Bulwark. V. 5. **Into Thine hand I commit my spirit,** in all the vicissitudes of life, in all the dangers of death, he places the life of his spirit into the hands of his heavenly

Father, as in the safest place of deposit, as also Jesus and Stephen did, Luke 23, 36; Acts 7, 59; **Thou hast redeemed me,** from all evils and dangers that beset the path of mortals here below, **O Lord God of truth,** whose Word and promise is secure at all times. Note that the spirit of faith is like the spirit of prophecy, speaking of things in the future with the certainty of fulfilment. V. 6. **I have hated them that regard lying vanities,** those who place their trust in vain idols; **but I trust in the Lord,** the emphasis being placed on the contrast, the "I" being stressed, as was the "Thou" in v. 4. V. 7. **I will be glad and rejoice in Thy mercy,** with exultant joy over God's act of grace upon him; **for Thou hast considered my trouble,** regarding it for the sake of relieving the sufferer; **Thou hast known my soul in adversities,** not ignored it, but taken note of its needs, v. 8. **and hast not shut me up into the hand of the enemy,** to be a miserable captive, subject to every form of indignity; **Thou hast set my feet in a large room,** in a wide place, where he would not be hindered by the enemies. With all these evidences of God's loving-kindness in mind, the psalmist again sounds his prayer. V. 9. **Have mercy upon me, O Lord,** being gracious to the unworthy, **for I am in trouble,** distressed and oppressed; **mine eye is consumed with grief,** wasted away with vexation, **yea, my soul and my belly,** his entire person, including both his spiritual and physical activities and experiences. V. 10. **For my life is spent,** consumed, eaten up, **with grief, and my years with sighing; my strength faileth because of mine iniquity,** by reason of the suffering which, as a punishment, followed his transgression, **and my bones are consumed,** wasted away with fear and dread. Note that David, and all believers with him, regards his sin as the real cause of his troubles. V. 11. **I was a reproach among all mine enemies,** rather, "Because of all mine adversaries I have become a reproach," on account of their continual nagging and jeering, **but especially among my neighbors, and a fear to mine acquaintance,** a burden to his nearest neighbors and a terror to all who knew him, on account of the reports spread about him, which laid every form of evil to his charge. **They that did see me without fled from me,** with an aversion due to the reports circulated about him. V. 12. **I am forgotten as a dead man out of mind,** consigned to oblivion by men, out of sight, out of mind; **I am like a broken vessel,** one that is perishing, about to be discarded as unfit. V. 13. **For I have heard the slander of many,** the whispering directed against his person; **fear was on every side,** terrors all around him; **while they took counsel against me, they devised to take away my life.** Thus his enemies were engaged, such intentions they harbored; that was the trouble in which David found himself, the experience of most believers, at one time or another.

CONFIDENCE AND TRIUMPH OF FAITH. — V. 14. **But I trusted in Thee, O Lord,** again spoken with emphasis, "But as for me, in Thee have I confided, O Jehovah." **I said, Thou art my God,** his highest Good, his safe Refuge. V. 15. **My times,** the entire course of the believer's life, **are in Thy hand,** not subject to blind fate, but to the gracious will of the heavenly Father. **Deliver me from the hand of mine enemies,** always stretched out to harm him, **and from them that persecute me,** torturing him with their pursuit. V. 16. **Make Thy face to shine upon Thy servant,** in merciful kindness; **save me for Thy mercies' sake,** all merit on the part of the believer being disowned. V. 17. **Let me not be ashamed, O Lord,** become an object of ridicule on account of his trust in Jehovah, **for I have called upon Thee; let the wicked be ashamed,** all mockery being heaped upon their head, **and let them be silent in the grave,** cut off from the land of the living and silenced in the realm of the dead below. V. 18. **Let the lying lips be put to silence,** forever become dumb in death, **which speak grievous things proudly and contemptuously against the righteous,** speaking arrogantly with pride and scorn, this attitude being characteristic of the unbelievers in their treatment of believers. V. 19. **Oh, how great is Thy goodness which Thou hast laid up,** as a precious treasure, **for them that fear Thee; which Thou hast wrought for them that trust in Thee before the sons of men!** The love of God is manifested to the soul in secret, in a hidden manner, but altogether satisfactory to the believer. V. 20. **Thou shalt hide them,** the believers, **in the secret of Thy presence,** in the protection which His face affords, **from the pride of man,** from the conspiracies of the wicked, concealing them as with a screen; **Thou shalt keep them secretly in a pavilion,** as a guest of Jehovah in the protecting shelter of His tent, **from the strife of tongues,** those of the wicked being engaged, as in warfare, in hurting the righteous. V. 21. **Blessed be the Lord; for He hath showed me His marvelous kindness,** working miracles for the sake of the believer, **in a strong city;** for the believer, by placing his trust in Jehovah, enters into a fortified city, which cannot be taken by the enemies. V. 22. **For I said in my haste,** while he was confused and as in a stupor from surprise, **I am cut off from before Thine eyes,** he had for a moment believed himself forsaken by God; **nevertheless, Thou heardest the voice of my supplications when I cried unto Thee,** the deliverance of the Lord putting his small faith to shame. V. 23. **O love the Lord, all ye His saints,** in return for the many evidences of His loving-kindness; **for the Lord preserveth the faithful,** Jehovah keeps the faith which He has promised, **and plentifully rewardeth the proud doer,** with the punishment which his pride deserves. V. 24. **Be of good courage, and He shall strengthen your heart,** strong and valiant of heart they shall be in their trust in Jehovah, **all ye that hope in the Lord,** confidently waiting for the final manifestation of His glory, a word which applies to the believers of all times. It may often seem as though nothing but darkness surrounded us, but the light of God's countenance is always upon us, the full manifestation of His unchanging love being revealed on the Last Day.

PSALM 32.

Of the Justification of a Poor Sinner.

A psalm of David, Maschil, a contemplation, written probably after David had been restored to the grace of God, a little more than a year after his great sin with Bathsheba, 2 Sam. 11, 27. The psalm pictures sin in the fulness of its terror and shows that no man may be just before God in his own person, being dependent entirely upon the grace and mercy of God in Christ Jesus. V. 1. **Blessed is he,** literally, "O the blessings of him," those which he possesses, **whose transgression is forgiven,** not condoned, but taken away, **whose sin is covered,** so that the just and holy God no longer sees it, as it were. In what sense this is possible is shown in the next verse. V. 2. **Blessed is the man unto whom the Lord imputeth not iniquity,** does not regard him as having committed the transgression, although sin in every form and manifestation cannot be undone, **and in whose spirit there is no guile,** no deceit and insincerity, which tries to cover up the wickedness, to excuse the transgression. Forgiveness of sins means that sin has lost its character as a debt and guilt still lying upon man by the fact that it was imputed to another, to the Redeemer. This remission of sins is here rightly called a blessing, for it is the greatest gift of God to sinful man. At the same time it should be noted that a full and free confession of sin does not merit forgiveness, but is a condition of remission in the sense that a denial of guilt shuts a person out from justification on the part of God. V. 3. **When I kept silence,** during that long year when he was conscious of his sin, but refused to acknowledge it, **my bones waxed old,** wasting away, withering like a flower during the time of drought, **through my roaring all the day long,** the howling and whining which went on in his inmost heart as the voice of his conscience drove him to despair. V. 4. **For day and night Thy hand was heavy upon me,** as long as he refused to turn to the Lord in true repentance; **my moisture is turned into the drought of summer,** all his vitality having left him. As long as sin is unforgiven, it devours the very marrow of the bones and kills all joy of life, like a canker or blight. **Selah.** Such is the condition of the unrepentant: the wrath of God rests upon them, giving them a foretaste of the terrible punishment which will strike them in hell. But all this finally had its effect upon David. V. 5. **I acknowledged my sin unto Thee,** in a full and free confession, **and mine iniquity have I not hid.** He had finally realized the guilt and damnableness of his crime; he had become conscious of the fact that he had transgressed against the great God in heaven. This sorrow of his heart he then made known. **I said, I will confess my transgressions unto the Lord,** openly acknowledging his iniquity, this state of mind being brought about by the visit of the prophet Nathan, 2 Sam. 12, 13; **and Thou forgavest the iniquity of my sin,** the guilt which he had heaped upon himself by his transgression. As soon as the first evidences of divine sorrow are present in the heart, forgiveness of sins is immediately dispensed by the Lord. He that is truly repentant longs for forgiveness and receives the forgiveness, as it has been gained for all men, with a believing heart. The comfort of forgiveness is eagerly accepted by a broken heart. **Selah.** David now sings a song of praise in honor of God for the forgiveness he has experienced, in which he now lives. V. 6. **For this shall every one that is godly,** every true believer, as a saint in the eyes of God, **pray unto Thee in a time when Thou mayest be found;** for all repentant, believing sinners constantly entreat the Lord to grant them His grace. **Surely in the floods of great waters,** when God in His anger dispenses His judgments, **they shall not come nigh unto him,** the righteous being spared such manifestations of God's anger, all their tribulations being mere merciful chastisements in the hand of God. With this assurance, David, and every believer with him, prays, v. 7. **Thou art my hiding-place,** God's mercy being the protection against the anger which strikes the unrepentant; **Thou shalt preserve me from trouble,** from all terror and fear of damnation; **Thou shalt compass me about with songs of deliverance;** because his soul is saved by the mercy of God, the believer sings songs of joy and exultation. **Selah.** The Lord now, on the basis of David's experience, gives some earnest advice to all whom His words can reach, especially to all sinners who have accepted His grace and are trying to walk in His ways. V. 8. **I will instruct thee and teach thee in the way which thou shalt go,** the eye of the Lord being directed upon every believer; **I will guide thee with Mine eye,** counseling him with His eye upon him. That is a consequence of the sinner's justification, the new obedience, his willingness to walk in the ways of the Lord. V. 9. **Be ye not as the horse or as the mule,** irrational brutes, **which have no understanding; whose mouth must be held in with bit and bridle, lest they come near unto thee,** that is, without the aid of such means, without force, it is impossible to control and direct brute animals. The obedience of the believers, repentant sinners as they are, is a ready and willing obedience. V. 10. **Many sorrows shall be to the wicked,** who are continually opposing the will of the Lord; **but he that trusteth in the Lord,** relying upon Him and following His guidance readily, **mercy shall compass him about,** the loving-kindness of Jehovah surrounding him on all sides and showing itself in many deeds of goodness, as wonderful pledges of His mercy. V. 11. **Be glad in the Lord and rejoice, ye righteous,** the grace of God which they have experienced being the motive for continual joy; **and shout for joy, all ye that are upright in heart,** thanking the Lord for all the blessings of His favor and compassion, as shown in the forgiveness of sins. Thus the entire life of the believers is spent in thanking the Lord for His grace and mercy, in humble preparation for the eternal rejoicing in heaven.

PSALM 33.

Praise to the Ruler of the World as the Protector of His People.

This entire psalm is a call to lively and joyful praise of God for His wonderful and glorious attributes and works, as displayed in creation, and of His general and special providence, in view of which the psalmist, in the name of all believers, professes trust and joy and invokes God's mercy. V. 1. **Rejoice in the Lord, O ye righteous,** those justified by the grace of God; **for praise is comely,** fitting, proper, **for the upright,** it is both their duty and their honor to praise the Lord; for silence on their part would be equivalent to a denial of His blessings. V. 2. **Praise the Lord with harp,** a kind of zither; **sing unto Him with the psaltery and an instrument of ten strings,** a ten-stringed harp or lute, which was also used in the Temple orchestra. V. 3. **Sing unto Him a new song,** one especially adapted to the occasion; **play skilfully with a loud noise,** with a vim, showing the eagerness of the heart to praise the glory of Jehovah in a song never heard before. V. 4. **For the Word of the Lord is right,** upright, true, not full of mistakes and contradictions; **and all His works are done in truth,** in faithfulness, the fulfilment always agreeing with His promises. V. 5. **He loveth righteousness and judgment;** He delights to show these attributes of His divine essence. **The earth is full of the goodness of the Lord,** of the many proofs of His kindness. V. 6. **By the Word of the Lord,** the great Word which was in the beginning with God, John 1, 1—3, **were the heavens made,** Prov. 8, 22—30; **and all the host of them by the breath of His mouth,** by the power of His Spirit, the reference obviously being to the third person of the Trinity. V. 7. **He,** the Triune God, **gathereth the waters of the sea together as an heap,** the mighty ocean being firmly held together by the almighty power of Jehovah; **He layeth up the depths in storehouses,** assigning to the vast extent of the ocean waters their place where they must stay. V. 8. **Let all the earth,** even the inanimate creatures, **fear the Lord; let all the inhabitants of the world,** especially men, who are endowed with reason and sense, **stand in awe of Him,** with a reverence verging on fear. V. 9. **For He spake,** with the almighty word of His command, **and it was done; He commanded, and it stood fast.** The reference is plainly to the story of creation: God said, Let there be; and there was, Gen. 1. God is furthermore to be praised on account of His almighty rule of the universe. V. 10. **The Lord bringeth the counsel of the heathen to naught,** making void their plans as actually devised; **He maketh the devices of the people,** the very thoughts and intentions of their hearts, **of none effect,** thus frustrating their wickedness. V. 11. **The counsel of the Lord standeth forever,** in contrast with the vain counsels and thoughts of men, **the thoughts of His heart to all generations,** abiding forever. V. 12. **Blessed is the nation whose God is the Lord,** Jehovah, as their Ruler, being also their greatest treasure; **and the people whom He hath chosen for His own inheritance,** as was the case in Israel at the time of David, the spiritual Israel, the Church of God, being His heritage in the highest sense of the word. V. 13. **The Lord,** as the great Ruler of the universe, **looketh from heaven,** with the eyes of His omniscience; **He beholdeth all the sons of men,** not one being hidden from His knowledge. V. 14. **From the place of His habitation He looketh upon all the inhabitants of the earth,** all their deeds being open to His gaze. V. 15. **He fashioneth their hearts alike,** He is the Former of their hearts all at once, both in the creation of each soul and in forming the thoughts of the heart under His providence; **He considereth all their works,** understanding exactly how they put their plans into execution. V. 16. **There is no king saved by the multitude of an host,** no matter what display of strength and arms he may make; **a mighty man is not delivered by much strength,** all this is useless without God. V. 17. **An horse is a vain thing for safety,** for a man to rely on; **neither shall He deliver any by His great strength;** as it is a delusion for help and victory, so it will disappoint him who absolutely relies upon it to carry him to safety. All this is subject to God's government. V. 18. **Behold, the eye of the Lord is upon them that fear Him,** the entire purpose of the world and of His government is realized in them, **upon them that hope in His mercy,** putting aside all trust in themselves; v. 19. **to deliver their soul from death,** sustaining them in all dangers which threaten their life, **and to keep them alive in famine.** These facts being set forth, the psalmist makes the application to the Church of God of all times. V. 20. **Our soul waiteth for the Lord,** trusting firmly in His help, no matter when it is manifested; **He is our Help and our Shield.** V. 21. **For our heart shall rejoice in Him because we have trusted in His holy name,** as the foundation of their faith, love, and hope, from which all salvation comes. V. 22. **Let Thy mercy, O Lord,** which alone gives the believers the courage to invoke the Lord, **be upon us, according as we hope in Thee,** their confident waiting and trusting and the divine answer being correlates. In this way the attitude of hope and trust is the attitude of the Church in all ages, sustained by the Word of God's grace.

PSALM 34.

Thanksgiving and Instruction of One Delivered out of Great Trouble.

A psalm of David when he changed his behavior before Abimelech, this being the title of the Philistine rulers, Gen. 20, 2, the name of this king of Gath being Achish; **who drove him away, and he departed,** 1 Sam. 21, 10—22, 1. Under the guidance of the Holy Spirit, David embodied the lessons of this incident in his life in the present hymn.

DAVID PRAISES GOD FOR HIS DELIVERANCE. — V. 1. **I will bless the Lord at all times,** in every season, David's own cheerfulness being so notable because his troubles at that time were by no means at an end, since he was obliged to hide in the cave Adullam, in the wilderness of Judah; **His praise shall continually be in my mouth,** for there is never an occasion when praise is not proper in the believer's mouth. V. 2. **My soul shall make her boast in the Lord,** glory in Jehovah, setting forth His majesty and goodness; **the humble,** that is, the sufferers, the pious who have been humbled in the school of sorrows, **shall hear thereof and be glad,** their own faith will be strengthened by the experiences of David. V. 3. **O magnify the Lord with me,** ascribing greatness to Him, in an act of praise, **and let us exalt His name together,** acknowledging His loving-kindness and tender mercies. V. 4. **I sought the Lord,** eagerly entreating Him for help, **and He heard me and delivered me from all my fears,** the evils and dangers which inspired terror in his heart. V. 5. **They,** all sufferers in the class of David, **looked unto Him,** in eager longing for salvation, **and were lightened,** they became bright, reflecting the beaming kindness of the heavenly Father; **and their faces were not ashamed,** they did not need to be abashed and blush with disappointment, with vain crying. V. 6. **This poor man cried,** this distressed one, the reference being to David in particular, but applying in all similar cases as well, **and the Lord heard him, and saved him out of all his troubles,** not merely from the danger threatening him in Gath. From this fact David draws a general conclusion: v. 7. **The Angel of the Lord,** that powerful minister of Jehovah, in whose person the Son of God so often revealed Himself in the Old Testament, who is always near to the believers with His mighty and gracious protection, **encampeth round about them that fear Him,** like an armed host, affording the safest protection, **and delivereth them,** setting them free from all dangers and oppressors. V. 8. **O taste,** trying it out as something extremely palatable, **and see,** enjoying it also with the eyes, **that the Lord is good,** the psalmist urging the believers to seek the experience, to make certain for themselves. **Blessed is the man that trusteth in Him,** makes Jehovah his refuge; for he who fears Him has all blessings in Him. V. 9. **O fear the Lord, ye His saints; for there is no want to them that fear Him,** they have the fulness of all they need. V. 10. **The young lions do lack and suffer hunger; but they that seek the Lord shall not want any good thing;** that is, it will sooner happen that the irrational animals, for whom the providence of God provides so regularly, Ps. 145, 16, will suffer hunger, than that those who strive after the true fellowship with God will be in any kind of need. So much all believers should learn from the deliverance which David experienced in Gath.

DAVID TEACHES TRUE PIETY. — V. 11. **Come, ye children,** the master addressing his disciples, **hearken unto me! I will teach you** the fear of the Lord. He himself had learned in the school of experience, under the guidance of God, and wanted to pass this information on to others. V. 12. **What man is he that desireth life,** prosperity in the best sense of the word, **and loveth many days,** a long life being considered a special blessing, **that he may see good?** That is, To whom will God show His goodness in richest measure, by showering blessings upon him? David describes such a person in a series of admonitions. V. 13. **Keep thy tongue from evil,** from all sins in speech, **and thy lips from speaking guile.** Cp. Jas. 1, 26; 3, 2—13. V. 14. **Depart from evil,** every form of transgression, **and do good; seek peace and pursue it,** aspiring after it with all zeal, Rom. 12, 9—18; 1 Pet. 3, 8—17. V. 15. **The eyes of the Lord are upon the righteous,** in gracious affection, **and His ears are open unto their cry,** always ready to answer their prayer. V. 16. **The face of the Lord,** set, in this case, in hard lines, **is against them that do evil,** opposed to their wicked ways, expressing His disapproval, **to cut off the remembrance of them from the earth,** so that they will be utterly destroyed. V. 17. **The righteous cry, and the Lord heareth,** answering those whose call comes forth from a heart acknowledging its own unworthiness, **and delivereth them out of all their troubles.** V. 18. **The Lord is nigh unto them that are of a broken heart,** whose self-righteousness and selfishness have been broken at the root by the thunderbolt of the Law; **and saveth such as be of a contrite spirit,** whose natural pride has been humbled into the dust, so that they have been led to the proper realization of their damnable sinfulness. People in whom the work of the Law has been done, who see in themselves nothing but unworthiness and damnableness, are in a condition to receive the glorious assurances of salvation, to receive the redemption in the Messiah. V. 19. **Many are the afflictions,** the distresses, snares, and persecutions, **of the righteous,** which he experiences at the hand of the wicked; **but the Lord delivereth him out of them all,** if not here in time, surely in eternity. V. 20. **He,** Jehovah, **keepeth all his bones,** the entire framework of his body; **not one of them is broken,** for without the will of the heavenly Father not even a hair of our heads may fall to the ground, Matt. 10, 30. V. 21. **Evil shall slay the wicked,** that being their final destiny; **and they that hate the righteous shall be desolate,** shall stand in the judgment of God and suffer as guilty. V. 22. **The Lord redeemeth the soul of His servants,** making them, finally, possessors of everlasting salvation; **and none of them that trust in Him shall be desolate,** since the guilt of their sins will not be imputed to them, and they will therefore not be condemned to everlasting punishment. With our sins imputed to Jesus Christ and His righteousness imputed to us, we are safe in the last Judgment, sure of eternal bliss and glory in heaven.

PSALM 35.

Prayer against the Godless.

A psalm of David, invoking God's aid against the ungodly, contrasting the hypocrisy, cunning, and malice of the wicked with the integrity and generosity of the righteous, on whose side he himself serves as example.

IMPRECATIONS UPON THE WICKED. — V. 1. **Plead my cause,** as in court proceedings, **O Lord, with them that strive with me,** impleading him for alleged wickedness; **fight against them that fight against me,** carrying their hatred to the point of making war on him. V. 2. **Take hold of shield and buckler,** the smaller one being used to protect the head, the larger to shelter the whole body, **and stand up for mine help,** to defend him against his enemies. V. 3. **Draw out also the spear,** as a weapon both of defense and of offense, **and stop the way against them that persecute me,** so that they cannot proceed. **Say unto my soul, I am thy Salvation,** an assurance on the part of God that He would deliver and save His servant, sustaining him in this extremity. V. 4. **Let them be confounded and put to shame that seek after my soul; let them be turned back,** in abject retreat, **and brought to confusion that devise my hurt,** planning evil against him. The heaping of words signifying the failure of the hopes and undertakings of the wicked shows that David prays for the utter frustration of all their intentions, for their complete overthrow. V. 5. **Let them be as chaff before the wind,** scattered to the four corners of the earth; **and let the Angel of the Lord chase them,** Jehovah Himself, in the person of this Angel, thrusting them down and destroying them. V. 6. **Let their way be dark and slippery,** literally, "darkness and slipperiness," where they could not even see nor get a good foothold as they fled from their punishment; **and let the Angel of the Lord persecute them,** pursuing them as He did the Egyptians when He terrified them in the Red Sea. V. 7. **For without cause,** without provocation on the part of David, while he was entirely innocent, **have they hid for me their net in a pit, (which) without cause they have digged for my soul.** That was David's complaint, that his enemies were hunting and pursuing his soul, his life, using every possible means for his destruction. V. 8. **Let destruction come upon him at unawares,** devastation striking all the enemies of David and Jehovah before they realized their danger; **and let his net that he hath hid catch himself; into that very destruction let him fall**, destroyed by the very punishment which he had intended for the righteous. This overthrow of the ungodly power would be followed by the joy of triumphant faith. V. 9. **And my soul shall be joyful in the Lord**, who by His revenge vindicated the cause of the righteous; **it shall rejoice in His salvation**, in the deliverance from their wiles which he had experienced. V. 10. **All my bones shall say, Lord, who is like unto Thee**, his body joining with his soul in praising the Lord, **which deliverest the poor**, the humble righteous person, **from him that is too strong for him, yea, the poor and the needy from him that spoileth him?** Cp. Ps. 10, 2. Note that a believer may well pray for the destruction of the wicked if he places the execution of the vengeance entirely in God's hands.

THE HYPOCRISY AND MALICE OF THE WICKED. V. 11. **False witnesses**, literally, "witnesses of violence," **did rise up**, with unjust accusations; **they laid to my charge things that I knew not**, of which he knew himself to be innocent. V. 12. **They rewarded me evil for good**, which he, on his part, was trying to show them, **to the spoiling of my soul**, to make his soul bereaved, to make him friendless, to isolate him. V. 13. **But as for me, when they were sick, my clothing was sackcloth**, in sympathetic mourning for their trouble; **I humbled my soul with fasting**, in making their sorrow his own; **and my prayer returned into mine own bosom**, for he was bowed forward so far, with his head lowered, that his voice sounded against his own bosom. Thus he had entreated for his enemies in the greatest earnestness and humility. V. 14. **I behaved myself as though he**, the enemy in distress, **had been my friend or brother; I bowed down heavily**, in dust and ashes, so that he appeared squalid and dirty, **as one that mourneth for his mother**, in the very deepest grief. V. 15. **But in mine adversity**, his halting, lameness, said of any deep distress, **they rejoiced, and gathered themselves together**, to witness the spectacle of his great trouble; **yea, the abjects**, contemptible, degraded persons, **gathered themselves together against me, and I knew it not**, people of whom he had till then not even taken notice; **they did tear me and ceased not**, attacked him with scorn and laughter, and were not silent; v. 16. **with hypocritical mockers in feasts**, those who love to make sport of a poor sufferer by cracking biting jokes at his expense, **they gnashed upon me with their teeth**, in a gesture of sneering contempt, probably also with stammering of distorted things. V. 17. **Lord, how long wilt Thou look on?** namely, without doing something to effect deliverance for him. **Rescue my soul from their destructions, my darling**, literally, "my only one," **from the lions**, from the wild and ravenous people who were treating him so contemptuously. V. 18. **I will give Thee thanks in the great congregation**, paying his vows of thanksgiving with all the other believers; **I will praise Thee among much people**, people of numbers and might. The congregation of believers may seem small and weak in the eyes of the world, but before the Lord and in His might they are invincible.

EARNEST PRAYER FOR RELIEF. — V. 19. **Let not them that are mine enemies wrongfully rejoice over me**, by their false and slanderous accusations; **neither let them wink with the eye**, in a gesture of cunning and contempt, **that hate me without a cause**, while he is wholly innocent. V. 20. **For they speak not peace**, their aim is not to bring quiet and happiness to the country; **but they devise deceitful matters against them that are quiet in the land**, against those who really love peace and seek the welfare of the country. V. 21. **Yea, they opened their mouth wide against me**, in a gesture of contempt, **and said, Aha, aha! our eye hath seen it**, namely, the gratification of their hopes that the believer would be in trouble. V. 22. **This Thou hast seen, O Lord**, the manner in which the enemies acted. **Keep not silence; O Lord, be not far from me!** in this great emergency, where He alone could provide help. V. 23. **Stir up Thyself**, rousing Himself, as though from sleep, making ready for energetic action, **and awake to my judgment, even unto my cause**, namely, to establish it as just, to vindicate him, **my God and my Lord.** V. 24. **Judge me, O Lord, my God, according to Thy righteousness; and let them not rejoice over me.** V. 25. **Let them not say in their hearts**, in their greed to devour, in their desire to destroy, **Ah, so would we have it! Let them not say, We have swallowed him up.** V. 26. **Let them be ashamed and brought to confusion together**, with all their evil intentions utterly frustrated, **that rejoice at mine hurt. Let them be clothed with shame and dishonor that magnify themselves**, puffing themselves up, **against me.** The righteous government of God is the only hope of the pious and the terror of the wicked. V. 27. **Let them shout for joy and be glad that favor my righteous cause**, or, who delight in my righteousness, glad that he should have his right; **yea, let them say continually, Let the Lord be magnified, which hath pleasure in the prosperity of His servant**, delighting in showing him His divine blessings. V. 28. **And my tongue shall speak of Thy righteousness**, in praising God's righteous government, **and of Thy praise all the day long.** God is the Champion of all those who are oppressed among His children, and they, in turn, make it their business to make known the honor of His holy name at all times.

PSALM 36.

The Curse of Estrangement from God and the Blessing of Fellowship with Him.

To the chief musician, for use in the liturgical services of the Temple, **a psalm of David, the servant of the Lord,** who here pictures to all other servants of Jehovah the darkness in which the ungodly dwell, and then the light in which the believers have their being. V. 1. **The transgression of the wicked saith within my heart,** rather, "A prompting of wickedness to the evil within the confines of his heart," **that there is no fear of God before his eyes.** That is the condition as David sees it: There is nothing but promptings to evil in the heart of the wicked and no evidence of fear and dread of God before their eyes. V. 2. **For he flattereth himself in his own eyes, until his iniquity be found to be hateful;** that is, vice, wickedness, evil, flatters the godless person in his own eyes, making sin pleasant and attractive, in order to plunge him into guilt by his hatred of the righteous, for that is the climax of his wickedness. V. 3. **The words of his mouth,** in the expression of this hatred against the godly, **are iniquity and deceit,** full of falsehood and lying; **he hath left off to be wise and to do good,** rejected all right principles of conduct. V. 4. **He deviseth mischief upon his bed,** using even the night for these meditations of wickedness; **he setteth himself in a way,** deliberately choosing a course, **that is not good; he abhorreth not evil,** the strongest way of saying that he delights in it. Such is the spiritual darkness of the ungodly. The psalmist now, by way of contrast, pictures Jehovah and those that believe in Him. V. 5. **Thy mercy, O Lord, is in the heavens,** rather, reaches up to the heavens; **and Thy faithfulness,** with which He keeps His promises of mercy, **reacheth unto the clouds,** filling the whole world. V. 6. **Thy righteousness is like the great mountains,** huge, massive, and certain; **Thy judgments are a great deep,** a mighty and powerful flood. **O Lord, Thou,** with such unbounded qualities of power, **preservest man and beast,** all creatures being included in His providence. V. 7. **How excellent is Thy loving-kindness,** how precious His mercy, **O God! Therefore the children of men put their trust under the shadow of Thy wings,** the believers finding full shelter in His protection, Deut. 32, 11; Ps. 91, 1. V. 8. **They shall be abundantly satisfied,** to the point of intoxication, **with the fatness of Thy house,** in connection with the sacrificial meals of the thank- and peace-offerings; **and Thou shalt make them drink of the river of Thy pleasures,** in a plentiful supply, as in a new, spiritual Eden, for God is the Fountainhead of richest blessings. V. 9. **For with Thee is the fountain of life,** the source of all true life, both physical and spiritual; **in Thy light shall we see light,** the light of everlasting grace from the countenance of God. The frequent connection of life and light in Scripture, Ps. 56, 14; Job 3, 20, also with reference to the coming of Christ, John 1, 4, shows that the redemption of salvation is meant. The believers, even here in time, are enjoying the benefits of the salvation gained through the work of Christ, and in yonder life they shall have it in joyful fulness, without any admixture of this earth's misery. Therefore the psalmist closes with a fervent prayer. V. 10. **O continue Thy loving-kindness unto them that know Thee,** letting them enjoy His merciful kindness also in the future, **and Thy righteousness to the upright in heart,** to act as a protective cover over them. V. 11. **Let not the foot of pride,** in an act of violence, **come against me, and let not the hand of the wicked remove me,** driving him away into banishment from the land of God's inheritance. V. 12. **There are the workers of iniquity,** the evil-doers, **fallen,** in the very act of violence they are overthrown; **they are cast down and shall not be able to rise,** so that the triumph of the righteous is complete. Such is ever the victory of faith, for it derives both light and life from God.

PSALM 37.

The Apparent Good Fortune of the Godless Compared with the Believers' True Happiness.

A psalm of David, rightly considered one of the most beautiful written by him, called by Luther the garment of the pious, bearing the inscription: "Here is the patience of the saints," Rev. 14, 12. V. 1. **Fret not thyself,** with excitement and anger, **because of evildoers, neither be thou envious against the workers of iniquity,** being vexed by their apparent good fortune and prosperity. V. 2. **For they shall soon be cut down like the grass,** fading away and perishing, **and wither as the green herb,** the tender grass and young vegetation of spring, whose beauty is but transient. These two verses having expressed the sentiment of the whole psalm, the two thoughts contained in them are further elaborated. V. 3. **Trust in the Lord,** every believer placing his full confidence in Jehovah alone, **and do good; so shalt thou dwell in the land,** the exhortation being to a quiet and peaceable life, **and, verily, thou shalt be fed,**

rather, practise faithfulness and uprightness in all dealings. V. 4. **Delight thyself also in the Lord,** considering Him the heart's highest desire; **and He shall give thee the desires of thine heart,** all the requests which accord with His gracious and good will. V. 5. **Commit thy way unto the Lord,** literally, "roll it upon Jehovah," heavy as it may seem with all its troubles and cares; **trust also in Him, and He shall bring it to pass,** perform all that is needed for the believer's true happiness. V. 6. **And He shall bring forth thy righteousness,** which is now unappreciated and in densest darkness, **as the light,** when the dawn spreads over the eastern sky and the morning sun dispels the darkness, **and thy judgment,** the right on the part of the believers, **as the noonday,** in full brightness before the eyes of all the world. V. 7. **Rest in the Lord,** being still before Jehovah with that calm resignation which knows itself secure in His hands, **and wait patiently for Him,** looking for His help in steadfast hope; **fret not thyself,** in anxious vexation, **because of him who prospereth in his way,** against the wicked in his good fortune, **because of the man who bringeth wicked devices to pass,** carrying out evil plans to harm the righteous. V. 8. **Cease from anger and forsake wrath,** jealously guarding against the sins of an evil temper; **fret not thyself in any wise to do evil,** for such would be the natural result if a believer would yield to his vexation; he himself would become guilty of sin. V. 9. **For evil-doers shall be cut off,** this result being certain without the sinful anger of the believer; **but those that wait upon the Lord,** steadfastly placing their trust in Him, **they shall inherit the earth,** enjoy true happiness even here in time, while sure of the blessings of eternity. V. 10. **For yet a little while, and the wicked shall not be,** wiped out by the avenging hand of God; **yea, thou shalt diligently consider his place,** wondering why it was so suddenly empty, **and it shall not be,** literally, "it is not," denoting the quick stroke of God's avenging justice. V. 11. **But the meek,** those who humbly rest their trust in God, **shall inherit the earth,** as the Lord repeats, Matt. 5, 5; **and shall delight themselves in the abundance of peace,** enjoying the happiness of true prosperity under the blessing of Jehovah. V. 12. **The wicked plotteth against the just,** with the intention of harming him at every opportunity, **and gnasheth upon him with his teeth,** in a gesture of unbridled fury. V. 13. **The Lord shall laugh at him,** making mockery of the unbeliever's futile anger; **for He seeth that His day,** the day of judgment and punishment, **is coming.** V. 14. **The wicked have drawn out the sword,** to commit murder, **and have bent their bow,** ready to let the death-dealing arrow fly, **to cast down the poor and needy,** with the weapons of violence, **and to slay such as be of upright conversation,** who conduct themselves in accordance with the will of Jehovah. V. 15. **Their sword,** by the dispensation of God, through His avenging power, **shall enter into their own heart, and their bows shall be broken.** V. 16. **A little that a righteous man hath,** though he be poor in this world's goods, **is better than the riches of many wicked,** which do not represent true prosperity, because they do not give contentment, do not afford them rest and satisfaction. V. 17. **For the arms of the wicked shall be broken,** so that these members of wickedness can neither harm others nor help themselves; **but the Lord upholdeth the righteous,** Jehovah being their everlasting Strength and Stay. V. 18. **The Lord knoweth the days of the upright,** carefully watches over them, lovingly orders all that befalls them; **and their inheritance shall be forever,** they will be given the blessings which He has intended for them, here in time and hereafter in eternity. V. 19. **They shall not be ashamed in the evil time,** objects of mockery because of their being forsaken by the Lord, **and in the days of famine they shall be satisfied,** their wants being supplied in accordance with God's gracious and good will. V. 20. **But the wicked shall perish,** this their ultimate fate being emphasized time and again, **and the enemies of the Lord shall be as the fat of lambs,** or, "as the splendor of the pastures," which vanishes so quickly; **they shall consume, into smoke shall they consume away,** as smoke dissolves and vanishes in the air. V. 21. **The wicked borroweth and payeth not again,** being deliberately dishonest in his dealings; **but the righteous showeth mercy and giveth,** glad to share the blessings given him by God with such as are in want. V. 22. **For such as be blessed of Him shall inherit the earth,** the blessing of Jehovah proving rich abundance for them; **and they that be cursed of Him shall be cut off,** their final lot being one of extreme want, of unhappiness, no matter how many treasures they have heaped up. V. 23. **The steps of a good man are ordered by the Lord,** firmly established, with Jehovah as his Guide; **and He delighteth in his way,** Jehovah has pleasure in the entire conduct and manner of living of the believer. V. 24. **Though he fall,** for even the righteous will occasionally stumble and become guilty of transgressions, **he shall not be utterly cast down,** stretched out to his full length, unable to rise again; **for the Lord upholdeth him with His hand,** sustaining him, offering him His almighty and gracious support, so that he can once more stand upright and proceed upon his way. V. 25. **I have been young and now am old,** the psalmist has the experience of a lifetime to draw from; **yet have I not seen the righteous forsaken,** abandoned past the point of help, **nor** his seed begging bread, suffering permanent want. Temporary abandonment and privation there may be, but the righteous are never really forsaken by Jehovah. V. 26. **He**, the righteous, the possessor of true righteousness by faith, **is ever merciful**, showing the faith of his heart in deeds of love, **and lendeth; and his seed is blessed**, the blessing of Jehovah resting upon his house and family. The conclusion drawn by David, therefore, is: v. 27. **Depart from evil and do good**, following the way of true righteousness; **and dwell forevermore**, that being God's blessing of mercy upon true piety. V. 28. **For the Lord loveth judgment**, He is right in all His dealings with men, **and forsaketh not His saints; they are preserved forever. But the seed of the wicked shall be cut off**, their entire posterity, following them in their wickedness, shall be destroyed. V. 29. **The righteous shall inherit the land and dwell therein forever**, possessors of true happiness. V. 30. **The mouth of the righteous speaketh wisdom**, for he is continually meditating upon such things as pertain to the highest wisdom, **and his tongue talketh of judgment**, intent upon the right in every situation. V. 31. **The Law of his God is in his heart**, providing the motive for his pious conduct; **none of his steps shall slide**, his entire conduct being guided by a certain rule and norm, since his will is regulated by the will of God. V. 32. **The wicked watcheth the righteous and seeketh to slay him**, to that end he has laid his plans. V. 33. **The Lord will not leave him in his hand**, will not give the righteous up to the evil intention of the wicked, **nor condemn him when he is judged**, the divine judgment will acquit him, even if men should declare him guilty. V. 34. **Wait on the Lord**, with quiet, steady confidence, **and keep His way, and He shall exalt thee to inherit the land**, this promise being given six times in this one psalm; **when the wicked are cut off, thou shalt see it.** V. 35. **I have seen the wicked in great power**, proud, ruthless, arrogant, **and spreading himself like a green bay-tree**, a tree in full foliage, teeming with strength. V. 36. **Yet he passed away**, rather, "lo, one passed by," spoken as of a casual passer-by, **and, lo, he was not**, gone without causing so much as a ripple; **yea, I sought him, but he could not be found.** "The paths of glory lead but to the grave." V. 37. **Mark the perfect man and behold the upright**, watching closely how the Lord deals with such a person; **for the end of that man is peace**, the man of peace receiving everlasting peace as the reward of God's mercy. V. 38. **But the transgressors shall be destroyed together; the end of the wicked**, their entire posterity, **shall be cut off.** V. 39. **But the salvation of the righteous**, their final deliverance from every evil, of body and soul, property and honor, **is of the Lord: He is their Strength in the time of trouble**, in every form of distress and oppression. V. 40. **And the Lord shall help them and deliver them; He shall deliver them from the wicked and save them because they trust in Him**, making Jehovah their sole refuge. The lesson of the psalm is beautifully summarized in the well-known hymn of Paul Gerhardt "Commit Whatever Grieves Thee," which has brought consolation to many a troubled heart.

PSALM 38.

Prayer for Relief from a Burden of Guilt.

A psalm of David, to bring to remembrance, to remind God of His great mercy toward poor sinners, the hymn probably being intended for that part of worship when the meat-offering was added to the sacrifice, for its sweet savor was to rise to Jehovah with the prayer of the faithful. V. 1. **O Lord, rebuke me not in Thy wrath**, although, as David knew, he well deserved it; **neither chasten me in Thy hot displeasure**, with the full rigor of divine justice. V. 2. **For Thine arrows stick fast in me**, the arrows of God's anger having sunk into his flesh, **and Thy hand presseth me sore**, in the misfortune or in the dread which was oppressing him. V. 3. **There is no soundness in my flesh because of Thine anger**, his body being ill in consequence of Jehovah's indignation over his sins; **neither is there any rest in my bones**, no proper health and peace, **because of my sin**, the results of which affected both body and mind with their afflictions. V. 4. **For mine iniquities are gone over mine head**, passing over him like an overwhelming flood; **as an heavy burden they are too heavy for me**, the burden bearing down upon his conscience exceeding his strength. V. 5. **My wounds**, the bruises which he, figuratively, bore by reason of his sins, **stink and are corrupt**, not only having an evil odor, but also running like an open, festering sore, **because of my foolishness**, this designation being chosen since all sin is folly and self-destruction. V. 6. **I am troubled**, bent over with the disease of his soul; **I am bowed down greatly**, as with a sickness which contracts the body in writhing pains; **I go mourning all the day long**, literally, "squalid," black with filth, on account of the ashes and the soiled garments indicating his mourning. V. 7. **For my loins**, usually representing robust strength, **are filled with a loathsome disease**, full of dry burning, as if gangrene were setting in; **and there is no soundness in my flesh,** all his former health had left him. V. 8. **I am feeble and sore broken,** chilled, benumbed, and utterly crushed; **I have roared,** with loud sighs and cries, **by reason of the disquietness of my heart,** which caused his lips to groan and moan. V. 9. **Lord, all my desire is before Thee,** Jehovah knows the longing which the sufferer feels in the midst of his misery; **and my groaning is not hid from Thee.** David refers to this fact in order to stimulate the mercy of the Lord. V. 10. **My heart panteth,** palpitating from violent agitation, as if barely surviving the trouble, **my strength faileth me; as for the light of mine eyes,** the strength of his vision, **it also is gone from me,** this condition resulting from extreme weakness of the whole body. V. 11. **My lovers and my friends,** those whose acquaintance and friendship he valued, **stand aloof from my sore,** on account of the stroke, or plague, which the Lord had laid upon him; **and my kinsmen stand afar off,** deserting him in this extremity. V. 12. **They also that seek after my life lay snares for me,** taking this opportunity when he is in trouble to show their spite; **and they that seek my hurt speak mischievous things,** planning his destruction, **and imagine deceits,** meditating upon malicious tricks, **all the day long.** V. 13. **But I, as a deaf man, heard not,** he deliberately shut his ears in order not to be provoked to a reply to their insulting speeches; **and I was as a dumb man that openeth not his mouth,** the consciousness of his guilt causing him to keep silence, to despair of ever helping himself, and to trust in Jehovah alone. V. 14. **Thus I was as a man that heareth not, and in whose mouth are no reproofs,** who does not venture to adduce any counter-evidence to justify himself. In this way a believer opens his heart and makes his complaint to the Lord in the midst of the trouble besetting him. V. 15. **For in Thee, O Lord, do I hope,** as the only one to whom he could safely turn in his great trouble; **Thou wilt hear,** an emphatic, trustful expectation, **O Lord, my God.** V. 16. **For I said, Hear me, lest otherwise they should rejoice over me,** the honor of the Lord's name demanding that He save His servant, lest the mockery strike Him also; **when my foot slippeth, they magnify themselves against me,** puffing themselves up and jeering at the simple faith of the believer, whose trust is shattered by his tribulations. V. 17. **For I am ready to halt,** on the point of falling with lameness, **and my sorrow is continually before me,** his feeling of guilt serving to keep his misery always before his eyes. V. 18. **For I will declare mine iniquity,** openly confessing his guilt; **I will be sorry for my sin,** filled with anxiety on its account. V. 19. **But mine enemies,** by way of contrast to his dejected state, **are lively,** full of vitality and vigor, **and they are strong; and they that hate me wrongfully are multiplied,** coming against him in ever-increasing numbers. V. 20. **They also that render evil for good are mine adversaries, because I follow the thing that good is,** the persecution of the pious on the part of the wicked being the ordinary, the usual thing in the world. But David, and every true believer with him, clings to his faith in Jehovah and in the pardoning mercy promised in the Gospel. V. 21. **Forsake me not, O Lord,** by giving him up to the will of his enemies or to the misery of utter despair; **O my God, be not far from me,** ready for his assistance. V. 22. **Make haste to help me, O Lord, my Salvation,** for in Him alone he could find deliverance from sin and its consequences. Such is the prayer of every believer when he feels the power of sin. And true repentance leads to faith; it despairs of itself, but keeps its trust in the Lord unshaken. And this confidence is not a vain trust.

PSALM 39.

The Believer's Attitude in View of the Apparent Happiness of the Godless.

To the chief musician, even to Jeduthun, or Ethan, the name of one of David's chief choristers, who was the leader of a family or choir of singers, active chiefly in the liturgical part of worship, **a psalm of David.** V. 1. **I said, I will take heed to my ways,** to his entire manner of thinking and acting, **that I sin not with my tongue,** namely, by murmuring and complaining over his own misfortune as compared with the good fortune of the wicked; **I will keep my mouth with a bridle,** a muzzle, to prevent his lamenting, **while the wicked is before me,** in his presence, while he was compelled to see the godless prosper in the fulness of his power, in apparent enjoyment of everything that was good. V. 2. **I was dumb with silence,** in trusting submission, **I held my peace, even from good,** away from prosperity, he shut his heart and mind off from everything and communed with God alone; **and my sorrow was stirred,** his fretting finally constrained him to cry out to the Lord. V. 3. **My heart was hot within me,** his emotions like a smothered flame, seeking for an outlet; **while I was musing, the fire burned,** bursting through all repression. **Then spake I with my tongue,** directing his complaint to the Lord. V. 4. **Lord, make me to know mine end,** give him the proper understanding of the vanity of this earthly life and the quickness with which it is cut off, **and the measure of my days, what it is,** that this measure may soon be filled up; **that I may know how frail I am,** a mortal being in the midst of perishable things. This thought is intended to stress, not so much the shortness of human life, as its utter vanity and therefore the folly of concerning one's self with the matters of this world to the exclusion of the one thing needful, the laying hold of God in faith and trust. V. 5. **Behold, Thou hast made my days as an handbreadth,** a mere span of life being assigned to each mortal; **and mine age is as nothing before Thee,** before the face of the eternal God. **Verily, every man at his best state,** even when he seems to be most firmly established, **is altogether vanity,** transitory and perishable. **Selah.** V. 6. **Surely every man walketh in a vain show,** an unsubstantial shadow like the image of himself cast on the ground by the light; **surely they are disquieted in vain,** only for a breath they make a noise, all their restless and noisy bustle with which they fret and stir themselves and elbow and jostle one another to obtain wealth and rank, is like a single breath; **he heapeth up riches,** that being the average person's chief concern in life, **and knoweth not who shall gather them,** dishonest adversaries or laughing heirs enjoying the fruit of his toil. With such contemplations the believer hushes the voice of his lamenting and extinguishes the fire of his murmuring. V. 7. **And now, Lord, what wait I for?** Turning away with relief from the contemplation of earthly vanity, the believer lets his eyes rest upon the Lord. **My hope is in Thee,** all his trust grounded in Jehovah alone, in whom he has the fulness of all true joys. V. 8. **Deliver me from all my transgressions,** which, as he knew, furnished abundant reasons for his own sufferings; **make me not the reproach of the foolish,** a target for the scorn of fools, whose mockery would, at the same time, bring disgrace upon the Lord. V. 9. **I was dumb, I opened not my mouth,** with reproachful lamenting directed against Jehovah, **because Thou didst it,** a confession with which he bows under the almighty hand of God. V. 10. **Remove Thy stroke away from me,** which seemed like a blow by the hand of divine anger; **I am consumed by the blow of Thine hand,** as the Lord set Himself in battle against him, knowing that he was doomed to destruction if the Lord should continue His course of chastisement. V. 11. **When Thou with rebukes dost correct man for iniquity,** sending forth His punishment upon the guilty, **Thou makest his beauty to consume away like a moth;** for just as garments disappear under the attack of moths, so the handsome appearance of man melts away under the stroke of divine chastisement. **Surely every man is vanity,** a mere breath, which disappears in a moment. **Selah.** V. 12. **Hear my prayer, O Lord,** his appeal for relief being addressed to the mercy of Jehovah, **and give ear unto my cry,** in a gracious, compassionate answer; **hold not Thy peace at my tears,** which flowed with the depth of his suffering; **for I am a stranger with Thee,** a mere guest in this world, **and a sojourner,** like a person who is not a citizen of a country, but lives there merely by concession, **as all my fathers were.** Just as the patriarchs did not hold citizenship in the country where they dwelled, so all believers do not consider this earth their true home, their citizenship being in heaven, Phil. 3, 20. V. 13. **O spare me,** turning from him the look of His angry face, **that I may recover strength,** being cheered in the midst of his troubles, **before I go hence and be no more.** Instead of being bound under wrath and chastened under displeasure, David longs for the face of God turned upon him in mercy, in order that he may give thanks and praise Him all his life. And so every believer, although oppressed with sin and sorrow, the anger of God and suffering, still turns to the heavenly Father in firm confidence, knowing that tribulation worketh patience; and patience, experience; and experience, hope; and hope maketh not ashamed, because the love of God is shed abroad in our hearts by the Holy Ghost which is given unto us, Rom. 5, 3—5.

PSALM 40.

Prophecy of Christ's Suffering and Prophetic Office.

To the chief musician, for performance in liturgical services, **a psalm of David,** the Messiah Himself speaking through his mouth and pen. Cp. Heb. 10, 5—7. V. 1. **I waited patiently for the Lord,** literally, "Waiting, I waited for Jehovah," the expression denoting the long siege of patient waiting for the help which the Messiah confidently expected; **and He inclined unto Me,** bowing down to Him in gracious tenderness, **and heard My cry,** as it was sent up to Him with such fervent insistence. V. 2. **He brought Me up also out of an horrible pit,** where He was wasting away with sufferings, **out of the miry clay,** into which He was sinking down, apparently to His destruction, **and set My feet upon a rock,** upon a solid foundation, **and established My goings,** making His steps firm, permitting Him to walk in security. In this way the Messiah's trust in the God of His salvation, in His heavenly Father, appeared even in the midst of His sufferings. V. 3. **And He hath**

put a new song in My mouth, a special psalm of thanksgiving intended particularly for this occasion, **even praise unto our God,** for this wonderful exhibition of His mercy; **many shall see it,** be informed of this wonderful deliverance, **and fear, and shall trust in the Lord,** with reverence and awe of His mercy and grace. From this fact a general truth is now deduced. V. 4. **Blessed is that man that maketh the Lord his trust,** who sets Jehovah as his confidence alone, **and respecteth not the proud,** turning to them for help, **nor such as turn aside to lies,** to the false idols and vanities of this life, to everything that men foolishly make the basis of their hope and trust outside of Jehovah. The speaker now, in the joy of His deliverance, includes Himself with the entire congregation of believers in exalting the mercies of Jehovah. V. 5. **Many, O Lord, My God, are Thy wonderful works which Thou hast done,** not only those pertaining to the creation, but especially to the redemption of the world, **and Thy thoughts,** the marvelous plans of His mercy, **which are to us-ward; they cannot be reckoned up,** set forth properly, **in order unto Thee,** on acount of their bewildering mass, or, there is none that can be compared to Thee. **If I would declare and speak of them, they are more than can be numbered.** Thus the Messiah, in a prophetic summary, declares the greatness of God, spreads the proper understanding of His name, and leads many to the knowledge of, and the belief in, Jehovah, the God of salvation. V. 6. **Sacrifice and offering Thou didst not desire,** God does not ask for, and takes no pleasure in, mere outward offerings, in a mechanical form of worship, whether such sacrifices are in the form of thank- and peace-offerings, intended to establish a closer fellowship with God, or in burnt offerings and sin-offerings, which are made to atone for sins; **Mine ears hast Thou opened,** literally, "ears hast Thou digged for Me," preparing His ears for hearing and heeding His will, in a true form of worship; **burnt offering and sin-offering hast Thou not required,** for all such outward forms of worship have value only in the measure of their flowing out of true faith, 1 Sam. 15, 22. V. 7. **Then said I, Lo, I come,** a solemn announcement of the Messiah's coming into the world, Mal. 3, 1; **in the Volume of the Book,** in the roll of parchment which is Holy Writ, the one wonderful Book of all times, John 5, 37, **it is written of Me:** v. 8. **I delight to do Thy will, O My God,** to carry out the pleasure of God's merciful counsel for the salvation of mankind; **yea, Thy Law is within My heart;** because the will of God filled His whole being, therefore the Messiah was ready to undertake the great task of preparing eternal redemption for all men. The entire ministry of Christ, but especially His great Passion, shows the perfection of His willing obedience. And now the Messiah, delivered out of the dreary pit of suffering and death and exalted on high, testifies to the Word of His truth in the past and in the present. V. 9. **I have preached righteousness in the great congregation,** declaring and proclaiming it through the mouth of His servants. **Lo, I have not refrained My lips, O Lord, Thou knowest,** He had not closed them up and kept them shut, but had made known God's faithfulness and salvation, His mercy and truth, John 1, 14, these being the benefits resulting from His completed Passion. V. 10. **I have not hid Thy righteousness within My heart,** namely, that which is by faith of Jesus Christ unto all and upon all them that believe, Rom. 3, 22; **I have declared Thy faithfulness and Thy salvation; I have not concealed Thy loving-kindness and Thy truth from the great congregation.** Having thus set forth the everlasting truth of the Gospel, the Messiah returns to the bitter complaint of the days of His suffering. V. 11. **Withhold not Thou Thy tender mercies from Me, O Lord; let Thy loving-kindness and Thy truth continually preserve Me.** It is the cry of a poor and stricken sinner whom the punishment of God has overtaken, who is tortured by the consciousness of his guilt; for Christ was the full Substitute for mankind, making the misery and the curse resting upon men His own. V. 12. **For innumerable evils have compassed me about,** attacking Him on all sides like countless hordes of bitter enemies; **Mine iniquities have taken hold upon Me,** having overtaken him like a victorious army, **so that I am not able to look up; they are more than the hairs of Mine head,** for they were the countless millions which had been committed by all men; **therefore My heart faileth Me,** it has forsaken Him, leaving Him weak and powerless in His misery. V. 13. **Be pleased, O Lord, to deliver Me; O Lord, make haste to help Me,** haste being necessary because He was in such depths of oppression. V. 14. **Let them be ashamed and confounded together that seek after My soul to destroy it,** for all the enemies of mankind were pursuing Him with all the curse, wrath, and damnation which the countless sins of men deserved; **let them be driven backward and put to shame,** covered with disgrace, **that wish me evil.** V. 15. **Let them be desolate for a reward of their shame,** utterly stunned and dazed, **that say unto Me, Aha, aha!** in sneering derision in an attempt to frustrate His work of redemption. The wonderful plans of God for our salvation are revealed in this passage in all their surpassing glory. The enemies cannot hinder the salvation of mankind, and all their attempts to do so result but in their own downfall. V. 16. **Let all those that seek Thee,** with hearts filled with faith, **rejoice and be glad**

in Thee, finding comfort in God, their Savior; **let such as love Thy salvation say continually, The Lord be magnified,** in a glorious hymn of thanksgiving. V. 17. **But I am poor and needy,** in misery on account of the load of human guilt resting upon Him; **yet the Lord,** the All-powerful, **thinketh upon Me,** taking care of Him in His trouble; **Thou art My help and My Deliverer; make no tarrying, O My God!** With the faith in Jesus Christ and His salvation for all mankind in our hearts, we may find comfort in all troubles of this earthly life and victoriously cope with all our enemies.

PSALM 41.

A Psalm of Thanksgiving and Trust in God.

To the chief musician, a psalm of David, composed probably during the time of persecution by Absalom and, if not Messianic throughout, is at least in part typical of the Messiah's suffering, John 13, 18; Acts 1, 16. V. 1. **Blessed is he that considereth the poor,** being properly attentive to the afflicted ones, observing the needy with loving sympathy; **the Lord will deliver him in time of trouble,** literally, "in the day of adversity," rewarding him in mercy for his deed of mercy. V. 2. **The Lord will preserve him and keep him alive; and he shall be blessed upon the earth,** be given true prosperity; **and Thou wilt not deliver him unto the will of his enemies,** giving him up to destruction. V. 3. **The Lord will strengthen him upon the bed of languishing,** support him upon his sick-bed, not let him sink down in death; **Thou wilt make all his bed in his sickness,** turning it into a couch of recovery and health. V. 4. **I said, Lord, be merciful unto me,** this always being the greatest concern of David, just as it stands out in the work of the great Son of David. **Heal my soul; for I have sinned against Thee,** that being the inward cause of his sufferings. V. 5. **Mine enemies speak evil of me,** wishing him evil and destruction, **When shall he die and his name perish?** V. 6. **And if he,** one of the adversaries whose enmity stood out above that of the rest, **come to see me, he speaketh vanity,** emptiness, hypocrisy; **his heart gathereth iniquity to itself,** all forms of mischief; **when he goeth abroad, he telleth it,** he makes known what he found out by his hypocritical behavior, by feigning a sympathetic interest. V. 7. **All that hate me whisper together against me,** in making use of the news brought by their spying confederate; **against me do they devise my hurt,** with deceitful plotting, in an evil conspiracy, such as that made by the leaders of the Jews after receiving from Judas the assurance of his readiness to betray Christ. V. 8. **An evil disease, say they, cleaveth fast unto him,** literally, "is welded to him," making it impossible for him to shake it off; **and now that he lieth, he shall rise up no more,** for the enemies blasphemously considered him marked and judged of God and therefore rejoiced that he was eliminated. V. 9. **Yea, mine own familiar friend,** literally, "the man of my peace," of his closest friendship and companionship, enjoying the sacred hospitality of his house, **in whom I trusted, which did eat of my bread, hath lifted up his heel against me,** not merely in a spurning gesture, but with the avowed purpose of kicking him aside. It is this verse which Jesus expressly applies to His betrayer, Judas Iscariot, John 13, 18. V. 10. **But Thou, O Lord, be merciful unto me,** David's usual plea for mercy, **and raise me up,** causing him to arise from his bed of sickness, from his depth of misery, **that I may requite them,** in executing judgment upon the wicked. V. 11. **By this I know that Thou favorest me,** that Jehovah has pleasure in him, **because mine enemy doth not triumph over me,** with shouts of victory, finding himself, rather, disappointed. V. 12. **And as for me, thou upholdest me in mine integrity,** the fact of his being innocent of deliberate wrongdoing, **and settest me before Thy face forever,** under God's watch and care, as an object of His trust and love throughout eternity. To the psalm has been added the doxology of the entire First Book of Psalms: v. 13. **Blessed be the Lord God of Israel,** the only true God, **from everlasting and to everlasting,** through all eternity. **Amen, and Amen;** yea, yea, this is most certainly true, and the firm confession of all believers.

PSALM 42.

An Exile's Longing for Zion.

To the chief musician, for performance in the liturgical part of the Temple-services, **Maschil,** a didactic poem, **for the sons of Korah,** written by some member of this Levitical family, or organization, 1 Chron. 6, 22—32, belonging to the Kohathite division of the tribe of Levi. Korah himself had perished in the punishment which followed his revolt, Num. 16, but his sons had not been included in the judgment, Num. 26, 11. Their descendants were afterward distinguished for their poetical and musical ability, eleven hymns of the psalter being credited to their authorship. They wrote altogether in the style of David, with a fervent love for the Sanctuary of the Lord.

V. 1. **As the hart panteth after the waterbrooks,** with an intense desire, with an overwhelming sense of want, **so panteth my soul after Thee, O God,** who is often set forth as a spring of living water for the refreshment of the exhausted. V. 2. **My soul thirsteth for God, for the living God,** the Source of all true life, who alone is able to restore the soul which finds itself in the depths of persecution, misery, and sorrow on account of sin. **When shall I come and appear before God?** in the regular acts of worship, at the times when all the faithful of Israel were required to come to the central Sanctuary, before the Lord, Ex. 23, 17; 34, 23. V. 3. **My tears have been my meat,** his substitute for food, his daily portion, **day and night, while they,** the sneering enemies, **continually say unto me, Where is thy God?** a question which, of course, implied that God had forsaken him, that he was foolish for placing his confidence in Jehovah. V. 4. **When I remember these things,** recalling the festive processions in which he has taken part, **I pour out my soul in me,** permitting it to dissolve in the pain which was filling him with misery; **for I had gone with the multitude,** it had been his custom to take his place in the procession, **I went with them to the house of God, with the voice of joy and praise,** singing psalms of thanksgiving, **with a multitude that kept holy-day.** This detailed picturing of the happiness of the past increased both his pain at being deprived of its pleasures and his longing to experience it once more. But in the midst of his complaint the inspired poet stops to admonish his fainting soul. V. 5. **Why art thou cast down,** bowed to the ground, **O my soul, and why art thou disquieted,** full of unrest and despondency, **in me?** No matter, however, what the affliction may be, there is one certain comfort. **Hope thou in God,** waiting steadfastly and confidently for His help; **for I shall yet praise Him for the help of His countenance,** the believer's faith trusting in a complete deliverance, holding the firm conviction that God's face would again be turned to Him in mercy. But a reaction once more sets in; there is an ebb, as well as a flow, of the tide of his joyful spirits. V. 6. **O my God, my soul is cast down within me,** in utter dejection; **therefore,** namely, to find new comfort in spite of this feeling of hopelessness, **will I remember Thee,** his thoughts going back to the Sanctuary of Jehovah, **from the land of Jordan,** from the country east of Jordan, where the exiled poet was sojourning, **and of the Hermonites,** the hills connected with Mount Hermon of the Antilebanon range, **from the hill Mizar,** in whose neighborhood he was making his temporary home. V. 7. **Deep calleth unto deep,** with the confused noise of deep waters in mighty agitation, **at the noise of Thy waterspouts,** when floods or cataracts of water come like a deluge; **all Thy waves and Thy billows are gone over me,** the floods of his sorrow, as sent by God, overwhelmed him. But even while the poet voices his complaint, he once more gains the proper trust in Jehovah. V. 8. **Yet the Lord will command His loving-kindness in the daytime,** a morning of salvation following the night of sorrow, **and in the night His song shall be with me,** the excitement of his joy keeping him awake to intone psalms of praise to Jehovah, his state of mind being one of constant happiness, **and my prayer unto the God of my life,** who does not deliver him to the pains of death. V. 9. **I will say unto God, my Rock,** a specimen of his prayer being given here, **Why hast Thou forgotten me? Why go I mourning,** in deep grief and sorrow, **because of the oppression of the enemy,** with its excruciating pain? V. 10. **As with a sword in my bones mine enemies reproach me,** with cruel taunts; **while they say daily unto me, Where is thy God?** Their mockery is blasphemous, for they not only decry the hope of the believer as foolish, but deny the very existence of a God who would help the afflicted in his troubles. And so, for the second time, the psalmist chides his despondent soul, v. 11. **Why art thou cast down, O my soul, and why art thou disquieted,** tossed and agitated like an angry sea, **within me? Hope thou in God; for I shall yet praise Him, who is the Health of my countenance,** his Help and Deliverance, who cheers him and drives away the clouds of sorrow from his face, **and my God,** to whom he clings despite the enemies' mockery, refusing to have doubt take the place of faith. Temptations caused by times of trouble can be overcome only by the believer's laying hold of God's grace as his one hope of salvation.

PSALM 43.

Conclusion of the Preceding Psalm.

The psalmist again opens with an appeal, followed by a vow of faithfulness to Jehovah and His worship. V. 1. **Judge me, O God,** vindicating his cause, **and plead my cause,** as the all-wise advocate against wickedness, **against an ungodly nation,** a generation of men not in God's favor. **O deliver me from the deceitful and unjust man,** who is full of falsehood and wickedness, devoid of every idea of right and justice. V. 2. **For Thou art the God of my strength,** his Refuge and

Stronghold by virtue of his trust in Him; **why dost Thou cast me off,** turning away from him in scorn, as from something loathsome? **Why go I mourning because of the oppression of the enemy?** Cp. Ps. 42, 9. V. 3. **O send out Thy light,** that of His grace and mercy tending toward the salvation of men, **and Thy truth,** the faithfulness which keeps His promises without fail; **let them lead me; let them bring me unto Thy holy hill,** where His Sanctuary had been erected, and to Thy tabernacles, where the Lord dwelled in the midst of His people, letting the light of His essence appear in the revelation of His love in the Messiah, John 1, 14. V. 4. **Then will I go unto the altar of God,** to the place of His worship, **unto God, my exceeding Joy,** in whom all the highest delights of the believer are personified; **yea, upon the harp will I praise Thee,** a small zither-like instrument used in divine worship, **O God, my God,** the emphasis again being placed upon the personal relation of the believer to his God, his highest Good. The believer having reached this point of assurance, he admonishes himself for the third time: v. 5. **Why art thou cast down, O my soul, and why art thou disquieted within me? Hope in God; for I shall yet praise Him, who is the Health of my countenance and my God.** All believers will guard against coming to their place of worship in a mechanical, dead manner, their hearts rather being united with God in the fellowship of true faith, exulting in Him as their greatest delight.

PSALM 44.

A Prayer in Times of National Distress.

To the chief musician for the sons of Korah, another hymn composed by a member of this family, **Maschil,** a didactic poem evidently written at a time when the nation was in great peril, the period of David's wars having been suggested when he was overthrowing the Ammonites and the Edomites took advantage of his absence to make a raid on Southern Canaan, 2 Sam. 10. The psalm finds its application in the life of all Christians, being particularly suitable for times of oppression by the enemies of the Church, when it seems that the heathen and tyrants will prevail. V. 1. **We have heard with our ears, O God,** in the form of instruction in vogue among the children of Israel, where every housefather informed his children regarding the great works of God, Ex. 10, 2; 12, 26; Deut. 6, 20; **our fathers have told us what work Thou didst in their days,** in the early history of Israel, **in the times of old;** v. 2. **how Thou didst drive out the heathen with Thy hand,** for it was not their own weapons and strength which gave them the victory, as the many specific instances recorded clearly show, but the almighty power of Jehovah, **and plantedst them,** giving to the fathers of Israel a permanent home in Canaan; **how Thou didst afflict the people,** the heathen inhabitants, **and cast them out.** V. 3. **For they,** the Israelites, **got not the land in possession by their own sword, neither did their own arm save them; but Thy right hand and Thine arm and the light of Thy countenance,** turned upon Israel in mercy, **because Thou hadst a favor unto them,** being disposed toward them in love. This is the first point which the inspired singer wishes to make, the fact of God's help in times past. This fact, moreover, inspires true confidence in Jehovah, the second point emphasized in the psalmist's prayer. V. 4. **Thou art my King, O God,** emphatically, "Even Thou Thyself art my King"; **command deliverances for Jacob,** for the small flock of the faithful, of the believers of all times. V. 5. **Through Thee will we push down our enemies,** as an angry ox charges and overthrows every one coming into his way; **through Thy name will we tread them under that rise up against us.** V. 6. **For I will not trust in my bow, neither shall my sword save me,** all confidence in one's own strength and ability is foolish. V. 7. **But Thou hast saved us from our enemies and hast put them to shame that hated us,** their opposition to Israel brought them nothing but disgrace, because God was the sole Help of His people. V. 8. **In God we boast all the day long,** making His almighty power the basis of their confident praise, **and praise Thy name,** His entire essence as revealed to men, **forever. Selah.** There follows a description of the desperate straits in which Israel found itself at that time, typical of the troubles which beset the Church of God, and a bitter complaint of neglect. V. 9. **But Thou hast cast us off,** that is, in spite of the trust which they reposed in Him it seemed that God was bent on their destruction, **and put us to shame,** a mockery before their enemies; **and goest not forth with our armies,** the various sections of Israel's army engaged in war. V. 10. **Thou makest us to turn back from the enemy,** in defeat and flight; **and they which hate us spoil for themselves,** gaining rich booty in the deserted camp of Israel. V. 11. **Thou hast given us like sheep appointed for meat,** to be used for food without offering resistance, **and hast scattered us among the heathen,** many members of Israel having been led away as slaves in the recent raids. V. 12. **Thou sellest Thy people for naught,** for a song, as though they were worthless, insignificant, as if He no longer cared for them, and dost not increase **Thy wealth by their price,** He did not go high in the price which He demanded in selling them into slavery. V. 13. **Thou makest us a reproach to our neighbors,** so that the surrounding nations would regard them with derision, **a scorn and a derision to them that are round about us.** V. 14. **Thou makest us a byword among the heathen,** their fate being bandied about in little verses of mockery, **a shaking of the head among the people,** in a gesture of sneering contempt. V. 15. **My confusion is continually before me,** the poet is always conscious of the disgrace resting upon him, **and the shame of my face hath covered me,** having taken hold of his entire being; v. 16. **for the voice of him that reproacheth and blasphemeth,** the taunting mockery of whose words cut so deeply; **by reason of the enemy and avenger,** whose face was full of malignant hatred. The counterpart of all this is found in the treatment accorded the true believers by the children of the world, and the cry of the faithful rises to the Lord at all times in similar strains. Yet they do not continue in vain lamentations, but turn to the Lord in confident prayer. V. 17. **All this is come upon us,** apparently in punishment; **yet have we not forgotten Thee, neither have we dealt falsely in Thy covenant,** to deserve such a fate as a punishment. V. 18. **Our heart is not turned back,** away from the will of God, **neither have our steps declined from Thy way,** to follow the path of error and denial of God, v. 19. **though Thou hast sore broken us in the place of dragons,** where jackals lived, out in the wastes of the desert, where this misfortune had come upon Israel, **and covered us with the shadow of death.** It is an emphatic declaration that Israel had not become apostate, continued also in the next sentence. V. 20. **If we have forgotten the name of our God or stretched out our hands to a strange god,** in open idolatry, v. 21. **shall not God search this out? For He knoweth the secrets of the heart,** and nothing can be hidden before His omniscience. Then there would be reason for His being angry, then He would rightly reject His children. But this is not the case. V. 22. **Yea, for Thy sake are we killed all the day long; we are counted as sheep for the slaughter.** That is the experience of the believers of all times on account of their adherence to God's Word, to the confession of His holy name. Cp. Rom. 8, 36. Therefore the believers are filled with the courage of faith, with the confidence which appeals to God with the certainty of being heard. V. 23. **Awake! Why sleepest Thou, O Lord?** this being the conclusion reached because of His failure to bring speedy deliverance to His children. **Arise, cast us not off forever!** V. 24. **Wherefore hidest Thou Thy face,** as though He had forgotten all His mercy, **and forgettest our affliction and our oppression,** as though indifferent to all their suffering? V. 25. **For our soul is bowed down to the dust; our belly cleaveth unto the earth,** their condition being one of the greatest oppression and humility. V. 26. **Arise for our help and redeem us for Thy mercies' sake,** the appeal, not to the justice, but to the mercy of God for the sake of the Redeemer, being the one argument which is bound to make an impression upon the Lord. Such is the daring quality of faith, which wins victories for every Christian and for the entire Christian Church.

PSALM 45.

The Anointed of God the Bridegroom of the Church.

To the chief musician, for use in public worship, **upon Shoshannim, for the sons of Korah, Maschil,** a didactic poem, **a song of loves.** One of the members of the Korahite family composed this wonderful song by the inspiration of the Holy Spirit, upon Shoshannim, that is, on or of the lilies, namely, in a figurative sense, partly explained in the words, "a song of loves," the plural referring to the bridal virgins and typifying the bride herself. The psalm is a song of the Bride, of the beloved of the great Bridegroom, the Messiah, and the plural is used because all the beloved of the King are united in the figure of the one who is His heart's delight, His Church. V. 1. **My heart is inditing a good matter,** the poet's heart is astir with the good word, the wonderful message, which he wants to set forth, the consoling Gospel-news: **I speak of the things which I have made touching the King,** dedicating his poem to the great King, the Messiah; **my tongue is the pen of a ready writer,** of a quick scribe, the thoughts, as inspired by the Holy Spirit, flowing into his pen in an uninterrupted stream. The King to whom he addresses his hymn has so filled his mind as to guide his pen in the glowing account which he here indites, a psalm of Christ, the Messiah, in His wonderful, eager love for His Bride, the Church. The King is now directly addressed. V. 2. **Thou art fairer than the children of men,** possessing beauty surpassing that of any mere son of man; **grace is poured into Thy lips,** charm and lovableness show themselves in His speech, in the beauty of His mercy and truth; **therefore God hath blessed Thee forever,** by virtue of the intimate relation between God and this King, the Messiah, divine blessings flow down upon Him and through His Gospel upon the world, streams of salvation and mercy issue from His mouth in the beautiful message of redemption. Because of this glory and beauty, because of this mercy and truth, all nations of the earth are blessed in Him. V. 3. **Gird Thy sword upon Thy thigh, O Most Mighty, with Thy glory and Thy majesty.** He is not only a fair and gracious King, but also a great Champion of His people, who went out to battle for the salvation of mankind, invincible in His glory and majesty, the attributes of the true and only God, Ps. 96, 6. With these same wonderful qualities He is now endowed as He sits at the right hand of God, Eph. 1, 21. 22. V. 4. **And in Thy majesty ride prosperously,** advancing as the victorious Hero, **because of truth and meekness and righteousness,** for it is a war in the interest of truth and of the sufferings of righteousness, undertaken because the righteous suffer great trouble and afflictions; **and Thy right hand shall teach Thee terrible things;** for as gentle and gracious as the King is toward those who bow under His merciful scepter, so majestic and terrible He is in dealing with His enemies. V. 5. **Thine arrows are sharp in the heart of the King's enemies; whereby the people fall under Thee.** The battle is briefly described. The King takes His whetted arrows and sends them forth into the ranks of the enemies, into their hearts, so that the people fall before Him, wounded to death, utterly vanquished. Thus the exalted Christ exerts His almighty power. No matter how often the truth is suppressed, no matter how severely the righteous suffer, they are assured of the assistance of their almighty Redeemer. Every victory won by Christ is a judgment and punishment upon the enemies, who will be finally disposed of on the last Great Day.

From the description of the King's majesty the writer now turns to a hymn of praise and worship. V. 6. **Thy throne, O God, is forever and ever,** the Messiah, true man, at the same time eternal God, Heb. 1, 8; **the scepter of Thy kingdom is a right scepter,** His dominion is one of rightness, of righteousness and justice. V. 7. **Thou lovest righteousness and hatest wickedness,** the King Himself, coequal with God, hates the evil and loves the good, He causes righteousness to be applied in the government of His kingdom by mercifully giving to all its citizens, through His Word, the merciful gift of His righteousness, which, in turn, causes them to eschew evil and love the truly good; **therefore God, Thy God, hath anointed Thee with the oil of gladness above Thy fellows.** The King, the Messiah, is here clearly addressed as God, worshiped as God. God has anointed Him who is Himself God. There is only one God, and yet a distinction is here made between God and God, between the Messiah and His God and Father. His God has anointed Christ with oil of gladness, with the Holy Ghost, who imparts joy in the Redeemer through the Word, Heb. 2, 11. 12; Is. 61, 1—3. Above His companions the Messiah is anointed, above all ordinary, merely human kings, priests, and prophets. He is anointed with the Holy Ghost without measure and therefore freely gives of this Spirit, filling the hearts of the poor and afflicted with glorious comfort, with the assurance of the forgiveness of their sins. V. 8. **All Thy garments smell of myrrh and aloes and cassia,** being perfumed with the most costly ointments and spices; **out of the ivory palaces, whereby they have made Thee glad,** rather, from the palaces of ivory the stringed instruments have gladdened Thee. The ivory palaces are the habitations in Messiah's kingdom. They are white, the color of innocence, purity, holiness, and the songs performed on the stringed instruments are the praises sung in honor of the King by the citizens of His kingdom, hymns of thanksgiving to His grace. V. 9. **King's daughters were among Thy honorable women,** precious and valued are the bridal virgins, the maidens of the bridal procession, the believers, who are also followers of the King; **upon Thy right hand did stand the queen in gold of Ophir,** the Bride, or Wife, of the King appearing in the midst of the bridal virgins chosen by His grace, and identified with them for the purposes of the lesson here conveyed. The gold of Ophir decorating the queen is a picture of the rich gifts of mercy which the Messiah has bestowed upon His Church. The paragraph thus treats of Christ, true God and man, King and Bridegroom, from whom the gifts of mercy, righteousness, and joy in the Holy Ghost go forth and are bestowed upon the members of His Church, but who also lets His enemies feel the power of His majesty.

The inspired singer now repeats the words with which the King, the Messiah, addresses His Bride. V. 10. **Hearken, O daughter,** called so by the Bridegroom because she is begotten and regenerated through the Gospel, 1 Pet. 1, 23, **and consider and incline thine ear,** becoming so absorbed in the words of His grace as to forget everything else, even the closest ties of human relationship; **forget also thine own people and thy father's house,** all for the sake of the Bridegroom and His love; v. 11. **so shall the King greatly desire thy beauty,** taking pleasure in her for the beauty of her obedience, her finest and most precious ornament; **for He is thy Lord,** who has made her His own by the shedding of His precious blood; **and worship thou Him,** giving Him the honor due Him as the great Lord and serving Him in the beauty of holiness. V. 12. **And the daughter of Tyre,** as the representative of the heathen world, **shall**

be there with a gift, bringing presents and attempting to gain the favor of the Bride; **even the rich among the people shall intreat thy favor,** seeking entrance into the kingdom of the Messiah. It is when the Bride, the Church, denies and forgets everything else, all the precious things of this world, that people outside the Church become interested. It is not by making concessions to the world that the Church gains members, but by being strictly exclusive, holding the treasure of the Gospel unpolluted. V. 13. **The King's daughter,** the Bride of Messiah, **is all glorious within,** clothed, as she is, with the garment of the Messiah's righteousness; **her clothing is of wrought gold,** of braided work of gold, with rich colored embroidery, the most costly garments, jewels of Christ's grace, spiritual and heavenly blessings. V. 14. **She shall be brought unto the King in raiment of needlework,** skilfully embroidered; **the virgins, her companions that follow her,** also such believers as have been gained from the heathen world, **shall be brought unto thee,** being identified with the Bride and received by Christ in the eternal palaces of heaven. V. 15. **With gladness and rejoicing shall they be brought; they shall enter into the King's palace,** into the everlasting glories of heaven. V. 16. **Instead of Thy fathers shall be Thy children, whom Thou mayest make princes in all the earth.** The King is here once more addressed. Instead of His fathers, the kings of the line of David who preceded Him, He will have sons, believers, citizens in His kingdom, His spiritual children; for His family will never die out, since He will always gain new adherents out of all nations, whom He will then set as princes over all the earth. All believers are kings and princes before Christ and His heavenly Father, they share in His glorious dominion, 1 Pet. 2, 9; Rev. 1, 6. And so the inspired singer finally, as a member and representative of Christ's Church on earth, extols the name of Messiah, the King. V. 17. **I will make Thy name to be remembered in all generations,** from generation to generation; **therefore shall the people praise Thee forever and ever.** Peoples, nations, believers, from every part of the earth, all the various members of the Church from all lands, give thanks to the King. And this song of thanksgiving, as it is begun here in time, will be continued without end, throughout eternity; for then the Bride, the Church, will forever be united with Christ, her Bridegroom, and her hallelujahs will sound forth in endless, glorious refrain.

PSALM 46.

The Church's Comfort and Security.

To the chief musician, for use in the Temple-services, **for the sons of Korah,** composed by a member of this talented family, **a song upon Alamoth,** for soprano voices, either for a chorus of virgins or for instruments in the treble clef, with a high pitch. It is a song of faith and trust, by which the Church of God is enabled to stand firm and secure in the midst of all enmity, in spite of the attacks of the armies of Satan. V. 1. **God is our Refuge,** under whose protection the Church and every individual believer is safe, **and Strength,** the Source and Fountain of all true strength, whose almighty power can overthrow all enemies, **a very present Help in trouble,** a Helper in the oppressions and anxieties, in the fightings and fears, with which the children of God must ever contend. V. 2. **Therefore,** because God is our great and invincible Champion, **will not we fear,** though ever inclined to do so on account of the smallness of our faith, **though the earth be removed,** be changed entirely, receive an entirely different form, **and though the mountains be carried into the midst of the sea,** sinking down into the depths from which they rose at the almighty power of God's word, Gen. 1, 9. 10; v. 3. **though the waters thereof roar,** as in fierce anger, and **be troubled,** rushing, foaming, and frothing like fermenting wine, **though the mountains shake with the swelling thereof,** as from the impact of a mighty tidal wave which threatens to undermine them. **Selah.** Such is the picture of the catastrophes which threaten the existence of the Church, but in whose midst the believers wait quietly for the Lord, knowing that the gates of hell shall not prevail against His Church. The reason for this simple trust is now given. V. 4. **There is a river,** a mighty stream, rich in water for purposes both of drinking and irrigating, **the streams whereof,** the various channels of which, **shall make glad the city of God, the Holy Place of the Tabernacles of the Most High,** where the great Ruler of the universe, the King of His Church, resides, that is, His strong city, with the walls and bulwarks of His salvation, Is. 26, 1. 2. It is the stream of the fulness of God's mercy, dividing into so many channels, in order to gladden the many congregations of the Church, wherever they may be found, including the fellowship with the Triune God in the beauty of His revelation. V. 5. **God is in the midst of her,** as her Protector and Savior; **she shall not be moved,** not be made to totter and fall; **God shall help her, and that right early,** literally, "before the face of morning," before break of day, no matter how dark the night of tribulation may have seemed. The help of Jehovah is sure in spite of all enemies. V. 6. **The heathen raged,** now foaming in terror over the deliverance which the Lord sends to His people, **the kingdoms were moved,** all their bulwarks tottering and falling with a mighty, booming noise; **He uttered His voice,** shouting in anger, **the earth melted,** dissolving before the devouring heat of His wrath, Amos 9, 5; Nah. 1, 5. V. 7. **The Lord of hosts,** the supreme Commander of all the heavenly armies, **is with us; the God of Jacob is our Refuge,** a high and safe Stronghold, which no enemies can storm and capture. **Selah.** Jehovah is with His Church, He is Immanuel, God-with-us, not only as trusted Ally, but as our Leader and Hero, before whose almighty power all enemies are as chaff before the wind. Therefore the challenging cry of the believers rings out: v. 8. **Come, behold the works of the Lord, what desolations He hath made in the earth,** in overthrowing the buildings and the enterprises of puny men, in punishing the world by bloody and destructive wars. V. 9. **He maketh wars to cease unto the end of the earth,** in the interest of His Holy City, in carrying out His plans for the deliverance of His saints; **He breaketh the bow and cutteth the spear in sunder; He burneth the chariot in the fire,** all instruments of the enemies employed in attacking the work of the Church, all the weapons of Satan intended for the overthrow of God's Zion. The kingdom of the Prince of Peace is established in the midst of all adversaries, and the Church Militant will become the Church Triumphant. The Church, therefore, issues a final solemn proclamation. V. 10. **Be still,** desist from making war upon Jehovah's Zion, **and know that I am God,** the God of the Church, the only true God; **I will be exalted among the heathen,** the great Victor on the field of encounter, **I will be exalted in the earth,** even the enemies being obliged to acknowledge His glory and majesty, forced to give Him the honor due Him as the Ruler of the universe. V. 11. **The Lord of hosts is with us; the God of Jacob is our Refuge. Selah.** That is the confident Amen of the Christian Church and of every believer, in the trust of a world-conquering faith; for "the kingdom ours remaineth." 2) With Christ on our side, we remain victors.

2) Cp. Doctrinal Essay, North Wisconsin District, 1921: *Der 46. Psalm.*

PSALM 47.

The Messiah in the Glory of His Exaltation.

To the chief musician, a psalm for the sons of Korah, written by one of their number at the inspiration of the Holy Ghost, as a prophecy of the victory and exaltation of Messiah to the right hand of Power. V. 1. **O clap your hands, all ye people,** the congregation of Jehovah being addressed with the summons to express their unbounded joy in a gesture of exultation which could not be repressed; **shout unto God with the voice of triumph,** in joyful acclaim of His majesty and glory. V. 2. **For the Lord most high is terrible,** to be feared, to be regarded with awe and reverence; **He is a great King over all the earth,** having dominion over all creatures, but ruling especially His Church with His grace and mercy. V. 3. **He shall subdue the people under us,** placing them in subjection to the Church by a spiritual victory, **and the nations under our feet,** the vanquished cheerfully joining the ranks of the victors in giving reverence to the King. V. 4. **He shall choose our inheritance for us,** the blessings imparted to His children by the manifestation of His grace, **the excellency of Jacob whom He loved,** the pride and glory of His Church, the bliss and joy of glorious perfection in heaven throughout eternity. **Selah.** All believers, whether they belong to Israel according to the flesh, or whether they have been gained from the ranks of heathendom, will share in the glorious blessings gained by Christ and enjoy their happiness, world without end. The reason for this wonderful outburst of joy is now given. V. 5. **God is gone up with a shout,** the holy singers in the spirit see God ascend up on high with jubilation, **the Lord with the sound of a trumpet,** for this was the instrument used on all joyful festivals of Israel. On account of this act of God-Jehovah the urgent cry now goes forth to men. V. 6. **Sing praises to God, sing praises,** psalms of joyful thanksgiving; **sing praises unto our King, sing praises,** for God on high and the King of His Church are here identified. V. 7. **For God is the King of all the earth,** the King, by His marvelous exaltation, has shown Himself the God of all the earth. **Sing ye praises with understanding,** bringing out the joyful feelings of their heart with the proper professional skill, to express their deepest feelings. V. 8. **God reigneth over the heathen,** the reign of the exalted Christ, in the Kingdom of Power, extends over the entire universe; **God sitteth upon the throne of His holiness,** at the right hand of Power in the heavenly places, Eph. 1, 20. V. 9. **The princes of the people are gathered together, even the people of the God of Abraham,** rather, to this people, the great and mighty ones of the earth joining the nation of Abraham's God, united with the spiritual Israel of all times; **for the shields of the earth belong unto God,** all weapons of war must be lowered before Him; **He is greatly exalted,** since He conquers with the power of His majestic mercy, through the Word of His grace. There can be no doubt, from the entire song, that the reference is to Jehovah-God, to the Messiah, in the exaltation following His deep humiliation. This exaltation was particularly emphasized before men in His visible ascension, followed by His sitting at the right hand of God, His heavenly Father. As a consequence and fruit of this exaltation He is continually adding new members to His spiritual Israel, to the congregation of believers, from all nations and peoples of the world, all of which unite in singing His praises, world without end.

PSALM 48.

Zion as a Type of the Christian Church.

A song and psalm for the sons of Korah, written by one of their number to set forth the privileges and blessings of God's dominion in His Church. V. 1. **Great is the Lord and greatly to be praised,** in setting forth His fame in psalms of thanksgiving, **in the city of our God,** where the Tabernacle and afterward the Temple stood, **in the mountain of His holiness,** where He dwells in the glory of His holiness. V. 2. **Beautiful for situation,** elevated for the sake of bringing out the beauty of its location on the hill, **the joy of the whole earth,** as it deserves to be according to the opinion of the spiritual Israel living there, **is Mount Zion, on the sides of the north,** where Moriah proper lifted its summit, **the city of the great King.** The entire description, though taken from the picture of Jerusalem, the location of which is singularly beautiful and impressive, is evidently typical of the holy Christian Church; for the name Zion or daughter of Zion, the city of God, is applied by the Holy Spirit to the congregation of believers of all times, as in Ps. 46. V. 3. **God is known in her palaces for a refuge,** having given evidence of His gracious protection and deliverance in so many troubles; the citadels of the spiritual Jerusalem are upheld by His divine power. V. 4. **For, lo, the kings,** the same enemies of Zion which are mentioned in Ps. 2, **were assembled, they passed by together,** in a confederacy to attack the city of God. V. 5. **They saw it,** after passing the boundary of the country and encamping against the Church, they became aware of the fact that Jehovah is its mighty Protector, **and so they marveled,** they were greatly astonished; **they were troubled and hasted away,** filled with terror at the revelation of God's omnipotence. V. 6. **Fear took hold upon them there,** trembling and quaking, **and pain, as of a woman in travail.** V. 7. **Thou breakest the ships of Tarshish,** the largest and most valuable merchant ships of those days, **with an east wind,** and so the mightiest enemies have no chance of overcoming him, they cannot cope with His almighty power. V. 8. **As we have heard,** in reports brought to them concerning former deliverances, **so have we seen in the city of the Lord of hosts,** who has all the heavenly armies under His command, **in the city of our God; God will establish it forever,** the gates of hell shall not prevail against the Church of Christ, Matt. 16, 18. **Selah.** The believers therefore, in congregation assembled, draw their conclusions to the strengthening of their faith in Jehovah. V. 9. **We have thought of,** by reflecting upon this deliverance and other manifestations of God's mercy, **Thy loving-kindness, O God, in the midst of Thy temple,** the grace and goodness revealed in His Church. V. 10. **According to Thy name, O God,** as it is proclaimed and glorified by the preaching of the Word, by setting forth the nature and the attributes of God, **so is Thy praise unto the ends of the earth,** wherever believers are gained by the preaching of the Gospel; **Thy right hand,** symbol of His dealings with His Church, **is full of righteousness,** which the Lord deals out and imputes to the believers, as they accept the redemption gained by the Savior, Jesus Christ. V. 11. **Let Mount Zion,** the spiritual Israel, **rejoice, let the daughters of Judah,** the congregation of believers, the children of the spiritual Judah, **be glad because of Thy judgments,** the decisions and acts of His just government in their favor. V. 12. **Walk about Zion,** taking the opportunity of examining the Church closely, both in its appearance and in its work, **and go round about her; tell the towers thereof,** counting the many means of defense which the Lord has given her in His Word. V. 13. **Mark ye well her bulwarks,** setting their hearts upon the fortifications of the Church, **consider her palaces,** the many fine congregations in which the Word and the Sacraments are in use in their original purity, **that ye may tell it to the generation following,** using all diligence that the faith of the fathers may be transmitted inviolate to the children, and that the hearts of the Christians may truly remain habitations of God through the Spirit. V. 14. **For this God,** who has revealed Himself to His Church in His Word, **is our God forever and ever; He will be our Guide even unto death,** or, in eternal youthfulness, to a world where there is no death, where all believers will be with Him in everlasting, deathless bliss.[3]

3) The last words of the psalm, in the Hebrew, may have reference to the kind of music to be used in playing this hymn, or they indicate the special form of verse employed.

PSALM 49.

Of the Vanity of Earthly Goods.

To the chief musician, for use in liturgical worship, **a psalm for the sons of Korah,** a hymn of instruction and consolation written by a member of the family of Korah, to show that mere earthly advantages do not bring lasting good fortune. V. 1. **Hear this, all ye people,** a solemn call for the most careful attention; **give ear, all ye inhabitants of the world,** all those living in this present time, in this age, which will soon pass away; v. 2. **both low and high,** the Hebrew distinguishing between the children of ordinary people, mankind in general, and the sons of people out of the ordinary, the excellent, the nobles, **rich and poor, together,** since all men should be interested in the subject broached here, regardless of station and fortune. V. 3. **My mouth shall speak of wisdom,** important and ponderous truths; **and the meditation of my heart,** as brought out in his whole instruction, **shall be of understanding,** such as goes to the root of matters, such as reveals their principles. V. 4. **I will incline mine ear,** in the attitude of the most careful attention, **to a parable,** a proverb and illustration of true wisdom revealed by God Himself; **I will open my dark saying,** the counsel of God, His providential dealings with men, which often seem to the believers like an inexplicable riddle, **upon the harp,** that is, he would accompany his explanations by a tune on the zither, his hymn being of a nature that others could also play it and find comfort in its instructions. V. 5. **Wherefore should I fear in the days of evil,** when misfortune strikes the believer, **when the iniquity of my heels,** the calamity inflicted by his oppressors, by bad men who abuse their power for such purposes, **shall compass me about?** It is the old complaint that the wicked surround the just, trying to attack them unawares and to inflict injury upon them. V. 6. **They that trust in their wealth,** as a means of insuring them lasting happiness, **and boast themselves in the multitude of their riches,** altogether vainglorious in their entire behavior, v. 7. **none of them,** the subject being generalized to include all men, **can by any means redeem his brother,** deliver him from the fate which will strike him on account of his sins, **nor give to God a ransom for him,** all the riches of the world are not sufficient to pay the guilt incurred by even one soul; v. 8. (**for the redemption of their soul is precious,** too costly to be paid for by anything which mere men may supply, **and it ceaseth forever,** it is bound to perish, to fail, the debt must remain forever unpaid, and all attempts to settle the indebtedness are futile;) v. 9. **that he should still live forever,** in an eternal life, without paying the penalty of death, **and not see corruption.** The passage plainly teaches the impossibility of redemption of any person in the world by the mutual assistance or by the united efforts of men, a fact which brands all so-called religions outside of Christianity as spurious and futile, for they all are unable to cope with the situation, Christianity alone affording a solution, namely, that of the vicarious suffering of Jesus Christ. V. 10. **For he,** every person in the world, including him whom men try to redeem by their own works, as in the supererogatory nonsense of the papists, **seeth that wise men die,** the so-called solid citizens of the state are subject to death, **likewise the fool and the brutish person,** in whom the animal desires occupy the first place, **perish, and leave their wealth to others.** How foolish, then, for the rich to imagine himself to be immortal on account of the wealth with which he impresses others. V. 11. **Their inward thought is that their houses shall continue forever and their dwelling-places to all generations,** not subject to misfortune and destruction, so that one generation after the other may pass forward into eternity without witnessing any change in their good fortune; **they call their lands after their own names,** that is, they celebrate their own names, they see to it that men praise and flatter them on account of their lands, their possessions. V. 12. **Nevertheless, man being in honor,** occupying the highest positions of honor and glory in this world, **abideth not,** passing away like a lodger who does not even await the full light of morning to continue his journey; **he is like the beasts that perish,** whose lives are suddenly, without warning, taken away. V. 13. **This their way is their folly,** it is the way all men fare who have such foolish confidence in themselves and in their riches; **yet their posterity approve their sayings,** the same thing happens to those who imitate them. **Selah.** V. 14. **Like sheep they are laid in the grave,** in spite of their alleged superiority and the greatness of their wealth; **death shall feed on them,** they are subject to its corruption; **and the upright shall have dominion over them in the morning,** the certain triumph of the righteous over the ungodly being a fact very soon, under the conditions brought about by the fulfilment of the Messianic promises; **and their beauty shall consume in the grave from their dwelling,** literally, "for their form is to be devoured by the kingdom of death," out of the dwelling which is theirs; they who proudly thought that they had built for eternity find themselves without a dwelling, their body rotting in the grave, and their memory being forgotten on earth. V. 15. **But God will redeem my soul from the power of the grave,** redeeming him from the hand or dominion of the realm of death; **for He shall receive me,** up into the glory of ever-

lasting life. Selah. The believers of the Old Testament, like the Christians to-day, held the belief in the resurrection of the body and in eternal life with God. The psalmist therefore makes the encouraging application. V. 16. **Be not thou afraid when one is made rich, when the glory of his house is increased,** when men praise him on account of his great wealth; v. 17. **for when he dieth, he shall carry nothing away,** he must leave all his wealth behind him; **his glory shall not descend after him,** for nothing is more evanescent than honor before men. V. 18. **Though while he lived, he blessed his soul,** flattering himself that he was truly happy and trying to enjoy life accordingly, Deut. 29, 18; Luke 12, 19; **and men will praise thee when thou doest well to thyself,** though men praise the wealthy person for enjoying life according to his own lights. V. 19. **He shall go to the generation of his fathers,** being cut off from the land of the living suddenly; **they,** all those included in this category, **shall never see light,** never enjoy the light of everlasting life. And so the poet closes his hymn with an apt conclusion: v. 20. **Man that is in honor,** enjoying wealth, good fortune, the esteem of men, **and understandeth not,** continuing in fleshly security, **is like the beasts that perish,** excluded from the hope of a higher and better life in heaven with God. All believers, therefore, will refrain from being offended by the apparent good fortune of the godless wealthy, knowing that their own happiness is secure in the hands of their heavenly Father.

PSALM 50.

Of the True Service of God.

A psalm of Asaph, one of the directors of the Temple-chorus at the time of David, distinguished for musical and poetical ability, 1 Chron. 26. The hymn shows how the grandeur and solemnity of the divine judgment should instruct men in the true worship and encourage them in true piety. V. 1. **The mighty God, even the Lord** (in the Hebrew: El Elohim Jehovah), the God of gods, Jehovah, the supreme God of earth and heaven, **hath spoken and called the earth from the rising of the sun unto the going down thereof,** as far as the earth extends, all its inhabitants are included in this mighty summons. V. 2. **Out of Zion,** where His Tabernacle and later His Temple stood, where He lived in the midst of His people, **the perfection of beauty,** the Church and congregation of God being the most beautiful object on earth, Ps. 48, 2. 3, **God hath shined,** sending out the brilliance of His majesty, more awe-inspiring than the rays of the sun. The psalmist is speaking of the majesty and glory of God's Word, especially the word of the Gospel, whose power and beauty goes forth to enlighten the earth. V. 3. **Our God shall come,** in this revelation of His divine essence, **and shall not keep silence,** bound to make known His glory before men everywhere; **a fire shall devour before Him,** especially in the words of the Law, **and it shall be very tempestuous round about Him,** fire and tempest being the heralds of God as the Judge of mankind. The fire threatens to devour the sinners, and the tempest of His wrath will scatter them like chaff before the wind. V. 4. **He shall call to the heavens from above,** the heavenly hosts being summoned as His servants, **and to the earth,** as witness, **that He may judge His people.** Cp. Deut. 4, 26; 30, 19; Is. 1, 2. V. 5. **Gather My saints together unto Me,** those who, by virtue of the righteousness imputed to them, are holy in His sight; **those that have made a covenant with Me by sacrifice,** the reference being to the division of the sacrificial animal, the two parties making the covenant passing between the divided portions, Gen. 15, 10. 18. V. 6. **And the heavens shall declare His righteousness,** the hosts of the heavens witnessing to the justice of all His sentences; **for God is Judge Himself. Selah.** Everything is now ready for the great scene of judgment: the court is about to open. V. 7. **Hear, O My people,** for He addresses those whom He wanted as His own, **and I will speak; O Israel, and I will testify against thee,** namely, for their failure to give Him the proper worship. **I am God, even thy God,** He bore the rightful title to act as judge over Israel. V. 8. **I will not reprove thee for thy sacrifices,** He had no complaint to make that they had not been offered, **or thy burnt offerings, to have been continually before Me,** rather, "and thy burnt offerings are over against Me always," they had omitted none of the sacrifices enjoined by the Law. V. 9. **I will take no bullock out of thy house nor he-goats out of thy folds,** God felt no interest in the sacrifices as brought by Israel; all outward ceremony of divine worship is futile without the true faith of the heart. V. 10. **For every beast of the forest is Mine,** all creatures being His, men could not offer Him anything which He did not already possess, **and the cattle upon a thousand hills.** V. 11. **I know all the fowls of the mountains,** all the birds that prefer to nest there; **and the wild beasts of the field are Mine,** all the animals that played in the valleys and lowlands. V. 12. **If I were hungry, I would not tell thee,** to plead for a sacrifice as food for Himself; **for the world is Mine and the fulness therof,** and there is no desire on His part which might be satisfied through sacrifice. V. 13. **Will I eat the flesh of bulls or drink the blood of goats?** Any believer bringing his offering should not do so under the delusion that he was doing something good to God personally, that he was obligating the Lord toward himself. The manner of true worship is now described. V. 14. **Offer unto God thanksgiving,** for true communion with Jehovah, **and pay thy vows unto the Most High,** Lev. 7, 11—18, namely, by bringing the homage of the heart, faith, penitence, and love, v. 15. **and call upon Me in the day of trouble,** after the right relation has thus been established by the proper worship. **I will deliver thee,** helping the worshiper out of all his difficulties, **and thou shalt glorify Me,** giving all praises to God alone for His every deliverance. That is the right relation which should obtain between the faithful here on earth and their heavenly Father. V. 16. **But unto the wicked God saith,** in a severe rebuke of hypocritical worship, **What hast thou to do to declare My statutes,** by imitating the behavior of the true believers, **or that thou shouldest take My covenant in thy mouth,** joining with the congregation in confessing the Word of God, v. 17. **seeing thou hatest instruction,** namely, the rebuke of hypocrisy and sin as contained in the Word, **and castest my words behind thee,** turning his back upon the divine instructions with a gesture of utter contempt? V. 18. **When thou sawest a thief, then thou consentedst with him,** taking pleasure in the form of wickedness practised against the Seventh Commandment and thus becoming guilty of the same crime, **and hast been partaker with adulterers,** in transgressing also the Sixth Commandment. V. 19. **Thou givest thy mouth to evil,** to slanderous talk of every kind, **and thy tongue frameth deceit,** deliberate falsehoods in order to take away the neighbor's good fame. V. 20. **Thou sittest and speakest against thy brother,** the nearest relative by blood not being safe against the tongue of the slanderer and reviler; **thou slanderest thine own mother's son,** the lowest and meanest form of betrayal. Throughout this passage the idea is brought out that God was amazed at the daring displayed by the hypocrite in being guilty of such transgressions and yet holding membership in the congregation of Jehovah. V. 21. **These things hast thou done, and I kept silence,** cp. Rom. 2, 21. 23; **thou thoughtest that I was altogether such an one as thyself,** conniving at such wicked behavior, because He did not punish the wickedness outright; **but I will reprove thee,** as soon as His patience which intended the sinner's salvation is exhausted, **and set them in order before thine eyes,** showing Himself in His awful majesty and in His revenging justice. V. 22. **Now consider this, ye that forget God,** those who depend upon an external righteousness of works and forget the need of true piety of the heart, **lest I tear you in pieces,** in a punishment of utter destruction, **and there be none to deliver,** for when God once begins to strike, it is impossible to escape. And so the conclusion is offered: v. 23. **Whoso offereth praise,** the true thanksgiving of a believing heart, **glorifieth Me,** the external worship in this case being an expression of the faith of the heart; **and to him that ordereth his conversation aright,** making his whole life conform with the rule of God's divine will, **will I show the salvation of God,** His presence and favor attending him at all times. All Christians will shun and abhor hypocrisy in every form and continually watch over their hearts, in order that all their worshiping of God may be the outflow of a heart grateful for His favor and love in Jesus Christ.

PSALM 51.

David's Penitential Prayer.

To the chief musician, for public performance, as an open confession of David's sin before the whole congregation, showing that his repentance was of the right kind, **a psalm of David, when Nathan, the prophet, came unto him, after he had gone in to Bathsheba,** 2 Sam. 11 and 12. For about one year after his terrible sin of adultery David had hardened his heart against repentance, although he had no rest in his conscience during this time, Ps. 32, 3. 4. It was when Nathan had thundered the accusation at David, "Thou art the man!" that the latter's resistance was broken and he confessed his sin. He received the word of absolution at once, but was constrained, as he realized the greatness of his transgression more and more, to plead with the Lord for His full mercy, as well as for the strength which would enable him to devote his whole life to the expiation of his guilt before men.

DAVID'S PLEA FOR MERCY. — V. 1. **Have mercy upon me, O God,** a confession of utter unworthiness and a cry of faith clinging to God as the only Hope of salvation, **according to Thy loving-kindness,** for He forgives sins only for His own sake, not for any merit in us; **according unto the multitude of Thy tender mercies blot out my transgressions,** God's grace and mercy alone being able to cleanse the believer from the greatness of his wickedness, in this case adultery, murder, and a year of hard-hearted refusal to acknowledge the transgression. V. 2. **Wash me throughly from mine iniquity,** which is like filth polluting the heart and conscience, **and cleanse me from my sin,** the term referring to the declaration of the priest by which one who was Levitically unclean was declared pure. God declares the sinner justified through the Word of the Gospel, if the latter but confesses his sin in true repentance. V. 3. **For I acknowledge my transgressions,** that is why he was approaching the Lord with such an urgent petition; **and my sin is ever before me,** it stood before his soul in all its horridness and heinousness. That is the curse attaching to sin, that man cannot forget it, that it rises up before him like a ghost that will not be laid, even though God has long forgiven and forgotten. Lest this condition drive a believer to the despair of Judas, he clings to the Lord, turning to Him again and again for mercy. V. 4. **Against Thee, Thee only, have I sinned and done this evil in Thy sight,** for every transgression of the Law, whether it be directed against the First or against the Second Table, is an infraction of the will of God and an insult to His dignity and holiness; for we are responsible to God alone, also in our conduct toward our neighbor, our apology to the neighbor for a wrong committed being a fruit of our repentance over against God; **that Thou mightest be justified when Thou speakest, and be clear when Thou judgest,** for every sin that is revealed and punished will in the end serve to set forth the holiness and justice of God, to glorify Him in the perfection of His essence. V. 5. **Behold, I was shapen in iniquity, and in sin did my mother conceive me;** for David, like all men, was sinful from the first moment of conception, flesh born of flesh, filled with all the corruption of mankind, all transgressions in thought, word, and deed being the result of the natural state of sinfulness, and the guilt of both laid upon every individual sinner. David thus made a full and unequivocal confession of the depth of his sin and of its full heinousness. V. 6. **Behold, Thou desirest truth in the inward parts,** without the slightest deceit and hypocrisy to mar the value of his confession of sin; **and in the hidden part Thou shalt make me to know wisdom,** namely, the true wisdom, which has its beginning in the fear of the Lord. The longing for a pure and wise heart is a characteristic of true repentance, and the prayer for this blessing is found with all believers throughout their lives. V. 7. **Purge me with hyssop,** a species of marjoram used in ceremonies of purification, Lev. 14, 4, **and I shall be clean,** declared justified in the eyes of God; **wash me, and I shall be whiter than snow,** looked upon as innocent of any wrong-doing on account of the forgiveness of sins pronounced upon him, Is. 1, 18. V. 8. **Make me to hear joy and gladness,** that is David's confident prayer now that his sins are forgiven, **that the bones which Thou hast broken may rejoice,** his entire body feeling the relief following the removal of the guilty feeling which rested upon his conscience. V. 9. **Hide Thy face from my sins,** turning it away, in order not to see it any longer and thus be incited to new anger and punishment, **and blot out all mine iniquities,** removing from His presence not only those on whose account he was suffering so severely, but those of his whole life, for a Christian must ask for forgiveness again and again, during his whole life, up to the hour of his death. But it must be the cry of faith clinging to God's promises of mercy.

NEW OBEDIENCE AS A FRUIT OF FAITH. — V. 10. **Create in me a clean heart, O God,** the believer's heart having been created anew in conversion, **and renew a right spirit within me,** establishing his heart and soul so that he was sure of his salvation, and that his mind would be centered upon God's Word, upon the performance of His will. V. 11. **Cast me not away from Thy presence,** for he had once felt the excruciating agony of being excluded from the mercy of God and feared a repetition of the experience, **and take not Thy Holy Spirit from me,** so that he would slip back into the impenitent condition of that one terrible year, persist in his opposition to God's gracious influence, and thus be lost. Every believer prays to the Lord to be preserved against the hardening of his heart which leads to rejection of the Gospel-message and to final destruction. V. 12. **Restore unto me the joy of Thy salvation,** for that is the height of the believer's happiness, if the Lord turns to him in grace, **and uphold me with Thy free spirit,** rather, the spirit of willingness will uphold me, namely, in the renewal of his whole life, in working true sanctification in him. V. 13. **Then will I teach transgressors Thy ways,** making known to them what God had done for him in delivering him from the misery of his sinful condition; **and sinners shall be converted unto Thee,** by reason of this open confession and instruction by the mouth of David, to which his gratitude for the mercy experienced would prompt him. V. 14. **Deliver me from blood-guiltiness,** not only that which was resting upon him on account of his murder of Uriah, but that of all severe transgressions, which are like enemies that try to oppress and enslave, **O God, Thou God of my salvation,** the mighty Lord of heaven being the only one who could help and deliver in such straits; **and my tongue shall sing aloud of Thy righteousness,** namely, that imputed to him by the grace of God in the Redeemer. V. 15. **O Lord, open Thou my lips,** God Himself giving him the necessary skill and ability to express his thanks in the proper manner, **and my mouth shall show forth Thy praise,** in an open and joyful song of praise for the grace vouchsafed him. V. 16. **For Thou desirest not sacrifice,** namely, as a mere external, mechanical act of worship,

else would I give it; Thou delightest not in burnt offering, such as is brought in a mere outward compliance with the letter of the Law, much as God is otherwise pleased to have the true faith of the heart shown in outward acts of worship. V. 17. **The sacrifices of God are a broken spirit**, one that is crushed by the consciousness of one's sinfulness; **a broken and a contrite heart**, one from which all self-righteousness has been removed by the realization of guilt, as shown in the demands of the Law, **O God, Thou wilt not despise**, in such a one, rather, He takes pleasure, with that He is delighted. Such sacrifices of the heart are then revealed in the corresponding sacrifices of the lips, in praises to God for the wonderful mercy vouchsafed in the forgiveness of sins. In conclusion, David includes himself with the entire congregation of believers. V. 18. **Do good in Thy good pleasure unto Zion**, showing His favor to the congregation of believers named after the Temple-mount; **build Thou the walls of Jerusalem**, namely, the spiritual walls of His Church, of the true people of God, the underlying thought being that the Lord would not permit the offense of David's transgression to take faith from the heart of any weak believer. V. 19. **Then shalt Thou be pleased with the sacrifices of righteousness, with burnt offering and whole burnt offering**, David being ready, in the consciousness of the righteousness imputed to him and in the eagerness to make known his change of heart, to bring sacrifices of every kind to expiate for his sins; **then shall they offer bullocks upon Thine altar**, as an act of thanksgiving for the mercy which he had received. A truly penitent person will offer to the Lord the sacrifices of his heart, of his lips, and of his hands, and the Lord will take pleasure in such offerings, if only the offense of heinous transgressions has first been removed.

PSALM 52.

The Punishment of Evil Tongues.

To the chief musician, for use in public worship, **Maschil**, a didactic anthem, a psalm **of David, when Doeg, the Edomite, came and told Saul, and said unto him, David is come to the house of Ahimelech**, the entire narrative being found 1 Sam. 19 to 22, especially chap. 21, 1—10 and 22, 1—10. This notice does not indicate the exact time when the psalm was composed, but the incident which occasioned it. V. 1. **Why boastest thou thyself in mischief**, for Doeg proudly set forth his connection with the wicked deed which he had performed at Gibeah, first in deceitfully betraying David and then in slaying eighty-five priests, **O mighty man?** It is not a real hero to which the name is here applied, but the word is a sarcastic designation of one whose craftiness was in his tongue. **The goodness of God endureth continually**, that is, in spite of all of Doeg's schemes the favor of God would continue to rest upon David, who therefore refused to consider his a lost cause. V. 2. **Thy tongue deviseth mischiefs**, planning wickedness and destruction of every kind; **like a sharp razor, working deceitfully**, or, "thou who workest deceit!" Doeg was ever engaged in undertakings of meanness against others, wickedness and deceit was his sphere of activity. V. 3. **Thou lovest evil more than good**, that is, in the place of good, he was altogether evil, **and lying rather than to speak righteousness**, his whole mind being devoted to falsehood and deceit. **Selah.** V. 4. **Thou lovest all devouring words**, literally, "words of swallowing," forms of speech by which he could harm and destroy others, **O thou deceitful tongue**, the entire person of Doeg being included in this appellation. V. 5. **God shall likewise destroy thee forever**, the divine vengeance being here set forth in retaliation for Doeg's wickedness; **He shall take thee away and pluck thee out of thy dwelling-place**, tearing down the tent of his habitation, leveling it with the ground, and removing even the tent-pins, **and root thee out of the land of the living**, in a total ruin of himself and all his possessions. **Selah.** V. 6. **The righteous also shall see**, namely, the ruin of the ungodly, **and fear**, with awe and respect for the avenging justice of the Lord, **and shall laugh at him**, deriding the ungodly for his folly, not with revengeful feelings, but with joy over the manner in which the Lord turns circumstances in their favor: v. 7. **Lo, this is the man that made not God his strength**, the triumph of the righteous being over the fallen oppressor, who thought he could go on indefinitely ignoring the Lord, **but trusted in the abundance of his riches**, believing that they could deliver him, **and strengthened himself in his wickedness**, in all his evil desires, believing himself to be safe from the vengeance of God. The fate of the righteous is shown by way of contrast. V. 8. **But I am like a green olive-tree in the house of God**, enjoying true prosperity in fellowship with the Lord; **I trust in the mercy of God forever and ever.** V. 9. **I will praise Thee forever, because Thou hast done it**, preserving David from all evil and making him partaker of the divine mercy; **and I will wait on Thy name**, hoping in the Lord as He has revealed Himself in His favor and grace; **for it is good before Thy saints**, every manifestation of God's mercy before the eyes of the believers being another proof of His goodness, inviting their unwavering faith.

PSALM 53.

Of the Corruption and Salvation of Men.

To the chief musician, for use in the liturgical part of public worship, **upon Mahalath,** in a sorrowful manner, agreeing with the general tone of the hymn, **Maschil,** a didactic poem, **a psalm of David.** This psalm, under the direction of the Holy Spirit, was evidently recast from Ps. 14, probably for a special occasion, and was for that reason included in the Psalter for the second time. Cp. Ps. 14 for the general explanation. V. 1. **The fool hath said in his heart, There is no God. Corrupt are they and have done abominable iniquity; there is none that doeth good.** V. 2. **God looked down from heaven upon the children of men to see if there were any that did understand, that did seek God.** V. 3. **Every one of them is gone back; they are altogether become filthy. There is none that doeth good, no, not one.** V. 4. **Have the workers of iniquity no knowledge, who eat up My people as they eat bread? They have not called upon God.** V. 5. **There were they in great fear,** filled with the terror of the Lord's judgment, **where no fear was,** when they had seen no reason to be terrified. The enemies had considered themselves secure, they were without fear or care, when the judgment of God suddenly broke upon them. **For God hath scattered the bones of him that encampeth against thee,** in a complete overthrow and ruin; **thou hast put them to shame, because God hath despised them,** this, by God's promise, being the glorious security of the children of Israel, of the congregation of believers, of all times: Because God is on their side, all enemies are confounded and disgraced; that is their eventual fate. V. 6. **Oh, that the salvation of Israel were come out of Zion! When God bringeth back the captivity of His people, Jacob shall rejoice, and Israel shall be glad.** This longing for deliverance by the hand of Messiah is found throughout the Old Testament, just as a similar longing for the final revelation of the last Great Day of the Lord characterizes the New Testament, 1 Cor. 16, 22; Rev. 22, 20.

PSALM 54.

Prayer and Consolation at the Time of Persecution.

To the chief musician on Neginoth, the music to be played on stringed instruments as the psalm was rendered in the liturgical service, **Maschil,** a didactic poem, **a psalm of David, when the Ziphims,** the inhabitants of the wilderness of Ziph in the southern part of Judah, **came and said to Saul, Doth not David hide himself with us?** This event, narrated 1 Sam. 23, 19; 26, 1, occasioned the writing of this hymn, a prayer for deliverance. V. 1. **Save me, O God, by Thy name,** this being the sum of all God's attributes as revealed to men, especially His grace, mercy, and truth, **and judge me by Thy strength,** another manifestation of His name or essence. David confidently asks that his case be taken up in the court of God, for he knows that he will be justified in the sight of the Lord. V. 2. **Hear my prayer, O God; give ear to the words of my mouth,** lending His ears, to that end, with the most careful attention. V. 3. **For strangers are risen up against me,** the reference being chiefly to the Ziphites, **and oppressors seek after my soul,** their object being to bring about his death; **they have not set God before them. Selah.** The Ziphites were not actuated by the fear of God in treacherously making known David's hiding-place, they were not performing a duty which their loyalty to Saul might have demanded of them, but proved themselves strangers, degenerate children of Abraham, and therefore of a wicked, violent, and cruel disposition. In these circumstances David turned to God as His only Helper. V. 4. **Behold, God is mine Helper,** taking his part against the enemies; **the Lord is with them that uphold my soul,** not merely one among many who support his soul in this extremity, but their only representative. V. 5. **He shall reward evil unto mine enemies,** paying the oppressors in their own coin. **Cut them off in Thy truth,** because of His faithfulness, on account of His promises to help the oppressed who trust in Him. V. 6. **I will freely sacrifice unto Thee,** with a glad heart and a willing hand, as true gratitude demands; **I will praise Thy name, O Lord; for it is good,** the revelation of God's essence in the case of David being that of His goodness. V. 7. **For He hath delivered me out of all trouble,** this deliverance being referred to the name of God; **and mine eye hath seen his desire upon mine enemies,** for such is the confidence of faith that it sees the fulfilment of prayer even while the prayer is being made. It is the same confidence of faith which is found in all Christians when they, in the midst of mighty enemies and oppressors, trust in the deliverance of the Lord, whether this come here in time or hereafter in eternity. They regard all His promises as already fulfilled.

PSALM 55.

A Complaint of False Friends.

To the chief musician on Neginoth, to be rendered with the accompaniment of stringed instruments in public worship, **Maschil, a psalm of David.** V. 1. **Give ear to my prayer, O God,** as usual, a strong expression for listening attentively; **and hide not Thyself from my supplication,** pretending to withhold His answer to David's earnest and importunate pleading. V. 2. **Attend unto me,** marking closely what he had to say, **and hear me. I mourn in my complaint,** reeling to and fro in painful meditation, which seemed to lead to no solution, **and make a noise,** groaning with pain, v. 3. **because of the voice of the enemy,** as he was compelled to hear it, **because of the oppression of the wicked,** the burden laid upon him by their hatred; **for they cast iniquity upon me,** the picture being that of a heavy load rolled down from a tower or mountain, making him moan and groan with its weight, **and in wrath they hate me,** acting against him with deceit and treachery. V. 4. **My heart is sore pained within me,** his inmost soul writhing with the agony laid upon him; **and the terrors of death are fallen upon me,** such as threatened death, taking away all hope of life. V. 5. **Fearfulness and trembling are come upon me,** like enemies attacking him, **and horror hath overwhelmed me,** its shades enveloping him and filling him with the deepest gloom. V. 6. **And I said, Oh, that I had wings like a dove!** a figure of powerful and rapid flight, **for then would I fly away and be at rest,** find a haven of security somewhere far from the oppression and treachery of the enemies. V. 7. **Lo, then would I wander far off,** flee to a great distance, **and remain in the wilderness,** the usual place of refuge for the persecuted and oppressed. **Selah.** V. 8. **I would hasten my escape,** hurrying with the greatest speed to a place of refuge, **from the windy storm and tempest,** for the rushing violence of the enemies intended his ruin. Such was the situation in which David found himself, not unlike that which sometimes threatens Christians even in our days; hence his pleading cry. V. 9. **Destroy, O Lord, and divide their tongues,** swallowing them up and confounding their speech and therefore also their counsels; **for I have seen violence and strife in the city,** Jerusalem having become a hotbed of anarchy under the influence of the conspirators. V. 10. **Day and night they go about it upon the walls thereof,** the enemies keeping a careful watch, spying upon the righteous; **mischief also and sorrow,** harm of every kind, **are in the midst of it.** V. 11. **Wickedness is in the midst thereof,** due to the treacherous agitation of the conspirators; **deceit and guile depart not from her streets,** from the open spaces or public concourses near the gates where the treacherous plans were passed on to others. V. 12. **For it was not an enemy that reproached me,** since in the case of an open adversary the situation would not have been so serious; **then I could have borne it,** for one expects no other treatment from an outspoken enemy, one endures his hostility; **neither was it he that hated me that did magnify himself against me,** seeking to carry out plans prompted by false ambition; **then I would have hid myself from him,** a course which he could not pursue with regard to a secret, treacherous foe, concerning whom one never knows when he will strike. V. 13. **But it was thou, a man mine equal,** whom David esteemed of the same rank with himself, **my guide and mine acquaintance,** rather, "my companion and my intimate friend," the reference probably being to Ahithophel, the Gilonite, 2 Sam. 15, 12. V. 14. **We took sweet counsel,** enjoying the intimacy of friendship, **together and walked into the house of God in company,** associating also in public, at the great festivals of Israel, when their close companionship was witnessed by all the people. Such conduct in betraying the love of a pure friendship fills David with righteous anger, causing him to call upon God for revenge. V. 15. **Let death seize upon them,** the treacherous friends, **and let them go down quick into hell,** into the realm of death, with a living body as in the case of Korah, Num. 16, 30; **for wickedness is in their dwellings and among them,** within the hearts. This was said without a feeling of personal hatred and vengeance, as a call for the punishment of God upon such as were wicked beyond the hope of correction. V. 16. **As for me,** placing his own person in emphatic opposition to his enemies, **I will call upon God,** in fervent and constant prayer; **and the Lord shall save me,** that being the firm conviction of his faith. V. 17. **Evening and morning and at noon,** the three principal periods of the day usually observed as special times of prayer, **will I pray** and cry aloud, complaining and moaning; **and He shall hear my voice.** V. 18. **He hath delivered my soul in peace from the battle,** or war, **that was against me,** granting him peace and security; **for there were many with me,** rather, "for with many are they against me," a multitude being arrayed against him. V. 19. **God shall hear and afflict them,** hearing their fierce tumult and answering them as the stern Judge, **even He that abideth of old,** the Refuge of the believers from everlasting to everlasting. **Selah. Because they have no changes,** were unwilling to turn from their evil conduct, their treacherous behavior, **therefore they fear not God.** It is such people whom the vengeance of the Lord will strike. V. 20. **He**, the treacherous friend described above, **hath put forth his hands against such as be at peace with him**, profaning the solemn covenant of intimate friendship; **he hath broken his covenant**, that of mutual faithfulness. V. 21. **The words of his mouth were smoother than butter**, with oily hypocrisy, **but war was in his heart; his words were softer than oil**, dripping smoothness and good will, **yet were they drawn swords**, his entire behavior being hypocrisy and deceit. For his own consolation David cries out: v. 22. **Cast thy burden upon the Lord**, the word referring to every believer's lot in life, whatever may be laid upon him according to the gracious will of his heavenly Father, **and He shall sustain thee; He shall never suffer the righteous to be moved**, preventing the believer's sinking to the ground under the burden assigned him. V. 23. **But Thou, O God, shalt bring them**, the false friends, **down into the pit of destruction**, to the pit or depth of the grave, a prey of an unwelcome death; **bloody and deceitful men**, who delight in treachery and violence, **shall not live out half their days**, not live half as long as ordinary conditions would seem to warrant. **But I will trust in Thee**, the believers of all times joining him in this implicit trust in God.

PSALM 56.

Comfort in the Midst of Persecution.

To the chief musician upon Jonath-elem-rechokim, the word not only denoting the melody according to which the hymn was to be sung, "The dove of silence of distant places," but also the subject of the psalm, David being the uncomplaining, meek dove, driven from home to wander in exile, **Michtam**, a poem of epigrams, **of David when the Philistines took him in Gath**, the event being recorded 1 Sam. 21, 10—12. V. 1. **Be merciful unto me, O God; for man would swallow me up**, panting for his soul with greedy desire, with snorts of rage; **he, fighting daily, oppresseth me.** The contrast is that of the majesty of God and the puny might of men. V. 2. **Mine enemies would daily swallow me up**, always lying in wait like beasts of prey; **for they be many that fight against me, O Thou Most High**, rather, "they fight in the pride of their hearts." V. 3. **What time I am afraid**, for there seems to be good reason for fear, **I will trust in Thee**, for in this trust he could successfully overcome his fear. V. 4. **In God I will praise His Word**, since it is according to His promise that believers are delivered from their enemies; **in God I have put my trust**, in His faithfulness and mercy; **I will not fear what flesh can do unto me**, or, more emphatically, "I trust in God, I do not fear; what can flesh," mere man, "do unto me?" Cp. Ps. 91, 1—3. V. 5. **Every day they wrest my words**, vexing his affairs, interfering with their proper care, harming his business; **all their thoughts are against me for evil**, their entire conduct being full of malice. V. 6. **They gather themselves together**, after the manner of cowardly adversaries, **they hide themselves**, to lie in wait, **they mark my steps, when they wait for my soul**, their object being to take his life. V. 7. **Shall they escape by iniquity?** literally, "By iniquity deliverance to them?" Will the ways of wickedness really bring lasting success? **In Thine anger cast down the people, O God**, namely, all the nations opposing Him. V. 8. **Thou tellest my wanderings**, counting how often and how far David had to flee before his enemies; **put Thou my tears into Thy bottle**, carefully measuring and preserving them as a record of his misery; **are they not in Thy book?** calculated and stored in the memory of the Lord. V. 9. **When I cry unto Thee, then shall mine enemies turn back**, the help of God coming with great readiness, at once; **this I know, for God is for me**, that "He is God on his side." V. 10. **In God will I praise His Word; in the Lord will I praise His Word.** V. 11. **In God have I put my trust; I will not be afraid what man can do unto me.** Cp. v. 4. V. 12. **Thy vows are upon me, O God**; he is under obligation to render thanks to the Lord; **I will render praises unto Thee**, as his duty of gratitude dictated. V. 13. **For Thou hast delivered my soul from death**, he already had numerous evidences of God's deliverance in his life; **wilt not Thou deliver my feet from falling that I may walk before God in the light of the living?** Instead of being brought to the realm of death as a result of the plans of the enemies, he knows that he will enjoy the light of God's face in the full enjoyment of the life preserved by the almighty power of the Lord, a foretaste of heavenly joy.

PSALM 57.

The True Confidence of Faith.

To the chief musician, Al-taschith, to be chanted according to the melody "Destroy not," which also referred to the critical circumstances connected with the event which occasioned the writing of the hymn, **Michtam,** a poem of epigrams, **of David when he fled from Saul in the cave,** 1 Sam. 22, 1; 24, 1—4. Its contents may well be used by every believer who finds himself in difficult straits on account of the persecution of his enemies. V. 1. **Be merciful unto me, O God, be merciful unto me,** for it is only the unmerited favor of God to which David appeals; **for my soul trusteth in Thee,** seeking refuge with the Lord alone; **yea, in the shadow of Thy wings,** a figure pointing out, in a most impressive manner, the full security under God's protection, Deut. 32, 11; Ps. 91, 1; Matt. 23, 37, **will I make my refuge, until these calamities,** the mischiefs put in operation by his enemies, **be overpast,** until there is no longer a sign of the ruinous danger threatening his life. V. 2. **I will cry unto God Most High,** the great Ruler of the universe; **unto God, that performeth all things for me,** always accomplishing His purposes for the deliverance of His children. V. 3. **He shall send from heaven,** in an extraordinary form of deliverance, if necessary, **and save me from the reproach of him that would swallow me up,** that is, even while the enemy pants after him in rage, snorting with greed to destroy him, David is sure of the Lord's deliverance. **Selah. God shall send forth His mercy and His truth,** His loving favor according to His faithful promise, as the messengers bringing deliverance, Ps. 25, 10; 36, 5. V. 4. **My soul is among lions,** surrounded by them on all sides, **and I lie even among them that are set on fire,** those greedy with desire for murder, the fact that he is ready to lie down to sleep in the midst of such dangerous circumstances showing the firmness of his trust in God, **even the sons of men, whose teeth are spears and arrows and their tongue a sharp sword,** instruments of destruction. V. 5. **Be Thou exalted, O God, above the heavens,** showing Himself in the sublimity of His majesty; **let Thy glory be above all the earth,** its light promising salvation to His children, but theatening death and destruction to His enemies. V. 6. **They have prepared a net for my steps,** to capture him unawares; **my soul is bowed down,** the enemies having bent it down to the ground with their oppressions; **they have digged a pit before me, into the midst whereof they are fallen themselves,** their sudden and utter overthrow as a result of their own wickedness being emphasized. **Selah.** V. 7. **My heart is fixed, O God,** ready, confident, fearless, **my heart is fixed,** in the certainty of victory; **I will sing and give praise,** both with voice and instrument. V. 8. **Awake up, my glory,** his soul, his whole being should be aroused to the proper frame of mind, to give praise; **awake, psaltery and harp,** or, harp and zither, which he loved to play to the glory of God. **I myself will awake early,** arousing the very dawn in his eagerness to sing praises, urging the sun to rise that he may begin his matin service. V. 9. **I will praise Thee, O Lord, among the people,** not only in his own private devotions, but out in public, where all men could hear his message of deliverance. **I will sing unto Thee among the nations,** going even beyond the bounds of Israel to bring his joyful news to all mankind. V. 10. **For Thy mercy is great unto the heavens,** towering up so high, filling the entire universe, **and Thy truth unto the clouds.** And therefore the psalmist repeats his address of praise: v. 11. **Be Thou exalted, O God, above the heavens; let Thy glory be above all the earth,** the God of Israel, of His Church, the one true God throughout eternity. Such is the spirit of praise which lives in the hearts of all believers.

PSALM 58.

A Cry for Vengeance upon the Subverters of Right.

To the chief musician, Al-taschith, to be sung to the same melody as the preceding psalm, **Michtam,** a poem in epigrammatic form, **of David.** V. 1. **Do ye indeed speak righteousness, O congregation?** He seems to be addressing a council, representatives of the government, princes, asking them whether they are dumb, whether they are unable to speak the truth, whether it is impossible for them to give a right decision. **Do ye judge uprightly, O ye sons of men?** Standing under God and pledged to uphold justice, were they forgetting its obligations? V. 2. **Yea, in heart ye work wickedness; ye weigh the violence of your hands in the earth,** giving decisions which are, in effect. measures of violence, without a show of right. The passage is highly sarcastic, implying that they indeed hold the balances of justice, their duty being to weigh out just awards, but that they abuse their right and substitute violence. V. 3. **The wicked are estranged from the womb,** full of wickedness against God from the very moment of their birth; **they go astray as soon**

as they be born, speaking lies, their character from the first being truly devilish and selfish, apparently incapable of any higher motives. V. 4. **Their poison,** that of their words and actions, **is like the poison of a serpent,** malignant, deadly; **they are like the deaf adder that stoppeth her ear,** one of the most dangerous reptiles of the Orient, intentionally dumb, v. 5. **which will not hearken to the voice of charmers, charming never so wisely,** no matter if the formulas are worded and the charm applied in the most careful manner. The wicked, in other words, are naturally, easily, malignantly, and stubbornly opposed to all that is good. V. 6. **Break their teeth, O God, in their mouth,** those which they use as instruments of violence. Ps. 57, 4; **break out the great teeth of the young lions, O Lord,** of the enemies who desired to take his life, so that they would be rendered harmless. The figure is now again changed. V. 7. **Let them melt away as waters which run continually,** of which not even a trace remains; **when he bendeth his bow to shoot his arrows,** the enemy being thought of as stepping on the bow to bend it and to fix his arrows for shooting, **let them,** all the enemies as represented by this one, **be as cut in pieces,** their arrows having no effect, as though they had their points cut off. V. 8. **As a snail which melteth, let every one of them pass away,** the figure used from the apparent melting away of a snail in slime; **like the untimely birth of a woman,** a miscarriage, **that they may not see the sun.** V. 9. **Before your pots can feel the thorns,** namely, the heat of the burning thorns used as fuel by caravans, **he shall take them away as with a whirlwind,** with a sudden and unexpected destruction, **both living and in his wrath,** literally, whether fresh or burning, that is, whether the meat in the pot at that time be raw or already in a state of roasting, whether their evil plans had but recently been made, or whether they were being carried out, there being a possible reference here to the rebellion of Absalom. V. 10. **The righteous shall rejoice when he seeth the vengeance,** over the fact that God uses the destruction of the wicked for his own deliverance; **he shall wash his feet in the blood of the wicked,** the Lord's slaughter of them being so great that their blood runs in streams, v. 11. **so that a man shall say,** with this bit of evidence before his eyes, **Verily, there is a reward for the righteous,** the Lord granting them this reward in mercy; **verily, He is a God that judgeth in the earth,** there is still a divinity judging on the earth, one higher than all the so-called gods of the heathen. The full revelation of this fact will be brought home to the believers on the Last Day, when the Lord's judgment will be pronounced on all men.

PSALM 59.

Prayer of an Innocent Person against Those who Seek His Soul.

To the chief musician, Al-taschith, again according to the melody "Destroy not," **Michtam,** a poem in epigrammatic form, **of David; when Saul sent, and they watched the house to kill him,** the event being recorded, 1 Sam. 19, 11—18. V. 1. **Deliver me from mine enemies, O my God,** tearing him out of their hands; **defend me from them that rise up against me,** moving him out of their reach, upon a height, to a stronghold. Note the call of trust: *my* God. V. 2. **Deliver me from the workers of iniquity and save me from bloody men,** such as come with murderous design and intent. V. 3. **For, lo, they lie in wait for my soul; the mighty,** those possessing power and influence in the world, **are gathered against me,** banded together for his destruction; **not for my transgression, nor for my sin, O Lord,** David feels himself innocent of any guilt which might have deserved such a persecution. V. 4. **They run and prepare themselves,** setting themselves in readiness to capture him, **without my fault; awake to help me and behold.** Jehovah, who seems asleep at this time of great emergency, is urged to rouse Himself, not to abandon him, but to meet him, as with an army of relief, to convince Himself of the great danger in which David found himself. V. 5. **Thou therefore, O Lord God of hosts,** the Commander of all the heavenly legions, **the God of Israel,** of the congregation of all those who truly believe in Him, **awake to visit all the heathen,** the expression including all the enemies of the kingdom of God; **be not merciful to any wicked transgressors,** namely, as long as they continue in their murderous designs against his life. **Selah.** V. 6. **They,** the particular enemies sent to capture him, **return at evening; they make a noise like a dog,** howling and snarling like the roaming Oriental dogs, the scavengers of their cities, **and go round about the city,** preying upon the dead and even upon the helpless and feeble. V. 7. **Behold, they belch out with their mouth,** as the dogs do with their growling and barking; **swords are in their lips,** Ps. 57, 4; **for who, say they, doth hear?** It is an impertinent challenge, for they believe themselves safe in their wicked undertaking; they ridicule the idea that God's punishment will strike them. V. 8. **But Thou, O Lord, shalt laugh at them,** in mockery and derision over their folly; **Thou shalt have all the heathen,** the enemies of Israel, **in derision,** for their puny efforts in trying to thwart His plans. V. 9. **Because of His strength will I wait upon Thee,** rather, "My Strength, Thee will I regard," confidently expecting his deliverance; **for God is my Defense,** his Stronghold in the midst of his enemies. V. 10. **The God of my mercy shall prevent me,** coming to meet him with the fulness of His grace; **God shall let me see my desire upon mine enemies,** those who were lying in wait to murder him. V. 11. **Slay them not, lest my people forget,** the lesson of their punishment being forgotten with their total removal; **scatter them,** leading them astray, driving them into the wilderness, **by Thy power and bring them down,** humbling them before all people, **O Lord, our Shield.** In this way the fate of the enemies would serve as a continual example of warning. V. 12. **For the sin of their mouth and the words of their lips,** everything they say being sin, blasphemy and slander, **let them even be taken in their pride; and for cursing,** against God, **and lying,** against David, **which they speak.** V. 13. **Consume them in wrath,** after a protracted miserable existence; **consume them, that they may not be, and let them know,** find out conclusively, **that God ruleth in Jacob unto the ends of the earth,** exercising dominion over His spiritual people wherever believers are found, 1 Sam. 17, 46. **Selah.** David, therefore, lifts up the eyes of his spirit and sees the fulfilment of his prayer. V. 14. **And at evening let them return; and let them make a noise like a dog and go round about the city,** v. 6, unable to satisfy their hunger, foiled in their attempts to do harm. V. 15. **Let them wander up and down for meat,** full of disquiet and pain on account of unsatisfied hunger, **and grudge if they be not satisfied,** remaining all night and watching greedily for food which is not forthcoming. V. 16. **But I will sing of Thy power,** contrasting his fate with that of the Lord's enemies; **yea, I will sing aloud of Thy mercy in the morning,** beginning the day with praising God; **for Thou hast been my Defense and Refuge in the day of my trouble.** V. 17. **Unto Thee, O my Strength,** by whose mighty power he had been delivered, **will I sing,** with music on the harp; **for God is my Defense,** his Stronghold and Fortress, **and the God of my mercy,** who furnished so many evidences of His gracious feeling toward David, many more than he deserved. David's praise is taken up by all believers, especially on account of their deliverance from the power of their great enemies, Satan, world, and flesh.

PSALM 60.

A Hymn of War and Victory.

To the chief musician upon Shushan-eduth, to be chanted in public worship according to the melody "The Lily of Testimony," this tune indicating also the contents of the psalm as referring to God's faithfulness in preserving His people and granting the armies of Israel victory, **Michtam of David,** a poem in epigrammatic form, **to teach; when he strove with Aram-naharaim,** that is, with Mesopotamia beyond the Euphrates, **and with Aram-zobah,** the Syria of Zobah, 2 Sam. 10, **when Joab returned and smote of Edom,** whose armies had invaded Canaan from the south, 2 Sam. 8, 13, **in the Valley of Salt,** near the southwestern end of the Dead Sea, **twelve thousand.** David, as king, was commander-in-chief of the armies of Israel, the victory therefore being credited to him, but Joab was the general of the army, and he dispatched his brother Abishai, the commander of this expedition, which, as it seems, slew twelve thousand Edomites in one battle and a total of eighteen thousand in the entire campaign, 2 Sam. 8, 13; 1 Chron. 18, 12. V. 1. **O God, Thou hast cast us off,** this being the conclusion David arrived at from the fact of Edom's invasion; **Thou hast scattered us,** literally, "broken us," that is, overwhelmed, overthrown them by this incursion of the enemies; **Thou hast been displeased,** the visitation having the appearance of an angry punishment on the part of God. **O turn Thyself to us again,** literally, "Give restoration to us," giving evidence once more of His grace and favor. V. 2. **Thou hast made the earth to tremble; Thou hast broken it,** the picture being that of all Canaan upset by an earthquake, to which this visitation was compared. **Heal the breaches thereof,** the losses caused by the enemy's inroads, which were like the rents torn by an earthquake; **for it shaketh,** the entire country resembling a tottering building, in danger of collapse. And still another picture David uses to set forth the plight of stricken Israel. V. 3. **Thou hast showed Thy people hard things,** laid a heavy burden upon them; **Thou hast made us to drink the wine of astonishment,** the wine of His wrath, which is intoxication, said of the commotion, of the internal confusion of spirit and of the bodily weakness, for all this had been brought about by the news of Edom's advance. At the same time, David did not yield to utter despair; he clung to his confidence in the Lord. V. 4. **Thou hast given a banner to them that fear Thee,** to which they could flee, around which they could rally, **that it may be displayed because of the truth,** lifted up to inspire Israel with new courage, so that they would trust in the sustaining power of His almighty hand and rely upon the faithful promises which God had made in His holiness. **Selah.** V. 5. **That Thy beloved,** the children of God's love, the people of Israel, **may be delivered, save with Thy right hand,** the symbol of His almighty power, **and hear me.** The plea having been made, David now continues in a strain of victory, anticipating the joy over the overthrow of the Edomites. V. 6. **God hath spoken in His holiness,** by which He upheld Israel's possession of the Promised Land. **I will rejoice,** exulting in the possession of the complete victory which was sure to come to Israel; **I will divide Shechem,** in the center of the country west of Jordan, as representing Canaan proper, **and mete out the Valley of Succoth,** east of Jordan, his measuring out of the land showing him to be in undisputed possession of it. V. 7. **Gilead is mine and Manasseh is mine,** representing the northeastern section of the country held by the children of Israel; **Ephraim also is the strength of mine head,** his helmet, for this tribe had obtained the right of the first-born, Gen. 48, 5. 19; 1 Chron. 5, 1; **Judah is my lawgiver,** his scepter, for the kings of Judah were of the family of David, the descendant of Judah, and they were the bearers of the Messianic promise, 1 Chron. 5, 2; v. 8. **Moab,** here mentioned by way of contrast, **is my wash-pot,** being obliged to perform the work of a servant in holding a wash-basin for the king; **over Edom will I cast out my shoe,** to indicate that this country was reduced to the rank of a slave; **Philistia, triumph thou because of me,** rather, "cry aloud," as one who has been overcome and is now wailing in anguish and terror. The victory being so certain, the conqueror is eager to start on his victorious march. V. 9. **Who will bring me into the strong city,** the capital of the Idumeans, the renowned fortress Petra? **Who will lead me into Edom?** V. 10. **Wilt not Thou, O God,** to whom he here confidently turns, **which hadst cast us off,** as he had complained in v. 1, **and Thou, O God, which didst not go out with our armies?** by permitting this reversal to strike them. V. 11. **Give us help from trouble,** affording them deliverance from the enemy; **for vain is the help of man,** this conviction being the basis of every trustful prayer. V. 12. **Through God we shall do valiantly,** sure of winning the victory; **for He it is that shall tread down our enemies.** "Israel conquers in God, and God, who is in Israel, will deservedly trample Edom under foot through Israel." (Delitzsch.) That is the nature of a true prayer, that it is certain of the best fulfilment by virtue of God's favor; for God's answer to the prayer of believers always accords with their best interests.

PSALM 61.

A Confident Prayer for Divine Aid.

To the chief musician upon Neginah, with the accompaniment upon stringed instruments, **a psalm of David.** V. 1. **Hear my cry, O God; attend unto my prayer,** the plea being all the more urgent since David at that time, probably on account of the rebellion of Absalom, was cut off from his usual privileges, particularly that of attending worship with the congregation. V. 2. **From the end of the earth,** places remote from the Sanctuary, to which he was now banished, **will I cry unto Thee when my heart is overwhelmed,** literally, "in the covering of my heart," while his heart was enveloped, or clouded, with anxiety and care. **Lead me to the rock that is higher than I,** one inaccessible to him by his own strength, and therefore also to the enemies, where he would be secure under God's protection. V. 3. **For Thou hast been a Shelter for me,** a Refuge in the midst of dangers, **and a strong Tower from the enemy,** affording that absolute safety which only God's power can grant. V. 4. **I will abide in Thy Tabernacle,** satisfied with the privilege of a guest in the tent of God's worship, **forever; I will trust in the covert of Thy wings,** the fine figure of absolute protection and safety again being used, Ps. 91, 1; Deut. 33, 27. **Selah.** V. 5. **For Thou, O God, hast heard my vows,** those connected with his prayer; **Thou hast given me the heritage of those that fear Thy name,** a part in the spiritual blessings of Israel. V. 6. **Thou wilt prolong the king's life,** adding to the days of his own life, **and his years as many generations,** or, "May his years be as generation and generation!" For David sees in spirit the royal line ending in Christ and thus enduring throughout eternity. V. 7. **He shall abide before God forever,** the king enthroned before God's face, enjoying the light of His favor; **O prepare mercy and truth,** Ps. 40, 11; 57, 3, **which may preserve him,** the grace of God, in accordance with His faithful promise, guarding him from his enemies and rebellious subjects. V. 8. **So will I sing praise unto Thy name forever,** extolling the essence of God and all His divine attributes and making them known by the proclamation of His Word, **that I may daily perform my vows,** the measure of his thanksgiving being the same as that of his prayers to the Lord. We Christians know how this prayer of David was heard, namely, that God preserved the throne of David through the darkness of many centuries, until the true light and salvation came in the person of Jesus Christ.

PSALM 62.

Trust in God in the Face of Great Danger.

To the chief musician, to Jeduthun, the special choirmaster being named who should take charge of this hymn for use in public worship, **a psalm of David,** apparently composed also during the period of great spiritual distress at the time of Absalom's rebellion. V. 1. **Truly my soul waiteth upon God,** literally, "Only silent submission to God my soul," that is, in the midst of the difficulties besetting him he rested in the promises of God, keeping down every murmur of dissatisfaction in his heart; **from Him cometh my salvation,** his deliverance from every danger. V. 2. **He only is my Rock and my Salvation,** a stronger expression than in v. 1, denoting the truth that, God being his, he already possesses deliverance from every evil, the certainty of salvation through His promises, wherefore he could stand immovably firm; **He is my Defense,** his high place of refuge, Ps. 9, 9; 18, 2; 59, 9. 17; **I shall not be greatly moved,** not be shaken much or totter greatly, at least not to the extent of being thrown to the ground. V. 3. **How long will ye imagine mischief against a man?** rushing, raving, storming upon him with lifted fist, in order to browbeat him. **Ye shall be slain, all of you,** rather, all of you break him down; **as a bowing wall shall ye be and as a tottering fence.** The reference is to him whom they wish to ruin, believing him to be like a wall inclined, like a fence overthrown. It is a fitting picture of the activity displayed by the enemies in trying to destroy David and all believers. V. 4. **They only consult to cast him down from his excellency,** to deprive him of his elevated office to which God had raised him; **they delight in lies,** the chief weapon of all detractors; **they bless with their mouth,** after the manner of hypocrites the world over, **but they curse inwardly,** counting upon their duplicity to carry the day for them. **Selah.** There is only one thing for the believer to do in such straits. V. 5. **My soul, wait thou only upon God,** being silent in submission to His will, the same figure of cheerful resignation being employed as in v. 1; **for my expectation is from Him,** in Him he hoped, knowing that His were thoughts only of good and not of evil. V. 6. **He only is my Rock and my Salvation,** the thought of v. 2. being repeated with emphasis; **He is my Defense; I shall not be moved,** his confidence being increased to the point where he knew himself to be altogether safe in the keeping of the Lord. V. 7. **In God is my salvation,** in God alone it rested, upon Him alone it depended, **and my glory,** he was fully satisfied if only God accepted him, this being of greater value than all approbation and praise of mere men; **the rock of my strength,** his very strongest support, **and my refuge is in God,** his faith being like an anchor which held so firmly in the rock-bottom of God's almighty power that he knew no one could harm him. Therefore he also admonishes the believers of all times to join him in this confidence of faith. V. 8. **Trust in Him at all times, ye people,** this cry being so general that it seems addressed to all men; **pour out your heart before him,** a strong figure for bringing all anxieties and troubles to His attention in prayer; **God is a Refuge for us. Selah.** V. 9. **Surely men of low degree,** all the ordinary sons of Adam, **are vanity,** a mere breath as compared with His almighty power, **and men of high degree,** the sons of those who are considered nobles on the earth, **are a lie,** a fraud, nothing real, **to be laid in the balance,** ascending up in the balances, without weight or value; **they are altogether lighter than vanity,** according to the standard of real worth they had nothing to commend them in the sight of God. Cp. Ps. 39, 5. Therefore he addresses a concluding warning to men in general. V. 10. **Trust not in oppression,** by which men of might hoped to enrich themselves, **and become not vain in robbery,** placing a foolish confidence in the results of small and great speculations; **if riches increase,** even by lawful gain, **set not your heart upon them,** clinging to them with a trust which belongs to God alone. V. 11. **God hath spoken once; twice have I heard this,** the number being used in order to give emphasis to his declaration, **that power belongeth unto God,** with God is almighty power, He is the only One who possesses it absolutely, man's ideas in this respect being a fatuous delusion. V. 12. **Also unto Thee, O Lord, belongeth mercy,** with God is grace, a fact which relieves the idea of His almighty power; **for Thou renderest to every man according to his work,** by His power He can show both mercy and justice. He who opposes the will of the almighty Lord will feel the power of His anger; he who submits to the will of the Lord will experience the power of His grace, through the Word. Cp. Rom. 2, 6—11; John 5, 29.

PSALM 63.

Morning Hymn of a Fugitive.

A psalm of David when he was in the wilderness of Judah, very likely at the time when he left Jerusalem at the approach of Absalom, for it was then that he spent a few days in the wilderness on the west side of the Dead Sea, a prey of the troubled anxiety which sapped his strength, 2 Sam. 15—17. V. 1. **O God, Thou art my God,** the psalm opening with a mighty word of personal faith;

early will I seek Thee, that is, earnestly, solicitously, at the rising of the dawn. **My soul thirsteth for Thee**, Ps. 42, 1, **my flesh longeth for Thee**, languishing with desire, **in a dry and thirsty land**, which made him weary, all his present circumstances filling him with a languid disgust, **where no water is**, for the desert aspect of the country increased his feeling of forsakenness, v. 2. **to see Thy power and Thy glory, so as I have seen Thee in the Sanctuary**, literally, "Thus have I in the Sanctuary looked for Thee to see Thy power and Thy glory." That had been the psalmist's custom in the past; that is what he missed so greatly at the present time. V. 3. **Because Thy loving-kindness is better than life**, that explained his longing, that the grace of God exceeded all this earthly life could offer, **my lips shall praise Thee**, extolling the grace which he had experienced in his whole life. V. 4. **Thus will I bless Thee while I live**, with the true gratitude of a believing heart; **I will lift up my hands in Thy name**, in the gesture of earnest supplication. V. 5. **My soul shall be satisfied as with marrow and fatness**, an image borrowed from a rich and splendid banquet, to show the possession of the most wonderful spiritual riches, **and my mouth shall praise Thee with joyful lips**, v. 6. **when I remember Thee upon my bed**, considering all the manifold evidences of God's favor as they showed in his whole life, **and meditate on Thee in the night-watches**, in earnest and prayerful meditation during the entire night. V. 7. **Because Thou hast been my Help**, coming to his assistance and rescue time and again, **therefore in the shadow of Thy wings will I rejoice**, the remembrance of God's mercy experienced in the past encouraging him to look with joy and confidence into the future. V. 8. **My soul followeth hard after Thee**, cleaving to Him as the one Helper in all the wide world; **Thy right hand upholdeth me**, lending just the right assistance to the psalmist to keep him from falling. V. 9. **But those that seek my soul to destroy it**, rather, "they" (emphatically) "to their own destruction shall seek my soul," that is, in trying to bring misfortune to David, they would fall a prey to their own designs, **shall go into the lower parts of the earth**, into the abysses of the earth, that is, to death and the grave. V. 10. **They shall fall by the sword**, whose hand or edge would dispose of them quickly; **they shall be a portion for foxes**, a prey of jackals, the wilderness scavengers of the Orient. V. 11. **But the king**, who was now being persecuted, **shall rejoice in God**, in the certain deliverance effected by Him; **every one that sweareth by Him**, with firm trust in His willingness and ability to help, **shall glory**, finally having occasion to boast of His deliverance; **but the mouth of them that speak lies**, the foes guilty of base treachery, **shall be stopped**, put to silence in death. Thus the trust of the believers is bound to be rewarded, since the God of their salvation has promised them the mighty deliverance of His arm. No matter what the present may offer, the future is safe, because it is in God's hands.

PSALM 64.

Invocation of God against the Deceit of Men.

To the chief musician, a psalm of David, composed at one of the periods of his life when he was annoyed above the ordinary by the trickery of men who professed to be his friends, but secretly sought to do him harm. V. 1. **Hear my voice, O God, in my prayer**, in his lamentation, in words of pain; **preserve my life from fear of the enemy**, from the danger producing this terror and from its evil effects upon his body and life. V. 2. **Hide me from the secret counsel of the wicked**, for that is the manner of the wicked, to conspire in secret, to form alliances of which no one knows anything, instead of fighting in the open; **from the insurrection of the workers of iniquity**, the noisy crowd of evil-doers, for, having perfected their secret counsels, they suddenly attack, trusting that they will be aided by the element of surprise in gaining their end; v. 3. **who whet their tongue like a sword**, to cut the reputation of the believers to pieces, **and bend their bows to shoot their arrows, even bitter words**, for these are like arrows wounding to death, v. 4. **that they may shoot in secret at the perfect**, those innocent of the charges made against them by the wicked; **suddenly do they shoot at him and fear not**, refusing to regard God, stifling the voice of their conscience. V. 5. **They encourage themselves in an evil matter**, using every means to secure their wicked object; **they commune of laying snares privily**, carefully going over each part of their plans to make them successful. **They say, Who shall see them?** foolishly believing that their secret scheming is not known to the Lord. V. 6. **They search out iniquities**, inventing, planning, evil acts; **they accomplish a diligent search**, completing the plan which they have conceived. **Both the inward thought of every one of them and the heart is deep**, literally, "and the inward part of a man and his heart is deep," the workshop of evil, the place where all the wicked designs are worked out, is hidden from the eyes of men like an abyss of dark mystery and brooding wickedness. While, however, they flatter themselves that their scheming is hidden from the eyes of men, the Lord knows their every thought. V. 7. **But God shall shoot at them with an arrow,** using a weapon like theirs, but with terrible effect; **suddenly shall they be wounded,** their wounds coming upon them before they are aware of it. V. 8. **So they shall make their own tongue to fall upon themselves,** they are made to fall, their own tongue overcomes them, the organ of their bodies with which they sought to harm others becomes the instrument bringing on the judgment to their own ruin; **all that see them shall flee away,** their partners in evil being terrified and others shaking their heads in a gesture indicating their mocking contempt of the wicked. V. 9. **And all men,** with this evidence of God's avenging justice before their eyes, **shall fear and shall declare the work of God,** understanding the punishment of the wicked as the act of God and no longer foolishly regarding it as a misfortune due to chance; **for they shall wisely consider of his doing,** noting cause and effect with a feeling of awe. V. 10. **The righteous shall be glad in the Lord,** happy in the knowledge that their trust is safe, **and shall trust in Him,** seek refuge in Him; **and all the upright in heart shall glory,** knowing that the shelter and protection of God's almighty hand are theirs. Every believer may make this fact his proud boast, especially for the purpose of encouraging his own heart over against the enmity of the children of the world.

PSALM 65.

Thanksgiving for the Blessings of the Lord.

To the chief musician, for performance in public worship, **a psalm and song of David,** composed for the purpose of praising God for His spiritual blessings upon His people and His kind providence over all the earth. V. 1. **Praise waiteth for Thee, O God, in Sion,** literally, "To Thee is silent resignation as praise," that is, the calm submission of the believer's heart is its tribute to the Lord, by which He is praised and exalted; **and unto Thee shall the vow be performed,** paid in recognition of His hearing prayer; for thereby the fellowship between God and the faithful was further established and strengthened. V. 2. **O Thou that hearest prayer,** this being the special attribute of God, **unto Thee shall all flesh come,** all creatures, but especially the believers, taking their refuge with Him, with a firm trust in His ability and in His willingness to help. V. 3. **Iniquities prevail against me,** cases or varieties of iniquity have overcome him as with a superior hostile power. **As for our transgressions,** the great burden of which belongs to the crosses of the believers, **Thou shalt purge them away,** freeing them from their burden and atoning for their guilt. It is here once more clearly stated that man cannot answer or atone for his sins; he must, in himself, perish under their burden; the forgiveness of God alone can lift the burden. V. 4. **Blessed is the man whom Thou choosest and causest to approach unto Thee that he may dwell in Thy courts.** It is a wonderful distinction to be chosen by God, to have one's true home and to be at home where He is enthroned and reveals Himself in His Word. **We shall be satisfied with the goodness of Thy house, even of Thy holy Temple,** having the unequaled, inestimable advantage of constant fellowship with God in the place of His worship. If that was true in the Old Testament, at the time of prophecy and type, how much more is it true now that we have the glory of the fulfilment before our eyes! V. 5. **By terrible things in righteousness wilt Thou answer us, O God of our salvation,** the awe-inspiring things being chiefly the mighty deeds and miracles of God in leading His people out of the bondage of Egypt, thereby answering the prayer of those who cried to Him; **who art the Confidence of all the ends of the earth and of them that are afar off upon the sea,** all the dwellers even in the most distant coasts and islands looking to Him for the benefits pertaining to this earthly life; v. 6. **which by His strength setteth fast the mountains, being girded with power,** He, as the true Master Workman, laying their foundation secure, for He brought them forth by His almighty power; v. 7. **which stilleth the noise of the seas,** its roaring when lashed by mighty storms, cp. Matt. 8, 26, **the noise of their waves, and the tumult of the people,** the passions of men, like the unbridled powers of nature also yielding to His almighty word. V. 8. **They also that dwell in the uttermost parts are afraid of Thy tokens,** the exhibitions of God's power, His mighty miracles, causing the dwellers of the distant coasts to tremble before Him. **Thou makest the outgoings of the morning and evening to rejoice,** the very ends of the earth with their inhabitants being filled with exuberant joy when the Lord stills the noise of wars. V. 9. **Thou visitest the earth and waterest it;** God's providential care is so obvious that He clearly attends to the wants of the land, arranges for its welfare, and moistens it with rain; **Thou greatly enrichest it with the river of God,** His rain being the brook of blessings referred to, **which is full of water,** richly supplied by the bounty of the Creator; **Thou preparest them corn,** the grain of all dwellers on the earth, **when Thou hast so provided for it,** so He prepares it, taking care of the crops and supplying plentiful harvests, God's provident care being evident throughout. V. 10. **Thou waterest the ridges thereof abundantly,** drenching the furrows of the land, as they have been prepared by the plow; **Thou settlest the furrows thereof,** packing down the ground around the seed; **Thou makest it soft with showers,** loosening the soil with copious rains; **Thou blessest the springing thereof,** the increase of the ground, the maturing crops. V. 11. **Thou crownest the year with Thy goodness,** the favor of His kind providence resting upon the year like a diadem or crown; **and Thy paths drop fatness,** that is, fruitfulness in overabundance follows the footsteps of the Lord or the track of His chariot. V. 12. **They drop upon the pastures of the wilderness,** that is, the very pastures of the steppe, the untilled meadow-lands, show rich fruitfulness; **and the little hills rejoice on every side,** girding themselves with joyfulness as with a garment. V. 13. **The pastures,** naked and sad without the providential care of God, **are clothed with flocks,** due to His goodness; **the valleys also are covered over with corn,** a rich stand of grain being in evidence everywhere; **they shout for joy, they also sing,** all men who realize the miracles of God's providence are constrained to shout with the exuberance of joy, to fill the earth with their songs of praise. Such are the blessings of peace and prosperity under the providence of the Lord.

PSALM 66.

Thanksgiving for the Miracles of God's Deliverance.

To the chief musician, for use in liturgical worship, **a song or psalm,** the name of the inspired poet not being mentioned. V. 1. **Make a joyful noise unto God, all ye lands,** the call being so general as to include all the inhabitants of the world. V. 2. **Sing forth the honor of His name,** exalting Him for the revelation of His essence and attributes; **make His praise glorious,** recognizing His majesty, giving honor to His renown, in order to spread His praise. V. 3. **Say unto God, How terrible,** to be regarded with awe and fear, **art Thou in Thy works!** Cp. Rev. 15, 3. 4. **Through the greatness of Thy power shall Thine enemies submit themselves unto Thee,** they fawn before Him with an unwilling, constrained, feigned homage, but are obliged, nevertheless, to submit. V. 4. **All the earth shall worship Thee,** the idea of the universal spread of the kingdom of God being in full accordance with the dispensation of God in all ages of the world, **and shall sing unto Thee,** accepting Him in adoring worship; **they shall sing to Thy name,** extolling the glory of God's essence and attributes. **Selah.** V. 5. **Come and see the works of God,** the invitation being extended to all men to convince themselves from facts illustrated in Israel's history; **He is terrible,** demanding awe and reverence, **in His doing toward the children of men.** V. 6. **He turned the sea into dry land,** the reference being to the miraculous drying up of the Red Sea, Ex. 14, 21; **they went through the flood on foot,** walking through the dry bed of the Jordan, whose waters were held back by God's power, Josh. 3, 17. **There did we rejoice in Him,** the whole congregation praising God with joy for these manifestations of His almighty favor. A conclusion is now drawn concerning the government of God at all times. V. 7. **He ruleth by His power forever,** His government being of everlasting duration; **His eyes behold the nations,** keeping watch over the affairs of all people in the world. **Let not the rebellious exalt themselves,** raising their heads in pride, with the notion that there is no one to see their wickedness or to punish it as it deserves. **Selah.** Once more the invitation of the believers rings out: v. 8. **O bless our God, ye people, and make the voice of His praise to be heard,** the need of an open confession of faith must never be forgotten; v. 9. **which holdeth our soul in life,** placing it out of the reach of danger, in the sphere of life, to enjoy its fulness in communion with God, **and suffereth not our feet to be moved,** to totter and stumble in a dangerous fall. V. 10. **For Thou, O God, hast proved us,** as an assayer tests ore for precious metals; **Thou hast tried us as silver is tried,** casting them, as it were, into a smelting furnace or pot, to remove all the dross adhering to them by sufferings directed by Him. V. 11. **Thou broughtest us into the net,** into an enclosed tower, into great straits; **Thou laidst affliction upon our loins,** the muscles of this part of the body coming into consideration in the carrying of heavy burdens. V. 12. **Thou hast caused men to ride over our heads,** in a subjugation with disgraceful treatment; **we went through fire and through water,** into perils of death in their most extreme forms, so that calamity seemed about to consume and overwhelm them; **but Thou broughtest us out into a wealthy place,** to the richest abundance of a blessed prosperity, thereby more than compensating them for the dangers to which they were submitted. An individual believer now takes up the strain of the psalm. V. 13. **I will go into Thy house with burnt offerings,** to make a sacrifice for the expiation of sins; **I will pay Thee my vows,** such gifts serving to bring about a closer fellowship between the believers and the covenant God, v. 14. **which my lips have uttered,** with a quick opening, due to the great extremity in which he found himself, **and my mouth hath spoken when I was in trouble,** the believer, under the stress of his difficulties, making a vow to the Lord to perform certain things if he were but delivered from the present emergency. V. 15. **I will offer unto Thee burnt sacrifices of fatlings,** lambs and bullocks, the chief animals of Old Testament sacrifice, **with the incense of rams,** as a free-will offering accompanying the burnt sacrifice; **I will offer bullocks with goats,** here again both classes of offerings being named side by side. **Selah.** V. 16. **Come and hear, all ye that fear God,** the believers of all times and in all places being addressed, **and I will declare what He hath done for my soul,** what the speaker had experienced in the form of spiritual blessings. V. 17. **I cried unto Him with my mouth,** with loud and urgent supplication, **and He was extolled with my tongue,** a hymn of praise being under his tongue in readiness for the deliverance of whose coming he felt sure. V. 18. **If I regard iniquity in my heart,** if he had knowingly been guilty of a transgression, **the Lord will not hear me;** for conscious and deliberate sinning cuts off the sinner from the communion with God; it is impossible for one burdened with such a feeling of guilt to pray in a manner acceptable to the Lord; v. 19. **but, verily, God hath heard me,** thus showing that the line of communication had not been broken by deliberate and wilful transgressions; **He hath attended to the voice of my prayer,** in mercifully granting his request. V. 20. **Blessed be God, which hath not turned away my prayer,** by rejecting it, by letting it pass by unheeded, **nor His mercy from me,** for the fulfilling of his petitions was due altogether and alone to the unmerited fatherly favor of the Lord. Christians must always be conscious of the fact that it is nothing but grace and mercy on the part of God which upholds them throughout their life. This serves to make their prayer confident.

PSALM 67.

A Psalm of Praise for the Conversion of the Gentiles.

To the chief musician on Neginoth, to be rendered in public services with the accompaniment of stringed instruments, **a psalm or song,** the inspired author himself not being known. V. 1. **God be merciful unto us,** looking upon the suppliants with grace and favor, **and bless us,** He, the only Giver of every good and every perfect gift, **and cause His face to shine upon us,** showing them the fulness of His favor, granting them His guiding presence, Num. 6, 25, **Selah;** v. 2. **that Thy way may be known upon earth,** the manner in which the Lord conducted Himself, especially with regard to the salvation of His people, **Thy saving health among all nations,** that is, the salvation as revealed to men in the Word of the Gospel. The prayer of the psalmist is that God would find ways and means to spread the glorious news of salvation to all mankind, that the message of Christ, the Messiah, be made known among the Gentiles everywhere. V. 3. **Let the people,** the nations throughout the earth, **praise Thee, O God; let all the people praise Thee.** V. 4. **O let the nations be glad and sing for joy,** with an exultation caused by the glorious knowledge of salvation; **for Thou shalt judge the people righteously,** the judging in this case being done according to His merciful and mild rule, with reference to the righteousness of the Messiah, revealed in the Gospel and accepted by faith, **and govern the nations upon earth,** in His wonderful Kingdom of Grace. **Selah.** V. 5. **Let the people praise Thee, O God; let all the people praise Thee,** having accepted Him as their Lord and Savior. V. 6. **Then shall the earth yield her increase,** it has, in fact, brought forth its fruit, in the person of the Redeemer with the fulness of His salvation, communicated to men by His gracious rule; **and God, even our own God,** truly ours by virtue of the fact that we are His children by faith in Christ Jesus, **shall bless us,** with all wonderful spiritual blessings in heavenly places in our Savior. V. 7. **God shall bless us, and all the ends of the earth,** all the inhabitants of the world, **shall fear Him,** regard Him with reverent awe as the mighty Author of salvation. It is a wonderful picture of missionary endeavor and success which is here drawn, full of encouragement and inspiration to all believers.

PSALM 68.

Of the Messiah's Exaltation.

To the chief musician, a psalm or song of David, the event which was the immediate cause for writing this powerful hymn, according to most commentators, being the placing of the Ark of the Covenant in the tent of David on Mount Zion, 2 Sam. 6, the general thought of the psalm being the celebration of God's entrance into His Sanctuary on Zion and His rule over the whole world. But the entire psalm is typical of the Messianic victories, certain sections being even directly prophetic, as Paul shows, Eph. 4, 8. References to contemporary history only are both forced and feeble. While it is true that the opening words of the psalm echo an exclamation from the early history of Israel, yet the expansion of the fundamental thought shows that a glorious victory of the Lord Jehovah over all His enemies and the establishment of His Kingdom of Grace is the fact which the inspired singer celebrates. Add to this the fact that the Lord is represented as blessing His people, as imparting spiritual benefits also to the heathen, a standing characteristic of Messianic prophecy, and the trend of the psalm must be admitted without question.

THE VICTORIES OF JEHOVAH. — V. 1. **Let God arise, let His enemies be scattered,** the ancient exclamation which signaled the departure of the Ark of the Covenant from a camp in the wilderness, Num. 10, 35, the prayer receiving its real significance in the application of its contents to the mighty leadership of Jehovah in the New Testament; **let them also that hate Him flee before Him,** as His countenance is directed against them in anger. V. 2. **As smoke is driven away,** vanishing into nothing, **so drive them away; as wax melteth before the fire, so let the wicked perish at the presence of God,** the very strongest pictures of human weakness and puny evanescence being used to show their helplessness before the face of the Lord. V. 3. **But let the righteous be glad,** since they, clothed with the righteousness of God, have every reason to rejoice before Him always; **let them rejoice before God,** since they can freely stand before His face by virtue of the redemption of Christ; **yea, let them exceedingly rejoice.** Note the heaping of synonymous expressions to indicate the exceeding exuberance of the happiness of faith. V. 4. **Sing unto God, sing praises to His name,** extolling His divine essence and attributes, as revealed in His Word; **extol Him that rideth upon the heavens,** rather, cast up a road for Him who driveth along through the steppes, the picture being taken from the custom of Oriental monarchs to have all obstructions removed from the route which they intended to follow, the filling up of low places being included in such preparations, **by His name JAH,** His name is Jehovah, for by this name He reveals Himself as the God of salvation, who manifests the power of His mercy toward all those who accept Him in faith, **and rejoice before Him,** since this name is for His people of all times a source of the greatest happiness. V. 5. **A Father of the fatherless,** taking care of orphans as their true Father, **and a Judge of the widows,** the mighty Advocate of those who have lost their natural protector on earth, **is God in His holy habitation,** both His holy justice and His almighty power coming into consideration in their defense. V. 6. **God setteth the solitary in families,** the forsaken will have a home given to them, Is. 58, 7; **He bringeth out those which are bound with chains,** liberating those who are bound, both expressions finding their fulfilment in the miraculous effect of the Gospel proclamation on the hearts of men, Is. 49, 8—10; 61, 1—3; Luke 4, 21. **But the rebellious dwell in a dry land,** where the parching heat of the sun torments them, where they are far from the land which is made fruitful by the waters of God's grace. The poet now refers to some examples of the miraculous leading of God, in order to emphasize His mercy toward His people in the Messianic period. V. 7. **O God, when Thou wentest forth before Thy people,** in the pillar of fire, when He led them through the wilderness, **when Thou didst march through the wilderness; Selah:** v. 8. **the earth shook,** in a mighty earthquake, **the heavens also dropped at the presence of God,** their heavy storm-clouds coming down to rest upon the mountain; **even Sinai itself was moved at the presence of God, the God of Israel,** Ex. 19, 16—19. The name "God of Israel" is most fitting in this connection, for from the event at Sinai dates the position of Israel as the covenant people. V. 9. **Thou, O God, didst send a plentiful rain,** said of the rich bestowal of spiritual gifts as experienced by Israel, the covenant nation, **whereby Thou didst confirm Thine inheritance when it was weary,** reviving them when they were parched with thirst, even as the mercy of God in the Gospel sustains the languishing at all times. V. 10. **Thy congregation hath dwelt therein,** in the inheritance, in the Land of Promise, like a herd of sheep under the gentle leadership of a good shepherd; **Thou, O God, hast prepared of Thy goodness for the poor,** as a Host liberal with His spiritual gifts and blessings toward the needy of the earth. V. 11. **The Lord gave the word,** that of authority, with which He intended to come to the aid of His people, the Word of Salvation. **Great was the company of those that published it,** the reference being to the choruses of women who usually celebrated the victories of Israel, Ex. 15, 20. 21; Judg. 11, 34. Even so in our days the victories of the Cross are celebrated in hymns sung by man and woman, young and old, all Christians joining in the choruses of thanksgiving in honor of the great blessings of God. V. 12. **Kings of armies,** hosts being mentioned in ironical contrast to Jehovah Sabaoth, **did flee apace,** in utter rout; **and she that tarried at home,** the woman in the tent, the mistress of the house, in this case the congregation, the Church of Christ, **divided the spoil,** dealing out richly to all her children the gifts of God's mercy, as assured by Messiah's victory. V. 13. **Though**

ye have lien among the pots, yet shall ye be as the wings of a dove covered with silver and her feathers with yellow gold, literally, "If you are encamped between cattle-pens, the wings of the dove are covered with silver, and her pinions with iridescent sheen of gold"; that is, the period of the Messiah is one of great spiritual prosperity, combined with a peaceful enjoyment of God's blessings, the riches granted by the Gospel being compared with the wonderful play of colors on the feathers of the dove as she preens them in the sun. V. 14. **When the Almighty scattered kings in it,** dispersing the attacking hosts of princes, **it was white as snow in Salmon,** the agreeable whiteness of the snow on the dark mountain picturing the relief which comes to the spiritual Israel with the victory over the enemies. V. 15. **The hill of God,** the abode of His Church, **is as the hill of Bashan; an high hill,** a mount full of peaks, **as the hill of Bashan.** V. 16. **Why leap ye, ye high hills?** the other many-peaked mountains looking with envy upon this abode of the Lord and His Church. **This is the hill which God desireth to dwell in; yea, the Lord will dwell in it forever,** and all the powers of darkness will not be able to overthrow the spiritual Zion. V. 17. **The chariots of God are twenty thousand,** many myriads, **even thousands of angels,** the innumerable hosts of the angels of God; **the Lord is among them, as in Sinai, in the Holy Place,** Deut. 33, 2. Thus the victorious might of Jehovah is set forth over against all the puny power of the kings of hosts, whose efforts to overthrow the Church of God are invariably frustrated, Matt. 16, 18.

THE EXALTATION AND REIGN OF MESSIAH. — V. 18. **Thou hast ascended on high,** to the height, referred by Paul to the ascension of Christ, Eph. 4, 8; for the Champion of His Church, having overcome all His enemies, now gives visible evidence of His victory by ascending in triumph to heaven; **Thou hast led captivity captive,** Satan and his hosts, who formerly held all mankind captive, now himself being bound with everlasting chains of darkness. **Thou hast received gifts for men,** among men, consisting of men, the reference being to the fact that the exalted Christ has chosen certain members of the human race as His own, men who are now subject to Him in the obedience of faith; **yea, for the rebellious also,** for even such as were formerly rebellious, unwilling to submit to the gentle rule of Messiah, are finally overcome by His mercy, **that the Lord God might dwell among them,** establishing His Church among the Gentiles also. For this establishment of the Messianic kingdom the psalmist now gives praise. V. 19. **Blessed be the Lord, who daily loadeth us with benefits, even the God of our salvation,** or, "Are we burdened, He, God, is our Help, He burdens Himself for us," thus helping us to bear the load which often seems too heavy for us. **Selah.** V. 20. **He that is our God,** again the language of trusting faith, **is the God of salvation,** of the many acts of deliverance which we experience in our lives; **and unto God the Lord belong the issues from death,** He has outlets, ways of escape, from death, He alone is able to rescue us from eternal death and to grant us the gift of eternal life; that is the privilege, the wonderful, mighty prerogative, of the exalted Christ. V. 21. **But God shall wound the head of His enemies,** break it to pieces, utterly destroy them, **and the hairy scalp of such an one as goeth on still in his trespasses,** whose defiant wildness refuses to bow to the authority of God. V. 22. **The Lord said, I will bring again from Bashan,** the wild fastnesses of the mountainous region east of Jordan, **I will bring My people,** rather, "the enemies," **again from the depths of the sea;** for whether they were hiding in the mountain forests or in the abysses of the Salt Sea, the Lord would search them out to mete out judgment to them; v. 23. **that thy foot,** that of the Church personified as one individual, **may be dipped in the blood of thine enemies,** which would flow copiously as the Lord struck them down in punishment, **and the tongue of thy dogs in the same,** the picture being taken from Oriental conditions, where the dogs licked up the blood of the slain, 1 Kings 22, 38. V. 24. **They,** the members of the Church of God, **have seen Thy goings, O God,** His triumphal march; **even the goings of my God, my King, in the Sanctuary,** as His procession moves on in holiness. V. 25. **The singers went before,** leading the triumphal procession, **the players on instruments followed after; among them were the damsels,** the virgins, **playing with timbrels,** moving along on either side, their hymns proclaiming the victory of the Messiah. V. 26. **Bless ye God in the congregations,** wherever the believers meet for worship, **even the Lord, from the fountain of Israel,** all the spiritual descendants of Abraham. V. 27. **There is little Benjamin with their ruler,** the conqueror of the enemies mentioned before, **the princes of Judah and their council,** the band of the leaders in Israel, **the princes of Zebulon, and the princes of Naphtali,** apparently a motley crowd, a great mass, but all united in the praise of the exalted Messiah; for in the spiritual Israel the high and the lowly, the rich and the poor, unite their voices in exalting the Lord, their King. V. 28. **Thy God hath commanded Thy strength,** giving to the Messiah, the exalted Christ, unlimited authority in His kingdom. **Strengthen, O God, that which Thou hast wrought for us,** so that His Church may have the benefit of His achievements. V. 29. **Because of Thy Temple at**

Jerusalem shall kings bring presents unto Thee, pledging the Messiah their obedience and allegiance, the prophet here looking forward to the spread of the Messianic kingdom among the Gentiles. V. 30. **Rebuke the company of spearmen,** the beast of the reed, the alligator, used as a symbol of Egypt and all heathendom, **the multitude of the bulls, with the calves of the people,** the entire hosts of enemy forces everywhere, **till every one submit himself with pieces of silver,** bringing tribute to the Messiah, unwilling though it may be, Phil. 2, 9—11. **Scatter Thou the people that delight in war,** their object being to make war on the Church. V. 31. **Princes shall come out of Egypt,** magnates submitting themselves to the rule of the Messiah. **Ethiopia shall soon stretch out her hands unto God,** offering tribute to the King of grace. V. 32. **Sing unto God, ye kingdoms of the earth; O sing praises unto the Lord,** the All-powerful, **Selah,** all nations giving Him the honor due His mighty name; v. 33. **to Him that rideth upon the heavens of heavens, which were of old,** the primeval or ancient heaven being thought of as the seat of God's majesty. **Lo, He doth send out His voice, and that a mighty voice,** sounding in a revelation of His almighty power. V. 34. **Ascribe ye strength unto God,** acknowledging the exalted Messiah as the almighty Ruler; **His excellency is over Israel,** the glory of His mercy upon His Church, **and His strength is in the clouds,** far above and beyond any possible interference on the part of puny men. V. 35. **O God, Thou art terrible out of Thy holy places,** to be regarded with fear and reverence; **the God of Israel is He that giveth strength and power unto His people,** to the assembly of believers in Him, to His Church on earth. **Blessed be God,** all glory due to Him alone for the marvelous revelation of the meaning and the fruit of Christ's exaltation. It is the Son of Man, elevated to the right hand of the eternal Father, to whom the Church, consisting of members both of Jew and Gentile nations, gives praise and glory as the eternal King of grace and glory.

PSALM 69.

The Messiah's Vicarious Suffering.

To the chief musician, for use in the public assembly of the congregation, **upon Shoshannim,** to be sung to the melody "On the Lilies." The psalm is referred to seven times in the New Testament, either by quotation or by unmistakable implication, as prophetical of Christ and the Messianic period. Cp. John 15, 25; 2, 17; Matt. 27, 34; John 19, 29.

LAMENT AND PRAYER. — V. 1. **Save Me, O God; for the waters are come in unto My soul,** the Messiah crying in the agony and distress, in the anguish of His sufferings, their flood threatening His very life. V. 2. **I sink in deep mire,** into the abyss of a swamp's sink-hole, **where there is no standing,** where He has lost His foothold; **I am come into deep waters, where the floods overflow Me,** overwhelming and submerging Him. V. 3. **I am weary of My crying,** with His calling for sympathy and help in His great trouble; **My throat is dried,** burned or scorched, parched and raw, by the excessive use of His voice; **Mine eyes fail while I wait for My God,** melting in tears, His eyes have become exhausted, worn out with straining in the unfulfilled hoping and longing for rescue at the hands of God. The Messiah now pictures the nature of His misery, the reason for His bitter complaint. V. 4. **They that hate Me without a cause,** while He is innocent of any wrong-doing, **are more than the hairs of Mine head,** having increased at such a rate that they outnumber the hairs which are commonly considered beyond numbering; **they that would destroy Me,** desiring to cut Him off from the land of the living, **being Mine enemies wrongfully, are mighty,** they make use of falsehood and deceit in trying to gain their object. **Then I restored that which I took not away,** literally, "What not I robbed, then I restored," that is, the Messiah not only alleges His personal innocence and sinlessness with great emphasis, but also states that He is being held to pay, to give compensation for, something which He did not rob, of which He did not despoil those seeking redress. The entire paragraph pictures the climax of Christ's sufferings. Both in Gethsemane and on Calvary the anguish of soul with which He was battling was of a nature exceeding all human experience and understanding. All His calling at that time availed Him nothing; He was obliged to drink the cup of God's wrath to the very dregs. His enemies, operating with the meanest falsehoods, set upon Him without reason, to take His life. But the supreme secret is found in the fact that He was called upon to replace, by means of this suffering, what He had not robbed. He bore the punishment of the sins of mankind; the guilt of transgressions as committed by countless human beings was charged to His account. It was a vicarious suffering which Jesus Christ endured, a vicarious satisfaction which He was called upon to render. God made Him to be sin for us who knew no sin, that we might be made the righteousness of God in Him, 2 Cor. 5, 21. It is as the Substitute of mankind that the Messiah now laments. V. 5. **O God, Thou knowest My foolishness,** the folly of the trespasses which

He here ascribes to Himself; **and My sins are not hid from Thee;** for so fully did He enter into His rôle as the Substitute of mankind that He stood before God in the nakedness of the guilt imputed to Him, as though it were really His own. V. 6. **Let not them that wait on Thee, O Lord God of hosts, be ashamed for My sake,** His prayer being that those who were depending upon Him for their salvation and thus putting their trust in the true God alone should not be disappointed in their hope; **let not those that seek Thee,** namely, by looking to the Messiah for their only deliverance, **be confounded for My sake, O God of Israel.** In the midst of His great offering our great High Priest did not neglect His intercession for the believers; while He was suffering as the greatest sinner who ever lived on earth, His one thought was for those whose transgressions He had taken upon Himself. V. 7. **Because for Thy sake,** by God's predetermined foreknowledge and counsel, **I have borne reproach,** Is. 53, 4. 10; **shame hath covered My face,** the full disgrace of the guilt of all mankind. V. 8. **I am become a stranger unto My brethren,** the members of His own nation regarding Him with aversion in His great Passion, **and an alien unto My mother's children,** His very relatives being among those who refused to accept Him as the promised Savior, John 1, 11; 7, 5. V. 9. **For the zeal of Thine house,** not only the outward building of the Temple, John 2, 17, but especially for the spiritual temple of Jehovah, for His holy Church, **hath eaten Me up,** consuming Him with anxiety; **and the reproaches of them that reproached Thee are fallen upon Me,** whatever objections were raised by the enemies to take away the honor of God, struck Him, the Messiah, with full force. V. 10. **When I wept,** in every bitter experience of His ministry, **and chastened My soul with fasting,** keeping under restraint, aloof from all wickedness, **that was to My reproach;** no matter what His behavior, some critic arose to condemn Him, Matt. 11, 19. V. 11. **I made sackcloth also My garment,** as one in deep mourning, abstaining from even the appearance of evil; **and I became a proverb to them,** His name and acts being bandied about jestingly. V. 12. **They that sit in the gate,** the nobles, the leaders of the people, **speak against Me; and I was the song of drunkards,** of drinkers of strong drink, the rabble of the taverns and streets joining in making mockery of Him, not only during His ministry, but especially when He hung on the cross. The Messiah now returns to the situation as pictured in the beginning of the psalm. V. 13. **But as for Me,** placing His own person in extreme opposition to that of His mocking enemies, **My prayer is unto Thee, O Lord, in an acceptable time;** He knew that the Father is well pleased with Him in spite of the degradation of His sufferings. **O God, in the multitude of Thy mercy hear Me,** answering Him favorably, **in the truth of Thy salvation,** since it was the will of God that not a single soul of the great host of sinners should be lost, but that salvation should be gained for all men. V. 14. **Deliver Me out of the mire,** the swamp of the evils which had been laid upon Him, **and let Me not sink; let Me be delivered from them that hate Me, and out of the deep waters,** the floods of His misery and anguish which threatened to engulf Him. V. 15. **Let not the water-flood overflow Me, neither let the deep,** the abyss of death, **swallow Me up, and let not the pit,** the cistern, or well, **shut her mouth upon Me,** the picture being that of a receptacle for rain-water in the steppe, whose opening was shut with a large stone. V. 16. **Hear Me, O Lord,** answering Him favorably; **for Thy loving-kindness is good,** comforting and gracious; **turn unto Me according to the multitude of Thy tender mercies,** drawing near to Him in unmerited favor; for He was not merely playing a part, but was actually laboring under the burden of sins placed upon Him. V. 17. **And hide not Thy face from Thy servant,** in unforgiving anger; **for I am in trouble,** in the distress and anguish of the guilt tormenting Him; **hear Me speedily,** an urgent cry for early deliverance, Ps. 22, 1. V. 18. **Draw nigh unto My soul,** for the purpose of rendering His divine assistance, **and redeem it; deliver Me because of Mine enemies,** who were upon Him to take His life. V. 19. **Thou hast known My reproach and My shame and My dishonor,** the result of the sin imputed to Him according to the divine counsel of love for the salvation of mankind; **Mine adversaries are all before Thee,** no one being more familiar with the enemies and their plans, with the devil and his host, than the omniscient God. The Messiah's lament grows in urgency as His distress increases. V. 20. **Reproach hath broken My heart,** the jeering slanders which struck Him from all sides crushed His soul; **and I am full of heaviness,** weak, failing under the burden; **and I looked for some to take pity,** waiting for sympathy and condolence in His unexampled misery, **but there was none; and for comforters,** men whose show of understanding kindness might serve to alleviate His anguish, **but I found none.** He had to tread the wine-press of God's wrath all alone. V. 21. **They gave Me also gall for My meat,** for food in the midst of His sufferings; **and in My thirst they gave Me vinegar to drink,** offering Him this astringent liquid when His body was racked with the most unbearable thirst. Such was the awful misery, the untold agony, the immeasurable anguish of Christ's suffering, in His capacity as the Substitute of mankind, as the Redeemer of the world.

PLEA FOR VENGEANCE. — V. 22. **Let their table become a snare before them,** spread for a banquet as it appeared, Ps. 23, 5, it should become a trap to the enemies; **and that which should have been for their welfare, let it become a trap,** literally, "and to the secure for a snare." Since no amount of seeking and calling could bring the enemies to their senses, since they persisted in rejecting Him and His Gospel, therefore the Messiah calls upon God to punish them as the hardness of their hearts deserved. V. 23. **Let their eyes be darkened,** in spiritual blindness, **that they see not, and make their loins,** commonly regarded as the seat of strength, **continually to shake,** in terror, dismay, and feebleness. V. 24. **Pour out Thine indignation upon them,** so that they would be submerged in the flood of righteous divine wrath, **and let Thy wrathful anger take hold of them,** overtaking them like a victorious enemy, for the purpose of enslaving and punishing them. V. 25. **Let their habitation be desolate,** their tents standing empty; **and let none dwell in their tents,** not one inhabitant remaining to relieve the horror of utter desolation. V. 26. **For they persecute Him whom Thou hast smitten,** pursuing the Messiah, stricken by the Lord as He was; **and they talk to the grief of those whom Thou hast wounded,** mockingly telling about the pains which the Lord's wounds caused Christ as He hung on the cross. V. 27. **Add iniquity unto their iniquity,** charging their trespasses to their account with full interest; **and let them not come into Thy righteousness,** by their own fault they would not become partakers of the salvation which was gained also for them. V. 28. **Let them be blotted out of the book of the living,** where the redemption of the Messiah would have entered their names for eternity, **and not be written with the righteous,** to whom the perfect righteousness of the Savior is imputed by faith. Such is the fate of those who consistently refuse to accept Jesus Christ and His salvation, who reject the counsel of God which has planned their righteousness. They have no one but themselves to blame if the righteousness of the Savior is not imputed to them, if their names are stricken from the book of life. Having disposed of His enemies in this manner, the Messiah returns to His complaint and prayer, but with a triumphant strain over the salvation of all believers. V. 29. **But I am poor and sorrowful,** miserable and in pain, because of the burden of sin and its punishment which He has taken upon Himself; **let Thy salvation, O God, set Me up on high.** He was sure of victory and of triumph, even in the midst of His suffering; He was sure that the deliverance of God would exalt Him. And therefore His song of praise and thanksgiving to God was made even then. V. 30. **I will praise the name of God with a song and will magnify Him with thanksgiving,** for the completion of the great work of atonement, the sacrifice of praise rising from His lips more sweetly than incense. V. 31. **This also shall please the Lord better than an ox or bullock that hath horns and hoofs,** for all external acts of worship, without the proper devotional attitude of the mind, as the outgrowth of true faith, are vain. Besides, the one sacrifice which our great High Priest brought is more acceptable in the eyes of Jehovah than all the offerings of brute beasts that were ever slaughtered, since with one sacrifice He has perfected forever them that are sanctified, Heb. 9. V. 32. **The humble shall see this and be glad,** the truly repentant and sorrowful rejoicing with their Redeemer over the fact of their salvation; **and your heart shall live that seek God,** literally, "ye who seek God," let live your heart, their souls being filled not only with gladness, but with a new and wonderful life, the life which has its source in God and brings the only lasting, satisfying happiness. V. 33. **For the Lord heareth the poor,** listening attentively and graciously to the voice of those who feel their need of salvation, **and despiseth not His prisoners,** those who have so long been bound by the fetters of sin and its consequences. Therefore the psalm ends with a triumphant burst of praise in honor of the salvation of God, as revealed and obtained in the Messiah. V. 34. **Let the heaven and earth praise Him, the seas and everything that moveth therein,** all creatures, the entire universe being called upon to give all honor to His merciful and holy name. V. 35. **For God will save Zion,** His Church, **and will build the cities of Judah,** all the congregations of the Messianic period being included here, **that they may dwell there and have it in possession,** all the blessings of Jehovah, as given through the redemption of Christ, being given to the believers through the means of grace. V. 36. **The seed also of His servants,** all the spiritual children of the many messengers of the Lord, who proclaim the redemption of Christ, **shall inherit it,** the blessings continuing in the Church as long as time endures; **and they that love His name shall dwell therein,** here in time in the Kingdom of Grace and its many cities, hereafter in eternity, in the Kingdom of Glory. After the days of the Church Militant will have been ended, the eternity of the Church Triumphant will begin, when the redeemed of the Lord will dwell with their exalted Head forevermore and praise His name, world without end.

PSALM 70.

Prayer for Help against the Enemies.

To the chief musician, as a prayer to be used in public worship, **a psalm of David, to bring to remembrance,** the hymn being intended for that part of the service when the meat-offering was added to the sacrifice; for its sweet smell was to rise to the nostrils of Jehovah together with the prayers of the faithful and plead for a gracious hearing. Cp. Ps. 40, 13—17. V. 1. **Make haste, O God, to deliver me,** from the sufferings and persecutions to which believers are subject; **make haste to help me, O Lord!** V. 2. **Let them be ashamed and confounded,** by being disappointed in their intention of harming the believer, **that seek after my soul; let them be turned backward,** baffled, their plans frustrated, **and put to confusion, that desire my hurt,** taking pleasure in doing evil. V. 3. **Let them be turned back for a reward of their shame,** as a punishment of their iniquity to their disgrace, **that say, Aha, aha!** in sneering derision. V. 4. **Let all those that seek Thee,** with truly believing hearts, **rejoice and be glad in Thee,** finding the true joy of faith in their confidence in Jehovah; **and let such as love Thy salvation,** with a proper appreciation of the blessings of redemption, **say continually, Let God be magnified,** exalted in hymns of thanksgiving. V. 5. **But I am poor and needy,** with the trouble which is the lot of all believers; **make haste unto me, O God,** for such is the proper importunate character of prayer. **Thou art my Help and my Deliverer; O Lord, make no tarrying!** It seems that the Messiah's prayer in Ps. 40 is here adapted to all believers, in order to teach them to place all their trust in life and death in the Lord alone, in the salvation gained through the work of the Redeemer, for in Him we have deliverance in all circumstances of life.

PSALM 71.

Prayer of an Aged Believer for God's Assistance.

PRAYER FOR DELIVERANCE. — V. 1. **In Thee, O Lord, do I put my trust,** resting secure in Jehovah's care; **let me never be put to confusion,** to become the laughing-stock of the enemies on account of his trust in Jehovah. V. 2. **Deliver me in Thy righteousness,** by which Jehovah keeps the gracious promise made to those who believe in Him, **and cause me to escape,** granting him freedom from all harm; **incline Thine ear unto me,** in close and merciful attention, **and save me,** as his Savior from all temporal and spiritual dangers. V. 3. **Be Thou my strong habitation,** literally, "a rock of dwelling," where one may live in the utmost security, **whereunto I may continually resort,** going there in calm trust whenever the need seems to demand it. **Thou hast given commandment to save me,** ordaining the salvation of all His believers; **for Thou art my Rock and my Fortress,** his Tower on the heights, inaccessible to the enemies. Cp. Ps. 31, 1—3. V. 4. **Deliver me, O my God, out of the hand of the wicked,** granting him freedom from him who would wickedly oppress him, **out of the hand of the unrighteous and cruel man,** the one employing injustice and violence in his dealing with others. V. 5. **For Thou art my Hope, O Lord God,** the All-powerful, Jehovah; **Thou art my Trust from my youth,** the firm foundation of the believer's confidence during his whole life. V. 6. **By Thee have I been holden up from the womb,** kept and sustained ever since his birth; **Thou art He that took me out of my mother's bowels,** protecting him, providing for him, granting him rich benefits throughout his life. **My praise shall be continually of Thee,** for the experiences of the past were a guarantee for the future. V. 7. **I am as a wonder,** a sign of the grace and protection of God, **unto many,** who find it impossible to believe the marvelous ways of the Lord in keeping His saints; **but Thou art my strong Refuge,** His almighty power warding off everything that might have brought real disaster to the believer. Cp. Ps. 22, 8—10. V. 8. **Let my mouth be filled with Thy praise and with Thy honor,** with statements giving all honor to God alone, **all the day.** V. 9. **Cast me not off in the time of old age,** for the faithfulness and kindness of God in youth and early manhood gives the believer courage to ask for His assistance in the declining years; **forsake me not when my strength faileth,** when the gradual dwindling of the vigor of maturity heralds the coming of death. V. 10. **For mine enemies speak against me,** taking new courage now that the believer has lost his youthful power and energy; **and they that lay wait for my soul,** eagerly watching for his destruction, **take counsel together,** v. 11. **saying, God hath forsaken him; persecute and take him, for there is none to deliver him.** The enemies of both body and soul make new efforts at the time when old age lays its hand upon the believer, their object being to get the faithful into their power. Therefore his cry must sound forth again and again, v. 12. **O God, be not far from me; O my God, make haste for my help.** Cp. Ps. 22, 11; 35, 4. 26; 38, 21. 22; 40, 13. 14. In this way the confident, persistent prayer of the believers, clinging to Him as His dear children, rises to the throne of grace, demanding the fulfilment of the Lord's promises.

WARNING AND THANKSGIVING. — V. 13. **Let them be confounded and consumed**, heaped with disgrace and delivered to utter ruin, **that are adversaries to my soul; let them be covered**, completely enveloped, **with reproach and dishonor that seek my hurt**, endeavoring to carry their wickedness into practise at every opportunity. V. 14. **But I**, in spite of such wicked counsels, **will hope continually and will yet praise Thee more and more**, knowing that there will be further occasion for expressing his thanksgiving. V. 15. **My mouth shall show forth Thy righteousness and Thy salvation all the day**, v. 2; **for I know not the numbers thereof**; the manifestations of God's attributes are so innumerable that one cannot keep count, and therefore the material for the praise of God is inexhaustible. V. 16. **I will go in the strength of the Lord God**, come forward with His mighty deeds, try to perform the impossible in enumerating them; **I will make mention of Thy righteousness, even of Thine only**, joyfully confessing it everywhere and upon all occasions. V. 17. **O God, Thou hast taught me from my youth**, namely, in His ways, as they agree with His holy will; **and hitherto have I declared Thy wondrous works**, namely, of the guidance of God in his whole life. V. 18. **Now also, when I am old and gray-headed**, showing the effects of old age in his appearance, **O God, forsake me not, until I have showed Thy strength**, the arm of the Lord, as the symbol of His almighty power and deeds, **unto this generation and Thy power to every one that is to come**, publishing the mighty works of Jehovah to all whom his voice may reach. V. 19. **Thy righteousness also, O God, is very high**, reaching even to the height of heaven, the highest point of creation, **who hast done great things**, which the psalmist feels constrained to proclaim even now. **O God, who is like unto Thee?** The God of Israel, the supreme God, is exalted in righteousness and might over all the universe. V. 20. **Thou, which hast showed me great and sore troubles**, by having him see and experience affliction and tribulation, **shalt quicken me again**, rather, "revive us again," for the poet now includes the entire congregation in his hymn of praise, **and shalt bring me up again from the depths of the earth**, the abysses of earth standing for threatening ruin. V. 21. **Thou shalt increase my greatness**, the prominence and authority of the psalmist's office in the kingdom, **and comfort me on every side**, chiefly by justifying him before the enemies. V. 22. **I will also praise Thee with the psaltery**, the lutelike instrument used to accompany singing, **even Thy truth, O my God**, the faithfulness with which the Lord keeps His promises; **unto Thee will I sing with the harp**, with the zither of David, **O Thou Holy One of Israel**. V. 23. **My lips shall greatly rejoice when I sing unto Thee**, composing and declaiming psalms in His honor; **and my soul, which Thou hast redeemed**, the deliverance from the troubles of this present life being the believer's guarantee of his final redemption. V. 24. **My tongue also shall talk of Thy righteousness all the day long**, v. 15; **for they are confounded, for they are brought unto shame, that seek my hurt**. That is the proper spirit of prayer, to anticipate the Lord's favorable answer and to praise Him in advance for all His blessings.

PSALM 72.

The Majestic Reign of the Messiah.

A psalm for Solomon, composed by Solomon; for he, under whose wise reign Israel reached the summit of its glory and power and was filled with the blessings of the Lord, sang this hymn in honor of the great King and His eternal glory and of the spiritual blessings of His dominion. V. 1. **Give the King Thy judgments, O God, and Thy righteousness unto the King's Son.** The Messiah is King and the Son of a King. To Him God gives, equips Him with, His righteousness, with His judgments. Every decision of this King, everything that He says and does, is right and acceptable with God. V. 2. **He shall judge Thy people with righteousness**, that is, the congregation of Jehovah, **and Thy poor**, those truly poor in spirit, **with judgment.** Because the Messiah is clothed with the righteousness of God as His own, therefore He is also able to dispense righteousness to the citizens of His kingdom, to impart it to those who believe in Him. It is His judicial sentence by and through which He declares His people to be righteous, justifies them with the righteousness which is perfect, which is acceptable in the sight of God. This is the right which God's people have before Him: their King declares them to be justified. The very ones who are poor and despised before the world, poor and humble also in the sight of God, are nevertheless honored by Him; they are partakers of His righteousness. So great and wonderful is this gift that the psalmist declares: v. 3. **The mountains shall bring peace to the people, and the little hills, by righteousness**, the blessings of God's mercy flowing down upon the believers, as it were, in streams. Righteousness is a gift coming down from above, bringing the peace of the heavenly Father with it and resulting in a calm satisfaction of mind, the believer being confident in the possession of the imputed righteousness. V. 4. **He shall judge the poor of the people,** those who feel their spiritual need; **He shall save the children of the needy,** those who depend upon Him alone, clinging to Him in true faith, accepting the righteousness imputed to them, **and shall break in pieces the oppressor,** crushing all those whose enmity oppresses His children. V. 5. **They shall fear Thee as long as the sun and moon endure, throughout all generations,** that is, the relation of the believers to their King is one of holy awe and reverence, by which they give Him the honor which is due Him, divine honor and glory. This is done before the sun, as long as the sun runs his course, and before the moon, as long as she stands in the sky, that is, to the end of time. V. 6. **He shall come down like rain upon the mown grass, as showers that water the earth,** literally, "like dewdrops, showers of rain on the earth," the point of resemblance being in the gentle, restoring freshness of a profuse fall of dew, of copious showers. Although the King has been exalted to the right hand of glory, exalted over all creatures and reigning over His congregation, yet His advent may be celebrated continually, for He is ever present in the midst of His Church in His means of grace, with righteousness, peace, and joy in the Holy Ghost, which are shed on us abundantly. V. 7. **In His days,** as the result of these rich spiritual blessings, **shall the righteous flourish,** blooming and thriving before Him in a life of sanctification flowing from faith, **and abundance of peace so long as the moon endureth,** literally, "until no longer the moon," throughout the present dispensation of grace. Because we are now, in the acceptable time, living before Him in the life of faith and enjoying the power of His grace in its effect upon our hearts and lives, therefore there is peace between us and God. And even after the moon has ceased shining, after the earth and all it contains have been destroyed, yea, then more than ever, will the believers have fulness of peace; in the world to come we shall possess and enjoy in everlasting bliss the peace of God which passes all understanding. V. 8. **He shall have dominion also from sea to sea,** His royal power extending over the whole earth, **and from the river unto the ends of the earth,** His dominion is enlarged, His power is spread, to the utmost ends of the universe, Eph. 1, 20—23. V. 9. **They that dwell in the wilderness,** the barbarians, the enemies of Christ and His Church, **shall bow before Him,** submitting themselves to His almighty power, since they refused to yield to His grace, Phil. 2, 10. 11; Matt. 26, 64; **and His enemies shall lick the dust,** be brought into full subjection to Him, forced to acknowledge Him as their Victor and Sovereign, since they refused to accept Him as their Redeemer. V. 10. **The kings of Tarshish,** Tartessus in Spain, an important commercial center, with many princes of finance, **and of the isles,** of the coasts of Europe, named as far-distant points, **shall bring presents,** the mighty ones of the very ends of the earth being named as doing homage before the Lord; **the kings of Sheba and Seba,** that is, of Arabia Felix and of Meroe in Egypt, **shall offer gifts,** people from heathen countries bringing tribute to His honor and acknowledging His sovereignty. V. 11. **Yea, all kings shall fall down before Him; all nations shall serve Him.** The King, by virtue of His having paid the ransom of His blood for the redemption of the whole world, has a right to expect the allegiance of all men. They are to acknowledge Him as their Savior and Lord. The psalmist mentions just those countries in which the Christian Church flourished for centuries. Many heathen from this entire territory along the coasts of the Mediterranean, including also princes and mighty men, acknowledged Christ as their Lord. But these heathen, at the same time, represent the entire heathen world; for the Lord has His children in all nations, the believers being the true representatives of the nations in the sight of God. The poet now gives the reason why so many heathen would turn to God, to Jehovah-Messiah: v. 12. **For He shall deliver the needy when he crieth; the poor also and him that hath no helper.** He has compassion with the spiritual poverty and want, with our weakness and helplessness; He saves the needy by His grace. When our hearts have been crushed by the blows of the Law, when our souls are bowed down to the ground by the realization of our sinfulness, then He comforts us with the beauty of His Gospel. V. 13. **He shall spare,** have pity on, **the poor and needy and shall save the souls of the needy,** delivering them from the damnation which threatens them. V. 14. **He shall redeem their soul from deceit and violence,** the word here used being the standing term of the Old Testament for redemption and deliverance of every kind; **and precious shall their blood be in His sight,** valuing their lives so highly that He pays the high price of His own blood for their redemption. Moreover, it is true in general that God will not forsake His children, even if the enmity of the world reaches the point where the blood of the believers is shed on account of their testimony of the truth. In life and in death Christ is their Redeemer, and He will finally avenge the blood of His children. Since these conditions obtain, therefore the kingdom of Christ will surely spread and extend over many nations. V. 15. **And He shall live,** the Possessor and the Giver of life, and to **Him shall be given of the gold of Sheba**, of the wealth of Arabia Felix, this being taken to represent the gifts of men as they throng to do homage to the Messiah. **Prayer also shall be made for Him continually**, in a service of worship before Him, which shall continue throughout eternity; **and daily shall He be praised**, the righteous blessing His name for the rich gifts of His grace. And now, with a glance at Canaan in the glory of its earthly products, Solomon speaks of the kingdom of Christ in terms of this rich plenty. V. 16. **There shall be an handful of corn in the earth upon the top of the mountains**, that is, the spiritual offspring of the Messiah will be as abundant as the grain of the lowlands, which clothed even the hills to their very tops; **the fruit thereof shall shake like Lebanon**, as the proud and mighty cedars of Lebanon; **and they of the city shall flourish like grass of the earth**, literally, "and they shall thrive from out the city as the grass of the earth," budding forth and bearing blossoms and fruit in rich and luscious abundance, for such are the conditions which obtain in Christ's Kingdom of Grace. V. 17. **His name shall endure forever**, exist, maintain itself, throughout eternity; **His name shall be continued as long as the sun**, or, "before the sun will flourish, propagate, His name." Wherever the Church is established, it grows from generation to generation through the power of His Word. It is for this reason that the name of the Messiah will last throughout eternity, the Church Militant merging into the Church Triumphant; as long as the sun continues in his course, His name will be proclaimed and bring forth fruit in abundance. **And men shall be blessed in Him**, blessing themselves in Him, calling themselves happy, fortunate, beyond description in the possession of His grace; **all nations shall call Him blessed**, praising the Lord Jehovah for all His wondrous deeds for the salvation of the world. In view of these unspeakably glorious facts which have been set forth briefly in his hymn, the inspired poet closes with a doxology: v. 18. **Blessed be the Lord God, the God of Israel, who only doeth wondrous things**, all glory and honor being given to Him alone; v. 19. **and blessed be His glorious name**, Himself with all His divine attributes, as He has revealed Himself to men in His Word, **forever; and let the whole earth be filled with His glory. Amen, and Amen.** As the Word of God had its course here in time, being proclaimed in every part of the earth, so the heavens will resound with the praises of His glory throughout eternity. This is most certainly true. The psalm closes with a note of the men who collected this second book of the psalter: v. 20. **The prayers of David, the son of Jesse, are ended**, this remark being apparently attached to an original collection of David's hymns.

PSALM 73.

Comfort and Warning Concerning the Offense Given by the Good Fortune of the Godless.

A psalm of Asaph, one of the choirmasters of David, 1 Chron. 6, 39; 25, 2.

A REFLECTION UPON THE APPARENT GOOD FORTUNE OF THE WICKED. — V. 1. **Truly, God is good to Israel**, only good, nothing but kindness and mercy, **even to such as are of a clean heart**, for all members of the spiritual Israel have their hearts cleansed by faith, so that they are honest and straightforward in all their dealings with the Lord. This is the poet's comfort in spite of the description of the apparent happiness of the unbelievers which now follows. V. 2. **But as for me**, his own person being set forward emphatically as an example, **my feet were almost gone**, almost he had stumbled and tottered; **my steps had well-nigh slipped**, he had been in great danger of losing his faith and giving way to doubt. V. 3. **For I was envious at the foolish**, filled with anger at the proud boasting of the ungodly, **when I saw the prosperity of the wicked**, when he noted the fact that they were living in peace, that nothing bothered them, that they enjoyed everything their hearts desired, and made it a point to tell everybody about it. V. 4. **For there are no bands in their death**, they are not plagued with sufferings which make them weary unto death; **but their strength is firm**, well nourished is their paunch, fatness being considered a sign of healthy strength, of stout vigor. V. 5. **They are not in trouble as other men**, they do not experience the misery of the ordinary mortal; **neither are they plagued like other men**, they are not bothered with so many inconveniences, they do not run up against so many difficulties; they find ways and means to avert disaster. V. 6. **Therefore**, because of their apparent immunity against life's usual troubles, **pride compasseth them about as a chain**, they lift up their necks proudly, they exhibit their pride like an ornament; **violence covereth them as a garment**, their whole nature is cruel and ruthless. V. 7. **Their eyes stand out with fatness**, this again being a picture of vigor due to prosperity; **they have more than heart could wish**, literally, "are revealed the imaginations of their hearts," that is, their proud thoughts appear in their speech and in their acts. V. 8. **They are corrupt**, given to mockery in their speech, **and**

speak wickedly concerning oppression, in their ungodliness they speak oppression, they plan to keep the upper hand over the believers; scoffing at the idea of trust in God, they oppress all such as hold this trust. **They speak loftily,** down from the height of their pride, with nothing but contempt for the hopelessly old-fashioned believers. V. 9. **They set their mouth against the heavens,** to blaspheme God, **and their tongue walketh through the earth,** with arrogant haughtiness, with meddlesome slander. Note: It is a composite picture which the psalmist draws in this paragraph, his object being not to portray the actions of each individual ungodly person, but to represent one wicked person as speaking for the mass of unbelievers on earth. V. 10. **Therefore his people return hither,** the multitude of the godless ever rallying round such an arrogant declaimer of blasphemies and slanders; **and waters of a full cup are wrung out to them,** prosperity being drained by them as they eagerly grasp at success and its enjoyments, or, further multitudes being gulped down by them, those who are duped by them joining with the seducers in their blasphemous speeches and conduct. V. 11. **And they say, How doth God know? And is there knowledge in the Most High?** They try to deceive themselves and others into the belief that God pays no attention to their wickedness in its various manifestations. They despise the wisdom of God in His eternal Word and arrogantly substitute the so-called assured results of scientific research. V. 12. **Behold, these are the ungodly,** as here briefly characterized they are found at all times, **who prosper in the world,** boasting of their success; **they increase in riches,** they possess everything which this world has to offer; they believe that they are secure forever, without a care to disturb their happiness.

THE BELIEVER'S TRUST AT THE REALIZATION OF THE TRUTH. — V. 13. **Verily, I have cleansed my heart in vain,** in view of the offense given by the prosperity of the ungodly, **and washed my hands in innocency,** making diligent efforts to live a holy life before the Lord. V. 14. **For all the day long have I been plagued,** buffeted with troubles on every hand, **and chastened every morning,** some new visitation of the Lord striking him with every new day. The psalmist, however, guards against such blasphemous utterances; he does not want to become guilty of speeches against the Lord. V. 15. **If I say, I will speak thus,** his thoughts being on the point of being uttered, **behold, I should offend against the generation of Thy children,** giving offense to the Lord's people by an act of perfidy against Jehovah, that is, he found himself in the position of Paul, Rom. 7, when he speaks of the quarrel in his members. V. 16. **When I thought to know this,** to get a satisfactory explanation of the riddle presented in the situation, **it was too painful for me,** his pondering remained a toil, did not offer him a satisfactory solution, v. 17. **until I went into the Sanctuary of God,** to the Tabernacle, or Temple, where the Word of the Lord was kept, which reveals also the mysteries of God's government of the world, so far as God wants the believers to know them; **then understood I their end,** then he found out what would be the final disposition of the ungodly, what fate God had in store for them. V. 18. **Surely Thou didst set them in slippery places,** they who believed themselves so safe and secure against misfortune were in reality in danger of slipping every moment; **Thou castedst them down into destruction,** bringing sudden ruin upon them. V. 19. **How are they brought into desolation, as in a moment! They are utterly consumed with terrors,** wasted away, reduced to nothing, by the horror of the fate which overtook them. V. 20. **As a dream when one awaketh,** from the moment when a person arouses himself from his sleep, so, **O Lord, when Thou awakest, Thou shalt despise their image.** A dream may seem real enough while it lasts, but upon awaking a person shakes it off with its effects, as lacking in material substance. Thus the ungodly, with all their show of prosperity, are nothing but a dream-picture in the eyes of God; there is no place for them in the eternal city of God, their fate is decided. V. 21. **Thus my heart was grieved, and I was pricked in my reins,** that is, if his heart should become embittered, if it should hurt him inside, in his inward parts, in his feelings; v. 22. **so foolish was I and ignorant; I was as a beast before Thee,** he would have been foolish and like an irrational animal before God if he had yielded to dissatisfaction and bitterness. But he shakes off the attack and states what his true comfort consists in. V. 23. **Nevertheless I am continually with Thee,** in spite of all the offense given by the unbelievers and their apparent good fortune; **Thou hast holden me by my right hand,** keeping the believer from falling, holding him secure with His almighty power. V. 24. **Thou shalt guide me with Thy counsel,** for God shows each of His children on which paths they should go forward, **and afterward receive me to glory,** when he has reached the goal, his soul's salvation, receiving the reward of mercy. Therefore every believer is constrained to call out with Asaph: v. 25. **Whom have I in heaven but Thee?** God is his highest Good; in Him there is complete satisfaction. **And there is none upon earth that I desire beside Thee,** he no longer finds true pleasure in this world and all its goods. V. 26. **My flesh and my heart faileth,** they faint, pine, dwindle away under the attacks of misery and tribulation; **but God is the Strength of my heart,** the dependable Rock of his faith, **and my Portion forever,** the inheritance which will give the believer eternal satisfaction and enjoyment. The psalmist therefore, in conclusion, offers a summary of his meditations. V. 27. **For, lo, they that are far from Thee shall perish,** they who have left God, have become estranged to Him by means of their pride and arrogance, will become victims of eternal destruction; **Thou hast destroyed all them that go a-whoring from Thee,** in spiritual adultery, in idolatry, by their disobedience and faithlessness. V. 28. **But it is good for me,** it is his greatest pleasure and happiness, **to draw near to God,** to be united with Him in the fellowship of faith; **I have put my trust in the Lord God that I may declare all Thy works,** that he may have reason to praise the works of God for his own salvation. In heaven we shall have the full revelation of the fact that it was the mercy and kindness of God which directed Him in His entire relation toward us, even during periods which seemed dark to us, which we could not explain at the time, and that the end and goal was the salvation of our souls and the glory of heaven.4)

4) For a detailed explanation of this psalm see *Lehre und Wehre,* 52 (1906), 495—510.

PSALM 74.

Prayer for the Preservation of the Church.

Maschil, a didactic poem, **of Asaph,** a prophetic psalm, foretelling some of the afflictions which would befall the Church of God, in the Old Testament as well as in the New. V. 1. **O God, why hast Thou cast us off forever?** this being the conclusion reached by the psalmist in considering the condition of the spiritual Israel as he saw it in spirit. **Why doth Thine anger smoke,** the smoking of the nostrils as with an inner fire being the picture frequently used in the Hebrew language to denote violent anger, **against the sheep of Thy pasture?** this being a common designation of the believers throughout the Bible. Cp. John 10. V. 2. **Remember Thy congregation,** not only thinking of it in mercy, but showing His favor in deeds of kindness, **which Thou hast purchased of old,** which had become His possession by the deliverance from the serfdom of Egypt; **the rod of Thine inheritance,** the tribe or nation of His possession, **which Thou hast redeemed,** this statement pointing both backward to the purchase out of Egypt's slavery and forward to the eternal redemption by Jesus Christ; **this Mount Zion,** His own holy Church of all times, **wherein Thou hast dwelt.** Note the climax in the terms to denote the relation of God to the people of His covenant. V. 3. **Lift up Thy feet,** in long and hurried steps, **unto the perpetual desolations,** the ruins of His spiritual Temple; **even all that the enemy hath done wickedly in the Sanctuary,** the desecrations of the Old Testament being due principally to idolatry, those of the New Testament consisting in false doctrine and the perversions of the means of grace. V. 4. **Thine enemies roar in the midst of Thy congregations,** in the place where God revealed Himself in the assembled congregation in His Word; **they set up their ensigns for signs,** heathen customs and ceremonies taking the place of the forms of worship instituted or approved by God. That this was done in the Chaldean and the Maccabean periods is a matter of historical fact; that it is being done to-day is evident to every observer. V. 5. **A man was famous according as he had lifted up axes upon the thick trees,** or, He, the enemy, shows himself, makes known himself, as one who raises axes on high in the thicket of the woods; v. 6. **but now they break down the carved work thereof,** the costly and artistic paneling of the Temple, **at once with axes and hammers,** in deliberate and ruthless vandalism, exactly as the present-day enemies attempt to desecrate the spiritual temple of the Lord. V. 7. **They have cast fire into Thy sanctuary,** deliberately burning the house of Jehovah; **they have defiled, by casting down, the dwelling-place of Thy name,** where the Lord revealed Himself to His people in the Word, **to the ground,** the profanation of all things holy being the delight of the Lord's enemies always. V. 8. **They said in their hearts, Let us destroy them together,** bringing the believers into subjection with cruelty and violence; **they have burned up all the synagogs of God in the land,** all the places of assembly, whether the schools of prophets are here meant or the synagogs proper as they existed after the Exile. V. 9. **We see not our signs,** the customs of regular worship had been discontinued; **there is no more any prophet,** this lament containing a true description not only of the last centuries of the pre-Christian era, but also of many other periods of the Church's life; **neither is there among us any that knoweth how long,** that is, how long the time of such persecution and tribulation would last. V. 10. **O God, how long shall the adversary reproach?** sneeringly state that Israel had been forsaken by God. **Shall the enemy,** by such jeering remarks, **blaspheme Thy name,** the entire revelation of the power and attributes of Jehovah, **forever?** V. 11. **Why withdrawest Thou Thy hand, even Thy right hand?** this being the symbol of God's almighty power. **Pluck it out of Thy bosom,** where it seemed that the Lord had hidden it; He should show

His might, the psalmist pleads, by sending destruction upon the enemies. V. 12. **For God is my King of old,** in spite of the gloominess of the present outlook the poet clings to this trust, **working salvation in the midst of the earth,** that is, throughout the habitable world He makes known and works His redemption. V. 13. **Thou didst divide the sea by Thy strength,** cleaving the Red Sea asunder for the passage of Israel; **Thou brakest the heads of the dragons in the waters,** the expression referring to the Egyptian tyrants. V. 14. **Thou brakest the heads of leviathan,** the crocodile, the most powerful animal of Egypt, **in pieces and gavest him to be meat to the people inhabiting the wilderness,** food for the wilderness dwellers, the wild beasts of the desert consuming the carcasses of the Egyptians after their overthrow in the Red Sea. Thus the monsters mentioned here are emblems of Egypt, whose power was overthrown by the might of Jehovah. V. 15. **Thou didst cleave the fountain and the flood,** in giving the Israelites water out of the rock, Ex. 17, 5; Num. 20, 11; **Thou driedst up mighty rivers,** the reference being chiefly to the passage of Jordan, Josh. 3, 13. V. 16. **The day is Thine, the night also is Thine,** He, as the great Sovereign, has fixed the laws governing their course; **Thou hast prepared the light and the sun,** the light-bodies being His creatures and subject to Him. V. 17. **Thou hast set all the borders of the earth,** not only by dividing it from the sea, but also by fixing the natural boundaries of nations; **Thou hast made summer and winter,** the seasons also being His creatures and therefore subject to His command. Thus the absolute, limitless power of God is described, this description serving as a basis of the supplication following. V. 18. **Remember this, that the enemy hath reproached, O Lord, and that the foolish people,** the enemies gone mad with their rejection of Jehovah, **have blasphemed Thy name,** v. 10. V. 19. **O deliver not the soul of thy turtle-dove,** the individual believer and the entire Church being included in this designation on account of the manner in which the dove seeks refuge when danger is near, **unto the multitude of the wicked,** the band which is so active in planning its destruction. **Forget not the congregation of Thy poor,** the meek sufferers for the sake of His name, **forever.** V. 20. **Have respect unto the covenant,** regarding His promise to uphold the fellowship between Himself and His people; **for the dark places of the earth,** the caves and hiding-places of the persecuted believers, **are full of the habitations of cruelty,** since it happened repeatedly in the history of the Church that the enemies searched out and killed the faithful even in the mountain fastnesses (period of the Maccabees, the Huguenot persecutions, etc.). V. 21. **O let not the oppressed return ashamed,** on account of the Lord's refusal to give him the assistance he craved; **let the poor and needy,** the afflicted members of His Church, **praise Thy name,** thanking Him for the deliverance which He was requested to provide. V. 22. **Arise, O God, plead Thine own cause,** for it was, after all, Jehovah's cause which was in danger on account of the action of the enemies; **remember how the foolish man reproacheth Thee daily,** Jehovah's own honor thereby being assailed. V. 23. **Forget not the voice of Thine enemies,** their sneering blasphemies; **the tumult of those that rise up against Thee,** in open rebellion against His sovereign rule, **increaseth continually,** rising up threateningly against the throne of the Most High. That is a prayer which is bound to have its effect, when the believers boldly point out to the Lord that it is His own interests in the world which are endangered on account of the attitude of the enemies.

PSALM 75.

The Church Praises the Nearness of God's Judgment.

To the chief musician, for use in the liturgical part of public worship, **Al-taschith,** according to the melody "Destroy Not," a psalm **or song of Asaph,** this hymn sounding like a continuation of the preceding psalm, the believers anticipating relief in view of God's righteous government. V. 1. **Unto Thee, O God, do we give thanks, unto Thee do we give thanks,** the repetition serving to emphasize the willingness of the congregation to acknowledge the blessings of Jehovah; **for that Thy name is near Thy wondrous works declare,** God's name, the revelation of His essence and attributes in His Word, is in the midst of His congregation; His wondrous works, the miracles of His grace, are recounted by believers everywhere. V. 2. **When I shall receive the congregation,** rather, the occasion, the time appointed in God's counsel for the execution of His judgment, **I will judge uprightly.** It is Jehovah Himself who here speaks. When the time selected by Him comes, then God will take hold of it with all energy, His judgment following the highest norm of righteousness. V. 3. **The earth and all the inhabitants thereof are dissolved,** when all men are discouraged and at the point of dissolution on account of oppression and violence of the wicked; **I bear up the pillars of it,** placing them upright once more, bringing back order into the confusion obtaining in the world. **Selah.** The Lord now sets forth the manner of His acting in doing away with chaotic conditions in the world. V. 4. **I said unto the fools**, to the vain boasters, **Deal not foolishly**, in boasting so proudly; **and to the wicked, Lift not up the horn**, this being an emblem of unjustified pride; v. 5. **lift not up your horn on high**, in displaying the instruments of violence, in brandishing them for the attack upon the righteous; **speak not with a stiff neck**, with insolence and presumption. V. 6. **For promotion cometh neither from the east nor from the west nor from the south**, from the mountainous desert, no earthly power can bring either oppression or redemption without God's will or permission. V. 7. **But God is the Judge**, stated with emphasis; **He putteth down one**, humiliating and treading under foot the wicked, **and setteth up another**, exalting the righteous. V. 8. **For in the hand of the Lord there is a cup**, that of God's wrath, cp. Is. 51, 17, **and the wine is red**, foaming and frothing with its strength; **it is full of mixture**, God Himself having prepared the fermenting liquid; **and He poureth out of the same**, serving it with His own hand while it is foaming; **but the dregs thereof, all the wicked of the earth shall wring them out and drink them**, the guilty being constrained to drink the entire cup of God's wrath without intermission, the mention of the dregs signifying the thoroughness with which God would carry out His punishment. This statement having been made, the psalmist again takes up the strain of his praise. V. 9. **But I will declare forever**, proclaiming the name of Jehovah; **I will sing praises to the God of Jacob**, the one true God. V. 10. **All the horns of the wicked**, their pride with their instruments of violence, **also will I cut off**, in the power of God, which is made perfect in his weakness; **but the horns of the righteous**, as instruments of righteous warfare, emblems of the right trust in God, **shall be exalted**. All the powers of the enemies are bound to be overthrown, while the Church of Christ will triumph at the last.

PSALM 76.

God the Protector of His Church.

To the chief musician on Neginoth, to be sung in public worship to the accompaniment of stringed instruments, **a psalm or song of Asaph**, another hymn commemorating God's deliverance of His people by a miraculous interposition of His power. V. 1. **In Judah**, where the central Sanctuary of Jehovah had been established, **is God known**, having revealed Himself to His people; **His name is great in Israel**, having been magnified by the proclamation of His servants throughout the nation. V. 2. **In Salem**, the city of Jerusalem, **also is His Tabernacle**, the dwelling of His tent, the central Sanctuary, **and His dwelling-place in Zion**, on whose summit the Tabernacle had been erected by David, the ancient tent of Moses being at that time still at Gibeon. V. 3. **There brake He the arrows of the bow**, literally, the lightnings of the bow, the weapons with which the enemies intended to attack the Church, **the shield and the sword and the battle**, war being used for the weapons of war. **Selah.** V. 4. **Thou art more glorious and excellent than the mountains of prey**, literally, "Full of splendor art Thou, glorious from the mountains of spoil," that is, the Lord is infinitely more glorious and splendid than all the powers of the enemy, of Satan and the world, who eagerly desire to spoil the Church, to rob it of its beauty. V. 5. **The stout-hearted are spoiled**, forced to deliver their weapons to the Lord, standing disarmed and disgraced, **they have slept their sleep**, fallen into the sleep of death; **and none of the men of might have found their hands**, they are helpless, they are unable to use their hands, to grasp their weapons for the purpose of continuing their warfare against the Church of God. V. 6. **At Thy rebuke, O God of Jacob**, at His almighty threat, by virtue of the power of His Word, **both the chariot and horse**, here used as types of the weapons and the attack of the enemies, **are cast into a dead sleep**, rendered helpless forever. Cp. Is. 43, 17. V. 7. **Thou, even Thou**, stated with the greatest emphasis, **art to be feared; and who may stand in Thy sight when once Thou art angry?** The answer is obvious: It is impossible for any man to stand before the almighty power of Jehovah; no enemy, no matter how powerful, can carry out his hostile designs without Jehovah's permission. V. 8. **Thou didst cause judgment to be heard from heaven**, Jehovah Himself speaking the decisive word against the tumult of the hostile world; **the earth feared and was still**, its tumult being constrained to die down into silence, v. 9. **when God arose to judgment, to save all the meek of the earth**, His people, suffering from the oppression of the enemies. **Selah.** V. 10. **Surely the wrath of man shall praise Thee**, bound finally to tend to the glorification of Jehovah, obliged, in its own despite, to show forth God's glory in its own ruin; **the remainder of wrath shalt Thou restrain**, or, while Thou girdest Thyself with the remainder of wrath, that is, after men have exhaused their rage against Jehovah, He makes use of His store of divine wrath, the result being the complete overthrow of all enemies, as pictured above. The psalmist, therefore, turns to the people of the Lord in a final admonition. V. 11. **Vow and pay unto the**

Lord, your God, being sure to fulfil what they promised Jehovah in recognition of His deliverance; **let all that be round about Him,** all the surrounding nations, **bring presents unto Him,** as a tribute to His almighty power, **that ought to be feared,** He being the essence of all that inspires reverence. V. 12. **He shall cut off the spirit of princes,** taking away their snorting, putting an end to their arrogance; **He is terrible to the kings of the earth,** feared, if not revered, by them all, for those who will not accept Him as their Redeemer must acknowledge Him the almighty Ruler of the universe. The enemies are judged; the Church is delivered, and the glory of God stands revealed before all men.

PSALM 77.

The Tribulation and Comfort of the Righteous.

To the chief musician, to Jeduthun, at that time in charge of the Temple music, **a psalm of Asaph,** the psalm picturing the relief experienced by believers in the midst of affliction, by calling to mind God's former and wonderful acts of deliverance. V. 1. **I cried unto God with my voice, even unto God with my voice,** in importunate supplication; **and He gave ear unto me,** in a gracious answer and act of deliverance. V. 2. **In the day of my trouble,** at the time when affliction beset him strongly, **I sought the Lord,** the All-powerful; **my sore ran in the night and ceased not,** rather, my hand is stretched out in the night, without being relaxed, he does not draw it back, he does not cease from crying to the Lord; **my soul refused to be comforted,** so thoroughly had his affliction discouraged him. V. 3. **I remembered God and was troubled,** groaning at the thought that Jehovah, once his Helper, had now apparently forsaken him; **I complained, and my spirit was overwhelmed,** so overcome that he could no longer think clearly. **Selah.** V. 4. **Thou holdest mine eyes waking,** holding the lids of his eyes open, depriving him of sleep on account of the misery which he felt; **I am so troubled that I cannot speak,** he is speechless from the excessive amount of his affliction. But his meditation now turns to the past. V. 5. **I have considered the days of old,** of ages long past, **the years of ancient times,** when the manifestations of God's power and mercy were so numerous. V. 6. **I call to remembrance my song in the night,** when a feeling of happy gratitude caused him to use even the night season for anthems of praise; **I commune with mine own heart,** meditating in the seclusion of his inmost soul, making comparisons with the past happiness and the present misery; **and my spirit made diligent search,** trying to become clear in his own mind regarding the ways of the Lord. A summary of his meditation is now given. V. 7. **Will the Lord cast off forever?** Can it be possible that He will utterly forsake the afflicted? **And will He be favorable no more,** never again showing His good pleasure in the afflicted soul trusting in Him? V. 8. **Is His mercy clean gone forever?** Has He forgotten all His merciful promises? **Doth His promise fail forevermore?** Surely such a course would not harmonize with the outstanding attributes of His essence. V. 9. **Hath God forgotten to be gracious,** to look upon His children with kind favor? **Hath He in anger shut up His tender mercies? Selah.** Note how closely these meditations agree with those in the experience of every believer. The psalmist now shakes off all feelings of doubt. V. 10. **And I said, This is my infirmity,** the suffering which was his lot in life; **but I will remember the years of the right hand of the Most High,** when the almighty power of Jehovah sustained him. V. 11. **I will remember the works of the Lord,** with praise and thanksgiving; **surely I will remember Thy wonders of old,** for there are miracles of God in the life of every believer, just as there are in the history of the Church. V. 12. **I will meditate also of all Thy work,** pondering upon them most carefully, **and talk of Thy doings,** by which God revealed His divine attributes to men. V. 13. **Thy way, O God, is in the Sanctuary,** literally, "in holiness"; everything that He does accords with the holiness of His essence. **Who is so great a God as our God?** His perfections place Him above all so-called gods and idols of the heathen. V. 14. **Thou art the God that doest wonders,** continually performing miracles of kindness and mercy; **thou hast declared Thy strength among the people,** revealing among the nations of the world His almighty power. V. 15. **Thou hast with Thine arm redeemed Thy people,** His uplifted, almighty arm providing deliverance to Israel, **the sons of Jacob and Joseph,** the latter being especially mentioned as bearers of the right of the first-born. **Selah.** V. 16. **The waters saw Thee, O God; the waters saw Thee,** namely, when He made ready to cleave the waters of the Red Sea; **they were afraid; the depths also were troubled,** being filled with awe and trembling before the power of the Creator, Ex. 14, 21. V. 17. **The clouds poured out water,** during a mighty thunderstorm revealing Jehovah's power; **the skies sent out a sound,** the entire firmament sounding; **Thine arrows also went abroad,** the lightnings being pictured as active and aggressive. V. 18. **The voice of Thy thunder was in the heaven,**

or "in the whirlwind"; **the lightnings lightened the world; the earth trembled and shook.** The entire passage seems to be an elaborate picture of the mighty phenomena preceding and accompanying the giving of the Law on Mount Sinai, all the powers of nature being used in the service of Jehovah, in the revelation of His incomparable majesty. V. 19. **Thy way is in the sea and Thy path in the great waters,** the trackless deep being obliged to offer Him a road, **and Thy footsteps are not known,** the full mysteries of His omnipotence and providence being beyond the comprehension of men. V. 20. **Thou leddest Thy people like a flock,** His hand both protecting and guiding them, **by the hand of Moses and Aaron,** His representatives before the children of Israel, Ex. 14, 29—31. All believers may rest assured that the God of Israel, Jehovah, will lead them, individually and collectively, through all the tribulations of this present time to everlasting salvation.

PSALM 78.

A Review of Israel's History as a Source of Consolation.

Maschil of Asaph, a didactic poem, intended to instruct the children of Israel in the wonderful ways of the Lord and to warn them against apostasy.

THE INTRODUCTION. — V. 1. **Give ear, O my people, to my law,** the religious teacher calling attention to his instruction which he is now about to begin; **incline your ears to the words of my mouth,** in the attitude of most careful attention. V. 2. **I will open my mouth in a parable,** in proverbial sayings; **I will utter dark sayings of old,** make statements which would appear as oracles or riddles if unexplained, or if the application to present conditions were omitted, v. 3. **which we,** the people of the older generation, **have heard and known, and our fathers have told us,** this being the custom in Israel, according to God's command, Deut. 6, 6. 7. 20—25. V. 4. **We will not hide them from their children,** by refusing to hand them down by word of mouth and by written record, **showing to the generation to come,** the children which are now growing up, **the praises of the Lord,** the acts of His government which redound to His glory, **and His strength,** in its various manifestations, **and His wonderful works that He hath done.** V. 5. **For He established a testimony in Jacob,** setting it up to be observed in the midst of His people, **and appointed a Law in Israel,** laying it down as a rule of life, **which He commanded our fathers, that they should make them known to their children,** Deut. 4, 9; v. 6. **that the generation to come might know them, even the children which should be born; who should arise and,** in turn, **declare them to their children;** v. 7. **that they might set their hope in God,** making Him the one foundation of their trust, **and not forget the works of God,** all the miracles by which He manifested Himself, **but keep His commandments,** observing all that He had ordered, v. 8. **and might not be as their fathers,** the reference being chiefly to those of the wilderness journey, **a stubborn,** faithless, disloyal, **and rebellious generation,** Ex. 32, 9; Deut. 21, 18; **a generation that set not their heart aright,** did not direct it to the service of God alone, **and whose spirit was not steadfast with God,** was not faithful toward Him. V. 9. **The children of Ephraim, being armed and carrying bows,** fully equipped for battle, **turned back in the day of battle;** although this tribe possessed the privileges, and therefore should have fulfilled the duties, of the first-born, by being leaders of the nation in everything that was good, its members showed their leadership rather in apostasy from God. V. 10. **They kept not the covenant of God,** they were backsliders almost from the start, permitting idolatry within their coasts almost immediately after the conquest of Canaan, **and refused to walk in His Law;** v. 11. **and forgat His works and His wonders that He had showed them,** not heeding the impressive lessons connected with the guidance of the Lord. So much is said, by way of introduction and summary, to prepare the way for the warning contained in the remainder of the hymn.

THE NARRATIVE OF GOD'S DEEDS. — V. 12. **Marvelous things did He in the sight of their fathers,** before the exodus, **in the land of Egypt, in the field of Zoan,** this being the residence of the Pharaohs at the time of the deliverance from Egypt, Num. 14, 22. The miracles performed by Moses were probably all done in or near this capital, and it is mentioned also at a later date because it was located in the most easterly portion of Egypt, in the part nearest to the land of Canaan. V. 13. **He divided the sea and caused them to pass through,** Ex. 14, 21; **and He made the waters to stand as an heap,** Ex. 15, 8. V. 14. **In the daytime also He led them with a cloud and all the night with a light of fire,** this pillar of fire being mentioned frequently in the account of the wilderness journey, Ex. 13, 21. 22. V. 15. **He clave the rocks in the wilderness,** on two different occasions, Ex. 17, 5; Num. 20, 11, **and gave them drink as out of the great depths.** V. 16. **He brought streams also out of the rock,** in performing the miracles just referred to, **and caused waters to run**

down like rivers. V. 17. **And they sinned yet more against Him by provoking the Most High in the wilderness,** with their continual rebellious murmurings. V. 18. **And they tempted God in their heart,** Matt. 15, 19, **by asking meat for their lust,** when they declared that their soul loathed the very sight of the manna, Num. 11, 4—6. V. 19. **Yea, they spake against God; they said, Can God furnish a table in the wilderness?** V. 20. **Behold, He smote the rock that the waters gushed out and the streams overflowed,** giving them water in rich abundance; **can He give bread also? Can He provide flesh for His people?** It was a blasphemous murmuring in the face of the great miracles performed for their benefit. V. 21. **Therefore the Lord heard this and was wroth,** Num. 11; **so a fire was kindled against Jacob, and anger also came up against Israel,** v. 22. **because they believed not in God,** had no faith in the covenant God, **and trusted not in His salvation,** the deliverance which He had promised them; v. 23. **though He had commanded the clouds from above and opened the doors of heaven,** v. 24. **and had rained down manna upon them to eat and had given them of the corn of heaven,** miraculous food, John 6, 31. V. 25. **Man did eat angels' food,** so called because it came down from heaven, Ps. 105, 40; **He sent them meat to the full,** all they needed to sustain their lives by the way. V. 26. **He caused an east wind to blow in the heaven, and by His power He brought in the south wind,** the exact direction of the wind therefore being southeast, Num. 11, 31. V. 27. **He rained flesh also upon them as dust,** in great abundance, **and feathered fowls like as the sand of the sea,** a day's journey wide around their camp and two cubits high; v. 28. **and He let it fall in the midst of their camp, round about their habitations.** V. 29. **So they did eat and were well filled,** falling upon the quails with the greatest greed; **for He gave them their own desire.** V. 30. **They were not estranged from their lust,** they were still indulging their desire to the full; **but while their meat was yet in their mouths,** v. 31. **the wrath of God came upon them and slew the fattest of them,** those physically in the best condition, **and smote down the chosen men of Israel,** those in the fulness of their strength, Num. 11, 33. V. 32. **For all this they sinned still,** refusing to let the punishments of the Lord lead them to repentance, **and believed not for His wondrous works,** even His miracles did not succeed in bringing about a lasting change of heart in them. V. 33. **Therefore their days did He consume in vanity,** literally, "He caused their days to vanish in a breath," **and their years in trouble,** with abrupt speed, for by His decision all the members of the nation which were forty years of age at the time of the exodus died in the wilderness. V. 34. **When He slew them, then they sought Him,** making a show at outward reformation, more from fear than from conviction; **and they returned and enquired early after God,** Num. 21, 7. V. 35. **And they remembered,** with a repentance of fear, **that God was their Rock,** Deut. 32, 15. 37, **and the high God their Redeemer,** from whom alone they might expect deliverance of body and soul. V. 36. **Nevertheless, they did flatter Him with their mouth,** trying to appease Him with a feigned change of heart, **and they lied unto Him with their tongues.** V. 37. **For their heart was not right with Him,** they were not sincere in their repentance, it was not a lasting sorrow which they felt, **neither were they steadfast in His covenant,** they did not prove themselves faithful. V. 38. **But He, being full of compassion,** of merciful patience, **forgave their iniquity and destroyed them not,** especially since Moses interceded for them time and again; **yea, many a time turned He His anger away and did not stir up all His wrath.** Cp. Num. 14, 20. V. 39. **For He remembered that they were but flesh,** weak and sinful mortals; **a wind that passeth away and cometh not again,** altogether evanescent. V. 40. **How oft did they provoke Him in the wilderness,** with rebellion upon rebellion, **and grieve Him in the desert,** troubling His loving fatherly heart with their unruly behavior. V. 41. **Yea, they turned back and tempted God,** testing out His kindness in a total of ten temptations, Num. 14, 22, **and limited the Holy One of Israel,** worrying, troubling, vexing Him with their rebellious conduct. V. 42. **They remembered not His hand,** outstretched as it had been for their deliverance, **nor the day when He delivered them from the enemy,** from the oppression of the Egyptians, v. 43. **how He had wrought His signs in Egypt and His wonders in the field of Zoan,** v. 12. the psalmist now turning to a recital of the plagues which God sent upon Pharaoh and the Egyptians in order to compel them to give Israel permission to leave, v. 44. **and had turned their rivers into blood,** in the first general plague, Ex. 7, 17, **and their floods, that they could not drink.** V. 45. **He sent divers sorts of flies among them,** the insect pests of the fourth plague, Ex. 8, 21—29, **which devoured them, and frogs,** in the second plague, Ex. 8, 2, **which destroyed them.** V. 46. **He gave also their increase unto the caterpillar,** literally, "the eater," the cricket, **and their labor unto the locust,** in the eighth plague, Ex. 10, 13—15. V. 47. **He destroyed their vines,** the growth of which was a very important industry in ancient Egypt, **with hail,** in the seventh plague, Ex. 9, 23—25, **and their sycomore-**

trees, the sycomore fig-trees of the Orient, **with frost,** great hailstones. V. 48. **He gave up their cattle also to the hail,** Ex. 9, 23, **and their flocks to hot thunderbolts,** for the play of lightning accompanying the hail was unparalled, Ex. 9, 22. 24. V. 49. **He cast upon them the fierceness of His anger, wrath, and indignation, and trouble, by sending evil angels among them,** that is, angels bringing all these misfortunes, destroying messengers of Jehovah. V. 50. **He made a way to His anger,** giving it free rein; **He spared not their soul from death, but gave their life over to the pestilence,** in the plague of murrain, Ex. 9, 6; v. 51. **and smote all the first-born in Egypt,** in the final plague, Ex. 12, 29; **the chief of their strength in the tabernacles of Ham,** in the habitations where the Egyptians, the descendants of Ham, dwelled; v. 52. **but made His own people to go forth like sheep,** under His protecting leadership, **and guided them in the wilderness like a flock,** Ps. 77, 21. V. 53. **And He led them on safely, so that they feared not,** there was no reason for worry or fear; **but the sea overwhelmed their enemies,** covering them, wiping them out. V. 54. **And He brought them to the border of His Sanctuary,** literally, "to the boundary of His holiness," the region or land in which His holiness was to rule, **even to this mountain, which His right hand had purchased,** the Holy Land itself. V. 55. **He cast out the heathen also before them,** under the leadership of Joshua, **and divided them an inheritance by line,** Josh. 13, 7, **and made the tribes of Israel to dwell in their tents,** every family in its own home, according to the allotment. V. 56. **Yet they tempted and provoked the most high God,** even after they were in possession of the Promised Land with all its blessings, Judg. 2, 11, **and kept not His testimonies,** all the regulations intended for the guidance of their conduct, v. 57. **but turned back,** aside from the prescribed path, **and dealt unfaithfully like their fathers,** they apostatized from their promised loyalty to Jehovah; **they were turned aside like a deceitful bow,** one which turns back and thus fails to shoot the arrow placed upon it. V. 58. **For they provoked Him to anger with their high places,** the altars on the hills devoted to idolatry, **and moved Him to jealousy with their graven images,** with the idols to which they turned in preference to Him. V. 59. **When God heard this, He was wroth,** filled with indignation, **and greatly abhorred Israel,** although not to the point of total rejection, v. 60. **so that He forsook the Tabernacle of Shiloh,** where it had first been erected after the conquest of the country, Josh. 18, 1; **the tent which He placed among men,** where He had promised to dwell and to reveal Himself to His people, for the Tabernacle was later erected near Gibeon, apparently on the hill between this town and Nob; v. 61. **and delivered His strength,** namely, the Ark of the Covenant, **into captivity,** by letting the Philistines capture it, 1 Sam. 4, **and His glory into the enemy's hand,** 1 Sam. 4, 21. 22. V. 62. **He gave His people over also unto the sword,** 1 Sam. 4, 10; **and was wroth with His inheritance,** with the people which belonged to Him by virtue of their deliverance. V. 63. **The fire,** namely, that of wars, **consumed their young men; and their maidens were not given to marriage,** no marriage anthems were intoned in their honor, for they were killed or dragged into exile during the troublous times of the judges. V. 64. **Their priests fell by the sword,** Hophni and Phinehas being examples, 1 Sam. 4, 11; **and their widows made no lamentation,** being kept from the customary rites of mourning by the terrors of war. But then came the change of Israel's fortunes. V. 65. **Then the Lord awaked as one out of sleep,** for it had seemed to Israel that He had slumbered while the heathen were enslaving His people, **and like a mighty man that shouteth by reason of wine,** filled with heroic courage by its proper enjoyment. V. 66. **And He smote His enemies in the hinder parts,** His blows raining down upon the backs, principally of the Philistines, who at that time were the chief enemies of Israel; **he put them to a perpetual reproach,** the disgrace recorded 1 Sam. 5, 6. V. 67. **Moreover, He refused the Tabernacle of Joseph,** taking it away from Shiloh, in the midst of the tribe of Ephraim, **and chose not the tribe of Ephraim,** v. 60, v. 68. **but chose the tribe of Judah,** the bearer of the Messianic promise, **the Mount Zion which He loved,** selecting Jerusalem as the city of His central Sanctuary. V. 69. **And He built his Sanctuary like high palaces,** firm as the heights of heaven, most excellent and glorious, **like the earth which He hath established forever,** founded most solidly. V. 70. **He chose David also His servant,** the ancestor of the Messiah, **and took him from the sheepfolds,** 1 Sam. 16, 11; v. 71. **from following the ewes great with young He brought him to feed Jacob, His people, and Israel, His inheritance,** the children of Israel being a type of the spiritual Israel, and David a type of the great Shepherd, the Messiah Himself, Is. 40, 11. V. 72. **So he fed them,** as their ruler, with all care and kindness, **according to the integrity of his heart,** striving after ever greater understanding of their needs, **and guided them by the skilfulness of his hands,** with the proper appreciation of all that was best for them. Herein also David prefigured the great King of the Church, whose understanding of our needs and wants resulted in our eternal redemption.

PSALM 79.

Prayer in the Midst of Oppression.

A psalm of Asaph, similar in tone and content to Ps. 74, though any special event which might have occasioned the writing of this hymn is not known. V. 1. **O God, the heathen are come into Thine inheritance,** the Holy Land, including both the city of the Sanctuary and the Temple itself, Ex. 15, 17, being referred to; **Thy holy Temple have they defiled,** by introducing some form of heathen pollution; **they have laid Jerusalem on heaps.** The psalmist, in prophetic spirit, sees Jerusalem laid waste and the Temple a heap of ruins, an event which came to pass when the city was taken by Nebuchadnezzar. V. 2. **The dead bodies of Thy servants have they given to be meat unto the fowls of the heaven,** the vultures feeding on the carcasses, **the flesh of Thy saints unto the beasts of the earth,** jackals and hyenas performing their gruesome work on the forsaken fields of battle. The description is typical of the desolation which has occasionally come upon the Church of Christ when the enemies have gained the upper hand. V. 3. **Their blood have they shed like water round about Jerusalem,** considering it utterly worthless, not feeling a single twinge of conscience on account of their violence; **and there was none to bury them,** all inhabitants being either dead or in exile. V. 4. **We are become a reproach to our neighbors,** objects of jeering on account of their trust in Jehovah, **a scorn and derision to them that are round about us,** whose blasphemy really struck the name of God, deriding Him as powerless to help the city of His Sanctuary. In like manner the enemies of the Church have ever behaved in times of persecution. V. 5. **How long, Lord? Wilt Thou be angry forever? Shall Thy jealousy burn like fire?** His zeal in punishing His people for their sins. V. 6. **Pour out Thy wrath upon the heathen that have not known Thee,** who were willingly estranged from Him, hostile to His Church, **and upon the kingdoms that have not called upon Thy name,** refusing to accept Jehovah as the only true God. V. 7. **For they have devoured Jacob,** the spiritual Israel, the Church of God suffering under the oppression of its enemies, **and laid waste his dwelling-place.** The enemies are purposely spoken of in the singular, in a collective sense; for no matter what form the enmity against Christ's Church takes, it always has the same object. V. 8. **O remember not against us former iniquities,** those of the forefathers, this statement including a confession of guilt, of apostasy in the past; **let Thy tender mercies speedily prevent us,** coming to meet the believers, in order to bring them proper assistance with the greatest haste; **for we are brought very low,** they were unable, without the mercy of God, to rise from their defeat. V. 9. **Help us, O God of our salvation,** in whom alone the believers of all times place their hope of redemption, **for the glory of Thy name,** for the performance of His merciful promises would redound to His glory; **and deliver us and purge away our sins for Thy name's sake;** for the granting of such remission always serves to set forth the most beautiful traits and attributes of God, His love, grace, and mercy. V. 10. **Wherefore should the heathen,** in taking note of the desolation of the Church, **say, Where is their God?** the doubt expressed in their derision being a form of blasphemy. **Let him be known among the heathen in our sight by the revenging of the blood of Thy servants which is shed,** that is, vengeance for the blood of the Lord's servants, as shed by the enemies, should come upon them in the sight of the believers, so that these would have evidence of the fact that God will not be mocked. V. 11. **Let the sighing of the prisoner,** the moaning of those kept in captivity by the enemies, **come before Thee; according to the greatness of Thy power,** the arm of His omnipotence stretched out in behalf of His children, **preserve Thou those that are appointed to die,** literally, "the children of slaughter"; for death is thought of as having fatherly authority to the extent of putting men to death; v. 12. **and render unto our neighbors,** the enemies spoken of throughout, **sevenfold into their bosom,** in exhausting His judicial punishment upon them, in making them feel the severity of His anger, **their reproach, wherewith they have reproached Thee, O Lord.** Thus would the Lord save His honor, reestablish His position of honor and power before the world. V. 13. **So we, Thy people and sheep of Thy pasture,** who have submitted themselves absolutely to the guidance of their great Shepherd, trusting implicitly in His power for protection, **will give Thee thanks forever; we will show forth Thy praise to all generations.** The same trust in Jehovah, together with the attitude of perpetual praise, must be found in all believers.

PSALM 80.

Prayer for the Deliverance of the Church.

To the chief musician upon Shoshannim-Eduth, to be rendered in public worship according to the melody "Lilies a Testimony," **a psalm of Asaph,** the hymn referring to the testimony of Jehovah before His people and speaking in a prophetic strain of the tribulation and deliverance of the Church of God. V. 1. **Give ear,** lending His ear in the attitude of most careful attention, **O Shepherd of Is-**

rael, Jehovah being the true Shepherd and Protector of the spiritual Israel, **Thou that leadest Joseph,** who here represents all believers, **like a flock,** Is. 40, 11; **Thou that dwellest between the cherubim,** the place above the mercy-seat where God revealed Himself to His people, Ex. 25, 22; Num. 7, 89, **shine forth,** making known His glory. V. 2. **Before Ephraim and Benjamin and Manasseh,** these three tribes, associated also Num. 2, 18—24, being named as representatives of Israel, in marching next to the Ark of the Covenant under the leadership of Jehovah, **stir up Thy strength,** which now seemed so sluggish, **and come and save us,** bringing assistance and salvation to His people. V. 3. **Turn us again,** bringing them back, delivering them out of all the misery with which they were contending, **O God, and cause Thy face to shine,** in the glory of His loving-kindness and tender mercies; **and we shall be saved,** this being the refrain sung by the congregation of believers for their own consolation. V. 4. **O Lord God of hosts,** the Ruler and General of all the heavenly forces, whom He freely used in His service, **how long wilt Thou be angry,** literally, "smoke," said of indignant snorting, **against the prayer of Thy people?** during their prayer, not heeding their prayer, their appeals not being able to penetrate the smoking clouds of wrath with which the Lord had surrounded Himself. V. 5. **Thou feedest them with the bread of tears,** they were unable to eat, their tears were their only food, Ps. 42, 4; **and givest them tears to drink in great measure,** all this being Oriental imagery to emphasize the severity of their affliction. V. 6. **Thou makest us a strife unto our neighbors,** the object of their taunts and attacks; **and our enemies laugh among themselves,** making mockery of Israel's plight. Therefore the Church's pleading cry sounds forth once more, v. 7. **Turn us again, O God of hosts, and cause Thy face to shine, and we shall be saved.** The believers now bring additional arguments to stress the need of speedy assistance. V. 8. **Thou hast brought a vine out of Egypt,** the congregation of the Lord; **Thou hast cast out the heathen,** expelling them out of Canaan, the land promised to Israel, **and planted it,** giving to His children the country where He expected them to live and flourish chiefly in their capacity as His Church. V. 9. **Thou preparedst room before it,** providing sufficient space for physical expansion, **and didst cause it to take deep root,** Israel being established firmly also as a nation, with the idea of the Lord's people foremost, **and it filled the land.** V. 10. **The hills were covered with the shadow of it, and the boughs thereof were like the goodly cedars,** Israel, as the Church of God, flourishing in its country, which is so largely mountainous, like the cedars of Lebanon. V. 11. **She sent out her boughs unto the sea,** for the Israelites occupied the land down to the Mediterranean Sea in the West, **and her branches unto the river,** the northeastern boundary being the Euphrates. V. 12. **Why hast Thou, then, broken down her hedges,** the picture of a vineyard with its sheltering hedge being retained, **so that all they which pass by the way do pluck her?** the hedge having been removed, any passer-by felt himself entitled to step in and rob. V. 13. **The boar out of the wood,** one of the neighboring nations, **doth waste it,** cutting it down with his tusks, **and the wild beast of the field,** the reference here probably being to the nomad tribes of Arabia, **doth devour it.** The entire country was helpless before the inroads of the enemies, and the Church was the chief sufferer. V. 14. **Return,** turning back His eyes which had been turned away in anger, **we beseech Thee, O God of hosts,** with His unlimited resources; **look down from heaven, and behold, and visit this vine,** once more taking an active interest in its welfare, supporting it in its present difficulty; v. 15. **and the vineyard,** the garden of the Church, **which Thy right hand,** emblem of almighty power, **hath planted, and the branch that Thou madest strong for Thyself,** protecting its stem, the stock of the Church, which He had chosen for the honor of His name, for the spread of His glory. V. 16. **It is burned with fire, it is cut down,** the reference being rather to the host of the enemy, which would be utterly destroyed by the avenging hand of the Lord; **they perish at the rebuke of Thy countenance,** this being the definite expectation of the believers. V. 17. **Let Thy hand,** in favor and protection, **be upon the man of Thy right hand,** supported by God's almighty power, **upon the son of man whom Thou madest strong for Thyself,** the reference being either to the Church as personified in each believer, or to the great Son of Man, the Messiah, Himself; for the prophetic character of the psalm is very marked. V. 18. **So will not we go back from Thee,** never forsaking the Lord of their salvation. **Quicken us,** blessing them with new spiritual life, **and we will call upon Thy name,** proclaiming the Lord as He has revealed Himself in His Word. With this assurance, which must be found in every prayer, the believers send up their appeal for the third time: v. 19. **Turn us again, O Lord God of hosts, cause Thy face to shine, and we shall be saved.** Such a prayer will bring to the believers the quickening grace, which enables them to persevere in the right worship.

PSALM 81.

A Joyful Salutation and God's Response.

To the chief musician upon Gittith, to be sung to the accompaniment of the zitherlike instrument which David brought along from the Philistine city of Gath, **a psalm of Asaph,** an antiphonal, festal hymn, probably for the celebration of the Passover, God Himself answering the praise of His people by reminding them of their obligations and picturing to them the happy consequences of obedience and loyalty to Him. V. 1. **Sing aloud unto God, our Strength,** letting exultation sound forth in His honor, to praise Him for His almighty protection; **make a joyful noise unto the God of Jacob,** the only true God, Jacob representing the Church of all times. V. 2. **Take a psalm,** the summons being addressed to the chorus of Levites to begin their songs of praise, **and bring hither the timbrel, the pleasant harp with the psaltery,** zither and harp being used largely in the Temple orchestra on account of the pleasing quality of their music. V. 3. **Blow up the trumpet in the new moon,** the horns, as blown by the priests, being the most prominent instruments on the Feast of the New Moon, the civil new year, on the first of Tishri, Num. 10, 10, **in the time appointed, on our solemn feast-day,** for trumpets were used on all the great festivals. V. 4. **For this was a statute for Israel,** pertaining to the precepts governing the covenant people, **and a law of the God of Jacob,** fixed by Him to regulate the customs of the feasts. V. 5. **This He ordained in Joseph,** this one tribe here representing the entire nation, **for a testimony, when He went out through the land of Egypt,** in preparing for the exodus of His people; for from that time dated the personal intercourse of Jehovah with His people; **where I heard a language that I understood not,** the psalmist speaking in the name of Israel, states that the fact of a strange language in the mouth of their oppressors in Egypt increased the burden of their slavery. The mention of these facts agreed with the object of the Hebrew festivals, which were to bring the great deeds of God to the remembrance of all believers. The Lord Himself now takes up the strain of the hymn. V. 6. **I removed his shoulder from the burden,** by setting His people free from the serfdom of Egypt; **his hands were delivered from the pots,** from the baskets which the children of Israel were forced to carry as hods in transporting building materials for the monuments of Pharaoh. V. 7. **Thou calledst in trouble,** when the Egyptians oppressed them, **and I delivered thee,** Ex. 2, 24. 25; **I answered thee in the secret place of thunder,** literally, the veil of the thunder, the pillar of cloud, from out of which God wrought His wonders at the passage of the Red Sea. **I proved thee at the waters of Meribah,** testing their faith by the miracle there performed, Ex. 17, 6. 7. **Selah.** V. 8. **Hear, O My people,** a most impressive appeal, **and I will testify unto thee; O Israel, if thou wilt hearken unto Me!** The Lord now states the terms of the solemn covenant between Himself and Israel. V. 9. **There shall no strange god be in thee,** every form of idolatry being an abomination before Him; **neither shalt thou worship any strange god.** V. 10. **I am the Lord, thy God, which brought thee out of the land of Egypt,** Ex. 20, 2; **open thy mouth wide,** to receive the great spiritual blessings due to the people of the covenant, **and I will fill it,** He alone being able to give the full and lasting satisfaction of peace and blessedness. V. 11. **But My people would not hearken to My voice,** as events after the giving of the Law showed; **and Israel would none of Me,** disobedience and self-will being its outstanding characteristics. V. 12. **So I gave them up unto their own hearts' lust,** their stubbornness, that being God's punishment upon the stubborn and rebellious of all times; **and they walked,** were engaged in and with, **their own counsels,** totally estranged to Jehovah. V. 13. **Oh, that My people had hearkened unto Me, and Israel had walked in My ways!** In that event their entire history would have had a different cast, and their fate would not have been so sad. V. 14. **I should soon have subdued their enemies,** whom they were too indifferent to drive out completely, Judg. 1 and 2, **and turned My hand against their adversaries,** to exterminate them altogether. V. 15. **The haters of the Lord should have submitted themselves unto Him,** brought into subjection by the almighty power of the Lord; **but their time,** that of the children of Israel, their pleasant relations with the covenant God, **should have endured forever.** V. 16. **He should have fed them also with the finest of the wheat,** with the richest blessings of His goodness and mercy; **and with honey out of the rock should I have satisfied thee.** Cp. Deut. 32, 1—47. Such is the earnest appeal of the Lord as it finds its application in the Church, also of the New Testament, a sermon which should be heeded especially in these last days of indifference and enmity toward God.

PSALM 82.

God as the Judge of Governments.

A psalm of Asaph, to set forth the majesty of the great Judge of the earth. V. 1. **God standeth in the congregation of the mighty,** in the assembly of God, firm and immovable in the midst of His Church, against which therefore the gates of hell cannot prevail; **He judgeth among the gods,** among the judges, the rulers of the earth; for every government receives its authority from God and is responsible to Him, who will call all the mighty ones of the earth to account for their manner of ruling. V. 2. **How long will ye judge unjustly,** engaging in, performing iniquity in ostensibly carrying out justice, **and accept the persons of the wicked,** favoring their faces, that is, pervert right and justice in their favor? **Selah.** Such perversion of justice was common in Oriental courts, where flattering courtiers were admitted to the presence of the sovereign and succeeded in gaining their ends, while others had to be content with remaining outside and having their case decided against them in their absence. V. 3. **Defend the poor and fatherless,** the orphans and those without political influence; **do justice to the afflicted and needy,** making it a point to see that they received the right due them. V. 4. **Deliver the poor and needy,** from the many forms of oppression practised by the mighty; **rid them out of the hand of the wicked.** The rulers are under obligation to see that justice is properly administered at all times and with regard to every station of mankind. V. 5. **They know not, neither will they understand,** that is, the rulers, in many cases, ignore the voice of their conscience, they wilfully set aside the obligation resting upon them; **they walk on in darkness,** deliberately blinding their eyes and hardening their hearts to the demands of their position; **all the foundations of the earth are out of course,** the entire order of things in the world is upset, their negligence causes anarchy to ensue and to overthrow law and order. V. 6. **I have said, Ye are gods,** He Himself has clothed them with their official dignity, they are never to forget that they are His representatives; **and all of you are children of the Most High,** they do not hold their office by an absolute right, but, as His sons, are responsible to Him for the entire discharge of their duties. V. 7. **But,** in spite of the prerogative which they hold by virtue of the grace of God, **ye shall die like men,** that is, like ordinary people, such as held no distinguishing positions during their lifetime, **and fall like one of the princes,** their fate would be that of the many other rulers whom the might of God had deposed from their high estate and laid into the grave. V. 8. **Arise, O God, judge the earth,** Himself exercising the functions of the great Judge, since men were performing this office so badly; **for Thou shalt inherit all nations,** it is in His power to take hold of the nations at any time, personally to take charge of the business of judging righteously. That is the constant prayer of the believers, that God would hinder all unrighteousness upon the earth, so that His children may lead a quiet and peaceable life in all godliness and honesty.

PSALM 83.

A Prayer for Help against the Enemies of the Church.

A song or psalm of Asaph, the last of his twelve hymns in the psalter, picturing the craft and rage of the enemies and invoking God's speedy destruction upon them. V. 1. **Keep not Thou silence,** content with resting, with being an idle spectator, **O God; hold not Thy peace and be not still, O God,** that is, inactive while such great dangers were threatening. V. 2. **For, lo, Thine enemies** (the enemies of the Church are God's enemies) **make a tumult; and they that hate Thee have lifted up the head,** in haughty pride and arrogance. V. 3. **They have taken crafty counsel,** laying their plans in secret and with guile, **against Thy people,** primarily Israel, but as typical of the spiritual Israel, **and consulted against Thy hidden ones,** the number of true believers always being so small, by comparison, that they disappear in the great mass of humanity, while, nevertheless, God protects them. V. 4. **They have said, Come and let us cut them off from being a nation,** exterminating them from among the nations, **that the name of Israel may be no more in remembrance,** the annihilation, as planned by them, being so complete that the very name of God's people would be forgotten in history. V. 5. **For they have consulted together with one consent,** their hearts and minds all being of the same opinion and purpose; **they are confederate against Thee,** their covenant against Israel being in reality a covenant against the God of Israel; v. 6. **the tabernacles of Edom,** that is, all the nomadic tribes belonging to this nation, **and the Ishmaelites; of Moab and the Hagarenes,** who roamed from the Persian Gulf to the desert country east of Gilead; v. 7. **Gebal,** the northern part of the mountains of Seir and therefore pertaining to Edom, **and Ammon,** Israel's ancient enemy east of Gilead, **and Amalek,** the last remnants of this desert tribe living within the territory of Edom or in remote parts of the Desert of Paran; **the Philistines,** on the Mediterranean, toward the southwest, **with the inhabitants of Tyre,** the Phenician nation; v. 8. **Assur also is joined with them,** the great kingdom of Assyria, which at that time had not yet reached the summit of its power; **they have holpen the children of Lot,** entered into an alliance with the Moabites and the Ammonites. **Selah.** Practically all the heathen nations surrounding Canaan were directly or indirectly interested in this plan of annihilating Israel, even as enemies of every description nowadays unite when the object of the confederacy is to fight the true Church. V. 9. **Do unto them as unto the Midianites,** who were practically annihilated at the time of Gideon, Judg. 7; 8, 11. 12; **as to Sisera, as to Jabin, at the brook of Kison,** at the time of Deborah and Barak, Judg. 4, v. 10. **which perished at Endor,** a town on the northern edge of the Plain of Jezreel, for it was there that the battle against the host of the Canaanites took place; **they became as dung for the earth,** their decaying carcasses forming manure, fertilizer, for the soil of Canaan. V. 11. **Make their nobles like Oreb and like Zeeb,** the two princes of the Midianites slain at the time of Gideon, Judg. 7, 25; **yea, all their princes as Zebah, and as Zalmunna,** slain by Gideon after their armies had been defeated, Judg. 8, 10—21; v. 12. **who said, Let us take to ourselves the houses of God in possession,** they had intended to overthrow the true religion. V. 13. **O my God, make them like a wheel,** like a whirlwind and whatever is carried away by a tornado, **as the stubble before the wind,** disappearing without leaving a trace behind. V. 14. **As the fire burneth a wood,** great forests being devoured in a short time, **and as the flame setteth the mountains on fire,** the mountains themselves melting away with their woody covering before the flame of God's wrath, v. 15, **so persecute them with Thy tempest and make them afraid,** completely overthrowing them, **with Thy storm.** V. 16. **Fill their faces with shame,** disgrace being heaped upon them by their overthrow, **that they may seek Thy name, O Lord,** acknowledging the exclusive divinity of Jehovah, whether willingly or under compulsion. V. 17. **Let them be confounded,** heaped with shame, **and troubled,** overthrown, **forever; yea, let them be put to shame, and perish,** fully convinced of their own vanity and that of their false gods, v. 18. **that men may know that Thou, whose name alone is JEHOVAH,** the God of revelation, **art the most high over all the earth,** admitted as such either in fear or in faith. Cp. Is. 37, 16—20; 2 Kings 19, 19. That is the comfort of the believers of all times, that the true God will, in the end, be revealed before all men, to their utter confusion and to His own glorification, as the most high God.

PSALM 84.

Longing for the Beauty of the Word of God.

To the chief musician upon Gittith, to be used in public worship with the accompaniment of a stringed instrument brought by David from the Philistine city of Gath, **a psalm for the sons of Korah,** one of the members of this family having been the author of this hymn praising the worship of the true God. V. 1. **How amiable are Thy tabernacles,** the places where God revealed Himself being both worthy of love and beloved by those who realize their importance, **O Lord of hosts!** The plural is used in speaking of God's habitations, because David had, at this time, erected a splendid tent on Mount Zion, which harbored the Ark of the Covenant, 2 Sam. 6, 17; 7, 2. But the old Tabernacle near Gibeon was still in use, one of the high priests being on duty there with regular priests and Levites as his assistants, 1 Chron. 22, 29; 2 Chron. 1, 3—5. V. 2. **My soul longeth,** with intensive desire, **yea, even fainteth,** exhausted and almost parched with spiritual thirst, **for the courts of the Lord,** where the congregation assembled for worship; **my heart and my flesh crieth out for the living God,** with jubilant rejoicing in the midst of their sorrow, at the prospect of being in the presence of the Lord once more. V. 3. **Yea, the sparrow hath found an house and the swallow a nest for herself, where she may lay her young,** brooding them with tender care, the reference being to the fact that small birds were permitted to build their nests within the precincts of the Temple without being disturbed, **even Thine altars, O Lord of hosts, my King, and my God.** Even as the birds considered the precincts of the Tabernacle their home, to which they always returned with longing and delight, so the singer regards the habitations of the Lord, the great sanctuaries of the people, as his home on earth and longs to return there, to find both protection and food in his fellowship with God. V. 4. **Blessed are they that dwell in Thy house,** enjoying their position as members of the household of God; **they will be still praising Thee,** no matter what outward afflictions tend to take away their feeling of happiness. **Selah.** While the poet waits for the removal of the obstructions which are keeping him from visiting the Sanctuary, he carries out the thought of the blessed fellowship with God, the believer's bond of union with Jehovah. V. 5.

Blessed is the man whose strength is in Thee, the might of the All-powerful being made perfect in his own weakness; **in whose heart are the ways of them,** in whose thoughts were not only the pilgrim routes to Jerusalem, as they led to the Sanctuary at the time of the great festivals, but also the ways of God's commandments, the following of which would keep the faithful in communion with Jehovah; v. 6. **who, passing through the Valley of Baca,** the vale of tears, the picture being that of the toilsome ascent to the hill upon which Jerusalem is situated, **make it a well,** the divine blessing accompanying the faithful everywhere and supplying the means by which they are refreshed on their journey; **the rain also filleth the pools,** the reference being to the first fruitful rain after the heat and drought of summer, which quickly changes the parched fields into green meadows. V. 7. **They go from strength to strength,** receiving an ever greater amount the nearer they approach the Holy City, **every one of them in Zion appeareth before God,** having reached his goal in safety. The prayer of the faithful, therefore, rises up to the throne of Jehovah in a mighty chorus: v. 8. **O Lord God of hosts, hear my prayer; give ear,** with close attention, **O God of Jacob! Selah.** It seems, however, that the psalmist, deprived of this glorious privilege of visiting the Tabernacle of the Lord with the congregation, now sends out an all the more fervent appeal. V. 9. **Behold, O God, our Shield,** the great Protector of His children, **and look upon the face of Thine anointed,** the reference here probably being to David during one of the periods when he was forced to flee from Jerusalem. V. 10. **For a day in Thy courts,** spent in worshiping with the congregation, **is better than a thousand,** such as are spent in the ordinary pursuits of life. **I had rather be a doorkeeper in the house of my God,** literally, "I prefer to lie upon the threshold," the smallest measure of God's blessing, the most remote connection with the privilege of partaking in His worship being such a wonderful experience, **than to dwell in the tents of wickedness,** in the midst of the greatest abundance supplied from earthly sources. V. 11. **For the Lord God is a Sun,** shining upon the believers with heavenly light and life, **and Shield,** protecting them against dangers of every kind; **the Lord will give grace and glory,** these gifts being the rays coming down from the divine Sun: grace, as the favor of God; glory, the honor He bestows. **No good thing will He withhold from them that walk uprightly,** making the entire conduct of their life accord with the will of the Lord. V. 12. **O Lord of hosts, blessed is the man that trusteth in Thee,** confidently expecting from the great King of heaven all good and all perfect gifts. The application of this psalm, both to the Christian's longing for the blessings contained in the means of grace and to his eager desire for the final revelation of God's glory, is obvious and, at the same time, most comforting.

PSALM 85.

A Prayer for the Welfare of the Country.

To the chief musician, for use in liturgical worship, **a psalm for the sons of Korah,** an inspired singer of this family praying to God for renewed blessings and rejoicing in the certainty of their being given. V. 1. **Lord, Thou hast been favorable unto Thy land,** showing His merciful kindness to the land of Canaan, the inheritance of Israel; **Thou hast brought back the captivity of Jacob,** the deliverance not only out of the serfdom of Egypt being meant, but also out of the many tribulations which had come upon the Lord's people till the time of David. V. 2. **Thou hast forgiven the iniquity of Thy people,** the entire history of Israel recounting this fact, **Thou hast covered all their sin,** this being the essence of the forgiveness of sins, not to ignore them, but to cover them. **Selah.** V. 3. **Thou hast taken away all Thy wrath,** withdrawing it, strong as the provocation continued; **Thou hast turned Thyself from the fierceness of Thine anger,** He still had occasion to let it burn against Israel, but had now caused it to retreat, no longer to be active. V. 4. **Turn us,** out of the captivity of sin and misery with which Israel was surrounded, **O God of our salvation,** who alone can give full deliverance from all bodily and spiritual tribulation, **and cause Thine anger toward us to cease,** bringing it to naught, withdrawing it entirely. V. 5. **Wilt Thou be angry with us forever?** Ps. 79, 5. **Wilt Thou draw out Thine anger to all generations?** prolonging it from generation to generation. V. 6. **Wilt Thou not revive us again,** giving them back the true enjoyment of life, in the assurance of His grace and in the power for sanctification flowing from His strength, **that Thy people may rejoice in Thee?** V. 7. **Show us Thy mercy, O Lord,** letting them see and enjoy it, **and grant us Thy salvation,** the idea of merit being excluded altogether. V. 8. **I will hear what God the Lord will speak; for He will speak peace unto His people,** the obstruction of their sins being removed, a cessation of enmity was made possible, **and to His saints,** that is, the godly, the believers in Him; **but let them not turn again to folly,** since deliberate sinning would once more provoke the anger of the Lord. V. 9. **Surely His salvation is nigh them that**

fear Him, the believers always having a feeling of reverence for the Lord of their salvation, **that glory may dwell in our land,** being at home once more, where it had become a stranger, once more giving to the believer the honor of being called the sons of God. V. 10. **Mercy and truth are met together,** grace and faithfulness meeting as friends and operating in harmony; **righteousness and peace have kissed each other,** the cooperation of these virtues making for the welfare of the land. V. 11. **Truth,** the covenant faithfulness following the return of God's merciful kindness upon the land of Israel, **shall spring out of the earth,** as a fruit of God's love; **and righteousness shall look down from heaven,** promising to God's children the richness of His imputed grace. V. 12. **Yea, the Lord shall give that which is good,** which brings true happiness to the country; **and our land shall yield her increase,** His blessings being apparent in both temporal and spiritual benefits. V. 13. **Righteousness shall go before Him,** as the herald proclaiming His coming; **and shall set us in the way of His steps,** following Him closely and carefully, so that it is once more generally known and observed throughout the land. In this way the Lord turns to the prayer of His saints, refreshing them after the experience of so much tribulation on their part, giving them hours of gladness before His face.

PSALM 86.

David's Prayer in the Midst of Persecution.

A prayer of David, the only hymn by the great king and prophet which was included by the collectors in this book of the psalter. We find here the same terms and phrases which are so familiar from the other psalms of David, particularly those written during the period of persecution. V. 1. **Bow down Thine ear,** in the attitude of the very closest attention, **O Lord, hear me; for I am poor and needy.** Cp. Ps. 40, 17. V. 2. **Preserve my soul,** in the midst of persecution and suffering; **for I am holy,** a saint of God, under His favor. **O Thou, my God, save Thy servant that trusteth in Thee,** clinging to Jehovah with the full confidence of his heart. Note the expression of faith in the emphatic "my God." V. 3. **Be merciful unto me, O Lord,** all claim of merit and worthiness being set aside by the psalmist; **for I cry unto Thee daily,** pleading for Jehovah's grace all day long. V. 4. **Rejoice the soul of Thy servant,** filling it with happy exultation; **for unto Thee, O Lord, do I lift up my soul,** raising it to the All-powerful in importunate and confident pleading. The reason for this bold approach is now given. V. 5. **For Thou, Lord, art good, and ready to forgive,** willing, not to ignore, but to remit sins; **and plenteous in mercy,** abundant in grace, **unto all them that call upon Thee,** in the true worship of the heart. V. 6. **Give ear, O Lord, unto my prayer,** the psalmist returning once more to his opening petition, **and attend to the voice of my supplications,** literally, "of my urgent pleading." V. 7. **In the day of my trouble I will call upon Thee,** that is, in every time of deep need; **for Thou wilt answer me,** this confidence being the necessary concomitant of a right prayer. V. 8. **Among the gods,** those designated with this honoring name by the ignorant heathen, **there is none like unto Thee, O Lord,** Jehovah being the only true God; **neither are there any works,** no matter what miracles are by the heathen falsely ascribed to their idols, **like unto Thy works.** V. 9. **All nations whom Thou hast made shall come and worship before Thee, O Lord,** the prophet, in this vision, seeing representatives of every people on earth bowing before Messiah's throne; **and shall glorify Thy name,** praising the true God as He has revealed Himself, chiefly in His Word. The universality of the one true, the revealed religion, now known as the Christian religion, is here plainly taught. V. 10. **For Thou art great and doest wondrous things,** the only miracles really worthy of the name being those performed by Jehovah; **Thou art God alone.** This being the case, the psalmist longs to be more closely united with God by the bands of faith. V. 11. **Teach me Thy way, O Lord,** pointing out how the believer may arrange his entire life in conformity with the will of Jehovah; **I will walk in Thy truth,** in line with the faithfulness of the covenant God; **unite my heart to fear Thy name,** uniting all the believer's powers to give the Lord his whole, undivided heart in showing Him reverence by a life of sanctification. V. 12. **I will praise Thee, O Lord, my God,** the All-powerful, **with all my heart; and I will glorify Thy name forevermore,** praising and proclaiming the perfections of God's essence and attributes as revealed in His Word. V. 13. **For great is Thy mercy,** God's unmerited favor, **toward me, and Thou hast delivered my soul from the lowest hell,** from the lowest regions of the realm of death, said of the extremely perilous situation in which David had found himself on account of the persecution of his enemies. V. 14. **O God, the proud,** insolent, arrogant persons, **are risen against me, and the assemblies of violent men,** a band of tyrants, **have sought after my soul,** to take his life, **and have not set Thee before them,** purposely ignoring Jehovah's attributes and His holy will, lest they be kept from their wickedness. V. 15. **But Thou, O Lord, art a God full of compassion,** as contrasted with the cruelty, insolence, and violence of the enemies, **and gracious, long-suffering, and plenteous in mercy and truth,** as He Himself had testified when passing before the face of Moses, Ex. 34, 6. V. 16. **O turn unto me,** with His face full of divine favor, **and have mercy upon me; give Thy strength,** the divine power being the source of all the believer's strength, **unto Thy servant, and save the son of Thine handmaid,** born into the inheritance of the children of God, possessing the blessings of the true worship of Jehovah from his birth. V. 17. **Show me a token for good,** an evidence of divine favor, a special measure of His blessings, **that they which hate me may see it and be ashamed,** covered with shame on account of the favor of the Lord so manifestly resting upon the faithful; **because Thou, Lord, hast holpen me and comforted me.** The same help and comfort on the part of God may freely be asked by all believers, for He is truly the God of every one who puts his faith in Him.

PSALM 87.

The Church of God the Spiritual Birthplace of the Nations.

A psalm or song for the sons of Korah, a triumphal hymn in the strain of these inspired singers, celebrating the glory of the Church as the means of spiritual blessings to all nations. V. 1. **His foundation,** that which Jehovah, the Lord of the Church, has laid, **is in the holy mountains,** the location of the Temple being given in the wide sense, for Jerusalem was situated on several hills, one of which became the hill of the Sanctuary. V. 2. **The Lord loveth the gates of Zion,** of the Temple situated on that mountain, as the emblem of His Church on earth, **more than all the dwellings of Jacob,** as the place of His habitation and of the revelation of His glory in the midst of His people. Note that the gates of Zion are mentioned to indicate the accessibility of the city to all men; for the means of grace administered by the Church are intended to bring salvation to all men. V. 3. **Glorious things are spoken of thee, O city of God. Selah.** The things which are said about the Church of God of all times redound to His glory, because they relate to Zion's increasing glory; and the miracles of God performed for the salvation of men are spoken in the city as well, that all its inhabitants may be confirmed in their faith. V. 4. **I will make mention of Rahab and Babylon to them that know Me,** literally, "I will call to remembrance Rahab," that is, Egypt, "and Babylon as those who know Me," publishing the fact that people even from these heathen nations came to the knowledge of the truth. **Behold Philistia,** the heathen country southwest of Canaan, **and Tyre,** that is, Phenicia, **with Ethiopia,** the country south of Egypt; **this man was born there,** that is, people from all these nations, from belligerent Philistia, from commercial Phenicia, from powerful Ethiopia, would be gained for Jehovah; always there would be some out of the heathen nations who would accept Jehovah as their Savior. V. 5. **And of Zion it shall be said,** of the Church itself the statement would be made, **This and that man was born in her,** added to her by his spiritual birth; **and the Highest Himself shall establish her,** God Himself having laid the foundations of the Church, it shall not be moved, Ps. 46. V. 6. **The Lord shall count, when He writeth up the people,** as one believer after the other is added to His register, **that this man was born there,** for the Lord knoweth them that are His, and He enters each individual name in the book of life, 2 Tim. 2, 19. **Selah.** V. 7. **As well the singers,** those praising the Lord with hymns of thanksgiving, **as the players on instruments,** those who leap and spring for joy in honor of the Lord, as David did when he brought the Ark of the Covenant to Mount Zion, **shall be there;** for the joy of the Church Militant will be continued in the exultation of the Church Triumphant. **All my springs are in thee;** for Jerusalem, or Zion, the Church of Christ, is the place where the true water of life springs up and flows for all men, inviting them all to partake of its riches to the salvation of their souls. These are some of the glorious facts which establish and maintain faith in the hearts of men, for which the believers give thanks to the Lord with exultant hearts, here in time and hereafter in eternity.

PSALM 88.

A Lament in the Midst of Suffering and Tribulation.

A song or psalm for the sons of Korah, written by a member of this illustrious family of musicians, **to the chief musician upon Mahalath Leannoth,** for use in public worship, but in a sorrowful manner, with muffled voices, **Maschil,** a didactic poem, **of Heman, the Ezrahite,** one of the four wise men at the time of Solomon, 1 Kings 4, 31, whose unusual musical gifts had caused him to be made a member of the Korahites, who were really more a guild than a family. V. 1. **O Lord God of my salvation,** in whom alone there is salvation for all men, a fact which makes it necessary for every individual to cling to Him in faith, **I have cried day and night,** without ceasing, **before Thee.** V. 2. **Let my prayer come before Thee,** placing no obstruction in its way, granting it a ready audience; **incline Thine ear unto my cry,** in the attitude of willing attention; v. 3. **for my soul is full of troubles,** filled up, surfeited, with evil, with suffering, **and my life,** in consequence of these evils, **draweth nigh unto the grave,** on the boundary of the realm of death. V. 4. **I am counted with them that go down into the pit,** those whose death is considered imminent. **I am as a man that hath no strength,** his utter loss of vitality contrasting with his former strength and energy; v. 5. **free among the dead,** that is, set free, or released, from the bonds of the living, **like the slain that lie in the grave, whom Thou rememberest no more,** they are no longer active in the history of men, apparently gone and forgotten for the time being; **and they are cut off from Thy hand,** no longer enjoying its guidance and help. V. 6. **Thou hast laid me in the lowest pit,** in the most remote parts of the realm of death, **in darkness, in the deeps,** for the kingdom of death was supposed to be in the depths below the ocean, in impenetrable darkness. All this is description of the almost indescribable affliction which had come upon the psalmist. V. 7. **Thy wrath lieth hard upon me,** pressing down upon him as with the force of mighty billows, **and Thou hast afflicted me with all Thy waves,** bowing down His wrath upon him, like the breakers of the seashore, **Selah.** V. 8. **Thou hast put away mine acquaintance far from me,** his closest friends drawing back from him with suspicion, knowing no other explanation for his condition than that of the righteous punishment of God, as in the case of Job; **Thou hast made me an abomination unto them,** so that they loathe the very sight of him; **I am shut up, and I cannot come forth,** his distress being so great that no way of escape opens before his eyes. V. 9. **Mine eye mourneth by reason of affliction,** failing and decaying in utter exhaustion. **Lord, I have called daily upon Thee,** day after day, without ceasing; **I have stretched out my hands unto Thee,** in a gesture of urgent pleading, imploring His compassion. V. 10. **Wilt Thou show wonders to the dead?** That is, Did God intend to wait till He had succumbed to death? **Shall the dead arise and praise Thee?** That is, God surely did not expect praise from ghosts. **Selah.** The thought is this, that the psalmist, while he was still alive, wanted to praise the Lord for his deliverance from all the misery afflicting him; therefore the Lord should not let his afflictions reach such a climax as to bring him to the realm of death; for then all opportunity for worshiping Him would be past. V. 11. **Shall Thy loving-kindness be declared in the grave or Thy faithfulness in destruction,** in the place of ruin? V. 12. **Shall Thy wonders be known in the dark?** in the darkness of the realm of death, **and Thy righteousness,** as He revealed and imparted it to the believers, **in the land of forgetfulness?** where the body, even of the believers, for the time being, loses the faculty of thinking, feeling, and acting. The question of a final resurrection is not broached here, the psalmist having before his eyes only the deliverance from the present troubles. V. 13. **But unto Thee have I cried, O Lord,** deliberately shaking off the thoughts of despair which threatened to overwhelm his trust in Jehovah; **and in the morning shall my prayer prevent Thee,** going forth to meet, to intercept, the Lord, before He could think of doing anything else. V. 14. **Lord, why castest Thou off my soul?** by apparently despising it with loathing. **Why hidest Thou thy face from me?** as though unwilling to help. Cp. Ps. 27, 9; 77, 7. V. 15. **I am afflicted and ready to die,** on the point of death on account of the many troubles laid upon him, **from my youth up; while I suffer Thy terrors, I am distracted,** in such extremes of anguish and despair that he could not regain his powers. V. 16. **Thy fierce wrath goeth over me,** the billows of God's wrath submerging him; **Thy terrors have cut me off,** thereby crushing him. V. 17. **They,** the terrors of God, which inspired such fears in his heart, **came round about me daily like water,** like an ocean flood; **they compassed me about together,** so that he saw no way of escape. V. 18. **Lover and friend,** all those who formerly were nearest and dearest to him, **hast Thou put far from me and mine acquaintance,** those whose confidence he had enjoyed, **into darkness,** so that they were no longer visible to him. "With this cry the harp drops from the poet's hand; he is silent and waits until God shall solve the enigma of his suffering." (Delitzsch.) As one commentator has it, this psalm may well be taken as typical of the immeasurable sufferings of Christ, the Messiah, when He became our Substitute in taking upon Himself the misery of humanity.

PSALM 89.

Of the Messiah and His Kingdom.

Maschil, a didactic poem, **of Ethan, the Ezrahite,** a descendant of Zerah, of the tribe of Judah, 1 Chron. 2, 6; 1 Kings 4, 31. He belonged to a great family, or guild, of singers, some of whom, at least, seem to have been trained in the schools of prophets. The psalm clearly substantiates the Messianic character of 2 Sam. 7, 12—29.

THE PROMISE MADE TO DAVID. — V. 1. **I will sing of the mercies of the Lord forever,** the poet immediately launching forth into his subject, the theme of his song, the merciful kindnesses of Jehovah; **with my mouth will I make known Thy faithfulness to all generations,** since it is this attribute, this manifestation of the divine essence, which causes Him to abide by the promises once made to those who believe in Him. The theme is now set forth somewhat more at length. V. 2. **For I have said, Mercy shall be built up forever,** firmly founded and erected in a structure which would never be overthrown; **Thy faithfulness shalt Thou establish in the very heavens,** never to be moved, these two manifestations of the Lord, merciful kindness and faithfulness, grace and truth, being the foundation upon which our salvation rests secure, John 1, 14. The psalmist now quotes the words of the Lord from 2 Sam. 7, or Jehovah Himself answers in an antiphonal strophe. V. 3. **I have made a covenant with My chosen, I have sworn unto David, My servant,** the Lord Himself assuring Him with a solemn oath, v. 4. **Thy Seed will I establish forever,** namely, in his dynasty, in the rulers out of his line, **and build up thy throne to all generations. Selah.** If this had been spoken of an earthly, temporal rule only, then this prophecy would have fallen to the ground, for in no kingdom of this world is there at the present time any ruler of the house of David. But Christ, who is truly a King, although His kingdom is not of this world, is the Seed of David whose rule will last throughout eternity. It is with reference to this promise that the praise of the psalmist sounds forth again. V. 5. **And the heavens shall praise Thy wonders, O Lord,** the miracles of love which he performed for the salvation of mankind; **Thy faithfulness also,** by which He would fulfil, and has fulfilled, His promises, **in the congregation of the saints,** all the angels rejoicing over the fact that God, in His infinite mercy and kindness, had found a way of delivering fallen mankind from the curse of damnation. Compare the song of the angels, Luke 2, 14. V. 6. **For who in the heaven can be compared unto the Lord,** in the immeasurable greatness of this miracle of His grace in providing a Savior for mankind? **Who among the sons of the mighty,** the greatest of His creatures, the mightiest rulers of the earth, **can be likened unto the Lord?** They cannot stand as His equals, there cannot even be a remote comparison. V. 7. **God is greatly to be feared,** very awesome, **in the assembly of the saints,** in the midst of His congregation, **and to be had in reverence of all them that are about Him,** the very angels trembling with awe in His presence. All believers regard Him, not with the fear of slaves, but with the trusting reverence due Him for the continual revelation of His greatness. V. 8. **O Lord God of hosts,** the mighty Ruler of the armies of heaven, **who is a strong Lord like unto Thee,** He alone possessing and wielding omnipotent power, **or to Thy faithfulness round about Thee?** For it is by virtue of this manifestation of His essence that the believers rely upon His Word with absolute confidence; it surrounds Him on all sides, it is like the rays of the sun shedding their brilliance in all directions. The majesty of God's omnipotence is now described. V. 9. **Thou rulest the raging of the sea,** when it tries to rise against His laws in insolent defiance; **when the waves thereof arise, Thou stillest them,** causing them to sink back in powerless rage. Before this almighty power, moreover, the proud arrogance of men is equally helpless. V. 10. **Thou hast broken Rahab in pieces,** crushed and wounded mighty Egypt at the time of Israel's deliverance from its slavery, **as one that is slain; Thou hast scattered Thine enemies with Thy strong arm.** All the enemies of the Lord and of His Church are mortally wounded and overthrown by the strength of His almighty arm. V. 11. **The heavens are Thine,** under His absolute power and control, **the earth also is Thine; as for the world and the fulness thereof,** all the creatures which it contains, **Thou hast founded them,** establishing and maintaining them by the Word of His power. V. 12. **The north and the south,** the entire expanse of the earth, **Thou hast created them; Tabor,** on the west side of Jordan, between the Sea of Galilee and the plain of Jezreel, **and Hermon,** in the extreme northeastern part of Palestine, **shall rejoice in Thy name,** even the inanimate creation showing its dependence upon Him by shouting for joy in His honor. V. 13. **Thou hast a mighty arm,** the singer here summarizing his description of God's majestic power; **strong is Thy hand, and high is Thy right hand,** the emblem of His irresistible power is exalted. The poet now turns to the manifestation of God's attributes as they chiefly appear in the work of redemption and in the relation of God to His children on earth. V. 14. **Justice,** that is, righteousness, **and judgment are the habitation of Thy throne,** the attributes upon which His kingdom is established; **mercy and truth shall go before Thy face.** The work of the redemption of the world is a revelation of God's righteousness and judgment. Because He cannot ignore and condone the sin of mankind, He caused the Messiah to take the burden of all men's iniquity upon Himself, and not only to bear it, but to take it away by a full vicarious expiation. Thus was His righteousness, the foundation of His throne, established. But at the same time the Lord keeps before His face, and manifests continually, His merciful kindness, in giving His only-begotten Son for the salvation of the world, and His faithfulness or truth, in fulfilling the promises made to the patriarchs and all the believers of the Old Testament. V. 15. **Blessed is the people that know the joyful sound,** all men who receive the Gospel-news of their salvation with a joyful sound of acceptance are truly blessed; **they shall walk, O Lord, in the light of Thy countenance,** as His grace shines forth upon them and warms them with the blessed assurance of their redemption in the Mesisah. V. 16. **In Thy name shall they rejoice all the day,** they have no righteousness and merit of their own to boast of, but they glory in the manifestation of God's love and mercy, **and in Thy righteousness shall they be exalted,** that is, by virtue of the righteousness imputed to them by Jehovah, by means of faith kindled in their hearts. V. 17. **For Thou art the glory of their strength,** that alone being the basis of their boasting before men, 2 Cor. 12, 9. 10; **and in Thy favor,** by the good pleasure of Jehovah shown them in the Messiah, **our horn shall be exalted,** they would receive the strength needed for the battle of life, against the forces of Satan and his allies. V. 18. **For the Lord is our Defense, and the Holy One of Israel is our King.** The confidence of the believers in the ultimate victory of their cause is so great because the Lord is on their side, both as their Shield in warding off the attacks of the enemies and as their peerless, undefiled Leader going on before them to victory.

THE RULE OF THE MESSIAH. — V. 19. **Then Thou spakest in vision to Thy holy one,** to His saint and servant, namely, the prophet Nathan, who acted as God's representative in dealing with David, 2 Sam. 7, **and saidst, I have laid help upon one that is mighty,** upon a great champion; **I have exalted one chosen out of the people,** the immediate reference being to David, the son of Jesse, but the implied reference to David's Son and David's Lord, the Messiah. It is a distinguishing mark of prophecy often to identify events and persons near at hand with those at a far distance according to human understanding. We must always remember that with the Lord there are no reckonings of time, that all events, as far as He is concerned, happen in an everlasting *now.* V. 20. **I have found David, My Servant; with My holy oil have I anointed Him,** v. 21. **with whom My hand shall be established; Mine arm also shall strengthen Him.** The Messiah, anointed with the oil of holiness, with the Holy Ghost, with the fulness of God's divinity, would be sustained throughout His ministry in His state of humiliation by the almighty power of God communicated to His human nature. V. 22. **The enemy shall not exact upon Him,** gaining power over Him, **nor the son of wickedness afflict Him;** although the son of iniquity, Satan, with his host, would attack the Messiah, he would not succeed in humbling Him, in gaining the victory over Him. V. 23. **And I will beat down His foes before His face and plague,** strike down, **them that hate Him;** all those who take the part of the arch-enemy of Christ and show lasting signs of hatred against the atonement of the Messiah would share the fate of their champion, of the murderer and liar from the beginning. V. 24. **But My faithfulness,** in fulfilment of all the promises of old, **and My mercy,** the merciful kindness by which the redemption of mankind would be effected, **shall be with Him; and in My name shall His horn,** emblem of aggressive strength, **be exalted,** as the Father would lay all His enemies at His footstool. V. 25. **I will set His hand also in the sea,** in the almighty power of the Deity communicated to His human nature, **and His right hand in the rivers,** imparting to Him the unlimited authority of divine power. Jesus Christ, even in the state of His humiliation, was the almighty God, the Creator and Preserver of the world. V. 26. **He shall cry unto Me,** the Messiah expressly calling God by this name, **Thou art My Father, My God, and the Rock of My salvation,** His Father by virtue of His eternal generation out of the essence of God, His God by virtue of His true humanity, and in this capacity also the Rock of His salvation, to whom He addressed Himself again and again in a plea for assistance in His work of expiating the sins of mankind. V. 27. **Also I will make Him My First-born,** God's only-begotten Son, Ps. 2, 7, **higher than the kings of the earth;** for the Messiah, as the almighty Ruler of the universe, is above them all. V. 28. **My mercy will I keep for Him forevermore,** preserving it for the Messiah as a treasure which He should enjoy in due time, with the completion of His work, **and My covenant shall stand fast with Him,** firm and unshakable. V. 29. **His seed also,** His spiritual offspring, those born again by faith in His atonement, **will I make to endure forever and His throne as the days of heaven,** the kingdom of His mercy and glory lasting through eternity. In the next section the close parallelism between this psalm and 2 Sam. 7, 12—29 is again apparent. V. 30. **If His children forsake My Law,** if the Messiah's spiritual offspring, those who have once accepted Jesus as their Savior, will then again reject His Word, **and walk not in**

My judgments, in refusing to lead a life in conformity with the rules of sanctification established by Him; v. 31. **if they break,** profane, **My statutes,** the precepts of His covenant, **and keep not My commandments,** the general obligations laid upon all men; v. 32. **then will I visit their transgression with the rod,** with a severe punishment for their defection, **and their iniquity with stripes,** His intention being to bring them to a realization of their sins. But this apostasy on the part of some believers will not change the counsel of God's love. V. 33. **Nevertheless My loving-kindness,** His merciful favor, **will I not utterly take from Him, nor suffer My faithfulness to fail,** the truth of His promises concerning the imparting of the blessings to all who believe in the Messiah would stand secure. V. 34. **My covenant will I not break,** that contained even in the first proclamation of the Gospel in the Garden of Eden and repeated so often since, **nor alter the thing that is gone out of My lips,** in setting forth before men the salvation in the Messiah. V. 35. **Once have I sworn by My holiness,** in a solemn oath by the essential purity of His essence, **that I will not lie unto David,** to whom this great Messianic promise had been given, v. 36. **His seed,** in the person of the Messiah, **shall endure forever, and His throne as the sun before Me,** that is, throughout eternity. V. 37. **It shall be established forever as the moon and as a faithful witness in heaven,** for steadfast testimony. **Selah.** This is a glorious assurance of the unchangeable nature of God's covenant with men, that He will never alter His Gospel promises.

LAMENT AND COMFORT. — V. 38. **But Thou hast cast off and abhorred,** rejected, **Thou hast been wroth with Thine Anointed.** The vicarious nature of the Redeemer's work is here stressed. So completely does He become the Substitute of man in the work of atonement that He can say He was rejected of God, that God was wroth with His Messiah. V. 39. **Thou hast made void the covenant of Thy Servant,** apparently spurning it in His anger; **Thou hast profaned His crown by casting it to the ground,** He Himself being bowed down to the dust in the extreme misery of His Passion. V. 40. **Thou hast broken down all His hedges,** the fences which kept the enemies from assailing Him; **Thou hast brought His strongholds to ruin,** the Proxy of mankind having all His fortifications taken from Him and reduced to ruins, thus giving all His adversaries an opportunity to work their will, as it seemed. V. 41. **All that pass by the way spoil Him,** He became the butt of the despoilers and detractors; **He is a reproach to His neighbors,** evidently a reference to the mockery attending the Lord's trials and His crucifixion. V. 42. **Thou hast set up the right hand of His adversaries,** apparently giving them the power to work their will against the Christ; **Thou hast made all His enemies to rejoice,** gladdened their hearts at the seeming success of their murderous plans. V. 43. **Thou hast also turned the edge of His sword,** apparently dulled the weapons with which He was battling, **and hast not made Him to stand in the battle;** it seemed that He was destined to lose in the tremendous conflict in which He was engaged for the benefit of mankind. V. 44. **Thou hast made His glory to cease and cast His throne down to the ground.** V. 45. **The days of His youth hast Thou shortened,** by the tremendous pressure of the burden of men's iniquity; **Thou hast covered Him with shame,** wrapping Him up in disgrace before men. **Selah.** Such was the Messiah's condition as He entered upon His great work of the redemption of mankind. The iniquities and the guilt of all men having been laid upon Him, He was held responsible for all, made strictly accountable for the debt which He had agreed to pay. The Messiah Himself is now introduced with a cry of distress. V. 46. **How long, Lord? Wilt Thou hide Thyself forever? Shall Thy wrath burn like fire?** Note that these words are practically a parallel to the Messiah's unexampled cry of distress and desolation, Ps. 22, 2. When He reached the climax of His suffering, it seemed to the great Sufferer that the Lord had definitely hidden His face from Him, that His anger would never cease from burning; it was the torture of hell which He endured. V. 47. **Remember how short My time is; wherefore hast Thou made all men in vain?** We have here only disjointed cries: "Remember — I — what the age? For what — vanity — hast Thou created the sons of man?" V. 48. **What man is he that liveth and shall not see death? Shall he deliver his soul from the hand of the grave,** from the realm of death? **Selah.** As the Representative of mankind, the Messiah was condemned to death, He must go down into the land of death, He must suffer even the pangs of eternal death. And yet He clings to His heavenly Father. V. 49. **Lord, where are Thy former loving-kindnesses which Thou swarest to David in Thy truth?** He places His confidence in the merciful kindnesses of the Lord, as contained in the Lord's faithful promises, sure to come upon Him in whom Jehovah, the heavenly Father, is well pleased. V. 50. **Remember, Lord, the reproach of Thy servants,** for He was bearing the reproach which should have struck others; **how I do bear in My bosom the reproach of all the mighty people,** literally, "all many peoples," as the Substitute of all mankind, v. 51, **wherewith Thine enemies have reproached, O Lord,** trying to heap disgrace upon Him, **wherewith they have reproached**

the footsteps of Thine Anointed, of the Lord's Messiah. Knowing that the Lord would be His Refuge in spite of all enemies and their mockery and would glorify Him by the pathway of the cross with all its agonies, the Messiah concludes His prayer with a burst of triumph, v. 52. **Blessed be the Lord forevermore. Amen, and Amen.** That was the end of the Messiah's vicarious work, blessing and honor and glory, of which all believers are partakers, here in time and hereafter in eternity.

PSALM 90.

The Mercy of God Man's Only Refuge.

A prayer of Moses, the man of God, the prophet who stood in the relation of an intimate friend to the God of Israel, who here contrasts man's frailty, the consequence of his sin, with God's eternity. This psalm is the oldest which has been preserved in the Psalter, the occasion for its writing probably being the incident recorded Num. 14, 22. 23. V. 1. **Lord,** the Majestic, the All-powerful, **Thou hast been our Dwelling-place,** a safe Habitation of refuge, **in all generations,** from one generation to the next, throughout the ages, the Messianic idea underlying the prayer. V. 2. **Before the mountains were brought forth,** by a process of divine generation, **or ever Thou hadst formed the earth and the world,** bringing them into existence in a manner exceeding human comprehension, by an absolute creative act, **even from everlasting to everlasting, Thou art God,** His divine being extending out of a limitless past and reaching forward to a boundless future, the eternal, unchanging Lord and Creator, in whom the trust of all believers may rest secure forever. V. 3. **Thou turnest man to destruction,** changing the proud strength and beauty of their bodies into crushed particles, into dust, **and sayest, Return, ye children of men,** one generation sinking down into the misery of the grave, and a new generation arising by His creative will. From the moment of our birth we bear in our bodies the germ of death; the contrast is between the omnipotence and unchangeableness of God and the frailty and vanity of man. V. 4. **For a thousand years in Thy sight are but as yesterday when it is past,** the eternal God, for whom, strictly speaking, time does not exist, regards them as nothing more than a disappearing moment, **and as a watch in the night,** as the third part of the night, which, even in the case of men, passes by unnoticed; for during sleep the consciousness of the passing of time is lost. All earthly time does not exist for the everlasting God; He is exalted above all the changes of puny men. V. 5. **Thou carriest them away as with a flood,** a heavy and devastating rain, whose swift destruction carries mortals away into the sleep of death; **they are as a sleep,** their whole life is a sleep or a dream, which is past and gone before a person fully realizes it; **in the morning they are like grass which groweth up,** the blossoming grasses which come to a quick maturity. V. 6. **In the morning it flourisheth,** the flowers of the prairies and meadows opening their blossoms in rapid succession, **and groweth up; in the evening it is cut down,** the scythe putting an end to the short-lived glory of the meadow-flowers, **and withereth.** Cp. 1 Pet. 1, 24; Ps. 103, 15. 16. V. 7. **For we are consumed by Thine anger,** withering away in the glow of its heat, **and by Thy wrath are we troubled,** destroyed by the intense heat of God's anger. Such is the impression which the destruction of one generation after the other is bound to make upon the thoughtful observer. V. 8. **Thou hast set our iniquities,** the open wickedness of deliberately leaving the paths of righteousness, **before Thee,** so that none of them is omitted or overlooked, **our secret sins in the light of Thy countenance;** for the secrets of all men's heart are open and uncovered before the eyes of His omniscience. Cp. Ps. 19, 13. Note: If we see our sins in the proper spirit of repentance, then God does not see them, for they are then covered by the garment of Christ's righteousness; but if we do not see our sins, then God surely will see them, for they remain uncovered before the light shining before Him, the light of His righteousness and holiness. V. 9. **For all our days are passed away in Thy wrath,** they are diminished, they vanish, because the anger of the Lord is manifested upon the sins; **we spend our years as a tale that is told,** like a murmuring, meaningless noise, which is not even brought out in a definite word. Thus the vanity of human life is again brought out. V. 10. **The days of our years are threescore years and ten,** literally, "The days of our years — in them seventy years," not worth mentioning, an insignificant sum; **and if by reason of strength,** that is, if a man possesses unusual vitality, **they be fourscore years,** if he actually reaches the age of eighty years, **yet is their strength,** even that about which men are wont to boast, **labor and sorrow,** vanity and foolishness, misery and grief. How foolish, then, for men to regard this life as the most desirable thing and to neglect the care for eternity! **For it is soon cut off,** the life of mortals glides past speedily, **and we fly away.** All the events of life move past our eyes in rapid flight; there is nothing stable, nothing lasting, in this world. Moses now draws his conclusion, summarizing the points contained in the previous paragraphs. V. 11. **Who knoweth the power of Thine anger?** this being as immeasurable as God Himself. **Even according to Thy fear, so is Thy wrath,** that is, Who fears the wrath of God in the proper measure? Who realizes what it means for his own fortunes? The great majority of people in the world go their heedless way, not knowing that death is hanging over their heads. But the believers are willing to learn their lesson. V. 12. **So teach us to number our days,** giving us the proper understanding that we realize the uncertainty of human life, knowing that every day may be our last day here on earth, **that we may apply our hearts unto wisdom,** for that is surely the essence of wisdom, to be prepared for death at all times. The prayer of Moses now changes to a fervent intercession. V. 13. **Return, O Lord, how long?** turning back His face in mercy, since it had been averted so long in anger. **And let it repent Thee concerning Thy servants,** His merciful kindness not permitting the threatened destruction to strike them. V. 14. **O satisfy us early with Thy mercy,** His grace being their first food at the very break of the dawn, and being supplied in all rich fulness, **that we may rejoice and be glad all our days;** for the happiness brought by the assurance of the grace of God is a lasting pleasure, its happy excess and wholesome surfeit both satisfying and stimulating desire. V. 15. **Make us glad according to the days wherein Thou hast afflicted us,** in proportion to the period of misery which drove them to repentance, **and the years wherein we have seen evil.** Cp. Ps. 51, 12. V. 16. **Let Thy work appear unto Thy servants,** making the wonderful deeds of His grace manifest before them, **and Thy glory unto their children,** that generations to come may also realize the glory of God as manifested in his salvation of men. V. 17. **And let the beauty of the Lord, our God,** the sweet favor of the Majestic and All-powerful, who is at the same time the God of our salvation, **be upon us,** resting upon the believers throughout their lives; **and establish Thou the work of our hands upon us,** letting His blessing attend the proclamation of God's glory in the work of redemption, as made by His children everywhere; **yea, the work of our hands, establish Thou it,** for only by and with the blessings of the Lord will the preaching of the Word, the proclamation of salvation, have success and the kingdom of the Lord on earth be built. Thus the prayer of Moses has significance and power for all periods of the Church's existence, until the very end of time.[5]

---

5) A complete exposition of this psalm is given in *Lehre und Wehre,* 65 (1919), January, March, April.

PSALM 91.

The Safety of the Believers in Every Emergency.

The author of this psalm is not mentioned in the Bible, but the contents and the spirit of the hymn suggest the name of David, the pestilence referred to probably being that described 2 Sam. 24. V. 1. **He that dwelleth in the secret place of the Most High,** sheltered in the fellowship of God by faith, abiding secure from all assaults, **shall abide under the shadow of the Almighty,** safe under the protection of His almighty wings. V. 2. **I will say of the Lord,** that is the boast of the believer, **He is my Refuge and my Fortress,** Jehovah, the God of grace, shielding him against the counsels and attacks of all enemies; **my God,** with the emphasis on the pronoun; **in Him will I trust,** every believer confidently and cheerfully yielding his life to the guiding hand of God. V. 3. **Surely He shall deliver thee,** so the psalmist assures every believer, **from the snare of the fowler,** from Satan, who, as a roaring lion, walketh about, seeking whom he might devour, **and from the noisome pestilence,** from the plague of destruction, the afflictions and temptations of Satan and his host. V. 4. **He,** Jehovah, the God of salvation, **shall cover thee with His feathers,** His wings forming a protecting wall about the believers, **and under His wings shalt thou trust,** knowing that the enemy cannot penetrate to the asylum of God's protection; **His truth,** the faithfulness of His promises of salvation, **shall be thy shield and buckler,** an unfailing protection against each and every danger. V. 5. **Thou shalt not be afraid for the terror by night,** of affliction and tribulation which is intensified by darkness, **nor for the arrow that flieth by day,** those with which the Evil One tries to wound the hearts and consciences of the believers, v. 6. **nor for the pestilence that walketh in darkness,** the destruction threatened by the various temptations assailing the believers, **nor for the destruction,** the severe plague, **that wasteth at noonday,** chiefly by the threats of the enemies of the Lord in the world. Against all such dangers the faithful are secure in the protection of their God and heavenly Father. V. 7. **A thousand shall fall at thy side and ten thousand at thy right hand,** overcome by the attacks of the enemies, submitting to the various secret and open attacks of the devil and the children of this world; **but it shall not come nigh thee,** not be able to harm those who cling to the protection of the Lord in firm faith. V. 8. **Only with thine eyes shalt thou behold and see**

the reward of the wicked, for the unbelievers will be taken by the enemy and will have to suffer for their wickedness. V. 9. **Because thou,** every believer, **hast made the Lord, which is my Refuge,** rather the psalmist speaks for himself, "For Thou, Jehovah, art my Refuge," **even the Most High, thy Habitation,** literally, "the Most High hast thou made thy Habitation," v. 1, v. 10. **there shall no evil befall thee,** coming upon the believer with sudden destruction, **neither shall any plague come nigh thy dwelling,** no stroke of misfortune and enmity which can bring us real harm, diminish our salvation and the blessings of God's grace. V. 11. **For He,** Jehovah, the God of salvation, **shall give His angels charge over thee,** placing the believers in their special care, as a guard against all evil, **to keep thee in all thy ways,** as long as the believers walk on the ways of God's will and good pleasure. V. 12. **They shall bear thee up in their hands, lest thou dash thy foot against a stone,** carefully carrying the believers over all obstructions of their faith and spiritual life, so that their salvation will never be really endangered. Every Christian lives the life and performs the work which God has intended for him. If death takes him away, it means that the goal set by God has been reached, so far as he is concerned, that all the difficulties and obstructions and afflictions of life are behind him. In the mean time, it is true, v. 13. **thou shalt tread upon the lion and adder; the young lion and the dragon shalt thou trample under feet,** overcome all the attacks of the powers of hell, no matter how fierce and insidious they are. The Lord now Himself takes up the strain of the psalm, substantiating what His servant has said. V. 14. **Because he hath set his love upon Me,** clinging to the Lord with the assurance of complete trust, **therefore will I deliver him,** from all afflictions and from the attacks of Satan and his host; **I will set him on high,** exalt him out of the enemy's reach, **because he hath known My name,** set his faith upon God, accepted His grace, mercy, and salvation. V. 15. **He shall call upon Me, and I will answer him,** coming to the believer's assistance no matter what difficulty he may find himself in; **I will be with him in trouble,** standing at his side even in the hour of death; **I will deliver him and honor him,** bringing him up to the glories of heaven. V. 16. **With long life,** that of eternity in and with God, **will I satisfy him,** in an everlasting enjoyment, **and show him My salvation;** for in heaven we shall see God face to face and know Him and all His wonderful blessings upon us, even as we are known.

PSALM 92.

A Sabbath Meditation.

A psalm or song for the Sabbath-day, used by the Jewish Church on the seventh day of the week, as one of the hymns of liturgical worship. V. 1. **It is a good thing,** a fine and proper custom, of benefit also to the worshiper, **to give thanks unto the Lord and to sing praises,** in joyful proclamation, **unto Thy name, O Most High,** making known Jehovah's perfections, especially in those attributes which are concerned in the salvation of mankind; v. 2. **to show forth Thy loving-kindness in the morning,** beginning to praise His grace with the very dawn of the morning, as the light of the Redeemer which penetrates the night of sin and condemnation, **and Thy faithfulness,** whereby He keeps the promises concerning our salvation, **every night,** for it is in the afflictions and terrors of the night that the thought of God's unswerving faithfulness upholds the spirit, v. 3. **upon an instrument of ten strings,** the ten-stringed harp, or lyre, **and upon the psaltery,** in joyful improvisations dictated by his happy mood; **upon the harp,** a smaller, zitherlike instrument, **with a solemn sound,** in an instructive composition. V. 4. **For Thou, Lord, hast made me glad through Thy work,** particularly by the acts of His creation and His providence; **I will triumph in the works of Thy hands,** exulting with a loud voice over the entire revelation of God, in both the works of creation and of redemption. V. 5. **O Lord, how great are Thy works! and Thy thoughts are very deep,** powerfully deep, beyond the understanding of man, unless enlightened by the Spirit of the Lord. V. 6. **A brutish man,** one whose understanding does not go beyond the intelligence of beasts, in knowing only the desires of this life, **knoweth not, neither doth a fool understand this,** he cannot really enter into the spirit of the universe, because he does not realize that, in all its manifestations, it is the work of the all-wise and almighty Creator. V. 7. **When the wicked spring as the grass,** apparently in the greatest good fortune, **and when all the workers of iniquity do flourish,** enjoying the fulness of all that this world has to offer; **it is that they shall be destroyed forever,** their punishment will overtake them in the world to come, in an eternity of damnation, if not before; v. 8. **but Thou, Lord, art most high forevermore,** exalted above all creatures in everlasting bliss, no matter what powerful and desperate efforts they make to overthrow His sovereignty. V. 9. **For, lo, Thine enemies, O Lord, for, lo, Thine enemies shall perish,** be destroyed utterly; **all the workers of iniquity shall be scattered,** literally, "be out of joint," become disorganized. V. 10. **But my horn,** emblem of powerful strength, and at the same time of stately grace, **shalt Thou exalt like the horn of an unicorn,** the reference probably being to the antelope, symbol of graceful strength; **I shall be anointed with fresh oil,** a picture representing the feeling of eventual complete victory which fills the heart of the believers. V. 11. **Mine eye also shall see my desire on mine enemies,** witnessing their complete overthrow, **and mine ears shall hear my desire of the wicked that rise up against me,** hearing that all their hopes of success have been disappointed. V. 12. **The righteous shall flourish like the palm-tree,** princess of the trees of the plains and valleys; **he shall grow like a cedar in Lebanon,** the proudest and mightiest of the trees of the mountains, emblem of evergreen strength. V. 13. **Those that be planted in the house of the Lord,** the believers having been transplanted from the desert of the world to the rich garden of the Lord's Church, **shall flourish in the courts of our God,** bringing forth the rich fruits of good works growing out of faith. V. 14. **They,** unlike ordinary plants, **shall still bring forth fruit in old age,** their spiritual vitality undiminished in spite of the many vicissitudes of life, because the remembrance of God's works of righteousness and grace is bound to renew their strength from day to day; **they shall be fat,** full of strength and vigor, **and flourishing,** yielding spiritual blossoms and fruit; v. 15. **to show that the Lord is upright,** straightforward and dependable in all His dealings; **He is my Rock,** the believer's place of refuge, **and there is no unrighteousness in Him,** He is righteous in all His ways. Cp. Deut. 32, 4. Thus the Christians praise the mercy and faithfulness of the Lord throughout their lives, in preparation for the endless songs of thanksgiving in heaven, where they will enjoy the realization of their hopes.

PSALM 93.

The Eternal Majesty of the Messiah.

Even the Jewish commentators applied this psalm to the times of the Messiah. It is a glorious song of praise to Jehovah, the second person of the Godhead, and to the majesty of His kingdom. V. 1. **The Lord reigneth,** He is King from everlasting to everlasting; **He is clothed with majesty;** according to His human nature He has been clothed with the majesty which was His, according to His divine nature, from eternity. **The Lord is clothed with strength,** almighty power, **wherewith He hath girded Himself,** the full possession of omnipotence being imparted to Him, to His humanity, and He, at the same time, girding Himself therewith; **the world also is stablished that it cannot be moved.** In His state of humiliation Christ did not always and not fully use the divine attributes communicated to Him, but with His exaltation came the establishment of His throne which made Him, true man, the Ruler of the universe, never to be moved from that exalted position. V. 2. **Thy throne is established of old,** literally, "from that time," since He was exalted to the right hand of the Father; and at the same time He, according to His divine nature, is from eternity; **Thou art from everlasting.** The two natures of Christ, the divine and the human, in His work of redemption, in His exaltation, are here referred to. V. 3. **The floods have lifted up, O Lord,** the streams of His adversaries have arisen, **the floods have lifted up their voice; the floods lift up their waves,** the enmity of all Christ's opponents being compared to the raging of swollen streams, to the rush of the mighty ocean as it pounds against the shore. V. 4. **The Lord on high is mightier than the noise of many waters, yea, than the mighty waves of the sea,** on His height, the undisturbed Ruler, sits Jehovah, Messiah, who reigns forever, in whose eyes the wild efforts of the mightiest enemies are but puny struggles of pygmies; He has them all in derision with their attempts to dethrone Him. V. 5. **Thy testimonies are very sure,** altogether trustworthy, they are the sure basis and foundation of the faith and security of the believers, the witness of God's eternal Word, of the Gospel of our salvation, sustains us; **holiness becometh Thine house, O Lord, forever,** this ornament and glory of Jehovah's house becoming the garment of every believer. Every one who places his trust in Jesus as the promised Messiah, the Redeemer of the world, is cleansed by virtue of the righteousness imparted to him by faith, has received the holiness of the Savior as his own, and stands before the Lord as a perfect child of His good pleasure through all eternity, assured of the fulness of heavenly blessings.

PSALM 94.

Against Tyrants in the Church.

The psalmist, whose name is not given, appeals to God in view of the oppression of the adversaries, who included not only the enemies from without, but also the tyrants within the external organization of the Church. V. 1. **O Lord God, to whom vengeance belongeth; O God, to whom vengeance belongeth, show Thyself.** The statement yielding all judicial power to the Lord alone is followed by the request that He should shine forth, make known His judicial authority by inflicting a righteous punishment upon the oppressors. V. 2. **Lift up Thyself,** arising, as from an indifferent attitude, **Thou Judge of the earth,** in the almighty exaltation of His judicial power; **render a reward to the proud,** punishing the arrogant pride of the adversaries. V. 3. **Lord, how long shall the wicked, how long shall the wicked triumph?** Note the force of the figure of repetition in emphasizing the insolence of the wicked and the increasing impatience of the believers in awaiting the interference of the Lord. V. 4. **How long shall they utter,** bubbling and sputtering, **and speak hard things,** spouting arrogance against the Lord, **and all the workers of iniquity boast themselves,** exalting themselves as though the Lord would not or could not keep them in check? V. 5. **They break in pieces Thy people, O Lord,** crushing the believers by their tyranny, **and afflict Thine heritage,** the Church of God being known by this designation, and the affliction including every form of oppression and hindering of the work of the Church. V. 6. **They slay the widow and the stranger and murder the fatherless,** such outrages being reported from almost every period of the Church's history. V. 7. **Yet they say, The Lord shall not see,** would deliberately ignore their wickedness, **neither shall the God of Jacob regard it,** that they might continue their insolent outrages unpunished. The psalmist now turns to the wicked in a sharp rebuke of their folly. V. 8. **Understand, ye brutish among the people,** on a level with the irrational beasts on account of their folly; **and ye fools, when will ye be wise?** For the arrogant behavior of the wicked showed a lack of ordinary common sense, of the simplest form of observation. V. 9. **He that planted the ear,** giving it its position and causing it to function as one of the senses of the body, **shall He not hear?** Would the wicked actually be so dense as to think that this Creator of the sense of hearing could not hear their insolent taunts? **He that formed the eye,** fashioning it to serve for the sense of sight, **shall He not see?** Did the tyrants believe that their acts of oppression were really unnoticed by the omniscient God? V. 10. **He that chastiseth the heathen,** punishing entire nations for their sins, **shall not He correct?** punishing the enemies for their wicked deeds. **He that teacheth man knowledge, shall not He know?** Before Him, the Source of all wisdom and knowledge, nothing is hidden. V. 11. **The Lord knoweth the thoughts of man,** He is familiar with even the inmost workings of the minds of men, **that they are vanity,** all their objects and intentions by nature being vain. Cp. 1 Cor. 3, 20. V. 12. **Blessed is the man whom Thou chastenest, O Lord,** correcting him in the manner in which a father chastises his child, **and teachest him out of Thy law,** giving him true understanding out of His eternal Word, v. 13. **that Thou mayest give him,** as a consequence of the saving knowledge thus gained, **rest from the days of adversity,** those of real evil, of being rejected from the face of the Lord, **until the pit be digged for the wicked,** until they receive their well-deserved punishment, the result being the relief of the faithful. V. 14. **For the Lord will not cast off His people,** the believers being His in spite of the present oppression, **neither will He forsake His inheritance,** His Church. V. 15. **But judgment shall return unto righteousness,** the latter being bound to be vindicated and set upright once more; **and all the upright in heart shall follow it,** eagerly hailing the restoration of right and justice after such a long period of oppression. V. 16. **Who will rise up for me,** in behalf of the petitioner, taking his part, **against the evil-doers? Or who will stand up for me against the workers of iniquity?** This rhetorical question emphasizes the answer given in the next verse. V. 17. **Unless the Lord had been my Help,** upholding and defending him in the midst of his troubles, **my soul had almost dwelt in silence,** namely, in that of death. V. 18. **When I said,** in a complaint and prayer to the Lord, **My foot slippeth,** when there was danger of his falling as a result of the enemy's oppression, **Thy mercy, O Lord, held me up,** sustaining him in the midst of all dangers. V. 19. **In the multitude of my thoughts within me,** as worries and anxious cares multiply in his heart, **Thy comforts delight my soul,** reassuring and refreshing it for cheerfully enduring the afflictions of this life. V. 20. **Shall the throne of iniquity have fellowship with Thee,** the judgment-seat of destruction, the tribunal of wicked rulers being allied with God, their boast being that God Himself sanctioned their oppression, **which frameth mischief by a law?** by abusing the divine right for iniquitous procedure, by using the name and Word of God as a cloak for their oppression. It has often been the case that tyrants quoted the Bible in support of their attacks on the Church, trying to defend their unjust measures by appealing to Holy Writ.

V. 21. **They gather themselves together against the soul of the righteous,** planning his destruction, **and condemn the innocent blood,** laying the penalty of the law upon the believers with a show of right. V. 22. **But the Lord is my Defense,** a Fortress against such attacks; **and my God is the Rock of my refuge,** protecting the believer against all enemies. V. 23. **And He shall bring upon them their own iniquity,** paying them back in their own coin, **and shall cut them off in their own wickedness,** destroy them for all the evil done by them; **yea, the Lord, our God, shall cut them off.** This psalm is clearly written for all periods of the Church's history and will therefore give consolation to the believers whenever they are beset by difficulties and persecutions.

PSALM 95.

Admonition to Praise Jehovah and Hear His Word.

By comparing verse 8 of this psalm with Heb. 4, 7, we find that it should be ascribed to David, either written by him personally or by one of his singers. V. 1. **O come, let us sing unto the Lord,** this appeal sounding again and again in Scripture on account of the natural inertia and sluggishness of men; **let us make a joyful noise,** in the highest exultation, **to the Rock of our salvation.** V. 2. **Let us come before His presence,** literally, "before His face," to His holy Sanctuary, **with thanksgiving and make a joyful noise unto Him with psalms,** hymns setting forth His wonderful attributes. V. 3. **For the Lord is a great God,** occupying a position of unique grandeur in this respect, **and a great King above all gods,** the idols falsely called gods by the heathen. V. 4. **In His hand,** by virtue of His essential creative power and omnipotence, **are the deep places of the earth,** the very depths of the ocean; **the strength of the hills,** the summits of the highest mountains, **is His also,** under His absolute government. V. 5. **The sea is His, and He made it,** the mighty ocean being a creature of His hand; **and His hands formed the dry land,** Gen. 1, 9. 10. His alone is the majesty of creative omnipotence and the government of the universe. V. 6. **O come, let us worship and bow down,** in humble adoration; **let us kneel before the Lord, our Maker,** to whom we also owe our being, life, and breath. V. 7. **For He is our God,** the emphasis being both upon "He" and upon "our"; **and we are the people of His pasture,** the flock nourished by Him, through His Word, **and the sheep of His hand,** the flock guided and protected by His almighty hand. **To-day, if ye will hear His voice,** the admonition calling upon all men to decide in favor of the Lord and His Word, v. 8. **harden not your heart, as in the provocation,** when the children of Israel contended with the Lord in the wilderness, at Meribah and Massah, Ex. 17, 7, **and as in the day of temptation in the wilderness,** when the conduct of the Israelites tested out the Lord's long-suffering and patience; v. 9. **when your fathers tempted Me, proved Me, and saw My work,** this summarizing the Lord's complaint, Num. 14, 22. V. 10. **Forty years long,** during the entire wilderness journey, **was I grieved with this generation,** vexed with the people whom He had chosen, **and said, It is a people that do err in their heart,** deliberately following the way of error and sin, **and they have not known My ways,** they refused to accept the Lord's precepts governing their conduct; v. 11. **unto whom I sware in My wrath,** a section of this solemn oath of Jehovah being quoted here, **that they should not enter into My rest.** Cp. Num. 14, 30. It was an emphatic declaration, supported by His oath, and it resulted in the death of all those who were above the age of forty at the time of the exodus from Egypt. As far as we Christians are concerned, Heb. 3, 7 to 4, 13 is, in effect, an application of this psalm to the condition in the Church of God at all times, a most searching passage, which we shall do well to heed in these last days of general apostasy.

PSALM 96.

A Hymn of the Kingdom of God.

V. 1. **O sing unto the Lord a new song,** one fitting the new appearance and form of things in the Messiah's kingdom; **sing unto the Lord, all the earth,** all creatures of the universe being included in the summons. V. 2. **Sing unto the Lord,** Jehovah, the mighty Messiah; **bless His name,** making known the attributes concerned with the redemption of mankind; **show forth His salvation from day to day,** in a continuous round of praise. V. 3. **Declare His glory among the heathen,** for the joyful news is not confined to the Jewish nation, **His wonders among all people,** for even in the Old Testament the missionary call sounded time and again. V. 4. **For the Lord is great,** unique in divine greatness, **and greatly to be praised,** most praiseworthy; **He is to be feared,** regarded with reverence and awe, **above all gods,** not as though the worship of idols were permissible beside that of Jehovah, but in the sense that He alone may and shall be worshiped as true God. V. 5. **For all the gods of the nations,** the idols, foolishly called gods by the blind heathen, **are idols,** literally, "nothingnesses"; **but the Lord made the heavens,** He alone is the almighty Creator. The contrast is most emphatic: the idols of men are non-existent, except in the foolish imagination of the heathen; Jehovah alone is the true God. V. 6. **Honor and majesty are before Him,** His attendants, as it were, declaring His mighty works throughout the earth; **strength and beauty are in His Sanctuary,** power and grace being particularly stressed in the relation of Jehovah and His Church, John 1, 14. The wonderful glory and majesty, as well as the kindness and mercy of Jehovah, having been set forth, the psalmist turns to all people with an urgent appeal to act upon this knowledge. V. 7. **Give unto the Lord, O ye kindreds of the people,** all the generations of earth-dwellers, **give unto the Lord glory and strength,** acknowledging Him as the possessor of these divine attributes. V. 8. **Give unto the Lord the glory due unto His name,** that which the revelation of His essence in His works and Word lays upon men as an obligation; **bring an offering,** a token of the acknowledgment of the heart, **and come into His courts,** the place of Jehovah's worship, where the congregation assembles to receive the means of grace. V. 9. **O worship the Lord in the beauty of holiness,** in the marriage garment of the New Testament parable, the holiness and righteousness imputed to the believers by faith; **fear before Him, all the earth,** giving Him the reverence of believing hearts. V. 10. **Say among the heathen,** in joyful proclamation of the essence and works of God, **that the Lord reigneth,** Jehovah alone being King of the universe; **the world also shall be established,** firmly founded, **that it shall not be moved,** no one being able to overthrow the Messiah's kingdom; **He shall judge the people righteously,** in uprightness and justice. With such ideal Messianic conditions obtaining, the psalmist launches forth in a last exultant admonition. V. 11. **Let the heavens rejoice, and let the earth be glad,** the very inanimate creation being called upon to join in the Church's hymn of praise; **let the sea roar,** with a voice of thanksgiving, **and the fulness thereof,** all it contains. V. 12. **Let the field be joyful,** all the meadows and prairies joining with the rest of creation, **and all that is therein; then shall all the trees of the wood rejoice,** the mighty forests singing their joyful hymns of praise to Jehovah, v. 13. **before the Lord; for He cometh, for He cometh to judge the earth,** to visit the earth with a wonderful judgment; **He shall judge the world with righteousness,** that gained by the Messiah for the entire lost and condemned world of sinners, **and the people with His truth,** the faithfulness of His gracious promises, as fulfilled in Messiah's coming. Thus were the glories of the Messianic period of grace sung before the believers of the Old Testament. How much more ought we Christians to sing of the glories of mercy and truth revealed to us and given to us in Jesus Christ and His redemption!

PSALM 97.

The Messiah the King of the Whole Earth.

There can be no doubt that the superscription of this psalm in Luther's Bible, "Of Christ and His Kingdom," is correct, that it is Jehovah, the second person of the Godhead, Jesus Christ, the Redeemer, of whom the inspired singer speaks. V. 1. **The Lord reigneth,** Jehovah is King, the almighty Ruler in His threefold kingdom; **let the earth rejoice,** Ps. 96, 11; **let the multitude of isles,** the many seacoasts, as the representatives of the heathen world, **be glad thereof.** The far coasts of the Mediterranean Sea were often used as a figure of the entire inhabited world, and this verse, therefore, is one of the great missionary texts of the Old Testament. V. 2. **Clouds and darkness are round about Him,** that is, His essence and attributes are so wonderful and mysterious as to make Him appear clothed in cloud and darkness, through which the human eye cannot penetrate; **righteousness and judgment are the habitation,** the foundation, **of His throne,** the fundamental principles of His rule. V. 3. **A fire goeth before Him,** as a manifestation of His almighty, consuming power, **and burneth up His enemies round about,** literally, "sets on fire His adversaries." V. 4. **His lightnings enlightened the world; the earth saw and trembled.** The psalmist probably has in mind the great disturbances in nature at the time of the giving of the Law on Mount Sinai, but he rightly ascribes the same majestic manifestations to Jehovah, the Messiah. V. 5. **The hills melted like wax at the presence of the Lord, at the presence of the Lord of the whole earth,** to whom unlimited dominion and sovereignty had been given. The Word of the Lord goes forth in mighty power; it either melts the hard hearts and works faith in them, or it brings the judgment of God upon the malicious rejecters of the message of salvation, becoming in them a savor of death unto death. He, the Messiah, is the Lord, the great All-ruler of all the earth. V. 6. **The heavens**

declare His righteousness, and all the people see His glory, are witnesses of the fact that the Gospel-truth is proclaimed in all the earth, and that nature itself loudly testifies to the unbounded power of Jehovah and to the evidence of His true deity. V. 7. **Confounded be all they that serve graven images,** brought to shame on account of the foolishness of their gross idolatry, **that boast themselves of idols,** of nothingnesses, of the creatures of their own imagination which they have placed instead of God. **Worship Him, all ye gods,** the very idols which have been set up as gods by foolish men are obliged to bow down and give all honor to the Messiah alone. Over against this cringing and unwilling acknowledgment stands the attitude of the Church of Christ. V. 8. **Zion heard and was glad,** filled with the happiness attending true faith; **and the daughters of Judah,** the congregation of believers, **rejoiced because of Thy judgments, O Lord;** for the fact that He carries out His gracious and good will, as well as His righteous and holy will, in His judgments upon men, proves His divine majesty. V. 9. **For Thou, Lord, art high above all the earth,** above all creation; **Thou art exalted far above all gods,** every creature which bears this name, by the foolishness of blind men. V. 10. **Ye that love the Lord, hate evil,** for this hatred of all that is wicked is a fruit of faith, Rom. 12, 5; **He preserveth the souls of His saints,** guarding and keeping them from the dangers which threaten their faith; **He delivereth them out of the hand of the wicked,** from the hatred and persecution of all their enemies. V. 11. **Light is sown for the righteous,** like seed which will always come up and sprout and bring fruit, no matter how bad the season, **and gladness for the upright in heart.** In spite of the dark days which are encountered from time to time, the light of the Gospel of God's mercy continues to shine upon the believers, giving them the happiness which exceeds any earthly satisfaction. Therefore the psalmist urges once more, in conclusion: v. 12. **Rejoice in the Lord, ye righteous,** Jehovah the Messiah being the Source and the Inspiration of all their happiness; **and give thanks at the remembrance of His holiness,** praising His holy name, proclaiming Him for the revelation of His mercy and truth in His Gospel. Thus the believers of all times, with joyful gratitude, hail the Messiah as their King.

PSALM 98.

Admonition to Praise the Messiah.

This is the only hymn in the Psalter which simply bears the superscription, **A psalm.** In view of the wonders of God's grace and righteousness, as revealed in the coming and in the work of the Messiah, the whole creation is invited to unite in praise to Jehovah. V. 1. **O sing unto the Lord a new song,** one of the newness of all things in consequence of the redemption of mankind through the work of the Messiah; **for He hath done marvelous things,** the miracles of His grace in bringing salvation to the world; **His right hand,** emblem of His almighty power, **and His holy arm,** upheld in the sinlessness of His perfection, **hath gotten Him the victory,** bringing help and salvation to men. God Himself intervened in favor of men; it was His miraculous interference through Him who is called Wonderful that brought deliverance to those who sat in the shadow and darkness of death. V. 2. **The Lord hath made known His salvation,** by the proclamation of the Gospel, both before and after the coming of the Messiah; **His righteousness,** that which found a way of bringing salvation by imputing the righteousness of the Redeemer to fallen mankind, **hath He openly showed in the sight of the heathen,** publicly displaying it before all men by having the Gospel-message proclaimed throughout the earth. V. 3. **He hath remembered His mercy and His truth,** His grace and faithfulness, the two divine attributes which were so conspicuously active in the work of salvation, **toward the house of Israel,** that is, the spiritual Israel, the believers of all times; **all the ends of the earth have seen the salvation of our God,** for it was gained for the whole world, John 3, 16. These facts having been set forth, the urgent admonition to praise follows. V. 4. **Make a joyful noise unto the Lord,** in exultant jubilation, **all the earth; make a loud noise,** in unrestrained happy shouting, **and rejoice, and sing praise.** V. 5. **Sing unto the Lord with the harp,** with the accompaniment of the zither, **with the harp and the voice of a psalm,** both vocal and instrumental music being placed in the service of Jehovah's praise. V. 6. **With trumpets and sound of cornet,** the horns used so frequently in divine worship, **make a joyful noise before the Lord, the King,** hailing the Messiah as their Sovereign. V. 7. **Let the sea roar and the fulness thereof,** the roaring suiting the fulness of the sea, expressing the great volume of joyful sound which should arise in honor of Jehovah; **the world, and they that dwell therein,** organic and inorganic, animate and inanimate creatures uniting in the praise of the Messiah. V. 8. **Let the floods clap their hands,** as a token of applause, an expression of joy used at the accession of kings; **let the hills be joyful together,** all these figures being purposely extravagant to denote the unbounded joy possessing the hearts of the believers, v. 9. **before the Lord; for He cometh to judge the earth,** in His great Messianic visitation; **with righteousness shall He judge the world and the people with equity,** in the uprightness and soundness of His principles of right. Whosoever accepts His righteousness in faith will be saved; he that believeth not will be damned, on account of his unbelief. Therefore let all believers rally to His banners with their faithful hymns of praise.

PSALM 99.

Praise of the Messiah, the Thrice Holy.

The psalmist, in this hymn of praise which fits so well into this series, sets forth the merciful government of God, particularly as exercised in and for His Church, in the work of the Messiah. V. 1. **The Lord reigneth,** Jehovah the Messiah is King; **let the people tremble,** venturing into His presence only with awe and reverence; **He sitteth between the cherubim,** the space between the outstretched wings of the golden cherubim on the mercy-seat being the place where the Lord revealed Himself to His people, Ex. 25, 22; Num. 7, 89. **Let the earth be moved,** inspired with fear by His lofty presence. V. 2. **The Lord is great in Zion,** in His holy Church, **and He is high above all the people,** in His capacity of King in His threefold kingdom. V. 3. **Let them praise Thy great and terrible name,** the awe-inspiring revelation of His majesty; **for it is holy,** emphatic in the Hebrew: "Holy is He," this being one line from the wonderful seraphic hymn, Is. 6, 1—4. V. 4. **The King's strength also loveth judgment,** His essential righteousness causes Him to exercise right at all times; **Thou dost establish equity,** uprightness and true justice in dealing with men at all times; **Thou executest judgment and righteousness in Jacob.** The reference is not merely to the theocratic government of God in the Old Testament, but to the Messiah's rule in His Kingdom of Grace, in which He freely gives to the members of this kingdom the righteousness which He gained for them, by virtue of which they may proudly lift up their heads in the judgment of the Lord. V. 5. **Exalt ye the Lord, our God,** for this manifestation of His grace, **and worship at His footstool,** prostrating themselves upon the steps leading up to His throne, in humble adoration, such places being found wherever the Lord finds two or three gathered together in His name; **for He is holy.** Again the words of the seraphic hymn ring out: "Holy is He!" The singer now, in casting about for a suitable comparison, looks back into the history of Israel. V. 6. **Moses,** who sometimes performed the functions of priest, Ex. 24; 40, 22. 23, **and Aaron among His priests, and Samuel among them that call upon His name,** 1 Sam. 7, 8. 9, these three being prominent representatives of the Old Testament Church; **they called upon the Lord,** their entire worship being an expression of their faith in Jehovah of Israel, **and He answered them,** thus recognizing them as His children by faith, with whom He was united in the fellowship which obtains between the Lord and all believers. V. 7. **He spake unto them,** to His entire people, **in the cloudy pillar; they kept His testimonies,** the true Israelites, the people of the Lord in the real sense of the word, observed all the commandments and precepts of Jehovah, **and the ordinance,** that of the covenant, **that He gave them.** V. 8. **Thou answeredst them, O Lord, our God; Thou wast a God that forgavest them,** the entire people of the children of Israel, **though Thou tookest vengeance of their inventions,** punishing them for their misdeeds, for their acts of rebellion. Forgiveness does not include the remission of the punishment which attaches to many sins; the chastening, rather, works greater humility. V. 9. **Exalt the Lord, our God,** giving Him the honor due to His majesty and power, **and worship at His holy hill,** on the mountain where He revealed Himself, that is, in the New Testament, wherever He comes to men in His Gospel, in His grace and truth; **for the Lord, our God, is holy,** again the emphatic: "For holy is Jehovah, our God." That is the song of praise which the Christians sing in honor of their Messiah and King, the thrice holy, world without end.

PSALM 100.

An Invitation to All Men to Serve the True God.

A psalm of praise, properly placed here to close this wonderful series of praise anthems, the summons here being to give thanksgiving to God, the Creator, Preserver, and Benefactor of men. V. 1. **Make a joyful noise unto the Lord,** with the voice of exultant singing, **all ye lands,** Ps. 98, 4. V. 2. **Serve the Lord with gladness,** not in the fear and terror of the Law, but with the joy flowing from true faith; **come before His presence with singing,** with shouts of homage to the mighty and merciful Ruler. V. 3. **Know ye that the Lord, He is God,** that is the basis of a proper understanding of the divinity, that Jehovah alone is the true God; **it is He that hath made us,** by His almighty, creative power, **and not we ourselves,** everything that we are and have is a gift of His goodness and grace, and we may well think of the entire explanation of the First and the Second Article of the Creed at this point; **we are His people,** the believers, the true spiritual Israel, **and the sheep of His pasture,** in the care of the great Good Shepherd. V. 4. **Enter into His gates with thanksgiving and into His courts with praise,** all men being invited to join the congregation of the Lord which has its place of worship in His temple, wherever His Word is preached; **be thankful unto Him,** for all the richness of His spiritual blessings, **and bless His name,** declaring the works performed by His wonderful attributes. V. 5. **For the Lord is good,** Ps. 25, 8; 34, 8; **His mercy,** the liberality of His divine favor, on the basis of the redemption, **is everlasting; and His truth,** the faithfulness of His promises and of His love, **endureth to all generations,** from one generation to the next, as long as the world will stand, every new generation of believers learning and proclaiming this wonderful song of praise in honor of Jehovah the Messiah, as it will be sung also throughout eternity.

PSALM 101.

The Principles of Right Government.

A psalm of David, in which he set forth the guiding rules of his life, especially those of his reign, showing, at the same time, his appreciation of God's mercy to him and celebrating Jehovah's kindness. V. 1. **I will sing of mercy and judgment,** of grace as given in the Gospel and appropriated by faith, and of justice, as shown by the Lord in dealing with the believers, the glorious example held before all rulers for careful emulation; **unto Thee, O Lord, will I sing,** for granting him His favor in establishing his rule on the foundation of grace and mercy and always keeping before the eyes of the king His example. V. 2. **I will behave myself wisely,** walking most circumspectly and carefully, **in a perfect way,** the way of uprightness. **Oh, when wilt Thou come unto me?** He desires the help of the Lord in his difficult office; he does not want to undertake anything without God's wisdom to guide him. **I will walk within my house,** conducting himself in all the affairs of his life, **with a perfect heart,** in the innocence of his heart, avoiding even the appearance of evil. V. 3. **I will set no wicked thing,** no worthless and vile matter, **before mine eyes,** opposite his eyes, as in the act of pleased contemplation **I hate the work of them that turn aside,** the committing of transgression and dissoluteness; **it shall not cleave to me,** he wants to keep himself scrupulously clean from all plans and purposes of Belial. V. 4. **A froward heart shall depart from me,** one false and perverse in all its plans; **I will not know a wicked person,** he will not indulge in, not even know, wickedness. V. 5. **Whoso privily slandereth his neighbor, him will I cut off,** destroying him, putting him to death for his sin; **him that hath an high look,** an arrogant and haughty bearing, **and a proud heart,** puffed up with insolent haughtiness, **will not I suffer,** him would David disown outright, not permitting him to remain in his vicinity. V. 6. **Mine eyes shall be upon the faithful of the land,** observing the trustworthy and making them his advisers, **that they may dwell with me; he that walketh in a perfect way,** on the way of uprightness, **he shall serve me;** he wanted only reliable and honest men as his servants. V. 7. **He that worketh deceit,** indulging in craft, **shall not dwell within my house,** not have a position there, not tarry or be established in that place; **he that telleth lies,** making it a habit to tell deliberate and malicious falsehoods, **shall not tarry in my sight,** such a one would not be permitted to remain at court. V 8. **I will early destroy all the wicked of the land,** the reference to the morning alluding either to the regular court session, which was held in the morning, or to a diligent, unremittent campaign against the wicked, **that I may cut off all wicked doers from the city of the Lord;** for he would not tolerate them in the holy place. The Church of Christ, the congregation of believers, also has the duty to remove from its midst all those who are open violators of God's holy will, since the toleration of wickedness reflects upon the organization which practises such false lenience, which the Lord wants to be a holy people.

PSALM 102.

Complaint of One in Great Trouble.

A prayer of the afflicted, one in great misery and distress, **when he is overwhelmed,** Ps. 61, 2, **and poureth out his complaint,** as from an inverted vessel, in a full stream, **before the Lord.** V. 1. **Hear my prayer, O Lord,** the Jehovah here named being the second person of the Godhead, as He was known and worshiped in the Old Testament also, Heb. 1, 10—12, **and let my cry come unto Thee,** by removing all obstructions which would hinder its free course. V. 2. **Hide not Thy**

face from me, in aversion or even indifference, **in the day when I am in trouble; incline Thine ear unto me**, in the attitude of favorable attention; **in the day when I call, answer me speedily**, a quick relief being required on account of the greatness of the need. V. 3. **For my days are consumed like smoke**, which passes upward and disappears, **and my bones are burned as an hearth**, the heat of fever glowing in his members and consuming him as the fuel on the hearth is consumed by the fire. V. 4 **My heart is smitten**, dried up, the supply of blood being insufficient, **and withered like grass**, on account of the heat of the inner affliction, **so that I forget to eat my bread**, the consequence of deep grief. V. 5. **By reason of the voice of my groaning**, on account of the effort attending his continual moaning and lamenting, **my bones cleave to my skin**, his extreme emaciation due to his agony. V. 6. **I am like a pelican of the wilderness; I am like an owl of the desert**, of ruined places, both of these being unclean birds according to the Levitical law. V. 7. **I watch**, passing the night in sleeplessness, **and am as a sparrow**, a small and despised bird, **alone upon the housetop**, the figures expressing extreme loneliness. V. 8. **Mine enemies reproach me all the day**, mocking him as one forsaken of God; **and they that are mad against me**, being filled with rage and fury, **are sworn against me**, making his name a byword, accompanying their most malignant curses against any one with a reference to the sufferer's condition. V. 9. **For I have eaten ashes like bread**, sitting in them as a sign of great mourning and strewing them upon his head and garments, **and mingled my drink with weeping**, cp. Ps. 42, 3, v. 10. **because of Thine indignation and Thy wrath**, Jehovah having given him proof of His anger over his trespasses; **for Thou hast lifted me up**, withdrawing the solid ground from beneath his feet, **and cast me down**, the figure being taken from a tempestuous wind which overthrows a person. V. 11. **My days are like a shadow that declineth**, lengthening as the sun draws near the western horizon, showing that the night of death is imminent; **and I am withered like grass**, like an uprooted plant which is bound to become dry. V. 12. **But Thou, O Lord, shalt endure forever**, whence the psalmist in the midst of his misery, addresses his confident prayer to Him, **and Thy remembrance unto all generations**, the eternal and unchangeable Ruler of the universe, whose promises stand secure forever. V. 13. **Thou shalt arise**, as one throwing off apparent indifference and lethargy, **and have mercy upon Zion**, upon His Church; **for the time to favor her**, to show her grace and kindness, **yea, the set time**, that is, that point of time to which the promise of Jehovah looked forward, **is come**. When affliction reaches its climax, then the help of the Lord is always nearest. V. 14. **For Thy servants**, the believers of all times, **take pleasure in her stones**, all of them being filled with fervent love for the Church, **and favor the dust thereof**, their loving desire clinging to the very ruins of the Church. This verse shows that the psalm was composed during the Babylonian exile, when the sympathetic attachment of the captive Jews turned with eagerness to the ruins of Jerusalem, the sanctuary of Jehovah. At the same time the situation is typical of many periods of affliction and ruin in the spiritual congregation of Christ, when the believers lament the troubled situation in the Church. V. 15. **So the heathen shall fear the name of the Lord**, men from all countries of the world learning to know Jehovah as He has revealed Himself, and worshiping Him in holy awe and reverence, **and all the kings of the earth**, even the rulers of Gentile nations, **Thy glory**. It is a picture of Messianic conditions which the prophet here draws. V. 16. **When the Lord shall build up Zion**, establishing His Church, **He shall appear in His glory**, in the glory of the Gospel as proclaimed throughout the world. V. 17. **He will regard the prayer of the destitute**, of the homeless exiles, **and not despise their prayer**, not reject their supplication for mercy. V. 18. **This shall be written for the generation to come**, making known the Gospel of Jehovah's salvation in future ages; **and the people which shall be created shall praise the Lord**, in the worship of true faith. V. 19. **For He hath looked down**, in an act of wonderful condescension, **from the height of His Sanctuary; from heaven did the Lord behold the earth**, observing closely the difficulties of His people, v. 20. **to hear the groaning of the prisoner**, the exiles of Judah serving to typify the spiritually afflicted in the Church at all times; **to loose those that are appointed to death**, by reason of bonds and captivity; v. 21. **to declare the name of the Lord in Zion**, in proclaiming the Gospel of His mercy, **and His praise in Jerusalem**, in the midst of His holy congregation, v. 22. **when the people are gathered together and the kingdoms to serve the Lord**, in that wonderful organization now known as the Christian Church. The psalmist now pictures the situation of the individual believer once more. V. 23. **He weakened my strength in the way**, Jehovah reduced his vitality by having him removed into exile; **He shortened my days**, and with him the entire people of the exile seemed doomed to death. V. 24. **I said, O my God, take me not away in the midst of my days**, death before the fulfilment of the average allotted life being considered a particularly severe punishment of the Lord; **Thy years are throughout all generations**, Jehovah's eternity standing out over against the weakness and vanity of man's life. V. 25. **Of**

old hast Thou laid the foundation of the earth, His creative power therefore being able to work deliverance also in this extremity; **and the heavens are the work of Thy hands,** a product of His act of creation. V. 26. **They shall perish,** namely, in connection with the great change which would take place on the Last Day, **but Thou shalt endure,** being established and changeless in the midst of the overthrow of the universe; **yea, all of them shall wax old like a garment,** Is. 51, 6; 2 Pet. 3, 10; **as a vesture shalt Thou change them, and they shall be changed,** Rev. 21, 1. V. 27. **But Thou art the same,** the eternal and changeless "I am," **and Thy years shall have no end.** Because Jehovah is the eternal Lord, therefore the psalmist concludes with a confident statement, v. 28. **The children of Thy servants shall continue,** the Christian Church continuing from one generation to the next, **and their seed shall be established before Thee,** as the community of believers reserved to eternal life. With this thought to sustain them, the Christians may cheerfully lift up their hearts to Jehovah, the God of their salvation, and trust in His deliverance.

PSALM 103.

Hymn to the Mercy of God.

A psalm of David, voicing his thankful acknowledgment of God's gifts and blessings upon himself, the conclusion calling upon all creatures to join in his song of praise. V. 1. **Bless the Lord, O my soul,** a most emphatic invitation and admonition, a joyful self-encouragement; **and all that is within me bless His holy name,** all the organs of the body being called upon to give thanks for the rich blessings of the Lord, to make known the revelation of His essence and all His attributes before men everywhere. V. 2. **Bless the Lord, O my soul, and forget not all His benefits,** all the deeds of His mercy and kindness for which He deserves well from all men; v. 3. **who forgiveth all thine iniquities,** the remission of sins being the fundamental blessing in the life of every Christian, and here not only one, but all sins being included in line for forgiveness; **who healeth all thy diseases,** those coming upon men as the consequence and punishment of sin, all internal and external sufferings; v. 4. **who redeemeth thy life from destruction,** delivering, even at a cost to Himself, that of giving His only-begotten Son, from misery and death itself; **who crowneth thee with loving-kindness and tender mercies,** the full wealth of His grace and mercy being given to the believer like a precious diadem on his head; v. 5. **who satisfieth thy mouth with good things,** giving His blessings in rich measure, **so that thy youth is renewed like the eagle's,** whose annual period of molt was used as a picture of rejuvenation through grace, Is. 40, 31. After this opening admonition there follows a description of God's gracious rule. V. 6. **The Lord executeth,** performing with loving care, **righteousness,** literally, "deeds of righteousness," **and judgment for all that are oppressed,** giving proof of His justice in favor of His people, over against all expressions of enmity on the part of the many adversaries of the believers. V. 7. **He made known His ways unto Moses,** by revealing and proclaiming Himself as the Lord of mercy in His march through the history of the world, Ex. 33, 13; 34, 6—8, **His acts unto the children of Israel,** in accordance with the promise given to Moses upon that occasion. V. 8. **The Lord is merciful and gracious,** the two attributes here represented being the outstanding features of His conduct toward His children at all times, **slow to anger,** waiting long and patiently for a sign of repentance before pouring out His wrath, **and plenteous in mercy,** His greatness in this respect being revealed to the believers throughout their lives. V. 9. **He will not always chide,** making man's behavior a cause for continual legal action, **neither will He keep His anger forever,** as though bearing a grudge against men. V. 10. **He hath not dealt with us after our sins,** for which we should have been punished with everlasting destruction, **nor rewarded us according to our iniquities,** with the penalty which we had really deserved. V. 11. **For as the heaven is high above the earth,** with its almost limitless reaches, **so great is His mercy toward them that fear Him.** V. 12. **As far as the east is from the west,** separated from it by an almost incomprehensibly great expanse, **so far hath He removed our transgressions from us,** and therefore also their penalty. The pictures illustrate the endless power and the utter unreservedness of God's grace. V. 13. **Like as a father pitieth his children,** showing them his fatherly mercy, **so the Lord pitieth them that fear Him,** His children through faith in Christ. V. 14. **For He knoweth our frame,** just how we are put together, our weakness and frailty; **He remembereth that we are dust,** for out of it was man originally formed, Gen. 2, 7. V. 15. **As for man, his days are as grass,** emblem of perishableness, 1 Pet. 1, 24; **as a flower of the field, so he flourisheth,** Job 14, 1. 2, its beauty of the very briefest duration. V. 16. **For the wind passeth over it,** the scorching wind coming up from the desert, **and it is gone,** withered and perished; **and the place thereof,** the spot of ground where it spent its brief existence, **shall know it no more.** Cp.

Is. 40, 7. 8; Job 7, 10. In wonderful contrast to this evanescent frailty of man stands the grace of Jehovah as revealed in the Gospel-message. V. 17. **But the mercy of the Lord is from everlasting to everlasting,** with an eternal power outlasting the frailty of all creatures, **upon them that fear Him,** trusting in Him by faith in the Messiah's redemption, **and His righteousness unto children's children,** shown and given to those who follow in the footsteps of their believing parents, Ex. 20, 6; 34, 7; Deut. 7, 9; v. 18. **to such as keep His covenant,** that of His grace, offered to all men in the Messiah, **and to those that remember His commandments to do them,** making their entire life conform to the rule of God's holy will. V. 19. **The Lord hath prepared His throne in the heavens,** established it firmly as the ever-blessed and all-powerful God, 1 Tim. 6, 15. 16, **and His kingdom ruleth over all,** since He is the King of kings and the Lord of lords, the Sovereign in His kingdom of power. V. 20. **Bless the Lord, ye His angels,** leaders of His invisible creatures, **that excel in strength,** they are heroes of strength, having been equipped by God with unusual might, **that do His commandments,** in acts of prompt obedience, **hearkening unto the voice of His word,** for to hear the Lord's command means, in their case, to execute it at once. V. 21. **Bless ye the Lord, all ye His hosts,** the great armies of the heavenly spirits; **ye ministers of His that do His pleasure,** that being the work of the angels, individually and collectively. V. 22. **Bless the Lord, all His works, in all places of His dominion,** the entire inanimate creation joining in His praise and thanksgiving; **bless the Lord, O my soul,** the last admonition of the psalmist repeating the thought with which he opened his powerful hymn. Truly, the believers of all times have every reason to praise and exalt the immeasurable mercy of the Lord as revealed to them in Jesus Christ, the Savior.

PSALM 104.

Praise of God for His Work in the Kingdom of Nature.

The psalmist, probably David, as in the preceding psalm, celebrates the glory of God in the works of His creation and providence. V. 1. **Bless the Lord, O my soul,** a powerful self-encouragement, like in the preceding psalm. **O Lord, my God, Thou art very great,** full of royal splendor and majestic glory; **Thou art clothed with honor and majesty,** these constituting the royal garment visible in all parts of the created universe; v. 2. **who coverest Thyself with light as with a garment,** shining forth in the light of His creation with His eternal power and Godhead. Gen. 1, 3—5; **who stretchest out the heavens like a curtain,** the firmament of the visible heavens being considered a tent-curtain reflecting His glory, Gen. 1, 6—8; Is. 40, 22; v. 3. **who layest the beams of His chambers in the waters,** the upper rooms of God's dwelling being regarded as founded on the waters beyond the firmament; **who maketh the clouds His chariot,** when He comes forth to bless with His rain and to threaten and destroy with His thunder and lightning, Is. 19, 1; **who walketh upon the wings of the wind,** in a glorious manifestation of His power; v. 4. **who maketh His angels spirits,** His own messengers being present in the blessing and destroying power of the winds; **His ministers a flaming fire,** for they are active in and through the forces of nature, they are vehicles of God's creative energy; v. 5. **who laid the foundations of the earth,** establishing its pillars, a poetic mode of expression, to denote the stability of the earth as suspended freely in space, Job 26, 7; 38, 4, **that it should not be removed forever,** until the Lord Himself would choose to make the change toward a new heaven and a new earth. V. 6. **Thou coveredst it with the deep,** with the waters of the original chaos, over which the Spirit of God moved at the time of creation, Gen. 1, 2, **as with a garment; the waters stood above the mountains.** V. 7. **At Thy rebuke they fled,** when His command separated the sea from the dry land; **at the voice of Thy thunder they hasted away.** V. 8. **They go up by the mountains; they go down by the valleys unto the place which Thou hast founded for them,** literally, "Up rose mountains, down sank valleys to the place which Thou didst establish for them," all this being done on that great third day of creation, Gen. 1, 9; for the mountains are as old as the earth and the waters, which originally covered it. V. 9. **Thou hast set a bound,** fixed them a definite boundary, **that they may not pass over, that they turn not again to cover the earth,** Job 38, 8—11; Jer. 5, 22. V. 10. **He sendeth the springs into the valleys,** their source being in the mountains above, **which run,** have their regular course, **among the hills,** in the brooks and rivers. V. 11. **They give drink to every beast of the field; the wild asses quench their thirst.** V. 12. **By them,** that is, along their course, **shall the fowls of the heaven have their habitation, which sing among the branches,** literally, "out from between the branches they give their voice." V. 13. **He watereth the hills from His chambers,** from His habitation above the firmament, in abundant rains; **the earth is satisfied with the fruit of Thy works,** the rain causing every form of vegetation to grow and mature in its season. V. 14. **He causeth the grass**

to grow for the cattle and herb, food plants of every kind, **for the service of man,** so that they may cultivate them and enjoy their fruits; **that He may bring forth food out of the earth,** by the blessings of His rain, v. 15, **and wine, that maketh glad the heart of man,** its proper use always being spoken of with approval in Holy Writ, **and oil to make his face to shine,** on account of the increased nutritive value which it gives to foods, **and bread which strengtheneth man's heart,** giving vigor and energy to man, these three, grain for bread, wine, and oil, being considered the chief articles of food in the Orient. V. 16. **The trees of the Lord,** the poet probably having in mind especially the cedars of Lebanon, **are full of sap, the cedars of Lebanon, which He hath planted;** v. 17. **where the birds make their nests; as for the stork,** or the heron, **the fir-trees,** or the cypresses, **are her house.** V. 18. **The high hills are a refuge for the wild goats,** called, for that reason, the mountain-goats, **and the rocks for the conies,** probably the rock-badger, a marmotlike animal, which has its home in rocky places. V. 19. **He appointed the moon for seasons,** to measure the seasons of the year; **the sun knoweth his going down,** as originally established by the Lord, Gen. 1, 14. V. 20. **Thou makest darkness, and it is night,** the night following upon day by His providential rule; **wherein all the beasts of the forest,** the beasts of prey, which spend the day in their dens, **do creep forth.** V. 21. **The young lions roar after their prey,** as they seek their food, **and seek their meat from God,** who gave them the instinct to hunt for their food in this manner. V. 22. **The sun ariseth, they gather themselves together,** withdrawing from the open spaces where they are in danger of meeting men, **and lay them down in their dens.** V. 23. **Man goeth forth unto his work,** the day being allotted to him, **and to his labor until the evening.** Cp. Job 24, 5; 37, 8; 38, 40. In the next section of the psalm the poet summarizes the miracles of God in the sea. V. 24. **O Lord, how manifold are Thy works! In wisdom hast Thou made them all,** being guided in His creative activity by His infinite all-wisdom; **the earth is full of Thy riches,** of His creatures. V. 25. **So is this great and wide sea,** spreading out so far, to the distant horizon, **wherein are things creeping innumerable, both small and great beasts.** V. 26. **There go the ships,** man venturing out on the ocean depths in pursuing his commercial activities; **there is that leviathan,** some sea-monster, probably the whale, **whom Thou hast made to play therein.** V. 27. **These,** all the millions of creatures, **wait all upon Thee,** looking to the providence of God, **that Thou mayest give them their meat,** the food which they need, **in due season,** at the proper time. V. 28. **That Thou givest them they gather,** from the various places where it is provided; **Thou openest Thine hand, they are filled with good,** plentifully supplied with all they need. V. 29. **Thou hidest Thy face,** refusing, for a time, to recognize and supply their need, **they are troubled,** terrified, immediately feeling themselves forsaken; **Thou takest away their breath,** depriving them of what they need to sustain their life; **they die and return to their dust,** Gen. 3, 19; Eccl. 12, 17. V. 30. **Thou sendest forth Thy Spirit,** the Holy Spirit, as active in the work of creation, Gen. 1, 3, **they are created, and Thou renewest the face of the earth,** with every new generation of creatures. V. 31. **The glory of the Lord shall endure forever,** as manifested in His work of creation; **the Lord shall rejoice in His works,** as He did when He found them very good, Gen. 1, 31. V. 32. **He looketh on the earth,** with a frown of anger, **and it trembleth,** in fear of His punishment; **He toucheth the hills, and they smoke,** set on fire at His will. Thus God could glorify His power in destruction if He so chose; therefore it is best for the believers to spend their lives in grateful praise of Him. V. 33. **I will sing unto the Lord as long as I live; I will sing praise to my God while I have my being.** V. 34. **My meditation of Him,** in considering all the miracles of His mercy and power, **shall be sweet,** acceptable to the Lord; **I will be glad in the Lord.** The same fine relation, according to the psalmist, ought to obtain everywhere, those who refuse to enter into fellowship with Jehovah being punished forever. V. 35. **Let the sinners,** those who refuse Him faith and service, **be consumed out of the earth, and let the wicked be no more. Bless thou the Lord, O my soul,** the final self-admonition of the psalmist. **Praise ye the Lord,** or, "Hallelujah!" giving full expression to the emotions of the poet, and calling upon the Church of God of all ages to join him in his hymn of praise.

PSALM 105.

Thanksgiving for God's Benefits.

After an exhortation to praise God, directed especially to the congregation of Israel, the psalmist offers his reasons for the admonition presented, in a summary of Israel's history from the calling of Abraham to the settlement in Canaan. V. 1. **O give thanks unto the Lord; call upon His name,** both in praising His glory and in proclaiming His essence and attributes; **make known His deeds among the people,** this proclamation among the nations serving as a missionary call. V. 2. **Sing**

unto Him, sing psalms unto Him, with the joyful accompaniment of music; **talk ye,** in willing discussions at home and abroad, **of all His wondrous works,** of all the miracles performed in the interest of Israel. V. 3. **Glory ye in His holy name,** boasting in His perfections, as His attributes show in His deeds; **let the heart of them rejoice that seek the Lord,** in true faith and trust. V. 4. **Seek the Lord and His strength,** desiring to possess it according to His gracious invitation and promise; **seek His face evermore,** to bask in the merciful light of His countenance. V. 5. **Remember His marvelous works that He hath done,** manifested in the past deliverances, as found in the history of Israel; **His wonders and the judgments of His mouth,** for His miracles showed Him in His decisions for the good and against the wicked, v. 6. **O ye seed of Abraham, His servant, ye children of Jacob, His chosen,** the text implying principally the spiritual descendants of Abraham and Jacob as they were found in the midst of the nation of Israel. After this preliminary exhortation the inspired poet briefly tells of some of Jehovah's notable deeds. V. 7. **He is the Lord, our God,** the Jehovah of salvation to all believers; **His judgments are in all the earth,** in love upon those who fear Him, in anger upon those who oppose Him. V. 8. **He hath remembered His covenant forever,** the merciful agreement by which Jehovah had accepted the children of Israel as His own, **the word which He commanded to a thousand generations,** for the promise by which Abraham and his descendants were designated as the Lord's people included the wider Messianic meaning and pertained to the chosen of the Lord of all times. V. 9. **Which covenant He made with Abraham,** Gen. 12, 2—7, **and His oath unto Isaac,** Gen. 26, 1—6; v. 10. **and confirmed the same unto Jacob for a law,** a covenant ordinance, **and to Israel,** here the second name of Jacob, Gen. 32, 38, **for an everlasting covenant;** v. 11. **saying, Unto thee will I give the land of Canaan,** Gen. 13, 14. 15; 15, 18, **the lot of your inheritance,** the expression denoting the land which is measured off with a cord, v. 12. **when they were but a few men in number,** Gen. 34, 30, **yea, very few, and strangers in it.** V. 13. **When they,** the patriarchs, the ancestors of God's chosen people, **went from one nation to another,** being obliged to change their dwelling-place often, Mesopotamia, Canaan, Philistia, and Egypt being the countries of their sojourn, **from one kingdom to another people,** v. 14. **He suffered no man to do them wrong,** not even after the revenge which Simeon and Levi took upon the Shechemites, Gen. 34; **yea, He reproved kings for their sakes,** as, Pharaoh and Abimelech, the kings of Egypt and Philistia, respectively, Gen. 12, 10—20; chaps. 26 and 31; v. 15. **saying, Touch not Mine anointed,** for so the patriarchs were called as the ancestors of kings, priests, and prophets, **and do My prophets no harm,** for all the patriarchs not only proclaimed the name of the Lord, but also foretold future events, especially in the blessings pronounced upon their children. V. 16. **Moreover, He called for a famine upon the land,** the one of the seven lean years at the time of Jacob, Gen. 41, 54; **He brake the whole staff of bread,** by withholding the chief source and supply of food, that of grain. V. 17. **He sent a man before them, even Joseph,** who himself acknowledges the guiding providence of God in the fact that he was sold into Egypt, Gen. 50, 20, **who was sold for a servant,** Gen. 37, 28. 36; v. 18. **whose feet they hurt with fetters,** when he was unjustly imprisoned, Gen. 39, 20; **he was laid in iron,** literally, "iron came on his soul," said either of the chains with which he was bound or of the feeling of misery which took hold of him in prison, v. 19. **until the time that his word came,** his own prediction of his exaltation being fulfilled, Gen. 42, 9; **the word of the Lord tried him,** for the revelation of God made to him proved his faith in the trials upon his own person. V. 20. **The king,** Pharaoh of the great famine, **sent and loosed him,** Gen. 41, 14, **even the ruler of the people, and let him go free.** V. 21. **He made him lord of his house,** after Joseph had interpreted his dreams, Gen. 41, 40, **and ruler of all his substance,** putting all his possessions, the entire rule of the country, into Joseph's power and retaining only the supreme sovereignty for himself, Gen. 41, 40—44, v. 22. **to bind his princes at his pleasure,** without any intervention and interference on the part of Pharaoh, **and teach his senators,** the ancient men, the counselors of the country, **wisdom.** V. 23. **Israel also came into Egypt,** as a consequence of the great famine and Joseph's exaltation, Gen. 46, 6; **and Jacob sojourned in the land of Ham,** this being a general designation of Egypt because it was settled by descendants of Ham. V. 24. **And He increased His people greatly,** blessing them with a very rapid growth, Ex. 1, 7; **and made them stronger than their enemies,** this fact being expressed in the fear expressed by the Pharaoh of the exile, Ex. 1, 9. 10. V. 25. **He turned their heart to hate His people, to deal subtilly,** with wicked craft, **with His servants.** Since they deliberately plotted meanness, the Lord held them to their wicked plans, in order thereby to bring about their own destruction. V. 26. **He sent Moses, His servant,** Ex. 3, 10, **and Aaron, whom He had chosen,** Ex. 4. 14. 30. V. 27. **They showed His signs among them,** which the Lord intended for strong admonitions addressed to the Egyptians and Pharaoh, **and wonders in the land of Ham,** in the great plagues. V. 28. **He sent darkness and made it dark,** Ex. 10, 21—23; **and they rebelled not against His word,** that is,

Moses and Aaron carried out the commands of God just as they had received them. V. 29. **He turned their waters into blood,** Ex. 7, 19—24, **and slew their fish.** V. 30. **Their land brought forth frogs in abundance,** Ex. 8, 1—15, **in the chambers of their kings,** Ex. 8, 3. V. 31. **He spake,** through the mouth of His representative, Moses, **and there came divers sorts of flies and lice in all their coasts,** Ex. 8, 16—19. V. 32. **He gave them hail for rain and flaming fire in their land,** Ex. 9, 22—25. V. 33. **He smote their vines also,** Ps. 78, 47, **and their fig-trees; and brake the trees of their coasts,** stripping them not only of their foliage, but even of their smaller twigs and branches. V. 34. **He spake, and the locusts came and caterpillars,** that is, grasshoppers, **and that without number,** Ex. 10, 12—20, v. 35. **and did eat up all the herbs in their land and devoured the fruit of their ground,** everything that was left after the hail. V. 36. **He smote also all the first-born in their land,** Ex. 12, 29, **the chief of all their strength,** for so the oldest sons were called, Gen. 49, 3. V. 37. **He brought them forth also with silver and gold,** freely given to them by the Egyptians, by the direction of the Lord, Ex. 12, 35. 36; **and there was not one feeble person among their tribes,** that is, unfit for the march through the wilderness, Ex. 13, 18. V. 38. **Egypt was glad when they departed,** rejoicing to be rid of their unlucky presence; **for the fear of them,** through the agency of the Lord, **fell upon them.** V. 39. **He spread a cloud for a covering,** for a bower or protecting screen against the heat of the sun, **and fire to give light in the night,** for that was the purpose of the pillar of fire, Ex. 13, 21. V. 40. **The people asked,** the true Israelites, the believers, among them, praying, the others demanding, **and He brought quails,** Ex. 16, 12—14; Num. 11, 31, **and satisfied them with the bread of heaven,** Ps. 78, 24. 25; John 6, 31, the miraculous feeding with manna. V. 41. **He opened the rock, and the waters gushed out,** in great abundance, Ex. 17, 6; Num. 20, 10. 11; **they ran in the dry places like a river,** Ps. 78, 15. 16. The Lord's reasons for these marvelous dealings with His people are given in conclusion. V. 42. **For He remembered His holy promise and Abraham, His servant,** His faithfulness to the word of His promise being His motive in showing such kindness to the children of Israel, Ex. 2, 24. V. 43. **And He brought forth His people with joy,** surely giving them occasion enough for rejoicing, **and His chosen with gladness,** with the voice of singing, Ex. 15, 1; v. 44. **and gave them the lands of the heathen,** whose land they occupied after the conquest of Canaan; **and they inherited the labor of the people,** of the heathen nations, Deut. 6, 10, taking possession of homes and cultivated lands which others had prepared with hard work, v. 45. **that they might observe His statutes,** the precepts of the covenant, **and keep His laws,** those pertaining to mankind in general, this being the second reason why the Lord showed Israel His favor, to induce them to show obedience to Him. **Praise ye the Lord,** this hallelujah being echoed by the true, spiritual Israel, the Church of God, at all times, for all the marvels of His gracious favor in and through Christ, the Redeemer.

PSALM 106.

God's Blessings in Spite of Israel's Unfaithfulness.

This psalm, whose author is not known, gives a detailed confession of the sins of Israel, as contrasted with the wonders of God's mercy, the conclusion being a supplication for God's favor. V. 1. **Praise ye the Lord,** for the attitude of praise should characterize the believers at all times. **O give thanks unto the Lord; for He is good,** He has revealed Himself to men in the beauty of His goodness; **for His mercy endureth forever,** the hand of His merciful kindness is always extended in a loving appeal to all men. V. 2. **Who can utter,** fully declare, sufficiently describe, **the mighty acts of the Lord,** as He manifested them in the power of His mercy, for the salvation of men? **Who can show forth all His praise,** the glory of His essence as He revealed Himself in history? V. 3. **Blessed are they that keep judgment,** observing the demands of right and justice, **and He that doeth righteousness at all times,** in accordance with the holy will of the Lord. V. 4. **Remember me, O Lord,** the psalmist here seeking the application of God's blessings to Himself, **with the favor,** the unmerited affection and good pleasure, **that Thou bearest unto Thy people: O visit with Thy salvation,** letting the inspired singer have the assurance that he also is included in the saving grace of the Lord, v. 5. **that I may see the good of Thy chosen,** taking part in the blessings which God had promised to Israel, the nation of His choice, **that I may rejoice in the gladness of Thy nation, that I may glory with Thine inheritance,** boasting of the favor of the Lord as shown in His many miracles in their behalf. Note that four different names are given to Israel in these two verses, all of them denoting the close fellowship which the Lord intended between Himself and them. But now follows the recital of Israel's trespasses. V. 6. **We have sinned with**

our fathers, the present generation following their fathers in wickedness, **we have committed iniquity, we have done wickedly,** all of them forming one mass of corruption and the terms denoting a rising gradation of sinning. Note the emphatic "we," which is essential for a full and free confession of sins. V. 7. **Our fathers understood not Thy wonders in Egypt,** they did not realize the Lord's purpose or the fulness of His divine favor; **they remembered not the multitude of Thy mercies, but provoked Him,** rather, they showed themselves rebellious, **at the sea, even at the Red Sea,** all the miracles of the Lord for their deliverance having been forgotten in this short space of time. V. 8. **Nevertheless He saved them,** in spite of their ungrateful behavior He delivered them, **for His name's sake,** without any merit or worthiness on their part, solely with the intention of keeping His glory untarnished, **that He might make His mighty power to be known,** and thus be exalted in the eyes of men everywhere. V. 9. **He rebuked the Red Sea also,** which apparently obstructed their way to liberty, **and it was dried up; so He led them through the depths,** the bed of the sea, **as through the wilderness,** ordinary plain country. V. 10. **And He saved them from the hand of him that hated them,** Pharaoh of the exodus, **and redeemed them from the hand of the enemy.** V. 11. **And the waters covered their enemies; there was not one of them left,** Ex. 14, 21—31. V. 12. **Then believed they His words,** for God constrained even such a hard-hearted people to turn to Him in momentary faith; **they sang His praise,** Ex. 15, 1—21. But the reaction came almost immediately. V. 13. **They soon forgat His works,** literally, "they made haste, they forgot," their flare of faith lasting barely three days; **they waited not for His counsel,** the plan which He had for their care, v. 14. **but lusted exceedingly in the wilderness,** demanding to be given their desire, **and tempted God in the desert,** trying Him out, wearing down His patience with their constant grumbling. Cp. 1 Cor. 10, 6. V. 15. **And He gave them their request,** sending them water, manna, quails, Ex. 15, 22—24; 16; 17, 2; Num. 11, **but sent leanness into their soul,** by consuming them with a very great plague, Num. 11, 33—35. V. 16. **They envied Moses also in the camp and Aaron, the saint of the Lord,** Num. 16, 1, the rebels desiring the places of authority for themselves. V. 17. **The earth opened and swallowed up Dathan and covered the company of Abiram,** Num. 16, 23—35. V. 18. **And a fire was kindled in their company; the flame burned up the wicked.** After this reference to the rebellion of Korah the psalmist returns to the early days of the wilderness journey. V. 19. **They made a calf in Horeb,** while Moses was on the mount with God, **and worshiped the molten image,** Ex. 32, 4. V. 20. **Thus they changed their glory,** Jehovah, the true God Himself, as He had manifested and proved Himself before the people, **into the similitude of an ox that eateth grass.** V. 21. **They forgat God, their Savior,** who had delivered them by such a signal deliverance, **which had done great things in Egypt,** in the ten plagues upon Pharaoh and his people; v. 22. **wondrous works in the land of Ham,** Egypt being called so because the descendants of Ham had settled there, **and terrible things,** which caused Him to be feared, **by the Red Sea.** V. 23. **Therefore He said that He would destroy them,** Ex. 32, 10; Num. 14, 12, **had not Moses, His chosen, stood before Him in the breach to turn away His wrath, lest He should destroy them,** for in one case the plague had already made great headway, Num. 16, 44—50. V. 24. **Yea, they despised the pleasant land,** when they rebelled after the report of the spies had been received, Num. 13 and 14, **they believed not His word,** Heb. 3, 18, v. 25. **but murmured in their tents,** Num. 14, 1—4, **and hearkened not unto the voice of the Lord.** V. 26. **Therefore He lifted up His hand against them to overthrow them in the wilderness,** v. 27. **to overthrow their seed also among the nations,** dispersing them with the effect of destroying their national identity, **and to scatter them in the lands,** a fate which Moses then averted, but which later struck the northern tribes. Cp. Deut. 9, 23—26. Another occasion is now cited. V. 28. **They joined themselves also unto Baal-peor,** Num. 25, in the immoral worship introduced by the Moabites, **and ate the sacrifices of the dead,** so called because the idols are dead, lifeless nothingnesses, as they are sometimes designated. V. 29. **Thus they provoked Him to anger with their inventions,** with their idolatrous and immoral doings; **and the plague brake in upon them,** Num. 25, 8. 9. V. 30. **Then stood up Phinehas,** the grandson of Aaron, **and executed judgment,** by summarily putting to death two flagrant malefactors; **and so the plague was stayed.** V. 31. **And that was counted unto him for righteousness unto all generations forevermore,** Num. 25, 11—13; for his deed was an act of faith and received the reward of faith. Still another event is here listed. V. 32. **They angered Him also at the waters of strife,** at Meribah and Massa, Num. 20, 3. 13, **so that it went ill with Moses for their sakes,** his disgust causing him to give way to doubt, at least for a moment, v. 33. **because they provoked His Spirit,** resisting and grieving the Spirit of the Lord, Ps. 78, 17. 40. 56, **so that he,** Moses, **spake unadvisedly with his lips,** thereby forfeiting his right to enter the Promised Land, Deut. 1, 37; 3, 26. Israel's disobedience continued even after they had taken possession of Canaan. V. 34. **They did not destroy the nations, concerning whom the Lord commanded them,** Deut. 7, 2. 16; Ex. 23, 32—34, v. 35. **but were mingled among the heathen,** permitting them to live in their midst and in many cases intermarrying with them, **and learned their works.** Cp. Judg. 1 and 2. V. 36. **And they served their idols,** the many cases of wholesale idolatry during the time of the judges and later being included here; **which were a snare unto them,** Ex. 23, 33. V. 37. **Yea, they sacrificed their sons and their daughters unto devils,** by letting them pass through the fire of Hinnom or actually offering them to Moloch, the abomination of the Moabites, Lev. 17, 7, v. 38. **and shed innocent blood, even the blood of their sons and of their daughters, whom they sacrificed unto the idols of Canaan; and the land was polluted with blood,** Num. 35, 33. 34. V. 39. **Thus were they defiled with their own works,** through the spiritual adultery of their idolatrous practises, Ex. 20, 43, **and went a-whoring with their own inventions,** with the doings dictated by their rejection of the true God. V. 40. **Therefore was the wrath of the Lord kindled against His people,** whom He had chosen for His own, **insomuch that He abhorred His own inheritance,** looking upon them with aversion and loathing. V. 41. **And He gave them into the hand of the heathen,** as stated throughout the Book of Judges and later; **and they that hated them ruled over them.** V. 42. **Their enemies also oppressed them,** not only by exacting tribute, but also by sending marauding parties into Canaan whenever it suited their fancy, **and they were brought into subjection under their hand,** in the great humiliation of being servants to the despised heathen. V. 43. **Many times did He deliver them; but they provoked Him with their counsel,** being self-willed and rebellious, **and were brought low for their iniquity,** the same circle of apostasy, servitude, deliverance, and relapse being found time and again during the four hundred years following the conquest of Canaan. V. 44. **Nevertheless He regarded their affliction when He heard their cry,** the reference here probably being to the time of Samuel and the century following; v. 45. **and He remembered for them His covenant,** Lev. 26, 41. 42, **and repented,** turning to them in sympathy, **according to the multitude of His mercies,** out of free grace and mercy, and not because of any merit or worthiness in them. V. 46. **He made them also to be pitied of all those that carried them captives,** as in the case of Jehoiachin, Ezra, Nehemiah, and Esther. In firm reliance upon this mercy of Jehovah the psalmist concludes with an appeal and a doxology. V. 47. **Save us, O Lord, our God, and gather us from among the heathen,** these words apparently pointing to the exile as the probable time when this psalm was written, **to give thanks unto Thy holy name and to triumph in Thy praise,** their boast being not of themselves, but of the wonderful attributes and works of Jehovah. V. 48. **Blessed be the Lord God of Israel from everlasting to everlasting,** throughout all eternity, **and let all the people,** especially all believers, all members of the Church of God, **say, Amen,** in joyful, believing assent. **Praise ye the Lord!** This hallelujah will be the chief content of the hymns in heaven, the song of the saved, while eternal ages run.

PSALM 107.

Thanksgiving for Deliverance from Various Troubles.

V. 1. **O give thanks unto the Lord, for He is good,** He reveals His gracious providence to all men in the various emergencies which come upon them; **for His mercy endureth forever,** His unmerited favor and kindness upon men lasts throughout eternity. V. 2. **Let the redeemed of the Lord say so,** the returned exiles, **whom He hath redeemed from the hand of the enemy,** from the power of oppression and misery, v. 3. **and gathered them out of the lands,** whither they had been led away captive, **from the east and from the west, from the north and from the south,** literally, "from the sea," the reference being either to Egypt or to Arabia. V. 4. **They wandered in the wilderness in a solitary way,** in loneliness and far from human habitations; **they found no city to dwell in,** where they would be received in a hospitable manner. V. 5. **Hungry and thirsty,** on account of the absence of both food and drink in the desert, **their soul fainted in them,** literally, "was muffled," grew dim, was near to extinction. V. 6. **Then they cried unto the Lord in their trouble, and He delivered them out of their distresses,** by a quick and complete deliverance. V. 7. **And He led them forth by the right way,** the true and proper road leading to deliverance, **that they might go to a city of habitation,** the reference being to Palestine, and specifically Jerusalem. V. 8. **Oh, that men,** that is, such as had the experiences here enumerated, **would praise the Lord for His goodness and for His wonderful works to the children of men,** that is, proclaiming their own wonderful deliverance to others and thus to exalt the Lord. V. 9. **For He satisfieth the longing soul,** the soul languishing for deliverance, **and filleth the hungry soul with goodness.** The application of this entire section to spiritual distress and religious persecution readily suggests itself, both the earnest crying for deliverance and the praise after deliverance being recommended.

The second paragraph treats of captives. V. 10. **Such as sit in darkness and in the shadow of death,** in miserable captivity, such as that of King Manasseh, **being bound in affliction and iron,** bound in pain and torture, especially by iron fetters of a shameful imprisonment, v. 11. **because they rebelled against the words of God,** proclaimed for their salvation, **and contemned the counsel of the Most High,** their rejection of God's gracious purposes in their behalf, combined with blasphemy, tending to frustrate His designs; v. 12. **therefore He brought down their heart with labor,** humiliating them by means of the distress which He laid upon them; **they fell down, and there was none to help,** it being the aim of God to bring them to a realization of their helplessness. V. 13. **Then they cried unto the Lord in their trouble,** having finally gained understanding, **and He saved them out of their distresses,** delivered them out of their anxious situation. V. 14. **He brought them out of darkness and the shadow of death and brake their bands in sunder.** V. 15. **Oh, that men,** that is, men having had such experiences, **would praise the Lord for His goodness and for His wonderful works to the children of men,** v. 8. V. 16. **For He hath broken the gates of brass,** in setting free the captives, **and cut the bars of iron in sunder,** this summary being like Is. 45, 2. The application of these words to men of all times who have resisted the work of the Holy Ghost, but have been brought to repentance by the visitation of the Lord, is again obvious.

The next section treats of those who foolishly bring misery upon themselves by wilful indulgence in sin. V. 17. **Fools because of their transgression,** men devoid of proper mentality, as they prove themselves to be by indulging in sins which invariably carry their own punishment with them, like immorality and intemperance, **and because of their iniquities, are afflicted.** A person yielding to every sensual and sensuous desire, setting aside all sanity and deliberately ruining his health and risking his reputation, will find himself subject to many burdens of punishment, even in this world. V. 18. **Their soul abhorreth all manner of meat,** foods which they formerly delighted in now fill their souls with disgust and loathing; **and they draw near unto the gates of death.** V. 19. **Then they cry unto the Lord in their trouble,** having been brought to the knowledge of their sin by the severity of the punishment which struck them, **and He saveth them out of their distresses,** delivering them out of the tight place into which their foolishness wedged them. V. 20. **He sent His Word and healed them,** the healing of the soul through the application of the Word being the chief step in the great Physician's treatment, **and delivered them from their destructions,** permitting them to escape out of the pits which their own lack of sense had dug for them. V. 21. **Oh, that men,** such as have had experiences of this kind, **would praise the Lord for His goodness and for His wonderful works to the children of men!** V. 8. V. 22. **And let them sacrifice the sacrifices of thanksgiving,** in seeking most earnestly to be united with Jehovah in the fellowship of faith and love, **and declare His works with rejoicing,** proclaiming the fact of their deliverance from the misery into which their own fault had plunged them. This attitude is all the more necessary in the case of such people, since their shame is usually known in a community, and they are obliged to live down their past.

In the next section are set forth the perils of seafaring. V. 23. **They that go down to the sea in ships,** launching forth on the deep after descending from the general elevation of the land, **that do business in great waters,** the allusion being to merchants with an oversea trade; v. 24. **these see the works of the Lord,** their own eyes observing the manifestation of God's mighty power on the ocean, **and His wonders in the deep,** since its limitless expanse fills the heart of man with awe in the presence of the greatness of God. V. 25. **For He commandeth,** as the Lord of the elements, **and raiseth the stormy wind,** literally, "makes the breath of the storm to stand," like an enemy threatening destruction, **which lifteth up the waves thereof,** or "His waves," those in His control. V. 26. **They mount up to the heaven,** their crests rising up like mountains, **they go down again to the depths,** in the deep troughs between the billows; **their soul is melted because of trouble,** that is, the hearts of the sailors are filled with dread. V. 27. **They reel to and fro,** as their frail craft is tossed about, **and stagger like a drunken man, and are at their wit's end,** altogether helpless in the turmoil of the elements. V. 28. **Then they cry unto the Lord in their trouble, and He bringeth them out of their distresses,** saving them in the emergency which threatened their ship and their lives. V. 29. **He maketh the storm a calm, so that the waves thereof are still,** presenting a smooth and untroubled surface. V. 30. **Then are they,** the sailors, **glad because they be quiet; so He bringeth them unto their desired haven,** to the port for which they were headed. V. 31. **Oh, that** men, after such experiences, **would praise the Lord for His goodness and for His wonderful works to the children of men!** V. 32. **Let them exalt Him also,** in telling of the wonderful deliverance they experienced, **in the congregation of the people,** in public assembly, in the place of worship, **and praise Him in the assembly of the elders,** in the open market-place, where the public meetings of the people were held. That this admonition applies to Christian sailors of all times is evident.

A further section describes the life of the tillers of the soil when they are deprived of the needed moisture in their fields, as well as when they receive an abundance of rain. V. 33. **He turneth rivers into a wilderness,** the earth's productiveness being changed to sterility by His withholding the sources of fertility, **and the water-springs into dry ground;** v. 34. **a fruitful land into barrenness,** into alkali deserts, **for the wickedness of them that dwell therein,** punishing the inhabitants for their sins. There are many examples of this fact in many parts of the world. On the other hand, the Lord sends bountiful blessings upon men. V. 35. **He turneth the wilderness,** the bare and apparently unfruitful desert, **into a standing water,** so that pools of water will be found there, **and dry ground into water-springs.** V. 36. **And there He maketh the hungry to dwell,** giving them dwellings, homes, in the former wilderness, **that they may prepare a city for habitation,** since the country proved rich enough to sustain a large population, v. 37. **and sow the fields and plant vineyards, which may yield fruits of increase,** the husbandman getting rich returns for his labors. V. 38. **He blesseth them also, so that they are multiplied greatly,** all the conditions surrounding them being favorable to such an increase; **and suffereth not their cattle to decrease.** Such are the blessings of the Lord which should be acknowledged by men with due thanks, both in proclaiming His goodness and in serving Him according to His will.

The final paragraph refers to such as are suffering under misrule and tyranny. V. 39. **Again, they are minished,** their prosperity being reduced by adverse circumstances, **and brought low through oppression, affliction, and sorrow,** brought upon them on account of the jealousy of those in power. V. 40. **He poureth contempt upon princes and causeth them to wander in the wilderness, where there is no way,** in pitiful exile. V. 41. **Yet setteth He the poor on high from affliction,** far from the reach of suffering, **and maketh him families like a flock,** this feature occurring time and again as an outstanding characteristic of God's blessing. V. 42. **The righteous,** those who are upright in heart, **shall see it and rejoice; and,** on the other hand, **all iniquity shall stop her mouth,** the arrogant for once being obliged to maintain silence at this evidence of God's favor. V. 43. **Whoso is wise and will observe these things,** he who will take note of these facts, profit by the example of others, **even they shall understand the loving-kindness of the Lord,** they will keep His merciful dealings in mind always. It is a lesson which cannot be learned too well or repeated too often, a lesson which all true Christians hold before their eyes every day, lest they forget their debt to the Lord and become lax in His service.

PSALM 108.

David's Thanksgiving and Prayer.

In this psalm David has used the material of former hymns of praise, the Holy Spirit making use of this new combination to bring out very strongly the features of praise and prayer. **A song or psalm of David,** vv. 1—5 being the same as Ps. 57, 7—11, and vv. 6—13 the same as Ps. 60, 5—12, only a few slight changes in the words having been made. V. 1. **O God, my heart is fixed,** in trustful reliance; **I will sing and give praise, even with my glory,** his entire soul with all its powers being engaged in this service. V. 2. **Awake, psaltery and harp,** for the purpose of early and energetic praise; **I myself will awake early.** V. 3. **I will praise Thee, O Lord, among the people, and I will sing praises unto Thee among the nations,** the missionary idea being expressed very clearly in this verse. V. 4. **For Thy mercy is great above the heavens,** extending beyond the limit of human understanding, **and Thy truth reacheth unto the clouds,** filling the entire universe. V. 5. **Be Thou exalted, O God, above the heavens and Thy glory above all the earth,** v. 6. **that Thy beloved may be delivered,** that is, the believer trusting in Jehovah; **save with Thy right hand,** emblem of almighty power, **and answer me.** V. 7. **God hath spoken in His holiness,** that being the guarantee in which the believer may trust. **I will rejoice, I will divide Shechem and mete out the Valley of Succoth.** V. 8. **Gilead is mine; Manasseh is mine; Ephraim also is the strength of mine head; Judah is my lawgiver;** v. 9. **Moab is my wash-pot; over Edom will I cast out my shoe; over Philistia,** now lying in a state of complete overthrow and subjection, **will I triumph.** V. 10. **Who will bring me into the strong city?**

Who will lead me into Edom? V. 11. Wilt not Thou, O God, who hast cast us off? And wilt not Thou, O God, go forth with our hosts? V. 12. Give us help from trouble; for vain is the help of man. V. 13. Through God we shall do valiantly; for He it is that shall tread down our enemies. It is a hymn setting forth the fulfilment of God's promises and as such is a fitting song for all believers, a hymn of triumph over all spiritual enemies, all of whom must finally submit to the Lord.

PSALM 109.

Lament of the Righteous Against Traitors and Enemies.

To the chief musician, for use in the liturgical part of worship, **a psalm of David,** in which he indeed may have reference to conditions of his own time, in his relation to Doeg, to Ahithophel, or to Shimei, but which at the same time is prophetical and typical of the relation in which Christ stood to the Jews and especially to Judas Iscariot, who betrayed Him. This is evident from the remarks of Peter at the election of Matthias, Acts 1, 16. 20. V. 1. **Hold not Thy peace,** as if God's silence were an indication of His indifference, **O God of my praise,** the object of his praise, of whose help he was so sure that he could proclaim His glory even in advance; v. 2. **for the mouth of the wicked and the mouth of the deceitful,** literally, "of deceit," said in an emphatic statement, **are opened,** that is, have the enemies opened, **against me,** as though in an effort to discredit him in court; **they have spoken against me with a lying tongue,** literally, "with a tongue of lies or falsehood," since their entire being was wrapped up in lying, since they knew nothing else. V. 3. **They compassed me about also,** coming against him from all sides, **with words of hatred, and fought against me without a cause,** without his having given provocation to them. V. 4. **For my love,** that is, in return for all the love which he has shown them, **they are my adversaries; but I give myself unto prayer,** literally, "I am prayer," that is, he gives forth his whole being in prayer, placing himself in the care of God in absolute trust. V. 5. **And they have rewarded me evil for good,** which he, on his part, showed toward them in all his dealings, **and hatred for my love.** Having thus set forth the wickedness of the adversaries, David singles out one of them, the type of Judas Iscariot, asking the Lord to punish him as he deserved. V. 6. **Set Thou a wicked man over him,** a power of punishment, an executioner, to drag him to judgment, **and let Satan,** in this case practically as the servant of God in carrying out the punishment fixed by Him, **stand at his right hand,** the usual position of the accusing witness. The court scene is further pictured. V. 7. **When he shall be judged, let him be condemned, and let his prayer become sin,** since it was not the crying of a penitent sinner, but of one in the depths of blasphemous despair. We are here reminded of the cry of Judas Iscariot: "I have sinned in that I have betrayed the innocent blood," Matt. 27, 4. V. 8. **Let his days be few,** his life coming to an end before the time normally set for its length; **and let another take his office,** this statement being directly applied by Peter to the apostleship lost by Judas Iscariot, Acts 1, 20. V. 9. **Let his children be fatherless,** orphaned by his violent death, **and his wife a widow,** his family sharing in the punishment of his guilt. V. 10. **Let his children,** who evidently followed their father in his wickedness, **be continually vagabonds,** wandering vagrants, **and beg; let them seek their bread also out of their desolate places,** prowling about at a distance from their ruined home. V. 11. **Let the extortioner,** the heartless creditor, **catch all that he hath,** as in a net or snare; **and let the strangers spoil his labor,** making that their plunder or booty over which he toiled with so much work. V. 12. **Let there be none to extend mercy unto him,** showing love to his children; **neither let there be any to favor his fatherless children.** V. 13. **Let his posterity be cut off,** by exterminating his family; **and in the generation following,** in the second generation, **let their name be blotted out,** so annihilated that not even a remembrance would be left. V. 14. **Let the iniquity of his fathers be remembered with the Lord, and let not the sin of his mother be blotted out.** V. 15. **Let them be before the Lord continually,** the iniquities of the father being unforgotten and unforgiven by the Lord, **that He may cut off the memory of them from the earth,** to the everlasting disgrace of the entire family, all of whose members, on account of their own wickedness, are burdened also with the guilt of their forbears, v. 16. **because that he,** the chief and representative enemy, **remembered not to show mercy, but persecuted the poor and needy man,** one who was already bowed down with suffering, **that he might even slay the broken in heart.** The Messianic character of this passage is seen from the corresponding section of Psalm 69, especially vv. 20—29. V. 17. **As he loved cursing, so let it come unto him,** it struck him with full force when he, in despair, took his own life; **as he delighted not in blessing, so let it be far from him.** His fate was the result of his own choice, made in spite of better knowledge and repeated warnings. V. 18. **As he clothed himself with cursing,** as one wrapping himself closely in it, happy in feeling it all about himself, **like as with his garment, so let it come into his bowels like water,** the curse penetrating into the innermost parts of his body, **and like oil into his bones,** saturating everything and bringing condemnation and punishment upon him. V. 19. **Let it be unto him as the garment which covereth him, and for a girdle wherewith he is girded continually.** All these imprecations are now summarized. V. 20. **Let this be the reward,** the well-deserved punishment, **of mine adversaries from the Lord, and of them that speak evil against my soul,** in repaying the love shown them with enmity in word and deed. They have brought the curse and punishment upon themselves, they have chosen the evil. The inspired singer now turns to lament and prayer. V. 21. **But do Thou for me, O God the Lord,** taking his part, showing him blessings, **for Thy name's sake; because Thy mercy,** the grace of Jehovah, the God of salvation, **is good,** the source and foundation of all true spiritual blessings, **deliver Thou me.** V. 22. **For I am poor and needy,** this being particularly descriptive of the Messiah in His suffering as our Substitute, **and My heart is wounded within Me,** as when He Himself complained that His soul was exceeding sorrowful, even unto death, Matt. 26, 38. V. 23. **I am gone like the shadow when it declineth,** toward evening, just before it is swallowed up by darkness; **I am tossed up and down as the locust,** driven away like grasshoppers before the wind, Ex. 10, 19. V. 24. **My knees are weak through fasting,** His deep grief causing Him to loathe all food; **and My flesh faileth of fatness,** emaciation following deep and sustained sorrow. V. 25. **I became also a reproach unto them,** Ps. 69, 11. 12; Matt. 27, 39—44; **when they looked upon Me, they shaked their heads.** V. 26. **Help Me, O Lord, My God,** the Messiah's own prayer being recorded here, as in Ps. 22 and 69; **O save Me according to Thy mercy,** v. 27. **that they,** the enemies, **may know that this is Thy hand, that Thou, Lord, hast done it,** His deliverance thus resulting in the glorification of Jehovah. V. 28. **Let them curse,** in a vain attempt to bring evil upon the Lord's servant, **but bless Thou,** since God's blessing more than offsets any curse on the part of men; **when they arise,** in order to carry out their evil designs, **let them be ashamed; but let Thy Servant rejoice,** knowing that the end of His suffering is near. V. 29. **Let Mine adversaries be clothed with shame,** on account of the fact that their evil plans miscarried, **and let them cover themselves with their own confusion, as with a mantle,** with the disgrace which their evil deeds brought upon them. V. 30. **I will greatly praise the Lord with My mouth,** for the deliverance which is bound to come; **yea, I will praise Him among the multitude,** in the midst of His congregation. V. 31. **For He shall stand at the right hand of the poor,** to wage war in His behalf, **to save Him from those that condemn His soul.** Thus God, the righteous Judge, would eventually pronounce the sentence of justification upon His Servant. Cp. Is. 53, 8.

PSALM 110.

A Psalm of Christ, Our King and High Priest.

A psalm of David, altogether prophetic in character, setting before the Church of the Old Testament the Messiah as the Lord of David. No other psalm, no other prophecy, is quoted so often in the New Testament as this psalm. Cp. Matt. 22, 44; Mark 12, 36; Luke 20, 42; Acts 2, 34; 1 Cor. 15, 25; Heb. 1, 13; 1 Pet. 3, 22. Compare also Ps. 45, 6. 7, where the same idea is brought out. V. 1. **The Lord said unto my Lord,** literally, "Declaration of Jehovah to my Lord," David here recording what he, in the spirit, heard Jehovah, the God of heaven, say to his Lord, the Messiah, **Sit Thou at My right hand,** emblem of the almighty power of God with which He shows forth His great miracles, especially those for the salvation of mankind, **until I make Thine enemies Thy footstool.** The Messiah, the Son of David, and at the same time David's Lord, born as a true man and living His life in lowliness and humility, is given a part in the divine power and rule, Himself in charge of God's government of the earth, exalted to that position according to His humanity. The climax of His kingly rule will be reached on the Last Day; for then the Lord Jehovah will crown His many victories in behalf of the Head of the Christian Church by vanquishing even the last enemy of mankind, death, 1 Cor. 15, 25. On that day the Kingdom of Grace will become the Kingdom of Glory, and Christ will rule as the King of Glory throughout eternity. V. 2. **The Lord shall send the rod,** the scepter, **of Thy strength,** stretching it out in the conquering power of His might, **out of Zion,** extending His Church on all sides, among all nations. The conquest of the enemies, the conversion of the heathen, is a proof of Christ's almighty power. **Rule Thou in the midst of Thine enemies.** In the very midst of His enemies Christ establishes His kingdom. V. 3. **Thy people shall be willing in the day of Thy power,** literally, "willingnesses" or "willing sacrifices" whenever He wants to mobilize them, whenever He wants them to carry forward His will, to spread the Gospel of His glory and salvation, **in the beauties of holiness from the womb of the morning; Thou hast the dew of Thy youth**, literally, "in the majesties of holiness, from the womb of the dawn to Thee is the dew of Thy young men." The people mobilized by the Lord, the soldiers enrolled under Messiah's banners, appear in the majesties of holiness, in the garments of the true priests, the symbol of purity, white linen, their garments cleansed by the blood of the Lamb. Thus they are a nation of priests, 1 Pet. 2, 9. In such numbers are they mobilized for spiritual warfare and ministry that the young men — the vigorous numbers making up the army — are like dew from the womb of the morning for multitude, a countless host. As the dew falls most strongly just at dawn, when the morning star arises, so the members of Christ's Church and army are brought forth when the heavenly light from the Day-star on high shines upon them, when they are converted by the power of the Spirit in the Word. The new spiritual life is bound to show in all the works of the Christians. The psalmist now pictures the majesty of the Messiah. V. 4. **The Lord**, Jehovah of heaven, **hath sworn**, in a solemn oath, **and will not repent**, the words of His oath being directed to the Messiah, **Thou art a Priest forever**, throughout eternity, **after the order of Melchizedek.** Jesus Christ is the great High Priest of His Church, who, by His atonement, by offering Himself as a sacrifice to God in the place of all men, as mankind's great Substitute, earned an everlasting redemption, the fruit of which is assured to all believers by His intercession for us at the throne of His Father. The priesthood is His after the order of Melchizedek, king of Salem, who was both king and priest in one person. The thought is carried out in great detail in the Epistle to the Hebrews, chap. 6, 20—7, 28. V. 5. **The Lord at Thy right hand**, the Messiah Himself, possessed of the full divine Godhead, also according to His human nature, **shall strike through kings in the day of His wrath**, crushing them, treading even the greatest and most powerful enemies under foot on the great Day of Judgment, when His anger will blaze forth. V. 6. **He shall judge among the heathen**, carrying out His sentence of wrath upon all such as persistently oppose His work; **He shall fill the places with the dead bodies**, the picture being that of a carnage of battle, with the dead and dying strewing the battle-field; **He shall wound the heads over many countries**, shattering "the head over much earth," the reference most likely being to Antichrist, of whom it is stated that the Lord shall consume him with the Spirit of His mouth and destroy him with the brightness of His coming, 2 Thess. 2, 8, so that he and all his adherents will receive their reward in everlasting damnation. At the same time the Victor will stand forth in His glory. V. 7. **He shall drink of the brook in the way; therefore shall He lift up the head.** He who was obliged to drink of the brook of suffering and tribulation in the state of His humiliation, especially in His last great Passion, will have His exaltation confirmed forever, before friends and enemies, on the great Last Day. It is nothing but victory, conquest, and triumph that falls to the lot of the Messiah. With His head raised up high above all His enemies, He shall never again be laid low, but shall hold the field forever, together with those who have accepted Him as their Savior and their King, in an everlasting victory and triumph.

PSALM 111.

A Psalm of Praise to Jehovah.

V. 1. **Praise ye the Lord**, or, "Hallelujah, praise Jehovah," the singer celebrating God's gracious dealings with His people, of which he gives a summary statement. **I will praise the Lord with my whole heart, in the assembly of the upright**, that is, in the intimate circle of believers, who form a company of confidential friends, **and in the congregation**, the true spiritual Israel of all times. V. 2. **The works of the Lord**, both of His providence and of His grace, **are great, sought out of all them that have pleasure therein**, that is, carefully studied by all who desire to understand them more perfectly. V. 3. **His work is honorable and glorious**, literally, "honor and majesty," to emphasize the fact that His entire essence finds expression in them; **and His righteousness**, especially as shown in the great work of redemption, **endureth forever.** V. 4. **He hath made His wonderful works to be remembered**, literally, "A remembrance He hath made to His miracles," setting them before men never to be forgotten; **the Lord is gracious and full of compassion**, His wonders showing in His goodness, love, and mercy. V. 5. **He hath given meat unto them that fear Him**, supplying them richly with food; **He will ever be mindful of His covenant**, the covenant between Israel and Jehovah being typical of that made with all believers in the Word of Grace. V. 6. **He hath showed His people**, the children of Israel, **the power of His works**, His almighty power being manifested in the manner in which He led and guided them, **that He may give them the heritage of the heathen**, as He did at the conquest of

Canaan. V. 7. **The works of His hands,** by which He manifests Himself to His people, **are verity and judgment,** truth and justice designating both their source and the manner in which they are performed before men; **all His commandments are sure,** whatever He ordains is trustworthy, dependable, as being intended for the highest benefit of mankind. V. 8. **They stand fast forever and ever,** established by His eternal decree, **and are done in truth and uprightness,** without hypocrisy, with only the highest good of His people in mind. V. 9. **He sent redemption unto His people,** the deliverance from the bondage of Egypt being typical of the great spiritual redemption which was gained by Christ for all men; **He hath commanded His covenant forever,** giving the assurance that the covenant of His mercy should never fail. **Holy and reverend is His name,** His entire essence and all His attributes filling all those who contemplate them with awe. V. 10. **The fear of the Lord is the beginning of wisdom,** the highest and best wisdom, for this world and for the world to come, flowing out of the reverence of God which is grounded in faith; **a good understanding,** a proper appreciation and recognition of the values in life, **have all they that do His commandments,** faithful in their duties according to His Word, the spiritual men being able to have the right judgment in all things. **His praise endureth forever,** that is, every one who fears the Lord with the reverence which is an outgrowth of faith may rightly be called happy and blessed, since he is in the most intimate relation with his heavenly Father, from whom every blessing flows.

PSALM 112.

A Psalm of the Happiness of the Believers.

V. 1. **Praise ye the Lord,** another hallelujah psalm, properly regarded as an exposition and application of the last verse of the preceding psalm, the object being to present the inner happiness of those who fear and obey God, as contrasted with the fate of the unbelievers. **Blessed,** living in true happiness, **is the man that feareth the Lord,** in the awe and reverence flowing from true faith, **that delighteth greatly in His commandments,** taking great pleasure, finding the highest happiness, in proper obedience to them. V. 2. **His seed,** his children or posterity, **shall be mighty upon earth,** literally, "a hero or champion," having authority and influence even in the temporal affairs of the state; **the generation of the upright,** his family, in so far as its members follow him in his godliness, **shall be blessed,** just as the Lord states in the summary of the Ten Commandments. V. 3. **Wealth and riches,** everything needed for a long and happy life, **shall be in his house,** even if the filthy lucre is not stacked up in heaps; **and his righteousness endureth forever,** his entire conduct is always in agreement with the divine requirements, because he has, by faith, accepted the righteousness imputed to him by virtue of the Messiah's work. V. 4. **Unto the upright there ariseth light in the darkness,** in the very midst of the valley of the shadow of death the sun of God's mercy shines upon them and guides them in the right way; **he is gracious and full of compassion and righteous,** every believer reflecting, in this respect, the virtues of His heavenly Father. V. 5. **A good man showeth favor and lendeth,** that is, happy is the man, it is well with him, who is benevolent and generous; **he will guide his affairs with discretion,** literally, "he will maintain his cause in judgment," his character will be so well established in the community that he will be safe against the schemes of enemies seeking to discredit him. V. 6. **Surely he shall not be moved forever,** his position being such that evil designs cannot harm him; **the righteous shall be in everlasting remembrance,** remembered with approval by all who were acquainted with him. V. 7. **He shall not be afraid of evil tidings,** not dread reports which threaten misfortune to himself and his house; **his heart is fixed,** set in firm confidence, **trusting in the Lord,** who will not permit any real evil to strike him. V. 8. **His heart is established,** firm in faith and trust, **he shall not be afraid, until he see his desire upon his enemies,** his oppressors laid low by the punishment of God. V. 9. **He hath dispersed,** showed proper generosity, **he hath given to the poor,** those really in need; **his righteousness endureth forever,** his righteous conduct, as grounded in, and flowing from, his faith in Jehovah; **his horn,** emblem of authority and might, **shall be exalted with honor,** lifted up high before all the world, with open appreciation of his moral worth. V. 10. **The wicked shall see it and be grieved,** on account of being disappointed in his evil designs; **he shall gnash with his teeth,** in impotent rage, **and melt away,** his final portion being everlasting destruction. **The desire of the wicked shall perish,** all his wicked scheming against the righteous will come to naught, be of no avail to him. This serves to cheer and encourage all believers in the midst of the world's hatred.

PSALM 113.

Praise of God's Mercy toward the Lowly.

V. 1. **Praise ye the Lord,** this being the third hallelujah psalm, setting forth the majesty of God, together with His mercy in dealing with the humble. It was used as the introduction to the great hallel sung by the Jews on their great festivals, particularly on the Passover. **Praise, O ye servants of the Lord,** all the faithful, all true believers, who delight in the true ministry of Jehovah, **praise the name of the Lord,** setting forth the glory of His essence and attributes, as shown in His Word and works. V. 2. **Blessed be the name of the Lord from this time forth and forevermore,** the entire Church, with all its members, singing His praises as Creator, Redeemer, and Sanctifier, throughout eternity. V. 3. **From the rising of the sun unto the going down of the same,** throughout the length and breadth of the world, **the Lord's name is to be praised,** all creatures being invited to join in this psalm. V. 4. **The Lord is high above all nations,** exalted above all human states with their puny rulers, **and His glory above the heavens,** over which He, too, is the absolute Sovereign. V. 5. **Who is like unto the Lord, our God, who dwelleth on high,** on the throne of His power, v. 6. **who humbleth Himself to behold the things that are in heaven and in the earth,** that is, who, from His exalted position of omniscience and omnipresence, watches most carefully over everything that happens in heaven and earth. V. 7. **He raiseth up the poor out of the dust,** out of the condition of extreme lowliness, **and lifteth the needy,** the miserable and despised, **out of the dunghill,** or ash-heap, as one cast off by men and making the refuse heap of the city his dwelling; v. 8. **that He may set him with princes, even with the princes of His people,** elevating him to a position in the nobility, the powerful people of the land. V. 9. **He maketh the barren woman to keep house,** taking from her the disgrace of childlessness, **and to be a joyful mother of children,** a blessing which is often emphasized in the Bible. **Praise ye the Lord!** It is the proper song for the believers of all times, and all the blessings here enumerated are gratefully acknowledged by them in hymns of praise and in willing ministry of the hands.

PSALM 114.

The God of Jacob the Deliverer out of Egypt.

A majestic song celebrating the care of God for His people at the time of the exodus from Egypt, when all the powers of nature were called to contribute for their benefit. V. 1. **When Israel,** God's chosen people, who had accepted the true God as their King, **went out of Egypt, the house of Jacob,** which had entered Egypt as a family and left it as a nation, **from a people of strange language,** that is, unintelligible, foreign, Hebrew being considered the sacred language, v. 2. **Judah,** the tribe which assumed the leadership and to whose tribe the capital was reckoned after the time of David, **was His Sanctuary and Israel,** the entire nation, as His Church, **His dominion,** His rule over them being acknowledged by all the true Israelites, Ex. 6, 7. V. 3. **The sea saw it and fled,** the Red sea opening up before the people, Ex. 14, 21; **Jordan was driven back,** Josh. 3, 13. 16; v. 4. **the mountains skipped like rams and the little hills like lambs,** the reference being to the quaking of Mount Sinai and the surrounding country at the time of the giving of the Law. V. 5. **What ailed thee, O thou sea, that thou fleddest? thou Jordan, that thou wast driven back?** the reference being to the two events that marked the beginning and the end of the wilderness journey. V. 6. **Ye mountains, that ye skipped like rams? and ye little hills, like lambs?** Why should all nature be in a turmoil with so many manifestations of His divine power? V. 7. **Tremble, thou earth, at the presence of the Lord,** that being the explanation of the agitation in nature at various times during the wilderness journey, **at the presence of the God of Jacob,** v. 8. **which turned the rock into a standing water,** on the two occasions when Moses, at the command of God, smote the rock and water gushed forth, **the flint into a fountain of waters,** Ex. 17, 6; Num. 20, 11. It is a source of great comfort to New Testament believers to know that the spiritual Rock on whom the children of Israel depended was Christ, 1 Cor. 10, 4. 9.

PSALM 115.

Vindication of God's Glory over against the Idols.

This psalm may have been a cry of Israel for the assistance of the Lord in the face of invading enemies, who placed their confidence in their heathen idols. V. 1. **Not unto us, O Lord, not unto us,** the repetition of the cry serving for emphasis, **but unto Thy name give glory,** so that His essence and His attributes might properly be proclaimed before all men, **for Thy mercy,** His free, unmerited favor, **and for Thy truth's sake,** on account of the faithfulness set forth in the promises of His Word. It is God's glory, and that alone, about which the faithful are ever concerned, not about their own honor. V. 2. **Wherefore should the heathen say,** in mockery on account of the sorry plight of God's people forsaken by their God, **Where is now their God?** This taunt was actually used by the messengers of Sennacherib, the Assyrian king, in his campaign against Hezekiah, Is. 36, 15—20. But while the psalmist records the mockery of the enemies, he also sets over against it the trust of the believers. V. 3. **But our God is in the heavens,** invisible indeed, but nevertheless ruling the world; **He hath done whatsoever He hath pleased,** for He alone is the almighty God, in contrast with the utter impotence of the idols of the heathen. V. 4. **Their idols are silver and gold,** carved images, manufactured out of precious metals, indeed, but without real existence, **the work of men's hands,** constructed, poured, carved, by weak and puny human beings, not even created, but made. V. 5. **They have mouths,** as fashioned by the artist making them, **but they speak not; eyes have they, but they see not;** v. 6. **they have ears, but they hear not; noses have they, but they smell not;** v. 7. **they have hands, but they handle not,** or, "their hands are there, yet they feel not"; **feet have they, but they walk not; neither speak they through their throat,** they cannot even mutter, utter an articulate sound. Note the pairing of the members and the effective way of grouping each pair, in order to bring out strongly the inanimate, dead character of the idols. Cp. Ps. 135, 15—17; Is. 44, 9—17; Jer. 10, 3—6. V. 8. **They that make them are like unto them,** devoid of proper understanding; **so is every one,** whether maker or worshiper, **that trusteth in them.** Idolatry lowers not only the religious and moral, but also the intellectual standard of a people. V. 9. **O Israel, trust thou in the Lord,** the admonition coming in all the more strongly after the contrast just presented; **He is their Help and their Shield,** safe to depend upon for purposes both of defense and of offense. V. 10. **O house of Aaron,** a name used for Israel as a people of priests and therefore applicable to all believers, **trust in the Lord; He is their Help and their Shield.** The general application is now made: v. 11. **Ye that fear the Lord,** no matter where and when, in either the Old or the New Testament, **trust in the Lord; He is their Help and their Shield,** on their side both for protection and for battle. V. 12. **The Lord hath been mindful of us,** turned His thoughts in mercy upon His children; **He will bless us; He will bless the house of Israel,** His people as a whole; **He will bless the house of Aaron,** His people as a congregation of priests. V. 13. **He will bless them that fear the Lord,** the Church of all times, **both small and great,** the prominent and the leaders in the Church together with the lowly. V. 14. **The Lord shall increase you more and more;** for the Church, by the blessing of Jehovah in the Word, is bound to grow, **you and your children.** V. 15. **Ye are blessed of the Lord,** richly supplied with the gifts of His goodness and mercy, **which made heaven and earth,** the worth and the greatness of His blessings being measured only by His immeasurable essence. V. 16. **The heaven, even the heavens, are the Lord's,** the throne of His power; **but the earth hath He given to the children of men,** to enjoy the fulness of His favor and to praise Him for His grace. V. 17. **The dead praise not the Lord, neither any that go down into silence,** into the realm of the dead; for then, for a season, their mouth is stilled, they are no longer physically able to join in the praise of Jehovah. All the more reason, then, for us, who are living, to be engaged in this necessary work. V. 18. **But we will bless the Lord from this time forth,** while still living here on earth, **and forevermore,** beyond the grave, after the Last Day, when soul and body will be reunited throughout eternity. **Praise the Lord,** our hallelujah sounding before the throne of the God of our salvation, world without end, in heaven's glorious halls.

PSALM 116.

Thanksgiving for Deliverance from Extreme Perils.

The psalmist proclaims the fact that he was saved from great dangers, celebrates his deliverance by giving praise to God alone, and pledges His public acknowledgment of his debt to Jehovah. V. 1. **I love the Lord because He hath heard my voice and my supplications,** the fact that God attended to His prayer and delivered him fills his heart with grateful love. V. 2. **Because He hath inclined His ear unto me,** in the attitude of willing attention, **therefore will I call upon Him as long as I live,** in prayers both of thanksgiving and of further supplication. He now pictures the situation in which he found himself, from which he was delivered. V. 3. **The sorrows,** literally, "the cords," of death **compassed me,** as in a net, **and the pains,** the oppressions, or straits, **of hell,** of the realm of death, **gat hold upon me; I found trouble and sorrow,** experiencing both in full measure. Cp. Ps. 18, 4. 5. V. 4. **Then called I upon the name of the Lord,** depending upon the promises in His Word: **O Lord, I beseech Thee, deliver my soul.** The psalmist now pictures the manner in which the Lord delivered him. V. 5. **Gracious,** full of merciful compassion, **is the Lord and righteous; yea, our God is merciful.** Cp. Ex. 34, 6. 7. V. 6. **The Lord preserveth the simple,** guarding them against evil designs of the enemies on every hand. **I was brought low,** thrown to the ground in utter helplessness, **and He helped me.** V. 7. **Return unto thy rest, O my soul,** being quiet and satisfied in the relief afforded by the Lord; **for the Lord hath dealt bountifully with thee,** showing kindness far beyond any man's merit. After this admonition to his own heart the poet turns back to his prayer. V. 8. **For Thou hast delivered my soul from death, mine eyes from tears, and my feet from falling,** these three expressions representing all calamities which may befall a man, and the deliverance therefore being complete in every way. V. 9. **I will walk before the Lord,** leading his whole life with the consciousness that he is in the presence of Jehovah and His omniscient eye, **in the land of the living;** instead of becoming a prey to death, he enjoys life and is able always to have his Savior before his eyes. V. 10. **I believed, therefore have I spoken,** literally, "for [this] I speak," in speaking he exercised his faith, his speaking was a proof of his faith, 2 Cor. 4, 13. **I was greatly afflicted,** but in spite of his affliction his faith manifested itself in the free confession of his mouth. V. 11. **I said in my haste,** in his trembling and terror, the result of his deep dejection, **All men are liars.** Forsaken by men, miserably neglected by those from whom he expected assistance in his troubles, he has learned to put all his trust in God alone, to depend upon Him in the midst of all calamities. V. 12. **What shall I render unto the Lord for all His benefits toward me?** How repay His manifold expressions of love and goodness? V. 13. **I will take the cup of salvation,** lifting up the cup of thanksgiving for his deliverance, the allusion probably being to this ceremony at the paschal meal, **and call upon the name of the Lord,** proclaiming Him and His attributes everywhere. V. 14. **I will pay my vows,** the special offerings made to express his gratitude to Jehovah, **now in the presence of all His people,** he was willing and eager to do so in public, that all men might be witnesses of his sacrifice, Num. 15, 3—5. V. 15. **Precious in the sight of the Lord,** esteemed very highly by Him, **is the death of His saints,** that is, He will not readily let death take them away from before Him. V. 16. **O Lord, truly I am Thy servant; I am Thy servant and the son of Thine handmaid,** wherefore, as a home-born servant, he claims the privileges of God's covenant love toward His people. **Thou hast loosed my bonds,** giving him the freedom of the people of God. Hence he once more expresses his gratitude. V. 17. **I will offer to Thee the sacrifice of thanksgiving and will call upon the name of the Lord.** V. 18. **I will pay my vows unto the Lord now in the presence of all His people,** v. 19. **in the courts of the Lord's house,** where the congregation assembled for public worship, **in the midst of thee, O Jerusalem. Praise ye the Lord,** all the believers of the New Testament joining in this hallelujah in honor of the God of their salvation and paying their vows to Him in cheerful service.

PSALM 117.

The Universal Kingdom of Messiah.

The shortest hymn in the Psalter, portraying, in a few words, the Church of God of all times in its relation to Jehovah, the God of salvation. The truth expressed in this psalm, that men from all nations would yet worship Jehovah, as the God who has revealed Himself in the fulness of His redemption for all mankind, is unfolded by Paul, Rom. 15, 11. V. 1. **O praise the Lord, all ye nations,** since He is the God of the Gentiles as well as of the Jews, Luke 2, 30—32; **praise Him, all ye people,** all the nations of the world, without exception. V. 2. **For His merciful kindness is great toward us,** His grace, as revealed in Jesus, the Messiah, is powerful, mighty, in forgiving sins and iniquities and in protecting the believers from everlasting damnation, as the consequence of their trespasses; **and the truth of the Lord endureth forever,** His faithfulness in fulfilling His promises is absolutely trustworthy, His Word, the Gospel-message, is thoroughly reliable. **Praise ye the Lord,** all believers joining in this great hallelujah, because grace and truth became their glorious possession in and with Jesus Christ, John 1, 14. 17, and the glory of this fact can never be sufficiently praised.

PSALM 118.

A Psalm for Festival Services.

This hymn, written altogether in the style of David, bears a liturgical character and was, in fact, used in the Jewish Church upon the occasion of the great festivals, as part of their great hallel, chanted during the time when the Temple-offerings were brought, as well as by the individual families in the intervals of the Passover-meal, although it may originally have been composed for use at the Feast of Tabernacles. Sections of the psalm were in such general use that the pilgrims going forth to meet Jesus at the time of His last entry into Jerusalem chanted them almost spontaneously, Matt. 21, 9; Mark 11, 9; Luke 19, 38. V. 1. **O give thanks unto the Lord, for He is good,** namely, in imparting His kindness in rich blessings upon the faithful; **because His mercy endureth forever.** Cp. Ps. 106, 1; 107, 1; 136, 1. V. 2. **Let Israel,** the entire nation, as the chosen people of God, **now say that His mercy endureth forever.** V. 3. **Let the house of Aaron,** not only the priests, but the entire Church, as a congregation of priests, **now say that His mercy endureth forever.** V. 4. **Let them now that fear the Lord,** all believers of all times, **say that His mercy endureth forever.** The urgent invitation having gone forth to the whole Church to join in praising the Lord, the psalmist now states the reason for his admonition. V. 5. **I called upon the Lord in distress,** when he was in straits, in such difficulties that he could turn neither to the right nor to the left; **the Lord answered me and set me in a large place,** where he had freedom of movement on every side, where he was no longer cramped and hindered on account of being beset by dangers and enemies. V. 6. **The Lord is on my side,** Rom. 8, 31; **I will not fear; what can man,** mere men, puny creatures, **do unto me?** V. 7. **The Lord taketh my part with them that help me,** as his assistance, Jehovah's help outweighing that of all other helpers; **therefore shall I see my desire upon them that hate me,** the enemies being bound to submit before His almighty power. The psalmist now urges the proper trust in Jehovah, as the One who is exalted in power above all men. V. 8. **It is better to trust in the Lord than to put confidence in man,** man at his best being but a weak and helpless creature. V. 9. **It is better to trust in the Lord than to put confidence in princes,** for their power, after all, is small, and their favor deceitful. V. 10. **All nations compassed me about,** or, "though all the heathen should surround me," **but in the name of the Lord,** trusting in the almighty power of Jehovah, **will I destroy them,** cut them down, exterminate them. V. 11. **They compassed me about; yea, they compassed me about,** though they attempt their attacks on all sides; **but in the name of the Lord I will destroy them,** he who makes the Lord his ally always having the balance of power in his favor. V. 12. **They compassed me about like bees,** or, "like wasps," who were particularly troublesome and vicious during harvest-time; **they are quenched as the fire of thorns,** which flares up with great force, but is as quickly extinguished; **for in the name of the Lord I will destroy them.** Sure of the assistance of Jehovah, the congregation is at all times possessed of a feeling of triumph. V. 13. **Thou hast thrust sore at me that I might fall,** the impersonal subject being used in the Hebrew, people have attempted in every possible way to wound and overcome the believer; **but the Lord helped me.** Therefore his song rings out with that of all the faithful. V. 14. **The Lord is my Strength,** affording the believer might to overcome, **and Song,** the subject of hymns of praise at all times, **and is become my Salvation,** delivering him from all enemies. V. 15. **The voice of rejoicing and salvation,** the happiness over the marvelous deliverance, as expressed in hymns of the congregation, **is in the tabernacles of the righteous,** in the homes of all believers, who have become partakers of the righteousness of the Messiah by the gift of God. **The right hand of the Lord doeth valiantly,** exalted in victory. V. 16. **The right hand of the Lord,** emblem of almighty power, **is exalted,** in a rule over all enemies; **the right hand of the Lord doeth valiantly,** in possession of victory. V. 17. **I shall not die,** thus being deprived of the privilege of praising Jehovah, **but live,** being preserved by God's mercy, **and declare the works of the Lord,** that being one of the glorious duties of all believers. V. 18. **The Lord hath chastened me sore,** in the anxieties and distresses to which the psalmist had referred in v. 5; **but He hath not given me over unto death.** Although the psalmist speaks in the singular, he is speaking in the name of the congregation, setting forth their common experience. V. 19. **Open to me the gates of righteousness,** this name being applied to the gates of the Temple, since they afforded an entrance to the place where God imparted His righteousness in His Word; **I will go into them,** together with all other members of the congregation, **and I will praise the Lord,** Jehovah of salvation; v. 20. **this gate of the Lord, into which the righteous shall enter,** the sacrificial acts on the part of the congregation, and the sacramental acts on the part of God's servants, uniting them with Him in the most intimate fellowship. V. 21. **I will praise Thee,** in the full consciousness of this wonderful union with Jehovah; **for Thou hast heard me and art become my Salvation.**

V. 22. **The stone which the builders refused,** rejecting it with scorn as useless, **is become the headstone of the corner,** the corner-stone upholding the entire building of the Lord's Temple. This is a direct prophecy, which, as Jesus says, was fulfilled in Himself, Matt. 21, 42; Mark 12, 10. 11; Acts 4, 11; 1 Pet. 2, 7; Is. 28, 16. The Jews rejected their Savior, refusing to acknowledge Him as the promised Messiah; but He, by the merciful counsel of the Lord, became the Corner-stone of the Christian Church, the Foundation upon which all believers rest their hope of salvation, Eph. 2, 20—22. V. 23. **This is the Lord's doing; it is marvelous in our eyes,** and its marvel grows with every new consideration of the manner in which our salvation was effected. V. 24. **This is the day which the Lord hath made,** the day, the period of grace and salvation extending down to the last day of the world, Is. 49, 8; 2 Cor. 6, 2; **we will rejoice and be glad in it.** Cp. Rev. 19, 7. V. 25. **Save now,** the hosanna of the multitudes on Palm Sunday, **I beseech Thee, O Lord! O Lord, I beseech Thee, send now prosperity,** true spiritual happiness, Matt. 21, 9. V. 26. **Blessed be he that cometh in the name of the Lord,** this cry of welcome, as used by the chorus of Levites in the Temple-services and by the inhabitants of Jerusalem in greeting their brethren from a distance, being used in an unusually appropriate manner in the case of Christ upon His entrance into the city; **we have blessed you out of the house of the Lord,** wishing them the wonderful blessings which are dispensed at the Temple. V. 27. **God is the Lord,** Jehovah is God, the only true God, **which hath showed us light,** with the spiritual enlightenment in His Word. **Bind the sacrifice with cords, even unto the horns of the altar,** the number of the offerings being so great upon festive occasions that the entire court was filled with the animals, so that some of them were led even to the space next to the altar of burnt offering, there to await their turn. This invitation is accepted by the worshiping multitude, in whose name the psalmist now answers. V. 28. **Thou art my God, and I will praise Thee,** with joyful thanksgiving; **Thou art my God, I will exalt Thee,** giving Him the honor due His holy name. V. 29. **O give thanks unto the Lord, for He is good; for His mercy endureth forever,** this same merciful favor being the sustaining power in the believers of all the world to this day.

PSALM 119.

The Christian's Golden ABC of the Praise, Power, and Value of God's Word.

This beautiful psalm, whose writer is not known, is divided into twenty-two sections of eight verses each. All the verses in the same paragraph open with the same letter of the Hebrew alphabet, all twenty-two letters of the Hebrew language thus being used. The outstanding characteristic of this wonderful psalm is the fact that in all but two verses (122 and 132) the Word of God is designated by some expression, such as commandments, judgments, statutes, precepts, testimonies, law, and others, all these terms being used here as synonyms, a fact which makes the psalm of direct value to all believers of all times, a manual of pious thought, especially for all teachers of the Word.

Aleph. OF THE BELIEVER'S CONDUCT IN ACCORDANCE WITH GOD'S WORD. — V. 1. **Blessed are the undefiled,** the blessed, sincere, irreproachable, **in the way,** in their entire conduct of life, **who walk in the Law of the Lord,** being guided by His Word in their entire life. V. 2. **Blessed are they that keep His testimonies,** the Word in which He testifies of Himself, for the truth and against sin, **and that seek Him with the whole heart,** desiring to have such a perfect knowledge of Him and His holy will that they will readily conform to it in all their actions. V. 3. **They also do no iniquity,** no deliberate wickedness; **they walk in His ways,** arrange their entire life in agreement with the manner prescribed in His Word. V. 4. **Thou hast commanded us to keep Thy precepts,** the directions which relate to the conduct of men in every circumstance of life, **diligently,** to observe them most carefully. V. 5. **O that my ways,** the behavior of the believer in every condition in which he finds himself, **were directed to keep Thy statutes,** the express laws relating to the various relations in life! V. 6. **Then shall I not be ashamed,** be brought to shame, heaped with disgrace, **when I have respect unto all Thy commandments,** those enjoining the good and forbidding the evil, to guard against both sins of commission and of omission. V. 7. **I will praise Thee with uprightness of heart,** without a trace of hypocrisy, **when I shall have learned Thy righteous judgments,** the decisions based upon God's justice, of approval as well as of condemnation. V. 8. **I will keep Thy statutes,** the commands of God's Word which are of permanent value for all men. **O forsake me not utterly,** for he who is forsaken of God is condemned to a life of unhappiness and to an eternity of woe. The prayer for faithfulness in making one's conduct agree with the Word of God must ever be in the mouth of every Christian.

Beth. OF THE DISTINGUISHING SIGNS OF AN IRREPROACHABLE LIFE. — V. 9. **Wherewithal shall a young man cleanse his way?** When will it be possible for a young person, surrounded with the many temptations of youth, 2 Tim. 2, 22, to be and remain clean in his conduct? **By taking heed thereto according to Thy Word,** by watching carefully over every step and applying the rule of God's Word to every situation with which he is confronted. The state of mind of such an earnest seeker after truth and holiness is now described. V. 10. **With my whole heart have I sought Thee,** earnestly desiring the closest fellowship with the Lord; **O let me not wander from Thy commandments,** so as to lose sight of the fundamental directions for conduct. V. 11. **Thy Word,** all that God had said in revealing Himself and His holy will to men, **have I hid in mine heart,** like a precious treasure which fills his entire inner life, **that I might not sin against Thee,** for sin cannot gain a foothold in a heart filled with the knowledge of God and with love for His Word. V. 12. **Blessed art Thou, O Lord,** the object of the believer's joyful praise; **teach me Thy statutes,** for the more a Christian knows of the precepts of God's holy will, the more he desires to learn the way of sanctification. At the same time he exercises himself in confession. V. 13. **With my lips have I declared,** he will solemnly proclaim, **all the judgments of Thy mouth,** especially those decisions of God's justice which approve of a righteous life and act as a constant spur to the faithful. V. 14. **I have rejoiced in the way of Thy testimonies,** in the manner in which God has revealed Himself and all His attributes, **as much as in all riches,** for therein the true wealth of the faithful consists, in the active possession and in the constant use of the Word of God. V. 15. **I will meditate in Thy precepts,** pondering them, mulling over them, trying to penetrate ever more deeply into their divine meaning, **and have respect unto Thy ways,** ever on the lookout for the paths which God's Word prescribes. V. 16. **I will delight myself,** find the greatest joy, full happiness, **in Thy statutes,** studying the rules of God's holy will in their relation to the conduct of every person in the world; **I will not forget Thy Word.** It is this rallying around the Bible which makes the individual and whole church organizations a power in the Lord.

Gimel. PRAYER FOR ENLIGHTENMENT UNTO A GODLY LIFE. — V. 17. **Deal bountifully with Thy servant,** giving him a rich measure of favor and of spiritual blessings, **that I may live and keep Thy Word,** observing the Word of God being the one great object of his life. But he realizes that he cannot, by his own reason and sense, penetrate into the beauties of Holy Writ. Therefore he cries out: v. 18. **Open Thou mine eyes,** the eyes of his spirit, of his understanding, **that I may behold wondrous things,** the inexpressible miracles of God's mercy and kindness, **out of Thy Law,** for it is only with eyes enlightened by the Spirit of God that a person may understand and realize the meaning of the Bible-truths. All our study of the Bible should be begun with, and accompanied by, this prayer for enlightenment. This is all the more necessary since we are strangers and pilgrims in this world, looking forward to the great revelation of God and to our eternal stay with God in our heavenly home. V. 19. **I am a stranger in the earth,** a pilgrim seeking the road which leads to the homeland; **hide not Thy commandments from me;** for without these heavenly directions of conduct our traveling in this strange world would be like that of a mariner without a compass and with the sky overcast. V. 20. **My soul breaketh for the longing,** is crushed and faint with eager desire, **that it hath unto Thy judgments at all times,** to meet with God's approval by following the directions of His Word. V. 21. **Thou hast rebuked the proud that are cursed, which do err from Thy commandments,** that is, the arrogant, who mocked the believer, have encountered the Lord's warning threat, since His curse will surely strike those who set aside His Word. V. 22. **Remove from me reproach and contempt,** that of the haughty and arrogant scoffers, who delight in heaping scorn upon the Christians for their trust in the Word of God; **for I have kept Thy testimonies,** observing the revelation of God and His essence for the truth and against sin, and following the guiding principles thus set forth. V. 23. **Princes also did sit and speak against me,** for it is a sad fact that the mighty and influential people of the earth are in the majority in taking sides against God's revelation in the Bible: **but Thy servant did meditate in Thy statutes,** deliberately ignoring the haughty criticism of the Bible, which will be apt to confuse even the believers if they pay too much attention to it, since every error in spiritual matters is more plausible to natural man than the revealed truth. V. 24. **Thy testimonials also are my delight and my counselors,** the constant study of Scriptures being his favorite occupation, and all its truths are like wise men whose advice fortifies the Bible-student against all opposition on the part of the enemies. This fact should encourage and incite every believer to study his Bible day after day and always to seek counsel from the pages of eternal wisdom.

Daleth. THE GRACE OF BEING CONFIRMED IN THE TRUTH. — V. 25. **My soul cleaveth unto the dust,** is often in great spiritual depression; **quicken Thou me,** daily filling him with new life and strength, **according to Thy Word,** it being the privilege of the believers to remind the Lord of His promises and to demand His assistance at such times of affliction. V. 26. **I have declared my ways,** stating that he would follow the paths of God's Word, **and Thou heardest me,** accepting his promise as a prayer for assistance; **teach me Thy statutes,** for it is at such a time that the positive and clear statements of the Word of God uphold the believer's determination. V. 27. **Make me to understand the way of Thy precepts,** to have a clear conception of the directions of God pertaining to man's conduct in all situations of life; **so shall I talk,** ponder, always think about, **of Thy wondrous works,** declaring the miracles of grace and kindness which God performed in his interest, this being the experience of all believers. V. 28. **My soul melteth for heaviness,** is dissolved in the heat of affliction; **strengthen Thou me according unto Thy Word,** setting him upright, so that he may walk with a firm tread and fear no dangers. V. 29. **Remove from me the way of lying,** of unfaithfulness, of denial of the truth, **and grant me Thy Law graciously,** the believer asking this only as a gift of mercy on the part of God, since he knows that he is in no way worthy of it. It is by the grace of God that we still have His Word, and we should appreciate it accordingly. V. 30. **I have chosen the way of truth,** of faithfulness to the Lord; **Thy judgments have I laid before me,** deliberately selecting them to direct his way of conduct in seeking the approval of the Lord. V. 31. **I have stuck unto Thy testimonies,** clinging to the revealed truth with all his heart; **O Lord, put me not to shame,** permitting him to become an object of mockery by withholding His strength and help from the believer in every emergency. V. 32. **I will run the way of Thy commandments,** not with slow and lagging steps, but with cheerful eagerness, **when Thou shalt enlarge my heart,** because God widens and expands the heart of the faithful with such virtues as are well-pleasing to Him, this including also the zeal for His Word and for true sanctification. Constant study and contemplation of God's Word will result in joyful service of God, in growth in all Christian virtues.

He. THE CONSTANCY OF THE BELIEVER UPHELD AND NOURISHED BY GOD'S WORD. — V. 33. **Teach me, O Lord, the way of Thy statutes,** just what His holy will wants the believer to do in every situation in life; **and I shall keep it unto the end,** sustained against apostasy by the power of God which flows from the Word. V. 34. **Give me understanding, and I shall keep Thy Law,** with a full and proper appreciation of its import; **yea, I shall observe it with my whole heart,** shunning and despising all half-hearted endeavors where the will of the Lord is concerned. V. 35. **Make me to go in the path of Thy commandments,** with the strictest attention to all their directions of conduct; **for therein do I delight,** rather than in honor and glory for himself before men. V. 36. **Incline my heart unto Thy testimonies,** bowing it down to a most careful observance of them, **and not to covetousness,** this being one of the vices which draws the heart away from the understanding of the truth. V. 37. **Turn away mine eyes from beholding vanity,** making them to pass by, causing them not to notice the many exhibitions of wickedness in the world, since the continued offense may make either callous and indifferent to evil or cause evil lust to arise in the heart, especially with reference to idolatry in its various forms; **and quicken Thou me in Thy way,** giving to the believer the proper spiritual life and power to overcome all temptations. V. 38. **Stablish Thy Word unto Thy servant,** setting it up firmly, making His promises to be fulfilled for the believer, **who is devoted to Thy fear,** literally, "which," that is, the Word of God, "is to those that fear Thee," it belongs to them, it works the proper fear of God in their hearts. V. 39. **Turn away my reproach which I fear,** namely, that of denying the Lord, or that of being unjustly accused of such denial; **for Thy judgments are good,** the decisions of God's justice, as revealed in His Word, would surely take from him the reproach of apostasy. V. 40. **Behold, I have longed after Thy precepts,** with an urgent desire to be directed by the Word of God in his entire conduct; **quicken me in Thy righteousness,** filling the believer with life from above and upholding him in all his difficulties, temptations, and trials.

Vau. THE NEED OF A FEARLESS CONFESSION OF THE DIVINE TRUTH. — V. 41. **Let Thy mercies,** the many manifestations of grace which every believer experiences, **come also unto me, O Lord, even Thy salvation,** the full deliverance which the Lord has promised to His believers, **according to Thy Word.** The psalmist seems to have particularly such cases in mind in which the faithful are attacked by unbelievers on account of their faith, when they need help to stand up under the vile attacks and to defend the truth. V. 42. **So shall I have wherewith to answer him that reproacheth me,** attacking him for his trust in the Lord; **for I trust in Thy Word.** The knowledge, based upon the clear statements of God's Word that every believer has salvation, is his means of defense against the enemy's insinuation that he cannot be sure of God's mercy. V. 43. **And take not the Word of Truth,** the believer's only weapon in his battle against unbelief, **utterly out of my mouth,** this punishment of the Lord having occasionally struck such as did not properly appreciate His merciful visitations; **for I have hoped in Thy judgments,** placing his trust in them alone. V. 44. **So shall I keep Thy Law,** cling to the instruction of God's Word in the strength given by the Word, **continually, forever and ever.** V. 45. **And I will walk at liberty,** not cramped, but in a space which permits freedom of movement, that being the condition in which all children of God find themselves as they follow the precepts of His holy will, not in the station of slaves forced to obey, but in that of children glad to obey; **for I seek Thy precepts.** V. 46. **I will speak of Thy testimonies,** of the Word of God, in which He has revealed Himself, which is the essence of truth, **also before kings,** as Jesus later told His disciples, Matt. 10, 18. 19, **and will not be ashamed,** not stand there as one disgraced by virtue of his allegiance to God's Word. V. 47. **And I will delight myself in Thy commandments,** finding the greatest pleasure in studying Holy Writ more and more, **which I have loved.** V. 48. **My hands also will I lift up unto Thy commandments which I have loved,** for prayer and confession must go hand in hand; **and I will meditate in Thy statutes,** never growing weary of pondering the saving and sustaining truths of God's Word. Such witnessing for the truth is well-pleasing to the Lord and will be rewarded by Him by His granting true willingness also to suffer for His sake if need be.

Zain. PATIENCE IN PERSECUTION AND CROSSES. V. 49. **Remember the word unto Thy servant,** the reference being to any of the wonderful promises of God in which He assures His servants of His assistance, **upon which Thou hast caused me to hope.** This is the proper importunity of prayer, to hold the Lord to His promises, Ps. 27, 8. V. 50. **This is my comfort in my affliction,** serving to console and uphold him in his misery; **for Thy Word hath quickened me,** filled him with new life and strength. The darker the days which come upon the believers, the more eagerly they watch for every ray of light from God's Word. V. 51. **The proud,** the arrogant and frivolous mockers, such as are always found where the true children of God are following the precepts of God's holy will, **have had me greatly in derision; yet have I not declined from Thy Law,** in fact, such mockery causes the believer to cling all the more closely to the Word of God. V. 52. **I remembered Thy judgments of old, O Lord,** in this case particularly the decisions of God concerning the condemnation of the godless, **and have comforted myself,** since the righteous judgments of the Lord according to His Word would be sure to be maintained. V. 53. **Horror hath taken hold upon me because of the wicked that forsake Thy Law,** that is, he is filled with indignation on account of their wickedness, a holy anger causes him to flare up in zeal for the honor of the Lord and to rebuke the unbelievers with merciless sharpness. At the same time the psalmist is determined to make the Word of God his one rule of life. V. 54. **Thy statutes have been my songs in the house of my pilgrimage,** that is, while the godless jeer with songs of mockery, he will uphold his courage with hymns of praise as long as he is in this earthly house of his pilgrimage, knowing that a complete change will take place in the heavenly home. V. 55. **I have remembered Thy name, O Lord, in the night,** the quiet of which is conducive to prayerful meditation, **and have kept Thy Law,** he has been faithful to the Word at all times. V. 56. **This I had,** that was his special privilege, **because I kept Thy precepts,** looking to the Word for directions to guide his conduct at all times. Thus the believers are ever rich and happy in the possession of the Word.

Cheth. TRUE PIETY THE CALLING OF THE BELIEVERS. — V. 57. **Thou art my Portion, O Lord; I have said that I would keep Thy words.** To realize at all times that God is his Portion, his Inheritance, and that for that reason he intends to observe the words of the Lord, this is the calling of the faithful, in this every one who is a child of God fulfils his destiny. V. 58. **I entreated Thy favor,** literally, "I appealed with supplications to Thy face," **with my whole heart,** begging for a manifestation of divine grace; **be merciful unto me according to Thy word,** the believer once more holding the Lord to His promise. V. 59. **I thought on my ways,** carefully examining them from all sides to see whether they were in agreement with God's Word, **and turned my feet unto Thy testimonies,** deciding quickly in favor of following the Word of God all alone. V. 60. **I made haste,** for the Lord delights in quick decisions in His favor, **and delayed not to keep Thy commandments,** always ready to exercise his piety in good works. V. 61. **The bands of the wicked have robbed me,** rather, "the cords of the wicked have surrounded me," that is, they have laid their snares for him as they do for all children of God who show that their profession of godliness is sincere; **but I have not forgotten Thy Law;** in fact, the remembrance of the Word of God gives to the believer his wonderful strength. V. 62. **At midnight,** as he meditates upon the wonderful manifestations of God's favor, **I will rise to give thanks unto Thee because of Thy righteous judgments,** to acknowledge with proper gratitude the judgments of God's righteousness. V. 63. **I am a companion of all them that fear Thee,** whose piety causes them to seek companionship of people of their own way of thinking, **and of them that keep Thy precepts.** All believers are united by their common faith, in a common cause. V. 64. **The earth, O Lord, is full of Thy mercy,** the evidences of His merciful blessings are everywhere to be found; **teach me Thy statutes;** for only the proper appreciation of the Word of God as the highest treasure given by God will cause one to realize the incomparable greatness of His mercy. All Christians are eager to possess the light, the consolation, and the strength of the Word of God.

Teth. THE REALIZATION THAT GOD'S HUMILIATION OF MAN IS SALUTARY. — V. 65. **Thou hast dealt well with Thy servant, O Lord, according unto Thy Word,** not with the intention of harming His servant, but of impressing upon him the fact that the believer's path is one of crosses and sorrows, as the Word of God so frequently states. A course in the school of suffering always works benefits to the children of God. V. 66. **Teach me good judgment and knowledge,** enabling him to distinguish carefully between good and evil; **for I have believed Thy commandments,** for it is only by following the path of God's Word with the greatest exactness that one is kept out of the mazes of error and sin. V. 67. **Before I was afflicted,** before God chose to lay the burden of suffering upon him, **I went astray; but now have I kept Thy Word.** It was the tribulation laid upon him which caused the psalmist to realize the hollow mockery of everything which this world offers, as well as the emptiness of his own righteousness. V. 68. **Thou art good and doest good,** even when God lays upon His children the burden of suffering, since His purpose is always one of kindness and mercy, **teach me Thy statutes,** for tribulation drives the believer into the Word. This appreciation of the Word is increased, moreover, on account of the lies which the godless are pleased to spread concerning the believers. V. 69. **The proud have forged a lie against me,** smearing falsehoods all at once over him, making the true nature of things hazy by daubing them over with false colors or pasting on deceit; **but I will keep Thy precepts with my whole heart,** in spite of all the falsehoods which are circulated about him and which cause men to look askance at him. V. 70. **Their heart is as fat as grease,** altogether without sensitiveness; it is impossible to make an impression upon the majority of the godless, to convince them of the wrong of their mockery; **but I delight in Thy Law,** his pleasure in studying the Word of God growing with every new attempt of the enemies to discredit him. V. 71. **It is good for me that I have been afflicted,** he now gratefully acknowledges the benefit which he has received from the afflictions laid upon him, **that I might learn Thy statutes,** for he might never have learned this important lesson if God had not taken him into the school of suffering. Therefore he concludes this section with a shout of triumph, v. 72. **The Law of Thy mouth is better unto me than thousands of gold and silver;** for he has now learned that all the wealth of the world cannot compare with the precious content of the Word, which is the true treasure of all Christians.

Jod. THE CONSOLATION OF GOD'S PROVIDENCE AND GOVERNMENT. — V. 73. **Thy hands have made me and fashioned me,** the special creation of man being referred to here, and the implication being that God will not destroy His noblest creature. **Give me understanding,** leading the believer back to the original knowledge of the heavenly Father, **that I may learn Thy commandments,** for the renewal of the image of God in the heart of the believers works in them righteousness and true holiness, so that their entire conduct agrees with the directions given in His Word. V. 74. **They that fear Thee will be glad when they see me,** rejoicing at the prosperity of the faithful, as they consider his cause their cause and glorify God for the revelation of His mercy, **because I have hoped in Thy Word,** for this hope never disappoints the believer. V. 75. **I know, O Lord, that Thy judgments,** His decisions of condemnation as well as of approval, **are right,** they served for his benefit, for his salvation, **and that Thou in faithfulness hast afflicted me,** dealing with him as a faithful Friend and Father, the chastisement which was laid upon him being just the right thing to turn him away from sin and from the allurements of this world. V. 76. **Let, I pray Thee, Thy merciful kindness be for my comfort,** to sustain him in the trials which his weak and sinful nature found so hard to endure, **according to Thy Word unto Thy servant,** another reminder of God's faithful promises, upon which he relies absolutely. V. 77. **Let Thy tender mercies come unto me,** the believer being unable, of his own reason and strength, to come to them or to earn them, **that I may live,** for the mercy of God is the source of all true life in man; **for Thy Law is my delight,** the Word of God's mercy sustains him. For this reason the psalmist now asks God to frustrate the plans of the enemies. V. 78. **Let the proud,** the arrogant mockers, **be ashamed; for they dealt perversely with me without a cause,** both by intimating that his sufferings were an evidence of his rejection by God and by trying to discredit him everywhere; **but I will meditate in Thy precepts,** continuing to fashion his conduct in accordance with the Word of God. V. 79. **Let those that fear Thee turn unto me,** realizing that the charges of his enemies are untrue, that God is not making him an example by punishing him in anger, **and those that have known Thy testimonies,** for all true believers will rally to his side in this emergency. V. 80. **Let my heart be sound,** perfect and sincere, **in Thy statutes,** making the Word his one rule of doctrine and life, **that I be not ashamed,** disgraced before the enemies on account of his trust and disappointed in his hope of salvation.

Caph. THE CONSOLATION OF GOD'S WORD IN THE MIDST OF GREAT TROUBLES. — V. 81. **My**

soul fainteth for Thy salvation, in the extreme longing brought about by a further attack of sorrow; **but I hope in Thy Word,** he refuses to let go this trust. V. 82. **Mine eyes,** strained with gazing for the coming of salvation, **fail for Thy Word,** on account of his waiting for the fulfilment of God's promises, **saying, When wilt Thou comfort me?** The assistance which he longed for seemed so slow in coming that he was filled with impatience and begged for a speedy revelation of God's mercy. V. 83. **For I am become like a bottle in the smoke,** a wine-skin shriveled up and blackened from being suspended high over the fireplace, the point of comparison being in the discarding of a useless article; **yet do I not forget Thy statutes,** he clings to God's Word, which alone has permanent value for a poor sinner. V. 84. **How many are the days of Thy servant?** This question arises in his heart on account of the shortness of human life, this fact causing him to fear that he may not live long enough to see himself vindicated before his enemies. **When wilt Thou execute judgment on them that persecute me?** He begs that God would interfere in his behalf very soon, since the enemies are showing an increased activity. V. 85. **The proud have digged pits for me,** plotting with the intention of destroying him, **which are not after Thy Law,** that is, although they pretend to be actuated only by the highest motives, in our days, for instance, by the welfare of the state, by the demands of a universal brotherhood, yet they have, in truth, no basis for their action in the Word of God. V. 86. **All Thy commandments are faithful,** altogether trustworthy and dependable; **they persecute me wrongfully,** with the usual false accusations as to his being an enemy of existing order and obstinately wanting his own way; **help Thou me.** V. 87. **They had almost consumed me upon earth,** their plans to destroy him had almost succeeded; **but I forsook not Thy precepts,** he would not give up his trust in the Word of God. V. 88. **Quicken me after Thy loving-kindness,** giving him new spiritual life and strength, both for enduring persecutions and for overcoming his enemies; **so shall I keep the testimony of Thy mouth,** for every new evidence of God's power in the life of the believers tends to strengthen their faith in the testimony of God for Himself, for the truth, against sin.

Lamed. THE IMPERISHABLE NATURE OF THE DIVINE WORD. — V. 89. **Forever, O Lord, Thy Word is settled in heaven;** like the essence of God, out of which it flowed, it is unchangeable and will endure throughout eternity. Cp. Matt. 24, 35; Luke 21, 33. V. 90. **Thy faithfulness is unto all generations,** remains the same from one generation to the next, absolutely trustworthy: **Thou hast established the earth, and it abideth,** standing as long as God's will so ordains. V. 91. **They continue this day according to Thine ordinances,** the earth and all it contains being subject to His Word, obliged to carry out the dictates of His will; **for all are Thy servants,** humbly obeying His unalterable laws. The trust in the eternal faithfulness of Jehovah has sustained the psalmist in his affliction. V. 92. **Unless Thy Law,** the Word of God with its divine instructions, **had been my delights,** the one thing affording him true happiness, **I should then have perished in mine affliction,** God's Word alone giving him strength to endure. V. 93. **I will never forget Thy precepts,** the special directions of God's holy will; **for with them Thou hast quickened me,** given him new spiritual life and endurance in the midst of his trials. V. 94. **I am Thine, save me,** delivering him from the difficulties which beset him; **for I have sought Thy precepts,** endeavoring earnestly to live up to all the directions which the Lord has laid down for the conduct of His children. V. 95. **The wicked have waited for me to destroy me,** their object being thereby to remove the Word which the servant of the Lord always quoted against them; **but I will consider Thy testimonies,** for the Word of God will abide in spite of all the efforts of the enemies to destroy it. V. 96. **I have seen an end of all perfection,** that is, no matter how perfect anything may seem here on earth, it has its limit or end, for absolute excellence is wanting where fallibility is natural; **but Thy commandment is exceeding broad,** the Word of God is not bound by the narrow limits of a human, earthly production. Man, be he never so wise, never outgrows the Word of God.

Mem. GOD'S WORD THE ESSENCE OF TRUE WISDOM. — V. 97. **Oh, how love I Thy Law!** the entire instruction in God's holy Word, as the revelation of His holy will. **It is my meditation all the day;** the longer he ponders upon it, the dearer it becomes to him. V. 98. **Thou through Thy commandments,** by which He directed the entire conduct of His servant, **hast made me wiser than mine enemies,** who believed themselves to be people of superior intelligence in possessing a large measure of this world's wisdom; **for they are ever with me,** the directions of God's words, which the psalmist made his companions, enabled him to vanquish the enemies in the field of knowledge, where they thought themselves supreme. V. 99. **I have more understanding than all my teachers,** those who taught a mere worldly wisdom; **for Thy testimonies are my meditation,** and with the knowledge which he had gained from studying the Word of God he was able to show the insufficiency of mere worldly knowledge. V. 100. **I understand more than the ancients,** those advanced in years, for age is no help against stupidity, if old people refuse to bow to the wisdom of God's Word, **because I keep Thy precepts**, the Bible being the basis and key of all true knowledge. V. 101. **I have refrained my feet from every evil way**, having gained the ability to mark and to shun wickedness in every form, **that I might keep Thy Word**, through which both knowledge and strength are given. V. 102. **I have not departed from Thy judgments**, making it a point to watch God's decisions of aproval and condemnation; **for Thou hast taught me.** The Word of God is very clear on that point; one must but do what it teaches. V. 103. **How sweet are Thy words unto my taste!** pleasant for spiritual edification; **yea, sweeter than honey to my mouth**, for such is the effect of the Gospel-promises upon every believer. V. 104. **Through Thy precepts**, as related to his entire conduct, **I get understanding**, practical knowledge in all matters pertaining to this world and to the world to come; **therefore I hate every false way**, he is able immediately to recognize any false tendency of the times and will promptly withdraw from anything which might implicate him, even as all Christians love the good and hate the evil.

Nun. TRUSTING IN THE LEADERSHIP OF GOD'S WORD. — V. 105. **Thy Word is a lamp unto my feet**, guiding his footsteps past the abysses of so many and severe dangers, **and a light unto my path**, not with a dim and uncertain illumination, but with a direct and clear ray, which makes every foot of the way unmistakable. Cp. 2 Pet. 1, 19. V. 106. **I have sworn**, with a solemn oath, **and I will perform it, that I will keep Thy righteous judgments**, observing with great care all those things which, according to God's righteousness, meet with His approval. V. 107. **I am afflicted very much**, bent down to the earth under the heavy burden of misery laid upon him; **quicken me, O Lord**, filling him with new spiritual life and strength, **according unto Thy Word.** V. 108. **Accept, I beseech Thee, the free-will offerings of my mouth, O Lord**, for such is the nature of all his prayers, vows, and confessions, freely flowing out from faith, **and teach me Thy judgments**, so that his knowledge of the Word may increase in proportion to his needs. V. 109. **My soul is continually in my hand**, he realizes that death may seize him at any time, and therefore is always prepared for it; **yet do I not forget Thy Law**, his constant remembrance of the Word of God, in fact, giving him the strength to meet death without flinching, if die he must. V. 110. **The wicked have laid a snare for me**, to destroy him unawares; **yet I erred not from Thy precepts**, not daring to wander away from his one certain source of comfort and strength, the Word of God. V. 111. **Thy testimonies have I taken as an heritage forever**, making them his most cherished possession, which he would not relinquish; **for they are the rejoicing of my heart**, they only work true happiness. V. 112. **I have inclined mine heart to perform Thy statutes alway, even unto the end**, for only he that endureth unto the end shall be saved, as our Lord Himself says, Matt. 24, 13.

Samech. THE NEED OF A FIRM STAND FOR THE TRUTH OF GOD'S WORD. — V. 113. **I hate vain thoughts**, literally, "wavering ones I hate," that is, those who are divided between two beliefs, those who waver in their loyalty, not knowing whether to turn to God or to false gods; **but Thy Law do I love.** People who are irresolute in their belief are, in a way, more dangerous than out-and-out enemies of the truth; for their unionistic attitude is apt to influence such as are weak in faith. The best plan, therefore, is to have nothing to do with such spirits, but cling to the Word of God alone. V. 114. **Thou art my Hiding-place**, affording him protection against the attacks of the enemies, **and my Shield; I hope in Thy Word**, confidently resting on its teachings and promises of grace and mercy. V. 115. **Depart from me, ye evil doers**, he wants nothing to do with such as deliberately indulge in wickedness; **for I will keep the commandments of my God;** resolved to do the will of God, he is sure of the Lord's protection in taking such a decided stand for the truth. V. 116. **Uphold me according unto Thy Word**, in agreement with the many promises of grace which are found in Scripture, **that I may live**, constantly drawing new life and strength from the Source of all life, through the agency of the Word; **and let me not be ashamed of my hope**, since, if the Lord would forsake His servant and not vindicate his cause, the enemies would have reason to sneer at him as being a fool on account of his trust. V. 117. **Hold Thou me up**, sustaining him in the natural weakness with which even believers are obliged to battle, **and I shall be safe**, sure of deliverance and salvation; **and I will have respect unto Thy statutes continually**, his faith receiving new nourishment with every new manifestation of God's help. V. 118. **Thou hast trodden down all them that err from Thy statutes**, rather, the Lord despises people of this kind who wander away from the truth of the Word, seeking to establish their own philosophy of religion; **for their deceit is falsehood**, that is, their net, which they weave in order to entrap the godly, is woven of deceit, and yet their expectation is vain. V. 119. **Thou puttest away all the wicked of the earth like dross**, the slag, or refuse, left in the smelters after the pure metals have been gained from the ore, such dross being discarded and dumped out; **therefore I love Thy testimonies**, for the very fulfilment of God's threat of punishment upon the ungodly draws the believer more closely to the Word. V. 120. **My flesh trem-**

bleth for fear of Thee, particularly when he witnesses the punishment of the Lord upon the wicked, and **I am afraid of Thy judgments,** this same holy awe and reverence of the righteous God serving the Christians of all times to keep their flesh in bounds and to shun evil in every form.

Ain. THE PROPER ESTIMATION OF GOD'S WORD IN THE MIDST OF OPPRESSION. — V. 121. **I have done judgment and justice,** performing and observing the rules of conduct which have been labeled with God's approval in His Word; **leave me not to mine oppressors.** Just as the consciousness of guilt aggravates any suffering, so the feeling of having performed one's duty yields at least a measure of comfort. V. 122. **Be surety for Thy servant for good,** becoming his advocate and so answerable for him against the slurs and accusations of the enemies; **let not the proud,** the arrogant mockers, **oppress me,** by making use of cruelty whenever opportunity offers and they feel that they have the power to use it. V. 123. **Mine eyes fail,** with anxious gazing, **for Thy salvation,** for the final deliverance promised to all believers, **and for the Word of Thy righteousness,** in which the righteousness of the Lord is promised to all those who accept it in faith. This is, of course, not a matter of merit on his part, as the psalmist says: v. 124. **Deal with Thy servant according unto Thy mercy,** according to His free grace and favor, the outflow of His love, **and teach me Thy statutes;** for every believer, having accepted the mercy of the heavenly Father, is anxious to show his appreciation of it by following the precepts of His holy will as closely as possible. V. 125. **I am Thy servant,** desiring nothing more than to occupy a position of the lowest service before Jehovah; **give me understanding,** a proper appreciation and insight, **that I may know Thy testimonies,** the Word in which God testifies of Himself, for the truth, against sin. V. 126. **It is time for Thee, Lord, to work,** all the signs and conditions of the times point to the urgent need of the Lord's interference; **for they have made void Thy Law,** set aside His Word as no longer possessing validity, just as the godless scoffers are trying to do in our days. A thorough and firm knowledge of the Word being all the more necessary when the enmity against it is so great, the psalmist adds: v. 127. **Therefore I love Thy commandments above gold, yea, above fine gold,** which might be his as the reward of denial of the truth. V. 128. **Therefore I esteem all Thy precepts concerning all things to be right,** he is bound to acknowledge all the directions of the Lord as good and praiseworthy, not only in matters of doctrine, but also in instructions pertaining to the everyday conduct of life; **and I hate every false way,** utterly rejecting every tendency which does not conform to the rule of the divine Word. It is true to this day that the Bible instructs the conscientious Christian in every question pertaining to his entire conduct, and therefore it should not only be consulted, but also followed with constant faithfulness.

Pe. THE NEED OF SPIRITUAL LIGHT IN THE MIDST OF GODLESSNESS. — V. 129. **Thy testimonies are wonderful,** elevated above everyday life and the common understanding, becoming more marvelous the longer one contemplates them; **therefore doth my soul keep them,** anxious to have the light of the Word fall into his dark heart and illumine it with rays of divine mercy and beauty. V. 130. **The entrance of Thy words giveth light,** that is, the opening, the unfolding, of His Word, as His Holy Spirit explains it to the heart of man, makes the words of divine wisdom clear; **it giveth understanding unto the simple,** to those without any pretense or show of learning in this world's wisdom, for that is not essential for the understanding of the fundamental divine truths. V. 131. **I opened my mouth and panted,** with great eagerness, as a traveler in a hot desert pants for a cooling breeze and for a refreshing draft of water; **for I longed for Thy commandments,** his desire was for the refreshment of God's Word. V. 132. **Look Thou upon me,** instead of averting His face in anger, **and be merciful unto me, as Thou usest to do unto those that love Thy name,** or, "according to the right of those that love Thy name." It is true that God's gift of grace is a gift of His free love, but it is true also that the believers may expect it of Him on the basis of His merciful promise. V. 133. **Order my steps in Thy Word,** making them firm in accordance with His promise, **and let not any iniquity have dominion over me,** which would cause him to stray from the path of rectitude and obedience to God. V. 134. **Deliver me from the oppression of man,** since it was bound to hinder him in his duties of obedience toward God; **so will I keep Thy precepts,** observing them with eager cheerfulness. V. 135. **Make Thy face to shine upon Thy servant,** with the assurance of His grace, Num. 6, 25, **and teach me Thy statutes,** His Word assuring the believer that he was truly a child of God. V. 136. **Rivers of waters run down mine eyes,** in deep grief and sorrow over the manner in which men reject the Lord and bring destruction upon themselves, **because they keep not Thy Law.** It is not overweening pride which causes the believers to speak to the godless in such an emphatic manner, but a sincere love for their soul's salvation.

Tzaddi. THE PROPER APPRECIATION OF THE WORD OF GOD. — V. 137. **Righteous art Thou, O Lord, and upright are Thy judgments,** for the right knowledge of God is gained from Scriptures and results in the proper worship of God. V. 138. **Thy testimonies that Thou hast commanded,** whose observance He has laid upon all men, **are righteous and very faithful,** literally, "righteousness and faithfulness," not falsehood and deceit, as the enemies of the Word falsely state. V. 139. **My zeal hath consumed me,** has brought him near to destruction, has almost robbed him of his life, **because mine enemies have forgotten Thy words.** All believers, filled with true zeal for God and His Word, consume themselves in fighting false doctrine and godless life. V. 140. **Thy Word is very pure,** like a precious metal which comes out of the assayer's refining without a trace of dross; **therefore Thy servant loveth it.** V. 141. **I am small and despised,** young and insignificant, without influential connections in the world, his opinions, therefore, being belittled and ridiculed by the wise and mighty of this world; **yet do I not forget Thy precepts,** they had not been able to shake his convictions concerning the Word. V. 142. **Thy righteousness is an everlasting righteousness,** outlasting all earthly cavil and enmity, **and Thy Law is the truth.** Cp. John 17, 17. V. 143. **Trouble and anguish have taken hold on me,** on account of the opposition of the enemies; **yet Thy commandments are my delights,** wherefore he continues to cling to them in spite of all affliction. V. 144. **The righteousness of Thy testimonies is everlasting,** they had proved their power in the past and would again do so in the future, upon this fact he could rely; **give me understanding, and I shall live,** be partaker of true spiritual life through the knowledge of the Word, the source from which all believers draw life and strength day after day.

Koph. CONSTANT PRAYER FOR FAITHFULNESS OVER AGAINST OPPOSITION. — V. 145. **I cried with my whole heart,** putting the full effort of his desire into his prayer; **hear me, O Lord! I will keep Thy statutes,** guarding the Word of the Lord as his precious treasure. V. 146. **I cried unto Thee; save me,** with a gracious deliverance, **and I shall keep Thy testimonies,** observing carefully what God testified of Himself and His works in His Word. V. 147. **I prevented the dawning of the morning,** being awake before the coming of dawn, **and cried; I hoped in Thy Word.** V. 148. **Mine eyes prevent the night-watches,** the coming of each of which finds him awake, **that I might meditate in Thy Word,** give himself to its undisturbed contemplation. V. 149. **Hear my voice according unto Thy loving-kindness,** on the basis of His mercy and grace alone, there being no merit on the psalmist's side which he might urge. **O Lord, quicken me according to Thy judgment,** reviving his heart by such declarations of gracious approval as served this purpose. V. 150. **They draw nigh that follow after mischief,** surrounding the Lord's servant with threats of violence; **they are far from Thy Law,** not guided by its precepts. V. 151. **Thou art near, O Lord,** with His help stepping between the psalmist and the enemies seeking to hurt him, **and all Thy commandments are truth,** especially those promises of the Word which proclaim deliverance to the oppressed. V. 152. **Concerning Thy testimonies,** on the basis of his knowledge as gained from the Word, **I have known of old that Thou hast founded them forever.** No matter how much time and effort the godless spend in trying to discredit the Word, the believers refuse to be led astray, since they know the eternal nature of God's Word.

Resh. THE INCREASING CONFIDENCE OF THE BELIEVER. — V. 153. **Consider mine affliction,** taking careful note of its severity, **and deliver me; for I do not forget Thy Law,** and he sets up his childlike obedience as a reason why God should regard his prayer favorably. V. 154. **Plead my cause,** God Himself acting as the great Advocate of His servant, **and deliver me; quicken me,** with new life and strength, **according to Thy Word.** V. 155. **Salvation is far from the wicked,** on account of their own obstinate disobedience; **for they seek not Thy statutes,** refusing to heed the Word of the Lord. V. 156. **Great are Thy tender mercies, O Lord,** to which the inspired singer appeals throughout the psalm, to the unmerited favor of the Lord; **quicken me according to Thy judgments,** reviving his soul with the wonderful and merciful decisions of approval found in His Word. V. 157. **Many are my persecutors and mine enemies,** their number increasing in proportion to his faithfulness to the Word; **yet do I not decline from Thy testimonies,** refusing to be turned aside from the Word, with its revelation of the great God and His love. V. 158. **I beheld the transgressors,** those who wilfully reject the Word, **and was grieved,** filled with loathing; **because they kept not Thy Word,** for this fact, with its accompanying unbelief, shuts them out from the mercies of God. V. 159. **Consider how I love Thy precepts,** marking well this love for the Word which is characteristic of all true children of God. **Quicken me, O Lord, according to Thy loving-kindness,** the appeal being again to God's mercy and grace alone. V. 160. **Thy Word is true from the beginning,** its sum, the whole body of revelation, the Bible, being the truth; **and every one of Thy righteous judgments endureth forever,** His decisions of approval encouraging His children in the midst of all the present tribulations and opening up vistas of eternal glory before them.

Schin (and *Sin*). THE BELIEVER'S FELLOWSHIP WITH GOD IN PRAYER. — V. 161. **Princes,** the mighty and influential ones of the earth, **have persecuted me without a cause,** although he had done nothing which might justly have provoked their hatred; **but my heart**

standeth in awe of Thy Word, in reverential fear of its marvelous strength and beauty. V. 162. **I rejoice at Thy Word,** instead of currying the favor of the wicked princes, he finds his greatest joy in the Word of his Lord, **as one that findeth great spoil,** being enriched by its possession beyond the dreams of avarice. V. 163. **I hate and abhor lying,** unfaithfulness to the covenant of God in any form; **but Thy Law do I love.** V. 164. **Seven times a day do I praise Thee,** in a continued course of devotional exercises, **because of Thy righteous judgments.** The hearts of the believers are temples of the Holy Spirit, in them the incense of their praise rises in continual adoration. V. 165. **Great peace have they which love Thy Law,** for in the midst of all the battles of life they have the assurance of the grace of God promised in the Word; **and nothing shall offend them,** causing the believers to stumble and fall, since they are upheld by the strength of God. V. 166. **Lord, I have hoped for Thy salvation,** longing for it as Jacob did of old, Gen. 49, 18, **and done Thy commandments,** obedient to the holy will of God, as laid down in His Word. V. 167. **My soul hath kept Thy testimonies,** observing them carefully, **and I love them exceedingly.** V. 168. **I have kept Thy precepts and Thy testimonies,** in an earnest effort to follow the way of sanctification; **for all my ways are before Thee.** All believers should strive to reach this level of calm assurance in urging the sincerity of their lives before the face of God.

Tau. CONCLUDING APPEAL. — V. 169. **Let my cry come near before Thee, O Lord,** with no obstructions to hinder it in its course; **give me understanding according to Thy Word,** since the Word alone is the source of all true knowledge. V. 170. **Let my supplication come before Thee,** be brought into His presence for favorable consideration; **deliver me according to Thy Word,** the psalmist's appeal time and again being to the mercy and to the promise of the Lord. V. 171. **My lips shall utter praise,** proclaiming His glory, **when Thou hast taught me Thy statutes,** leading him ever more deeply into the glories of His Word. V. 172. **My tongue shall speak of Thy Word,** being constrained so to do by the miracles related in the Word; **for all Thy commandments are righteousness,** in full agreement with eternal right and truth. V. 173. **Let Thine hand help me,** literally, "Be Thy hand for my help"; **for I have chosen Thy precepts,** thereby placing himself entirely on the side of the Lord, with the right to expect help from Him. V. 174. **I have longed for Thy salvation, O Lord;** thus his eagerness once more causes him to exclaim; **and Thy Law is my delight,** he finds his greatest pleasure in the knowledge of the Word. V. 175. **Let my soul live,** in full fellowship with the heavenly Father, to whom he has appealed in his wonderful prayer, **and it shall praise Thee, and let Thy judgments help me,** sustaining him in all trials and leading him safely to the home of the Father. V. 176. **I have gone astray like a lost sheep,** apparently all forsaken in the midst of a host of enemies; **seek Thy servant,** to bring him back to rest and shelter; **for I do not forget Thy commandments.** On the side of men there is ever erring and getting lost; on the part of God there is ever seeking and finding and taking home to the enjoyment of eternal blessings.[6)]

6) Cp. *Syn.-Ber.*, Nord-Wis.-Dist., 1919, 9–75.

PSALM 120.

Prayer for Deliverance from Slander and Deceit.

A song of degrees, literally, "of ascents," the first of fifteen psalms designated by that name, the reference being either to the fact that these hymns were used by the pilgrims on their three annual journeys to Jerusalem, or to the peculiar structure of these psalms, since every new verse or strophe builds up on the preceding in form and thought. The writer here, while acknowledging the mercy of God, prays for relief from a slanderous foe. V. 1. **In my distress,** when he was in tribulation at some former time, **I cried unto the Lord,** turning to Him alone for deliverance, **and He heard me,** graciously affording help, for it pleases Him to have His children cry to Him. V. 2. **Deliver my soul, O Lord, from lying lips and from a deceitful tongue,** literally, "from a lip of lying, from a tongue of malice," the contention of the psalmist being implied that he is innocent of the charges falsely brought against him. He now turns directly to the base slanderer. V. 3. **What shall be given unto thee,** by way of righteous punishment, **or what shall be done unto thee,** being added to the measure of the first punishment, **thou false tongue?** He himself gives the answer, v. 4. **Sharp arrows of the mighty,** inflictions of a most destructive kind, **with coals of juniper,** the charcoal made of the wood of the broom-tree retaining its heat longest; a picture, therefore, of long-continued heat of affliction. V. 5. **Woe is me that I sojourn in Mesech,** a region between the Black and the Caspian Sea, **that I dwell in the tents of Kedar,** of barbarous Arabia! The point of comparison in both cases is the wild and rude character of the people of these regions; such was also the nature of the slanderers of the psalmist, which made it appear to him that he had been inadvertently set down in the midst of barbarians. V. 6. **My soul hath long dwelt with him that hateth peace,** people who were maliciously hostile and took every occasion to do him harm. V. 7. **I am for peace,** his entire attitude showed his love of peace, his willingness to maintain peace, his desire for peace; **but when I speak,** protesting this readiness to live at peace with all men, if possible, **they are for war,** they deliberately choose to regard his attitude as hostile and act accordingly. Thus the unbelievers everywhere pounce upon the slightest excuse for acts of hostility against the faithful, often even inventing an excuse for the occasion.

PSALM 121.

The Guardian Care of the Lord.

A song of degrees, full of believing fervor due to the consciousness of the fellowship of God with His children on earth. V. 1. **I will lift up mine eyes,** in anxious, yet trustful desire and longing, **unto the hills,** regarded as the throne of Jehovah, **from whence cometh my help,** or, in the form of a question, "From whence will come my help?" a most emphatic declaration of trust in the almighty power of God and in His willingness to help His children. V. 2. **My help cometh from the Lord, which made heaven and earth,** His creative power being a pledge of His ability to rescue those who trust in Him from all dangers. In order to strengthen this trust still more, the psalmist now addresses his own soul. V. 3. **He will not suffer thy foot to be moved,** to stagger with weakness; **He that keepeth thee will not slumber,** His watchful care never ceases, is never diminished. V. 4. **Behold,** an exclamation expressing and inducing further assurance, **He that keepeth Israel shall neither slumber,** in an occasional short nap, **nor sleep,** in total forgetfulness of His children. His is a sleepless vigilance, as the history of Israel abundantly shows. The assurance of the believers is therefore expressed in a series of positive statements setting forth the fatherly care of the Lord. V. 5. **The Lord is thy Keeper; the Lord is thy Shade upon thy right hand,** literally, "over the hand of thy right side," said of a complete overshadowing and protecting. V. 6. **The sun shall not smite thee by day,** its withering heat producing illness or even death, **nor the moon by night,** for in the case of many people, and in a number of countries, the effect of the moon's rays on the uncovered head is similar to that of the direct light of the sun. The injurious influences proceeding from sun and moon are representative of all dangers by day and night, against all of which the ever-watchful eye of God grants protection. V. 7. **The Lord shall preserve thee from all evil,** no matter of what kind it may be and from which side it may threaten; **He shall preserve thy soul,** the life of the soul being the believer's highest possession. V. 8. **The Lord shall preserve thy going out and thy coming in,** the believer's whole life, with all its occupations and undertakings, **from this time forth and even forevermore,** in time and eternity; for no danger can harm him who rests in the shadow of the eternal love of the heavenly Father, relying on the merciful promises of His Word.

PSALM 122.

A Hymn of Love for the Church of God.

A song of degrees of David, expressing the sacred joy of the faithful in being able to participate in the services of the Temple and to feel the appeal of the capital city, this psalm being particularly appropriate for a festival journey. V. 1. **I was glad when they said unto me, Let us go into the house of the Lord.** The psalmist expresses his joy over the invitation to join the festal train; he now remembers the happiness that filled his heart when he was asked to be one of those making up a caravan of pilgrims to Jerusalem. V. 2. **Our feet shall stand within thy gates, O Jerusalem,** or, "Our feet stood still in thy gates," rooted to the spot for some minutes with astonishment at the glorious beauty of Jerusalem which was presented to their eyes. V. 3. **Jerusalem is builded as a city that is compact together,** built up without gaps and unsightly open spaces, one house next to the other, presenting a solid community, v. 4. **whither the tribes go up, the tribes of the Lord,** the faithful members of all Israel being required to journey to Jerusalem three times a year, for the great festivals, **unto the testimony of Israel,** that is, according to the rule and ordinance of God, **to give thanks unto the name of the Lord,** for that was the chief function of the congregation and all its members at the festival seasons. V. 5. **For there are set thrones of judgment, the thrones of the house of David;** for Jerusalem was not only the seat of the Sanctuary of Israel, but also the capital city of the nation, where the highest government officials resided, where, above all, the administration of justice was the original and chief duty of the monarch in times of peace. The psalmist, having thus painted a picture of Jerusalem, the capital, which also contained the Sanctuary of the nation, is constrained to send up a prayer for its continued well-being. V. 6. **Pray for the peace of Jerusalem,** as a city of peace, welfare, prosperity, and happiness; **they shall prosper that love thee,** their welfare being involved in that of their capital city. V. 7. **Peace be within thy walls,** both externally and inwardly, **and prosperity within thy palaces,** the blessing of Jehovah resting upon all inhabitants. V. 8. **For my brethren and companions' sakes,** with whom he includes himself by virtue of the communion of saints, the fellowship obtaining between all believers, **I will now say, Peace be within thee,** for the welfare and prosperity of the Church is that of all its members. V. 9. **Because of the house of the Lord, our God,** the Temple, or Tabernacle, as the center of Israel's worship, the symbol of the true religion over against those without, **I will seek thy good,** for the welfare of the Jewish Church was largely dependent upon the safety and prosperity of the city of the Sanctuary. Even so the spiritual welfare and happiness of all believers is bound up with the fortunes of the Church, for which reason this special petition for peace is included in the General Prayer read in many of our churches every Sunday.

PSALM 123.

Trust in the Lord in the Midst of Anguish.

A song of degrees, setting forth the psalmist's earnest prayer for mercy on account of the distress which has beset him. V. 1. **Unto Thee lift I up mine eyes,** in humble, but confident expectation of help, **O Thou that dwellest in the heavens,** enthroned as the almighty Sovereign, for whom it is a small matter to come to the assistance of His children on earth. V. 2. **Behold, as the eyes of servants look unto the hand of their masters, and as the eyes of a maiden,** of a servant-girl, **unto the hand of her mistress,** watching and interpreting the slightest gesture and sign correctly, **so our eyes wait upon the Lord, our God, until that He have mercy upon us,** for that is the firm expectation of the believers, as they desire mercy only and urge no merit on their part. "The servants of God should look to His directing hand to appoint them their work; to His supplying hand, to give them their portion in due season; to His protecting hand, to right them when wronged; to His correcting hand, 1 Pet 5, 6; to His rewarding hand." V. 3. **Have mercy upon us, O Lord, have mercy upon us,** this call being, as one commentator has it, the constant **Kyrie** of all believers; **for we are exceedingly filled with contempt,** heaped with scorn by the proud enemies and oppressors. V. 4. **Our soul is exceedingly filled with the scorning of those that are at ease,** the enemies who believe themselves to be secure, **and with the contempt of the proud,** despots who sought to oppress them in every possible manner. Thus the Church has ever, in the midst of persecution, turned to the Lord alone, resting its hope of deliverance in His mercy.

PSALM 124.

The Lord the Deliverer of His Church.

A song of degrees of David, setting forth the assistance and deliverance of Jehovah in the midst of great dangers. V. 1. **If it had not been the Lord who was on our side,** if it had not been for His merciful and almighty protection, **now may Israel say,** that is, all believers, as constituting together the spiritual Israel; v. 2. **if it had not been the Lord who was on our side when men rose up against us,** as they will time and again in the interest of unbelief, v. 3. **then they had swallowed us up quick,** gulping the believers down while they were still alive, **when their wrath was kindled against us,** flaming up in ferocious hatred; v. 4. **then the waters had overwhelmed us, the stream had gone over our soul,** the result being a quick drowning; v. 5. **then the proud waters had gone over our soul,** that is, the insolent enemies would have accomplished their destruction; for the situation was such as to place them beyond all human help; it was an extremity in which only the assistance of the Lord sustained them. V. 6. **Blessed be the Lord,** to Him alone all praise and glory, **who hath not given us as a prey to their teeth,** not permitting the enemies to carry out their evil designs. V. 7. **Our soul is escaped as a bird out of the snare of the fowlers; the snare is broken,** by the merciful providence of the Lord, **and we are escaped.** Both figures, that of rapacious wild beasts eager to sing their teeth into their prey and that of fowlers placing their snares for unwary birds, show, on the one hand, the greatness of the danger, on the other, however, the miracle of God's deliverance. Therefore the psalmist concludes: v. 8. **Our help is in the name of the Lord,** in reliance upon His glorious essence and all His attributes, as they are revealed and proclaimed in His Word, **who made heaven and earth,** for the almighty Sovereign of the universe is, at the same time, our merciful Father in Jesus, our Redeemer, whose deliverance and assistance we enjoy.

PSALM 125.

Jehovah a Sure Defense against Apostasy.

A song of degrees, setting forth the manner in which God honors the trust of His people, both by protecting them and by leaving the hypocrites to the doom of the wicked. V. 1. **They that trust in the Lord shall be as Mount Zion,** established as firmly as the mount of God's holy Church, **which cannot be removed, but abideth forever,** the gates of hell being unable to prevail against it, Matt. 16, 18. V. 2. **As the mountains are round about Jerusalem,** the entire chain of mountains upon several of whose summits the capital was located, **so the Lord is round about His people from henceforth even forever,** a wall of defense against all enemies. The figure of the psalmist emphasizes the impregnable nature of the Church's protection both against attack and against temptation. V. 3. **For the rod of the wicked shall not rest upon the lot of the righteous,** that is, the scepter of wickedness, as an emblem of superior power, would not abide upon the inheritance of Israel, upon the Holy Land, and therefore also not upon the Church, **lest the righteous put forth their hands unto iniquity,** namely, under the pressure brought to bear upon them by the tyrants, causing the believers finally to join the oppressors, in order to find relief, a situation which has been found all too often in the history of the Church. V. 4. **Do good, O Lord, unto those that be good and to them that are upright in their hearts,** who are not given to hypocrisy and have not turned aside under the stress of temptation. V. 5. **As for such as turn aside unto their crooked ways,** leaving the right road and striking out in false paths and devious byways of their own choosing, **the Lord shall lead them forth with the workers of iniquity,** with whom their hypocritical and wicked behavior causes them to be classed; **but peace shall be upon Israel,** the full prosperity of spiritual blessings will rest upon those who are truly members of the Church of God, the true Israel, Gal. 6, 16. Everlasting punishment is the end of the hypocrites and the oppressors; everlasting peace is the reward of those who place their trust in the Lord with unwavering confidence.

PSALM 126.

Sowing in Tears, Reaping in Joy.

A song of degrees, admonishing the believers to praise the Lord for the many evidences of His favor and to pray for its continued manifestation. V. 1. **When the Lord turned again the captivity of Zion,** restoring His people to the Land of Promise after the long years of exile, **we were like them that dream.** Whether this is a prophecy or a statement of historical fact, it sets forth the indescribable bliss of those who were privileged to return to the Land of Promise. V. 2. **Then was our mouth filled with laughter,** in an excess of jubilation, **and our tongue with singing,** with shouts of exultation; **then said they among the heathen,** who were informed of the decree of Cyrus permitting the Jews to return to their home country, **The Lord hath done great things for them.** This word is caught up by the faithful, as expressing their gratitude in the proper manner, v. 3. **The Lord hath done great things for us,** in providing this deliverance, altogether without their merit and worthiness, **whereof we are glad.** But while the first band of returned exiles thus voiced its happiness in hymns of praise to the Lord, others were still sighing for deliverance: v. 4. **Turn again our captivity, O Lord,** giving them also an opportunity to return to the Land of Promise, **as the streams in the south,** as the dry watercourses of the Plains of Judah were renewed with the opening of the rainy season and the entire country burst into blossoms. At the same time even these remaining exiles look forward to a joyful return to the country of their fathers. V. 5. **They that sow in tears,** almost with despair in their hearts, the allusion probably being to the tearful return of the exiles and to the rebuilding of the Temple amidst the tears of the people, **shall reap in joy,** the harvest bringing the Lord's rich blessings. V. 6. **He that goeth forth and weepeth,** walking back and forth in his grief, **bearing precious seed,** patiently scattering his seed, hopefully laboring in the work given him by the Lord, **shall doubtless come again,** returning from his labors, **with rejoicing, bringing his sheaves with him,** God Himself having crowned his patient and hopeful efforts with rich success. It is the same thought which is expressed by St. Paul when he writes: "Let us not be weary in well-doing; for in due season we shall reap if we faint not," Gal. 6, 9. At the same time the entire psalm is typical of the deliverance which awaits all the children of God, when God will turn the captivity of this vale of tears and give to all believers the reward of mercy by permitting them to share in the harvest of the deeds made possible by His mercy, in the blessings which He dispensed from His throne.

PSALM 127.

The Divine Blessing Needed for Human Enterprises.

A song of degrees for Solomon, a hymn written by him probably in connection with the building of the Temple, but applicable to all similar conditions of life, the believers realizing their dependence upon Jehovah in all things. V. 1. **Except the Lord build the house,** Himself watching over the erection of every building executed by men and prospering their labors, **they labor in vain that build it,** there being so many possibilities of failure if the blessing or consent of the Lord is missing; **except the Lord keep the city,** Himself the Watchman and Guardian prospering the precautionary measures of the citizens, **the watchman waketh but in vain,** no matter with what degree of faithfulness he applies himself to his appointed work. V. 2. **It is vain,** to no object and purpose, **for you to rise up early, to sit up late,** lengthening the day by artificial means, toiling and moiling with worry and care, always taking thought for this life and its needs, Matt. 6, 25—34, **to eat the bread of sorrows,** thinking only of the hardships connected with the obtaining of one's daily bread; **for so He giveth His beloved sleep,** that is, while the believer reposes securely in God's protection, free from trouble and care on account of his trust in the providence of his heavenly Father, the Lord prepares to reward this trust by giving him all that he needs for his own good, as a free reward of His kindness and mercy. This blessing of the Lord upon the believers is now set forth by an unusually evident example. V. 3. **Lo, children are an heritage of the Lord,** sons are bequeathed by the Lord as a special gift and blessing, **and the fruit of the womb is His reward,** given to parents as an evidence of His favor, this fact being stressed time and again in Scripture as a standing reproof to the many blind and foolish people of our days who enter into marriage only for selfish reasons and consider children an unwelcome burden. V. 4. **As arrows,** weapons of defense, **are in the hand of a mighty man, so are children of the youth,** begotten while the parents are still in the vigor of their age, Gen. 37, 3, and therefore themselves grown to manhood and womanhood before the senile decline of the parents. V. 5. **Happy is the man that hath his quiver full of them,** to whom the Lord has granted a house full of children; **they shall not be ashamed,** they will not meet with disgrace, **but they shall speak with the enemies in the gate,** that is, in the place where business was transacted and differences were adjusted. Not only will children, if properly brought up, be a support of their parents when these have attained old age, but they will also make it their business to protect the rights of their parents against all detractors — a beautiful picture serving as an admonition to both parents and children, an example which should be heeded far more.

PSALM 128.

The Happiness of the Pious.

A song of degrees, setting forth the temporal blessings of true piety. Cp. Zech. 8. V. 1. **Blessed is every one that feareth the Lord,** his entire life being arranged in conformity with God's holy will, in childlike reverence; **that walketh in His ways,** his entire behavior agreeing with the Word of the Lord. V. 2. **For thou shalt eat the labor of thine hands,** being, by God's blessing, supplied with the fruits of his industry, especially the produce of garden and field; **happy shalt thou be, and it shall be well with thee,** real good fortune being found in a house which thus enjoys the blessing of Jehovah, where temperance and frugality are combined with contentment, and no one is compelled to eat the bread of charity. V. 3. **Thy wife shall be as a fruitful vine by the sides of thine house,** not on the outside, however, in club and society life, but in the rear, the inner rooms of the house, not a mere clinging vine, but a sturdy plant, leaning on her husband and happy in the midst of her family; **thy children like olive-plants round about thy table,** known for their luxuriant strength and promising rich returns at the time of their maturity. V. 4. **Behold that thus shall the man be blessed,** with the rich blessings of God's kindness, **that feareth the Lord,** whose faith works in him the true reverential regard for Jehovah and the willingness to walk in the path of His will. V. 5. **The Lord shall bless thee out of Zion,** the throne of His gracious presence in the midst of His people, just as He now lives in the midst of His congregation, in His Word and Sacraments; **and thou shalt see the good of Jerusalem all the days of thy life,** witnessing both the temporal and the spiritual blessings which the Lord grants to His Church and its members. Every true believer takes part in the well-being of the Church, the gift which God dispenses in His mercy. V. 6. **Yea, thou shalt see thy children's children,** a long and happy life being considered one of the Lord's special blessings, **and peace upon Israel,** rather, in the form of a prayer: "Peace be upon Israel," that is, God is invoked to grant the blessing of peace to His Church and to all its members, according to the promise of His Word, the blessings of this peace then resting also on the homes.

PSALM 129.

The Victory of the Church over Her Enemies.

A song of degrees, describing the deliverances of the people of God in the past and therefore confidently asserting the overthrow of the enemies in the future as well. V. 1. **Many a time have they afflicted me from my youth,** with severe oppressions, **may Israel now say,** the reference being especially to the bondage of Egypt; v. 2. **many a time have they afflicted me from my youth,** the thought being repeated for the sake of emphasis, with not only Egypt in mind, but also the Philistines, the Midianites, the Moabites, the Syrians, and the Babylonians; **yet they have not prevailed against me,** it had not been possible for the enemies to carry out their purpose of subduing Israel and exterminating it as a nation. V. 3. **The plowers plowed upon my back,** a figure of scourging expressing the most severe physical punishment; **they made long their furrows,** with relentless cruelty, for the picture is that of a strip of land which the farmer works with great thoroughness. Such had been the condition of Israel in the past. V. 4. **The Lord is righteous,** also in His judgment upon the wicked; **He hath cut asunder the cords of the wicked,** with which they tried to hold Israel in captivity. From the deliverance thus experienced the psalmist draws a conclusion regarding the future, expressed in the form of a prayer to Jehovah. V. 5. **Let them all be confounded,** covered with shame and disgrace, **and turned back,** hindered from accomplishing their wicked designs, **that hate Zion** (the members of the spiritual Israel), who attempt to hinder the work of the Church of all times. V. 6. **Let them be as the grass upon the housetops,** the grass that sprouts in the thin soil blown or carried on the flat roofs of Oriental houses, **which withereth afore it groweth up,** since it lacks sufficient nourishment and moisture and therefore cannot endure the heat of the sun for any length of time, v. 7. **wherewith the mower filleth not his hand,** since it is not worth while to pluck the few stalks, **nor he that bindeth sheaves his bosom,** the amount being too small to carry home and the quality poor. V. 8. **Neither do they which go by say,** with the ancient greeting used especially by workers in the harvest, **The blessing of the Lord be upon you,** whereupon the workers answered, **We bless you in the name of the Lord,** Ruth 2, 4. For the wicked, the enemies of the Church, of the believers, there will be no joyful harvest, but they will wither and die. The righteous, however, joyfully exchanging greetings, will be able to bring in all the harvest which they have sown, to be stored in the eternal granaries of heaven.

PSALM 130.

Prayer for Forgiveness of Sins.

A song of degrees, known of old as *De Profundis*, from its opening words in the Latin version, a sinner's cry to Jehovah for forgiveness and mercy. V. 1. **Out of the depths have I cried unto Thee, O Lord,** these depths being those of sin with its resulting distress, calamity, and peril, represented by an abyss of deep waters, whose waves have passed over the writer. V. 2. **Lord, hear my voice,** the appeal being to the All-powerful to grant deliverance; **let Thine ears be attentive to the voice of my supplications,** in a careful and merciful attention to his pleading. V. 3. **If Thou, Lord, shouldest mark iniquities,** observing them, bearing them in mind, imputing them to the sinner, **O Lord, who shall stand?** No human being could stand up fearlessly before the all-seeing eye of the All-powerful, the great Judge of all the earth, the consciousness of guilt rather causing every person in the world to sink to the ground before the Lord in the most severe self-condemnation. The verse expresses in the strongest possible manner the utter impossibility of any man to stand before Jehovah in his own merit and righteousness. V. 4. **But there is forgiveness with Thee,** the unmerited grace and mercy of the Lord being the only hope of sinful mortals, their only chance of deliverance and salvation, **that Thou mayest be feared,** for the assurance of God's mercy, far from producing a feeling of smug satisfaction and licentious leanings, rather makes for holiness. It is not that the believers who are assured of the forgiveness of the Lord presume upon His mercy, but that they walk before Him with all the greater awe. V. 5. **I wait for the Lord,** in confident expectation of His deliverance and assistance, **my soul doth wait,** with all the intensity of a painful longing, **and in His Word do I hope,** relying upon the promises there set forth. V. 6. **My soul waiteth for the Lord,** turned in longing toward the All-powerful, **more than they that watch for the morning,** those unable to rest on account of illness or misery, in whose case the rising of the dawn will be a release from pain; **I say, more than they that watch for the morning,** the repetition again emphasizing the eager longing of the heart anxious to see the deliverance of the Lord. The psalmist is sure that redemption will be forthcoming, not only for him, but for all the faithful. V. 7. **Let**

Israel hope in the Lord, waiting for salvation from Him; **for with the Lord there is mercy,** He is the only One able to dispense redemption, **and with Him is plenteous redemption,** mercy in all its fulness, enough for the sins of the whole world. Where sin abounded, grace did much more abound, Rom. 3, 20. V. 8. **And He shall redeem Israel from all his iniquities,** the prophet here looking forward to the propitiation of Christ, whereby He earned and obtained eternal redemption for us, Heb. 9, 12. Cp. Luke 1, 68—75; 2 Tim. 4, 18, this redemption being transmitted to us by faith.

PSALM 131.

Humble Submission to God.

A song of degrees of David, in which he expresses his feelings when exercising his royal authority and teaches proper submissiveness to the heavenly Father. V. 1. **Lord, my heart is not haughty,** filled with arrogant pride on account of his elevation from the lowly position of shepherd to that of the king of Israel, **nor mine eyes lofty,** for the pride of the heart finds its expression chiefly in the eyes; **neither do I exercise myself in great matters,** with the officious meddling of such as think that no important matter can be decided and carried out without their assistance, **or in things too high for me,** for the proud in heart disdain to engage in the trivial matters of every-day life, believing themselves to be called for great and decisive matters only. The characterization of the proud is brief, but inclusive and fitting. V. 2. **Surely I have behaved and quieted myself,** the figure being that of a weaned child clinging with perfect contentment to his mother, **as a child that is weaned of his mother,** and therefore perfectly satisfied; **my soul is even as a weaned child.** "As the weaned child no longer cries, frets, and longs for the breast, but lies still and is content, because it is with its mother, so the poet's soul is weaned from all discontented thoughts, from all fretful desires for earthly good, waiting in stillness upon God, finding its satisfaction in His presence, resting peacefully in His arms." The closing admonition, therefore, is a fitting addition: v. 3. **Let Israel hope in the Lord from henceforth and forever,** looking to Him alone for help and assistance, for sustenance and strength; for He resisteth the proud, but giveth grace to the humble in every circumstance of life, no matter what it may be.

PSALM 132.

Prayer for the House of God and the House of David.

A song of degrees, showing that the mercies of God, so richly promised to David, 2 Sam. 7, 12—29, would find their real fulfilment in the Messiah, the blessings of the Gospel thereby being dispensed to all believers. V. 1. **Lord, remember David and all his afflictions,** the troubles, anxieties, and vexations which attended his efforts for the welfare of the Church; v. 2. **how he sware unto the Lord and vowed unto the mighty God of Jacob,** cp. Gen. 49, 24: v. 3. **Surely I will not come into the tabernacle of my house nor go up into my bed,** himself enjoying good fortune and taking his ease; v. 4. **I will not give sleep to mine eyes or slumber to mine eyelids,** denying himself all rest, v. 5. **until I find out a place for the Lord,** a permanent sanctuary, **an habitation for the mighty God of Jacob,** that is, a place where God might dwell in the midst of Israel. The historical reference is the following: The Philistines had captured the Ark of the Covenant, 1 Sam. 4, 17, but had been glad to get rid of it again. Since the time of Samuel it had been in the house of Abinadab at Kirjath-jearim, 1 Sam. 7, 1. During the time of Saul it had not been missed, but David felt differently about it. He wanted to provide a permanent resting-place for the ark, a sanctuary for all Israel. He erected a tabernacle on Mount Zion and brought the Ark of the Covenant to this tabernacle, 2 Sam. 6. But when he proposed to build a Temple to Jehovah he was told that this boon would not be granted him, but that his son would be given permission to erect the Temple. The psalmist now continues in the name of the congregation: v. 6. **Lo, we heard of it at Ephratah,** that is, at Bethlehem, where David had grown up; **we found it in the fields of the wood,** at Kirjath-jearim, for there the ark had been stored all these years, until David took it up to the capital. V. 7. **We will go into His tabernacles,** to the Sanctuary, or Temple, now completed; **we will worship at His footstool,** that is, facing the place where the Ark of the Covenant was resting, since on its lid the Lord revealed Himself to His servants, Ex. 25, 22; Num. 7, 89. Their summons to worship is now seconded by the cry of Moses, Num. 10, 35: v. 8. **Arise, O Lord, into Thy rest,** to occupy the finished Temple as His Sanctuary, **Thou and the ark of Thy strength,** as the central object of His worship. V. 9. **Let Thy priests,**

who were ordinarily clothed in white linen, to typify the purity which should characterize their office, **be clothed with righteousness,** that imputed to them by virtue of their faith in the Messiah; **and let Thy saints shout for joy,** singing hymns of praise to the Lord for the blessings of grace imparted to them through the work of the priests. V. 10. **For Thy servant David's sake,** who was the servant of the Lord, to whom the Lord had pledged the Messianic promise, 2 Sam. 7, 12—16, **turn not away the face of Thine anointed,** by continuing the house and throne of David till the coming of the great Son of David. V. 11. **The Lord hath sworn in truth unto David,** in that same great Messianic prophecy; **He will not turn from it,** since faithfulness and truth are His attributes: **Of the fruit of thy body will I set upon thy throne.** V. 12. **If thy children will keep My covenant and My testimony that I shall teach them, their children shall also sit upon thy throne forevermore,** the culmination of his dynasty coming in Jesus, the Messiah, David's Son and David's Lord. Cp. 2 Sam. 7, 12—16; Ps. 89, 3—5; Acts 2, 30. With this Messianic promise is connected the special mercy whereby the Lord had selected Jerusalem as His Sanctuary. V. 13. **For the Lord hath chosen Zion; He hath desired it for His habitation,** for the prosperity of the kingdom was closely connected with that of the Church, the capital and the Sanctuary therefore being in the same city. V. 14. **This is My rest forever,** Jerusalem the Lord's permanent Sanctuary, not like Shiloh, which He had rejected; **here will I dwell, for I have desired it.** From this Sanctuary the Lord dispenses His blessings. V. 15. **I will abundantly bless her provision,** by supplying her temporal needs in rich measure; **I will satisfy her poor with bread.** This may refer also to spiritual blessings, as the next verse does with express words, v. 16. **I will also clothe her priests with salvation,** not only imputing it to them, but also making them instruments and bearers of the message of redemption, **and her saints,** to whom the same message of salvation would be communicated, **shall shout aloud for joy,** in being assured of their redemption. V. 17. **There will I make the horn of David,** symbol of aggressive power, **to bud,** thus enlarging his power; **I have ordained a lamp for Mine anointed,** David himself being the light of Israel, 2 Sam. 21, 17. V. 18. **His enemies will I clothe with shame,** heap disgrace upon them; **but upon himself shall his crown flourish,** for the Son of David, the Messiah, will have an eternal kingdom, Luke 1, 32. 33. This is truly also a New Testament psalm, and faith may now freely take the righteousness and salvation obtained through the work of the Messiah, Rom. 10, 10—13, for the King of Grace is ever mindful of His own.

PSALM 133.

The Blessing of Brotherly Unity.

A song of degrees of David, in which he sets forth the blessings of true unity as it should obtain between brothers, friends, and members of the same church or church-body. Cp. Eph. 4, 3—6. V. 1. **Behold,** the psalmist's purpose being to set before our eyes the picture which he has in mind by inspiration of the Lord, **how good and how pleasant,** a source of delight and bliss, **it is for brethren to dwell together in unity,** in full agreement with the brotherliness which their confession of the same doctrine demands. The suggestion for this thought was probably found in the spirit of unity which was expressed at the great festivals of the Jews, when the members of their Church assembled from even the remotest sections of Canaan, all united by the bonds of their common faith. V. 2. **It is like the precious ointment,** the oil of anointing, Ex. 30, 25, **upon the head,** where it was poured in the act of consecration, Lev. 8, 12, **that ran down upon the beard, even Aaron's beard; that went down to the skirts of his garments,** the emphasis being upon the type of the high-priesthood in the fulness of its divine consecration as illustrating the possibility of even an external union by means of religious customs; v. 3. **as the dew of Hermon,** whose snow-covered heights yielded a heavy precipitation of moisture throughout the surrounding country, **and as the dew that descended upon the mountains of Zion,** both of them bringing refreshment and blessings, just as the manifestation of brotherly unity results in blessings for the Church and its members; **for there the Lord commanded the blessing,** fixing Jerusalem as the point from which His blessings went forth, **even life forevermore,** for it is eternal life which is brought to men by the labors of the spiritual Zion, by the Church's proclamation of the Gospel, for this is His divine order till the end of time.

PSALM 134.

The Office of the Servants of the Church.

A song of degrees, probably used, by its original purpose, as the greeting of the worshiping multitudes at the opening of a great festival, the priests answering the song of greeting with the assurance of God's blessing. V. 1. **Behold, bless ye the Lord,** giving all praise and honor to Him, **all ye servants of the Lord, which by night stand in the house of the Lord,** the reference being either to the Temple chorus at the vesper service or to those officials of the tribe of Levi, both Levites and priests, who had charge of the Temple during the night, being responsible for the safety of all Temple property and making everything ready for the worship of the next day. V. 2. **Lift up your hands in the Sanctuary,** in a gesture of appeal, **and bless the Lord,** the admonition being not to forsake the acts of worship and devotion while engaged in the duty of watching. The congregation having sent its greeting up to the Temple mount or to the Court of the Priests, the chorus of priests answers with a blessing, v. 3. **The Lord that made heaven and earth,** the almighty Sovereign of the universe, **bless thee out of Zion,** from the place of His residence among His people, just as He now sends forth His blessings through the work of the Church, whose pastors, missionaries, and teachers bring the Gospel to men everywhere, the object being to make them wise unto salvation by faith in Christ Jesus, the avowed purpose of all Gospel-preaching.

PSALM 135.

The Hallelujah of the Congregation and Its Servants.

A hymn setting forth the wonderful relation of God to His Church, His almighty power over all the world, and His mercy in delivering His people, as contrasted with the vanity of idol worship. V. 1. **Praise ye the Lord,** a mighty hallelujah, as the keynote of the entire psalm. **Praise ye the name of the Lord,** as He has manifested it in all His attributes; **praise Him, O ye servants of the Lord,** all the members of His Church being eager to minister unto Him. V. 2. **Ye that stand in the house of the Lord, in the courts of the house of our God,** that is, the priests and Levites, as the ministers of the Lord in a special sense, v. 3. **praise the Lord; for the Lord is good,** manifesting His kindness to all men, but especially to His Church; **sing praises unto His name, for it is pleasant,** it is the delight of the believers to make the praise of the Lord their constant business. V. 4. **For the Lord hath chosen Jacob,** the patriarch and the people descended from him, **unto Himself,** to be His nation in a special sense, **and Israel for His peculiar treasure,** Ex. 19, 5, just as He now gathers those whom He has chosen in Christ Jesus to be His royal priesthood, 1 Pet. 2, 9. 10. The name and the attributes of the Lord are now proclaimed in detail. V. 5. **For I know that the Lord is great,** the Possessor of immeasurable greatness, **and that our Lord,** the All-powerful whom we worship as God, **is above all gods,** all those foolishly designated as gods by blind and idolatrous men. His incomparable creative majesty is now pictured. V. 6. **Whatsoever the Lord pleased,** whatever suited the convenience of His almighty will, **that did He in heaven and in earth, in the seas and all deep places,** in the abysses of the ocean; for over all these places His almighty power rules. V. 7. **He causeth the vapors to ascend from the ends of the earth,** fashioning them into clouds; **He maketh lightnings for the rain,** for the two usually occur together in a thunderstorm; **He bringeth the wind out of His treasuries,** out of His storehouses, since He has absolute power over the winds of the earth. But not only His creative and providential power makes Him worthy of praise, but also the deliverance which He effected in Egypt. V. 8. **Who smote the first-born of Egypt, both of man and beast,** from the heir apparent down to the calf of the lowliest herder, Ex. 12, 12. V. 9. **Who sent tokens and wonders into the midst of thee, O Egypt,** in the great plagues which preceded the exodus of the children of Israel, **upon Pharaoh and upon all his servants,** Ex. 7—10. Moreover, the Lord is praiseworthy on account of His conquest of the Land of Promise. V. 10. **Who smote great nations and slew mighty kings,** all those of Canaan and the country east of Jordan, Num. 21, 24—35; v. 11. **Sihon, king of the Amorites, and Og, king of Bashan, and all the kingdoms of Canaan,** Deut. 3 and 4; v. 12. **and gave their land for an heritage, an heritage unto Israel, His people,** so that they could possess the land as though it had been bequeathed to them. On the basis of these great works of the Lord the congregation now lifts up its voice in praise. V. 13. **Thy name, O Lord, endureth forever,** lasting throughout eternity, long after the names of all idols are forgotten; **and Thy memorial, O Lord, throughout all generations,** from one generation to the next, not only while the world stands, but beyond the confines of time, world without end. V. 14. **For the Lord will judge His people,** obtaining justice for them over against the oppression of the enemies, **and He will repent Himself concerning His servants,** change His manner of dealing with them to continual kindness, proving Himself the living and gracious God over against the vanity of idols invented by men. V. 15. **The idols of the heathen are silver and gold,** fashioned from precious metals by the hand of the silversmith, **the work of men's hands,** made by puny men. V. 16. **They have mouths, but they speak not; eyes have they, but they see not;** v. 17. **they have ears, but they hear not, neither is there any breath in their mouths,** not even a trace of life and breath, the expression emphasizing the lifelessness and helplessness of the idols. Cp. Ps. 115, 4—8. V. 18. **They that make them are like unto them,** just as stupid spiritually, for the practise of idolatry brutalizes men; **so is every one that trusteth in them,** altogether without understanding in spiritual matters and destined for perdition. The summons, therefore, goes out once more: v. 19. **Bless the Lord, O house of Israel,** the entire congregation of believers; **bless the Lord, O house of Aaron,** all the priests of the Church; v. 20. **bless the Lord, O house of Levi,** all the Levites, that is, all the ministers of the Church, no matter of what degree; **ye that fear the Lord,** all the believers of all times, **bless the Lord.** V. 21. **Blessed be the Lord out of Zion,** from the center of true worship, **which dwelleth at Jerusalem,** His praise being extolled through this proclamation of His name far and wide over the earth. **Praise ye the Lord,** the psalm closing, as it began, with a joyful hallelujah in honor of the one true Lord and God, whose blessings are sent forth everywhere in the Gospel-message.

PSALM 136.

Exhortation to Give Thanks to God.

An antiphonal hymn, which takes up the theme of the preceding psalm and was intended to be sung in alternation by the choir and the congregation, the former chanting the invitation and the latter responding with the call, stating the reason for the hymn of praise. V. 1. **O give thanks unto the Lord, for He is good,** exhibiting His goodness in all His works for the benefit of His children; **for His mercy,** His free favor and unmerited lovingkindness, **endureth forever.** V. 2. **O give thanks unto the God of gods,** the Sovereign, whose creative and providential power is over every rank of government and everything that is worshiped falsely; **for His mercy endureth forever.** V. 3. **O give thanks to the Lord of lords,** in whose hands is all power, the direction of all affairs of the universe; **for His mercy endureth forever.** V. 4. **To Him who alone doeth great wonders,** all help and interference on the part of any creature being excluded; **for His mercy endureth forever.** V. 5. **To Him that by wisdom,** by the application of divine knowledge and understanding, **made the heavens; for His mercy endureth forever.** V. 6. **To Him that stretched out the earth above the waters,** the water of the world being partly visible, in the oceans, and partly invisible, in the underground streams and springs; **for His mercy endureth forever.** V. 7. **To Him that made great lights,** Gen. 1, 14; **for His mercy endureth forever:** v. 8. **the sun to rule by day,** to have dominion in controlling the division of time; **for His mercy endureth forever:** v. 9. **the moon and stars to rule by night,** Gen. 1, 16; **for His mercy endureth forever.** The deliverance out of the bondage of Egypt is next proclaimed: v. 10. **To Him that smote Egypt in their first-born,** Ex. 12, 29; **for His mercy endureth forever;** v. 11. **and brought out Israel from among them,** Ex. 12, 51; **for His mercy endureth forever;** v. 12. **with a strong hand and with a stretched-out arm,** with a manifestation of His majesty and power; **for His mercy endureth forever.** V. 13. **To Him which divided the Red Sea into parts,** when Moses, at His command, stretched out his staff over the sea, Ex. 14, 21. 22; **for His mercy endureth forever;** v. 14. **and made Israel to pass through the midst of it,** the waters standing on either side like walls; **for His mercy endureth forever;** v. 15. **but overthrew Pharaoh and his host in the Red Sea,** literally, "shaking them," as one would shake small particles in a bottle, the figure picturing the utter annihilation of the enemies; **for His mercy endureth forever.** V. 16. **To Him which led His people through the wilderness,** during the forty-year journey, Deut. 8, 15; **for His mercy endureth forever.** V. 17. **To Him which smote great kings,** such as possessed great power, mighty armies; **for His mercy endureth forever;** v. 18. **and slew famous kings,** such as were celebrated far and wide for their power; **for His mercy endureth forever:** v. 19. **Sihon, king of the Amorites; for His mercy endureth forever;** v. 20. **and Og, the king of Bashan; for His mercy endureth forever;** v. 21. **and gave their land for an heritage; for His mercy endureth forever;** v. 22. **even an heritage unto Israel, His servant; for His mercy endureth forever.** Cp. Ps. 135, 10—12; Deut. 2, 32—3, 11. V. 23. **Who remembered us in our low estate,** either in the bondage of Egypt or in the captivity of

Babylonia; **for His mercy endureth forever;** v. 24. **and hath redeemed us from our enemies,** snatching them suddenly out of the hands of their adversaries; **for His mercy endureth forever.** V. 25. **Who giveth food to all flesh,** His providential care embracing all His creatures; **for His mercy endureth forever.** The psalmist therefore sums up his exhortation in one final call: v. 26. **O give thanks unto the God of heaven,** the great Ruler of the heavens and therefore the Sovereign of the earth as well; **for His mercy endureth forever.** It is a wonderful prayer of thanksgiving, which the Church and all its members will gladly send up to the throne of grace at all times.

PSALM 137.

Song of Grief of the Captive Jews.

The unknown poet here records the deep grief and mourning of the Jews during the Babylonian captivity and includes a prayer for the destruction of their enemies, since their enmity was a challenge to the God of Israel. V. 1. **By the rivers of Babylon,** along the banks of which many of the Jews had settled for the period of the captivity, **there we sat down,** their deep grief having driven them away into the solitude of the country, **yea, we wept when we remembered Zion,** for the anxiety of the believing Jews did not concern the loss of their temporal goods so much as that of the Sanctuary, the visible sign of the true worship. V. 2. **We hanged our harps,** otherwise used to accompany joyous and festal songs, **upon the willows in the midst thereof,** to indicate that all their joyful hymns were hushed. The silent and pensive sitting among the weeping willows by the side of the gently flowing streams agrees well with the feeling of homesickness which filled the hearts of the captives. V. 3. **For there they that carried us away captive required of us a song,** either out of curiosity or in derision; **and they wasted us,** those who had inflicted pain upon them, their oppressors, **required of us mirth,** an expression of happiness, **saying, Sing us one of the songs of Zion.** The enemies did not realize how tactless they were, and did not care whether the compliance of the Jews with their request would agree with their depressed feelings or not. They had heard of the wonderful hymns of the Jews and insisted upon being entertained by them. But the resentment and the bitterness of the captives kept them from complying with the request addressed to them. V. 4. **How shall we sing the Lord's song in a strange land?** Their sacred songs were, in their minds, inseparably connected with the worship of the Temple, the Sanctuary in Jerusalem, and it seemed to them a desecration to strike up their psalms for the entertainment of their captors; it was opposed to their religious and moral feelings. After this descriptive part of the psalm the poet launches forth in a lyric strain expressive of the feelings which filled the hearts of the captive Jews. V. 5. **If I forget thee, O Jerusalem,** the Sanctuary with the worship of Jehovah, **let my right hand forget her cunning,** the power of motion in general, and especially her skill with the harp. V. 6. **If I do not remember thee, let my tongue cleave to the roof of my mouth,** in an agony of thirst and suffering; **if I prefer not Jerusalem above my chief joy,** literally, "if I do not place Jerusalem above the summit of my joy," that is, if he, and all believing Jews with him, did not consider the Sanctuary of Jehovah the source of his greatest delight in life. It is an expression of homesick longing which properly pictures the deep remorse and grief of the captives. The poet now, in holy anger, turns to call God's wrath down upon the enemies of Israel, who were, at the same time, the enemies of Jehovah. V. 7. **Remember, O Lord, the children of Edom,** who had been particularly active in the destruction of Jerusalem, Amos 1, 11; Joel 4, 19, for which reason they had been threatened with divine vengeance, Jer. 49, 7. 8, **in the day of Jerusalem,** at the time of its downfall; **who said, Raze it, raze it, even to the foundation thereof,** not permitting one stone to remain upon the other, for such were their vindictive feelings. But Babylon was also included in the poet's execration. V. 8. **O daughter of Babylon, who art to be destroyed,** literally, "that art destroyed," for in the prophetic mind her destruction was already begun, **happy shall he be that rewardeth thee as thou hast served us.** Cp. Is. 47, 6. V. 9. **Happy shall he be that taketh and dasheth thy little ones against the stones,** so that no new generation, rising from the ruins, would restore her shattered world power, Is. 14, 21. 22. It is not personal vindictiveness that is speaking here, but the prophet of the Lord, in the name of the Lord; for the divine justice upon the blaspheming enemies must be carried out. Naturally, this psalm finds its application in the Christian Church of all times, for it is equivalent to a prayer that God would deliver us from every evil work and preserve us unto His heavenly kingdom.

PSALM 138.

Thanksgiving for God's Salvation.

A psalm of David, in which he describes the greatness of God's benefits and assures himself and others of His continued presence and faithfulness. V. 1. **I will praise Thee with my whole heart,** without reserve or hypocrisy; **before the gods,** the princes or mighty ones of the earth, **will I sing praise unto Thee.** The true God is to be exalted above all creatures, no matter how great their power and authority. V. 2. **I will worship toward Thy holy Temple,** for the prayers of the faithful Jews were made with their faces toward Jerusalem and the Temple, **and praise Thy name for Thy loving-kindness,** the unmerited favor shown to David, **and for Thy truth,** in keeping His promises; **for Thou hast magnified Thy Word above all Thy name,** literally, "for Thou hast made great above all Thy name Thy Word," that is, the promise of God, 2 Sam. 7, 12—16, exceeded all other revelations of Himself in its greatness and in its application to the salvation of men. V. 3. **In the day when I cried,** requesting strength and help for bearing his burdens, **Thou answeredst me and strengthenedst me with strength in my soul,** so that his whole soul was charged with a feeling of power enabling him to sustain all his trials with cheerful fortitude. V. 4. **All the kings of the earth shall praise Thee, O Lord,** being influenced thereto by the experience of David, **when they hear the words of Thy mouth,** particularly the great Messianic promise to which David chiefly refers, which would surely be fulfilled. V. 5. **Yea, they shall sing in the ways of the Lord,** setting forth the wonderful manner in which the Lord deals with those who put their trust in Him; **for great is the glory of the Lord,** that which He exhibits in fulfilling His purposes of redemption. V. 6. **Though the Lord be high,** exalted above all creatures, **yet hath He respect unto the lowly,** He observes them with the intention of coming to their aid; **but the proud He knoweth afar off,** He is fully familiar with their ways and deserts, even though they think that they are not responsible to any one; He will in due time show them the extent of their liability to Him. V. 7. **Though I walk in the midst of trouble,** surrounded with trials and tribulations of every description, **Thou wilt revive me,** loosing the bands which threaten to draw him down to destruction, and filling him with new life and strength. **Thou shalt stretch forth Thine hand against the wrath of mine enemies,** holding it back from accomplishing its purpose, **and Thy right hand shall save me,** giving him deliverance from all his difficulties. V. 8. **The Lord will perfect,** carry to a successful completion, **that which concerneth me,** all that He had undertaken in delivering David from all the trials besetting him; **Thy mercy, O Lord,** which was the guaranty upon which David relied, **endureth forever; forsake not the works of Thine own hands,** letting them lie uncompleted, for they include not only all those pertaining to the person of David and the fact of his elevation to the dignity of king, but especially that by which the glorious promise of the Son of David and His work of redemption would be realized, the glorious fact upon which the faith of all believers is based. With Him on their side they are never forsaken.

PSALM 139.

The Omniscience, Omnipresence, and Omnipotence of God.

To the chief musician, for performance in the liturgical part of public worship, **a psalm of David,** in which he first describes the chief attributes of God and then adds a prayer for a pure heart and a faultless conduct. David addresses himself, first of all, to the omniscient God, vv. 1—6. V. 1. **O Lord, Thou hast searched me,** making a careful survey of his innermost heart and mind, **and known me,** having a full understanding of all the motives which prompted his every thought and act. V. 2. **Thou knowest my downsitting and mine uprising,** every movement which every person in the world makes; **Thou understandest my thought afar off,** being familiar with it even before the desire is fully formed or the idea takes shape. V. 3. **Thou compassest my path and my lying down,** literally, "my walking and my lying down Thou siftest," that is, the Lord proves it out, He weighs it even before it happens and while the act is going on, **and art acquainted with all my ways,** his entire conduct being uncovered before the eyes of God's omniscience. V. 4. **For there is not a word in my tongue,** uttered or unuttered, **but, lo, O Lord,** stated with emphasis, **Thou knowest it altogether,** in every respect, both as to motive and performance. V. 5. **Thou hast beset me behind and before,** so that there is no way for him to escape from the Lord's surveillance, **and laid Thine hand upon me,** holding him in bounds, guarding against an unbridled use of freedom, for the consciousness of the omniscience of God will act as a curb against an undue assertion of what men claim as their rights. The contemplation of these facts causes David to cry out: v. 6. **Such knowl-**

edge is too wonderful for me, it is beyond the reach of man's mind; **it is high, I cannot attain unto it;** it is beyond man's comprehension, it is an article of faith.

David next sets forth the omnipresence of God, vv. 7—12. V. 7. **Whither shall I go from Thy Spirit?** the Spirit of God and God Himself being identified in all their acts. **Or whither shall I flee from Thy presence?** in a strenuous effort to escape from the Lord after some act challenging the vengeance of the Lord. Is it possible to find a place where His presence is not found, to which His arm does not extend? V. 8. **If I ascend up into heaven, Thou art there,** for there is the throne of His majesty; **if I make my bed in hell,** the realm of the dead, **behold, Thou art there.** Cp. Amos 9, 2; Job 26, 6. V. 9. **If I take the wings of the morning,** or, "of the dawn," as it rises upward with the speed of wings and spreads over the eastern heaven, **and dwell in the uttermost parts of the sea,** in the most remote part of the universe, v. 10. **even there shall Thy hand lead me,** with the guiding power of omnipresent providence, **and Thy right hand shall hold me,** for God is everywhere. V. 11. **If I say,** as criminals are wont to do, since vice and crime seek the cover of night, **Surely the darkness shall cover me,** making him invisible to the eyes of the Lord, **even the night shall be light about me,** for with God, who Himself is the Source of light, there is no distinction between day and night, His eye pierces the darkness of created night as though it were the brightest noonday. V. 12. **Yea, the darkness hideth not from Thee,** it cannot produce a darkness which His eye cannot penetrate; **but the night shineth as the day,** emitting light at His command; **the darkness and the light are both alike to Thee,** literally, "as is darkness, so is light," it makes no difference to Him whose omnipresence is aided by His omniscience, before whom nothing in all the universe is hidden.

David now describes the creative power and providence of God and adds a prayer extolling the Lord and appealing for a just trial. V. 13. **For Thou hast possessed my reins,** that is, formed, framed, fashioned the organs of his body in creation; **Thou hast covered me in my mother's womb,** that is, plaited or weaved the body before birth, as the bones, sinews, and flesh took shape. V. 14. **I will praise Thee, for I am fearfully and wonderfully made,** in a manner which produces awe and reverence at the miracle of creation. **Marvelous are Thy works,** those of creation in general, **and that my soul knoweth right well,** being impressed with these miracles on every hand. V. 15. **My substance,** that is, the bones, the framework of the body, **was not hid from Thee when I was made in secret and curiously wrought in the lowest parts of the earth,** literally, "wrought in various colors," on account of the veining of the body and the different colors of its various organs and parts, the reference to God's creative act in the case of each human being including a reference to the original creation of man out of the dust of the earth. V. 16. **Thine eyes did see my substance, yet being unperfect,** while he was still in the form of an embryo, **and in Thy book all my members were written,** or rather, all the days of his life, **which in continuance were fashioned, when as yet there was none of them,** that is, among the days planned in God's counsel there was also one which was destined for the creation of David, in other words, beginning, development, and completion of all creatures take place according to God's creative counsel. The contemplation of this power of God, as revealed in the act of God's creation of man, fills the poet's heart with adoring praise. V. 17. **How precious also are Thy thoughts unto me, O God!** weighty, important, full of deep significance. **How great is the sum of them,** how overpowering in their total amount! the human mind being unable to grasp their great number and meaning. V. 18. **If I should count them,** attempting to keep account of them, **they are more in number than the sand,** innumerable for a mere human being. **When I awake,** having fallen asleep in the futile attempt to form an adequate picture of their number, **I am still with Thee,** still engaged in the contemplation of God, the incomprehensible, still thinking about His counsels and dealings. V. 19. **Surely Thou wilt slay the wicked, O God,** to whom the believer's faith in the Lord is a source of mockery; **depart from me therefore, ye bloody men,** those whose consciences are burdened with blood-guilt. V. 20. **For they speak against Thee wickedly,** having evil designs in their hearts, **and Thine enemies take Thy name in vain,** speaking of Him, mentioning Him, with craftiness and deceit, such enmity against God always resulting in sins and crimes of every kind. V. 21. **Do not I hate them, O Lord,** rather, "Should not I hate those," **that hate Thee? And am not I grieved with those that rise up against Thee?** abhorring the adversaries of Jehovah with perfection of hatred. V. 22. **I hate them with perfect hatred,** with the very extremity of abhorrence, but without personal bitterness or self-exaltation; **I count them mine enemies;** for those whom God considers His adversaries must be so considered by His believers. V. 23. **Search me, O God, and know my heart,** to prevent all deception of self; **try me and know my thoughts,** testing them out for their sincerity; v. 24. **and see if there be any wicked way in me,** literally, "a way of grief," namely, that leading to punishment for sins committed, **and lead me in the way everlasting,** that agreeing with His will, the way of righteousness, which endures forever, for that is the desire of all believers.

PSALM 140.

Prayer for Deliverance from Malicious Enemies.

To the chief musician, for performance in public worship, **a psalm of David,** in which he presents to the Lord the usual complaint, adding to this a fervent prayer and confident hope of relief. V. 1. **Deliver me, O Lord, from the evil man; preserve me from the violent man,** one who delights in inflicting injuries, v. 2. **which,** that is, such people as a class, **imagine mischiefs in their heart,** ever planning evil and wickedness; **continually are they gathered together for war,** stirring up strife at every opportunity. V. 3. **They have sharpened their tongues like a serpent,** so that the sting of it is as deadly as that of a snake; **adders' poison is under their lips,** to be poured into the wounds made by their fangs as they slander their victim. **Selah.** V. 4. **Keep me, O Lord, from the hands of the wicked,** for they will not hesitate to vent their spite by outright acts of violence; **preserve me from the violent man, who have purposed to overthrow my goings,** literally, "to upset my steps, "either by tripping or by kicking, the figure picturing the malicious manner in which the ungodly try to bring harm upon the faithful. V. 5. **The proud have hid a snare for me and cords; they have spread a net by the wayside,** very near to the path which the believer must go, so that he will likely be caught; **they have set gins,** traps and pitfalls, **for me. Selah.** Cp. Ps. 10, 7; 31, 13; 58, 4. With all this malice and mischief before his eyes the psalmist now makes a declaration of his trust in the Lord. V. 6. **I said unto the Lord,** to Jehovah, the God of mercy, **Thou art my God,** the essence of true faith being expressed in the confident possessive "my," with which the believer defies all enemies; **hear the voice of my supplications, O Lord,** the appeal by which he places himself entirely into the care of his heavenly Father. V. 7. **O God the Lord,** the All-powerful, **the Strength of my salvation,** the one Stronghold in which the believers are sure of deliverance, **Thou hast covered my head in the day of battle,** literally, "in the day of armor," namely, when this is carried into battle; for it is then that the Lord is the Helmet of the faithful, protecting them from all harm. The psalmist does not depend upon his own strength in the emergency in which he finds himself, but on God alone. V. 8. **Grant not, O Lord, the desires of the wicked,** by which he intends to destroy the believers; **further not his wicked device,** so that his plans meet with success; (lest) **they exalt themselves. Selah.** V. 9. **As for the head of those that compass me about,** if they lift up their heads to carry out their wicked plans, **let the mischief of their own lips cover them,** that is, the trouble or suffering which they intend for others shall recoil upon their own heads, as a well-deserved punishment. V. 10. **Let burning coals fall upon them,** be cast upon them in perils of a terrible nature; **let them be cast into the fire,** into everlasting destruction; **into deep pits,** abysses filled with water, **that they rise not up again.** The entire passage emphasizes the heinousness of the sin of slander and the severity of its just punishment. V. 11. **Let not an evil speaker,** literally, "a man of tongue," one who steadily engages in slander, **be established in the earth,** be tolerated anywhere; **evil shall hunt the violent man,** who engages in such vicious practises, **to overthrow him,** overtaking him quickly and making an end of him. Once more, in conclusion, the psalmist states his confident belief in the God of his salvation. V. 12. **I know that the Lord will maintain the cause of the afflicted,** bringing it to a successful issue in spite of all attempts of the wicked, **and the right of the poor,** because those who lack this world's goods are usually also without influence to fight malicious attacks. V. 13. **Surely the righteous shall give thanks unto Thy name,** for the deliverance which is bound to come; **the upright shall dwell in Thy presence,** here in time, in the enjoyment of the means of grace, and hereafter in eternity, when they will be beyond the reach of malice and wickedness.

PSALM 141.

Evening Psalm in the Midst of Trials.

A psalm of David, a prayer for deliverance from afflictions and from the enemies who cause them. V. 1. **Lord, I cry unto Thee,** with the consciousness of the emergency besetting him; **make haste unto me,** since the need is so great; **give ear unto my voice,** paying speedy attention to it, **when I cry unto Thee.** The anguish-stricken soul, filled with distress, frets as though God were far from him, and therefore calls Him to draw near in mercy. V. 2. **Let my prayer be set forth before Thee as incense,** like the clouds of burning incense which rose up before the face of Jehovah in the Temple, as the officiating priest offered it at the golden altar in the Holy Place, Ex. 30, 8; Rev. 8, 3, **and the lifting up of my hands,** in the attitude of fervent prayer, **as the evening sacrifice,** which, if graciously accepted by the Lord, fitly closed the day and left the worshiper with a sense of peace and security in the hands of

Jehovah, Ex. 29, 38—42. The picture is that of prayers which are acceptable to our heavenly Father and heard. At the same time every believer is striving for perfection and needs the help of God in fighting his own evil nature. V. 3. **Set a watch, O Lord, before my mouth,** to keep it from expressing sinful thoughts; **keep the door of my lips,** guarding them from uttering complaints which would be equivalent to accusations against the Lord. V. 4. **Incline not my heart to any evil thing,** permitting it to follow its natural tendency in this respect, **to practise wicked works with men that work iniquity,** joining them in the wickedness in which they are so thoroughly at home; **and let me not eat of their dainties,** not taste and partake of the sensuous enjoyments of those who have gained their possessions unjustly. But the believer is willing also to accept the reproof of his brethren in the faith. V. 5. **Let the righteous smite me,** even with severe rebukes, **it shall be a kindness,** that is, the correcting should be done with the proper degree of gentleness; **and let him reprove me, it shall be an excellent oil, which shall not break my head,** his head would not refuse it, that is, far from resenting a fellow-Christian's reprimand, every believer will rather welcome it as aiding him in his course of sanctification; **for yet my prayer also shall be in their calamities,** that is, the believer meets the malice of the enemies with prayer, their shameful practises with intercessions to the Lord. V. 6. **When their judges,** that is, the rulers and leaders of the enemies, **are overthrown in stony places,** cast down into utter destruction, **they shall hear my words; for they are sweet.** The time would come, David declares, when the people would overthrow the wicked rulers, the rebellious leaders, and execute them; then they would welcome once more their true king's messages. V. 7. **Our bones are scattered at the grave's mouth, as when one cutteth and cleaveth wood upon the earth,** or, "as one draws furrows and loosens the soil," that is, although the enemies should apparently succeed in gaining the upper hand to the extent of stretching out the believers at the door leading to the realm of death, yet would they rise up once more, as the seed springs up out of the soil prepared for it, much as it seems to be cut up by the plowing. V. 8. **But mine eyes are unto Thee,** fixed upon Him in confident hope, **O God the Lord,** the All-powerful; **in Thee is my trust; leave not my soul destitute,** pouring it out, depriving it of its hold on His mercy. V. 9. **Keep me from the snares which they have laid for me,** which are like hands stretched out to catch and overthrow the believer, **and the gins of the workers of iniquity,** wherewith they intend to trap the faithful. V. 10. **Let the wicked fall into their own nets,** as a well-deserved punishment for their malicious persecution of the believer, **whilst that I withal escape,** all the wicked attempts of the godless thus coming to naught. So will all pious Christians finally be redeemed from every evil work to enjoy the redemption gained for them, world without end, the bliss of eternity being rightly called a deliverance.

PSALM 142.

Cry for Help in Great Extremity.

Maschil, a didactic poem, one teaching an important lesson, **of David; a prayer when he was in the cave,** either in that of Adullam, 1 Sam. 22, or in that of Engedi, 1 Sam. 24, teaching all believers the manner of praying to the Lord when trouble has reached its highest point. V. 1. **I cried unto the Lord with my voice,** in a loud appeal for help; **with my voice unto the Lord did I make my supplication,** with great earnestness and importunity, imploring His merciful assistance and deliverance. V. 2. **I poured out my complaint before Him,** depositing all his worries and cares at one time, Ps. 37, 5; **I showed before Him my trouble,** making known to Him all that was bothering him, all his distress. V. 3. **When my spirit was overwhelmed within me,** fainting away with the severity of his distress, **then Thou knewest my path,** the entire conduct of David lying open before the omniscient eyes of Jehovah, with all its weaknesses, indeed, but also with the underlying sincerity which characterized him. **In the way wherein I walked,** which his duty bade him walk, **have they privily laid a snare for me,** to effect his destruction. V. 4. **I looked on my right hand,** the place of a protector, **and beheld, but there was no man that would know me,** no friend upon whom he could depend without reserve; **refuge failed me,** there seemed to be no place in which he was secure; **no man cared for my soul,** he felt himself utterly forsaken of men, for even the faithful ones who shared his exile occasionally did not understand him, 1 Sam. 24, 1—7; 26, 5—11. Since, then, he had no other refuge, his helpless soul was driven to the Lord alone. V. 5. **I cried unto Thee, O Lord; I said, Thou art my Refuge and my Portion in the land of the living,** by providing him the safe stronghold of His almighty power and the assurance of His grace and mercy in the midst of his afflictions. V. 6. **Attend unto my cry,** his appeal once more ringing out; **for I am brought very low,** he has reached the point of extreme weakness; **deliver me from my persecutors; for they are stronger than I,** they had the upper hand at that time and tried their best to carry out their wicked intention of destroying David. V. 7. **Bring my soul out of prison,** out of this extremity of sorrows in which he found himself, **that I may praise Thy name,** in grateful appreciation of what the Lord had done for him. **The righteous shall compass me about,** coming to him and surrounding him in sympathetic joy; **for Thou shalt deal bountifully with me,** his final triumph being a certainty beyond the shadow of a doubt in his mind, since he relied upon the promise of his merciful heavenly Father. Thus the sorrows of this present world teach all believers to have their hearts attuned to the praise of the Lord always, in setting forth His bounty.

PSALM 143.

A Prayer of Repentance and a Sigh for Mercy.

A psalm of David, which sets forth the fundamental facts concerning sin and grace, for which reason it was reckoned by Luther with the Pauline psalms. V. 1. **Hear my prayer, O Lord; give ear to my supplications,** in which he implores the Lord's help and mercy; **in Thy faithfulness,** by which God keeps His promises, **answer me, and in Thy righteousness,** which He shows in relieving those who walk before Him in obedience to His holy will. V. 2. **And enter not into judgment with Thy servant,** dealing with him according to His strict and absolute justice; **for in Thy sight,** before the all-seeing eye of the omniscient God, **shall no man living be justified,** not one human being can stand before God in his own righteousness, allege the perfection of his life and conduct. It is only by realizing and acknowledging his sinfulness without reserve and throwing himself entirely upon the mercy of the Lord that any person can expect justification, namely, by means of the righteousness of Christ imputed to him. V. 3. **For the enemy hath persecuted my soul,** seeking to obtain the highest good which he possessed; **he hath smitten my life down to the ground,** almost succeeding in his evil intention; **he hath made me to dwell in darkness, as those that have been long dead,** that is, David's enemies intended his utter destruction, they wanted him to sleep the sleep of eternal death, and he realized that he would remain without deliverance, unless God Himself in mercy would take up his defense. V. 4. **Therefore is my spirit overwhelmed within me,** being faint by reason of the long duration of his trials; **my heart within me is desolate,** not only forsaken, but almost rigid and motionless with fear and terror. V. 5. **I remember the days of old,** when Jehovah was so evidently on his side; **I meditate on all Thy works,** thinking over the many manifestations of God's mercy and salvation in his life; **I muse on the work of Thy hands,** God's guidance being so evident in the history of Israel. V. 6. **I stretch forth my hands unto Thee,** in a gesture denoting both helplessness and absolute reliance upon the mercy of the Lord; **my soul thirsteth after Thee as a thirsty land,** languishing with desire for His help, as a thirsty land for rain. **Selah.** V. 7. **Hear me speedily, O Lord,** for haste was essential in this great emergency; **my spirit faileth,** almost consumed with languishing. **Hide not Thy face from me,** in anger, **lest I be like unto them that go down into the pit;** repudiated by God, there is only one alternative, eternal destruction. With this fate following an angry demonstration on the part of God, the psalmist once more turns to Him in a fervent appeal, v. 8. **Cause me to hear Thy loving-kindness in the morning,** so that with the dawn of the new day the night of tribulation might be definitely ended; **for in Thee do I trust,** Ps. 90, 14. **Cause me to know the way wherein I should walk,** that which finds the full approval of the Lord; **for I lift up my soul unto Thee,** in longing for salvation and in firm confidence of faith. V. 9. **Deliver me, O Lord, from mine enemies; I flee unto Thee to hide me,** that is, he flees to the Lord as his true Refuge, seeking safety with Him alone. In possession of salvation, however, the Lord's servant desires to be in possession of sanctification also. V. 10. **Teach me to do Thy will,** to conduct himself in all his dealings in accordance with God's good pleasure; **for Thou art my God,** and the heart of the believer, joined with that of his heavenly Father, his highest good, in the most intimate fellowship, seeks only to conform in his whole life to the standard of God's holy will. **Thy Spirit is good; lead me into the land of uprightness,** or, "Thy good Spirit," whose work is done in the hearts of the believers through the means of grace, "lead me in a level land," where the roads have been prepared by the Lord Himself, Is. 26, 7; Ps. 23, 3. V. 11. **Quicken me, O Lord, for Thy name's sake,** in order that the name of God, especially His mercy and love, might be magnified in consequence of His act of deliverance; **for Thy righteousness' sake bring my soul out of trouble,** out of all distress and tribulation with which David was then contending. V. 12. **And of Thy mercy,** both by reason of His mercy and in order to make it known, **cut off mine enemies and destroy all them that afflict my soul,** by oppressions as described in this psalm; **for I am Thy servant,** and in helping him the Lord would magnify His own glory. Thus the hope of all believers and their constant prayer is in the mercy of God.

PSALM 144.

Thanksgiving and Prayer for Deliverance.

A psalm of David, in which he praises God for help experienced in the past and confidently implores His assistance against the enemies of the nation, as well as His blessing for continued prosperity. V. 1. **Blessed be the Lord, my Strength,** his Rock or Refuge, with whom he is safe, **which teacheth my hands to war and my fingers to fight,** giving the king instruction and assistance in waging a just war; v. 2. **my Goodness,** rather, my Mercy, since it was the Lord's unmerited favor which sustained David, **and my Fortress,** his mountain Stronghold, where he is beyond the reach of his enemies; **my high Tower, and my Deliverer,** who was able to snatch him out of the midst of troubles; **my Shield,** to protect him from attacks, **and He in whom I trust,** in whose care he knew himself to be definitely out of harm's way; **who subdueth my people under me,** making Israel realize that David's authority was his by divine investment. It is the feeling of his own unworthiness which moves David to cry out, in view of God's mercy upon him: v. 3. **Lord, what is man that Thou takest knowledge of him,** by conferring such wonderful favors, **or the son of man,** an ordinary, frail human being, **that Thou makest account of him!** The very fact that God pays any attention to him at all fills David with a sense of his own insignificance, since it contrasts his own nothingness, and that of mankind generally, with the greatness of such a gracious God. V. 4. **Man is like to vanity,** like a breath which is gone before it is noticed; **his days are as a shadow that passeth away,** Ps. 102, 11. All the firmer, then, must be the believer's trust in God. V. 5. **Bow Thy heavens, O Lord,** bringing them nearer, as it were, for speedy help, **and come down,** manifesting His almighty power; **touch the mountains,** with the hand of His majesty extended from the heights of heaven, **and they shall smoke,** the volcanoes revealing His omnipotent power. V. 6. **Cast forth lightning,** in a mighty thunderstorm, **and scatter them; shoot out Thine arrows,** for the lightnings were considered the arrows of the majestic God, **and destroy them.** V. 7. **Send Thine hand from above,** extending it in His almighty power; **rid me,** saving him from drowning, **and deliver me out of great waters from the hand of strange children,** the heathen enemies, the barbarians, v. 8. **whose mouth speaketh vanity,** making statements without the foundation of truth, **and their right hand is a right hand of falsehood,** since it is raised in swearing falsely. The entire picture is that of the powers of the world, the enemies of the Lord and of His people, assembled to work harm to the Church, but overthrown by the manifestation of God's almighty power. Relying upon this fact, the psalmist lifts up his voice in a song of praise. V. 9. **I will sing a new song unto Thee,** one composed for this special occasion, **O God; upon a psaltery,** a sort of harp or lute, **and an instrument of ten strings,** a lyre then in common use, **will I sing praises unto Thee.** V. 10. **It is He that giveth salvation unto kings,** granting them deliverance from great dangers; **who delivereth David, His servant, from the hurtful sword,** that which had caused him evil and misfortune. V. 11. **Rid me,** snatching him away from the danger, **and deliver me from the hand of strange children, whose mouth speaketh vanity, and their right hand is a right hand of falsehood,** this repetition of the appeal just made serving to emphasize the great need of the Lord's interference, v. 12. **that our sons may be as plants grown up in their youth,** thriving in the strength of their youth; **that our daughters may be as corner-stones, polished after the similitude of a palace,** graceful as the architectural ornaments, glistening with gold and brilliant colors, which were found in the reception-halls of Oriental houses, the figure stressing both the strength and the charm of the young women; v. 13. **that our garners may be full, affording all manner of store,** grain of every kind; **that our sheep may bring forth thousands and ten thousands in our streets,** out in the open meadows; v. 14. **that our oxen may be strong to labor,** prolific, bringing forth strong calves; **that there be no breaking in nor going out,** no enemy making a breach in the city walls, no city forced to surrender; **that there be no complaining in our streets,** no lamenting on account of indignities inflicted by cruel conquerors. It is a fine description of happiness and prosperity under the blessing of God. V. 15. **Happy is that people that is in such a case,** whose condition is such as here described; **yea, happy is that people whose God is the Lord;** for that, after all, is the greatest blessing, the highest distinction, surpassing all mere earthly blessings, if a people has the right to call Jehovah their God, their heavenly Father, chosen by Him as His children and blessed with all spiritual blessings in heavenly places in Christ.

PSALM 145.

A Psalm of Praise for the Blessings Due to the Messiah's Exaltation.

David's psalm of praise, dedicated to Messiah for His mighty, righteous, and gracious government of all men, and of His Church in particular. V. 1. **I will extol Thee,** exalting Him high above all mere men, **my God, O King,** Messiah being the King over all by virtue of His exaltation to the right hand of God; **and I will bless Thy name forever and ever,** singing the praises of His divine essence and attributes not only here in time, but throughout eternity. V. 2. **Every day will I bless Thee,** the repetition bringing out the necessity of the constant praise in honor of God and Messiah, the King; **and I will praise Thy name forever and ever.** The song of praise now follows. V. 3. **Great is the Lord and greatly to be praised,** greatness, unsearchable majesty, being the sum of His essence; **and His greatness is unsearchable,** literally, "and to His greatness not is there a search," it cannot be fathomed and comprehended by finite man. V. 4. **One generation shall praise Thy works to another and shall declare Thy mighty acts,** that being the effect which a contemplation of God's greatness, as manifested in His works of creation and redemption, is bound to have upon men, fathers teaching their children and thus keeping the consciousness of God's greatness and majesty alive in their minds. V. 5. **I will speak of the glorious honor of Thy majesty and of Thy wondrous works,** meditating upon the excellent superlative beauty of God's glory and celebrating the redemption through the promised Messiah, the most wonderful theme for prayerful and thankful meditation which can be suggested. V. 6. **And men shall speak of the might of Thy terrible acts,** as the holy God performs His righteous judgments upon the children of men; **and I will declare Thy greatness,** for that is the effect which the acts of God's justice have upon the believers, causing them to set forth the majesty of the Lord. V. 7. **They shall abundantly utter the memory of Thy great goodness,** announcing and proclaiming it, keeping the remembrance of it alive in the minds of men, **and shall sing of Thy righteousness,** shouting for joy over the manifestation of this attribute of God, in dealing with us on the basis of Christ's perfect atonement, thereby giving us evidence of His unfailing interest in the welfare and in the salvation of mankind. V. 8. **The Lord is gracious and full of compassion,** His mercy being revealed in and through Jesus Christ, the Messiah of the world; **slow to anger and of great mercy,** His mercy serving, as it were, as a check upon His anger, keeping it from breaking forth upon us. That is the most wonderful fact in the Bible, that God is great in mercy, full of love and kindness toward us in and through Jesus Christ, our Savior. This Gospel-message is brought out still more strongly in the second part of the psalm. V. 9. **The Lord is good to all, and His tender mercies are over all His works,** manifested to all His creatures, the evidence of this goodness filling the believers with all the greater joy since it tends to confirm them in their trust in Jehovah, in their confidence in His love. V. 10. **All Thy works shall praise Thee, O Lord,** all creatures showing their gratitude to Jehovah by proper thanksgiving, **and Thy saints shall bless Thee;** for the obligation resting upon the believers to give Him grateful credit for the salvation granted to them is greater even than that of men in general with reference to the goodness of God. V. 11. **They shall speak of the glory of Thy kingdom,** especially the Kingdom of Grace, the Church; for it is there that His glory is revealed in the most remarkable way, **and talk of Thy power,** proclaiming with all earnestness His might, as illustrated so frequently in the history of the Church, v. 12. **to make known to the sons of men His mighty acts,** the works of redemption gained for all mankind, **and the glorious majesty of His kingdom,** in spreading the Gospel and its glorious truths throughout the nations. V. 13. **Thy kingdom is an everlasting kingdom,** standing firm through all eternity, the Kingdom of Grace merging into the Kingdom of Glory, the Church Militant into the Church Triumphant, **and Thy dominion endureth throughout all generations,** in the power and mercy of His ruling. V. 14. **The Lord upholdeth all that fall,** literally, "Is holding up Jehovah for all that are falling," keeping them through the Word of His grace, **and raiseth up all those that be bowed down,** rather, "for all those who are bowed down," hearts broken and contrite on account of the realization of their guilt. Cp. Matt. 11, 28. However, it is not only in the Kingdom of Grace that the Messiah's power is exerted, but also in the Kingdom of Power. V. 15. **The eyes of all wait upon Thee,** looking to the Lord for their sustenance, **and Thou givest them their meat in due season,** supplying them with food as they are in need of it. V. 16. **Thou openest Thine hand,** which is like the true horn of plenty, **and satisfiest the desire of every living thing,** His bounty supplying in rich measure what they actually need for their maintenance. To these acts of God's providential care are added those of His government. V. 17. **The Lord is righteous in all His ways and holy in all His works;** being sinless, without a flaw, in His essence, His acts also are of a nature that no justified complaint can be lodged against Him with regard to any of His dealings with men. V. 18.

The Lord is nigh unto all them that call upon Him, to all that call upon Him in truth, their prayer being prompted by, and flowing from, true faith, and being strictly free from all hypocrisy and doubt. V. 19. **He will fulfil the desire of them that fear Him; He also will hear their cry and will save them,** probably not always in the manner in which they had imagined their deliverance, but always in agreement with their longing and therefore in true fulfilment of the prayer of faith, Matt. 21, 22; Mark 11, 24; Jas. 5, 16; 1 John 3, 22. V. 20. **The Lord preserveth all them that love Him,** whose faith finds its expression in childlike love and trust in Him; **but all the wicked will He destroy,** for His avenging wrath is bound to strike all those who persist in their wickedness. All these wonderful facts having been set forth concerning the Lord, the psalmist is constrained to summarize his praise in conclusion: v. 21. **My mouth shall speak the praise of the Lord,** making it his business to extol Him everywhere and at all times; **and let all flesh,** joining the psalmist in his grateful anthem, **bless His holy name forever and ever,** glorifying Him for all the various ways in which He manifested Himself for the benefit of mankind in general and of His Church in particular; for the believers are looking forward to everlasting salvation in heaven.

PSALM 146.

A Hallelujah to the True Helper.

This psalm, whose author is not known, is the first of the five Hallelujah Psalms with which the psalter closes, an invitation to praise the Lord for the merciful and faithful exercise of His power, especially in acts of kindness to the needy. V. 1. **Praise ye the Lord! Praise the Lord, O my soul,** this invitation, addressed to himself, placing the poet in the right mood to continue his hymn with all the vigor of a heart charged with the consciousness of God's fatherly grace and kindness. V. 2. **While I live, will I praise the Lord,** the believer's whole life being filled with songs of thanksgiving to Him whose compassion is new every morning. **I will sing praises unto my God while I have any being,** singing psalms to Him with the most joyful accompaniment upon musical instruments to express the ecstasy of his heart in some adequate manner. V. 3. **Put not your trust in princes,** in any of the mighty ones of the earth, **nor in the son of man,** in any frail human being, **in whom there is no help,** Ps. 60, 11. V. 4. **His breath goeth forth,** or, "when his breath ascends," mortal as he is, when he must yield up his spirit, **he returneth to his earth,** from which the substance of man's body was originally taken, "earth to earth, ashes to ashes, dust to dust," Job 14, 1. 2; **in that very day his thoughts perish,** all his plans are overthrown, whence it follows that reliance upon human beings is foolish. V. 5. **Happy is he that hath the God of Jacob,** the one true, almighty, and eternal God, **for his help, whose hope is in the Lord, his God,** who looks up to the Lord in firm trust, with the feeling of fellowship, of possession; v. 6. **which made heaven and earth, the sea and all that therein is,** who is, in short, the almighty Creator of the universe; **which keepeth truth forever,** fulfilling all His promises with regard to the welfare of men; v. 7. **which executeth judgment for the oppressed,** proving Himself the Champion of those who are suffering from oppression; **which giveth food to the hungry,** supplying all men with their daily bread, manifesting Himself as the Provider of all those who look to Him for maintenance. The thought is now brought out in a series of direct statements. **The Lord looseth the prisoners,** taking from them the yoke and the fetters of their captivity; v. 8. **the Lord openeth the eyes of the blind,** giving them sight; **the Lord raiseth them that are bowed down,** bearing the heavy burden of trials and sorrows; **the Lord loveth the righteous,** the believers to whom His righteousness has been imputed by faith and who strive to walk in His paths; v. 9. **the Lord preserveth the strangers,** who were usually regarded with suspicion and treated with scorn; **He relieveth the fatherless and the widow,** widows and orphans being so often in need of a protector; **but the way of the wicked He turneth upside down,** directing their steps, on their persistently crooked way, toward the destruction of hell. All this, of course, is typical of the manner in which the Lord deals in spiritual matters, the application being made very frequently in the New Testament. Therefore the psalmist concludes: v. 10. **The Lord shall reign forever,** delighting most to rule in love, **even thy God, O Zion,** the congregation of believers, the Church of God, **unto all generations.** The eternal duration of Jehovah's kingdom is also the pledge of its glorious perfection, as the Church Triumphant. **Praise ye the Lord!** Hallelujah to Him now and in eternity!

PSALM 147.

Hallelujah to the God of Zion.

A Hallelujah Psalm, setting forth God's providential care toward all creatures, but especially toward His people, His holy congregation. V. 1. **Praise ye the Lord,** the entire congregation of believers raising its voice to that end; **for it is good to sing praises unto our God,** with whom the believers are joined in the most intimate fellowship and proudly declare their possession of Him; **for it is pleasant, and praise is comely,** it is fitting and appropriate for the faithful to be engaged in singing psalms of praise, a welcome duty. Some of the facts which incite the believers to praise Jehovah are now enumerated. V. 2. **The Lord doth build up Jerusalem;** as He built the earthly Jerusalem in the time of Nehemiah, so He builds the spiritual Jerusalem, His holy congregation, at all times; **He gathereth together the outcasts of Israel,** those who are scattered abroad. V. 3. **He healeth the broken in heart,** those in great distress on account of bitter experiences in their lives, **and bindeth up their wounds,** literally, "their griefs," or "pains." V. 4. **He telleth the number of the stars; He calleth them all by their names,** bringing them forth, by creative action, in numbers agreeing with His almighty intention. The connection of thought is, of course, that He who is familiar with the last detail of creation, knows all the griefs of His children and is easily able to help. Cp. Is. 40, 26. 27. V. 5. **Great is our Lord and of great power,** fully able to help and to save, no matter how severe the difficulties may seem; **His understanding is infinite,** His wisdom can be defined by human beings neither in its depth nor in its fulness, it cannot be figured out by finite minds. V. 6. **The Lord lifteth up the meek,** those who are suffering in humility He raises up from their lowly position; **He casteth the wicked down to the ground,** and the higher they exalt themselves, the greater will be their downfall. All this is comfort to the Church and to every believer, no matter how strange the experiences which befall the faithful. The psalm, therefore, changes its tone to one of joyful summons. V. 7. **Sing unto the Lord with thanksgiving,** in giving all honor to His almighty power and mercy; **sing praise upon the harp,** or "zither," **unto our God;** v. 8. **who covereth the heaven with clouds,** to provide moisture to the earth in due season, **who prepareth rain for the earth, who maketh grass to grow upon the mountains,** far from the cultivated fields of the farmer. V. 9. **He giveth,** as a result and expression of His providential care, **to the beast,** to the animals of the wilderness, **his food and to the young ravens which cry,** which feel their dependence upon His might and care. How much more will the Lord attend to the wants of His children! V. 10. **He delighteth not in the strength of the horse,** which is often used as a type of powerful agility; **He taketh not pleasure in the legs of a man,** in man's physical strength and muscular power. These natural powers will not in themselves save a man nor achieve victory for him. V. 11. **The Lord taketh pleasure in them that fear Him,** who, realizing their own weakness and vanity, feel their full dependence upon Him, reverently trusting in His unmerited favor, **in those that hope in His mercy.** Such trust meets with the pleasure of Jehovah and is therefore followed by security and blessing in city, house, and country. V. 12. **Praise the Lord, O Jerusalem; praise thy God, O Zion,** the summons going out to the entire congregation of Jehovah. V. 13. **For He hath strengthened the bars of thy gates,** Neh. 7, 1—4, protecting His Church against all invaders and enemies; **He hath blessed thy children within thee,** for rich spiritual blessings are dispensed by the Lord through the means of grace in the Church. V. 14. **He maketh peace in thy borders,** enabling His congregation to be built up without the disturbing and distracting influences of steady warfare, **and filleth thee with the finest of the wheat,** with the richest of blessings, Ps. 81, 16. V. 15. **He sendeth forth His commandment upon earth,** as He did at the time of creation, Gen. 1; Ps. 33, 6—9; **His word runneth very swiftly,** in order to accomplish His purposes as speedily as possible. The effect of His almighty commands is now shown. V. 16. **He giveth snow like wool,** the snowflakes coming down like small particles of wool; **He scattereth the hoarfrost like ashes,** all objects being powdered with the congealed dew or fog. V. 17. **He casteth forth His ice like morsels,** namely, in the form of hail; **who can stand before His cold?** All these are small things for the almighty power of Jehovah. V. 18. **He sendeth out His word,** His command, **and melteth them,** the ice, snow, and hail; **He causeth his wind to blow,** as in the case of the foehn of the Alps or the chinook of the northwestern prairies, **and the waters flow,** the congealed masses dissolving beneath the warmth of the spring breezes. But all these manifestations of His almighty power, great as they are, nevertheless are but secondary to the revelations of God's kindness and mercy to His people. V. 19. **He showeth His Word unto Jacob,** the Gospel of His salvation revealed in Law and prophecy, **His statutes and His judgments unto Israel,** thereby separating and distinguishing this people as a peculiar nation, even as the spiritual Israel is holy to Him through the Gospel. V. 20. **He hath not dealt so with any nation,** that is, no heathen nation was chosen by Him in this same manner; and as for **His judgments,** the precepts of His divine justice, as laid down in His written Word, **they have not known them.** It was Israel's privilege to possess the historical, written revelation of the one true God, to this people alone were entrusted the oracles of the Lord, whose gist are the Messianic promises. **Praise ye the Lord!** "The joyful hallelujah is not sounded because these other nations do not possess such a positive knowledge of God's judgments, but because Israel does possess it. It is declared abundantly in other places that this knowledge of Israel shall be the means of making salvation the common property of the whole world of nations." (Delitzsch.)

PSALM 148.

Hallelujah by All Creatures to the God of Salvation.

A song of praise, even more extensive in its scope than the preceding, all heavenly creatures being called upon to join with the beings on earth to give all honor and glory to Jehovah, especially for exalting His people. V. 1. **Praise ye the Lord,** the hallelujah being addressed at once to the highest sphere of creation. **Praise ye the Lord from the heavens,** all the inhabitants of the heavens being called upon to send forth their voices in joyful praise of Jehovah; **praise Him in the heights,** from the heights of heaven. V. 2. **Praise ye Him, all His angels,** the messengers of the supreme Ruler of the universe; **praise ye Him, all His hosts,** the armies of the God of Sabaoth. V. 3. **Praise ye Him, sun and moon,** the largest and most important light-bearers; **praise Him, all ye stars of light,** created to give light upon the earth. V. 4. **Praise Him, ye heavens of heavens,** the very highest heaven, or the fulness of the heavens, as the abode of Almighty God, **and ye waters that be above the heavens,** beyond the firmament, Gen. 1, 7. V. 5. **Let them praise the name of the Lord,** setting forth in grateful songs His wonderful essence and attributes; **for He commanded, and they were created,** Gen. 1, 1. 6; Ps. 33, 6. 9. V. 6. **He hath also stablished them forever and ever,** firmly set them in their place, subject only to the power of His changing hand; **He hath made a decree which shall not pass;** for the laws of nature, as fixed by God, are not subject to change at the whim of the creatures, but the stars must pursue their course, the sun must rise at his appointed time, and all other creatures are guided altogether by the will of the Lord, as manifested in the decrees governing all nature. The psalmist now turns to the creatures of the earth. V. 7. **Praise the Lord from the earth, ye dragons,** the mighty monsters of the sea, **and all deeps,** the great oceans; v. 8. **fire and hail; snow and vapors,** especially the smoke of volcanoes, all of these being phenomena which impressed the people of Canaan all the more since they occur but rarely in that country; **stormy wind fulfilling His word,** for even the destructive agencies of nature are subject to His command or go forth only by His permission; v. 9. **mountains and all hills; fruitful trees,** those of the orchards, **and all cedars,** representing the forest trees; v. 10. **beasts,** the wild animals, **and all cattle,** the domestic animals; **creeping things,** all reptiles and amphibians, **and flying fowl;** v. 11. **kings of the earth,** the individual kings of the various nations, **and all people,** human beings as divided into nations; **princes and all judges of the earth,** those in charge of the administration of justice; v. 12. **both young men and maidens; old men and children,** men of every age and of both sexes: v. 13. **let them praise the name of the Lord,** proclaiming Him as He has revealed Himself in the works of creation; **for His name alone is excellent,** so exalted that no other name may approach His in excellence, incomparable in majesty; **His glory is above the earth and heaven,** His glorious testimony of Himself extends beyond the boundaries of the visible world into infinite space, which He fills. V. 14. **He also exalteth the horn of His people,** establishing the power of His Church, **the praise of all His saints,** for His gift of strength tends to the renown of His people, **even of the children of Israel,** the spiritual Israel, His Church, **a people near unto Him,** united with Him by the bonds of a wonderful fellowship through faith in His love and mercy. **Praise ye the Lord,** in preparation of the more perfect praise which will arise when we shall be delivered from the bondage of corruption into the glorious liberty of the children of God, Rom. 8, 21.

PSALM 149.

Hallelujah to the God of Victory.

A song of praise exhorting particularly the chosen people, the true believers, to praise God for favors of the past, as well as for future victories, which His promise assures them. V. 1. **Praise ye the Lord,** this being the constant occupation of the faithful, their most delightful pastime. **Sing unto the Lord a new song,** one composed under the pressure of new, youthful energy, as the congregation enters upon a new era of growth and prosperity, and **His praise in the congregation of saints,** in the midst of those who have remained faithful to the true God and are impelled to make known the faith of their hearts in open avowal to Him. V. 2. **Let Israel,** the congregation of believers, **rejoice in Him that made him,** who has once more renewed His covenant with His children and established them as His people; **let the children of Zion,** the members of the Church, **be joyful in their King,** in Christ, the Messiah, Ruler of the Kingdom of Grace. V. 3. **Let them praise His name in the dance,** in ecstatic marching and rhythmic leaping, as we read of Miriam and of David, Ex. 15, 20. 21; 2 Sam. 6, 14; **let them sing praises unto Him with the timbrel,** a small kettle-drum, **and harp,** or zither, their hymns accompanied with the most joyful instrumental music. V. 4. **For the Lord taketh pleasure in His people,** accepting their offerings and thereby declaring Himself well pleased with them; **He will beautify the meek with salvation,** adorning those who come to Him with sorrowful, repentant hearts, with faith, hope, joy, and peace. V. 5. **Let the saints be joyful in glory,** on account of the honor granted them by virtue of their adoption as children of God; **let them sing aloud upon their beds,** the change from mourning and lamentation being so great that the day is too short to express the happiness possessing their hearts, for which reason they continue their hymns of praise even after they have retired for the night. V. 6. **Let the high praises of God be in their mouth,** literally, in their throat, to indicate the bubbling over of the joy of their hearts in hymns glorifying Jehovah, **and a two-edged sword in their hand,** signifying their willingness to defend the truth of their belief against the whole world, true soldiers of the Cross, v. 7. **to execute vengeance upon the heathen,** at that time a part of Israel's duty, **and punishments upon the people,** the fleshly warfare having now been replaced by the warfare of the Word, attended by the victories of the Gospel; v. 8. **to bind their kings with chains and their nobles with fetters of iron;** v. 9. **to execute upon them the judgment written,** the proclamation of the Gospel continuing to have the effect of taking captive the hearts of even mighty and learned ones of this world and convincing them of the truth of the Gospel, Is. 53, 12; 49, 23; Rev. 3, 8. 9. **This honor have all His saints,** the glory of being a soldier of the Cross not being confined to the regularly ordained pastors and missionaries, but being the privilege of all Christians, as they are inspired with missionary energy flowing from the Word and go forth to win the Lord's battles. **Praise ye the Lord!** Cp. 2 Cor. 2, 14—17.

PSALM 150.

Concluding Hymn of Praise.

The last Hallelujah Psalm is a fitting doxology for the whole Book of Psalms, proclaiming the place, theme, mode, and extent of God's praise. V. 1. **Praise ye the Lord! Praise God in His Sanctuary,** in the places set aside for His worship here on earth, no matter where they may be; **praise Him in the firmament of His power,** which was considered the foundation of the heavens. Earthly and heavenly places of dwelling and worship are mentioned together to indicate the universal extent of God's worship. V. 2. **Praise Him for His mighty acts,** the miraculous exhibitions of His creative power; **praise Him according to His excellent greatness,** or "abundance of greatness," the absolute and limitless manifestation of His attributes. V. 3. **Praise Him with the sound of the trumpet,** or cornet, as used by the Jews to announce religious assemblies, Num. 10, 1—10; **praise Him with the psaltery,** a kind of lute, **and harp,** or zither. V. 4. **Praise Him with the timbrel,** a form of tambourine, **and dance,** rather, the pipe; **praise Him with stringed instruments and organs,** the latter being a series of graduated pipes used by shepherds. V. 5. **Praise Him upon the loud cymbals,** or castanets; **praise Him upon the high-sounding cymbals,** the larger form, with deeper and fuller tones. Musical instruments of every kind, wood instruments, string instruments, and instruments of percussion — a full orchestra is needed if one would even attempt adequately to sing the praises of Jehovah. V. 6. **Let everything that hath breath praise the Lord,** all living beings joining with their voices to proclaim the glory of His name. **Praise ye the Lord!** "There is nothing in the Psalter more majestic or more beautiful than this brief, but most significant *finale,* in which solemnity of tone predominates, without, however, in the least disturbing the exhilaration which the close of the Psalter intended to produce, as if in emblematical allusion to the triumph which awaits the Church and all its members when, through much tribulation, they shall enter into rest."

THE PROVERBS.

INTRODUCTION.

The third poetical book of the Old Testament is that of the Proverbs of Solomon, not a collection of popular sayings or a product of human speculation and observation, but a book setting forth the principles of true wisdom and making the divine truths the object of believing contemplation. The scope of the wise sayings in this book is to direct all men, but especially the believers, so to order their life and conduct as to please God and promote their welfare here on earth. And there is one outstanding feature in this book, namely, the revelation of the true Source and Fountain of wisdom, the Son of God. He who knows and accepts the Son of God, Jesus Christ, by faith, will bring his entire conduct in life in agreement with the true reverence and fear of the Lord over against the foolishness and blindness of such as despise this true wisdom, the sum of all instruction in the Word of God.

The entire book is ascribed to Solomon, although the last chapters, which were added to the collection at a later time, have as their authors Agur, the son of Jakeh, and King Lemuel. Of Solomon it is stated that he spoke three thousand proverbs, 1 Kings 4, 32. Some of these Solomonic proverbs were gathered together in our book, as the superscriptions of the various sections show: "The proverbs of Solomon, the son of David," chap. 1, 1; "The proverbs of Solomon," chap. 10, 1; "These are the proverbs of Solomon, which the men of Hezekiah, king of Judah, copied out," chap. 25, 1.

The three superscriptions also indicate the divisions of the book. The first section, chaps. 1 to 9, inclusive, contains a description and recommendation of true wisdom, directed especially to young people. The second section, chaps. 10 to 24, is more loosely constructed, the pearls of wisdom following one another in a most telling manner. The third section, chaps. 25 to 29, contains such proverbs as were selected by a committee of prophets at the time of Hezekiah. The book closes with three additions, chap. 30, 1—33; 31, 1—9; 31, 10—31.

The practical wisdom contained in the Book of Proverbs is intended by the Lord for the instruction of all men of all times and should be heeded in this sense also by the Christians of the New Testament. It is the Lord Himself who speaks to men in these sayings, and therefore they are profitable for doctrine, for reproof, for correction, for instruction in righteousness, that a man of God may be perfect, thoroughly furnished unto every good work, 2 Tim. 3, 15—17.[1]

1) Cp. Fuerbringer, *Einleitung in das Alte Testament*, 53—55.

CHAPTER 1.

Wisdom Defined and Introduced in Person.

THE TITLE AND THE INTRODUCTION. — V. 1. **The proverbs of Solomon, the son of David, king of Israel,** 1 Kings 1, 39; 2, 12, a proverb, in this connection, designating a maxim or aphorism rather than a popular proverbial saying; v. 2. **to know,** to become most intimately acquainted with, **wisdom and instruction,** the latter word referring to education, moral training, the practical side of wisdom, by which it finds its application in every-day life; **to perceive the words of understanding,** enabling one to discern between good and evil; v. 3. **to receive the instruction of wisdom, justice, and judgment, and equity,** a training to a reasonable, intelligent condition, to understand what is in agreement with duty and right and uprightness in one's entire behavior; v. 4. **to give subtilty,** cleverness, prudence, discernment, **to the simple,** to all who are too easily inclined to yield to the allurements of sin, **to the young man,** who is still inexperienced, **knowledge and discretion,** the thoughtfulness, circumspection, and caution which weighs every matter carefully and never plunges headlong into danger. The author now shows that writings of this nature will be appreciated by such as are trying to shape their conduct in life in accordance with the will of God. V. 5. **A wise man will hear,** realizing the value of such instruction and therefore yielding a willing ear, **and will increase learning,** adding to the stock already at his disposal, not haughtily insisting that he knows it all; **and a man of understanding,** one who has some insight into the demands of the proper Christian conduct, **shall attain unto wise counsels,** gladly accepting and adopting all the measures which prudent knowledge suggests; v. 6. **to understand a proverb and the interpretation,** that is, enigma, figurative speech, readily to see and apply the lessons contained in the maxims of this book; **the words of the wise and their dark sayings,** the lessons which they clothe in such figures and parabolic utterances that they require careful study. No true wisdom is easily acquired, least of all that pertaining to a God-fearing conduct in life.

A FUNDAMENTAL TRAIT OF WISDOM IS THE

AVOIDANCE OF WICKEDNESS. — V. 7. **The fear of the Lord,** the reverence of Jehovah flowing from childlike faith in Him, **is the beginning of knowledge,** the basis of all true wisdom, both in understanding the Word and will of the Lord and in applying this understanding in one's entire conduct, in every situation of life; **but fools despise wisdom,** learning and knowledge of every kind, **and instruction,** the moral training which follows understanding. V. 8. **My son, hear the instruction of thy father,** his discipline, his teaching, as applied to all matters and conditions of life, **and forsake not the law of thy mother,** setting aside her doctrine, her instructive precepts; v. 9. **for they shall be an ornament of grace unto thy head,** a lovely wreath, or diadem, adorning the head, **and chains about thy neck,** the teachings of wisdom being like a necklace of pearls imparting grace and charm to the wearer. The general admonition is now followed by a specific warning. V. 10. **My son, if sinners,** habitual transgressors of the law, criminals, **entice thee,** literally, "open the way," making it seem inviting and alluring, **consent thou not,** an outright refusal being the only way to cope with such a situation. V. 11. **If they say, Come with us, let us lay wait for blood,** without any reason for revenge, merely out of the lust for slaying; **let us lurk privily for the innocent without cause,** like the huntsman hidden near a game trail; v. 12. **let us swallow them up alive as the grave,** their murder bringing them down to the realm of the dead, **and whole,** while they are living in uprightness and in full possession of God's blessings, **as those that go down into the pit,** who descend into the grave, their plans thus contemplating a most heinous crime, cold-blooded murder; v. 13. **we shall find all precious substance,** rich booty of all kinds, robbery following murder; **we shall fill our houses with spoil,** namely, in this career of ruthless killing and robbing; v. 14. **cast in thy lot among us,** joining them on an equal basis, also in the division of the booty; **let us all have one purse,** one treasury in which they would all share. Such a proposal might place glittering prospects before the eyes of inexperienced youth, and therefore the warning is repeated with great emphasis: v. 15. **My son,** the tender form of address being very effective in influencing a young person for good, **walk not thou in the way with them,** every form of association with the wicked being dangerous; **refrain thy foot from their path,** the mention of a single member of the body increasing the impressiveness of the passage; v. 16. **for their feet run to evil and make haste to shed blood,** wherefore all godly people will shun the pathway of crime. V. 17. **Surely in vain the net is spread in the sight of any bird,** literally, "in the eyes of everything possessing wings," that is, if even a bird will flee from the net which is openly spread in his sight, how much more should a God-fearing young person shun the allurement of crime held out with such boldness! V. 18. **And they lay wait for their own blood,** it is their own lives which are finally taken, either on account of treachery in their own ranks or because murder will certainly be punished at last; **they lurk privily for their own lives,** being caught in the net which they spread for others. V. 19. **So are the ways of every one that is greedy of gain,** that is the fate of all those who choose a career of crime in serving the vice of avarice, **which taketh away the life of the owners thereof,** unjust gain invariably bringing punishment upon the criminal. The love of money is the root of all evil, drawing men into many foolish and hurtful lusts, which drown them in destruction and perdition, 1 Tim. 6, 9. 10.

THE INVITATION OF WISDOM. — V. 20. **Wisdom,** the essence of divine knowledge and true understanding, as set forth throughout the Book of Proverbs, **crieth without,** on the street, in public places, not ashamed of her teaching, but openly seeking the welfare of all; **she uttereth her voice in the streets,** on the principal thoroughfares; v. 21. **she crieth in the chief place of concourse,** where there are crowds of people in noisy surging, **in the openings of the gates,** where market was held in Oriental cities, which served as their public square; **in the city,** on the inner side of the gates, **she uttereth her words, saying,** v. 22. **How long, ye simple ones,** inexperienced and ingenuous people, easily influenced by temptation, **will ye love simplicity and the scorners delight in their scorning,** their open denial and rejection of the truth, **and fools,** who consider themselves above instruction, **hate knowledge?** V. 23. **Turn you at my reproof,** from the evil and perverse way which they were then following. **Behold, I will pour out my Spirit unto you,** in abundant fulness and refreshing power; **I will make known my words unto you,** for the Spirit of the Lord is given in and through His Word. There is a pause here, as though wisdom were waiting for the simple, the scorners, and the fools to accept her invitation. But no answer being forthcoming, a stern rebuke is added. V. 24. **Because I have called, and ye refused,** paying no attention to the kind invitation; **I have stretched out My hand,** in a gesture of eager beseeching, **and no man regarded;** v. 25. **but ye have set at naught all My counsel,** refusing to make use of it and to follow it, **and would none of My reproof,** absolutely declining to consider it, v. 26. **I also will laugh at your calamity,** in holy mockery at their distress; **I will mock when your fear cometh,** when terror would overwhelm them; v. 27. **when your fear cometh as desolation,** like a tempest sweeping everything before it, and your destruction cometh as a whirlwind; when distress and anguish cometh upon you, their oppressing and cramping effect being the result of men's refusing to accept the precepts of true wisdom. V. 28. **Then shall they call upon Me**, praying for wisdom to meet the emergency in which they would find themselves, **but I will not answer; they shall seek Me early**, with the rising of the dawn, with great diligence, **but they shall not find Me**, cp. Amos 8, 11—13. V. 29. **For that they hated knowledge**, when it was offered to them, **and did not choose the fear of the Lord**, the basis and source of all true wisdom; v. 30. **they would none of My counsel**, did not yield to its kind insistence; **they despised all My reproof**, v. 31. **therefore shall they eat of the fruit of their own way**, experiencing the evil consequences of their foolish and wicked action, **and be filled with their own devices**, get their fill of their evil planning even to the point where it sickens them. V. 32. **For the turning away of the simple**, when they turned away from discipline and forsook wisdom, **shall slay them, and the prosperity of fools**, their carnal security, their idle, easy rest, which renders them too proud to seek understanding, **shall destroy them**; for a man's rejection on the part of God is the consequence either of his rejection of the Word or his indifference to its teaching. V. 33. **But whoso hearkeneth unto Me**, yielding a glad obedience, **shall dwell safely, and shall be quiet from fear of evil**, at ease and without fear in the midst of dangers threatening on all sides. Such is the quiet security of the believers, since it is grounded, not in their own wisdom and understanding, but in the eternal wisdom of God, the everlasting Word.

CHAPTER 2.

Invitation to Seek Wisdom.

ADVANTAGES IN ACCEPTING WISDOM. — V. 1. **My son**, so Wisdom, as the proper teacher of all men cries out, **if thou wilt receive my words and hide my commandments with thee**, laying them up in store, guarding them as a precious treasure, v. 2. **so that thou incline thine ear unto wisdom**, yielding a ready obedience, **and apply thine heart to understanding**, ready to accept it, to make use of the right discrimination in every situation in life; v. 3. **yea, if thou criest after knowledge**, calling and inviting it, **and liftest up thy voice for understanding**, in order to be able to distinguish between good and evil, between wise and foolish; v. 4. **if thou seekest her as silver**, with the same eagerness, **and searchest for her as for hid treasures**, with the avidity which avarice induces in a person digging for gold or jewels, v. 5. **then shalt thou understand the fear of the Lord**, making this childlike reverence for Jehovah, the outflow of faith, one's most valuable possession, **and find the knowledge of God**, for the fear of God is the basis of all true wisdom, and its object is God Himself. V. 6. **For the Lord giveth wisdom**, granting it as a gift of His free favor; **out of His mouth cometh knowledge and understanding**, it is a matter of revelation in His Word. The ability of having the right judgment in the various situations in life and of discriminating properly in applying this knowledge is a gift of the Lord. V. 7. **He layeth up sound wisdom for the righteous**, preserving it after the manner of a treasure or a jewel; **He is a buckler to them that walk uprightly**, for wisdom shields all those who exercise themselves in a blameless conduct. V. 8. **He keepeth the paths of judgment**, protecting the ways of justice, the conduct of those who try to behave in agreement with the demands of justice, **and preserveth the way of His saints**, guiding and guarding them from foolish and wicked behavior. V. 9. **Then shalt thou understand righteousness and judgment and equity**, all parts of the duty included in a godly conduct toward God and man; **yea, every good path**, for it is only with the wisdom gained from the Word of God, as the source of true wisdom, that a person's conduct will be in accordance with His will.

WISDOM PRESERVES FROM FOLLY. — V. 10. **When wisdom entereth into thine heart**, not as a transient guest, but for the purpose of making it a permanent residence, **and knowledge is pleasant unto thy soul**, affording the only genuine pleasure and satisfaction, v. 11. **discretion shall preserve thee**, that is, proper reflection, a careful consideration, will serve to keep the prudent from foolish steps, **understanding shall keep thee**, enabling one to judge rightly in any given situation, v. 12. **to deliver thee from the way of the evil man**, from wicked conduct, **from the man that speaketh froward things**, uttering perverse and malicious speeches; v. 13. **who**, that is, such people in general, **leave the paths of uprightness**, where their conduct was in agreement with the Word and will of God, **to walk in the ways of darkness**, being habitually active in the pursuit of wickedness; v. 14. **who rejoice to do evil, and delight in the frowardness**, the maliciousness and deceitfulness, **of the wicked**; v. 15. **whose ways are crooked**, literally, "who with respect to their ways are crooked," **and they froward**, full of malice and deceit, **in their paths**; v. 16. **to deliver thee from the strange woman**, the unknown, foreign, unattached, her existence and way of conduct being full of dangers to youth, **even from the stranger which flattereth with her words,** making use of wanton speeches, v. 17. **which forsaketh the guide of her youth,** her lawful husband, **and forgetteth the covenant of her God,** which demands purity and chastity from every woman. V. 18. **For her house inclineth unto death,** sinking down to destruction, **and her paths unto the dead,** the shadowy forms of those who dwell in the kingdom of the dead, said, in this case, of everlasting damnation. V. 19. **None that go unto her return again,** being swallowed up by the destruction which is her punishment, **neither take they hold of the paths of life,** they forfeit their chance to reach the ways of life once more. Over against the temptation from such wicked men and wanton women is placed the companionship of godly people. V. 20. **That thou mayest walk in the way of good men,** following their conduct, **and keep the paths of the righteous,** that being the object of this admonition. V. 21. **For the upright shall dwell in the land,** enjoying earthly prosperity, as the blessing of the Lord, **and the perfect shall remain in it.** V. 22. **But the wicked shall be cut off from the earth,** utterly destroyed, **and the transgressors shall be rooted out of it,** this punishment being all the greater in the case of the Israelites because their land was the Land of Promise and a removal from it was equivalent to total rejection by the Lord. But the same facts, in substance, apply to men at this time, and therefore the warning of wisdom should be heeded most carefully.

CHAPTER 3.

Exhortation to Various Virtues.

OBEDIENCE, FAITH, AND LIBERALITY URGED. — V. 1. **My son, forget not my law,** the teaching of wisdom, **but let thine heart keep my commandments,** sincerely observing all instructions of God's Word; v. 2. **for length of days and long life and peace,** literally, "years of life and peace," **shall they add to thee,** earthly prosperity and happiness following the application of knowledge gained from the divine Law. V. 3. **Let not mercy and truth,** both on the part of men and on the part of God, **forsake thee,** loving sympathy and companionship being one of the prime factors in our moral life; **bind them about thy neck,** like a costly chain or necklace, from which was suspended the seal-ring; **write them upon the table of thine heart,** the emphasis being both upon the inward motives and upon the outward expression and adornment in the way of virtues. V. 4. **So shalt thou find favor,** gracious acceptance, **and good understanding,** good reputation, good success, **in the sight of God and man,** the good opinion on the part of men corresponding to the favorable judgment on the part of God, and both serving for the success of the believer. This being a gracious gift on the part of God, the godly person is warned: v. 5. **Trust in the Lord with all thine heart,** committing oneself entirely to the grace and faithfulness of Jehovah, **and lean not unto thine own understanding,** in false and blameworthy self-confidence. V. 6. **In all thy ways acknowledge Him,** by reposing one's trust in Him and relying entirely upon His wisdom, **and He shall direct thy paths,** for the benefit and well-being of His child. V. 7. **Be not wise in thine own eyes,** puffed up with an imagined superiority on account of possible greater learning, since the wisdom of this world is not essential before God; **fear the Lord,** such reverence for Jehovah serving to set aside one's own wisdom, **and depart from evil,** this course being natural in the case of a child of God, to whom all wickedness is undesirable and loathsome. V. 8. **It shall be health to thy navel,** considered as the center of the entire body, **and marrow to thy bones,** refreshing the entire organism with vigor and strength; for such is the effect of a good conscience and of an honest endeavor to serve the Lord in faith. V. 9. **Honor the Lord with thy substance,** with the riches which one enjoys as His blessing, repaying Him from the gifts granted by Him, **and with the first-fruits of all thine increase,** the yield of one's work and the harvest of one's land, for mere lip-service is not sufficient, the Lord demanding tangible evidence of the faith which His children profess to possess; v. 10. **so shall thy barns be filled with plenty,** as a reward of God's gracious favor and fatherly kindness, **and thy presses,** rather, the vats where the wine was stored, **shall burst out with new wine,** overflowing with rich abundance by the blessing of God, with which He would acknowledge the willingness of His children. But the opposite also holds true: As we should not forget the Lord in days of plenty, so we should not be estranged from Him in evil days. V. 11. **My son, despise not the chastening of the Lord,** the correction which He deals out in the school of life; **neither be weary of His correction,** regarding it with loathing and aversion; v. 12. **for whom the Lord loveth He correcteth,** and so the person subject to His discipline thereby receives a proof of His love; **even as a father the son in whom he delighteth,** or, "holds him dear as a father his son," in whose case the lack of discipline is rightly referred to a want of fatherly love. Cp. Job 5, 17; Heb. 12, 5. 6.

THE HAPPINESS OF POSSESSING TRUE WISDOM. — V. 13. **Happy is the man that findeth wisdom,** obtaining it with eagerness and holding it securely, **and the man that getteth understanding,** drawing or digging it out, even with much labor. V. 14. **For the merchandise of it,** the act of gaining or acquiring wisdom, **is better than the merchandise of silver,** such as men are eager to accumulate, **and the gain thereof than fine gold,** even though it be of the finest and purest kind. V. 15. **She is more precious than rubies,** or corals, gems of the greatest costliness; **and all the things thou canst desire are not to be compared unto her,** wisdom surpassing them all by far. Cp. Job 28, 18. V. 16. **Length of days is in her right hand,** as a reward to those who accept and exercise true wisdom; **and in her left hand riches and honor,** all the blessings of true prosperity being dispensed by her. V. 17. **Her ways are ways of pleasantness,** with never a disagreeable feature to mar one's enjoyment of true wisdom, **and all her paths are peace,** without the strife and alarm found where human wisdom is proclaimed. V. 18. **She is a tree of life to them that lay hold upon her,** her fruit preserving life, so that living is a blessing; **and happy is every one that retaineth her,** keeping a firm hold upon this wonderful species of knowledge learned from the Word of God. V. 19. **The Lord by wisdom hath founded the earth,** by means of His personal, essential wisdom, which He has also revealed in His Word; **by understanding hath He established the heavens,** preparing them with proper discrimination and judgment. V. 20. **By his knowledge the depths are broken up,** the seas did divide, breaking forth from the chaotic mass of formless matter and occupying their fixed places, **and the clouds drop down the dew,** the rain still falling in agreement with His laws. From the majesty with which the work of creation portrays the wisdom of the Lord the author now deduces admonitions which should be heeded by all the godly. V. 21. **My son, let not them depart from thine eyes,** namely, these words of instruction, lest they escape in a moment when vigilance is relaxed; **keep sound wisdom and discretion,** or "thoughtfulness and circumspection," prudence properly applied in all affairs of life; v. 22. **so shall they be life unto thy soul and grace,** or charm, **to thy neck,** like an ornament, a fine bit of jewelry. V. 23. **Then shalt thou walk in thy way safely,** free from anxiety and care, secure in the Lord's protection, **and thy foot shall not stumble,** on account of some obstruction with which the enemies attempt to bring the godly to fall. V. 24. **When thou liest down, thou shalt not be afraid,** be filled with anxious trembling; **yea, thou shalt lie down, and thy sleep shall be sweet,** untroubled by any notion of impending danger, like that of a child. V. 25. **Be not afraid of sudden fear,** such an alarm as would tend to fill the heart with terror, **neither of the desolation of the wicked when it cometh,** who would come sweeping along like a destructive tempest. V. 26. **For the Lord shall be thy Confidence,** a safe place of refuge, **and shall keep thy foot from being taken,** in the snares which the godless are always spreading for the feet of the unwary for which reason the believers are all the more under obligations to make use of the true wisdom in keeping their feet on the right path.

WARNING AGAINST EVIL. — V. 27. **Withhold not good from them to whom it is due,** to whom it belongs by reason of his need, whether he really deserves it or is so destitute that he can no longer help himself, **when it is in the power of thine hand to do it.** V. 28. **Say not unto thy neighbor, Go and come again, and to-morrow I will give,** thus putting him off and discouraging him, **when thou hast it by thee.** Cp. Jas. 2, 15. 16. V. 29. **Devise not evil against thy neighbor,** by meditating upon wickedness and contriving it, **seeing he dwelleth securely by thee,** without suspicion. V. 30. **Strive not with a man without cause,** thus increasing litigation, both within the Church and without, **if he have done thee no harm,** both the taking of the initiative in quarreling and of seeking revenge for a supposed insult being condemned here. V. 31. **Envy thou not the oppressor,** the man of violence or mischief, no matter how successful his methods may seem, **and choose none of his ways,** in the hope of rising in the world by such methods. V. 32. **For the froward,** the malicious person, the deceiver, **is abomination,** an abhorrence, **to the Lord,** wherefore his lot will be that of everlasting destruction; **but His secret is with the righteous,** literally, "toward the upright His secret compact," they enjoy His friendship, the intimate fellowship with Him. V. 33. **The curse of the Lord is in the house of the wicked,** in spite of all outward semblance of prosperity and happiness; **but He blesseth the habitation of the just,** His blessing abiding with them. V. 34. **Surely He scorneth the scorners,** that is, if there is a person who believes himself entitled to scorn, He heaps scorn upon him; **but He giveth grace unto the lowly,** to the humble, who seek only His grace and mercy and claim no merit and worthiness for themselves. V. 35. **The wise shall inherit glory,** they will finally be given the honor which their attitude merits; **but shame shall be the promotion of fools,** that will be the reward which they will carry away with them, the portion properly pertaining to them. That is the consolation of the righteous, that in the end they will be honored by the Lord in the presence of the whole world; this thought enables them to bear many of the afflictions of this present time.

CHAPTER 4.

The Weight of Parental Counsel.

ADMONITIONS CONCERNING WISDOM. — V. 1. **Hear, ye children,** the affectionate address being intended to arouse attention in his readers, **the instruction of a father,** one who, for that reason, had the experience needed to teach others, **and attend to know understanding,** to make it their property. V. 2. **For I give you good doctrine,** teachings which he had received from his father, the value of which had been proved, which he could therefore hand over to the younger generation with words of warm commendation; **forsake ye not my law,** by setting his advice aside, by neglecting it. V. 3. **For I was my father's son,** an object of special care and tender regard in David's eyes, **tender and only beloved in the sight of my mother,** the one whom she surrounded with particular love. V. 4. **He taught me also and said unto me,** David thus proving himself a wise teacher, **Let thine heart retain my words,** holding them fast for the purpose of following them always; **keep my commandments and live,** for by observing them he would become the possessor of true life and enjoy its advantages. V. 5. **Get wisdom, get understanding,** that being the sum total of David's instruction; **forget it not,** clinging to it as a most valuable possession; **neither decline from the words of my mouth,** literally, "forget not, turn not aside from, the sayings of my mouth," as they were offered in the maxims which Solomon heard time and again. V. 6. **Forsake her not,** the wisdom which was here so highly praised, **and she shall preserve thee,** serve as a protection against bad influences and uphold true life; **love her, and she shall keep thee,** this being the reward dispensed by wisdom. V. 7. **Wisdom is the principal thing,** the highest and most desirable possession; **therefore get wisdom,** this being suggested as the guiding rule of life; **and with all thy getting,** at the price of all one's possessions, no matter how much it costs, **get understanding,** the prudence and discretion needed for a virtuous life. V. 8. **Exalt her, and she shall promote thee,** this being the wonderful exchange made by wisdom in rewarding her followers; **she shall bring thee to honor when thou dost embrace her,** wisdom being personified here as a beloved and honored wife, queen of the home. V. 9. **She shall give to thine head an ornament of grace,** a graceful or charming wreath, for so wisdom serves to adorn its possessor; **a crown of glory shall she deliver to thee,** a glorious diadem, which bestows dignity. V. 10. **Hear, O my son, and receive my sayings, and the years of thy life shall be many,** a long and happy life being one of the rewards granted to him who uses knowledge aright. V. 11. **I have taught thee in the way of wisdom,** in the conduct which is in agreement with the precepts of true wisdom; **I have led thee in right paths,** literally, "in the paths of straightness," following the standard of right always. V. 12. **When thou goest, thy steps shall not be straitened,** be hindered and confined by obstructions, **and when thou runnest, thou shalt not stumble,** rather have ample room for a full and free stride. V. 13. **Take fast hold of instruction,** the moral training given by wisdom; **let her not go; keep her; for she is thy life,** by bestowing long life and happiness upon those who are devoted to her. That is the sum of instruction which should be given to all young people in an appropriate and effective manner.

WARNING AGAINST WICKEDNESS. — V. 14. **Enter not into the path of the wicked,** to join them in their godless conduct, **and go not in the way of evil men,** such behavior being incompatible with true wisdom. V. 15. **Avoid it, pass not by it,** not only by ignoring, but by utterly rejecting the way of evil, **turn from it and pass away,** if one should inadvertently have strayed into such paths. V. 16. **For they,** the wicked, **sleep not except they have done mischief,** the fact that they have not committed some trespass keeps the sleep from their eyes; **and their sleep is taken away unless they cause some to fall,** by betraying others and leading them into sin. V. 17. **For they eat the bread of wickedness and drink the wine of violence,** of violent deeds, they seem to derive their strength from wicked acts, their means of subsistence are obtained in that manner. V. 18. **But the path of the just is as the shining light,** like the growing brightness of dawn as it heralds and ushers in the day, **that shineth more and more unto the perfect day,** growing brighter with each succeeding minute, the comparison of the moral conduct of the righteous with the light of the rising sun being most appropriate; for he goes forward to ever greater clearness and perfection, not only in his inward knowledge, but also in its outward manifestation. V. 19. **The way of the wicked is as darkness,** directly opposite to that of the righteous; **they know not at what they stumble,** they flounder around in immorality, going from bad to worse in their behavior. V. 20. **My son, attend to my words; incline thine ear unto my sayings,** the admonition and warning going out once more, with a special reference to the ruinous consequences which the forgetting and ignoring of wisdom is sure to bring about. V. 21. **Let them not depart from thine eyes,** so that they escape when vigilance is relaxed for so much as a moment; **keep them in the midst of thine heart,** so that this treasure will not be lost. V. 22. **For they are life**

unto those that find them, cp. chap. 3, 2. 16; 4, 13, **and health to all their flesh,** to their whole body, since observing them results not only in moral and mental, but also in physical advantages, by a healthful reaction. V. 23. **Keep thy heart with all diligence,** literally, "more than every object of watching guard thy heart," the seat of moral life; **for out of it are the issues of life,** as Jesus also points out, Matt. 12, 35; 15, 19. V. 24. **Put away from thee a froward mouth,** deceitful and malicious speaking, **and perverse lips,** those misdirected toward evil, **put far from thee.** V. 25. **Let thine eyes look right on,** straight ahead, without any self-seeking, **and let thine eyelids look straight before thee,** intent upon the duties of each day and hour. V. 26. **Ponder the path of thy feet,** making it straight, avoiding errors and sins, **and let all thy ways be established,** the entire conduct guided by wise forethought. V. 27. **Turn not to the right hand nor to the left,** to by-paths of evil; **remove thy foot from evil,** withdrawing it at once in case of danger. The entire admonition may fitly be summarized in the words of the Lord: "Watch and pray that ye enter not into temptation; the spirit indeed is willing, but the flesh is weak," Matt. 26, 41.

CHAPTER 5.

The Evils of Unchastity.

Warning against Wantonness. — V. 1. **My son, attend unto my wisdom,** giving heed to its precepts, **and bow thine ear,** in the attitude of the most careful listening, **to my understanding,** both the possession of knowledge and the proper exercise of discrimination in applying it to the various situations of life being urged, v. 2. **that thou mayest regard discretion,** the reflection and consideration needed for circumspect behavior, **and that thy lips may keep knowledge,** preserving its instructions word for word and repeating them often, lest they be forgotten. This is placed in contrast to the seductions of the wanton woman. V. 3. **For the lips of a strange woman,** of a harlot, **drop as an honeycomb,** with seductive invitations, **and her mouth is smoother than oil,** in framing flattering and alluring speeches; v. 4. **but her end,** her future, the reward which is sure to strike her, **is bitter as wormwood,** the universal emblem of poisonous bitterness, **sharp as a two-edged sword,** such is the final result of yielding to her seductions. V. 5. **Her feet go down to death,** whither she leads all those who have yielded to her blandishments; **her steps take hold on hell,** the course of her life ends in everlasting destruction. V. 6. **Lest thou shouldest ponder the path of life,** or, "Far from treading the pathway of life," **her ways are movable,** her steps stray from that which is right and good, **that thou canst not know them,** rather, she knows not whither and does not seem to care, the result being that all who attempt to follow her will be stricken with a dizziness which will prevent them from seeing and considering in a normal manner. V. 7. **Hear me now, therefore, O ye children, and depart not from the words of my mouth,** this admonition being based upon the picture just drawn and introducing the following warning. V. 8. **Remove thy way far from her,** for safety, in the case of this temptation, does not lie in attempting to give battle, but in fleeing and keeping one's distance, **and come not nigh the door of her house,** thereby risking and inviting temptation, v. 9. **lest thou give thine honor unto others,** for there is not only the exposure of the fornicator to be considered, but also the fact that the harlot and her favorites will succeed in taking the respect of men from their victim, **and thy years unto the cruel,** the wanton woman and the procurers employed by her, who calmly and cruelly ruin the health of those who are seduced by them and take their riches into the bargain; v. 10. **lest strangers be filled with thy wealth,** enjoying their fill in consuming the labor and strength of their victim, **and thy labors,** what a man has worked for with hard labor, **be in the house of a stranger,** the harlot being so designated because originally all that plied her trade were foreigners, v. 11. **and thou mourn at the last,** groaning in distress when it is too late, **when thy flesh and thy body are consumed,** this being the punishment which will eventually strike the libertine, v. 12. **and say, How have I hated instruction,** as here given, **and my heart despised reproof,** by which earnest men, true friends, tried to keep him from the path of lewdness; v. 13. **and have not obeyed the voice of my teachers nor inclined mine ear to them that instructed me!** Such is the vain lament of the ruined sinner over his neglect of warning and his sad fate in being brought to public disgrace. V. 14. **I was almost in all evil in the midst of the congregation and assembly,** literally, "Almost I had been in the extremity of evil in the midst of assembly and congregation," that is, he had just barely escaped the height of ruin, open condemnation in the midst of the congregation, which might have resulted in severe punishment for him. Such is the way of sin, to hold alluring temptations before the eyes of the unwary and then to plunge him into the greatest misery, the victim's repentance often coming too late.

Chastity Contrasted with Unchastity. — V. 15. **Drink waters out of thine own cistern and running waters out of thine own**

well, seeking the satisfaction of permitted desire and intercourse only and alone within the bounds of holy wedlock. V. 16. **Let thy fountains be dispersed abroad and rivers of waters in the streets**, in the proper enjoyment of marital love. V. 17. **Let them be only thine own**, that is, the waters of this fountain in lawful wedlock, **and not strangers' with thee**, in illegitimate intercourse. V. 18. **Let thy fountain be blessed**, the children of lawful wedlock being gifts of the Lord, **and rejoice with the wife of thy youth.** Cp. Deut. 24, 5; Eccl. 9, 9. V. 19. **Let her be as the loving hind and pleasant roe**, or the graceful gazelle, emblems of the graceful, fascinating, lively nature of a young wife; **let her breasts satisfy thee at all times**, her bosom charming her husband, **and be thou ravished always with her love**, said of the ecstatic joy of the loving husband which meets with the glad approval of God within holy wedlock. V. 20. **And why wilt thou, my son, be ravished with a strange woman**, with a wanton harlot, professing the same delight in her company which he might and should lawfully have with the wife given him by the Lord, **and embrace the bosom of a stranger?** of one in whose case such familiarity is excluded by the prohibition of the Sixth Commandment. V. 21. **For the ways of man are before the eyes of the Lord, and He pondereth all his goings**, His omniscience marking the conduct of every person and noting every unchaste desire, thought, word, and act. V. 22. **His own iniquities shall take the wicked himself**, overtake every evil-doer, **and he shall be holden with the cords of his sins**, as fetters holding him captive and keeping him securely for the final punishment. V. 23. **He shall die without instruction**, for want of correction, because he would not accept it, **and in the greatness of his folly he shall go astray**, thus bringing destruction upon himself. Such is the way of the libertine, a few years of forbidden voluptuousness followed by everlasting condemnation.

CHAPTER 6.

Of Various Sins against the Second Table.

WARNING AGAINST FOOLISH SURETYSHIP, IDLENESS, AND MALICE. — V. 1. **My son, if thou be surety for thy friend**, pledging himself or giving security for the debts of another, **if thou hast stricken thy hand with a stranger**, giving his hand to any neighbor in need, to any debtor as a sign of binding oneself for his debts, Job 17, 3, v. 2. **thou art snared with the words of thy mouth**, or, "if thou art entangled with the sayings of thy mouth," **thou art taken**, held captive, **with the words of thy mouth**, held to his promise, this referring to the situation arising when the debtor finds himself unable to meet his obligations. V. 3. **Do this now, my son, and deliver thyself**, tearing himself loose from the entanglement, **when thou art come into the hand of thy friend**, or, "since thou hast come into the hand of thy neighbor," this being the unfortunate consequence of the pledge lightly given. **Go, humble thyself**, rather, "stamp with thy foot," in an emphatic demand, **and make sure thy friend**, importuning him with great earnestness to fulfil his obligations, to tend to the payment of the debt before it is too late. V. 4. **Give not sleep to thine eyes nor slumber to thine eyelids**, the most strenuous, ceaseless endeavors being demanded by the situation. V. 5. **Deliver thyself as a roe from the hand of the hunter**, literally, "from his," the debtor's, "hand," bending every effort, with anxiety and exertion, **and as a bird from the hand of the fowler.** Prompt and energetic action will be necessary to avoid serious trouble. The author now sets forth the kind of person who is most apt to require surety, the connection of thought probably being this, that the man who went security might be considered as speaking to the lazy debtor in this manner: v. 6. **Go to the ant**, the proverbial emblem of industry, **thou sluggard; consider her ways**, carefully observing how she makes provision for herself, **and be wise**, learning wisdom from the irrational insect; v. 7. **which, having no guide, overseer, or ruler**, none of the officials who were and are required in Oriental countries to oversee the average workman, v. 8. **provideth her meat**, her winter's supply of food, **in the summer and gathereth her food in the harvest**, in the heat of late summer, storing it away carefully for the time of need. V. 9. **How long wilt thou sleep, O sluggard?** lying abed in laziness. **When wilt thou arise out of thy sleep?** And now the conduct of the lazy is graphically described, v. 10. **Yet a little sleep, a little slumber**, an ironical imitation of the sigh of the sluggard, **a little folding of the hands to sleep!** But what is the result? V. 11. **So shall thy poverty come as one that traveleth**, not merely a vagrant, but a footpad, **and thy want as an armed man**, one armed with a shield, prepared for both offense and defense, so that the sluggard is overwhelmed before he has seriously thought of warding off danger. — The mention of the footpad, or robber, now results in the description of violent and malicious men. V. 12. **A naughty person**, morally worthless, **a wicked man**, the heedless man being a vile deceiver, **walketh with a froward mouth**, exercising himself in perverseness of speech, so addicted to malicious falsehood that he is a stranger to truth. V. 13. **He winketh with his eyes,** as a signal to his companions to join him in some act of malice, **he speaketh with his feet,** giving signs with a similar intention, **he teacheth with his fingers,** hinting with them in a form of sign language understood by his fellows; v. 14. **frowardness is in his heart,** malicious plans of every description, **he deviseth mischief continually,** in agreement with his wicked nature; **he soweth discord,** throwing out matters of dispute, stirring up strife, fomenting quarrels. V. 15. **Therefore shall his calamity come suddenly,** a crushing weight of destruction overtaking him before he is aware of it; **suddenly shall he be broken without remedy,** without a chance to escape, when the measure of his sins is full. In this connection the author enumerates some of the things which challenge the punishment of the Lord. V. 16. **These six things doth the Lord hate, yea, seven are an abomination unto Him,** He regards them all with loathing and abhorrence: v. 17. **a proud look,** a haughty and supercilious behavior, **a lying tongue,** the organ of speech being named here for the false person, **and hands that shed innocent blood,** cp. Is. 59, 7, v. 18. **an heart that deviseth wicked imaginations,** always planning mischief, **feet that be swift in running to mischief,** unable to restrain their eagerness for every form of wickedness, v. 19. **a false witness that speaketh lies,** literally, "breatheth out lies," since he is addicted to that habit, **and he that soweth discord among brethren,** turning friends and relatives against one another. Against all these sins the inspired writer warns the believers of all times, since Satan, as a roaring lion, walketh about, seeking whom he may devour.

WARNING DEPICTING THE CONSEQUENCES OF UNCHASTITY. — V. 20. **My son, keep thy father's commandment,** the function of parents consisting also in this, that they guide and guard their growing children with reference to the dangers here described, **and forsake not the law,** the instruction and the precepts, **of thy mother.** V. 21. **Bind them continually upon thine heart,** keeping them in loving remembrance, **and tie them about thy neck,** like a string of precious jewels. The fundamental idea is this, that the entrance of evil thoughts should be prevented by supplying good material for contemplation always, since an idle mind is the devil's workshop. V. 22. **When thou goest, it shall lead thee,** that is, the instruction of the parents would be the guide of the growing children; **when thou sleepest,** even in dreams, **it shall keep thee; and when thou awakest, it shall talk with thee,** the instruction of true wisdom filling the thoughts with proper material and directing all the conduct of a person. V. 23. **For the commandment is a lamp, and the Law is light,** its instruction serving not only to enlighten the heart and mind of man, but also to guide him on his way, Ps. 119, 105; **and reproofs of instruction are the way of life,** because they serve for discipline and correction, bidding a person do the right and forsake the wrong, thereby urging him onward on the way of sanctification; v. 24. **to keep thee from the evil woman,** the woman of vileness and wantonness, **from the flattery of the tongue of a strange woman,** the speech of the harlot being smooth and oily in its allurement. V. 25. **Lust not after her beauty in thine heart,** for the inward unchastity is also sinful and has evil consequences; **neither let her take thee with her eyelids,** with the wanton and captivating glances with which she tries to ensnare her victims. V. 26. **For by means of a whorish woman a man is brought to a piece of bread,** brought to utter poverty as a result of satisfying her demands, **and the adulteress will hunt for the precious life,** lying in wait to destroy a man's soul, since her victim loses liberty, purity, honor, and dignity by submitting to her advances. It is a most serious matter which is here broached, and therefore the prophet tries to bring home his lesson with proper emphasis. V. 27. **Can a man take fire in his bosom,** attempt to carry it in that manner, **and his clothes not be burned?** V. 28. **Can one go upon hot coals,** upon fiery, glowing coals or cinders, **and his feet not be burned?** The answer, of course, will be a most emphatic *no.* V. 29. **So he that goeth in to his neighbor's wife,** in adulterous intimacy; **whosoever toucheth her shall not be innocent,** that is, he shall most assuredly be guilty. V. 30. **Men do not despise a thief,** literally, "heap contempt and shame upon him," although they do insist upon his punishment, **if he steal to satisfy his soul when he is hungry,** that is, when only the greatest extremity of hunger causes him to steal in order to get something to eat; v. 31. **but if he be found, he shall restore sevenfold; he shall give all the substance of his house,** be held responsible for his theft with all that he possesses, even beyond the ordinary four- and fivefold restoration, Ex. 21, 37; 22, 1; Luke 19, 8. V. 32. **But whoso committeth adultery with a woman lacketh understanding,** he is deficient both in moral principle and prudence, he risks more than any reasonable man would chance; **he that doeth it destroyeth his own soul,** it is only the self-destroyer, closely related to the suicide, who would be so foolish, since men judge the adulterer much more harshly. V. 33. **A wound and dishonor shall he get,** namely, from the enraged husband and his relatives; **and his reproach shall not be wiped away,** it is an extreme case of self-defamation. V. 34. **For jealousy is the rage of a man,** in this way the wrath of the injured husband burns, with fierce raging; **therefore he will not spare in the day of vengeance,** when the facts of the crime become known and have been proved. V. 35. **He will not regard any ransom,** with which the guilty man might seek to placate him and keep him from demanding the limit of punishment; **neither will he rest content though thou givest many gifts,** he will not be found willing to forego his strict right of revenge. Such is the warning held before the adulterer, the force of which is by no means spent in our days.

CHAPTER 7.

Condemnation of Fornication and Adultery.

On account of the terrible devastation wrought by sins of adultery and by every gratification of sexual desires outside of holy wedlock, affecting not only the sinners themselves, but the entire social body, Solomon continues his warning in this entire chapter in a very concrete and effective manner, the subject being introduced with the usual impressive admonitions to heed and follow true wisdom. V. 1. **My son, keep my words,** observing his sayings, **and lay up my commandments with thee,** like a precious treasure, to be used with discretion. V. 2. **Keep my commandments and live,** true life following the exercise of true wisdom, **and my law as the apple of thine eye,** literally, "as the little man of thine eye," emblem of a very precious possession, guarded with the greatest care. V. 3. **Bind them upon thy fingers,** like an ornament or ring, to serve as a constant reminder; **write them upon the table of thine heart,** for the remembering was to be not only in the mind, but in the heart, in true and eager love. V. 4. **Say unto wisdom, Thou art my sister,** with whom he should be united in the bonds of confidential fellowship; **and call understanding thy kinswoman,** in order to enjoy her counsel always, no mere distant acquaintance being sufficient, but a familiarity of relationship which would be of real value, v. 5. **that they may keep thee from the strange woman,** the harlots in Israel being originally foreigners, **from the stranger which flattereth with her words,** her object being to allure and seduce with smooth speeches. The author now brings an illustration from life in order to substantiate his argument. V. 6. **For at the window of my house I looked through my casement,** through the lattice-work found on Oriental windows which face the street, v. 7. **and beheld among the simple ones,** those inexperienced in matters of this life, in the ways of men, **I discerned among the youths,** the youngsters, those in the dangerous age when they resent instruction, **a young man void of understanding,** clearly lacking in judgment, v. 8. **passing through the street near her corner,** where harlots were accustomed to linger for the purpose of accosting; **and he went the way to her house,** the very slow sauntering, strolling, or pacing being a sign of imprudence, v. 9. **in the twilight, in the evening, in the black and dark night,** the heaping of expressions fitting the actions of the young man as belonging to the works of darkness; v. 10. **and, behold, there met him a woman with the attire of an harlot,** the Hebrew expression referring either to indecent exposure or to a decorating of the bosom to draw attention to its charms, **and subtile of heart,** hypocritical and two-faced, simulating faithfulness and love in the presence of her husband, but flattering strange men in wanton abandonment. (V. 11. **She is loud,** stormily excited, **and stubborn,** ungovernable; **her feet abide not in her house,** where her duty to her husband should have kept her; v. 12. **now is she without, now in the streets, and lieth in wait at every corner,** her progress from before her own door to the street and then to the intersection of streets being graphically portrayed.) V. 13. **So she caught him and kissed him,** such kisses being the very essence of unchastity, **and with an impudent face said unto him,** literally, "she put on a bold face in inviting him," v. 14. **I have peace-offerings with me; this day have I paid my vows,** that is, she had, on the day which was just coming to a close or had closed with sundown, brought a thank-offering to the Lord, the rule being that the flesh must be eaten at a sacrificial meal on the second day, at the latest, Lev. 7, 16. It was this meal which she wanted the young man to share with her, in the privacy of her own chambers. V. 15. **Therefore came I forth to meet thee, diligently to seek thy face,** the flattery consisting in her singling out this victim, as though he alone had been in her thoughts, whereas practically any other man would have answered her purpose just as well, **and I have found thee.** V. 16. **I have decked my bed with coverings of tapestry,** with beautiful and costly upholstering and pillows, **with carved works, with fine linen of Egypt,** that is, with variegated coverlets of Egyptian linen. V. 17. **I have perfumed my bed with myrrh, aloes, and cinnamon,** sprinkling it with sweet-smelling spices. V. 18. **Come, let us take our fill of love until the morning; let us solace ourselves with loves,** the intoxicating quality of illicit love being brought out very strongly. V. 19. **For the goodman,** of whom the wife speaks in a cold and distant manner, **is not at home, he is gone a long journey,** the implication being that he is far enough away and they need fear no discovery; v. 20. **he hath taken a bag of money with him,** this showing that his business was important and took some time, **and will come home at the day appointed,** he had named the day of the next full moon as the day of his return. In this way the wanton woman met all possible objections of her victim in advance. V. 21. **With her much fair speech she caused him to yield,** she brought him around, she broke down his resistance, **with the flattering of her lips she forced him,** the young man being no match for the skilful and enticing rhetoric which the adulteress knew to employ. V. 22. **He goeth after her straightway,** at once, with passionate promptness, the text indicating that this is always the case in similar situations, **as an ox goeth to the slaughter or as a fool to the correction of the stocks,** that is, as one who has lost his right mind is caught and fettered, v. 23. **till a dart strike through his liver,** an arrow dividing his vital organs; **as a bird hasteth to the snare and knoweth not that it is for his life,** the young man of the story and all victims like him not realizing that their life, their soul's welfare, is at stake. V. 24. **Hearken unto me now therefore, O ye children, and attend to the words of my mouth,** this exhortation receiving added weight on account of the story to which it is attached. V. 25. **Let not thine heart decline to her ways,** those of the harlot, **go not astray in her paths.** V. 26. **For she hath cast down many wounded,** many are those who have fallen victims to her wiles; **yea, many strong men have been slain by her,** both in body and soul. V. 27. **Her house is the way to hell,** literally, "ways of hell her house," **going down to the chambers of death.** That is the inevitable consequence of an immoral life: eternal destruction in the abyss of hell.

CHAPTER 8.

Of the Messiah, the Personal Wisdom.

THE RICHNESS OF WISDOM'S GIFTS. — V. 1. **Doth not Wisdom cry,** calling aloud to men to hear, **and understanding put forth her voice,** in an effort to reach all men? V. 2. **She standeth in the top of high places,** on the top of high places along the way, easily to be seen by all who pass by, **by the way in the places of the paths,** at the cross-roads. V. 3. **She crieth at the gates,** standing where the roads converge and many people come together, **at the entry of the city, at the coming in at the doors,** at the outside of the gateway, where multitudes were wont to assemble. V. 4. **Unto you, O men, I call, and My voice is to the sons of man,** the implication being that not one human being is excepted from the message herewith proclaimed. The sum of the proclamation is now offered: v. 5. **O ye simple, understand wisdom,** in order to be able to apply it properly, **and ye fools, be ye of an understanding heart,** using prudence and discrimination in all situations of life. V. 6. **Hear; for I will speak of excellent things,** stated in plain terms, but with noble and princely contents, **and the opening of My lips shall be right things,** uprightness in every respect. V. 7. **For My mouth shall speak truth,** literally, "My palate meditateth truth," reflecting upon it, considering it always, **and wickedness is an abomination to My lips.** V. 8. **All the words of My mouth are in righteousness; there is nothing froward or perverse in them,** nothing twisted or distorted, such as might lead men astray. V. 9. **They are all plain to him that understandeth,** so that the way of salvation is clear, **and right to them that find knowledge,** teaching them the duties of sanctification. V. 10. **Receive My instruction and not silver,** for true wisdom is to be preferred above the greatest wealth of this world, **and knowledge rather than choice gold.** V. 11. **For wisdom is better than rubies,** the finest coral jewelry, **and all the things that may be desired are not to be compared to it.** Cp. chap. 3, 14. 15. This entire section clearly speaks of the divine wisdom in a most peculiar sense, as personified in the person of the Word of God, Jesus Christ, for He it is who, in His revealed Word, teaches all men the true understanding of His person and office and the way to salvation. V. 12. **I, Wisdom, dwell with prudence,** skill in making use of every situation in life in the proper manner is His constant companion, **and find out knowledge of witty inventions,** of sagacious counsels, He Himself having this ability by virtue of His essential Godhead and teaching it in His Word. V. 13. **The fear of the Lord is to hate evil,** or "the fear of Jehovah hates wickedness," that being the result and outflow of faith; **pride and arrogancy,** a proud and supercilious behavior, **and the evil way,** wickedness in any form, **and the froward mouth,** crafty and malicious speech, **do I hate.** V. 14. **Counsel is Mine,** that basic knowledge, the essential wisdom, which is able to give real advice, **and sound wisdom,** that is, penetration, which goes to the bottom of things and tests them for their soundness and strength; **I am Understanding; I have strength,** that is, the energy necessary to put wisdom in action. V. 15. **By Me kings reign,** making use of wisdom in their rule, **and princes decree justice,** for its full and proper administration is possible only by means of the knowledge from on high. V. 16. **By Me princes rule and nobles, even all the judges of the earth,** the officials of the government of every degree. V. 17. **I love them that love Me,** exercising this love in all the circumstances of life, **and those that seek Me early,** as they do for the first evidences of the dawn in the East after a dark night, **shall find Me,** John 5, 39. V. 18. **Riches and honor,** of the true and lasting kind, **are with Me; yea, durable,** that is, increasing, **riches and righteousness,** the latter especially being the lasting possession of those who cling to the personal Wisdom in true faith. V. 19. **My fruit is better than gold, yea, than fine gold,** the riches which the believers obtain from Christ exceeding the wealth of Croesus in desirability, **and My revenue than choice silver,** exceeding it in costliness and real worth. V. 20. **I lead in the way of righteousness,** literally, "I am walking," that being the standard of His conduct, **in the midst of the paths of judgment,** all His dealings being in agreement with the demands of divine justice, v. 21. **that I may cause those that love Me to inherit substance,** true and lasting blessings; **and I will fill their treasures,** giving them possessions which outlast this world, the happiness of those who are united with Christ by the bonds of love, who receive the fulness of His merciful gifts and the blessings of His grace in His Word, which teaches true wisdom. Having thus spoken of His work, of His office, Christ next gives information concerning His person.

THE ORIGIN AND THE BLESSINGS OF THE PERSONAL WISDOM. — V. 22. **The Lord possessed Me,** brought Me into being, the reference being to the eternal begetting of the Father by which the Son was brought forth from eternity, Ps. 2, 7, **in the beginning of His way,** as a revelation of His innermost essence, **before His works of old,** before the creation of the world. V. 23. **I was set up from everlasting,** ordained, inaugurated, established, **from the beginning, or ever the earth was,** from the primordial times of the earth, the eternity of the personal Word being asserted again and again. V. 24. **When there were no depths, I was brought forth,** when the great oceans had not yet been made; **when there were no fountains abounding with water,** that is, the hidden springs from which the floods of the deep broke forth, Gen. 7, 11. V. 25. **Before the mountains were settled,** placed in position by the Creator, as He laid the foundation of the earth, **before the hills, was I brought forth,** v. 26. **while as yet He had not made the earth nor the fields,** literally, "the open spaces," the deserts, as distinguished from the habitable part of the earth, **nor the highest parts of the dust of the world,** literally, "the first of the dust particles of the world," that is, the first clods of the earth. V. 27. **When He prepared the heavens, I was there; when He set a compass upon the face of the depth,** the horizon all around serving as a circular boundary with reference to human eyes; v. 28. **when He established the clouds above,** fixing and securing them in their place, to prevent a sudden outpouring of their contents; **when He strengthened the fountains of the deep,** subduing them, setting their bounds, keeping them in check by His laws; v. 29. **when He gave to the sea His decree,** setting its bounds after the division of water and dry land, Gen. 1, 9. 10, **that the waters should not pass His commandment,** no farther than He permitted them to go; **when He appointed the foundations of the earth,** settling its foundation pillars in the work of creation: v. 30. **then I was by Him, as one brought up with Him,** as the Artist, Director, or Overseer of the work, Himself actively engaged in the creation of the earth; **and I was daily His delight,** that is, there was delight day after day on account of the wonderful relation between the Father and the Son in their creative activity, **rejoicing always before Him,** v. 31. **rejoicing in the habitable part of His earth,** the land where man lived; **and My delights were with the sons of men,** Gen. 1, 10. 12. 18. 31. Thus the divine attributes of the personal Wisdom, His eternity, His omnipotence, are set forth, while at the same time it is emphasized that He was even then interested in all the sons of men, that they were the special objects of His loving care. He therefore closes this message of revelation of Himself with another admonition, v. 32. **Now, therefore, hearken unto Me, O ye children; for blessed are they that keep My ways,** fashioning their entire conduct in life in agreement with the instruction given in the Word of God. V. 33. **Hear instruction and be wise, and refuse it not,** rejecting it in foolish rebellion. V. 34. **Blessed is the man that heareth Me,** in willing obedience, **watching daily at My gates,** eager to find out more and more about the fundamental truths of true wisdom, **waiting at the posts of My doors.** V. 35. **For whoso findeth Me findeth life,** wisdom teaching him the fulness of true life, **and shall obtain favor of the Lord,** gaining it, bearing it away as a reward of grace. V. 36. **But he that sinneth against Me wrongeth his own soul,** bringing everlasting harm upon it. **All they that hate Me love death,** their behavior showing that they prefer destruction, that they deliberately plunge into their own misfortune. Christians, in seeking true wisdom, will follow the advice of the eternal Word, their Lord Jesus Christ, and thus be made wise unto salvation by faith in Him alone, 2 Tim. 3, 16. 17.

CHAPTER 9.

Wisdom Contrasted with Folly.

THE BANQUET OF WISDOM. — V. 1. **Wisdom,** the divine and true wisdom, as it is exercised and exhibited here on earth among men, **hath builded her house,** to dwell in the midst of men. **She hath hewn out her seven pillars,** the reference being to the pillars of the inner court, which bear the upper stories, the number seven referring to the chief attributes of wisdom, the gifts of the Holy Spirit, Is. 11, 2. V. 2. **She hath killed her beasts,** slaughtering them in preparation for the great feast which she had planned; **she hath mingled her wine,** by adding spices of various kinds to enhance the flavor; **she hath also furnished her table,** set the table for the banquet. V. 3. **She hath sent forth her maidens,** bearing the invitations; **she crieth upon the highest places of the city,** so that the calls of invitation may be heard by all inhabitants and visitors. The message, as proclaimed by the messengers in the name of wisdom, is now given: v. 4. **Whoso is simple,** inexperienced, not yet acquainted with the dangers and temptations of life, **let him turn in hither,** to partake of wisdom's banquet; **as for him that wanteth understanding,** that is, who lacks the proper insight, **she saith to him,** v. 5. **Come, eat of my bread and drink of the wine which I have mingled,** the gifts which she freely offers. V. 6. **Forsake the foolish and live,** because the leaving of the company of fools and scorners is the first step in the right direction on the road to life, **and go in the way of understanding,** moving straight ahead on the way by which men obtain true knowledge. This demand, to abandon intercourse with the enemies of wisdom, is now further substantiated. V. 7. **He that reproveth a scorner,** trying to correct him, **getteth to himself shame,** his efforts are met with insults and mocking rejection, **and he that rebuketh a wicked man getteth himself a blot,** that is, his labor of love has the reward of bringing him into discredit with men, of heaping disgrace upon him. V. 8. **Reprove not a scorner,** the warning being not to attempt instruction and correction while the scorner is in his mood of opposition, **lest he hate thee; rebuke a wise man, and he will love thee,** his willingness to accept a deserved correction showing the soundness of his wisdom. Only a fool is always in the right; a wise man knows that to err is human. V. 9. **Give instruction to a wise man,** for he is willing to learn, and every correction serves for his further training, **and he will be yet wiser; teach a just man,** showing him how he may make still further progress in righteousness of life, **and he will increase in learning,** he will add to his store of knowledge and make proper use of it. V. 10. **The fear of the Lord is the beginning of wisdom,** the basis and source of all true wisdom, **and the knowledge of the Holy,** of Him who is the essence of holiness, **is understanding,** since it acts as a spur to ever greater efforts in holiness of life. V. 11. **For by me,** through the knowledge and strength given by true wisdom, **thy days shall be multiplied,** and **the years of thy life shall be increased,** a long and happy life being the reward of the use of true wisdom. V. 12. **If thou be wise, thou shalt be wise for thyself,** he who makes use of wisdom having the greatest benefit therefrom himself; **but if thou scornest, thou alone shalt bear it,** for the foolish must pay the price of their folly, sooner or later. It pays to learn the wisdom of the Word of God and be guided by it in every vicissitude of life.

THE BANQUET OF FOLLY. — V. 13. **A foolish woman is clamorous,** literally, "A simple, noisy woman is folly," devoid of sense, but raising all the more clamor, boisterous, excited, and wanton; **she is simple and knoweth nothing,** utter ignorance being characteristic of folly. V. 14. **For she sitteth at the door of her house,** like a harlot watching for passers-by, Gen. 38, 14, **on a seat in the high places of the city,** the lofty throne of the city being named in irony to show what measures are adopted by folly to gain adherents for herself, v. 15. **to call passengers who go right on their ways,** unwary travelers who are using the highways, intent upon their business: v. 16. **Whoso is simple, let him turn in hither,** to partake of the banquet of her folly, to be steeped ever more thoroughly in foolishness; **and as for him that wanteth understanding,** lacking in this essential part of a proper life, **she saith to him,** v. 17. **Stolen waters are sweet,** that is, forbidden pleasures, as praised by folly, especially in the form of immoral acts, illicit intercourse, seem pleasant enough for the time being, **and bread eaten in secret is pleasant,** literally, "bread of secrecy," because both the unjust gain and the forbidden enjoyment are emphasized, Cp. chap. 3, 15—20. V. 18. **But he,** the person who hearkens to the invitation of folly, **knoweth not that the dead are there,** the children of death, who are moving forward to the horrors of the realm of death and everlasting destruction, **and that her guests are in the depths of hell.** That is the end of folly and of all who accept her invitation, while the faithful, who follow the call of wisdom, will attain to true prosperity and live a life of true usefulness and happiness in the world.

CHAPTER 10.

From chapter 10 to chapter 25 of the Book of Proverbs there are no connected discourses, but only individual maxims of Solomon, loosely strung together, the sense of each being complete in one or two verses. Any division in this entire section is more or less arbitrary, although it may be said that the parallelism of members in chapters 10 to 15 is generally antithetic and in chapters 16 to 22 synthetic, and there are certain other characteristics and relations of thought which show the transition from one idea to another. — V. 1. **The proverbs,** maxims of instruction, **of Solomon. — A wise son maketh a glad father,** one who follows the precepts of wisdom makes his father glad or happy; **but a foolish son,** one who rejects the instruction of true wisdom, **is the heaviness of his mother,** causing her grief and distress. V. 2. **Treasures of wickedness,** such as have been gained by any form of wickedness, **profit nothing,** they cannot bring lasting happiness nor avert a sudden and unhappy death; **but righteousness,** righteous living, merciful love and charity, **delivereth from death,** since it shows the presence of faith in the heart. V. 3. **The Lord will not suffer the soul of the righteous to famish,** actually to suffer want; **but He casteth away the substance of the wicked,** repelling their greedy desire, often leaving their craving for wealth unfulfilled. V. 4. **He becometh poor that dealeth with a slack hand,** doing his work with an idle hand, too lazy to exert himself; **but the hand of the diligent maketh rich,** under the blessing of God prosperity and even wealth will be given to him who works with industry and energy. V. 5. **He that gathereth in summer,** in the time of harvest, **is a wise son,** literally, "that doeth wisely"; **but he that sleepeth in harvest,** thus losing the best opportunity for storing the fruits of the land, **is a son that causeth shame,** bringing ruin upon himself and upon his aged parents. V. 6. **Blessings are upon the head of the just,** as a merciful reward of God's bounty and in acknowledgment of his righteous conduct in life; **but violence covereth the mouth of the wicked;** although he hides the violence of his heart by keeping silence, he cannot escape its curse; the fact that he covers in himself ruin for others turns the blessing away from him. V. 7. **The memory of the just is blessed,** he is spoken of with esteem, mentioned with praise after his death; **but the name of the wicked shall rot,** the figure pointing to the disgust and loathing which the mention of his name will excite in all men after his death. V. 8. **The wise in heart will receive commandments,** showing himself ready to be instructed and guided in the right way; **but a prating fool,** a person of foolish lips, **shall fall,** be overthrown, bring about his own ruin. V. 9. **He that walketh uprightly,** in purity or piety of life, **walketh surely,** with the confidence flowing from a good conscience; **but he that perverteth his ways,** adopting hidden or crooked ways of conducting himself in order to gain his aims and objects, **shall be known,** made manifest in his real nature, exposed for what he is in his heart. V. 10. **He that winketh with the eye,** as a malicious and mocking sign to his confederates to watch him or to join him in some act of insult, **causeth sorrow,** injury and grief; **but a prating fool shall fall,** eventually destruction will come upon him who is foolish of lips. V. 11. **The mouth of a righteous man is a well of life,** on account of the cheerful and helpful utterances which proceed from it; **but violence covereth the mouth of the wicked,** he hides it for a while, but revenge will surely overtake him and give him the proper punishment for his malice. V. 12. **Hatred stirreth up strifes,** so that constant quarrels and disputes are the result; **but love covereth all sins,** by treating transgressions in a kind manner, as diseases of the soul, by being ready to forgive, by endeavoring to gain the sinner from the error of his ways and have him turn to the paths of righteousness, Jas. 5, 20; 1 Cor. 13, 4; 1 Pet. 4, 8. V. 13. **In the lips of him that hath understanding wisdom is found,** his utterances will naturally reveal his possession of real wisdom; **but a rod is for the back of him that is void of understanding,** that is, he well deserves the punishment which strikes him as the result of his folly. V. 14. **Wise men lay up knowledge,** like treasures which are to be put to a good use; **but the mouth of the foolish is near destruction,** because his foolish suggestions are always breaking forth and bringing misfortune to himself and others, like the sudden collapse of a house. V. 15. **The rich man's wealth is his strong city,** it serves as his bulwark in adversity and enables him to go forward with confidence and energy; **the destruction of the poor is their poverty,** for they are dependent upon, and influenced by, even the slightest misfortune, that is, poverty well deserved on account of foolish and improvident conduct always causes such poor people to sink more deeply in folly and moral need. V. 16. **The labor of the righteous tendeth to life,** his earnings, his income, will be used by him in such activities as will bring him true happiness in living; **the fruit of the wicked [tendeth] to sin,** for he squanders his income for sinful purposes and brings ruin upon himself. V. 17. **He is in the way of life,** on the highway to the true enjoyment of life, **that keepeth instruction,** heeding and accepting correction; **but he that refuseth reproof,** turning from it, impatient of being led aright, erreth, goes astray and may lead others astray. V. 18. **He that hideth hatred with lying lips,** deliberately deceiving others as to the real condition of his heart, being hypocritical falsehood personified, **and he that uttereth a slander,** spreading abuse and base detraction concerning his neighbor, **is a fool,** for slander is one of the most odious of vices, making a person loathsome and despised in the sight of God and men. V. 19. **In the multitude of words there wanteth not sin,** that is, one given to excessive talking on any and every subject will easily become guilty of transgression; **but he that refraineth his lips,** showing discretion in speech, **is wise,** for silence is golden. Cp. Jas. 3, 2; Matt. 12, 36. V. 20. **The tongue of the just,** the speech of the righteous, **is as choice silver,** his words and advice are of great value; **the heart of the wicked is little worth,** it is a trifle, it is no good. V. 21. **The lips of the righteous feed many,** the counsel of their wholesome instruction serving as nourishment for heart and intellect; **but fools die for want of wisdom,** bringing misfortune and destruction upon themselves by their persistent rejection of true understanding. V. 22. **The blessing of the Lord,** by which He gives prosperity and wealth, **it maketh rich,** for in this case there is no taint of ill-gotten wealth, **and He addeth no sorrow with it,** rather, "and not does labor add beside it," that is, all anxious worrying and striving for this world's goods will not bring true prosperity and happiness, Ps. 127, 2; Matt. 6, 25—34. V. 23. **It is as sport to a fool to do mischief,** that is, the practise of any form of iniquity is his delight, it agrees with his perverted sense of humor; **but a man of understanding hath wisdom,** that is his delight, therein he finds his pleasure. V. 24. **The fear of the wicked,** that which he dreads, **it shall come upon him,** cp. Is. 56, 4; Job 3, 25; **but the desire of the righteous shall be granted,** the good things for which they longed are given them by the Lord. V. 25. **As the whirlwind passeth,** rather, "When a storm sweepeth by," **so is the wicked no more,** taken away like chaff; **but the righteous is an everlasting foundation,** set firmly against all storms of adversity. V. 26. **As vinegar to the teeth,** affecting the enamel and tending to make the teeth feel dull, **and as smoke to the eyes,** affecting the sensitive membranes and interfering with sight, **so is the sluggard to them that send him,** a source of constant vexation and worry. V. 27. **The fear of the Lord prolongeth days,** adding to their number; **but the years of the wicked shall be shortened,** their span of life will not reach the normal length. V. 28. **The hope of the righteous shall be gladness,** their expectation is fulfilled, bringing them true happiness; **but the expectation of the wicked shall perish,** they will be disappointed in their hopes of lasting fortune. V. 29. **The way of the Lord is strength to the upright,** a bulwark for the innocent or pious; for as long as they follow it, they are safe; **but destruction shall be to the workers of iniquity,** that is their final lot. V. 30. **The righteous shall never be removed,** not lose his home or be banished from his country; **but the wicked shall not inhabit the earth,** they will not remain in possession of the land. V. 31. **The mouth of the just bringeth forth wisdom,** that being the fruit of his lips, the outgrowth of the faith of his heart; **but the froward tongue,** that given to malice and deceit, **shall be cut out,** like an unfruitful tree or a dangerous shrub. V. 32. **The lips of the righteous know what is acceptable,** they are familiar with it, they are continually meditating upon it; **but the mouth of the wicked speaketh frowardness,** only such things as are full of distortion, malice, and deceit. He who follows the precepts of God's eternal wisdom in His Word will avoid both foolishness and deceit.

CHAPTER 11.

V. 1. **A false balance,** literally, "balances of deceit," **is abomination to the Lord,** cheating in business is loathsome to Him; **but a just weight,** literally, "a stone of fulness," a complete measure, for the Jews commonly used stones as weights in their balances, **is His delight.** V. 2. **When pride cometh,** that is, when a person becomes self-conceited and arrogant, **then cometh shame,** for such a person is beyond teaching and is bound finally to make a fool of himself; **but with the lowly is wisdom,** they are not beyond learning, and therefore grow wise. V. 3. **The integrity of the upright,** their innocence and rectitude, **shall guide them; but the perverseness of transgressors shall destroy them,** for their malicious transgressions eventually plunge them into ruin. V. 4. **Riches profit not in the day of wrath,** when God prepares to judge the earth; **but righteousness delivereth from death,** true righteousness of life will be found acceptable in the Last Day. V. 5. **The righteousness of the perfect,** of him whose conduct is beyond reproach, **shall direct his way,** make it plain and open, enabling him to walk in the security of a good conscience; **but the wicked shall fall by his own wickedness,** their own lusts proving a snare to them. V. 6. **The righteousness of the upright shall deliver them,** being accepted as an adequate defense in the court of God; **but transgressors shall be taken in their own naughtiness,** caught in the trap which they set for others. V. 7. **When**

a wicked man dieth, his expectation shall perish, all his hopes come to naught, his longing for wealth and honor and the gratification of his lusts is cut off, **and the hope of unjust men perisheth,** literally, "the expectation of wickedness," for death puts an end to all desires of this kind. This verse implies, also, that death cuts off all hopes, every person being judged according to the way in which death finds him; there is no purgatory and therefore no deliverance from purgatory. V. 8. **The righteous is delivered out of trouble,** the Lord Himself being his Deliverer, 2 Tim. 4, 18, **and the wicked cometh in his stead,** taking the place of the righteous in the midst of trouble. V. 9. **An hypocrite with his mouth destroyeth his neighbor,** for with his flattering he hides his real intention until he accomplishes his evil purpose; **but through knowledge shall the just be delivered,** his shrewdness enables him to unveil the schemes of the flatterer and to escape their evil effect. V. 10. **When it goeth well with the righteous,** when they are prosperous and happy, **the city rejoiceth,** all the inhabitants receiving the benefit of their prosperity; **and when the wicked perish, there is shouting,** because both their oppression and their bad example are removed. V. 11. **By the blessing of the upright,** by the good wishes, prayers, and honest work of the righteous, **the city is exalted,** attaining to ever greater prosperity and power; **but it is overthrown by the mouth of the wicked,** ruined as a result of the bold, slanderous, and blasphemous speeches of the ungodly. V. 12. **He that is void of wisdom despiseth his neighbor,** that is, he who mocks his neighbor lacks in heart and mind; **but a man of understanding holdeth his peace,** withholding his judgment, guarding against hasty condemnation and a self-righteous exaltation of self. V. 13. **A talebearer revealeth secrets,** his conduct in going about tattling and slandering results in the betrayal of many a thing which had better remained hidden; **but he that is of a faithful spirit,** one who proves himself trustworthy, one upon whom people can depend, **concealeth the matter,** secrets which were committed to him, things whose publication will result only in heartaches and not in edification. A different matter is that broached Matt. 18, 15—20. V. 14. **Where no counsel is,** no wise direction or leadership, **the people fall,** decay and ruin come upon the whole country; **but in the multitude of counselors there is safety,** that is, it is bound to serve for the benefit of a people if intelligent counselors are always available to the government. V. 15. **He that is surety for a stranger shall smart for it,** he will fare extremely ill on account of his rash act; **and he that hateth suretyship,** avoiding both the persons who are too ready to give their hands in pledge and the methods lightly adopted by them, **is sure,** he places himself beyond danger. V. 16. **A gracious woman retaineth honor,** her amiable and pleasant disposition, her grace and charm, give her an honored and powerful standing in the community; **and strong men retain riches,** making use of decision and energy in holding outward wealth, which, after all, cannot compare with the blessing of a high regard in the eyes of others. V. 17. **The merciful man doeth good to his own soul,** that is, if he practises benevolence, manifests true goodness toward others, he thereby benefits his own soul, the Lord Himself granting him this as a reward; **but he that is cruel troubleth his own flesh,** for God visits a cruel and hardhearted conduct with a severe penalty. V. 18. **The wicked worketh a deceitful work,** the acquisitions which he gains are delusive, they are neither real nor lasting; **but to him that soweth righteousness shall be a sure reward,** for in scattering the seed of a righteous conduct he prepares for the harvest of God's merciful reward. V. 19. **As righteousness tendeth to life,** or, "genuine righteousness," flowing from the fulness of a heart sound in faith, will result in a truly happy life, bringing happiness to all who practise it; **so he that pursueth evil pursueth it to his own death,** that is the consequence of his act. V. 20. **They that are of a froward heart,** full of crookedness and malice, **are abomination to the Lord; but such as are upright in their way,** pure and straightforward in their conduct, **are His delight,** with them He is well pleased. V. 21. **Though hand join in hand,** literally, "hand in hand," as a pledge or guarantee, that is, most assuredly, **the wicked shall not be unpunished; but the seed of the righteous shall be delivered,** the generation of the righteous, all who practise righteousness, will escape punishment. V. 22. **As a jewel of gold in a swine's snout,** a nose-ring such as is worn in the Orient, **so is a fair woman which is without discretion,** without a sense of propriety and modesty, her beauty corresponding to the golden nose-ring and her immodesty to the swine's coarseness, in either case a disgusting sight to behold. V. 23. **The desire of the righteous is only good,** they want only such things as are pleasing to the Lord; **but the expectation of the wicked is wrath,** a presumption which challenges the wrath of God and brings destruction upon themselves. V. 24. **There is that scattereth,** practising cheerful liberality with the goods given him in life, **and yet increaseth,** since the blessing of the Lord more than compensates for the money spent in benevolences; **and there is that withholdeth more than is meet,** not even giving his share for the alleviation of bodily and spiritual suffering, **but it tendeth to poverty,** in spite of his careful hoarding his possessions decrease, so that he saves only to poverty. V. 25. **The liberal soul shall be made fat,** being rewarded with blessings from the Lord; **and he that watereth shall be watered also himself,** that is, God will reward with a corresponding refreshing him who refreshes and restores others by deeds of kindness. V. 26. **He that withholdeth corn,** as is done to this day in the so-called dealing in "futures" and in "corners in wheat," **the people shall curse him,** for such speculative manipulations raise the price of the necessities of life; **but blessing shall be upon the head of him that selleth it,** not holding it for purposes of speculation, but disposing of it as there is need. V. 27. **He that diligently seeketh good procureth favor,** that is, who is diligent toward all things that are good earnestly desires the favor of the Lord; **but he that seeketh mischief, it shall come unto him,** he will be punished by that which he practised. V. 28. **He that trusteth in his riches,** placing his confidence in his outward possessions, **shall fall,** for such trust is a species of idolatry; **but the righteous shall flourish as a branch,** like a green leaf, like luxurious foliage. V. 29. **He that troubleth his own house,** his avarice causing him to withhold from the members of his household their earnings or their rightful keep, **shall inherit the wind,** gain nothing and come to nothing; **and the fool shall be servant to the wise of heart,** the very same miser who treated his household so niggardly coming to such straits that he is a servant to one who was not guilty of the same foolishness. V. 30. **The fruit of the righteous,** all his deeds, as an outflow of the faith of his heart and the integrity of his life, **is a tree of life,** a fountain of blessing to all who come into contact with him; **and he that winneth souls is wise,** or, "the wise man winneth souls," gaining them for the service of the Lord and for the cause of truth. V. 31. **Behold, the righteous shall be recompensed in the earth,** that is, if even he will not reach a stage when he will be free from suffering in this world, **much more the wicked and the sinner,** the ungodly will assuredly be subject to much severer punishment and will deserve the full measure of retribution which will strike them. It is a strong argument and admonition for righteousness of life.

CHAPTER 12.

V. 1. **Whoso loveth instruction,** including all moral training, **loveth knowledge,** for that is the fruit of such training; **but he that hateth reproof is brutish,** for in resenting correction a person places himself on the level of beasts in stupidity. V. 2. **A good man obtaineth favor of the Lord,** is an object of Jehovah's good pleasure; **but a man of wicked devices will He condemn,** for He loathes planning which intends the neighbor's harm. V. 3. **A man shall not be established by wickedness,** the prosperity of such a one will not be lasting, nor will it give him true happiness; **but the root of the righteous shall not be moved;** as their faith is rooted in Jehovah, their foundation is secure. V. 4. **A virtuous woman,** a wife of moral power and probity, as shown in her pious activity in the home, **is a crown to her husband,** an emblem of honor and glory before the whole world; **but she that maketh ashamed,** causing him shame by her misconduct, **is as rottenness in his bones,** like a gnawing worm, a canker slowly undermining and destroying. V. 5. **The thoughts of the righteous are right,** just and pious, leading to words and deeds which are also righteous; **but the counsels of the wicked are deceit,** the manner in which they influence and direct others is deceitful and is bound to work harm. V. 6. **The words of the wicked are to lie in wait for blood,** they intend malice and violence, their thoughts find expression in bloodthirsty and murderous ways; **but the mouth of the upright shall deliver them,** namely, those whose life is threatened by the wicked with their murderous designs. V. 7. **The wicked are overthrown and are not,** they come to an end like the ungodly inhabitants of Sodom and Gomorrah; **but the house of the righteous shall stand,** sustained in the midst of all storms by the power of Jehovah. V. 8. **A man shall be commended according to** (literally, "in the presence of") **his wisdom,** in proportion to the insight he shows in all matters of life; **but he that is of a perverse heart shall be despised,** his crooked and malicious dealings meeting with the contempt and condemnation which they deserve. V. 9. **He that is despised and hath a servant is better,** rather, "Better is the lowly that serveth himself," being of small means and not too proud to be found engaged in performing the work of a servant about the house, **than he that honoreth himself and lacketh bread,** his pride of birth or caste keeping him from honest work. V. 10. **A righteous man regardeth the life of his beast,** taking proper care of his domestic animals; **but the tender mercies of the wicked are cruel,** they are utterly devoid of sympathy and compassion. V. 11. **He that tilleth his land shall be satisfied with bread,** his industry ordinarily being rewarded in this manner; **but he that followeth vain persons,** vanity, idleness, laziness, **is void of understanding,** lacks the very principles of ordinary common sense. V. 12. **The wicked desireth the net of evil men,** rather, the spoil, that which is taken in the net; that is, one wicked person tries to deprive the other of his ill-gotten gains, their selfishness causing them to consume one another; **but the root of the righteous yieldeth fruit;** since all their acts flow from faith, they are filled with a power which impels them forward in righteous conduct. V. 13. **The wicked is snared by the transgression of his lips,** his own speeches prove a dangerous snare to him, so that he is overthrown; **but the just shall come out of trouble,** escaping from the net which was placed for his feet. V. 14. **A man shall be satisfied with good by the fruit of his mouth,** his own wise, benevolent, and charitable discourse results in blessings to him; **and the recompense of a man's hands,** what he deserves for his works, **shall be rendered unto him,** the justice of God being shown in rewards as well as in acts of punishment. V. 15. **The way of a fool is right in his own eyes,** in his own judgment, making it practically impossible to convince him of the contrary; **but he that hearkeneth unto counsel is wise,** or, "the wise listens to sound advice," it is one of his characteristics. V. 16. **A fool's wrath is presently known,** his indignation breaks out suddenly, often without a careful examination of the difficulty which caused it; **but a prudent man covereth shame,** he exercises prudent self-control, he keeps his temper well in hand always. V. 17. **He that speaketh truth showeth forth righteousness;** breathing the atmosphere of the love of truth, he utters that which is strictly just; **but a false witness deceit,** he breathes and speaks lies. V. 18. **There is that speaketh like the piercings of a sword,** his speeches being as rude and sharp as knife thrusts, their intention being to hurt and injure; **but the tongue of the wise is health,** healing, intended to overcome the effect of sharp speeches and to bind up the wounds inflicted by foolish babblers. V. 19. **The lip of truth shall be established forever,** for truth, although trodden to the earth, will ever rise again; **but a lying tongue is but for a moment,** the falsehood being readily exposed and therefore losing its power. V. 20. **Deceit is in the heart of them that imagine evil,** for they can rarely carry out their evil intentions without malignity and deceit; **but to the counselors of peace is joy,** those who give wholesome counsel, and the peacemakers, cause rejoicing. V. 21. **There shall no evil happen to the just,** the very sufferings coming upon them in God's wise government being but blessings in disguise, Ps. 91, 10; Rom. 8, 28; **but the wicked shall be filled with mischief,** evil, misfortune, and calamity striking them. V. 22. **Lying lips are abomination to the Lord,** He loathes liars and deceivers; **but they that deal truly,** practising uprightness always, **are His delight.** V. 23. **A prudent man concealeth knowledge,** not showing off his knowledge upon every occasion; **but the heart of fools proclaimeth foolishness,** they are bound to expose their nonsense by their forward manner. V. 24. **The hand of the diligent shall bear rule,** he will reach a position of power and influence; **but the slothful shall be under tribute,** being obliged to serve, to hold a subordinate position, all his life. V. 25. **Heaviness in the heart of man maketh it stoop,** it is readily bowed down by trouble and grief; **but a good word maketh it glad,** so that he straightens up from his grief and gains new courage. V. 26. **The righteous is more excellent than his neighbor,** rather, guideth his friend aright, being concerned about his welfare, in a true spirit of altruism; **but the way of the wicked seduceth them,** their own foolishness and wickedness leading them astray. V. 27. **The slothful man roasteth not that which he took in hunting,** literally, "catcheth not his prey," being too lazy to make use of his opportunities; **but the substance of a diligent man is precious,** his industry is a valuable possession and grasps the opportunities offered him. V. 28. **In the way of righteousness is life,** it leads to the possession and enjoyment of true life; **and in the pathway thereof there is no death,** no misfortune of any kind, for it is only the devious way that leads to destruction.

CHAPTER 13.

V. 1. **A wise son heareth his father's instruction,** is the object and product of his father's corrective training; **but a scorner heareth not rebuke,** no matter how earnestly he is reproved, it makes no impression upon him. V. 2. **A man shall eat good,** himself enjoy the benefits, **by the fruit of his mouth,** as the result of his speaking always with the benefit of others in mind; **but the soul of the trangressors shall eat violence,** they are satisfied only if they can exercise violence upon others and thus satisfy their appetite for spoil. V. 3. **He that keepeth his mouth,** that no evil, sinful speeches issue therefrom, **keepeth his life; but he that openeth wide his lips,** permitting the evil thoughts of his heart to issue in the form of malignant speeches, **shall have destruction,** bringing it upon himself as the inevitable consequence of his foolish or sinful indiscretion. V. 4. **The soul of the sluggard desireth,** he is always ready to discourse on what he wants and ought to have, **and hath nothing,** he has no success, because he is too lazy to work for it; **but the soul of the diligent shall be made fat,** as a result of their industry they possess in abundance what they need. V. 5. **A righteous man hateth lying,** deceitful language as well as deceitful matters; **but a wicked man is loathsome,** all his acts being done in baseness, **and cometh to shame,** literally, "maketh offensive," he brings disgrace upon every one with whom he comes in contact. V. 6. **Righteousness keepeth him that is upright in the way,** protecting those whose conduct is straightforward, being itself a gift of the Lord; **but wickedness overthroweth the sinner,** since his sin becomes a snare to his feet and plunges him into destruction. V. 7. **There is that maketh himself rich,** making a pretense of wealth, trying to impress others with the greatness of his resources, **yet hath nothing,** all his show being idle boasting, empty vaunting; **there is that maketh himself poor,** making no show of his wealth, which does not necessarily infer deceitful concealment, **yet hath great riches.** Cp. chap. 12, 9. V. 8. **The ransom of a man's life,** that with which he may buy immunity for himself and possibly even save his life, **are his riches; but the poor heareth not rebuke,** that is, no warning or threatening will have any effect in his case, because he has nothing to give up to the robber or blackmailer. V. 9. **The light of the righteous rejoiceth,** burning brightly and cheerfully; he enjoys true happiness no matter what befalls him; **but the lamp of the wicked shall be put out,** they shall not enjoy true prosperity. V. 10. **Only by pride cometh contention,** for those who are arrogantly ambitious always fear rivalry and therefore are always picking quarrels; **but with the well-advised,** those who are willing to accept counsel, **is wisdom.** V. 11. **Wealth gotten by vanity,** gained by deceit and fraud, **shall be diminished,** since the blessing of the Lord does not rest upon it; **but he that gathereth by labor,** by hard, steady, and honest work, **shall increase.** V. 12. **Hope deferred maketh the heart sick,** since the unfulfilled longing is too great a strain for a person; **but when the desire cometh, it is a tree of life,** giving new vigor and strength, renewing a person's youth. V. 13. **Whoso despiseth the Word shall be destroyed,** even if a person thinks he can mock the will and Word of the Lord, he is still bonded to it and cannot escape the obligation laid on him; **but he that feareth the commandment shall be rewarded,** he will enjoy blessing and peace. V. 14. **The law of the wise is a fountain of life,** his teaching being like a spring which yields new understanding and strength every day, **to depart from the snares of death,** for wisdom enables him to recognize and to avoid such snares. V. 15. **Good understanding giveth favor,** that is, proper prudence, true culture, causes men to have a high and kindly regard for those who possess it; **but the way of transgressors is hard,** the selfishness of the ungodly and malicious causes them to be hard, utterly lacking in sympathy, and therefore also desolate and unfruitful. V. 16. **Every prudent man dealeth with knowledge,** with a careful weighing of all facts as presented to him; **but a fool layeth open his folly,** exposing it, spreading it before the eyes of all men, showing off his folly. V. 17. **A wicked messenger falleth into mischief,** causing his errand to fail; **but a faithful ambassador is health,** like healing medicine to a smarting wound or like a tonic to the weary person, his faithful energy yielding such pleasant benefits. V. 18. **Poverty and shame shall be to him that refuseth instruction,** declining to accept correction and moral training; **but he that regarded reproof,** observing it carefully, accepting it willingly, **shall be honored.** V. 19. **The desire accomplished is sweet to the soul,** if it is fulfilled and appeased, the resulting gratification is most pleasant; **but it is abomination to fools to depart from evil,** because they desire only the morally objectionable and refuse to consider anything else. V. 20. **He that walketh with wise men,** making them his companions and listening to their counsel, **shall be wise; but a companion of fools shall be destroyed,** or, "he who attendeth fools tendeth to folly," and therefore becomes base, partaking of their meanness. V. 21. **Evil pursueth sinners,** as their well-merited punishment; **but to the righteous good shall be repayed,** that is, God rewards him in mercy for his efforts on the way of sanctification. V. 22. **A good man leaveth an inheritance to his children's children,** his estate being transmitted to them complete, as a result of God's blessing upon him; **and the wealth of the sinner is laid up for the just,** the latter eventually becoming the possessor of that which the sinner squanders. V. 23. **Much food is in the tillage of the poor,** that is, he who with much labor clears and breaks up land, tilling it with all diligence, will be rewarded with a rich harvest; **but there is that is destroyed for want of judgment,** for lack of uprightness, attempting to gain by fraud and violence what he ought to obtain by lawful labor. V. 24. **He that spareth his rod hateth his son,** for it is not love, but the lack of love, which causes parents to forget and set aside their parental power and duty in correcting their children, if necessary, with the rod; **but he that loveth him chasteneth him betimes,** applying correction in the measure required by the occasion, chap. 3, 12; 23, 13. 14; 29, 15. V. 25. **The righteous eateth to the satisfying of his soul,** the Lord granting him enough to satisfy all his needs; **but the belly of the wicked shall want,** not only because the Lord often punishes their wickedness with a lack of the necessities of life, but because their enjoyment of them is often not attended with true happiness.

CHAPTER 14.

V. 1. **Every wise woman buildeth her house,** literally, "Woman's wisdom buildeth her house," the reference being to the prudence and foresight of the wise housekeeper, who manages well; **but the foolish plucketh it down with her hands,** her mismanagement results in ruin. V. 2. **He that walketh in his uprightness feareth the Lord,** for the fear of Jehovah is the guiding principle in the life of the upright; **but he that is perverse in his ways despiseth Him,** that is, his contempt of the Lord shows in his crooked and malicious conduct, which no amount of outward religious activity can cover. V. 3. **In the mouth of the foolish is a rod of pride,** that is, he bears with himself the rod which will punish his pride, or his pride shows itself in speeches which hurt and injure others; **but the lips of the wise shall preserve them,** so that no word of folly is spoken by them to the injury of others, chap. 10, 13. 14. V. 4. **Where no oxen are, the crib is clean,** the manger is empty, that is, he who is too lazy or too indolent to use the proper means for acquiring possessions under God's blessings will find that he makes no progress in life; **but much increase is by the strength of the ox,** although it requires work to keep him. V. 5. **A faithful witness will not lie,** he will not utter falsehoods to bolster up a weak case; **but a false witness will utter lies,** will habitually make use of them in gaining his ends. Cp. chap. 12, 17; 6, 19. V. 6. **A scorner seeketh wisdom and findeth it not,** for his mockery of true wisdom, of the truth contained in the Word of God, closes the road of real enlightenment to him, no matter how much superficial culture he seems to possess; **but knowledge is easy unto him that understandeth,** if he is earnestly concerned about knowing the truth of the Word, it is readily given to him. V. 7. **Go from the presence of a foolish man,** it being a matter of wisdom for a person to keep his distance from such a one, **when thou perceivest not in him the lips of knowledge,** remembering that he has never yet uttered a truly sensible word. V. 8. **The wisdom of the prudent is to understand his way,** to observe where he is going, to pay close attention to his conduct; **but the folly of fools is deceit,** self-deception, since they are wilfully blind to the demands of every situation in which they find themselves, and so invite punishment and destruction upon themselves. V. 9. **Fools make a mock at sin,** literally, "the sacrifice mocks the fools"; for even if such ungodly people offer up burnt offerings for expiation and atonement, it is useless, it fails of its object, since it is not acceptable to God; **but among the righteous there is favor,** the relation among the upright being one of mutual good-fellowship and love, which prevents their becoming guilty of gross transgressions. V. 10. **The heart knoweth his own bitterness,** it is best acquainted with its own trouble and resents interference; **and a stranger doth not intermeddle with his joy,** for no outsider is able fully to enter into the feelings of the heart. This saying does not conflict with Rom. 12, 15, but is directed against officious intrusion and an unsympathetic prying into the affairs of one's neighbors. V. 11. **The house of the wicked shall be overthrown,** no matter how permanent they believe it to be; **but the tabernacle of the upright,** their tent, their temporary dwelling, for they do not regard it as their permanent home, **shall flourish,** the blessing of the Lord resting upon it. V. 12. **There is a way which seemeth right unto a man,** the way of sin, at the outset, being apparently straight and smooth, **but the end thereof,** what it finally leads to, **are the ways of death,** for transgression invariably leads to mortal ruin. V. 13. **Even in laughter the heart is sorrowful,** that is, a person may hide a deep sorrow under a superficial joyousness; **and the end of that mirth is heaviness,** for trouble will invariably cut short such outward manifestations of joy and bring sorrow in the end. V. 14. **The backslider in heart,** he who is of a perverse, malicious heart, who has departed from God in his heart, **shall be filled with his own ways,** he will be surfeited with the consequences of his own perverseness, he will have to suffer the ruinous results of his sinful acts; **and a good man shall be satisfied from himself,** literally, "out of himself," his good conscience affording him the satisfaction of knowing that his behavior is in agreement with the demands of true piety. V. 15. **The simple,** the inexperienced, **believeth every word,** without examining its truth, he is driven to and fro without any judgment of his own; **but the prudent man looketh well to his going,** watching every step, not attempting anything without the most careful consideration. V. 16. **A wise man feareth and departeth from evil,** dreading its power and preferring to keep his distance; **but the fool rageth,** in carnal presumption and insolence, **and is confident,** foolishly believing himself to be able to avoid the consequences of his sinful folly, rushing wildly into his own destruction. V. 17. **He that is soon angry,** losing his temper at the slightest provocation, **dealeth foolishly,** working only folly, with evil consequences to himself; **and a man of wicked devices is hated,** since he, with his malicious craft and hypocritical subtlety, is even more dangerous than he who flies into a passion at the slightest provocation. V. 18. **The simple inherit folly,** that is the portion of those who will not learn wisdom, who will not be guided by the experiences of others; **but the prudent are**

crowned with knowledge, they embrace, they accumulate, knowledge as a precious possession. V. 19. **The evil bow before the good**, humbling themselves as a result of the punishment which they incurred for their sins, **and the wicked at the gates of the righteous**, like beggars humbly praying for some gift of charity. V. 20. **The poor is hated even of his own neighbor**, for the loss of wealth immediately changes the attitude of false friends, who now find their impoverished neighbor obnoxious; **but the rich hath many friends**, such as profess friendship for him as long as they partake of his bounty. V. 21. **He that despiseth his neighbor sinneth**, that is, he who neglects a friend to whom he owes love, especially if he is in need; **but he that hath mercy on the poor**, showing true compassion to the poor and wretched, **happy is he**, since he himself may expect benefit from his act. V. 22. **Do they not err that devise evil**, who foolishly go astray and bring misfortune upon themselves? **But mercy and truth**, in the favor of God and the fulfilment of all His promises of love, **shall be to them that devise good**, always planning how they may be of assistance to such as are in need. V. 23. **In all labor there is profit**, if a person is really diligent and earnest in his work, results will show; **but the talk of the lips**, idle talk, not backed up by honest toil, **tendeth only to penury**, brings the one who practises it to want. V. 24. **The crown of the wise is their riches**, their possessions, gained by dint of hard work, serve to honor them; **but the foolishness of fools is folly**, no matter how much show and pomp he makes, how anxiously he strives to offer a magnificent appearance. V. 25. **A true witness**, one who fearlessly utters the truth, **delivereth souls**, from the death which threatened them as a result of false charges brought against them; **but a deceitful witness**, one full of crafty malice, **speaketh lies**, constantly breathing them out. V. 26. **In the fear of the Lord is strong confidence**, it gives a strong security, a safe reliance; **and his children shall have a place of refuge**, for since they follow the upright conduct of their parents, the Lord protects them in like manner. V. 27. **The fear of the Lord is a fountain of life**, the source of all true spiritual life, **to depart from the snares of death**; for where there is no fear of God, there is transgression, and transgression leads to everlasting death. V. 28. **In the multitude of people is the king's honor**, it serves for his glory, for the establishment of his name, if he reigns wisely and successfully over a large nation; **but in the want of people is the destruction of the prince**, where the people of a country are few and scattered on account of some weakness in the sovereign's rule, such a condition brings about the downfall of the ruler, his reign will soon come to an end. V. 29. **He that is slow to wrath**, he who is able to control himself, who has himself well in hand at all times, **is of great understanding**, he will always have a clear mind to discriminate properly; **but he that is hasty of spirit**, rash and quick-tempered, **exalteth folly**, is bound to carry foolishness to excess, to make a fool of himself. V. 30. **A sound heart is the life of the flesh**, literally, "life of the members is a heart of composure"; for it is the tranquil spirit which is able to judge calmly and correctly, weighing all factors dispassionately; **but envy the rottenness of the bones**, for every form of passionate, violent zeal sets aside calm consideration, indulges in foolish acts, and results in harm to the quick-tempered person's health and spiritual well-being. V. 31. **He that oppresseth the poor reproacheth his Maker**, mocks God Himself, who is the Champion of the poor and downtrodden; **but he that honoreth Him**, having the proper regard for the Lord, **hath mercy on the poor**, this being the natural result of the fear and love of Jehovah. Cp. chap. 17, 5; 19, 17. V. 32. **The wicked is driven away in his wickedness**, that is, if misfortune, ruin, and death strike the ungodly person, he is swept away suddenly, thrust out of this life violently; **but the righteous hath hope in his death**, he is confident even in the hour of death, for the future beyond the grave holds no terrors for him, since he places his trust in the mercy of the Lord alone. V. 33. **Wisdom resteth in the heart of him that hath understanding**, it is quietly safe there, and the wise person carefully guards and increases it; **but that which is in the midst of fools is made known**, they are always eager and loud in giving their opinion, since they believe themselves to be wise, but they thereby reveal their lack of true understanding, they make known the emptiness of their minds. V. 34. **Righteousness exalteth a nation**, the exercise of true moral uprightness in every department of a nation's activity will set such a nation up on high, tend to give it material prosperity, for God rewards civil righteousness in such a manner; **but sin is a reproach to any people**; if it is openly countenanced in a nation, the consequence is shame, disgrace, injury, decrease, destruction. V. 35. **The king's favor is toward a wise servant**, he will naturally prefer and reward one who is discreet and prudent in his work; **but his wrath is against him that causeth shame**, it will strike the base and give him his well-merited punishment.

CHAPTER 15.

V. 1. **A soft answer turneth away wrath,** a word spoken in gentleness when people are about to fly into a passion, is like oil on troubled waters; **but grievous words,** such as are offensive and violent, **stir up anger,** making it more passionate and embittered. V. 2. **The tongue of the wise useth knowledge aright,** presenting it in well-arranged form, clothing it in an attractive manner; **but the mouth of fools poureth out foolishness,** in great and loathsome quantities, its utterances being noisy, confused, and without sense, nothing but folly. V. 3. **The eyes of the Lord are in every place,** His omniscience seeing everything that goes on in the world, **beholding the evil and the good,** watching their every act, familiar with their desires, words, and acts. V. 4. **A wholesome tongue,** literally, "gentleness of tongue," **is a tree of life,** that is, a person who, in true humility, uses gentle, pacifying, soothing speech will do his share toward a better appreciation and use of life, will cause people with whom he comes into contact to enjoy it more properly; **but perverseness therein,** that is, transgression with the tongue, its abuse for the purpose of stirring up contention, **is a breach in the spirit,** it wounds the spirit of men, it causes heartache and grief. V. 5. **A fool despiseth his father's instruction,** he reveals his folly by refusing to be corrected; **but he that regardeth reproof,** always willing to accept correction, **is prudent,** shows the proper discretion. Cp. chap. 19, 25; 1 Sam. 23, 22. V. 6. **In the house of the righteous is much treasure,** such prosperity being the blessing of the Lord; **but in the revenues of the wicked is trouble,** the income of the ungodly results in desolation; for the more they have, the more they spend in the service of sin. V. 7. **The lips of the wise disperse knowledge,** casting it out over the country like good seed, which will return a rich harvest; **but the heart of the foolish doeth not so;** having no wisdom, he cannot spread any, he is not set in the right direction and is therefore utterly incompetent to teach others. V. 8. **The sacrifice of the wicked is an abomination to the Lord,** for it is brought in ungodliness and hypocrisy; **but the prayer of the upright,** by which they worship God in spirit and in truth and enter into true fellowship with Him, **is His delight.** V. 9. **The way of the wicked is an abomination unto the Lord,** He loathes their entire conduct; **but He loveth him that followeth after righteousness,** who makes it his business to search after, to pursue with great eagerness, that righteousness of life which pleases Jehovah. V. 10. **Correction is grievous unto him that forsaketh the way,** that is, a sharp punishment will strike him who leaves the path pointed out by the will of the Lord; **and he that hateth reproof,** namely, the rebuke of God's Word, **shall die,** for death is the wages of sin. V. 11. **Hell and destruction are before the Lord,** the realm of the dead, the place of eternal perdition, is uncovered before Him; He knows them, though they be hidden from the eyes of men; **how much more, then, the hearts of the children of men?** Jehovah knows the hearts of all men, they are all uncovered before His eyes, Jer. 17, 10; Heb. 4, 13. V. 12. **A scorner,** one who makes it a point to mock at everything that is holy, **loveth not one that reproveth him,** for his foolish pride resents correction; **neither will he go unto the wise,** because there he must expect censure; so he prefers the company of those who applaud his folly. V. 13. **A merry heart maketh a cheerful countenance,** for when the spirit is joyous, it brightens the face; **but by sorrow of the heart the spirit is broken,** if grief has taken possession of the heart, the powers of the mind are also influenced, clearness of thought is gone, and the shock proves generally disastrous to the whole spiritual life. V. 14. **The heart of him that hath understanding seeketh knowledge,** for he is anxious always to increase in true wisdom, as it applies to the various situations in life; **but the mouth of fools feedeth on foolishness,** literally, "the face of fools pastures on folly," delighting in it, as an animal eagerly feeds on grass in the pasture. V. 15. **All the days of the afflicted are evil,** for the inward burden of their grief makes every day sad for them; **but he that is of a merry heart,** refusing to be burdened or bowed down by sorrow, **hath a continual feast,** his life being like a constant festival. V. 16. **Better is little with the fear of the Lord,** the proper contentment with the blessings of the Lord, small as they may be outwardly, **than great treasure and trouble therewith,** for the possession of riches brings cares and worries, which often are very unpleasant, 1 Tim. 6, 6. V. 17. **Better is a dinner of herbs,** a portion of the very simplest food, **where love is,** where a person is in the midst of his loved ones, **than a stalled ox,** one fattened by hand-feeding, **and hatred therewith,** on account of the envy, jealousy, and hatred of people with whom one dines. Not the richness of the repast brings happiness, but the circumstances which attend it. V. 18. **A wrathful man,** one unable to keep his temper, **stirreth up strife,** his way of acting is bound to result in quarrels; **but he that is slow to anger appeaseth strife,** himself refusing to become excited and always making use of conciliatory speeches. V. 19. **The way of the slothful man is as an hedge of thorns,** since he is always meeting with obstructions and hindrances; **but the way of the righteous is made plain,** like an open highway, for his diligence and the blessing of the Lord combine in making the accomplishment of life's tasks easy. V. 20. **A wise son maketh a glad father,** chap. 10, 1; **but a foolish man despiseth his mother,** such neglect and contempt of his mother proving him to be a fool of a man, not only on account of the transgression of the Fourth Commandment involved, but because the wisdom and love of a mother serves for the best guidance. V. 21. **Folly is joy to him that is destitute of wisdom,** to him who lacks proper sense; **but a man of understanding walketh uprightly,** going straight forward on the way of duty, permitting no foolishness to interfere with his faithfulness. V. 22. **Without counsel, purposes are disappointed,** plans are sure to fail if they have not been considered carefully and from every angle in advance; **but in the multitude of counselors they are established,** for when they are worked out in this manner, with advice from every quarter, the chances are that all difficulties are taken into account. V. 23. **A man hath joy by the answer of his mouth;** if he has succeeded in giving the right advice, it naturally pleases him; **and a word spoken in due season,** one which just hits the nail on the head, thus solving the difficulty, **how good is it,** how welcome, pleasing, and salutary! V. 24. **The way of life is above to the wise,** he directs his course upward, aiming at a higher degree of sanctification with every new day, his eye set on the reward held out by the mercy of God, **that he may depart from hell beneath,** he shuns the way which leads to everlasting perdition. V. 25. **The Lord will destroy the house of the proud,** visiting him, his family, and all his possessions with punishment; **but He will establish the border of the widow,** not permit the boundary line of her property to be moved, that is, safeguard her possessions. V. 26. **The thoughts of the wicked are an abomination to the Lord,** He loathes evil plans, He will not tolerate wicked purposes; **but the words of the pure are pleasant words,** literally, "but pure are words of pleasantness"; if untainted by hypocrisy, they are sweetly consoling, full of consolation for troubled souls, and therefore precious in the sight of Jehovah. V. 27. **He that is greedy of gain,** his covetousness causing him to seek unjust gain, **troubleth his own house,** for his actions are bound to bring unpleasant consequences to his own family; **but he that hateth gifts,** being above the meanness of bribery, **shall live,** enjoying life and prosperity. V. 28. **The heart of the righteous studieth to answer,** carefully considering and reflecting before giving an opinion or suggesting advice; **but the mouth of the wicked poureth out evil things,** in a full and murky stream, without consulting conscience and right. V. 29. **The Lord is far from the wicked,** so that they cannot reach Him with their hypocritical form of worship; **but He heareth the prayer of the righteous,** they have free access to the throne of mercy, and He gladly fulfils their desires. V. 30. **The light of the eyes rejoiceth the heart,** when the eyes shine with a friendly luster, the influence thereby exerted upon the heart of one's neighbor is such as to impart some of the cheer to him; **and a good report,** joyful news, **maketh the bones fat,** gives refreshment and strength to the whole body. V. 31. **The ear that heareth the reproof of life,** a censure or correction which points out the way to life, **abideth among the wise,** belongs to their circle on account of the wisdom thus gained. V. 32. **He that refuseth instruction,** trying to withdraw from correction, paying no heed to it, **despiseth his own soul,** valuing it but lightly, not knowing or caring that the true enjoyment of life depends upon his accepting reproof; **but he that heareth reproof getteth understanding,** and thereby shows that he regards his soul properly. V. 33. **The fear of the Lord is the instruction of wisdom,** it offers the training which leads to true wisdom; **and before honor is humility,** that is, true humility will open the way to true honor, for God giveth grace to the humble.

CHAPTER 16.

V. 1. **The preparations of the heart in man and the answer of the tongue is from the Lord,** literally, "To man," that is, pertaining to man, "the plannings of the heart, but from Jehovah the answer of the tongue." The mind of a man may be engaged in attempting to solve a problem, in setting up various plans or schemes to reach a right conclusion, but the best solution is that which is given by the Lord, who finally leads the thoughts according to His will and causes them to be expressed in words in agreement with His plans. V. 2. **All the ways of a man are clean in his own eyes,** in his own judgment; **but the Lord weigheth the spirits,** He has ways and means to try all men according to their real moral worth, and His judgment is not fallible like that of men. V. 3. **Commit thy works unto the Lord,** rolling them in His direction, for Him to take care of, Ps. 37, 5, **and thy thoughts shall be established,** He Himself will give the proper and blessed direction to the believer's plans and purposes. V. 4. **The Lord hath made all things for Himself,** according to His all-wise plans; **yea, even the wicked for the day of evil,** for even the works of the ungodly are included in His government, although His punishment will finally overtake them, the evil thus serving for His glorification. V. 5. **Every one that is proud in heart is an abomination to the Lord,** He loathes such as exalt themselves; **though hand join in hand,** that is, most assuredly, **he shall not be unpunished.** V. 6. **By mercy and truth iniquity is purged,** loving and faithful conduct toward one's neighbor, however, not being named as the reason for the expiation of sin, but as an invariable expression of a penitent and believing heart, cp. Luke 7, 47; **and by the fear of the Lord,** which is shown in the virtues of mercy and truth, **men depart from evil,** that is, the believer thereby escapes moral evil, sin in all its forms. V. 7. **When a man's ways please the Lord,** when Jehovah finds that a person's conduct, the objects which he has in mind, and the means which he uses to accomplish them, are in accordance with His will, **He maketh even his enemies to be at peace with him,** causing them to abandon their hostile attitude and even to take his part. V. 8. **Better is a little with righteousness,** small possessions gained and kept with a good conscience, **than great revenues,** a large income and great wealth, **without right,** having been gained by oppression and iniquity. V. 9. **A man's heart deviseth his way,** reflecting most carefully on his conduct, considering as best he can what might be best for him to do; **but the Lord directeth his steps,** the result and the end are the Lord's, and the best suggestion is that a Christian from the beginning place himself under God's guidance; for "man proposes, but God disposes." V. 10. **A divine sentence is in the lips of the king,** he, in his position as sovereign, makes his decision as the representative of Jehovah; **his mouth transgresseth not in judgment,** he may not use his power for his own private interests by arbitrarily setting aside true justice. V. 11. **A just weight and balance are the Lord's,** literally, "The scale and balances of justice belong to Jehovah," His sovereign will directs their proper use, He wants business to be carried on without cheating; **all the weights of the bag are His work,** the stones which were commonly used as weights and carried by the merchant in a sack were, by the direction of God, to be honest weight. V. 12. **It is an abomination to kings,** it makes them objects of loathing and contempt, **to commit wickedness,** the setting aside of right and justice causes both God and men to despise them; **for the throne is established by righteousness,** regal power is sustained by righteousness in its constant application, not by the arbitrariness of the despot. V. 13. **Righteous lips are the delight of kings,** true sovereigns are pleased to have men among their counselors who will frankly state the truth in righteousness; **and they love him that speaketh right,** that is, if they themselves are God-fearing men, they will prefer to have such men among their advisers. V. 14. **The wrath of a king is as messengers of death,** if he becomes enraged, he has many means and instruments at his disposal to carry out his sentence of death; **but a wise man will pacify it,** he will quietly offer such arguments as will allay and soothe the wrath of the king. V. 15. **In the light of the king's countenance is life,** when he is graciously disposed, he dispenses favors which make life pleasant for his subjects; **and his favor is as a cloud of the latter rain,** that which preceeded harvest, the point of comparison being the enlivening strength. V. 16. **How much better is it to get wisdom than gold!** its value being so immeasurably greater, **and to get understanding rather to be chosen than silver!** If a person should gain the wealth of the whole world, such an acquisition could not compare with that of true wisdom. V. 17. **The highway of the upright,** their entire conduct, **is to depart from evil,** they avoid it by following the highway of strict piety; **he that keepeth his way preserveth his soul,** for it is by a careful following of God's will and Word that a person keeps his soul from spiritual and eternal death. V. 18. **Pride goeth before destruction,** for self-exaltation blinds a person against dangers and against the growing resentment of other people and thus hastens his fall, **and an haughty spirit before a fall,** the herald of the proud person's overthrow. V. 19. **Better it is to be of an humble spirit with the lowly,** to abide with those who are in trouble, content to lead a life of obscurity, **than to divide the spoil with the proud,** enjoying the ill-gotten gains of false ambition. V. 20. **He that handleth a matter wisely,** giving careful heed to the Word of God in every situation in life, **shall find good,** obtain true prosperity; **and whoso trusteth in the Lord,** being united with Him in the personal, confidential relation of faith, **happy is he,** the possessor of true blessedness. V. 21. **The wise in heart shall be called prudent,** regarded as possessing true discernment, **and the sweetness of the lips increaseth learning,** that is, where one makes use of grace, of a pleasant and attractive manner, in teaching, he will have easy access to ever-widening circles of hearers. V. 22. **Understanding,** proper insight and watchful discretion, **is a well-spring of life unto him that hath it,** a source of life and power to its possessor; **but the instruction of fools is folly,** their folly, serving for their correction, being a source of all possible disadvantages; for a lack of reason is its own punishment, destroying a person's own happiness. V. 23. **The heart of the wise teacheth his mouth,** for wisdom of heart and mind is shown in sensible speech, **and addeth learning to his lips,** giving greater emphasis and weight to his teaching. V. 24. **Pleasant words are as an honeycomb, sweet to the soul and health** to the bones; for the spirit of friendliness inspired by love is evident in them, to strengthen the hearer. V. 25. **There is a way that seemeth right unto a man,** when his conduct, in his own judgment, is good and fitting, **but the end thereof are the ways of death;** his judgment being wrong, his error leads him into destruction. Cp. chap. 14, 12. V. 26. **He that laboreth, laboreth for himself,** his spirit or soul, under the pressure of life's necessities, impels him to work earnestly for his daily bread; **for his mouth craveth it of him,** drives him forward, compels him, goads him on, for it is the Lord's rule that man must work in order to gain the necessities of life. V. 27. **An ungodly man diggeth up evil,** his worthlessness causing him to dig pits for others; **and in his lips there is as a burning fire,** his words and statements are like a scorching fire or iron, whose searing heat destroys everything. V. 28. **A froward man,** one who makes use of malice, **soweth strife,** for his conduct is bound to create enmity; **and a whisperer,** a backbiter, **separateth chief friends,** causing close friends to be divided, for such is the effect of slander skilfully disseminated. V. 29. **A violent man enticeth his neighbor,** deliberately and maliciously persuading him to his hurt, **and leadeth him into the way that is not good,** where he will be in a position to execute the ruin which he planned. V. 30. **He shutteth his eyes,** to keep away any good influence, **to devise froward things,** to meditate mischief and craftiness; **moving his lips, he bringeth evil to pass,** the act or gesture of pressing together the lips being evidence of malice, and so he carries out his wicked intentions. V. 31. **The hoary head,** the white hair of an old person, **is a crown of glory,** like a splendid diadem, a shining ornament, **if it be found in the way of righteousness,** for only then will an old person be regarded with approval by the Lord. V. 32. **He that is slow to anger,** keeping himself well in hand always, controlling his temper, **is better than the mighty,** a champion fighter, who is always engaged in battle; **and he that ruleth his spirit,** holding his temper in leash, **than he that taketh a city,** for not quarreling and fighting upon the slightest provocation is the sign of greatness of mind, but a meekness which is able to control a person's feelings and gains its point by its very unshakable tranquility. V. 33. **The lot is cast into the lap,** apparently at random; **but the whole disposing thereof is of the Lord,** the decision rests with Him, for even those events which seem to us most fortuitous and subject only to chance are ordered and governed by God.

CHAPTER 17.

V. 1. **Better is a dry morsel,** without even the customary wine or diluted vinegar, **and quietness therewith,** harmony among all those at the table, **than an house full of sacrifices,** a great amount of the meat and other sumptuous foods served at sacrificial meals, **with strife,** hatred breaking out in quarrels, this being the danger when the rich went to excesses in their banquets. V. 2. **A wise servant shall have rule over a son that causeth shame,** the degenerate, profligate heir of the house, who squanders his fortune, becoming poor to the point of enforced servitude, while the former slave, through diligence and thrift, would become master, **and shall have part of the inheritance among the brethren,** that is, having squandered his own patrimony, the foolish son, though the first-born, would be obliged to divide the inheritance among the other heirs, while he himself receives not another cent. V. 3. **The fining-pot is for silver and the furnace for gold,** their nature and purity in either case being brought out by the process to which they are submitted; **but the Lord trieth the hearts,** testing the worth of both their nature and their contents, familiar with even the hidden desires of men. V. 4. **A wicked doer giveth heed to false lips,** literally, "Wickedness attends to lips of violence," for lies, deceit, and violence agree with the sentiments of a wicked heart; **and a liar giveth ear to a naughty tongue,** finding his pleasure in evil talk, which agrees with his own base thoughts and encourages him in his wickedness. V. 5. **Whoso mocketh the poor,** treating him with contempt on account of his lowly position, **reproacheth his Maker,** for the Lord gave the poor his station in life; **and he that is glad at calamities,** rejoicing over the misfortunes which befall others, **shall not be unpunished.** Cp. chap. 14, 31. V. 6. **Children's children are the crown of old men,** it is a blessing of the Lord and a source of honor and pride to the gray-headed if they see their offspring to the third generation, for the happiness of the younger generation is reflected in the life of the older; **and the glory of children are their fathers,** for the rule works both ways, and pious children share in the honor enjoyed by their parents. V. 7. **Excellent speech,** fine and high talk, in an assuming, dictatorial way, **becometh not a fool; much less do lying lips a prince,** for true nobility will have nothing to do with deceitfulness and crafty speeches. V. 8. **A gift is as a precious stone,** literally, "a stone of loveliness," of charming grace, **in the eyes of him that hath it,** the reference apparently being to the case of one who is stimulated by the prospect of a rich gift or bribe and therefore works with all the greater earnestness; **whithersoever it turneth**, that is, to whomsoever the gift comes, **it prospereth**, making prosperous, securing for its giver supporters and friends. V. 9. **He that covereth a transgression**, in a kindly and charitable manner avoiding the spread of evil reports, **seeketh love**, exercising it in a proper manner; **but he that repeateth a matter**, referring to certain transgressions time and again, keeping the memory of them alive, causing people to point the finger of scorn at the transgressor, **separateth very friends**, for suspicion and ill will is bound to destroy friendship. V. 10. **A reproof entereth more into a wise man**, makes a deeper and more lasting impression, has better consequences, **than an hundred stripes into a fool**, for the fool is callous and cannot be influenced. V. 11. **An evil man seeketh only rebellion**, that is, he who rebels against the Lord in wilful transgression of His Law has evil in mind; **therefore a cruel messenger shall be sent against him**, that is, evil will be punished with inexorable severity. V. 12. **Let a bear robbed of her whelps meet a man rather than a fool in his folly**, for a malignant fool is a greater menace to society and mankind in general than an angry bear. V. 13. **Whoso rewardeth evil for good**, in an excess of ingratitude, **evil shall not depart from his house**, for misfortune is the penalty of such acts of base ingratitude. V. 14. **The beginning of strife is as when one letteth out water**, as the breaking forth of waters through a dam or dike; one never knows to what proportions the flood will grow; **therefore leave off contention before it be meddled with**, cease before the mischief is set a-going; for, as in the case of a flood, one never knows how much damage will eventually be done. V. 15. **He that justifieth the wicked, and he that condemneth the just**, with an utter disregard of the demands of justice, **even they both are abomination to the Lord**, God regards either case with equal loathing. V. 16. **Wherefore is there a price in the hand of a fool to get wisdom**, believing that money will purchase knowledge or earthly gold, understanding, **seeing he hath no heart to it?** this fact being the real difficulty so far as the fool is concerned and shutting him out from true wisdom. V. 17. **A friend loveth at all times**, the good will among comrades being constant always, ever on the same level, **and a brother is born for adversity**, or, but the brother is born of adversity, for it is at such times that friendship and the proper brotherly relation receive their test. V. 18. **A man void of understanding**, lacking in common sense, **striketh hands**, pledging himself and his goods foolishly, **and becometh surety in the presence of his friend**. Cp. chap. 6, 1—5; 11, 15. V. 19. **He loveth transgression that loveth strife**, for a quarrelsome disposition is usually combined with wickedness of heart; **and he that exalteth his gate seeketh destruction**, putting on the airs of the wealthy by building a lofty gateway to his house, thereby inviting jealousy and enmity and leading to his own ruin. Pride is the most common cause of ruinous quarrels. V. 20. **He that hath a froward heart**, one that is crooked and malicious, **findeth no good**, will never prosper; **and he that hath a perverse tongue**, a wayward tongue, one which is not consistent, but winds and twists to suit the occasion, **falleth into mischief**, plunging himself into a well-deserved punishment. V. 21. **He that begetteth a fool doeth it to his sorrow**, he is most unfortunate to have a fool for his son; **and the father of a fool hath no joy**. Cp. chap. 10, 1; 18, 13. V. 22. **A merry heart doeth good like a medicine**, cheerfulness is conducive to health and well-being; **but a broken spirit**, one afflicted with grief and distress, **drieth the bones**, taking the very marrow and strength out of the body. V. 23. **A wicked man taketh a gift out of the bosom**, rather, "A bribe from the bosom," one given secretly and stealthily, "the wicked will receive," **to pervert the ways of judgment**, that being the object of bribes. V. 24. **Wisdom is before him that hath understanding**, it is very near to him, it guides and directs him always, leading him along one definite road always; **but the eyes of a fool are in the ends of the earth**, engaged with things in a dim and shadowy distance, his thoughts straying about without definite aim. V. 25. **A foolish son is a grief to his father**, causing him sorrow and mourning, **and bitterness to her that bare him**, by the vexation which he causes. V. 26. **Also, to punish the just is not good**, it is against the principles of justice to have the righteous bear any kind of punishment, **nor to strike princes for equity**, smiting the noble contrary to right, under the pretense of right and justice openly to dispense injustice. V. 27. **He that hath knowledge spareth his words**, is chary of speech, refrains from garrulity; **and a man of understanding is of an excellent spirit**, rather, he that is of a quiet temper, a man who has himself in hand always, shows that he is sensible. V. 28. **Even a fool, when he holdeth his peace, is counted wise, and he that shutteth his lips is esteemed a man of understanding**, this being an admonition to the foolish at least to abstain from making known his lack of wisdom and thus to maintain a reputation for common sense, if he can do nothing more.

CHAPTER 18.

V. 1. **Through desire a man, having separated himself, seeketh and intermeddleth with all wisdom,** rather, "After his own desire seeketh the odd person, against all sound counsel he setteth himself," that is, he who goes his own way out of selfish opposition to everything that is established among men seeks only his own selfish interest in life. V. 2. **A fool hath no delight in understanding, his pleasure not being set that way, but that his heart may discover itself,** display the wisdom which he imagines to be there, for he believes it to be his duty to let the world know his greatness in this respect. V. 3. **When the wicked cometh, then cometh also contempt,** for such a person considers himself above submission to others and therefore is lacking in both reverence and forbearance, **and with ignominy reproach,** for the wicked must display his assumed superiority by treating all those not in his favor with studied contempt. V. 4. **The words of a man's mouth are as deep waters,** hard to fathom and exhaust, if he really has something to say, **and the well-spring of wisdom as a flowing brook,** literally, "a bubbling brook," a fountain of wisdom, rich in content and life-giving in quality. V. 5. **It is not good to accept the person of the wicked,** to favor him in any way, especially in a court case, **to overthrow the righteous in judgment,** so that he loses his case on account of the partiality of the judge. V. 6. **A fool's lips enter into contention,** bring on a quarrel, **and his mouth calleth for strokes,** he challenges and provokes the punishment which strikes him. V. 7. **A fool's mouth,** on account of his quarrelsome disposition, **is his destruction,** it brings ruin upon him, **and his lips are the snare of his soul,** his rash language causes trouble for himself. V. 8. **The words of a talebearer are as wounds,** rather, as sweet morsels, or, as pastime, eagerly grasped and swallowed by those who listen to slander, **and they go down into the innermost parts of the belly,** gladly accepted and remembered. V. 9. **He also that is slothful in his work,** who does not apply himself to it with all diligence, **is brother to him that is a great waster,** a squanderer; the two are closely related, since in either case possessions are lost. V. 10. **The name of the Lord is a strong tower,** he who relies upon Jehovah as He has revealed Himself in His Word has a stronghold of safest protection; **the righteous,** he who by faith places his confidence in the Lord, **runneth into it and is safe,** gains a high and sheltered position, where the enemies can do him no harm. V. 11. **The rich man's wealth is his strong city and as an high wall in his own conceit,** his own foolish imagination; for it is not a tower like the name of the Lord. V. 12. **Before destruction the heart of man is haughty,** pride going before the fall, **and before honor is humility,** preceding it like a herald showing the way. Cp. chap. 16, 18; 15, 33. V. 13. **He that answereth a matter before he heareth it,** before a careful hearing of both sides enables him to reach a right and just conclusion, **it is folly and shame unto him,** for an opinion not based upon sound investigation is worse than worthless, Eccl. 11, 8. V. 14. **The spirit of a man will sustain his infirmity,** a strong and courageous mind supporting him in bodily sickness or weakness; **but a wounded spirit,** one bowed and broken by adversity, **who can bear?** It is a more difficult matter to bear up under the infirmities of the soul, the griefs, sorrows, troubles, and tribulations which affect the inner life than to overcome the effects of bodily weakness. V. 15. **The heart of the prudent getteth knowledge,** working for its possession, ready for its reception, **and the ear of the wise seeketh knowledge,** eager to serve the heart and the inner life in the acquisition of true wisdom. V. 16. **A man's gift,** sent before him to procure favor for him, **maketh room for him,** giving him ready access to the one whose favor he is seeking, **and bringeth him before great men,** for it opens the doors of the mighty before him, this being true not only in the Orient, but also in the midst of our Western civilization. V. 17. **He that is first in his own cause seemeth just,** that is, a person believes himself to be altogether in the right in any disputed matter before he has heard the other side; **but his neighbor cometh and searcheth him,** makes him submit to a new examination concerning the matter at issue, thereby bringing the truth to light and reversing the original opinion. V. 18. **The lot,** as used by the Jews according to law, **causeth contentions to cease,** for the Lord Himself guided the result, **and parteth between the mighty,** deciding the matter between them and thus preventing bloody quarrels. V. 19. **A brother offended is harder to be won than a strong city,** for if he has been estranged by some deliberate offense, by a breach of faith, he will look upon every attempt at adjustment with suspicion; **and their contentions are like the bars of a castle,** quarrels between former friends are the most stubborn obstructions to a reconciliation. V. 20. **A man's belly shall be satisfied with the fruit of his mouth,** his whole body will have to bear the consequences of his speeches; **and with the increase of his lips shall he be filled,** it will come back to him as it has gone forth from his mouth. V. 21. **Death and life are in the power of the tongue,** that is, the one or the other will be the fate of man, in agreement with the manner in which he used his tongue; **and they that love it shall eat the fruit thereof,** experiencing in themselves the effects of its good use and of its abuse. V. 22. **Whoso findeth a wife,** the words implying an earnest and wise search, **findeth a good thing,** for a virtuous wife is a true helpmeet for man, **and obtaineth favor of the Lord,** for such a wife is abundant evidence of the Lord's merciful kindness and truly belongs in the Fourth Petition. V. 23. **The poor useth intreaties,** his poverty and the lowliness of his station compelling him to show all meekness in dealing with those in power; **but the rich,** depending upon the respect which is universally given to great possessions, **answereth roughly,** feeling himself privileged to do so on account of his wealth. V. 24. **A man that hath friends must show himself friendly,** rather, a man who has all the world for his friend will fail in true friendship, for he will hardly stand up for well-defined principles; **and there is a friend that sticketh closer than a brother,** one who will be tested in adversity and found sound, for the proof of friendship is if it stands the test of trouble.

CHAPTER 19.

V. 1. **Better is the poor that walketh in his integrity,** in innocence of heart and righteousness of conduct, **than he that is perverse in his lips,** full of malice in his speech, **and is a fool,** for his riches will not save him from this condemnation. V. 2. **Also, that the soul be without knowledge,** where the soul lacks knowledge and insight, **it is not good,** for that fact keeps it from all energy and progress; **and he that hasteth with his feet,** going ahead without proper consideration, in foolish rashness, to obtain some outward blessing, **sinneth,** since his zeal is not according to knowledge. V. 3. **The foolishness of man perverteth his way,** he himself is to be blamed if he is thrown prostrate and brought to ruin; **and his heart fretteth against the Lord,** murmuring against Jehovah when he has no one but himself to blame. V. 4. **Wealth maketh many friends,** for people seek the favor of the wealthy, in the hope of obtaining some benefit for themselves; **but the poor is separated from his neighbor,** it is the way of the world to leave the impoverished to his own resources and to ignore him. V. 5. **A false witness shall not be unpunished,** his lies being recorded in God's records, **and he that speaketh lies,** constantly breathing them out, **shall not escape,** an emphatic way of saying that he shall surely perish. V. 6. **Many will intreat the favor of the prince,** literally, "stroke his face," flatter him; **and every man is a friend to him that giveth gifts,** with the expectation of sharing in his generosity. These facts are stated as in agreement with men's conduct everywhere and do not imply the approval of the Lord. V. 7. **All the brethren of the poor do hate him,** his own relatives treating him with an utter want of charity; **how much more do his friends go far from him!** for his acquaintances are not even bound by the ties of relationship and therefore withdraw with less compunction. **He pursueth them with words,** eager to hear at least some words of encouragement and friendly interest, **yet they are wanting to him,** that is, no one cheers him with words of kindness; even so much is denied him. V. 8. **He that getteth wisdom,** proper understanding and common sense, **loveth his own soul,** for this love is demonstrated and proved by the acquiring of wisdom; **he that keepeth understanding shall find good,** have true fortune and happiness. V. 9. **A false witness shall not be unpunished, and he that speaketh lies shall perish.** Cp. v. 5. V. 10. **Delight is not seemly for a fool,** a life of luxury does not become him, **much less for a servant to have rule over princes,** this being possible at courts where the favorites of the sovereign ingratiate themselves and eventually direct the affairs of the realm. V. 11. **The discretion of a man deferreth his anger;** if he always follows the dictates of prudence, he will delay his anger and show all due patience with the erring; **and it is his glory,** it adds to his honorable reputation, **to pass over a transgression,** not by condoning and ignoring it, but by keeping it from becoming public property, to be made a morsel of defaming tongues. V. 12. **The king's wrath is as the roaring of a lion,** striking terror to the hearts of men as he prepares to fall upon his prey; **but his favor is as dew upon the grass,** pleasant and refreshing. V. 13. **A foolish son is the calamity of his father,** his mischievous and sinful acts are like stroke upon stroke, they strike his father with a steady beating; **and the contentions of a wife,** her quarrelsome nagging and brawling, **are a continual dropping,** like water dropping from the eaves with a steady, maddening monotony. V. 14. **House and riches are the inheritance of fathers,** it is possible to get into possession of them by the fact of one's being an heir; **and a prudent wife is from the Lord,** a special gift of His kindness. V. 15. **Slothfulness casteth into a deep sleep,** causing a man to sink into stupor and lethargy, sapping the last bit of his energy, **and an idle soul shall suffer hunger,** that being the result of sloth. V. 16. **He that keepeth the commandment,** namely, that of God's Law, **keepeth his own soul,** for such conduct is conducive to spiritual life; **but he that despiseth his ways,** taking no heed to keep them in agreement with the Word of God, **shall die**, for destruction is the punishment of such disobedience. V. 17. **He that hath pity upon the poor**, showing him charity in the right spirit, **lendeth unto the Lord**, money given to the poor is deposited in the savings-bank of Jehovah; **and that which he hath given**, in helping out the poor and needy, **will He pay him again.** Cp. Matt. 25, 40; Luke 6, 30—35. V. 18. **Chasten thy son while there is hope**, correcting him, if necessary, by corporal punishment, **and let not thy soul spare for his crying**, literally, "and to his death do not lift up thy soul"; wisdom and love must know and observe the proper measure of punishment, knowing, at the same time, that there is a cruel kindness, which kills by withholding seasonable correction. V. 19. **A man of great wrath**, one who cannot control his temper, **shall suffer punishment; for if thou deliver him, yet thou must do it again**, that is, to interfere with a wrathful man with the purpose of saving him from his own foolishness usually makes matters worse; he must learn to govern himself. V. 20. **Hear counsel and receive instruction**, in effecting the moral training which every person needs for true wisdom, **that thou mayest be wise in thy latter end**, in the future; for the conduct of the truly wise will grow nearer perfection as they grow in years. V. 21. **There are many devices in a man's heart**, he may have many ideas and plans; **nevertheless, the counsel of the Lord, that shall stand;** it is He who disposes, leading the affairs of all men according to His will. V. 22. **The desire of a man is his kindness**, that is, the worth of his show of liberality depends upon his good will, upon the genuineness of his beneficence or altruism; **and a poor man is better than a liar**, one who is unable to help, but is sincere in desiring to do so, is better than one who, with riches at his command, professes to be unable to help. V. 23. **The fear of the Lord tendeth to life**, it shows and points the way to the true life in the Lord; **and he that hath it shall abide satisfied; he shall not be visited with evil**, because Jehovah will protect, promote, and in every way bless such a man. V. 24. **A slothful man hideth his hand in his bosom**, rather, he plunges it into the wide dish which contained the principal food of the family, **and will not so much as bring it to his mouth again**, too lazy even to eat. V. 25. **Smite a scorner**, who is beyond rebuke, in whose case no admonition will bring fruit, **and the simple will beware;** although inexperienced, he will learn a lesson by constraint; **and reprove one that hath understanding**, who is eager to learn prudence, and **he will understand knowledge**, he will immediately accept the correction and act accordingly. V. 26. **He that wasteth his father**, attacking him violently, abusing him in words and possibly also in deeds, **and chaseth away his mother**, making life unbearable for her in her own home, **is a son that causeth shame and bringeth reproach**, his conduct causing grief to his parents not only by his disregard of their authority, but also by the fact that men will point the finger of scorn at them. V. 27. **Cease, my son, to hear the instruction that causeth to err from the words of knowledge**, rather, "to depart from the sayings of understanding," for teaching which is not wholesome and in accord with the Word of God leads to destruction. V. 28. **An ungodly witness**, one who is worthless, vain, and wicked in the sight of God, **scorneth judgment**, scoffing at the righteous punishment which is threatened; **and the mouth of the wicked devoureth iniquity**, he desires mischief most passionately, he cannot get enough. V. 29. **Judgments are prepared for scorners**, their verdict of condemnation is ready, **and stripes for the back of fools**, for their punishment also is inevitable, since the just God will not be mocked.

CHAPTER 20.

V. 1. **Wine is a mocker**, excessive indulgence in it produces scorn and blasphemy in the drinker, **strong drink is raging**, it robs a man of clear thinking and proper self-possession; **and whosoever is deceived thereby is not wise**, that is, if he is led astray thereby, so that he reels and staggers under its influence, he shows the lack of wisdom and will never attain to true wisdom. V. 2. **The fear of a king**, the terror spread by his anger, **is as the roaring of a lion**, chap. 19, 12; **whoso provoketh him to anger sinneth against his own soul**, foolishly risks and even forfeits his own life. V. 3. **It is an honor for a man to cease from strife**, to dwell and remain far from quarrels, neither to provoke nor to promote them; **but every fool will be meddling**, foolishly starting quarrels. V. 4. **The sluggard will not plow by reason of the cold**, the disagreeable weather furnishing him a welcome excuse to keep him from tilling the soil; **therefore shall he beg in harvest and have nothing**, that is, when he looks for grain in the season of harvest, his field has borne none, that being the reward of sloth. V. 5. **Counsel in the heart of man is like deep water**, for his plans are hidden in his innermost heart; **but a man of understanding**, one who knows how to deal with men, **will draw it out**, he will judge the actions of men according to their motives and objects and draw the right conclusions. V. 6. **Most men will proclaim every one his own goodness,** literally, "Many a man meets a man of his pleasantness," for an outward show of pleasantness, an amiable exterior, is not unusual; **but a faithful man,** one upon whom one may depend in time of need, **who can find?** Such faithfulness is rare. V. 7. **The just man walketh in his integrity,** he who in his innocence conducts himself uprightly, righteously, **his children are blessed after him,** if they follow him in his righteousness, the Lord's blessing rests upon them to a thousand generations, Ex. 20, 6; Deut. 7, 9. V. 8. **A king that sitteth in the throne of judgment,** dispensing justice in his capacity of sovereign, **scattereth away all evil with his eyes,** he searches out, he sifts by winnowing, and so separates the evil from the good, the right from the wrong. V. 9. **Who can say, I have made my heart clean,** purifying it to the point of moral perfection, **I am pure from my sin?** The answer is clearly given in the question and stated, Eccl. 7, 20. V. 10. **Divers weights,** stones as they were used for weights in balances, **and divers measures,** the reference being not only to the vessels used in dry measure, but to every kind of measure, **both of them are alike abomination to the Lord;** deception in business, cheating in trade, is sinful and loathsome in His sight. V. 11. **Even a child is known by his doings,** reveals his nature and character by his acts, **whether his work be pure, and whether it be right,** there is no innocence in childhood, and children will be held responsible by God for their acts. V. 12. **The hearing ear and the seeing eye, the Lord hath made even both of them;** therefore He, the omniscient Creator of the senses, will demand a reckoning of their use on the Last Day. V. 13. **Love not sleep,** that associated with slothfulness, **lest thou come to poverty,** that being the result of sloth; **open thine eyes,** with the proper energy, industry, and vigor, **and thou shalt be satisfied with bread,** for so is diligent activity rewarded. V. 14. **It is naught, it is naught, saith the buyer,** he insists that the goods offered him are bad, worthless, in order to beat down the price; **but when he is gone his way,** having gotten the better of the deal, **then he boasteth,** setting forth the shrewdness with which he drove his bargain, such conduct also being a form of dishonesty. V. 15. **There is gold and a multitude of rubies,** or pearls, such trinkets are found in abundance in the world; **but the lips of knowledge are a precious jewel,** they are rare indeed in the world. V. 16. **Take his garment that is surety for a stranger,** for one so foolish and inconsiderate might as well hand it over at once, since he will surely lose it, **and take a pledge of him for a strange woman,** or, "for strange people," for such suretyship is always ill-advised. V. 17. **Bread of deceit is sweet to a man,** what he gains by such means may seem pleasant and enjoyable to him at first; **but afterwards his mouth shall be filled with gravel,** it will be most disagreeable and grievous to him. V. 18. **Every purpose is established by counsel,** definite plans should be formulated only after a careful consultation with such as are in a position to advise; **and with good advice make war,** after considering all emergencies and possibilities. Cp. Luke 14, 31. V. 19. **He that goeth about as a talebearer,** making it his business to carry gossip and slander, **revealeth secrets; therefore meddle not with him that flattereth with his lips.** Cp. chap. 11, 13; 13, 3. V. 20. **Whoso curseth his father or his mother,** in a bold and blasphemous transgression of the Fourth Commandment, **his lamp shall be put out in obscure darkness,** the picture being that of hopeless destruction of property and life, a condemnation under the wrath of God. V. 21. **An inheritance may be gotten hastily at the beginning,** wayward and ungodly children being so eager that they even drive their parents out of their possession; **but the end thereof shall not be blessed,** the blessing of God will not rest upon such unfilial and wicked behavior. V. 22. **Say not thou, I will recompense evil,** avenging evil with evil after the manner practised by the ungodly; **but wait on the Lord,** placing the outcome entirely in His hands, **and He shall save thee.** Cp. Ps. 27, 14; Rom. 12, 17—19. V. 23. **Divers weights are an abomination unto the Lord, and a false balance is not good.** Cp. v. 10. V. 24. **Man's goings are of the Lord,** he is dependent upon the Lord in all his actions, he is directed by the manner of God's disposal; **how can a man, then, understand his own way?** It is impossible for him to decipher the ways in which God directs him, he cannot uncover the secrets of God's government. V. 25. **It is a snare to the man who devoureth that which is holy,** if he is overhasty in making a vow to the Lord and in devoting some of his substance to the Temple-service, **and after vows to make enquiry,** that is, when it was too late, the result usually being that the rash vow is broken. V. 26. **A wise king scattereth the wicked,** sifting and winnowing them, as the chaff is separated from the grain, **and bringeth the wheel over them,** as the wheel of the threshing-cart separated the wheat-kernels from the hulls when it was passed over the stalks spread out on the threshing-floor. V. 27. **The spirit of man is the candle of the Lord,** the spiritual and moral powers of man, under the direction of Jehovah, penetrate into his innermost being, **searching all the inward parts of the belly.** V. 28. **Mercy and truth preserve the**

king, they are the attributes or virtues which make **his reign successful, and his throne is upholden by mercy,** by gracious kindness and favor. V. 29. **The glory of young men is their strength,** for they are in the first flush of their manhood, and their physical power is at its best; **and the beauty of old men is the gray head,** which gives dignity to their appearance. V. 30. **The blueness of a wound cleanseth away evil,** literally, "Wounding stripes purge away evil"; **so do stripes the inward parts of the belly,** for a proper measure of severe discipline penetrates to the depths of the heart and removes the desire for evil, all punishment, rightly administered, having this object.

CHAPTER 21.

V. 1. **The king's heart is in the hand of the Lord as the rivers of water,** the thoughts and plans of the mightiest rulers, sovereign as they may seem, are like ditches and canals in which men lead water where they desire; **He turneth it whithersoever He will;** no matter what the mighty may fatuously ascribe to themselves in the way of absolute authority, there is One whose government directs even their actions in agreement with His will. V. 2. **Every way of a man is right in his own eyes,** he is inclined to self-satisfaction, which may lead him astray; **but the Lord pondereth the hearts,** He weighs them and thus determines the direction which their plans should take. Cp. chap. 16, 2. V. 3. **To do justice and judgment,** to exercise the principles of righteousness and justice in all our dealings, **is more acceptable to the Lord than sacrifice,** for all outward acts of worship are hollow sham without true piety of the heart. V. 4. **An high look and a proud heart,** literally, "haughtiness of eyes and pompousness of heart," **and the plowing of the wicked,** either the light, the prosperity, or the whole business, all that the ungodly do, **is sin,** and therefore makes them guilty in the eyes of the Lord. V. 5. **The thoughts of the diligent tend only to plenteousness;** because they are industrious and thrifty, they have success; **but of every one that is hasty, only to want;** for haste, that is, rashness, lack of proper planning, makes waste. V. 6. **The getting of treasures by a lying tongue,** by means of misrepresentations and concealment of the truth, **is a vanity tossed to and fro of them that seek death,** like a fleeting breath, a vanishing haze; for their prosperity has no sound foundation, leading them, instead, to destruction. V. 7. **The robbery of the wicked,** the violence which they try to exert in working harm to others, **shall destroy them,** they are swept away as the result of their own wickedness, **because they refuse to do judgment,** that which is just and right before the Lord. V. 8. **The way of man is froward and strange,** literally, "Twisted is the way of the guilt-laden," for the vicious man has only wickedness in mind; **but as for the pure,** one who is clean in his conduct, **his work is right,** in agreement with the will of God. V. 9. **It is better to dwell in a corner of the housetop,** seated alone and forsaken on the parapet of the Oriental flat roof, exposed to every form of weather, **than with a brawling woman,** one always nagging and quarreling, **in a wide house;** for though the house be large enough for several families, it is not large enough to afford peace where the one or the other spouse is addicted to such unpleasant behavior. V. 10. **The soul of the wicked desireth evil,** since that is his only delight in life; **his neighbor findeth no favor in his eyes,** his selfishness makes him utterly devoid of mercy and compassion. V. 11. **When the scorner is punished, the simple is made wise,** since he profits by the example of warning; **and when the wise is instructed, he receiveth knowledge,** no severe correction or punishment being necessary in his case, since he accepts teaching readily. Cp. chap. 19, 25. V. 12. **The righteous man wisely considereth the house of the wicked,** the reference evidently being to God, who marks the house of the ungodly, noting every sign of wickedness, every deed of violence; **but God overthroweth the wicked for their wickedness,** He plunges them into misfortune and destruction. V. 13. **Whoso stoppeth his ears at the cry of the poor,** deliberately and hard-heartedly ignoring their appeals for help, **he also shall cry himself, but shall not be heard,** thus being punished in the manner in which he transgressed. V. 14. **A gift in secret pacifieth anger,** a gift brought concealed in the bosom and presented at the proper moment; **and a reward in the bosom,** a gift of bribery, **strong wrath,** for the more liberal the present, the more readily will it influence the one who receives it. V. 15. **It is joy to the just to do judgment,** they love right and delight in performing its demands always; **but destruction shall be to the workers of iniquity,** that is, the exercise of justice strikes terror to the heart of those who are active in wickedness. V. 16. **The man that wandereth out of the way of understanding,** deliberately choosing the way of error, **shall remain in the congregation of the dead,** shall rest there, as in his everlasting home. V. 17. **He that loveth pleasure,** the delights of costly luxuries, **shall be a poor man; he that loveth wine and oil,** perfumed oil used as a cosmetic, **shall not be rich**, for his property and earnings will be squandered for useless baubles and dangerous luxuries. V. 18. **The wicked shall be a ransom for the righteous**, for by the punishment which he suffers he atones, in a way, for the errors of the pious or is substituted by God for his intended victim, as Haman was for Mordecai, **and the transgressor for the upright.** Cp. Josh. 7, 26; Esther 7, 9. V. 19. **It is better to dwell in the wilderness**, far from the habitations of men, **than with a contentious and an angry woman.** Cp. v. 9. V. 20. **There is treasure to be desired and oil in the dwelling of the wise**, because he will carefully lay up and increase wealth; **but a foolish man spendeth it up**, he is a spendthrift and a waster. V. 21. **He that followeth after righteousness and mercy**, eagerly desiring and practising these virtues, **findeth life**, the true spiritual life whose source is in God, **righteousness**, such as is acceptable in the sight of God, **and honor**, as the Lord bestows upon His children, for they are valued highly in His eyes, no matter how despised they may be in this world. V. 22. **A wise man scaleth the city of the mighty**, for a wise man will find and suggest ways of taking even a strong fortress, defended by numerous and strong warriors, Eccl. 9, 14. 15, **and casteth down the strength of the confidence thereof**, the bulwarks upon which the defenders relied. V. 23. **Whoso keepeth his mouth and his tongue**, that is, he who can control them properly, both in refraining from speech and in speaking at the right time and to some definite purpose, **keepeth his soul from troubles**; for a garrulous fool is always making difficulties for himself. V. 24. **Proud and haughty scorner**, a puffed-up jackanapes, **is his name, who dealeth in proud wrath**, in an excess of insolence, with mockery of everything that is holy. V. 25. **The desire of the slothful**, his natural appetites and needs, for which he refuses to provide, **killeth him**, for want of diligence he dies of want; **for his hands refuse to labor**; too lazy to work, he is bound to starve. V. 26. **He coveteth greedily all the day long**, his needs clamor to be met; **but the righteous giveth and spareth not**, his industry providing not only for his own needs, but for those in actual need as well. V. 27. **The sacrifice of the wicked is abomination**, no amount of mechanical, outward acting will take the place of worship in spirit and in truth; **how much more when he bringeth it with a wicked mind**, for transgression, while his heart is still filled with wickedness, the outward sacrifice being intended to cover up the lack of repentance. This verse applies to all outward, mere mechanical worship, to all the churchgoing of hypocrites. V. 28. **A false witness shall perish**, chap. 19, 5. 9; **but the man that heareth speaketh constantly**, being modest and lending a ready ear to instruction, he is able to render reliable testimony, not being obliged to cease for uncertainty or a muddled condition of his mind. V. 29. **A wicked man hardeneth his face**, trying to hide his wicked thoughts and intentions behind a bold exterior; **but as for the upright, he directeth his way**, carefully weighing and testing every step, and thus establishing his conduct under all circumstances. V. 30. **There is no wisdom nor understanding nor counsel against the Lord**, all human wisdom which would set itself over against the truth of God's eternal Word is folly. V. 31. **The horse is prepared against the day of battle**, that is, men may make all arrangements and preparations for war, deeming the victory as good as gained; **but safety is of the Lord**, it is in His hand to give victory or defeat, it rests with Him to decide the issues, 1 Sam. 17, 47.

CHAPTER 22.

V. 1. **A good name is rather to be chosen than great riches**, it is much more precious, Eccl. 7, 1, **and loving favor rather than silver and gold**, that is, the kind regard of the wise and good is to be preferred to all outward possessions. V. 2. **The rich and poor meet together**, they are found side by side, in agreement with God's order in the world; **the Lord is the Maker of them all**, whence it follows that the poor should not envy the rich, and the rich should not oppress the poor. V. 3. **A prudent man foreseeth the evil and hideth himself**, for his prudence takes into account all possibilities; **but the simple**, the inexperienced, those who are too foolish to learn, **pass on and are punished**, they suffer the consequences of their foolishness. V. 4. **By humility and the fear of the Lord**, coming to men as a result of these virtues, **are riches and honor and life**, for outward prosperity, the respect of men, and inner growth are the rewards given to believers by the Lord. V. 5. **Thorns and snares are in the way of the froward**, they are often placed in the way of those who are crooked in their thinking and dealing, or they are naturally found along the paths frequented by them; **he that doth keep his soul**, in conducting himself according to the precepts of true morality and piety, **shall be far from them**, he will have no such things to hinder him in his way. V. 6. **Train up a child in the way he should go**, carefully imparting to him the instruction which he needs for the right formation of pious habits, the method of instruction following the age and the peculiarity of the child; **and when he is old, he will not depart from it,** his moral habits having been established by constant and proper training, he will naturally conduct himself always in a manner becoming a Christian. V. 7. **The rich ruleth over the poor,** his wealth giving him a large measure of power, especially if the poor are dependent upon him for loans, **and the borrower is servant to the lender,** for indebtedness is bound to interfere with the feeling, if not with the fact, of freedom. V. 8. **He that soweth iniquity,** unrighteousness and wickedness in any form, **shall reap vanity,** misfortune and calamity; **and the rod of his anger shall fail,** the staff of his haughty wrath with which he so often tried to intimidate men, is bound to vanish, his tyranny will come to an abrupt end. V. 9. **He that hath a bountiful eye,** one which reflects kindness, friendliness, and charity, **shall be blessed; for he giveth of his bread to the poor;** as he dispenses blessing, he will receive blessing. V. 10. **Cast out the scorner,** the one whose mockery is directed against godliness in every form, **and contention shall go out,** for blasphemous taunts engender quarrels; **yea, strife and reproach shall cease,** with the removal of the blasphemer. V. 11. **He that loveth pureness of heart, for the grace of his lips the king shall be his friend,** literally, "He who loves purity, integrity, of heart, and to whom is grace of lips, the king is his friend," he will stand high in the counsels of the mighty of the earth. V. 12. **The eyes of the Lord preserve knowledge,** for His eyes are fixed in protecting care upon those who observe the norm of true knowledge as found in His Word, **and He overthroweth the words of the transgressor,** all the proposals and plans by which the wicked intends to harm the believer. V. 13. **The slothful man saith,** eagerly making use of every shadow of an excuse to abstain from work, senseless though it may be, **There is a lion without, I shall be slain in the streets,** so he prefers not to take any chances, but continues to indulge his laziness. V. 14. **The mouth of strange women,** for so the harlots were commonly designated in the midst of God's people, **is a deep pit,** on account of the alluring and seductive language which they use in pursuing their intended victims; **he that is abhorred of the Lord shall fall therein,** in just punishment of his wickedness, the curse of Jehovah thereby going into effect. V. 15. **Foolishness is bound in the heart of a child,** the reference being not merely to silly pranks and senseless escapades, but to the sinfulness of a child's nature, which shows itself in evil words and acts; **but the rod of correction,** which the Lord has entrusted to parents, as His representatives, for the use of which they are responsible to Him, **shall drive it far from him,** judicious punishment properly administered will put the dread of evil in the heart of the child. V. 16. **He that oppresseth the poor to increase his riches,** his oppression results in ill-gotten wealth for himself, **and he that giveth to the rich shall surely come to want,** such an act will result in nothing but loss to himself. In either case, selfishness is the ruling motive, and in either case the punishment of God will strike the transgressor. V. 17. **Bow down thine ear,** inclining it in the attitude of the most careful attention, **and hear the words of the wise, and apply thine heart unto my knowledge,** that presented by the inspired author in this new section of the Book of Proverbs. V. 18. **For it is a pleasant thing if thou keep them within thee,** the words of the wise serving to give true delight; **they shall withal be fitted in thy lips,** abiding there and exerting their authority. V. 19. **That thy trust may be in the Lord I have made known to thee this day, even to thee,** for it is the author's object to teach the fear of Jehovah by his precepts. V. 20. **Have not I written to thee excellent things in counsels and knowledge,** most excellent maxims of proper behavior, v. 21. **that I might make thee know the certainty,** the strict correctness or verity, **of the words of truth, that thou,** equipped with this knowledge, **mightest answer the words of truth to them that send unto thee?** The reference is to the parents, who have sent their son to the teacher of wisdom and expect him to become proficient in the principles of true wisdom. After this introductory admonition to heed the precepts of truth the author offers maxims of pious conduct. V. 22. **Rob not the poor,** depriving him of his property by force or by a show of right, **because he is poor,** unable to procure assistance, **neither oppress the afflicted in the gate,** the place where local cases were usually decided by the elders or judges of the city; v. 23. **for the Lord will plead their cause,** conducting the case of the poor and afflicted, as their Advocate and Champion, **and spoil the soul of those that spoiled them,** taking the side of the wronged and vindicating the poor by punishing the violation of right and justice on the part of the powerful. V. 24. **Make no friendship with an angry man,** a man of violent temper, **and with a furious man thou shalt not go,** one who cannot control himself. v. 25. **lest thou learn his ways,** be infected by his vice, **and get a snare to thy soul,** for a violent temper is a fatal net to him who is subject to its attacks. V. 26. **Be not thou one of them that strike hands,** by hastily pledging himself for the debts of another, **or of them that,** in a frivolous manner, **are sureties for debts.** V. 27. **If thou hast nothing to pay,** being called upon to make good his pledge, **why should he take away thy bed**

from under thee? the bed having been pledged as a guarantee for the payment of the debt here concerned. Cp. chap. 6, 1—4; 11, 15; 17, 18; 20, 16. V. 28. **Remove not the ancient landmark,** set to mark the boundaries, **which thy fathers have set.** Cp. chap. 15, 25. V. 29. **Seest thou a man diligent in his business?** one who is skilful, apt, diligent. **He shall stand before kings,** being invited to serve them with his counsel and with his ability; **he shall not stand before mean men,** ordinary, obscure persons, for the services of such a man would be considered too valuable to be of benefit to a small circle only.

CHAPTER 23.

V. 1. **When thou sittest to eat with a ruler,** with a person of influence and power, **consider diligently what is before thee,** keeping in mind throughout the dinner that it is a mightier and loftier one at whose invitation one is present, v. 2. **and put a knife to thy throat, if thou be a man given to appetite,** keeping the usual gluttonous appetite in leash by the strongest warnings and threats, restraining the least sign of self-indulgence. V. 3. **Be not desirous of his dainties,** craving the finest food on the table; **for they are deceitful meat,** literally, "bread of deception," it is a deceptive meal, the object of the powerful person not being to dispense free hospitality, but to make use of his guest in some manner. V. 4. **Labor not to be rich,** the vanity of such an ambition being obvious; **cease from thine own wisdom,** having enough common sense not to make the acquisition of riches the chief aim in life. V. 5. **Wilt thou set thine eyes upon that which is not,** looking eagerly for, craving eagerly after, something which has no lasting substance? **For riches certainly make themselves wings,** they are not a dependable possession; **they fly away as an eagle toward heaven,** they are as unstable as a bird of the air, whence it follows that he who trusts in them is foolish. V. 6. **Eat thou not the bread of him that hath an evil eye,** of a jealous and covetous man, **neither desire thou his dainty meats,** which are held out before his guest as a sort of bait, not with open kindliness, but with a hidden purpose, for the envious person's selfishness will not permit him to dispense true hospitality; v. 7. **for as he thinketh in his heart, so is he,** his true nature does not appear on the outside, but his calculating meanness counts every bite his guest takes. **Eat and drink, saith he to thee,** with apparent politeness and cordial hospitality; **but his heart is not with thee,** he is not sincere, it is all sham and deceit, planned with selfish calculation. V. 8. **The morsel which thou hast eaten shalt thou vomit up,** namely, afterwards, upon finding out about the host's deception, **and lose thy sweet words,** those spoken in acknowledgment of the supposed hospitality. V. 9. **Speak not in the ears of a fool; for he will despise the wisdom of thy words.** V. 10. **Remove not the old landmark,** the boundary which was placed when the land was first divided to the several families, **and enter not into the fields of the fatherless,** for the purpose of changing the boundary marks or committing other acts of violence; v. 11. **for their Redeemer,** their Avenger, the one who champions their cause, **is mighty;** for it is the Lord Himself who acts as their vindicator; **He shall plead their cause with thee,** appearing as the Advocate of the defenseless and, at the same time, as the Judge of the violators. V. 12. **Apply thine heart unto instruction,** paying willing attention to correction, **and thine ears to the words of knowledge,** those which teach prudence and circumspection. V. 13. **Withhold not correction from the child; for if thou beatest him with the rod, he shall not die,** that is, the punishment may be bitter, even for the parent, but that fact dare not interfere with the plain duty imposed by the Lord. V. 14. **Thou shalt beat him with the rod,** with severe punishment, if necessary, **and shalt deliver his soul from hell,** for the correction will result in blessing to the child, in keeping him from worse transgressions and thus becoming a victim of death in sins. Cp. chap. 3, 27; 19, 18; 22, 15. V. 15. **My son, if thine heart be wise,** as the result of wholesome teaching here offered, **my heart shall rejoice, even mine,** for such is the effect of successful teaching upon the instructor. V. 16. **Yea, my reins,** his whole inner being, **shall rejoice when thy lips speak right things,** in an outward manifestation of the wisdom of the heart. V. 17. **Let not thine heart envy sinners,** for their apparent happiness and prosperity; **but be thou in the fear of the Lord all the day long;** that is the proper object of emulation, after which one ought to strive with all his heart. V. 18. **For surely there is an end,** the end, the Day of Judgment, will surely come; **and thine expectation shall not be cut off,** God will then fulfil the hopes of the righteous and give them the joys of immortal life with Him. V. 19. **Hear thou, my son, and be wise, and guide thine heart in the way,** by directing it to go straight forward on the right way, in conduct becoming a believer, a child of God. V. 20. **Be not among winebibbers,** those given to intemperance in drinking, **among riotous eaters of flesh,** for these two forms of intemperance are usually found together; v. 21. **for the drunkard and the glutton shall come to poverty,** all his property being dissipated in riotous living; and **drowsiness,** the laziness and apathy into which the intemperate man is bound to sink in consequence of his excesses, **shall clothe a man with rags,** bring him to the very depths of poverty. V. 22. **Hearken unto thy father that begat thee,** in ready obedience to all his commands, **and despise not thy mother when she is old,** it being the tendency of young people to be ashamed of their aged parents and no longer to heed their counsel. V. 23. **Buy the truth,** not minding the hard labor and sacrifice required to gain it, **and sell it not,** since it is precious beyond all riches of the world; **also wisdom and instruction and understanding,** these synonyms including both the knowledge in itself and its application in all situations of life. V. 24. **The father of the righteous shall greatly rejoice,** being filled with happiness on account of the fact that his son turned out so well and is an honor to his father; **and he that begetteth a wise child,** one who has acquired true wisdom and understanding, **shall have joy of him,** this fact will make his old age pleasant. V. 25. **Thy father and thy mother shall be glad, and she that bare thee shall rejoice,** this fact being urged in order to stimulate the children in true pious conduct. Cp. chap. 10, 1; 15, 20; 27, 11. V. 26. **My son, give Me thine heart,** Wisdom herself here pleading with the young person to be devoted to her at all times, **and let thine eyes observe My ways,** following the conduct, the principles, and the rules of life which are prescribed by true wisdom, as summarized in the Word of God. V. 27. **For a whore,** as opposed to the person of wisdom, **is a deep ditch, and a strange woman,** the outsider, the harlot, **is a narrow pit,** one yielding to her seductions will find it hard to escape from her power. V. 28. **She also lieth in wait as for a prey,** like a highwayman, **and increaseth the transgressors among men,** multiplying the number of those who yield to her seductive arts and commit the sin of fornication or adultery. Cp. chap. 7, 5—23. V. 29. **Who hath woe? Who hath sorrow,** or grief? The Hebrew notes the moaning by giving the sighs Ah! and Alas! **Who hath contentions?** being most easily involved in quarrels. **Who hath babbling?** said of senseless mutterings and mouthings. **Who hath wounds without cause?** inflicted in drunken brawls. **Who hath redness of eyes?** the characteristic bloated, bleary, and flushed condition of the face which marks the drunkard and the habitual drinker. V. 30. **They that tarry long at the wine,** being engaged regularly in drinking it; **they that go to seek mixed wine,** the strong spiced liquor whose inebriating effects were even worse than that of wine. The admonition, therefore, is spoken: v. 31. **Look not thou upon the wine when it is red,** observing its tempting color with longing eyes, **when it giveth his color in the cup,** literally, "when it showeth its eye," in an inviting sparkle, **when it moveth itself aright,** when it glides down the throat smoothly and pleasantly. V. 32. **At the last it biteth like a serpent,** its ruinous and destructive influence becoming evident afterward, **and stingeth like an adder,** whose venom had a most deadly effect. V. 33. **Thine eyes,** under the influence of the liquor, as it clouds the senses, **shall behold strange women,** rather, strange things, all objects being doubled, or uncertain, or swaying, in the vision of the drunken man, **and thine heart shall utter perverse things,** foolish talk. V. 34. **Yea, thou shalt be as he that lieth down in the midst of the sea,** down in its depths, unconscious of his surroundings, **or as he that lieth upon the top of a mast,** asleep in a most perilous position, reeling, staggering to and fro, in momentary danger of being hurled into the waves. V. 35. **They have stricken me, shalt thou say,** the language of the drunken man being well imitated, **and I was not sick,** he did not feel the pain of it; **they have beaten me, and I felt it not,** he was not aware of it; **when shall I awake?** He is anxious to get over the effect of the present debauch. **I will seek it yet again;** for he who is addicted to the vice of intemperance is bound as with chains, he is a willing slave. The entire description is remarkably true to life and is intended to fill the reader with the deepest aversion and loathing for the sin of drunkenness, which changes men into brute beasts and often degrades them even below the level of animals.

CHAPTER 24.

V. 1. **Be not thou envious against evil men,** desiring their company on account of their apparent prosperity and good fortune, **neither desire to be with them,** to be one of their number, to be accepted into their ranks. Cp. chap. 23, 17. V. 2. **For their heart studieth destruction,** they are constantly meditating upon oppression and violence, **and their lips talk of mischief,** their expressed purpose being to harm others. V. 3. **Through wisdom is an house builded,** not only the dwelling, but the occupants of the house being included in the designation, **and by understanding it is established,** in this way only do people get a home in the true sense of the word; v. 4. **and by knowledge shall the chambers be filled with all precious and pleasant riches,** the words describing not a miserly hoarding of money, but a condition of the household which speaks of a comfortable prosperity. V. 5. **A wise man is strong,** full of strength, exerting a powerful influence; **yea, a man of knowledge,** one making use of proper circumspection and caution, **increaseth strength,** develops and extends his influence, makes use of his power in the proper manner. V. 6. **For by wise counsel thou shalt make thy war,** carry it forward to a successful issue, **and in multitude of counselors,** all of whom contribute good advice, **there is safety,** matters are sure to go forward favorably. Cp. chap. 20, 18; 11, 14; 15, 22. V. 7. **Wisdom is too high,** altogether unattainable, **for a fool; he openeth not his mouth in the gate,** he cannot be consulted by the leading men of the city as they deliberate upon the welfare of the community, their place of assembly being in the gate of the city or immediately inside the gate, where the open space was set aside for public meetings. V. 8. **He that deviseth to do evil,** with whom mischief and wrong is self-evident, who is the master of wickedness, **shall be called a mischievous person,** his evil reputation will soon be well established. V. 9. **The thought of foolishness,** literally, "the meditation of folly," **is sin,** that is, even when folly tries to perform something with prudent reflection, the result is the same, a transgression of God's holy Law, **and the scorner is an abomination to men,** his mockery makes him an object of loathing. V. 10. **If thou faint in the day of adversity,** in times when anxiety and distress seem to obstruct progress, **thy strength is small,** for it is necessary to keep up courage, to develop moral courage and capacity of resistance, in order to perform anything worth while in life. V. 11. **If thou forbear to deliver them that are drawn unto death,** rather, "Deliver those who are taken to death," **and those that are ready to be slain,** the appeal being directed particularly to such as witnessed the deeds of religious fanatics, who then, as now, often made it a point to interfere with the business of the government and to demand the severest punishments for such as had incurred their displeasure; v. 12. **if thou sayest, Behold, we knew it not,** the one addressed trying to salve his conscience with a poor excuse, **doth not He that pondereth the heart consider it? And He that keepeth thy soul,** familiar with the innermost thoughts of the mind, **doth not He know it? And shall not He render to every man according to his works?** The last is a direct statement: He will requite man according to his deeds, His retributive justice cannot be avoided by a profession of ignorance. Cp. chap. 31, 8. 9. V. 13. **My son, eat thou honey because it is good, and the honeycomb, which is sweet to thy taste,** this figurative admonition serving to introduce the praise of the loveliness and agreeableness of true wisdom. V. 14. **So shall the knowledge of wisdom be unto thy soul,** altogether agreeable and full of rich nourishment and therefore well worth acquiring; **when thou hast found it, then there shall be a reward, and thy expectation shall not be cut off,** the future will show that the acquiring of wisdom was well worth while. V. 15. **Lay not wait, O wicked man,** with the intention of performing mischief and malice, **against the dwelling of the righteous; spoil not his resting-place,** where he is leading a quiet and peaceable life in all godliness and honesty; v. 16. **for a just man falleth seven times,** for misfortunes often seem to single him out, he has his full share of them, **and riseth up again,** endowed with new strength by the Lord; **but the wicked shall fall into mischief,** stumble into destruction, their fate being everlasting misfortune. V. 17. **Rejoice not,** in malignant joy, **when thine enemy falleth, and let not thine heart be glad when he stumbleth,** since delight in another's hurt is just as objectionable as outright violence, v. 18. **lest the Lord see it and it displease Him,** as all evidences of malice are bound to do, **and He turn away His wrath from him,** that is, from the enemy, His punishment striking the person of malignant spirit instead. V. 19. **Fret not thyself because of evil men,** becoming enraged with envy on account of their apparent good fortune, **neither be thou envious at the wicked,** whose prosperity often seems so great; v. 20. **for there shall be no reward to the evil man,** he will have no lucky future or end; **the candle of the wicked shall be put out,** a picture of eventual unhappiness and destruction. V. 21. **My son, fear thou the Lord and the king,** the government established by Jehovah, 1 Pet. 2, 17; Rom. 13, 1, **and meddle not with them that are given to change,** those who are always dissatisfied with the government and therefore are always planning revolutions; v. 22. **for their calamity,** the misfortune sent upon them by God, **shall rise suddenly,** striking them with unexpected suddenness; **and who knoweth the ruin of them both?** For those who rebel against the constituted and existing government thereby rebel against the Lord. — V. 23. **These things also belong to the wise,** the proverbs, or maxims, now following are ascribed to wise men, from this point to the end of the chapter. **It is not good to have respect of persons in judgment,** literally, "to observe faces," that is, to be partial, no matter for what reason. V. 24. **He that saith unto the wicked, Thou art righteous,** rendering a verdict in favor of the guilty, **him shall the people curse,** since perversion of justice in even one case affects the welfare of all, **nations shall abhor him;** v. 25. **but to them that rebuke him shall be delight,** the judges who do their duty in punishing evildoers shall be rewarded, **and a good blessing shall come upon them,** the Lord Himself dispensing rich and manifold gifts of His kindness and mercy. V. 26. **Every man shall kiss his lips that giveth a right answer,** rather, "A kiss upon the lips does he bestow who returns well-pleasing words," that is, a faithful and favorable answer, especially before a court of justice, is like a most agreeable caress. V. 27. **Prepare thy work without and make it fit for thyself in the field,** by tilling the soil and laboring for a plentiful harvest first; **and afterwards build thine house,** which includes the establishment of a family and household, the summary being: Provide necessaries first, then comforts. V. 28. **Be not a witness against thy neighbor without cause,** without reason and need, out of pure animosity; **and deceive not with thy lips,** rather in the form of a question, "And shouldest thou practise deception with thy lips?" a very emphatic way of reproving such an intention. V. 29. **Say not, I will do so to him as he hath done to me,** the eagerness for revenge governing one's actions; **I will render to the man according to his work.** Cp. Matt. 5, 43—45; Rom. 12, 17. V. 30. **I went by the field of the slothful,** where he could well observe the effect of sloth, **and by the vineyard of the man void of understanding,** one too lazy to work because he lacked in wisdom; v. 31. **and, lo, it was all grown over with thorns,** the entire field, for want of cultivation, had produced noxious weeds, **and nettles had covered the face thereof, and the stone wall thereof was broken down,** another sign of utter neglect. V. 32. **Then I saw and considered it well,** observing the lesson taught by that neglected field; **I looked upon it and received instruction,** laying down the admonition conveyed by the scene of desolation in a maxim for others. V. 33. **Yet a little sleep, a little slumber, a little folding of the hands to sleep,** that being the thought governing the actions of the slothful; v. 34. **so shall thy poverty come as one that traveleth, and thy want,** the need of money and of all necessaries of life, **as an armed man,** literally, "one armed with a shield." Cp. chap. 6, 10. 11.

CHAPTER 25.

True Wisdom the Highest Good of Kings and Subjects.

V. 1. **These are also proverbs of Solomon,** maxims composed by the wise son of David, by inspiration of God, **which the men of Hezekiah, king of Judah, copied out,** evidently from collections where they were being preserved, the king being very anxious to have the literature of the "Golden Age" passed on to posterity in a form which would be as complete as possible. V. 2. **It is the glory of God to conceal a thing,** He, whose essence is unsearchable and whose wisdom is past finding out, cannot be grasped by finite minds; **but the honor of kings is to search out a matter,** to make careful inquiry and get the right understanding of every case that is brought before them for judicial decision. God's judgments are often advisedly hidden before the eyes of men, the king's judgments must always be open and clear. V. 3. **The heaven for height,** for it extends to immeasurable distances, **and the earth for depth,** since its abysses are unbelievably deep, **and the heart of kings is unsearchable,** their intentions cannot be figured out by ordinary subjects, whence it follows that it is foolish for men to flatter themselves with possessing the favor of the mighty, true wisdom consisting in guarding oneself in both words and deeds and in letting true worth make its impression. V. 4. **Take away the dross from the silver,** the impurities from the ore, **and there shall come forth a vessel for the finer,** the metal being pure enough to be used for the finest vessels made by the goldsmith. V. 5. **Take away the wicked from before the king,** by a judicial action which removes such dross from before the ruler's eyes, **and his throne shall be established in righteousness,** a wise and beneficent government resulting from energetic administration of justice. V. 6. **Put not forth thyself in the presence of the king,** in showing off or boasting, **and stand not in the place of great men,** with insolent coolness; v. 7. **for better it is that it be said unto thee, Come up hither,** to a place of greater honor in the table-round, **than that thou shouldest be put lower in the presence of the prince whom thine eyes have seen,** so that such a one would be humbled before the entire assembly. Cp. Luke 14, 8—11. V. 8. **Go not forth hastily to strive,** rushing forth at the slightest provocation with quarrelsome intent, **lest thou know not what to do in the end thereof, when thy neighbor hath put thee to shame,** for it is easy to pick a quarrel, but its terrible consequences are often past estimation. V. 9. **Debate thy cause with thy neighbor himself,** if a cause of action has arisen without a person's fault, let the controversy be carried on in an honorable manner; **and discover not a secret to another,** betraying one's confidence to a third person and thus making use of unfair methods, v. 10. **lest he that heareth it put thee to shame,** any person hearing of the treachery earnestly reproving and upbraiding the one making use of such dishonest practises, **and thine infamy turn not away,** for the disgrace attending such treachery clings to it indefinitely and prevents men from trusting him at any time. V. 11. **A word fitly spoken,** with proper wisdom and tact, **is like apples of gold in pictures,** in a framework, on a groundwork, **of silver,** the reference being to decorations such as were employed on ceilings and pillars, where everything is supposed to harmonize well and not to offend the eye. V. 12. **As an earring of gold and an ornament of fine gold,** a pendant usually worn on the neck, **so is a wise reprover,** one who teaches with wise tact, **upon an obedient ear,** that is, the listening ear, ready to accept instruction, is better than one hung with gold. V. 13. **As the cold of snow in the time of harvest,** used for the cooling of drinks on a hot summer's day, **so is a faithful messenger to them that send him; for he refresheth the soul of his masters,** since he performs his work well and brings back a cheering message. V. 14. **Whoso boasteth himself of a false gift,** of a liberality which he does not practise, **is like clouds and wind without rain,** which also promise much and yield nothing. V. 15. **By long forbearing is a prince,** that is, a judge sitting in a case, **persuaded,** a persistent, gentle patience very often succeeding in gaining its point, **and a soft tongue breaketh the bone,** wearing down the most stubborn resistance by its gentleness. V. 16. **Hast thou found honey? Eat so much as is sufficient for thee,** as much as the body may well use for food, **lest thou be filled therewith,** be surfeited, **and vomit it,** for that is the consequence of intemperance and overindulgence. V. 17. **Withdraw thy foot from thy neighbor's house,** making the visits rare, few and far between, **lest he be weary of thee,** tired of the company imposed upon him, **and so hate thee,** on account of the importunity displayed. V. 18. **A man that beareth false witness against his neighbor is a maul and a sword and a sharp arrow,** since his words wound and crush with unmerciful cruelty. V. 19. **Confidence in an unfaithful man,** credulous reliance upon a false person, **in time of trouble,** when one is in need of a trustworthy friend, **is like a broken tooth and a foot out of joint,** worthless as they are, they provoke all the more by the infliction of pain. V. 20. **As he that taketh away a garment in cold weather,** such a laying aside of warm clothing on a cold day being manifestly a senseless way of doing things, **and as vinegar upon niter,** the result being the destruction of the soda on account of the chemical reaction produced, **so is he that singeth songs to an heavy heart,** for songs of mirth in a house of mourning are contradictory and useless, Rom. 12, 15. V. 21. **If thine enemy be hungry, give him bread to eat,** readily sharing food with him, **and if he be thirsty, give him water to drink;** v. 22. **for thou shalt heap coals of fire upon his head,** kindness softening the heart as metals are melted by heaping glowing coals upon them, **and the Lord shall reward thee.** Cp. Matt. 5, 44; Rom. 12, 20. V. 23. **The north wind driveth away rain,** blowing from the north, it produces rain, it blows up a rain-storm; **so doth an angry countenance a backbiting tongue,** for if the tongue is busy spreading slander, it produces troubled faces, worried looks, angry frowns. V. 24. **It is better to dwell in the corner of the housetop than with a brawling woman and in a wide house.** Cp. chap. 21, 9. V. 25. **As cold waters to a thirsty soul,** producing the same feeling of refreshment, **so is good news from a far country,** that concerning an absent friend or relative. V. 26. **A righteous man falling down before the wicked,** wavering before the craft of the wicked, lacking moral firmness, **is as a troubled fountain and a corrupt spring,** from either of which pure and healthy water cannot be obtained; for the transgression of a just person is more far-reaching in its evil effects than that of one known to be ungodly. V. 27. **It is not good to eat much honey,** it is so overrich in nourishment that its excessive use will produce a feeling of repugnance; **so for men to search their own glory is not glory,** literally, "and seeking their difficulties is difficulty," that is, pondering problems which have no solution is injurious. V. 28. **He that hath no rule over his own spirit,** one unable to control his temper, **is like a city that is broken down,** its defenses having been leveled, **and without walls,** such a man is open to all assaults upon his morality and freedom, the enemies can easily cause him to transgress.

CHAPTER 26.

Warnings against Dishonorable Conduct.

CONCERNING FOOLS AND SLUGGARDS. — V. 1. **As snow in summer and as rain in harvest,** either possibility being suggested as something altogether unfitting, not to be expected, **so honor is not seemly for a fool,** it is not proper that he should have it, he is altogether unworthy of it. V. 2. **As the bird by wandering,** the sparrow flitting along, **as the swallow by flying,** the aimlessness of their ordinary flight being the point of comparison, **so the curse causeless shall not come,** that is, if it is undeserved, it will not be fulfilled, and the person against whom it is directed has no cause for worry. V. 3. **A whip for the horse, a bridle for the ass,** both being necessary in the case of irrational brutes in order to keep them under control, **and a rod for** the fool's back, for only by force can he be directed in the proper way. V. 4. **Answer not a fool according to his folly,** by putting oneself on a level with him in speech and actions, **lest thou also be like unto him,** be placed in the same class with him by decent and intelligent people. V. 5. **Answer a fool according to his folly,** a sharp and decisive answer being framed to meet foolish remarks, **lest he be wise in his own conceit,** filled with the notion that he really possesses wisdom. V. 6. **He that sendeth a message by the hand of a fool,** expecting him to represent his interests in a proper manner, **cutteth off the feet,** he puts himself in a helpless condition, he harms his own cause, **and drinketh damage,** harms, or injures, himself, he is bound to suffer abuse. V. 7. **The legs of the lame are not equal,** they drag or dangle, they render him helpless in his walk; **so is a parable in the mouth of fools,** it is altogether awkward for him to use a proverb or maxim, as he cannot apply it properly. V. 8. **As he that bindeth a stone in a sling,** as we might say, as one who plays with a loaded gun, **so is he that giveth honor to a fool,** for no fool is more dangerous than he who finds himself in a position of honor and authority. V. 9. **As a thorn goeth up into the hand of a drunkard,** a branch of a thornbush in the hands of such a person being a dangerous weapon, since one never knows who will be injured in the inebriate's uncertain striking, **so is a parable in the mouth of fools,** he works more harm than profit with his wrong applications. V. 10. **The great God that formed all things both rewardeth the fool and rewardeth transgressors,** rather, literally, "Much produceth all, and both the reward and the rewarder of the fool pass away," that is, diligence brings reward, but folly brings destruction. V. 11. **As a dog returneth to his vomit, so a fool returneth to his folly,** repeating it again and again, not aware of the loathsomeness of his action. Cp. 2 Pet. 2, 22. V. 12. **Seest thou a man wise in his own conceit,** in a false estimate of his knowledge and abilities? **There is more hope of a fool than of him,** for a person with false self-assurance is a hopeless case. V. 13. **The slothful man saith,** eagerly inventing excuses to keep himself from work, **There is a lion in the way; a lion is in the streets.** Cp. chap. 22, 13. V. 14. **As the door turneth upon his hinges,** never, however, moving from its place, **so doth the slothful upon his bed,** moving indeed, but not leaving his place and therefore making no progress in life. V. 15. **The slothful hideth his hand in his bosom,** rather, he dips it into the large bowl on the table with the intention of getting food for himself; **it grieveth him to bring it again to his mouth,** he is actually too lazy to bring it up to his mouth, chap. 19, 24. V. 16. **The sluggard is wiser in his own conceit,** in his own estimate of himself, **than seven men that can render a reason,** giving wise answers, proper information concerning questions placed before them. True humility is one of the chief Christian virtues.

CONCERNING BUSYBODIES. — V. 17. **He that passeth by and meddleth with strife belonging not to him,** becoming excited over a dispute which is really none of his business, is **like one that taketh a dog by the ears,** deliberately provoking trouble for himself. V. 18. **As a madman who casteth firebrands,** or fiery darts, **arrows, and death,** deadly missiles of all kinds, v. 19. **so is the man that deceiveth his neighbor,** using craft against him, deliberately hurting him with bitter speeches, **and saith, Am not I in sport?** Gentle teasing and irony may well be permissible, but there is a limit to everything, and joking must never become pointed raillery with a personal sting. V. 20. **Where no wood is, there the fire goeth out,** for want of fuel; **so where there is no talebearer,** whose slanderous remarks always add further fuel for quarrels, **the strife ceaseth,** it is quieted for want of material to keep it going. V. 21. **As coals are to burning coals and wood to fire,** keeping the blaze steady, **so is a contentious man to kindle strife,** always to stir it up anew. V. 22. **The words of a talebearer are as wounds, and they go down into the innermost parts of the belly.** Cp. chap. 18, 8. V. 23. **Burning lips,** such as are fervent with demonstrations of regard, **and a wicked heart,** showing that the glow of the lips is repulsive hypocrisy, **are like a potsherd covered with silver dross,** impure silver covering an earthen vessel, the comparison serving to bring out the falseness of such actions. V. 24. **He that hateth, dissembleth with his lips,** or, "With his lips the hater dissembleth," **and layeth up deceit within him;** v. 25. **when he speaketh fair,** making his voice and speech pleasant, **believe him not; for there are seven abominations in his heart,** hateful and loathsome plans and projects engage his attention, Matt. 12, 45. V. 26. **Whose hatred is covered by deceit,** since he has managed to keep it secret for a while, **his wickedness shall be showed before the whole congregation,** exposed before the entire assembly convened for judgment. V. 27. **Whoso diggeth a pit shall fall therein,** this being the form which the punishment of God will take; **and he that rolleth a stone,** with the intention of harming another, **it will return upon him,** in just retribution. V. 28. **A lying tongue hateth those that are afflicted by it,** it is not a case of merely repeating a slander in a thoughtless manner, but a deliberate expression of hatred; **and a flattering mouth worketh ruin,** for if men are duped by flattery, it brings misfortune upon them. Careful uprightness is required of every true child of God.

CHAPTER 27.

Warning against Self-Praise and Presumption.

EXALTATION OF SELF LEADS TO FOLLY. — V. 1. **Boast not thyself of to-morrow,** by proudly setting forth the assured success of one's schemes in the future; **for thou knowest not what a day may bring forth,** the future with both its successes and failures being entirely in the hands of God. V. 2. **Let another man praise thee, and not thine own mouth; a stranger, and not thine own lips;** for a person's praise of his own virtues and good deeds has no value and is, in addition, repulsive to others. V. 3. **A stone is heavy and the sand weighty,** literally, "weight of stone and heaviness of sand"; **but a fool's wrath is heavier than them both,** both unreasonable and excessive, a burden to himself and others. V. 4. **Wrath is cruel, and anger is outrageous,** literally, "Raving is anger and wrath is overflowing," like a flood which carries everything before it; **but who is able to stand before envy?** jealousy being worse to contend with than outright anger with open warfare. V. 5. **Open rebuke is better than secret love,** that is, censure applied openly and honorably is much to be preferred to such a pretense of love as dissembles and refuses to rebuke a neighbor's fault where principles of true love would require it. V. 6. **Faithful are the wounds of a friend,** that is, he, in the earnest concern for his neighbor's true welfare, may sometimes give a sharp reproof; **but the kisses of an enemy,** when he feigns friendship, **are deceitful,** full of treachery and craft. V. 7. **The full soul,** one already satisfied with food, with no appetite remaining, **loatheth an honeycomb,** inviting and appetizing as it otherwise may be; **but to the hungry soul every bitter thing is sweet,** for "hunger is the best cook." V. 8. **As the bird that wandereth from her nest,** deserting her home in a spirit of restlessness, **so is a man that wandereth from his place,** roaming about in a spirit of adventure instead of cultivating proper domestic tastes. V. 9. **Ointment and perfume rejoice the heart,** both of them being used by the Oriental host in honoring his guests; **so doth the sweetness of a man's friend by hearty counsel,** if the counsel really proceeds from a sincere heart, it is pleasant beyond all outward indications of affection. V. 10. **Thine own friend and thy father's friend forsake not,** for they are reliable, having been found tried and true; **neither go into thy brother's house in the day of thy calamity,** since a relationship by blood is not so close and intimate, in many cases, as one founded upon true friendship; **for better is a neighbor that is near,** with whom one is connected by the bonds of friendship, **than a brother far off,** with whom one may no longer have many things in common. The ties of blood may be less reliable than those of genuine friendship.

WISDOM AND HUMILITY GO HAND IN HAND. V. 11. **My son, be wise and make my heart glad,** the inspired author again addressing all his readers in the tone of fatherly admonition, **that I may answer him that reproacheth me,** since the wise behavior of a pupil will enable the teacher to stop the reviling of an enemy who would mock at his teaching. V. 12. **A prudent man foreseeth the evil,** he is able to judge the signs of the times, **and hideth himself; but the simple pass on and are punished,** they come to harm because they take no steps to avoid it. Cp. chap. 22, 3. V. 13. **Take his garment that is surety for a stranger,** foolishly pledging himself, **and take a pledge of him for a strange woman,** rather, "on account of strange things." Cp. chap. 20, 16. V. 14. **He that blesseth his friend with a loud voice, rising early in the morning,** in an attempt to appear most friendly and sincere and thus to hide his real feeling, **it shall be counted a curse to him,** it will so be charged against him on account of his hypocrisy and insincerity. V. 15. **A continual dropping in a very rainy day,** when the drip of the spouts persists with maddening monotony, **and a contentious woman,** one always nagging and quarreling, **are alike,** namely, in their disagreeable effect upon others. V. 16. **Whosoever hideth her,** that is, whoever attempts to restrain such a woman, **hideth the wind,** it is just as foolish to try to shut out the wind, **and the ointment of his right hand, which bewrayeth itself,** rather, "and his right hand encounters oil," something which always slips out of his grasp; for it is impossible to put a stop to the shrew's scolding. V. 17. **Iron sharpeneth iron,** namely, when a file is used; **so a man sharpeneth the countenance of his friend,** namely, by the stimulation of his conversation and the encouragement of his example. V. 18. **Whoso keepeth the fig-tree,** giving it the care which it needs, **shall eat the fruit thereof,** thus finding his labor rewarded; **so he that waiteth on his master,** having the proper regard for him, cultivating the spirit of loyal service in his employ, **shall be honored,** his faithfulness being properly rewarded. V. 19. **As in water face answereth to face,** the surface of the water acting as a mirror which reflects all objects, **so the heart of man to man,** being mirrored in that of his fellow, a true knowledge of men being gained best by a thorough study of self. V. 20. **Hell and destruction are never full,** the grave and the realm of the dead are insatiable, they never have enough; **so the eyes of man,** of him who has given way to covetousness, **are never satisfied,** the avaricious man never has enough. V. 21. **As the fining-pot for silver and the furnace for gold,** both of them serving to bring out the purity of the metals tried in them, **so is a man to his praise,** he is tested, his real character is disclosed, by his glorying or boasting, whether this is concerned with praiseworthy or with blameworthy and trivial things, or, according to the opinion in which he is held by honorable people. Cp. chap. 12, 8. V. 22. **Though thou shouldest bray a fool in a mortar among wheat with a pestle,** stamping him into little bits in a crucible in an effort to find at least a grain of sense, **yet will not his foolishness depart from him,** since it pervades every atom of his being. V. 23. **Be thou diligent to know the state of thy flocks,** literally, "the face of thy sheep," their condition, **and look well to thy herds,** as a careful manager must do. V. 24. **For riches are not forever,** they are unstable and must therefore be carefully looked after; **and doth the crown endure to every generation?** Even the king is not sure that his royal dignity and power will descend in his family, so uncertain and vain is all human possession; whence it behooves man all the more to make use of care and circumspection. V. 25. **The hay appeareth, and the tender grass showeth itself, and herbs of the mountains are gathered,** the careful and provident manager insuring a sufficient supply for his herds, so that they do not lack food. V. 26. **The lambs are for thy clothing,** their fleece furnishing wool for garments, **and the goats are the price of the field,** their value being so great that the money obtained by their sale will pay for the farm. V. 27. **And thou shalt have goats' milk enough for thy food, for the food of thy household,** the family and the house-servants, **and for the maintenance for thy maidens,** the female slaves which were always found in large establishments. Prosperity is a blessing of the Lord, but that does not exclude diligence and care on the part of every person, for prayer and industry must go hand in hand.

CHAPTER 28.

Warning against Unscrupulous Dealing.

THE CONSEQUENCES OF IMPIETY. — V. 1. **The wicked flee when no man pursueth,** their bad conscience making them timid; **but the righteous,** filled with the consciousness of their uprightness and therefore possessing a good conscience, **are bold as a lion,** their courage being upheld by their trust in God. V. 2. **For the transgression of a land many are the princes thereof,** that is, when the spirit of rebellion once takes hold of a country, there will be many men aspiring to be rulers, and many changes of policy in government are harmful; **but by a man of understanding and knowledge,** a ruler who makes use of the proper circumspection, foresight, and wisdom, **the state thereof shall be prolonged,** the rule of the one good prince will continue long. V. 3. **A poor man that oppresseth the poor,** an upstart who has enriched himself at the expense of his subjects, **is like a sweeping rain,** a heavy, driving shower, **which leaveth no food,** the flood either drowning out or carrying away the growing crops. V. 4. **They that forsake the Law praise the wicked,** who makes it a practise to ignore the Law in his own interest, his selfishness being supreme; **but such as keep the Law contend with them,** those who are on the side of law and order naturally are opposed to all lawbreaking. V. 5. **Evil men understand not judgment,** for their wickedness confuses their ideas of morality; **but they that seek the Lord,** and thereby make His Word the standard of their life, **understand all things,** according to the rule of the Word they have no trouble in determining what is right. V. 6. **Better is the poor that walketh in his uprightness,** in integrity of life, in agreement with God's holy will, **than he that is perverse in his ways,** walking in crooked ways, in conduct either hypocritical or downright wicked, **though he be rich,** for the possession of riches will not condone wickedness. Cp. chap. 19, 1. V. 7. **Whoso keepeth the Law,** observing carefully all instruction which he receives, **is a wise son,** chap. 10, 1; 29, 3; **but he that is a companion of riotous men,** loving the company of profligates and wasters, **shameth his father.** V. 8. **He that by usury and unjust gain,** by interest exacted from an impoverished neighbor and by exactions in natural products, by exercising a cold and grasping avarice, **increaseth his substance,** growing rich at the expense of the poor, **he shall gather it for him that will pity the poor,** for by God's government some other person, probably an heir, will get hold of it who will show greater compassion toward the poor. V. 9. **He that turneth away his ear from hearing the Law,** deliberately ignoring the way prescribed by the Word of God and disobedient to His will, **even his prayer shall be abomination,** because his prayer cannot possibly be made in spirit and in truth. V. 10. **Whoso causeth the righteous to go astray in an evil way,** seducing him to ungodly and sinful conduct, **he shall fall himself into his own pit,** be ruined in the manner intended for others; **but the upright shall have good things in possession,** the Lord's blessing resting upon their efforts. V. 11. **The rich man,** who is also wicked and therefore foolish, **is wise in his** own conceit, in his own blind estimation of himself, chap. 26, 16; **but the poor that hath understanding**, who makes use of wise discrimination, **searcheth him out**, he knows and sees through the weaknesses of the foolish rich and despises his way of doing things. V. 12. **When righteous men do rejoice**, exulting over the victory of the righteous cause, **there is great glory**, for they show their triumph openly; **but when the wicked rise, a man is hidden**; for when they are in power, they push all others aside and trample them under foot. V. 13. **He that covereth his sin shall not prosper**, for to harden one's heart and conceal one's wickedness is of no avail before the omniscient and righteous God; **but whoso confesseth and forsaketh them**, in open and true repentance, **shall have mercy**, for God is glad to accept in love him who is humbly penitent. V. 14. **Happy is the man that feareth alway**, conducting himself with holy dread and awe, lest he in some manner transgress the will of the Lord; **but he that hardeneth his heart shall fall into mischief**, for a deliberate serving of sin leads to destruction. V. 15. **As a roaring lion and a ranging bear**, wild beasts full of ravenous cruelty, **so is a wicked ruler over the poor people**; for so a cruel and bloodthirsty tyrant is fitly described. V. 16. **The prince that wanteth understanding**, lacking proper discernment, **is also a great oppressor**, he abounds in oppression, not realizing that his attitude hurts his position; **but he that hateth covetousness**, the influential man avoiding all unjust gain, **shall prolong his days**; for so does the kindness of the Lord reward him. V. 17. **A man that doeth violence to the blood of any person**, literally, "burdened with the blood of a soul," weighted down by the load of his guilt, **shall flee to the pit**, in an attempt to escape the terrors which possess him; **let no man stay him**, trying to recover him who is lost beyond all hope. Such a person has deliberately chosen his lot and has no one but himself to blame if destruction descends upon him.

THE ADVANTAGES OF INTEGRITY. — V. 18. **Whoso walketh uprightly**, in the integrity of pious conduct, **shall be saved**, delivered or helped by the Lord; **but he that is perverse in his ways**, trying to hide his wickedness under the mantle of hypocrisy, **shall fall at once**, be brought to sudden ruin. V. 19. **He that tilleth his land**, working in the sweat of his face, **shall have plenty of bread**, as the reward of his labor; **but he that followeth after vain persons**, being engaged in all kinds of vain and foolish pursuits, leading the life of an idle drone, **shall have poverty enough**, be surfeited with it. Cp. chap. 12, 11. V. 20. **A faithful man**, one using the strictest fidelity and uprightness in all his dealings, **shall abound with blessings**, given to him by the Lord in recognition of his faithful conduct; **but he that maketh haste to be rich**, thereby becoming guilty of dishonorable dealings, **shall not be innocent**, his guilt, rather, being charged to his account with a full reckoning. V. 21. **To have respect of persons is not good**, that is, to let one's judgment be guided by personal considerations; **for for a piece of bread**, for a very small bribe, **that man**, one readily hired by a bribe, **will transgress**, a trifle will sway his judgment. V. 22. **He that hasteth to be rich hath an evil eye**, one showing the covetous nature of his heart, **and considereth not that poverty shall come upon him**; for riches are perishable, and God will bring him to want before he realizes his plight. V. 23. **He that rebuketh a man**, earnestly bringing his backsliding tendency to his attention, **afterwards shall find more favor than he that flattereth with the tongue**, for a person saved from a foolish step by a word of warning will esteem the fearless reprover and despise the fawning flatterer. V. 24. **Whoso robbeth his father or his mother**, simply apropriating goods belonging to them, **and saith, It is no transgression**, trying to make light of sin, **the same is the companion of a destroyer**, to be ranked with, and treated like, highwaymen. V. 25. **He that is of a proud heart**, rather, the covetous man, with his grasping ways, **stirreth up strife**, excites quarrels; **but he that putteth his trust in the Lord**, trusting in His goodness and bounty for all good gifts, **shall be made fat**, with a rich reward of God's kindness. V. 26. **He that trusteth in his own heart**, guided solely by first impressions and impulses, without careful reasoning and weighing of all facts, **is a fool**, for the feelings are an uncertain foundation of actions; **but whoso walketh wisely**, taking into account the course suggested by wisdom, **he shall be delivered**, from foolish moves and resulting harm. V. 27. **He that giveth unto the poor**, practising charity in the right manner, **shall not lack**, the Lord Himself preserving him from want; **but he that hideth his eyes**, deliberately closing them against evidence of need, in an utter lack of sympathy, **shall have many a curse**, namely, the curses of the poor whom he neglects. V. 28. **When the wicked rise**, attaining to positions of power and influence, **men hide themselves**, fearing oppression; **but when they perish, the righteous increase**, since they no longer are oppressed by tyrants, they can once more form a numerous and strong party. It is for this reason that we pray for a good government, that we may lead a quiet and peaceable life in all godliness and honesty.

CHAPTER 29.

Warning against Stubbornness and Rebellion.

DESCRIPTION OF STUBBORNNESS AND DISOBEDIENCE. — V. 1. **He that, being often reproved, hardeneth his neck,** shaking off the reproofs with deliberate stubbornness, **shall suddenly be destroyed, and that without remedy,** for when the patience of God is exhausted, He will shut the door to repentance and bring ruin upon the offender. V. 2. **When the righteous are in authority,** when they increase in numbers, when they are in the majority, **the people rejoice,** for such a condition serves to further the welfare of a nation; **but when the wicked beareth rule, the people mourn,** grieving on account of the harm which is bound to strike the country under the administration of the ungodly. Cp. chap. 28, 12. V. 3. **Whoso loveth wisdom rejoiceth his father,** who will, of course, share in the reward which the application of wisdom brings, chap. 10, 1; **but he that keepeth company with harlots spendeth his substance,** thus bringing disgrace upon himself and upon all his relatives. V. 4. **The king by judgment,** by maintaining the cause of righteousness and justice, **establisheth the land,** so that it is in good condition, so that safety and prosperity are assured to all its citizens; **but he that receiveth gifts,** is influenced in his administration by bribes which are offered him, **overthroweth it,** for in such a manner good government is bound to be perverted. V. 5. **A man that flattereth his neighbor spreadeth a net for his feet,** for all his fine talk lacks sincerity, serving merely as a veil of hypocrisy to keep his victim from realizing the peril into which he is being led. V. 6. **In the transgression of an evil man there is a snare,** he is caught in his own wickedness; **but the righteous doth sing and rejoice,** not only for a moment, but constantly, on account of the good fortune which is the reward of virtue. V. 7. **The righteous considereth the cause of the poor,** regarding them as entitled to certain rights in life; **but the wicked regardeth not to know it,** he refuses to listen to reason and to consider the right of the poor, he has neither compassion nor justice in his make-up. V. 8. **Scornful men bring a city into a snare,** literally, "Men of mockery set on fire a city," namely, by exciting the passions and the party spirit of the people upon every occasion; **but wise men turn away wrath,** they work to subdue passions and to prove themselves peacemakers always. V. 9. **If a wise man contendeth with a foolish man,** trying to gain a point for his own cause, **whether he rage or laugh, there is no rest,** that is, the fool will either fly into a rage or pretend to find the matter extremely funny, so that it is impossible to argue with him in a sane manner. V. 10. **The bloodthirsty hate the upright,** since the conduct of the righteous is a constant reproof to them; **but the just seek his soul,** their aim being to uphold and preserve the upright. V. 11. **A fool uttereth all his mind,** he is ready, upon the slightest occasion, to give vent to angry spite; **but a wise man keepeth it in till afterwards,** he does not permit his angry feeling to get the better of him, but controls himself always. V. 12. **If a ruler hearken to lies,** permitting his judgment to be swayed by lying flattery and exaggerated misrepresentations, **all his servants are wicked,** for since their master does not heed the truth, they are educated and trained in falsehood. V. 13. **The poor and the deceitful man,** literally, "the usurer," the unmerciful creditor, **meet together,** they live side by side, as incongruous as it often seems; **the Lord lighteneth both their eyes,** they both owe their blessings to His kindness. Cp. Matt. 5, 45. V. 14. **The king that faithfully judgeth the poor,** with proper attention to his duty, so that he renders always a true judgment, **his throne shall be established forever.** Cp. chap. 20, 28; 25, 5.

THE SOURCE OF EVIL SHOWN. — V. 15. **The rod and reproof,** properly and judiciously administered to a child, **give wisdom,** lay the foundation for the attainment of true morality; **but a child left to himself,** without proper discipline, left to his own will, **bringeth his mother to shame,** whose foolish indulgence is often to blame for the degeneration of her children. V. 16. **When the wicked are multiplied,** when they are in the majority in a community or state, **transgression increaseth,** for not only do they themselves grow in impudence, but they influence others as well and cause them to transgress; **but the righteous shall see their fall,** be witness of the punishment laid upon the godless by the Lord. V. 17. **Correct thy son,** with proper reproof and punishment, **and he shall give thee rest,** bring a feeling of quiet satisfaction to the parent's heart; **yea, he shall give delight unto thy soul,** so that the parent may have constant enjoyment. V. 18. **Where there is no vision, the people perish;** if revelation is scarce, if the Word of God is precious, if men do not properly judge circumstances with relation to their ultimate effects, the people become wild, untractable, grow beyond discipline; **but he that keepeth the Law, happy is he,** sure to come under the blessing of Jehovah. V. 19. **A servant will not be corrected by words,** being in need often of sharper correction; **for though he understand, he will not answer,** he will pay no attention to an ordinary statement or reproof. V. 20. **Seest thou a man that is hasty in his words?** one who speaks before he thinks. **There is more hope of a fool than of him.**

Cp. chap. 26, 12; Eccl. 9, 18. V. 21. **He that delicately bringeth up his servant from a child,** causing the slave to believe himself more than his station really permits him to be, **shall have him become his son at the length,** or, his end will be contention, for rebellion on the part of the slave will naturally follow. V. 22. **An angry man,** one readily yielding to his temper, **stirreth up strife,** chap. 15, 18, **and a furious man,** one who gives way to angry passions, **aboundeth in transgression,** that being the inevitable consequence of such a disposition. V. 23. **A man's pride shall bring him low,** for self-exaltation comes before the fall; **but honor shall uphold the humble in spirit.** Cp. Matt. 23, 12; Luke 14, 11; 1 Pet. 5, 5. V. 24. **Whoso is partner with a thief hateth his own soul,** the concealer, being on the same level with the criminal, must expect to share his punishment; **he heareth cursing and bewrayeth it not,** he hears the imprecation or objurgation of the judge, Lev. 5, 1, warning him to tell the truth, but he refuses to reveal the crime, and so the penalty descends upon him. V. 25. **The fear of man bringeth a snare,** many a person having yielded to sin under the constraint of such terror; **but whoso putteth his trust in the Lord shall be safe,** both by overcoming temptation and by escaping the evils attending transgression. V. 26. **Many seek the ruler's favor,** literally, "his face," they try to gain his good will by every form of attention; **but every man's judgment cometh from the Lord,** who is not swayed by fawning or flattery, but always judges a righteous judgment. V. 27. **An unjust man is an abomination to the just,** on account of his utter lack of uprightness; **and he that is upright in the way,** in his entire conduct, **is abomination to the wicked,** because the behavior of the righteous is a constant accusation of the ungodly, a fact which they resent very strongly. There can be no union between the godly and the ungodly, between believers and unbelievers. To be a friend of the world is equivalent to being an enemy of God.

CHAPTER 30.

The Maxims of Agur, the Son of Jakeh.

GOD'S WORD AS THE SOURCE AND DISPENSER OF ALL WISDOM. — V. 1. **The words of Agur, the son of Jakeh,** a wise man, otherwise unknown, some of whose maxims were added to the proverbs of Solomon as the first supplement, **even the prophecy,** the prophetic utterance: **the man spake unto Ithiel, even unto Ithiel and Uchal,** literally, according to the best texts: "I have steadfastly endeavored, I have constantly vexed myself, O God," v. 2. **surely I am more brutish than any man,** or, "for a man I am lacking in sense," for which reason he finds himself unable to fathom the divine nature, **and have not the understanding of a man,** that which a man should possess in order to have an insight into the attributes of the Lord. V. 3. **I neither learned wisdom nor have the knowledge of the Holy,** since to know God is the center of all true wisdom. It is impossible for mere man to fathom the mysteries of the divine essence. V. 4. **Who hath ascended up into heaven or descended? Who hath gathered the wind in his fists? Who hath bound the waters in a garment? Who hath established all the ends of the earth?** All these great acts of creation and preservation are fully understood by the Creator alone. **What is His name, and what is His Son's name, if thou canst tell?** It is a most emphatic way of saying that no human being is able to uncover the secrets of God's essence. Instead, therefore, of foolishly and vainly puzzling over the incomprehensible nature of God, the believers should turn to Him in simple trust of faith. V. 5. **Every word of God is pure,** purified, rendered free from all impurities of human beings; **He is a shield unto them that put their trust in Him,** making Him their refuge at all times. V. 6. **Add thou not unto His words,** since the revelation of God in the Bible is fully adequate and sufficient for the needs of all men, **lest He reprove thee,** convicting the intermeddler of his blasphemous conduct, **and thou be found a liar,** for all precepts and commandments of men become lies when intermingled with the Word of God and placed on a level with it. V. 7. **Two things have I required of Thee,** in an earnest prayer; **deny me them not before I die,** the poet's entreaty being for a constant enjoyment of these blessings during his whole life: v. 8. **Remove far from me vanity and lies,** deceit and lying words, every form of transgression of the Eighth Commandment; **give me neither poverty nor riches,** both extremes being dangerous for the average human being; **feed me with food convenient for me,** literally, "of my lot or portion," as much as God found best to assign to him, as much as he needed, v. 9. **lest I be full,** surfeited by an overabundance, **and deny Thee,** in the notion that he no longer needed the care of Jehovah, **and say, Who is the Lord?** such being the danger on the one side, **or lest I be poor,** in the abyss of severe want, **and steal, and take the name of my God in vain,** such mockery and blasphemy being found in the mouth of such as believe themselves ill-treated in this world or not properly recognized by the Lord. V. 10. **Ac-**

cuse not a servant unto his master, by slanderous reports, **lest he curse thee,** for the wrong done to him, **and thou be found guilty,** obliged to pay the penalty of the transgression. V. 11. **There is a generation,** a detestable class of people, **that curseth their father and doth not bless their mother,** thus becoming guilty of one of the most atrocious forms of ungodliness. V. 12. **There is a generation that are pure in their own eyes,** proud in their own estimate of self, puffed up in their own conceit, **and yet is not washed from their filthiness,** they are blind against their own shortcomings and transgressions, Rev. 3, 17. V. 13. **There is a generation, O how lofty are their eyes! and their eyelids are lifted up,** in haughty contempt of others. V. 14. **There is a generation whose teeth are as swords and their jaw-teeth,** specifically the canines, **as knives, to devour the poor from off the earth, and the needy from among men,** without the slightest show of compassion. This insatiable oppression is now characterized by a bold comparison. V. 15. **The horse-leech hath two daughters, crying, Give, give!** never being satisfied with what they have already gotten. **There are three things that are never satisfied, yea, four things say not, It is enough:** v. 16. **the grave,** although the number of dead are placed into it in endless succession, **and the barren womb,** where conception and birth is not possible, **the earth is not filled with water,** though tons of rain fall in every shower, **and the fire that saith not, It is enough,** being known as the most insatiable of the ancient elements. V. 17. **The eye that mocketh at his father,** pride and contempt being shown especially in the eye, **and despiseth to obey his mother,** in deliberate waywardness and disobedient scorn, **the ravens of the valley shall pick it out,** when the unburied corpse becomes carrion, **and the young eagles shall eat it,** such being the punishment of the Lord upon those who despise His representatives on earth and therefore set aside His authority.

DEDUCING TRUTHS FROM COMMON EXPERIENCE. — V. 18. **There be three things which are too wonderful for me,** beyond the explanation of an ordinary mind, **yea, four which I know not,** cannot understand, which are incomprehensible: v. 19. **the way of an eagle in the air,** both its manner and the fact that the air shows no trace of his having passed through; **the way of a serpent upon a rock,** which also leaves no marks; **the way of a ship in the midst of the sea,** whose wake is swiftly obliterated by the waves; **and the way of a man with a maid,** for such intercourse also leaves no traces which are immediately and directly apparent. Even so can hypocrisy conceal the real condition of the heart and mind, at least for a while. V. 20. **Such is the way of an adulterous woman,** who eagerly makes use of such concealment; **she eateth,** enjoying the sinful act, **and wipeth her mouth,** boldly professing innocence, **and saith, I have done no wickedness,** feeling sure that she is safe against detection. V. 21. **For three things the earth is disquieted,** trembling as under an unbearable burden, **and for four which it cannot bear:** v. 22. **for a servant,** a man of the lowest condition and status in life, **when he reigneth,** when he suddenly finds himself elevated to the position of ruler and then follows his caprice; **and a fool when he is filled with meat,** since he, being surfeited, becomes insolent; v. 23. **for an odious woman when she is married,** for an old maid, disagreeable in disposition, is apt to repay the contempt which she suffered from others in the same coin, and with full interest; **and an handmaid,** a house slave or nurse, **that is heir to her mistress,** such a piece of good fortune tending to make her insolent and presumptuous in her behavior. V. 24. **There be four things which are little upon the earth,** inconspicuous and therefore ordinarily overlooked, **but they are exceeding wise:** v. 25. **The ants are a people not strong,** not powerful in size, **yet they prepare their meat in the summer,** their diligence and thrift laying up a store for the time of need; v. 26. **the conies,** the cliff-badgers of Palestine, **are but a feeble folk,** also lacking in strength, **yet make they their houses in the rocks,** thus exhibiting a shrewdness which is worthy of imitation; v. 27. **the locusts have no king, yet go they forth all of them by bands,** their swarms migrating in perfect harmony and order; v. 28. **the spider,** rather, the gecko, a poisonous spotted lizard, **taketh hold with her hands,** being able to cling to, and even move forward upon, the flat surfaces, **and is in kings' palaces,** able to adapt herself to every situation. These virtues, as taught by the animals mentioned, are to be applied by men in their domestic, social, and political life. V. 29. **There be three things which go well,** creatures that move with a stately bearing, **yea, four are comely in going,** showing dignity and power in every stride: v. 30. **a lion, which is strongest among beasts,** commonly acknowledged as the king of wild beasts, **and turneth not away for any,** being a stranger to fear; v. 31. **a greyhound,** slender in his loins and possessed of great and graceful speed; **an he-goat also,** known for strength and courage; **and a king against whom there is no rising up,** who exercises the authority of calling his men to battle and with becoming dignity marches at their head. V. 32. **If thou hast done foolishly in lifting up thyself,** self-exaltation being evidence of unusual denseness, **or if thou hast thought evil,** in wicked plotting against a neighbor, **lay thine hand upon thy mouth,** refraining from further speech and thus from further sinning. V. 33. **Surely the churning of milk,** the Oriental method being that of squeezing and wringing in a skin or bottle of leather, **bringeth forth butter, and the wringing of the nose,** if it is pressed too hard, **bringeth forth blood; so the forcing of wrath,** when one or both parties to a quarrel are highly irritated, **bringeth forth strife,** the proper course for a Christian therefore being that of refraining from anger and provocation and of living peaceably with all men, Rom. 12, 18.

CHAPTER 31.

The Proverbs of Lemuel.

OF PROPER KINGLY DEPORTMENT.—V. 1. **The words of King Lemuel,** concerning whom nothing is otherwise known, **the prophecy that his mother taught him,** the words of instruction in the form of proverbial sayings which she imparted to him. V. 2. **What, my son!** an impassioned exclamation addressed to her son to keep him from choosing ways of evil. **And what, the son of my womb!** the expression being intended to show the depth of the true mother's attachment. **And what, the son of my vows!** the mother regarding her son as one dedicated to the Lord from his birth. Having thus given evidence of her loving interest, the mother of Lemuel added some specific admonitions. V. 3. **Give not thy strength unto women,** in a life of luxury, dissipation, and immorality, **nor thy ways to that which destroyeth kings,** to the women who ruin kings by leading them into licentiousness. V. 4. **It is not for kings, O Lemuel, it is not for kings, to drink wine,** to be given to drink, to be enslaved by the inebriating cup, **nor for princes strong drink,** they must never be under the influence of intoxicants, v. 5. **lest they drink and,** with their senses and intellect enfeebled by alcohol, **forget the law, and pervert the judgment of any of the afflicted,** so that all the poor, helpless, and needy would be obliged to forego justice, that justice no longer could be obtained. V. 6. **Give strong drink unto him that is ready to perish,** to those who are afflicted, heavy in heart, full of anxiety, who are on the point of expiring, **and wine unto those that be of heavy hearts,** who are bowed down under the crushing weight of calamities which have befallen them. V. 7. **Let him drink and forget his poverty,** the effect of the intoxicant being to give him a brighter view of life, **and remember his misery no more.** Not intemperance, but a moderate and proper use of wine and strong drink as gifts of God is here advocated, while total abstinence is recommended to those who occupy positions of authority and power. V. 8. **Open thy mouth for the dumb,** those unable to maintain their own cause, **in the cause of all such as are appointed to destruction,** or for the right of all orphan children, who are deprived of their natural protector. V. 9. **Open thy mouth, judge righteously,** so that judgment is rendered in behalf of those under oppression, **and plead the cause of the poor and needy.** The virtues of mercy and justice should properly be combined in every person holding a position of authority and influence.

THE ABC OF THE VIRTUOUS WOMAN. — V. 10. **Who can find a virtuous woman?** the emphatic question pointing to the meaning: How splendid it would be for every man to have such a wife! **For her price is far above rubies,** beyond the worth of pearls and all treasures of the home, in so far as they pertain to this life. V. 11. **The heart of her husband doth safely trust in her,** he may rely absolutely upon her prudence and skill in the home, **so that he shall have no need of spoil,** he shall not fail of gain, since she watches over the income of the family. V. 12. **She will do him good,** in a constant show of affection, **and not evil all the days of her life,** her love not being subject to moods. Her diligence, wisdom, and shrewdness are now portrayed. V. 13. **She seeketh wool and flax,** or linen, busying herself with these materials in order to produce garments, **and worketh willingly with her hands,** taking pleasure in performing the work which every day offers. V. 14. **She is like the merchants' ships,** in selling her products and obtaining new ware and gain; **she bringeth her food from afar,** providing all the necessities of the house in ample time. V. 15. **She riseth also while it is yet night,** she is up and at her work before daylight, **and giveth meat to her household,** distributing food to all its members, for an early breakfast, **and a portion to her maidens,** so that the meals are ready at a certain time and no time is lost. V. 16. **She considereth a field,** carefully contemplating its worth for purchase, **and buyeth it,** since her thrift has enabled her to lay aside the purchase money, **with the fruit of her hands,** with the money she has earned by her own labor, **she planteth a vineyard,** investing her money wisely. V. 17. **She girdeth her loins with strength,** showing vigor in every undertaking, **and strengtheneth her arms,** both her diligence and the energy displayed by her increasing continually. V. 18. **She perceiveth that her merchandise is good,** she is aware that her gain is regular, a fact which spurs her on to renewed effort; **her candle goeth not out by night,** if necessary she will work far into the night in order to accomplish her purpose. V. 19. **She layeth her hands to the spindle, and her hands hold the distaff,** she uses the spinning-wheel in the proper and effective manner, she lacks neither the skill nor the willingness to work with her own hands. At the same time, it is not selfishness or avarice which inspires the virtuous woman. V. 20. **She stretcheth out her hand to the poor,** spreading out both hands with gifts for the unfortunate; **yea, she reacheth forth her hands to the needy,** always ready to help such as are truly in need. V. 21. **She is not afraid of the snow for her household,** having used the proper foresight, she need not fear the cold of winter for those dependent upon her; **for all her household are clothed with scarlet,** heavy woolen material, both warm and of prosperous appearance. V. 22. **She maketh herself coverings of tapestry,** coverlets and hangings to decorate her home; **her clothing is silk and purple,** made of fine Egyptian byssus and of cloth dyed with reddish-purple from Phenicia. Moreover, her influence extends beyond the confines of her home. V. 23. **Her husband is known in the gates,** where the most influential citizens were wont to assemble, **when he sitteth among the elders of the land,** an important and famous personage. V. 24. **She maketh fine linen,** shirts and underclothes, **and selleth it; and delivereth girdles unto the merchant,** literally, to the Canaanite, for the Phenician merchants were the most prominent at that time. V. 25. **Strength and honor are her clothing,** making her independent of all petty annoyances and worries and permitting her to look into the future with simple confidence; **and she shall rejoice in time to come,** not in foolish self-confidence, but in the consciousness of having made the best possible preparations for the maintenance of herself and her household. V. 26. **She openeth her mouth with wisdom,** for that is all her heart knows; **and in her tongue is the law of kindness,** her speech is altogether amiable and full of love. V. 27. **She looketh well to the ways of her household,** wisely arranging and superintending the work of all the servants, **and eateth not the bread of idleness,** being busy both in superintending and in joining hands with the rest in working. V. 28. **Her children arise up,** wherever they present themselves, **and call her blessed,** praising the mother to whom they owe so much; **her husband also, and he praiseth her,** in the words now quoted, v. 29. **Many daughters have done virtuously,** many women have shown virtue, Ruth 4, 11, **but thou excellest them all.** The author now gives a summary of his remarks. V. 30. **Favor,** that is, grace acquired and shown by a woman, **is deceitful,** it has no real, lasting value, **and beauty is vain,** it is a breath, a vanity, it is no measure of a woman's real worth; **but a woman that feareth the Lord, she shall be praised,** that is the highest praise which can be bestowed upon a woman at any time. V. 31. **Give her of the fruit of her hands,** namely, the praise which she so richly deserves; **and let her own works praise her in the gates,** that is, in the place where the elders, the representatives of the people, assemble, the foremost men of the nation acknowledging such a woman's excellency. This hymn, called the Abc of a virtuous woman, on account of the fact that it is an acrostic in the original Hebrew, each succeeding verse beginning with the next letter of the Hebrew alphabet, is well worthy to be memorized by every Christian woman, and especially every Christian wife, as containing the ideal of the Lord Himself.

ECCLESIASTES, OR THE PREACHER.

INTRODUCTION.

Luther writes, in the introduction to his exposition of this book: "This book is one of the most difficult books of all Holy Scriptures, into whose depths no one, till now, has fully penetrated; yea, rather, through improper explanations of many it has been so corrupted that it is almost a greater task to cleanse and liberate our author from the dreams of those people, which they have brought into the text, than to show the true meaning. There was, however, a twofold reason why this book was unusually dark to others. The one is that they did not see the purpose and the scope of the author. . . . The other reason is based upon their ignorance of the Hebrew language and upon a certain peculiar manner of expressing himself which the author has, one which deviates from the ordinary usage of language and differs widely from our own manner of speaking. The consequence has been that this book, which in many respects is worthy of being in the hands of all men daily, with which, moreover, the leaders of a community should particularly be familiar, . . . has been deprived of its name and dignity and been cast aside in miserable contempt, so that we to-day have neither the use nor the effect of it. . . . Therefore our first endeavor must be to mark the scope of the book, what it intends to accomplish and what is its object."1)

The scope and general character of the book is indicated by its divisions, four discourses being clearly included: On the vanity of human wisdom and earthly pleasures, chaps. 1. 2; on the proper use of earthly goods and pleasures, chaps. 3—5; on the vanity of riches and the achievement of true wisdom, chaps. 6—8; on the proper rules of conduct, as based on true wisdom, chaps. 9—12. The author plainly teaches that a person may well enjoy the earthly gifts of God, in proper piety, on the one hand, and in true charity, on the other, without clinging to the vain gifts of this world, but rather in true love to the Word of God and in constant remembrance of the Judgment which is coming.

The title of the book is Ecclesiastes, a word derived from the Greek translation of the Old Testament, the meaning of the word being Preacher, as the author plainly calls himself. The description of the opening sentence, "The words of the Preacher, the son of David, king in Jerusalem," will properly apply to no one but Solomon, to whom the book has been ascribed from the earliest times. All the arguments of modern higher critics have not been able to shake the authenticity of the book. The only question, one which was considered by Luther also, is this, whether Solomon personally wrote the words as contained in this book, or whether the discourses were penned by one of Solomon's scribes. They appear to have been spoken by Solomon in his old age, and that with the intention of repairing as much as possible the damage he had done by his evil example (1 Kings 11, 1—8), and to warn others against those sins and follies which he had committed.2)

1) Luther, 5, 1377.

2) Cp. Fuerbringer, *Einleitung in das Alte Testament*, 55—58; *Concordia Bible Class*, April, 1919, 62. 63.

CHAPTER 1.

Of the Vanity of the Earthly Wisdom of Man.

GENERAL INTRODUCTION. — V. 1. **The words of the Preacher,** in the sense of one who, from the rich stock of his knowledge, gives wise and profitable instruction, the reference being to Solomon, **the son of David, king in Jerusalem,** the capital of the entire kingdom of Israel and Judah at that time. The fact that Solomon does not mention his given name is easily accounted for by the fact that the entire book breathes the spirit of repentance, together with admonitions and warnings, such as are to be expected from an aged and experienced man rather than from a king. V. 2. **Vanity of vanities,** the most utter vanity, **saith the Preacher,** thereby announcing the theme of his entire book, **vanity of vanities; all is vanity,** that is, all earthly nature and everything pertaining to temporal things has been perverted, in consequence of sin, so that it no longer serves the original purpose of God, but the vain objects of sin. V. 3. **What profit,** what lasting value, what enduring advantage, **hath a man of all his labor,** the toil and exertion with which he fatigues himself, **which he taketh under the sun?** The author does not say that man's labor is useless, but that, in itself, it has no enduring, eternal value. While the sun runs his course with unfailing regularity, the doings of men seem altogether changeable and variable. The work of their hands is good, if done in the Lord's service, but the misery and the hardships connected with it set the imprint of vanity upon their entire life. V. 4. **One generation passeth away,** sinking down into the dust of death, **and another generation cometh,** replacing those who are laid in the grave; there is a continual going and coming; **but the earth abideth forever,** it stands the same, as long as the Lord so decrees, in the midst of the turmoil of changing centuries, calmly remaining while generations come and go. V. 5. **The sun also ariseth, and the sun goeth down,** steadily pursuing his course, and **hasteth to his place where he arose,** to come up again in the east, governing time as the Lord ordered, Gen. 1, 16. V. 6. **The wind goeth toward the south, and turneth about unto the north,** following certain fixed laws of the universe; **it whirleth about continually,** in an ever-returning change, **and the wind returneth again according to his circuits,** in courses whose general regularity has been learned even by human observers. V. 7. **All the rivers run into the sea, yet the sea is not full,** it does not overflow on account of the immense masses of water which it constantly receives; **unto the place from whence the rivers come, thither they return again,** in a constant evaporation and condensation, the cycle of ocean, clouds and fog, rain and dew, springs, creeks, and rivers continuing without intermission. V. 8. **All things are full of labor,** full of trouble, weariness, fatigue on account of the curse following sin, Gen. 3, 19; **man cannot utter it,** the endlessness and burden of human troubles cannot be told by human tongue, it is beyond man's ability to express it; **the eye is not satisfied with seeing, nor the ear filled with hearing,** the senses become wearied in trying to master the endless succession of impressions and phenomena which press upon them from all sides in the course of this sinful existence. V. 9. **The thing that**

hath been, that which has happened time and again in the past, **it is that which shall be; and that which is done is that which shall be done,** occurring over and over again in human experience; **and there is no new thing under the sun,** no matter how men may change their environment and place the newest achievements of science and invention into their service, the misery and the toil of life is ever the same, and the abuse of God's gifts and the transgression and the dissatisfaction of man's heart are ever the same. V. 10. **Is there anything whereof it may be said, See, this is new?** Has human nature and the misery of human life changed since the fall of man? **It hath been already of old time, which was before us,** always, within the memory of man. V. 11. **There is no remembrance of former things,** men forget the lessons which the insufficient records of the past teach them; **neither shall there be any remembrance of things that are to come with those that shall come after,** for the impressive warnings of even the greatest cataclysms in the history of the world have gone unheeded. Cp. Matt. 24, 37—39.

THE UNRELIABILITY OF EARTHLY WISDOM. — V. 12. **I, the Preacher, was king over Israel in Jerusalem,** over the entire nation, as Solomon states in looking back over his long reign. V. 13. **And I gave my heart to seek and search out by wisdom,** applying the wisdom given him by the Lord with all zeal, **concerning all things that are done under heaven,** the motives, acts, and lives of men everywhere; **this sore travail,** namely, the zealous searching, the steady and ceaseless endeavor to inquire into the works of men, **hath God given to the sons of man to be exercised therewith,** it is a part of the labor laid upon mankind by the Lord, the acquiring of knowledge is a difficult task. Now Solomon states the result of his studies; v. 14. **I have seen all the works that are done under the sun,** in a careful observation of the ways of men; **and, behold, all is vanity and vexation of spirit,** efforts which bring about no lasting good, for all the affliction of mind with which men strive to go forward cannot bring them lasting good fortune and true happiness. What this world only has to offer will always fall short of the mark. V. 15. **That which is crooked cannot be made straight,** human beings cannot alter what has been determined by God, even as they cannot, by their own reason and strength, change their sinful hearts to such as are well-pleasing to God; **and that which is wanting cannot be numbered,** if it is missing, it cannot be accounted for, what is wholly defective cannot be supplied. V. 16. **I communed with mine own heart,** in a careful contemplation or consideration of the difficulty presented, **saying, Lo, I am come to great estate,** being possessed of incalculable wealth, **and have gotten more wisdom than all they that have been before me in Jerusalem,** for the Lord had conferred upon Solomon a most extraordinary amount of wisdom, 2 Chron. 1, 12; **yea, my heart had great experience of wisdom and knowledge,** he not only possessed a great measure of wisdom from the beginning, but he also grew in circumspection and caution from day to day and from year to year. V. 17. **And I gave my heart to know wisdom,** on its positive side, **and to know madness and folly,** the error and foolishness of men, to estimate it properly; **I perceived that this also,** namely, the activity of striving after such knowledge, **is vexation of spirit,** a miserable and troublesome exertion. V. 18. **For in much wisdom is much grief,** lack of knowledge or deliberate ignorance saving a person many a disagreeable meditation on the weakness and meanness of human nature; **and he that increaseth knowledge increaseth sorrow,** for he will have an understanding of conditions as they actually exist, he will be able to judge things as they are, and the realities of this world, due to sin, are always disagreeable and vexatious. It takes much trust in the Lord to overcome the offense of this world.

CHAPTER 2.

The Vanity of Earthly Pleasure and Luxury.

SOLOMON'S OWN EXAMPLE. — V. 1. **I said in mine heart,** in considering carefully the possibility of enjoyment, **Go to, now, I will prove thee with mirth,** to find out whether he would feel happy and contented in enjoyment of the senses; **therefore enjoy pleasure,** sensual delights of every kind; **and, behold, this also is vanity,** it affords no true happiness. V. 2. **I said of laughter,** of the joy and cheerfulness which he madly attempted to reach, **It is mad,** foolish, it affords no real satisfaction; **and of mirth, What doeth it?** It accomplishes nothing of value, it avails nothing in the attainment of real, lasting good. V. 3. **I sought in mine heart to give myself unto wine,** to comfort himself by its use, either with the object of nourishing the body or to have the sensual pleasure afforded by the exhilaration produced by the stimulant, **yet acquainting mine heart with wisdom,** that is, to keep wisdom and discretion as the guiding principles of his life; **and to lay hold on folly,** to seize and enjoy the pleasures of the flesh, to find out whether they would satisfy, **till I might see what was that good for the sons of men,** what course they had best pursue in going through life, **which they should do under the heaven all the days of their life.** Solomon did what so many people have tried out since his time; instead of accepting the statements of God's Word concerning that which is good and beneficial to them, they determine to try out for themselves what is good and so are obliged to learn through many bitter and painful experiences. Solomon, having the means, took every opportunity for his experiment. V. 4. **I made me great works,** building magnificent structures and piling up evidences of wealth on every hand; **I builded me houses,** 1 Kings 7 to 10; **I planted me vineyards,** Song of Sol. 8, 11; v. 5. **I made me gardens and orchards,** pleasure-grounds near his various residences, **and I planted trees in them of all kind of fruits,** in rich variety, including many from foreign countries; v. 6. **I made me pools of water,** artificial lakes for purposes of irrigation, **to water therewith the wood that bringeth forth trees,** this being necessary on account of the extent and the magnificence of his parks; v. 7. **I got me servants and maidens,** slaves of both sexes, **and had servants born in my house,** such slaves usually being distinguished for loyalty to their master; **also I had great possessions of great and small cattle above all that were in Jerusalem before me,** as God had promised him, 2 Chron. 1, 12; v. 8. **I gathered me also silver and gold, and the peculiar treasure of kings and of the provinces,** 1 Kings 9, 28; 10, 24—29; **I gat me men singers and women singers,** such as were common at Oriental courts for the entertainment of the court and of the royal guests, **and the delights of the sons of men, as musical instruments, and that of all sorts,** in great abundance, as befitted his station and wealth. V. 9. **So I was great,** possessed of riches and power, **and increased more than all that were before me in Jerusalem,** as the historical accounts fully substantiate, 1 Kings 9 to 11; **also my wisdom remained with me,** it stood by him in all his experimenting to find happiness, it never left his side, for he was honestly concerned about finding true satisfaction in this life, if possible. V. 10. **And whatsoever mine eyes desired I kept not from them, I withheld not my heart from any joy,** he tried them all out to see whether he could obtain true profit from any of them; **for my heart rejoiced in all my labor,** it was an agreeable pursuit, he felt that he would surely find what he was seeking; **and this was my portion of all my labor,** he found this a recompense for all his troubles and sorrows. V. 11. **Then I looked on all the works that my hands had wrought,** he carefully surveyed the results of his experiment, **and on the labor that I had labored to do,** which he had planned and carried out with so much pains; **and, behold, all was vanity and vexation of spirit,** there was no lasting satisfaction in the possession and enjoyment of all earthly goods and pleasures, **and there was no profit under the sun.** V. 12. **And I turned myself to behold wisdom, and madness, and folly,** to compare them, to consider their relative value, chap. 1, 17; **for what can the man do that cometh after the king?** Solomon surely had the best chance to make his experiment in happiness, and if he had not succeeded, any one else would have still smaller chance of success. **Even that which hath been already done,** the same foolish mistakes having been made by men from the beginning. V. 13. **Then I saw that wisdom excelleth folly as far as light excelleth darkness,** he recognized the absolute worth of wisdom, he found that the one excluded the other, that folly is vain, empty, and unsubstantial. V. 14. **The wise man's eyes are in his head,** he uses them with proper observation and understanding; **but the fool walketh in darkness,** deliberately closing his eyes and his understanding to the advantages of true spiritual knowledge; **and I myself perceived also that one event happeneth to them all,** they are all subject to death and decay. V. 15. **Then said I in my heart,** in considering this apparent puzzle, **As it happeneth to the fool, so it happeneth even to me,** literally, "I also, it will happen to me"; **and why was I then more wise?** The possession of great knowledge in itself, without being placed into service, is of little value. **Then I said in my heart that this also is vanity,** namely, that so far as death in itself is concerned, the same fate awaits them both. V. 16. **For there is no remembrance of the wise more than of the fool forever,** people forget the one as rapidly as the other; **seeing that which now is in the days to come shall all be forgotten,** that is ordinarily and generally the case, the few exceptions tending to confirm the rule. **And how dieth the wise man? As the fool,** they must both yield up the spirit in the same manner. V. 17. **Therefore I hated life,** he was filled with weariness and loathing toward all that this life has to offer; **because the work that is wrought under the sun is grievous unto me,** the contemplation of it all fills the observer with a sense of oppression; **for all is vanity and vexation of spirit.** V. 18. **Yea, I hated,** regarded with disgust and aversion, **all my labor which I had taken under the sun,** with which he had exerted himself; **because I should leave it unto the man that shall be after me,** his successor thus reaping the fruit for which he had labored, a fact which, for the moment, made his own work appear so useless. V. 19. **And who knoweth whether he shall be a wise man or a fool?** since so much depends upon the attitude of men. Solomon himself, having disregarded his father's dying charge, was filled with misgivings concerning the manner in which Rehoboam, his son by an idolatrous Ammonitess, Naamah, would conduct himself, a foreboding which was only too fully justified. **Yet shall he have rule over all my labor wherein I have labored, and wherein I have showed myself wise under the sun. This is also vanity.** There is a serious suggestion here for all Christian parents to discard all selfishness and sentimentality and to train their children in the fear and admonition of the Lord.

THE VANITY OF LABOR IN ITSELF. — V. 20. **Therefore I went about to cause my heart to despair of all the labor which I took under the sun,** he was inclined to regard his life as a failure, if viewed from this standpoint alone. V. 21. **For there is a man whose labor is in wisdom, and in knowledge, and in equity,** who possesses wisdom, applies it to the circumstances of every-day life, and uses the proper ability in so doing; **yet to a man that hath not labored therein shall he leave it for his portion,** another will reap what he sowed. **This also is vanity and a great evil,** for it seems to place wisdom and its proper application at a disadvantage. V. 22. **For what hath man of all his labor, and of the vexation of his heart,** the hard work with which he applies wisdom and knowledge in all his transactions, **wherein he hath labored under the sun?** V. 23. **For all his days are sorrows, and his travail grief,** that seems to be the only result and reward of all his labor; **yea, his heart taketh not rest in the night,** since he is troubled with anxiety and kept awake by worry. **This is also vanity.** Solomon therefore states his conclusion, so far as this life in itself is concerned. V. 24. **There is nothing better for a man than that he should eat and drink and that he should make his soul enjoy good in his labor,** cheerfully making use of all the blessings which God bestows on His children and accepting them with a grateful heart. **This also I saw, that it was from the hand of God,** namely, the feeling of quiet and appreciative contentment in the midst of all the wearing vicissitudes of life. V. 25. **For who can eat, or who else can hasten hereunto,** to the enjoyment of God's gifts, **more than I?** Christians may profit by the sad experiment which Solomon made without paying the high price which the Jewish king had to pay for the wisdom so gained. V. 26. **For God giveth to a man that is good in His sight,** who lives before Him in the fear of God, **wisdom, and knowledge, and joy,** as a reward dealt out by His mercy; **but to the sinner,** the godless, the unbeliever, **he giveth travail,** misery and tribulation, **to gather and to heap up, that he may give to him that is good before God,** unconsciously, of course, and in spite of himself. Solomon, conducting himself with piety, enjoyed his wealth in agreement with God's blessing upon him; the same king, forsaking the precepts of the Lord, became unhappy, while the riches which he had heaped up became the prey of the Egyptian king, 2 Chron. 12. **This also is vanity and vexation of spirit,** but the lesson which it teaches should be heeded well by all believers.

CHAPTER 3.

Of Earthly Care and Happiness.

THE DEPENDENCE OF MAN UPON THE COURSE OF NATURE. — V. 1. **To everything,** all that men undertake or do on earth, **there is a season, and a time to every purpose under the heaven,** under the government and providence of God: v. 2. **a time to be born,** literally, "to bear," **and a time to die,** as the Lord has arranged; **a time to plant, and a time to pluck up that which is planted,** these seasons being beyond the control of men; v. 3. **a time to kill,** by inflicting mortal wounds, **and a time to heal; a time to break down, and a time to build up;** v. 4. **a time to weep, and a time to laugh; a time to mourn,** on account of some grief or bereavement, **and a time to dance,** to leap for joy; v. 5. **a time to cast away stones,** where they encumber the ground, **and a time to gather stones together,** as for building purposes; **a time to embrace,** to show one's love and affection, **and a time to refrain from embracing,** for to show affection to excess is surfeiting; v. 6. **a time to get,** to obtain possession of, **and a time to lose,** deliberately to dispose of some object for some special reason, or cheerfully to give it up as the will of God indicates; **a time to keep, and a time to cast away,** without any care for the future; v. 7. **a time to rend,** as when garments were torn under the influence of great grief, **and a time to sew; a time to keep silence,** not only in the silence of mourning, but on general principles, **and a time to speak,** for its omission may amount to a denial of the truth; v. 8. **a time to love,** this being the summary of the Law, **and a time to hate; a time of war,** when men think it necessary to shed blood in such a manner, **and a time of peace.** All these activities are carried out by men in the course of their lives, they occupy a certain period of time; not as though the Lord looked upon them all with approbation, but that He knows of them and uses all events for the furtherance of His will. It is not blind chance which rules the world, but "there's a Divinity that shapes our ends," and we Christians gladly submit to His guidance. V. 9. **What profit hath he that worketh,** being engaged in the one or the other of the activities enumerated above, **in that wherein he laboreth?** There is no lasting happiness and satisfaction to be found on this earth. V. 10. **I have seen the travail which God hath given to the sons of men to be exercised in it,** the misery which is the lot of all human beings. V. 11. **He hath made everything beautiful in his time,** for the enjoyment of men during the short period of their lives, in the proper season; **also He hath set the world in their heart,** so that they might understand it as reflecting the wisdom and goodness of God, **so that no man can find out the work that God maketh from the beginning to the end,** this being the restriction which is placed upon man's knowledge, the inability to gain a correct and adequate insight into the divine plan of the world and the unsearchable essence of God.

THE NATURE OF HUMAN HAPPINESS. — V. 12. **I know that there is no good in them,** in the works of God given to men, **but for a man to rejoice,** in a cheerful use of the blessings of the Lord, **and to do good in his life,** to himself and to others in the proper use of God's gifts, for this is one essential part of true human happiness. V. 13. **And also that every man should eat and drink, and enjoy the good of all his labor, it is the gift of God,** and should be acknowledged as such with the proper thanksgiving. V. 14. **I know that, whatsoever God doeth, it shall be forever,** for His works are established and upheld by His almighty power; **nothing can be put to it,** by the weak attempts of frail human beings, **nor anything taken from it,** they cannot interfere with His government; **and God doeth it that men should fear before Him,** for the contemplation of God's works brings about a feeling of awe and reverence, together with the knowledge that the omniscience of God is familiar with even those things which men often believe hidden from His eyes. V. 15. **That which hath been is now,** it was established by God's creative act; **and that which is to be hath already been,** in agreement with God's plans before the creation of the world; **and God requireth that which is past,** literally, "God seeketh that which was driven away," restoring that which seemed changed and crowded out by the cycle of events in the history of the world. V. 16. **And, moreover, I saw under the sun the place of judgment,** where the judges and rulers of men should dispense justice only, **that wickedness was there; and the place of righteousness, that iniquity was there,** perversion of justice by persons in authority being all too common. V. 17. **I said in mine heart,** in meditating upon a possible change in the unfortunate conditions obtaining, **God shall judge the righteous and the wicked,** if not on this side of the grave, then in the last great Judgment; **for there is a time there,** in heaven above, **for every purpose and for every work,** for God is still supreme Sovereign in the universe. V. 18. **I said in mine heart concerning the estate of the sons of men,** fallen mankind in general, **that God might manifest them,** that is, sift, test, prove them, **and that they might see that they themselves are beasts,** so far as their physical life and its end is concerned, they are on a level with brutes, that being the curse of vanity, the result of sin. V. 19. **For that which befalleth the sons of men befalleth beasts; even one thing befalleth them: as the one,** according to their bodily, physical nature only, **dieth, so dieth the other; yea, they have all one breath,** their physical life is of the same kind; **so that a man hath no preeminence above a beast,** so far as his outward, physical life comes into consideration; **for all is vanity.** V. 20. **All go unto one place,** to the realm of death; **all are of the dust, and all turn to dust again,** Gen. 3, 19. V. 21. **Who knoweth the spirit of man that goeth upward, and the spirit of the beast that goeth downward to the earth?** How can we expect the ordinary person, without the illumination of the Word, to distinguish between the death of a human being and an animal? For it certainly seems as though there is no difference, death ensuing as soon as the breath stops. V. 22. **Wherefore I perceive that there is nothing better than that a man should rejoice in his own works,** take pleasure and delight in the labor which falls to his lot in life; **for that is his portion,** so much is allotted to him in this life; **for who shall bring him to see what shall be after him?** The lesson for the believers is this, that they do not chase after shadows, thereby losing the reality, but that they enjoy the blessings of God with a carefree heart, leaving the future in the hands of their heavenly Father.

CHAPTER 4.

Various Evils and Misfortunes of Mankind.

PERSONAL MISFORTUNES. — V. 1. **So I returned and considered all the oppressions that are done under the sun,** turning his reflections from the vanity of human life to the violence practised by many men; **and behold the tears of such as were oppressed, and they had no comforter,** no one to dry their tears by healing their injuries; **and on the**

side of their oppressors there was power, that being the way of tyrants everywhere, **but they had no comforter,** the repetition of this phrase emphasizing the desperate and hopeless condition of the poor and downtrodden. V. 2. **Wherefore I praised the dead which are already dead,** and thus beyond the reach of tyranny and oppression, **more than the living which are yet alive,** and therefore always in danger of becoming victims of violence. V. 3. **Yea, better is he than both they, which hath not yet been, who hath not seen the evil work that is done under the sun,** for, not having been born, he has been spared the pain of witnessing the many evidences of oppression and tyranny which are always found in the world. This is not an expression of unbelieving pessimism, but a statement of fact which will cause the believers to turn all the more eagerly to the comforts of the Christian religion. V. 4. **Again, I considered all travail and every right work,** the prosperity coveted by men, the source and motive of so much of the oppression found in the world, **that for this,** namely, for his apparent success, **a man is envied of his neighbor,** this also resulting in a condition of misfortune. **This is also vanity and vexation of spirit,** for such emulation and striving is bound to result in misfortune to men. V. 5. **The fool foldeth his hands together,** too lazy to exert himself, **and eateth his own flesh,** using up his fortune and ruining himself by his idleness, having no one but himself to blame for his misfortune. V. 6. **Better is an handful,** a small amount of this world's goods, **with quietness,** to be enjoyed in peace, **than both the hands full,** a large measure of riches, **with travail and vexation of spirit,** for riches, if obtained only by anxious labor and retained only with care and sorrow, are a misfortune and cannot be conducive to happiness.

Evils of Social and Civil Life. — V. 7. **Then I returned,** fixing his attention upon another point that needed explanation, **and I saw vanity under the sun.** V. 8. **There is one alone, and there is not a second,** the reference being to a man without relatives or friends; **yea, he hath neither child nor brother,** no one bound to him by natural ties, the necessity being laid upon him, therefore, to gain friends by other means; **yet is there no end of all his labor; neither is his eye satisfied with riches,** he continues to crave new treasures, although there is no object in it for him; **neither saith he, For whom do I labor, and bereave my soul of good?** He never stops to think that his heaping up of treasures is pure folly. **This is also vanity,** an empty and useless performance, **yea, it is a sore travail.** V. 9. **Two are better than one,** for friendship, marriage, association in religious communion will tend to oppose selfishness; **because they have a good reward for their labor,** the advantage resulting from such associating with others being shown in the next verses. V. 10. **For if they fall, the one will lift up his fellow,** a second one always being present to aid the one stumbling; **but woe to him that is alone when he falleth; for he hath not another to help him up,** he lacks the friendly sympathy and assistance enjoyed by one who is united with others by the ties of friendship or a common cause. V. 11. **Again, if two lie together, then they have heat,** the reference being to traveling companions obliged to pass the night out in the open air, the chilliness of the Palestinian nights being proverbial; **but how can one be warm alone?** A poorer traveler particularly, with only his over-garment as a cover, would probably suffer severely. The expression brings out the benefits of warm sympathy derived from social ties. V. 12. **And if one prevail against him,** if an individual person finds himself obliged to submit to the attacks of some criminal, **two shall withstand him,** their combined strength overcoming the assailant; **and a threefold cord is not quickly broken.** In union is strength, but such union must be based upon unity. V. 13. **Better is a poor and a wise child,** one which, although in the depths of poverty, yet uses proper knowledge and circumspection and is willing to be guided by proper counsel, **than an old and foolish king,** one presumably with great wealth at his command, **who will no more be admonished,** believing himself beyond good advice of every kind. V. 14. **For out of prison he cometh to reign,** that is, some person in the very lowest station is elevated to the highest position of authority in the land; **whereas also he that is born in his kingdom,** a prince by birth, **becometh poor.** Joseph becomes ruler of Egypt, Jehoahaz is led away to Egypt in shame and disgrace. V. 15. **I considered all the living which walk under the sun,** observing the great number of adherents which the poor person elevated to power in the country had gained, **with the second child that shall stand up in his stead,** taking the place of the old and foolish king who was dethroned for his refusal to take advice. V. 16. **There is no end of all the people, even of all that have been before them,** the entire mass of subjects hail the usurper with joy and expect great things from him; **they also that come after shall not rejoice in him,** he may disappoint the expectations which are placed in him, or his popularity may suddenly wane. Whether Solomon had a certain instance in mind or not, the truth of his observation has often been shown in history, as Luther and other commentators point out. **Surely this also is vanity and vexation of spirit,** coming under the heading of the many things in life which give no lasting satisfaction and happiness.

CHAPTER 5.

The Advancement of Earthly Happiness.

PROPER WORSHIP OF GOD. — V. 1. **Keep thy foot when thou goest to the house of God,** carefully watching lest it stray aside from the path leading to the Lord's Temple and such a person's heart be affected with thoughts which interfere with true devotion, **and be more ready to hear,** rather, "approach to hear," to listen to and to heed the Word of God, **than to give the sacrifice of fools,** as is done in thoughtless and hypocritical worship; **for they consider not that they do evil,** they do not realize how deeply they offend the Lord with their irreverent behavior. V. 2. **Be not rash with thy mouth,** quick to speak, especially in thoughtless prayer, **and let not thine heart be hasty to utter anything before God,** since prayer demands an attitude of true devotion; **for God is in heaven,** exalted above all levity and thoughtless form of worship, **and thou upon earth,** immeasurably beneath the majesty of the almighty Sovereign of the earth; **therefore let thy words be few,** not indulging in heathenish babbling, Matt. 6, 7. V. 3. **For a dream cometh through the multitude of business,** when a person is engrossed with the cares and anxieties of his work, his dreams are apt to mislead him into a land of make-believe; **and a fool's voice is known by multitude of words,** he believes the efficacy of prayer depends upon the amount of language expended, whereas it depends upon the sincerity of the mind resting upon the true devotion of faith. V. 4. **When thou vowest a vow unto God,** such vows among the Jews being included in the precepts of their religion, Num. 30, 2; Deut. 23, 21—23, **defer not to pay it,** this admonition being directed against hasty and ill-considered vows; **for He hath no pleasure in fools,** God wants no vows to be made in a spirit of levity, without regarding their sanctity; **pay that which thou hast vowed,** Ps. 66, 13. 14. V. 5. **Better is it that thou shouldest not vow,** Deut. 23, 22, not make rash promises supported by an obligation before the Lord, **than that thou shouldest vow and not pay,** provided the vow is in agreement with the great precepts of God's Word, especially the command of love. V. 6. **Suffer not thy mouth to cause thy flesh to sin,** for the sensual nature of man is stimulated by the sins of the tongue; **neither say thou before the angel,** before the priest, as the representative of the Lord, **that it was an error,** the object being to escape the consequences of an unfulfilled vow; **wherefore should God be angry at thy voice,** which has thus become guilty of lying, **and destroy the work of thine hands?** The punishment of God, in a case of this kind, is shown not only in the failure of undertakings, but also in the overthrowing of projects already established. V. 7. **For in the multitude of dreams,** foolish fancies concerning God's requirements of men in worship, **and many words,** hasty and ill-considered, **there are also divers vanities,** they are unreliable and do not fit a person for the duties which the Word of God lays upon him; **but fear thou God,** for the fear of God, as the basis of all true wisdom, will guide the steps of man aright on the way of true sanctification.

ABSTAINING FROM VICES AND FOSTERING VIRTUES. — V. 8. **If thou seest the oppression of the poor,** chap. 4, 1, **and violent perverting of judgment and justice in a province,** chap. 3, 16, **marvel not at the matter,** for such things are to be expected in this wicked world, 1 Pet. 4, 12, wherefore the believers should also not be worried about the eventual trend of justice; **for He that is higher than the highest regardeth, and there be higher than they,** above all the rulers of this world is the great Sovereign of them all, who will finally adjudicate all matters which now often seem mingled in a hopeless muddle. V. 9. **Moreover, the profit of the earth,** the increase or produce of the land, **is for all; the king himself is served by the field,** and therefore the great Lord of all will finally punish all those who abused their authority and robbed the poor of their share in this world's goods. V. 10. **He that loveth silver shall not be satisfied with silver,** for the covetous is never satisfied, never happy; **nor he that loveth abundance with increase,** having his heart set on a multitude of possessions, for the more he has, the more he wants; **this is also vanity,** for it cannot yield true happiness. V. 11. **When goods increase, they are increased that eat them,** for with increasing wealth comes the demand for more servants, and they and other dependents are consumers rather than producers; **and what good is there to the owners thereof,** what benefit have they of all their possessions, **saving the beholding of them with their eyes?** a feeling of pleasure which cannot permanently satisfy. V. 12. **The sleep of a laboring man is sweet,** sound and healthful, **whether he eat little or much,** whether he has a generous supply of food or must be satisfied with nourishment just sufficient to sustain life; **but the abundance of the rich will not suffer him to sleep,** rich foods together with worry over his possessions drive the sleep from the eyes of the wealthy. V. 13. **There is a sore evil which I have seen under the sun, namely, riches kept for the owners thereof to their hurt,** carefully taken care of by guardians, but later a snare to the possessors, plunging them into many evil and hurtful lusts. V. 14. **But those riches perish by evil travail,** they are lost by the various misfortunes attending wealth; **and he begetteth a son, and there is nothing in his hand,** he is an heir of poverty. V. 15. **As he came forth of his mother's womb, naked shall he return to go as he came, and shall take nothing of his labor, which he may carry away in his hand,** whatever treasures he has gained he must leave behind. Cp. Job 1, 21; Ps. 49, 17; 1 Tim. 6, 7. V. 16. **And this also is a sore evil,** not only the fact that the rich must leave all his wealth behind, but that he is subject to death, as are all human beings, **that in all points as he came, so shall he go,** departing without a cent; **and what profit hath he that hath labored for the wind?** for he stored up his wealth without use and benefit, since he must leave all behind. V. 17. **All his days also he eateth in darkness,** always under a gloomy cloud, never sure of the continuance of his wealth, **and he hath much sorrow and wrath with his sickness,** nothing but annoyance and dissatisfaction on account of the anxiety connected with the acquiring and maintaining of his riches. V. 18. **Behold that which I have seen,** the conclusion which he reaches also in this chapter: **It is good and comely for one to eat and to drink, and to enjoy the good of all his labor that he taketh under the sun all the days of his life, which God giveth him,** without avarice on the one hand, and without care and worry on the other; **for it is his portion,** which he should use properly while living in this world. V. 19. **Every man also to whom God hath given riches and wealth,** as a blessing bestowed by God's loving-kindness, **and hath given him power to eat thereof, and to take his portion,** in a lawful use of his wealth, **and to rejoice in his labor,** enjoying the fruit thereof according to God's will; **this is the gift of God,** to be accepted and used in that sense only, and not after the manner of the avaricious fool who hoards his riches and spoils his chances for happiness. V. 20. **For he shall not much remember the days of his life,** for the memory of any earthly enjoyment is brief; **because God answereth him in the joy of his heart,** vouchsafing to him such happiness in this life as will enable him to sojourn amidst the disappointments of this earth with a heart resting in trust in the heavenly Father, that being the ideal which the believer should keep before his eyes always.

CHAPTER 6.

Of the Vanity of Earthly Riches.

V. 1. **There is an evil which I have seen under the sun, and it is common among men,** it weighs heavily upon a great many unfortunate people; v. 2. **a man to whom God hath given riches, wealth, and honor,** even to the point of luxury, all the highest gifts known to man here on earth, **so that he wanteth nothing for his soul of all that he desireth,** lacking nothing of things which are commonly considered most desirable by men, **yet God giveth him not power to eat thereof,** either on account of illness or by reason of excessive and oppressive cares, **but a stranger eateth it,** the heirs of such a man rioting and reveling in the enjoyment of the goods for which they did not labor; **this is vanity, and it is an evil disease,** it is like a severe illness which deprives a person of all joy in life. V. 3. **If a man beget an hundred children,** the possession of a great many children being considered a most extraordinary blessing of the Lord, **and live many years,** in a long and happy life, **so that the days of his years be many,** the full sum allotted to men, **and his soul be not filled with good,** not having the satisfaction of a real enjoyment of God's blessings in the status of a child of God, **and also that he have no burial,** being deprived of honor even in his death, this being considered a great disgrace in Oriental countries; **I say that an untimely birth is better than he,** it would have been better for him if he had never been born. V. 4. **For he cometh in with vanity,** naked, poor, into an empty existence, **and departeth in darkness,** into a future which holds no hope for him, **and his name shall be covered with darkness,** assigned to utter forgetfulness and oblivion, in an unhonored death. V. 5. **Moreover he hath not seen the sun,** he has never had any enjoyment of life, **nor known anything,** shut out from everything that might bring happiness; **this hath more rest than the other,** that is, the unborn child is less troubled with the annoyances of life than the miser. V. 6. **Yea, though he live a thousand years twice told,** more than twice as long as the oldest patriarchs from Adam to Noah, **yet hath he seen no good,** his own gloomy covetousness depriving him of any true enjoyment of life; **do not all go to one place?** for the realm of the dead is bound to receive all men without exception. V. 7. **All the labor of man is for his mouth,** his chief concern in this life being the satisfaction of his hunger and of the sensual enjoyment of food, **and yet the appetite is not filled,** the soul is not satisfied, for a person living for this world only will never have his fill of sensual delights. V. 8. **For what hath the wise more than the fool?** He who strives after real knowledge seems to have no advantage, according to outward appearances, over one who lives only for the satisfaction of his sensual nature. **What hath the poor that knoweth to walk before the living?** That is, What advantage has the wise person, who strives for true humility, who leads a quiet and retired life, over him who disregards all considerations of this kind and boldly lives for his own interest alone? V. 9. **Better is the sight of the eyes,** the pleasant and sensible enjoyment of that which this life offers, **than the wandering of the desire,** when a person, dissatisfied with his lot, is ever planning something great for himself; **this is also vanity and vexation of spirit,** such restlessness and dissatisfaction brings only misery. V. 10. **That which hath been is named already,** men have, in the past, inquired into its nature, **and it is known that it is man,** that is, man is vanity, all his vaunted greatness is nothing; **neither may he contend with Him that is mightier than he,** God being the absolute Sovereign of the universe, whom no one can withstand. V. 11. **Seeing there be many things that increase vanity,** on account of the many trials, dangers, and changes of fortune with which man must contend, **what is man the better?** namely, in possessing wealth or the means for enjoying sensual delights. V. 12. **For who knoweth what is good for man in this life, all the days of his vain life which he spendeth as a shadow?** How can any mere human being, himself subject to change and decay, decide just what special condition of fortunes will be most beneficial to him? **For who can tell a man what shall be after him under the sun?** The future of every person's existence and fortunes is not in his own hands, but under the direction of God, to whom all believers will therefore entrust themselves, with all that they have, in childlike confidence.

CHAPTER 7.

Instruction Concerning True Happiness.

CONTEMPT OF THE WORLD AND THE SPIRIT OF CALM RESIGNATION. — V. 1. **A good name,** an excellent reputation before men and a high regard in the sight of God, **is better than precious ointment,** which was highly valued in the Orient for its refreshing odor; **and the day of death than the day of one's birth,** for at birth a person's fate is as yet unknown, while on the day of death life with all its vanities lies behind. To the believer particularly death means a deliverance from all evil, Phil. 1, 23. V. 2. **It is better to go to the house of mourning,** where people, lamenting for some deceased relative or friend, meditate upon the vanity of life, **than to go to the house of feasting,** where banqueting and carousing is indulged in and the serious side of life is ignored; **for that,** the fact that every house eventually becomes a house of mourning, **is the end of all men,** wherefore all men should keep it in mind; **and the living will lay it to his heart.** V. 3. **Sorrow,** a proper, mournful regard of the vanity of this world, **is better than laughter,** that is, worldly and boisterous merriment, which deliberately ignores the serious side of life; **for by the sadness of the countenance,** by a proper, serious contemplation of the vanities of life, **the heart is made better,** it will then observe a cheerfulness based upon understanding and not upon frivolousness. V. 4. **The heart of the wise is in the house of mourning,** that is, with all outward cheerfulness he never forgets the sober side of life and its problems; **but the heart of fools is in the house of mirth,** given to senseless merriment, which ignores the true conditions. V. 5. **It is better to hear the rebuke of the wise,** whereby some foolish behavior is censured, **than for a man to hear the song of fools,** the boisterous and suggestive, coarse and ribald songs which thoughtless and wicked people love, by which they attempt to forget the facts of life. V. 6. **For as the crackling of thorns under a pot,** where they are nevertheless consumed by the fire, **so is the laughter of the fool,** it agrees well with the apparent merriment of the thorns as they feed the fire; **this,** the senseless, boisterous merriment of fools, **also is vanity.** V. 7. **Surely oppression,** various forms of tyranny practised by fools in high and low places, **maketh a wise man mad,** either by making him call in question the wisdom of God's providence or by leading him into some transgression by which he seeks revenge; **and a gift,** a bribe offered to the wise man, **destroyeth the heart,** so that even he yields to corruption. V. 8. **Better is the end of a thing,** when a person knows just how he will succeed or has succeeded, **than the beginning thereof,** when one does not yet know how an affair will turn out; **and the patient in spirit,** long-suffering both in enduring wrong and in awaiting the outcome of some incident, **is better than the proud in spirit,** in whose case haughtiness is combined with a violent temper. V. 9. **Be not hasty in thy spirit to be angry,** easily insulted, holding a grudge for a long time, impatient in adversity; **for anger resteth in the bosom of fools,** with them only is an irritable disposition found. V. 10. **Say not thou, What is the cause that the former days were better than these?** the reference being to such as criticize and carp without attempting to improve present conditions. **For thou dost not enquire wisely,** literally, "on the basis of wisdom," **concerning this,** for the truly wise will try to improve conditions as he finds them. V. 11. **Wisdom is good with an inheritance,** that is, if compared with earthly possessions, or when joined with an ample estate, for the wise man, if wealthy, will use his wealth in accordance with the will of God, especially for the advantage of such as are in need; **and by it there is profit to them that see the sun,** wisdom combined with wealth will result in various benefits for the living. V. 12. **For wisdom is a defense,** literally, "a shadow," **and money is a defense,** both of them serve for protection in adversity; **but the excellency of knowledge is that wisdom giveth life to them that have it,** it is the more precious of the two blessings. V. 13. **Consider the work of God,** with the proper calmness of spirit; **for who can make that straight which He hath made crooked?** A man's impatience will not straighten out what to him seems foolish and adverse in human destiny. V. 14. **In the day of prosperity be joyful,** enjoying God's blessings with due thankfulness, **but in the day of adversity consider,** regard most carefully, let your thoughts run along these lines; **God also hath set the one over against the other,** He sends evil days as well as good, **to the end that man should find nothing after him,** in order that the future be hidden and remain hidden from man, for if the veil were lifted which hides the future, men would consider themselves independent of the divine dispensation.

A SPIRIT OF SORROW OVER SIN AND ITS ALLUREMENTS. — V. 15. **All things have I seen in the days of my vanity,** Solomon had taken note of everything possible while enjoying the empty life of this world; **there is a just man that perisheth in his righteousness,** his plans were failures, and he himself died in misfortune because he placed the emphasis upon a mere outward show of perfection only, **and there is a wicked man that prolongeth his life in his wickedness.** Cp. Ps. 73, 3—12. V. 16. **Be not righteous overmuch,** with a mere external, Pharisaic righteousness; **neither make thyself overwise,** in pretending to be a teacher of wisdom, while the substance is still lacking; **why shouldest thou destroy thyself?** for the curse of God is sure to strike arrogance and hypocrisy. V. 17. **Be not overmuch wicked,** not as though a little wickedness were permissible, but because an excess of malice is particularly disgusting; **neither be thou foolish,** in deliberately ignoring God and the wisdom of His Word; **why shouldest thou die before thy time?** for death is the consequence and punishment of foolishness and wickedness. V. 18. **It is good that thou shouldest take hold of this,** properly considering and thus avoiding the two extremes set forth; **yea, also from this withdraw not thine hand,** keeping it in mind always; **for he that feareth God shall come forth of them all,** avoiding both a false righteousness, with its hypocrisy, and bold immorality, with its challenge of God. V. 19. **Wisdom strengtheneth the wise more than ten mighty men which are in the city,** for true wisdom, which flows from the fear of God, is more effective in protecting its owner than all outward show of might. V. 20. **For there is not a just man upon earth that doeth good, and sinneth not,** not one who can truly claim perfection, they are all under the condemnation of sinfulness. Cp. Prov. 20, 9; 1 Kings 8, 46; Rom. 3, 23. V. 21. **Also take no heed unto all words that are spoken,** by being idly curious and anxious about what people say; **lest thou hear thy servant curse thee,** the vain listener being disgraced by the remarks of his own servant; v. 22. **for oftentimes also thine own heart knoweth that thou thyself likewise hast cursed others,** conscience being a stern accuser and bringing home many a sin which one has practically forgotten. V. 23. **All this,** the rules of life and the practical counsels here offered, **have I proved by wisdom,** his experience being dearly bought; **I said, I will be wise; but it was far from me,** he had not yet reached the true and perfect wisdom for which he was aspiring. V. 24. **That which is far off and exceeding deep, who can find it out?** True wisdom, as contained in the Word of God and flowing out of the fear of God, is not a matter of mere human comprehension. V. 25. **I applied mine heart to know,** literally, "I turned, I and my heart," **and to search and to seek out wisdom and the reason of things,** by examining, comparing, and judging the facts offered, **and to know the wickedness of folly, even of foolishness and madness,** literally, "wickedness, stubbornness, yea, stupidity, madness," the climax showing the utter vanity and futility of opposition to the Word of God, especially in deliberate sins; v. 26. **and I find more bitter than death the woman whose heart is snares and nets,** who uses words and glances to inveigle her victims, **and her hands as bands,** since she uses them in voluptuous embraces; **whoso pleaseth God shall escape from her,** by His special mercy; **but the sinner,** unwilling to accept the correction of the Word of God, **shall be taken by her,** delivered to her seductions in just punishment of his disobedience. V. 27. **Behold, this have I found, saith the preacher,** this is the result of his experiences, **counting one by one,** comparing one thing with another, **to find out the account,** to reach a definite conclusion; v. 28. **which yet my soul seeketh, but I find not: one man among a thousand have I found,** namely, one realizing the futility of human wisdom; **but a woman among all those**

have I not found, since moral weakness and proneness to temptation is ascribed to her sex in other parts of Scriptures as well. Cp. Gen. 3, 16; 2 Cor. 11, 3; 1 Tim. 2, 12—14. V. 29. **Lo, this only have I found, that God hath made man upright,** good, in perfect righteousness and holiness, Gen. 1, 26. 27; 5, 1; **but they have sought out many inventions,** their nature has been corrupted by malicious tricks and conceits, by disobedience to God's holy Law, by which they have brought the curse of vanity upon the entire human race.

CHAPTER 8.

True Wisdom a Rare Quality.

IN CIVIL RELATIONS. — V. 1. **Who is as the wise man?** equal to him in the right understanding of things. **And who knoweth the interpretation of a thing?** The advantages of true wisdom are again emphasized. **A man's wisdom maketh his face to shine,** a sunny countenance being the reflection of a wise and serene mind, **and the boldness of his face shall be changed,** for the truly cultured person avoids all coarseness, cultivating, instead, a proper form of benign conduct. V. 2. **I counsel thee to keep the king's commandment,** such obedience being the course followed by true wisdom, **and that in regard of the oath of God,** for by such an oath the subject vows allegiance to the king. A willing loyalty is not only expedient, it is demanded by God, it comes within the Fourth Commandment. V. 3. **Be not hasty to go out of his sight,** in disobedience or slavish terror; **stand not in an evil thing,** literally, "in an evil word," that is, it behooves the subject to be modest, yet firm, in the presence of the ruler, even if he speak an angry word; **for he doeth whatsoever pleaseth him,** the author, of course, having in mind the absolute authority of Oriental monarchs. It is surely a proof of great wisdom if a person can so conduct himself before such a potentate as to hold his own, giving way neither to terror nor to obstinacy. V. 4. **Where the word of a king is, there is power,** for so his rule is established; **and who may say unto him, What doest thou?** V. 5. **Whoso keepeth the commandment,** obeying the commands of the government in power as the representatives of God on earth, **shall feel no evil thing,** for naturally no punishment for transgression of the laws will strike him; **and a wise man's heart discerneth both time and judgment,** he knows that there is a time of punishment upon every evil and therefore avoids transgressions. V. 6. **Because to every purpose there is time and judgment, therefore the misery of man,** namely, of him who disregards the truth and warning contained in this fact, **is great upon him,** he is visited with heavy misfortune. V. 7. **For he knoweth not that which shall be,** since he neglected to heed the warning and did not properly weigh the consequences of his acts; **for who can tell him when it shall be?** The destiny of the judgment strikes such a person with great suddenness, because he has failed to note the accepted time and the day of salvation, 2 Cor. 6, 2. V. 8. **There is no man that hath power over the spirit to retain the spirit,** no human being can hold and control the breath of life; **neither hath he power in the day of death,** he must yield up his life when it is required of him; **and there is no discharge in that war,** as in the case of military service, no one is exempt from obedience to the call which death sends forth; **neither shall wickedness deliver those that are given to it,** the godless cannot hope to escape from the penalty of temporal and eternal death.

OVER AGAINST TYRANNY AND INJUSTICE. — V. 9. **All this have I seen and applied my heart unto every work that is done under the sun,** in seeking proper explanations of all the various circumstances in life, the question of tyranny also engaged his attention; **there is a time wherein one man ruleth over another to his own hurt,** for in exercising oppression the tyrant damages his own cause, 1 Kings 12. V. 10. **And so I saw the wicked buried,** in an honorable burial, **who had come and gone from the place of the holy,** where they sat as God's representatives, **and they,** the godly people, **were forgotten in the city where they had so done,** namely, in living an honorable and upright life; **this is also vanity,** namely, the unequal distribution of destinies in human life. V. 11. **Because sentence against an evil work is not executed speedily,** many flagrant offenses going unpunished on account of the slowness or the miscarriage of justice, **therefore the heart of the sons of men is fully set in them to do evil,** for in such circumstances criminals will feel safe in assuming that punishment will not strike them. V. 12. **Though a sinner do evil an hundred times, and his days be prolonged,** so that, to all intents, he is safe in his sinning, **yet surely I know,** in spite of the apparent evidence to the contrary, **that it shall be well with them that fear God, which fear before Him,** the godly finally receiving the recognition which God intends for them; v. 13. **but it shall not be well with the wicked, neither shall he prolong his days, which are as a shadow,** the punishment of God is bound finally to strike him; **because he feareth not before God,** Ps. 73,

18—20. V. 14. **There is a vanity which is done upon the earth,** a circumstance which shows the emptiness of the present life, **that there be just men,** true children of God, **unto whom it happeneth according to the work of the wicked; again, there be wicked men to whom it happeneth according to the work of the righteous,** this strange commingling and interchange of fortunes being one of the riddles of the universe; **I said that this also is vanity,** it seemed to emphasize the futility of this world. V. 15. **Then I commended mirth,** a proper and godly cheerfulness, **because a man hath no better thing under the sun than to eat, and to drink, and to be merry,** in the right use of God's gifts and blessings; **for that shall abide with him of his labor the days of his life, which God giveth him under the sun,** it is the one sure thing to be enjoyed from earthly work. V. 16. **When I applied mine heart to know wisdom, and to see the business that is done upon the earth,** the travail and trouble caused by his anxious search for the grounds and aims of human action, fate, and life; **(for also there is that neither day nor night seeth sleep with his eyes,** in his anxiety knowing no rest;) v. 17. **then I beheld all the work of God,** he made this observation with regard to all the works of God, **that a man cannot find out the work that is done under the sun,** he is unable to solve all the mysteries which present themselves to him; **because, though a man labor to seek it out, yet he shall not find it,** the mystery being beyond human understanding; **yea, farther: though a wise man think to know it, yet shall he not be able to find it,** and all human speculations regarding the motives of God in the government of the world are futile. Full and absolute trust is required on the part of God's children.

CHAPTER 9.

Puzzling Facts in the Government of the World.

CONCERNING HUMAN DESTINY. — V. 1. **For all this I considered in my heart,** in applying himself to learn true wisdom, **even to declare all this, that the righteous, and the wise, and their works,** their fate or destiny, **are in the hand of God,** that human effort with all its results depends entirely upon God; **no man knoweth either love or hatred by all that is before them,** that is, he cannot tell whether happiness or unhappiness will be his lot, for his future is hidden by a veil which he cannot penetrate. V. 2. **All things come alike to all,** the destiny of all men is decided by the Lord; **there is one event to the righteous, and to the wicked,** the same Providence governing the lives of both; **to the good, and to the clean, and to the unclean,** in the moral sense; **to him that sacrificeth,** fulfilling the outward obligations of divine worship, **and to him that sacrificeth not; as is the good, so is the sinner; and he that sweareth as he that feareth an oath,** the one who is rash and frivolous with his oath and he who holds it sacred. V. 3. **This is an evil among all things that are done under the sun, that there is one event unto all,** that they are all subject to the same destiny, as it seems to the observer; **yea, also the heart of the sons of men is full of evil,** since they all apparently are in the power of death in the same manner, **and madness is in their heart while they live,** since they have their inevitable lot before their eyes, **and after that they go to the dead,** which seems to be the aim of existence and the end of all men, their ultimate fate. V. 4. **For to him that is joined to all the living there is hope,** and so the condition of the living is still to be preferred, one should not give way to a sinful hopelessness; **for a living dog is better than a dead lion,** that is, no matter how lowly is a person's position in life, his condition is preferable to that of even the most honored person who has been claimed by death and can therefore no longer labor nor enjoy the fruits of his labor. V. 5. **For the living know that they shall die,** the consciousness of their inevitable fate gives them at least so much superiority over the dead; **but the dead know not anything, neither have they any more a reward,** their fate is decided for the present, they are beyond reward; **for the memory of them is forgotten,** in most cases their very name becoming a hollow, meaningless sound in a few years. V. 6. **Also their love, and their hatred, and their envy,** all the sentiments which actuated them in life, **is now perished,** the activities connected with these attributes have ceased; **neither have they any more a portion forever in anything that is done under the sun,** their bodies are in the grave, and all communication with the world of the living has ceased. Note that both the doctrine of purgatory and the vagaries of spiritism are here denied. V. 7. **Go thy way, eat thy bread with joy, and drink thy wine with a merry heart,** this being the conclusion which the author reaches on the basis of his contemplations; **for God now,** at the present time, here in this world, **accepteth thy works.** Note that the text presupposes food gained by each person by his own efforts. V. 8. **Let thy garments be always white,** in token of joy; **and let thy head lack no ointment,** for its absence would have been considered a sign of grief. V. 9. **Live joyfully**

with the wife whom thou lovest, the lawfully wedded spouse, **all the days of the life of thy vanity, which He hath given thee under the sun, all the days of thy vanity,** Prov. 5, 15—19; 18, 22; **for that is thy portion in this life, and in thy labor which thou takest under the sun,** that is, a proper enjoyment of God's blessings will compensate the believer for the toil and labor which is the inevitable lot of men in life. V. 10. **Whatsoever thy hand findeth to do,** whatever task falls to man's lot in life, whether in daily labor or in any other undertaking begun in the name of the Lord, **do it with thy might,** with vigor and energy; **for there is no work, nor device, nor knowledge, nor wisdom in the grave, whither thou goest.** It is necessary for the believers to work the works of their heavenly Father while it is day; the night cometh when no man can work, John 9, 4.

WISDOM STILL TO BE SOUGHT. — V. 11. **I returned and saw under the sun,** throughout the world, in all circumstances and conditions of men, **that the race is not to the swift nor the battle to the strong,** that is, by their own absolute determination and effort, **neither yet bread to the wise,** whose wisdom might be expected to provide food for himself in large amounts, **nor yet riches to men of understanding,** who would presumably know how to acquire them, **nor yet favor to men of skill,** although one might expect that a man of ability should be hailed with acclaim; **but time and chance happeneth to them all,** all the success of human endeavor depends upon circumstances and powers beyond their control, which, in turn, are in the hands of God. V. 12. **For man also knoweth not his time,** he knows neither when death will overtake him nor the hour when some special work is expected of him; **as the fishes that are taken in an evil net,** their fate suddenly overtaking them, **and as the birds that are caught in the snare,** altogether unawares; **so are the sons of men,** all weak and sinful mortals, **snared in an evil time, when it falleth suddenly upon them,** the unexpected suddenness of the capture being the point of comparison. V. 13. **This wisdom have I seen also under the sun, and it seemed great unto me:** v. 14. **There was a little city, and few men within it,** to serve as its defenders against an enemy; **and there came a great king against it,** quite naturally in command of a large force, **and besieged it, and built great bulwarks against it,** in order to prepare for the storming of the city; v. 15. **now, there was found in it a poor wise man, and he by his wisdom delivered the city,** several instances of this kind being recorded in history; **yet no man,** in the extremity of the siege, **remembered that same poor man,** whose cleverness might well have found a way of saving the city, if he had been given a chance. V. 16. **Then said I, Wisdom is better than strength,** that fact being universally conceded; **nevertheless the poor man's wisdom is despised, and his words are not heard,** his counsel is ignored. V. 17. **The words of wise men are heard in quiet more than the cry of him that ruleth among fools,** the superiority of wisdom being established in spite of the fact that it is often neglected, for those who give heed to its advice will surely receive benefit, while even a king who listens to folly does so to his own hurt. V. 18. **Wisdom is better than weapons of war,** it is more desirable than the greatest physical and martial strength; **but one sinner,** placing himself in opposition to the counsels of wisdom, cp. Josh. 7, 1—12, **destroyeth much good,** his folly quickly undoing the measures proposed by wisdom. It should be noted in this entire chapter that Solomon does not teach hopeless pessimism and fatalism, but a tender and mournful realism, relieved by his admonition to make use of the proper cheerfulness in enjoying the blessings of the Lord in this life.

CHAPTER 10.

The Course of Wisdom.

IN THE MIDST OF PRESUMPTION AND ARROGANCE. — V. 1. **Dead flies,** literally, "flies of death," that is, such as fall into a mixture and, in decomposing, taint it with their rottenness, **cause the ointment of the apothecary to send forth a stinking savor,** so that its value is lost; **so doth a little folly,** even a small show of sinful weakness, **him that is in reputation for wisdom and honor,** the one weakness spoils everything. V. 2. **A wise man's heart is at his right hand,** that is, he uses his understanding in the proper, expert way; **but a fool's heart at his left,** lacking wisdom, he bungles everything that he undertakes. V. 3. **Yea, also, when he that is a fool walketh by the way,** tending to the ordinary business of life, **his wisdom faileth him,** he gives abundant proof of his stupidity and folly, **and he saith to every one,** by his every word and act, **that he is a fool.** V. 4. **If the spirit of the ruler rise up against thee,** in an angry outburst, **leave not thy place,** that is, forget not thy position as subject, remember always that it is a ruler with whom thou dealest, control thy temper; **for yielding pacifieth great offenses,** it prevents transgressions which otherwise might result. V. 5. **There is an evil which I have seen under the sun, as an error which proceedeth from the ruler,** a mistake often made by people possessing authority: v. 6. **Folly is set in great dignity,** foolish and incompetent persons are given posts of honor and authority, **and the rich,** not the foolishly wealthy, but the noble, distinguished, and wise, **sit in low place,** they are deprived of their rightful positions of authority and honor. V. 7. **I have seen servants,** men whose station in life was among the lowly, **upon horses,** like mighty lords, **and princes,** men qualified for the highest positions, **walking as servants upon the earth,** as a result of some foolish ruler's caprice. V. 8. **He that diggeth a pit,** indulging in dangerous work, **shall fall into it,** that is, he who courts danger must expect it to strike him; **and whoso breaketh an hedge,** or a stone fence, in whose crevices reptiles make their homes, **a serpent shall bite him.** It is a matter of record that the one who tries to injure his neighbor is often seriously hurt by the very injury which he intended for his neighbor. V. 9. **Whoso removeth stones,** either in tearing down an old building or in working in a stony field, in a dangerous occupation, **shall be hurt therewith,** he must expect injuries of this kind; **and he that cleaveth wood shall be endangered thereby,** since the ax-head may strike him. V. 10. **If the iron be blunt,** the wood-chopper having neglected to tend to it in time, **and he do not whet the edge, then must he put to more strength,** for splitting wood with a dull ax requires greater exertion; **but wisdom is profitable to direct,** namely, to a successful issue. If a person wants to force matters by main strength, he will probably do so to his own harm; but if he uses proper discrimination, he will succeed without difficulty.

In the Midst of Foolish Talking and Slothfulness. — V. 11. **Surely the serpent will bite without enchantment,** that is, unless it is kept under enchantment by music or the sound of the voice properly modulated; **and a babbler is no better.** As one may escape the sting of the serpent by the application of charms, so he may avoid the harm of defamation by wise discretion. V. 12. **The words of a wise man's mouth are gracious,** full of pleasant graciousness and therefore always most welcome; **but the lips of a fool will swallow up himself,** he will injure himself by his foolish talk, Prov. 10, 8. 14. 21. 32; 15, 2. V. 13. **The beginning of the words of his mouth is foolishness,** as soon as he opens his mouth, it is with silly twaddle; **and the end of his talk is mischievous madness,** it works injury not only to himself, but mischief also to others. V. 14. **A fool also is full of words,** he is talkative with empty loquacity; **a man cannot tell what shall be; and what shall be after him, who can tell him?** And yet a fool will usually have most to say about future events, of what he intends to do and accomplish. V. 15. **The labor of the foolish wearieth every one of them,** the slightest exertion is too much for his lazy bones, **because he knoweth not how to go to the city;** he does not know the road straight ahead of him, he is ignorant of the simplest matters of every-day life. V. 16. **Woe to thee, O land, when thy king is a child,** lacking mature judgment and discretion, a thoughtless fool, **and thy princes eat in the morning,** in excessive gluttony and feasting at the time when they should be dispensing justice. V. 17. **Blessed art thou, O land, when thy king is the son of nobles,** not so much by birth, as by wisdom and virtue, **and thy princes eat in due season,** at the proper time and in the proper way, **for strength and not for drunkenness,** in intemperate feasting, whereby the mind is blunted and the body corrupted. V. 18. **By much slothfulness,** due to the owner's idleness, **the building decayeth,** no repairs being made, **and through idleness of the hands the house droppeth through,** the roof leaking and the rain penetrating to the interior of the house. V. 19. **A feast is made for laughter,** for foolish rioting, **and wine maketh merry,** the foolish rulers engaged therein neglecting the building of the government; **but money answereth all things,** that is, the reveling rulers believe that money will buy anything and cover up the criminality of their behavior. V. 20. **Curse not the king, no, not in thy thought,** in the innermost consciousness, the danger being that this state of mind will be revealed, **and curse not the rich in thy bed-chamber,** in the foolish hope that it will not become known; **for a bird of the air shall carry the voice, and that which hath wings shall tell the matter,** that is, the betrayal will be brought about in ways which are almost past understanding, whence it follows that strict prudence must govern the conduct of him who is truly wise. The believer who observes the Eighth Commandment will guard against every form of evil, even in thoughts, not for fear of earthly punishment, but for love of God.

CHAPTER 11.

The Way to True Happiness.

PRACTISING BENEVOLENCE. — V. 1. **Cast thy bread upon the waters,** in practising benevolence freely, without the hope of profit or immediate return, Matt. 5, 46. 47; Luke 6, 35—38; **for thou shalt find it after many days,** God will return a rich harvest at the time appointed by Him, Gal. 6, 9. 10; 2 Cor. 9, 6—9; 1 Tim. 6, 18. 19. V. 2. **Give a portion to seven and also to eight,** ready to dispense charity to many; **for thou knowest not what evil shall be upon the earth,** when the tables may be turned by some misfortune, and the giver himself may find himself in need of help. V. 3. **If the clouds be full of rain, they empty themselves upon the earth,** when periods of misfortune are due to happen, evil will come in full measure; **and if the tree fall toward the south or toward the north, in the place where the tree falleth, there it shall be.** Just so it is with gifts of benevolence: their fruit is not lost, although they do not always come to light in the manner intended. Or, as Luther says, man is like a tree which is bound to fall one way or the other, and will be judged according to the way he falls in death. V. 4. **He that observeth the wind,** in timid anxiety and hesitation, **shall not sow,** for while he waits for favorable weather, he misses the proper period for action; **and he that regardeth the clouds,** with the same over-anxious watchfulness, **shall not reap.** The Christian must sow the seed of good works regardless of the promise of returns. V. 5. **As thou knowest not what is the way of the spirit,** or of the wind, concerning whose various vagaries men are just as puzzled as ever, in spite of the progress made by the science of meteorology, cp. John 3, 8, **nor how the bones do grow in the womb of her that is with child,** in the mystery of creation or generation, Ps. 139, 14. 15, **even so thou knowest not the works of God, who maketh all,** the works of His almighty power are unfathomable by the mind of finite men. V. 6. **In the morning sow thy seed,** in all the works of one's regular occupation, but especially in acts of benevolence and charity, **and in the evening withhold not thine hand,** not growing weary in the appointed tasks and in well-doing, Gal. 6, 9. 10, **for thou knowest not whether shall prosper,** the blessing may rest upon the early or upon the late labor, **either this or that, or whether they both shall be alike good,** both producing substantial and enduring good. The conduct advised by the author, therefore, is that of steady faithfulness in the appointed tasks.

REJOICING WITH TREMBLING. — V. 7. **Truly, the light is sweet,** life is most agreeable and beautiful if spent in the manner urged by the author in the first part of this chapter, **and a pleasant thing it is for the eyes to behold the sun,** if one is engaged in godly pursuits; v. 8. **but if a man live many years and rejoice in them all,** in the manner set forth in Holy Writ, Phil. 4, 4, **yet let him remember the days of darkness,** the long night of death; **for they shall be many. All that cometh is vanity,** this world, with all it offers, is empty and futile in comparison with the eternal realities which await the true believers. V. 9. **Rejoice, O young man, in thy youth,** the general admonition of the preceding verses being addressed to young people in particular, as living in that period of life which is especially favorable to cheerful enjoyment, **and let thy heart cheer thee in the days of thy youth,** with the proper happiness in the midst of the turmoil and troubles of this present world, **and walk in the ways of thine heart,** in seeking enjoyment of the right kind, such as is acceptable to the Lord, **and in the sight of thine eyes,** in innocent pleasures and pastimes, the eyes being trained for proper observance of God's rules of conduct; **but know thou that for all these things God will bring thee into Judgment,** wherefore a most careful and circumspect conduct, a most godly caution, is required at all times. It is necessary to serve the Lord with fear and to rejoice with trembling, Ps. 2, 11; Phil. 2, 12. V. 10. **Therefore remove sorrow,** a false sorrow, a gloomy sanctimoniousness, **from thy heart and put away evil from thy flesh,** namely, in the form of a melancholy asceticism which is not in agreement with the cheerfulness required by the Christian religion; **for childhood and youth are vanity,** both early infancy and the dawn of the days, that is, adolescence, are in themselves futile and empty without the cheering presence of the Word of God.

CHAPTER 12.

The Duty of Fearing God in Every Age of Life.

AN APPEAL TO THE YOUNG. — V. 1. **Remember, now, thy Creator in the days of thy youth,** with a feeling of reverence and gratitude for the many blessings received, the product of true faith in the heart, **while the evil days come not,** those of advanced age, **nor the years draw nigh when thou shalt say, I have no pleasure in them,** when the vigor of youth and maturity is replaced by the feeling of decay and the feebleness of senility;

v. 2. **while the sun, or the light,** the refreshing beauty of the morning light, **or the moon, or the stars be not darkened,** when the light of youthful life is darkened by the shadows of advancing old age, **nor the clouds return after the rain,** one misfortune or calamity following another; v. 3. **in the day when the keepers of the house,** all the members and organs of the body, especially the hands and feet, **shall tremble, and the strong men shall bow themselves,** bent over with the weight of age, the legs no longer standing upright, but crooked and misshapen with the various ailments of age, **and the grinders cease because they are few,** the teeth, particularly the molars, having decayed and fallen out, **and those that look out of the windows,** the eyes admitting light to the body, **be darkened,** as sight becomes feeble, v. 4. **and the doors shall be shut in the streets,** the mouth, with the upper and lower lips, no longer being able to perform its function of speaking well, **when the sound of the grinding is low,** the voice, breathing out from the wall of the teeth, lacking the power and force of youth, **and he shall rise up at the voice of the bird,** his voice being reduced to the low, whispering sound of old men, **and all the daughters of music shall be brought low,** the ears, growing deaf, no longer enjoy the singing as in former days; v. 5. **also when they shall be afraid of that which is high,** since their strength will no longer permit their climbing, **and fears shall be in the way,** they are readily overcome with timidity, they no longer have the courage to overcome perils and obstacles, **and the almond-tree shall flourish,** whose white blossoms in the midst of winter were a fitting symbol of old age with its silvery hair, **and the grasshopper shall be a burden,** when even the least weight becomes distressing, **and desire shall fail,** when interest in almost everything languishes and dies, **because man goeth to his long home,** he is rapidly approaching death and the grave, which will hold him for many years, **and the mourners,** having come to give him an honorable burial, **go about the streets;** v. 6. **or ever the silver cord,** that by which the lamp of life was supposed to be suspended, **be loosed,** the thread of life being severed, **or the golden bowl,** conceived to be holding the oil of life, **be broken, or the pitcher be broken at the fountain,** the body, particularly with its organs of respiration, being compared to a vessel for drawing water regularly, **or the wheel,** with which the water was raised from the reservoir, **broken at the cistern,** the reference being to the breaking down of the whole mechanism of the body in death. V. 7. **Then shall the dust,** out of which man was formed at the beginning, Gen. 2, 7, **return to the earth as it was,** Gen. 3, 19, **and the spirit,** namely, of every one that died in the true faith, **shall return unto God, who gave it;** for into the hands of God all His children commend their souls at all times. Note: This paragraph is one of the most beautiful poetical passages in the entire Bible and deserves to be studied for its form as well as for its contents, the earnest and searching admonition contained in its lofty sentences.

THE CONCLUSION OF THE BOOK. — V. 8. **Vanity of vanities, saith the Preacher,** who now summarizes the teaching of the entire book; **all is vanity,** the entire human life in itself is empty and futile. V. 9. **And moreover, because the Preacher was wise,** speaking on the basis of many years' experience, with the wisdom given him from on high, **he still taught the people knowledge,** dispensing it orally whenever opportunity offered; **yea, he gave good heed,** he considered, weighed, marked carefully, **and sought out and set in order,** after such careful meditation and reflection, **many proverbs,** which were transmitted in writing to serve a wider circle. V. 10. **The Preacher sought to find out acceptable words,** setting forth his maxims in a pleasant, appealing way; **and that which was written was upright,** simple and straightforward, **even words of truth,** unmistakable in their meaning. V. 11. **The words of the wise are as goads,** their inspired character causing them to pierce deeply into the mind, **and as nails fastened by the masters of assemblies,** uniting the individual statements in collections, or books, **which are given from one shepherd,** a single wise and inspired teacher directing the editing of the book, as we see in the case of Solomon's books. V. 12. **And further, by these,** by the proverbs and maxims of wisdom, **my son, be admonished,** Solomon here speaking with fatherly affection. **Of making many books there is no end,** the number of useless and even dangerous books having increased to such an extent as to make them an outright menace; **and much study is a weariness of the flesh,** aimless reading, particularly of harmful books, weakens mind and body. V. 13. **Let us hear the conclusion of the whole matter,** over against the unsystematic devouring of books resulting in mental and spiritual indigestion: **Fear God and keep His commandments; for this is the whole duty of man,** sanctification flowing out of reverence of faith. V. 14. **For God shall bring every work into Judgment,** everything being revealed before Him on the Last Day, **with every secret thing,** which men foolishly and fatuously believed they could hide before His omniscience, **whether it be good, or whether it be evil.** "Wherefore, beloved, seeing that ye look for such things, be diligent that ye may be found of Him in peace, without spot, and blameless," 2 Pet. 3, 14.

THE SONG OF SOLOMON.

INTRODUCTION.

The Song of Solomon, or the "Song of Songs," as it is called in the opening verse, is a prophetic poem, which sets forth in an allegorical or mystical manner the relation between Christ, the one Bridegroom of our souls, to His Church, the bride. An allegory is a narrative describing real or supposed facts for the purpose of presenting certain higher truths or principles than the narrative in itself, taken literally, could have taught; it is "a figurative sentence or discourse, in which the principal subject is described by another subject resembling it in its properties and circumstances. The real subject is thus kept out of view or barely indicated, and we are left to collect the intentions of the speaker or writer from the resemblance of the secondary to the primary subject." The Song of Solomon depicts, under the allegory of the bridal love of Solomon and Shulamite, the mutual love of the Lord and His Church. The representation of Christ as the Bridegroom and the Church as the bride is a favorite allegory, or picture, in the Bible. Cp. Ps. 45; Hos. 2, 19. 20; Matt. 9, 15; John 3, 29; Eph. 5, 25—29. The poem shows a beautiful progression of thought, the heart of the believer declaring: 1) Jesus is mine, He belongs to me. 2) I am Christ's, I belong to Him. 3) In spite of all obstacles our union of love will be established throughout eternity. If we follow the outline of the book strictly, we may distinguish two divisions, each with three sections: the eager longing of the lovers, chap. 1, 2—2, 7; the mutual seeking and finding, 2, 8—3, 5; the meeting, 3, 6—5, 1; the separation and the second meeting, 5, 2—6, 9; the mutual praise of the lovers, 6, 10—8, 4; the eternal covenant of loyalty, 8, 5—14.

In studying this book, which presents difficulties in more than one respect, it should be noted that whoever does not understand God's revealed plan of salvation and has not experienced the love of Christ nor love to Christ in his heart, to him this book will remain a sealed book, and he will probably become guilty of the error made by the majority of modern critics, who find in the Song of Solomon nothing but a collection of Oriental love-songs.[1])

1) Cp. *Concordia Bible Class*, April, 1919, 63. 64; Fuerbringer, *Einleitung in das Alte Testament*, 58—60; *Lehre und Wehre*, 1908, Maerz ff.

CHAPTER 1.

The Church's Longing for Christ.

The Song of Songs, which is Solomon's. This superscription clearly names Solomon as the author of the prophetic poem contained in this book, and the many references throughout the book fully substantiate his authorship. V. 2. **Let Him kiss me with the kisses,** with one of the kisses, **of His mouth; for Thy love is better than wine,** that is, sweeter and more pleasant in every way. V. 3. **Because of the savor of Thy good ointments,** rather, "As to odor, Thy ointments are good," **Thy name is as ointment poured forth,** one taken from its box or vial; **therefore do the virgins love Thee,** their attention being arrested by His costly perfume's diffusing a wide fragrance. V. 4. **Draw me, we will run after Thee,** all the hearts devoted to the King hastening after Him with eager longing; **the King hath brought me into His chambers,** into the royal palace. **We will be glad and rejoice in Thee, we will remember,** and therefore duly praise, **Thy love more than wine,** for its pleasant, agreeable qualities. **The upright love Thee,** or, "they love Thee rightly," with the best of reasons. V. 5. **I am black,** browned by exposure to the sun, **but comely,** still attractive and engaging, **O ye daughters of Jerusalem, as the tents of Kedar,** those of the Bedouins, darkened by the heat of the sun, yet, at the same time, **as the curtains of Solomon,** the precious hangings, the beautiful tapestry with which the wealthy king decorated his house. V. 6. **Look not upon me, because I am black, because the sun hath looked upon me,** thereby causing her tanned appearance. **My mother's children were angry with me; they made me the keeper of the vineyards,** giving her the position of a servant; **but mine own vineyard have I not kept,** she had not been faithful to her chief charge. V. 7. **Tell me, O Thou whom my soul loveth, where Thou feedest,** pasturing His sheep, **where Thou makest Thy flock to rest at noon,** the sheep being given an opportunity to rest during the heat of the day; **for why should I be as one that turneth aside by the flocks of Thy companions?** straying away from His presence in desolation, to be disgraced. The King's answer to this question is immediately given: v. 8. **If thou know not,** if she is really lacking in knowledge, as she states, **O thou fairest among women, go thy way forth by the footsteps of the flock,** following its tracks, **and feed thy kids beside the shepherds' tents,** in the rôle of shepherdess. V. 9. **I have compared thee, O my love, to a**

company of horses in Pharaoh's chariots, which fitly represented his royal power. V. 10. **Thy cheeks are comely with rows of jewels,** with strings of pearls, **thy neck with chains of gold,** little disks of precious metal or corals pierced and strung together. V. 11. **We will make thee borders of gold with studs of silver,** golden chains studded with silver ornaments. The bride now answers upon the King's praise: v. 12. **While the King sitteth at His table,** while the meal was in progress, **my spikenard,** an aromatic perfume made from an Oriental herb, **sendeth forth the smell thereof,** a delightful and pleasant odor. V. 13. **A bundle of myrrh,** which was kept in a small sack or receptacle and carried in the bosom, **is my Well-beloved unto me; He shall lie all night betwixt my breasts.** V. 14. **My Beloved is unto me as a cluster of camphire,** the cyprus-flower of India, cultivated for its strong perfume, **in the vineyards of Engedi,** where Solomon had probably brought some of the Indian plant. V. 15. **Behold, thou art fair, my love,** or companion, friend; **behold, thou art fair; thou hast doves' eyes,** or, "thine eyes are doves," as lustrous and shimmering as the iridescence on the plumage of doves. And the bride answers: v. 16. **Behold, Thou art fair, my Beloved, yea, pleasant,** sweet and charming; **also our bed is green,** they were sitting on a couch in a shady grassplot or in a summer-bower. V. 17. **The beams of our house are cedar,** rather, our houses, **and our rafters of fir,** rather, our wainscoting of cypress, which is of a reddish hue, hard, durable, and fragrant.

The interpretation of this chapter, at least in its general outlines, is not difficult in the light of clear passages of the Bible. The woman Shulamith, the Church, feels the need of her Bridegroom's love, although she realizes that she is not worthy of His caresses, wherefore she pleads for but one kiss of His mouth. Her desire restores the relation of true faith, and therefore she praises the blessings of His companionship, especially the fact that His name, He Himself breathes a savor of life unto life, which causes all the members of the Church to be inflamed with love toward the heavenly Bridegroom. At the same time, the bride is fully conscious of her own weakness, which is shared by all the members of the Church. Therefore she pleads that Christ Himself would draw her by the power of His love, for He is the Way, the Truth, and the Life. She realizes and confesses her own lack of righteousness, so that her appearance is indeed like that of filthy rags. Moreover, men, her own relatives in this world, hate and despise her; they inveigle her into the business of this world, so that she neglects her own vineyard, the work in the Church. That is her guilt, by reason of which she feels forsaken and desolate in herself; she cries out for the love of Christ, unworthy in herself though she is. And the mercy of Christ answers her. Rebuking her for her lack of knowledge, He nevertheless gives her the advice she needs, He admonishes her to seek true rest and food on the green pastures of the Gospel. At the same time He acknowledges her as His bride, He praises her as His pride and His might, He wants to decorate her with the riches of His merciful blessings. The Church agrees to this promise, confessing, at the same time, that the perfume of His love delighted her as long as He was with her, but that without His presence the finest jewelry had no value. This confession having restored the proper relation between Christ and the Church, especially since she praised His gifts of grace only and not her own worthiness, He now praises her beauty, her holiness and purity, while she, in turn, points out the happiness of being united with Him in true bridal love, this fact holding true of all the members of Christ's Church, no matter in which earthly homes they may be at the present time. Every Christian congregation, according to her true essence and nature, consists of elect, saints, beloved of Christ.

CHAPTER 2.

The Mutual Love of Christ and the Church.

THE BRIDE PROTESTS THE FERVOR OF HER LOVE. — V. 1. **I am the rose of Sharon,** the wild flowers of this plain being noted for their beauty, **and the lily of the valleys,** the elegant red lily of Palestine being referred to. The Bridegroom readily agrees to this comparison. V. 2. **As the lily among thorns, so is My love among the daughters,** surpassing them to such an extent that their dingy stalks were not even noticed. And the bride, inflamed by His praise, calls out: v. 3. **As the apple-tree among the trees of the wood,** surpassing them all in desirability, **so is my Beloved among the sons. I sat down under His shadow with great delight,** literally, "In His shadow delighted I to sit," more than satisfied with His companionship, **and His fruit was sweet to my taste,** she enjoyed all His gifts and blessings. V. 4. **He brought me to the banqueting-house,** the apartment set apart for the drinking of wine, the banquet-hall, **and His banner over me was love,** which protected and comforted her at all times. V. 5. **Stay me with flagons,** rather, with grapes or raisin-cakes, a refreshing confection of the Orient; **comfort me**

with apples, whose refreshment also was delightful; **for I am sick of love,** her love is so ardent that she feels weak from its powerful reaction upon her entire body and therefore needs refreshment of some kind. V. 6. **His left hand is under my head,** in a fond caress, **and His right hand doth embrace me.** V. 7. **I charge you, O ye daughters of Jerusalem,** in a very strong objurgation, 1 Sam. 17, 55; 2 Sam. 11, 11, **by the roes and by the hinds of the field,** fit symbols of tender and ideal love, **that ye stir not up nor awake my Love till he please,** literally, "awaken love till it please," all frivolous coquetry in the relation toward Christ being excluded.

The meaning is again clear. The Church praises the beauty which she has received from the Lord, and He not only agrees to her description, but even places her in contrast to the base growths of false churches, which try to sap the life of the Church with their doctrines of works. In an ecstatic monolog the bride now sets forth the excellencies of Christ, the safety of His protection, the richness of His blessings, the thought of which so fills her heart with bliss that it cannot contain it all. It is the great mystery of the relation between Christ and His Church, Eph. 5, 32. At such times, which are occasionally granted to the Church, the Lord does not wish her to be disturbed. The Church is in His keeping, even as she jealously watches over every indication of a false expression of affection toward Him.

The Mutual Call of Love. — V. 8. **The voice of my Beloved!** So Shulamith calls out, anxiously awaiting the coming of the Bridegroom. **Behold, He cometh, leaping upon the mountains, skipping,** or bounding, **upon the hills,** in an excess of youthful vigor and strength. V. 9. **My Beloved is like a roe,** the Palestinian gazelle, **or a young hart. Behold, He standeth behind our wall,** that of her home; **He looketh forth at the windows,** that is, through the windows, **showing Himself through the lattice,** eagerly searching for His bride. V. 10. **My Beloved spake and said unto me,** or, "speaks and says to me," **Rise up, My love,** My companion, **My fair one, and come away,** leaving the house. V. 11. **For, lo, the winter,** the season of clouds, the time of rain, **is past, the rain is over and gone,** so that the inclemencies of the season no longer keep people in the houses; v. 12. **the flowers appear on the earth,** they are seen in the land with the coming of spring; **the time of the singing of birds is come,** for the mating songs of the various birds called for a similar response on the part of men, **and the voice of the turtle,** that is, the turtle-dove, the harbinger of spring, **is heard in our land;** v. 13. **the fig-tree putteth forth her green figs,** rather, "spices its fruit," for the latent figs of autumn now matured, **and the vines with the tender grape,** being in blossom, **give a good smell,** fill the air with their rich fragrance. **Arise, My love,** My companion, **My fair one, and come away.** V. 14. **O My dove, that art in the clefts of the rock,** secure and protected, **in the secret places of the stairs,** the ladders of rock or the cliffs, **let Me see thy countenance,** her entire form, **let Me hear thy voice; for sweet is thy voice, and thy countenance is comely.** And the bride yields to His entreaties, saying, v. 15. **Take us the foxes, the little foxes, that spoil the vines,** injuring the roots and gnawing the young shoots; **for our vines have tender grapes,** literally, "our vineyards are in bloom." V. 16. **My Beloved is mine,** the bride has the full right to Him and all His gifts and blessings, **and I am His,** in a happy surrender of faith; **He feedeth among the lilies,** wherever He abides, joy and loveliness are about Him. V. 17. **Until the day break,** namely, that of eternity, **and the shadows,** those of this present world with its manifold troubles, **flee away, turn, my Beloved,** to visit and remain with the bride, **and be Thou like a roe or a young hart upon the mountains of Bether,** on cleft mountains, symbols of youthful vigor and strength.

The Church, having gained inner strength through the blessings of the Gospel, is now ready to heed the call of Christ. She sees Him approaching in the full vigor of His merciful power, He comes to visit her, to call her forth to enjoy the beauties which He has prepared, and to be active in His interest. He tells her that the period of afflictions is past for the time being, that a new and favorable time of grace has dawned. His invitation and appeal is clothed in the gentlest and most appealing words, irresistible to the heart filled with true faith. And the Church responds by calling upon its own members, especially its pastors and teachers, to stop the destructive work of false prophets, who make use of every new awakening in the Church to do damage to Christ's vine. At the same time the Church affirms her loyalty to Christ and her trust in His love and power, knowing that His merciful presence is in the midst of His believers. And all this is done in the certainty of the Lord's final return to lead His bride to the eternal marriage-feast in heaven.

CHAPTER 3.

Reverses and New Hopes for the Church.

THE CHURCH IN DIFFICULTIES. — V. 1. **By night on my bed I sought Him whom my soul loveth,** she contemplated ways and means of finding Him whom she had apparently lost; **I sought Him, but I found Him not,** the Lord's visitation of grace had seemingly come to an end. V. 2. **I will rise now and go about the city in the streets,** on the market-places, **and in the broad ways,** the chief avenues of the city; **I will seek Him whom my soul loveth. I sought Him, but I found Him not.** V. 3. **The watchmen that go about the city,** the nightly guardians of the public safety, **found me; to whom I said, Saw ye Him whom my soul loveth?** literally, "Whom my soul loves, have ye seen?" the question being inserted without introduction, even without the common particle of questioning, to show the extreme anxiety of her heart. V. 4. **It was but a little that I passed from them,** she had scarcely passed from the watchmen, **but I found Him whom my soul loveth; I held Him,** grasping Him in an eager embrace, **and would not let Him go until I had brought Him into my mother's house and into the chamber of her that conceived me,** that being the thought which she had, to lead her Bridegroom into the women's apartments, to open her home and her heart to Him. V. 5. **I charge you, O ye daughters of Jerusalem, by the roes,** the gazelles, **and by the hinds of the field, that ye stir not up nor awake My love till he please,** "till it please," chap. 2, 7, for the words are evidently those of the Bridegroom, who in His joy over this renewed proof of the bride's love, has her comfort and encouragement in mind.

The Church Militant is here described as she appears in the midst of the storms, battles, and trials of this world. Night has fallen after the beautiful spring day described in the previous section, and the Church is surrounded by so many and such grievous difficulties that she deems herself forsaken by the Lord. He, on His part, hides His mercy for a while, in order to stimulate her to the most careful search. She finds nothing but empty spaces, a dead religion of works, a spiritless piety, many and serious offenses. Even the watchmen, the leaders of the Church, are infected with the general lethargy and take no interest in the search for the Lord, in a living Christianity. History shows that this condition obtained more than once, not only in the ancient Church, but in the modern as well. But the Lord has not utterly forsaken His bride; He permits Himself to be found, He turns back His countenance in mercy to His Church. His conduct thus stimulates the faith and love of the Church, and she declares her allegiance to Him in terms of the highest affection, while He, on His part, grants her a period of rest and refreshment, lest she be tempted above that she is able, 1 Cor. 10, 13.

THE CHURCH'S VICTORIOUS PROGRESS. —V. 6. **Who is this that cometh out of the wilderness,** ascending from the lower level of a wilderness to the city set on a mountain, **like pillars of smoke, perfumed with myrrh and frankincense, with all powders of the merchant?** The cavalcade of Shulamith is preceded and followed by clouds of perfumed smoke, which mark her progress. V. 7. **Behold His bed,** the traveling litter, howdah, or palanquin, such as are used in the Orient for long journeys, **which is Solomon's,** which the Bridegroom has placed at the disposal of His bride; **threescore valiant men are about it,** as a protecting body-guard, **of the valiant of Israel.** V. 8. **They all hold swords, being expert in war,** skilful in the use of their weapons; **every man hath his sword upon his thigh,** ready for immediate use, **because of fear in the night,** lest any danger come near enough to the bride to disturb her rest. V. 9. **King Solomon made himself a chariot,** a bridal wagon or sedan-chair, **of the wood of Lebanon,** of the finest cedar-wood. V. 10. **He made the pillars thereof of silver,** designed chiefly as ornaments, but supporting the canopy, **the bottom thereof,** that is, the floor, **of gold, the covering of it,** fine hangings or tapestries, **of purple, the midst thereof being paved with love, for the daughters of Jerusalem,** that is, its interior, the sides and the top of the finest material, being embroidered by the women of Jerusalem, as a labor of love. V. 11. **Go forth, O ye daughters of Zion, and behold King Solomon with the crown wherewith his mother crowned him in the day of his espousals and in the day of the gladness of his heart.**

Here the Church is pictured, not as she usually appears to the casual beholder, but as she is in reality in the sight of the Lord. She is moving forward and upward through the wilderness of this world to the eternal City above, a great multitude from all nations and tongues and peoples. She is surrounded by a cloud of prayers, expressing her steadfast confession of faith, her patience in suffering, and her work in love, a sweet savor in the nostrils of the Lord. And the Lord has provided an appropriate conveyance for her, a bridal wagon of singular beauty, surrounded by His mighty, ministering heroes, the angels of His power. Yea, more; for every one who belongs to the army of the bride He has a special chariot, in which He has the soul of His believers carried into the eternal home of heaven. There each believer serves as a jewel, enhancing the beauty of the King, and all the believers together will be a diadem, a crown of beauty, when the marriage of the Lamb is celebrated and we behold His glory, world without end.

CHAPTER 4.

The Church's State of Grace.

The Comeliness of the Church. — V. 1. **Behold, thou art fair, My love,** so the Bridegroom tells the Church; **behold, thou art fair; thou hast dove's eyes,** or, "thy eyes are doves," gleaming in iridescent beauty, **within thy locks,** or "behind the veil"; **thy hair is as a flock of goats that appear,** or repose, **from Mount Gilead,** the country east of Jordan known for its fine cattle. The point of comparison is to be found in the glossy blackness and luxuriant abundance of Shulamith's hair as well as in its silky softness and delicacy. V. 2. **Thy teeth are like a flock of sheep that are even shorn, which came up from the washing,** regular and snow-white; **whereof every one bear twins, and none is barren among them,** the upper and the lower set of teeth being perfect and exactly corresponding to each other. V. 3. **Thy lips are like a thread of scarlet,** their crimson forming a beautiful contrast to the dazzling whiteness of her teeth, **and thy speech is comely,** rather, "thy mouth is lovely," both in shape and in speech; **thy temples are like a piece of a pomegranate,** whose cut segment offers a soft red mingled with creamy white, **within thy locks.** V. 4. **Thy neck is like the tower of David builded for an armory, whereon there hang a thousand bucklers, all shields of mighty men.** The reference here is to graceful and powerful stateliness, enhanced by splendid ornaments. V. 5. **Thy two breasts are like two young roes that are twins,** fawns, twins of a gazelle, **which feed among the lilies,** of delicate and exquisite beauty. This declaration on the part of the Bridegroom causes Shulamith to respond: v. 6. **Until the day break,** rather, "until the day cools," until the approach of evening, **and the shadows flee away,** rapidly lengthening toward the east, **I will get me to the mountain of myrrh and to the hill of frankincense,** where she could commune with God in undisturbed solitude. And the King answers, in joyful approval: v. 7. **Thou art all fair, My love; there is no spot in thee.**

We have here a fine description of the inner beauty of the Church, as Christ sees it, the purity, holiness, majesty, and glory which is known to Him, because wrought by Him. The Church and all its members should be distinguished by guilelessness, wisdom, faithfulness. Having received the riches of His grace, the believers have the finest apparel and ornaments, and their praise of the mercy of God received by them is lovely, their teaching wholesome and edifying. Moreover, the Church is in possession of eternal youth and offers a majestic appearance, while, at the same time, she is a true mother to all her children, who desire the sincere milk of the Word, that they may grow thereby. With such loveliness ascribed to her, the Church naturally vows to the Lord that she will keep her beauty unsullied, that it will be her steady endeavor to worship Him in spirit and in truth, whereupon He once more assures her that, through the merits of His righteousness transmitted to her, she is without spot, or wrinkle, or any such thing, holy and without blemish in His eyes, Eph. 5, 27, clean through the Word which He has spoken to her, John 15, 3.

The Ravishing Love of the Church. — V. 8. **Come with Me from Lebanon, My spouse,** His affianced bride, **with Me from Lebanon,** here representing a mountainous and inhospitable country. **Look from the top of Amana, from the top of Shenir and Hermon,** all three peaks being in the Anti-Lebanon range, **from the lions' dens, from the mountains of the leopards,** or panthers, where beasts of prey proved a constant menace to the traveler. V. 9. **Thou hast ravished My heart,** robbing Him of His heart by the miracle of her beauty, **My sister,** as the adopted child of His heavenly Father, **My spouse; thou hast ravished My heart with one of thine eyes,** literally, with one from thy eyes, that is, with a glance of love, **with one chain of thy neck,** with the sparkle and charm of the necklace as she turned to look at Him. V. 10. **How fair is thy love,** pleasant and acceptable, **My sister, My spouse! How much better is thy love than wine,** sweet to the taste and pleasant in every way, **and the smell of thine ointments than all spices!** V. 11. **Thy lips, O My spouse, drop as the honeycomb,** distilling sweetness; **honey and milk are under thy tongue,** in the loveliness of her speech; **and the smell of thy garments is like the smell of Lebanon,** whose fragrance, the balsamic odor of cedars, was proverbial in Palestine. V. 12. **A garden enclosed is My sister, My spouse,** one locked against intruders, open only to the owner; **a spring shut up, a fountain sealed,** the meaning being that the place where the sparkling water wells from the ground is inaccessible to all but the Bridegroom Himself. V. 13. **Thy plants are an orchard of pomegranates, with pleasant fruits,** all her acts being charming and excellent; **camphire,** or cyprus flowers, **with spikenard,** from which precious perfume was made, v. 14. **spikenard and saffron,** from which an agreeably pungent liquid perfume was made; **calamus,** used for similar purposes, **and cinnamon, with all trees of frankincense; myrrh and aloes,** a fine aromatic balsam, **with all the chief spices,** all of these being important articles of trade, since they were used also for the holy anointing oil, Ex. 30, 23. 31; v. 15. **a fountain of gardens, a well of living waters,** fed by inexhaustible springs, **and streams from Lebanon,** fed by its perpetual snows, cool and refreshing. The bride, wrought up to the highest pitch of excitement by this fulsome praise in the mouth of the Bridegroom, exclaims, v. 16. **Awake, O north wind,** cool and refreshing, **and come, thou south,** warm and moist, but usually not boisterous; **blow upon my garden that the spices thereof may flow out,** its perfume be wafted in every direction. **Let my Beloved come into His garden and eat His pleasant fruits,** enjoy the companionship and the charms of His bride.

This section contains both a warning and the highest praise. It is necessary for all believers to deny the world with all its blandishments and to be united with Christ alone, through the strength given in His Word. At the same time Christ openly states that the believers, looking upon Him with the eyes of faith, increase His love toward them. Therefore He praises the loveliness of the Church in extravagant terms, especially since the ointment of the Holy Spirit in the bosom of the Church fills the air with lovely fragrance, while her prayer drops from her lips like the most excellent honey, and her confession of Him is as pleasant as milk and honey. Moreover, the Church, in the midst of the world, is a closed garden, in which rich fruits ripen for the delectation of the heavenly Bridegroom, and where the refreshing waters of the Sacraments flow. The Church, in fact, is in every way full of spiritual power and fruitfulness, filled with the fruits of righteousness, which are by Jesus Christ, unto the glory and praise of God, Phil. 1, 11. Having heard the praise of Christ, the Church pleads for His gracious presence in her midst, for it is only when He Himself accepts the worship of His believers that the purpose of the Church can be realized; only then can she fulfil her duty in the right manner.

CHAPTER 5.

Christ's Call to the Drowsy Church.

THE CHURCH AROUSED FROM SLEEP. — V. 1. **I am come into My garden, My sister, My spouse,** this being the King's answer to Shulamith's invitation, chap. 4, 16; **I have gathered My myrrh with My spice; I have eaten My honeycomb with My honey; I have drunk My wine with My milk,** all expressions showing the measure with which the King enjoyed the fruits of His singular garden. **Eat, O friends,** the wedding-guests being addressed; **drink, yea, drink abundantly, O beloved,** partaking to repletion of the rich gifts provided by the King's bounty and by His garden. The reference is plain. When the heavenly Gardener comes into the garden of His Church, the enjoyment is mutual, since He rejoices in her faith and in the works of her faith, and the Church, with all her members, is refreshed by the rich blessings of His grace.

The next paragraph pictures a period of spiritual depression, together with a merciful visitation of the Lord, the bride herself relating the events in their order. V. 2. **I sleep, but my heart waketh,** unable to shake off the half-conscious drowsiness which came upon her; **it is the voice of my Beloved that knocketh, saying, Open to Me, My sister, My love, My dove, My undefiled,** the one of whom He is sure that she is wholly devoted to Him in love, as His terms of endearment show; **for My head is filled with dew and My locks with the drops of the night,** the fall of dew being very heavy in Palestine. V. 3. **I have put off my coat,** the tunic or undergarment, which served as a covering in the night; **how shall I put it on? I have washed my feet,** as custom requires it where only sandals are worn; **how shall I defile them?** She had become so indifferent to her Bridegroom that she eagerly adopted the slightest excuse, as though she no longer relished His company. V. 4. **My Beloved put in His hand by the hole of the door,** through which the bolt could be reached from the outside if no other locks were employed, **and my bowels were moved for Him,** she was greatly excited, or agitated, in sympathy for Him, she began to repent of her indifference. V. 5. **I rose up to open to my Beloved,** once more thoroughly aroused in love and longing; **and my hands dropped with myrrh,** best token of her reawakened love, **and my fingers with sweet-smelling myrrh,** whose perfume was sure to please the King, **upon the handles of the lock,** as she eagerly attempted to push back the bolt. V. 6. **I opened to my Beloved,** ready now to appreciate His visitation of love; **but my Beloved had withdrawn Himself and was gone,** apparently tired of waiting, ready to extend His merciful call to some one else; **my soul failed when He spake,** when He had spoken before, this also explaining her long inaction. **I sought Him, but I could not find Him,** He had withdrawn His gracious presence; **I called Him, but He gave me no answer.** V. 7. **The watchmen that went about the city found me; they smote me, they wounded me; the keepers of the walls,** whose business it was to protect the inhabitants of the city, **took away my veil from me,** an act which was an indignity offered to an Oriental girl at any time, and here doubly so, since the veil was the bride's greatest pride and the sign of her exalted state. V. 8. **I charge you, O daughters of Jerusalem,** adjuring them most earnestly, **if ye find my Beloved, that ye tell Him that I am sick of love,** her longing had now become overwhelmingly great, due to the very indifference professed by the Lord.

This paragraph correctly pictures the spiritual sleep which sometimes falls upon a single congregation or upon a whole section of the Church. There may still be some feeling of duty and a corresponding battling against the benumbing influence of sleep, but in the eyes of God such a community is dead, even while it has the name that it is living, Rev. 3, 1. When the Lord comes to such a church to admonish and incite her to true watchfulness, she is often unwilling to be disturbed. She would prefer to go her lukewarm way, without true life and spirituality. And so the Lord, after an urgent call and attempt to arouse the Church, withdraws His merciful presence. Meanwhile the Church arouses herself to the remembrance of the many evidences of grace and love which she has received at His hands, and so she, on her part, now tries to hold Him back from leaving her. She is again filled with the sweet savor of good works flowing from true faith; her heart eagerly seeks Him; she realizes that His condemnation Rev. 3, 17—19 applies to her. Having been deprived of His presence, she searches most diligently. But the very men who should have aided her in finding the Bridegroom now abuse the Church, while she loudly protests her love for the Bridegroom. Compare the words of the Lord, John 7, 33. 34: "Yet a little while am I with you, and then I go unto Him that sent Me. Ye shall seek Me and shall not find Me; and where I am, thither ye cannot come." If at such times the individual congregation or the Church as such relies only upon the grace of the Lord, there is the best hope for the future.

THE CHURCH PRAISES HER BRIDEGROOM. — V. 9. **What is thy Beloved more than another beloved,** to place Him so high in praise, **O thou fairest among women?** so the "daughters of Jerusalem," introduced for the sake of the liveliness of the presentation, ask Shulamith. **What is thy Beloved more than another beloved that thou dost so charge us?** namely, by admonishing them to assure Him of her lasting love and devotion. And the bride answers, v. 10. **My Beloved is white and ruddy,** fair and with the color of health, **the chiefest among ten thousand,** distinguished above a myriad, an unequaled Champion. V. 11. **His head is as the most fine gold,** not only from the red luster of His crown, but by reason of preciousness, **His locks are bushy,** like the waving fronds of the date-palm, **and black as a raven.** V. 12. **His eyes are as the eyes of doves by the rivers of waters,** full of lustrous brightness, **washed with milk,** to enhance their beauty, **and fitly set,** literally, "sitting in fulness," like a precious gem in the setting of a ring. V. 13. **His cheeks are as a bed of spices,** or balm, in the luxuriant growth of the beard, **as sweet flowers,** elevated beds or mounds of spice plants; **His lips like lilies,** the red lilies of Palestine, **dropping sweet-smelling myrrh.** V. 14. **His hands are as gold rings,** each finger being a cylinder of gold, **set with the beryl,** or encased in turquoises; **His belly is as bright ivory overlaid with sapphires,** or, "his body a figure of ivory veiled with sapphires," so spoken of either from the delicate blue veining or from the girdle studded with these precious gems. V. 15. **His legs are as pillars of marble, set upon sockets,** or bases, **of fine gold,** the references probably being to the costly sandals worn by the King; **His countenance is as Lebanon,** His entire appearance and bearing is majestic, **excellent as the cedars,** choice and stately as the finest trees of the forest. V. 16. **His mouth is most sweet,** literally, "His palate is sweetnesses"; **yea, He is altogether lovely,** literally, "lovelinesses," the plural indicating the excess of pleasurable qualities. **This is my Beloved, and this is my Friend, O daughters of Jerusalem.**

This is the ecstatic description which the Church gives of the Bridegroom with whose love she is ravished, she herself being once more addressed with the honoring name of "the fairest among women," since the Church is, by virtue of His grace, without spot, or blemish, or any such thing. Her praise of the King is in the same strain which caused the inspired writers to call out: "Thou art fairer than the children of men; grace is poured out into Thy lips; therefore God hath blessed Thee forever," Ps. 45, 2. The entire description shows Christ as true man, but at the same time, in the fulness of His divinity, with majesty and stateliness in His entire appearance, and loveliness and sustaining power in His words. Beauty and strength, delicacy and might, are combined in His person, and therefore the sight of Him does not cause fear and terror, but inspires love and confidence. The entire description fits only Him who, while indeed true man, is at the same time God over all, blessed forever. It is the indescribable majesty of His deity which is here set forth in pictures and parables, in order that we might know Him with the eyes of faith, until we shall finally see Him as He is and be with Him in everlasting joy and happiness.

CHAPTER 6.

The Confession of the Church Rewarded.

THE FURTHER CONFESSION AND CHRIST'S ANSWER. — The bride having answered the first question of the "daughters of Jerusalem" for a description of her soul's Bridegroom, they now ask about her relation to this marvelous King. V. 1. **Whither is thy Beloved gone, O thou fairest among women?** Surely if He is such a paragon of excellence, the place of the bride is always at His side! **Whither**

is thy Beloved turned aside, as though spurning her love, **that we may seek Him with thee?** For even outsiders are sometimes impressed with the message of the Church. The bride answers, accordingly, v. 2. **My Beloved is gone down into His garden,** to which she invited Him, but from which she foolishly absented herself, **to the beds of spices, to feed in the gardens and to gather lilies.** But she immediately adds, in a burst of joyful confidence, which knows that the present estrangement cannot last: v. 3. **I am my Beloved's, and my Beloved is mine; He feedeth among the lilies.** This confession of love and of trustful confidence is immediately rewarded by the King when He says: v. 4. **Thou art beautiful, O My love,** with a surpassing fairness, **as Tirzah,** the beautiful city of the northern kingdom which Jeroboam chose for his residence, 1 Kings 14, 17, **comely as Jerusalem,** the capital city praised above all other cities of the world, **terrible as an army with banners,** a victorious host, carrying everything before it. V. 5. **Turn away thine eyes from Me,** which were just then fixed upon Him with a look of the deepest longing, **for they have overcome Me,** exciting and inspiring a feeling of the same intense love in His heart; **thy hair is as a flock of goats that appear from Gilead,** chap. 4. 1. V. 6. **Thy teeth are as a flock of sheep which go up from the washing, whereof every one beareth twins, and there is not one barren among them.** V. 7. **As a piece of a pomegranate are thy temples within thy locks.** Cp. chap. 4, 2. 3. V. 8. **There are threescore queens and fourscore concubines and virgins without number,** these idealized figures being introduced here only for the sake of comparison, to bring out all the more strongly the uniqueness of the bride's position. V. 9. **My dove, My undefiled is but one,** perfect in her relation to Him; **she is the only one of her mother, she is the choice one of her that bare her,** the only one of her kind. **The daughters saw her and blessed her; yea, the queens and the concubines, and they praised her.**

Events move rapidly in this paragraph. The Church had indeed for a time been deprived of the merciful presence of her Lord, He had withheld His gracious visitation from her. But she was sure of His return, for she was still united with Him in faith; she could not lose the Bridegroom of her soul. This confession of faith causes the Lord once more to sing the praises of His bride, whose beauty He compares to, and exalts above, the fairest cities of the land, and whose victorious march makes her unconquerable. He is filled with the most burning love for her and therefore lauds her qualities in a wonderful burst of song. The former relation of the most intimate love between Christ and the Church has been restored after her repentance. He wants all people of the world to know that His Church, His Kingdom of Grace, ranks highest in His estimation, that for her sake He makes and deposes kings and emperors, so that even these outsiders must acknowledge her superiority and glory, Eph. 1, 21—23; 1 Pet. 2, 9.

CHRIST'S LOVE TOWARD THE CHURCH. — The King's wonderful description of the bride's beauty causes the "daughters of Jerusalem" to call out in admiration: v. 10. **Who is she that looketh forth,** suddenly arising from the background, **as the morning,** like the rising dawn, **fair as the moon, clear as the sun, and terrible as an army with banners,** moving forward with victorious power? The answer of the bride is given with becoming humility: v. 11. **I went down into the garden of nuts,** the beautiful park of the King, **to see the fruits of the valley,** or "to inspect the shrubs of the valley," **and to see whether the vine flourished and the pomegranates budded.** V. 12. **Or ever I was aware, my soul made me like the chariots of Amminadib,** literally, "I knew it not that my soul had made me chariots of my noble people," that the King had displayed her pomp and power before the whole world. But the "daughters of Jerusalem" now clamor to see her beauty, v. 13. **Return, return, O Shulamite,** so they may observe her from all sides; **return, return, that we may look upon thee,** for they had never realized before what beauty was found in this bride of the King. Now the inspired author inserts a question, to test the interest which the "daughters of Jerusalem" may have in the bride. **What will ye see in the Shulamite?** And they promptly answer, **As it were the company of two armies,** that is, the angel hosts of Mahanaim, Gen. 32, 2. They regard the bride to be as magnificent and stately as the angel hosts whom Jacob saw near Peniel, between Jabbok and the Jordan.

Here we see the bride, filled with new courage and zeal for her work, ready to fulfil her ministry, imposing and impressive, even to outsiders, in her victorious progress, as the praise given her shows. She, however, disclaims any special merit, stating that it was reward enough for her to be permitted to see and admire the work of God's hands. Yet the others insist that the work of the Church, if rightly viewed, reminds them of the blessed ministry of angels, with whose assistance the messengers of the Church carry out the duty entrusted to them. That is the glory connected with the work of the Church at all times.

CHAPTER 7.

The Victorious Progress of the Church.

THE BEAUTY OF THE CHURCH'S PROGRESS. — V. 1. **How beautiful are thy feet,** literally, "thy steps," **with shoes, O prince's daughter,** as the bride proceeds on her way in stately majesty. **The joints of thy thighs,** the swing or motion of her hips in walking, **are like jewels,** like the regular swinging of a pendant chain, **the work of the hands of a cunning workman,** only an artist of the highest rank being able to work such perfection. V. 2. **Thy navel is like a round goblet,** a mixing-bowl, **which wanteth not liquor,** or, "Let not mixed wine," such as was mixed with wine or spices, "be wanting"; **thy belly is like an heap of wheat,** a rounded pile of grain, **set about with lilies.** V. 3. **Thy two breasts,** organs of nourishment, **are like two young roes that are twins,** twin gazelles, figures of graceful strength. V. 4. **Thy neck is as a tower of ivory,** in whiteness and symmetry; **thine eyes like the fish-pools in Heshbon,** blue basins mirroring the rays of the sun, **by the gate of Bath-rabbim,** Heshbon itself being called the "daughter of many," since it was a populous commercial city; **thy nose is as the tower of Lebanon, which looketh toward Damascus,** the point of comparison being its straightness, making for a handsome profile. V. 5. **Thine head upon thee is like Carmel,** a lofty and beautiful mountain, **and the hair of thine head like purple,** with its dark luster and silkiness. **The King is held in the galleries,** fettered in love by the beauty of her curls. V. 6. **How fair and how pleasant art thou, O love, for delights,** charming and amiable in her caresses! V. 7. **This thy stature is like to a palm-tree,** with its towering stateliness, **and thy breasts to clusters of grapes,** rather, the clusters of fruit of the palm-tree. V. 8. **I said, I will go up to the palm-tree,** that being His present intention, **I will take hold of the boughs thereof; now also thy breasts shall be,** or, "Let thy breasts be," **as clusters of the vine and the smell of thy nose like apples,** the King desiring to revel in the beauty and sweetness of His bride; v. 9. **and the roof of thy mouth,** the sweetness of the palate referring to the loveliness of her kisses, **like the best wine for My beloved, that goeth down sweetly,** or smoothly, **causing the lips of those that are asleep to speak,** gliding down gently and causing the drinker to fall into gentle slumber.

Here we see how the Lord regards His Church on her progress through the world, in performing the work of her calling, of the evangelization of nations. The Church is full of generative power, and her children receive the rich food of the means of grace. At the same time she is strong in the defense of the truth, trying the spirits and ever on the watch for dangers from without and within. Although the Church is a populous city, yet no impurity is found in her: she consists of saints, she is a holy, Christian Church. Her majesty is evident to all, and spiritual blessings go forth from her in richest measure, so that the King is ravished with her appearance and with her caresses, Is. 62, 4. The Bridegroom eagerly longs for the time when He will be united with the bride in heavenly bliss, Eph. 5, 32; Rev. 19, 7—9.

THE BRIDE'S ANSWER TO THE LORD. — Even at the end of the last paragraph the bride had caught up the words of the Bridegroom, stating, on her part, that the Word of her message, of the Gospel-truth, was like wine which caused the most pleasant dreams. She now continues, in reciprocating His affectionate speech: v. 10. **I am my Beloved's, and His desire is toward me,** a joyful exclamation showing how sure she is of His love, and how safe she feels in its possession. She, therefore, invites the Bridegroom: v. 11. **Come, my Beloved, let us go forth into the field,** out into the open country; **let us lodge in the villages,** the Church lodging not only in one place, but wherever a congregation with the pure Word is organized. V. 12. **Let us get up early to the vineyards,** figures of rich fruitfulness; **let us see if the vine flourish,** whether it has sprouted, **whether the tender grape appear,** that is, whether its blossoms have opened, **and the pomegranates bud forth; there will I give Thee my loves,** opening her heart without reserve and giving Him the full love of the chaste bride. V. 13. **The mandrakes,** whose odor was supposed to stimulate love, **give a smell, and at our gates are all manner of pleasant fruits,** the reference being to the store-rooms for dried fruits and vegetables over the doors of the houses, **new and old, which I have laid up for Thee, O my Beloved,** for only the richest products will properly express the fulness of her affection for the King.

While the Church longs for the consummation of the heavenly marriage, she nevertheless does not neglect her work in this world. She wants the Bridegroom to go out with her into the wide world, to visit and observe the growth of the many congregations, to witness the results of her work. For this labor in the vineyard of the Lord is the true evidence of her love. In her mind there is no doubt that there are many sweet-smelling plants throughout the world, the elect of the Lord, whose souls He will gather as noble fruits of the Church's toil. Like excellent fruits these fruits are stored in the home of the Church, to be kept for the day when the work of the bride will be ended and the marriage of the Lamb will be celebrated.

CHAPTER 8.

The Joys of the Heavenly Marriage.

THE LONGING CRY OF THE CHURCH. — V. 1. **O that Thou wert as my brother,** literally, "as a brother to me," **that sucked the breasts of my mother! When I should find Thee without,** out in the open country, the far reaches of the world, **I would kiss Thee; yea, I should not be despised,** or, "yet none would despise me." V. 2. **I would lead Thee and bring Thee into my mother's house, who would instruct me,** rather, "Thou wouldest instruct me"; **I would cause Thee,** in return for such instruction, **to drink of spiced wine of the juice of my pomegranate,** the full and true love of her heart. V. 3. **His left hand should be under my head, and His right hand should embrace me,** chap. 2, 6. V. 4. **I charge you,** so the Bridegroom calls out once more, **O daughters of Jerusalem, that ye stir not up nor awake My love, until he please,** rather, "until it please," chap. 2, 7.

Although the work of the Church is done willingly and faithfully, yet it is done under difficulties. And therefore she cries out to Him who is her Brother, with whom, by virtue of His humanity, she is connected with the closest ties, that she hopes soon to find and meet Him outside this present world. In the Great Beyond she will no longer be subject to disgraceful behavior on the part of her enemies; she will be at home, in the city of her eternal rest. Together with Christ, whose work in and with the Church will be brought to an end with the conversion of the last elect, she will enjoy the bliss of eternity. There He will give His Church the full understanding of all things, 1 Cor. 13, 12. There her heart will be given to Him in the perfection of bliss ineffable. So sure is the Church of this fulfilment of her hopes that she speaks of them as being present; she is even now possessing everything contained in the promises of her Bridegroom. And he, in turn, insists upon granting to His Church every possible moment and hour of rest and respite, that she may enjoy His love all the more in the halls of heaven.

THE BLISSFUL UNION IN HEAVEN. — V. 5. **Who is this that cometh up from the wilderness, leaning upon her Beloved?** supported by Him as they, united in love, approach their home above. **I raised Thee up under the apple-tree,** stimulating His jealous zeal; **there Thy mother brought Thee forth; there she brought Thee forth that bare Thee,** namely, that Brother who now was her Husband. Therefore she makes a powerful appeal: v. 6. **Set me as a seal upon Thine heart,** like a signet-ring worn on a cord over the heart, **as a seal upon Thine arm; for love,** in its essence, in the absoluteness of its perfection, **is strong as death; jealousy is cruel as the grave,** hard and unyielding in persistence; **the coals thereof are coals of fire, which hath a most vehement flame,** its fiery flames are a blaze of Jehovah. V. 7. **Many waters cannot quench love,** as found in Jehovah, **neither can the floods drown it,** the rivers washing it away. **If a man would give all the substance of his house for love,** hoping to buy or gain it with such a price, **it would utterly be contemned,** for all the riches of this world are insufficient and inadequate to pay for it. V. 8. **We have a little sister, and she hath no breasts; what shall we do for our sister in the day when she shall be spoken for?** when suitors for her hand would appear. V. 9. **If she be a wall, we will build upon her a palace of silver; and if she be a door, we will enclose her with boards of cedar,** to prevent access. V. 10. **I am a wall,** so Shulamith answers, **and my breasts like towers; then was I in His eyes as one that found favor;** because she had kept her charms intact, she found peace in the love of the King. V. 11. **Solomon had a vineyard at Baal-hamon,** the "city of tumult"; **he let out the vineyard unto keepers,** placing it in the charge of several at once; **every one for the fruit thereof was to bring a thousand pieces of silver,** the full product of the vineyard. Answering this statement of the bride, the King says: v. 12. **My vineyard, which is Mine, is before Me,** in the person of the bride. That is as it should be, the bride says: **Thou, O Solomon, must have a thousand, and those that keep the fruit thereof two hundred,** as a payment for their faithful work. In conclusion the Bridegroom once more issues His kind invitation: v. 13. **Thou that dwellest in the gardens, the companions hearken to thy voice; cause Me to hear it.** And the bride answers in the eagerness of her love: v. 14. **Make haste, my Beloved, and be Thou like to a roe or to a young hart upon the mountains of spices,** those known for the scent of their balsam. It is the last fond cry of the Church as she looks forward to the delights of heaven.

We have here both a climax and a summary. The Church, accompanied by Christ, her Bridegroom, is pictured as approaching the end of her course, nearing her heavenly home, where the marriage will take place. The Church, in reviewing her history, reminds Christ of the time when her conduct provoked Him to a jealous zeal. But as she was lying there, in the misery of her sinful condition, Christ came, being born into the lowliness and curse of this earthly life, in order to deliver mankind, and especially those that are His own, from the condemnation which men had brought upon themselves. Her consideration of these blessings causes the Church to exclaim that she is the seal of His love and His power. She adds an overwhelming cry of praise concerning the love of Jehovah as shown in the sending of the Messiah for the salvation of mankind, His love being the supernatural strength and divine persistence, a blaze of perfect and enduring affection for all lost and condemned sinners. The great floods of the world's sins and misery were not able to extinguish this love as revealed in Jesus Christ, altogether unmerited as it was on the part of men.

The Bridegroom, in turn, reviews the history of His relation to the Church. He found the Church when she was still without comeliness and beauty, Ezek. 16, 7, and immediately had compassion upon her. When suitors of a false kind approached her, when the false wisdom of this world tried to influence her, when the lusts of the world tried to insinuate themselves into her favor, He sheltered her. This the Church acknowledges with gratitude; she has been kept faithful and well — ornamented by virtue of His mercy. At the same time she meditates upon the vineyard which the heavenly Solomon had in the midst of the world, the city of turmoil, in which He had His watchmen, apostles, preachers, and teachers, who delivered its fruits to the Lord. Christ answers that He has His vineyard before His eyes, that the bride is His kingdom of glory and perfection. To this she assents, reminding Christ, at the same time, of the reward of mercy which the faithful watchmen should have, Luke 8, 23. In conclusion the situation as at present existing is once more pictured in a single glance. The Church is still living in gardens, in many congregations scattered over the world; there she must still proclaim the message of salvation in preparing many souls for the bliss of heaven. Therefore she prays to the Lord to hasten the course of His Word far and wide in the world, in order that the last elect may soon be won for the truth and the heavenly marriage take place. When that day comes, all believing hearts, united in the Church as the bride of Christ, will meet the great Bridegroom of their souls and be with Him in everlasting joy and happiness.

THE BOOK OF THE PROPHET ISAIAH.

INTRODUCTION.

Among the people of God of the Old Covenant who were actively engaged in His ministry were not only the priests, who were chiefly in charge of public worship, although they also did some teaching, but also the prophets, the official spokesmen of God to the children of Israel and others, whose work consisted not only in foretelling future events, but, in general, in uttering the message of God entrusted to them, whether this pertained to an exposition of the will of God, to an application of the Law to the circumstances of their time, or to an unveiling of the future, particularly of the glories of the Messianic period. The prophets were also called seers, men of God, messengers of Jehovah, servants of the Lord, in short, organs and instruments of the Lord in making Himself, His person and His will, known to men. They performed their work either in prophetical speech, spoken or written, or by the narration of visions and dreams vouchsafed to them by the Lord, or by symbolical acts signifying certain events in the coming history of God's people.

Among the men whose prophetical writings have been preserved in the canon of the Bible, Isaiah, the son of Amoz, stands first. Of the circumstances of his life little is known. He seems to have descended from a noble family, according to Jewish tradition a side-line of the reigning family of David. Isaiah was married and lived in Jerusalem, his two sons, by God's command, bearing names with symbolical meanings. He began his activity as prophet in the year in which King Uzziah died, 758 B. C., and appears to have been active for some sixty years. Beside his book of prophecy Isaiah also wrote a historical work, 2 Chron. 26, 22. According to an ancient tradition, which, however, cannot be verified, Isaiah suffered martyrdom under King Manasseh.

The period of Isaiah's activity is that of the Kings Uzziah, Jotham, Ahaz, and Hezekiah. In the first part of this period the kingdom of Judah was in a most flourishing condition, 2 Kings 14, 21—15, 7. At this time the double kingdom once more had the extent which it had possessed in the days of David and Solomon. But with the accession of Ahaz came a period of disintegration and decay: gross idolatry, human sacrifices, desecration of the Temple, turning to the Assyrians for help, who, in turn, became a scourge of the country. With the accession of Hezekiah things took a turn for the better, since he restored the Temple services, celebrated the Passover, renounced the covenant with the Assyrians, and was miraculously delivered from the power of the Assyrian king. But when he gave himself to pride and made overtures to the Babylonians, he paved the way for the later ascendency of this world power and for the fall of the southern kingdom.

Isaiah stands midway between Moses and Christ. He was, at the same time, the great preacher of repentance and the evangelist of the Old Testament. To the godless he proclaimed the wrath of the Lord, the inevitable destruction, with an earnestness and impressiveness which is overwhelming in its force; to the believers, the small remnant, he preaches the comforting message of the deliverance of mankind through the Messiah, the Servant of Jehovah.

The Book of Isaiah is clearly divided into two parts, chaps. 1 to 39 and 40 to 66, both parts being grouped about certain historical facts, the first being the hypocritical apostasy of Ahaz and the subsequent invasion of Sennacherib, the second the foolish act of Hezekiah in showing the envoys of the Babylonian king the treasures of his house and thus inviting the world power to covet the riches of Judah. The first group of prophecies concerns not only Judah and Jerusalem, but also the chief foreign countries and nations, chiefly Assyria, Babylon, Moab, Syria, Egypt, and Tyre. The second group is known as the Book of Consolations and pictures the restoration of the remnant of Israel, the Messianic King, and the final glory of the Church.[1]

[1] Cp. *Concordia Bible Class*, May, 1919, 66—68; Fuerbringer, *Einleitung in das Alte Testament*, 60—66; Stoeckhardt, *Der Prophet Jesaia*, III—XIII.

I 1—39
1) 1-6 Intro
2) 7-12 Immanuel
3) 13-23 Judgment
4) 24-27 World Judgment
5) 28-33 Israel's Decay
6) 34-35 " Restoration
7) 36-39 Historical
II 40-66
1) 40-48 Return of remna[nt]
2) 49-57 Redemption fr[om] ...
3) 58-66 Glorification of C...

CHAPTER 1.

The Opening Vision.

THE ADDRESS. — V. 1. **The vision of Isaiah** ("The Lord will save"), **the son of Amoz, which he saw,** by special enlightenment and inspiration of the Lord, **concerning Judah,** the southern kingdom, **and Jerusalem,** the capital of Judah, the site of the Temple, and therefore the center of theocratic worship, **in the days of Uzziah,** also known as Azariah, 2 Kings 14, 21, **Jotham, Ahaz, and Hezekiah, kings of Judah.** V. 2. **Hear, O heavens, and give ear, O earth,** the witnesses who were present at the giving of the Law, Deut. 4, 36, were to hear the complaint of the Lord, as He entered into judgment with His people after seven centuries, cp. Deut. 32, 1; **for the Lord hath spoken,** the very words of Jehovah, the self-existing and unchangeable God, being quoted here, **I have nourished,** brought to maturity, to adult age, **and brought up children, and they have rebelled against Me,** for so Israel, the first-born son of God, Ex. 4, 22, had rewarded the blessings received at the hand of God during these many years since the deliverance out of the serfdom of Egypt. Rebellion against God, apostasy from God: that is the chief characteristic in the history of Israel since the days of Solomon. V. 3. **The ox knoweth his owner and the ass his master's crib,** the very unthinking brutes acquiring a certain attachment for their master, so that they will not voluntarily leave him; **but Israel doth not know,** does not realize, **My people doth not consider,** does not meditate and reflect upon it, continues in deliberate ignorance of its Lord and Provider. V. 4. **Ah! sinful nation,** going its way of wilful error, **a people laden with iniquity,** with guilt and corruption of right, burdened with transgressions, **a seed of evil-doers,** a brood of such as prefer wickedness to the holiness required of them, **children that are corrupters,** themselves subject to spiritual decay and infecting others with their corruption; **they have forsaken the Lord,** they are guilty of apostasy in heart and mind, **they have provoked the Holy One of Israel unto anger,** they have gotten into the habit of blaspheming and mocking or rejecting with scorn, Him who is spotlessly pure and who chose these people to be a holy nation unto Himself; **they are gone away backward,** following their own corrupt ways, especially in sins of idolatry. Such is the sevenfold woe of the Lord, which may rightly be applied wherever apostasy is found in His Church, also in our days.

THE DESOLATION OF ZION. — V. 5. **Why,** that is, to what end and purpose, **should ye be stricken any more? Ye will revolt more and more,** or, "while ye are revolting more and more." The case was such that Israel heaped rebellion upon blasphemy, always becoming subject to more severe forms of punishment, and yet no beneficial result showed. **The whole head is sick and the whole heart faint,** that is, the entire nation, leaders and followers, within and without, were suffering from the consequences of the many wounds received at the hands of God. V. 6. **From the sole of the foot even unto the head,** that is, the whole body of the people, from the lowest to the highest and most honorable, **there is no soundness in it,** not a healthy spot, **but wounds,** gaping as from the stroke of a sword, **and bruises,** contusions as from the blows of fists, **and putrefying sores,** from which the pus must be drawn; **they have not been closed,** by pressing the gaping edges together, both to remove all foreign matter and to cause an even healing, **neither bound up,** by a cool and softening bandage, **neither mollified with ointment,** to hasten the healing process. In other words, when the prophets tried to heal the various wounds and bruises of Israel by using the knife of the Law, by calling the people to repentance, in order to apply the cooling ointment of the Gospel afterwards, the people resented the treatment and hindered the healing; they refused the assistance of the Lord and repudiated His mercy. The prophet now abandons his figurative language for a concrete description of the situation in Judah and Jerusalem at that time. V. 7. **Your country is desolate,** it has been made a desert by the inroads of the enemies, **your cities are burned with fire,** laid waste by plundering hordes; **your land, strangers devour it in your presence,** that is, the fruits of the ground, of fields and orchards, were taken by the invaders, **and it is desolate,** turned into a wilderness, **as overthrown by strangers,** conditions such as barbarians usually bring about. V. 8. **And the daughter of Zion,** the city of Jerusalem with its inhabitants, **is left as a cottage in a vineyard,** the shack of a watchman, offering meager shelter, **as a lodge in a garden of cucumbers,** a similar shelter in a truck-garden, temporary and frail, **as a besieged city,** for the devastated country is inhabited by enemies, and therefore the inhabitants of Jerusalem were practically cut off from all outside intercourse. V. 9. **Except the Lord of hosts,** Jehovah Sabaoth, in whose hands, after all, are the destinies of all people and especially of His Church Militant, **had left unto us a very small remnant,** some who had escaped the general desolation behind the walls of Jerusalem, **we should have been as Sodom, and we should have been like unto Gomorrah,** visited by a total destruction. Thus far God's judgment upon the backsliding Jews had proceeded. But the climax of His punishment had not yet struck Jerusalem; there were still such as had escaped. Let all sinners everywhere heed the warning of the Lord, lest the final judgment strike them.

REBUKE OF HYPOCRITICAL WORSHIP. — V. 10. **Hear the Word of the Lord, ye rulers of Sodom,** for as such Jehovah addresses the princes of Jerusalem; **give ear unto the Law of our God, ye people of Gomorrah,** whose conduct was characterized by pride, the lust of the flesh, and lack of mercy. The thought underlying this turn of the prophet's solemn appeal is this, that the Jews might have desired to object to his rebuke by pointing to the apparent splendor of the Temple-worship. V. 11. **To what purpose is the multitude of your sacrifices unto Me? saith the Lord,** for the people were still observing the letter of the Law with great exactness, depending upon this outward fulfilment of God's command as sufficient to gain and retain His good will toward them. **I am full of the burnt offerings of rams,** He is surfeited with their dead worship, **and the fat of fed beasts; and I delight not in the blood of bullocks, or of lambs, or of he-goats,** such sacrifices indeed having been commanded by the Lord, but not in a lifeless, mechanical form of worship, for such hypocritical conduct is ever an abomination to the Lord. V. 12. **When ye come to appear before Me,** namely, in person, to attend any of the festivals of the Jewish Church, **who hath required this at your hand to tread My courts?** The presence of a person's body in the place of worship, without worship in spirit and in truth, is of no value, for all hypocrites and Christians in name only trample the Lord's courts and waste the Church's property without benefit to themselves. V. 13. **Bring no more vain oblations,** offerings of vanity and lying, the reference being to such as were made of flour, principally in the form of fried and boiled cakes; **incense is an abomination unto Me,** namely, if brought by a mere mechanical act; **the new moons and Sabbaths, the calling of assemblies,** as it was solemnly done at the direction of the priests and rulers, **I cannot away with; it is iniquity, even the solemn meeting,** rather, "I cannot endure iniquity and solemn assembly," namely, as practised by these people. V. 14. **Your new moons and your appointed feasts My soul hateth,** they are a matter of loathing to Him on account of the total lack of spirituality in the people; **they are a trouble,** a grievous burden, **unto Me; I am weary to bear them,** He must soon shake them off and reward the hypocrites according to their deserts. V. 15. **And when ye spread forth your hands,** in a gesture which is a caricature of true prayer, **I will hide Mine eyes from you,** His eyes, as it were, finding themselves unable to look upon such hypocrisy; **yea, when ye make many prayers,** in the foolish belief that mere lip-service is sufficient before Him, **I will not hear; your hands are full of blood,** for the people of Jerusalem and Judah were guilty of violence and injustice before God, by which they had become murderers in His eyes. Those who do not serve the Lord in spirit and in truth also lose all true love and mercy over against their neighbor, and therefore the sighing of the afflicted becomes an obstruction between them and the Lord and hinders the effect of their prayers.

SUGGESTING THE ONLY WAY OF RELIEF. — V. 16. **Wash you,** in a true and thorough cleansing of the heart, **make you clean,** namely, from the polluting effect of their wicked behavior; **put away the evil of your doings from before Mine eyes,** so that it will no longer be within the range of His vision, these three admonitions being the negative demands made by the Lord; **cease to do evil,** withdrawing from its influence, overcoming it by a steady wrestling against its influence; v. 17. **learn to do well,** not the mere knowing, but the doing being emphasized; **seek judgment,** doing that which is right in the eyes of God, **relieve the oppressed,** aiding them in obtaining justice, **judge the**

fatherless, plead for the widow; for orphans and widows, those deprived of their natural protectors, are in the ward of God, under His protection, in a special sense. Thus the Lord demands repentance, a change of life. From this it does not follow that man, by his own reason and strength, is able to change his heart and mind in the sight of God, but the Lord's admonitions are a powerful factor in bringing about such a change. The Lord now pictures the situation as it obtains. V. 18. **Come now and let us reason together, saith the Lord,** the case being brought to trial before His tribunal, the children of Israel standing before Him as condemned culprits. **Though your sins be as scarlet,** blood-red with guilt, **they shall be white as snow; though they be red like crimson,** the color apparently fast and fixed beyond the possibility of fading, **they shall be as wool.** Such is the remarkable sentence of the Lord. His people, though laden with guilt, are not condemned to everlasting damnation, but God gives and imputes to them perfect righteousness. Here the meaning of justification becomes clear, for God declares the ungodly, the guilty, to be innocent, clean, holy, and righteous in His sight. Cp. Rom. 4, 5. And this righteousness is obtained and transmitted through the redemption gained by the blood of Christ. The sentence of God is passed regardless of the attitude of man; it is spoken for His own sake, by virtue of the perfect righteousness and the complete atonement of Jesus Christ. But the sentence of God is now proclaimed to sinners in order that they may accept and believe His offer of grace and salvation. V. 19. **If ye be willing and obedient,** hearing and believing His joyous verdict concerning the forgiveness of sins, **ye shall eat the good of the land,** become partakers of salvation, of eternal life; v. 20. **but if ye refuse and rebel,** despising and rejecting the grace of God obtained by the vicarious suffering of Christ, **ye shall be devoured with the sword,** become victims of eternal destruction; **for the mouth of the Lord hath spoken it.** "He that believeth not shall be damned." Mark 16, 16.

THE LORD'S COMPLAINT AGAINST JERUSALEM. V. 21. **How is the faithful city,** Jerusalem with its representative inhabitants, formerly excelling in faithfulness to Jehovah, **become an harlot,** given to spiritual adultery or idolatry! **It was full of judgment,** justice in agreement with the Law of God being practised in the city; **righteousness lodged in it,** being at home there at one time; **but now murderers,** for violence, tyranny, oppression are transgressions of the Fifth Commandment. V. 22. **Thy silver,** the princes and rulers, which formerly distinguished the city, **is become dross, thy wine,** the leaders and nobles, **mixed with water,** that is, the judges and rulers of the city had turned from integrity and sincerity to moral impurity; v. 23. **thy princes are rebellious,** obstinately opposing God and His covenant, **and companions of thieves,** thinking only of ways and means to satisfy their greed; **every one loveth gifts,** expecting bribes, **and followeth after rewards,** openly seeking money for selling right to the highest bidder; **they judge not the fatherless,** that is, they do not see to it that orphans receive justice, **neither doth the cause of the widow come unto them,** so that they might receive that which is due to them. Such is ever the case in times of apostasy; for it is then that tyranny and oppression, faithlessness and blasphemy, reign, and the efforts of the few believers seem to count almost for nothing. V. 24. **Therefore saith the Lord, the Lord of hosts, the Mighty One of Israel,** He who possesses absolute power over all the fortunes and actions of men, **Ah! I will ease Me of Mine adversaries,** have the satisfaction of punishing them for their attitude against Him, **and avenge Me of Mine enemies,** by punishing them in His wrath and thus working satisfaction to His holiness; v. 25. **and I will turn My hand upon thee,** namely, against Jerusalem, the faithless, sinful city, **and purely purge away thy dross,** melting it out with lye, removing the obstinate and wicked leaders, **and take away all thy tin,** the lead mixed with the precious metal, the ungodly in high and low places; v. 26. **and I will restore thy judges as at the first,** men possessing the integrity of the original days, **and thy counselors as at the beginning,** in the golden period of Israel's history. **Afterward thou shalt be called The City of Righteousness, the Faithful City,** where true righteousness and dependable loyalty would be found always. We have here a reference to the true Israel of the New Testament, to the Church of Jesus Christ, in the perfection of its nature as wrought by Jesus Christ. V. 27. **Zion shall be redeemed with judgment,** through the redemption of the Messiah, **and her converts with righteousness,** for with the guilt of mankind laid upon Christ and the full atonement demanded of Him, the way is paved for the complete appeasing of God's wrath, the basis of justification. V. 28. **And the destruction of the transgressors and of the sinners shall be together,** for rejecting the Lord, **and they that forsake the Lord,** refusing to change their evil mind, **shall be consumed,** this being the fate of all obstinate sinners at all times. V. 29. **For they shall be ashamed of the oaks,** or terebinths, **which ye have desired,** they will be brought to shame on account of the groves where they practised idolatry, and **ye shall be confounded for the gardens that ye have chosen,** where idolatry and other vices held full sway. V. 30. **For ye shall be as an oak whose leaf fadeth,** dying for want of nourishment, **and as a**

garden that hath no water, whose flowers and fruits are bound to die. V. 31. **And the strong shall be as tow,** that is, the well-to-do will be as a lamp-wick, **and the maker of it as a spark,** rather, his work as a spark, for the idol causes a consuming fire, which devours the idolaters themselves, **and they shall both burn together, and none shall quench them.** When the final Judgment comes and the fate of men has been decided, then the verdict of condemnation will strike the ungodly, and their worm will not die, neither will their fire be quenched, and they will be an abomination to all flesh.

CHAPTER 2.

The Kingdom of Christ Revealed.

THE GENTILES CALLED TO THE KINGDOM.—V. 1. **The word,** the prophetic oration, **that Isaiah, the son of Amoz, saw concerning Judah and Jerusalem,** the revelation here recorded extending to the end of the fourth chapter. V. 2. **And it shall come to pass in the last days,** in the Messianic age, which precedes the end of the world, **that the mountain of the Lord's house,** that is, Zion or Jerusalem, the kingdom of God, **shall be established in the top of the mountains,** towering high above every human and, especially, every idolatrous organization, **and shall be exalted above the hills; and all nations shall flow unto it,** seeking the city of God in large streams. This is said of the Church in the time of the New Testament, when it is established in every part of the world, high above all false religions and churches, its beauty serving as a lodestone drawing men from all nations to seek the true God. V. 3. **And many people shall go and say,** in encouraging one another to seek the truth of the Gospel, **Come ye and let us go up to the mountain of the Lord, to the house of the God of Jacob,** to become members of the true Church, such zeal in coming and inviting others being a sign of real conversion; **and He will teach us of His ways,** literally, "out of His ways," so that the instruction will be most thorough, **and we will walk in His paths,** in the willing obedience of faith; **for out of Zion,** from the midst of God's holy congregation, **shall go forth the Law,** the word here designating the law of the New Covenant, the Gospel of God's mercy, and **the Word of the Lord,** of Jehovah, the God of grace, **from Jerusalem.** This explains the manner in which the Gentiles come to the city of God, to His holy Church, namely, by and through the preaching of the Gospel, which is brought to them and accepted by them. V. 4. **And He shall judge among the nations and shall rebuke many people,** stating His decisions, performing the functions of King and Judge in governing the people under His spiritual rule; **and they,** under the influence of the Lord's Spirit, who lives in them, **shall beat their swords into plowshares,** the broad knives fastened to the shaft of the plow by Oriental farmers, **and their spears into pruning-hooks,** that is, vine-dressers' knives. **Nation shall not lift up sword against nation, neither shall they learn war any more,** for in the Church of God as it really exists, under the government of the Prince of Peace, there is nothing but peace, unity, and love. It is a wonderful description of the Messianic kingdom and its beauties which is here given. V. 5. **O house of Jacob,** the children of Israel, specifically the inhabitants of Judah and Jerusalem being here addressed, **come ye and let us walk in the light of the Lord,** an urgent appeal to heed the prophetic message, to know the Lord as He has revealed Himself in the Word, and to give proof of this knowledge in their entire conduct and life. V. 6. **Therefore Thou hast forsaken Thy people, the house of Jacob,** rather, "For Thou hast rejected," since this fact, the deliberate transgressions of Israel, had caused God to let them walk in the foolishness of their minds, **because they be replenished from the East,** admitting the idolatrous influences of the Orient, **and are soothsayers, like the Philistines,** accepting this abomination from their neighbors to the southwest, **and they please themselves in the children of strangers,** going hand in hand with them, making covenants with them, in a most intimate friendship. Because Israel had so acted, therefore the Lord had rejected them, and for that reason the appeal of the prophet went forth that they should return to the light of the Lord. But the apostasy of the people is further described. V. 7. **Their land also is full of silver and gold, neither is there any end of their treasures; their land is also full of horses, neither is there any end of their chariots,** this heaping up of material wealth being contrary to the divine prohibition, Deut. 17, 14—17; v. 8. **their land also is full of idols,** for idolatry had entered the land with the wealth gained through commerce with the surrounding heathen nations; **they worship the work of their own hands, that which their own fingers have made,** the words expressing the disgust and the contempt of the Lord for such practises; v. 9. **and the mean man,** the lowly among the people, **boweth down,** as a result and punishment of the idolatrous practises in use among the children of Israel, **and the great man,** the nobles and leaders among the people, **humbleth himself,** is humbled by God. **Therefore forgive them not,** literally, "and not wilt Thou forgive them." Worldliness, idolatry, rejection of God, challenges the holiness of the Lord, causes His righteousness to pronounce judgment, and therefore on the last Great Day, all admonitions having been fruitless, His punishment will strike the wilful transgressors.

THE MAJESTY OF GOD IN HIS FINAL REVELATION. — V. 10. **Enter into the rock,** as people hide before a cruel enemy, **and hide thee in the dust,** as the travelers in the wilderness throw themselves down when the simoom, or sirocco, bears down upon them, **for fear of the Lord and for the glory of His majesty.** When the terror of God will strike the world, when the Lord will be revealed in the glory of His majesty, then all wilful sinners, all idolaters, all servants of mammon, and all rebellious men, who have let the love of the world fill their hearts, will be filled with terror and heaped with shame. V. 11. **The lofty looks of man shall be humbled,** every gesture indicating pride will be forgotten, **and the haughtiness of men shall be bowed down,** humbled into the dust, **and the Lord alone shall be exalted in that day,** standing secure in the perfection of His essence. V. 12. **For the day of the Lord of hosts,** the final Day of Judgment, **shall be upon every one that is proud and lofty, and upon every one that is lifted up,** the day being, as it were, kept in reserve by the Lord, to come as a surprise upon the haughty despisers of His grace; **and he,** every proud sinner, **shall be brought low,** cp. Joel 1, 15; 3, 4; v. 13. **and upon all the cedars of Lebanon that are high and lifted up,** pictures and emblems of the proud sinners, **and upon all the oaks of Bashan,** the rich pastureland east of Jordan, v. 14. **and upon all the high mountains, and upon all the hills that are lifted up,** every creature that excels in majesty and beauty in the world, v. 15. **and upon every high tower, and upon every fenced wall,** products of men's ambition and pride, v. 16. **and upon all the ships of Tarshish,** the finest instruments of commerce in the ancient days, **and upon all pleasant pictures,** works produced to satisfy man's lust of the eyes. In short, what human art and human science have produced under the incentive of human ambition, pride, and haughtiness will be destroyed in that great Day of Judgment. V. 17. **And the loftiness of man shall be bowed down,** since all the objects of man's pride will be destroyed, **and the haughtiness of men shall be made low; and the Lord alone shall be exalted in that day,** the highest and most glorious in the majesty of His essence. V. 18. **And the idols He shall utterly abolish,** literally, "they will be changed," they will vanish away, their vanity will be apparent before all men. V. 19. **And they,** the idolaters, **shall go into the holes of the rocks and into the caves of the earth,** in cellars or cisterns dug into the ground, **for fear of the Lord and for the glory of His majesty, when He ariseth to shake terribly the earth.** Cp. Luke 23, 30. V. 20. **In that day,** under the influence of a repentance which comes too late, **a man shall cast his idols of silver and his idols of gold, which they made each one for himself to worship, to the moles and to the bats,** into the first convenient crevice, in an effort to rid himself of their incriminating presence; v. 21. **to go into the clefts of the rocks, and into the tops of the ragged rocks,** his terror driving him to seek safety anywhere and everywhere, **for fear of the Lord,** namely, dread of the inevitable punishment, **and for the glory of His majesty, when He ariseth to shake terribly the earth,** to spread terror throughout the world, for His wrath will find His enemies in the most remote corners and hiding-places of the earth. V. 22. **Cease ye from man, whose breath is in his nostrils,** all men are admonished not to place their trust in man, weak and powerless as he is in all that he undertakes, dependent upon a breath which quickly disappears; **for wherein is he to be accounted of?** All human props may and will be taken away in the twinkling of an eye. It is good at all times to trust in the Lord and not to put confidence in man, especially in view of the coming Judgment, which will show the vanity of man's pride and of all his accomplishments.

CHAPTER 3.

The Confusion and Judgment of Sin.

GOD'S THREAT OF PUNISHMENT. — V. 1. **For, behold, the Lord, the Lord of hosts,** a most solemn designation of the almighty Ruler of the universe, **doth take away from Jerusalem,** as the capital and center, **and from Judah,** the entire southern kingdom, **the stay and the staff,** He is engaged in this act, it is a judgment which is continuing, **the whole stay of bread and the whole stay of water,** the heaping of synonyms indicating the seriousness of the situation and the Lord's responsibility for sending famine and depriving the people of the things upon which they depended, v. 2. **the mighty man and the man of war,** the military power of the nation, **the judge, and the prophet, and the prudent,** the diviner, **and the ancient,** those whose counsel was based upon experience, v. 3. **the captain of fifty,** the smallest unit of the Jewish army, **and the honorable man,** the preferred favorite of the king, **and the counselor, and the cunning artificer,** the state engineer and inventor, one versed in mechanical and military arts, **and the eloquent orator,** the expert enchanter. No definite order is observed in the enumeration of these officers, the specific Jewish being named together with the heathen, in order to show how easily the Lord can overthrow all their pomp and power. V. 4. **And I will give children to be their princes,** weak and inexperienced young men, **and babes shall rule over them,** incompetent and wanton youngsters, exercising power as they please. V. 5. **And the people shall be oppressed, every one by another, and every one by his neighbor,** all respect for the God-given rights of others having vanished; **the child shall behave himself proudly against the ancient,** without the slightest regard for his superiors, **and the base against the honorable,** not only by ignoring all distinction of rank, but by setting aside the government instituted by God. In other words, tyranny is followed by mob-rule, and this, in turn, by anarchy, so that everything is in a turmoil, every semblance of governmental control has vanished. V. 6. **When a man shall take hold of his brother of the house of his father, saying, Thou hast clothing,** having saved at least a decent suit of clothes in the general overthrow, **be thou our ruler and let this ruin,** what is left of the former nation, **be under thy hand,** in order to see whether there is still some chance of relief in this great emergency, v. 7. **in that day shall he,** refusing to take this obligation upon himself, **swear, saying,** calling out loudly in protest, **I will not be an healer,** in trying to save the wreck; **for in my house is neither bread nor clothing,** he is just as poor and ragged as the others; **make me not a ruler of the people,** rather, with greater emphasis, "You shall not make me a ruler." The entire description sets forth the disintegration, the decay, of the nations preceding the end. V. 8. **For Jerusalem is ruined, and Judah is fallen,** outward and inward decay is evident, **because their tongue and their doings are against the Lord,** their apostasy and blasphemy have reached the limit, **to provoke the eyes of His glory,** the glorious appearance of His holy essence, for they challenge the wrath of the Lord by deliberately planning and executing evil. V. 9. **The show of their countenance,** their whole appearance, the boldness expressed in their entire conduct, **doth witness against them,** their vices being imprinted upon their foreheads; **and they declare their sin as Sodom,** boasting of it without the slightest evidence of shame, **they hide it not. Woe unto their soul! for they have rewarded evil unto themselves,** they are bound to bring punishment upon themselves. With a few strokes the prophet draws a picture of wantonness and moral filth, which fills the reader with loathing of such depths of wickedness. V. 10. **Say ye to the righteous,** to the few who are still found in the midst of the general decay, **that it shall be well with him; for they shall eat of the fruit of their doings,** their good works, the fruit of their faith, do follow them, Rev. 14, 13. V. 11. **Woe unto the wicked! it shall be ill with him,** his will be a lamentable fate; **for the reward of his hands,** that which he earned by his evil deeds, **shall be given him.** The godless will have no one to blame but themselves when everlasting destruction comes upon them.

THE VANITY OF THE WOMEN OF JERUSALEM. V. 12. **As for My people,** still looked upon by the Lord with loving regard, **children,** incompetent and ruthless youngsters, **are their oppressors, and women,** subject to whims and moods, **rule over them. O My people, they which lead thee cause thee to err,** the leaders becoming misleaders, **and destroy the way of thy paths,** devouring it by their false, erroneous preaching, so that the way of divine truth is no longer visible. V. 13. **The Lord standeth up to plead,** to take up the case of the world, **and standeth to judge the people,** all the nations of the world, to convict them of their wickedness. V. 14. **The Lord will enter into judgment with the ancients of His people,** who were supposed to be their leaders, **and the princes thereof,** to whose guidance He had intrusted Israel; **for ye have eaten up the vineyard,** crushing the Church of God; **the spoil of the poor,** of whom the Church largely consists, **is in your houses,** due to the persecution of the rulers. V. 15. **What mean ye that ye beat My people to pieces,** crushing them with the most severe tyranny, **and grind the faces of the poor?** in trampling them under foot, **saith the Lord God of hosts.** That is a special sign of the time preceding the Last Judgment: oppression and persecution of the Church of God, and for this the Lord will punish the wicked in full measure. However, it is not only the princes and rulers of the people who have brought God's judgment upon themselves, but also the women of the land. V. 16. **Moreover, the Lord saith, Because the daughters of Zion are haughty and walk with stretched-forth necks,** proudly thrown back, **and wanton eyes,** winking in feigned innocence, but with hidden invitation, **walking and mincing,** with affected, tripping steps, as **they go and making a tinkling with their feet,** the ankle-chains, which brought about the mincing steps, also producing a delicate ringing, v. 17. **therefore the Lord will smite with a scab the crown of the head of the daughters of Zion,** where long hair now is decorated handsomely, will be found nothing but loathsome uncleanness, **and the Lord will discover their secret parts,** exposing them to shame and disgrace before the whole world. V. 18. **In that day the Lord will take away the bravery,** the adornment, **of their tin-**

kling ornaments about their feet, the ankle-rings with their chains, **and their cauls,** braided ornaments fastened to the forehead, **and their round tires like the moon,** half-moon-shaped decorations fastened about the neck, v. 19. **the chains,** the ear-pendants, **and the bracelets,** or chains worn on wrist or arm, **and the mufflers,** fluttering veils, v. 20. **the bonnets,** turban-shaped diadems, **and the ornaments of the legs,** the step-chains connecting the ankle-bracelets, **and the head-bands,** beautiful girdles, **and the tablets,** perfume capsules, the favorite odor being musk, **and the earrings,** small amulets with verses of magic, v. 21. **the rings,** usually seal-rings, **and nose-jewels,** suspended from the septum of the nose, v. 22. **the changeable suits of apparel,** the finest street dresses, **and the mantles,** roomy tunics with sleeves, **and the wimples,** costly shawls, **and the crisping-pins,** beautifully worked hand-bags or boxes, v. 23. **the glasses,** small metal mirrors, **and the fine linen,** shirtlike garments of the finest India linen, **and the hoods,** colored turbans, **and the veils,** mufflerlike throws for the neck, a total of twenty-one objects being named without special order, to indicate the contempt which the Lord felt for the vanity of women in making such toilet articles their chief concern, to the neglect and detriment of more important matters. V. 24. **And it shall come to pass that instead of sweet smell,** the delicate perfume of balsam, **there shall be stink and instead of a girdle a rent,** nothing but a rope to hold the garments together, **and instead of well-set hair,** such as was artistically curled and built up, **baldness, and instead of a stomacher,** the splendid mantles now worn, **a girding of sackcloth, and burning,** a mark such as was branded upon slaves, **instead of beauty.** The entire passage is surcharged with a holy sarcasm and may therefore well serve to warn many of the modern girls and women who find their greatest delight in objects such as are named here. V. 25. **Thy men shall fall by the sword,** the defenders of Jerusalem a prey of war, **and thy mighty in the war.** V. 26. **And her gates,** where the chief men of the city were wont to discuss the welfare of the city, **shall lament and mourn,** because the seats of the men are empty; **and she,** the daughter of Zion, the city itself, **being desolate, shall sit upon the ground,** a picture of desolation. Chapter 4, 1. **And in that day,** due to the fact that the men have fallen in battle, **seven women shall take hold of one man,** in an unnatural denial of womanly modesty, **saying, We will eat our own bread and wear our own apparel,** not depending upon him for support; **only let us be called by thy name,** that they might be known as his wives, **to take away our reproach,** for it was considered a disgrace not to be married and bear children. Such are the scenes which preceded the fall of Jerusalem, and similar scenes will precede the end of the world.

CHAPTER 4.

Christ the Sanctuary of the Believers.

THE INVITING COMELINESS OF THE BRANCH OF JEHOVAH. — V. 2. **In that day,** in the Messianic period preceding the end of the world, **shall the Branch of the Lord,** the great Son of David, the Messiah Himself, Is. 11, 1; 53, 2; Zech. 3, 8, **be beautiful and glorious,** literally, "ornament and glory," emphasizing these attributes as essential in the miraculous person of Christ, **and the Fruit of the earth,** the Savior Himself, product of the human race, growing up out of the house of David according to the counsel of God, **shall be excellent and comely,** literally, "splendor and brilliant glory," **for them that are escaped of Israel,** included in the great deliverance which came through Jesus Christ. V. 3. **And it shall come to pass that he that is left in Zion and he that remaineth in Jerusalem,** the elect of the Lord, **shall be called holy,** consecrated to the Lord and serving Him in a holy life, **even every one that is written among the living in Jerusalem,** those who are appointed by God unto eternal life, Acts 13, 48, whether they be of Jews or Gentiles, v. 4. **when the Lord shall have washed away the filth of the daughters of Zion,** namely, the moral uncleanness and sinfulness which no amount of outward ornament can cover before His eyes, **and shall have purged the blood of Jerusalem,** the outstanding acts of wickedness and guilt, **from the midst thereof by the Spirit of judgment and by the Spirit of burning,** His Holy Spirit both rebuking the evil and destroying all wickedness by a thorough winnowing and sifting, for conversion is entirely and alone His work. V. 5. **And the Lord will create upon every dwelling-place of Mount Zion and upon her assemblies,** wherever there are congregations of believers, **a cloud and smoke by day and the shining of a flaming fire by night,** these being the vehicle and sign of the merciful presence of Jehovah in the midst of His people; **for upon all the glory,** in every place of glory where believers are assembled in His name, **shall be a defense,** a covering, or canopy, the Lord Himself, as the King of Grace, having His throne in every congregation and causing it, by the gifts of His mercy, to be a glory, a place where His glory shines forth. V. 6. **And there shall be a tabernacle for a shadow in the daytime from the heat,** Christ Himself dwelling in their midst, **and for a place of refuge and for a covert,** where one may hide in safety, **from storm and from rain;** for Christ is the Protector of His Church against the manifold dangers with which it is surrounded. In this way the Branch of the Lord serves for glory to His elect, and the believers cheerfully trust themselves to His keeping.

CHAPTER 5.

The Judgment of Destruction upon Jehovah's Vineyard.

THE DISAPPOINTMENT OF THE VINEYARD. — V. 1. **Now will I sing to my Well-beloved a song of my Beloved,** the prophet singing to Jehovah, concerning the Lord, but at the same time expressing the thoughts of the Lord, **touching His vineyard,** that of His Church at the time of the prophet. **My Well-beloved hath a vineyard in a very fruitful hill,** literally, "on the horn, or summit, of a son of oil," the vineyard being situated on a hill and having most fertile soil; v. 2. **and He fenced it,** rather, spaded or hoed it thoroughly, **and gathered out the stones thereof,** which hindered the proper cultivation of the ground, **and planted it with the choicest vine,** a very fine Oriental variety of grape, called sorek, **and built a tower in the midst of it,** this being the usual watch-tower, **and also made a wine-press therein,** the lower trough into which the grape-juice flowed from the wine-press proper; **and He looked that it should bring forth grapes,** the fruit of the excellent vine which He had planted there, **and it brought forth wild grapes,** the sour product of the wild vine or of a similar plant. V. 3. **And now, O inhabitants of Jerusalem and men of Judah,** to whom the prophet is specifically addressing himself, appealing to them as to judges in this difficult situation, **judge, I pray you, betwixt Me and My vineyard,** making their decision on the basis of the facts presented to them, which were visible to even the casual onlooker. V. 4. **What could have been done more to My vineyard that I have not done in it?** The Lord had shown His people mercy, goodness, and truth in so many ways that He had, as it were, exhausted His love in their behalf. He had not reached the limit of His grace in dealing with them, but matters had certainly reached a stage where they could expect no more at His hand. **Wherefore, when I looked that it should bring forth grapes, brought it forth wild grapes?** Surely if the Lord now abandoned this vineyard, the people themselves must admit that they had fully deserved such treatment, that they had but themselves to blame for their destruction, as the Lord now states. V. 5. **And now go to; I will tell you what I will do to My vineyard,** the Judge Himself announcing the punishment which He had decided upon: **I will take away the hedge thereof,** one of thorns and briers being the usual protection of vineyards in the Orient, **and it shall be eaten up, and break down the wall thereof,** as a second means of keeping out marauders, **and it shall be trodden down,** the emphatic statement of the original being "for a treading down"; v. 6. **and I will lay it waste,** for a complete ruin; **it shall not be pruned,** to remove the superfluous shoots, **nor digged,** to loosen the ground for the admission of air to the roots; **but there shall come up briers and thorns,** making the growth of vines of the right and welcome kind impossible; **I will also command the clouds that they rain no rain upon it.** V. 7. **For the vineyard of the Lord of hosts is the house of Israel and the men of Judah His pleasant plant,** literally, "the plant of His pleasure"; **and He looked for judgment,** that the people would do what is right and good, **but behold oppression,** the infringement of rights by graft and other forms of wickedness; **for righteousness,** that is, an outward dealing according to the demands of a righteous conduct, **but behold a cry,** namely, that of the people who suffer wrong. The explanation of the parable is here briefly indicated. Israel was the vineyard of the Lord, separated by Him from all nations, placed into a rich and fruitful land and endowed with unsurpassed blessings in every respect, among them the nobles of the people, the patriarchs, the kings, the priests, the prophets. The watch-tower of God in the midst of His people was the government of David and of His house. But this vineyard had bitterly disappointed the Lord in His expectations, so that He finally sent His punishment in full measure, not only the Babylonian captivity, but the ultimate overthrow of the Jewish nation and Church in the year 70 A. D. Cp. Ps. 80; Matt. 21, 33—46. Let the Christian Church and all those who profess to be members of the Church take warning, for the Lord searches the reins and hearts and at all times expects true fruits of righteousness from all those who are called after His name.

A SIXFOLD WOE UPON THE JEWISH TRANSGRESSORS. — V. 8. **Woe unto them that join house to house,** in a greed for wealth which is never satisfied, **that lay field to field,** their covetousness causing them to add one piece of property to another, **till there be no place,** no room for any one else, **that they,** literally, "ye," for the prophet here turns directly to the

Jews, **may be placed alone in the midst of the earth,** thus violating the statutes both concerning the inheritance of real estate and the year of jubilee, Num. 27, 9—11; Lev. 25, 10—13. V. 9. **In mine ears said the Lord of hosts,** the great Ruler of the universe Himself making it known to His prophet, **Of a truth many houses shall be desolate, even great and fair,** the beautiful homes of the rich, **without inhabitant,** as a punishment upon their greed. V. 10. **Yea, ten acres of vineyard shall yield one bath,** one bucket of wine, about seven and one half gallons, **and the seed of an homer,** about eight bushels, **shall yield an ephah,** a little more than three pecks, the land thus producing only about one-tenth of the amount of seed sown in the spring, that is, a starvation harvest. V. 11. **Woe unto them that rise up early in the morning that they may follow,** eagerly pursue, **strong drink,** a kind of brandy prepared from dates, apples, pomegranates, honey, and barley; **that continue until night,** protracting their session of debauchery until the cool of the evening and beyond, **till wine inflame them,** putting them into a condition where they are ready for all the works of darkness. Note that the moderate use of even intoxicating beverages is not in itself condemned, but every form of excess, as the further description shows. V. 12. **And the harp,** or zither, **and the viol,** a guitar-like instrument, **the tabret,** the tambourine, **and pipe,** a kind of flute, **and wine are in their feasts,** of these their banquets consist, this is all they have in mind in planning and executing their drinking-bouts; **but they regard not the work of the Lord,** they were deaf to the message of Jehovah in nature, in history, especially in the preaching of His prophets, **neither consider the operation of His hands,** in preparing the punishment of righteousness for all the guilty. **V. 13. Therefore My people,** as the Lord still affectionately calls them, **are gone into captivity,** the visitation of the Babylonian captivity being pictured as already taking place, **because they have no knowledge,** not only because they hardened their hearts against all understanding, but because the calamity, for this reason, also caught them unawares; **and their honorable men are famished,** literally, "become starvelings," people suffering hunger, **and their multitude dried up with thirst,** a vivid description of Israel as it was driven into exile. Such is ever the consequence when the luxury-loving people of this world deliberately exclude the understanding of spiritual things from their hearts. V. 14. **Therefore hell,** in this case the realm of death in so far as they were subject to punishment in the place reserved for the wicked, **hath enlarged herself and opened her mouth without measure,** to receive the great number of victims; **and their glory,** the splendor of their wickedness, **and their multitude, and their pomp,** the tumult and noise of their drunken shouting, **and he that rejoiceth,** those finding their enjoyment in the excesses of this world, **shall descend into it.** Then all the laughter and shouting of the children of this world will be changed to cries of woe, accompanied by weeping and gnashing of teeth. V. 15. **And the mean man shall be brought down, and the mighty man shall be humbled,** men of every rank and station being included in the Lord's condemnation, **and the eyes of the lofty shall be humbled,** so that they are no longer lifted up in pride; v. 16. **but the Lord of hosts,** He who exerts unlimited authority over the world and all its fortunes, **shall be exalted in judgment,** the very overthrow of the wicked redounding to His glory, **and God that is holy shall be sanctified in righteousness,** give evidence of His holiness in exercising justice upon the ungodly. V. 17. **Then shall the lambs feed after their manner,** as on their usual pasturage, **and the waste places of the fat ones shall strangers eat,** the nomad tribes of the desert again occupying the land which had been held by similar people in ancient days. Thus the land of Canaan would become a monument of God's punitive justice, as a result of Israel's apostasy. V. 18. **Woe unto them that draw iniquity with cords of vanity,** their first excuses to themselves being like hair-strings, but their increasing callousness finally causing them boldly to draw their guilt to them as with heavy cords, **and sin, as it were, with a cart-rope,** they hitch it to them like draft-horses dragging a heavy wagon, laying themselves to the traces with all their might, utterly ignoring the thought of a day of vengeance; v. 19. **that say, Let Him make speed and hasten His work that we may see it,** that is, the threatened retribution, **and let the counsel of the Holy One of Israel draw nigh and come that we may know it!** Their blasphemous mockery is like that of which the Apostle Peter writes, 2 Pet. 3, 3—13, and will surely draw down upon them the punishment of the Lord. And so far as the mockers of our day are concerned, the time will come when they, overcome with terror at the revelation of God's judgment upon them, will call upon the mountains to fall upon them and to the hills to cover them. V. 20. **Woe unto them that call evil good and good evil,** thus reversing all principles of true morality; **that put darkness for light and light for darkness,** particularly in palliating the wickedness of sin, in representing avarice, luxury, the lust of the flesh as harmless faults; **that put bitter for sweet,** by condemning the godly, the children of God, as enemies of mankind, **and sweet for bitter,** by glossing over transgression and thus leading men into everlasting destruction. V. 21. **Woe unto them that are wise in their own eyes,** arrogant in their self-conceit, an offense which is rebuked also by St. Paul, Rom. 12, 16,

and prudent in their own sight, such people being beyond the necessity of learning, their lack of humility causing them to reject all instruction that is brought to their notice, especially the message of the Lord's servants. V. 22. **Woe unto them that are mighty to drink wine, and men of strength to mingle strong drink,** champions of dissolute living, selling justice in order to obtain the means to indulge in the service of mammon and luxury; v. 23. **which justify the wicked for reward,** openly seeking bribes, and, in fulfilling the promises made on the strength of such gifts, **take away the righteousness of the righteous from him,** deciding against him in court and thus frustrating the ends of justice. Note that all the sins which are here condemned with such harsh words are found in our day and age and will surely be subject to the Lord's punishment, as in the days of Isaiah. V. 24. **Therefore, as the fire devoureth the stubble, and the flame consumeth the chaff,** in a sudden and thorough destruction, **so their root,** the supposed firm hold of these transgressors, **shall be as rottenness,** moldy and decayed, **and their blossom,** their outward prosperous appearance, **shall go up as dust,** flying away like small particles, **because they have cast away the Law of the Lord of hosts,** in a deliberate, blasphemous rejection, **and despised the Word of the Holy One in Israel,** through which He wanted to call them to repentance. V. 25. **Therefore is the anger of the Lord kindled against His people, and He hath stretched forth His hand against them and hath smitten them,** the scene again being painted before the eyes of the people, in order to urge them to repentance; **and the hills did tremble,** under the blow delivered by Jehovah, as from a mighty earthquake, **and their carcasses were torn in the midst of the streets,** lying there as dung, even as it had happened before, 2 Chron. 28, 6. **For all this,** although the punishment of the Lord has repeatedly gone forth, **His anger is not turned away, but His hand is stretched out still.** So great was the apostasy in Israel that the wrath of the Lord was not yet appeased, especially since the nation showed no signs of true repentance; it was the wrath of the final Judgment. V. 26. **And He,** in delivering the last great blow, **will lift up an ensign to the nations from far,** as a signal and invitation for them to attack Israel, **and will hiss unto them from the end of the earth,** the figure being taken from the work of the bee-keeper, who coaxes the bees from their hives by a hissing sound; **and, behold, they shall come with speed swiftly,** most eager to carry out the Lord's will upon Israel. V. 27. **None shall be weary nor stumble among them; none shall slumber nor sleep, neither shall the girdle of their loins be loosed,** to retard their movements, **nor the latchet of their shoes be broken,** all this being descriptive of their tireless activity, their unwearied zeal, and their readiness for battle; v. 28. **whose arrows are sharp and all their bows bent,** ready to send the arrows to their mark; **their horses' hoofs shall be counted like flint,** a most important attribute for a campaign of war carried to such distances, **and their wheels like a whirlwind,** for their rolling resembled the sound of an advancing tempest; v. 29. **their roaring shall be like a lion,** a fearful battle-cry, **they shall roar like young lions,** eager for their prey; **yea, they shall roar and lay hold of the prey,** Israel becoming an easy victim, **and shall carry it away safe, and none shall deliver it,** no one being strong enough to come to Israel's aid in this emergency laid upon it by the Lord. V. 30. **And in that day they shall roar against them like the roaring of the sea,** the surf breaking on the precipitous shore with a fearful thunder; **and if one look unto the land,** seeking a firm foothold, **behold darkness and sorrow, and the light is darkened in the heavens thereof,** literally, "darkness — distress and light — night in the clouds of heaven above," that is, tribulation and relief would change off quickly in the fate of Israel; but the final result would be the blackest night, shutting out all light. That, in brief, is the outline of Israel's history until the exile, not only the conquest of Nebuchadnezzar, but that of the Romans in the year 70 A. D. as well.

CHAPTER 6.

Vision of Jehovah in His Temple.

JEHOVAH REVEALED IN HIS GLORY. — V. 1. **In the year that King Uzziah died,** that is, in the last year of this king's successful reign, 2 Kings 15, 1—7; 2 Chron. 26, in the year 758 B. C., **I saw also the Lord,** the All-powerful, **sitting upon a throne, high and lifted up,** the prophetic vision, beyond the range of the normal ability of human senses, permitting the prophet to see the revelation of God, not face to face, — for God dwells in an inaccessible light, — but in a manner which uncovered the divine glory to his inner mind, **and his train filled the Temple,** that is, His kingly robe with its majestic train, fitting emblem of the divine glory, covered and filled the heavenly Sanctuary. V. 2. **Above it stood the seraphim,** heavenly spirits of the highest rank, ministers of the Lord serving as guardians of the throne. **Each one had six wings,** in accordance with their nature as heavenly beings; **with twain he covered his face,** for even the seraphim cannot endure the sight of the essential holiness of God, **and with twain**

he covered his feet, for even the angels, with a proper feeling of humility and modesty, prefer to keep their forms covered before the eyes of the Most Holy One, **and with twain he did fly,** floating about the throne of the Lord. V. 3. **And one cried unto another,** in a wonderful antiphonal chorus, **and said, Holy, holy, holy, is the Lord of hosts,** thrice holy not only on account of the supreme excellence of His essential holiness, but also on account of the Triunity of persons, each of which is the possessor of the divine holiness in its fulness and glory; **the whole earth is full of His glory,** literally, "filling the whole earth is His glory"; for all men on earth will see the revelation of His divine majesty, all His works, in creation, redemption, sanctification, will serve to magnify Him as the supreme and only God. Cp. Rev. 4, 8. V. 4. **And the posts of the door,** the foundations of the sills, or thresholds, the heavenly temple with its portals down to the lowest foundation, **moved at the voice of him that cried,** the powerful sound of the entire chorus, **and the house was filled with smoke,** as from the incense of all the prayers of the saints, uniting with the angels above to give praise and adoration to the great Lord of heaven, Rev. 5, 8; 8, 3. 4. V. 5. **Then said I,** overcome with awe and terror at the tremendous impressiveness of the scene, **Woe is me! for I am undone,** lost, threatened with death and destruction, **because I am a man of unclean lips,** the feeling of his own sinfulness coming over him all the more strongly in view of the perfect holiness which he had just seen, **and I dwell in the midst of a people of unclean lips,** descendant and member of a generation of sinners; **for mine eyes have seen the King, the Lord of hosts,** between whom and man is not only the gulf separating the Creator from His creatures, but the greater abyss between the holy God and the world of sinners. Cp. Ex. 33, 20. V. 6. **Then flew one of the seraphim unto me, having a live coal in his hand, which he had taken with the tongs from off the altar,** the altar of incense evidently being referred to; v. 7. **and he laid it upon my mouth,** he caused the glowing coal to come into contact with the prophet's lips, **and said, Lo, this hath touched thy lips; and thine iniquity is taken away and thy sin purged,** atoned for. The act of the angel evidently had a symbolical meaning, first of all with reference to the atonement made in and through the person of Jesus Christ, the work of redemption carried out in accordance with the Triune God's counsel. Not only, however, is the prophet, sinful man as he was, assured of the grace of God, but the Lord also imparts special strength to him and fits him to be the instrument of His inspiration.

THE MISSION OF THE PROPHET. — V. 8. **Also I heard the voice of the Lord,** of the All-powerful, the great Ruler of the universe, **saying, Whom shall I send?** the call being for volunteers to proclaim the atonement set forth in the vision just vouchsafed the prophet. **And who will go for Us?** the persons of the Trinity here consulting together in this very important matter. **Then said I, Here am I; send me.** The prophet, in the spirit of voluntary service wrought by the Lord, a principal requisite for the proper and effective ministry of the Word, is ready to undertake the task. V. 9. **And He said, Go and tell this people,** to which He no longer refers as His people, but as strangers, in the third person, **Hear ye indeed,** constantly within reach of the Word of God, **but understand not,** the words making no impression upon mind and heart; **and see ye indeed,** namely, the great works of God by which He reveals Himself to mankind, **but perceive not,** not really grasping their significance or applying them to their own condition. The judgment of God is now proclaimed as carried out upon the Jews during eight centuries and more. V. 10. **Make the heart of this people fat,** insensitive to impressions for good, so that feeling, reason, and will would become callous, **and make their ears heavy,** the hearing of the mind becoming impaired beyond the possibility of understanding, **and shut their eyes,** namely, those of the spirit, **lest they see with their eyes, and hear with their ears, and understand with their heart, and convert,** that is, be converted, **and be healed.** Note that the members or organs spoken of are given in inverted order in the second part of the sentence, to increase its impressiveness. It is the judicial hardening, the judgment of obduration, which is here described, for if people deliberately and maliciously reject God's offers of salvation, He may punish them in the manner here described, so that the message which otherwise works salvation becomes to them a savor of death unto death. Cp. 2 Cor. 2, 16; Matt. 13, 14. 15; Mark 4, 12; Luke 8, 10; John 12, 40; Acts 28, 26. 27. It is not that God works obduration, but He surrenders the godless to their evil will; He withdraws from their hearts with His Holy Spirit. V. 11. **Then said I, Lord, how long?** that is, how long would this hardening continue? **And He answered, Until the cities be wasted,** altogether desolate, **without inhabitant, and the houses without man,** without a protector, **and the land be utterly desolate,** literally, "made desolate a desert," v. 12. **and the Lord have removed men far away,** by having them led away into exile, **and there be a great forsaking in the midst of the land.** V. 13. **But yet in it shall be a tenth, and it shall return and shall be eaten,** literally, "And if there is yet in it a tenth, it will once more become subject to devouring"; as a teil-

tree, a terebinth, **and as an oak, whose substance is in them,** a mere stump being left, **when they cast their leaves,** when they are felled, **so the holy seed shall be the substance thereof,** the stump or stem. Thus the obduration upon Israel would continue until the last wrath would come upon Israel, resulting in its destruction. And yet, after the trunk would be hewn down, the stump which remained would bring forth new shoots, a people consecrated to God. As in Israel, so in all the nations of the world the Lord has His holy seed, people who by His grace accept the Gospel and are saved.

CHAPTER 7.

Ahaz Given the Promise of Deliverance.

GOD PROMISES HELP AGAINST SYRIA AND EPHRAIM. — V. 1. **And it came to pass in the days of Ahaz, the son of Jotham, the son of Uzziah, king of Judah,** 2 Kings 15, 37; 16, 5. 6; 2 Chron. 28, 5. 6, **that Rezin, the king of Syria, and Pekah, the son of Remaliah, king of Israel,** who had formed an alliance, 2 Kings 15, 37, **went up toward Jerusalem to war against it, but could not prevail against it.** According to the historical accounts this war took place about 743—739 B. C., with the preliminary advantage entirely on the side of the allies; for Rezin took the harbor of Elath on the Elanitic Gulf, and Pekah gained a victory over a large army of Judah. Nevertheless, Jerusalem was not taken, very likely because the allies did not even find occasion to lay siege to it; their plans were overthrown. V. 2. **And it was told the house of David,** the reigning monarch of that line, in this case Ahaz, **saying, Syria is confederate with Ephraim,** depending upon the northern kingdom as a faithful ally, its armies having joined Israel's forces to strengthen them, or being supported by them. **And his heart was moved and the heart of his people,** both King Ahaz and all the people of Judah being frightened by the invasion, **as the trees of the wood are moved with the wind,** their terror being intensified by their feeling of guilt. V. 3. **Then said the Lord unto Isaiah,** Himself taking charge of affairs in this emergency, **Go forth now to meet Ahaz, thou and Shear-jashub** ("A remnant returns"), **thy son, at the end of the conduit of the upper pool,** one of the reservoirs where the water of the city was stored, chap. 36, 2, **in the highway of the fuller's field,** which was also situated west of the city, near the pool, this highway apparently being the main caravan road leading from Jerusalem to Joppa; v. 4. **and say unto him,** who was probably engaged in having the fortifications strengthened, **Take heed and be quiet,** perfectly unconcerned and without worry; **fear not, neither be faint-hearted,** literally, "and thy heart, not be it soft with despondency," **for the two tails of these smoking firebrands,** burned-out and quenched stumps of torches, **for the fierce anger of Rezin with Syria,** with his whole great army, **and of the son of Remaliah,** as Pekah, king of Israel, is contemptuously called. All the enemies of God and of His Church are always helpless before His almighty power. V. 5. **Because Syria,** or Aram, with its confederates, **Ephraim, and the son of Remaliah,** the northern kingdom and its ruler, **have taken evil counsel against thee, saying,** v. 6. **Let us go up against Judah and vex it,** throw it into consternation, fill it with terror, **and let us make a breach therein for us,** take the capital, **and set a king in the midst of it, even the son of Tabeal,** an unknown man, to be the vassal king of Judah, for such was the plan of the allies: v. 7. **thus saith the Lord God, It shall not stand,** they would not carry out their plan, **neither shall it come to pass,** since He Himself had decided to hinder it. V. 8. **For the head of Syria,** its capital and metropolis, **is Damascus, and the head of Damascus is Rezin; and within threescore and five years shall Ephraim,** the northern kingdom, which had relied upon Syria, **be broken that it be not a people,** that it would cease to exist as a nation. V. 9. **And the head of Ephraim,** its capital and stronghold, **is Samaria, and the head of Samaria is Remaliah's son.** The meaning of this somewhat enigmatic saying is evidently this, that both Syria and the kingdom of Israel would be confined to the territory now occupied by them, since their schemes of conquest would utterly fail. Moreover, Ephraim, the northern kingdom, was destroyed within the next sixty-five years, Shalmanezer of Assyria taking the majority of the people into exile in the year 722 B. C., and the downfall of the country being completed with the settling of colonists from Asia, about 675 B. C., 2 Kings 17, 24; Ezra 4, 2. The prophet closes his encouraging message with the words, **If ye will not believe, surely ye shall not be established,** that is, if Judah, both its king and its people, would not firmly cling to God's Word and promise, it would also cease to exist, it would be destroyed. This word has a general application: He who does not believe will not be able to stand before the judgment of God.

THE SON OF THE VIRGIN PROMISED. — V. 10. **Moreover, the Lord,** through the prophet Isaiah, **spake again unto Ahaz,** who had not answered upon the consoling message of the Lord's messenger, since he had already made arrangements to get the assistance of Assyria,

saying, in an earnest endeavor to have him place his trust in the help of the Lord, v. 11. **Ask thee a sign of the Lord, thy God,** this offer to perform a miracle being intended to confirm the promise just made; **ask it either in the depth,** in the underworld, in hell, **or in the height above,** in heaven. The Lord permitted Ahaz to attach his faith to a condition named by himself, so that every excuse of unbelief would be taken from him. V. 12. **But Ahaz,** in wicked unbelief and disgusting hypocrisy, **said, I will not ask, neither will I tempt the Lord.** Having already decided upon enlisting Assyria's help, he rejected the offer of Jehovah with a hypocritical pretext. This was the very climax of obduration. When unbelief assumes the garments of piety, the effect is much more loathsome than open blasphemy and mockery. V. 13. **And he,** Isaiah, through whom the Lord was addressing the apostate king, **said, Hear ye now, O house of David,** not only the present monarch being addressed, but all his followers as well: **Is it a small thing for you to weary men,** making the prophet, who had labored so long and faithfully in trying to win him for the truth, both disgusted and weary, **but will ye weary my God also?** so that He also becomes filled with weariness and turns from the reprobate people in disgust and delivers them into the destruction they so deliberately sought. V. 14. **Therefore the Lord Himself,** in a significant revelation of His almighty power, **shall give you a sign,** cause a miracle to happen which would have abiding significance. **Behold,** an exclamation calling attention to the extraordinary prophecy now following, **a virgin,** literally, "the virgin," that certain virgin whom the Lord had even now selected for this purpose, not merely an unwed woman of marriageable age, but an undefiled maiden, Ps. 68, 25; Matt. 1, 25, **shall conceive,** without the carnal knowledge of man, **and bear a son,** the event being represented as happening now, in the everlasting present of the eternal God, **and shall call His name Immanuel,** which is correctly interpreted by Matthew as meaning, "God with us." This name characterizes the person, the essence, and the work of the Messiah. The son of the virgin, conceived and born a true human being, yet without sin, is at the same time true, almighty, eternal God. It is the great mystery of godliness: God manifest in the flesh, the true Savior, Protector, and Helper of all men. V. 15. **Butter,** the thick curdled milk, which is a favorite in the Orient, **and honey shall He eat, that He may know to refuse the evil and choose the good,** such would be His food beginning with the age of discretion and throughout His life, partaking, as a true human being, of the food of a desolate country. V. 16. **For before the Child shall know to refuse the evil and choose the good,** before He would reach the age of adolescence, **the land that thou abhorrest shall be forsaken of both her kings,** rather, "desolate will be the land, of the face of whose two kings thou hast a horror," the judgment of the Lord having been carried out upon it. The time of this event is more exactly fixed in the next verses. V. 17. **The Lord shall bring upon thee, and upon thy people, and upon thy father's house, days that have not come from the day that Ephraim departed from Judah,** when the northern tribes seceded after the death of Solomon; **even the king of Assyria,** this kingdom being here introduced as the representative of the great world powers which finally overthrew Judah. The disintegration began at that time and continued for centuries. V. 18. **And it shall come to pass in that day,** at the time when He would send His judgment upon Judah, **that the Lord shall hiss for the fly that is in the uttermost part of the rivers of Egypt,** the various canals of the Nile, **and for the bee that is in the land of Assyria,** calling them to come and do His bidding, for these insects are evidently types of the armies of the heathen nations which subjugated Judah. V. 19. **And they shall come and shall rest, all of them, in the desolate valleys,** rather, in the valleys of the declivities, **and in the holes of the rocks,** in the clefts of the mountains, **and upon all thorns and upon all bushes,** in all the rich meadow-lands, with the object of devouring and destroying everything in sight. V. 20. **In the same day shall the Lord shave with a razor that is hired,** through an army which He placed in His service, to carry out His will, **namely, by them beyond the river, by the king of Assyria, the head, and the hair of the feet; and it shall also consume the beard,** the land being depopulated and the entire body of the nation destroyed by the heathen power summoned by the Lord. V. 21. **And it shall come to pass in that day that a man shall nourish a young cow and two sheep,** glad to have kept these animals, a small remnant of the herds which he formerly possessed; the land no longer being cultivated, the people took their recourse to stock-raising and dairying; v. 22. **and it shall come to pass for the abundance of milk that they,** the few animals left him, **shall give he shall eat butter; for butter and honey,** which was abundant in the wild state, **shall every one eat that is left in the land,** for that was the food of a land which had practically been turned into a wilderness by the enemies. V. 23. **And it shall come to pass in that day,** at the time when Jehovah's judgment would be carried out, **that every place shall be, where there were a thousand vines at a thousand silverlings,** valued at about 64 cents apiece, **it shall even**

be for briers and thorns, which would overrun the former rich vineyards. V. 24. **With arrows and with bows shall men come thither,** to hunt wild beasts in the former orchards, **because all the land shall become briers and thorns.** V. 25. **And on all hills that shall be digged with the mattock,** which ordinarily were hoed and cultivated, **there shall not come thither the fear of briers and thorns,** that is, no one will venture there for fear of not being able to cope with the thorns; **but it shall be for the sending forth of oxen,** who would make the devastated lands their playground, **and for the treading of lesser cattle.** Thus the history of Judah and Jerusalem, till the coming of the promised Messiah, is sketched in a few bold lines. At that time the former glory of Judah had departed, and the proud nation had become subject to a heathen world power. Christ Himself, although the eternal Son of God, was born into the lowliness of this bondage. He is, to this day, with the Gospel proclaimed by His messengers, a savor of life unto life to those who accept Him, but a savor of death unto death to those who reject Him.

CHAPTER 8.

A Sign, a Rebuke, and an Exhortation.

A Double Prophetic Sign. — V. 1. **Moreover the Lord said unto me,** apparently not long after the event related in the last chapter, **Take thee a great roll,** evidently a large writing-tablet of the kind usually employed, **and write in it with a man's pen,** the stylus making impressions on the wax covering the tablet in such a way that the ordinary man could read the script, **concerning Maher-shalal-hash-baz** ("Make speed to the spoil — Hasten to the prey"). The inscription, as made by Isaiah, was purposely enigmatic, the purpose being to arouse the interest and curiosity of the people, to make them feel that the announcement contained in these mysterious words was very important. V. 2. **And I took unto me faithful witnesses to record,** the Lord Himself choosing them through the prophet to be present and to testify to Isaiah's preparing the tablet, **Uriah, the priest,** 2 Kings 16, 10, **and Zechariah, the son of Jeberechiah.** These men could later, when the prophecy was fulfilled, vouch for the fact that Isaiah had written concerning the future. But in close connection with this event there was another. V. 3. **And I went unto the prophetess,** to his own wife, **and she conceived and bare a son. Then said the Lord to me, Call his name Maher-shalal-hash-baz,** the same mysterious words which had been written on the tablet almost a year before, the word signifying either "Make speed to the spoil — Hasten to the prey," or, "The spoil hastens — Robbery hastens forward." V. 4. **For before the child shall have knowledge to cry, "My father," and, "My mother,"** that is, before the passing of another year, **the riches of Damascus and the spoil of Samaria shall be taken away before the king of Assyria,** so that all their wealth would be borne as a trophy before the king of Assyria. This happened about the year 739 B. C., Syria being entirely overthrown, together with that part of the northern kingdom which was east of the Jordan — the sad beginning of Israel's destruction.

A Rebuke and an Exhortation. — V. 5. **The Lord spake also unto me again,** in a series of prophecies whose final object was rich comfort to the true believers in Judah, **saying,** v. 6. **Forasmuch as this people refuseth the waters of Shiloah,** the spring and tiny brook which sprang up at the foot of the Temple-mount and, with another spring, fed the pool Siloam, **that go softly,** with none of the boisterousness of a large stream, such as the Euphrates, the people despising the quiet manner in which the kingdom of God works in the midst of men, **and rejoice in Rezin and Remaliah's son,** the latter statement referring chiefly to the people of the northern kingdom with their trust in the strength of men and in the power of huge armies, v. 7. **now, therefore, behold, the Lord bringeth up upon them the waters of the river,** that is, the Euphrates, typical of the entire heathen power bent upon the destruction of Israel, **strong and many, even the king of Assyria and all his glory,** his powerful host; **and he shall come up over all his channels and go over all his banks,** like a mighty river overflowing at the time of the spring freshets; v. 8. **and he shall pass through Judah,** penetrating to its remotest ends; **he shall overflow and go over, he shall reach even to the neck,** threatening Judah's very life; **and the stretching out of his wings,** as the streams leave the main channel of the river on either side, **shall fill the breadth of thy land, O Immanuel,** the people in whose midst the Messiah would be born. Thus the judgment would begin in Israel and progress southward to encompass Judah as well, threatening its existence. Therefore the end of the sentence is a call for help addressed to Immanuel, the Messiah, not to forsake His people, but to remember them in mercy. V. 9. **Associate yourselves, O ye people,** rather, "Be wicked, rage, raise tumults," as much as ye please, **and ye shall be broken in pieces,** for all enemies directing their attacks against the people of God will finally be destroyed; **and give ear, all ye of far countries,** the nations inhabiting distant parts of the earth; **gird yourselves,** in preparing for battle, **and ye shall be broken in pieces.** The double imperative in the Hebrew and the repetition of the command makes it all the more impressive; it places the majesty of God in contrast to the feeble endeavors of men to overthrow His power. V. 10. **Take counsel together,** against the Lord and against His people, Ps. 2, 2, **and it shall come to naught; speak the word,** in discussing the attack, **and it shall not stand,** it will most certainly be frustrated; **for God is with us.** With Immanuel on their side, the children of God have a refuge against all enemies. Even if all the powers of this world combine to attack the Church, they are bound to suffer defeat. V. 11. **For the Lord spake thus to me with a strong hand,** literally, "while His hand became strong," while His Spirit came upon the prophet with power, **and instructed me that I should not walk in the way of this people, saying,** namely, in warning the prophet and those who adhered to his people against the great mass of reprobates in Israel and Judah, v. 12. **Say ye not, "A confederacy," to all them to whom this people shall say, "A confederacy,"** literally, "Do not call conspiracy all that this people calls conspiracy," the prophet and his disciples and adherents should not be filled with apprehension on account of the conspiracy and confederation of Syria with the northern kingdom; **neither fear ye their fear nor be afraid,** they should not join the unbelieving people in their dread of the enemies. V. 13. **Sanctify the Lord of hosts Himself,** giving Him the honor, setting Him apart for adoration as the almighty Ruler of the universe, **and let Him be your fear and let Him be your dread,** standing in awe of Him and taking care not to make Him angry by a show of little faith, for He wants the believer's full confidence, his undivided trust. V. 14. **And He shall be for a sanctuary,** a safe, sheltering, holy asylum to all believers; **but for a stone of stumbling and for a rock of offense to both the houses of Israel,** causing them to fall, **for a gin,** a trap set in the way, **and for a snare to the inhabitants of Jerusalem,** namely, to those who do not truly fear Him. V. 15. **And many among them,** all those who persist in their enmity toward the Lord, **shall stumble,** by their own fault, **and fall, and be broken, and be snared, and be taken.** To him who deliberately rejects Jesus and His mercy the very Gospel-message becomes a savor of death unto death, as the application of this word by Simeon, Luke 2, 34, by Paul, Rom. 9, 33, to the obdurate Jews of their day, and by Peter, 1 Pet. 2, 7. 8, to the unbelievers in general shows. This fact will tend all the more to make the believers serve the Lord with fear and to rejoice with trembling.

WARNING AGAINST FALSE TESTIMONY. — V. 16. **Bind up the testimony,** so the Lord says to Immanuel, the Messiah, or directly to Isaiah, **seal the Law among My disciples,** so that the Word of the Lord is sealed and kept safe through the power of the Savior exerted through the Gospel-message. V. 17. **And I will wait upon the Lord,** so Immanuel — or the prophet — calls out in cheerful confidence, **that hideth His face from the house of Jacob,** by rejecting the great mass of unbelievers among the people, **and I will look for Him,** trusting in the riches of His mercy, in the certainty of the salvation of His chosen people. V. 18. **Behold, I and the children whom the Lord hath given Me,** all those who have accepted the Messiah in true faith, who belong to the elect of the Lord, **are for signs and for wonders in Israel,** placed before the eyes of all men, of the whole world, as a remarkable evidence of God's love, **from the Lord of hosts, which dwelleth in Mount Zion.** Jesus, through His Word, as proclaimed by the mouth of His servants, gains those whom the Father has given Him and will, on the Last Day, present this entire host to the Father in the temple of heaven. Cp. Heb. 2, 13. We are kept by the power of God, through faith, unto salvation. The prophet now adds a strong warning against necromancy and spiritism. V. 19. **And when they,** the unbelieving people, **shall say unto you,** in endeavoring to coax the faithful away from the truth of the revealed Word, **Seek unto them that have familiar spirits,** asserting that they possess the ability of interviewing departed souls, **and unto wizards that peep and that mutter,** said of the murmuring noises made in imitation of the shades in the realm of death and of the whispering of magical formulas which they claimed to have received from disembodied spirits, just as the modern tribe of spiritists does: **Should not a people,** so the Lord indignantly asks, **seek unto their God?** turning to Him for counsel and assistance in every emergency in life, **for the living to the dead?** How can men be so foolish as to seek help from the dead? as the spiritists insist that they are quoting the spirits of the departed. Over against this blasphemous foolishness the Lord places His urgent summons: v. 20. **To the Law and to the testimony!** Turn to the Word and the promises of the Lord alone; trust in His Gospel, in the glorious assurance of salvation contained therein; make the clear exposition of His Word the one guide of your lives! **If they,** the unbelieving majority, **speak not according to this word,** if they do not join in this call and invitation nor heed its summons, **it is because there is no light in them,** the dawn of salvation will not arise for them. He who sets aside, ignores, rejects, the Word of God destroys himself, has no hope for time and for eternity. V. 21. **And they,** the unbelievers, **shall pass through it,** walking about in the land, **hardly bestead,** oppressed both from within and without, **and hungry,** in the very depths of misery; **and it shall come to pass that when they shall be hungry,** in the midst of tribulation besetting them on every hand, **they shall fret themselves,** be filled with a helpless rage, **and curse their King and their God,** blaspheming the Lord and His Messiah, **and look upward.** V. 22. **And they shall look unto the earth,** seeking alleviation and deliverance from their affliction, **and behold trouble and darkness, dimness of anguish,** not one ray of relief and salvation penetrating the night of their suffering; **and they shall be driven to darkness,** cast out into utter darkness. Such is the punishment of God upon the unbelievers, upon those who reject the Messiah, even here on earth; how much more terrible, then, will the condemnation of eternity be into which the present punishment will merge!

CHAPTER 9.

The Promise of the Messiah in the Midst of Spiritual Darkness.

THE BIRTH OF THE GOD-MAN PROMISED. — V. 1. **Nevertheless the dimness shall not be such as was in her vexation,** literally, "Not is darkness to him to whom is affliction," that is, the land now oppressed with darkness and afflictions will be delivered from its oppression, **when at the first He lightly afflicted the land of Zebulun and the land of Naphtali,** for this country west and northwest of the Sea of Galilee had from the earliest days suffered severely from various heathen invasions, **and afterward did more grievously afflict her,** rather, but at a later time He will bring honor, **by the way of the sea, beyond Jordan, in Galilee of the nations.** The meaning of this somewhat involved sentence, then, is this, that the inhabitants of Upper and of Lower Galilee, including also the thickly settled sections on both sides of the Sea of Galilee, would first suffer severely from Assyrian and other invaders, the reference being especially to Tiglath-Pileser IV, 2 Kings 15, 29, but should later, in the time of the Messiah, be singled out for unusual honors in having the Savior devote so much time to its deliverance. V. 2. **The people that walked in darkness,** namely, these same inhabitants of Galilee of the Gentiles, those who had been oppressed with spiritual darkness, **have seen a great light,** the prophet, speaking as the mouthpiece of the eternal and omniscient God, views the Messianic period as present even now, for so certain is the fulfilment of God's promise; **they that dwell in the land of the shadow of death,** in the darkness of heathendom, **upon them hath the light shined,** namely, that of salvation, of the wonderful spiritual blessings of the Savior. As the evangelist shows, Matt. 4, 12—17, this prophecy was literally fulfilled during the Galilean ministry of Jesus, when He made Capernaum His headquarters and from there set forth on His journeys, not only throughout Galilee, but also into the country east of Jordan. V. 3. **Thou hast multiplied the nation,** so the prophet addresses the Lord in a direct hymn of praise, since He, beginning with Galilee, extended the circle of believers in Him until His Church was spread over the whole world, **and not increased the joy,** or, "to whom Thou didst not magnify the joy," the reference once more being to the time of great sorrow and distress under heathen conditions; **they joy before Thee according to the joy in harvest,** when the sacrificial feasts were eaten by grateful worshipers, Deut. 12, 7; 14, 26, **and as men rejoice when they divide the spoil,** after a victorious campaign against their enemies. V. 4. **For Thou hast broken the yoke of his burden,** the spiritual slavery with which the people were burdened, **and the staff of his shoulder,** the reference being to the cudgel of the overseer in striking the back of the slave, **the rod of his oppressor,** with which the people were kept in subjection, **as in the day of Midian,** Judg. 7, 15—22. Even as the Lord, at the time of Gideon, had delivered Israel from the oppression of the Midianites in a miraculous manner, so He effected a deliverance from everlasting bondage, from spiritual slavery, so the Messiah overcame all the enemies of mankind and now divides the spoil among the believers everywhere. V. 5. **For every battle of the warrior is with confused noise and garments rolled in blood; but this shall be with burning and fuel of fire,** literally: "For every greave" (armor, especially to protect the feet and legs) "of him who girds on his armor with noise, and the soldier's cloak rolled in blood, it shall become a burning, food for the fire." With the coming of the Messiah spiritual oppression and slavery, wrath, punishment, and judgment will be brought to an end, for His deliverance is a perfect, an everlasting salvation. V. 6. **For unto us a Child is born, unto us a Son is given,** the eternal Word being made flesh for us, not only in our stead, but for our benefit, for the eternal salvation of all believers; **and the government shall be upon His shoulder,** the absolute and unlimited power, the divine authority in its fullest sense, rests upon Him, He is, from His birth, in complete possession of the eternal power and Godhead; **and His name shall be called Wonderful,** not only His birth, but His entire essence being a miracle, **Counselor,** for He not only knows the right and proper counsel in every difficulty of body and soul, He also carries out His plans for the benefit of men, **The Mighty God,** for the Messiah, true man as He is, is at the same time above all, God blessed forever, altogether identical with Jehovah, **The Everlasting Father**, Himself the living, eternal God, whose fatherly love and faithfulness surrounds all believers with a care far surpassing human understanding, **The Prince of Peace**, the true Shiloh, Gen. 49, 10, who has restored the right relation between God and man, making peace by abolishing in His flesh the enmity which existed since the fall of man, Eph. 2, 14. 15. V. 7. **Of the increase of His government**, in extending the boundaries of His spiritual kingdom, **and peace there shall be no end**, that is, He brings about a condition of eternal peace between God and man, **upon the throne of David and upon his kingdom**, for the kingdom of Christ is the kingdom of David, continued and established in the spiritual sense, **to order it and to establish it with judgment and with justice from henceforth even forever**; for the fact that Christ endured the judgment, the punishment of sin, that He satisfied the justice of God, brought about the foundation of His kingdom, upon the fact of His atonement He builds up His Church. **The zeal of the Lord of hosts**, the eagerness of His love in seeking the salvation of mankind, **will perform this.** All this was fulfilled in the Son of Mary, of whom the angel says: "He shall be great and shall be called the Son of the Highest; and the Lord God shall give unto Him the throne of His Father David, and He shall reign over the house of Jacob forever, and of His kingdom there shall be no end. . . . That Holy Thing which shall be born of thee shall be called the Son of God." Luke 1, 32—35.

JEHOVAH'S HAND STRETCHED OUT IN JUDGMENT. — V. 8. **The Lord sent a word into Jacob**, a warning against His people, **and it hath lighted upon Israel**, falling from heaven like a morsel intended for the whole nation. God revealed His intention to His servant, and by the preaching of the prophet it reached the place for which it was intended. V. 9. **And all the people shall know, even Ephraim and the inhabitant of Samaria**, the northern kingdom with its capital being emphatically mentioned first, as being leaders in disobedience and haughtiness, **that say in the pride and stoutness of heart**, v. 10. **The bricks are fallen down, but we will build with hewn stones; the sycomores are cut down, but we will change them into cedars**, that is, they intended to replace their former lowly dwellings of dried clay and the cheap wood of the sycomore fig-tree by splendid palaces of stone and costly cedar-wood. It is the height of presumption and blasphemous pride if men scorn the punishment of the Lord. V. 11. **Therefore the Lord shall set up the adversaries of Rezin against him**, namely, the Assyrians, who, according to God's plan, conquered Syria and then advanced upon the northern kingdom, **and join his enemies together**, rather, Jehovah will stir up Ephraim's enemies against him; v. 12. **the Syrians before**, for as allies of the Assyrians they would attack Israel from the east, **and the Philistines behind**, for these ancient enemies made use of every opportunity to wreak vengeance upon Israel and Judah, cp. 2 Chron. 28, 16—19; **and they shall devour Israel with open mouth**, eating with a full mouth, pillaging the land almost to the point of destruction. Thus the Lord punishes the pride of unrepentant sinners. **For all this His anger is not turned away, but His hand is stretched out still.** The misfortunes here described were but the beginning of the great destruction which would strike the entire nation for its disobedience, and so the Lord would not withdraw His chastening hand. V. 13. **For the people turneth not unto Him that smiteth them, neither do they seek the Lord of hosts.** The object of His punishment, therefore, is not realized, they refuse to repent of their sins and thus give Him a new cause for punishing them. V. 14. **Therefore the Lord will cut off from Israel**, in wreaking His final vengeance upon the rebellious people, **head and tail, branch and rush, in one day**, in one great destruction. The prophet explains the figure used in this connection: v. 15. **The ancient and honorable**, the princes and nobles of the people, **he is the head; and the prophet that teacheth lies, he is the tail.** The false prophets considered themselves leaders among the people, but they are here told, with bitter irony, that they are morally the basest of the people, the vilest part of the nation. V. 16. **For the leaders of this people cause them to err**, thereby showing themselves utterly unfit for leadership; **and they that are led of them are destroyed**, literally, "swallowed up," namely, by the error and its peril, just as the humble rush must perish if submerged and covered with a flood of filthy water. V. 17. **Therefore the Lord shall have no joy in their young men**, the All-powerful, who formerly granted success to the arms of Israel's young men, would withdraw His assistance, **neither shall have mercy on their fatherless and widows**, who formerly had been the special objects of His fostering care; **for every one is an hypocrite and an evildoer**; that is, corrupt, atrociously bad, inclined to every form of wickedness, **and every mouth speaketh folly**, blasphemous foolishness and villainy. And so once more the warning cry rings forth: **For all this His anger is not turned away, but His hand is stretched out still**, ready to apply further punishment. V. 18. **For wickedness burneth as the fire**, challenging God to continue in His course of punishment, bringing forth its own destruction; **it shall devour the briers and thorns**, the great mass of the lowly people, who have become weeds and thistles on the face of the earth, **and shall kindle in the**

thickets of the forest, of the standing timber, of the upper classes of Israel, **and they shall mount up,** the fire lifting them up in a heavy column, **like the lifting up of smoke.** Thus the fire of God's wrath, growing out of the nation's wickedness, would bring destruction upon the entire people, the picture being that of a devastating forest-fire. V. 19. **Through the wrath of the Lord of hosts is the land darkened,** burned out to ashes, utterly destroyed, **and the people shall be as the fuel of the fire,** to be devoured without mercy; **no man shall spare his brother,** for selfishness takes account only of its own safety, disregarding all considerations of charity, patriotism, and kinship. V. 20. **And he** (impersonal subject), that is, every man, **shall snatch on the right hand and be hungry,** like a beast snapping in every direction; **and he shall eat on the left hand, and they shall not be satisfied; they shall eat every man the flesh of his own arm,** the members of his own family and tribe: v. 21. **Manasseh, Ephraim; and Epraim, Manasseh,** in a form of civil war in which every man's hand would be turned against his neighbor; **and they together shall be against Judah,** for the hatred which obtained between Israel and Judah continued in the nation even as late as the siege of Jerusalem by the Romans, when their murderous selfishness reached its climax. **For all this His anger is not turned away, but His hand is stretched out still;** for if sinners will not heed His warning here in time, His destruction will be upon them throughout eternity.

CHAPTER 10.

Assyria Threatened, Israel Comforted.

WOE UPON TYRANTS. — V. 1. **Woe unto them that decree unrighteous decrees,** in tyrannical legislation, **and that write grievousness which they have prescribed,** making and enforcing laws which bring unbearable oppressions to the poorer people of the land, v. 2. **to turn aside the needy from judgment,** that is, to deprive them of their rights, of the justice due them, **and to take away the right from the poor of My people,** wilfully and maliciously taking it from them, **that widows may be their prey, and that they may rob the fatherless,** the tyrants making themselves possessors of the property of the defenseless. They have reached the very heights of oppression and injustice. V. 3. **And what will ye do in the day of visitation,** when God will visit their injustice upon them, **and in the desolation,** the sudden storm, crash, and collapse, **which shall come from far?** It is here hinted that God would send the enemy, who should avenge the poor by destroying their oppressors, from a far country. **To whom will ye flee for help?** this being a reference to Israel's custom of seeking help from foreign nations. **And where will ye leave your glory?** that is, the treasures, valuables which they had piled up in practising injustice and in treading down the poor. V. 4. **Without Me,** rather, Nothing remains but that **they shall bow down under the prisoners,** their lot being even worse than that of other captives, **and they shall fall under the slain,** trodden under foot by others, hewn down in cold blood by their captors. Such is the lot of those who were formerly honorable and powerful, but abused their authority by tyrannical measures. **For all this His anger is not turned away, but His hand is stretched out still,** for it is impossible to escape the punishment of the Lord when once He sets out to avenge the wrongs committed against the poor and defenseless.

WOE AGAINST ASSYRIA. — V. 5. **O Assyrian, the rod of Mine anger, and the staff in their hand is Mine indignation,** literally, "Woe to Asshur (which is) the rod of My wrath, and the staff, that in their hand, Mine indignation." The Lord here pronounces a woe upon Assyria; for whereas He wanted to use this nation merely as His instrument in punishing Israel, the Assyrians took the opportunity to gratify their own lust for conquest and bloodshed. V. 6. **I will send him against an hypocritical nation,** one that is impure, corrupt, and wicked, **and against the people of My wrath will I give him a charge,** bidding Assyria smite Israel for its sins, **to take the spoil, and to take the prey, and to tread them down like the mire of the streets,** destroy their power, render them utterly helpless. So much the charge of the Lord to Assyria included, not, indeed, as if the Lord had sent this command by some messenger, but that He places even the heathen nations into His service to carry out His plans, to punish the disobedient. V. 7. **Howbeit he,** that is, Assyria, **meaneth not so,** does not hold the same idea that the Lord holds, **neither doth his heart think so, but it is in his heart to destroy and cut off nations not a few,** that is, Assyria was driven only by the thought of conquest and destruction and therefore was guilty before God, even while carrying out His plans. The plans of sinners are no less to be condemned, though they by them unwittingly fulfil God's designs. The selfish and blameworthy pride of Assyria is now described. V. 8. **For he saith, Are not my princes altogether kings?** Assyria was a world-power, and even its provinces had the extent and the might of kingdoms, so that their governors could well rank with kings. V. 9. **Is not Calno,** a large city on the Tigris,

as Carchemish, an important commercial center on an island in the Euphrates? **Is not Hamath**, an important city and formerly a capital on the Orontes, **as Arpad**, a city in Syria proper? **Is not Samaria as Damascus?** Three pairs of cities are named in such a way that boasting Assyria emphasizes the great ease with which its conquests were made. V. 10. **As my hand hath found the kingdoms of the idols**, conquering those upon whom the people of Judah looked down as idol-worshipers, **and whose graven images did excel them of Jerusalem and of Samaria**, being more plentiful than they and therefore supposedly better able to defend their cities; v. 11. **shall I not, as I have done unto Samaria and her idols**, which had been destroyed in the sacking of the city, **so do to Jerusalem and her idols?** The God of Jerusalem, so the speaker boastfully asserts, would no more be able to protect this city than the gods of the other cities had succeeded in doing. Cp. chap. 36, 18—20; 37, 11—13. This blasphemous boast could not remain unpunished, as the Lord now shows. V. 12. **Wherefore it shall come to pass that when the Lord hath performed His whole work upon Mount Zion and on Jerusalem**, Assyria being His instrument of chastisement upon those whom He had chosen for His people, and a remnant of whom remained true to Him in the general apostasy and now bowed under His chastening hand, **I will punish the fruit of the stout heart of the king of Assyria**, the blasphemous pride which showed itself in his boasting, **and the glory of his high looks**, literally, "the haughtiness of the loftiness of his eyes," the description showing the self-complacent nature of his assumed glory. V. 13. **For he saith, By the strength of my hand I have done it, and by my wisdom**, ascribing his success entirely to his own ability; **for I am prudent**, always making use of proper understanding; **and I have removed the bounds of the people**, changing their boundaries to suit himself, **and have robbed their treasures**, taking at will everything that they had accumulated, **and I have put down the inhabitants like a valiant man**, butting down those occupying thrones like a mighty hero or an angry steer; v. 14. **and my hand hath found as a nest the riches of the people**, locating them with an experienced hand; **and as one gathereth eggs that are left**, forsaken by the mother bird, **have I gathered all the earth, and there was none that moved the wing**, in defense, **or opened the mouth, or peeped**, in terrified protest. All nations had bowed in dumb resignation under the hand of the mighty Assyrian, and for this he took all credit to himself. But the prophet counters with a reproof of bitter irony: v. 15. **Shall the ax boast itself against him that heweth therewith? Or shall the saw magnify itself against him that shaketh it**, drawing it to and fro in severing the wood? It is just as foolish for a tool to boast over against the workman as for the king of Assyria to ascribe to himself all the might which he possesses only by divine permission. **As if the rod should shake [itself against] them that lift it up, or as if the staff should lift up itself, as if it were no wood**, literally, "as if a staff should lift up" (that which is) "not wood," that is, the person handling it. That rod or staff should lift up or shake those who have hold of them presents the very extreme of absurd presumption. So it was utterly absurd for the king of Assyria, who, although unknown to himself, carried out God's punishment upon Israel, to ascribe to himself the wisdom and power, the design and success of this campaign. The very evil in the world is used by God to serve His objects. Cp. Gen. 50, 20. The punishment upon Assyria is now pronounced: v. 16. **Therefore shall the Lord**, the All-powerful, **the Lord of hosts**, who commands the untold legions of heaven, **send among his fat ones leanness**, consuming the mighty ones of Assyria, **and under his glory He shall kindle a burning like the burning of a fire**, to consume it in a moment, with a mighty crackling and hissing. V. 17. **And the Light of Israel**, the Holy One of Israel Himself, **shall be for a fire and His Holy One for a flame; and it shall burn and devour his thorns and his briers in one day**, the Assyrian nation being devoured in one great destruction, v. 18. **and shall consume the glory of his forest and of his fruitful field**, the majesty of his leaders and the wealth of his merchants, **both soul and body**, in a complete destruction; **and they shall be as when a standard-bearer fainteth**, rather, as when a consumptive pines away, hurrying forward to an early death. V. 19. **And the rest of the trees of his forest**, the few that have survived the devastation of the fire, **shall be few, that a child may write them**, put down the number which he easily counted. Thus the Lord, even in the midst of His enemies, has some few whom He has chosen, who are saved in the general destruction which will come upon the unbelievers.

THE REDEMPTION OF THE REMNANT OF ISRAEL. — V. 20. **And it shall come to pass in that day**, the time to which the entire Old Testament looked forward, the Messianic period, **that the remnant of Israel, and such as are escaped of the house of Jacob**, the true spiritual Israel, the people of God, whom He has chosen from among the nations, **shall no more again stay upon him that smote them**, placing their confidence in Assyria, the nation to whom the kings of both Israel and Judah turned time and again, **but shall stay upon the Lord, the Holy One of Israel, in truth**, making Him alone the full basis of their trust. V. 21. **The remnant shall return, even the remnant of Jacob, unto the mighty God**, being converted to

God in Jesus Christ, together with the elect from the heathen nations. V. 22. **For though thy people, Israel, be as the sand of the sea,** a countless multitude, **yet a remnant of them shall return,** unfortunately only a remnant, the great mass being blinded and obdurate, Rom. 9, 27; **the consumption decreed shall overflow with righteousness,** literally, "destruction is firmly decided upon, righteousness coming along as a flood." God's punitive justice overflows and submerges the unrepentant mass of the people in the judgment of destruction decreed upon it. V. 23. **For the Lord God of hosts shall make a consumption, even determined,** literally, "and that which is decreed," **in the midst of all the land.** There is no escaping the wrath of the Lord when once He sets the machinery of destruction in motion, when He begins to carry out His decree of everlasting punishment upon His enemies, for the judgment upon Israel is merely a preliminary act and the beginning of the Last Judgment. V. 24. **Therefore,** because the Lord will judge and destroy the unbelieving world, **thus saith the Lord God of hosts,** in a call full of reassuring comfort, **O My people that dwellest in Zion,** the true Church of God, dwelling in His merciful presence, **be not afraid of the Assyrian,** the oppressor typifying all the enemies of the Lord and His Church; **he shall smite thee with a rod,** with tyrannical behavior, **and shall lift up his staff against thee,** like an overseer of slaves, **after the manner of Egypt,** when the children of Israel were in the house of bondage and suffered severely from their oppressors. In the midst of all these afflictions the believers should not let fear and terror possess their hearts. V. 25. **For yet a very little while,** 1 Pet. 1, 6, **and the indignation shall cease,** God's people being delivered from the enmity of the godless, **and Mine anger in their destruction,** rather, "My wrath has the object to destroy them," the enemies of His Church, to wear them down to nothing. V. 26. **And the Lord of hosts shall stir up a scourge for him,** brandishing it over Assyria, **according to the slaughter of Midian at the rock of Oreb,** when Gideon's forces annihilated the army of the Midianites, Judg. 7, 25; **and as His rod was upon the sea,** namely, when Moses stretched out his hand over the Red Sea and parted it for the safe passage of the children of Israel, Ex. 14, 26, **so shall He lift it up after the manner of Egypt,** lifting Assyria up and dashing it to pieces as He destroyed the forces of Pharaoh. V. 27. **And it shall come to pass in that day,** in the time of the Messiah's reign, **that his burden shall be taken away from off thy shoulder and his yoke from off thy neck,** the Lord Himself taking away the oppression of Assyria, of all the enemies of the Church, **and the yoke shall be destroyed because of the anointing,** rather, on account of the fat. The picture is that of an ox who becomes so fat and strong in spite of the yoke laid upon him that he breaks the yoke on his neck to pieces. Thus the Church is to overcome the world by strength from within. Thus the deliverance of the Church is described as it begins in and with Immanuel, and as it is completed on the Last Day, the day of redemption. The prophet now, in a very vivid picture, describes the progress of the Assyrians in attacking Jerusalem, and their complete destruction by Jehovah. V. 28. **He,** the Assyrian and his army, **is come to Aiath,** hardly ten miles northeast of Jerusalem, **he is passed to Migron,** a hamlet still nearer to the capital; **at Michmash he hath laid up his carriages,** leaving the baggage in order to move forward with greater speed; v. 29. **they are gone over the passage,** a deep, rough ravine, now known as the Wady-es-Suweinit; **they have taken up their lodging at Geba,** rather, "Let Geba be our lodging!" halting only for the night; **Ramah,** the home of Samuel, **is afraid; Gibeah of Saul is fled,** its inhabitants forsaking their city in terror. V. 30. **Lift up thy voice,** crying in consternation over the impending calamity, **O daughter of Gallim,** the inhabitants of another village in the path of the Assyrian army; **cause it to be heard unto Laish,** the shrieks of terror echoing far and wide through the country. **O poor Anathoth!** only three-fourths of an hour distant from Jerusalem and therefore bound to suffer from the enemies. V. 31. **Madmenah is removed,** the people forsaking their homes; **the inhabitants of Gebim gather themselves to flee.** V. 32. **As yet shall he remain at Nob that day,** a hill to the north of Jerusalem, overlooking the city, which the enemy would reach that very day; **he shall shake his hand against the mount of the daughter of Zion, the hill of Jerusalem,** all ready for the attack which would surely bring ruin to the capital. Thus Assyria, typifying the army of the ungodly, the enemies of the Church, is here pictured as going forward to the attack with an irresistible force, and the doom of the city, of the Church of Christ, seems to be impending. But here the Lord interferes. V. 33. **Behold, the Lord,** the All-powerful, **the Lord of hosts, shall lop the bough with terror,** cutting them down as branches are felled with an ax; **and the high ones of stature shall be hewn down, and the haughty shall be humbled,** all their plans being foiled at the very moment when they seemed to mature according to calculation. V. 34. **And He,** the Lord in His avenging wrath, **shall cut down the thickets of the forest with iron,** with a sharp instrument of destruction, **and Lebanon,** the name under which all the hostile forces are comprehended, **shall fall by a Mighty One,** by Him who possesses the majesty of the almighty and eternal God, who is both the Defender and the Deliverer of His Church. It is He also, who on the last day will change the Church Militant into the Church Triumphant.

CHAPTER 11.

The Kingdom and Government of the Messiah.

THE MESSIAH, THE BRANCH OUT OF THE STEM OF JESSE. — V. 1. **And there shall come forth a Rod,** a fresh shoot or twig, **out of the stem of Jesse,** out of the dead stock, the stump, of the former proud tree of the house of David, **and a Branch shall grow out of his roots,** Zech. 3, 8; 4, 12; Jer. 23, 5; 33, 15, the root-stock being all that was left of the former grandeur of David's house, the renewal of his family by this singular Scion would indeed be a miracle; v. 2. **and the Spirit of the Lord shall rest upon Him,** the sevenfold Spirit, Himself God from eternity, lighting or settling upon Him, Ps. 45, 7, with the fulness of His divine power, **the Spirit of wisdom,** which searches all things, even the secrets of God, **and understanding,** able to make the proper distinction concerning all things, **the Spirit of counsel,** by whom the Messiah is endowed to be the Counselor, **and might,** for Christ is the mighty God, Is. 7, 6, **the Spirit of knowledge,** by means of which He is familiar with all the mysteries of God, **and of the fear of the Lord,** which culminates in both adoration and communion, Christ, according to His human nature, praying to His heavenly Father and seeking His fellowship, but according to His divine nature united with Him in an everlasting union, which now exists according to both natures; v. 3. **and shall make Him of quick understanding in the fear of the Lord,** literally, His pleasant savor is in the fear of Jehovah, He is highly pleased when men bring to Him the sacrifice of their fear of God; **and He shall not judge after the sight of His eyes, neither reprove after the hearing of His ears,** rendering judgment not according to external appearances, rather according to His understanding of the heart and soul; v. 4. **but with righteousness shall He judge the poor,** His Savior's-interest turning especially to the lowly, to those who bear the enmity of the world on account of their faith with the proper meekness, **and reprove with equity for the meek of the earth,** taking the part of those who are persecuted for their confession's sake; **and He,** in His care for the poor small crew of His Church, **shall smite the earth with the rod of His mouth,** rebuking in a most emphatic manner the hostility of the ungodly world, **and with the breath of His lips,** His Word, which bears almighty power, **shall He slay the wicked,** overthrowing the power of Satan even here in time, revealing his true character by the preaching of the Gospel, His last condemnation being reserved for the final Judgment. V. 5. **And righteousness shall be the girdle of His loins and faithfulness,** upon which His believers may rely with full confidence, **the girdle of His reins,** holding up His clothes at His hips. Even as the girdle confined the wide garments of the ancients and enabled them to work, run, and fight without hindrance, so the Messiah furthers His cause and makes use of His full strength by righteousness and truth. The conditions of His reign are now described. V. 6. **The wolf also shall dwell with the lamb, and the leopard shall lie down with the kid; and the calf and the young lion and the fatling together; and a little child shall lead them,** a figurative representation of ideal spiritual conditions. V. 7. **And the cow and the bear shall feed,** all the bloodthirstiness of the latter forgotten; **their young ones shall lie down together; and the lion shall eat straw like the ox,** his nature so completely changed that he is no longer a carnivorous, but a herbivorous animal. V. 8. **And the sucking child,** the unweaned infant, **shall play on the hole of the asp,** on the entrance of the adder's cave, **and the weaned child shall put his hand on the cockatrice's den,** or, stretch out his arm to touch the sparkling eye of the basilisk, the poisonous serpents having lost all their vicious habits. All this poetic description is now explained: v. 9. **They shall not hurt nor destroy in all My holy mountain,** all the members of the Messiah's kingdom, whose former state was characterized by the comparison with the various animals named above, would lose and lay aside their hostile habits toward one another; **for the earth shall be full of the knowledge of the Lord, as the waters cover the sea.** Knowledge of Jehovah, love and fear of God, is the motive in all acts of the believers; because they fear the Lord in truth, because they know Him the one true God, and Jesus Christ, whom He has sent as the Savior of the world, therefore they, the inhabitants of His holy mountain, the members of His holy Church, give expression of their faith in their entire conduct; therefore they, in the midst of the general hatred and hostility of the world, live together in peace and love.

THE SPREAD OF THE MESSIAH'S KINGDOM. — V. 10. **And in that day there shall be a root of Jesse,** that same wonderful Scion, the Son of David spoken of in v. 1, **which shall stand for an ensign of the people,** a standard raised up to attract the attention of the nations everywhere, directing them to the redemption obtained by the Messiah; **to it shall the Gentiles seek,** believers from all nations being gathered about Him; **and His rest shall be glorious,** that is, after the battle and turmoil of this present world the Church Militant will be changed into the Church Triumphant, and the rest of eternity will be the glory of the Savior, His people both giving Him eternal glory and partaking of His glory.

V. 11. **And it shall come to pass in that day,** in the Messianic period of the New Testament, **that the Lord shall set His hand again the second time,** stretching it out as once before when He led His chosen people out of Egypt, **to recover the remnant of His people which shall be left,** not only the believers of Israel and Judah, but those from all the nations of the world, **from Assyria,** the mighty nation in the valley of the Euphrates, **and from Egypt,** the empire toward the southwest, **and from Pathros,** Upper Egypt, **and from Cush,** or Ethiopia, **and from Elam,** Southern Media, **and from Shinar,** Southern Mesopotamia, **and from Hamath,** the country or province on the Orontes, north of Palestine, **and from the islands of the sea,** an expression which refers to the entire coast of the Mediterranean and the adjacent countries. V. 12. **And He shall set up an ensign for the nations,** around which all the believers might rally, **and shall assemble the outcasts of Israel,** those of His spiritual people, **and gather together the dispersed of Judah from the four corners,** wings or edges, **of the earth,** so that they will march under His banner, united in spirit, though outwardly separated by race and language and customs. V. 13. **The envy also of Epraim shall depart,** this hostility having been the chief factor in keeping up the division of the nation during the time of the kings in the Old Testament, **and the adversaries of Judah shall be cut off: Epraim shall not envy Judah, and Judah shall not vex Ephraim,** that is, the Israel of the New Testament, the spiritual Israel, the Church of Christ, is a perfect and harmonious union, its various parts living together in perfect love. V. 14. **But they shall fly upon the shoulders of the Philistines toward the west,** this nation being the embodiment of the fiercest hostility in the early history of Israel; **they shall spoil them of the east together,** the Bedouin hordes of Arabia; **they shall lay their hand upon Edom and Moab,** conquering the country of these ancient enemies; **and the children of Ammon shall obey them,** literally, "their obedience." These pictures, taken from the wars of Israel, show the manner in which the Lord, through His Church, will judge and destroy His enemies. The Last Day especially will spell their doom, and the believers, the soldiers of the Lord, will be present to celebrate the victory. V. 15. **And the Lord shall utterly destroy the tongue of the Egyptian sea,** the fork of the Arabian Gulf known as the Red Sea, as at the time when the children of Israel left the house of their bondage; **and with His mighty wind shall He shake His hand over the river,** over the Euphrates, **and shall smite it in the seven streams,** separating it into seven shallow brooks, **and make men go over dry-shod,** walking through its bed on sandals. In Old Testament references and figures the Lord here promises to the spiritual people of God a wonderful salvation, like that out of Egypt or out of the captivity of Assyria. V. 16. **And there shall be an highway for the remnant of His people,** cast up or purposely built for the believers in the Lord's Church, **which shall be left, from Assyria,** permitting the captives to return to their inheritance; **like as it was to Israel in the day that he came up out of the land of Egypt.** This redemption of His people out of the hand of all enemies and oppressors is the last great deed of the exalted Messiah, and its completion will usher in the peace and glory of eternity. In this way the despised Branch out of the house of David established His kingdom, which, although jeered at on all sides, will still conquer in the end.

CHAPTER 12.

Israel's Song of Its Redemption.

V. 1. **And in that day,** when the redemption of the spiritual Israel, of the Church of Christ, shall be completed, **thou shalt say,** the Church Triumphant breaking forth in a paean of praise, **O Lord, I will praise Thee; though Thou wast angry with me,** in a just wrath over the natural sinfulness of those whose redemption was perfected, **Thine anger is turned away,** through the atonement made by Christ, **and Thou comfortedst me,** the fact of the salvation gained in Christ is the highest consolation of the believers in time and eternity. V. 2. **Behold, God is my Salvation,** literally, "Behold the God of my salvation," Him who planned and carried out the redemption of a world lost in sin; **I will trust,** placing full reliance upon His promise of help, **and not be afraid,** not being brought to shame on account of the confidence resting in Him; **for the Lord JEHOVAH is my Strength,** giving full evidence of His power in redeeming His people, **and my Song,** the object of His Church's endless praise; **He also is become my Salvation,** the blessings of which are now enjoyed by the elect of God. V. 3. **Therefore with joy shall ye draw water out of the wells of salvation,** partaking of its benefits richly and endlessly. "At the Feast of Tabernacles water was drawn from the fountain of Siloam for a drink-offering. From the priest that so brought it with solemnity into the Temple, another took it, and, while pouring out the water, used the words of our text." V. 4. **And in that day,** while enjoying the fulness of the redemption, **shall ye say,** the prophet here addressing all the members of the Church of Christ, **Praise**

the Lord, call upon His name, loudly proclaiming the miracles of His mercy, **declare His doings among the people,** making them known throughout the earth, **make mention that His name is exalted,** thus giving all glory to Him alone. V. 5. **Sing unto the Lord, for He hath done excellent things,** proving His excellence and majesty in the various acts of His redemption; **this is known in all the earth,** it should be announced to all mankind. V. 6. **Cry out and shout, thou inhabitant of Zion,** the Church of God receiving her name from the mountain where the house of true divine worship was located; **for great is the Holy One of Israel in the midst of thee,** as the Giver of victory and the Fountain of life. Thus this wonderful hymn, modeled after so many psalms of praise in the Old Testament, especially that sung upon the delivery of the children of Israel at the hands of Pharaoh, Ex. 15, 1—18, sets forth the joy of the redeemed of the Lord, of the Church Triumphant, when entering upon the blessings of eternal redemption.

CHAPTER 13.

The Burden of Babylon.

General Introduction to the Prophecies of Wrath. — V. 1. **The burden of Babylon,** the sentence of judgment revealed by special inspiration of the Lord, **which Isaiah, the son of Amoz, did see:** v. 2. **Lift ye up a banner upon the high mountain,** raising the standard of battle upon a deforested peak, where it may be visible from all sides, **exalt the voice unto them,** calling in urgent invitation, **shake the hand,** in a beckoning gesture, **that they may go into the gates of the nobles,** summoned to celebrate a victorious battle, a war against the enemies which would result in a glorious triumph. V. 3. **I have commanded My sanctified ones,** Jehovah Himself summoning the warriors consecrated to His work, **I have also called My mighty ones for Mine anger,** the heroes who should carry out the purposes of His wrath, **even them that rejoice in My highness,** boasting of the victory won in His might. V. 4. **The noise of a multitude in the mountains, like as of a great people,** a turmoil as when masses of people, great armies, congregate; **a tumultuous noise of the kingdoms of nations gathered together,** an exceptionally large and powerful host. **The Lord of hosts,** the Commander-in-chief of all heavenly forces, **mustereth the host of the battle,** ready to carry out His plan of punishment upon the heathen. V. 5. **They come from a far country, from the end of heaven,** from beyond the horizon, where the earth appears to be bounded by the sky, **even the Lord, and the weapons of His indignation, to destroy the whole land,** literally, "to overturn the whole earth," for the entire world, then known, would feel the ravages of the war of destruction determined upon by Jehovah. The prophet now turns directly to the heathen nations, with Babylon in the lead: v. 6. **Howl ye,** in consternation and terror; **for the day of the Lord is at hand,** when He intends to carry out His judgment; **it shall come as a destruction from the Almighty,** all the enemies being included in this threat and all opposition being declared useless from the start. V. 7. **Therefore shall all hands be faint,** hanging down limp and without strength, **and every man's heart shall melt,** like water, said of an utter lack of courage, of complete hopelessness; v. 8. **and they shall be afraid,** terrified in bewilderment; **pangs and sorrows shall take hold of them,** their terror showing in convulsive movements; **they shall be in pain as a woman that travaileth,** Joel 2, 6; **they shall be amazed one at another,** staring with all evidences of extreme terror, **their faces shall be as flames,** alternately reddening and blanching as their fear drives the blood back and forth in the body. V. 9. **Behold, the day of the Lord cometh,** the day of His vengeance, **cruel both with wrath and fierce anger,** consuming with its heat, **to lay the land desolate; and He shall destroy the sinners thereof out of it,** for the Lord here has the whole earth in mind. V. 10. **For the stars of heaven and the constellations thereof shall not give their light,** the figure of utter darkness pointing to the severity of the punishment; **the sun shall be darkened in his going forth,** ceasing to shine as soon as it rises, **and the moon shall not cause her light to shine.** All this, as in Joel 3, 4 and Amos 5, 8, indicates that all hope would be vain. V. 11. **And I will punish the world for their evil and the wicked for their iniquity; and I will cause the arrogancy of the proud to cease,** so that the voice of boasting is no longer heard, **and will lay low the haughtiness of the terrible,** putting down the tyrants and stopping their violence. V. 12. **I will make a man more precious than fine gold,** humankind becoming rarer on earth than the choicest gold, **even a man than the golden wedge of Ophir,** noted for the purity and the rich amounts of the gold it produced. In this manner would the Lord visit the world with His anger, to punish and annihilate it in the extremity of His wrath. V. 13. **Therefore I will shake the heavens,** namely, for the purpose of punishing the earth and making men scarce on it, **and the earth shall remove out of her place,** being crowded aside, as it were, by the immensity of God's indignation, **in the wrath**

of the Lord of hosts and in the day of His fierce anger. All creatures that are not objects of His punishment are bound to become its instruments, for He is determined to make this chastisement a type and a beginning of the final Judgment upon a godless world.

Against Babylon in Particular. — V. 14. **And it,** namely, Babylon, **shall be as the chased roe,** the timid gazelle, which is so easily startled, **and as a sheep that no man taketh up,** like a panic-stricken flock which simply cannot be brought together again. **They shall every man turn to his own people and flee every one into his own land,** that is, the great mass of strangers gathered in the great world market, Babylonia, would, at her fall, scatter in all directions, every one anxious to reach the protection of his own country. V. 15. **Every one that is found,** not having sought safety in flight, **shall be thrust through, and every one that is joined unto them,** rather, intercepted in flight, **shall fall by the sword,** for it is a general slaughter which will come upon the mixed population of Babylon. V. 16. **Their children also shall be dashed to pieces before their eyes,** their parents witnessing their murder; **their houses shall be spoiled,** everything plundered, **and their wives ravished,** for war ever brutalizes men, in many cases placing them below the level of beasts. The punishment in general having been described, the prophet now proceeds to mention particulars. V. 17. **Behold, I will stir up the Medes against them,** the Medo-Persians being the world power which conquered Babylon, **which shall not regard silver; and as for gold, they shall not delight in it,** that is, it would be impossible to bribe them, to buy them off, and thus save the city whose destruction was firmly determined upon by the Lord. V. 18. **Their bows also shall dash the young men to pieces,** a very vivid description of the effect which would attend the wholesale slaughter; **and they shall have no pity on the fruit of the womb,** not sparing even the unborn children, 2 Kings 8, 12; 15, 16; Hos. 14, 1; Amos 1, 13; **their eye shall not spare children,** for the enemies would be devoid of all pity. V. 19. **And Babylon, the glory of kingdoms,** an ornament of beauty in the midst of conquered nations, **the beauty of the Chaldees' excellency,** to which they all pointed with pride as the greatest capital of the world, **shall be as when God overthrew Sodom and Gomorrah,** utterly destroyed, an eternal wilderness. V. 20. **It shall never be inhabited, neither shall it be dwelt in from generation to generation; neither shall the Arabians,** the Bedouin nomads, **pitch tent there; neither shall the shepherds make their fold there,** total desolation should reign there forever. V. 21. **But wild beasts of the desert shall lie there,** making their dens in the midst of the ruins; **and their houses shall be full of doleful creatures,** the howling jackals probably being meant; **and owls shall dwell there,** rather, ostriches, **and satyrs,** or wild goats, thought to be possessed of demons, **shall dance there.** V. 22. **And the wild beasts of the islands,** probably hyenas, **shall cry in their desolate houses,** in the ruined palaces of the city, **and dragons in their pleasant palaces,** jackals or wolves being among the inhabitants of the stone heaps remaining. **And her time is near to come, and her days shall not be prolonged,** the threatened ruin would come in a comparatively short time. And so it came to pass, for the destruction of Babylon, begun by Darius Hystaspes, continued by Xerxes, was completed by Seleucus Nicator in the fourth century before Christ, so that even before the birth of Christ the historian Strabo describes the ruins of proud Babylon in words which are strangely like those of the prophet here recorded.

CHAPTER 14.

Israel's Deliverance and God's Judgment upon Babylon, Assyria, and Philistia.

The Deliverance of Israel. — V. 1. **For the Lord will have mercy on Jacob,** it is His love for His spiritual people, for His Church, which caused Him to bring the judgment of destruction upon Babylon, **and will yet choose Israel,** in accordance with His divine plan of salvation, **and set them in their own land,** His Church being rightly called a peculiar people, 1 Pet. 2, 9; **and the strangers,** people who are not members of Israel according to the flesh, **shall be joined with them,** in the great communion of saints, **and they shall cleave to the house of Jacob,** to be reckoned members of God's people. V. 2. **And the people shall take them and bring them to their place,** nations considering it a privilege to serve the believers; **and the house of Israel shall possess them in the land of the Lord for servants and handmaids,** the former enemies of the Lord being glad to serve Him in this manner; **and they,** the members of the spiritual Israel, the believers, **shall take them captives whose captives they were,** in returning good for evil in a most remarkable manner; **and they shall rule over their oppressors,** namely, with the rule of the Gospel-message. V. 3. **And it shall come to pass in the day that the Lord**

shall give thee rest from thy sorrow and from thy fear and from the hard bondage wherein thou wast made to serve, for the spiritual afflictions were included with those of the body in the Babylonian captivity, v. 4. **that thou shalt take up this proverb,** a song of triumph, **against the king of Babylon and say, How hath the oppressor ceased! the golden city ceased!** literally, "Ended is the driving despot, ended the exacting" (of gold), or "the oppression"; for the greatest burden which Babylon laid upon the people under her dominion was that of tribute. V. 5. **The Lord hath broken the staff of the wicked and the scepter of the rulers,** since it was used only for tyrannous oppression. V. 6. **He who smote the people in wrath with a continual stroke,** namely, the scepter of the tyrant, **he that ruled the nations in anger, is persecuted, and none hindereth,** rather, "he subjugated in anger nations by hounding on without sparing," for such is the way of the enemies of God's people at all times. V. 7. **The whole earth is at rest and is quiet,** now that the enemy is overthrown, the peace of God's kingdom being pictured; **they break forth into singing,** the believers praising the Lord for His deliverance. V. 8. **Yea, the fir-trees,** or cypresses, **rejoice at thee,** at the tyrant's misfortune, **and the cedars of Lebanon,** for their wood had been exported to the East for centuries, so that the great forests had practically disappeared, **saying, Since thou art laid down,** Babylon having fallen, **no feller is come up against us,** to strip the mountainsides of their forests. At the same time, however, while things have grown quiet on earth and the Church is enjoying peaceful growth, the realm of the dead and of the damned is in turmoil. V. 9. **Hell from beneath is moved for thee,** the place of eternal torment being stirred, **to meet thee at thy coming; it stirreth up the dead for thee,** the specters or giants inhabiting hell, **even all the chief ones,** literally, "the leaders" or "great goats," **of the earth,** as many as are in the dominion of darkness; **it hath raised up from their thrones all the kings of the nations.** All these dwellers in the realms of everlasting torment are pictured as astonished and excited at the prospect of seeing the king of Babylon enter their place of abode, their words of greeting now being given by the prophet. V. 10. **All they shall speak and say unto thee,** not in contempt and mockery, but in honest astonishment, **Art thou also become weak as we,** void of all strength? **Art thou become like unto us?** V. 11. **Thy pomp is brought down to the grave,** all Babylon's earthly glory and majesty destroyed, **and the noise of thy viols,** the sound of the harps which accompanied his feasts of merrymaking on earth; **the worm,** the flesh-eating maggot, **is spread under thee, and the worms cover thee,** the most repulsive creatures, symbols of decay, taking the place of the precious Babylonian carpets, tapestries, and coverings to which the king had been accustomed here on earth. V. 12. **How art thou fallen from heaven, O Lucifer, son of the morning!** literally, "O day-star, son of the dawn," the reference being to the high and influential position occupied by the Babylonian ruler. **How art thou cut down to the ground,** like a giant tree which has been felled, **which didst weaken the nations,** in conquering and subduing them. V. 13. **For thou hast said in thine heart,** in the pride of Nebuchadnezzar, Dan. 4, 30, **I will ascend into heaven, I will exalt my throne above the stars of God,** the residences of the spirits of God; **I will sit also upon the mount of the congregation, in the sides of the North,** this being said according to the idea of the Babylonians, who placed the sacred mountain of the gods in the far North; v. 14. **I will ascend above the heights of the clouds,** considered the chariots and thrones of the ancient deities; **I will be like the Most High,** many of the emperors of old regarding themselves as the sons or the offspring of God and laying claim to divine honors. This pride is, in the final analysis, at the bottom of all enmity against Christ and His Church, for every one who opposes God, His Word and His work, thereby exalts himself above the majesty of Him who will not give His glory to another. The song of the specters in the realm of the damned is now merged into the prophecy of the Lord: v. 15. **Yet thou shalt be brought down to hell, to the sides of the pit,** his reception in the place of everlasting destruction having just been pictured. V. 16. **They that see thee,** after the great downfall which has been so graphically pictured, **shall narrowly look upon thee and consider thee,** musing upon the terrible fate which struck their former companion or acquaintance, **saying, Is this the man that made the earth to tremble, that did shake kingdoms,** as the great Babylonian empire often did; v. 17. **that made the world as a wilderness and destroyed the cities thereof; that opened not the house of his prisoners?** showing no pity in dismissing them to their homes. Because the king of Babylon was guilty on every count here brought forward, for that reason he himself was pitilessly dealt with and now lay there as a deserted carcass, his empire sharing his fate. V. 18. **All the kings of the nations, even all of them, lie in glory, every one in his own house,** their bodies, properly prepared for burial, lying in state in the tombs of their ancestors. V. 19. **But thou art cast out of thy grave like an abominable branch,** like a worthless twig or parasite, which hinders the growth of the tree, **and as the raiment of those that are slain, thrust**

through with a sword, that go down to the stones of the pit, for the garments of the fallen soldiers that were slashed to pieces and smeared with blood were not saved by their friends nor considered welcome plunder by their enemies, but were thrown into the pit with the carcasses; **as a carcass trodden under feet,** not even given the honor of a burial. V. 20. **Thou shalt not be joined with them in burial,** his punishment reaching even beyond his death, **because thou hast destroyed thy land and slain thy people,** making it the instrument of his tyrannical lust of conquest; **the seed of evil-doers shall never be renowned,** his race becoming extinct as godless and cursed. V. 21. **Prepare slaughter for his children for the iniquity of their fathers,** to which they agreed and on whose account his dynasty shall be destroyed, **that they do not rise, nor possess the land, nor fill the face of the world with cities,** thereby once more establishing their dominion and regaining their former power. V. 22. **For I will rise up against them, saith the Lord of hosts,** here speaking directly through the prophet, **and cut off from Babylon the name, and remnant,** all the descendants that are left, **and son, and nephew, saith the Lord.** V. 23. **I will also make it,** the site of Babylon, **a possession for the bittern,** or an animal something like the porcupine which inhabits the wastes of the Euphrates Valley, **and pools of water,** swamps resulting from the annual overflow of the river; **and I will sweep it with the besom of destruction,** treating it like a heap of rubbish, **saith the Lord of hosts.** As noted at the end of chapter 13, this prophecy was literally fulfilled, as the accounts of Babylonian excavations show.

PROPHECIES AGAINST ASSYRIA AND PHILISTIA. — V. 24. **The Lord of hosts,** the Commander of all the forces of heaven, **hath sworn, saying, Surely as I have thought,** as He had disposed or planned, **so shall it come to pass,** this prophecy preceding that against Babylon in point of human time; **and as I have purposed, so shall it stand,** this prophecy being practically a continuation of chap. 10, 34; v. 25. **that I will break the Assyrian in My land,** overthrowing his power within the boundaries of Judah, **and upon My mountains tread him under foot,** for the turning-point in the Assyrian fortunes came at Libnah, in the foothills of the Judean mountains, with the destruction of Sennacherib's forces, 2 Kings 19. **Then shall his yoke depart from off them,** namely, the inhabitants of Judah, **and his burden depart from off their shoulders,** so that the design of the invader could not be accomplished. V. 26. **This is the purpose that is purposed upon the whole earth,** in the counsel of the Lord, in whose hand is the government of the whole earth; **and this is the hand that is stretched out upon all the nations,** and every decree of the Lord has significance for all men. V. 27. **For the Lord of hosts hath purposed, and who shall disannul it?** No power of the world can prevent its execution. **And his hand is stretched out, and who shall turn it back?** No man can turn Him aside from the acts which He has determined upon. — V. 28. **In the year that King Ahaz died,** about 727 B. C., **was this burden,** this sentence of judgment upon the Philistines, who just at this time prepared to regain their ancient power: v. 29. **Rejoice not thou, whole Palestina,** that is, Philistia, **because the rod of him that smote thee is broken,** the Philistines being of the opinion that the alliance of Syria and the Northern Kingdom, as a consequence of which Ahaz and Judah had become vassals of Assyria, 2 Kings 16, 5—9, had resulted in breaking the power of Judah, which had only just before that been asserted by Uzziah, 2 Chron. 26, 6; **for out of the serpent's root shall come forth a cockatrice,** that is, an adder, a still more poisonous serpent, **and his fruit shall be a fiery flying serpent,** the reference probably being to Hezekiah, who promptly smote the Philistines and definitely brought about their destruction, 2 Kings 18, 8. V. 30. **And the first-born of the poor shall feed, and the needy shall lie down in safety,** that is, the inhabitants of Judah would enjoy peace and safety under the reign of Hezekiah, over against Philistia; **and I will kill thy root with famine,** thus eradicating the Philistines as a people, **and he,** Hezekiah, **shall slay thy remnant,** thereby carrying out God's punishment upon the ancient enemies of Judah. V. 31. **Howl, O gate!** the strong fortifications of the Philistine cities being meant. **Cry, O city!** Ashdod and Gaza having retained much of their ancient glory. **Thou, whole Palestina, art dissolved,** melting away to nothing; **for there shall come from the North a smoke,** namely, the Assyrian hordes with their ruthless devastations, **and none shall be alone in his appointed times,** literally, "and none is by himself in his armies," the Assyrian soldiers knowing neither weariness nor insubordination, but all filled with that one idea — the lust of conquest. V. 32. **What shall one, then, answer the messengers of the nation?** What answer do the messengers of the nation bring? What report did the ambassadors of various heathen nations make when they returned to their own countries after viewing the results of God's punishment of Philistia and His protection of Judah? **That the Lord hath founded Zion, and the poor of His people shall trust in it,** the troubled refugees being safe within its walls. In this way the Lord protects those who believe in Him against all enemies, He Himself being their Refuge and Strength.

CHAPTER 15.

Prophecy against Moab.

V. 1. **The burden,** the sentence of judgment, **of Moab,** the nation descended from the elder daughter of Lot, occupying the country southeast of the Dead Sea. **Because in the night Ar of Moab is laid waste and brought to silence,** made desolate and annihilated; **because in the night Kir of Moab is laid waste and brought to silence!** It is a call of astonishment at, and horror over, the sudden and fearful destruction of these two leading cities of the nation. V. 2. **He,** rather the impersonal one, standing collectively for all the inhabitants of Moab, **is gone up to Bajith,** to the house of the temple, **and to Dibon,** a city not far from the Arnon, **the high places, to weep,** before the altars of the country's idols. **Moab shall howl over Nebo and over Medeba,** rather, "on Nebo and Medeba of Moab howling is going on"; for in these two towns in the hills toward the west they had sanctuaries. **On all their heads shall be baldness and every beard cut off,** mutilated, as a sign of deep mourning, Lev. 21, 5. V. 3. **In their streets they shall gird themselves with sackcloth,** thus exhibiting their grief openly; **on the tops of their houses,** which are flat in the Orient, **and in their streets every one shall howl, weeping abundantly,** being dissolved in tears. V. 4. **And Heshbon,** a former Amorite city, but regarded as belonging to Moab, **shall cry, and Elealeh,** near Heshbon, within the boundaries of Reuben; **their voice shall be heard even unto Jahaz,** another town of this district; **therefore the armed soldiers of Moab shall cry out,** impelled thereto by the greatness of the horror; **his life shall be grievous unto him,** literally, "his soul trembles for him," the entire nation being shaken by the bitterness of the punishment. The situation is such as to fill the heart of the prophet with pity. V. 5. **My heart shall cry out for Moab; his fugitives shall flee unto Zoar, an heifer of three years old,** literally, "whose bolts (extended) to Zoar, the three-year-old heifer," that is, the locks or fortified boundaries of Moab reached as far as Zoar, the city of Lot's refuge, on the peninsula extending into the southeastern end of the Dead Sea; **for by the mounting up of Luhith with weeping shall they go it up,** that is, the Moabite fugitives were ascending the incline of Luhith, in the southwestern part of their country, with bitter weeping; **for in the way of Horonaim,** on the road leading down to this town in the valley, Jer. 48, 5, **they shall raise up a cry of destruction,** bewailing the impending fall of the city. V. 6. **For the waters of Nimrim,** known for the freshness of their springs, **shall be desolate,** filled with earth or rubbish by the invaders; **for the hay is withered away, the grass faileth, there is no green thing,** the entire land being devastated, the vegetation drying up for want of care, and the crops apparently even burned up by the foes. V. 7. **Therefore,** on account of the destruction of their land, **the abundance they have gotten,** above and beyond their needs, **and that which they have laid up,** by careful saving, **shall they carry away to the brook of the willows,** a small stream on their southern boundary, which the Moabite fugitives forded in order to find refuge with the people of Idumea. V. 8. **For the cry is gone round about the borders of Moab,** thus filling their entire country; **the howling thereof unto Eglaim,** a town near the Dead Sea, **and the howling thereof unto Beer-elim,** in northeastern Moabitis, that is, the cry of distress reaches from one end of the country to the other. V. 9. **For the waters of Dimon,** the river Arnon, **shall be full of blood; for I will bring more upon Dimon,** further misfortune, **lions upon him that escapeth of Moab, and upon the remnant of the land,** the reference being either to another enemy among foreign nations or to wild animals whom the Lord would send to complete the devastation of the land. He here calls out to all men: "Be not deceived, God is not mocked!"

CHAPTER 16.

Further Prophecies Concerning Moab.

THE CONDITIONS OF DELIVERANCE. — V. 1. **Send ye the lamb to the ruler of the land from Sela to the wilderness, unto the mount of the daughter of Zion,** Moab here, having found refuge in Petra of Idumea, being admonished to send its tribute of lambs to the ruler of the land, to the king reigning at Jerusalem, the road to this capital, whose most important section was Mount Zion, leading through the wilderness south and west of the Dead Sea. To submit to Judah, in both the physical and the spiritual sense, was Moab's only hope. V. 2. **For it shall be that, as a wandering bird cast out of the nest,** like birds aimlessly fluttering, like a nest whose occupants have suddenly been turned out, **so the daughters of Moab shall be at the fords of Arnon;** for here, at the boundary of their land, they assemble in huddled bands, looking for help and deliverance. To this appeal the prophet answers: v. 3. **Take counsel, execute judgment,** planning deliverance instead of oppression, as heretofore; **make thy shadow as the night in the midst of the noonday,** thereby concealing all those who trust in this shadow as completely as if the darkness of night enclosed them; **hide the outcasts,** those who are driven from home without cause; **bewray not him that wandereth,** betraying him into the hands of the enemies. V. 4. **Let Mine outcasts dwell with thee, Moab; be thou a covert to them from the face of the spoiler,** thus giving shelter to all people who might become fugitives from Judah in the uncertain circumstances obtaining at that time. The reason for this admonition is now given. **For the extortioner is at an end,** the great world-power which made it a practise to destroy and tread under foot was itself overcome, **the spoiler ceaseth,** destruction is no longer to be found, **the oppressors are consumed out of the land.** Jerusalem was delivered from the Assyrian affliction, which represented, at the same time, all the forces of evil arrayed against the Church of God. V. 5. **And in mercy shall the throne,** that of Judah, of the Messiah, **be established,** prepared and confirmed; **and He,** the Messiah Himself, **shall sit upon it in truth in the tabernacle of David,** one in whom the truth of the Lord's promise is fulfilled, one who Himself is the Truth, **judging, and seeking judgment, and hasting righteousness,** for those are the principles of His government. There is only one way for Moab to escape the threatening everlasting Judgment, and that is by throwing itself upon the mercy of this King.

MOAB'S PRIDE AND RUIN. — The Lord's invitation was issued to Moab also, for He wants all men to be saved and to come to the knowledge of the truth. The appeal, however, was unavailing, and therefore the prophecy of punishment is once more resumed. V. 6. **We have heard of the pride of Moab,** its conceit and foolish dependence upon its own strength, Jer. 48, 14—29; **he is very proud; even of his haughtiness and his pride and his wrath,** his senseless anger against Israel; **but his lies shall not be so,** his false boasts would soon be shown to be vain. V. 7. **Therefore shall Moab howl for Moab,** lamenting its own ruin; **every one shall howl; for the foundations of Kir-hareseth,** the ruins of its strongest fortress, **shall ye mourn,** for this citadel of brick would be razed, or its grape-cakes would no more be available; **surely they are stricken,** rather, the people of Moab, utterly stricken by this calamity, would lament. V. 8. **For the fields of Heshbon languish and the vine of Sibmah,** their richest products being ruined by the invaders; **the lords of the heathen have broken down the principal plants thereof,** all the fine plants of the vine whose culture was so extensively carried on in this country; **they,** namely, the grape-vines, **are come even unto Jazer,** in the northern part of the country; **they wandered through the wilderness,** extending to the desert on the east; **her branches are stretched out, they are gone over the sea,** spreading out over the Dead Sea, to Engedi and Hebron. All these rich gifts of God's goodness were appointed to destruction. V. 9. **Therefore I will bewail with the weeping of Jazer the vine of Sibmah,** the prophet's tears joining in pity and in lament with those of the rich districts of Moab; **I will water thee with my tears, O Heshbon, and Elealeh,** weeping on account of the hardness of heart shown by the Moabites, which resulted in such a terrible punishment; **for the shouting for thy summer fruits and for thy harvest is fallen,** rather, "for the vintage-shout (*hedad*) is fallen on thy fruits and on thy vintage," namely, the invader, whose shout of triumph accompanied his trampling the harvest of fruits and grapes into the ground. V. 10. **And gladness is taken away and joy out of the plentiful field,** out of the garden-land; **and in thy vineyards there shall be no singing, neither shall there be shouting,** as when the harvest was gathered in times of peace; **the treaders shall tread out no wine in their presses; I have made their vintage-shouting to cease.** The destruction wrought by the enemy has brought about the end of all happy harvesting; for what he does not destroy outright he plunders. V. 11. **Wherefore my bowels,** his whole heart, **shall sound like an harp for Moab,** like the sounding-board of a stringed instrument, which vibrates with the depth of his emotion, **and mine inward parts for Kir-haresh.** But the most pitiful aspect of the entire situation is now given: v. 12. **And it shall come to pass, when it is seen that Moab is weary on the high place,** when its people have lamented themselves weary, **that he shall come to his sanctuary to pray,** turning to the high place consecrated to his god Chemosh and tormenting himself to utter fatigue; **but he shall not prevail,** for the god in whom he foolishly trusts is nothing but a dead idol. Such is ever the result when men place their confidence in an idol of their own invention. V. 13. **This is the word that the Lord hath spoken concerning Moab since that time,** that is, the prophecy recorded till now had been some time before. The accurate time of its fulfilment is now added by the prophet: v. 14. **But now the Lord hath spoken, saying, Within three years, as the years of an hireling,** very carefully measured, **and the glory of Moab shall be contemned,** covered with shame, **with all that great multitude,** the whole mass of its inhabitants; **and the remnant shall be very small and feeble,** in no sense large, there would be but an insignificant remainder of the former mighty nation. The ruins of the places mentioned in this prophecy, whose names have been preserved even to this day, testify to both the inspiration of prophecy and the punitive justice of God.

CHAPTER 17.

Prophecy against Damascus.

DAMASCUS AND EPHRAIM THREATENED. — V. 1. **The burden of Damascus,** the capital of Syria being mentioned first because it was at the head of the league which Israel had joined as a strong ally. Even during the reign of Ahaz the Assyrian ruler Tiglath-pileser had carried away the people of Damascus to Kir, 2 Kings 16, 9; but now a further overthrow is foretold: **Behold, Damascus is taken away from being a city,** no longer to be found in the number of cities, **and it shall be a ruinous heap,** in a catastrophe of destruction which, for the time being, left the city deserted, although it afterward recovered. V. 2. **The cities of Aroer,** the two cities of this name in the country east of the Jordan, with the towns under their jurisdiction, **are forsaken; they shall be for flocks,** an open pasturage, **which shall lie down, and none shall make them afraid,** there being no one there to drive them off. The prophecy is now extended to include the northern kingdom. V. 3. **The fortress also shall cease from Ephraim,** since its fortified cities would be taken, **and the kingdom from Damascus and the remnant of Syria,** so that both of them would no longer rank as independent nations; **they,** that is, those who are left of Syria, **shall be as the glory of the children of Israel,** to be led into captivity, **saith the Lord of hosts,** the mighty ruler of the heavenly armies. V. 4. **And in that day it shall come to pass that the glory of Jacob,** especially the kingdom of Ephraim and all who relied upon it, **shall be made thin,** be weakened and pine away, **and the fatness of his flesh shall wax lean,** the picture being that of a man rapidly falling away under the influence of a severe fever. The power and wealth which both kingdoms had once more gained under the reign of Jeroboam II and Uzziah melted away to almost nothing. V. 5. **And it shall be as when the harvestman gathereth the corn and reapeth the ears with his arm,** literally, "and his arm reapeth the ears"; **and it shall be as he that gathereth ears in the Valley of Rephaim,** the fertile plain southwest of Jerusalem, toward the country of the Philistines. Cp. 2 Sam. 5, 18—22. The picture is that of a farmer going into a field of grain and gathering an armful of stalks with his left hand, while he cuts off the grain below with a sickle in his right hand. V. 6. **Yet gleaning grapes shall be left in it,** in the land of Israel, **as the shaking of an olive-tree, two or three berries in the top of the uppermost bough, four or five in the outmost fruitful branches thereof, saith the Lord God of Israel.** In harvesting olives, the trees were first shaken, whereupon a few berries within reach were knocked down with sticks, but those which hung in the tree-tops, beyond reach, remained hanging. Thus only a few poor inhabitants would be left in Israel. V. 7. **At that day shall a man look to his Maker,** instead of trusting in fortresses and in the strength of man's arm, as heretofore, **and his eyes shall have respect to the Holy One of Israel,** for the small remnant of Israel and also of Judah, the spiritual Israel, returned to the true God and His worship. V. 8. **And he shall not look to the altars, the work of his hands,** which the children of Israel had formerly devoted to idolatry, **neither shall respect that which his fingers have made, either the groves,** the Asherah-idols picturing one of the Semitic goddesses, very often identified with Venus, **or the images,** those of Baal, the sun-god, so that all the hosts of heaven were included in this idol-worship. Cp. 2 Kings 21, 7; 23, 5. It is the mercy of the Lord which preserves at least a remnant of people everywhere, in the midst of an almost universal apostasy, like brands snatched from the burning.

A WOE UPON ISRAEL'S ENEMIES. — V. 9. **In that day shall his strong cities,** namely, those of Ephraim, the northern kingdom, **be as a forsaken bough and an uppermost branch,** literally, "like the forsaken places in the forests and mountain summits," ruined strongholds in remote parts of the country, **which they left because of the children of Israel,** which the Canaanites deserted in retiring before the children of Israel; **and there shall be desolation,** all the great fortresses of Israel sharing the fate of these ruined castles. The prophet now addresses Ephraim directly: V. 10. **Because thou hast forgotten the God of thy salvation,** the only one who can bring true redemption, **and hast not been mindful of the Rock of thy strength,** Jehovah being the one true Rock of Ages, Deut. 32, 15. 18, **therefore shalt thou plant pleasant plants and shalt set it with strange slips.** V. 11. **In the day shalt thou make thy plant to grow, and in the morning shalt thou make thy seed to flourish; but the harvest shall be a heap in the day of grief and of desperate sorrow.** It was because the northern kingdom, on the whole, had left the true God that its people had, literally, "planted plantings of pleasantness," had taken up the various sensuous heathen cults and had then planted a strange vine in their garden, namely, by becoming allies of the king of Damascus. The new plant had then been carefully fenced in, namely, by shrewd political schemes, so that the strange plant grew to maturity very rapidly, like a hothouse plant, for the alliance brought about a plan to attack Judah. But the whole scheme was frustrated by the action of Jehovah, who promptly reserved the garden of Ephraim as a heap, heaped up in the harvest, in the day of grief. Such is the consequence of the denial of the Lord and of fraternizing with the enemies of God. While Jehovah, however, used Assyria as His tool in punishing Ephraim, the great world-power itself would not escape His avenging power. V. 12. **Woe to the multitude of many people,** with the turmoil and tumult of their advance, **which make a noise like the noise of the seas; and to the rushing of nations, that make a rushing like the rushing of mighty waters!** The enemies of Israel, who are also types of the enemies of the Church, are pictured as being in a state of seething unrest, anxiously striving to harm the Lord's people. V. 13. **The nations shall rush like the rushing of many waters,** in an apparently irresistible tidal wave; **but God shall rebuke them, and they shall flee far off,** rather, it, the threatening tide of hostility, **and shall be chased as the chaff of the mountains before the wind,** the picture being taken from the open threshing-floors of the Orient, which were usually situated in elevated places, **and like a rolling thing before the whirlwind,** like whirling dust or particles of straw from the threshing-floor, as the wind picks them up and flings them away. V. 14. **And behold at evening-tide trouble,** horror falling upon the approaching enemies; **and before the morning he is not,** before ever the day dawns, they are destroyed. **This is the portion of them that spoil us, and the lot of them that rob us.** Thus the Lord will finally carry out His sentence of punishment upon all enemies of His Church and its work.

CHAPTER 18.

Prophecy against Ethiopia.

V. 1. **Woe to the land shadowing with wings, which is beyond the rivers of Ethiopia,** the land of Cush in the upper reaches of the Nile, the land of whirring wings, where tropical insects are found in great numbers, v. 2. **that sendeth ambassadors by the sea,** traversing the waters of that far country, **even in vessels of bulrushes upon the waters,** light and fleet boats made of the papyrus-reed, **saying, Go, ye swift messengers, to a nation scattered and peeled,** rather, extended far and polished, gleaming, or shining, **to a people terrible from their beginning hitherto,** a handsome, ruling, and victorious people, one of great hidden beauty and power; **a nation meted out and trodden down, whose land the rivers have spoiled,** literally, "a nation of line, line," and treading under foot, under the command of Ethiopic kings, whose rule often bordered upon oppression, and whose land was carried down the Nile in the annual inundations. This entire powerful nation is stirred up by the messengers of the kings, full of excitement on account of the danger of the Assyrian invasion. V. 3. **All ye inhabitants of the world and dwellers on the earth, see ye,** always on the lookout for important happenings, **when he lifteth up an ensign on the mountains,** really, with an impersonal subject, when one does this, when this happens; **and when he bloweth a trumpet, hear ye.** The signals for the combat having been given, all the people concerned should be watching, for something of great moment will happen. V. 4. **For so the Lord said unto me, I will take My rest, and I will consider in My dwelling-place,** calmly looking on, apparently without the intention of interfering, **like a clear heat upon herbs,** while it is pleasantly warm in the sunlight, **and like a cloud of dew in the heat of harvest,** while the plants, refreshed by the heavy dew of the harvest season, grow to maturity. It seems that the Lord is letting things go on as they please, that He is not actively interested in the affairs of the world; but it only seems so to such as do not know Him. V. 5. **For afore the harvest, when the bud is perfect,** after the blossom has withered, **and the sour grape is ripening in the flower,** while the fruit is slowly maturing, **He shall both cut off the sprigs with pruning-hooks and take away and cut down the branches.** Then the Lord would overthrow their present plans and prevent them from forming any future ones. V. 6. **They shall be left together unto the fowls of the mountains,** the birds of prey feeding on their carcasses, **and to the beasts of the earth,** to the foxes, hyenas, and jackals; **and the fowls shall summer upon them, and all the beasts of the earth shall winter upon them,** finding abundance of food the year around on the field of battle. V. 7. **In that time,** in the Messianic period, **shall the present,** namely, a tribute or sacrificial gift, **be brought unto the Lord of hosts,** the true God, **of a people scattered and peeled and from a people terrible from their beginning hitherto,** cp. v. 2; **a nation meted out and trodden under foot, whose land the rivers have spoiled, to the place of the name of the Lord of hosts, the Mount Zion,** the Church of Jesus Christ. In the very midst of a prophecy describing the punishment meted out by God we have this Messianic promise. The Christian Church gained a foothold in Ethiopia and Abyssinia at a very early date and flourished there for many centuries.

CHAPTER 19.

Prophecies Concerning Egypt.

A THREAT OF DESTRUCTION. — V. 1. **The burden of Egypt**, including both Lower and Upper Egypt: **Behold, the Lord rideth upon a swift cloud**, coming on light clouds as His chariots, in order to pass sentence, **and shall come into Egypt; and the idols of Egypt shall be moved at His presence**, trembling with terror at their approaching fall and doom, **and the heart of Egypt shall melt in the midst of it**, namely, for fear of the impending punishment. Thus the prophet summarizes his entire prophecy upon Egypt. V. 2. **And I will set the Egyptians against the Egyptians**, inciting them to civil war and anarchy such as we are told of by secular historians; **and they shall fight every one against his brother and every one against his neighbor; city against city and kingdom against kingdom.** All this was fulfilled at the beginning of the seventh century before Christ, about the time before Nebuchadnezzar's invasion, when Egypt was divided into twelve kingdoms and into forty-two nomes, or districts, between some of whom there was always dissension, and real peace was not established even after Psammetichus had become sole ruler of the country. V. 3. **And the spirit of Egypt shall fail in the midst thereof**, so that the courage of the Egyptians would, literally, "be emptied out"; **and I will destroy the counsel thereof**, swallowing all their plans, so that the rulers would be helpless in the situation; **and they shall seek to the idols**, appealing to them for help, **and to the charmers**, literally, "the murmurers, or mutterers," those who professed to be in touch with the spirit world, **and to them that have familiar spirits**, the spiritists of those days, **and to the wizards**, those actually in league with the Evil One. Then, as now, people who refused to accept the true God resorted to superstitious rites and to the assistance of the spirits of darkness. V. 4. **And the Egyptians will I give over into the hand of a cruel lord**, the reference being either to one of their own tyrannical rulers or to the Assyrian conquerors; **and a fierce king shall rule over them, saith the Lord, the Lord of hosts.** Three Pharaohs, namely, Psammetichus, Necho, and Hophra, oppressed the Egyptians so severely that the land never recovered from their tyranny. V. 5. **And the waters shall fail from the sea**, the Nile itself being so called on account of its great width at the time of its annual overflow, which, however, would not take place now, **and the river shall be wasted and dried up**, this condition being a calamity for Egypt, since it depended entirely upon irrigation. V. 6. **And they shall turn the rivers far away**, rather, "and the rivers shall produce a stench," being reduced to stagnating pools; **and the brooks of defense shall be emptied and dried up**, that is, the canals of the Nile, especially in its delta and in the irrigation systems, would carry no more water; **the reeds and flags**, principally the papyrus-plants depending altogether upon the moisture of the river, **shall wither.** V. 7. **The paper-reeds by the brooks**, literally, "the naked places," the meadows on the Nile, **by the mouth of the brooks**, along the banks of the river, **and everything sown by the brooks**, the grain-fields along the very edge of the Nile, **shall wither, be driven away**, scattered by the wind in the form of dust, **and be no more.** V. 8. **The fishers also shall mourn**, because they would be thrown out of employment, **and all they that cast angle into the brooks**, that is, the Nile, **shall lament, and they that spread nets upon the waters shall languish**, since the rich fisheries of the Nile would no longer exist. V. 9. **Moreover, they that work in fine flax, and they that weave networks**, white cotton cloth, **shall be confounded**, since neither flax nor cotton would grow, and this important industry would thus be made impossible. V. 10. **And they shall be broken in the purposes thereof, all that make sluices and ponds for fish**, literally, "and shall be her foundations ruins, all laborers for hire swamps of the soul," that is, the upper castes of the nation would lose their power, and the poorest people of the country would give way to hopelessness and despair. V. 11. **Surely the princes of Zoan**, or Tanis, a city of Lower Egypt, at one time the capital of the country, **are fools, the counsel of the wise counselors of Pharaoh is become brutish**, the priestly counselors of the Egyptian king had lost all their wisdom. **How say ye unto Pharaoh, I am the son of the wise, the son of ancient kings?** In spite of the fact that they boasted their descent from wise and ancient counselors, even of royalty, they were unable to offer advice in the present crisis. V. 12. **Where are they? Where are thy wise men? And let them tell thee now**, in a certain prophecy, **and let them know what the Lord of hosts hath purposed upon Egypt.** But the challenge remains unanswered. V. 13. **The princes of Zoan are become fools, the princes of Noph**, of Memphis, on the western bank of the Nile, capital of Lower Egypt, **are deceived; they have also seduced Egypt**, led its people astray by their false claims and foolish counsel, **even they that are the stay of the tribes thereof**, upon whom the people depended for leadership. The explanation for this condition is now given. V. 14. **The Lord hath mingled a perverse spirit in the midst thereof**, for the false wisdom of the leading castes acted like a spirit of intoxication; **and**

they have caused Egypt to err in every work thereof, as a drunken man staggereth in his vomit, unable to find his way out. V. 15. **Neither shall there be any work for Egypt which the head or tail, branch or rush, may do,** that is, no person in Egypt, whether of the ruling or of the serving class, whether lofty or humble, will be able to do anything to stop the general destruction. Such is the effect of the Lord's judgment upon Egypt.

A PROMISE OF BLESSING. — V. 16. **In that day shall Egypt be like unto women,** on account of the greater timidity which usually characterizes the weaker sex; **and it shall be afraid and fear because of the shaking of the hand of the Lord of hosts which He shaketh over it,** His judgments and punishments thus being scattered by means of the invaders of Egypt. V. 17. **And the land of Judah shall be a terror unto Egypt,** either because the mere mention of the name struck terror to their hearts at this time, or because Judah was now allied with Assyria against the king of Egypt, **every one that maketh mention thereof,** namely, of Judah, **shall be afraid in himself because of the counsel of the Lord of hosts which He hath determined against it,** for they all dreaded the punishment which they felt was now inevitable. But in the very midst of the threatened destruction a ray of hope shone upon those who turned to the Lord in true repentance. V. 18. **In that day shall five cities in the land of Egypt speak the language of Canaan,** that is, accept the true, revealed religion, **and swear to the Lord of hosts,** pledging themselves to Him with a sacred oath; **one shall be called The City of Destruction,** literally, "Ir-ha-heres," which may have been the city of the sun, or Heliopolis. The prophecy of Jeremiah, chap. 43, 13, also means to point to the destruction of this or a similar city. V. 19. **In that day shall there be an altar to the Lord in the midst of the land of Egypt, and a pillar at the border thereof,** probably an obelisk, **to the Lord.** The reference is either to the establishment of the religion of Jehovah in Egypt in the second century before Christ, when Alexandria became the center of Egyptian Jewry, or, better still, to the foothold which the Christian religion gained in Egypt at a very early date in the new era. V. 20. **And it shall be for a sign and for a witness unto the Lord of hosts in the land of Egypt,** so that their contemporaries could see the evidence of their worship and their descendants have this proof of their religion; **for they shall cry unto the Lord because of the oppressors, and He shall send them a savior, and a great one, a mighty warrior, and he shall deliver them,** the reference probably being to Alexander the Great, whose coming was a deliverance to Egypt in various ways. V. 21. **And the Lord shall be known to Egypt, and the Egyptians shall know the Lord in that day,** namely, when Jehovah would visit Egypt in mercy and cause the truth to be proclaimed to its people, **and shall do sacrifice and oblation,** perform the acts of true worship to the only God; **yea, they shall vow a vow unto the Lord and perform it,** pledging themselves to Jehovah and His service. V. 22. **And the Lord shall smite Egypt,** in order to bring its people to repentance; **He shall smite and heal it,** for His purpose is always one of mercy; **and they shall return even to the Lord,** His punishment having taken the right effect, **and He shall be intreated of them and shall heal them.** Cp. Lev. 26, 44; Deut. 32, 36. V. 23. **In that day shall there be a highway out of Egypt to Assyria,** permitting free and friendly communication, **and the Assyrian shall come into Egypt and the Egyptian into Assyria, and the Egyptians shall serve with the Assyrians,** proselytes and Jews from both countries meeting at Jerusalem and elsewhere for the worship of Jehovah. V. 24. **In that day shall Israel be the third with Egypt and with Assyria,** the believers of the three countries being joined by the one faith, **even a blessing in the midst of the land,** since blessings would go forth from them to the inhabitants of other countries all over the world; v. 25. **whom the Lord of hosts shall bless, saying, Blessed be Egypt, My people,** admitted to all the spiritual privileges formerly held by Israel alone, **and Assyria, the work of My hands,** His workmanship in the spiritual sense, **and Israel, Mine inheritance,** still designated thus as the actual son of the household of God and head of His family. Altogether, we have here a splendid example of the spread of the true religion under the merciful direction of God, especially in Messianic times.

CHAPTER 20.

The Symbol of Egypt's and Ethiopia's Fall.

V. 1. **In the year that Tartan,** the commander-in-chief of the Assyrian armies, 2 Kings 18, 17, **came unto Ashdod,** one of the cities of Philistia which had revolted against the Assyrian supremacy (**when Sargon, the king of Assyria,** who succeeded Shalmaneser at just about the time when Samaria was taken by the Assyrians, **sent him), and fought against Ashdod, and took it,** in the second last decade of the eighth century before Christ (in 711 B. C., according to the Assyrian annals), v. 2. **at the same time spake**

the Lord by Isaiah, the son of Amoz, in the year when the siege of Ashdod began, **saying, Go and loose the sackcloth,** the loose outer garment of coarse cloth which Isaiah wore, **from off thy loins and put off thy shoe from thy foot. And he did so, walking naked,** that is, with only his tunic or shirtlike garment, **and barefoot,** presenting the appearance of one who had been robbed or spoiled, stripped of his possessions, like a beggar or captive of war. The very dress of Isaiah called attention to his message of repentance. V. 3. **And the Lord said, Like as My servant Isaiah hath walked naked and barefoot three years,** to bring home with great emphasis the lesson which the Lord wished to convey, **for a sign and wonder upon Egypt and upon Ethiopia,** for a portentous type against the double kingdom, v. 4. **so shall the king of Assyria lead away the Egyptians prisoners, and the Ethiopians captives, young and old, naked and barefoot,** as foretold by the symbolic act of Isaiah, **even with their buttocks uncovered,** as a sign of extreme disgrace, 2 Sam. 10, 4. 5, **to the shame of Egypt.** V. 5. **And they,** the inhabitants of Palestine, also the Jews, who looked to Egypt as a possible ally against Assyria, **shall be afraid and ashamed of Ethiopia, their expectation,** finding themselves disappointed in their hopes of help from this quarter, **and of Egypt, their glory,** of whose power they had boasted and on whose strength they had relied. V. 6. **And the inhabitants of this isle,** of the coastal country along the Mediterranean, including Philistia, Phenicia, and the kingdom of Judah, **shall say in that day, Behold, such is our expectation, whither we flee for help to be delivered from the king of Assyria,** that is, such was the lot of those to whom they looked for help and deliverance from the power of Assyria; **and how shall we escape?** The nation which they considered strong and mighty had proved itself powerless against the common enemy; how, then, could the weaker states hope to escape? It is but another instance of the folly of men in placing their trust in the power of flesh and believing that they can escape the Lord.

CHAPTER 21.

Prophecies against Babylon, Edom, and Arabia.

THE ORACLE AGAINST BABYLON. — V. 1. **The burden of the desert of the sea,** the valley and plain of the Euphrates and Tigris, where the Babylonian nation had its home. This country had been alternately a desert and a sea, depending upon the season of the year. Great dikes and levees built by Semiramis had served to control the water and make it available for irrigation purposes, but the razing of these dikes again converted the plain into a swampy sea. Cp. Jer. 51, 13. 36. **As whirlwinds in the south pass through,** coming up with irresistible force, from the deserts of Arabia, **so it cometh from the desert, from a terrible land,** said of the enemy forces which would conquer the land of Babylon. V. 2. **A grievous vision is declared unto me,** one which he could endure and record only with difficulty on account of its importance and consequences; **the treacherous dealer dealeth treacherously,** the enemies of Babylon repaying her in her own coin, by a military stratagem overthrowing her, **and the spoiler spoileth. Go up, O Elam,** a nation bordering on Persia on the west, and often named together with the latter country; **besiege, O Media,** the country which first conquered Babylon; **all the sighing thereof,** namely, that which was caused by the tyrannical Babylon, **have I made to cease,** by giving the victory to her adversaries. V. 3. **Therefore,** on account of the calamities which would come upon Babylon, **are my loins filled with pain,** with trepidation, as in the case of spasms; **pangs have taken hold upon me, as the pangs of a woman that travaileth; I was bowed down at the hearing of it,** writhing in pain; **I was dismayed at the seeing of it,** prevented from seeing at the horror of it all. V. 4. **My heart panted,** beating wildly, **fearfulness affrighted me,** with a terrifying, numbing force; **the night of my pleasure,** the darkness of night, which ordinarily was pleasant to the prophet on account of the bodily rest and the conduciveness to quiet contemplation associated with it, **hath He turned into fear unto me,** namely, on account of the horrible vision connected with it in this instance. V. 5. **Prepare the table, watch in the watch-tower, eat, drink,** the prophet in the spirit witnessing and describing a carousal in Babylon. **Arise, ye princes, and anoint the shield,** to keep it from becoming rusty and to cause strokes of the enemy to glide off. Thus matters were going on in Babylon, and during all this time its destruction was imminent. V. 6. **For thus hath the Lord said unto me, Go, set a watchman, let him declare what he seeth,** this watchman being the prophet's substitute in declaring the vision. V. 7. **And he saw a chariot with a couple of horsemen,** a whole army of mounted soldiers riding two abreast, **a chariot of asses, and a chariot of camels,** the various mounts thus being described, as the enemy rode forward to the attack, their pack-animals remaining behind with the baggage. **And he hearkened diligently with much heed,** with the closest application, his object being to get more information concerning the Persian invaders. V. 8. **And he cried,** in growing impatience, **A lion,** properly, "as a lion," with a lionlike voice, **My lord, I stand continually upon the watch-tower in the daytime, and I am set in my ward whole nights,** in sleepless vigilance, in order to find out about the army which he saw passing on its way to attack the country of Babylon; v. 9. **and, behold,** even while he was voicing his complaint, he makes a discovery, **here cometh a chariot of men, with a couple of horsemen,** a small troop of men riding in pairs. **And he answered and said,** the watchman hearing the triumphant cry even from a distance as the little band rides forword, **Babylon is fallen, is fallen,** the army which had gone down before having been victorious; **and all the graven images of her gods He hath broken unto the ground,** Jehovah Himself having proved His almighty power over against all idolatry. V. 10. **O my threshing and the corn of my floor,** literally, "son of my threshing-floor," the reference being to Israel, as being subject to the severe punishment of Babylon, in which the love of the Lord, however, interferes and guides. **That which I have heard of the Lord of hosts, the God of Israel, have I declared unto you.** Israel, the object of divine punishment, which was administered to him through the exile, is here given the comfort that Jehovah Himself is concerned about His people's welfare and will hold back the wrath in due time.

AGAINST EDOM AND ARABIA. — V. 11. **The burden of Dumah,** that is, Idumea, the land of Edom, the land of the night and stillness of death: **He calleth to me out of Seir,** which is the country of Edom, between the Dead Sea and the Elanitic Gulf of the Red Sea, **Watchman, what of the night?** Is there any hope for the dawn of deliverance? **Watchman, what of the night?** the repetition of the call showing the eagerness of the people of Idumea to be delivered from the night of their calamity which, as the text implies, has now come upon them. V. 12. **The watchman,** that is, the prophet to whom they turned in their affliction, **said, The morning cometh and also the night,** that is, no sooner would the morning dawn than it would be devoured once more by night and destruction; **if ye will enquire, enquire ye,** namely, in vain, as long as they continued in their enmity against the Lord. **Return, come!** For only by being converted to the God of Israel would they escape the threatened misfortune. This prophecy was exactly fulfilled, for Idumea was plunged from one affliction into the next, with barely a dawn of better days to relieve the night. The way of salvation for Edom as for all other people is that of repentance. V. 13. **The burden upon Arabia,** concerning the punishment which would strike this great country of many nomadic tribes: **In the forest in Arabia shall ye lodge,** in the thick undergrowth, or *mesquite,* of the wilderness, as in our own Southwest, **O ye traveling companies of Dedanim,** caravans of the nomadic tribes in the northwestern part of the peninsula. V. 14. **The inhabitants of the land of Tema,** a province with its capital city in this section of Arabia, **brought water to him that was thirsty,** to the fugitives of Dedan; **they prevented with their bread him that fled,** thus anticipating the wants of those who were in need and giving them the food which they needed for their support now that they were fugitives before the enemy. V. 15. **For they fled from the swords,** as the enemy advanced upon Dedan, **from the drawn sword and from the bent bow and from the grievousness of war,** which was rolling over them like a mighty giant. V. 16. **For thus hath the Lord said unto me, Within a year, according to the years of an hireling,** most carefully measured, chap. 16, 14, **and all the glory of Kedar shall fail,** the name here including all the tribes of Arabia, which represented a nation, but only in a loose federation; v. 17. **and the residue of the number of archers,** the remnant of the Arab warriors, noted for their skill with the bow, **the mighty men of the children of Kedar,** celebrated for their warlike nature, **shall be diminished,** only a very few of them remaining; **for the Lord God of Israel hath spoken it.** In His hands are the fortunes of all nations, and His Word is the eternal truth.

CHAPTER 22.

Prophecy Concerning Jerusalem and Some of Its Chief Inhabitants.

THE ORACLE OF THE VALLEY OF VISION. — V. 1. **The burden of the Valley of Vision,** literally, "of the Valley of Visions," that is, Jerusalem, where God vouchsafed revelations and visions in larger number than elsewhere, for which reason Jerome called the city the nursery of prophets: **What aileth thee now,** the people of Jerusalem being addressed here collectively, as one person, **that thou art wholly gone up to the housetops?** the former insolence of the inhabitants having been changed to terror and panic. V. 2. **Thou that art,** rather, "wert," **full of stirs,** of noisy and joyful tumult and excitement, **a tumultuous city, a joyous city,** a fortress filled with jubilating people, **thy slain men are not slain with the sword,** in open and honorable warfare, **nor dead in battle,** rather by the famine and pestilence caused by the siege of the city which the prophet sees before the eyes of his mind. The reference is probably to the time of Sennacherib, when the Assyrians overran the country and a secret understanding with Egypt was being prepared. V. 3. **All thy rulers,** the officers of the Jewish army, **are fled together, they are bound by the archers,** taken captive with ease, because they are without weapons, they do not even draw a bow to defend themselves; **all that are found in thee are bound together, which have fled from far,** having come a long distance to find security in the capital, but sadly disappointed in their hopes. All this fills the prophet with deep grief. V. 4. **Therefore said I, Look away from me,** leaving him alone in his deep mourning; **I will weep bitterly,** literally, "that I may be bitter in my weeping." **Labor not to comfort me,** such attempts being resented by him, **because of the spoiling of the daughter of my people,** since Jerusalem, the daughter of Zion, is so deeply humiliated by the enemy. V. 5. **For it is a day of trouble,** of noisy tumult, **and of treading down, and of perplexity by the Lord God of hosts in the Valley of Vision,** in the entire city of Jerusalem, **breaking down the walls, and of crying to the mountains,** the mournful cries reechoing among the hills. V. 6. **And Elam,** the warriors of the country east of the lower Tigris, later a province of Persia, **bare the quiver with chariots of men and horsemen,** as a part of the Assyrian army, **and Kir,** another country subject to Assyria, between the Caspian and the Black Sea, **uncovered the shield,** by taking off its leather covering in preparation for the battle. Thus the coming of Israel's enemies is described. V. 7. **And it shall come to pass that thy choicest valleys,** the most fruitful sections of Judah, **shall be full of chariots, and the horsemen shall set themselves in array at the gate,** ready to storm the city. Meanwhile the people of the city are aroused to the danger which is threatening them. V. 8. **And He,** the Lord God, **discovered the covering of Judah,** taking from the inhabitants of the country the veil which caused their blindness, **and thou,** Judah, **didst look in that day to the armor of the house of the forest,** examining the weapons stored in the great armory built by Solomon, 1 Kings 7, 2; 10, 17. 21. V. 9. **Ye have seen also the breaches of the City of David,** where the fortifications were in poor condition, **that they are many; and ye gathered together the waters of the lower pool,** getting ready to withstand a siege. Cp. 2 Kings 20, 20; 2 Chron. 32, 3—5. V. 10. **And ye have numbered the houses of Jerusalem,** examining them for purposes of defense, **and the houses have ye broken down to fortify the wall,** repairing the breaches of the walls with the stones from the houses razed with that object in mind. V. 11. **Ye made also a ditch between the two walls,** those of the city proper and of the fortress, **for the water of the old pool,** also known as the upper pool, west of the city, thus making careful provisions for all emergencies, as they thought; **but ye have not looked unto the Maker thereof, neither had respect unto Him that fashioned it long ago;** in their calculations and plans they disregarded the Lord altogether, although it was He at whose command the defenses were originally made and who caused the fountains to flow; it was He also who was preparing a severe punishment upon Jerusalem. V. 12. **And in that day did the Lord God of hosts,** the mighty Commander of the heavenly armies, **call to weeping, and to mourning, and to baldness,** the artificial baldness which was a sign of grief, **and to girding with sackcloth,** urging the people to give evidence of the sorrow and grief of their hearts in this manner; v. 13. **and, behold,** instead of such repentance and mourning, **joy and gladness, slaying oxen, and killing sheep, eating flesh, and drinking wine,** in obstinate and reckless revelry: **Let us eat and drink, for to-morrow we shall die,** such being the invitation with which the sinful Jews urged one another to a shameful disregard of the Lord's call through His faithful prophets. V. 14. **And it was revealed in mine ears by the Lord of hosts,** who, in His word to the prophet, makes Himself known, reveals His will, **Surely this iniquity shall not be purged from you till ye die,** death being the sentence of God upon the wilful sinner, **saith the Lord God of hosts.** The idea of death, eternal death, as a form of punishment, is by no means found only in the New Testament, but is plainly shown in the Old Testament as well.

THE ORACLE AGAINST SHEBNA.—V. 15. **Thus saith the Lord God of hosts,** beginning another oracle with the mention of His majestic title, **Go, get thee unto this treasurer,** the privy councilor, or minister of the interior, in the kingdom, 1 Kings 4, 6; 18, 3, **even unto Shebna, which is over the house,** the present incumbent of the office in the king's palace, **and say,** v. 16. **What hast thou here, and whom hast thou here, that thou hast hewed thee out a sepulcher here,** up in the City of David, **as he that heweth him out a sepulcher on high,** namely, on the height of Zion, **and that graveth an habitation for himself in a rock?** The prophet should inquire what business Shebna had in taking an honor for himself which was highly coveted and accorded by the people only to a man like Jehoiada, 2 Chron. 14, 16, for unusual services to the nation. V. 17. **Behold, the Lord will carry thee away with a mighty captivity,** literally, "will whirl thee out with a whirl as a man," that is, with the force of a strong man, **and will surely cover thee,** taking hold of him, wrapping him up, rolling him together tightly. V. 18. **He will surely violently turn and toss thee like a ball,** all wound together like a ball of string, **into a large country,** into a wide and open prairie; **there shalt thou die, and there the chariots of thy glory shall be the shame of thy lord's house,** that is, the shame which the house of his master would suffer through his fault would be the only thing which would accompany him to the grave. V. 19. **And I will drive thee from thy station,** depose him from his office, **and from thy state,** the high position which Shebna now held, **shall he,** the king who executes the will of the Lord, **pull thee down.** V. 20. **And it shall come to pass in that day,** when Shebna would be deposed, **that I will call My servant Eliakim, the son of Hilkiah,** who may have been the same as Azariah, 1 Chron. 6, 13; v. 21. **and I will clothe him with thy robe and strengthen him with thy girdle,** investing him with the official dress, **and I will commit thy government,** all the authority of his office, **into his hand; and he shall be a father to the inhabitants of Jerusalem and to the house of Judah,** performing the duties of his office in such a way as to have the welfare of all the people in mind always. V. 22. **And the key of the house of David will I lay upon his shoulder,** as an emblem of his power and authority; **so he shall open, and none shall shut; and he shall shut, and none shall open,** his decisions as to admission to the king's palace ordinarily being final. V. 23. **And I will fasten him as a nail in a sure place,** like a peg in the wall where one may hang things, so that they are secure; **and he shall be for a glorious throne to his father's house,** an ornament to his family, just as a fine chair is for a room. V. 24. **And they shall hang upon him all the glory of his father's house,** he being the bearer of the honor for the whole family, **the offspring and the issue,** the offshoots of the family, high and low, **all vessels of small quantity, from the vessels of cups, even to all the vessels of flagons,** the humble and lowly in his relationship, as well as the honorable, receiving their share of the honor laid upon him. The prophecy here takes a contemptuous turn, as the Lord considers these hangers-on who want to share the glory of Eliakim. V. 25. **In that day,** when the judgment would strike also this house, **saith the Lord of hosts, shall the nail that is fastened in the sure place,** this same Eliakim, **be removed and be cut down and fall; and the burden that was upon it,** the entire relationship, **shall be cut off,** losing rank and all its advantages; **for the Lord hath spoken it,** in an admonition which was intended to warn Eliakim, lest he permit such conditions to creep in and thus bring disaster upon himself as well as his relatives. The Lord at all times resisteth the proud, but giveth grace to the humble.

CHAPTER 23.

The Oracle Concerning Tyre.

THE FALL OF TYRE. — V. 1. **The burden of Tyre,** the proud Phenician metropolis, which withstood the attacks of several Assyrian armies and endured a siege of thirteen years by Nebuchadnezzar, but was destroyed by Alexander the Great after a siege of seven months: **Howl, ye ships of Tarshish,** the great merchant vessels of that day, named after the city of Tartessus in Spain with which much of the world's commerce was carried on; **for it,** Tyre, the center of the world's markets, **is laid waste, so that there is no house,** not one of them being left in the city on the mainland after the siege of Nebuchadnezzar, **no entering in,** neither into buildings nor even into the harbor after Alexander had destroyed the city on the island; **from the land of Chittim,** the island of Cyprus, whose capital was Citium, **it is revealed to them,** the sailors and merchants of Tyre, returning from a long voyage, receiving the news of the city's destruction at this, their last landing-place before reaching Phenicia. V. 2. **Be still,** namely, with amazement and horror, **ye inhabitants of the isle,** those of the coast country of Phenicia in general and of New Tyre in particular; **thou whom the merchants of Zidon,** the second great commercial city of Phenicia, **that pass over the sea, have replenished,** both by founding the city and by making it one of the world's chief markets. V. 3. **And by great waters,** by maritime trade and transportation, **the seed of Sihor,** "dark-colored," applied to the Nile, **the harvest of the river,** the products of the rich lowlands of Egypt, **is her revenue,** that with which Tyre traded not only along the Mediterranean coast, but far inland as well; **and she is a mart of nations,** what was gathered in her became profitable merchandise to all nations. V. 4. **Be thou ashamed,** trembling with the disgrace of it all, **O Zidon,** Phenicia in general; **for the sea hath spoken, even the strength of the sea,** the fortress of Tyre, which was located on an island at some distance from the coast, **saying, I travail not nor bring forth children, neither do I nourish up young men nor bring up virgins.** Tyre, bereaved of all her children by war, was like a childless woman. There was nothing but rock and sea left where formerly the rich city had stood. V. 5. **As at the report concerning Egypt,** when the sad news concerning the fall of Tyre shall reach Egypt, **so shall they be sorely pained at**

the report of Tyre, because this meant not only a severe reduction in the trade of Egypt, but also the removal of one of the bulwarks against the enemy. Moreover, those who escaped from Tyre would have to flee to the remote corners of the earth. V. 6. **Pass ye over to Tarshish,** the commercial metropolis of Spain, the colony where the last Phenician ships might be found; **howl, ye inhabitants of the isle,** all those living along the coast of the Mediterranean, the fugitives with the inhabitants, since they all were included in the calamity which had come upon Tyre. V. 7. **Is this your joyous city, whose antiquity is of ancient days?** That was the end of all her proud self-glorification. **Her own feet shall carry her afar off to sojourn,** rather, "whose feet carried her afar to settle," not only over her trade routes, but also in locating colonies in distant countries. The doom of Tyre having been pictured thus, the prophet proceeds to preach the glory of Jehovah. V. 8. **Who hath taken this counsel against Tyre, the crowning city,** which dispensed crowns to the rulers of its colonies, **whose merchants are princes, whose traffickers are the honorable of the earth?** The wealth of these men, together with their connections in distant lands, gave them a position of power and influence like that of rulers. V. 9. **The Lord of hosts hath purposed it,** He who has the fortunes of all men in His hands, **to stain the pride of all glory,** to profane, to bring shame upon that which the Tyrians wrongfully elevated, **and to bring into contempt all the honorable of the earth,** so that both they and their temples and idols would be disgraced and humiliated. The result is that the colonies gain their independence. V. 10. **Pass through thy land as a river,** overflowing it like the Nile, without interference and hindrance from fallen Tyre, **O daughter of Tarshish,** the Spanish colony of Tyre; **there is no more strength,** literally, "not is there any more a dam." The fate of Tyre is now further described for the benefit of the colonies: v. 11. **He, Jehovah, stretched out His hand over the sea,** as the One who has absolute power over all the forces of nature; **He shook the kingdoms,** putting them in commotion to carry out His plans. **The Lord hath given a commandment against the merchant city,** literally, "against Canaan," which here designates Phenicia only, **to destroy the strongholds thereof,** chiefly the bulwarks of Tyre. V. 12. **And He said, Thou shalt no more rejoice, O thou oppressed virgin, daughter of Zidon,** Tyre and all Phenicia being disgraced now as a result of the conquest. **Arise, pass over to Chittim,** emigrating to Cyprus, since the home country was in the hands of the enemies; **there also shalt thou have no rest,** for the colony would not welcome the former oppressors. V. 13. **Behold the land of the Chaldeans,** whence the destroyers came; **this people was not,** who at first did not figure in history, **till the Assyrian founded it for them that dwell in the wilderness,** for a section of the Assyrian empire had at first been assigned to them for settlement; **they set up the towers thereof,** that is, the Babylonians erected their siege-towers against Tyre, **they raised up the palaces thereof,** rather, "utterly destroyed its castles"; **and he brought it to ruin,** its bulwarks were overthrown. V. 14. **Howl, ye ships of Tarshish; for your strength is laid waste.** Cp. v. 1. Thus the Lord punishes those who exalt themselves and are proud in their idolatrous hearts.

THE RESTORATION OF TYRE. — V. 15. **And it shall come to pass in that day,** at the time when this prophecy would be fulfilled, **that Tyre shall be forgotten seventy years,** the length of the Chaldean supremacy, **according to the days of one king,** the reference to this period being as of a time during which the lot of Tyre will be uniformly bad. **After the end of seventy years shall Tyre sing as an harlot,** the fate of Tyre will be according to the song of the harlot, a portion of which is now quoted: v. 16. **Take an harp,** or zither, **go about the city, thou harlot that hast been forgotten; make sweet melody,** with pleasant playing, **sing many songs that thou mayest be remembered,** the trade of Tyre being compared with the business of a harlot because both serve mammon and, in part, the lowest desires of the flesh. The methods of Tyre are now represented as having success. V. 17. **And it shall come to pass after the end of seventy years that the Lord will visit Tyre,** in mercy, to give her another opportunity to repent, **and she shall turn to her hire,** the gain of her trade being compared to the price of prostitution, **and shall commit fornication with all the kingdoms of the world upon the face of the earth,** because she would court merchants from all nations and admit any one for the sake of gain. V. 18. **And her merchandise and her hire shall be holiness to the Lord,** by a disposition of God of which probably many of the Tyrians were not aware; **it shall not be treasured nor laid up,** concealed for her own use; **for her merchandise shall be for them that dwell before the Lord,** His disciples, **to eat sufficiently, and for durable clothing,** to be taken care of in the proper manner, with changes of raiment according to the custom of the time. There seems to be no doubt that this prophecy refers to the Christian era. We know that Jesus visited the neighborhood of Tyre, Matt. 15, 21, that Paul found disciples there, Acts 21, 3—6, that it afterward was a powerful Christian bishopric, its cathedral being one of the most splendid of the early days. Other phases of the prophecy concerning Tyre are given by other prophets.

CHAPTER 24.

The Judgment upon the Earth.

The four chapters, 24 to 27 inclusive, form one continuous poetical prophecy, remarkable both for form and for content. It is a great chorus in four movements, describing the end of the world, the revelation of Jehovah, the establishment of the Church of Christ, and the glorious growth of the communion of saints. This chorus embraces every form and style of poetry, from the most elevated heavenly hymn to the most simple and appealing folk-song. "This entire *finale* is a great hallelujah to chapters 13 to 23, its contents hymnic, its form musical, and this to such a degree that, as in chap. 25, 6, the prophecy is like text and score together. Only Isaiah is such an incomparable master of language." (Delitzsch.)

THE DESTRUCTION OF THE SURFACE OF THE EARTH. — V. 1. **Behold, the Lord maketh the earth empty,** depopulating it, taking away its inhabitants, **and maketh it waste,** by a final devastation, **and turneth it upside down,** changing its form and appearance, **and scattereth abroad the inhabitants thereof,** thereby making it desolate. V. 2. **And it shall be, as with the people, so with the priest,** all sharing the same calamities alike; **as with the servant, so with his master; as with the maid, so with her mistress; as with the buyer, so with the seller; as with the lender, so with the borrower; as with the taker of usury,** the creditor, **so with the giver of usury to him,** the debtor. They are alike in the midst of this great catastrophe; no favored class shall escape. V. 3. **The land shall be utterly emptied,** made altogether desolate, **and utterly spoiled,** consumed by plundering; **for the Lord hath spoken this word,** and according to His word things would come to pass. V. 4. **The earth mourneth and fadeth away,** like a flower that is stepped upon and wilted, **the world languisheth and fadeth away; the haughty people of the earth,** the most prominent persons, **do languish,** in utter despair. V. 5. **The earth also is defiled under the inhabitants thereof,** affected with the blood-guiltiness of its inhabitants, **because they have transgressed the laws, changed the ordinance, broken the everlasting covenant,** that is, men disregarded the revelation of God in the works of creation, ignored the admonitions of conscience, set aside the agreement made at the time of Noah: all mankind has returned to the baseness of the time before the Flood. V. 6. **Therefore hath the curse devoured the earth,** with the fire of the divine wrath, **and they that dwell therein are desolate,** compelled to do the most bitter penance; **therefore the inhabitants of the earth are burned and few men left,** namely, the small remnant of those who are true to Jehovah. V. 7. **The new wine mourneth,** the grape-juice as extracted from the fruit becoming vapid, **the vine languisheth,** because there is none to cultivate it, **all the merry-hearted do sigh.** V. 8. **The mirth of tabrets,** or tambourines, used to accompany merry songs, **ceaseth, the noise of them that rejoice endeth, the joy of the harp,** or zither, **ceaseth.** V. 9. **They shall not drink wine with a song,** as in the days of peace and prosperity; **strong drink,** date-wine or a brandylike liquor, **shall be bitter to them that drink it.** All the former incentives to joy are removed, and utter desolation prevails. The world with her lust is judged and therefore also the leading city of the world, in which this lust was concentrated. V. 10. **The city of confusion is broken down,** there is nothing but ruin and desolation; **every house is shut up that no man may come in,** the entrance being choked up by ruins; everything is chaos. V. 11. **There is a crying for wine in the streets,** lamentation on account of the destruction of vineyards out in the fields; **all joy is darkened, the mirth of the land is gone.** V. 12. **In the city is left desolation,** only chaos and ruin to be found there, **and the gate is smitten with destruction,** battered down. Cp. Matt. 24, 6—8; Mark 13, 7. 8; Luke 21, 9—11.

THE DESTRUCTION OF THE MASS OF THE EARTH. — V. 13. **When thus it shall be in the midst of the land among the people,** as described in the first part of the chapter, **there shall be as the shaking of an olive-tree,** when the few olives remaining at the close of the harvest are struck down with a stick, **and as the gleaning grapes when the vintage is done,** for only a small remnant, the true children of God, would be left. V. 14. **They shall lift up their voice,** namely, those who are delivered in the general destruction, **they shall sing for the majesty of the Lord,** by whose glorious power they have been preserved, **they shall cry aloud from the sea,** from the Mediterranean, as the western body of water, the cry of the believers thus going forth toward the East and toward the West. V. 15. **Wherefore glorify ye the Lord,** so the song of the redeemed reads, **in the fires,** in the countries of light, in the Eastern countries, **even the name of the Lord God of Israel in the isles of the sea,** in the Western countries. The meaning is: "Whereever ye be scattered, whether in the far East or in the remote West, glorify the Lord." This urgent invitation is not issued in vain. V. 16. **From the uttermost part of the earth have we heard songs,** all the believers joining in the praise of Jehovah, **even glory to the Righteous,** literally, "Praise to the Just!" **But I said,** the prophet cried out in remembering the afflictions of the final Judgment, **My leanness, my leanness, woe unto me!** for he felt his powers wasting away as the result of the extraordinary terror taking hold upon him. **The treacherous dealers have dealt treacherously; yea, the treacherous dealers have dealt very treacherously.** He saw perfidy and faithlessness exercised on every hand, and in the highest degree. V. 17. **Fear and the pit and the snare are upon thee, O inhabitant of the earth.** The Hebrew text here has an alliteration by means of which the very sound of the words conveys the dreadfulness of the judgment. V. 18. **And it shall come to pass that he who fleeth from the noise of the fear,** the shouting which produces terror, **shall fall into the pit,** forgetting all caution under the influence of a blind fear, **and he that cometh up out of the midst of the pit,** scrambling out of its confining depth, **shall be taken in the snare,** all chances for escape thus being cut off; **for the windows from on high are open,** through which the Lord's instruments of punishment are sent down to the earth, **and the foundations of the earth do shake,** its very supports tottering and preparing to fall. V. 19. **The earth is utterly broken down,** deep gashes appear on its surface, **the earth is clean dissolved,** burst open, **the earth is moved exceedingly,** shaken to pieces. The picture shows the earth with deep clefts, which quickly widen down to its innermost recesses, until finally the whole fabric collapses. V. 20. **The earth shall reel to and fro like a drunkard and shall be removed like a cottage,** it swings back and forth like a hammock; **and the transgression thereof,** which has caused this punishment to come upon the earth, **shall be heavy upon it,** pressing her down to the ground; **and it shall fall and not rise again,** the total destruction of the earth in its present form being pictured. V. 21. **And it shall come to pass in that day,** at the time of the final Judgment, **that the Lord shall punish the host of the high ones that are on high and the kings of the earth upon the earth,** the angels being regarded as presiding over the kingdoms of the world and being held responsible for the manner in which matters are taken care of on earth. Cp. 1 Cor. 6, 3. V. 22. **And they shall be gathered together as prisoners are gathered in the pit, and shall be shut up in the prison,** 2 Pet. 2, 4; Jude 6; Rev. 20, 1—3; **and after many days shall they be visited,** for the final punishment which would then be carried out upon them. V. 23. **Then the moon shall be confounded,** covering her face in shame, **and the sun ashamed,** shrinking back in disgrace, **when the Lord of hosts shall reign in Mount Zion and in Jerusalem,** in the final great victory over all His enemies, **and before His ancients gloriously,** the leaders of the believers, together with the entire Church of the saints, partaking of His eternal glory in heaven, Rev. 21, 23; 22, 5.

CHAPTER 25.

A Song of Salvation and Triumph.

THANKSGIVING FOR GOD'S BENEFITS. — V. 1. **O Lord, Thou art my God,** the God of the covenant, the God of salvation, Cp. Ps. 31, 15; 40, 6; 143, 10. **I will exalt Thee,** in songs of thanksgiving, **I will praise Thy name,** as the revelation of His wonderful essence; **for Thou hast done wonderful things, Thy counsels of old,** those pertaining to the deliverance of His people, **are faithfulness and truth;** for the Lord has kept, and is keeping, His promises concerning the redemption of mankind. V. 2. **For Thou hast made of a city an heap,** laid the wicked world city in ruins, **of a defensed city a ruin,** as described in the preceding chapter, **a palace of strangers to be no city,** the fortifications, the citadels being used for the entire city; **it shall never be built.** V. 3. **Therefore shall the strong people glorify Thee,** men of various nations being brought to the knowledge of Jehovah, **the city of the terrible nations,** despots and tyrants, **shall fear Thee,** Gentiles everywhere coming to the knowledge of the true God. V. 4. **For Thou hast been a strength to the poor,** Matt. 5, 3, **a strength to the needy in his distress, a refuge from the storm,** so that its fury could do no harm, **a shadow from the heat,** that of various afflictions caused by the hostility of men, **when the blast of the terrible ones is as a storm against the wall,** for thus the furious snorting and raging of the violent enemies appears. V. 5. **Thou shalt bring down the noise of strangers, as the heat in a dry place, even the heat with the shadow of a cloud; the branch of the terrible ones shall be brought low,** literally, "As the burning of the sun in a dry land Thou didst suppress the raging of the barbarians, as the burning of the sun by a shadow of a cloud the triumphant song of violent ones must cease"; that is, Just as Jehovah causes the glowing heat of the sun to be cut off by a sheltering bank of clouds, so He is able to quell instantaneously all the raging and the triumph of hosts of enemies. V. 6. **And in this mountain,** the spiritual Zion, as the dwelling-place of Jehovah in the midst of His people, **shall the Lord of hosts make unto all people,** all the inhabitants of the earth being included in His gracious will, **a feast of fat things,** of the richest foods, **a feast of wines on the lees,** left on the lees to increase its strength, **of fat things full of marrow,** rich in strength-building properties, **of wines on the lees well refined,** properly drawn and filtered. The entire verse, in the Hebrew, is a most poetical and musical song, full of praises for the richness of God's grace in the spiritual food prepared for His children in the Gospel. V. 7. **And He will destroy in this mountain,** the habitation of His holy Church, **the face of the covering cast over all people and the veil that is spread over all nations,** namely, that of their spiritual blindness, brought upon them by their own natural depravity. Cp. 2 Cor. 3, 15. V. 8. **He will swallow up death in victory,** completely abolish it with all its power, 2 Tim. 1, 10; Rev. 20, 14; **and the Lord God will wipe away tears from off all faces,** Rev. 21, 4; **and the rebuke of His people shall He take away from off all the earth,** thus removing the cause of all troubles with which men are suffering; **for the Lord hath spoken it.** In this manner the final victory of the Church is pictured, the happy perfection of all the saints in the glory of heaven. Cp. 1 Cor. 15, 28. 54. After the final victory over death the people of God, delivered from its power, will praise the Lord throughout eternity.

PRAISE FOR THE SUBJECTION OF MOAB. — V. 9. **And it shall be said in that day,** namely, the day of final deliverance, at the end of time, **Lo, this is our God,** He upon whom we can place our confidence in unwavering certainty; **we have waited for Him, and He will save us,** they depended upon Him to save them and were not disappointed. **This is the Lord; we have waited for Him; we will be glad and rejoice in His salvation,** which the believers will experience and enjoy at that time. V. 10. **For in this mountain shall the hand of the Lord rest,** not only to protect Zion, His Church, but also to effect her revenge, **and Moab,** representing the sneering enemies of the Church, **shall be trodden down under Him, even as straw is trodden down for the dunghill,** to be saturated and rotted by the water of the dung-pit. V. 11. **And he shall spread forth his hands in the midst of them,** Moab, representing the hostile forces of the world, trying to save himself by a desperate struggle, **as he that swimmeth spreadeth forth his hands to swim,** in an unavailing effort. **And He,** Jehovah, **shall bring down their pride together with the spoils of their hands,** in spite of all artful attempts of Moab to effect his own deliverance. V. 12. **And the fortress of the high fort of thy walls,** the strongholds of Moab, **shall He bring down,** utterly overthrowing them, **lay low, and bring to the ground, even to the dust.** Thus all the enemies of the Lord will finally be destroyed with the everlasting destruction of the wrath of the just God, while the city of God, the congregation of believers, will triumph with Him in all eternity.

CHAPTER 26.

Israel's Final Song of Deliverance.

THE CHURCH'S SONG OF PRAISE. — V. 1. **In that day,** at the time of the final deliverance of the ransomed of God, **shall this song be sung in the land of Judah,** by the believers who have been preserved by the power of the Lord: **We have a strong city,** namely, the city of God, Ps. 46, 4, His holy Church; **salvation will God appoint for walls and bulwarks,** His redemption is established as a strong wall of exterior and interior defense, so that no enemy is able to penetrate inside and take away the blessings of the redeemed. V. 2. **Open ye the gates,** so the cry sounds down from the heavenly host, **that the righteous nation which keepeth the truth,** which was faithful to the Lord and His Word to the end, **may enter in.** All those who keep the covenant of faith are welcomed in the heavenly mansions. V. 3. **Thou,** namely, Jehovah, **wilt keep him in perfect peace whose mind is stayed on Thee,** the peace of God which passeth all understanding resting upon all those who belong to the spiritual Israel and cling to Him in true faith, **because he trusteth in Thee;** and the Lord rewards such trust with a double measure of peace. V. 4. **Trust ye in the Lord forever,** thus the chorus from heaven once more admonishes; **for in the Lord JEHOVAH,** the God of salvation, **is everlasting strength,** He is the Rock of Ages, whose strength overcomes all enemies; v. 5. **for He bringeth down them that dwell on high,** casting down even the world-powers which presume to oppose Him; **the lofty city,** representing the wickedness of the unbelievers everywhere, **He layeth it low,** as shown in chapter 21; **He layeth it low, even to the ground; He bringeth it even to the dust,** chap. 25, 12. V. 6. **The foot shall tread it down, even the feet of the poor, and the steps of the needy,** the very ones who formerly were trodden down by the tyrants of this world. V. 7. **The way of the just is uprightness,** that being the basis of his entire conduct; **Thou, Most Upright,** namely, God, **dost weigh the path of the just,** literally, "dost roll his path," thereby making it possible for him to conduct himself uprightly. Thus all glory for the believer's life of sanctification is given to God alone. V. 8. **Yea, in the way of Thy judgments,** so the new strophe of the hymn begins, **O Lord, have we waited for Thee,** expecting Him to give proof of His justice over against all enemies; **the desire of our soul is to Thy name and to the remembrance of Thee,** namely, that He would reveal Himself in a deed which would cause men to call Him by His right name and to spread the right knowledge of Him. So deeply does this matter affect the prophet that he continues his hymn in the name of every individual believer. V. 9. **With my soul have I desired Thee in the night,** in the time of affliction, which deprived him of rest; **yea, with my spirit within me will I seek Thee early,** confident that the morning would bring a happy deliverance; **for when Thy judgments are in the earth,** His punishments being intended to call sinners to repentance, **the inhabitants of the world will learn righteousness,** that conduct which is in agreement with the Word of God, the life of sanctification. Only the enemies of God, by a deliberate rejection of His grace, are excluded from this course. V. 10. **Let favor be showed to the wicked, yet will he not learn righteousness,** a righteous, God-pleasing conduct; **in the land of uprightness,** where everything is done in harmony with the will of God, **will he deal unjustly,** being in no way in sympathy with the ideals of the just and good, **and will not behold the majesty of the Lord,** namely, in consequence of his wilful rejection of God's grace, on account of the perversity of his mind, which despises the goodness of God. If a man is lost, he has only himself to blame.

CONCLUDING SCENES FROM THE WORLD'S HISTORY.—V. 11. **Lord, when Thy hand is lifted up,** to punish the foes of His people, **they will not see,** they deliberately close their eyes against the manifestation of His majesty; **but they shall see and be ashamed for their envy at the people,** heaped with disgrace as they see the zeal of Jehovah for His people; **yea, the fire of Thine enemies shall devour them,** rather, "fire will devour Thine adversaries." That is the judgment of God upon the wicked, by which they would be both surprised and confused. V. 12. **Lord, Thou wilt ordain peace for us,** firmly establishing the condition of peace in the midst of His congregation; **for Thou also hast wrought all our works in us,** the believers' life of sanctification being a gift of the Lord and therefore acceptable in His sight. V. 13. **O Lord, our God, other lords beside Thee have had dominion over us,** for various despots of the world attempt time and again to tyrannize the believers; **but by Thee only will we make mention of Thy name,** for Jehovah has overthrown the tyrants and enabled His children to worship Him as their Lord. V. 14. **They,** the enemies, **are dead, they shall not live,** they cannot return to their former power; **they are deceased, they shall not rise,** the enemies of God cannot hope to be delivered from the everlasting destruction to which they are condemned; **therefore hast Thou visited and destroyed them and made all their memory to perish.** That is the lot of the Lord's adversaries. Over against that we have the blessings which He sends upon His own people. V. 15. **Thou hast increased the nation, O Lord, Thou hast increased the nation,** for the Lord causes the number of His children to grow; **Thou art glorified,** by this act of mercy; **Thou hadst removed it far unto all the ends of the earth,** for thus far the Church of God, by His own promise, is to be extended. V. 16. **Lord, in trouble have they visited Thee,** thus the prophet once more cries out with reference to the night of affliction; **they poured out a prayer,** all the more fervent because it is made in secret, **when Thy chastening was upon them,** rendering them almost speechless with its severity. This is true to this day with regard to the consciousness of sin with its depressing effects. V. 17. **Like as a woman with child that draweth near the time of her delivery is in pain and crieth out in her pangs, so have we been in Thy sight, O Lord.** The more unendurable the affliction seemed, the nearer was the time of deliverance. V. 18. **We have been with child, we have been in pain, we have,** as it were, **brought forth wind,** this being ever the result of man's sinfulness, of his life without God, which is all vanity; **we have not wrought any deliverance in the earth,** for by their own reason and strength men cannot produce salvation; **neither have the inhabitants of the world fallen,** literally, "no inhabitants of the world will drop," that is, no new spiritual births can be brought out by the efforts of men, without the power of God. But in the hand of the Lord the matter assumes a different aspect: v. 19. **Thy dead men shall live,** by the power of God's mercy; **together with my dead body shall they arise,** delivered by the might of God. **Awake and sing, ye that dwell in dust; for Thy dew is as the dew of herbs,** the divine glory imparting its heavenly power to the moldering dust of men, **and the earth shall cast out the dead.** The earth is forced to give up its victims, and the awakened believers join the number of those who are living the true life of the Spirit by the power of God. V. 20. **Come, my people, enter thou into thy chambers,** hiding while God takes vengeance upon the ungodly, **and shut thy doors about thee,** to be secure from disturbance; **hide thyself, as it were, for a little moment, until the indignation be overpast,** until the judgment of God has gone forth upon His enemies. V. 21. **For, behold, the Lord cometh out of His place to punish the inhabitants of the earth for their iniquity; the earth also shall disclose her blood,** reveal the murders committed, **and shall no more cover her slain,** everything being laid open before the eyes of the Judge of the world. Thus the chapter shows the deliverance and the resurrection of the believers in the midst of the judgment pronounced and carried out upon the ungodly.

CHAPTER 27.

The Care of the Lord for His Vineyard.

The Downfall of the Worldly Powers. — V. 1. **In that day,** at the time when God's judgments will be carried out upon the world, **the Lord with His sore and great and strong sword,** His well-tempered, powerful, and irresistible weapon, **shall punish leviathan, the piercing serpent,** the fleeing dragon, **even leviathan, that crooked serpent,** whose mighty coils threaten to crush everything they enfold; **and He shall slay the dragon that is in the sea,** the reference being to the three great world-powers, Assyria, along the Tigris, Babylonia, along the Euphrates, and Egypt, representing all the forces which are hostile to the Lord and His people. V. 2. **In that day sing ye unto her,** the Church of God, **A vineyard of red wine,** literally, "A desirable vineyard — sing [antiphonally] to it!" V. 3. **I, the Lord, do keep it,** as the almighty Watchman; **I will water it every moment,** thus combining watchful with loving care; **lest any hurt it, I will keep it night and day,** so that no enemy may attack and harm it. V. 4. **Fury is not in Me,** the Lord feels nothing but the most sincere love for His Church; **who would set the briers and thorns against Me in battle?** literally, "Would that were given Me, that I had before Me, thorns and briers in battle!" the reference being to His warfare against the wicked of the world. **I would go through them, I would burn them together,** with martial impetuosity the Lord would stride in against them and destroy them. V. 5. **Or let him take hold of My strength,** let him make his peace with God, the only alternative by which the wicked may escape the threatened punishment, **that he may make peace with Me; and he shall make peace with Me.** To take refuge with God and make peace with Him is the only advisable course for all those who have ever opposed Him. The prophet now adds to this song, as an explanation for the sake of his readers: v. 6. **He shall cause them that come of Jacob to take root,** literally, "In the coming days Jacob shall take root," the Church of God being established. **Israel shall blossom and bud,** the believers being active in good works, **and fill the face of the world with fruit,** Rom. 11, 12. The believers of all times are rich in good works, to the glory of God.

The Gathering of the Church. — V. 7. **Hath He,** Jehovah, in His visitation of mercy, **smitten him,** Israel, His people, **as He smote those that smote him?** literally, "with the stroke of his smiter," after the manner of the enemies who vented their spite upon Israel, **or is he slain according to the slaughter of them that are slain by him?** V. 8. **In measure, when it shooteth forth, Thou wilt debate with it,** literally, "in a small measure [that of a *seah*], by sending her away, Thou punishest her," the reference being to Israel's exile; **He stayeth His rough wind in the day of the east wind,** literally, "He breathes with His rough breath on the day of the east wind"; that is, the Lord, at the time of the captivity, sent His breath with great force to purify the country. Not the destruction of Israel, but its salvation, was intended. V. 9. **By this, therefore,** by the punishment of the exile, **shall the iniquity of Jacob be purged,** his guilt expiated, purification brought about; **and this is all the fruit to take away his sin,** the punishment, if properly effective, shall have the following result: **when he maketh all the stones of the altar as chalk-stones that are beaten in sunder, the groves and images shall not stand up,** really, "so that the places of Ashtoreth and the images of the sun shall not rise again." Israel is shown the condition under which it will be acceptable to God. By dashing to pieces the stones of their idolatrous altars and destroying both the idols and their pedestals, the people of the land will give evidence of the fruit of the expiation that has been rendered and of the forgiveness that has been received. All this is stated in emphatic contrast to the fate which overcame the city of wickedness, the representative of hostility against God. V. 10. **Yet the defensed city,** the center of worldly power, **shall be desolate and the habitation forsaken and left like a wilderness,** without inhabitants; **there shall the calf feed, and there shall he lie down, and consume the branches thereof,** the foliage of the bushes covering the ruined city. V. 11. **When the boughs thereof are withered, they shall be broken off,** the twigs of the dry shrubs falling off; **the women come and set them on fire,** gathering them for fuel; **for it is a people of no understanding,** namely, of the ways of God, that is why this desolation comes upon them. **Therefore He that made them will not have mercy on them, and He that formed them will show them no favor.** All who oppose Him are His enemies and are treated accordingly. V. 12. **And it shall come to pass in that day that the Lord shall beat off,** as the harvester does the sheaves with a flail, **from the channel of the river unto the stream of Egypt,** from the Euphrates to the brook on the boundary of Egypt now known as the Wadi el-Arish, **and ye shall be gathered one by one, O ye children of Israel,** as the result of such harvesting, the picture being taken from the land of Canaan and the deliverance of the children of Israel. V. 13.

And it shall come to pass in that day that the great trumpet shall be blown, the signal of the final Judgment, **and they shall come which were ready to perish in the land of Assyria,** here representing all the hostile forces of the world, **and the outcasts in the land of Egypt,** just as the Lord says, Matt. 8, 11, **and shall worship the Lord in the holy mount at Jerusalem.** Israel's return from exile is a type of the restoration of all the redeemed and their inheritance of the heavenly home.

CHAPTER 28.

Concerning Samaria and Jerusalem.

Chapters 28 to 33 in the Book of Isaiah contain a cycle of prophecies and proclamations concerning the relation of Judah to Assyria in the time of King Hezekiah. Ahaz had sinned in seeking protection against Syria and Israel not in the Lord, but in Assyria, thereby making Assyria a scourge of Judah. Hezekiah, otherwise a pious king, erred in seeking protection against Assyria by appealing to Egypt and entering into an alliance with this heathen nation. All this is described at length in these chapters and the planning and scheming without the Lord condemned. At the same time, like flashes of sunlight on a dark day, Messianic promises are found in the midst of the gloomy denunciations of the prophet.

THE LORD REBUKES AND COMFORTS. — V. 1. **Woe to the crown of pride, to the drunkards of Ephraim,** that upon which they prided themselves in their contempt of the Lord, **whose glorious beauty,** like that of a wreath or garland put on during a drunken feast, **is a fading flower, which are,** rather, which is, for the reference is to the crown or garland worn by the drunken fools of Samaria, **on the head of the fat valleys of them that are overcome with wine.** The picture is that of Samaria, the capital of the Northern Kingdom, situated on a beautiful hill, surrounded with rich, terraced valleys like wreaths, but with its leaders slaves of wine, overcome by the vice of drunkenness. The picture is purposely painted dark, as a warning to the inhabitants of the Southern Kingdom. V. 2. **Behold, the Lord hath a mighty and strong one,** namely, the Assyrian conqueror, **which as a tempest of hail and a destroying storm,** a shower of destruction, **as a flood of mighty waters overflowing, shall cast down to the earth with the hand,** overthrowing boastful Ephraim with its proud capital, Samaria. V. 3. **The crown of pride, the drunkards of Ephraim,** the wreath which the drunkards of Ephraim, the rulers of the Northern Kingdom, wear with such arrogant haughtiness, **shall be trodden under feet;** v. 4. **and the glorious beauty, which is on the head of the fat valley, shall be a fading flower, and as the hasty fruit before the summer,** that is, it will happen to the fading flower of Ephraim's beauty, which is on the head of the fertile valley, as it does to the early fig, **which, when he that looketh upon it seeth, while it is yet in his hand,** just as soon as he has gotten hold of it, **he eateth it up.** The ruin of Samaria took place in hardly more than four or five years, and there was as yet no intimation of its destruction when the prophet wrote these words. But the reference to the overthrow of the false glory of Samaria leads to the mention of the divine, the Messianic beauty. V. 5. **In that day,** with the dawn of the Messianic era, **shall the Lord of hosts be for a crown of glory and for a diadem of beauty unto the residue of His people,** namely, to the believers of the true Israel, especially in the New Testament, the small number from all nations and peoples who accept the Messiah, v. 6. **and for a spirit of judgment to him that sitteth in judgment,** to have righteousness and justice prevailing throughout the land, **and for strength to them that turn the battle to the gate,** both in repelling an attack of the enemies and in directing the battle against the stronghold of the adversaries. The believers have power both to withstand the evil and to wage an offensive war against those who are its exponents. After this beautiful interlude the Lord turns to the people of Judah with a similar earnest warning. V. 7. **But they also have erred through wine,** the rulers of Judah being addicted to the same vice as those of Samaria, **and through strong drink are out of the way,** reeling and staggering in their drunkenness; **the priest,** to whom the use of intoxicating liquors was strictly forbidden, **and the prophet have erred through strong drink,** cp. Lev. 10, 9; Ezek. 44, 21, **they are swallowed up of wine,** altogether overcome by the vice, **they are out of the way through strong drink; they err in vision,** at the very time when they should be under the influence of the Spirit of God alone, **they stumble in judgment,** their befuddled minds causing them to make wrong applications and interpretations of the Law. V. 8. **For all tables are full of vomit and filthiness,** the result of their beastly drunkenness, **so that there is no place clean.** The prophet paints the picture of their besottedness before the eyes of these leaders of the people, in order to hold the filth of their vice up before them as in a mirror. He now introduces the drunken adversaries in person, with all their scoffing comment of his warnings. V. 9. **Whom shall he teach knowledge?** so they sneeringly ask. **And whom shall he make**

to understand doctrine? presuming to teach them knowledge. **Them that are weaned from the milk and drawn from the breasts.** They would have him know that they are no unweaned children, and that they are tired of his schoolmastery ways. They now try to heap ridicule and mockery upon him by stammering about his endless preaching and dinning in their ears. V. 10. **For precept must be upon precept, precept upon precept; line upon line, line upon line,** that is, rule upon rule; **here a little and there a little,** the gist of their attempted reproach being that the prophet was wearying their souls with a mass of little rules and precepts, directions and warnings in wearisome repetition, and without a right plan and order. V. 11. **For with stammering lips and another tongue will He,** namely, Jehovah, **speak to this people,** namely, by a foreign and hostile people, whose language would indeed seem strange and barbarous to them, the Assyrian invaders. V. 12. **To whom He said,** or, "He who said to them," **This is the rest wherewith ye may cause the weary to rest,** for that is what the Lord in His Word offers to weary souls longing for salvation; **and this is the refreshing; yet they would not hear,** they despised and rejected the Word of the Lord. V. 13. **But the Word of the Lord was unto them,** that is, it shall now truly be, **precept upon precept, precept upon precept; line upon line, line upon line; here a little and there a little,** namely, in stammering sounds and a tedious repetition which would come upon them as a judgment from on high, **that they might go,** unwilling though it may be, **and fall backward and be broken and snared and taken,** snared and captured by the enemy. Thus many a person, who in our days is sneering at the Word of God as an endless repetition of a jumble of rules and orders of life, will find himself judged and condemned to an eternity of damnation by that very Word; for "he that believeth not shall be damned."

THE FALSE AND THE TRUE REFUGE. — V. 14. **Wherefore hear the word of the Lord, ye scornful men,** those who despised and mocked the prophet's warning, **that rule this people which is in Jerusalem,** the capital being named for the entire Southern Kingdom. V. 15. **Because ye have said,** in some further mockery which is now recorded, **We have made a covenant with death,** confident that death itself could not harm them, **and with hell,** the realm of the dead, **are we at agreement,** hoping to be safe against its power on account of their alliance with Egypt; **when the overflowing scourge,** the Assyrian army, **shall pass through, it shall not come unto us, for we have made lies our refuge, and under falsehood have we hid ourselves,** concealing their real intention and purposes by the use of cunning policy, of fine diplomacy, the same procedure being found in all unbelievers to this day: v. 16. **therefore thus saith the Lord God,** in another beautiful statement concerning the true foundation of the believer's trust, **Behold, I lay in Zion for a foundation,** as the Rock upon which His Church is firmly founded, **a Stone, a tried Stone,** one who is Himself approved, and by whom the hearts of all men are tested, **a precious Corner-stone,** one laid where two walls meet, which serves to connect them firmly, **a sure Foundation,** literally, "a Corner-stone of preciousness and a founded Foundation," to emphasize the solidity of this foundation. **He that believeth shall not make haste,** he who relies on Him shall not be confounded or flee in hasty alarm, for this Cornerstone is Jesus Christ Himself, the Rock of Ages for His Church. Cp. Matt. 21, 42; Acts 4, 11; Rom. 9, 33; 10, 11; Eph. 2, 20; 1 Pet. 2, 6—8. V. 17. **Judgment also will I lay to the line and righteousness to the plummet,** the acts of Jehovah being regarded as the erecting of a building against the scorners according to the strictest vengeance of His Law; **and the hail shall sweep away the refuge of lies,** as the shovel cleared away the ashes from the altar in the Temple, **and the waters shall overflow the hiding-place,** thereby both exposing and sweeping away the fabric of lies built by the leaders of Judah. V. 18. **And your covenant with death shall be disannulled,** its writing obliterated and the covenant nullified, **and your agreement with hell,** with the realm of death, **shall not stand,** these enemies rather overcoming them; **when the overflowing scourge shall pass through,** when the flood of the Assyrian army would come along, **then ye shall be trodden down by it,** literally, "ye shall be to it a treading down," signifying a complete subjection. V. 19. **From the time that it goeth forth it shall take you,** one Assyrian campaign after the other would be successful; **for morning by morning shall it pass over,** in one wave of invasion after the other, **by day and by night; and it shall be a vexation only to understand the report,** the scoffers would now hear a preaching in act, which would be naught but terror. V. 20. **For the bed is shorter than that a man can stretch himself on it, and the covering narrower than that he can wrap himself in it,** that is, the people of Jerusalem would find that the Egyptian covenant in which they hoped to find safety and rest would prove altogether insufficient. V. 21. **For the Lord shall rise up as in Mount Perazim, He shall be wroth as in the Valley of Gibeon,** when, at the time of David, as an ally of Israel, He overthrew the armies of the Philistines and afforded deliverance to His people, 2 Sam. 5, 20; 1 Chron. 14, 11—15, **that He may do His work, His strange work,** for it would surely appear strange to other nations to see Jehovah punishing His own children in this manner, **and bring to pass His** act, **His** strange act, whereby He destroys His own people. V. 22. **Now, therefore,** so the prophet, in conclusion, warns the scoffers, **be ye not mockers, lest your bands be made strong,** namely, the fetters of their submission to Assyria; **for I have heard from the Lord God of hosts a consumption,** that He intended a general destruction, **even determined upon the whole earth.** Therefore quick repentance was in order, lest the punishment of the Lord consume them all.

THE CHASTISEMENT OF THE LORD OF HOSTS. V. 23. **Give ye ear and hear My voice; hearken and hear My speech,** close attention being demanded all the more since the illustration which now follows concerning the work of the farmer is not explained any further. V. 24. **Doth the plowman plow all day to sow?** Does he continue the same process in endless repetition? **Doth he open and break the clods of his ground?** by the process of harrowing. To keep on with the same work all the time would manifestly be absurd. V. 25. **When he hath made plain the face thereof,** prepared the top of the ground, so that it is even, **doth he not cast abroad the fitches,** rather, the black cumin, **and scatter the cumin,** the ordinary kind, **and cast in the principal wheat,** planting the best grain in rows, **and the appointed barley,** in a place by itself, **and the rye,** or spelt, **in their place?** apparently along the edge of the field, in order to protect the nobler grains against wild animals and stray cattle. V. 26. **For his God doth instruct him to discretion,** to do his work with understanding, **and doth teach him.** It was God who taught the rules of husbandry to man, Gen. 3, 23. V. 27. **For the fitches are not threshed with a threshing-instrument,** the threshing-sledge, **neither is a cart-wheel,** the broad wheel of the threshing-wagon, **turned about upon the cumin,** for either one of these seeds would be crushed by such a process; **but the fitches,** the black cumin, **are beaten out with a staff and the cumin with a rod,** the threshing-staff, or flail, being used in their case V. 28. **Bread-corn is bruised,** rather, "Is the bread-corn bruised?" Would a farmer be foolish enough to continue the process of threshing until the grain is crushed? The answer implied is, No; **because he will not ever be threshing it, nor break it with the wheel of his cart, nor bruise it with his horsemen,** as the horses trod out the grain from the husks. V. 29. **This also cometh forth from the Lord of hosts, which is wonderful in counsel and excellent in working,** that is, this parable teaches the wisdom of God in the higher plane, the manner in which He deals with His harvest on earth. The Lord punishes, but only in order to bless; He threshes, but not with crushing blows, not with the purpose of destroying. His object in sending tribulation is to separate the moral chaff from the wheat and to obtain the fulness of the harvest.

CHAPTER 29.

The Tribulation and Delivery of Ariel.

THE WOE UPON ARIEL. — V. 1. **Woe to Ariel, to Ariel,** a name signifying either "lion of God" or, more likely, "mountain of God,"[2] **the city where David dwelt!** which is still distinguished by that fact. **Add ye year to year,** another year to the present year; **let them kill sacrifices,** so that another cycle of festivals will be completed, that is, after the end of the present year another full church-year would elapse, but then the catastrophe would surely strike Jerusalem. V. 2. **Yet I will distress Ariel,** at the time indicated, **and there shall be heaviness and sorrow,** sighing and groaning; **and it shall be unto Me as Ariel,** Jerusalem would prove herself a place where the judgment of the Lord would be carried out. V. 3. **And I will camp against thee round about,** the enemies carrying out His plans in their siege of the city, **and will lay siege against thee with a mount,** with fortifications fully manned, every soldier determined to take the city, **and I will raise forts against thee,** earthworks or entrenchments. V. 4. **And thou shalt be brought down and shalt speak out of the ground,** as though covered with earth, her voice faint and hollow, **and thy speech shall be low out of the dust,** muffled and hard to understand, **and thy voice shall be as of one that has a familiar spirit, out of the ground,** like that of a ventriloquist imitating the speech of spirits, **and thy speech shall whisper out of the dust,** as one would imagine the voice of a dead person to sound out of the grave. Note the heaping of the expressions to emphasize the intention of the Lord. But the time of tribulation would not last long. V. 5. **Moreover, the multitude of thy strangers,** of the enemies of Zion, **shall be like small dust,** utterly crushed, **and the multitude of the terrible ones shall be as chaff that passeth away,** carried off by the wind without a trace to show that they were there; **yea, it shall be at an instant suddenly,** the destruction coming upon them in a moment. V. 6. **Thou,** Jerusalem, **shalt be visited,** but graciously, with a view to deliverance, **of the Lord of hosts,** the mighty Commander of the heavenly armies, **with thunder, and with earthquake, and great noise, with storm and tempest, and**

---

2) Cp. *Amer. Journal of Archeology,* XXVI (1922), 97.

the flame of devouring fire, all the forces of nature being employed by the Lord in overthrowing the haughty invaders. V. 7. **And the multitude of all the nations that fight against Ariel,** the mount of the Lord, typical of His holy Church, **even all that fight against her and her munition,** her mountain fortress, **and that distress her, shall be as a dream of a night vision,** with nothing tangible to boast of, with no victory won. V. 8. **It shall even be as when an hungry man dreameth, and, behold, he eateth,** the dream being so very vivid; **but he awaketh, and his soul is empty,** no real food having passed his lips; **or as when a thirsty man dreameth, and, behold, he drinketh; but he awaketh, and, behold, he is faint,** with his thirst unquenched, **and his soul hath appetite,** he is still longing for a cooling drink. **So shall the multitude of all the nations be that fight against Mount Zion.** They had thought it would be an easy matter to conquer Jerusalem, but they find themselves bitterly disappointed. The whole attempt of Assyria upon Jerusalem would be as if it had not been, would be as empty and unreal as the fabric of a dream. The same will finally be true of all the enemies of the real Mount Zion, of the Church of God. But since the people of Jerusalem would not accept the words of the prophet in firm faith, in glad acclaim, therefore he continues with sharp reproof. V. 9. **Stay yourselves and wonder,** stopping in foolish astonishment and unbelieving amazement; **cry ye out and cry,** rather, "blind yourselves and become blind," said of those who deliberately harden themselves against the influence of the joyful message brought to their attention; **they are drunken, but not with wine,** a spiritual paralysis having taken hold upon them; **they stagger, but not with strong drink,** their intoxication being due to their spiritual stupidity. And since they were thus closing their hearts against the influence of the Lord, He would punish them with that same stupidity which they were cultivating. V. 10. **For the Lord hath poured out upon you the spirit of deep sleep,** with which they were stupefied, **and hath closed your eyes,** blinding them against the light of understanding; **the prophets and your rulers, the seers, hath He covered,** the very leaders who were supposed to teach the people were afflicted with blindness. V. 11. **And the vision of all,** that which was revealed by the vision of the true prophets concerning all things, **is become unto you as the words of a book that is sealed,** of a roll of parchment sealed so that the writing is not visible, **which men deliver to one that is learned, saying, Read this, I pray thee; and he saith, I cannot, for it is sealed,** and unless the roll is opened, it is impossible for the writing to be seen; v. 12. **and the book is delivered to him that is not learned,** an illiterate person, **saying, Read this, I pray thee; and he saith, I am not learned.** In either event, the writing will not be revealed, the teaching of God is hidden from them, just as it is from the hearts and minds of all such as harden their hearts against His teaching.

THE COUNSEL OF GOD. — V. 13. **Wherefore the Lord said, Forasmuch as this people,** the men of the Southern Kingdom, the children of Judah, **draw near Me with their mouth and with their lips do honor Me,** in a mere outward form of worship, **but have removed their heart far from Me,** faith being lost entirely, **and their fear toward Me is taught by the precept of men,** their outward morality being based wholly upon the rules of conduct in vogue among men, not upon the way of sanctification prescribed by God, cp. Matt. 15, 8. 9, v. 14. **therefore, behold, I will proceed to do a marvelous work among this people, even a marvelous work and a wonder,** by an exceptional act of judgment; **for the wisdom of their wise men shall perish,** so that the counsel and help of those upon whom Judah depended would no longer appear, **and the understanding of their prudent men shall be hid,** their leaders becoming dull and stupid without knowing it. V. 15. **Woe unto them that seek deep to hide their counsel from the Lord,** trying to conceal their object from the eyes of God, as even Hezekiah did at times, **and their works are in the dark,** as they think, hidden from the omniscience of the Lord, **and they say, Who seeth us, and who knoweth us?** V. 16. **Surely your turning of things upside down shall be esteemed as the potter's clay,** the sentence being like an exclamation: "Alas upon your perversion! As clay is the potter to be considered?" **For shall the work,** the vessel as it comes from the potter's hands, **say of him that made it, He made me not? Or shall the thing framed,** that which is formed by the artist's skill, **say of him that framed it, He had no understanding?** The leaders of Judah were turning things upside down, ignoring God and even placing themselves in His stead. V. 17. **Is it not yet a very little while and Lebanon shall be turned into a fruitful field, and the fruitful field shall be esteemed as a forest?** The reference is to the time of the Messiah, when the hearts of men, moral deserts without the Lord, will be reclaimed so as to bear fruits of righteousness. V. 18. **And in that day shall the deaf,** those whose ears had, by their natural perversity, been closed to the voice of the Lord, **hear the words of the Book,** of the written revelation, **and the eyes of the blind,** those suffering with spiritual blindness, **shall see out of obscurity and out of darkness,** for the Lord Himself would enlighten the eyes of their understanding. V. 19. **The meek also shall**

increase their joy in the Lord, the godly among the afflicted finding their one satisfaction in communion with Him, **and the poor among men shall rejoice in the Holy One of Israel.** Cp. Matt. 5, 3; Luke 6, 20. V. 20. **For the terrible one is brought to naught, and the scorner is consumed,** both the tyrants and the mockers, the enemies of Jehovah being laid low, **and all that watch for iniquity are cut off,** their wickedness in watching for opportunities to commit iniquity being duly punished, v. 21. **that make a man an offender for a word,** unjustly condemning him, no matter what his cause may be, **and lay a snare for him that reproveth in the gate,** one who has a matter at issue in the courts, which were commonly held in the gates of the cities, **and turn aside the just for a thing of naught,** bringing lying accusations against him, this being the way of the world everywhere. V. 22. **Therefore, thus saith the Lord who redeemed Abraham,** by calling him away from his father's house, out of the midst of idolatry, **concerning the house of Jacob,** the congregation of people chosen by Him, **Jacob shall not now be ashamed, neither shall his face now wax pale,** the Church of the Lord no longer being subject to shame and disappointment. V. 23. **But when he seeth his children, the work of Mine hands,** a new generation of sincere believers in Him, **in the midst of him,** as a new congregation and assembly of saints, **they shall sanctify My name, and sanctify the Holy One of Jacob, and shall fear the God of Israel,** the lesson of Judah's punishment and of the overthrow of the Lord's enemies serving to make the hearts more willing to accept the doctrines of the Lord. V. 24. **They also that erred in spirit,** those whose spirit had forsaken the way of the Lord, **shall come to understanding,** namely, that of God's will and ways, **and they that murmured shall learn doctrine,** receive the discipline or instruction of the Lord. God desires His children of all times to learn the true wisdom from Him, to hear and heed His Word and be found on the ways of sanctification.

CHAPTER 30.

Woe Concerning the Covenant with Egypt.

THE ALLIANCE WITH EGYPT AND THE REBELLIOUS PEOPLE. — V. 1. **Woe to the rebellious children,** stubborn, obstinate, refractory people, **saith the Lord, that take counsel,** making plans of their own, **but not of Me,** without consulting Him, **and that cover with a covering,** weave an alliance, form a league, **but not of My Spirit,** not suggested or commanded by the Holy Spirit speaking through the Lord's messengers, **that they may add sin to sin!** The alliance of Judah with Egypt was not only undertaken without the consent of the Lord, but was connected with idolatrous acts. V. 2. **That walk to go down into Egypt and have not asked at My mouth; to strengthen themselves in the strength of Pharaoh,** making the king of Egypt their refuge, **and to trust in the shadow of Egypt!** They sought protection from a heathen ruler, whereas Jehovah, the true God, lived in their midst. V. 3. **Therefore shall the strength of Pharaoh be your shame,** they would be disappointed and disgraced when he and the desired refuge would fail them, **and the trust in the shadow of Egypt your confusion,** for the help and protection which they expected would not be forthcoming. V. 4. **For his princes,** the ambassadors sent by Judah, **were at Zoan,** having arrived there to confer with Pharaoh, **and his ambassadors came to Hanes,** these two cities being the royal seats of Egypt at that time. V. 5. **They were all ashamed of a people that could not profit them,** that is, disgrace would strike the people of Judah for taking this course in seeking help from Egypt, which could be of no real benefit to them, **nor be an help nor profit, but a shame and also a reproach.** That would be the result, the well-merited punishment which would come upon Judah for forsaking the trust in Jehovah alone. The prophet here interrupts his testimony of warning in order to insert an oracle directed against Egypt. V. 6. **The burden of the beasts of the South,** of the hippopotamus, as the emblem of Egypt: **Into the land of trouble and anguish,** through the desert between Palestine and Egypt, with its many disagreeable and dangerous features, **from whence come the young and old lion, the viper and fiery flying serpent,** these animals representing some of the great dangers of the wilderness, **they,** the ambassadors of Judah, **will carry their riches,** the treasures with which they intend to buy Egypt's help, **upon the shoulders of young asses and their treasures upon the bunches of camels,** upon their humps, their strongest pack-animals being pressed into service for this purpose, **to a people that shall not profit them,** who would leave them in the lurch at the very time when they would need assistance most. V. 7. **For the Egyptians shall help in vain and to no purpose,** their help will be vapor and emptiness, an unusually strong expression to designate the helplessness of Egypt; **therefore have I cried concerning this, Their strength is to sit still.** That was the Lord's name for Egypt: Boastfulness that sits still, unable to be of service, in spite of all its arrogant promises. In connection with this divine oracle the prophet now receives his special commission, v. 8. **Now go, write it before them in a table,** a writing-tablet, such as was in general use in those days, **and note it in a book,** entering the complete prophecy on a parchment roll for a permanent record, **that it may be for the time to come forever and ever,** to the most remote future, v. 9. **that this is a rebellious people,** v. 1, **lying children,** unfaithful to Jehovah, with whom they had entered into a covenant as His children, **children that will not hear the Law of the Lord,** setting aside all His revealed instruction; v. 10. **which say to the seers, See not,** in an attempt to hinder the servants of the Lord in their teaching of God's Word, **and to the prophets,** the teachers appointed by God, **Prophesy not unto us right things; speak unto us smooth things,** blandishments, flatteries, **prophesy deceits,** things that tickle the vanity of the people, since the latter have itching ears, 2 Tim. 4, 3. V. 11. **Get you out of the way,** namely, that prescribed by the command of God, **turn aside out of the path,** forsaking the Lord altogether, **cause the Holy One of Israel to cease from before us,** for they wanted to hear no more of His holiness, that attribute being the one which sinners dread most. So the people not only rejected the Lord themselves, but demanded that His true servants join them in their apostasy. V. 12. **Wherefore thus saith the Holy One of Israel,** that same God against whom they were rebelling, **Because ye despise this word,** regarding His warning with the deepest aversion, **and trust in oppression and perverseness, and stay thereon,** for they placed their trust in acts of violence, by means of which they exacted the money needed to purchase the aid of Egypt, v. 13. **therefore this iniquity shall be to you as a breach ready to fall, swelling out in a high wall,** the bulging out of the wall indicating that it was about to topple over, **whose breaking cometh suddenly, at an instant.** Thus the ruin of Judah would overtake the nation with great suddenness because of their idolatrous alliance with Egypt. V. 14. **And He,** Jehovah, in His judgment upon the apostate nation, **shall break it as the breaking of the potters' vessel that is broken in pieces,** intentionally smashed into fragments; **He shall not spare, so that there shall not be found in the bursting of it a sherd to take fire from the hearth,** a fragment of the broken vessel large enough to serve for this purpose, **or to take water withal out of the pit,** to be used for drawing water from a cistern. The Lord's threat contemplates an utter overthrow of the disobedient nation. It is ever thus: If the Lord's warnings are not heeded, He sends His punishments with great severity.

TRUST IN JEHOVAH REWARDED; OVERTHROW OF THE LORD'S ENEMIES. — V. 15. **For thus saith the Lord God, the Holy One of Israel, In returning and rest,** by turning back to the Lord in true repentance and trusting in Him all alone, **shall ye be saved,** finding deliverance from all the dangers which beset them; **in quietness and in confidence,** leaving it to the Lord alone to guide and direct them in all their affairs, **shall be your strength,** that being the secret of the power possessed by all believers; **and ye would not,** the unbelievers, by their own stubbornness, deprive themselves of the great blessings to be found in association with the Lord through His Word. V. 16. **But ye said, No; for we will flee upon horses,** their boast being that they could not wait to meet the enemy on swift horses; **therefore shall ye flee;** namely, in trying to escape the victorious onslaught of their adversaries; **and, We will ride upon the swift,** anxious to risk the battle on runners, horses noted for their speed; **therefore shall they that pursue you be swift,** the Lord giving the victory to their enemies. V. 17. **One thousand shall flee at the rebuke of one; at the rebuke of five shall ye flee,** overcome by terror, in disgraceful flight, cp. Lev. 26, 8; Deut. 32, 30, **till ye be left as a beacon upon the top of a mountain,** a solitary signal staff, **and as an ensign on an hill,** only a tiny remnant being left after the Lord has carried out His punishment. V. 18. **And therefore will the Lord wait,** the miserable condition of Israel causing Him to turn toward His people once more, **that He may be gracious unto you, and therefore will He be exalted,** withdrawing Himself, removing, hiding behind the veil of His holiness and majesty, for the time being, as it were, **that He may have mercy upon you; for the Lord is a God of judgment,** He is bound to execute justice. **Blessed are all they that wait for Him,** for the time when He once more reveals His mercy. In a little wrath God hides His face for a moment, but with everlasting kindness will He have mercy on us. Is. 54, 8. Cp. Jer. 30, 11; 46, 28. V. 19. **For the people shall dwell in Zion at Jerusalem,** the Church of God being preserved in the midst of all dangers and enemies; **thou shalt weep no more,** the spiritual Israel, the people of the Lord, should not give way to excessive mourning; **He,** Jehovah, **will be very gracious unto thee at the voice of thy cry,** the repentant cry for mercy; **when He shall hear it, He will answer thee,** with an act of mercy. V. 20. **And though the Lord give you the bread of adversity,** of distress, **and the water of affliction,** such as His merciful chastisement often lays upon His children, Rom. 8, 18—25, **yet shall not thy teachers be removed into a corner any more, but thine eyes shall see thy teachers,** who would no longer find it necessary to hide, as in the days of Ahab of Israel or of Ahaz of Judah; v. 21. **and thine ears shall hear a word behind thee,** the guiding voice of God, through His servants, **saying, This is the way, walk**

ye in it, this being a word of warning, **when ye turn to the right hand, and when ye turn to the left,** thus keeping them in the paths of righteousness. V. 22. **Ye shall defile also,** as a result of the good teaching of the prophets, **the covering of thy graven images of silver,** the plating used to cover the body of their images, **and the ornament of thy molten images of gold; thou shalt cast them away,** scattering them, **as a menstruous cloth,** as something filthy and loathsome; **thou shalt say unto it, Get thee hence,** throwing it out as trash. V. 23. **Then,** after such evidences of repentance on the part of the people, **shall He give the rain of thy seed,** so that the grain which had been sown would have a good stand, **that thou shalt sow the ground withal; and bread of the increase of the earth,** of everything that the earth produces for the food of man, **and it shall be fat and plenteous,** full of rich nourishment. **In that day shall thy cattle feed in large pastures,** in meadows the size and richness of which insure abundant pasturage. V. 24. **The oxen likewise and the young asses that ear the ground,** that is, which plow and till the farmland, **shall eat clean provender,** a mash of grain and chopped herbs, made more palatable by the addition of salt, the superior quality of the straw used being emphasized by the words, **which hath been winnowed with the shovel,** a large, flat shovel for the larger legumes and grains, **and with the fan,** a five- or six-pronged fork used for tossing up the grain and thus cleaning it of chaff. V. 25. **And there shall be upon every high mountain and upon every high hill,** barren as they otherwise were, **rivers and streams of waters in the day of the great slaughter,** when the punishment of God will strike His enemies, **when the towers fall,** namely, those of all fortifications of men erected over against the city of God. V. 26. **Moreover, the light of the moon shall be as the light of the sun,** equal to it in brightness, **and the light of the sun shall be sevenfold, as the light of seven days, in the day,** the time to which the entire Old Testament looked forward, **that the Lord bindeth up the breach of His people,** the calamity which had struck them on account of their sins, **and healeth the stroke of their wound.** The entire passage pictures the spiritual splendor of the Messianic era. V. 27. **Behold, the name of the Lord,** revealing His holy and righteous nature and His almighty majesty for the purpose of judgment, **cometh from far,** like an immense storm or a devastating prairie fire arising above the horizon, **burning with His anger, and the burden thereof is heavy,** settling down like a heavy pall of smoke upon the entire landscape; **his lips are full of indignation and his tongue as a devouring fire;** v. 28. **and His breath, as an overflowing stream,** with all the impetous force of a spring freshet, **shall reach to the midst of the neck,** so that only his head extends above the division of waters, **to sift the nations with the sieve of vanity,** the result of the Lord's sifting being nothingness, destruction; **and there shall be a bridle in the jaws of the people, causing them to err,** the reference being either to wild horses, which must be kept in subjection with force, or to the manner in which prisoners were sometimes fettered, the prisoners in either case being forced into destruction, as a just punishment upon them. Over against this destruction we have the deliverance of Israel, the people of God. V. 29. **Ye shall have a song, as in the night when a holy solemnity is kept,** the solemn festal hymn of the Passover Festival, **and gladness of heart, as when one goeth with a pipe to come into the mountain of the Lord, to the Mighty One of Israel.** In other words, Israel, the Church of God, is in the midst of its glorious worship, while round about it Jehovah is carrying out His punishment upon the adversaries of His people. "God is in the midst of her, she shall not be moved; God shall help her, and that right early." Ps. 46, 5. V. 30. **And the Lord shall cause His glorious voice,** raised in a majestic battle-cry, **to be heard and shall show the lighting down of His arm,** as it descends upon the scoffers, **with the indignation of His anger and with the flame of a devouring fire, with scattering,** as of that accompanying a cloudburst, **and tempest,** a heavy rain, **and hailstones,** all the destructive forces of nature. V. 31. **For through the voice of the Lord shall the Assyrian be beaten down, which smote with a rod,** this destruction of the world-power being a type of the punishment which strikes all the enemies of the Church of God. V. 32. **And in every place where the grounded staff shall pass,** where the avenging rod, as decreed by God, will strike, **which the Lord shall lay upon him,** in punishing and destroying the world-power, **it shall be with tabrets and harps,** with trimbrels and zithers, that is, while the people of God rejoice over their deliverance; **and in battles of shaking will He fight with it,** with uplifted arm Jehovah will wage war. V. 33. **For Tophet is ordained of old,** a dreadful altar being prepared for the slaughter; **yea, for the king it is prepared,** for the ruler of the world power; **He,** Jehovah, **hath made it deep and large,** so that there is room for many victims upon the place of slaughter; **the pile thereof is fire and much wood,** ready for the great sacrifice; **the breath of the Lord, like a stream of brimstone, doth kindle it,** in a sudden and terrible destruction, in the last great act of the Lord's avenging punishment. The believers are secure in the hands of God, though all the powers of earth and hell be arrayed against them.

CHAPTER 31.

The Folly of Judah's Trust in Egypt.

EGYPT CANNOT PROTECT ISRAEL AGAINST THE LORD'S WRATH. — V. 1. **Woe to them that go down to Egypt for help,** making it a practise to turn to this world-power for assistance, **and stay on horses and trust in chariots, because they are many,** the chief strength of the Egyptian army being represented by their cavalry, which boasted some very powerful war-chariots, **and in horsemen, because they are very strong,** there being a powerful multitude of them; **but they look not unto the Holy One of Israel, neither seek the Lord!** They forsake the God of the covenant in order to put their trust in mere men. V. 2. **Yet He also is wise,** said in divine irony, for God is wise in essence, far wiser than the Egyptians, and in comparison with Him the Jews had surely proved themselves fools in forsaking His mighty counsel and protection, **and will bring evil,** executing punishment upon those who ignore Him, **and will not call back His words,** He will not take back the threats which He had uttered against the Egyptian alliance, **but will arise against the house of the evil-doers and against the help of them that work iniquity,** both the Jews who sought assistance and the Egyptians who were ready to give assistance being condemned together. V. 3. **Now, the Egyptians are men, and not God,** that is, on the one hand were finite, powerless creatures, on the other the almighty God; **and their horses flesh and not spirit,** not endowed with the power of spirit beings, but only weak and perishable flesh. **When the Lord shall stretch out His hand,** make use of His almighty power, **both he that helpeth shall fall,** namely, Egypt, **and he that is holpen,** namely, Judah, **shall fall down,** the helper stumbling and he who accepts the help being carried down to the ground in his fall, **and they all shall fail together.** V. 4. **For thus hath the Lord spoken unto me,** in a word which partakes of the nature of both a warning and a promise to Judah, His people, **Like as the lion and the young lion roaring on his prey,** growling over an animal which he has stolen from the herd and is in the act of tearing to pieces, **when a multitude of shepherds is called forth against him,** there being an allusion here to the help solicited from Egypt, **he will not be afraid of their voice nor abase himself,** shrinking back or slinking away in fear, **for the noise of them,** not permitting himself to be deprived of his prey, **so shall the Lord of hosts come down to fight for Mount Zion and for the hill thereof,** for the congregation of His children. Thus the visitation of the Lord becomes a chastisement of love to His people, for He will finally deliver them from every evil work.

JEHOVAH PROTECTS THOSE WHO FEAR HIM. V. 5. **As birds flying,** fluttering over a brood of fledglings, **so will the Lord of hosts defend Jerusalem,** hovering over its inhabitants with anxious care; **defending also He will deliver it, and passing over He will preserve it,** as the destroying angel passed over the blood-marked houses of the children of Israel in Goshen at the time of the first Passover, Ex. 12, 13. 23. 27. V. 6. **Turn ye unto Him,** the God of the covenant, the God of love, **from whom the children of Israel have deeply revolted.** The result of such true repentance is now pictured: v. 7. **For in that day,** when the Lord visits His people, especially with the dawning of the Messianic era, **every man shall cast away his idols of silver and his idols of gold,** renouncing idolatry in every form, **which your own hands have made unto you for a sin,** whereby they contracted guilt in great measure. V. 8. **Then shall the Assyrian,** representative of the world-power hostile to the true Lord, **fall with the sword, not of a mighty man,** that of a human champion, **and the sword, not of a mean man,** of a human adversary, **shall devour him; but he shall flee from the sword,** namely, the weapon employed by the Lord, **and his young men shall be discomfited,** become subject to slavery, the former masters being humiliated most deeply. V. 9. **And he shall pass over to his stronghold for fear,** that is, the king of Assyria, hitherto the strong refuge of his people, would flee in terror, **and his princes shall be afraid of the ensign,** scattered in wild confusion before the onslaught of Jehovah, **saith the Lord, whose fire is in Zion and His furnace in Jerusalem,** the light of His divine presence shining forth from His holy congregation. With God in her midst, with the illuminating light of His Word and with the destroying power of His wrath over against His enemies, the Church of God of all times is secure.

CHAPTER 32.

The Blessings of Messiah's Kingdom.

A GOVERNMENT OF RIGHTEOUSNESS. — V. 1. **Behold, a King shall reign in righteousness,** namely, He who is Himself the Lord, our Righteousness, Jer. 23, 6, **and princes,** all those who hold positions of authority in the kingdom of Christ, in His Church, **shall rule in judgment,** applying justice in accordance with the will of the Lord. V. 2. **And a Man,** or *the* Man, namely, the great Son of Man,

Jesus Christ, **shall be as an hiding-place from the wind,** a Shelter against windstorms, **and a Covert from the tempest,** a Protector against oppression; **as rivers of water in a dry place,** giving refreshment to the souls of the poor and wretched, **as the shadow of a great rock in a weary land,** where dense shade brings welcome relief to the heated traveler. This sounds the merciful invitation of the Savior, extended to all those that are heavy laden, to come unto Him and find rest for their souls, Matt. 11, 28—30. V. 3. **And the eyes of them that see shall not be dim, and the ears of them that hear shall hearken,** that is, the spiritual understanding of the Lord's people will be in proper order for realizing and appreciating the blessings of God's mercy. V. 4. **The heart also of the rash,** such as judge hastily and superficially concerning the great facts of man's redemption, **shall understand knowledge,** so as to weigh religious truth aright, **and the tongue of the stammerers,** those who do not think and speak clearly on divine matters, but are always confused, **shall be ready to speak plainly,** in proper agreement with the Word of God. V. 5. **The vile person shall be no more called liberal,** a fool, given to wickedness as he is, will no longer be called noble, **nor the churl said to be bountiful,** the swindler will no longer be called a baron. In the outward, visible form of the kingdom of Christ the fraudulent person, the hypocrite, may deceive himself and others, but in the estimation of Christ such a person will be given the position which his hypocrisy deserves. V. 6. **For the vile person will speak villainy,** the wicked mocker cannot but give expression to the mockery of his heart, **and his heart will work iniquity, to practise hypocrisy,** profligacy and malice, **and to utter error against the Lord,** arguments of unbelief and impiety, which are intended to mislead, **to make empty the soul of the hungry,** taking away the foundation of belief which will satisfy the needs of the spiritually hungry, **and he will cause the drink of the thirsty to fail,** namely, of him who hungers and thirsts after the righteousness of the Lord. V. 7. **The instruments also of the churl,** of the fraudulent, of the hypocrite, **are evil; he deviseth wicked devices,** plots of every kind, **to destroy the poor with lying words,** to bring destruction upon the afflicted with words of falsehood, **even when the needy speaketh right,** when he pleads with full justice, when his claims are just. V. 8. **But the liberal deviseth liberal things, and by liberal things shall he stand,** that is, a person of noble mind and of high moral character will not only conceive noble things, but will also persevere in them, will carry them out, with the approval of the righteous King.

Desolation and Restoration. — V. 9. **Rise up, ye women that are at ease,** who lived a life of self-indulgence, without regarding the dangers of their times; **hear my voice, ye careless daughters,** heedless of the larger issues of life; **give ear unto my speech.** V. 10. **Many days and years shall ye be troubled,** literally, "days upon a year," that is, an indefinite number of days, at the most a year, **ye careless women; for the vintage shall fail, the gathering shall not come,** there would be no harvest of fruit, since the enemy would occupy all the land about Jerusalem. V. 11. **Tremble, ye women that are at ease,** resting in smug self-satisfaction; **be troubled, ye careless ones,** who fondly imagined that the circumstances to which they were accustomed would never change; **strip you and make you bare,** laying aside the costly garments in which they delighted, **and gird sackcloth upon your loins,** as a sign of trouble, sorrow, and mourning. V. 12. **They shall lament for the teats, for the pleasant fields, for the fruitful vine,** rather, "Upon their breasts they will strike over the fields of pleasantness or desire, over the vine of fruitfulness," deeply grieving on account of the desolation which had come upon their fertile land. V. 13. **Upon the land of my people,** which formerly had been a type of unexampled fruitfulness, **shall come up thorns and briers; yea, upon all the houses of joy,** which were so abundant in the capital city, **in the joyous city.** The prophet, as in chapter 3, has in mind women who have never known any want, but have continually lived in abundance and luxury. His purpose was to frighten them out of their secure and proud repose and to make them realize the condition in which their land was on account of the sins of its inhabitants. V. 14. **Because the palaces,** in which the rich were then living, **shall be forsaken; the multitude of the city shall be left,** the noisy din of the large city, that is, the city with its noisy multitude, forsaken; **the forts and towers,** Ophel, the rocky prominence of Moriah with its watchtower, **shall be for dens forever,** homes of wild animals, **a joy of wild asses, a pasture of flocks,** all this being a picture and type of spiritual desolation which had taken hold of the Jewish people, v. 15. **until the Spirit be poured upon us from on high,** in the time of the Messiah, **and the wilderness be a fruitful field, and the fruitful field be counted for a forest,** that is, men now barren of true religion would become fruitful as a result of the regeneration wrought in them, while those already converted would bring forth fruit in such rich abundance as to make their former life seem like a wilderness by comparison. V. 16. **Then judgment shall dwell in the wilderness,** the justice of God being acknowledged where it was formerly unknown, **and righteousness remain in the fruitful field,** since the believers grow both in the knowledge of the Lord and in good works. V. 17. **And the work of righteousness,** the condition which is produced by the application of the Lord's righteousness in all the affairs of the Church, **shall be peace,** a security resting upon the foundation of God's protection; **and the effect of righteousness,** its reward, **quietness and assurance forever,** a firm reliance upon the mercy and grace of the Lord. V. 18. **And my people shall dwell in a peaceable habitation,** from which all strife would be far removed, **and in sure dwellings, and in quiet resting-places,** dwelling in the most fortunate and desirable circumstances of peace and security; v. 19. **when it shall hail, coming down on the forest,** when the forest shall fall under a storm of hail, **and the city shall be low in a low place,** the reference being to the overthrow of all hostile world-powers as the Church of the Messiah is established. V. 20. **Blessed are ye that sow beside all waters,** scattering their seeds in the fertile lowlands everywhere, **that send forth thither the feet of the ox and the ass,** letting their beasts of burden roam freely on account of the great abundance of the harvest. This is again a picture of the prosperity and security of the Church under the blessing of the Lord in the New Testament: the world-powers, all spiritual enemies vanquished and the city of God with the fields of His Word happy and prosperous.

CHAPTER 33.

The Fifth Woe.

THE PUNISHMENT STRIKES THE ADVERSARY. V. 1. **Woe to thee that spoilest, and thou wast not spoiled,** the hostility of the Assyrian invader being a type of the world-power's enmity toward the Church of God; **and dealest treacherously,** in invading the country for the purpose of robbery, **and they dealt not treacherously with thee,** the hostile act being altogether unprovoked. **When thou shalt cease to spoil,** when the measure of damage which the plans of God included had been reached, **thou shalt be spoiled; and when thou shalt make an end to deal treacherously, they shall deal treacherously with thee.** The text clearly indicates that the punishment of him who had been unpunished would certainly come upon him. The prophet's threat now turns into a pleading petition to the Lord. V. 2. **O Lord, be gracious unto us!** For the grace and mercy of the heavenly Father is the believers' only stay. **We have waited for Thee,** trustfully expecting the help which He alone can give; **be Thou their arm every morning,** for the danger is new every day, **our salvation also in the time of trouble,** bringing deliverance as the severest affliction looms up before the people. This intercessory prayer is made with the proper confidence, and therefore the prophet in spirit sees the fulfilment of his desire. V. 3. **At the noise of the tumult,** as Jehovah makes ready to punish the enemy, **the people fled,** as before the onset of a powerful army; **at the lifting up of Thyself the nations were scattered,** their armies fleeing in hopeless confusion. V. 4. **And your spoil,** so the prophet tells the adversaries, **shall be gathered like the gathering of the caterpillar,** that is, the treasures which the invaders had robbed would be abandoned by them, to be collected by the Jews with the same eagerness exhibited by the wingless locust as it devours the vegetation; **as the running to and fro of locusts shall He run upon them,** as when hordes of grasshoppers clear off a harvest-field to the very last blade of grass. The consequence of all this would be that Jehovah is exalted. V. 5. **The Lord is exalted,** He who occupies the throne on high is given all glory for His triumph over the world-power, for executing righteousness and justice in the world; **for He dwelleth on high,** His victory is a glorious exhibition of His divine power; **He hath filled Zion with judgment and righteousness.** Cp. chap. 32, 15. 16. V. 6. **And wisdom and knowledge shall be the stability of thy times and strength of salvation,** literally, "And there shall be security, a firm and lasting prosperity, of thy times, a treasure of salvation, of wisdom and knowledge"; that is, the times, the period here referred to, will be characterized by an absence of all disturbing and unstable elements, as the effect of the treasure of salvation given to the believers, and by wisdom and knowledge from on high; **the fear of the Lord is his treasure,** the treasure-trove of Judah, out of it all the other spiritual gifts and graces flow, as they are enumerated in this verse. Cp. chap. 11, 2. V. 7. **Behold, their valiant ones shall cry without,** namely, the men of rank sent to the Assyrian general at Lachish, to offer presents and sue for peace, 2 Kings 18, 14. 18. 37; **the ambassadors of peace shall weep bitterly,** since their proposals were treated with duplicity and scorn. V. 8. **The highways lie waste,** travel had been discontinued on account of the desolation spread by the invaders, **the wayfaring man ceaseth,** for the life of no traveler was safe on the roads; **he,** the enemy, **hath broken the covenant,** in accepting the ransom offered, yet refusing to retire to fulfil its stipulations, **he hath despised the cities,** his superior forces making a mockery of their resistance; **he regardeth no man,** rather sacrificing human lives without the slightest compunction. V. 9. **The earth mourneth and languisheth,** on account of the wickedness committed on its surface and in consequence of the devastation wrought by the invading hordes. **Lebanon is ashamed and hewn**

down, its mighty forests withered; **Sharon,** the fertile plain along the Mediterranean, south of Mount Carmel, **is like a wilderness,** for it was through its rich fields that the invaders marched; **and Bashan and Carmel,** the two fruitful elevations in the eastern and western part of the Promised Land, **shake off their fruits,** so that their great forests stand bare. This condition, which the Lord had apparently viewed sitting down, as though He were not interested in the devastation, He wants to change with a mighty arm. V. 10. **Now will I rise, saith the Lord,** getting up from the throne of His might; **now will I be exalted,** showing Himself in the might of His greatness; **now will I lift up Myself,** as a champion preparing for battle. He now addresses the enemies directly. V. 11. **Ye shall conceive chaff,** dry grass or hay, since the plans which they laid were not fresh and full of life, but utterly dry, without strength and sap, **ye shall bring forth stubble,** to which their futile ideas might well be compared; **your breath,** their own snorting anger, as they fretted and fumed, **as fire, shall devour you,** so that they would be destroyed as a result of their own foolish counsels. V. 12. **And the people shall be as the burnings of lime,** which consumes itself as it comes in contact with water; **as thorns cut up,** which burn with a bright flame, with loud crackling, and much smoke, **shall they be burned in the fire.** Thus are the adversaries of the Lord consumed by the fire of His anger, while His salvation shelters those who place their confidence in Him alone.

THE SINNERS ALARMED, THE PIOUS COMFORTED. — V. 13. **Hear, ye that are far off,** all the distant nations of the world, **what I have done; and, ye that are near,** the Jews and the nations near them, **acknowledge My might,** so Jehovah calls out through His herald. V. 14. **The sinners in Zion,** those who falsely professed the religion of Israel, though their heart was not in their worship, **are afraid,** terrified because their hypocrisy is about to be revealed; **fearfulness hath surprised the hypocrites,** who were often addicted to secret idolatry while they continued their outward membership in the true Church. **Who among us shall dwell with the devouring fire?** Such is the cry of the sinners as they contemplate the devouring fierceness of Jehovah's anger. **Who among us shall dwell with everlasting burnings?** They themselves realize and must admit it that they cannot endure the flames of God's divine anger which is bound to strike them in righteous judgment. The prophet himself, on the basis of Ps. 15; 24, 3—6, answers their question: v. 15. **He that walketh righteously,** practising the proper righteousness of life in every respect, **and speaketh uprightly,** without a trace of hypocrisy; **he that despiseth the gain of oppressions,** repudiating the very idea of enriching himself by means which savor of blackmail, **that shaketh his hands,** interlocking them tightly, **from holding of bribes,** his act being conducive to that end, helping him to refrain from accepting bribe money, **that stoppeth his ears from hearing of blood,** refusing to listen to any plan which involves revenge, hatred, or violence, **and shutteth his eyes from seeing evil,** sanctioning wickedness or yielding to lust, in short, one who "rejoiceth not in iniquity" in any form, 1 Cor. 13, 6, v. 16. **he shall dwell on high,** in places inaccessible to the foe, **his place of defense shall be the munitions of rocks,** the fastnesses of the mountains, where he dwells under the protection of Jehovah; **bread shall be given him; his waters shall be sure,** he will have both food and drink in rich abundance. Thus the prophet draws a sketch of one who, under the guidance and by the power of Jehovah, does not need to fear the judgment of wrath which will come upon those who delight in wickedness. The description causes the prophet to forget the sordid present and to look forward to the time when the congregation of the Lord would consist entirely of such desirable members. V. 17. **Thine eyes shall see the King in His beauty,** the Messiah in the glory of His redemptive work; **they shall behold the land that is very far off,** for the Messiah's kingdom would extend over the whole earth. V. 18. **Thine heart,** once more conscious of the mournful condition of the present, so unlike the future glorious state, **shall meditate terror,** considering what fearful things have been left behind. **Where is the scribe?** the man who supervised the paying of tribute according to the assessments entered in his books. **Where is the receiver?** the weigher, who weighed the valuables received as tribute and was most exacting in his demands. **Where is he that counted the towers?** making a plan of the city, which was to be taken by storm. All these officers in the employ of the enemy were well known to the Jews, the mere mention of whose names filled their hearts with terror. But the prophet comforts his people with reassuring words: v. 19. **Thou shalt not see a fierce people,** for the terrible enemies will then have disappeared forever, **a people of a deeper speech than thou canst perceive,** whose language is difficult to understand; **of stammering tongue,** indistinguishable to those not familiar with the dialect, **that thou canst not understand.** It is a picture of happy deliverance which the prophet paints before the eyes of the true Israel. V. 20. **Look upon Zion, the city of our solemnities,** where Jehovah dwells and the people assemble for worship, to praise the Lord and to keep His feasts; **thine eyes shall see Jerusalem a quiet habitation, a tabernacle that shall not be taken down,** as was the case with the Tabernacle in the wilderness; **not one of the stakes thereof shall ever be removed, neither shall any of the cords thereof be broken,** both the tent-pins and the guy-ropes remaining intact forever. The reference is to the security and stability of the Church of God, as established upon the foundation of Jesus Christ, the entire passage reminding one strongly of Ps. 46. V. 21. **But there the glorious Lord will be unto us a place of broad rivers and streams,** that is, by virtue of the indwelling of God in the midst of His people the Church would be like a great city, which is both defended and watered by rich streams, **wherein shall go no galley with oars, neither shall gallant ship,** one of the mighty sail-ships which ventured out on the mighty ocean, **pass thereby,** Jehovah Himself being the defense of His people and protecting them against all enemies. V. 22. **For the Lord is our Judge,** who watches over His people's rights and honor; **the Lord is our Lawgiver,** He who wields the general's staff in their midst; **the Lord is our King,** His throne of power and mercy being established in their midst; **He will save us,** to Him they could confidently look for deliverance from all harm and danger. And so the chapter concludes with a description of the City of God, the Church of Christ, its present distress being contrasted with its future glory. V. 23. **Thy tacklings are loosed,** Jerusalem being considered a ship whose cables and rigging have been torn by adverse winds; **they could not well strengthen their mast,** for the mast had no hold without the cables, **they could not spread the sail,** for the same reason, their vessel thus practically being at the mercy of wind and waves. **Then is the prey of a great spoil divided,** immense booty is distributed, at the very moment of the greatest helplessness the Lord grants victory; **the lame take the prey,** the very cripples being able to share in the plunder. V. 24. **And the inhabitant shall not say, I am sick,** not one of them shall be subject to illness or weakness; **the people that dwell therein shall be forgiven their iniquity,** this, in fact, being the secret of their strength. And thus the Church of God is constituted — it consists of people who have come to the full realization of their own helplessness, who are deeply repentant, and who, as a consequence, have received the gift of the forgiveness of their sins and draw upon the Lord alone for all their strength. That is the abiding comfort of all believers.

CHAPTER 34.

Judgments upon Idumea.

Isaiah is rightly called the evangelist of the Old Testament. Throughout his book of prophecies he refers to conditions as they would obtain in the time of the Messiah. In chapters 34 and 35 also, which form the conclusion of the first half of his book, he makes use of New Testament ideas and pictures. For this reason these chapters, at the same time, strike the introductory chords to the great Book of Consolations, chap. 40—66.

Introductory Proclamation. — V. 1. **Come near, ye nations, to hear, and hearken, ye people!** the prophet's proclamation being so great and momentous that he summons all nations to give attention. **Let the earth hear and all that is therein,** all creatures being concerned in this weighty announcement; **the world,** the entire circle of the inhabited globe, **and all things that come forth of it.** The invitation is like Ezek. 6, 3; Deut. 32, 1; Ps. 50, 4; Micah 6, 1. 2. V. 2. **For the indignation of the Lord is upon all nations,** His is a great wrath, which will result in punishment upon all His enemies, **and His fury upon all their armies,** upon which they, in the excess of their insolence, rely; **He hath utterly destroyed them,** doomed them, by a solemn curse, to destruction, **He hath delivered them to the slaughter,** appointed them to be slain. V. 3. **Their slain also shall be cast out,** left to lie unburied, **and their stink,** the odor of decay, **shall come up out of their carcasses, and the mountains shall be melted with their blood,** washed away as by a mighty torrent. Cp. Matt. 24, 29; 2 Pet. 3, 7. 10. 12; Rev. 6, 13. 14. V. 4. **And all the host of heaven,** all the stars and heavenly bodies, **shall be dissolved, and the heavens shall be rolled together as a scroll,** in the manner in which parchment-rolls were formerly rolled together; **and all their host shall fall down,** as the firmament of the heavens passes away, **as the leaf falleth off from the vine,** upon its fading in the autumn, **and as a falling fig from the fig-tree,** immature and useless. The prophet clearly has in mind the final dissolution of the universe, the end of the present dispensation, for which reason Peter makes use of the same picture in describing the end of the world, 2 Pet. 3, 10—12.

Idumea as a Type of Hostility against God. — V. 5. **For My sword shall be bathed in heaven,** intoxicated, as it were, as it prepares to execute His punishment; **behold, it shall come down upon Idumea,** as in a drunken frenzy, **and upon the people of My curse,** those doomed to experience His condemnation, **to judgment.** The Lord has an unparalleled slaughter and sacrifice in mind, to be carried out upon Edom, the apostate brother nation of Israel, and upon all those who followed Edom in his enmity against the chosen of the Lord. V. 6. **The sword of the Lord is filled with blood,** glutted with heavy slaughter; **it is made fat with fatness,** as it engages in bringing sacrifice, **and with the**

blood of lambs and goats, with the fat of the kidneys of rams, those parts being named which were especially devoted to God in the sacrifices, 2 Sam. 1, 22; **for the Lord hath a sacrifice in Bozrah,** the capital of Auranitis, east of Jordan, for thus far Edom had extended its dominion at that time, **and a great slaughter in the land of Idumea,** whose territory extended from the southern end of the Dead Sea to the Elanitic Gulf. V. 7. **And the unicorns,** the Asiatic buffaloes, **shall come down with them, and the bullocks with the bulls,** representing the sacrificial animals of the herds, the powerful men in Edom to be slain with the ordinary people; **and their land shall be soaked with blood and their dust made fat with fatness,** the entire country, as it were, glutted, drunken with the great amount of blood and fat of the slain. V. 8. **For it is the day of the Lord's vengeance and the year of recompenses for the controversy of Zion,** the time when Jehovah will retaliate on those who have contended with Zion, in order to give justice to Zion, the people of His choice. Cp. chap. 43, 4; Deut. 32, 35. 41. V. 9. **And the streams thereof,** of Idumea, **shall be turned into pitch,** in agreement with the volcanic and sulphurous character of the country near the Dead Sea, **and the dust thereof into brimstone,** which is still found in large quantities in that neighborhood, **and the land thereof shall become burning pitch,** a place where a fearful fire would rage. V. 10. **It shall not be quenched night nor day, the smoke thereof shall go up forever; from generation to generation it shall lie waste,** as the result of the terrible volcanic upheavals by which its fertility was destroyed; **none shall pass through it forever and ever.** The first act of the final destruction is shown in the fact that to this day one may travel for days through former Idumea without finding one inhabited city, and the final act will come with the fire of eternity. Cp. Rev. 14, 11; 18, 18; 19, 3. V. 11. **But the cormorant,** the pelican, **and the bittern,** the porcupine, **shall possess it; the owl also and the raven shall dwell in it,** the description of the desolation wrought agreeing with that in other parts of the prophets, chap. 13, 20—22; 14, 23; Zeph. 2, 14; **and He,** Jehovah, **shall stretch out upon it the line of confusion,** His measuring-line being used with deliberate intent in working ruin, **and the stones,** the weights at the end of the plumb-lines, **of emptiness,** resulting in utter destruction. With the same rigorous exactness which marks the carpenter's construction the Lord carries out His program of destruction, thus reducing Edom to a state of desolation. V. 12. **They shall call the nobles thereof to the kingdom, but none shall be there,** literally, "As to her nobles, there are none there that call out a monarchy," that is, none are left to elect a new king or to succeed to the throne, **and all her princes shall be nothing,** none being there, none could be elected by the nobility to assume the power of a reigning monarch. V. 13. **And thorns shall come up in her palaces,** growing up in the midst of their ruins, **nettles and brambles in the fortresses thereof,** where formerly magnificent castles stood; **and it shall be an habitation of dragons,** wild cats or dogs, **and a court for owls,** a place where ostriches will find their food. V. 14. **The wild beasts of the desert shall also meet with the wild beasts of the island,** the marten rivaling the jackal in his attempts to find food, **and the satyr,** spirit of the desert, **shall cry to his fellow; the screech-owl,** a night-specter believed to be dwelling in the wilderness, **also shall rest there and find for herself a place of rest,** for this evil spirit felt at home in the midst of desolation. V. 15. **There shall the great owl,** rather, the arrow-snake, **make her nest, and lay, and hatch, and gather under her shadow,** cherishing her young in the shadow of the ruins; **there shall the vultures also be gathered, every one with her mate.** In short, all the animal dwellers of the wilderness, whose shaggy appearance by day and whose melancholy cries by night made them objects inspiring fear and superstition, would be found in the desolate wastes of the former rich Idumean cities. Moreover, the people who would then compare prophecy and fulfilment would find that they agree most exactly. V. 16. **Seek ye out of the Book of the Lord,** the prophecies as preserved by the command of Jehovah, who inspired them, **and read,** such searching being commanded to this day; **no one of these shall fail,** every point brought out in the prophecy would find its fulfilment, **none shall want her mate,** the corresponding prediction; **for My mouth, it hath commanded, and His spirit,** His breath, as God inspired His servants to write, **it hath gathered them,** so that the prophecy came to pass literally. V. 17. **And He,** Jehovah, **hath cast the lot for them,** for all the wild beasts of the desert, **and His hand hath divided it unto them by line,** distributed it to them, given it to them for a possession; **they shall possess it forever, from generation to generation shall they dwell therein,** these doleful creatures occupying the land which had been the pride of Edom. Thus Jehovah ever is the Protector of His children over against all enemies.

CHAPTER 35.

The Joyful State of Christ's Kingdom.

We have, in this chapter, a beautiful and majestic picture of the flourishing condition of Christ's kingdom, of the glorious future awaiting those who belong to the mountain of Zion, the redeemed of the Lord. V. 1. **The wilderness and the solitary place,** the desert and the steppe, **shall be glad for them,** that is, what formerly was a moral wilderness would be totally changed; **and the desert shall rejoice and blossom as the rose,** the Oriental narcissus, or crocus, which rapidly covers the waste places of the steppes after the beginning of the rainy season, making the whole surface of the land appear like a carpet of flowers. V. 2. **It shall blossom abundantly and rejoice even with joy and singing,** in an ecstasy of delight over the blessings of the Lord; **the glory of Lebanon,** with its mighty forests, **shall be given unto it, the excellency of Carmel,** the mountain famed for its beauty, **and Sharon,** the valley south of Carmel, famed for its luxurious vegetation, **they shall see the glory of the Lord and the excellency of our God,** namely, with the coming of the Messianic era. Therefore the prophet addresses words of cheer and comfort to the afflicted believers: v. 3. **Strengthen ye the weak hands,** the reference being to the firm grasp with which the believers should hold to the hope of their calling, **and confirm the feeble knees,** so that they will stand upright, keeping their ground against all enemies. V. 4. **Say to them that are of a fearful heart,** agitated and terrified by the dangers besetting them on every hand, **Be strong, fear not; behold, your God will come with vengeance,** to revenge His children upon their enemies, **even God with a recompense,** to punish every one according to his deserts; **He will come and save you,** for in punishing the enemies of His people the Lord delivers and saves those that are His. V. 5. **Then the eyes of the blind,** said of the spiritual blindness of natural man, **shall be opened,** to see the beauty of the Savior, **and the ears of the deaf shall be unstopped,** so that those who have never understood the sweet message of salvation will heed and believe it. V. 6. **Then shall the lame man,** who by reason of his self-righteousness was unable to walk the way of God's commandments, **leap as an hart,** in eager willingness to do the Lord's bidding, **and the tongue of the dumb,** of him who formerly knew nothing of the Gospel and therefore confessed nothing, **sing,** in hymns of thanksgiving to the God of his salvation; **for in the wilderness shall waters break out and streams in the desert,** for the grace and mercy of God in the New Testament era flows in rich streams to those who thirst for His forgiveness. Cp. Ps. 65, 9. 10. V. 7. **And the parched ground shall become a pool,** the mirage shall become a real lake, that is, the civic righteousness of men, their acts and works, which now only seem good, will then truly be good because flowing from the motive of faith in Christ, **and the thirsty land springs of water,** made fruitful by the power of love in the Word; **in the habitation of dragons,** in the dens of jackals, **where each lay, shall be grass with reeds and rushes,** an oasis of the Lord in the midst of a world filled with enmity toward Him. V. 8. **And an highway shall be there and a way,** a causeway such as was used by armies, the valleys being filled up and all obstructions removed, **and it shall be called The Way of Holiness,** the holy way, where the saints of the Lord were found; **the unclean shall not pass over it,** only those consecrated by the Lord; **but it shall be for those,** such as have, by the grace of God, found the way of sanctification; **the wayfaring men, though fools, shall not err therein,** that is, even the most unlearned will be able to follow the way of salvation as set forth in the Word of God. V. 9. **No lion shall be there,** the lion being named as one of the fiercest representatives of the animal world, **nor any ravenous beast shall go up thereon; it shall not be found there,** every one who walks on this way being under the special protection of God; **but the redeemed shall walk there,** those who have accepted the redemption of God in Christ Jesus and rely upon it in firm faith. V. 10. **And the ransomed of the Lord,** those whom the Messiah has delivered from the natural slavery of sin and from the consequent condemnation of death, **shall return and come to Zion with songs and everlasting joy upon their heads,** this joy being visible in their entire aspect, especially in the appearance of their faces; **they shall obtain joy and gladness, and sorrow and sighing shall flee away;** for the Christian religion is the most cheerful religion, the absolute religion also for this reason, that it alone announces to sinners the full and free love of God in Christ Jesus. In this manner these two chapters are in the fullest sense of the word Messianic prophecies, finding their application wherever the kingdom of Christ is established. Cp. Phil. 4, 4.

CHAPTER 36.

The Assyrians Threaten Jerusalem.

The three chapters now following form the historical appendix to the first part of the book of the prophet Isaiah, serving chiefly to make the prophecies concerning Assyria more intelligible. The events here told are narrated in practically the same form as in 2 Kings 18, 13—20, 11, but stress certain features of the story for the purposes which the inspired author had in mind.

RABSHAKEH'S MOCKERY. — V. 1. **Now, it came to pass in the fourteenth year of King Hezekiah that Sennacherib, king of Assyria, came up against all the defensed cities of Judah,** all those which were fortified with walls and towers, **and took them,** their number, according to an Assyrian account of the expedition, being forty-six. The Assyrian attack was directed primarily against Phenicia, Philistia, Edom, and Moab, but the enemies also overran the country of Judah. V. 2. **And the king of Assyria sent Rabshakeh,** the commander-in-chief of his army, **from Lachish,** a fortress in the southwestern part of Canaan, which the Assyrians wished to take preliminary to their descent upon Egypt, **to Jerusalem unto King Hezekiah with a great army,** a large detachment of his troops. **And he,** the general of the Assyrian king, **stood by the conduit of the upper pool in the highway of the fuller's field,** on an eminence overlooking the city from the west, chap. 7, 3. Hezekiah, in anticipation of Sennacherib's invasion, had stopped up the fountains outside of the city and conducted the water of the fountain of Gihon and that of the upper pool in a new conduit between the two walls. V. 3. **Then came forth unto him,** as emissaries of the king of Judah, **Eliakim, Hilkiah's son, which was over the house,** the royal chamberlain, and **Shebna, the scribe,** the king's secretary, and therefore an important state officer, and **Joah, Asaph's son, the recorder,** he who kept the royal archives. V. 4. **And Rabshakeh said unto them, Say ye now to Hezekiah, Thus saith the great king, the king of Assyria, What confidence is this wherein thou trustest?** Just on whom and on what did Hezekiah depend to deliver him and his city at this time? V. 5. **I say, sayest thou, (but they are but vain words,** upon which it is not safe to **rely), I have counsel and strength for war,** that is, empty bragging is his talk concerning preparation for war; **now, on whom dost thou trust that thou rebellest against me?** namely, by refusing to surrender Jerusalem in addition to the ransom paid. V. 6. **Lo, thou trustest in the staff of this broken reed, on Egypt,** as Rabshakeh contemptuously calls the ally of Judah, **whereon if a man lean, it will go into his hand and pierce it. So is Pharaoh, king of Egypt, to all that trust in him,** the Assyrian general naturally deriding and mocking the strength of Assyria's rival for world supremacy. V. 7. **But if thou say to me, We trust in the Lord, our God,** in Jehovah, the God of Israel, **is it not He whose high places and whose altars Hezekiah hath taken away and said to Judah and to Jerusalem, Ye shall worship before this altar?** Hezekiah had indeed done away with all the high places in Judah, even with those erected in honor of Jehovah, but that had been done only in the interest of the one central Sanctuary in Jerusalem and was therefore no interference with the authority of Jehovah. V. 8. **Now, therefore, give pledges, I pray thee,** giving sufficient security, and thus entering upon a wager, **to my master, the king of Assyria, and I will give thee two thousand horses, if thou be able on thy part to set riders upon them.** In other words, Rabshakeh wanted to bet the king of Judah that he could not produce two thousand men trained to serve in the cavalry of an army. V. 9. **How, then, wilt thou turn away,** resist and cause to retire, **the face of one captain of the least of my master's servants and put thy trust on Egypt for chariots and for horsemen?** The course which Hezekiah was following, so his argument ran, was ridiculous, suicidal; for Judah, even with the help of Egypt, had no chance of winning. V. 10. **And am I now come up without the Lord against this land to destroy it?** This argument was intended to be particularly effective in breaking down the *morale* of the Jews. **The Lord said unto me, Go up against this land and destroy it.** This was a bold shot, without foundation, but apt to terrify all those within hearing, so that they would refuse to follow Hezekiah any longer. A similar trick is used by the enemies of the Church in our day, when they insist that they are acting only in its interest as their evil plans are put into execution.

RABSHAKEH'S EFFORTS TO BRING ABOUT REVOLT. — V. 11. **Then said Eliakim and Shebnah and Joah,** the representatives of the king of Judah, **unto Rabshakeh, Speak, I pray thee, unto thy servants in the Syrian language,** in the Aramaic tongue, as spoken by the Assyrians, **for we understand it, and speak not to us in the Jews' language,** in the pure Hebrew, as spoken in and near Jerusalem, **in the ears of the people that are on the wall,** since they feared that the suggestions made by the Assyrian envoys might have a bad effect upon the inhabitants of the city. This remonstrance, however, exposed the fears of the Jewish leaders, for which reason the enemies were quick to take advantage of it. V. 12. **But Rabshakeh said, Hath my master sent me to thy master and to thee to speak these words,** on a secret mission? **Hath he not sent me to the men that sit upon the wall, that they may eat their**

own dung and drink their own piss with you? The messengers of Sennacherib purposely spoke in the Hebrew tongue and with a loud voice, in order to hold before the defenders of the city the fate which awaited them if they would not yield, namely, that of a most terrible starvation, which would drive them to the last extreme in providing food and drink for themselves. V. 13. **Then Rabshakeh,** suiting his actions to his words, **stood and cried with a loud voice in the Jews' language and said, Hear ye the words of the great king, the king of Assyria!** V. 14. **Thus saith the king, Let not Hezekiah deceive you; for he shall not be able to deliver you,** to save them from the fate which was in store for them in case they refused to surrender. V. 15. **Neither let Hezekiah make you trust in the Lord,** this being the chief weapon of the believers of all times, **saying, The Lord will surely deliver us; this city shall not be delivered into the hand of the king of Assyria,** this evidently being the gist of Hezekiah's assurances, and rightly so. V. 16. **Hearken not to Hezekiah; for thus saith the king of Assyria, Make an agreement with me by a present,** that is, Enter into a relation of mutual congratulations with me, the reference being to a surrender with the ratification of peace, at which time people congratulated one another, **and come out to me,** abandoning and surrendering the city; **and eat ye every one of his vine and every one of his fig-tree,** this being the Assyrian's promise to all inhabitants of Jerusalem who would side with him, **and drink ye every one the waters of his own cistern,** in a peaceful and undisturbed enjoyment of his own land and its products, v. 17. **until I come and take you away to a land like your own land, a land of corn and wine, a land of bread and vineyards.** Upon his return from Egypt, which Sennacherib believed he could overcome without difficulty, the Assyrians intended to follow their usual policy of deporting the inhabitants and thus keeping them in subjection most effectively. V. 18. **Beware lest Hezekiah persuade you, saying, The Lord will deliver us,** this challenge now being supported by a third consideration. **Hath any of the gods of the nations,** of the heathen countries round about, **delivered his land out of the hand of the king of Assyria?** V. 19. **Where are the gods of Hamath,** the capital of the country between the Lebanon and the Anti-Lebanon, **and Arphad,** a city still nearer the Syrian frontier? **Where are the gods of Sepharvaim?** the southernmost city of Mesopotamia, on the left bank of the Euphrates. **And have they,** the idols of the heathen, **delivered Samaria out of my hand?** V. 20. **Who are they among all the gods of these lands that have delivered their land out of my hand that the Lord should deliver Jerusalem out of my hand?** One commentator aptly remarks that the speaker forgets his own assertion here, v. 10, according to which he had come up against Judah *with* the Lord. "Liars need good memories." V. 21. **But they,** the men of Judah, also those on the wall, **held their peace and answered him not a word,** for a single incautious remark might have worked great harm; **for the king's commandment was, saying, Answer him not.** V. 22. **Then came Eliakim, the son of Hilkiah, that was over the household, and Shebna, the scribe, and Joah, the son of Asaph, the recorder,** the three envoys of Judah, **to Hezekiah with their clothes rent,** as a sign of deep grief and sorrow, **and told him the words of Rabshakeh.** Their obedience is rightly regarded as an example for others to follow.

CHAPTER 37.

The Pride and Overthrow of the King of Assyria.

THE EFFECT OF SENNACHERIB'S BOAST UPON HEZEKIAH. — V. 1. **And it came to pass, when King Hezekiah heard it,** namely, the report of his envoys, **that he rent his clothes and covered himself with sackcloth,** the depth of his grief and distress being shown by the fact that he wrapped himself in the vestments of mourning, **and went into the house of the Lord,** seeking help in the place in which God had promised to hear the prayers of His faithful people, 1 Kings 8, 29. V. 2. **And he sent Eliakim, who was over the household,** the royal chamberlain, **and Shebna, the scribe,** a high state officer, **and the elders of the priests,** a committee of priests selected on account of their age and experience, **covered with sackcloth,** in the same garments of mourning as the king had donned, **unto Isaiah, the prophet, the son of Amoz,** thus indicating the importance of the prophet's position at that time. V. 3. **And they said unto him, Thus saith Hezekiah, This day is a day of trouble,** of great affliction, **and of rebuke,** the king recognizing here a reproof of the Lord on account of the sins of his people, **and of blasphemy,** namely, of the blasphemous utterances of Rabshakeh; **for the children are come to the birth, and there is not strength to bring forth,** the mother's labor being inadequate to complete the birth, the reference being to the situation in the nation, which was threatened with destruction on account of its own weakness. V. 4. **It may be the Lord, thy God, will hear the words of Rabshakeh, whom the king of Assyria, his master, hath sent to reproach the liv-**

ing God, and will reprove the words which the Lord, thy God, hath heard, namely, the blasphemous statements that Jehovah, after all, was no more than the gods of the surrounding nations, a mistake which others had made before, 1 Kings 20, 23; **wherefore lift up thy prayer for the remnant that is left,** namely, Jerusalem and its inhabitants, everything else having been conquered by the invaders. V. 5. **So the servants of King Hezekiah came to Isaiah.** V. 6. **And Isaiah said unto them,** when they had presented their message, **Thus shall ye say unto your master, Thus saith the Lord, Be not afraid of the words that thou hast heard, wherewith the servants,** literally, "the youths," a disparaging designation characterizing their empty boasting, **of the king of Assyria have blasphemed Me,** that being the real and grievous offense committed by Rabshakeh's embassy. V. 7. **Behold, I will send a blast upon him,** influence his judgments and actions by a spirit which will guide him according to the plans of the Lord, **and he shall hear a rumor,** an evil report, **and return to his own land,** instead of attacking Jerusalem, as he evidently intended to do; **and I will cause him to fall by the sword in his own land,** by the hand of assassins, as related at the end of the chapter. V. 8. **So Rabshakeh returned,** marching back to the camp of his master without having accomplished his end, **and found the king of Assyria warring against Libnah,** a fortified city somewhat nearer to Jerusalem; **for he had heard that he was departed from Lachish,** withdrawing before the Egyptian advance. V. 9. **And he heard say concerning Tirhakah, king of Ethiopia,** at that time master of the entire country of Egypt, **He is come forth to make war with thee,** this being the report which, according to Isaiah's promise, was to influence Sennacherib to abandon his campaign. **And when he heard it, he sent messengers to Hezekiah, saying,** in a second attempt to get possession of Jerusalem and thus to strengthen his cause against Egypt, v. 10. **Thus shall ye speak to Hezekiah, king of Judah, saying, Let not thy God, in whom thou trustest, deceive thee, saying, Jerusalem shall not be given into the hand of the king of Assyria.** His attempt to intimidate the inhabitants of Jerusalem having failed, Sennacherib hoped to influence Hezekiah himself and cause him to yield. V. 11. **Behold, thou hast heard what the kings of Assyria have done to all lands by destroying them utterly,** this being a typical example of the boastfulness which characterizes the royal tablets of the Assyrian kings; **and shalt thou be delivered?** V. 12. **Have the gods of the nations,** namely, those subdued up to that time, **delivered them which my fathers have destroyed, as Gozan,** a province and city on the boundary of Mesopotamia and Armenia, **and Haran,** in Mesopotamia proper, **and Reseph,** in the valley of the Euphrates, on the western side, **and the children of Eden which were in Telassar?** a Mesopotamian locality on the east side of the Tigris. V. 13. **Where is the king of Hamath and the king of Arphad and the king of the city of Sepharvaim,** chap. 36, 19, **Hena, and Ivah?** the latter being cities in Babylonia. V. 14. **And Hezekiah received the letter from the hand of the messengers,** that is, the sheets upon which the message was penned, **and read it. And Hezekiah went up unto the house of the Lord and spread it before the Lord,** unrolled the parchment-scroll of writing. He thus brought the blasphemy to the attention of the Lord. V. 15. **And Hezekiah prayed unto the Lord, saying,** v. 16. **O Lord of hosts,** Commander of the heavenly armies, **God of Israel, that dwellest between the cherubim,** for that was the place from which the Lord communed with Moses, where He dwelt in the midst of His people, Ex. 25, 22; Num. 7, 89, **Thou art the God, even Thou alone, of all the kingdoms of the earth,** the one and only supreme Ruler of the universe; **Thou hast made heaven and earth,** and by virtue of His creation they are subject to Him. V. 17. **Incline Thine ear, O Lord,** in the gesture of close attention, **and hear; open Thine eyes, O Lord, and see,** both of them, as it were, being focused upon conditions as they obtained in Judah at that time, **and hear all the words of Sennacherib, which hath sent to reproach the living God,** to heap contempt upon Him. V. 18. **Of a truth, Lord, the kings of Assyria have laid waste all the nations and their countries,** the nations and their land, v. 19. **and have cast their gods into the fire; for they were no gods, but the work of men's hands, wood and stone,** dead and helpless idols; **therefore they have destroyed them,** this fact explained the easy victory of the Assyrians. V. 20. **Now, therefore, O Lord, our God,** upon whom Hezekiah and his people based their firm trust for deliverance, **save us from his hand, that all the kingdoms of the earth may know that Thou art the Lord, even Thou only,** the appeal thus being that the Lord should rescue His honor. That is the strongest argument which we may plead before the Lord in prayer, that He must hear us for the sake of His holy name, lest His honor be attacked with a show of right by the enemies.

Isaiah's Prophecy and Its Fulfilment. — V. 21. **Then,** after Hezekiah had laid his matter before the Lord in prayer, **Isaiah, the son of Amoz, sent unto Hezekiah, saying, Thus saith the Lord God of Israel, Whereas thou hast prayed to Me against Sennacherib, king of Assyria:** v. 22. **this is the word which the Lord hath spoken concerning him,** and therefore the plan which would be carried into effect: **The virgin, the daughter of Zion,** Jerusalem with its inhabitants, as representing the Church of God, **hath despised thee and laughed thee to scorn; the daughter of Jerusalem hath shaken her head at thee,** namely, in derision, as she looked after the Assyrian, who was forced to retreat without having accomplished his object. The reason for this change of fortunes is now stated: v. 23. **Whom hast thou reproached and blasphemed, and against whom hast thou exalted thy voice,** in boastful mockery, **and lifted up thine eyes on high?** in a gesture of supercilious contempt. **Even against the Holy One of Israel.** That is where Sennacherib had made his mistake, in directing his blasphemous scorn against the true God, who is jealous of His honor. V. 24. **By thy servants,** Rabshakeh and his companions, **hast thou reproached the Lord and hast said, By the multitude of my chariots am I come up to the height of the mountains, to the sides of Lebanon,** thus relying entirely upon his own strength; **and I will cut down the tall cedars thereof,** the finest trees of the mighty forests, **and the choice fir-trees thereof,** the splendid cypresses to be found there; **and I will enter into the height of his border, and the forest of his Carmel,** the most luxuriant part of his forest. The reference, as has been repeatedly noted, is not only to the occupation of the Lebanon district by the Assyrian forces, but there is also a hint here of Sennacherib's plan to conquer Jerusalem with its Temple, whose buildings were largely constructed of cedars and cypresses from Lebanon. V. 25. **I have digged and drunk water,** so the boast of Sennacherib went on, **and with the sole of my feet have I dried up all the rivers of the besieged places,** that is, where water was lacking, he had his men provide it, and where streams hindered his progress, he had but to call upon the resources at his command and the waters were diverted. Over against this proud boasting of the Assyrian concerning his own might the prophet explains that he was but the tool in the hands of God. V. 26. **Hast thou not heard long ago how I have done it,** the Lord Himself having planned this punishment for the purposes of His mercy, **and of ancient times, that I have formed it?** everything being ordered in accordance with His plans. **Now have I brought it to pass that thou shouldest be to lay waste defensed cities into ruinous heaps,** the Lord having decided upon their destruction in order to call their inhabitants to repentance, if possible. V. 27. **Therefore their inhabitants were of small power,** helpless before the invaders; **they were dismayed and confounded,** rendered powerless by terror; **they were as the grass of the field and as the green herb, as the grass on the housetops,** with but a thin layer of soil, **and as corn blasted before it be grown up,** such vegetation being unable to withstand even a moderate amount of blasting winds. The prophecy now turns directly against Sennacherib. V. 28. **But I know thy abode,** namely, when he is at home, **and thy going out, and thy coming in, and thy rage against Me,** the entire course of Sennacherib's life being known to the Lord, also the preparations for the present campaign and its success hitherto. V. 29. **Because thy rage against Me and thy tumult,** his proud self-confidence, **is come up into Mine ears, therefore will I put My hook in thy nose,** as one controls an unruly beast, **and My bridle in thy lips,** so that he must submit, though unwillingly, **and I will turn thee back by the way by which thou camest.** The prophet's message now turns to Hezekiah: v. 30. **And this shall be a sign unto thee,** a token whose fulfilment would assure him of the truth of the entire prophecy, **Ye shall eat this year such as groweth of itself,** volunteer grain; **and the second year that which springeth of the same,** for the Assyrian invasion had not only destroyed the harvest of the last year, but had also made it impossible to put out the new crop; **and in the third year,** that is, about one year after the present prophecy, **sow ye,** this being done in the fall of the year, **and reap, and plant vineyards, and eat the fruit thereof,** everything being restored to its usual order by that time. V. 31. **And the remnant that is escaped of the house of Judah,** those who survived after Sennacherib's invasion, **shall again take root downward and bear fruit upward,** be firmly settled once more, for the kingdom of Judah lasted for another century after this prophecy; v. 32. **for out of Jerusalem shall go forth a remnant,** those who had found shelter in the city before the advance of the Assyrians, **and they that escape out of Mount Zion. The zeal of the Lord of hosts shall do this.** There is more than a hint here concerning the rejuvenation of the Messianic period. The Lord now abandons His figurative language and makes a direct statement. V. 33. **Therefore thus saith the Lord concerning the king of Assyria, He shall not come into this city,** not subdue it, **nor shoot an arrow there,** he will not even begin his threatened siege of the city, **nor come before it with shields,** for the purpose of storming it, **nor cast a bank against it,** the usual trenches of siege warfare. V. 34. **By the way that he came, by the same shall he return,** without accomplishing his object, **and shall not come into this city, saith the Lord.** V. 35. **For I will defend this city to save it for Mine own sake,** to defend His own honor against the bragging of Sennacherib, **and for My servant David's sake,** the establishment of whose kingdom was connected with the safety of his capital. Cp. 2 Kings 20, 6. V. 36. **Then the Angel of the Lord,** the Son of God, who bears this name throughout the Old Testament, **went forth and smote in the camp of the Assyrians a hundred and fourscore**

and five thousand, the calamity being in the nature of a pestilence or some other similar visitation. **And when they,** the survivors, **arose early in the morning, behold, they,** the Assyrians, **were all dead corpses,** their army had been practically annihilated. V. 37. **So Sennacherib, king of Assyria, departed,** he abandoned his campaign, **and went and returned, and dwelt at Nineveh,** the capital of his empire. V. 38. **And it came to pass, as he was worshiping in the house of Nisroch, his god,** one of the chief idols of Assyria, an eagle-headed human figure, **that Adrammelech and Sharezer, his sons, smote him with the sword,** his own offspring becoming guilty of assassination; **and they escaped into the land of Armenia,** where they, according to some accounts, established kingdoms of their own. **And Esarhaddon, his son, reigned in his stead,** who is mentioned Ezra 4, 2. "Such was the end of the haughty Sennacherib, who had dared to blaspheme the God of Israel. He who had boasted that no god or people could resist him must fall before the swords of his sons. He that regarded himself unconquerable by the help of his idols must suffer death in the temple, in the presence of his idol!" (Lange.) Thus the Lord ever upholds the honor of His holy name.

CHAPTER 38.

Hezekiah's Illness, Recovery, and Song of Praise.

Hezekiah's Illness and Recovery. — V. 1. **In those days,** at the time of the Assyrian invasion or shortly after, **was Hezekiah sick unto death,** with an illness which was ordinarily mortal. **And Isaiah, the prophet, the son of Amoz, came unto him,** evidently by a direct command of the Lord, **and said unto him, Thus saith the Lord, Set thine house in order,** literally, "Give charge concerning thy house"; he was to make arrangements especially concerning his successor to the throne and regarding the disposition of his goods; **for thou shalt die and not live,** this announcement being in agreement with the ordinary course of the disease. It is advisable for a believer always to have everything in readiness, so that, no matter when the Lord may call him hence, his earthly effects may be in order and those dependent upon him provided for. V. 2. **Then Hezekiah turned his face toward the wall,** in a movement which showed that he wished to be undisturbed with his thoughts, that he wished to be undistracted for communion with God, **and prayed unto the Lord,** v. 3. **and said,** in the fervent appeal of a child of God. **Remember now, O Lord, I beseech Thee, how I have walked before Thee in truth,** without uncertainty and hypocrisy, **and with a perfect heart,** which aimed to serve Him in sincerity, **and have done that which is good in Thy sight,** according to the standard of Ps. 15 and also Matt. 5, 21. 22. **And Hezekiah wept sore,** for it seemed hard for him to die in the fulness of his manhood, without an heir, and with his country in a dangerous position. V. 4. **Then came the word of the Lord to Isaiah, saying,** v. 5. **Go and say to Hezekiah, Thus saith the Lord, the God of David, thy father,** for whose sake He gave so many evidences of His goodness and mercy to many of the kings of Judah, **I have heard thy prayer, I have seen thy tears; behold, I will add unto thy days fifteen years,** by a gracious dispensation. V. 6. **And I will deliver thee and this city out of the hand of the king of Assyria,** so that he would undertake no further campaigns against it; **and I will defend this city.** V. 7. **And this shall be a sign unto thee from the Lord that the Lord will do this thing that He hath spoken,** a token which will prove the truth of this prophecy: v. 8. **Behold, I will bring again the shadow of the degrees which is gone down in the sun-dial of Ahaz ten degrees backward.** This dial seems to have been built up in semicircular form, in a series of steps, the size of which was such as to make them visible from the king's rooms. **So the sun returned ten degrees, by which degrees it was gone down.** The sun not only stood still, but it actually moved backward for a short distance, by the command of the Lord. The sickness of Hezekiah was not the plague, but a fever with an eruption of ulcers or boils. The present account is much abbreviated, as a comparison with 2 Kings 20 shows, but all the essential points are included. One commentator here makes the remark: "How often our wishes, when gratified, prove curses! Hezekiah lived to have a son; that son was the idolater Manasseh, the chief cause of God's wrath against Judah and of the overthrow of the kingdom."

Hezekiah's Hymn of Praise. — V. 9. **The writing of Hezekiah, king of Judah, when he had been sick and was recovered of his sickness,** a psalm of thanksgiving composed and written by him: v. 10. **I said in the cutting off of my days,** rather, in the tranquillity of my days, at the time of his life and reign when he could look forward to an undisturbed enjoyment of his kingly position, **I shall go to the gates of the grave,** the kingdom of death had opened before him in his illness; **I am deprived of the residue of my years,** of the rest of his life according to the natural, average length of life. V. 11. **I said, I shall not see the Lord, even the Lord, in the land of the living,** enjoy the gifts of His goodness here on earth, Ps. 27, 13; **I shall behold man no more with the inhabitants of the world,** no longer enjoy the companionship of men among the denizens of the realm of death. V. 12. **Mine age is departed,** broken off, removed, folded up, **and is removed from me as a shepherd's tent,** which is quickly pitched and as quickly taken down; **I have cut off, like a weaver, my life,** rolling it together as the craftsman folds the finished garment; **He will cut me off with pining sickness,** as the thread is cut off which tied the loom to the weaver's beam; **from day even to night wilt Thou make an end of me.** While Hezekiah, as it were, was rolling up his life, as he lived it, on the weaver's beam, the Lord threatened, by His cutting off, to interrupt his labor suddenly, and so rapid was the progress of the sickness that it seemed about to do its work in one day. V. 13. **I reckoned till morning,** composing himself till the next day, **that, as a lion, so will He break all my bones,** rather, for He was breaking my bones, and it was only with difficulty that he kept himself from despair; **from day even to night wilt Thou make an end of me,** it seemed that he could not endure the agony till evening. V. 14. **Like a crane or a swallow, so did I chatter, I did mourn as a dove,** murmuring and groaning with querulous notes, with broken sounds expressive of pain; **mine eyes fail with looking upward,** with painful longing, and yet lifted up to the Lord. **O Lord, I am oppressed,** as a debtor hard pressed by his creditor; **undertake for me,** literally, "be surety for me," so that he would be delivered from this oppression. V. 15. **What shall I say?** Hezekiah finds himself at a loss for words adequately to express his appreciation of the deliverance afforded him. **He hath both spoken unto me, and Himself hath done it,** the Lord's performance agreeing exactly with His promise; **I shall go softly all my years in the bitterness of my soul,** or: "Shall I walk along softly all the years of my life after the bitterness of my soul?" The answer is, of course, that God granted him just this, to have such relief after his bitter experience. V. 16. **O Lord, by these things men live, and in all these things is the life of my spirit,** namely, by the blessings of God's goodness and mercy; **so wilt Thou recover me and make me to live,** preserving his life by His almighty power. V. 17. **Behold, for peace I had great bitterness,** that is, unto deliverance was bitterness for me, bitterness, what he considered the bitter distress of death makes his deliverance stand out all the more brightly; **but Thou hast in love to my soul delivered it from the pit of corruption, for Thou hast cast all my sins behind Thy back,** this forgiveness of sins being the reason for God's gracious deliverance of the king, being the ground for His act of mercy. V. 18. **For the grave cannot praise Thee, death cannot celebrate Thee,** people in the realm of death have no opportunity to sing His praises; **they that go down into the pit cannot hope for Thy truth,** place their trust in His faithfulness. V. 19. **The living, the living, he shall praise Thee, as I do this day,** the great contrast between the mournful past and the joyful present being brought out here; **the father to the children shall make known Thy truth,** the faithfulness of God in keeping His promises. V. 20. **The Lord was ready to save me,** to give him deliverance from the evil which beset him; **therefore we will sing my songs to the stringed instruments,** with their accompaniment, **all the days of our life in the house of the Lord,** the hymn probably being used for public worship at stated times, especially on the anniversary of Hezekiah's recovery. To tarry in the house of the Lord and to bring Him the sacrifices of our lips and hands is the only proper way of showing our thankfulness for favors received from Him. V. 21. **For Isaiah had said,** at the time when he had promised the king that he would recover from his illness, **Let them take a lump of figs,** a remedy often used to bring relief in case of swellings, but here merely a secondary feature in the miraculous cure, **and lay it for a plaster upon the boil, and he shall recover.** V. 22. **Hezekiah also had said,** when Isaiah delivered to him the Lord's promise, **What is the sign that I shall go up to the house of the Lord?** He had been given the sign, and his recovery had taken place. His prayer had been heard, and so his heart overflowed in grateful melody to the God of all good gifts, a fine example for believers of all times.

CHAPTER 39.

The Babylonian Embassy and Its Consequences.

Encouraged by the reverses which the Assyrian forces suffered in Syria, one of the viceroys of Babylon, the Chaldean Merodach-baladan, made himself, for a number of years, independent of the Assyrian power and attained to a position of some influence in the Eastern Empire. He was naturally most desirous of establishing himself more firmly and therefore sought also the friendship of Judah with its mighty king. V. 1. **At that time Merodach-baladan, the son of Baladan, king of Babylon,** and formerly one of the Assyrian viceroys, **sent letters and a present to Hezekiah, for he had heard that he had been sick and was recovered.** He was by no means prompted by friendliness in sending this embassy, but was guided by political motives, by the desire to form as strong an alliance as possible against the Assyrian power. V. 2. **And Hezekiah**, flattered by the attention shown him by this mighty power, **was glad of them**, pleased by their visit, **and showed them the house of his precious things**, where he stored all the highest valuables which he had acquired in the course of his reign, **the silver, and the gold, and the spices**, various aromatic fruits, **and the precious ointment**, probably the fine variety used for the anointing of priests and kings, **and all the house of his armor**, his arsenal, **and all that was found in his treasuries; there was nothing in his house nor in all his dominion**, for all this had been brought to Jerusalem at the approach of the enemies, **that Hezekiah showed them not.** But this friendliness toward representatives of a heathen nation was not in conformity with the will of the Lord. V. 3. **Then came Isaiah, the prophet**, acting in his usual capacity as God's messenger, **unto King Hezekiah and said unto him, What said these men, and from whence came they unto thee?** The very presence of these ambassadors and the reception they received at the hands of Hezekiah proved that the king of Judah was once more preparing to become affiliated with a heathen nation. **And Hezekiah said**, with a certain amount of evasion, **They are come from a far country unto me, even from Babylon**, the argument implied in his answer being that it certainly devolved upon him to show hospitality to men who came from such a great distance. V. 4. **Then said he**, Isaiah, again speaking by the command of the Lord, **What have they seen in thine house? And Hezekiah answered, All that is in mine house have they seen; there is nothing among my treasures that I have not showed them.** The king here made an open confession of his folly, submitting to the scrutiny of the propet without flinching. It is the attitude which should always be found in men when the Lord searches the hearts and minds. V. 5. **Then said Isaiah to Hezekiah, Hear the word of the Lord of hosts**, the almighty Commander and Ruler of all men and all things: v. 6. **Behold, the days come that all that is in thine house**, all the material riches which he had amassed, of which he had shown himself so proud and vain, at least in a measure, **and that which thy fathers have laid up in store until this day**, everything that had escaped being paid as tribute, especially the precious metals inside the Temple, **shall be carried to Babylon; nothing shall be left, saith the Lord.** This was the first direct prophecy foretelling the Babylonian captivity. V. 7. **And of thy sons that shall issue from thee, which thou shalt beget**, his direct descendants, **shall they take away**, this being true even of his son Manasseh, but particularly of the last kings of his line; **and they shall be eunuchs**, court officers, chamberlains, **in the palace of the king of Babylon.** Cp. Dan. 1, 2. 3. 7. V. 8. **Then said Hezekiah to Isaiah, Good is the word of the Lord which thou hast spoken.** He readily bowed to the decree of the Lord, as pronounced upon him. **He said moreover, For there shall be peace and truth in my days**, that is, for the rest of his reign, at least, Judah would not be harassed by the enemies, and all the allies would keep their word and not precipitate a crisis, for all of which the king was duly thankful to the Giver of all good gifts. That is a sign of true repentance, if a sinner bows to the will of the Lord, finding cause for thanksgiving in every show of mercy which may be revealed to him.

CHAPTER 40.

The Word of Comfort and the God of Comfort.

The last part of the book of the prophet Isaiah has fitly been called the Book of Comfort, for in its beautiful language and in its exalted visions the Gospel of salvation is so clearly taught that it often seems as though John himself were speaking. The preacher and the prophet are combined in the message brought out by Isaiah to such an extent as to make us feel that voices from the world beyond are singing a glorious hymn of praise.

THE GOSPEL OF COMFORT. — V. 1. **Comfort ye, comfort ye, My people, saith your God.** Note the repetition of the charge, with the emphasis implied, the significance of the address in the plural as including the Gospel-messengers of all times, and the inviting designations "My" people and "your" God. In the very charge of Jehovah there is contained a tender call to the believers of all times to find true comfort and consolation in the message of salvation. V. 2. **Speak ye comfortably to Jerusalem**, literally, "to the heart of Jerusalem," addressing words of consolation to all members of the spiritual Zion, the Church of God, **and cry unto her**, in a sermon of sweetest assurance, **that her warfare is accomplished**, that the tribulation to which His people are subjected would soon be ended, **that her iniquity is pardoned**, namely, in and through the Messiah, whose coming is so clearly foretold in this series of prophecies; **for she hath received of the Lord's hand double for all her sins**, that is, the severe punishment which the Lord's people had to endure for their sins was to be replaced in richest measure by evidences of His grace and mercy. That is the strange and wonderful manner in which the Lord deals with His children always — He substitutes acts of love and mercy for the well-merited condemnation. The prophet now shows in what way his threefold message would be realized. V. 3. **The voice of him that crieth in the wilderness,** of the herald of the great King Messiah, **Prepare ye the way of the Lord,** in the very midst of the spiritual wilderness in which men find themselves by nature, they should make ready a road on which their King might come into their hearts, **make straight in the desert a highway for our God.** V. 4. **Every valley shall be exalted,** the hearts that have been humbled by the hammer-blows of the Law being lifted up, **and every mountain and hill shall be made low,** the proud and self-righteous spirits being taught to despair of their own virtue; **and the crooked shall be made straight,** the hindrances laid flat, **and the rough places plain,** all obstructions due to sin and objection to the Lord and His Word being removed by the message of the New Testament; v. 5. **and the glory of the Lord shall be revealed,** namely, chiefly in the coming of His only-begotten Son, full of grace and truth, John 1, 14, **and all flesh shall see it together,** all men having an opportunity to become acquainted with the Gospel of salvation, Matt. 24, 14; **for the mouth of the Lord hath spoken it.** The paragraph deals with the call to repentance with which the Messianic era opened, particularly in the preaching of John the Baptist, Matt. 3, 1—3; Mark 1, 2. 3; Luke 3, 2—6; John 1, 23, but finds its application also in all true preaching of the New Testament, which is essentially a proclamation of sin and grace. The prophet now introduces a dialog between a heavenly voice and that of the ideal prophet concerning the proclamation which is to be made. V. 6. **The voice,** some one with authority speaking from heaven, **said, Cry,** call out, announce! **And he,** a voice on earth representing all true preachers of righteousness, **said, What shall I cry?** What are to be the contents of his preaching? And the answer comes down from heaven, **All flesh is grass,** all human beings are mortal, transitory, perishable, subject to death and decay, **and all the goodliness thereof,** all the outward show and pomp of men, **is as the flower of the field,** barely reaching an early maturity before it withers. V. 7. **The grass withereth, the flower fadeth, because the Spirit of the Lord bloweth upon it,** for it is He who gives them their being, and it is He who causes their decay; **surely the people is grass,** even the covenant nation. Cp. Ps. 104, 29. 30; Eccl. 8, 8; Rom. 6, 23; Ps. 90. V. 8. **The grass withereth, the flower fadeth,** the repetition being made for the sake of impressing this great truth upon all minds; **but the Word of our God shall stand forever,** in the midst of the death and decay of this world, in the midst even of the final great cataclysm which will usher in the end of the present earth, the Word of the Lord abides without change and modification, throughout eternity. The prophet, therefore, urges Zion, the Church of the Lord, to make known this Word with rejoicing, v. 9. **O Zion, that bringest good tidings,** the congregation of the Lord being regarded as an evangelist proclaiming the message of the Gospel, **get thee up into the high mountain,** from where her voice could be heard far and wide. **O Jerusalem, that bringest good tidings,** the parallelism bringing out the urgency of the call, **lift up thy voice with strength,** in triumphant strains, in a cheerful announcement; **lift it up, be not afraid,** faint-hearted on account of the feeling of unworthiness; **say unto the cities of Judah,** to all those who have experienced tribulation similar to that of the mother, **Behold your God!** The picture is that of the deliverance from the Babylonian captivity, but its application throughout presupposes New Testament conditions. V. 10. **Behold, the Lord God will come with strong hand,** the almighty Ruler making use of His omnipotence, **and His arm shall rule for Him,** in triumphing over all enemies. **Behold, His reward is with Him,** namely, that which He gained in the severe battle which He undertook, **and His work before Him,** the spoils which He has brought back, with which He intends to bless His people. One of these blessings is now described. V. 11. **He shall feed His flock,** take the proper care of all His children in the faith, **like a shepherd,** in His capacity as the one true Shepherd of their souls; **He shall gather the lambs,** the young, weak, and inexperienced, **with His arm,** picking them up since they are unable to walk, **and carry them in His bosom,** with the most tender care, **and shall gently lead those that are with young,** lest the ewes be harmed by being overdriven. This entire introductory section, with its four strophes outlining the last part of the book, pictures the coming of the Messiah in all the beauty of its comfort, calls to repentance, emphasizes the certainty of His salvation, and proclaims the victory of the Lord and the glorification of the believers.

JEHOVAH THE SUPREME RULER. — The connection of thought between this section and the foregoing one is this, that the majesty and glory of God over against the idolatry of the heathen nations guarantees the security and the deliverance of the believers of all times. V. 12. **Who hath measured the waters in the hollow of his hand?** fixing the quantity of all the water in ocean, seas, and streams, **and meted out heaven with the span,** the measure between the thumb and middle finger, **and comprehended the dust of the earth in a measure,** the third part of an ephah, **and weighed the mountains in scales and the hills in a balance?** Before the exalted Lord and Ruler of the universe the whole earth and all it contains are insignificant, amount to nothing or next to nothing, yet it was His good pleasure to weigh them out and to adjust them in their proper relation. V. 13. **Who hath directed the Spirit of the Lord?** Who can measure and understand Him, **or,** being **His counselor, hath taught Him?** advising Him on the basis of his understanding of the Lord's mind. Cp. Rom. 11, 34. The fundamental principle of education is here stated: Understanding the pupil and giving him instruction, teaching him to discriminate and to perform the works of His government properly. It is preposterous that God should need or seek the counsel of any man. V. 14. **With whom took He counsel, and who instructed Him,** so that He learned discrimination, **and taught Him in the path of judgment, and taught Him knowledge,** so that He could apply His wisdom in the right manner, **and showed to Him the way of understanding?** so that His knowing could be translated into the right kind of doing. This thought is even more outside of the pale of possibility, for the Lord is immensely exalted above all human beings even at the highest point of their enlightenment, as the text shows in the next section. V. 15. **Behold, the nations are as a drop of a bucket,** clinging to the bottom of the bucket when it is emptied, **and are counted as the small dust of the balance,** like a grain of sand in the pan. **Behold, He taketh up the isles as a very little thing,** like a mote that is carried upward. The prophet uses the very strongest comparisons to indicate the immeasurable distance by which even the imagination of man stays behind and fails to reach the exaltation of Jehovah. V. 16. **And Lebanon is not sufficient to burn,** to supply fuel enough for worthy sacrifices to the glory of God, **nor the beasts thereof sufficient for a burnt offering,** the untold number of animals with which these forests abounded would not be enough fittingly to honor Him by their sacrifice. V. 17. **All nations before Him are as nothing,** their entire sum and substance totaling only so much before Him; **and they are counted to Him less than nothing and vanity.** Therefore the prophet inserts the question which, at the same time, introduces the new section of this chapter, v. 18. **To whom, then, will ye liken God?** Why try to make comparisons, which, at best, are so utterly inadequate and futile? **Or what likeness will ye compare unto Him?** How foolish to try to represent Him by one of the idols whom the prophet now proceeds to describe. V. 19. **The workman melteth a graven image,** casting it in molds, **and the goldsmith spreadeth it over with gold,** in a plating of the more precious metal, **and casteth silver chains,** as ornaments on the figure. V. 20. **He that is so impoverished that he hath no oblation,** that is, the heathen priest who is supported by such gifts, **chooseth a tree that will not rot,** the most durable wood; **he seeketh unto him a cunning workman to prepare a graven image,** to set it up in the proper manner, **that shall not be moved,** so that the idol would fall to the ground. Note the irony of the prophet which is in evidence throughout, followed by disgust, which shows itself in a number of questions expressing great displeasure. V. 21. **Have ye not known? Have ye not heard?** The facts which the prophet has in mind could and should be well known to all whom the prophet's words might reach. **Hath it not been told you from the beginning? Have ye not understood from the foundations of the earth?** God alone has established the earth and laid its foundations and no idol ever even approached Him, much less was worthy of being compared with Him. This God is now described by the prophet. V. 22. **It is He that sitteth upon the circle of the earth,** highly exalted above the globe of this puny world, **and the inhabitants thereof are as grasshoppers,** so insignificant and despicable in comparison with Him; **that stretcheth out the heavens as a curtain,** the reference being to the awning which is drawn over the court of Oriental houses for shelter in rain or hot weather, **and spreadeth them out as a tent to dwell in;** v. 23. **that bringeth the princes to nothing,** their power being helpless before Him; **He maketh the judges of the earth as vanity,** nothingness, an empty show. V. 24. **Yea, they shall not be planted; yea, they shall not be sown; yea, their stock shall not take root in the earth,** that is, hardly have they, in their own opinion, gained a foothold, believing themselves to be safe without the Lord, **and He shall also blow upon them, and they shall wither, and the whirlwind shall take them away as stubble,** as chaff in a tornado, absolutely helpless before Him who is the Ruler of the universe. Therefore the Lord now bids men consider His incomparable majesty and glory. V. 25. **To whom, then, will ye liken Me or shall I be equal? saith the Holy One.** It is a vain and fruitless task even to compare the wisdom and power of individuals and of nations with that of the Lord; for He is the Possessor of limitless power and wisdom. V. 26. **Lift up your eyes on high,** namely, to the heights of heaven, to the starry firmament, **and behold who hath created these things,** all the heavenly bodies, **that bringeth out their host by number,** like a shepherd leading his sheep to the meadow. **He calleth them all by names by the greatness of His might, for that He is strong in power; not one faileth,** He takes care, by virtue of His might and of His goodness, that not one is left behind. How readily will He, therefore, will His love and goodness, surround His children everywhere with His protection! Cp. Ps. 147, 4; Matt. 10, 30. V. 27. **Why sayest thou, O Jacob, and speakest, O Israel,** all the believers everywhere, when evil days come upon them, **My way is hid from the Lord, and my judgment is passed over from my God?** the complaint often being made by Christians that the Lord takes no interest in them, that He disregards their case, that He neglects them, passing by their distress without noticing it. The reproachful question is followed by an emphatic statement, also in the form of a question, v. 28. **Hast thou not known?** It surely had been proclaimed often enough. **Hast thou not heard that the everlasting God,** who is unchangeable from eternity to eternity, **the Lord,** the covenant God, **the Creator of the ends of the earth,** that is, of the whole world with all that it contains, **fainteth not, neither is weary?** He never so much as begins to abandon His vigilant care for His children, much less will He fail in it. **There is no searching of His understanding,** it cannot be fathomed by the finite mind of any human being. This fact, then, should inspire His people with the strongest confidence. V. 29. **He giveth power to the faint,** sustaining them when they are about to sink down; **and to them that have no might He increaseth strength,** that is, to those who are utterly helpless He imparts power. V. 30. **Even the youths,** those in the prime of their young manhood, **shall faint and be weary,** namely, when depending on their own strength, **and the young men,** those excelling in youthful vigor and energy, **shall utterly fall,** for mere human might and power is, after all, subject to weariness and decay. V. 31. **But they that wait upon the Lord,** putting all their trust in Him alone, **shall renew their strength,** gaining new spiritual power from day to day; **they shall mount up with wings as eagles,** the birds who have ever been types of almost limitless strength, Ps. 103, 5; **they shall run and not be weary; and they shall walk and not faint,** finishing their course with the strength imparted to them from on high, victorious to the last. 2 Tim. 4, 7.

CHAPTER 41.

The God of History and of Prophecy.

THE GLORY OF THE LORD AND THE VANITY OF THE HEATHEN. — V. 1. **Keep silence before Me, O islands,** since the Lord is about to argue His case before the leaders of the Gentile world, **and let the people,** all those on the side of the enemies, **renew their strength,** gather all the resources at their command, in order, if that be possible, to gain the advantage in the argument; **let them come near,** stepping before the tribunal of the great Judge. **Then let them speak,** arguing their case; **let us,** the Lord and His enemies, **come near together to judgment,** to have their matter adjudicated in court. It is a majestic challenge on the part of the great God. V. 2. **Who raised up the righteous man from the East, called him to his foot, gave the nations before him, and made him rule over kings?** literally, "Who stirs, raises up from the East him (whom) justice calls to her footprints, gives nations before him, and lets him step upon kings?" It is God who calls a great deliverer from the Eastern empire, a man who is ready to follow in the footsteps of the covenant faithfulness, and whom the Lord causes to subdue nations and kings. **He gave them as the dust to his sword and as driven stubble to his bow,** or, in the form of a question, "Who makes them as dust by His sword, as wind-driven stubble through His bow?" all the enemies of the Lord being destroyed before Him. V. 3. **He pursued them and passed safely,** without hindrance; **even by the way that he had not gone with his feet,** that is, the conquerer whom the Lord calls will carry on his pursuit of the Lord's enemies with such energy as to disregard all obstructions, no matter of what kind they may be. V. 4. **Who hath wrought and done it,** undertaking and also finishing the work which He had set before Him, **calling the generations from the beginning? I, the Lord, the First and with the last: I am He.** Jehovah, who called all the generations of man into being and will do so until the end of time, raises up also this deliverer as the champion of His cause. We now have a description of the impression which the argument of Jehovah made upon the enemies. V. 5. **The isles,** the leaders among the heathen, **saw it and feared,** filled with terror before the deliverer appointed by the Lord; **the ends of the earth,** all the inhabitants of the world, **were afraid, drew near, and came,** huddling together for mutual defense, with a show of opposition. V. 6. **They helped every one his neighbor,** they attempt to assist one another in the work which they now undertake; **and every one said to his brother, Be of good courage,** trying to give him moral support, for they intend to supply gods for their defense against Jehovah. V. 7. **So the carpenter,** the craftsman in wood and metal, **encouraged the goldsmith,** the man who cast the idols, **and he that smootheth with the hammer him that smote the anvil, saying, It is ready for the soldering,** saying of the soldered mass, It is good; **and he fastened it with nails that it should not be moved.** Although the picture, as put together, seems solid enough, yet the workmen, for safety's sake, put in a few nails to hold it upright, a fine bit of irony characterizing the vanity of idolatry and the helplessness of the idol worshipers, who trust in the work of man's hands.

THE LORD'S PROMISE OF A FUTURE VICTORY. V. 8. **But thou, Israel, art My servant,** as Jehovah, in a section replete with love and consolation, assures His children, **Jacob, whom I have chosen, the seed of Abraham, My friend,** His servants, the people of His covenant, of old, especially the spiritual descendants of him who had the honor of being known as the friend of God. V. 9. **Thou, whom I have taken from the ends of the earth and called thee from the chief men thereof,** from its most remote corners, **and said unto thee, Thou art My servant; I have chosen thee and not cast thee away.** Note how excellently this description fits the believers of the New Testament, and how fully the glory of our calling into His kingdom is given to Jehovah alone. Therefore the Lord's encouraging words gain in beauty with every new reading; every word, in fact, as one commentator puts it, breathes the most fervent love. V. 10. **Fear thou not, for I am with thee,** with His merciful power; **be not dismayed,** filled with anxiety, **for I am thy God,** who freely gives His heart, His grace, His salvation, to His children; **I will strengthen thee,** so that no one can overthrow him; **yea, I will help thee,** upholding him who is in himself too weak to withstand the enemy; **yea, I will uphold thee with the right hand of My righteousness,** for the righteousness of God, which is imputed to men by faith, is the element which sustains him in the midst of all dangers and enemies of this world and keeps him safe for the final deliverance from every evil. V. 11. **Behold, all they that were incensed against thee,** who gave expression to their wrath, **shall be ashamed and confounded,** by the defeat and destruction which would strike them; **they shall be as nothing, and they that strive with thee shall perish,** since the Lord Himself would do battle for His people. V. 12. **Thou shalt seek them and shalt not find them, even them that contended with thee,** daring to attack the Lord's people; **they that war against thee shall be as nothing and as a thing of naught,** so utterly exterminated that not a trace of them could be found. V. 13. **For I, the Lord, thy God, will hold thy right hand,** thereby imparting His almighty strength, **saying unto thee, Fear not, I will help thee.** Cp. Deut. 33, 26. 29. The encouragement now increases in fervency. V. 14. **Fear not, thou worm Jacob,** trodden under foot as he now seems, **and ye men of Israel,** the poor small crew who hold to the Lord: **I will help thee, saith the Lord,** that is His majestic saying, **and thy Redeemer (is) the Holy One of Israel,** the mighty Deliverer and Vindicator of His people at all times, He who is zealous for His own honor and for the safety of His children. V. 15. **Behold, I will make thee a new sharp threshing instrument having teeth,** the sledge used in the Orient to cut up the straw for fodder and to separate the grain from the hull, sometimes used to put captives to death; **thou shalt thresh the mountains, and beat them small, and shalt make the hills as chaff,** the very world-powers being compelled to yield to the army of the Lord. V. 16. **Thou shalt fan them,** as the husbandman winnows his grain, **and the wind shall carry them away,** like useless chaff, **and the whirlwind,** the strong tempest, **shall scatter them; and thou,** seeing this marvelous victory over the mighty enemies, **shalt rejoice in the Lord and shalt glory in the Holy One of Israel,** properly giving all honor to Him who is the zealous Deliverer of His people. Not only will the enemies be overthrown, however, but the Church of God will find divine refreshment in the midst of the tribulation of this world. V. 17. **When the poor and needy seek water,** spiritual comfort and strength, **and there is none, and their tongue faileth for thirst,** their heart parched, exhausted with the heat of the affliction, **I, the Lord, will hear them,** their sighs and their prayers; **I, the God of Israel, will not forsake them,** not permit them to perish in their misery. V. 18. **I will open rivers in high places,** in dry rocks, as He did in the wilderness, **and fountains in the midst of the valleys,** so that the headsprings will yield abundantly. **I will make the wilderness a pool of water and the dry land springs of water.** In the midst of Israel's great spiritual trouble the Lord Himself would send refreshment for their souls in the Word of His grace. V. 19. **I will plant in the wilderness the cedar, the shittah-tree,** the acacia, or Egyptian thorn, **and the myrtle, and the oil-tree,** the wild olive, valued as an ornamental tree; **I will set in the desert the fir-tree,** the cypress, **and the pine,** the Oriental elm, **and the box-tree together,** the pine, the former desert becoming a garden of the Lord, v. 20. **that they may see, and know, and consider, and understand together,** become thoroughly saturated with the knowledge, **that the hand of the Lord hath done this and the Holy One of Israel hath created it.** In this manner the copious spiritual refreshment which would fall to the lot of those sighing for comfort would serve for the glory of Jehovah, just as it is His mercy, and His mercy alone, which to this day is the cause of our salvation and of all spiritual blessings which we enjoy.

THE COMING OF THE DELIVERER. — V. 21. **Produce your cause, saith the Lord,** presenting their case for the court's consideration; **bring forth your strong reasons, saith the King of Jacob,** their arguments for the correctness of their position that they had a right to continue in their idolatry, in their enmity against

God. V. 22. **Let them bring them forth and show us what shall happen; let them show the former things,** the events of the very nearest future, **what they be, that we may consider them,** laying their argument to heart, turning to it as a strong support of their cause, **and know the latter end of them, or declare us things for to come,** understand the consequences of events and acts which would take place in the future. The enemies are urged from every angle to bring proof in support of their position as idolaters, but such clear proof as would demand acknowledgment. V. 23. **Show the things that are to come hereafter,** at any time in the future, for prophecy is one of the strongest proofs of divinity, **that we may know that ye are gods,** duly accept them as such; **yea, do good or do evil,** anything at all that will at least show life, **that we may be dismayed and behold it together,** concede that they had done wrong in opposing the claims of the idols, and be filled with fear. The entire section is built up in an ironical manner of speaking which greatly heightens the effect of the prophet's argument: the living God over against the helpless, the dead idols! V. 24. **Behold, ye are of nothing, and your work of naught; an abomination is he that chooseth you,** such is the conclusion which one is bound to reach from the premises presented: the idolater like his idol under the condemnation of the Lord. All the more prominently and emphatically, therefore, Jehovah stands out as the God of history and of prophecy, who directs the affairs of the whole world according to His divine will. V. 25. **I have raised up one from the North, and he shall come,** serving as the instrument of the Lord; **from the rising of the sun shall he call upon My name,** proclaiming the true God, as Cyrus did when he issued his decree permitting the Jews to return to their country, 2 Chron. 36, 23; Ezra 1, 1. 2; **and he shall come upon princes as upon mortar,** treading them under foot as the clay of the streets, **and as the potter treadeth clay,** the feature of contempt entering very strongly at this point. V. 26. **Who hath declared from the beginning that we may know,** proved His divinity by foretelling the future, **and beforetime, that we may say, He is righteous,** he is in the right? **Yea, there is none,** namely, among the enemies, the idolaters, and their idols, **that showeth; yea, there is none that declareth; yea, there is none that heareth your words;** there was not one real prophet among them. V. 27. **The first shall say to Zion, Behold, behold them,** or, "I let Zion have the first one who says, Behold, there it is"; **and I will give to Jerusalem one that bringeth good tidings;** that is, the idols were unable to foretell the future, but Jehovah, the true God, predicted the happening just as it came to pass, His messengers telling what He would surely perform in the future. Thus the godhead of Jehovah was fully proved. V. 28. **For I beheld, and there was no man;** even among them, the enemies, **and there was no counselor,** not one true prophet, **that, when I asked of them, could answer a word,** or in the form of a question: "And if I ask them, do they so much as answer?" It is a most emphatic way of saying that all the claims of the idolaters are fraudulent and empty. V. 29. **Behold, they are all vanity,** emptiness, nothingness; **their works are nothing; their molten images are wind and confusion,** utter desolation. They that make them are like unto them; so is every one that trusteth in them. Ps. 115, 8.

CHAPTER 42.

The Mediator of Israel and the Savior of the Heathen.

THE TRUE SERVANT OF THE LORD. — V. 1. **Behold My Servant,** the designation here used in its most restricted sense, of the Messiah, **whom I uphold,** having established Him in His office, the Lord is now also confirming Him, standing behind Him with the fulness of His divine power; **Mine Elect,** chosen or selected for a special purpose, **in whom My soul delighteth,** whom He regards with unmixed pleasure, Matt. 3, 17; Luke 9, 35; 2 Pet. 1, 17; **I have put My Spirit upon Him,** chap. 11, 2. **He shall bring forth judgment to the Gentiles,** namely, the rights and the privileges of the New Covenant, of the Gospel of mercy in Jesus Christ, for it is in this message that God declares us to be righteous in and through the merits of our Savior. V. 2. **He shall not cry, nor lift up, nor cause His voice to be heard in the street,** the expressions being heaped in the form of a climax, in order to emphasize the meekness and humility of Jesus of Nazareth, which He applied throughout His work. V. 3. **A bruised reed,** the fragile stem of a plant which has been bent to the point of breaking off, **shall He not break, and the smoking flax,** a wick which is at the point of becoming extinguished, **shall He not quench,** not put out entirely, that is, the Savior would make use of true pastoral mildness in dealing with hearts which are broken and contrite, not only by not driving them to despair, but by seeking them and caring for them with His full Savior's love. **He shall bring forth judgment unto truth,** bringing it to the Gentiles, making it known to them in deed and in truth, working faith in their hearts. V. 4. **He shall not fail nor be discouraged,** not give way to weakness in all the great work which He has undertaken, till **He have set judgment in the earth,** till His righteous cause gains the victory; **and the isles shall wait for His Law,** the longing of the heathen for a deliverance from this present world, unconscious and inarticulate as it is, being satisfied only in the redemption earned and offered by Christ. That this entire paragraph was fulfilled in the person and work of Jesus is plainly stated Matt. 12, 18—21. V. 5. **Thus saith God the Lord,** the covenant God, **He that created the heavens and stretched them out,** like an immense curtain suspended on nothing; **He that spread forth the earth,** for man's use and delight, **and that which cometh out of it,** all its plants and products of the soil; **He that giveth breath unto the people upon it,** Acts 17, 25, **and spirit,** reason and personality, **to them that walk therein,** to all its inhabitants: v. 6. **I, the Lord, have called Thee,** namely, the Messiah, whom He here addresses in words of encouragement, **in righteousness,** in His zeal for the salvation of Israel, in the merciful expression of His love for fallen mankind, by virtue of which the true righteousness is imputed to all believers, **and will hold Thine hand,** take a firm and reassuring grasp, transmitting His divine power, **and will keep Thee and give Thee for a covenant of the people,** as the Mediator of the covenant made with the patriarchs, **for a Light of the Gentiles,** to bring true spiritual light to the Gentiles; v. 7. **to open the blind eyes,** those stricken by the blindness of the natural sinfulness and enmity against God, **to bring out the prisoners,** those held by the fetters of sin, **from the prison, and them that sit in darkness,** namely, in the darkness which fills the heart of all men by nature, Eph. 5, 8, **out of the prison-house.** All of this was fulfilled in Jesus, as the New Testament so abundantly testifies, this section being quoted or used by the evangelists and apostles at least fifteen times. That this work of the Servant of Jehovah will be carried out successfully is vouched for by the name and the honor of God Himself. V. 8. **I am the Lord,** Jehovah, the Unchangeable One; **that is My name,** Ex. 3, 14; **and My glory will I not give to another, neither My praise to graven images.** The honor of His holy name, over against the false claims of the idols and their servants, demanded this solemn pledge. If He does not send the promised Mediator of the covenant to bring salvation to Jews and Gentiles alike, then He has lost the right to be called Jehovah and to be adored as the true God. V. 9. **Behold, the former things are come to pass,** namely, the deliverance of Israel at the time of their passage through the Red Sea, Ex. 14 and 15, **and new things do I declare,** the fulfilment of former promises being the guarantee that those herewith uttered will also come to pass; **before they spring forth, I tell you of them.** "All the promises of God in Him are yea, and in Him Amen, unto the glory of God by us." 2 Cor. 1, 20.

THE JOY OVER THE JUDGMENT OF CONDEMNATION UPON THE UNGODLY. — V. 10. **Sing unto the Lord a new song,** Ps. 33, 3; 40, 3, a hymn of praise in honor of the new things promised, a psalm lauding His mercy in the Savior, **and His praise from the end of the earth,** so that the whole earth resounds with it, **ye that go down to the sea,** the seafaring inhabitants of the isles and coasts of the Mediterranean Sea, **and all that is therein,** all the marine animals being called upon to join in this praise of the Lord; **the isles and the inhabitants thereof,** that is, all the people of the earth. V. 11. **Let the wilderness and the cities thereof,** the great Arabian Desert with its commercial centers, **lift up their voice, the villages,** the fortified camps, **that Kedar doth inhabit,** the second son of Ishmael, Gen. 25, 13, being named as representative of the nomad tribes of the East; **let the inhabitants of the rock,** of mountainous Idumea, **sing; let them shout from the top of the mountains,** with a voice which carries far and wide. V. 12. **Let them give glory unto the Lord and declare His praise in the islands,** the entire exhortation being summarized here. V. 13. **The Lord,** in carrying out His counsel of salvation, **shall go forth as a mighty man,** like a hero; **He shall stir up jealousy,** the indignation and fury in His own heart, **like a man of war,** an invincible warrior; **He shall cry, yea, roar,** with a fearful battle-cry; **He shall prevail against His enemies,** boasting of His victory over all His enemies. The entire section is built up so that there can be no question of Jehovah's final triumph. The Lord now takes up His proclamation in person once more. V. 14. **I have long time holden My peace,** not interfering with the ways of men; **I have been still and refrained Myself,** purposely holding Himself back; now, when patience and forbearance could no longer be practised, **will I cry like a travailing woman, I will destroy and devour at once,** groan, pant, and gasp. V. 15. **I will make waste mountains and hills,** thereby destroying the enemies, **and dry up all their herbs,** as a preliminary act of the final annihilation; **and I will make the rivers islands, and I will dry up the pools,** thereby making their land uninhabitable. The final Judgment of the world is always included in prophecies like that here given, where one act of the preliminary punishment is sketched. But while the enemies feel the wrath of the Lord, the believers feel the riches of His blessing. V. 16. **And I will bring the blind,** those who realize the condition of blindness with which they are suffering, **by a way that they knew not,** which they never would and could find on account of the natural perverseness of their hearts, John 9, 39—41; **I will lead them in paths that they have not known,** Ps. 32, 8; **I will make darkness light before them,** so that they will not stumble and fall, **and crooked things straight,** removing all obstructions and making level paths everywhere, all this proclaiming the sure deliverance of the children of God. **These things will I do unto them and not forsake them,** for the Lord is ever by the side of those who believe in Him. By way of contrast He now refers to the unhappy condition of the idolaters, of the ungodly. V. 17. **They shall be turned back,** reeling in a stupor of disappointment, **they shall be greatly ashamed,** heaped with disgrace, **that trust in graven images, that say to the molten images, Ye are our gods.** That is ever the lot of the idolaters, no matter whether their idolatry is openly practised or held in secret only. The religion of Jesus Christ is the only true, the absolute religion.

THE WRATH OF GOD UPON ISRAEL. — V. 18. **Hear, ye deaf, and look, ye blind, that ye may see,** so the prophet now addresses the people of Israel in general, on account of their spiritual callousness, which is rapidly turning into hardness of heart. V. 19. **Who is blind but My servant?** the reference here being to Israel itself, **or deaf, as My messenger that I sent?** not hearing a word of the message which the Lord entrusted to him to be given to the Gentiles. **Who is blind as he that is perfect,** one whom the Lord had regarded as His friend, **and blind as the Lord's servant,** this very fact making the blindness almost unexplainable and causing the Lord to refer to it so continually. Cp. John 9, 41. V. 20. **Seeing many things, but thou observest not; opening the ears, but he heareth not.** Israel has reached a point where most of its members are unable to understand although they have both eyes and ears open; the many miracles of God's grace are overlooked or speedily forgotten. All this in spite of the wonderful exhibitions of grace which the Lord gave them time and again. V. 21. **The Lord is well pleased for His righteousness' sake; He will magnify the Law and make it honorable,** literally, "It pleased Jehovah for the sake of His righteousness; great He made His instruction and glorious," revealing Himself in His Word for the sake of His covenant faithfulness; yet they did not understand. V. 22. **But this is a people robbed and spoiled,** Israel, in spite of all the Lord's efforts, lying on the ground helpless; **they are all of them snared in holes, and they are hid in prison-houses,** the very ones who were called to the liberty of the children of God; **they are for a prey, and none delivereth; for a spoil, and none saith, Restore.** The very people who, as the friend and messenger of Jehovah, should enjoy the most perfect freedom is being held in the most disgraceful captivity. This unnatural condition should surely open their eyes. V. 23. **Who among you will give ear to this? Who will hearken and hear for the time to come?** realizing the gravity of the situation properly and being guided by it. V. 24. **Who gave Jacob for a spoil and Israel to the robbers?** Was it merely the work of chance? **Did not the Lord, He against whom we have sinned?** the prophet here identifying himself with the disobedient people of his nation. **For they would not walk in His ways, neither were they obedient unto His Law,** they were very emphatic in their refusal to be guided by His Word and will. V. 25. **Therefore He hath poured upon him the fury of His anger and the strength of battle,** the fury of warfare; **and it hath set him,** Israel, the Lord's people, **on fire round about; yet he knew not,** did not realize even then what the Lord intended them to feel; **and it burned him, yet he laid it not to heart,** even the Lord's punishment did not make them wise. The prophet's complaint is the same as that which was made by Jesus when He looked upon the city of Jerusalem and wept over it with the exclamation that the matters conducive to her welfare were hidden from her eyes. Luke 19, 42.

CHAPTER 43.

Jehovah's Merciful Love and Covenant Faithfulness.

JEHOVAH'S LOVE PROTECTS AND GATHERS HIS PEOPLE. — V. 1. **But now, thus saith the Lord that created thee, O Jacob, and He that formed thee, O Israel,** not only in the act of creation, but in the sense of making the descendants of Jacob His own peculiar people, a distinction which has now been transferred to the spiritual Israel, the Church of God, **Fear not,** namely, after the stern reproofs of the last chapter and on account of the natural feeling of sinfulness and unworthiness, **for I have redeemed thee,** His main activity ever consisting in His ransoming His children from the power of their enemies; **I have called thee by thy name,** thereby expressing the relation of intimate friendship which He wanted to exist; **thou art Mine,** His incomparable love causing Him to regard Israel as His precious possession, which He treasures with all the power of His eternal mercy. V. 2. **When thou passest through the waters,** through great dangers, **I will be with thee; and through the rivers, they shall not overflow thee,** as when Israel went dry-shod through the bed of Jordan, although it was the period of the annual floods, Josh. 3, 15; **when thou walkest through the fire, thou shalt not be burned, neither shall the flame kindle upon thee,** the most extreme perils would not be able to harm those who placed their trust in Him, the God of their salvation. V. 3. **For I am the Lord, thy God, the Holy One of Israel, thy Savior,** the outstanding names of the true God in the Old Testament, the very mention of which is a guarantee of His friendship, especially that of Savior, 1 Tim. 1, 1. **I gave Egypt for thy ransom, Ethiopia,** the southern part of Egypt, **and Seba,** the province of Meroe, between the White and the Blue Nile, **for thee,** the ungodly being given as ransom for the just, to punish them for their iniquities in opposing the true God, Prov. 21, 18. V. 4. **Since thou wast precious in My sight,** valued most highly by the great God, **thou hast been honorable,** esteemed greatly in His sight, **and I have loved thee,** this being the climax of His kind assurances; **therefore will I give men for thee and people for thy life,** sacrificing the ungodly in order to deliver them that are His, as stated in the previous verse. So eager is the Lord to impress the greatness of His love upon the minds of His children that He repeats His reassuring statements. V. 5. **Fear not, for I am with thee,** the pronoun "I" being placed with special emphasis; **I will bring thy seed from the East and gather thee from the West,** the spiritual Israel, the Church of God, being collected from the members of all nations; v. 6. **I will say to the North, Give up, and to the South, Keep not back,** the form of the admonition including a very willing yielding on the part of the distant peoples, all under the influence of the Lord's merciful invitation. **Bring My sons from far and My daughters from the ends of the earth,** the prophecy having in mind the sum total of the believers gained through the proclamation of His message, v. 7. **even every one that is called by My name,** as an evidence of their belonging to Him in faith; **for I have created him,** Israel, as representing the Church of God of all times, **for My glory,** that the work of the Church might redound to His honor and glory; **I have formed him,** by a process of careful education; **yea, I have made him,** prepared him for the purposes of His mercy. Of the saints of the Lord, whom He has called, sanctified, and kept in the faith, not one will remain behind on the Last Day; all will enter into the joy of their Lord.

Jehovah the True God and Only Savior. V. 8. **Bring forth the blind people that have eyes and the deaf that have ears,** namely, to appear before the tribunal; for in spite of their spiritual blindness the children of Israel have had the opportunity to observe certain facts with their senses, to which they may now testify. V. 9. **Let all the nations be gathered together and let the people be assembled,** the Gentiles from all over the world; **who among them can declare this and show us former things?** The heathen are challenged either to prophesy in the same manner as the Lord or to bring proof of the fact that events have come to pass according to their prediction. **Let them bring forth their witnesses that they may be justified,** namely, by submitting adequate proofs which others would be bound to acknowledge; **or,** in case they are unable to do this, **let them hear and say, It is truth,** namely, that presented on the Lord's side. V. 10. **Ye are My witnesses, saith the Lord, and My Servant whom I have chosen,** for the purpose of bringing Israel to the knowledge of the only true God, **that ye may know and believe Me,** by virtue of the testimony of their own eyes, **and understand that I am He,** have a clear and convincing comprehension. **Before Me there was no god formed,** He alone was God from eternity, **neither shall there be after Me,** since He is in exclusive possession of the deity. V. 11. **I, even I, am the Lord,** the isolation of the sentence bringing out its emphasis all the more strongly, **and beside Me there is no savior,** He is the only one who can bestow deliverance from sin, death, and the power of the devil, the one in whom the salvation of mankind is found. V. 12. **I have declared,** announced in advance, **and have saved,** in accordance with His prophecy, **and I have showed,** let them hear another prediction, **when there was no strange god among you; therefore ye are My witnesses, saith the Lord, that I am God,** they had had a sufficient number of incontrovertible proofs and could testify accordingly. V. 13. **Yea, before the day was, I am He,** literally, "from this day," that is, He would be the same unchangeable God in the future as in the past, **and there is none that can deliver out of My hand; I will work, and who shall let it?** Who would be strong enough to hinder or frustrate His plans? The works of the Lord speak for Him, reveal Him, as in the past, so in the future.

Proof that Jehovah is the Holy One. — V. 14. **Thus saith the Lord, your Redeemer,** their Vindicator and Deliverer, **the Holy One of Israel,** whose outstanding attribute in dealing with His people is holiness: **For your sake I have sent to Babylon and have brought down all their nobles,** causing the Babylonians to be driven away as fugitives, **and the Chaldeans,** the original inhabitants of Babylonia, **whose cry is in the ships,** literally, "together with the Chaldeans on the ships of their exulting," over which they rejoiced with loud cries as the witnesses of their wealth and the bulwarks of their power. V. 15. **I am the Lord, your Holy One, the Creator** of **Israel**, who chose and established Israel as His people, **your King**, their Ruler, Provider, and Protector. V. 16. **Thus saith the Lord, which maketh a way in the sea**, as when He led Israel through the Red Sea, **and a path in the mighty waters**, whose almighty power is unchanged through the ages, v. 17. **which bringeth forth the chariot and horse**, the cavalry being considered the most powerful part of an army in those days, **the army and the power**, the might of the enemies' host; **they shall lie down together, they shall not rise**, being overcome completely; **they are extinct, they are quenched as tow**, as Pharaoh's army was buried in a watery grave. V. 18. **Remember ye not the former things**, when the Lord, in the past, performed such great things, **neither consider the things of old**, for what the Lord intended to do for His people in the future made all that which lay in the past seem insignificant by comparison. V. 19. **Behold, I will do a new thing**, unusual, remarkable in its wonderful character; **now it shall spring forth; shall ye not know it?** The challenge intends to call their attention to His action, of which He now speaks. **I will even make a way in the wilderness and rivers in the desert**, thereby performing a miracle which was unheard of among men. V. 20. **The beast of the field**, all the wild animals of the desert, **shall honor Me, the dragons**, or jackals, **and the owls**, the ostriches, the reference being to the Gentiles who are still in the wilderness of their sinfulness, **because I give waters in the wilderness and rivers in the desert to give drink to My people, My chosen**, the believers having the refreshing waters of the Word of mercy to sustain them on their way through the desert of this world. V. 21. **This people**, the spiritual Israel, **have I formed for Myself**, made them His own by His creative and educative activity in their behalf; **they shall show forth My praise**. That is the end and object of the Christians' life, to glorify the heavenly Father for the deeds of His mercy, as they have been enabled to do by His strength granted them through His call.

ISRAEL'S SALVATION THE WORK OF JEHOVAH'S MERCY. — V. 22. **But thou hast not called upon Me, O Jacob**, they had not chosen the true God; **but thou hast been weary of Me, O Israel**, they had in no way exerted themselves on His account, His election of them as His peculiar people rather being an act of His free love and mercy. V. 23. **Thou hast not brought Me the small cattle of thy burnt offerings**, to atone for the general condition of sinfulness and to dedicate themselves to Jehovah; **neither hast thou honored Me with thy sacrifices**, in order to establish and maintain the relation of dependence brought about by the mercy of God imparted in the Word. **I have not caused thee to serve with an offering**, the unbloody sacrifice which expressed the praise of God on the part of His saints, **nor wearied thee with incense**, which signified the prayers of the believers. Before the Lord called the patriarchs and designated their descendants as the people sanctified to Him, they had not sought Him, His selection of Abraham and of the children of Israel being a matter of His free grace and mercy alone. V. 24. **Thou hast bought Me no sweet cane with money**, the sweet-smelling plant used in preparing the sacred oil, imported at a great price, **neither hast thou filled Me with the fat of thy sacrifices**, never tiring themselves out in acts of worship, just as there was no merit on their part in being called into the relation of the covenant; on the contrary: **but thou hast made Me to serve with thy sins**, causing Him much trouble after He had accepted them into the relation of His children, **thou hast wearied Me with thine iniquities**, their constant transgression of His holy Law causing Him great distress and vexation. V. 25. **I, even I, am He that blotteth out thy transgressions for Mine own sake**, by an act of His boundless mercy, in order that His name might not be blasphemed among the heathen, **and will not remember thy sins**, this being the essence of forgiveness, that He remits the specific breach of faith as well as the general deviation from the path of His holy will. V. 26. **Put Me in remembrance**, Israel reminding the Lord of His acts of mercy by a recital of the same; **let us plead together**, in order to establish their case, if they thought they were in a position to say anything in their own favor; **declare thou, that thou mayest be justified**, be established as righteous in the face of God's accusation. V. 27. **Thy first father**, the ancestor of the children of Israel, **hath sinned, and thy teachers have transgressed against Me**, the very ones who should have transmitted the will of God to the people. V. 28. **Therefore**, because they made themselves unworthy of the honor given them in their office, **I have profaned the princes of the Sanctuary**, degrading the high priests, treating them as no longer consecrated, **and have given Jacob to the curse and Israel to reproaches**. Israel alone was to blame for its present misfortune. The fact that the Lord intended to bring salvation was due entirely to His grace and mercy. Hos. 13, 9.

CHAPTER 44.

The Evidences of Jehovah's Love.

The Reassurance of God's Covenant Faithfulness. — V. 1. **Yet now hear,** namely, over against the lamentable condition pictured at the end of the last chapter, **O Jacob, My servant, and Israel, whom I have chosen,** the assurances of the Lord's affection serving as a tender invitation to the true members of His people: v. 2. **Thus saith the Lord that made thee and formed thee from the womb,** who had chosen and established Israel as His people of old, **which will help thee,** with a steady assistance, with unvarying certainty of protection: **Fear not, O Jacob, My servant, and thou, Jesurun,** the upright and pious one, a term of endearment which the Lord used of Israel, Deut. 32, 15, **whom I have chosen,** the fact of God's merciful election being emphasized time and again. V. 3. **For I will pour water upon him that is thirsty,** those in need of spiritual refreshment, Matt. 5, 6, **and floods upon the dry ground; I will pour My Spirit upon thy seed,** the children of the Church, **and My blessing,** that of His mercy in the Word, **upon thine offspring;** v. 4. **and they,** the spiritual children of Israel, **shall spring up as among the grass,** in rich luxuriance, **as willows by the watercourses,** like the juicy and strong poplars along the banks of the Euphrates, the reference being to the luxuriant spiritual growth of the newly converted, with the fervor of their first love. V. 5. **One shall say, I am the Lord's,** proud of his privilege in being permitted to worship the true God; **and another shall call himself by the name of Jacob,** praising the name of the patriarch, as the ancestor of the spiritual Israel; **and another shall subscribe with his hand unto the Lord,** mentioning the name of Jehovah as an honorary title, magnifying it above all other names, **and surname himself by the name of Israel,** glorifying this designation because it confers such a high honor upon all who wear it. V. 6. **Thus saith the Lord, the King of Israel,** whose relation to His people is one of dignity combined with love, **and his Redeemer,** He who delivers from all enemies, **the Lord of hosts,** who is clothed with mighty power: **I am the First, and I am the Last,** the one true God from everlasting to everlasting; **and beside Me there is no god,** He is the exclusive possessor of the eternal deity. V. 7. **And who, as I, shall call, and shall declare it, and set it in order for Me,** the Lord's challenge being to all men to produce one equal to Him in prophetic wisdom, **since I appointed the ancient people?** As long as the world is in existence, there has never been any other who, like Himself, could foretell the future. **And the things that are coming and shall come, let them show unto them,** for that would be a proof substantiating their claim of being on a level with God or with His inspired prophets. But since Israel was still suffering with lack of confidence in the true God and, in a measure at least, showed their superstitious fear concerning the power of the heathen nations, therefore Jehovah once more gives them a joyful assurance: v. 8. **Fear ye not, neither be afraid,** with mistrust toward Jehovah, on the one hand, and dread of the heathen gods, on the other. **Have I not told thee from that time and have declared it?** namely, the utter vanity of the heathen idols. **Ye are even My witnesses,** who must admit the truth of this assertion. **Is there a** [true] **God beside Me?** The emphatic question is answered with equal definiteness, **Yea, there is no** [other true] **God; I know not any,** even the omniscient God being unable to name one. The attitude of men with respect to this one true God decides their eternal fate.

The Vanity of Idolatry over against Jehovah. — V. 9. **They that make a graven image,** those who manufacture idols, **are all of them vanity,** nothingness, desolation; **and their delectable things,** the idols for which they profess such a deep affection, **shall not profit,** not being able to help them in any way; **and they are their own witnesses; they see not nor know,** the idol-worshipers themselves testifying that their gods are both blind and ignorant, **that they,** the idolaters, **may be ashamed,** for their attitude condemns them. V. 10. **Who hath formed a god or molten a graven image that is profitable for nothing?** The answer which is implied would clearly state: No one while he is in his right mind. V. 11. **Behold, all his fellows,** the entire guild of idol-makers, **shall be ashamed, and the workmen,** those who direct the work, **they are of men,** themselves creatures and therefore unable to make a real god. **Let them all be gathered together, let them stand up,** to make an issue of their claim to recognition before the true God; **yet they shall fear, and they shall be ashamed together,** the hollowness and emptiness of their doing will be exposed before all witnesses. This is followed by a concrete, detailed description of idol-manufacture as practised in those days, full of the keenest ironical allusions. V. 12. **The smith with the tongs both worketh in the coals and fashioneth it with hammers,** rather, in the impersonal form of the original, "One fashioneth iron with the cold-chisel, and causeth it to glow in coals, and with hammers formeth it," **and worketh it with the strength of his arms; yea, he is hungry, and his strength faileth; he drinketh no water and is faint.** He is so busily engaged that he neglects even eating and drinking, until he becomes utterly exhausted. A similar energy is shown in the case of wooden idols. V. 13. **The carpenter stretcheth out his rule,** again impersonal, "One felleth trees, draweth his line," in order to cut a piece of wood of the required size; **he marketh it out with a line, he fitteth it with planes,** marking off the figure with a stylus, **and he marketh it out with the compass,** so that the outside wood may be removed exactly, **and maketh it after the figure of a man, according to the beauty of a man,** for the idols were given the most handsome appearance, in many instances, **that it may remain in the house,** be enclosed permanently in a small place, whereas the true God does not live in houses made by men. V. 14. **He heweth him down cedars and taketh the cypress and the oak,** rather, "In order to have the finest wood, he chooseth the holm-oak and the common oak," both of them distinguished for the excellence of their wood, **which he strengtheneth for himself among the trees of the forest,** carefully nurturing such a tree among the giants of the forest; **he planteth an ash,** a fir or cedar, **and the rain doth nourish it,** so that, in the course of years, it reaches its proper size, the description of the long wait tending to show the ridiculous aspect of the idolater's activity. V. 15. **Then shall it be for a man to burn,** that is, ordinarily such a tree will yield fuel; **for he will take thereof and warm himself; yea, he kindleth it and baketh bread; yea, he maketh a god and worshipeth it;** as he does the one thing, so he does the other, not realizing how utterly foolish the latter act is in comparison with the former; **he maketh it a graven image and falleth down thereto,** in the usual act of adoration. The contrast is brought out still more emphatically in the next sentences. V. 16. **He burneth part thereof in the fire,** for fuel to keep him warm; **with part thereof he eateth flesh,** using it for cooking; **he roasteth roast and is satisfied,** feeling perfectly content; **yea, he warmeth himself and saith, Aha!** an exclamation expressing the height of comfort, **I am warm, I have seen the fire,** felt its pleasant effect; v. 17. **and the residue thereof he maketh a god, even his graven image,** what he calls his god; **he falleth down unto it, and worshipeth it, and prayeth unto it, and saith, Deliver me, for thou art my god,** this prayer being the very climax of foolish behavior, which, however, the idolaters do not realize. V. 18. **They have not known nor understood,** they do not realize the inconsistency of their conduct; **for He hath shut their eyes,** rather, their eyes are daubed shut, **that they cannot see, and their hearts that they cannot understand,** that they do not learn true wisdom. Cp. Rom. 1, 18—21. V. 19. **And none considereth in his heart,** so much as thinks over his act, **neither is there knowledge nor understanding to say,** in reflecting upon his own conduct, **I have burned part of it in the fire; yea, also, I have baked bread upon the coals thereof,** upon the glowing bed of coals; **I have roasted flesh and eaten it, and shall I make the residue thereof an abomination? Shall I fall down to the stock of a tree?** to the figure which the tree yielded, the idol which it, in a manner of speaking, produces. The idolaters become utterly callous to the rank inconsistency of their behavior, to the unreasonableness of their worship. V. 20. **He feedeth on ashes; a deceived heart hath turned him aside,** or, more emphatically, "He who watcheth over ashes — a foolish heart has led him astray," **that he cannot deliver his soul,** his idolatry leads him into eternal damnation, **nor say, Is there not a lie in my right hand?** Spiritual blindness is always, in the first instance, self-inflicted; he that persists in it is eternally lost. On the other hand, the believers, the children of God, the true members of the spiritual Israel, are in happy possession of their deliverance, of the forgiveness of their sins. V. 21. **Remember these,** namely, what the Lord is about to say, **O Jacob and Israel,** His people, **for thou art My servant,** not a foolish idol-manufacturer; **I have formed thee, thou art My servant,** by virtue of his having been chosen by Jehovah. **O Israel, thou shalt not be forgotten of Me,** the admonition, Forget Me not! coming with emphasis at the end of this sentence. V. 22. **I have blotted out, as a thick cloud,** so that they are completely erased, **thy transgressions,** even such as meant a severing of the covenant relations, **and, as a cloud, thy sins,** that is, in the same way as the sun dissolves and drives away the darkness of a heavy cloud. **Return unto Me, for I have redeemed thee;** with Him, in His redemption, is life and salvation. This promise causes the prophet to address a rousing admonition to the entire creation. V. 23. **Sing, O ye heavens, for the Lord hath done it,** the deliverance has been gained; **shout, ye lower parts of the earth,** everything beneath the skies; **break forth into singing, ye mountains,** as the most prominent parts of the landscape, **O forest and every tree therein; for the Lord hath redeemed Jacob and glorified Himself in Israel,** wherefore all the creatures of the universe should sing praises to this miracle of His redemption. To the believing heart there is no limit to the songs of praise and adoration arising to the throne of grace.

THE PROMISE TO HAVE JERUSALEM REBUILT. This section, according to a careful analysis, belongs to the next chapter, for it takes up the deliverance of Israel as effected in consequence of the decree of Cyrus. V. 24. **Thus saith the**

Lord, thy Redeemer, and He that formed thee from the womb, cp. v. 2: **I am the Lord that maketh all things,** the supreme Ruler and Guide of the universe, the Sovereign of the world and all it contains; **that stretcheth forth the heavens alone,** chap. 40, 22; 42, 5; **that spreadeth abroad the earth by Myself,** without assistance, v. 25. **that frustrateth the tokens of the liars,** of the vain talkers, especially the necromancers, **and maketh diviners mad,** so that they appear as fools with their false prophecies; **that turneth wise men backward,** so that they are relegated to the background, **and maketh their knowledge foolish,** exhibiting their ignorance before the whole world; v. 26. **that,** by way of contrast, **confirmeth the word of His servant,** establishing the prophetic message which His prophets proclaimed, **and performeth the counsel of His messengers,** so that not one of His words falls to the ground; **that saith to Jerusalem, Thou shalt be inhabited,** rising once more out of the ruins, **and to the cities of Judah,** which had likewise been plundered and sacked, **Ye shall be built, and I will raise up the decayed places thereof;** v. 27. **that saith to the deep,** in another exhibition of His power, **Be dry, and I will dry up thy rivers,** to serve His purpose at all times; v. 28. **that saith of Cyrus,** the prophecy here giving the exact words of the Lord's command to him as it came to pass more than a century later, **He is My shepherd,** the designation referring to his leadership of nations, **and shall perform all My pleasure,** namely, in bringing about the deliverance of Israel; **even saying to Jerusalem, Thou shalt be built, and to the Temple, Thy foundation shall be laid.** This prophecy was literally fulfilled; for the rebuilding of the city of Jerusalem and of the Temple took place in accordance with the express command of Cyrus. That his name is mentioned so many years in advance need cause no more surprise than the fact that Josiah's work of reformation was predicted at the time of Jeroboam I, more than three centuries intervening between prophecy and fulfilment. The God of prophecy is the omniscient God, before whom nothing is hidden.

CHAPTER 45.

The Fact of Israel's Deliverance a Powerful Appeal to All Nations.

THE DELIVERANCE BY CYRUS A PROOF OF JEHOVAH'S POWER. — V. 1. **Thus saith the Lord to His anointed,** the king set apart by the Lord's providence, for His special purpose, **to Cyrus, whose right hand I have holden,** to sustain and strengthen him in the work of his calling, **to subdue nations before him,** Cyrus being victorious by Jehovah's strength; **and I will loose the loins of kings,** taking off the girdle which enabled them to go forth into battle, the Lord's action thus rendering them defenseless, **to open before him the two-leaved gates,** those of all cities against which he would make war; **and the gates shall not be shut,** no city daring to withstand him: v. 2. **I will go before thee and make the crooked places straight,** removing all obstructions and hindrances; **I will break in pieces the gates of brass and cut in sunder the bars of iron,** as those of the city of Babylon, for the city was taken in spite of its strong defenses; v. 3. **and I will give thee the treasures of darkness,** those kept in subterranean vaults, **and hidden riches of secret places,** where they were stored for safe-keeping, **that thou mayest know that I, the Lord, which call thee by thy name,** namely, to enter His service, **am the God of Israel,** in whose interest Cyrus was chiefly to be active. V. 4. **For Jacob My servant's sake and Israel, Mine elect,** for the purpose of delivering His people, **I have even called thee by thy name,** for this special work; **I have surnamed thee, though thou hast not known Me,** long before there was any idea of saving knowledge in the heart of Cyrus, if, indeed, it may be assumed that he was at least temporarily a believer. V. 5. **I am the Lord, and there is none else,** Jehovah's absolute deity being stressed once more; **there is no** (other true) **God beside Me. I girded thee,** giving him strength for battle and victory, **though thou hast not known Me;** v. 6. **that they may know from the rising of the sun and from the West,** throughout the habitable world, **that there is none beside Me,** the very heathen realizing, with a sort of instinctive feeling, that God Himself was directing the campaigns of Cyrus. **I am the Lord, and there is none else.** V. 7. **I form the light,** He made it at the beginning of the world, **and create darkness,** by withdrawing light, which is His creation; **I make peace and create evil,** both good fortune and misfortune being sent by Him; **I, the Lord, do all these things.** The Lord Himself has ever guided the events of the world's history in order to carry out the plans of His loving-kindness and tender mercy.

REBUKING THE REPROBATE PEOPLE. — V. 8. **Drop down, ye heavens, from above,** in fertilizing rain, **and let the skies,** the clouds of the firmament, **pour down righteousness,** the fulness of spiritual salvation. **Let the earth open and let them bring forth salvation,** that coming down from above being eagerly received by the earth, **and let righteousness spring up together,** in luxuriant growth; **I, the Lord, have created it.** The reference is to faith and its fruits as brought forth under the influence of the Word of God's grace and mercy, especially in Messianic times — the ideal condition in the world. But Israel, full of doubt and mistrust on account of the misery of its captivity, murmured against God in spite of His promise of deliverance. This attitude the Lord takes into account in this section. V. 9. **Woe unto him that striveth with his Maker,** an individual person trying to call the great God of heaven and earth to account! **Let the potsherd strive with the potsherds of the earth,** that is, man with his equal. **Shall the clay say to him that fashioneth it,** arguing with the potter, **What makest thou? or thy work, He hath no hands?** not possessing enough strength and skill to produce something worth while. The very idea of such an occurrence is preposterous, but the murmuring of the people against the Lord no less so. The Lord therefore rebukes this presumption in a solemn statement. V. 10. **Woe unto him that saith unto his father, What begettest thou? or to the woman, What hast thou brought forth?** Applied to the Lord, these questions would challenge both His authority and His power. Therefore He now makes a majestic statement concerning His glory and supremacy. V. 11. **Thus saith the Lord, the Holy One of Israel, and his Maker,** He who has chosen and established Israel as His peculiar people, **Ask Me of things to come concerning My sons and concerning the work of My hands command ye me,** literally, "The future demand of Me; concerning My sons and the creatures of My hands command Me!" Will they dare to go to this extent? Has this pass been reached? It is the very strongest condemnation of Israel's presumption. V. 12. **I have made the earth and created man upon it,** making him with His own hands; **I, even My hands, have stretched out the heavens,** like a great tent, **and all their host have I commanded,** His omnipotence as well as His wisdom being in evidence everywhere. V. 13. **I have raised him,** Cyrus, **up in righteousness,** in accordance with His covenant with Israel, **and I will direct all his ways,** removing all obstructions which might hinder him; **he shall build My city,** Jerusalem, **and he shall let go My captives,** the exiled Jews, **not for price nor reward, saith the Lord of hosts.** When Cyrus issued His decree concerning the return of the Jews to their country, he acted under the impulse of the divine will; for God directs the conduct of men everywhere, so that they act in accordance with His will.

The Glorification of Israel an Appeal to the World. — V. 14. **Thus saith the Lord,** in foretelling the overthrow of the Gentiles everywhere, **The labor of Egypt,** that which the Egyptians had gained by their labor, **and merchandise of Ethiopia,** what the Ethiopians gathered by their commercial activities, **and of the Sabeans, men of stature,** the inhabitants of Meroe in Upper Egypt being known far and wide on account of their great size, **shall come over unto thee, and they shall be thine,** freely submitting themselves; **they shall come after thee, in chains they shall come over,** as though bound hand and foot, **and they shall fall down unto thee,** acknowledging Israel as their superior, **they shall make supplication unto thee, saying, Surely God is in thee, and there is none else, there is no** (other true) **God.** Israel is here declared to be the nation of the one true God. V. 15. **Verily, thou art a God that hidest Thyself, O God of Israel, the Savior,** that is, the God of Israel, whom even the heathen must acknowledge as the only God, keeps Himself hidden, His essence is above and beyond human reason. Cp. Rom. 11, 33; 1 Cor. 2. V. 16. **They shall be ashamed and also confounded, all of them,** the Lord Himself says concerning the makers and worshipers of idols; **they shall go to confusion together that are makers of idols,** heaped with shame and disgrace on account of the foolishness of their actions. Note that throughout this section the heaping of synonymous expressions emphasizes the point which the Lord wishes to make. V. 17. **But Israel,** as typifying and representing the Church of God, **shall be saved in the Lord with an everlasting salvation,** namely, in the spiritual Israel, the kingdom of the Messiah, by the redemption of Christ; **ye shall not be ashamed nor confounded world without end,** be shielded forever from the disgrace which will strike the unbelievers. This assurance is now further substantiated. V. 18. **For thus saith the Lord, that created the heavens; God Himself, that formed the earth and made it; He hath established it; He created it not in vain, He formed it to be inhabited,** or, with the emphasis of the original tongue: "For thus saith Jehovah, the Creator of the heavens — He is God! The Former of the earth and its Maker — He has prepared it! Not empty He created it, for inhabiting He prepared it." **I am the Lord, and there is none else.** The work of creation is a mighty and convincing proof for the deity of Jehovah. But the same holds true of the Word of His revelation. V. 19. **I have not spoken in secret, in a dark place of the earth,** as the diviners, the necromancers, and the oracle-mongers of the heathen were wont to do; **I said not unto the seed of Jacob, Seek ye Me in vain,** on the basis of an empty promise. **I, the Lord, speak righteousness,** proclaiming the salvation assured by the covenant between Him and Israel; **I declare things that are right,** unmixed with hypocrisy and wickedness. The Word of God reveals Him with regard to both His essence and His attributes; in it and by it we have free access to the redemption made by Christ Jesus. Therefore the Lord's challenge to the heathen goes forth once more, bidding them appear before the tribunal of justice: v. 20. **Assemble yourselves and come; draw near together**, in an organized body, for a formal hearing, **ye that are escaped of the nations**, the campaigns of Cyrus being regarded as brought to a close in this connection, and the mass of remaining heathen being addressed. **They have no knowledge that set up the wood of their graven image and pray unto a god that cannot save**, they are lacking in understanding, as may be seen from the fact that they carried away their idols in their hasty flight, appealing to gods that could not help them. V. 21. **Tell ye and bring them near**, show proofs; **yea, let them take counsel together**, to consider whether they have any evidence to offer which would equal the testimony of Jehovah for His own divinity: **Who hath declared this from ancient time?** namely, the prophecy of Israel's elevation above the heathen. **Who hath told it from that time?** even from the time of the patriarchs, Gen. 12, 18; 22, 17. **Have not I, the Lord? And there is no** (true) **God else beside Me**, He has brought abundant proofs for His deity; **a just God**, faithful to His covenant, **and a Savior**, the only one in whom all men have salvation; **there is none beside Me.** On the basis of this clear proof, therefore, the invitation goes forth: v. 22. **Look unto Me and be ye saved, all the ends of the earth**, the turning to the Lord in true repentance being followed by the imparting of salvation, or, more exactly, as His call produces repentance, it also works faith, thereby granting salvation full and free, and His call goes out to all men: **For I am God, and there is none else**, a declaration which is repeated time and again in order to convince the idolaters, to cause them to accept the true God. V. 23. **I have sworn by Myself**, the most solemn formula which can be used, **the word is gone out of My mouth in righteousness and shall not return**, since it expresses His covenant faithfulness, **That unto Me every knee shall bow**, in acknowledging His sovereignty, **every tongue shall swear**, most solemnly affirming the conviction of the heart. Cp. Phil. 2, 10. 11. V. 24. **Surely, shall one say**, namely, such as turn to the Lord in true repentance and faith, **in the Lord have I righteousness and strength**, the salvation of the covenant, the Messianic redemption, the strength of the Holy Spirit. **Even to Him shall men come, and all that are incensed against Him shall be ashamed**, that is, those who refuse to accept Him in faith will be obliged to acknowledge Him as their Judge; those who will not believe shall be damned. V. 25. **In the Lord shall all the seed of Israel**, the spiritual seed, believers from all nations of the earth, **be justified**, possess the salvation assured by the covenant, **and shall glory**, giving praise and honor to God for His grace and mercy.

CHAPTER 46.

A Reproof of Israel's Idolatrous Tendency.

THE FALL OF BABYLON'S IDOLS. — V. 1. **Bel**, the highest deity of Babylon, **boweth down**, is fallen, **Nebo**, another Babylonian idol, the tutelary deity of the reigning house of Chaldea, **stoopeth**, collapsing, or falling prostrate, namely, in the plundering of the city; **their idols were upon the beasts and upon the cattle**, when the beasts of burden dragged them away as a part of the conqueror's booty. **Your carriages were heavy loaden, they are a burden to the weary beast**, that is, the statues of their idols, otherwise carried about by the priests in solemn procession, were seen by the prophet as loaded upon pack-animals, which dragged along, weary with the heavy load. V. 2. **They**, the idols, **stoop, they bow down together**, they are entirely collapsed; **they could not deliver the burden**, they were unable to save the burden of their own statues, they could not bring them to a place of safety, **but themselves are gone into captivity**, the very gods of the Babylonians captured and led away into exile, a sarcastic thrust at their helplessness. This introduction prepares the way for a sharp reproof of Israel for its idolatrous leanings. V. 3. **Hearken unto Me, O house of Jacob and all the remnant of the house of Israel**, all those whom the Lord has chosen to be His own peculiar people, **which are borne by Me from the belly, which are carried from the womb**, sustained and protected by the loving-kindness of the Lord since the time when He chose them as His people; v. 4. **and even to your old age I am He**, the same faithful, dependable God; **and even to hoar hairs will I carry you**, to the most advanced age of their history, to the very end of their national existence. **I have made, and I will bear**, the fact of His having sustained them in the past being their guarantee for the future; **even I will carry and will deliver you**, this deliverance being the surest proof of His divinity. V. 5. **To whom will ye liken Me, and make Me equal, and compare Me, that we may be like?** Cp. chap. 40, 18. 25. The heaping of expressions again stresses the uniqueness of the true God, the fact that He alone merits the designation of God. How is it possible for Israel even to think of placing the true God on a level with the heathen idols after the manifestations of His power and mercy which they have witnessed? To make this thought stand out still more clearly, the vanity of the idolaters is once more described. V. 6. **They lavish gold out of the bag,** paying it out in large quantities, or producing it in heaps as material for the craftsman, **and weigh silver in the balance,** cheerfully opening their treasures, **and hire a goldsmith, and he maketh it,** the precious metal which is delivered to him, **a god; they fall down,** in foolish adoration of the idol, **yea, they worship.** V. 7. **They bear him,** lifting their idol up from the place where he was cast, **upon the shoulder, they carry him, and set him in his place,** on the pedestal, in the niche intended for him, **and he standeth,** a dead thing unable to move; **from his place shall he not remove; yea, one shall cry unto him,** trusting to obtain help from the idol, **yet can he not answer nor save him,** the worshiper who places his confidence in him, **out of his trouble.** Thus the helplessness, nothingness, of the idols is once more set before the people.

A Reproof of Israel's Refusal to Believe the Divine Promises. — V. 8. **Remember this,** keeping in mind what the Lord was now about to proclaim, **and show yourselves men,** renouncing the childishness of idolatry; **bring it again to mind, O ye transgressors,** those who were forgetting the covenant and forsaking the true God. V. 9. **Remember the former things of old,** the miracles of God which happened in the earliest history of Israel, chap. 43, 18; **for I am God, and there is none else; I am God, and there is none like Me,** this point being made again over against the danger of idolatrous practises, v. 10. **declaring the end from the beginning and from ancient times the things that are not yet done,** the foretelling of future events in the manner in which it was done by Jehovah being one of the chief proofs of His divinity, **saying, My counsel shall stand, and I will do all My pleasure,** namely, as now set forth: v. 11. **calling a ravenous bird,** a falcon, eagle, or bird of prey, **from the East,** this being Cyrus himself, **the man that executeth My counsel from a far country; yea, I have spoken it, I will also bring it to pass,** actually setting His plan in motion; **I have purposed it, I will also do it,** so that it will be an accomplished fact. The unquestioned authority of the Lord is combined with His ability to carry out His plans, to realize His projects, something in which He differed most radically from the dead idols. V. 12. **Hearken unto Me, ye stout-hearted,** those who were willingly hardening their hearts against the influence of the Lord, **that are far from righteousness,** who have excluded themselves from the salvation promised in the Lord's covenant. V. 13. **I bring near My righteousness,** the salvation of Israel; **it shall not be far off, and My salvation shall not tarry,** He would surely bring deliverance to those who believe in Him, to the everlasting disgrace of the reprobates, **and I will place salvation in Zion for Israel, My glory.** Salvation in Zion, glory and honor in Israel, in the midst of His Church, all of this sets forth the happy condition of the Messianic period.

CHAPTER 47.

The Fall of Proud Babylon.

The Humiliation of the Daughter of Babylon. — V. 1. **Come down and sit in the dust,** degraded to the lowest depth, **O virgin daughter of Babylon,** the city and country being regarded as a virgin queen; **sit on the ground, there is no throne,** the seat of empire being lost to the former proud ruler, **O daughter of the Chaldeans! For thou shalt no more be called tender and delicate,** the reference being to the luxury and debauchery and prostitution practised in connection with the religious rites of the Babylonians and at other times. V. 2. **Take the millstones,** those of the hand-mill, as turned by female slaves, **and grind meal,** the grain being fed in through the center opening above and ground to flour by the revolving of the upper stone; **uncover thy locks,** taking off the veil, probably together with the plaited hair, as worn by Oriental women, its removal being considered a mark of the deepest degradation, **make bare the leg,** removing the long outer garment worn especially by women of rank, **uncover the thigh,** gathering up even the inner garment, **pass over the rivers,** like a slave girl being taken into captivity. V. 3. **Thy nakedness shall be uncovered, yea, thy shame shall be seen,** a figurative expression for exposing the hidden wickedness of Babylonia. **I will take vengeance,** for all the evil shown to His people Israel, **and I will not meet thee as a man,** not pardon or spare any man, but overthrow all the enemies. At this point the prophet causes the congregation of believers to insert a glad hallelujah. V. 4. **As for our Redeemer, the Lord of hosts is His name,** whose power is unlimited in carrying out His purposes, **the Holy One of Israel,** zealous for the welfare of His people. The prophet, in beginning the second strophe of the chapter, once more addresses Babylon directly. V. 5. **Sit thou silent,** namely, in captivity, **and get thee into darkness,** into the darkness of the dungeon, **O daughter of the Chaldeans; for thou shalt no more be called The Lady of Kingdoms,** the queen and mistress of the world, a position which Babylon enjoyed for less than a century. V. 6.

I was wroth with My people, so the Lord explains the Babylonian captivity, which is hereby also prophesied, **I have polluted Mine inheritance,** taking away the consecration which Israel possessed as His people, **and given them into thine hand,** it was an act of the Lord's punishment, not a matter of Babylonia's strength. **Thou didst show them no mercy,** treating the exiled Jews with the utmost cruelty; **upon the ancient hast thou very heavily laid thy yoke,** not sparing even the aged, but submitting them to indignities with the rest. V. 7. **And thou saidst,** flattering herself in her own mind, **I shall be a lady forever,** haughtily considering her position beyond attack from every side, in an insolence which was an insult to God, **so that thou didst not lay these things to thy heart,** she did not consider the extent of her own cruelty, **neither didst remember the latter end of it,** namely, the consequences of such actions. The pride of the average sinner causes him to disregard or to discount the punishment which follows; it is a species of blindness which leads to destruction.

Babylon's Vain Attempt to Avert the Threatened Destruction. — V. 8. **Therefore hear now this, thou that art given to pleasures,** living in wantonness, luxury, and licentiousness, **that dwellest carelessly,** the feeling of false security being characteristic of the people of Babylon in that day, **that sayest in thine heart, I am, and none else beside me,** an expression of unbounded haughtiness; **I shall not sit as a widow,** believing that the Babylonian men, the soldiers of its army, could never be overcome, **neither shall I know the loss of children,** by being bereaved of her inhabitants in the war; v. 9. **but these two things shall come to thee in a moment in one day,** with frightful suddenness, **the loss of children and widowhood,** a total bereavement; **they,** these two great trials, **shall come upon thee in their perfection,** in full measure, **for the multitude of thy sorceries and for the great abundance of thine enchantments,** witchcraft in its various forms being one of the outstanding features in many of the ancient nations, as recent excavations also show, for magicians and astrologers are frequently mentioned, and formulas of magic were in general use. V. 10. **For thou hast trusted in thy wickedness,** deeming herself secure in spite of her cruelty and tyranny; **thou hast said, None seeth me. Thy wisdom,** particularly that of various magical arts, **and thy knowledge,** especially the science of mathematics, which was pretty well developed in Babylon, **it hath perverted thee,** turned the heads of the Chaldeans; **and thou hast said in thine heart, I am, and none else beside me,** imagining herself the mistress of the earth, indulging in self-deification. V. 11. **Therefore shall evil come upon thee,** in the Lord's punishment, **thou shalt not know from whence it riseth,** not being able to banish it; **and mischief,** misfortune, destruction, **shall fall upon thee, thou shalt not be able to put it off,** to lay down ransom-money to be delivered from it; **and desolation shall come upon thee suddenly,** as when a destructive storm comes rushing headlong, **which thou shalt not know,** against which all Babylon's might and wisdom would be powerless. V. 12. **Stand now with thine enchantments,** the various magical formulas employed, **and with the multitude of thy sorceries, wherein thou hast labored from thy youth,** this having ever been a characteristic of Babylon, as far as its history goes back; **if so be thou shalt be able to profit, if so be thou mayest prevail!** It is a bitterly sarcastic challenge: Apply all your magical arts; maybe they will help, they may even instil fear and terror in the heart of Jehovah! V. 13. **Thou art wearied in the multitude of thy counsels,** driven to despair by the fruitless quest for means and methods to meet the threatened punishment and to avert it. **Let now the astrologers,** those versed in astronomy, but connecting with their activity that of fortune-telling, **the star-gazers,** the professional observers of the movements of the sidereal bodies, **the monthly prognosticators,** men who determined the time of the new moon and gave advice concerning lucky days, **stand up and save thee from these things that shall come upon thee,** rather, those who at new moons make known, by means of them, the things that shall come upon thee. The challenge is held in an even more sarcastic vein than in the foregoing verse. V. 14. **Behold, they,** all the wizards and necromancers and astrologers, **shall be as stubble, the fire shall burn them,** so that they will be totally destroyed; **they shall not deliver themselves from the power of the flame,** as the wrath of God comes upon them to their destruction; **there shall not be a coal to warm at,** the stubble burning down to dead ashes, **nor fire to sit before it,** total destruction having come upon Babylon. V. 15. **Thus shall they,** these men upon whom the Babylonians depended, **be unto thee with whom thou hast labored, even thy merchants, from thy youth,** for the astrologers and wizards and magicians did a flourishing business at the expense of the citizens of Babylonia; **they shall wander every one to his quarter,** reeling to and fro in the effort to save his life, if possible; **none shall save thee.** Such would be the fate of proud Babylon, as it usually is the fate of all those who place their trust in witchcraft and necromancy in its various forms. The warning may be fitly appended also here: "Be not deceived, God is not mocked; for whatsoever a man soweth, that shall he also reap."

CHAPTER 48.

The Deliverance out of Babylon.

A TESTIMONY CONCERNING THE HOUSE OF JACOB. — V. 1. **Hear ye this, O house of Jacob,** the form of address purposely being cold and distant, **which are called by the name of Israel,** presuming upon this right, **and are come forth out of the waters of Judah,** being physical descendants of the patriarchs, indeed, but lacking in spirituality and faith, **which swear by the name of the Lord,** the gracious God of the covenant, **and make mention of the God of Israel,** who intended to make Israel His true, peculiar people, His children indeed, their attitude, however, being such as to make the prophet add, **but not in truth nor in righteousness,** that is, not in the faithfulness demanded by the covenant, but with a false and lying heart. This hypocrisy of the people is further characterized: v. 2. **For they call themselves of the Holy City,** boasting of their outward connection with Jerusalem, **and stay themselves upon the God of Israel; The Lord of hosts is His name.** They defiantly claimed the assistance of the almighty God for themselves, merely on account of their outward relation to the Lord's people, forgetting that God is also the Holy One and a devouring fire upon all hypocrites. Jehovah Himself now takes up the message: v. 3. **I have declared the former things from the beginning,** making known the miracles of His deliverance before they came to pass; **and they went forth out of My mouth, and I showed them,** brought them about; **I did them suddenly, and they came to pass,** so unexpectedly, so entirely at variance with the results of human planning, that men were bound to recognize the hand of God. V. 4. **Because I knew that thou art obstinate,** hard of head and of heart, **and thy neck is an iron sinew,** inflexible, **and thy brow brass,** insisting upon going forward on its own sinful way, refusing to be guided by the Lord's will, v. 5. **I have even from the beginning declared it to thee; before it came to pass I showed it thee,** the argument being that He who can both foretell the future and then bring His prophecy to pass must be divine; **lest thou shouldest say, Mine idol hath done them, and my graven image and my molten image hath commanded them,** ascribing to these false gods an interference with the affairs of the world which was excluded by the Lord's proof of prophecy and fulfilment. V. 6. **Thou hast heard,** Israel having had plenty of opportunity to investigate. **See all this,** convincing themselves by personal observation; **and will not ye declare it?** Are men, in view of the fact that prophecy and fulfilment harmonize so perfectly, not bound to acknowledge the true God? The answer implied is that they certainly ought to agree to this if they would but speak the truth. Not only, however, has Israel sinned in this respect, but they are hardening their hearts also against further proclamations of truth. **I have showed thee new things from this time,** imparting this information at this time, namely, the revelation concerning the deliverance by Cyrus, **even hidden things, and thou didst not know them,** for the uncovering of the future is a matter pertaining to the omniscient God alone. V. 7. **They are created now,** brought into being, **and not from the beginning; even before the day when thou heardest them not,** having no information concerning them by themselves, **lest thou shouldest say, Behold, I knew them,** thus discounting the statements now made as not out of the ordinary. V. 8. **Yea, thou heardest not; yea, thou knewest not; yea, from that time that thine ear was not opened,** their ears being as little opened now as ever, their hardness of heart continuing as bad as ever; **for I knew that thou wouldest deal very treacherously,** full of perfidy and iniquity, **and wast called a transgressor from the womb,** the allusion being to the strategy of Jacob, of which even Esau complained, Gen. 27. The descendants of Jacob had inherited the bad qualities of their ancestor without assuming those attributes which made Jacob the servant of God. V. 9. **For My name's sake will I defer Mine anger,** not letting the judgment of wrath descend upon the apostate people, **and for My praise,** on account of His jealousy for His own honor, **will I refrain for thee, that I cut thee not off.** Because of His promise and covenant Jehovah did not exterminate the disobedient people at this time, but gave them another opportunity for repentance. V. 10. **Behold, I have refined thee,** with the heat of tribulation, **but not with silver,** they had not yet assayed well; **I have chosen thee in the furnace of affliction,** proving them out, trying them, to find their worth. V. 11. **For Mine own sake, even for Mine own sake, will I do it,** lest His name be desecrated; **for how should My name be polluted?** The heathen would ascribe the extermination of Israel to the inability of their God to protect them. **And I will not give My glory unto another,** this honor depending upon His deliverance of His people in accordance with His selection and the promises given to the patriarchs.

AN URGENT INVITATION TO BELIEVE THE LORD'S WORD. — V. 12. **Hearken unto Me, O Jacob and Israel, My called,** the form of address once more being in the usual cordial style used by the Lord in speaking to the people of His choice, here identical with His Church; **I am He: I am the First, I also am the Last,** this fundamental truth being repeated also here, where Jehovah prepares to preach salvation. V. 13. **Mine hand also hath laid the foundation of the earth, and**

My right hand hath spanned the heavens, stretching them out like a tent; cp. chap. 40, 28; 42, 5; 44, 24; 45, 12. 18; **when I call unto them,** in the work of creation, **they stand up together,** and this same power is evident in all His works. V. 14. **All ye, assemble yourselves and hear,** this challenge going forth to the Lord's adversaries, to the heathen; **which among them,** among those whom He here calls upon, **hath declared these things?** Not one of the opponents nor any of their gods could have predicted what the Lord intended to perform through Cyrus. **The Lord hath loved him,** and therefore chosen Cyrus to carry out His will; **He,** Jehovah, **will do His pleasure on Babylon, and His arm shall be on the Chaldeans,** to punish them. V. 15. **I, even I, have spoken,** the one true God, who has just described Himself once more as the almighty and eternal Creator; **yea, I have called him; I have brought him, and he shall make his way prosperous,** being successful in the undertaking which Jehovah bade him perform. The Lord now once more turns directly to Israel: v. 16. **Come ye near unto Me, hear ye this. I have not spoken in secret from the beginning,** revealing His will and intention concerning the mission of Cyrus very plainly, without the slightest ambiguity; **from the time that it was,** when He first determined upon this course, **there am I,** the only One able to control the destinies of individuals and nations according to His divine will. **And now the Lord God and His Spirit hath sent me,** that is, the salvation, the deliverance brought about by Cyrus itself, announces that it is here, ready to be performed and applied. And this salvation, which typifies the final great redemption, is now proclaimed and set before the eyes of all men, being offered in particular, however, to Israel at this time. V. 17. **Thus saith the Lord, thy Redeemer, the Holy One of Israel,** the names which Jehovah has applied to Himself throughout this section: **I am the Lord, thy God, which teacheth thee to profit,** imparting the knowledge of that which is beneficial, truly profitable, spiritual advantages, **which leadeth thee by the way that thou shouldest go,** on paths of salvation, Ps. 32, 8. V. 18. **O that thou hadst hearkened to My commandments,** willing now to be attentive; **then had thy peace,** the harmonious relation between the people and the God of salvation, **been as a river,** carrying blessings in richest measure, **and thy righteousness as the waves of the sea,** the salvation promised in the Lord's covenant overwhelming His people by its greatness and power; v. 19. **thy seed also,** the spiritual descendants of Israel, the believers everywhere, **had been as the sand and the offspring of thy bowels like the gravel thereof,** the Messianic idea of the great extent of Jehovah's kingdom being set forth here; **His name,** that of Israel, **should not have been cut off nor destroyed from before Me.** On the basis of all this the Lord now issues an invitation to His people to accept and enjoy the redemption prepared for them: v. 20. **Go ye forth of Babylon,** leaving the house of bondage, **flee ye from the Chaldeans with a voice of singing,** over the deliverance which they received; **declare ye, tell this, utter it even to the end of the earth,** the expressions being heaped to show the very height of exultant joy; **say ye, The Lord hath redeemed His servant Jacob,** the people thereby being received once more into the original relation toward Jehovah. V. 21. **And they thirsted not when He led them through the deserts; He caused the waters to flow out of the rock for them,** Ex. 17, 6; **He clave the rock also, and the waters gushed out,** Num. 20, 11, the reference to these miracles of Jehovah in the wilderness being intended to emphasize the deliverance out of Babylon, in both the real and the figurative sense; for all believers are led in a similar manner, receiving the spiritual refreshment prepared by the Lord unto the salvation of their souls. Over against their happiness the unhappy condition of the Lord's enemies stands out all the more glaringly. V. 22. **There is no peace, saith the Lord,** in a solemn declaration, **unto the wicked.** Those who refuse to accept the salvation prepared by Him for all men will never know anything of the peace which passeth all understanding, the joyful assurance of their redemption through the merits of their Savior.

CHAPTER 49.

The Covenant Faithfulness of the Lord in the Deliverance of Israel.

THE TESTIMONY OF JEHOVAH'S SERVANT. — V. 1. **Listen, O isles, unto Me, and hearken, ye people, from far,** the entire heathen world being called upon to give attention to the proclamation here being made: **The Lord hath called Me from the womb,** designating the Servant of Jehovah for His special service from the very hour of His birth; **from the bowels of My mother hath He made mention of My name,** the words plainly indicating that an individual is speaking, and not the entire nation of Israel, He who has received the definite name of the Messiah of Israel, for only He, properly speaking, is the Servant of Jehovah. V. 2. **And He hath made My mouth like a sharp sword,** in the proclamation of His Word, Heb. 4, 12; Rev. 2, 12; **in the shadow of His hand hath He**

hid Me, as an instrument prepared for His service, and **made Me a polished shaft**, an arrow of unsullied purity; **in His quiver hath He hid Me**, to be used at the time appointed by Him, v. 3. **and said unto Me, Thou art My Servant, O Israel, in whom I will be glorified**, the Messiah being the true Israel, He who battled with God and with men and remained victorious and was therefore elevated to the divine glory and majesty. Cp. Phil. 2, 9—11. V. 4. **Then I said**, the Messiah speaking here in His rôle of true human being, in the weakness which beset Him in Gethsemane, **I have labored in vain, I have spent My strength for naught and in vain**, being oppressed with sorrow and the fear of death in the midst of His work of atonement; **yet surely**, in spite of that feeling of depression and terror, **My judgment is with the Lord**, the cause which He represented was that of Jehovah, **and My work with My God**, the fruit and result of His labors being in the hand of His almighty Father. It is the same thought which we find in the story of Gethsemane: If it be possible, take this cup from Me; yet not My will, but Thine, be done. V. 5. **And now, saith the Lord that formed Me from the womb to be His Servant**, as stated in verse 1, **to bring Jacob again to Him**, namely, the true spiritual children of Jacob, **Though Israel be not gathered**, rather, "and that Israel may be gathered to Him," for this is one of the purposes for which the Servant of Jehovah is prepared, **yet shall I be glorious in the eyes of the Lord, and My God shall be My Strength**, the second object of the Servant's calling being to equip Him for His work by the strength of the Lord. V. 6. **And He**, Jehovah, **said, It is a light thing that Thou shouldest be My Servant to raise up the tribes of Jacob and to restore the preserved of Israel**, those whom the Lord had chosen for His own out of the descendants of the patriarchs, cp. Matt. 15, 24; **I will also give Thee for a light to the Gentiles**, chap. 60, 3, **that Thou mayest be My Salvation unto the end of the earth**, the Servant of Jehovah being the Savior of the whole world, the heathen being fellow-citizens with the saints and of the household of God. Although the children of Israel were the chosen people of the Lord, His first-born son, it remains true, nevertheless, that there is no difference between the Jew and the Greek; for the same Lord over all is rich unto all that call upon Him, Rom. 10, 12. V. 7. **Thus saith the Lord, the Redeemer of Israel**, the almighty and merciful Vindicator of His people, **and His Holy One**, who is zealous for His honor, **to Him whom man despiseth**, whom people generally hold in contempt, **to Him whom the nation abhorreth**, whom they regard as an abomination, **to a Servant of rulers**, one who is treated like a slave by the tyrants among men, as history relates of Jesus, **Kings shall see and arise**, namely, when He appears in view, **princes also shall worship**, being obliged to show Him due honor, **because of the Lord that is faithful**, since they are bound to realize that the Lord is standing behind His Servant and upholding His cause, **and the Holy One of Israel, and He shall choose Thee**, on account of the zeal of Jehovah for His chosen people. V. 8. **Thus saith the Lord**, once more in answer to the complaint voiced in verse 4, **In an acceptable time have I heard Thee**, in the Messianic period, when His grace and mercy would be evident in an extraordinary measure, **and in a day of salvation have I helped Thee**, at the time when help came out of Zion upon the spiritual Israel; **and I will preserve Thee**, keeping Him from destruction in the hours of the greatest trials, **and give Thee for a covenant of the people**, as a Mediator of His covenant of grace, **to establish the earth**, the entire land of Canaan, as the type of the spiritual Israel's heritage, **to cause to inherit the desolate heritages**, so that all believers become partakers of the blessings originally given to Israel (these blessings, chiefly of a spiritual nature, were wilfully despised by the great majority of them, but are now, in the Messianic era, to be the lasting possession of all true Israelites), v. 9. **that Thou mayest say to the prisoners, Go forth, to them that are in darkness**, namely, the darkness of sinfulness and unbelief, **Show yourselves**. The reference is to the spiritual deliverance, which is the fruit of the Gospel-message. Cp. chap. 42, 22. **They shall feed in the ways**, the entire number of those who are partakers of the salvation in Christ enjoying the blessings offered by Him, **and their pastures shall be in all high places**, the richest spiritual food in the very midst of the vanities of this world. V. 10. **They shall not hunger nor thirst**, having food and drink for their souls in abundance in the Word of His grace; **neither shall the heat nor sun smite them**, the tribulations of this world being unable permanently to harm them; **for He that hath mercy on them shall lead them, even by the springs of water shall He guide them**, the assurances of His loving-kindness and tender mercy serving to refresh the souls in every circumstance of life. V. 11. **And I will make all My mountains a way, and My highways shall be exalted**, all obstructions and difficulties will be removed, so that the Lord's children will have their pathway to heaven made smooth. V. 12. **Behold, these**, those who belonged to the Lord by virtue of their salvation, **shall come from far; and, lo, these from the North and from the West, and these from the land of Sinim**, probably China, for the Lord has His own in every country of the world. For that reason the prophet inserts a powerful admonition to the whole creation to break forth in thanksgiving for the evidence of the Lord's mercy in the salvation of His people. V. 13. **Sing, O heavens, and be joyful, O earth,** all creatures everywhere raising their voices in grateful anthems, **and break forth into singing, O mountains; for the Lord hath comforted His people,** refreshing and healing them in the midst of their afflictions, **and will have mercy upon His afflicted,** giving them direct and concrete evidence of His love in the Messiah. All this, however, redounds to the glory of the Lord's Servant, since He alone receives all the credit for every soul which is saved by His mercy, as our hymns to this day expressly state.

THE GLORIFICATION OF ZION BY JEHOVAH'S SERVANT. — V. 14. **But Zion,** the capital of the chosen people as type of the Church of God, **said, The Lord hath forsaken me,** the God of the covenant having apparently turned against her, **and my Lord hath forgotten me,** her Bridegroom and Husband was utterly estranged from her. It is an expression of the deepest affliction of the soul, which is obsessed by the fear and terror of hell. Upon this the Lord Himself answers with words of glorious consolation, v. 15. **Can a woman forget her sucking child,** the tiny infant in her arms; **that she should not have compassion on the son of her womb?** It is the strongest comparison which the Lord can find for human understanding. But His love and mercy surpass even the intense love of the fondest mother. **Yea, they may forget,** it may so happen that a human mother will so far forget herself and deny the call of natural affection, **yet will I not forget thee,** the heavenly Father's love is so inexpressibly great and burning that He actually finds it impossible not to feel the compassion of love toward those that are His. V. 16. **Behold, I have graven thee upon the palms of My hands,** as a token that the picture of the Lord's pity is indelibly impressed upon His heart and mind, that He has it before the eyes of His mind always; **thy walls are continually before Me,** He has them before Him in their proper and correct reconstruction; He sees His Church as a beautiful and perfect building, a habitation of His Holy Spirit. V. 17. **Thy children shall make haste,** hurrying to the side of their mother as though they could not come fast enough to save and to glorify her; **thy destroyers and they that made thee waste shall go forth of thee,** leaving Zion in undisturbed possession of her city. V. 18. **Lift up thine eyes round about and behold,** so the Lord's consoling admonition proclaims, **all these,** the people gained for the Lord by the proclamation of the Gospel, **gather themselves together and come to thee,** to join the Church. **As I live, saith the Lord,** with a solemn oath of reassurance, **thou shalt surely clothe thee with them all,** like a bride putting on her rich garments, **as with an ornament, and bind them on thee as a bride doeth,** as she girds her robes about her. The Church is pictured with a host of her children about her, their great number serving as her choicest ornament. V. 19. **For thy waste and thy desolate places and the land of thy destruction,** the land of Judah with its many sacked cities and ruined farms being a type of the Church's desolation in consequence of the Babylonian captivity, **shall even now be too narrow by reason of the inhabitants, and they that swallowed thee up shall be far away,** the destroyers of the land being crowded out of the land by the increasing number of Jerusalem's children, by the growing number of believers in the Messianic era. V. 20. **The children which thou shalt have,** the spiritual offspring of Zion, **after thou hast lost the other,** those that were born to her during the time of the exile, **shall say again in thine ears,** this would surely come to pass once more that they would clamor, **The place is too strait for me,** too narrow for their increasing number; **give place to me that I may dwell,** providing enough room for those who would be born anew by the Spirit of God in the Word. V. 21. **Then shalt thou say in thine heart,** in joyful surprise, **Who hath begotten me these, seeing I have lost my children,** before and during the Babylonian captivity, **and am desolate,** a captive, **and removing to and fro?** Zion was childless and unfruitful, rejected of her Lord and left by the wayside; she thought she had been utterly forsaken. **And who hath brought up these?** the children which now come with the demand that they be given sufficient room to spread out in the land. And once more her surprised question is sounded, **Behold, I was left alone; these, where had they been?** The Church cannot grasp the mercy of the Lord as it is revealed in this rich blessing. The Lord now gives a most solemn answer: v. 22. **Thus saith the Lord God,** the all-powerful Ruler and Sovereign of the universe, **Behold, I will lift up Mine hand to the Gentiles,** in a signal which bids them come, **and set up My standard to the people,** a guide directing them in the right way; **and they shall bring thy sons in their arms,** the spiritual children of Israel born in the midst of heathenism, **and thy daughters shall be carried upon their shoulders,** in eager submission to the rule of the King of Peace. V. 23. **And kings shall be thy nursing fathers,** protecting and nurturing the Church, **and their queens thy nursing mothers,** fostering the cause of the believers in every conceivable manner; **they shall bow down to thee with their face toward the earth,** in the attitude of submission and worship, **and lick up the dust of thy feet,** giving due homage to the Church on account of the obvious protection which the Lord gives to those that trust in Him; and thou shalt know, by the powerful proof thus given, that **I am the Lord,** the evidence to that effect being continuous and overwhelming; **for they shall not be ashamed that wait for Me,** this being a promise which applies to the believers of all times. Moreover, the Lord now answers an objection which might be made in view of the fact that the children of Zion were still in the power of the enemies: v. 24. **Shall the prey be taken from the mighty or the lawful captive,** the entire band of captives, **delivered?** this being the somewhat dubious question put by the more timid, who see nothing of the promised deliverance. V. 25. **But thus saith the Lord, Even the captives of the mighty,** those whom the enemies thought they were holding most securely, **shall be taken away, and the prey of the terrible shall be delivered; for I will contend with him that contendeth with thee,** overcoming those who made war on His chosen people, **and I will save thy children,** therefore the future is so secure. V. 26. **And I will feed them that oppress thee with their own flesh,** in revenging the wrongs done to His people; **and they shall be drunken with their own blood, as with sweet wine,** in a slaughter brought upon them by Jehovah; **and all flesh,** all people of the world, **shall know that I, the Lord, am thy Savior and thy Redeemer, the Mighty One of Jacob,** invincible in His power. Thus the Lord promises to bring Zion to the knowledge of His grace and love by imparting His salvation, while His judgment upon the enemies of His Church causes them to acknowledge His sovereign power and covenant faithfulness.

CHAPTER 50.

The Defection of Israel Atoned for by the Servant of Jehovah.

The opening of this chapter continues the picture of the Lord and His Church, represented by Zion, His bride, whom He seeks with the faithfulness of His eternal love. V. 1. **Thus saith the Lord,** in addressing the Jewish nation in general, all members of which were presumably members also of the Lord's Church, **Where is the bill of your mother's divorcement,** the reference being to the document which the Jewish Law provided for, Deut. 24; Jer. 3, 1, **whom I have put away?** The mother, Zion-Jerusalem, is here distinguished from her children or such as were commonly recognized as her children. **Or which of My creditors is it to whom I have sold you?** The picture is that of the sale of children to creditors, to be kept in peonage until the debt had been paid off by the labor of the children. Cp. 2 Kings 4, 1. **Behold, for your iniquities,** their many guilty actions, **have ye sold yourselves, and for your transgressions,** their many breaches of faith and of the covenant, **is your mother put away,** being obliged to bear the wickedness of her children to which she had yielded. V. 2. **Wherefore, when I came, was there no man,** namely, to listen to the message of His prophets? **when I called, was there none to answer?** to assent to the preaching by which He intended to save their souls. The Jews had persisted in their disobedience and hardened their hearts against the Lord's merciful offers. **Is My hand shortened at all that it cannot redeem?** Did He no longer possess almighty power to save His people? **Or have I no power to deliver? Behold, at My rebuke I dry up the sea,** as when He made a path through the Red Sea for the children of Israel, **I make the rivers a wilderness; their fish stinketh because there is no water, and dieth for thirst.** Cp. Ex. 14, 21; 7, 18. 21. V. 3. **I clothe the heavens with blackness,** as in Egypt, Ex. 10, 21, **and I make sackcloth their covering,** the garment of mourning, whose color was dark. Since the Lord was the absolute Master of the elements, it was an easy matter for Him to protect Israel from the wrath of the enemies and to overthrow the tyrants everywhere. Yea, more: this was only a minor consideration, for the Lord had a complete salvation for His people in mind through the obedience of His Servant, who is now introduced as speaking. V. 4. **The Lord God hath given Me the tongue of the learned,** one versed in the art of the orator, **that I should know how to speak a word in season to him that is weary,** to him that is of a broken and contrite spirit, Matt. 11, 28. It is rightly said of the Messiah, Christ the Lord, "Never man spake as this man," John 7, 46. Cp. Matt. 7, 29. **He wakeneth morning by morning, He wakeneth Mine ear to hear as the learned,** to have the proper spiritual understanding of the Lord's will and to yield a glad obedience to it. Cp. Ps. 40, 6—8; Heb. 10, 5—7. V. 5. **The Lord God hath opened Mine ear,** to listen with cheerful willingness, **and I was not rebellious, neither turned away back,** not even when His soul was sorrowful even unto death and His human nature was trembling with the severity of the afflictions which He suffered. Cp. Ps. 22, 12—21; 1 Pet. 2, 22. V. 6. **I gave My back to the smiters,** in the terrible scourgings to which He was subjected in His great Passion, Matt. 26, 67. 68; 27, 26 ff.; John 19, **and My cheeks to them that plucked off the hair,** in the indignities heaped upon Him, which would arouse a storm of indignation in any other human being;

I hid not My face from shame and spitting, accepting both blasphemous mockery and actions with the spirit of divine humility which characterized Him throughout His sufferings. V. 7. **For the Lord God**, the all-powerful Jehovah, the God of the covenant, to whom He has appealed time and again, **will help Me, therefore shall I not be confounded**, the assistance given to His soul by the strength of Jehovah keeping Him from being submerged in misery and shame; **therefore have I set My face like a flint**, meeting all mockery with the conquering power of His unflinching will, **and I know that I shall not be ashamed**, His vindication would finally be brought about. V. 8. **He is near that justifieth Me**, His innocence being established in the last great Judgment; **who will contend with Me?** The guilt of all mankind was indeed imputed to Him, but in His own person He was ever the Holy One of God, whom no man could convict of sin. **Let us stand together**, appearing before the tribunal of the almighty Judge of the universe; **who is Mine adversary?** Let him who believes that he has a case against the Messiah step forward. **Let him come near to Me.** It is a defiant challenge which the Servant of Jehovah sends forth in the consciousness of His innocence. V. 9. **Behold, the Lord God will help Me**, standing at His side against all enemies; **Who is he that shall condemn Me?** namely, by bringing a charge which may be substantiated. **Lo, they**, the adversaries, **all shall wax old as a garment**, falling into dust as it rots; **the moth shall eat them up**, such is their fate, since they have dared oppose the Holy One of God. V. 10. **Who is among you that feareth the Lord**, in the proper respect for His majesty, but not in slavish dread, **that obeyeth the voice of His servant**, which is the Word of God, **that walketh in darkness and hath no light?** this being the lot of such as side with the Lord. **Let him trust in the name of the Lord**, in the midst of all tribulation, **and stay upon his God**, since in Him is full and complete security for all believers. V. 11. **Behold, all ye that kindle a fire**, the adversaries who persist in their hatred of the Lord, **that compass yourselves about with sparks**, the reference being to the tying up of tarred tow around arrows, these being shot into a besieged city for the purpose of setting houses on fire; **walk in the light of your fire and in the sparks that ye have kindled**, to be consumed by the fire which they themselves had lighted. **This shall ye have of Mine hand**, namely, as their lot and punishment; **ye shall lie down in sorrow**, in the extremity of pain, in the tortures of hell. He that believeth shall be saved; he that believeth not shall be damned.

CHAPTER 51.

The Realization of Zion's Salvation.

THE CERTAINTY OF DELIVERANCE. — V. 1. **Hearken unto Me, ye that follow after righteousness**, earnestly seeking to obtain it, **ye that seek the Lord**, in true repentance over their sins, as yet not daring to show a happy faith; **look unto the rock whence ye are hewn**, namely, Abraham, before the promise of the Lord regarding the birth of Isaac was fulfilled, **and to the hole of the pit whence ye are digged**, this cistern of the rock being Sarah, as the context shows. The nation of Israel was called into being by a miracle of God, who gave to Abraham and Sarah the son of promise. V. 2. **Look unto Abraham, your father, and unto Sarah, that bare you**, the ancestors of the Jewish people and, in a wider sense, of the spiritual Israel; **for I called him alone**, when he was but one, **and blessed him and increased him**, the conclusion which follows being that the same God is able to deliver and restore His people at all times. V. 3. **For the Lord shall comfort Zion**, building up His city anew; **He will comfort all her waste places**, letting her arise from her ruins; **and He will make her wilderness like Eden and her desert like the garden of the Lord**, new life and new glory following His blessing; **joy and gladness shall be found therein, thanksgiving and the voice of melody**, all this instead of the former misery. Cp. Rev. 7; 14; 21. V. 4. **Hearken unto Me, My people**, the invitation going forth once more and with increased emphasis, **and give ear unto Me, O My nation**, in the attitude of most careful attention; **for a law shall proceed from Me**, His Word issuing for the instruction of men, **and I will make My judgment**, that which is right and good according to His will, **to rest for a light of the people**, so that it would be a power for the conversion and salvation of all men. Cp. Luke 2, 32; Acts 26, 18. The promised renewal is that of the New Testament, which merges into that of heaven. That the interval of time does not exist in the omniscience of God is evident also from the following expressions: v. 5. **My righteousness is near**, which includes all the mercies promised in the covenant made with His people; **My salvation is gone forth**, is already an established fact, **and Mine arms shall judge the people**, His merciful power directing their thoughts to the salvation of the Messiah. **The isles shall wait upon Me**, to receive the deliverance of the Lord out of the misery of their sins, **and on Mine arm**, which obtains mercy for them, **shall they trust**, the heathen thus coming to the knowledge of their Savior. This certainty is now further emphasized. V. 6. **Lift up your eyes to the heavens,** with its impression of endless stability, **and look upon the earth beneath,** with its uninterrupted succession of generations, both appearing to the human mind as established securely; **for the heavens shall vanish away like smoke, and the earth shall wax old like a garment,** both of them bound for destruction on account of their inherent vanity, in spite of their apparent permanence, **and they that dwell therein shall die in like manner,** like a snap of the finger; **but My salvation shall be forever, and My righteousness,** His mercy promised in His covenant, **shall not be abolished,** it will endure throughout eternity. Moreover, the enemies will find themselves unable to hinder the establishment of the Lord's salvation. V. 7. **Hearken unto Me, ye that know righteousness,** choosing the mercy of the Lord's covenant, **the people in whose heart is My Law,** who delight in the instruction given in His Word; **fear ye not the reproach of men, neither be ye afraid of their revilings,** which were then, as now, poured out upon the believers for their trust in the salvation promised by the Lord; v. 8. **for the moth shall eat them up like a garment, and the worm shall eat them like wool,** bring about their destruction, put them out of the way; **but My righteousness shall be forever and My salvation from generation to generation,** His redemption means an eternal deliverance to all who trust in Him. Instead of continuing the comforting message from the mouth of the Lord, the prophet now, in an eminently dramatic manner introduces the listening believers as speaking, their prayer serving to substantiate the statements which have just been made. V. 9. **Awake, awake, put on strength,** exhibiting His almighty power, **O arm of the Lord,** as in carrying out a difficult piece of work; **awake, as in the ancient days, in the generations of old,** as when He delivered His people from the bondage of Egypt. **Art Thou not it that hath cut Rahab,** the crocodile, as the symbol of Egypt, **and wounded the dragon,** the sea-serpent? another symbol of Egypt. V. 10. **Art thou not it which hath dried the sea, the waters of the great deep, that hath made the depths of the sea a way for the ransomed to pass over?** The reference is to the deliverance of Israel at the Red Sea, when Pharaoh's might was overthrown. The thought which is implied is this: Even as the Lord overthrew the armies of the enemies in the past, so He can vanquish and annihilate the enemy's hosts at all times. V. 11. **Therefore the redeemed of the Lord shall return and come with singing unto Zion,** their deliverance from the captivity of Babylon being a picture of the salvation of mankind from the bondage of Satan; **and everlasting joy shall be upon their head,** like the wreath of a bride; **they shall obtain gladness and joy,** the very summary of bliss, **and sorrow and mourning shall flee away,** be removed forever. Such is the happy condition of the redeemed of the Lord of all times, a fact which they cannot realize too thoroughly or trust in too implicitly.

THE LOOSING OF THE EXILES.—V. 12. **I, even I, am He that comforteth you,** so Jehovah Himself announces in taking up the topic of the chapter once more. **Who art thou that thou shouldest be afraid of a man that shall die,** why should Zion as such or any individual believer fear any mortal enemy, **and of the son of man which shall be made as grass,** withering after a very brief life, v. 13. **and forgettest the Lord, thy Maker,** the almighty Creator of the universe, **that hath stretched forth the heavens,** chap. 40, 22; 42, 5, **and laid the foundations of the earth,** established it most firmly; **and hast feared continually every day because of the fury of the oppressor,** of the tyrant among men, of whom Babylon is a type, **as if he were ready to destroy? And where is the fury of the oppressor?** This rebuke of the Lord may well be applied in the case of all His children; for their occasional fear of the enemies is equivalent to a lack of trust in the power of Jehovah. The rage of the tyrant is unable to hinder the deliverance which God has planned for those who believe in Him. V. 14. **The captive exile hasteneth that he may be loosed,** literally, Soon the one bowed down (as captive) shall be loosed, the heavy fetters which bore him down to the ground being removed, **and that he should not die in the pit, nor that his bread should fail,** that is, he should be delivered from prison and have all the bread that he needs. V. 15. **But I am the Lord, thy God,** the gracious Sovereign, **that divided the sea,** whipping it into fury, **whose waves roared. The Lord of hosts is His name,** He who has command of both the heavenly and the earthly powers, He who directs the elements at His will. V. 16. **And I have put My words in thy mouth,** entrusting them to His people, **and I have covered thee in the shadow of Mine hand,** sustaining Israel in faith and in His grace, **that I may plant the heavens and lay the foundations of the earth,** as the Creator of the universe, **and say unto Zion,** with whom He is united by the bonds of His merciful love, **Thou art My people.** The entire description pictures the perfection of the new order which was to be established by Christ in His spiritual kingdom. V. 17. **Awake, awake, stand up, O Jerusalem,** this call being intended for the time immediately after the taking of Jerusalem by Nebuchadnezzar, **which hast drunk at the hand of the Lord the cup of His fury,** namely, in the punishment meted out by the Babylonian army. **Thou hast drunken the dregs of the cup of trembling,** the terror brought about by the wrath of the Lord,

and wrung them out, drained the dregs to the last drop. The misery of the situation is intensified by the fact that the sufferer is all alone in her tribulation. V. 18. **There is none to guide her among all the sons whom she hath brought forth**, none to direct her while she was in this helpless state of drunken terror; **neither is there any that taketh her by the hand**, to uphold and strengthen her, **of all the sons that she hath brought up**. It is impossible to bring salvation to mankind by a mere outward morality, by a mere social uplift as it is proclaimed in our days. The wrath of God over the sins of mankind may be appeased only by the atonement of the Savior, which turns the wrath into grace. V. 19. **These two things are come unto thee**, things of two kinds which are presently mentioned; **who shall be sorry for thee?** Not one showed sympathy with Zion in her deep disgrace. The two varieties of affliction are now named. **Desolation and destruction**, on the one hand, **and the famine and the sword**, on the other, the first pair striking the city, the second its inhabitants; **by whom shall I comfort thee?** There was none to comfort her in her misery. V. 20. **Thy sons have fainted**, all the inhabitants of Jerusalem being overcome; **they lie at the head of all the streets**, at the intersection of all thoroughfares, **as a wild bull in a net**, as a gazelle which is helplessly enmeshed; **they are full of the fury of the Lord, the rebuke of thy God**, for this invariably brings about death and destruction. But now the Lord turns to Jerusalem with the fulness of His mercy. V. 21. **Therefore hear now this, thou afflicted**, one who has experienced the depths of misery and tribulation, **and drunken, but not with wine**, the wrath of God alone being the cause of her miserable condition: v. 22. **Thus saith thy Lord**, the Husband and Sovereign of Jerusalem, **the Lord**, the God of the covenant, **and thy God, that pleadeth the cause of His people**, taking their part against the tyrants, **Behold, I have taken out of thine hand the cup of trembling**, the terror being induced by the wrath of the Lord over the sins of His people, **even the dregs of the cup of My fury**, which Zion was just represented as draining; **thou shalt no more drink it again**, since the Lord now promised His merciful deliverance, v. 23. **but I will put it into the hand of them that afflict thee**, who had brought all this tribulation upon her, **which have said to thy soul, Bow down that we may go over**, their backs thus serving to be trampled under foot by the enemies, **and thou hast laid thy body as the ground and as the street**, like a pavement, **to them that went over**. So great had been the humiliation of Zion-Jerusalem, representing the Church of God. But the Lord was determined to bring salvation to His people through the work of the Messiah.

CHAPTER 52.

The Redemption of Jerusalem.

THE PROMISE OF REDEMPTION.—V. 1. **Awake, awake! Put on thy strength, O Zion**, arousing herself from her dejection and assuming the proper confidence in view of the happy message which is now proclaimed; **put on thy beautiful garments, O Jerusalem, the Holy City**, in view of her coming elevation and glorification, for the restoration of Jerusalem was a type of the renewal of the Church of God in the Messianic era; **for henceforth**, after the consecration by the redemption of the Messiah, **there shall no more come into thee the uncircumcised and the unclean**, any one not in communion with the God of the covenant. In the Zion of the New Testament the Lord Himself reigns in an uninterrupted rule of mercy, the outward membership of hypocrites not being regarded as a true membership. V. 2. **Shake thyself from the dust**, where she had occupied the seat of mourners, **arise and sit down, O Jerusalem**, on the throne which was properly her place; **loose thyself from the bands of thy neck, O captive daughter of Zion**, who is here still regarded as an exile nation, but with the fetters of her captivity broken. V. 3. **For thus saith the Lord, Ye have sold yourselves for naught**, He Himself having given them into the power of their enemies, but without receiving anything in return; **and ye shall be redeemed without money**, since the Lord would not offer the enemy tyrants any money to release His people. The Lord intended to use His almighty power in bringing deliverance to His people, in overthrowing the hosts of the enemy. V. 4. **For thus saith the Lord God**, the all-powerful Jehovah, **My people went down aforetime into Egypt to sojourn there**, to enjoy the privilege of guests, not to be placed into bondage, this feature being added by the Egyptians against Jehovah's will; **and**, at a later date, **the Assyrian oppressed them without cause**, without justification, in inexcusable tyranny. V. 5. **Now, therefore, what have I here**, in the case of the Babylonian exile, **saith the Lord, that My people is taken away for naught?** He received no return for His act in permitting the Chaldeans to take Israel captive. **They that rule over them make them to howl**, their oppressors making boisterous noises, **saith the Lord, and My name continually, every day, is blasphemed**, since the enemies would not acknowledge His hand as He shaped events in their favor, but blasphemously ascribed their success to themselves and to their idols. V. 6. **Therefore My people shall know My name,** in view of such behavior on the part of the oppressors; **therefore they shall know in that day that I am He that doth speak,** powerful for the deliverance of His people and for the overthrow of all enemies; **behold, it is I,** the Lord is known for fulfilling His promises. It is the same Lord upon whose power and mercy we depend in all vicissitudes of life, knowing that He is the one true God.

The Messengers of Redemption. — V. 7. **How beautiful upon the mountains are the feet of him that bringeth good tidings,** namely, those of the salvation of Israel, of Zion, **that publisheth peace,** announcing that all devastating warfare is now ended, **that bringeth good tidings of good,** preaching with glad acclaim, **that publisheth salvation,** making the fact of redemption known throughout the nation, **that saith unto Zion, Thy God reigneth,** He has entered upon His rule. During the exile, indeed, the Lord had given the heathen power over the kingdoms of the world and even over Israel, but now that His people is delivered from the bondage of Babylonia, He has once more established His Kingdom of Grace over Israel, just as He has once more assumed the reins of the world government, never to relinquish them again. The picture which is here drawn is one of perfect Messianic conditions, the beauty of the Messianic era with its wonderful Gospel proclamation. V. 8. **Thy watchmen shall lift up the voice,** as they see the messengers approaching; **with the voice together shall they sing, for they shall see eye to eye,** very plainly and unmistakably, **when the Lord shall bring again Zion,** when He Himself shall return to His city. Such shouts of rejoicing are now inserted in order to emphasize the full extent of the deliverance gained. V. 9. **Break forth into joy, sing together, ye waste places of Jerusalem,** the ruins of the city themselves being regarded as mourning on account of the downfall of the city; **for the Lord hath comforted His people,** placing them once more into their ancient heritage, **He hath redeemed Jerusalem,** tearing it out of the hands of the enemies. V. 10. **The Lord hath made bare His holy arm,** in preparing for a mighty punishment, **in the eyes of all the nations,** before the eyes of the unbelieving, mocking enemies; **and all the ends of the earth shall see the salvation of our God,** being obliged to witness in what manner the Lord brings deliverance to His people. The description now goes back to the first moments of the deliverance from Babylon. V. 11. **Depart ye, depart ye,** the Lord urges the returning Jews, **go ye out from thence,** from the midst of idolatrous Babylon, **touch no unclean thing,** anything connected with idolatry; **go ye out of the midst of her; be ye clean, that bear the vessels of the Lord,** namely, those belonging to the Temple, which the exiles took back with them to Jerusalem. Cp. Ezra 1, 7—11. The expression refers to the need of consecration in the Lord's work in all times, under all circumstances. V. 12. **For ye shall not go out with haste, nor go by flight,** in a precipitate hurry, as at the time of the exodus from Egypt; **for the Lord will go before you,** their Ruler Himself being their guide, **and the God of Israel will be your rearward,** bringing up the rear and thus sheltering them on both sides and giving them the full security needed in all their ways. Thus the believers are ever and everywhere secure against the evil plans of their enemies, the Lord Himself being their Guide and their Protector.

CHAPTER 53.

(Chapter 52, 13—53, 12.)

The Suffering of Jehovah's Servant.

The closing verses of chapter 52, according to the somewhat unsatisfactory division of the chapters in this instance, present a summary of the entire next chapter, setting forth the unparalleled humiliation of the Servant of Jehovah, followed by His triumphant exaltation. V. 13. **Behold, My servant shall deal prudently,** prospering His cause, bringing it to a successful conclusion in spite of its great difficulty; **He shall be exalted and extolled,** to a position of triumphant power, **and be very high.** The entire verse has been understood by Lutheran commentators as referring to the resurrection, the ascension, and the sitting at the right hand of God on the part of the Messiah. V. 14. **As many were astonied at thee,** filled with astonishment and aversion; **His visage was so marred, more than any man, and His form more than the sons of men,** that is, His entire appearance had been so disfigured by the extremity of the sufferings to which He was subjected that it was almost beyond comprehension how a human being could endure such an excess of misery; v. 15. **so,** on the other hand, **shall He sprinkle many nations,** cause the heathen to shrink apart with terror, as when a heavy weight dropped into water causes it to splash in all directions; **the kings shall shut their**

mouths at Him, rendered speechless by the sudden appearance of Jehovah's Servant on the last day, Matt. 24, 30; Rev. 6, 15. 16; **for that which had not been told them shall they see, and that which they had not heard shall they consider,** since they find that to be coming true which they considered impossible. After this introductory summary the prophet sets forth his message in greater detail. Chapter 53, 1. **Who hath believed our report?** Who puts faith in that which he hears from us, the messengers of the Lord? **And to whom is the arm of the Lord revealed?** The evangelist of the Old Testament, in an ineffably sad strain, deplores the natural lack of interest in the great central message of salvation. The report is indeed made, it goes forth and may be heard, but the arm of the Lord, in the revelation of the mighty power of His grace, is hidden from the great majority of men. The way of salvation, through the suffering of the Messiah, does not appeal to their self-righteousness, to the vanity of their hearts. V. 2. **For He,** the Servant of Jehovah, **shall grow up before Him,** the Lord, **as a tender plant and as a root out of a dry ground,** a shoot springing up from beneath a dead stump. **He hath no form,** no attractiveness, **nor comeliness; and when we shall see Him, there is no beauty that we should desire Him.** In the midst of Israel's spiritual wilderness and desolation, from the well-nigh dead stump of the house and family of David, the Messiah came forth, like a shoot springing up from the roots of a tree-stump. But this remarkable happening had little or no influence on the children of Israel. For He had no attractive form; there was nothing in Him to strike the eye of natural man and to draw him to the Servant of the Lord. V. 3. **He is despised and rejected of men,** forsaken by them all, **a man of sorrows and acquainted with grief,** fully acquainted with sicknesses and the misery of this earthly life; **and we hid, as it were, our faces from Him. He was despised, and we esteemed Him not,** ignoring Him, passing Him by. He stood all alone throughout His life, despised, rejected, forsaken of men, He who was acquainted with life's sorrows, who alone could have compassion on men's weakness. Men, in contempt of Him, turned the other way and ignored Him, just as they do to this day. V. 4. **Surely He hath borne our griefs and carried our sorrows,** the sufferings and pains which we should have endured; **yet we did esteem Him stricken, smitten of God, and afflicted,** bowed down with suffering. V. 5. **But He was wounded for our transgressions,** for the crimes by which we had become guilty in the sight of God, **He was bruised for our iniquities,** for the debts which we had incurred; **the chastisement of our peace was upon Him, and with His stripes we are healed,** literally, "by His stripes healing to us." V. 6. **All we like sheep have gone astray; we have turned every one to his own way;** and, in the mean time, while we were yet sinners and godless, **the Lord hath laid on Him the iniquity of us all.** While mankind, as a whole, was indifferent to Him, rejected and despised Him, He was wonderfully active in our behalf. With emphasis it is stated, "Surely our griefs He has carried, the sufferings which we deserved He has borne in our stead." While we, all men, in the blindness of our self-righteousness, stood back and considered the Sufferer smitten, struck, and afflicted by God, He was taking upon Himself the blame for our crimes, the guilt of our iniquities. Our transgressions were charged to His account, and He was engaged in paying them off. In order that we might again be at peace with God, He took upon Him our chastisement; in order that we might not suffer the bruises and stripes which we had so richly merited, He permitted them to be laid upon Himself. Yea, while we were going astray in our own blindness and wilfulness, every one turning to the way which suited his evil nature best, God laid even these crimes and all other iniquities upon Him. Such is the wonderful message of Christ's vicarious suffering. V. 7. **He was oppressed,** sorely ill-treated, **and He was afflicted,** He bowed Himself down, offering a willing back to the burden placed upon it; **yet He opened not His mouth; He is brought as a lamb to the slaughter, and as a sheep before her shearers is dumb, so He openeth not His mouth,** not one cry of protest passing His lips. V. 8. **He was taken from prison and from judgment,** through force and judicial sentence, **and who shall declare His generation? For He was cut off out of the land of the living,** that is, who of the people of His time deplored the fact that He was torn away out of the land of the living? the answer being: Practically not one. **For the transgression of My people was He stricken,** the curse of the judgment came upon Him. V. 9. **And He made His grave with the wicked and with the rich in His death,** rather, "but with the rich He was in His death"; **because He had done no violence, neither was any deceit in His mouth.** Christ is the true sacrificial Lamb brought to the slaughter, a sheep dumb before her shearers. But He attained to the object which He had in mind in this suffering, for which He came into this world; for misery and judgment exhausted themselves in His case. He fought His way through to an endless length of life. This involved, of course, that He was torn away from the land of the living. Because His vicarious obedience demanded this sacrifice, the curse came upon Him for His people's crime. Yet in the very hour after His death He received recognition. Men had planned His interment with the wicked; they thought they could break His legs and treat Him like the criminals that were crucified with Him, casting His body into some convenient pit. Instead of that, however, He was with the rich in His death, buried like a wealthy man, in Joseph's grave. And this because He had done no violence, and in His mouth there was no deceit: He was the Holy One of God. V. 10. **Yet it pleased the Lord to bruise Him; He hath put Him to grief,** laid sickness and sorrow upon Him. **When Thou shalt make His soul an offering for sin,** literally, "when His soul shall have been offered as a sacrifice of trespass," **He shall see His seed, He shall prolong His days, and the pleasure of the Lord shall prosper in His hand.** Here the mystery of the treatment accorded by God to the sinless Servant is set forth. His sufferings, His bruises, were divinely inflicted; He bore the sicknesses of mankind by the determinate counsel and foreknowledge of God. His very soul, His life, was offered as a vicarious sacrifice of trespass, in voluntary surrender, a complete ransom. But now comes the fruit and the glory of the mystery; for the Servant, having died, sees His offspring, His spiritual children, born to Him as the result of the Gospel-message. Having died, He prolongs His days, for now He lives forevermore. Having died and being now once more alive, He carries into effect the divine purpose, His kingdom advancing throughout the world, through the effect of His power. V. 11. **He shall see the travail of His soul and shall be satisfied,** feel satisfaction and true refreshment; **by His knowledge shall My righteous Servant justify many, for He shall bear their iniquities.** V. 12. **Therefore will I divide Him a portion with the great,** apportion to Him the many, **and He shall divide the spoil with the strong,** the mighty ones becoming subject to Him, **because He hath poured out His soul unto death, and He was numbered with the transgressors, and He bare the sin of many, and made intercession for the transgressors,** being their Mediator even to-day. The work of redemption ends with the Servant's satisfied contemplation of His atoning work, of the consequences of the travail of His soul. Now the knowledge of Him, that is, His Gospel, through which we learn to know Him as the Savior of the world, makes men righteous. It is a grand view of His work which He has before His eyes: the many made partakers of His work, of His atonement, since His sin-bearing is the basis of our righteousness. And so the prophecy ends with a note of conquest and triumph. Not only has God apportioned to His Servant the many, but God's power and that of His Servant are placed side by side, gathering men, even the mighty of the earth, as their spoil. The fact that He poured out His life in death, that He bore the sins of many, is now the everlasting foundation of His work as our Advocate with the Father; on the basis of that He makes continual intercession for us. Such is Christ's work of vicarious atonement, as it was preached to the believers of the Old Testament, as we now know it to have been fulfilled.

CHAPTER 54.

The Fruit of the Messiah's Sufferings.

THE LORD'S PROMISE TO RELIEVE ZION'S BARRENNESS. — V. 1. **Sing, O barren, in joyful shouting, thou that didst not bear,** the Jewish Church being for a while forsaken of God and therefore destitute of spiritual children; **break forth into singing and cry aloud, thou that didst not travail with child,** while the affliction of the dispersion was upon her; **for more are the children of the desolate,** of her who had for a time been forsaken by the Lord, her Husband, **than the children of the married wife, saith the Lord.** During the exile the house of David was rejected by God, the worship of Jehovah in Jerusalem had ceased, and prophecy had been reduced in amount. Therefore the message of salvation was heard by a few only, and no new believers were gained. With the restoration of Israel, however, and especially in the Messianic era, this condition would once more be changed in such a manner that Zion would have a greater number of spiritual children than ever. V. 2. **Enlarge the place of thy tent,** to make room for the increased number of spiritual children, **and let them,** the servants, **stretch forth the curtains of thine habitations,** the various sections which made up the large tent of the wealthy; **spare not,** do not hold back; **lengthen thy cords,** to accommodate the increased area of the tent, and **strengthen thy stakes,** substituting stronger pins for those used till now; v. 3. **for thou shalt break forth on the right hand and on the left,** on account of the rapid increase in children of the Gospel; **and thy seed shall inherit the Gentiles, and make the desolate cities to be inhabited,** the picture being taken from the former warfare against the heathen and signifying the spiritual conquest of the Gentile world through the preaching of the Gospel. V. 4. **Fear not,** in doubt as to the truth and certainty of the promise given, **for thou shalt not be ashamed,** not experience another rejection at the hand of the Lord; **neither be thou confounded,** made the object of ridicule and contempt, **for thou shalt not be put to shame; for thou shalt forget the shame of thy youth,** the time of the bondage in Egypt, **and shalt not remember the reproach of thy widowhood any more,** the time of the Babylonian captivity. V. 5. **For thy Maker is thine Husband,** or "Thy Husband is He who made thee," the almighty Lord of the universe; **the Lord of hosts is His name,** the great God of the covenant; **and thy Redeemer the Holy One of Israel,** who in the zeal of His love for His people overthrows the power of the enemies. **The God of the whole earth shall He be called,** whose absolute power and authority are a guarantee to the Church of its future greatness and glory. God is ever and in all places the Redeemer and Vindicator of His people, a strong Rock of refuge to those that trust in Him.

THE LORD'S PROMISE OF ETERNAL LOVE AND FAITHFULNESS. — V. 6. **For the Lord hath called thee as a woman forsaken and grieved in spirit,** one who had been rejected and therefore sat mourning, **and a wife of youth,** surrounded by the love of her husband, **when thou wast refused, saith thy God.** This assurance was given to Zion by Him who, although He had once cast her aside, yet is her God and will forever remain her God. V. 7. **For a small moment have I forsaken thee,** forsaking her at a time of great excitement of mind, under stress of a momentary anger; **but with great mercies will I gather thee,** drawing her to Him again in the overwhelming power of His love. V. 8. **In a little wrath I hid My face from thee for a moment,** while His anger, as it were, burned with a sudden flame; **but with everlasting kindness will I have mercy on thee,** in a flood of tenderness and grace, **saith the Lord, thy Redeemer,** He who is ever the Vindicator of His people. V. 9. **For this is as the waters of Noah unto Me,** namely, the present flood of wrath which had struck Israel; **for as I have sworn that the waters of Noah,** the Deluge with its general destruction, **should no more go over the earth,** an oath which, as all men knew, had been kept all these centuries, **so have I sworn that I would not be wroth with thee nor rebuke thee,** giving vent to His anger in various punishments. V. 10. **For the mountains shall depart and the hills be removed,** although the most awful cataclysms of nature should occur, so that the very foundations of the earth are shaken, **but My kindness shall not depart from thee,** so that the wonderful union and communion of love between Christ and His Church would be disturbed or disrupted, **neither shall the covenant of My peace be removed,** that of the Messianic promise, as first given to Abraham and then repeated throughout the Old Testament, **saith the Lord that hath mercy on thee.** The depth and the certainty of God's love is thus set forth in a manner which makes this promise basic for the faith of all Christians of all times. What was written here is written for our comfort; we should believe these promises and rejoice in them always.

THE LORD'S PROMISE OF PERFECT SECURITY FOR THE CHURCH. — V. 11. **O thou afflicted,** one full of misery and sorrow, **tossed with tempest,** like the chaff from the threshing-floor, **and not comforted,** still lying in desolation, **behold, I will lay thy stones with fair colors,** building up the city walls and houses in such a way as to lay the stones in colored mortar to enhance the beautiful effect, **and lay thy foundations with sapphires,** as a plinth for the whole city. V. 12. **And I will make thy windows of agates,** the parapets of houses and walls of jewels, **and thy gates of carbuncles,** stones which are both beautiful and terrifying, **and all thy borders,** the walls proper, **of pleasant stones,** of such whose beauty makes them desirable. It is a fine description of the manner in which the Lord builds His Church on earth. Cp. Eph. 2, 19—22. V. 13. **And all thy children,** the inhabitants of the Lord's city, **shall be taught of the Lord,** His disciples knowing Him by faith; **and great shall be the peace of thy children,** namely, the peace which passes all understanding, which comes to the believers by virtue of the fact that the enmity between God and man has been removed by the atoning work of the Messiah. V. 14. **In righteousness shalt thou be established,** clothed with salvation, firmly grounded in the righteousness imputed by faith; **thou shalt be far from oppression,** fearing no danger and misfortune, **for thou shalt not fear,** literally, "Far be it from thee to fear"; **and from terror, for it shall not come near thee,** nothing would be able to bring further desolation. V. 15. **Behold, they shall surely gather together, but not by Me,** that is, If some of the enemies, in spite of all, should attempt to harm Zion, it would be against the Lord's counsel and will; **whosoever shall gather together against thee shall fall for thy sake,** being overcome and induced to join the party of the Lord. V. 16. **Behold, I have created the smith that bloweth the coals in the fire and that bringeth forth an instrument for his work,** drawing it out of the fire as his labor requires; **and I have created the waster to destroy.** The physical strength for the making of weapons of war comes from the Lord, but at the same time He has reserved to Himself the power to destroy these same weapons. V. 17. **No weapon that is formed against thee shall prosper,** none being able to attack the Church with lasting success;

and every tongue that shall rise against thee in judgment thou shalt condemn, the Church remaining victorious also against the efforts of all science falsely so called to disprove the truth of the Gospel. **This is the heritage of the servants of the Lord,** namely, that they can conquer all the enemies, **and their righteousness is of Me, saith the Lord,** He alone being the Source of their salvation. This promise is Jehovah's powerful Amen at the end of this chapter, a source of comfort to the believers of all times.

CHAPTER 55.

Jehovah's Gospel Invitation.

THE HEATHEN INVITED TO THE BANQUET OF GRACE. — V. 1. **Ho, every one that thirsteth,** the earnest attention of all who feel their need being solicited, **come ye to the waters! And he that hath no money,** nothing of real value to offer in exchange, **come ye, buy and eat; yea, come, buy wine and milk without money and without price.** The Hebrew text brings out even more strongly than can be done in an English translation the idea of a gracious giving on the part of the Lord. The rich nourishment, the refreshing sweetness of His spiritual blessings are offered in the Gospel altogether free and for nothing. Everything else in the world costs something, must be paid for in money or labor, or in some act representing compensation for value received; only the mercies of David, the salvation in Christ, cost absolutely nothing. The substance of this verse is contained in Matt. 11, 28—30. V. 2. **Wherefore do ye spend money for that which is not bread?** exerting themselves in a vain effort to gain the true, lasting peace of mind by acts of their own righteousness, **and your labor for that which satisfieth not?** All the efforts of men to find true satisfaction and happiness in things which this world has to offer are vain and useless. **Hearken diligently unto Me, and eat ye that which is good, and let your soul delight itself in fatness.** The spiritual eating of the believers is done through their hearing of the Word, for God has placed His whole salvation in His Word, in the Gospel, and the highest consolation, joy, and bliss is to be found in Him. V. 3. **Incline your ear,** in the attitude of eager attention, **and come unto Me,** the invitation being issued time and again to emphasize its urgency; **hear,** with a willing acceptance, **and your soul shall live,** by and in the life in the Lord; **and I will make an everlasting covenant with you,** unlike the temporal covenant made on Sinai, **even the sure mercies of David,** the Messianic promises given to David and his descendants, culminating in the great Son of David, Jesus Christ. Cp. Ps. 89, 34—37. V. 4. **Behold, I have given Him for a Witness to the people,** the Messiah Himself testifying of the grace of God, **a Leader and Commander to the people,** the exalted Ruler, with endless authority and power. This King is now directly addressed, v. 5. **Behold, thou shalt call a nation that thou knowest not,** namely, into His kingdom, to be included in His government of peace, **and nations that knew not thee,** Gentiles of the farthermost parts of the earth, **shall run unto thee because of the Lord, thy God, and for the Holy One of Israel,** for the purpose of carrying out the counsel of God and therefore for His glorification, since He is zealous for His kingdom; **for He hath glorified thee.** The purpose of God in sending the Messiah as His witness is to procure for Him the honor and glory due Him as the King of this great, blessed, and eternal God. In giving to others the honor and beauty provided for them through the work of the Messiah, the Lord glorifies the Messiah Himself. The fact that the believers are saved redounds to His glory.

ISRAEL CALLED TO REPENTANCE. — V. 6. **Seek ye the Lord,** so the Lord now calls out to Israel through the proclamation of His prophet, **while He may be found,** while the time of grace is still present with them; **call ye upon Him while He is near,** while His salvation is so close at hand in the Word of His grace, while the opportunity for repentance is still held out. V. 7. **Let the wicked forsake his way,** no longer, in contempt of God, pursuing the way of his own lusts and desires, **and the unrighteous man his thoughts,** his evil inclinations and intentions, **and let him return unto the Lord,** to the God of the covenant, **and He will have mercy upon him,** forgive all his iniquities, **and to our God, for He will abundantly pardon,** literally, "He makes much to forgive," He is most ready to forgive, His mercy is limitless. Cp. Rom. 5, 20; Is. 1, 18; 1 Tim. 1, 13—17. V. 8. **For My thoughts are not your thoughts, neither are your ways My ways, saith the Lord,** for the thoughts of the wicked are evil and lead into everlasting destruction, whereas the ways of the Lord are good, righteous, and holy, and lead into everlasting salvation. V. 9. **For as the heavens are higher than the earth,** separated by an infinitely great distance, **so are My ways higher than your ways and My thoughts than your thoughts.** At the same time it is true that, although the weight of man's sins, the foolishness of wicked ways, is so great as to make them seem unpardonable, yet God does not cease to let His Word be proclaimed in richest measure. V. 10. **For as the**

rain cometh down and the snow from heaven, according to the regular course of nature, **and returneth not thither,** namely, without carrying out the designs of God, **but watereth the earth,** the moisture being absorbed by the soil, **and maketh it bring forth and bud,** so that it grows and matures in due time, **that it may give seed to the sower,** for next year's seed-corn, **and bread to the eater,** the human family thus being provided with food from year to year, v. 11. **so shall My Word be that goeth forth out of My mouth,** proceeding thence to fulfil the purpose set by the Lord; **it shall not return unto Me void,** without giving to men at least some spiritual benefit, **but it shall accomplish that which I please,** what He chooses to have done, **and it shall prosper in the thing whereto I sent it,** for it is the Word filled with His almighty power, and the omnipotent God Himself is active in and through it. The Gospel is a power of God unto salvation, Rom. 1, 16. 17. V. 12. **For ye,** the people of the Lord, now in shameful captivity, **shall go out with joy and be led forth with peace,** to leave their captivity behind and to return home to Zion. **The mountains and the hills shall break forth before you into singing, and all the trees of the field shall clap their hands,** all creatures, as it were, rejoicing over the salvation enjoyed by the children of God, since it culminates in the bliss of heaven. V. 13. **Instead of the thorn,** symbol of sin and misery, **shall come the fir-tree, and instead of the brier shall come up the myrtle-tree,** both of these trees being representative of the finest products of faith in good works; **and it shall be to the Lord for a name, for an everlasting sign that shall not be cut off,** a monument of glory to Jehovah which would last throughout eternity. All sinners in the whole world, who rely upon the promise of the Lord in His Word, will find that these promises will be fulfilled in their case, eternal salvation and glorification being theirs through His grace.

CHAPTER 56.

True Repentance Necessary for Admission to the Kingdom of God.

ADMONITION AND COMFORT TO THE AFFLICTED. V. 1. **Thus saith the Lord,** the same God of the covenant who has spoken in the foregoing powerful appeals, **Keep ye judgment,** equity or righteousness in living in conformity with the demands of the covenant with Jehovah, **and do justice,** following the ordinances of His will, the admonition presupposing a neglect in this respect on the part of the Lord's people; **for My salvation is near to come and My righteousness to be revealed,** namely, in the glories of the Messianic revelation. It is the same message which was proclaimed by John the Baptist: "Repent, for the kingdom of heaven is at hand." Matt. 3, 8; 4, 17. V. 2. **Blessed is the man that doeth this,** weak and mortal as he is in his own person, **and the son of man,** offspring of sinful and mortal parents, **that layeth hold on it,** namely, in observing the covenant made upon Sinai, **that keepeth the Sabbath from polluting it,** since it was the day when the blessed communion between God and His people was stressed most strongly, **and keepeth his hand from doing any evil.** In urging the keeping of the Sabbath and the observing of the demands of righteousness the prophet is not insisting upon a mere outward mechanical observance of the Law, but desires a return to the ancient covenant faithfulness. V. 3. **Neither let the son of the stranger that hath joined himself to the Lord,** the non-Israelite, the proselyte from among the Gentiles, **speak, saying, The Lord hath utterly separated me from His people,** since people of his class were not admitted to the same privileges as native Israelites; **neither let the eunuch say, Behold, I am a dry tree,** for even if he could have become a member of the Jewish Church, his family would immediately have become extinct in the nation. Over against these laments the Lord gives His gracious reassurance: v. 4. **For thus saith the Lord unto the eunuchs that keep My sabbaths, and choose the things that please Me, and take hold of My covenant,** observing the will and command of the Lord in every respect, thereby giving evidence of the proper condition of their hearts; v. 5. **even unto them will I give in Mine house and within My walls,** the Temple as symbolizing His Church, **a place and a name better than of sons and of daughters,** of those who claimed recognition on the basis of their external membership in the Jewish nation only; **I will give them an everlasting name, that shall not be cut off,** namely, by accepting them fully into the grace of His Messianic kingdom. V. 6. **Also the sons of the stranger,** of the non-Israelite, of the Gentile, **that join themselves to the Lord to serve Him,** in the true worship of faith, **and to love the name of the Lord, to be His servants,** in an inner and truly cordial service, **every one that keepeth the Sabbath from polluting it and taketh hold of My covenant,** v. 7. **even them,** no matter from what nation they come, **will I bring to My holy mountain,** to Zion with its Temple, as representing His holy Church, **and make them joyful in My house of** prayer, by refreshing them with the blessings of His grace; **their burnt offerings and their sacrifices shall be accepted upon Mine altar,** their entire worship being pleasing to Jehovah; **for Mine house shall be called an house of prayer for all people,** not only the Jews, but the Gentiles as well being included in the membership of His Church. Cp. Eph. 2, 19. V. 8. **The Lord God which gathereth the outcasts of Israel,** those who were dispersed among the nations, **saith, Yet will I gather others to him,** to Israel, to the true people of Jehovah, **beside those that are gathered unto him.** The Gentiles are not excluded from the kingdom of the Lord, as Jesus Himself plainly tells the Jews, John 10, 16.

THE NEGLECT OF JEHOVAH'S FLOCK BY ITS SHEPHERDS. — V. 9. **All ye beasts of the field, come to devour, yea, all ye beasts in the forest!** It is an ironical call to the enemies of the Church to take advantage of Israel's helplessness, since she is lying there without protection, her shepherds living a life of ease and indulgence. V. 10. **His watchmen,** the men on the lookout in the watch-tower of city or fold, in this case the prophets of Israel, **are blind,** the false teachers deliberately blinding themselves against the needs of the people; **they are all ignorant,** lacking in true spiritual understanding, **they are all dumb dogs, they cannot bark,** like shepherd dogs too lazy or indifferent to raise the alarm at the coming of the wolves; **sleeping, lying down,** idle dreamers and sluggards, **loving to slumber,** delighting in self-indulgence. Instead of feeding the flock of the Lord with the Word of God entrusted to them, the false prophets of all times have only their own comfort, the enrichment of their own lazy selves, in mind. Physical laziness usually goes together with intellectual and spiritual relaxation. V. 11. **Yea, they are greedy dogs, which can never have enough,** the covetousness of false prophets having become proverbial, **and they are shepherds that cannot understand,** that is, they want to be shepherds, they desire so to be regarded, and yet they have no insight into the demands of their position, they do not realize that their actions give the lie to the title which they bear; **they all look to their own way,** following the desire of their own evil heart, **every one for his gain, from his quarter,** to the very end of the gain which they may get out of their position, every one intent upon getting as much as possible out of the people and out of his office. V. 12. **Come ye, say they,** in the spirit which always characterizes their self-indulgence, **I will fetch wine, and we will fill ourselves with strong drink,** in an orgy of bestial drinking; **and to-morrow shall be as this day and much more abundant,** literally, "great, much more in excess," a strong expression denoting the habitual and intentional indulgence in intoxicants, with all its accompanying bestiality. Chap. 57, 1. **The righteous perisheth,** namely, while the false teachers are forsaking their duties, **and no man layeth it to heart,** no one is aware of the fact that the hand of God interferes in graciously taking the believing Israelite out of this world before the great Judgment descends upon it; **and merciful men are taken away,** by a sudden death, apparently before their time, **none considering that the righteous is taken away from the evil to come.** V. 2. **He shall enter into peace,** namely, the one to whom Jehovah thus shows His mercy; **they shall rest in their beds,** slumbering safely in the chambers of their graves, **each one walking in his uprightness.** This fact, rightly considered, is a source of comfort in every form of bereavement among the faithful, since the Lord, by taking His believers away from this vale of tears, spares them many a bitter experience to which they are subject as long as they sojourn in this sinful world.

CHAPTER 57.

Destruction to the Apostates, Salvation to the Repentant.

JEHOVAH REJECTS ALL IDOLATERS. — V. 3. **But draw near hither,** so the Lord now calls to the apostates, **ye sons of the sorceress,** men addicted to sorcery, to superstitious practises which were connected with the worship of false gods, **the seed of the adulterer and the whore,** in whose case idolatry is inherent, their second nature, the expression being the very strongest reproof to the unbelieving and apostate Jews, who depended upon their external membership in Israel to give them a safe standing in the eyes of Jehovah. V. 4. **Against whom do ye sport yourselves?** in malignant joy, in insulting sneers. **Against whom make ye a wide mouth and draw out the tongue?** in malicious mockery. These gestures of derision on the part of the unbelievers were directed not only against the pious members of the nation in general, but in particular against the righteous, who, as the apostates thought, were cut off so soon on account of some fault in them. **Are ye not children of transgression, a seed of falsehood,** thoroughly steeped in iniquity, v. 5. **enflaming yourselves with idols under every green tree,** burning with lust toward their idolatrous images in the terebinth groves, **slaying the children in the valleys under the clifts of the rocks?** as a sacrifice to Molech, the abomination of the Moabites. This shows that some of the people, even after the Babylonian exile, once more became addicted to idolatry and its abominations. V. 6. **Among the smooth stones of the stream,** the stone formations hollowed out and polished in grotesque images by the action of the water, **is thy portion,** there the idolaters in Israel brought their sacrifices; **they, they are thy lot,** upon these dead rocks the idolaters relied; **even to them hast thou poured a drink-offering, thou hast offered a meat-offering,** giving to them the worship which belongs to Jehovah alone. **Should I receive comfort in these?** The Lord cannot be quiet any longer, He can no longer keep silence; He is obliged to forsake His mercy and to interfere with His wrath. V. 7. **Upon a lofty and high mountain hast thou set thy bed,** in spiritual adultery; **even thither wentest thou up to offer sacrifice,** in the heathen worship of Baal and Ashtaroth, for this required altars, pillars, and Asherah-idols on all prominent hills. V. 8. **Behind the doors also and the posts,** within the house devoted to idolatry, **hast thou set up thy remembrance,** the memorial tablet reminding the apostates of their idols; **for thou hast discovered** (uncovered) **thyself to another than Me and art gone up,** namely, to the couch of sin; **thou hast enlarged thy bed and made thee a covenant with them,** agreeing upon a price of shame; **thou lovedst their bed where thou sawest it,** delighting in the filthiness of the spiritual adultery thus openly practised, the shamelessness thus brazenly paraded. V. 9. **And thou wentest to the king with ointment and didst increase thy perfumes,** playing the coquette with the world-power because she doubts the ability of the Lord to help her, **and didst send thy messengers far off,** in a special embassy to gain the good will of the powerful emperor, **and didst debase thyself even unto hell,** in a total loss of pride and character. V. 10. **Thou art wearied in the greatness of thy way,** by the many trips made in the interest of her lust; **yet saidst thou not, There is no hope,** in a proper realization of the fruitlessness of her quest; **thou hast found the life of thine hand,** still being able to sustain life by a steady application of energy, **therefore thou wast not grieved,** she did not relax in her efforts to gain the heathen emperor's good will. The Lord now asks the reasons for her faithless intrigues. V. 11. **And of whom hast thou been afraid or feared that thou hast lied and hast not remembered Me, nor laid it to thy heart?** In spite of her faithlessness she is utterly callous and indifferent; she is apparently lost to every good influence. **Have not I held My peace even of old,** being patient in spite of her apostasy, holding back wrath and punishment, **and thou fearest Me not?** Jehovah had not treated Israel so as to cause any one in the nation to live in terror of Him; the apostates had no excuse for their action. The entire section pictures the tireless seeking of the renegade people after the vanity of idolatry and of heathen customs — surely a sad waste of energy! Therefore Jehovah now, in a burst of holy irony, calls them to task. V. 12. **I will declare thy righteousness,** such as it is, **and thy works,** in breaking the covenant; **for they shall not profit thee,** all the idolatrous acts being duly exposed. V. 13. **When thou criest,** in vexation over disappointed hopes, **let thy companies,** all the agencies upon which she had relied, **deliver thee; but the wind shall carry them all away,** a single breath of the Lord being sufficient to overthrow all her allies, **vanity shall take them. But he that putteth his trust in Me shall possess the land and shall inherit My holy mountain,** the picture of the occupation of Canaan and Zion being a type of the possession and government which pertains to the believers by the merciful gift of Jehovah.

JEHOVAH GRANTS SALVATION AND PEACE TO THE REPENTANT. — What the Lord had indicated at the end of the last paragraph He now elaborates upon. V. 14. **And shall say,** that is, a voice is heard to say, **Cast ye up, cast ye up,** in leveling the path; **prepare the way, take up the stumbling-block out of the way of My people,** so they have free access to the deliverance of Jehovah. V. 15. **For thus saith the High and Lofty One that inhabiteth eternity,** He who occupies the throne of His majesty forever, **whose name is Holy,** He who dwells in the inaccessible light of perfect sanctity; **I dwell in the high and holy place,** in absolute exaltation and holiness, **with him also that is of a contrite and humble spirit,** bowed down and humbled by deep repentance, **to revive the spirit of the humble,** by an infusion of new spiritual life, **and to revive the heart of the contrite ones,** so that they are filled with new life and courage, with hope and confidence in Jehovah. V. 16. **For I will not contend forever,** in rebuking and punishing, **neither will I be always wroth,** being filled with anger which may overflow at any moment; **for the spirit should fail before Me,** He wants to dismiss His anger, **and the souls which I have made,** showing mercy to those that are of a contrite heart, since He has created them for life. The fact of creation is often made the basis of the mercy shown by God upon His works. V. 17. **For the iniquity of his covetousness,** on account of the guilt of Israel, **was I wroth and smote him,** for the sin of avarice, the love of money, is properly called a root of all evil. **I hid Me and was wroth, and he went on frowardly in the way of his heart,** hardening himself against every influence for the better. V. 18. **I have seen his ways,** the many paths of misfortune which Israel chose to go, **and will heal him,** taking the proper care of the wounds which are the consequence of sin; **I will lead him also,** namely, on the paths of righteousness, Ps. 23, 3, and **restore comforts unto him and to his mourners,** so that, although the misery of this earthly life will remain, the sinners will feel the consolation of God's mercy in His Word. V. 19. **I create the fruit of the lips, Peace, peace! to him that is far off and to him that is near, saith the Lord; and I will heal him,** that is, by sending out the Gospel-message into all the world the Lord offers the redemption gained by the Messiah, the healing of the Sun of Righteousness, to all men. Over against the deliverance of the righteous the prophet places the fate of the unbelievers. V. 20. **But the wicked are like the troubled sea,** their rejection of the Lord's salvation causing them to become like a storm-tossed ocean, **when it cannot rest, whose waters,** churning up the very floor of the sea, **cast up mire and dirt,** in endless sinning. V. 21. **There is no peace, saith my God, to the wicked,** a hidden fear of the wrath of the Lord driving them about from one expedient to another, but only increasing their wickedness and heaping upon them new guilt. The ungodly may seem happy enough on the outside, as Asaph writes in Ps. 73, but their heart is not at rest, and they will be cast down into destruction.

CHAPTER 58.

Deliverance Comes to the Truly Repentant.

A Sharp Reproof of Hypocrisy. — V. 1. **Cry aloud,** so the Lord calls out to the prophet in bidding him rebuke the hypocritical conduct of the people, **spare not,** in an indulgence which in this case would amount to a sinful weakness, for which reason a crying at the top of the voice is demanded, **lift up thy voice like a trumpet,** with the far-sounding signal of the trumpets used on the great festivals of the Jewish Church, **and show My people their transgression,** the breach of covenant of which they had become guilty, **and the house of Jacob their sins,** for the Lord's mercy had chosen the entire nation and He still sought all its members with the same fervent love which He had shown them of old. V. 2. **Yet they seek Me daily,** the very Lord whom they have rejected, **and delight to know My ways,** pretending an earnestness which they are far from feeling, inquiring into the reason for God's manner of dealing with them, **as a nation that did righteousness,** as though they were a nation practising the covenant righteousness required of them, **and forsook not the ordinance of their God,** just as if they had upheld their end of the covenant; **they ask of Me the ordinances of justice,** literally, "the judgments of righteousness," namely, that the Lord should interfere in their behalf; **they take delight in approaching to God,** pleading for their own deliverance and the destruction of their enemies. V. 3. **Wherefore have we fasted, say they,** in the spirit of self-righteousness, which caused them to act as though God had been placed under obligations by their fasting, **and Thou seest not?** the Lord ignoring them on account of their hypocrisy. **Wherefore have we afflicted our soul,** by the hardships of fasting, **and Thou takest no knowledge?** the intimation being that Jehovah was not appreciating their efforts sufficiently. But the Lord has His answer ready and sets them right with emphasis. **Behold, in the day of your fast ye find pleasure,** seeking advantage for themselves by their show of piety, **and exact all your labors,** oppressing the men who worked for them even while they were professing an unusual degree of holiness. V. 4. **Behold, ye fast for strife and debate,** while they were practising their wicked oppression, they made a great show of their supposed piety, **and to smite with the fist of wickedness,** not hesitating even to strike blows in tyrannizing their laborers; **ye shall not fast as ye do this day to make your voice to be heard on high.** Their fasting was nothing but hypocritical show, lacking the essence of the practise; for proper fasting presupposes a heart filled with repentance, pleading with the Lord for forgiveness and mercy. V. 5. **Is it such a fast that I have chosen? a day for a man to afflict his soul?** Could the Lord accept their fasting as an expression of repentance? **Is it to bow down his head as a bulrush,** affecting a sorrow which he was far from feeling, **and to spread sackcloth and ashes under him?** to make that his bed. **Wilt thou call this a fast and an acceptable day to the Lord?** All external evidences of sorrow and mourning mean nothing if the heart and mind are not affected, if they do not flow out of a repentant heart. The fasting which pleases the Lord is of an entirely different kind. V. 6. **Is not this the fast that I have chosen: to loose the bands of wickedness,** to release the oppressed laborers, **to undo the heavy burdens,** which these tyrants had laid upon their men as upon pack-animals, **and to let the oppressed go free, and that ye break every yoke?** Note the heaping of synonymous expressions in order to emphasize the necessity of desisting from works of tyranny and of practising true works of mercy. V. 7. **Is it not to deal thy bread to the hungry,** to share it with him who is in need, **and that thou bring the poor that are cast out,** those without a home, without a roof to call their own, **to thy house; when thou seest the**

naked that thou cover him, by providing him with clothing, **and that thou hide not thyself from thine own flesh?** every human being in need of help being our neighbor. The true proof of repentance consists in discontinuing wickedness and oppression in every form and in practising mercy toward all men.

THE BLESSINGS FOLLOWING TRUE REPENTANCE. — V. 8. **Then,** namely, when a person acts in accordance with the suggestion made in the first part of the chapter, **shall thy light break forth as the morning,** like the dawn of the Orient, which speedily covers the sky, **and thine health shall spring forth speedily,** the spiritual healing going on with great rapidity; **and thy righteousness,** the deliverance promised in the covenant, **shall go before thee,** as the pillar of Jehovah did at the time of the wilderness journey; **the glory of the Lord shall be thy rearward,** to protect him against any attack from that quarter. This is nothing else than the glory of God in the face of Jesus Christ, the Messiah Himself. Cp. 2 Cor. 4, 6; 1 Cor. 10, 4. V. 9. **Then,** namely, when this wonderful fellowship obtains, **shalt thou call, and the Lord shall answer,** with a ready assistance; **thou shalt cry,** appealing to Him for help, **and He shall say, Here I am,** indicating His presence and readiness to help with the customary answer. **If thou take away from the midst of thee the yoke,** removing every form of oppression, **the putting forth of the finger,** in a threatening gesture, **and speaking vanity,** things which would prove harmful to the neighbor; v. 10. **and if thou draw out thy soul to the hungry,** opening his heart in true mercy, **and satisfy the afflicted soul,** offering it the desired relief, **then shall thy light rise in obscurity,** in the midst of the darkness of this vale of tears, **and thy darkness,** what seems to be the worst form of affliction, **be as the noonday,** filled with the glorious light of God's kindness and mercy; v. 11. **and the Lord shall guide thee continually,** throughout life, **and satisfy thy soul in drought,** whenever a time of spiritual want comes, **and make fat thy bones,** strengthening a man's frame for endurance; **and thou shalt be like a watered garden,** a park with luxuriant growth, **and like a spring of water whose waters fail not,** such as do not disappoint the traveler by being dried up at the crucial time. V. 12. **And they that shall be of thee,** their descendants, the members of their nation, **shall build the old waste places,** changing ruins into inhabited dwellings; **thou shalt raise up the foundations of many generations,** all the cities of the Holy Land, but especially Jerusalem; **and thou shalt be called The Repairer of the Breach, The Restorer of Paths to Dwell In,** both activities making the dwelling in the Promised Land possible once more. V. 13. **If thou turn away thy foot from the Sabbath,** the Sabbath being regarded as holy ground, which no unholy foot dared touch, **from doing thy pleasure on My holy day,** whatever pleases the natural heart of man, **and call the Sabbath a delight,** refreshment for the soul, **the holy of the Lord, honorable,** keeping it sacred in the manner commanded by the Lord, **and shalt honor Him, not doing thine own ways, nor finding thine own pleasure, nor speaking thine own words,** in vanity and foolishness: v. 14. **then shalt thou delight thyself in the Lord,** finding the soul's true refreshment in Him; **and I will cause thee to ride upon the high places of the earth,** once more to occupy the hills of their homeland, **and feed thee with the heritage of Jacob, thy father,** enjoying all the blessings promised to that patriarch; **for the mouth of the Lord hath spoken it,** a solemn formula to assure men of the fulfilment of God's promises. Even as Israel, the Church of the Old Testament, could come to the enjoyment of Jehovah's heritage only by true repentance, so the believers of the New Testament fitly keep the admonition of the Lord before their eyes, "Repent ye, for the kingdom of heaven is at hand."

CHAPTER 59.

The Sins Which Hinder Deliverance.

INIQUITIES SEPARATE FROM GOD. — V. 1. **Behold, the Lord's hand is not shortened that it cannot save,** it was not want of power on His part which delayed deliverance; **neither His ear heavy that it cannot hear,** it was not unwillingness on His part to hear the people's prayer for help; v. 2. **but your iniquities,** the sins by which they loaded guilt upon themselves, **have separated between you and your God,** erecting a barrier which made it impossible for the Lord to come to their aid, **and your sins have hid His face from you that He will not hear,** that His wrath over their disobedience will keep Him from granting their request. V. 3. **For your hands are defiled with blood and your fingers with iniquity,** on account of the oppression practised against their own neighbors, against the people of their own nation; **your lips have spoken lies,** in giving voice to the falseness and wickedness of their hearts, **your tongue hath muttered perverseness,** the intention to commit knavery appearing in their very mumbling, in their whispered comments. V. 4. **None calleth for justice,** praying to the Lord in truth and righteousness, **nor any pleadeth for truth,** literally, "in faithfulness," in reliance upon the sound condition of heart and mind, that is, there is none who is sincere in faith and life; **they trust in vanity,** in a perfection of self which they imagine, **and speak lies,** believing that they can impress the Lord and hide their hypocrisy before Him; **they conceive mischief and bring forth iniquity,** the evil plans which they have laid serving to bring about their own destruction. V. 5. **They hatch cockatrice's eggs,** those of the basilisk serpent, whose venom was deadly, **and weave the spider's web,** to entrap their victims; **he that eateth of their eggs dieth, and that which is crushed,** namely, any one of these poisonous eggs, **breaketh out into a viper,** splitting open to emit the venomous reptile. V. 6. **Their webs shall not become garments,** they cannot be woven like the threads of the silk-worm, **neither shall they cover themselves with their works,** with the fabrications of their wickedness; **their works are works of iniquity,** bringing destruction wherever they are found, **and the act of violence is in their hands,** that is what their hands are engaged in, what they love to perform. V. 7. **Their feet,** as instruments of sin, **run to evil,** to deeds which result in mischief, **and they make haste to shed innocent blood,** the crime of murder being the chief wickedness in which they delight; **their thoughts are thoughts of iniquity,** seeking evil as their object, making it their purpose; **wasting and destruction are in their paths,** as the result of their wicked counsel. V. 8. **The way of peace they know not,** they have no idea of what really pertains to their peace, **and there is no judgment in their goings,** they can expect no sentence granting them deliverance and salvation on the part of God; **they have made them crooked paths,** so that they are bound to lead to destruction, **whosoever goeth therein shall not know peace,** shall not enjoy the salvation which will be given to the faithful believers. St. Paul uses this section to describe the unbelievers in general, and the description fits the great mass of people to this day. Rom. 3, 14—18.

INIQUITIES MAKE BLIND AND HELPLESS. — V. 9. **Therefore is judgment far from us,** the Jews themselves complaining that the sentence of deliverance is not spoken in their behalf, **neither doth justice,** deliverance and salvation, **overtake us,** they cannot reach them, cannot help them; **we wait for light,** for good fortune and happiness, **but behold obscurity,** misfortune and destruction; **for brightness, but we walk in darkness,** in the very midst of disaster. V. 10. **We grope for the wall like the blind, and we grope as if we had no eyes,** seeking for a way out of the dungeon of misery; **we stumble at noonday as in the night,** increasing their misery and sorrow in their fruitless groping for light; **we are in desolate places as dead men,** as dead people in the midst of healthy and strong men. While the true believers enjoy life in the fellowship with Jehovah, the hypocrites and wicked people are on their way to eternal destruction. V. 11. **We roar all like bears,** moaning and growling for food, **and mourn sore like doves,** with plaintive calls; **we look for judgment,** for the sentence of deliverance, **but there is none, for salvation, but it is far off from us,** by their own fault. V. 12. **For our transgressions are multiplied before Thee,** in their breaches of the covenant faithfulness, **and our sins testify against us,** as witnesses of their guilt; **for our transgressions,** by which they denied the covenant faithfulness, **are with us,** are in evidence before the eyes of all men; **and as for our iniquities, we know them,** bound to acknowledge and confess them; v. 13. **in transgressing,** unfaithful to the covenant, **and lying against the Lord,** trying to cover their perfidy with hypocrisy, **and departing away from our God,** in a denial of the covenant Lord, **speaking oppression and revolt,** in rebellion against Jehovah, **conceiving and uttering from the heart words of falsehood,** untrue and destructive speeches, which encourage rebellion. V. 14. **And judgment,** the deliverance which the Lord would otherwise grant, **is turned away backward, and justice,** the sentence of deliverance, **standeth afar off,** so that salvation will not come to these reprobates; **for truth is fallen in the street, and equity cannot enter,** both faithfulness and probity being out of the question, not being permitted to testify openly. V. 15. **Yea, truth faileth,** faithfulness is forsaken; **and he that departeth from evil,** taking an open stand against perfidy and wickedness, **maketh himself a prey,** becomes the object of violence on every side. This is the experience which all believers may have at one time or another, that their witnessing for the truth brings upon them the hatred of the wicked.

THE LORD MAKING READY FOR JUDGMENT AND REDEMPTION. — V. 15b. **And the Lord saw it,** namely, the desperate condition of His people, **and it displeased Him that there was no judgment,** that no one interfered to punish and to deliver. V. 16. **And He saw that there was no man,** no hero, no champion to work deliverance, **and wondered that there was no intercessor,** none to interpose in behalf of the oppressed people; **therefore His arm brought salvation unto him,** to Israel, **and His righteousness, it sustained him,** He gave evidence of His zeal for the salvation of them whom He had chosen for His own, for He is the Redeemer of His Church. The Lord called upon His omnipotence and His mercy, as the expression of His covenant faithfulness, in bringing salvation to His faithful people. V. 17. **For He put on righteousness,** the mercy promised to His people, **as a breastplate and an helmet of salvation**

upon His head, with which He intended to hearten Himself in His struggle for the redemption of mankind; **and He put on the garments of vengeance for clothing and was clad with zeal as a cloak,** His wrath upon His enemies causing Him to attack them in fury, to let His judgment go forth upon them. V. 18. **According to their deeds,** as they had richly deserved, **accordingly He will repay: fury to His adversaries,** by which they would be consumed, **recompense to His enemies; to the islands,** the heathen nations of the shores and islands of the Mediterranean, **He will repay recompense,** making them the object of His avenging fury. V. 19. **So shall they,** men in every part of the world, **fear the name of the Lord,** with the reverence of true faith, **from the West and His glory from the rising of the sun,** many heathen being filled with the knowledge of the merciful redemption of the Lord. **When the enemy shall come in like a flood, the Spirit of the Lord shall lift up a standard against him,** literally, "For He will come like an enclosed stream whom the breath of Jehovah drives." The Lord, who is coming, is the rushing stream, and He is urged forward by the Spirit of revenge and of salvation, bringing destruction to His enemies and salvation to those who accept Him in faith. V. 20. **And the Redeemer shall come to Zion,** the promised Messiah making His appearance in the fulness of time, **and unto them that turn from transgression in Jacob,** such as had left the covenant faithfulness, but had turned back to the Lord with a repentant heart, **saith the Lord.** Although, under the circumstances, the redemption of Jacob seems almost unbelievable, yet the promise of the Lord is there to assure this deliverance; for whosoever turns to Him in true repentance will become partaker of the salvation gained for the whole world. V. 21. **As for Me, this is My covenant with them, saith the Lord,** this explains why He had not rejected the entire nation outright: **My Spirit that is upon thee,** upon Israel, especially in its representative leaders and prophets, **and My words which I have put in thy mouth, shall not depart out of thy mouth,** the Word of salvation remaining with His Church forever, **nor out of the mouth of thy seed,** the spiritual seed of Israel, **nor out of the mouth of thy seed's seed, saith the Lord, from henceforth and forever.** The Lord kept His covenant faithfulness to the end, the entire history of the Church, both before and after the coming of the Messiah being proof of that fact. His mercy includes not only all the true descendants of the patriarchs in Israel, but embraces heathen from every nation in the world as well.

CHAPTER 60.

The Glorification of Zion through the Personal Glory of Jehovah.

THE GLORY OF THE MESSIAH UPON THE GENTILES. — V. 1. **Arise, shine; for thy light is come, and the glory of the Lord is risen upon thee.** V. 2. **For, behold, the darkness shall cover the earth and gross darkness the people,** the expression referring to the murky darkness of a cloudy day; **but the Lord shall arise upon thee, and His glory shall be seen upon thee.** Here the evangelist of the Old Testament addresses himself to the congregation of believers, first of all among His own people, the faithful in Israel. It is a cry which goes forth, in undiminished power, to the Church of all times. As one who has been sluggish and asleep the Church is bidden, "Arise!" As one who has hidden her light from men she is commanded, "Shine," be a light, show the power of a real light! The reason for this summons is the opening of the Messianic period: "For come is thy Light," the Day-star from on high, the Messiah. In Him the glory of Jehovah has arisen upon the Church, like the sun arising in all his splendor and majesty. While the earth as a whole is covered by the darkness signifying the lack of the proper knowledge of God and a total abandonment to sin and iniquity, while a dark and cloudy thickness surrounds the people and lies like a pall upon them, the light which arose upon the Church, upon those who waited for the coming of the Messiah, stands out, by way of contrast, in all the greater beauty and glory, shining upon those who have waited for His coming during all the long centuries since the first Gospel-message was proclaimed. V. 3. **And the Gentiles shall come to thy light and kings to the brightness of thy rising,** where the rays of the Sun of Righteousness were illuminating the world. V. 4. **Lift up thine eyes round about and see: All they gather themselves together, they come to thee; thy sons shall come from far, and thy daughters shall be nursed at thy side.** V. 5. **Then thou shalt see and flow together,** be bright with joy, shine with exultation, and **thine heart shall fear and be enlarged,** swell with delight, **because the abundance of the sea shall be converted unto thee, the forces of the Gentiles shall come unto thee,** with all their wealth and power. V. 6. **The multitude of camels shall cover thee, the dromedaries,** the young camels, **of Midian and Ephah. All they from Sheba shall come; they shall bring gold and incense; and they shall show forth the praises of the Lord,** blessing the name of Jehovah, setting forth His glory. Here the universal power and extent of Messiah's reign is pictured. Although in His own person He was sent only to the lost sheep of the house of Israel, He was still the Salvation of all men to the ends of the earth. And His power was to be exerted through His Church as His agent and instrument, as the bearer and proclaimer of the Gospel-message. The Church, bearing the light of the Gospel, should know that Gentiles, a great multitude from the midst of the heathen world, would walk in this light, even kings, some of the mighty of the earth, in the brightness of her coming up, as she would shine forth like the sun in glory. Knowing this, the Church should use her eyes, should see the Gentiles gathering themselves from every part of the world. From afar off her new sons, born through the power of the Gospel, would come, and at her side, in her midst, her newly gained daughters would be nourished and brought up by the study of the Word. This fact should then again react upon the Church. It should arouse her to more fervent efforts, to shine with ever greater brightness, with awe and an enlarged heart. For the multitudes of the heathen along the shores of the Great Sea would be converted and join her forces, the flower and might of the Gentiles would enroll under Messiah's banner. From Midian, in the far Southeast, from Ephah and Sheba in the Arabian wilderness, from the ends of the earth they would come, overcome by the might of the Messiah in His Word and gladly sacrificing of their earthly goods to Him, as they bless and extol the name of Jehovah. Cp. Matt. 2. V. 7. **All the flocks of Kedar**, in the south of Arabia Deserta, the chief possession of its inhabitants, **shall be gathered together unto thee**, as a gift of worship, **the rams of Nebaioth**, the most excellent of the flocks of the sons of Ishmael in Arabia Petraea, **shall minister unto thee**, be used as sacrificial animals; **they shall come up with acceptance on Mine altar**, as acceptable gifts, well-pleasing to the Lord, **and I will glorify the house of My glory**, the Temple where He lived in the fulness of His glory, as revealed to men. We have here a picture of the manner in which men from every part of the world are gained for the truth of the Gospel and thereupon honor the Lord with the gifts of their hands. V. 8. **Who are these that fly as a cloud?** so the prophet asks in directing the eyes of the Church to the West, **and as the doves to their windows?** the mass of people seeking the Lord's Sanctuary being represented as an almost numberless multitude. The answer is given in a beautiful verse: v. 9. **Surely the isles**, the inhabitants of the coasts and islands of the Mediterranean Sea, **shall wait for Me and the ships of Tarshish**, here representing their owners, **first**, as the first among the Gentiles to acknowledge Jehovah, **to bring thy sons from far**, in great haste, **their silver and their gold with them, unto the name of the Lord, thy God**, in order to give Him honor and praise for the blessings of salvation vouchsafed them, **and to the Holy One of Israel**, whose zeal against all enemies has resulted in the highest benefit to them, **because He hath glorified thee**, making them partakers of His divine glory. V. 10. **And the sons of strangers**, the Gentiles of whom the entire chapter is speaking, **shall build up thy walls**, so that Jerusalem may rise out of her ruins, a picture of the restoration of the Church, **and their kings shall minister unto thee**, many of the mighty ones of the earth bowing under the scepter of the Messiah and becoming affiliated with His Church; **for in My wrath I smote thee**, in permitting the Chaldeans to lead Judah into captivity, **but in My favor have I had mercy on thee.** Cp. chap. 54, 7. 8. V. 11. **Therefore thy gates shall be open continually, they shall not be shut day nor night**, since the gifts of God's mercy are dispensed in the Church without ceasing, until the end of time, **that men may bring unto thee the forces of the Gentiles**, large armies of heathen from every part of the world, **and that their kings may be brought**, as willing converts to Zion's King. Cp. Luke 14, 23. V. 12. **For the nation and kingdom that will not serve thee shall perish**, be utterly destroyed; **yea, those nations shall be utterly wasted**, by the Lord's judgment of punishment for their enmity against Him. In accordance with this prophecy the Lord visited His Church with the glory of His mercy and brought about the conversion of many Gentiles, all of whom place themselves with all their gifts in the service of the Church.

THE HAPPINESS ATTENDING THE GLORIFICATION OF THE MESSIAH. — V. 13. **The glory of Lebanon**, the wonderful forest growth which adorned its mountains, **shall come unto thee**, men of excellence everywhere devoting themselves to the service of the Lord and His Church, **the fir-tree, the pine-tree, and the box together**, the cypress, ilex, and cedar, the finest trees of Lebanon's forest, **to beautify the place of My Sanctuary, and I will make the place of My feet glorious**, so that Zion, the city of God, the Church of Jehovah, will immediately be recognized as a dwelling of the Lord. V. 14. **The sons also of them that afflicted thee**, of the former oppressors and enemies of the Church, **shall come bending unto thee**, in humble submission to Jehovah; **and all they that despised thee shall bow themselves down at the soles of thy feet**, in a gesture of complete surrender; **and they shall call thee The City of the Lord**, of Jehovah, the covenant God, **The Zion of the Holy One of Israel**, who is a jealous God and zealous of His own honor and of that of His Church. Thus the confession of the mouth agrees with the outward behavior and conduct. V. 15. **Whereas thou hast been forsaken and hated**, chap. 54, 1, **so that no man went**

through thee, an expression increasing the picture of complete desolation, **I will make thee an eternal excellency,** the highest expression of unparalleled magnificence, **a joy of many generations,** so that many people would delight in her. V. 16. **Thou shalt also suck the milk of the Gentiles,** enjoy the gifts brought by them, **and shalt suck the breast of kings,** have the use of the most precious treasures of earth, **and thou shalt know that I, the Lord, am thy Savior and thy Redeemer, the Mighty One of Jacob,** He to whose unvarying faithfulness and almighty power Zion owes all that she is and has. In this way the glorification of the Church by the Lord will cause her former enemies and oppressors to give her reverence and love. V. 17. **For brass I will bring gold, and for iron I will bring silver, and for wood, brass, and for stones, iron,** replacing the former inexpensive building materials with the most precious metals, with the most durable materials, so that the city would be both well protected and beautifully ornamented; **I will also make thy officers peace and thine exactors righteousness,** so that the government of Zion would be peace and the salvation of righteousness, security within and safety without, so that there is no further need of rulers. V. 18. **Violence shall no more be heard in thy land,** on account of the fact that the members of the Church will be united by the bands of the most cordial love, **wasting nor destruction within thy borders,** the enemies no longer being permitted to work their evil will without hindrance; **but thou shalt call thy walls Salvation and thy gates Praise,** the place of walls and gates being taken by the deliverance and redemption of Jehovah and by the reputation which Zion would have throughout the world. That this has been fulfilled in the Church of the New Testament is evident from the fact that the enmity of the world has not only not succeeded in overcoming the Church, but has even resulted in a condition which gives the Church a certain standing in the midst of the so-called Christian nations. V. 19. **The sun shall be no more thy light by day, neither for brightness shall the moon give light unto thee,** Zion no longer being in need of these external, physical light bodies; **but the Lord shall be unto thee an everlasting Light, and thy God thy Glory,** namely, in and through the Word of His grace, from which the Church derives all her light. V. 20. **Thy Sun,** the Lord Himself, **shall no more go down, neither shall thy Moon withdraw itself,** disappearing by setting, **for the Lord shall be thine everlasting Light,** in an uninterrupted continuity, Jas. 1, 17, **and the days of thy mourning shall be ended.** Ceaseless happiness, endless joy and delight, is the lot of the Church under the gracious rule of the Lord. Cp. Rev. 7, 17. V. 21. **Thy people also shall be all righteous,** as the nature of the covenant of mercy demands, by virtue of the righteousness imputed to them; **they shall inherit the land forever,** Matt. 5, 5, **the branch of My planting, the work of My hands,** a true garden of Jehovah, owing everything to His grace, **that I may be glorified,** for this is the final aim and object of His expressions of mercy. V. 22. **A little one,** the smallest and most insignificant member of Zion, **shall become a thousand and a small one a strong nation,** equaling a great many enemies in might; **I, the Lord, will hasten it in His time.** When the period fixed by His eternal counsel has come, His plans go into effect with a suddenness which overwhelms all those who are not on His side, who are not upheld by His power. Therefore all believers should be careful to discern the signs of the times and know what pertains to their peace.

CHAPTER 61.

The Lord's Year of Jubilee.

The chapter opens with a powerful description of the office of the Servant of Jehovah, of the Messiah Himself. V. 1. **The Spirit of the Lord God,** of the all-powerful Ruler, the covenant God, whose name is Jehovah, **is upon Me, because the Lord hath anointed Me to preach good tidings,** a joyful message, the Gospel proclamation, **unto the meek,** to those subject to spiritual misery; **He hath sent Me to bind up the broken-hearted; to proclaim liberty to the captives and the opening of the prison to them that are bound;** v. 2. **to proclaim the acceptable year of the Lord,** literally, "a year of good pleasure to Jehovah," **and the day of vengeance of our God; to comfort all that mourn;** v. 3. **to appoint unto them that mourn in Zion, to give unto them beauty,** an ornamental headdress, the groom's turban, **for ashes, the oil of joy for mourning, the garment of praise for the spirit of heaviness,** of distress and discouragement; **that they might be called trees of righteousness, the planting of the Lord, that He might be glorified,** the fact that the believers have become partakers of His mercy redounding to His praise. It is the Messiah Himself who is speaking here, for so He interprets the passage in His great sermon at Nazareth, Luke 4, 18—21. It is repeatedly stated in Scripture that the Messiah has the Spirit of Jehovah, that He has been anointed with the Holy Ghost without measure. The anointing on the part of Jehovah, however, concerns not merely an acknowledgment and acceptance of Christ's person, but includes the laying of a charge upon Him, giving Him an office to perform. It is Christ's prophetic office which here stands out so plainly, His work of bringing the Gospel to poor sinners. That is the essence of His work, to announce the joyful message, the glorious news of salvation, to all men. God has commissioned Him to bind up the broken in heart, the poor, lost, repentant sinners, to proclaim liberation to those who have been taken captive by sin and Satan, to tell those who are bound that they are to be free, that their prison-doors have been opened, to announce that a year, an endless period, of good pleasure and favor of Jehovah has come, a day in which He will avenge His own wrongs and those of His people upon His enemies. For the purpose of His work is to bring comfort and joy to the mourners, to replace the ashes on their head with the turban and tiara of joy, like that worn by a happy bridegroom, to put on the oil of gladness and adornment after the period of deep mourning, when they were in the power of Satan. Where formerly the spirit of distress and uneasiness ruled, the garment of praise to Jehovah shall be donned. All this will result in making the believers trees of righteousness, characterized by the fruits of righteousness in them which are the result of faith. For all this is not their own doing, a matter of self-righteous glorification, but they are the planting of Jehovah, who lives in them, and it is through His favor and mercy that they will be glorified before Him. Such is the office of the Messiah, Jesus Christ, the Lord. V. 4. **And they shall build the old wastes,** so that Zion will rise out of its ruins, **they shall raise up the former desolations,** the places of the Holy Land which lay waste from the time before the Exile, **and they shall repair the waste cities,** building them up new, **the desolations of many generations,** the parts of the country which have been a wilderness from ancient times. In this way the true Israelites, the believers, are regarded as the restorers of their Zion. But they are joined by others, as the text shows. V. 5. **And strangers,** members of the Gentile nations who have been converted to the true God, **shall stand and feed your flocks, and the sons of the alien shall be your plowmen and your vine-dressers,** voluntarily providing for the needs of the Church by the work and the time which they devote to the support of the ministry of the Word in its various forms. V. 6. **But ye,** all the members of the Church of God, **shall be named the priests of the Lord,** every one of whom has direct access to the Lord, without special intercession; **men shall call you the ministers of our God,** all of them being active in His service, deeming it an honor to fulfil His will; **ye shall eat the riches of the Gentiles,** being supported also by the material help which the former heathen willingly offered, **and in their glory shall ye boast yourselves,** so that honor and distinction would come to the Church because of the conversion and service of these Gentiles. V. 7. **For your shame ye shall have double,** the disgrace not only being balanced by the honor given them, but the glory being twice as great as the former shame, **and for confusion,** instead of the infamy which had been heaped upon Israel, the Lord's Zion, **they shall rejoice in their portion,** the believers once more enjoying the inheritance which is theirs in agreement with the Lord's promises. **Therefore in their land they shall possess the double,** the twofold mercy of Jehovah, a much greater amount of His mercy than has been revealed heretofore; **everlasting joy shall be unto them,** this marking the condition of the believers' heart as a consequence of the Lord's blessing. V. 8. **For I, the Lord, love judgment, I hate robbery for burnt offering,** because Jehovah is a God who loves equity and hates robbery and unrighteousness in every form, **and,** or "therefore," **I will direct their work in truth,** secure the fruit of their labor, **and I will make an everlasting covenant with them.** The Lord's people, having been replaced into their inheritance, shall never again become a prey of unrighteousness, but Jehovah will place it beyond the oppression of all enemies. V. 9. **And their seed,** the spiritual children of Israel, the Church of the Lord, **shall be known among the Gentiles,** regarded with respect, **and their offspring among the people,** those of the world in general; **all that see them shall acknowledge them, that they are the seed which the Lord hath blessed,** the Church receiving this recognition even from the outsiders and from outspoken enemies. And so Israel, the congregation of the redeemed saints, breaks forth into a song of praise to Jehovah, the covenant God. V. 10. **I will greatly rejoice in the Lord,** the Inspiration and Source of all true spiritual joy; **my soul shall be joyful in my God,** on account of the deliverance which the believers have experienced; **for He hath clothed me with the garments of salvation,** with the righteousness of the Messiah imputed by faith; **He hath covered me with the robe of righteousness,** so that the believer's sinfulness is no longer visible before the eyes of the holy God, **as a bridegroom decketh himself with ornaments,** winding his turban after the manner of priests, to give expression to his joy, **and as a bride adorneth herself with her jewels.** Thus the Church, and every member of the Church, is adorned with the beauty of the righteousness of the Lord. V. 11. **For as the earth bringeth forth**

her bud, causing the seed to sprout and come up, **and as the garden causeth the things that are sown in it to spring forth,** in accordance with the laws of nature fixed by God, **so the Lord God will cause righteousness and praise to spring forth before all the nations,** so that all men must acknowledge these virtues as existing in the midst of the Church. The God who causes the laws of nature to control the round of the seasons also makes the word of His mercy to come true, so that His salvation is fulfilled.

CHAPTER 62.

Zion the Bride of Jehovah.

The prophecy concerning the glory of Zion's perfection here reaches the highest point of exaltation: *the congregation of the redeemed as the bride and spouse of the Lord.* V. 1. **For Zion's sake will I not hold My peace,** so the Lord calls out through His prophet, in His eagerness to picture the glory which would pertain to Zion in the new dispensation, **and for Jerusalem's sake I will not rest,** He will not feel satisfied, He will not abate in His zeal, **until the righteousness thereof,** the salvation guaranteed by His covenant, **go forth as brightness,** like the light of the dawn, **and the salvation thereof as a lamp,** a torch or cresset, **that burneth,** dispelling the gloom and darkness of ignorance. V. 2. **And the Gentiles shall see thy righteousness,** the salvation intended to be revealed to the whole world, **and all kings thy glory,** the mighty ones of the earth noting the revelation of God's mercy upon His Zion; **and thou shalt be called by a new name which the mouth of the Lord shall name,** this in itself being a distinction which shows the exceeding greatness of God's love to lost and condemned mankind. V. 3. **Thou shalt also be a crown of glory,** a glorious diadem, **in the hand of the Lord,** under His gracious protection, **and a royal diadem,** a turban of the finest material, **in the hand of thy God,** ready to be placed upon His head. Cp. Mal. 3, 17; Rev. 6, 2; 19, 12. V. 4. **Thou,** Jerusalem, representing the Church of Christ, **shalt no more be termed Forsaken,** as a wife deserted by her husband; **neither shall thy land any more be termed Desolate,** as a mother forsaken by her children; **but thou shalt be called Hephzi-bah** (My delight is in her), **and thy land Beulah** (Thou art married), as a testimony of the relation existing between the Church and Jehovah, her Lord; **for the Lord delighteth in thee,** as the first name states, **and thy land shall be married,** as the second name says, not only ownership, but also protection by Jehovah being implied. V. 5. **For as a young man marrieth a virgin, so shall thy sons marry thee,** the land being returned to the possession of the children of Zion, the Church coming into her own; **and as the bridegroom rejoiceth over the bride,** with a chaste and exalted delight, **so shall thy God rejoice over thee,** for He delights in glorifying His Church, in entering into the most intimate fellowship with her. Having thus stated His relation to His Zion, the Lord now urges the watchmen of His Church to insist upon His fulfilling His promise. V. 6. **I have set watchmen upon thy walls, O Jerusalem,** the prophets and teachers who were to be on the lookout for the enemies, lest disaster overtake His flock, **which shall never hold their peace day nor night,** being engaged continually in promoting the glorification of Zion; **ye that make mention of the Lord,** the inhabitants of Zion, including the children of strangers who had joined them, **keep not silence.** All those who confess their faith in the Lord, teachers and hearers, should give themselves and the Lord no rest until their glorification is accomplished, as the text continues: v. 7. **And give Him no rest till He establish, and till He make Jerusalem a praise in the earth,** so that His Church will be an object of praise and of reverence throughout the world. V. 8. **The Lord hath sworn by His right hand and by the arm of His strength,** in a most solemn oath, with the definite assurance that His almighty power is able to carry out His will, **Surely I will no more give thy corn to be meat for thine enemies,** as had been the case whenever the enemies invaded the land, **and the sons of the stranger shall not drink thy wine for the which thou hast labored,** enjoy the fruits of the Church's labor; v. 9. **but they that have gathered it shall eat it,** the believers enjoying what they had worked for with such trouble, **and praise the Lord, and they that have brought it together shall drink it in the courts of My holiness,** in connection with sacrifices of thanksgiving made in honor of the Lord. The believers are the only truly happy people in the world, and they enjoy the blessings of the Lord with due thankfulness. Moreover, they invite all the children of Zion to share their happiness and the name given them by Jehovah. V. 10. **Go through, go through the gates,** so the members of the Church appeal to the strangers without, asking them to assemble in their own cities and make ready for the final great home-coming; **prepare ye the way of the people,** removing all obstacles and hindrances; **cast up, cast up the highway,** preparing the road as for the movement of a large army; **gather out the stones; lift up a standard for the people,** so that they all might gather under the banner of the Cross. V. 11. **Behold, the**

Lord hath proclaimed unto the end of the world, so that all nations could hear the glorious message, **Say ye to the daughter of Zion, Behold, thy salvation cometh,** namely, in the person of the Messiah. **Behold, His reward is with Him and His work before Him,** for He brings the trophies of His victory over all the enemies of mankind and offers them to His believers. V. 12. **And they shall call them,** the children of Zion, the believers, **the holy people, the redeemed of the Lord,** those who have received and are enjoying the salvation prepared for them; **and thou,** Zion herself, **shalt be called "sought out,"** many people being eager to partake of the deliverance which the Church enjoys, **a city not forsaken,** one whose streets are always alive with people desiring to receive the benefit of the salvation offered to all men in the Gospel-message which she proclaims. This inner glory of the Church is hers even here in time, in the midst of the tribulations of these latter days, and it will be hers without cover or measure in the eternal home above.

CHAPTER 63.

Messiah Coming as the Avenger of His People.

THE APPROACH OF THE DELIVERER. — V. 1. **Who is this,** so the prophet, in a burst of triumphant ecstasy, asks, **that cometh from Edom,** where the scene of the great judgment is laid, **with dyed garments from Bozrah?** this city being the ancient capital of Idumea. The garments of the Hero are pictured as being brilliant, scarlet, namely, with blood, as the next verses show: **this that is glorious in His apparel, traveling in the greatness of His strength?** coming along with proud bearing and stately stride. The Champion Himself answers, **I that speak in righteousness,** proclaiming the covenant of salvation, **mighty to save,** He in whom the redemption of the world is personified, He who carried out God's plan of salvation. Again the prophet asks, v. 2. **Wherefore art Thou red in Thine apparel and Thy garments like him that treadeth in the wine-fat?** He was fascinated by the bespattered dress of the Champion and desired to know whence these spots came. The Champion promptly answers: v. 3. **I have trodden the wine-press alone,** as the questioner rightly concluded, **and of the people there was none with Me,** of the entire world of men there was not one to give Him companionship, to stand by His side in the great battle; **for I will tread them in Mine anger and trample them in My fury,** rather, "I have trodden them in Mine anger and trampled them in My rage"; **and their blood shall be sprinkled upon My garments, and I will stain all My raiment,** all His clothing was splashed with the blood of the enemies, soiled all over. V. 4. **For the day of vengeance is in Mine heart,** He had definitely decided to avenge Himself upon the nations, **and the year of My redeemed is come,** the time had come when He would deliver those whom He had chosen for His own, an allusion to the great Year of Jubilee with its manifold forms of deliverance. The Champion now explains the excess of His fury in the battle which He fought. V. 5. **And I looked,** when He found Himself surrounded by enemies on every hand, **and there was none to help; and I wondered,** with a feeling akin to horror, **that there was none to uphold. Therefore Mine own arm brought salvation unto Me,** in overthrowing the enemies, **and My fury, it upheld Me,** giving Him the assistance He needed to obtain the victory. V. 6. **And I will tread down the people in Mine anger and make them drunk in My fury,** His wrath and rage being considered the weapons with which He had waged war so successfully, **and I will bring down their strength to the earth.** It is a wonderfully poetical description of the last great Judgment of the Lord, the day of His vengeance. Cp. chap. 34, 8; Rev. 19 and 20.

THE LORD'S LOVING-KINDNESS IN THE PAST AND HIS PEOPLE'S PRAYERS. — V. 7. **I will mention the loving-kindnesses of the Lord,** so the pious believer sings, **and the praises of the Lord,** His glorious deeds, **according to all that the Lord hath bestowed on us,** to which the hymn of thanksgiving must properly correspond, **and the great goodness toward the house of Israel which He hath bestowed on them according to His mercies,** which is the source of all His acts of goodness, **and according to the multitude of His loving-kindnesses.** The grace and mercy of the Lord to this day is our chief motive for singing His praises. V. 8. **For He said, Surely they are My people,** chosen by Him as His own, **children that will not lie,** who will not become guilty of disloyalty; so, as a result of this confidence in them, **He was their Savior,** who brought them permanent deliverance. V. 9. **In all their affliction He was afflicted,** in all their tribulation there was no overwhelming affliction for them, **and the angel of His presence saved them,** or, "No messenger (or angel) — with His own countenance He helped them," that is, in the last instance, through the redemption of the Messiah; **in His love and in His pity He redeemed them,** cp. Ex. 32 and 33; Num. 14; **and He bare them and carried them all the days of old,** namely, during the days of the wilderness journey. V. 10. **But they rebelled,** as the story of those days so abundantly shows, **and vexed His Holy Spirit,** the third person of the Godhead thus being spoken of as present during the days of the wilderness sojourn; **therefore He was turned to be their enemy,** as when He sent the fiery serpents and brought other severe punishments upon them, **and He fought against them,** also at a later time, when He permitted their enemies to overthrow them. V. 11. **Then he,** or men in general, especially the children of Israel themselves, **remembered the days of old, Moses and his people,** they reminded themselves of that deliverance, **saying, Where is He that brought them up out of the sea,** when Israel passed through the Red Sea, **with the shepherd of His flock?** Moses himself being represented as an excellent shepherd and guide of the people. **Where is He that put His Holy Spirit within him?** namely, in the midst of the Lord's flock, the reference being to the power of the Spirit imparted to Moses and the other princes of the people; cp. Num. 11, 17. 25; 14, 24; 27, 18; Deut. 34, 9; v. 12. **that led them by the right hand of Moses with His glorious arm,** so that Moses was not left to shift for himself, but had the almighty power of the Lord to serve him, **dividing the water before them,** Ex. 14, 21; Josh, 3, 16, **to make Himself an everlasting name?** the Lord's glory being promoted by this proof of His almighty power; v. 13. **that led them through the deep,** when they passed streams in safety, **as an horse in the wilderness, that they should not stumble?** or, "As horses in the plains they did not stumble," V. 14. **As a beast goeth down into the valley, the Spirit of the Lord caused him,** namely, Israel, **to rest,** namely, in the Land of Promise, **so didst Thou lead Thy people to make Thyself a glorious name.** Having thus pictured the manner in which the people in days of old turned to their almighty Deliverer and by Him were brought to the promised haven of rest, the believer now makes an appeal to the almighty power and the mercy of the Lord over against the present difficult situation. V. 15. **Look down from heaven and behold from the habitation of Thy holiness and of Thy glory,** to which He had apparently retired, leaving His people to their fate; **where is Thy zeal and Thy strength,** the mighty deeds which He had exhibited so often in days of old, **the sounding of Thy bowels,** the abundance of His sympathy, **and of Thy mercies toward me? Are they restrained?** It is a powerful appeal: Do not restrain them; do not hold back at this time! To this the petitioner adds a confident statement: v. 16. **Doubtless Thou art our Father,** that being the reason for the trustful prayer, **though Abraham be ignorant of us, and Israel acknowledge us not,** both of them being up in heaven and no longer cognizant of affairs of this life. **Thou, O Lord, art our Father,** by virtue of creation and redemption, **our Redeemer; Thy name is from everlasting,** or, "Our Redeemer from everlasting, that is Thy name." Jehovah is known in Israel as the God who saves and redeems in truth, in whom all believers, all His children, may and shall safely trust. V. 17. **O Lord, why hast Thou made us to err from Thy ways,** why did He permit this going astray, **and hardened our heart from Thy fear?** so that the judgment of hardening goes into effect upon those who despise His grace and mercy. **Return for Thy servants' sake,** on account of the relation of the covenant which obtained between the Lord and His people, **the tribes of Thine inheritance,** whom He Himself had chosen to be partakers of His blessings. One of the most effective forms of praying is that of taking the Lord aside, as it were, and reminding Him of His promises, to hold Him to His Word.

CHAPTER 64.

(Chapter 63, 18—64, 12.)

A Prayer out of the Depths.

A PLEA FOR GOD'S INTERFERENCE. — V. 18. **The people of Thy holiness have possessed it but a little while,** rather, "Down to a small remnant they," the enemies, "possess Thy holy people," using the inheritance of Israel to their own advantage. **Our adversaries have trodden down Thy Sanctuary,** not only the Temple proper, but the entire Holy City. V. 19. **We are Thine; Thou never barest rule over them, they were not called by Thy name,** or, in a circumscription suggested by the original, We have become as those over whom Thou hast not ruled, who are not called by Thy name, a complaint which places the present miserable position of Israel into the strongest contrast with the former happiness. Chap. 64, 1. **Oh, that Thou wouldest rend the heavens,** so the suppliant now begs the Lord, **that Thou wouldest come down,** bursting forth to execute vengeance, suddenly descending on Thy people's foes, **that the mountains might flow down at Thy presence,** the mightiest of His creatures being overcome by the revelation of His majesty, v. 2. **as when the melting fire burneth,** consuming brushwood in the twinkling of an eye, **the fire causeth the waters to boil,** literally, "as fire makes the water swell and seethe," **to make Thy name known to Thine adversaries,** with a powerful rage, **that the nations may tremble at Thy presence,** at the majestic revelation of His omnipotence. V. 3. **When thou didst terrible things which we looked**

not for, such as the visible coming of the Lord to the final Judgment will be, **Thou camest down, the mountains flowed down at Thy presence**, with an unparalleled exhibition of His unexcelled might, transcending all human fantasy. V. 4. **For since the beginning of the world men have not heard nor perceived by the ear, neither hath the eye seen, O God, beside Thee**, any God beside the one true God, **what He hath prepared for him that waiteth for Him**, or, "who intercedes for those who rely upon Him in faith," interfering in behalf of His children. St. Paul uses this verse, 1 Cor. 2, 9, in order to describe the mystery of the Gospel-message.

AN APPEAL TO JEHOVAH TO FORSAKE HIS WRATH. — V. 5. **Thou meetest**, in a friendly and kindly manner, **him that rejoiceth and worketh righteousness**, happy in observing the covenant faithfulness, **those that remember Thee in Thy ways**, doing His will with joyful willingness. **Behold, Thou art wroth**, He became angry, **for we have sinned. In those is continuance**, the persistence in sin being a punishment in itself, **and we shall be saved**, or, "how could we have been saved?" The people having hardened their hearts, the Lord gave them up to their obstinacy, so that their deliverance seemed impossible. V. 6. **But**, or in consequence of this sad situation, **we are all as an unclean thing**, like the uncleanness of leprosy, **and all our righteousnesses**, all the deeds which men might consider righteous and laudable, **are as filthy rags**, loathsome objects, an abomination in His sight; **and we all do fade as a leaf; and our iniquities, like the wind, have taken us away**, as dried leaves are heaped up for destruction. V. 7. **And there is none that calleth upon Thy name**, since unbelief and despair has taken hold of all hearts, **that stirreth up himself to take hold of Thee**, the great majority of the people being overwhelmed by a feeling of dumb resignation which excluded faith; **for Thou hast hid Thy face from us, withdrawn** His grace, **and hast consumed us because of our iniquities**, delivering them into the hand, into the power, of their iniquities, so that their guilt prepared the way to their destruction. Now, however, the suppliant once more changes His prayer to an urgent appeal: V. 8. **But now, O Lord**, in spite of the seriousness of the situation, **Thou art our Father**, He Himself had begotten them in mercy; **we are the clay and Thou our Potter**, who chose and molded the people for His purposes, **and we all are the work of Thy hand**, both Israel's history and position being in the guidance of Jehovah. V. 9. **Be not wroth very sore, O Lord**, not to the last extremity nor for eternity, **neither remember iniquity forever. Behold, see, we beseech Thee, we are all Thy people**, the believers relying upon the fact of their having been chosen by the Lord as His own. V. 10. **Thy holy cities are a wilderness**, this being a special appeal to the Lord to preserve His honor; **Zion is a wilderness, Jerusalem a desolation**, all of which ought deeply to affect His heart and arouse Him to a holy zeal in changing conditions. V. 11. **Our holy and our beautiful house, where our fathers praised Thee**, the Temple in which the true worship had taken place, **is burned up with fire**, consumed by its flames; **and all our pleasant things**, the customs and everything connected with the cultus of the Jews, **are laid waste**, defiled by the heathen bands. V. 12. **Wilt Thou refrain Thyself for these things, O Lord?** holding back from coming to the assistance of His people. **Wilt Thou hold Thy peace and afflict us very sore?** continuing the act of humiliating His people to the very limit. We have here a powerful appeal to the boundless mercy of the Lord, together with the firm confidence that He will not let destruction overtake His people. Even so the believers of all times trust in the covenant mercy of Jehovah and appeal to His fatherly love in all their prayers.

CHAPTER 65.

Rejection of the Apostates. Salvation of the Pious.

THE LORD'S REFUSAL. — V. 1. **I am sought of them that asked not for Me**, the Gentiles being represented as having access to the Lord and His mercy, although they were not members of God's covenant people; **I am found of them that sought Me not**, His free grace and mercy being revealed to all men without any merit or worthiness on their part. **I said, Behold Me, behold Me! unto a nation that was not called by My name**, that did not belong to Israel according to the flesh. The universality of the Gospel-message is here set forth in unmistakable terms. By way of contrast the Lord now describes the behavior of Israel. V. 2. **I have spread out My hands all the day**, during the entire period when His covenant relation with Israel was in force, **unto a rebellious people**, stiff-necked and stubborn in all its actions, **which walketh in a way that was not good**, utterly at variance with God's holy will, **after their own thoughts**, which were always evil and therefore led to destruction; cp. Rom. 11, 7; v. 3. **a people that provoketh Me to anger continually to My face**, with a bold impertinence that challenged the wrath of the Lord; **that sacrificeth in gardens**, in groves, after the manner of the heathen, **and burneth**

incense upon altars of brick, like the idol-worshipers of Babylonia; v. 4. **which remain among the graves and lodge in the monuments,** passing the night in hidden recesses, for the purposes of necromancy and Spiritism, **which eat swine's flesh,** a custom which was expressly forbidden in the Ceremonial Law, Lev. 11, 7, **and broth of abominable things is in their vessels,** cp. Lev. 7, 18; 19, 7; v. 5. **which say, Stand by thyself,** thus declaring their rejection of Jehovah, **come not near to me; for I am holier than thou.** Thus the idolaters give voice to the thoughts of their hearts, with whom they no longer desire to be identified, since they consider themselves members of a better religious class than His worshipers represent. **These are a smoke in My nose,** most disagreeable to Him, **a fire that burneth all the day,** causing consuming wrath to be kindled in Him. V. 6. **Behold, it is written before Me,** so that He has it before His eyes all the time. **I will not keep silence,** this being God's answer upon their final appeal, chap. 64, 12, **but will recompense, even recompense into their bosom,** with a thoroughness which they would not be apt to forget, v. 7. **your iniquities and the iniquities of your fathers together, saith the Lord,** so that the guilt of both would be laid upon them, Ex. 20, 5, **which have burned incense upon the mountains,** in an excess of idolatry which had so often been rebuked by the Lord, **and blasphemed Me upon the hills,** where the worship of Baal, Ashtaroth, and other heathen idols was carried on. **Therefore will I measure their former work into their bosom,** letting them bear the full burden of their transgressions. As it was true then, so it is true to-day: "God is not mocked; for whatsoever a man soweth, that shall he also reap." Gal. 6, 7.

A REMNANT SAVED. — V. 8. **Thus saith the Lord,** in a parable setting forth His mercy upon His chosen people, **As the new wine is found in the cluster,** as one, upon examining imperfect, unripe grapes, still finds juice in some of the berries, **and one saith, Destroy it not, for a blessing is in it,** a wholesale destruction would include the good with the evil, **so will I do for My servants' sakes,** for those who are still in truth His children in faith, **that I may not destroy them all,** the wheat with the tares, Matt. 13, 29. V. 9. **And I will bring forth a seed out of Jacob,** reserve to Himself out of the people taken away into the Babylonian exile the nucleus of a Church of the New Testament, **and out of Judah an inheritor of My mountains,** since the Messiah, the Ruler of His Church, would be a descendant of this tribe, cp. Micah 5, 1; **and Mine elect shall inherit it, and My servants shall dwell there,** all the believers being united in the spiritual Jerusalem under the government of the Prince of Peace. V. 10. **And Sharon,** the fruitful plain along the Mediterranean, **shall be a fold of flocks,** rich meadow-land, **and the Valley of Achor,** near the city of Jericho, sloping toward the Dead Sea, **a place for the herds to lie down in,** where caravans might find a resting-place, **for My people that have sought Me,** the entire section picturing the happy condition of the believers as recipients of the Lord's blessings. But the Lord now once more turns to the apostates with a further rebuke. V. 11. **But ye are they that forsake the Lord, that forget My holy mountain,** the place of His habitation, where He was worshiped, **that prepare a table for that troop,** for Gad, the idol of happiness and good fortune, **and that furnish the drink-offering unto that number,** to Meni, who may have been the corresponding goddess. The exiles had been addicted to the service of these idols during their captivity at Babylon and had brought the idolatrous practises connected with their cult back with them to Judea, as the prophet saw in spirit. V. 12. **Therefore will I number you to the sword,** deliver them to the extremity of a violent death, and **ye shall all bow down to the slaughter,** to the slaughtering-bench instead of to the loaded banquet-table at the feast of idols; **because, when I called, ye did not answer,** when the Lord sought out those who ignored Him, they continued in their attitude of indifference; **when I spake, ye did not hear,** setting aside His Word with an utter disregard of His rights, **but did evil before Mine eyes and did choose that wherein I delighted not.** In other words, they proved themselves the enemies of the Lord in every way. V. 13. **Therefore, thus saith the Lord God,** the all-powerful Ruler of the universe, **Behold, My servants,** the believers, **shall eat,** enjoy the fulness of God's blessings, **but ye shall be hungry; behold, My servants shall drink, but ye shall be thirsty; behold, My servants shall rejoice, but ye shall be ashamed,** being deprived of all advantages which pertain to the children of God; v. 14. **behold, My servants shall sing for joy of heart,** in the happiness which goes with the certainty of being children of a gracious Father, **but ye shall cry for sorrow of heart,** when despair takes hold of them, **and shall howl for vexation of spirit,** when their courage fails them altogether. V. 15. **And ye shall leave your name for a curse unto My chosen,** so that the Lord's people would pronounce curses upon the name of the idolaters whenever they think of it; **for the Lord God shall slay thee and call His servants by another name,** so that they would no longer be obliged to bear the name of the apostates to their reproach, v. 16. **that he who blesseth himself in the earth,** calling down some blessing upon his head, **shall bless himself in the God of truth,** literally, "in the God of Amen," in Him who fulfils all His promises to His children and executes His threats upon His enemies; **and he that**

sweareth in the earth shall swear by the God of truth, because the former troubles are forgotten, with all the doubts which they tended to create in the hearts of the believers, **and because they are hid from Mine eyes,** so that they have disappeared entirely. This thought fitly introduces the next paragraph, where the new order of things is described in language which is both beautiful and majestic.

THE NEW HEAVEN AND THE NEW EARTH. — V. 17. **For, behold, I create new heavens,** the plural being applied to the abode of the blessed in many passages of the Bible, **and a new earth,** cp. Rev. 21; **and the former,** that which was here infested with sin and its curse, **shall not be remembered nor come into mind,** the very remembrance of the sorrows of this present world being erased by the overwhelming mercies of God. V. 18. **But be ye,** the partakers of the glories in this new earth, **glad and rejoice forever in that which I create; for, behold, I create Jerusalem a rejoicing and her people a joy,** so that the believers of all times are engaged in praises of Him always, in honor of His works of mercy. V. 19. **And I will rejoice in Jerusalem and joy in My people,** in the Church which He Himself founded, this joy of the Lord being apparent throughout the entire Bible; **and the voice of weeping shall be no more heard in her nor the voice of crying,** the tears over the misery of this earthly life being dried up in the merciful light of God's countenance. V. 20. **There shall be no more thence,** in the kingdom of the Messiah, **an infant of days,** a babe taken away after just a few days of earthly life, **nor an old man that hath not filled his days,** reaching the full measure of years in accordance with God's creative plan; **for the child shall die an hundred years old,** one passing away at this age being considered still a young man; **but the sinner being an hundred years old shall be accursed,** he who would otherwise be torn away by the avenging justice of God at about half the usual age now being spared till he reaches the age of at least a hundred years, the patience of the Lord being so much greater than before. The fact that the Lord, in the time of the New Testament, shows such wonderful long-suffering in dealing with transgressors, individuals as well as nations, is one of the chief marks distinguishing this age from the time before the Messiah's coming. V. 21. **And they shall build houses and inhabit them,** enjoying the blessings of the Lord in a quiet and peaceable life; **and they shall plant vineyards and eat the fruit of them,** this expression being used throughout the Old Testament of undisturbed happiness. V. 22. **They shall not build and another inhabit; they shall not plant and another eat,** so that they will be deprived of the fruit of their labor; **for as the days of a tree are the days of My people,** all of them being blessed with a ripe age, as of a cedar or oak, **and Mine elect,** those whom His mercy has chosen to be His children, **shall long enjoy the work of their hands.** All of these expressions are figurative and portray the rich beauties of the blessings enjoyed in the Lord's kingdom. V. 23. **They shall not labor in vain,** without result or lasting reward, **nor bring forth for trouble,** their children inheriting nothing but misery; **for they are the seed of the blessed of the Lord,** begotten of the Lord and blessed by Him, **and their offspring with them,** partakers of the same benefits, which the children enjoy with their parents. V. 24. **And it shall come to pass that before they call,** the cry having hardly left their lips, **I will answer,** being so desirous of extending assistance and deliverance to them, **and while they are yet speaking, I will hear,** such being the extent of His good pleasure in His children. V. 25. **The wolf and the lamb shall feed together,** pasturing in the same meadow, **and the lion shall eat straw like the bullock,** forgetting his ferocious nature; **and dust shall be the serpent's meat,** or, "and even the serpent whose food is the dust". **They shall not hurt nor destroy in all My holy mountain, saith the Lord.** The description, as of conditions before the Fall, while the peace of Paradise was still in force, sets before the eyes of all believers the glorious peace of the Messianic kingdom, in which men, without the ferociousness of their sinful nature, will be at peace with one another and serve and worship the Lord with entire unanimity of mind.

CHAPTER 66.

The Passing of the Old and the Rise of the New Church.

THE ABOMINATIONS OF A DEAD WORSHIP AND THE BIRTH OF THE NEW CHURCH. — V. 1. **Thus saith the Lord, The heaven is My throne, and the earth is My footstool,** a majestic declaration of His almighty power and rule; **where is the house that ye build unto Me, and where is the place of My rest?** The Lord desires neither the Temple nor the worship of such as have forsaken Him; they are an abomination in His sight. V. 2. **For all those things hath Mine hand made,** everything that men might offer to Him was His even by virtue of His creation, **and all those things have been, saith the Lord,** heaven and earth with all their creatures having been brought into being by the word of His power, wherefore the hypocrites and believers in name only have nothing upon which they might pride themselves; **but to this man will I look,** such a one the Lord will regard with favor, **even to him that is poor and of a contrite spirit,** whose heart is filled with genuine repentance, **and trembleth at My Word,** who stands in awe of God's holy Word and will and shuns a dead orthodoxy as well as a religion of works. Upon such a person the Lord looks with merciful compassion, him He accepts with a full and free expression of His grace. The loathing which the Lord feels with regard to a mere external observance of the forms of religion is now set forth. V. 3. **He that killeth an ox,** in an act of sacrifice which is nothing but a dead custom, **is as if he slew a man; he that sacrificeth a lamb as if he cut off a dog's neck,** as if he insulted the Lord by the sacrifice of a dog; **he that offereth an oblation,** a drink-offering, **as if he offered swine's blood,** the sacrifice of which was forbidden in the Law of God; **he that burneth incense,** with a heart not turned to the Lord in true faith, **as if he blessed an idol.** The Lord feels nothing but the deepest loathing and horror of the sacrifices and the worship of the apostate Jews. **Yea, they have chosen their own ways,** different from those prescribed by God's holy will, **and their soul delighteth in their abominations,** that being their condition of mind. V. 4. **I also will choose their delusions,** picking out and appointing to them misfortune, **and will bring their fears,** all the misery that men dread, **upon them; because when I called,** bidding them come to repentance, holding out to them the riches of His grace, **none did answer; when I spake, they did not hear, but they did evil before Mine eyes and chose that in which I delighted not.** Cp. chap. 65, 6. 7. 12—15. Thus the Lord sets forth and rebukes the abomination of a dead worship. He now turns to the believers, His children, and announces to them the full glory of the Gospel comfort. V. 5. **Hear the word of the Lord, ye that tremble at His Word,** in a wholesome awe, in the reverence engendered by a childlike faith: **Your brethren that hated you,** the hypocrites and godless people whom the Lord has just exposed, **that cast you out for My name's sake,** for in opposing the Lord they also became open enemies of His confessors, **said,** in giving expression to the bitter mockery of their hearts, **Let the Lord be glorified,** let Him reveal Himself in a miracle of punishment upon them! These scorners would find that the Lord would indeed glorify Himself upon them. **But He shall appear to your joy, and they shall be ashamed,** so Jehovah comforts His people. The sentence may also be constructed to read, in the jeering call of the unbelievers, Let the Lord by all means glorify Himself, that we may see your joy! the Lord's retort being: They shall be brought to shame. The revelation of Jehovah's glory in founding and establishing His Church in the Messianic era is now described. V. 6. **A voice of noise from the city,** of a great uproar, **a voice from the Temple,** the seat of Jehovah, **a voice of the Lord that rendereth recompense to His enemies,** on the great day of vengeance, the time of deliverance of His children, which is so often referred to in Isaiah's prophecies. V. 7. **Before she,** Zion, the bride, the Church of the Lord, **travailed, she brought forth; before her pain came, she was delivered of a man child.** V. 8. **Who hath heard such a thing? Who hath seen such things?** The event to which the Lord has reference is unheard of. **Shall the earth be made to bring forth in one day?** Is a whole land or nation thus brought into being? **Or shall a nation be born at once? For as soon as Zion travailed,** with the first show of labor, **she brought forth her children.** V. 9. **Shall I bring to the birth and not cause to bring forth?** so that the birth is not completed, **saith the Lord. Shall I cause to bring forth and shut the womb? saith thy God.** This description fits all the great crises in the history of the Church, the birth of the Christian Church, the reformation of the Church in the sixteenth century. When traditions and customs obscure the true life of the Church and bring about a condition of dead orthodoxy or of false teaching, the Lord comes with His mighty, merciful intervention and brings about a rebirth, which renews His Church to an extent that makes it almost a new creation. What the Lord has once undertaken He carries out to His own glory and that of His Church.

THE HAPPINESS OF THE NEW TESTAMENT CHURCH. — V. 10. **Rejoice ye with Jerusalem,** so the prophet calls out to all believers, **and be glad with her, all ye that love her; rejoice for joy with her, all ye that mourn for her,** all those who formerly shared her misery and tribulation, v. 11. **that ye,** as the spiritual children of Zion, **may suck and be satisfied with the breasts of her consolations,** enjoying her spiritual blessings and treasures to the full; **that ye may milk out,** drain the riches of the Gospel mercies, **and be delighted with the abundance of her glory.** V. 12. **For thus saith the Lord,** Himself the covenant God, **Behold, I will extend peace to her like a river,** in great quantities, **and the glory of the Gentiles,** all the power and the gifts which they possess, **like a flowing stream,** which threatens to overflow its banks; **then shall ye suck,** drinking in full measure; **ye shall be borne upon (her) sides, and be dandled upon (her) knees,** the Lord Himself taking His children into His arms and extending to them the fulness of His mercy. V. 13. **As one whom his mother comforteth,** like a mother consoling her grown-up boy with true maternal sympathy, **so will I comfort** you; and ye shall be comforted in Jerusalem, whose glory is now the means of the divine consolation. V. 14. **And when ye see this,** realizing, to some extent, the riches of God's mercy, **your heart shall rejoice, and your bones shall flourish,** be filled with new life and strength, **like an herb; and the hand of the Lord shall be known toward His servants,** in love and kindness, **and His indignation toward His enemies,** who would feel His wrath in an everlasting punishment. V. 15. **For, behold, the Lord will come with fire,** with a devastating punishment, **and with His chariots like a whirlwind, to render His anger with fury and His rebuke with flames of fire,** for fire is mentioned throughout the Bible as an instrument of God's avenging anger. V. 16. **For by fire and by His sword will the Lord plead with all flesh,** carrying out the sentence of His justice upon all men; **and the slain of the Lord shall be many,** because all unbelievers make themselves the objects of His wrath and heap damnation upon themselves. V. 17. **They that sanctify themselves and purify themselves in the gardens behind one tree in the midst,** that is, the idol-worshipers who anxiously observe all the ceremonies of cleansing under the direction of some priest or master, **eating swine's flesh, and the abomination,** some other forbidden meat, **and the mouse,** also Levitically unclean, Lev. 11, 29, **shall be consumed together,** by the judgment of His wrath, **saith the Lord.** V. 18. **For I know their works and their thoughts,** or, "so far as their works and their ideas are concerned." **It shall come that I will gather all nations and tongues; and they shall come and see My glory,** which would be revealed in the Lord's judgment upon the reprobate Jews, this warning being intended to prepare the way for the spread of the Gospel among the heathen. V. 19. **And I will set a sign among them,** performing a miracle in their midst, **and I will send those that escape of them unto the nations,** these messengers being the few who escaped His great punishment upon the apostates, brands snatched from the burning, **to Tarshish,** Tartessus in Spain, in the extreme West, **Pul,** in Northeastern Africa, between Egypt and Ethiopia, **and Lud,** the Libyans of Africa, **that draw the bow,** renowned warriors, **to Tubal,** in Asia Minor, south of the Caucasus, **and Javan,** the Ionians of Greece and Asia Minor, **to the isles afar off that have not heard My fame, neither have seen My glory;** in short, His Gospel-message was to be carried into all the world; **and they,** the Lord's ambassadors, **shall declare My glory among the Gentiles.** V. 20. **And they shall bring all your brethren,** the so-called dispersion among the heathen, **for an offering unto the Lord out of all nations,** these being brought to Him as a precious gift, **upon horses, and in chariots, and in litters,** low and comfortable wagons, **and upon mules, and upon swift beasts,** dromedaries, **to My holy mountain Jerusalem, saith the Lord, as the children of Israel bring an offering in a clean vessel into the house of the Lord.** V. 21. **And I will also take of them for priests and for Levites, saith the Lord,** there being no difference in the Church of Christ between Jews and Gentiles, all of them being of equal rank as spiritual priests before the Lord. V. 22. **For as the new heavens and the new earth which I will make,** the new creation of which He spoke chap. 65, 17, **shall remain before Me, saith the Lord, so shall your seed and your name remain,** namely, that of the believers, the spiritual children of Israel, gathered from Jews and Gentiles alike. V. 23. **And it shall come to pass that from one new moon to another and from one Sabbath to another,** with clocklike regularity, **shall all flesh come to worship before Me,** all the members of the new, wonderful kingdom of the Messiah, **saith the Lord.** V. 24. **And they shall go forth,** namely, the members of the Church of the Lord, represented as coming out of the Temple of Jehovah, engaged in His worship, **and look upon the carcasses of the men that have transgressed against Me,** as the people of Jerusalem had a view of the carcasses in the Valley of Hinnom; **for their worm shall not die, neither shall their fire be quenched, and they shall be an abhorring unto all flesh.** Thus the punishment which comes upon the enemies of the Lord will be both a source of satisfaction to the believers and an example of warning. Cp. Matt. 13, 42. To this day and hour the words of the Lord hold true: "He that believeth and is baptized shall be saved, but he that believeth not shall be damned." Mark 16, 16.

THE BOOK OF THE PROPHET JEREMIAH.

INTRODUCTION.

The prophet Jeremiah, a native of Anathoth, a town situated a little over three miles northeast of Jerusalem, within the boundaries of Benjamin, was born shortly before Josiah became king. He was a member of a priestly family, and God called him to be a prophet when he was still a very young man. He witnessed the great reformation in the eighteenth year of Josiah, whose death he lamented. During the early years of Jehoiakim's reign he was in danger of losing his life on account of his faithful preaching. He was threatened even by his townsmen and opposed by his own family. He was obliged to endure many other indignities and adversities, not only under the reign of Jehoiakim, but also under that of Zedekiah, the climax of his sufferings being reached when the armies of the Chaldeans approached the city. After the capture of Jerusalem, Jeremiah was taken in chains as far as Ramah, but released by Nebuchadnezzar's general. He lived with Gedaliah, the governor of the country, for a while, but after the assassination of Gedaliah was carried to Egypt by force. He continued to preach and prophesy in Egypt, predicting the conquest of the country by Nebuchadnezzar and warning the Jews to abstain from idolatry. He seems to have died in Egypt, according to tradition having been stoned to death by his own countrymen.

As the brief outline of Jeremiah's life shows, the period of Jewish history in which he lived was the critical time preceding the nation's doom. Only one of the five kings under whom Jeremiah prophesied was a pious ruler. The people became guilty of gross idolatry and, as they relapsed into paganism, of immoral practises. Covetousness, dishonesty, murder, adultery, stealing, false swearing, and other sins were prevalent throughout the nation. Year after year Jeremiah came with messages from God, whose mercy and compassion sought to turn His people to repentance, but the moral corruption was too great, and the people refused to obey. They preferred to listen to various false prophets, who predicted peace and prosperity. But though the work of Jeremiah, to all outer appearances, was vain, it resulted, in fact, in a clearing of the situation, since, as a consequence, the true Israelites were preserved in faith. In spite of all the trying experiences, therefore, which Jeremiah, naturally of a mild, sensitive, and retiring disposition, had to undergo, he remained faithful to his task as a prophet of the one true God. He ever found comfort and strength in the promise which the Lord had given him at the beginning of his labors: "Be not afraid of their faces; for I am with thee to deliver thee. . . . They shall fight against thee, but they shall not prevail against thee."

The arrangement of the Book of Jeremiah is topical rather than chronological. It may be divided into two large groups. The first division contains the introduction and the prophecies concerning Judah, together with some historical matter, chaps. 1—45; the second division contains ten prophetical discourses concerning nine foreign nations, together with a final historical account concerning the destruction of Jerusalem and the release of Jehoiachin. A more detailed division of the book yields the following outline: prophecies belonging for the most part to the reign of Josiah, chaps. 1—6; prophecies belonging probably chiefly to the reign of Jehoiakim, chaps. 7—21; prophecies probably belonging to the reign of Jehoiachin, chaps. 22 and 23; prophecies and events in the reign of Zedekiah, chaps. 24—39; history and prophecies under Gedaliah's administration and in Egypt, chaps. 40—44; group of prophecies against heathen nations, chaps. 46—51; historical conclusion, chap. 52. As stated above, however, this division is only general.

There are several notable prophecies in the Book of Jeremiah, some of them being veritable gems of epigrammatic utterance. But the most beautiful passages are the Messianic prophecies concerning the Lord, our Righteousness. Cp. chap. 23, 5. 6; 30, 9; 33. The prophecy of the New Covenant refers to the days of the New Testament, which began with the coming of Christ. Chap. 31, 31—34.[1])

1) Cp. the introduction in Fuerbringer, *Einleitung in das Alte Testament*, 67—70; *Concordia Bible Class*, May, 1919, 68—71; Sampey, *Syllabus for Old Testament Study*, 222—240.

CHAPTER 1.

THE SUPERSCRIPTION. — V. 1. **The words of Jeremiah, the son of Hilkiah, of the priests that were in Anathoth, in the land of Benjamin,** this being one of the four cities within the territory of Benjamin allotted to the Kohathites, Josh. 21, 18; v. 2. **to whom the word of the Lord came in the days of Josiah, the son of Amon, king of Judah, in the thirteenth year of his reign.** V. 3. **It came also in the days of Jehoiakim, the son of Josiah, king of Judah, unto the end of the eleventh year of Zedekiah, the son**

of Josiah, king of Judah, unto the carrying away of Jerusalem, that is, of its inhabitants, **captive in the fifth month.** Note that Jeremiah expressly claims divine authority and inspiration for his prophecies, insisting that it is the Word of the Lord which he recorded. He omits the names of Jehoahaz and Jehoiachin from his list, since they reigned only three months each, and his title intends to specify in a general way only. "Since Jeremiah labored from the thirteenth year of Josiah, consequently eighteen years under Josiah, and eleven years each under Jehoiakim and Zedekiah, he ministered altogether, including the six months under the kings omitted, forty years in the midst of the theocracy." Jeremiah was a member of a lowly family, and yet the Lord called him to a very important position as chief adviser of kings. God often chooses the weak, base, and despised things to confound the mighty. 1 Cor. 1, 27—29.

THE CALL AND COMMISSION OF THE PROPHET. V. 4. **Then,** namely, at the time designated in the introduction, **the word of the Lord came unto me, saying,** v. 5. **Before I formed thee in the belly, I knew thee,** before ever his conception had taken place, the Lord had destined him to be His prophet; **and before thou camest forth out of the womb, I sanctified thee,** separating and consecrating him, setting him apart for the sacred office, **and I ordained thee a prophet unto the nations,** not only to the people of Judah and Jerusalem, but to other nations as well. Jeremiah's choice of his calling was not the result of meditation and reflection, of a false enthusiasm and ecstasy, but of a supernatural revelation, of a selection on the part of God, which was in no way influenced by any ability or disposition on the prophet's part. V. 6. **Then said I,** with some realization of the difficulty and danger of the divine commission, **Ah! Lord God, behold, I cannot speak, for I am a child,** a young man below the age at which the Israelites took an active part in public work. The sensitive nature of Jeremiah shrank back from a position which would expose him to public criticism. The work of the ministry is a good work, 1 Tim. 3, 1, but it is attended by difficulties which the average person appreciates only in rare instances. Well may a timid person shrink back from its ordeal. V. 7. **But the Lord said unto me, Say not, I am a child,** in an effort to make his youth and inexperience an excuse for refusing to follow the Lord's call; **for thou shalt go to all that I shall send thee, and whatsoever I command thee thou shalt speak.** It was not a matter to be argued, but the Lord, by a categorical declaration of His will, commissioned Jeremiah. No matter to which nations and princes the Lord would bid him go, he was cheerfully to declare God's counsel and will, regardless of any show of hostility. V. 8. **Be not afraid of their faces,** in an excess of awe which would interfere with the effectiveness of his message; **for I am with thee to deliver thee, saith the Lord.** He thus imparted the necessary courage to His servant to enable him to stand before the mighty of the world. Cp. Matt. 10, 16—22. V. 9. **Then the Lord put forth His hand and touched my mouth,** this, of course, being a symbolical act experienced by Jeremiah in a vision, its meaning being that God Himself would give His servant the right utterance, would inspire him to proclaim His message in its full truth. **And the Lord said unto me, Behold, I have put My words in thy mouth.** The Lord made the individuality of Jeremiah the instrument of His eternal wisdom in making His will known to men. V. 10. **See, I have this day set thee over the nations and over the kingdoms,** the naturally timid and fearful prophet being appointed to their oversight, **to root out, and to pull down, and to destroy,** to extirpate, exterminate, and eliminate, **and to throw down,** to pronounce the divine judgment upon His enemies, **to build and to plant,** by announcing God's mercy and grace to all who heeded His call. The conditions in Judah were such at that time as to provoke threatenings and rebukes on the part of the Lord rather than promises of grace and mercy. V. 11. **Moreover, the word of the Lord came unto me, saying, Jeremiah, what seest thou?** Jehovah wanted to give His prophet some signs confirming his call. **And I said, I see a rod of an almond-tree,** a shoot or branch of the tree which was the first to awaken to life after the winter's sleep and was therefore a symbol of wakefulness. V. 12. **Then said the Lord unto me, Thou hast well seen; for I will hasten My word to perform it,** literally, "wakeful (or intent) shall I, on My part, be with regard to My words to do them," the allusion to the wakeful tree thus being justified. V. 13. **And the word of the Lord came unto me the second time, saying, What seest thou?** a second vision being vouchsafed the prophet. **And I said, I see a seething pot,** one of the large kettles used to prepare vegetables for many guests; **and the face thereof is toward the north,** so that its contents threaten to be emptied from that side. V. 14. **Then the Lord said unto me, Out of the north an evil shall break forth,** out of a great and wide opening, **upon all the inhabitants of the land.** A boiling kettle is an Oriental symbol of a raging war, and since Babylon was regarded by the people of Judah as situated toward the north, it was clear that the Lord prophesied the Babylonian invasion. V. 15. **For, lo, I will call all the families,** the tribes or clans, **of the kingdoms of the North, saith the Lord,** all the great chieftains of the Chaldeans uniting in an effort to overthrow Judah; **and they shall come, and they shall set every one his throne at the entering of the gates of Jerusalem,** the conquering princes establishing their tribunals of justice in the place set aside for this purpose of old, thereby taking over the administration of the land, **and against all the walls thereof round about and against all the cities of Judah,** thereby laying siege to all the fortified cities of the land in a successful campaign. V. 16. **And I will utter My judgments against them,** the wicked inhabitants of the land, **touching all their wickedness,** pronouncing their condemnation and doom, **who have forsaken Me and have burned incense unto other gods and worshiped the works of their own hands.** Thus the Lord, by His stern judgments and punishments, would visit His wrath upon the apostate Jews for their idolatry, the sin which, like the unbelief of to-day, is the essence and summary of disobedience. The symbols having been explained, the Lord now adds an admonition to Jeremiah to fulfil the duties of his office with fearless zeal. V. 17. **Thou, therefore, gird up thy loins,** like a soldier or a man on a journey, to remove every hindrance in traveling, **and arise and speak unto them all that I command thee,** the fact of his being the Lord's messenger and representative once more being stressed; **be not dismayed at their faces,** shrinking back before them, **lest I confound thee before them,** so that he would be rejected, crushed, and overcome before them. V. 18. **For, behold, I have made thee this day a defensed city,** one fortified most strongly, **and an iron pillar, and brazen walls against the whole land,** enduing him with strength which no power of the enemies would be able to overcome, **against the kings of Judah, against the princes thereof, against the priests thereof, and against the people of the land,** all of whom would unite to oppose his message and warning. V. 19. **And they shall fight against thee,** a fact of which Jeremiah was to be aware from the outset, **but they shall not prevail against thee; for I am with thee, saith the Lord, to deliver thee,** this assurance serving as the source of the prophet's strength in the coming trials. It has happened more than once in the history of the Church that practically a single man was obliged to stand against the enmity of the mighty ones of the earth and of the masses of people as well, but that he maintained his righteous cause in the power of the Lord.

CHAPTER 2.

God's Faithfulness and Israel's Faithlessness.

ISRAEL'S LACK OF FAITHFULNESS. — V. 1. **Moreover, the word of the Lord came to me, saying,** this being an introduction both to the first prophetic discourse and to the whole cycle of Jeremiah's prophetic messages, v. 2. **Go and cry in the ears of Jerusalem,** the expression "in the ears" showing that the prophet should preach to the people living in this center of idolatry with clamoring insistence, **saying, Thus saith the Lord: I remember thee, the kindness of thy youth,** the love which Israel bore the Lord in Egypt and at the time of the Exodus, or the merciful kindness which Israel experienced from the earliest days of its history, **the love of thine espousals,** at the period between the Exodus from Egypt and the formal establishment of the covenant upon Mount Sinai, **when thou wentest after Me in the wilderness, in a land that was not sown,** with no strange god in evidence in the midst of the arid desert. V. 3. **Israel was holiness unto the Lord,** consecrated to Him and to His service, **and the first-fruits of His increase,** the people chosen by Him as the first among all nations, produced as the first in the garden of His love and mercy. **All that devour him shall offend,** all those who dared to prey upon Israel became guilty before the Lord; **evil shall come upon them, saith the Lord.** His punishment descended upon the Amalekites, the Amorites, and upon all other nations that interfered with His plans of love toward His chosen people. Such were the manifestations of Jehovah's mercy and kindness to Israel, and therefore His rebuke certainly came with good reason. V. 4. **Hear ye the word of the Lord, O house of Jacob, and all the families of the house of Israel,** individually and collectively, the whole nation, all of them being in the same condemnation. V. 5. **Thus saith the Lord, What iniquity have your fathers found in Me,** what wrong done to them by Jehovah, **that they are gone far from Me,** deserting Him for the false gods of the heathen, **and have walked after vanity,** the nothingnesses of their idols, **and are become vain?** The worshipers of idols become just as vain and worthless as their empty gods, and are therefore despised and condemned by God in the same degree. Cp. Deut. 7, 26; Ps. 115, 8; 2 Kings 17, 15; Rom. 1, 21. V. 6. **Neither said they, Where is the Lord that brought us up out of the land of Egypt, that led us through the wilderness,** that of Sinai, Paran, and Arabia, **through a land of deserts and of pits,** where chasms and sink-holes abounded, endangering the lives of man and beast, **through a land of drought and of the shadow of death,** as the way led under overhanging rocky precipices, **through a land that no man passed through and where no man dwelt?** Israel is thus pictured as having utterly forgotten the Lord's protection and blessings, wherefore the Lord asks such reproachful questions. V. 7. **And I brought you into a plentiful country,** a well-cultivated and fruitful land, **to eat the fruit thereof and the goodness thereof,** to enjoy all the blessings it offered to the full; **but when ye entered, ye defiled My land,** namely, by becoming addicted to idolatry, **and made Mine heritage an abomination,** so that He was filled with loathing for the land which He had chosen for them. V. 8. **The priests said not, Where is the Lord?** The very ones who were supposed to expound the Law ignored the very Giver of the Law. **And they that handle the Law knew Me not,** the teachers who were occupied with it as the subject of their profession paid no attention to the Lord. **The pastors also,** the princes of the people, who were supposed to be its shepherds both in a civil and in a spiritual sense, **transgressed against Me,** being themselves in rebellion against the Chief Shepherd, **and the prophets prophesied by Baal,** in his name and by his authority, **and walked after things that do not profit,** that are vain and worthless beside the eternal truths of God's will. V. 9. **Wherefore I will yet plead with you, saith the Lord,** by citing them before His tribunal and pronouncing judgment upon them, **and with your children's children will I plead,** since they follow their parents in all their wicked ways. V. 10. **For pass over the isles of Chittim,** applied first of all to the island of Cyprus, but later to the entire coast of the Mediterranean, especially to Greece, **and see, and send unto Kedar,** the descendants of Ishmael in the Arabian Desert, **and consider diligently, and see if there be such a thing.** The children of Israel were bidden to search both the West and the East for an instance in which a heathen nation had become guilty of such foolish behavior as exhibited by them. V. 11. **Hath a nation changed their gods, which are yet no gods?** In spite of the fact that their idols were false gods, the heathen at least had the pride and the decency of clinging to their gods. **But My people have changed their glory for that which doth not profit,** exchanging their possession of Jehovah, the true God, for vain idols, with less consistency than that shown by the ignorant and despised heathen. In astonishment and horror the Lord cries out: v. 12. **Be astonished, O ye heavens, at this,** at the unspeakable wickedness of their behavior, **and be horribly afraid,** be filled with shuddering loathing, **be ye very desolate, saith the Lord,** exceedingly aghast at the monstrous spectacle thus presented. V. 13. **For My people have committed two evils,** thus exceeding even the heathen with their one transgression of foolish idolatry: **they have forsaken Me, the Fountain of living waters,** the only true and living God, **and hewed them out cisterns,** whose waters lack the freshness and the sparkle of spring- or well-water, **broken cisterns, that can hold no water.** Putting aside the one and only Source of spiritual life and power, they placed their trust in gods which belied even the outward appearance that men had given them. The same foolish and harmful course is pursued by all those who in our days deny the inspiration of the Bible, the deity of Christ, and other fundamental doctrines and turn to man-made doctrines instead.

ISRAEL'S PUNISHMENT AND ITS CAUSE. — V. 14. **Is Israel a servant? Is he a homeborn slave? Why is he spoiled?** The question, whether asked by the prophet or directly by God, expresses surprise that the nation which was once God's favorite should now be left at the mercy of the enemy like a worthless slave. Whence this change in fortunes? Whence this unhappy condition? V. 15. **The young lions roared upon him and yelled,** raising their voices in a roar of triumph, **and they made his land waste; his cities are burned without inhabitant.** This is the condition of Israel which the prophet sees in spirit, the picture of the devastation wrought by beasts of prey being particularly fitting to describe the desolation of the land of Israel after the overthrow by the Chaldeans. V. 16. **Also the children of Noph,** of Memphis, the capital of Lower Egypt at that time, **and Tahapanes,** of Daphne, a city on the frontier of Egypt toward Palestine, **have broken the crown of thy head.** The Egyptians also took the opportunity of spoiling Judah when the nation had become weak under the reign of Jehoiakim; for the taking away of the natural covering of the hair, to which reference is here made, was symbolic of an entire sweeping away of the people. V. 17. **Hast thou not procured this unto thyself,** the Israelites having brought this calamity upon themselves, **in that thou hast forsaken the Lord, thy God, when He led thee by the way?** on the good path of His will, on the road of righteousness. V. 18. **And now, what hast thou to do in the way of Egypt to drink the waters of Sihor?** For Israel had sent to Egypt for help against Assyria and Babylon. **Or what hast thou to do in the way of Assyria to drink the waters of the river,** Euphrates? in endeavoring, at times, to enter into a league with this heathen nation. This reliance upon the power of men was a mark of decay, of a lack of trust in God, of a denial of Jehovah. V. 19. **Thine own wickedness shall correct thee,** their sin bearing with it its own punishment, **and thy backslidings shall reprove thee,** for the very allies whose help they sought became the instruments of Israel's destruction. **Know therefore and see that it is an evil thing and bitter that thou hast forsaken the Lord, thy God,** this they were to find out to their cost, and that

My fear, the reverence which the nation as such should have had toward Jehovah, **is not in thee, saith the Lord God of hosts.** Wherever the fear of God does not guide and direct the conduct of men, they are bound to pay for their defection and apostasy sooner or later.

The Sin of Idolatry. — V. 20. **For of old time I have broken thy yoke and burst thy bands,** rather, "For from ancient times thou hast broken thy yoke and burst thy bands," namely, the laws and ordinances of God; **and thou saidst, I will not transgress,** literally, "I will not serve," thus obstinately refusing obedience to the Lord, **when upon every high hill and under every green tree thou wanderest,** where the sanctuaries of idolatry were always found, **playing the harlot,** the act of adultery, as practised in connection with heathen rites, being figurative of shameless idolatry. V. 21. **Yet I had planted thee a noble vine,** the finest and most fruitful of the Holy Land, **wholly a right seed,** cp. Deut. 32, 32; Ps. 80, 8. 9; Is. 5, 1; **how, then, art thou turned into the degenerate plant of a strange vine unto Me?** After all the pains which the Lord had taken with Israel it certainly was a matter which could not be laid to His charge that Israel had turned out so badly. V. 22. **For though thou wash thee with niter,** an alkali having the properties of lye, used for washing, **and take thee much soap,** the potash which, mixed with oil, was used for washing clothes, **yet thine iniquity is marked before me,** is a stain before the eyes of the Lord, **saith the Lord God.** All the efforts of men are not sufficient to purge away the ugly spots of sin on their hearts. V. 23. **How canst thou say, I am not polluted,** denying the guilt of her wickedness, **I have not gone after Baalim?** the plural being used to characterize the many forms which this god took among the various nations. **See thy way in the valley,** considering the course which she had followed, **know what thou hast done. Thou art a swift dromedary,** a young she-camel, **traversing her ways,** literally, "braiding (or twisting) her ways," doubling and turning back and forth in her lust; v. 24. **a wild ass used to the wilderness,** not to be tamed, **that snuffeth up the wind at her pleasure,** both to cool her ardor and to direct her way; **in her occasion,** her anxiety to accomplish her purpose, **who can turn her away? All they that seek her will not weary themselves,** have no need to tire themselves out in finding her; **in her month,** at the season of the year when this impulse is strongest, **they shall find her,** for she will readily be found, since she acts under the uncontrollable impulse of her instinct. With the same fierceness and disregard of consequences Israel was addicted to her idolatry. V. 25. **Withhold thy foot from being unshod,** in running so violently after idolatry as to wear out her shoes, **and thy throat from thirst,** as a result of her excessive exertion in seeking strangers and their idolatrous customs; **but thou saidst, There is no hope, no;** it is useless to argue, since she is firmly resolved to go on on her sinful course; **for I have loved strangers,** strange gods in place of the one true God, **and after them will I go,** determined to persist in her wickedness. V. 26. **As the thief is ashamed when he is found,** put to shame by the evidences of his guilt, **so is the house of Israel ashamed; they, their kings, their princes, and their priests, and their prophets,** leaders and people in the same condemnation, v. 27. **saying to a stock,** to a tree or log, **Thou art my father,** hailing the dead creature as god; **and to a stone, Thou hast brought me forth; for they have turned their back unto Me and not their face,** that is their transgression; **but in the time of their trouble they will say, Arise and save us.** When affliction and trouble bring them to their senses, then they will turn to Jehovah for help. Cp. Luke 15, 16—18. Over against this insulting behavior the Lord tells them: v. 28. **But where are thy gods that thou hast made thee? Let them arise if they can save thee in the time of thy trouble; for according to the number of thy cities are thy gods, O Judah!** Idolaters of all times and places have had the same experience, namely, that idols of every kind cannot deliver from trouble, no matter how great their number.

The Guilt Established. — V. 29. **Wherefore will ye plead with Me?** contending with the Lord as though He had no right to punish them. **Ye all have transgressed against Me, saith the Lord,** forsaking Him in rebellious wickedness. V. 30. **In vain have I smitten your children,** in endeavoring to bring them to their senses; **they received no correction,** they would not permit themselves to be guided on the right path; **your own sword hath devoured your prophets like a destroying lion.** Cp. 2 Chron. 36, 16; Neh. 9, 26; Matt. 23, 29. 31. V. 31. **O generation!** Children of perverseness now living! **See ye the word of the Lord,** which is hereby brought before them with the demand that they regard it. **Have I been a wilderness unto Israel,** where all the necessaries of life are wanting, **a land of darkness?** so that they would seem to be under the shadow of death when in His care. **Wherefore say My people, We are lords,** proudly strutting about as though they were their own masters; **we will come no more unto Thee?** fatuously boasting that they no longer were in need of Him. V. 32. **Can a maid forget her ornaments or a bride her attire?** the precious girdle with which she adorned herself on her wedding-day. **Yet My people have forgotten Me days without number.** Israel should have clung to her God, her highest and most precious Ornament and Possession, by whom she had been so richly blessed. Instead of that she forsook Jehovah, not only once, in an unguarded moment, but continually. V. 33. **Why trimmest thou thy way to seek love?** Israel decking herself like a harlot to accomplish her ends. **Therefore hast thou also taught the wicked ones thy ways.** As wicked as the Gentiles were in themselves, Israel was able to give them instruction in wickedness. V. 34. **Also in thy skirts is found the blood of the souls of the poor innocents,** of holy men and prophets who dared to reprove Israel for her sins. **I have not found it by secret search,** such a careful scrutiny was not necessary in this case, **but upon all these,** on account of the sin of idolatry, which finally led to the murder of the Lord's servants. V. 35. **Yet thou sayest,** with brazen boldness, **Because I am innocent, surely His anger shall turn from me. Behold, I will plead with thee,** citing Israel before the tribunal of His judgment, **because thou sayest, I have not sinned,** in a self-righteous denial of her guilt. V. 36. **Why gaddest thou about so much to change thy way?** in forming alliances with her heathen neighbors. **Thou also shalt be ashamed of Egypt,** whose vassal Israel was for a while, **as thou wast ashamed of Assyria,** after King Ahaz had sent there for help, 2 Chron. 28, 16—21. V. 37. **Yea, thou shalt go forth from him,** from all heathen allies, **and thine hands upon thine head,** as a sign of deep mourning; **for the Lord hath rejected thy confidences,** the heathen nations in whom Israel trusted, **and thou shalt not prosper in them,** have no success in the stays on which she relied. All such as are Christians in name only and rely upon the enemies of the Lord will finally find themselves forsaken by their supposed friends and subject to the punishments of the Lord.

CHAPTER 3.

God's Mercy over against Judah's Wickedness

THE POSSIBILITY OF RETURN. — V. 1. **They say,** literally, "Saying," God Himself being the subject of the sentence, **If a man put away his wife, and she go from him and become another man's, shall he return unto her again?** Such dismissals were sometimes practised among the Jews, but it was then unlawful for a man to take back his former wife, Deut. 24, 1—4. **Shall not that land be greatly polluted?** on account of the abomination connected with such practises. **But thou hast played the harlot with many lovers,** none of them being her lawful husband; **yet,** in spite of the fact that it is not in accordance with legal regulations, **return again to Me, saith the Lord,** for He was ready to show mercy even under such adverse conditions. V. 2. **Lift up thine eyes unto the high places,** the scene of her former idolatries, **and see where thou hast not been lien with,** in spiritual adultery. **In the ways hast thou sat for them,** like a common prostitute, Gen. 38, 14. 21; Prov. 7, 12, **as the Arabian in the wilderness,** who lies in wait to attack travelers; **and thou hast polluted the land with thy whoredoms and with thy wickedness.** V. 3. **Therefore,** as a punishment for such idolatrous behavior, **the showers have been withholden, and there hath been no latter rain,** which was absolutely necessary for maturing the crops in Palestine, cp. Lev. 26, 19; **and thou hadst a whore's forehead,** showing brazen boldness, **thou refusedst to be ashamed,** to feel shame and repentance over the course which she had pursued. On the contrary, Israel speaks in a confident and presumptuous voice to the Lord, even in a tone of gentle rebuke for the undeserved severity exhibited by Him. V. 4. **Wilt thou not from this time cry unto Me, My Father, Thou art the Guide of my youth!?** She uses the endearing term "Companion of my youth," in speaking to the Lord, as though to win Him back. V. 5. **Will He reserve His anger forever? Will He keep it to the end?** Israel implies that her misfortune, by which she was receiving an everlasting mark, was due entirely to the Lord's unreasonable anger. But the answer of the Lord is, **Behold, thou hast spoken and done evil things as thou couldest.** While speaking these words of pleading endearment, Israel had continued on the way of wickedness. Such is ever the way of hypocrisy, to profess an affection for the Lord which these false people are far from feeling.

THE CALL TO RETURN. — V. 6. **The Lord said also unto me in the days of Josiah, the king,** an account which the prophet here inserts on account of the application, **Hast thou seen that which backsliding Israel hath done?** Israel being called apostasy outright to emphasize the seriousness of her defection. **She is gone up upon every high mountain and under every green tree and there hath played the harlot,** in committing idolatry or spiritual adultery, the sanctuaries of idols being located in such places. V. 7. **And I said after she had done all these things,** these were the thoughts which filled the Lord's heart, **Turn thou unto Me,** this being the underlying thought in all prophetic admonition. **But she returned not,** the northern kingdom consistently rejecting the Lord's call. **And her treacherous sister Judah saw it,** being influenced by Israel's evil example. V. 8. **And I saw, when for all the causes whereby backsliding Israel com-**

mitted adultery **I had put her away and given her a bill of divorce,** a writing of dismissal, namely, at the time when the northern kingdom was led away into the Assyrian captivity; **yet her treacherous sister Judah feared not,** was not filled with a wholesome respect for the Lord's punishment, **but went and played the harlot also,** was also given to idolatry. V. 9. **And it came to pass through the lightness of her whoredom,** the ease with which she practised her infamous wickedness, **that she defiled the land and committed adultery with stones and with stocks,** with idols of wood and stone, so that the entire land was profaned before the Lord, the entire section inhabited by the northern tribes being polluted by the idolatrous customs so readily accepted by its people. V. 10. **And yet for all this,** although she had the deterring example of Israel before her eyes always, **her treacherous sister Judah hath not turned unto Me with her whole heart, but feignedly, saith the Lord.** The reformation in the eighteenth year of Josiah was not general or thorough; it was only a straw-fire without lasting consequences. V. 11. **And the Lord said unto me, The backsliding Israel hath justified herself more than treacherous Judah,** she was righteous by comparison with the overwhelming guilt of the latter, who possessed the unusual advantages of the Temple and the center of worship in her midst. V. 12. **Go and proclaim these words toward the North,** because Israel had been carried away captive in that direction, **and say, Return, thou backsliding Israel, saith the Lord,** a loving invitation addressed to the northern tribes, which was also to arouse the zeal of Judah, **and I will not cause Mine anger to fall upon you,** not continue to frown upon them in wrath and displeasure; **for I am merciful, saith the Lord,** preferring to show grace and mercy rather than indignation, **and I will not keep anger forever.** But there is one condition upon the fulfilment of which the Lord must insist: v. 13. **Only acknowledge thine iniquity,** freely confessing her transgressions and her guilt, **that thou hast transgressed against the Lord, thy God,** against whom, in the last analysis, every sin is directed, **and hast scattered thy ways to the strangers under every green tree,** wandering back and forth in her apostasy, **and ye have not obeyed My voice, saith the Lord.** V. 14. **Turn, O backsliding children, saith the Lord, for I am married unto you,** literally, "I am Lord and Husband to you"; **and I will take you one of a city and two of a family,** or tribe, collecting the true Israelites from the cities and nations where they are scattered, one by one, **and I will bring you to Zion,** at the time of the New Testament or Messianic kingdom; v. 15. **and I will give you pastors,** leaders in both the spiritual and the civil domain, as Zerubbabel and Nehemiah, **according to Mine own heart, which shall feed you with knowledge and understanding,** the New Testament teachers of the Gospel-message being foremost in this respect. V. 16. **And it shall come to pass, when ye be multiplied and increased in the land, in those days, saith the Lord,** in the days when the spiritual Israelites would be gathered in the kingdom of the Messiah, **they shall say no more, The Ark of the Covenant of the Lord,** attaching the real importance of religion to the possession of this sacred vessel, **neither shall it come to mind,** they would, in fact, not even miss it; **neither shall they remember it, neither shall they visit it, neither shall that be done any more,** it would not be made again. The ark was, in fact, not restored after the Babylonian captivity, the Lord thus signifying that the time of types and shadows was soon to come to an end. V. 17. **At that time,** in the Messianic period, **they shall call Jerusalem the throne of the Lord,** where He revealed Himself to His people, but no longer in a cloud and in a pillar of fire; **and all the nations,** namely, in their representatives, the true believers, **shall be gathered unto it, to the name of the Lord, to Jerusalem,** because the name of the Lord, the Word of His grace, would be proclaimed in the midst of His holy congregation; **neither shall they walk any more after the imagination of their evil heart,** in obstinacy or stubbornness. V. 18. **In those days the house of Judah shall walk with the house of Israel,** all true Israelites being united in the Church of Christ, **and they shall come together out of the land of the North,** from all the countries of the dispersion, **to the land that I have given for an inheritance unto your fathers,** to enjoy the Gospel-blessings together. V. 19. **But I said,** the Lord here beginning His statement of the manner in which Israel may come to the knowledge of her sins, **How shall I put thee among the children,** adopting those into His family once more who had forsaken Him for idols, **and give thee a pleasant land, a goodly heritage of the hosts of nations?** in enjoying the blessings of the Messianic era. **And I said, Thou shalt call Me, My Father,** returning once more to the true God; **and shalt not turn away from Me,** fully restored to the favor of Jehovah. Once more, however, the Lord sets forth the faithlessness of the people of His choice. V. 20. **Surely as a wife treacherously departeth from her husband,** forsaking the companion of her youth, **so have ye dealt treacherously with Me, O house of Israel, saith the Lord.** Upon this final accusation of the Lord the sorrow of the people and their confession of sins is brought out with dramatic intensity. V. 21. **A voice was heard upon the high places,** the very scene of their idolatries becoming the scene of their open confession of their transgressions, **weeping and supplications of the children of Israel,** a public proclamation of their penitence; **for they have perverted their way, and they have forgotten the Lord, their God,** a fact which they now acknowledge with deep sorrow. So the Lord calls to them: v. 22. **Return, ye backsliding children, and I will heal your backslidings.** And they, full of eager desire, answer: **Behold, we come unto Thee; for Thou art the Lord, our God.** Moreover, they now concede: v. 23. **Truly, in vain is salvation hoped for from the hills and from the multitude of mountains,** it is a delusion and a snare to expect help from the priests of the mountain sanctuaries; **truly, in the Lord, our God, is the salvation of Israel,** He alone can bring about the deliverance of His people. V. 24. **For shame hath devoured the labor of our fathers from our youth,** namely, the idols, whose worship brought shame and disgrace upon their worshipers; **their flocks and their herds, their sons and their daughters,** for not only did their service require a steady stream of sacrifices, but their worship also brought down upon the people the punishment of the Lord, by which their children were torn from their side. V. 25. **We lie down in our shame,** as the penitent seats himself in dust and in ashes, **and our confusion covereth us; for we have sinned against the Lord, our God, we and our fathers, from our youth even unto this day, and have not obeyed the voice of the Lord, our God.** A full and unequivocal confession of sins, a complete acknowledgment of guilt, is the first step in true repentance. "He that covereth his sins shall not prosper; but whoso confesseth and forsaketh them shall have mercy." Prov. 28, 13.

CHAPTER 4.

The Judgment upon Judah for Not Returning.

A LAST CALL TO RETURN. — V. 1. **If thou wilt return, O Israel, saith the Lord, return unto Me,** or, "if thou wilt return unto Me," the repetition serving to emphasize the anxious, merciful call of the Lord, **and if thou wilt put away thine abominations out of My sight,** so that they no longer fill Him with loathing, **then shalt thou not remove,** no longer waver, no more be an unsettled wanderer, running from one sanctuary of idolatry to the next. V. 2. **And thou shalt swear, The Lord liveth, in truth,** not in hypocrisy, as formerly, **in judgment, and in righteousness,** in a just cause and with genuine uprightness of heart; **and the nations,** under the influence of this confession, **shall bless themselves in Him, and in Him they shall glory,** thereby becoming partakers of the blessings which were promised in the Messianic prophecies from the time of the patriarchs. The sincere conversion of Judah would have this effect upon the Gentiles, for such an open confession is a powerful argument for the truth. Cp. Luke 22, 32. V. 3. **For thus saith the Lord to the men of Judah and Jerusalem,** the capital being mentioned particularly as the center of Jewish worship, **Break up your fallow ground,** that of their hearts, which is like wild land overgrown with weeds, where cleansing is effected only by deep and repeated plowing, **and sow not among thorns,** in not removing hypocrisy and other evil growths. V. 4. **Circumcise yourselves to the Lord and take away the foreskins of your heart,** the natural corruption which seriously interfered with the proper attitude toward the Lord, cp. Deut. 10, 16; 30, 6; Rom. 2, 29; Col. 2, 11, **ye men of Judah and inhabitants of Jerusalem,** a sincere repentance being required of all of them, **lest My fury come forth like fire and burn that none can quench it, because of the evil of your doings.** Just as the Lord required a circumcision of the heart in those days in addition to the circumcision of the body, so He insists upon the baptism with the Spirit in our days, lest we offend Him by insincerity.

DESCRIPTION OF THE JUDGMENT UNDER THREE EMBLEMS. — V. 5. **Declare ye in Judah,** announcing it, making it known widely, **and publish in Jerusalem and say, Blow ye the trumpet in the land,** as a signal calling the inhabitants to arms; **cry, gather together,** and say, rather, "cry fully," that is, with a loud voice, shouting, **Assemble yourselves and let us go into the defensed cities,** into their strongest fortresses. V. 6. **Set up the standard toward Zion,** raising their banners as a signal to make the city of God their refuge; **retire, stay not,** flee, do not try to make a stand! **For I will bring evil from the North and a great destruction,** namely, by the invasion of the enemy. V. 7. **The lion is come up from his thicket,** Nebuchadnezzar, like an angry lion, leaving his lair, Babylon, with his army of Chaldean soldiers, **and the destroyer of the Gentiles,** he who subdued many nations, **is on his way; he is gone forth from his place to make thy land desolate,** by ravaging it with fire and sword; **and thy cities shall be laid waste, without an inhabitant.** Cp. chap. 2, 15. V. 8. **For this,** on account of the impending destruction, **gird you with sackcloth,** the garment of deep mourning, **lament and howl; for the fierce anger of the Lord is not turned back from us.** Cp. Is. 9, 12. 17. 21. The people who had expected to return to the Lord on the basis of their hypocritical behavior, their feigned repentance, would find themselves sorely disappointed. V. 9. **And it shall come to pass at that day, saith the Lord,** at the time when this judgment would come upon Judah, **that the heart of the king shall perish,** the rulers whose position demanded that they devise means of defense would be utterly at a loss in this emergency, unable to provide help, **and the heart of the princes; and the priests shall be astonished,** amazed at the turn of events, **and the prophets shall wonder,** be filled with horror. So all the leaders are helpless and without presence of mind. V. 10. **Then said I, Ah, Lord God!** the prophet here recording the impression which the declaration of the Lord made upon him; **surely Thou hast greatly deceived this people and Jerusalem,** in permitting the false prophets to lead the people astray, willing as they were to be duped, **saying, Ye shall have peace,** that being the common assurance of the deceiving prophets, **whereas the sword reacheth unto the soul.** Cp. 1 Kings 22, 22. If people persist in opposing Him, the Lord finally delivers them to the certain consequences of such opposition and brings their punishment upon them in this manner. V. 11. **At that time,** when the judgment of the Lord will strike the idolaters, **shall it be said to this people and to Jerusalem,** the center of Jewish religious life, **A dry wind,** the simoom, or desert wind, with its destructive breath, **of the high places in the wilderness,** sweeping down from the high places and across the desert, **toward the daughter of My people,** the children of God's chosen nation, **not to fan nor to cleanse,** not the gentle breeze which ordinarily carried off the chaff as the threshed grain was winnowed. V. 12. **Even a full wind from those places,** more violent than any such light breezes, **shall come unto Me,** as the Lord's instrument for working His punishment; **now also will I give sentence against them,** passing judgment upon the idolaters and executing the same. V. 13. **Behold, he,** the enemy with his army, **shall come up as clouds,** those of sand and dust blown up by the tempest, **and his chariots shall be as a whirlwind; his horses are swifter than eagles,** in bringing destruction to the land of Israel. **Woe unto us! for we are spoiled,** thus the exclamations of the despairing Israelites are recorded. But the Lord has still another emblem of the expected judgment, which He proceeds to hold before the eyes of Judah and Jerusalem. V. 14. **O Jerusalem, wash thine heart from wickedness,** for a mere outward change of behavior is not sufficient, heart and mind and soul must undergo a complete transformation, **that thou mayest be saved,** for only he who truly repents may partake of the Lord's deliverance. **How long shall thy vain thoughts lodge within thee?** It was high time for all sinful thoughts to be dismissed. V. 15. **For a voice declareth from Dan,** in the extreme northern part of Canaan, where the advance of the enemy would be felt first, **and publisheth affliction from Mount Ephraim,** this being an evidence that the foe is coming nearer and nearer, and that there is great danger in delaying repentance. V. 16. **Make ye mention to the nations,** calling the attention of the neighbors to the Lord's judgment. **Behold, publish against Jerusalem that watchers come from a far country,** people who would witness the catastrophe upon Jerusalem, **and give out their voice against the cities of Judah,** in a shout of triumph or derision. V. 17. **As keepers of a field,** the men whose duty it was to frighten away wild animals from the cultivated land, lest they work harm, **are they against her round about,** as watchers who have surrounded a harmful animal and are making ready to dispatch it, **because she hath been rebellious against Me, saith the Lord.** This God further affirms by turning directly to Judah once more. V. 18. **Thy way and thy doings have procured these things unto thee,** she had only herself to blame if the punishment struck her with full force; **this is thy wickedness,** the fruit and consequence of her evil doing, **because it is bitter,** in its effect upon others as well as upon the sinners themselves, **because it reacheth unto thine heart,** inflicting deadly wounds. Such is ever the result of sin: sweet and attractive as it seems at first, it strikes deadly wounds, as the sinner usually finds out to his great regret.

THE DESOLATION FOLLOWING THE LORD'S JUDGMENT. — The prophet here, in a most dramatic manner, introduces Israel as lamenting over the calamity which has struck the nation. V. 19. **My bowels, my bowels!** the whole inner part of the man quaking with terror. **I am pained at my very heart!** or, I feel the pain of a severe cramp — the chambers of my heart! **My heart maketh a noise in me,** moaning with the severity of the affliction; **I cannot hold my peace because thou hast heard, O my soul, the sound of the trumpet, the alarm of war,** the shout of battle, as the enemy advances to subdue the land of Israel. V. 20. **Destruction upon destruction is cried,** blow upon blow is reported; **for the whole land is spoiled,** rendered desolate by the enemy; **suddenly are my tents spoiled and my curtains,** those out of which the tent was made, **in a moment,** in the twinkling of an eye. V. 21. **How long shall I see the standard,** the banner of the advancing enemy, **and hear the sound of the trumpet?** How long would this state of things continue? When would the reports of calamities and disasters cease? The answer of the Lord gives them the proper enlightenment. V. 22. **For My people is foolish,** without the right knowledge of God, **they have not known Me,** still more emphatic in the Hebrew, "Me have they not known"; **they are sottish children,** silly and unreasonable,

and they have none understanding, no discernment; **they are wise to do evil, but to do good they have no knowledge,** thereby showing themselves to be the opposite of the ideal held before men in Rom. 16, 19. V. 23. **I beheld the earth, and, lo, it was without form and void,** as in the beginning of creation, the prophet thus picturing the dismal waste which would follow the Chaldean invasion, **and the heavens, and they had no light;** here also a return to chaos. V. 24. **I beheld the mountains, and, lo, they trembled,** because the very foundations of the earth were moved, **and all the hills moved lightly,** as heavy bodies which shake with the slightest disturbance. V. 25. **I beheld, and, lo, there was no man,** the land itself was stripped of its inhabitants, **and all the birds of the heavens were fled,** preferring to shun the dead wastes beneath them. Note that this description presupposes the account of Genesis 1. V. 26. **I beheld, and, lo, the fruitful place was a wilderness,** Carmel, the part of Canaan renowned for its fertility, a desert, **and all the cities thereof were broken down,** sharing in the general devastation, **at the presence of the Lord,** whose sentence of judgment would thereby be carried out, **and by His fierce anger.** V. 27. **For thus hath the Lord said,** thus has Jehovah spoken, **The whole land shall be desolate,** be turned into a desert; **yet will I not make a full end,** He would not bring about a total annihilation at this time. V. 28. **For this shall the earth mourn,** lamenting on account of the desolations just described, which destroyed its fruitfulness, **and the heavens above be black,** wearing the garment of mourning, **because I have spoken it, I have purposed it,** the sentence as carried out rested upon His decree, **and will not repent, neither will I turn back from it,** the ruin had definitely been determined upon on account of the persistent transgressing of the people. V. 29. **The whole city,** or, "every city," all the cities of the land, **shall flee for the noise of the horsemen and bowmen,** as the invading army draws near; **they shall go into thickets,** their hiding-places, **and climb up upon the rocks,** seeking refuge before the attacking hordes; **every city shall be forsaken and not a man dwell therein.** Cp. Judg. 6, 2; 1 Sam. 13, 6. V. 30. **And when thou art spoiled,** rather, "But thou, O destroyed one," **what wilt thou do?** How escape the threatened destruction? **Though thou clothest thyself with crimson,** in garments of the most expensive material, **though thou deckest thee with ornaments of gold,** in decking herself for the purpose of coquetting with heathen nations, **though thou rentest thy face with painting,** applying antimony black to the eyelids, in order to increase the luster of the eyes, a custom still followed by harlots and vain women in the Orient and elsewhere, **in vain shalt thou make thyself fair,** all arts exercised to procure the aid of foreign nations would be useless; **thy lovers will despise thee,** no longer attracted by such artifices, **they will seek thy life.** V. 31. **For I have heard a voice as of a woman in travail and the anguish as of her that bringeth forth her first child,** heartrending wails and moans, **the voice of the daughter of Zion,** of the Lord's own chosen people, **that bewaileth herself, that spreadeth her hands, saying,** panting in her agony, **Woe is me now! for my soul is wearied because of murderers,** as one who yields to murderers, unable to withstand any longer. Such is the usual fate of men who disregard the warnings and pleadings of the Lord: when it is too late, they begin to mourn and lament, bewailing their fate. But as far as God is concerned, love is still with Him even in the might of His anger.

CHAPTER 5.

The Causes of the Threatened Judgments.

Lack of Truth and Faith in Public Life. V. 1. **Run ye to and fro through the streets of Jerusalem,** searching the lanes of the city, **and see now, and know, and seek in the broad places thereof,** in the wider streets and intersections of streets, where many people come together, **if ye can find a man, if there be any that executeth judgment,** carrying out justice and righteousness, **that seeketh the truth,** to possess and practise faithfulness in all intercourse with all his fellow-men, **and I will pardon it,** grant His pardon to the city. Jerusalem was so corrupt in those days that among all the leaders of the people, the counselors, the priests, the false prophets, not one just person was found, and therefore the attitude and the testimony of the faithful few, such as Baruch and Zephaniah, disappeared in the general depravity. V. 2. **And though they say,** in a form of assurance which had become habitual with them, even as with many thoughtless people in our days, **The Lord liveth, surely they swear falsely.** The oath under such circumstances had no validity, it was just as insincere as their profession of the worship of Jehovah. V. 3. **O Lord, are not Thine eyes upon the truth?** Does not Jehovah seek faithfulness and sincerity in all things? Is He not ever the God of truth? **Thou hast stricken them, but they have not grieved,** they do not feel the pain, the punishment makes no impression upon them; **Thou hast consumed them,** destroying them as a nation, **but they have refused to receive correction,** to accept the

Lord's discipline; **they have made their faces harder than a rock; they have refused to return.** Such is the perversity of deliberate wrong-doing that it hardens the heart of the sinner against every influence for good, producing such a degree of callousness that every effort of the Lord is vain. It is in such cases that His judgment of hardening the heart of the sinner is often enacted. V. 4. **Therefore I said, Surely these are poor,** the prophet here interrupting himself to voice an objection to the Lord; **they are foolish,** acting foolishly on account of their ignorance; **for they know not the way of the Lord nor the judgment of their God.** The prophet assumes that only the untaught poor are guilty of such depravity, and that a better state of affairs may be expected in the higher ranks of society. V. 5. **I will get me unto the great men,** those of the so-called higher classes, **and will speak unto them; for they have known the way of the Lord and the judgment of their God,** that is, Surely one might expect to find better knowledge among these people, considering their position. **But these have altogether broken the yoke and burst the bonds.** Matters were worse here than in the so-called lower class of people; for education, wealth, and rank alone are no guarantee against wickedness. The entire class had defiantly set aside the Law of God and despised the restrictions laid down in His holy will. V. 6. **Wherefore a lion out of the forest shall slay them and a wolf of the evenings,** one of those found in the great steppes and deserts, **shall spoil them, a leopard shall watch over their cities,** lurking for his prey near by, the strongest, the most ravenous, and the swiftest of the beasts of prey being chosen as types to represent the formidable character of the Babylonian invaders; **every one that goeth out thence shall be torn in pieces, because their transgressions are many, and their backslidings are increased,** their acts of rebellion against God had become a great multitude. That is the feature which ever makes sin so reprehensible: it always amounts to a rebellion against God, the Father of all mankind.

FAITHLESSNESS AND TREACHERY. —V. 7. **How shall I pardon thee for this?** It would obviously be inconsistent with God's holiness to overlook the transgressions of Israel, to let their wickedness go unpunished. **Thy children have forsaken Me and sworn by them that are no gods,** or, more emphatic, "by that which is no god," worshiping a creature of their own imagination. **When I had fed them to the full,** in distributing the blessings of His bounty, or, "I bound them by the oath of allegiance and loyalty," but **they then committed adultery,** transgressing the Sixth Commandment in the most flagrant manner, probably in connection with the idolatrous customs which they accepted, **and assembled themselves by troops in the harlots' houses,** rushing forward in companies in their eagerness to commit this beastly sin. V. 8. **They were as fed horses in the morning,** fat and dissolute stallions; **every one neighed after his neighbor's wife,** inflamed with sinful lust. V. 9. **Shall I not visit for these things,** punishing the guilty ones to the limit, **saith the Lord, and shall not my soul be avenged on such a nation as this?** How could His anger be withheld under such circumstances? The Lord therefore turns to the Chaldeans, calling upon them to carry out His punishment upon Israel. V. 10. **Go ye up upon her walls and destroy,** scaling them in a successful attack upon them; **but make not a full end,** so that Judah's existence would forever be at an end; **take away her battlements,** or, "hew off her branches," remove her tendrils, namely, the chief men of the nation, **for they are not the Lord's,** and therefore are altogether unprofitable. V. 11. **For the house of Israel and the house of Judah,** the entire nation of God's chosen people, **have dealt very treacherously against Me, saith the Lord,** their faithlessness being the Lord's chief reason for complaint. V. 12. **They have belied the Lord,** denying Jehovah, the God of the covenant, **and said, It is not He,** insisting that He was not the true and only God, **neither shall evil come upon us, neither shall we see sword nor famine,** thus both denying and challenging the threat of the Lord regarding the punishment which He had threatened for apostasy of every kind; v. 13. **and the prophets shall become wind,** their warnings, in the estimation of the scoffers, being nothing but idle threats, **and the Word is not in them,** the unbelieving rebels declaring that God did not speak through those prophets who rebuked their wickedness; **thus shall it be done unto them,** that is, their evil predictions would be fulfilled in no one but themselves. This attitude called for a most emphatic declaration on the part of Jehovah. V. 14. **Wherefore, thus saith the Lord God of hosts,** the mighty Captain of the heavenly armies, **Because ye speak this word, behold, I will make My words in thy mouth fire,** Jeremiah being given a sharp and scathing message to the rebellious people whom the Lord here puts far from Him, **and this people wood,** fuel which is easily kindled, **and it shall devour them,** they would be consumed as a consequence of the denunciation which Jeremiah would make by God's command. V. 15. **Lo, I will bring a nation upon you from far, O house of Israel, saith the Lord,** this being the specific manner in which His punishment of destruction would be carried out. **It is a mighty nation, it is an ancient nation,** one of great antiquity in history, a **nation whose language thou knowest not,** a factor which made the enemies all the more formidable, **neither understandest what they say.** The language spoken by the Chaldeans at that time was totally unlike that derived from any Semitic stem, but very much like ancient Persic. V. 16. **Their quiver is as an open sepulcher,** on account of the death-dealing arrows which it contained, **they are all mighty men,** distinguished for their strength and bravery. V. 17. **And they shall eat up thine harvest,** the standing grain, **and thy bread, which thy sons and thy daughters should eat,** which was intended for their food; **they shall eat up thy flocks and thine herds; they shall eat up thy vines and thy fig-trees,** everything that in any manner yielded food; **they shall impoverish thy fenced cities,** destroying all of Israel's proud fortresses, **wherein thou trustedst, with the sword.** V. 18. **Nevertheless, in those days,** when this severe punishment strikes the nation, **saith the Lord, I will not make a full end with you,** He would not yet bring total annihilation upon them. Thus the Lord is gracious and merciful and long-suffering, and abundant in goodness and truth, ever more ready to show kindness than to bring His punishment upon the guilty. It is a most powerful appeal to all men to heed the voice of His admonitions.

BLINDNESS OF HEART, INGRATITUDE, DECEIT, AND VIOLENCE. — V. 19. **And it shall come to pass, when ye shall say, Wherefore doeth the Lord, our God, all these things unto us?** when they finally reach the point that they make inquiry concerning the punishment striking them, **then shalt thou answer them, Like as ye have forsaken Me and served strange gods in your land,** in idolatrous worship, **so shall ye serve strangers in a land that is not yours.** Cp. Deut. 28, 47. 48. This was the Lord's retribution, which repaid the idolatrous people in kind. V. 20. **Declare this in the house of Jacob and publish it in Judah, saying,** for the benefit of the whole nation, v. 21. **Hear now this, O foolish people and without understanding,** lacking in spiritual insight, **which have eyes and see not, which have ears and hear not,** who are afflicted with spiritual blindness and dulness, who have hardened their hearts against every influence for good: v. 22. **Fear ye not Me? saith the Lord; will ye not tremble at My presence,** standing in awe and reverence before Him, **which have placed the sand for the bound of the sea,** defining the shore-line, **by a perpetual decree that it cannot pass it,** being held in check by the barriers erected by the Creator; **and though the waves thereof toss themselves,** in rage and fury, **yet can they not prevail; though they roar, yet can they not pass over it?** The immense body of the ocean with its turbulent waves, the wildest and most irresistible force of nature, is yet held in check by the power of the one true God; who, then, will not fear Him? V. 23. **But this people hath a revolting and rebellious heart,** not only apostate, but positively hostile to the Lord; **they are revolted,** breaking loose from their affiliation with the Lord, **and gone,** far away from Him who is the one Hope of their deliverance. V. 24. **Neither say they in their heart,** in repenting of their evil ways, **Let us now fear the Lord, our God, that giveth rain, both the former,** shortly after the crop has been sown, from October to December, **and the latter,** which falls before harvest, in March and April, **in his season; He reserveth unto us the appointed weeks of the harvest,** whence it follows that His goodness ought to lead men to repentance and to a proper fear of Him. V. 25. **Your iniquities have turned away these things,** the blessings of God's goodness, **and your sins have withholden good things from you,** acting as a barrier against the flow of God's gifts. V. 26. **For among My people are found wicked men,** evil and godless persons; **they lay wait,** they spend their time in lurking, **as he that setteth snares,** as fowlers crouch when laying their snares; **they set a trap, they catch men,** namely, for the purpose of destroying them. V. 27. **As a cage is full of birds, so are their houses full of deceit,** filled with treasures gained by fraud; **therefore they are become great and waxen rich,** their unrighteous wealth giving them a position of honor before the world. V. 28. **They are waxen fat,** from a life of laziness and indulgence, **they shine,** with the sleekness due to their luxurious living; **yea, they overpass the deeds of the wicked,** exceeding the ordinary measure of wickedness, as presented in the case of the Gentiles; **they judge not the cause,** they do not carry out the principles of right and justice, **the cause of the fatherless,** although the care of widows and orphans was especially enjoined in Scripture, **yet they prosper, and the right of the needy do they not judge,** they not only prosecute the fatherless, but they take no steps to defend the rights of the poor. Therefore the Lord once more asks His searching question, v. 29. **Shall I not visit for these things? saith the Lord? Shall not My soul be avenged on such a nation as this?** Cp. v. 9. V. 30. **A wonderful and horrible thing is committed in the land,** something fearful and horrible has happened, chap. 18, 13; 23, 14; Hos. 6, 10. V. 31. **The prophets prophesy falsely,** proclaiming lies, **and the priests bear rule by their means,** literally, "by their hands," that is, at their side, under the guidance of the false prophets, lording it over the people by such shady methods; **and My people love to have it so,** are altogether satisfied with such deception, their sound sense having left them to such an extent that they do not react against oppression and injustice; **and what will ye do in the end thereof?** Under such circumstances the judgment is inevitable, is bound to be the fatal issue of this sinful course; and who will be able to avert it? The attitude of the men of Noah's time and of people in every crisis of the world's history is found also in our days, in spite of the earnest warning which the Lord issues in so many passages of the Bible. Cp. 1 Cor. 10, 1—13; 2 Pet. 3, 5—10.

CHAPTER 6.

The Judgment is Firmly Decided Upon.

THE ADVICE TO FLEE FROM JERUSALEM. — V. 1. **O ye children of Benjamin,** here addresssed particularly because Jerusalem was situated on the border of their territory and because Jeremiah wanted to appeal especially to the members of his own tribe in the capital city, **gather yourselves to flee out of the midst of Jerusalem,** to escape the impending doom, **and blow the trumpet in Tekoa,** the birthplace of the prophet Amos, south of Jerusalem, the signal being intended to call the people together for flight, **and set up a sign of fire,** as a warning of approaching danger, **in Beth-haccerem,** another village south of Jerusalem, situated on a lofty hill; **for evil appeareth out of the North,** with the invading armies of the Chaldeans, **and great destruction.** Since the enemy was approaching from the North, the inhabitants of Jerusalem and the surrounding country would naturally flee toward the south. After this warning call the prophet describes the situation in Judah. V. 2. **I have likened the daughter of Zion to a comely and delicate woman,** literally, "The comely and delicate one! I destroy the daughter of Zion," laying waste the city and the entire country, as a rich and luxuriant meadow is laid waste by senseless cropping. V. 3. **The shepherds with their flocks shall come unto her,** the hostile armies under their cruel generals; **they shall pitch their tents against her round about; they shall feed every one in his place,** ruthlessly pasturing and treading down the territory which he occupies. The invaders are now pictured as encouraging one another in the attack upon Jerusalem. V. 4. **Prepare ye war against her,** literally, "sanctify war," the reference being to the solemn ceremonies with which a campaign of war was opened; **arise and let us go up at noon,** their zeal to attack being so great that even the unfavorable hour of noon could not detain them. **Woe unto us! for the day goeth away, for the shadows of the evening are stretched out,** and they fear that the approach of night will suspend their operations against Judah and Jerusalem. But even so they will not permit this fact to interfere with their assault, since they cry out: v. 5. **Arise and let us go by night,** in spite of the night and all unfavorable circumstances, **and let us destroy her palaces,** all her lofty buildings including her fortifications. V. 6. **For thus hath the Lord of hosts said,** either the prophet or the enemies inserting this statement in explanation of the assault made on Jerusalem, **Hew ye down trees and cast a mount against Jerusalem,** constructing breastworks for the siege. **This is the city to be visited,** where punishment is well applied; **she is wholly oppression in the midst of her,** literally, "she is altogether violence in her inside," wherefore she is altogether to be punished. V. 7. **As a fountain casteth out her waters,** a well causing its water to flow in a steady and uninterrupted quantity, **so she casteth out her wickedness,** which springs forth in a steady stream; **violence and spoil,** injustice and plunder, **is heard in her,** because she was given to these forms of wickedness; **before Me,** namely, Jehovah, **continually is grief and wounds,** so that He is a witness of their acts of violence and is deeply offended by their wickedness. V. 8. **Be thou instructed, O Jerusalem,** so the Lord addresses her in a tender appeal, **lest My soul depart from thee,** unwilling as His love is to take this step, **lest I make thee desolate, a land not inhabited,** this warning being repeated here once more, in order to cause her to return to her senses. An appeal of this kind may often be a means of preventing the misery and ruin of a sinful people.

THE PROPHET VOICES THE FURY OF THE LORD. — V. 9. **Thus saith the Lord of hosts, They,** namely, the invaders whose approach was here prophesied, **shall thoroughly glean the remnant of Israel as a vine,** not hastily nor superficially, but with the greatest thoroughness, as the divine judgment is ever executed. **Turn back thine hand as a grape-gatherer into the baskets,** going back to the vines again and again in order to get even the last of the berries, said of the repeated invasions of the Chaldeans, at each of which they carried away captives to Babylon. V. 10. **To whom shall I speak and give warning,** so the prophet now voices his objection, **that they may hear?** Of what use is all remonstrance under such circumstances? **Behold, their ear is uncircumcised,** closed against all admonitions by their own carnal-mindedness, **and they cannot hearken,** owing to the hardness of their hearts, brought on by their stubborn opposition. **Behold, the Word of the Lord is unto them a reproach,** a mockery and a derision; **they have no delight in it.** V. 11. **Therefore I am full of**

the fury of the Lord, so that its abundance must voice itself, like a stream overflowing its banks; **I am weary with holding in,** restraint was no longer a virtue; **I will pour it out upon the children abroad,** those playing in the streets and lanes, **and upon the assembly of young men together; for even the husband with the wife shall be taken, the aged,** the one who is just growing old, **with him that is full of days.** Thus the sentence of the Lord would strike all classes of people and every age without exception, the whole nation being included in the outpouring of His wrath. V. 12. **And their houses shall be turned unto others,** transferred to them as the spoils of war, **with their fields and wives together.** Cp. Deut. 28, 30; **for I will stretch out My hand upon the inhabitants of the land, saith the Lord,** namely, for the purpose of chastising them. V. 13. **For from the least of them even unto the greatest of them,** all classes of people, those of no influence as well as the powerful and mighty, **every one is given to covetousness,** the love of money suppressing every good intention, every laudable pupose; **and from the prophet even unto the priest,** the very leaders and teachers of the people, **every one dealeth falsely,** practising falsehood and deception. V. 14. **They have healed also the hurt of the daughter of My people slightly,** touching upon the faults and transgressions of the body politic in a superficial manner only, **saying, Peace, peace! when there is no peace.** The prophets and priests, the leaders of the people, who were, by God's command, the watchmen of the nation, ignored this duty in the interest of their own selfishness. Instead of exposing the evils, the wickedness, and idolatry of the people, they glossed over the conditions, treating the ulcerous growths of the body politic as insignificant bruises, after the manner of similar weak characters the world over. V. 15. **Were they ashamed when they had committed abomination?** rather, "They are put to shame because they have wrought abominable things." **Nay, they were not at all ashamed, neither could they blush;** they were devoid of all sense of decency, of all feeling of shame. **Therefore they shall fall among them that fall,** with the rest of the people that are doomed to destruction; **at the time that I visit them they shall be cast down, saith the Lord.** Words having proved unavailing, the Lord will now execute His vengeance in deeds which will bring home the lessons which He intended to convey. The false leaders of any Church will deceive only themselves if they hope to escape the wrath which will strike the people under their care due to their own defection in attending to their duty.

THE IMPENDING JUDGMENT ANNOUNCED. — V. 16. **Thus saith the Lord,** rather, "Thus has Jehovah spoken," namely, in the ancient days, when He had shown the children of His chosen people the way of salvation, **Stand ye in the ways and see,** looking around on all sides, **and ask for the old paths,** diligently inquiring for the paths traveled in ancient times, **where is the good way,** the path of salvation, **and walk therein, and ye shall find rest for your souls,** a secure resting-place, with protection from all injury. The picture is taken from the predicament of travelers who have lost the right road and are now anxiously inquiring for the path from which they have wandered. **But they said, We will not walk therein,** the Jews stubbornly and rebelliously refused to walk the way of salvation pointed out to them by Jehovah. V. 17. **Also I set watchmen over you,** seers and prophets, whose duty it was to point out threatening calamities to the people and thus to lead them to repentance, **saying, Hearken to the sound of the trumpet,** which was blown for the purpose of rallying the children of Israel around the banner of the true God. **But they said, We will not hearken,** thus rejecting in the most stubborn fashion even the last warning of Jehovah. V. 18. **Therefore hear, ye nations,** the Gentile people everywhere, **and know, O congregation,** either the entire assembly of the nations which are here summoned, or the faithful few in Israel who still formed the Church of Jehovah, **what is among them,** what punishment the Lord is about to inflict. And the prophet now addresses himself to a still greater circle of witnesses. V. 19. **Hear, O earth! Behold, I,** Jehovah Himself, as He brings out with emphasis, **will bring evil upon this people, even the fruit of their thoughts,** the result of their counsels, the consequence of their evil scheming, **because they have not hearkened unto My words nor to My Law, but rejected it.** V. 20. **To what purpose cometh there to Me incense from Sheba,** that from the coasts and islands of Southern Arabia, **and the sweet cane,** the calamus, **from a far country?** the root of which was used in the preparation of the anointing-oil. All external worship without faith of the heart and the obedience of love is an abomination to the Lord, who hates sham and hypocrisy in every form. Cp. Is. 1, 11; Amos 5, 21. **Your burnt offerings are not acceptable nor your sacrifices sweet unto Me,** because the Lord was not deceived by outward appearances which were not in agreement with the true condition of the heart. V. 21. **Therefore, thus saith the Lord, Behold, I will lay stumbling-blocks before this people,** the devices of the enemies which would bring about their ruin, **and the fathers and the sons together,** both being equally guilty, **shall fall upon them; the neighbor and his friend shall perish,** all the people without exception being doomed to feel Jehovah's sentence on account of the depravity which was so generally prevalent. V. 22. **Thus saith the Lord, Behold, a people cometh from the north country, and a great nation shall be raised from the sides of the earth,** from its remotest regions, the expression being vague in agreement with the indefinite geographical notions to be found among the Jews at that time. The Chaldean hordes, of course, are meant. V. 23. **They shall lay hold on bow and spear,** as weapons of offense, of powerful attack; **they are cruel and have no mercy,** giving no quarter, determined on merciless extinction; **their voice roareth like the sea,** in their angry or triumphant battle-cry; **and they ride upon horses, set in array as men for war,** fitted out most perfectly for the planned invasion, **against thee, O daughter of Zion,** against Jerusalem and the land of Judah. V. 24. **We have heard the fame thereof,** the report which was spread about their prowess, **our hands wax feeble,** sinking down without a show of resistance; **anguish hath taken hold of us and pain as of a woman in travail.** V. 25. **Go not forth into the field,** in venturing outside of the walls of Jerusalem, **nor walk by the way,** along the roads of Judah; **for the sword of the enemy and fear is on every side.** All these facts are set forth as the basis of another appeal. V. 26. **O daughter of My people,** the nation which the Lord has chosen for His own, **gird thee with sackcloth,** the garment of repentance, **and wallow thyself in ashes,** in an excess of sorrow and grief; **make thee mourning, as for an only son, most bitter lamentation,** such as was expressed by beating the breast; **for the spoiler shall suddenly come upon us.** V. 27. **I have set thee for a tower and a fortress among My people,** literally, "as a prover," or explorer, and an assayer, one who separates the metal from the dross, **that thou mayest know and try their way,** testing it out for truth and solid worth. V. 28. **They are all grievous revolters,** mutineers and betrayers in the highest degree, **walking with slanders,** deliberately seeking opportunities to indulge in slandering and reviling others; **they are brass and iron,** debased and hardened in their opposition to the Lord; **they are all corrupters,** having only destruction in mind. The prophet continues his figure of the base metals. V. 29. **The bellows are burned,** in the long process which was intended to purify the people and produce some amount of gold, **the lead is consumed of the fire,** or, "out of its fire comes lead," instead of the precious metal which the Lord had a right to expect; **the founder melteth in vain,** there were no such results as one might have expected; **for the wicked are not plucked away,** the great mass of the people are dross, worthless metal. V. 30. **Reprobate silver shall men call them,** silver so thoroughly mixed with the baser metals as to be worthless for all ordinary purposes, **because the Lord hath rejected them.** All those whom the Lord has tried in the oven of His test, whom He has found wanting in the qualities which should be found in a true believer, will finally be cast out as base metal.

CHAPTER 7.

A Warning against False Confidence and Hypocritical Worship.

GOD'S REQUIREMENT AND PROMISE. — V. 1. **The word that came to Jeremiah from the Lord,** the fact that he received his messages by inspiration of God being brought out time and again, **saying,** v. 2. **Stand in the gate of the Lord's house,** very likely that which led from the outer court to the Court of Israel, **and proclaim there this word,** where the worshiping multitudes from the entire country might hear him, **and say, Hear the word of the Lord, all ye of Judah, that enter in at these gates to worship the Lord.** The address seems to indicate that the sermon here recorded was held at one of the great festivals of the Jews, when great throngs visited the capital and the Temple. V. 3. **Thus saith the Lord of hosts, the God of Israel,** He whose power and mercy the children of Israel had so often experienced, **Amend your ways and your doings,** their habits of living and the individual acts of their life, **and I will cause you to dwell in this place,** permitting them to continue their residence in Jerusalem, the seat of the Lord's Temple. V. 4. **Trust ye not in lying words,** in those words of falsehood which were so often dinned in their ears by their wicked leaders, **The Temple of the Lord, the Temple of the Lord, the Temple of the Lord, are these!** the various buildings making up the entire Temple. The repetition of the proud cry is intended to picture the sublime self-assurance of the people under the leadership of the false prophets. V. 5. **For if ye throughly amend your ways and your doings,** making a decided stand for a behavior in complete accordance with the holy will of God; **if ye throughly execute judgment between a man and his neighbor,** so that justice is exercised in all conditions of life, toward all men; v. 6. **if ye oppress not the stranger, the fatherless, and the widow,** the three points which were emphasized time and again in the Law of God, **and shed not innocent blood in this place,** throughout Jerusalem and Judah, **neither walk after other gods to your hurt,** idolatry invariably challenging the punishment of the Lord, provoking Him to righteous anger: v. 7. **then will I cause you to dwell in this place**, permitting them to continue as inhabitants of Jerusalem and Judah, **in the land that I gave your fathers, forever and ever**, for a long period of uninterrupted possession. The Lord is eager to show His kindness and mercy to all those who will hearken to Him; His blessings, also in temporal goods, are upon those that fear Him.

THE WARNING EXAMPLE OF SHILOH. — V. 8. **Behold, ye trust in lying words**, those of the false prophets, the hypocritical leaders, **that cannot profit**, which brought only harm and the curse upon them. V. 9. **Will ye steal, murder, and commit adultery, and swear falsely, and burn incense unto Baal**, the chief idol of the heathen nations round about, **and walk after other gods whom ye know not**, who have never manifested and proved themselves as the true God did, by His words and works, v. 10. **and come and stand before Me in this house**, in brazen hypocrisy, cp. Ezek. 23, 39, **which is called by My name, and say, We are delivered to do all these abominations?** They believed that, in spite of the threats announced by the prophet, they had nothing to fear, that the calamities which Jeremiah insisted were impending would not strike them, that their hypocritical behavior would have no evil consequences. But the Lord has His rejoinder ready. V. 11. **Is this house, which is called by My name**, the Temple where Jehovah revealed Himself, **become a den of robbers in your eyes?** a place where they feel safe with their loot, a refuge where they hope to plan further abominations. **Behold, even I have seen it, saith the Lord**, namely, the fact that this abuse of the Temple is taking place. V. 12. **But go ye now unto My place which was in Shiloh, where I set My name at the first**, namely, when the Tabernacle was erected there, Deut. 12, 11; Josh. 18, 1, **and see what I did to it for the wickedness of My people Israel.** Because the northern nation persisted in its idolatrous practises, the Lord not only took away the Tabernacle from Shiloh, but He also brought a complete destruction upon the entire country of the ten tribes. This fact is intended as an example of warning to Judah. V. 13. **And now, because ye have done all these works, saith the Lord**, becoming guilty of the various forms of wickedness which He has enumerated in His reproofs, **and I spake unto you, rising up early**, in His earnest zeal for their welfare, **and speaking, but ye heard not, and I called you, but ye answered not**, being wilfully disobedient and stubborn, v. 14. **therefore will I do unto this house, which is called by My name, wherein ye trust**, placing their confidence in the external building, **and unto the place which I gave to you and to your fathers, as I have done to Shiloh.** As the Lord had ceased to dwell in the midst of the disobedient Israelites, when He took from them His sanctuary, so He would cease to dwell at Jerusalem. V. 15. **And I will cast you out of My sight**, completely disowning them, **as I have cast out all your brethren**, descendants of the same forefather, Abraham, **even the whole seed of Ephraim**, the ten tribes. The evidences of the goodness of the Lord are intended at all times to lead men to repentance.

THE IDOLATRY AND DISOBEDIENCE OF THE JEWS. — V. 16. **Therefore pray not thou for this people**, the Lord expressly forbidding the prophet to make intercession for the reprobate nation, **neither lift up cry nor prayer for them, neither make intercession to Me; for I will not hear thee.** As strong as the prayers of the righteous are in holding back the wrath of God, the time will come when they are unavailing, due to the hardness of men's hearts, which provokes the punishment of the Lord. V. 17. **Seest thou not what they do in the cities of Judah and in the streets of Jerusalem?** The wickedness which Jeremiah was obliged to witness wherever he looked was bound to convince him that the course of the Lord was right, that He was fully justified in rejecting all prayers made in behalf of the apostate Jews. The extent of their idolatry is now described. V. 18. **The children gather wood, and the fathers kindle the fire, and the women knead their dough to make cakes to the queen of heaven**, the female goddess Ashtoreth, or Astarte, the counterpart of the male idol Baal, in whose honor the cakes, made of honey, fine flour, and other ingredients, bore a round, flat surface to resemble the disk of the moon, **and to pour out drink-offerings**, the libations made as sacrifices, **unto other gods that they may provoke Me to anger**, the expression implying design on their part, the deliberate intention to arouse His wrath. V. 19. **Do they provoke Me to anger? saith the Lord.** Do they truly believe that they can aggrieve Him by such acts? Will they reduce the bliss which He enjoys? **Do they not provoke themselves**, bringing grief and sorrow upon their own heads, **to the confusion of their own faces?** That is ever the consequence of sin: the perfect blessedness of God is not reduced by man's transgression, but his own peace of mind is disturbed, and he loads grief and sorrow upon himself. V. 20. **Therefore, thus saith the Lord God**, Jehovah, the All-powerful: **Behold, Mine anger and My fury shall be poured out upon this place**, upon Jerusalem, as the center of His nation and from there over the entire land, **upon man, and upon beast**, on the cattle owned by them, **and upon the trees of the field, and upon the fruit of the ground**, that resulting from its tilling by the hand of man; **and it,** the fury of the Lord, **shall burn and shall not be quenched,** the very irrational and inanimate creation being included in the Lord's punishment, in order to strike terror to the heart of men. V. 21. **Thus saith the Lord of hosts, the God of Israel,** still the Lord of those who are truly His Israel, His people, but who here addresses the apostate nation: **Put your burnt offerings unto your sacrifices,** the former, which were required to be wholly burned, being mingled with the latter, of which only parts were placed on the altar of burnt offerings, **and eat flesh.** It is a cry of disgust: So far as I am concerned, you may treat the one the same as the other; they are both equally loathsome to Me, since I despise your entire worship. V. 22. **For I spake not unto your fathers nor commanded them in the day that I brought them out of the land of Egypt concerning burnt offerings or sacrifices,** it was not His object to establish a mere external worship without true piety of the heart, v. 23. **but this thing commanded I them, saying, Obey My voice, and I will be your God, and ye shall be My people,** that being the fundamental principle upon which the entire relation between God and Israel was built up, **and walk ye in all the ways that I have commanded you that it may be well unto you.** All the Jewish rites and ceremonies presupposed faith and obedience on the part of the people. God required no sacrifice, unless it was the outgrowth of obedience grounded in faith. The actual claims of the Moral Law always preceded the ordinances pertaining to the outward form of worship. Cp. 1 Sam. 15, 22. V. 24. **But they hearkened not,** they ignored the Lord and His precepts entirely, **nor inclined their ear,** they did not even attempt to listen, **but walked in the counsels and in the imagination,** the stubbornness, **of their evil heart and went backward and not forward,** literally, "they were to the back and not to the face," that is, they turned their backs to the Lord. V. 25. **Since the day that your fathers came forth out of the land of Egypt unto this day,** beginning with Moses, the servant of Jehovah, **I have even sent unto you all My servants, the prophets, daily rising up early and sending them,** with unremitting diligence and eager kindliness; v. 26. **yet they hearkened not unto Me nor inclined their ear, but hardened their neck,** like a stubborn ox under the yoke, Deut. 31, 27; **they did worse than their fathers,** the later generations, particularly that now addressed, being much farther removed from the true service of Jehovah than the generation of the Exodus. V. 27. **Therefore thou shalt speak all these words unto them, but they will not hearken to thee,** Jeremiah would have as little success as the other prophets had had; **thou shalt also call unto them, but they will not answer thee,** being utterly indifferent to the Word of the Lord. V. 28. **But thou shalt say unto them, This is a nation that obeyeth not the voice of the Lord, their God,** being therefore classed with the Gentile nations, **nor receiveth correction,** hardened to the point that all rebukes make no impression upon them; **truth is perished,** all reliability, all fidelity is lost, **and is cut off from their mouth.** There is a fine bit of sarcasm in this phrase, for the Jews confessed the Lord with their mouths only, and not with their hearts. The use of God's name for the purpose of mouth-worship only is a flagrant offense against the Second Commandment and is bound to bring down the wrath of God upon the offenders.

THE JUDGMENT PRONOUNCED. — V. 29. **Cut off thine hair, O Jerusalem,** shearing it off as the sign of the deepest mourning, Jerusalem here being considered a virgin consecrated to the Lord, **and cast it away and take up a lamentation on high places,** on account of the uncleanness and desecration of her guilt; **for the Lord hath rejected and forsaken the generation of His wrath,** the people against whom His indignation has been aroused, against whom His anger is burning. V. 30. **For the children of Judah have done evil in My sight, saith the Lord,** things which are loathsome before His eyes; **they have set their abominations,** altars for the host of heaven and graven images of various idols, 2 Kings 21, 4—7, **in the house which is called by My name to pollute it.** Cp. chap. 32, 34. V. 31. **And they have built the high places of Tophet,** idolatrous altars with their sanctuaries at this point, **which is in the Valley of the Son of Hinnom,** southwest of Jerusalem, **to burn their sons and their daughters in the fire,** in the terrible child sacrifices made in honor of Moloch; **which I commanded them not, neither came it into My heart,** He had not even thought of permitting such abominations, much less of sanctioning them, His prohibibtion being strictly against such practises. Cp. Deut. 17, 3; 12, 31. V. 32. **Therefore, behold, the days come, saith the Lord, that it shall no more be called Tophet, nor the Valley of the Son of Hinnom,** or Ben-hinnom, **but the Valley of Slaughter,** a name applied to it as the result of the great number of burials of Jews slaughtered in the siege of the city; **for they shall bury in Tophet till there be no place,** all available space being occupied by the graves of the fallen. V. 33. **And the carcasses of this people shall be meat for the fowls of the heaven,** the birds of prey, particularly the buzzards, feeding on the unburied corpses, **and for the beasts of the earth, and none shall fray them away,** no person being present then to frighten them away from their loathsome repast. V. 34. **Then will I cause** to cease from the cities of **Judah and from the streets of Jerusalem the voice of mirth and the voice of gladness, the voice of the bridegroom and the voice of the bride,** the reference being made to the joyous processions in the Orient in which the bride and the bridegroom are led through the streets, accompanied by bands of musicians and singers; **for the land shall be desolate.** So completely was the punishment of the Lord carried out upon reprobate Judah for having rejected Him and His mercy.

CHAPTER 8.

The Calamity of the Jews on Account of Their Persistent Impenitence.

RETRIBUTION UPON THE JEWS. — V. 1. **At that time, saith the Lord,** namely, when the sentence of God upon Jerusalem would be carried into effect, **they shall bring out the bones of the kings of Judah, and the bones of his princes, and the bones of the priests, and the bones of the prophets,** of all the rulers and leaders of the people, **and the bones of the inhabitants of Jerusalem out of their graves,** the Babylonians defiling even the resting-places of the dead in carrying out the judgment upon Judah; v. 2. **and they shall spread them before the sun and the moon and all the host of heaven,** exposing them under the open sky to the influence of these heavenly bodies, **whom they have loved, and whom they have served, and after whom they have walked, and whom they have sought, and whom they have worshiped,** the many synonyms serving to bring out the accumulation of their idolatrous practises, the extremity of the foolish zeal with which they worshiped the host of heaven. **They shall not be gathered nor be buried; they shall be for dung upon the face of the earth,** the decomposing flesh and the skeletons serving as fertilizer of the fields. But the lot of the survivors would be still worse. V. 3. **And death shall be chosen rather than life by all the residue of them that remain of this evil family, which remain in all the places whither I have driven them, saith the Lord of hosts,** literally, "shall prefer death to life in all places of the survivors whither I have driven them, saith Jehovah Sabaoth," the people in exile and captivity among the heathen being thus called to repentance even now.

THE JEWS PERSIST IN WICKEDNESS. — V. 4. **Moreover, thou shalt say unto them, Thus saith the Lord, Shall they fall and not arise? Shall he turn away and not return?** or, "Shall a man fall and not get up again? Shall one wander off and not return to the right path?" It is a natural instinct and inclination of men to get up after a fall, to search for the right path if one has lost his way. V. 5. **Why, then, is this people of Jerusalem slidden back by a perpetual backsliding?** Why do they persist so obstinately in their perverse ways? **They hold fast deceit,** clinging to their hypocritical behavior, **they refuse to return,** they stubbornly cling to the error of their ways. V. 6. **I hearkened and heard,** listening carefully for some evidence of repentance, **but they spake not aright,** they were far from confessing any wrong on their part; **no man repented him of his wickedness, saying, What have I done?** aghast at the evidences of his guilt. **Every one turned to his course,** to his own wicked ways, **as the horse rusheth into the battle,** with a mad impetuousness which cannot be restrained. V. 7. **Yea, the stork in the heaven knoweth her appointed times,** the regular migration seasons; **and the turtle,** that is, the turtle-dove, **and the crane and the swallow observe the time of their coming,** returning with unfailing certainty from their winter quarters to their summer homes; **but My people,** those whom the Lord had originally chosen to be His children, **know not the judgment of the Lord,** thus showing less understanding than the irrational birds. Cp. Is. 1, 3. V. 8. **How do ye say, We are wise, and the Law of the Lord is with us?** They prided themselves upon their possessing the Law, Rom. 2, 17; but this fact alone served rather to emphasize their dead orthodoxy, since they ignored the very teachings which they so emphatically proclaimed. **Lo, certainly in vain made He it; the pen of the scribes is in vain,** the false teachers, who spread their lies with word of mouth and pen, were spreading falsehood, even while they professed to be zealous for the truth. Their false pen converted the Law of God into a lie, just as the false teachers of all times have done. V. 9. **The wise men are ashamed,** put to shame and reproach, **they are dismayed,** confounded, **and taken. Lo, they have rejected the Word of the Lord, and what wisdom is in them?** Having despised and set aside the only norm of doctrine and life, the only source of true wisdom, they could not lay claim to any kind of knowledge and understanding any more, they were fools in the sight of God. V. 10. **Therefore,** on account of the wickedness thus shown by the false teachers, **will I give their wives unto others and their fields to them that shall inherit them; for every one, from the least even unto the greatest, is given to covetousness; from the prophet even unto the priest every one dealeth falsely.** V. 11. **For they have healed the hurt of the daughter of**

My people slightly, saying, Peace, peace! when there is no peace. V. 12. **Were they ashamed when they had committed abomination? Nay, they were not at all ashamed, neither could they blush; therefore shall they fall among them that fall, in the time of their visitation they shall be cast down, saith the Lord.** Cp. chap. 6, 12—15. The punishment of the Lord will ever strike the false teachers, if not here in time, then at the Last Judgment.

Further Description of the Impending Punishment. — V. 13. **I will surely consume them, saith the Lord,** making a clean sweep of them all; **there shall be no grapes on the vine nor figs on the fig-tree,** both of these plants representing unfruitful Israel, **and the leaf shall fade.** As it had been at the time of Isaiah, Is. 5, 2, and as it later was at the time of Christ, Matt. 21, 19, so it was emphatically stated of Israel in the last years before the Chaldean invasion that the Lord was deeply disappointed in the fruit which He expected of the people as such. **And the things that I have given them shall pass away from them,** rather, "I will give them to those who shall overrun them," overwhelming and subduing them in the invasion which was here predicted. V. 14. **Why do we sit still?** So the prophet hears the people of Judah cry out in view of the impending calamity. **Assemble yourselves,** so they are represented as urging one another, **and let us enter into the defensed cities,** seeking security behind their buttressed walls, **and let us be silent there,** to perish after but a little respite; **for the Lord, our God, hath put us to silence,** having definitely determined their destruction, **and given us water of gall to drink,** a poisonous draught, which would surely result in their extermination, **because we have sinned against the Lord,** a realization which came to them when it was too late. V. 15. **We looked for peace,** still expecting deliverance, **but no good came,** their hope of blessing being utterly vain; **and for a time of health,** when healing would come to them, **and behold trouble!** So all the promises of the false prophets upon which the people had depended were found to be vain. V. 16. **The snorting of his,** the invader's, **horses was heard from Dan,** on the extreme northern border of Canaan, the prophet here seeing the Chaldean hordes advancing to subdue the country; **the whole land trembled at the sound of the neighing of his strong ones,** of the proud chargers of the Chaldean cavalry; **for they are come and have devoured the land and all that is in it,** the food and the treasures and everything of value, **the city and those that dwell therein.** V. 17. **For, behold, I will send serpents, cockatrices, among you,** reptiles of a most poisonous kind, **which will not be charmed,** rendered harmless by soothing music, **and they shall bite you, saith the Lord.** The Chaldeans are here represented as cruel and destructive enemies, whose power no means could counteract. With this fate of his beloved nation before his eyes, the prophet breaks forth in a bitter lamentation. V. 18. **When I would comfort myself against sorrow, my heart is faint in me,** literally, "O my exhilaration in sorrow! My heart very ill!" His sorrow was so great that he despaired of finding consolation. He hears the bitter complaint of his people, v. 19. **Behold the voice of the cry of the daughter of My people because of them that dwell in a far country,** a lament from the people in exile in distant lands: **Is not the Lord in Zion? Is not her King in her?** namely, to deliver His people from their captivity and to lead them back to Jerusalem. But the divine justice asks in turn, **Why have they provoked Me to anger with their graven images and with strange vanities,** with foreign gods? so that He was compelled, as it were, to carry out His punishment upon them. V. 20. **The harvest is past,** so the people continue to lament, **the summer is ended, and we are not saved.** As the farmer who expects a good harvest and is disappointed sees only failure and ruin before his eyes, so Israel despaired of deliverance. V. 21. **For the hurt of the daughter of my people am I hurt,** so the prophet once more cries out in bitter grief; **I am black,** deeply sad and mournful, his face expressing dark despair; **astonishment hath taken hold on me,** a horror and dread of the ultimate consequences. V. 22. **Is there no balm in Gilead?** the reference being to a balsam which was in wide use in the Orient for the cooling and healing of wounds. **Is there no physician there?** Because this balsam, found chiefly in the country east of Jordan, drawn from the terebinth-tree and similar plants, was considered so very healthful, many persons established themselves in that territory and practised the profession of physician. But for the wound of the daughter of Zion no physician of the body was sufficient. **Why, then, is not the health of the daughter of My people recovered?** Why could not the healing of her illness proceed? For the wounds of the soul, for the illness of sin, there is no healing except by the Word of God's grace.

CHAPTER 9.

Jeremiah's Lament for the Foolishness of the Jews and Their Punishment.

THE DECEIT OF THE PEOPLE.—V. 1. **Oh, that my head were waters**, an inexhaustible reservoir, **and mine eyes a fountain of tears**, flowing in an endless stream, **that I might weep day and night for the slain of the daughter of my people**, those who have become victims of their own foolishness in transgressing the Law of the Lord. Although the apostate Jews had fully deserved the punishment which came upon them, the prophet was still filled with deep compassion for them. At the same time his feeling of right and duty causes him to draw back in horror from every contact with them. V. 2. **Oh, that I had in the wilderness**, far from the wicked capital and the haunts of men, **a lodging-place of wayfaring men**, a traveling lodge or caravansary, such as are found in the Orient, **that I might leave my people and go from them!** He preferred the loneliness and filth of a desert dwelling to the companionship of his own people, who had forsaken the Lord. **For they be all adulterers, an assembly of treacherous men**, who practise falsehood and deceit. V. 3. **And they bend their tongues like their bow for lies**, so that lies are the arrows which they send to their mark, **but they are not valiant for the truth upon the earth**, they do not make adequate and proper use of fidelity in their dealings with others; **for they proceed from evil to evil and they know not Me, saith the Lord**, one wickedness being heaped upon the other. Therefore the Lord issues His warning in the form of a command: v. 4. **Take ye heed every one of his neighbor**, even of those who profess to be friends, **and trust ye not in any brother**, the very ties of blood-relationship being insufficient to withstand the general perfidy; **for every brother will utterly supplant**, literally, "trip up by the heel," cp. Gen. 27, 36, **and every neighbor will walk with slanders**, go about for tale-bearing. Cp. Micah 7, 5. 6. V. 5. **And they will deceive every one his neighbor**, over-reaching him, trying to get the advantage of him, **and will not speak the truth; they have taught their tongue to speak lies**, the tongue, as it were, being almost compelled, as though unwilling to become guilty of so much wickedness, **and weary themselves to commit iniquity**, going to much pains to that end, for sin is a hard master. V. 6. **Thine habitation is in the midst of deceit**, so God tells Jeremiah in characterizing the entire nation; **through deceit they refuse to know Me, saith the Lord**, their ignorance of Jehovah being wilful and obstinate. V. 7. **Therefore, thus saith the Lord of hosts**, the mighty ruler of the heavenly armies, **Behold, I will melt them and try them**, test them in the fire of tribulation, as the refiner tests metals in his furnace; **for how shall I do for the daughter of My people?** There is nothing remaining for Jehovah to do but this. V. 8. **Their tongue is as an arrow shot out**, a sharp and deadly missile; **it speaketh deceit**, that being the burden of the Lord's complaint throughout this passage; **one speaketh peaceably to his neighbor with his mouth**, professing nothing but kindness and good will for him, **but in heart he layeth his wait**, setting his ambush to harm and kill his neighbor. V. 9. **Shall I not visit them for these things? saith the Lord**, letting His punishment come upon them for their treacherous and deceitful behavior. **Shall not My soul be avenged on such a nation as this?** Cp. chap. 5, 9. 29. God's righteousness and holiness demand that He visit the iniquity of wilful sinners upon them.

THE DESOLATION OF THE LAND.—V. 10. **For the mountains will I take up a weeping and wailing**, the prophet once more taking up his lament, **and for the habitations of the wilderness**, for the pastures of the steppes, **a lamentation because they are burned up**, singed by the sun's excessive heat, no one remaining to tend and to irrigate them, **so that none can pass through them**, much less inhabit them; **neither can men hear the voice of the cattle**, their contented lowing in luscious pastures; **both the fowl of the heavens and the beast are fled; they are gone**, the land being deserted by every form of life. Upon this complaint Jehovah answers. V. 11. **(And) I will make Jerusalem heaps**, a shapeless ruin, **and a den of dragons**, or jackals; **and I will make the cities of Judah desolate, without an inhabitant**, the standing expression for the very height of desolation. The application of the prophet now follows. V. 12. **Who is the wise man that may understand this?** Who will heed and apply this lesson, this warning, in a proper manner? **And who is he to whom the mouth of the Lord hath spoken that he may declare it**, explain it to his countrymen, **for what the land perisheth and is burned up like a wilderness that none passeth through?** Evidently there is not one who possesses this divine wisdom. V. 13. **And the Lord said**, in answering the question which has just been proposed, **Because they have forsaken My Law which I set before them and have not obeyed My voice**, the message brought by the true prophets, **neither walked therein**, not making the Word of the Lord their one rule of life, v. 14. **but have walked after the imagination of their own heart**, following their own sinful desires in all the acts of their lives, **and after Baalim**, the idols of the heathen, **which their fathers taught them**, whose idolatry they made their own, thus becoming guilty of the same transgressions:

v. 15. **therefore thus saith the Lord of hosts, the God of Israel,** the almighty and only God, **Behold, I will feed them, even this people, with wormwood,** a bitter and poisonous food, **and give them water of gall to drink,** poison-water, cp. chap. 8, 14. V. 16. **I will scatter them also among the heathen,** in shameful captivity and exile, **whom neither they nor their fathers have known,** as an adequate punishment for their transgression; **and I will send a sword after them till I have consumed them,** a large number of them thus being destroyed, especially among those who sought the shelter of Egypt, against the warning of God. Cp. chap. 44, 27. V. 17. **Thus saith the Lord of hosts, Consider ye and call for the mourning women,** those hired to give expression to their grief by plaintive cries and a general mournful behavior, found also in the New Testament, Matt. 9, 23, **that they may come, and send for cunning women that they may come,** for those most skilful in lamentation were required in this instance; v. 18. **and let them make haste and take up a wailing for us,** for the whole nation of Judah, **that our eyes may run down with tears and our eyelids gush out with waters,** in the strongest expression of excessive sorrow. V. 19. **For a voice of wailing is heard out of Zion,** in a lamentation over the city's pitiful fate, but without a true repentance of the heart, **How are we spoiled,** laid waste by the enemy! **We are greatly confounded,** heaped with shame and disgrace, **because we have forsaken the land,** having been compelled to leave it, **because our dwellings have cast us out,** or, "because the enemy has driven us out." V. 20. **Yet hear the word of the Lord, O ye women, and let your ear receive the word of His mouth,** in ready obedience to the suggestion which He here makes, **and teach your daughters wailing and every one her neighbor lamentation,** so that the older generation of mourning women might quickly be replaced, and that there might always be a sufficient number of professional mourners in view of the coming slaughter. V. 21. **For death is come up into our windows,** unexpectedly, stealthily, like a thief in the night, **and is entered into our palaces,** for the soldiers of the invading army, finding the doors barred, would gain admission through openings which are not so firmly barred, **to cut off the children from without,** those playing out in the streets and in the open places, **and the young men from the streets.** Thus death would take its harvest both in the houses and outside, in the streets and market-places. V. 22. **Speak,** this being addressed to the prophet, in continuing the command of verse 20, **Thus saith the Lord, Even the carcasses of men shall fall as dung upon the open field,** there to rot away, **and as the handful after the harvestman,** the grain ready to be gathered into sheaves, **and none shall gather them,** there would be neither a gathering of the bundles nor the labor of gleaners to take care of this grain. The words imply utter destruction, an utter casting aside on the part of Jehovah.

THE WAY OF ESCAPE REJECTED. — V. 23. **Thus saith the Lord,** in once more picturing to the apostate Jews the one way of salvation, **Let not the wise man glory in his wisdom,** as though that were sufficient to bring him redemption, **neither let the mighty man glory in his might,** trusting in his strength and power to deliver him, **let not the rich man glory in his riches,** as though they could protect him from the threatening destruction, v. 24. **but let him that glorieth glory in this,** make this fact the one and only foundation of his boasting, **that he understandeth and knoweth Me,** that he has learned to know the true God, the Triune God and the Father of our Lord and Savior Jesus Christ, the one Messiah of the world, **that I am the Lord which exercise loving-kindness,** His grace and mercy occupying first place in His attitude over against us, **judgment, and righteousness,** in the expression of His holiness and faithfulness in His Word, whether in reward or in punishment, **in the earth,** in His entire relation toward mankind; **for in these things I delight, saith the Lord,** He Himself is active in exercising His bliss in them, and He is anxious to have His children and all men walk in them. V. 25. **Behold, the days come, saith the Lord, that I will punish all them which are circumcised with the uncircumcised,** literally, "every circumcision in foreskin," that is, He would visit in anger all men whose heart was not turned to Him in the true obedience of faith, whether they had submitted to the rite of circumcision or not: v. 26. **Egypt, and Judah, and Edom, and the children of Ammon, and Moab,** the Jews with all the nations surrounding them, **and all that are in the utmost corners, that dwell in the wilderness,** literally, "all having their hair," that is, their beard, "clipped at the corners," a custom in use among the heathen nations, but expressly forbidden to the Israelites, Lev. 19, 27; 21, 5; **for all these nations are uncircumcised,** they had not accepted the rite by which the Jews were distinguished as the chosen people of the Lord under the covenant made with the patriarchs, **and all the house of Israel are uncircumcised in the heart,** that is, in their case the outward observance of the formerly significant rite had lost its meaning, since they had not turned to the Lord in true repentance. Without such change of heart the rite of acceptance into the outward membership in Israel was of no avail, just as the Sacrament of Baptism has no value in the case of those who do not believe. A mere outward observance of the customs of religion will not bring men to true fellowship with the Lord.

CHAPTER 10.

A Warning against Idolatry.

THE NOTHINGNESS OF IDOLS. — V. 1. **Hear ye the word which the Lord speaketh unto you, O house of Israel!** those who now survived as the representatives of the former great nation. V. 2. **Thus saith the Lord, Learn not the way of the heathen,** in becoming accustomed to their idolatrous worship, **and be not dismayed at the signs of heaven,** filled with the fear which caused the Gentile nations to associate various perils with the movements of comets, with the occurrence of eclipses, and other phenomena; **for the heathen are dismayed at them,** since they revered supernatural powers in the various constellations. This warning is now further substantiated by a description of idolatrous customs. V. 3. **For the customs of the people are vain,** literally, "the precepts of the nations," what they fix for people to follow, "are breath, nothingness"; **for one cutteth a tree out of the forest,** literally, "for wood is it," that is what the object of their worship amounts to, "hewn out of the forest," **the work of the hands of the workman, with the ax.** That is a fair sample of the objects of worship chosen by the heathen — a log felled in the woods and fashioned by an ax. V. 4. **They deck it with silver and with gold,** with ornaments of precious metals; **they fasten it with nails and with hammers that it move not,** for that is the only way in which the idol, supposed to be a god, can retain his upright position. V. 5. **They,** the idols, **are upright as the palm-tree,** they are like a statue of turned work, resembling a palm-tree, **but speak not,** Ps. 115, 5, for all their possessing a mouth; **they must needs be borne, carried about from one place to another, because they cannot go,** they are unable to walk. **Be not afraid of them,** standing in awe of any power which they are said to possess; **for they cannot do evil,** they can do no one any harm, **neither also is it in them to do good,** they cannot bring blessings or benefits upon any of their worshipers, since they are simply dead. Cp. Is. 41, 7—10. 23. V. 6. **Forasmuch as there is none like unto Thee, O Lord,** literally, "not a particle of anything," this being the strongest possible denial of any power in any other god besides Jehovah; **Thou art great, and Thy name is great in might,** His essence is made known in works of His almighty power. V. 7. **Who would not fear Thee, O King of nations? For to Thee doth it appertain,** to Him alone does it properly pertain, namely, that He is to be feared, is to be respected and revered by all men, **forasmuch as among all the wise men of the nations and in all their kingdoms there is none like unto Thee.** No matter where a person searches for a god who might stand a comparison with Jehovah, the quest will be useless: He alone is the one becoming object of worship. V. 8. **But they are altogether brutish and foolish,** the heathen are all alike in their stupidity, they have sunk to the level of brutes because they have severed their connection with the true God; **the stock is a doctrine of vanities,** or, "the instruction of vanities is — wood"; the very idols from whom, according to their lights, they hope to receive instruction are wood and therefore unable to give understanding. V. 9. **Silver spread into plates is brought from Tarshish,** from Tartessus in Spain, whose gold mines were well known in the ancient world, **and gold from Uphaz,** or Ophir, 1 Kings 9, 27, **the work of the workman,** beaten into the form of a thin covering by the goldsmith, **and of the hands of the founder,** the artist in precious metals; **blue and purple is their clothing,** made of the finest cloth, Ex. 25, 4; **they are all the work of cunning men,** of craftsmen possessing a very high degree of skill. The thought evidently is this: No matter how the idolaters strive to give their statues the semblance of living and mighty beings by ornamenting them in this fashion, they still remain idols and cannot be elevated to the position of gods. V. 10. **But the Lord,** Jehovah, the covenant God, **is the true God,** His whole essence being truth over against the nothingness of the idols, **and an everlasting King,** Ruler of the universe forever; **at His wrath the earth shall tremble,** shrinking back in terror before His living wrath, **and the nations shall not be able to abide His indignation,** to endure even the smallest expression of His anger. V. 11. **Thus shall ye say unto them,** the Jews being given an argument in the very tongue of Aramaic idolaters who were trying to seduce them to commit idolatry, **The gods that have not made the heavens and the earth,** those upon whom the heathen relied in their foolishness, **even they shall perish from the earth,** disappear into nothingness, **and from under these heavens.** The import, then, of the Lord's warning is this: not only should the Jews feel no fear of the heathen idols, but they should declare to the Gentiles that their supposed gods would soon be forgotten. Over against the weakness and nothingness of the heathen idols the almighty power of the one true God is now once more proclaimed, v. 12. **He hath made the earth by His power, He hath established the world by His wisdom,** Ps. 136, 5. 6; 93, 1, **and hath stretched out the heavens by His discretion,** spreading out the firmament by His unlimited skill and understanding. V. 13. **When He uttereth His voice,** when He causes it to thunder, **there is a multitude of waters in the heavens,** or, "a heaving of waters in the heavens," as the clouds come rolling along in heavy masses, **and He caus-**

eth the vapors to ascend from the ends of the earth, to form the clouds of the storm; He maketh lightnings with rain and bringeth forth the wind out of His treasures, out of His storehouses. Thus thunder, lightning, clouds, rain, and storm are named as evidences of Jehovah's almighty powers in the tempest. V. 14. **Every man is brutish in his knowledge,** they are all stupid in their skill and understanding, as they fashion their idols; **every founder is confounded by the graven image,** every artist who makes idols is put to shame by the work of his own hands; **for his molten image is falsehood,** their casting, what they fashion, is a lie, **and there is no breath in them,** they lack all evidence of life. V. 15. **They are vanity,** a vapor, nothingness, **and the work of errors,** of deceit and mockery, causing their worshipers to be mocked and derided when the nothingness of the idols becomes evident; **in the time of their visitation they shall perish,** that is, when God shall punish the idol-worshipers, the idols themselves shall likewise perish. V. 16. **The Portion of Jacob is not like them,** that is, Jehovah, the Portion of the true Church forever, does not in any way resemble the dead idols against which He warns His people; **for He is the Former of all things,** the Fashioner of the universe, **and Israel is the rod of His inheritance,** the tribe or nation which He has chosen as His possession. **"The Lord of hosts" is His name,** He alone is the almighty God, to whom the armies of the heavens, the angels and all the heavenly host, are subject, the Lord and Ruler of the whole world from everlasting to everlasting.

THE PROPHET'S LAMENTATION AND PRAYER. V. 17. **Gather up thy wares out of the land, O inhabitant of the fortress,** literally, "Collect thy bundle from the earth, thou that sittest in the distress of the siege," the summons being issued to the entire nation of the Jews, in preparation for their being led into exile. V. 18. **For thus saith the Lord, Behold, I will sling out the inhabitants of the land at this once,** both the suddenness and the violence of their removal to Babylon being brought out, **and will distress them,** bring them into dire straits, **that they may find it so,** feel and experience the bitterness of His oppression. V. 19. **Woe is me for my hurt!** so the prophet cries out in the name of Judah, bewailing its calamity. **My wound is grievous,** incurable! **But I said, Truly, this is a grief,** the desolation of the land and the captivity of the people being the suffering which Judah now had to endure, **and I must bear it.** This is a yielding to the inevitable, not a frank declaration of guilt. V. 20. **My tabernacle is spoiled, and all my cords are broken,** the picture being that of a tent which is being ruined, due to the fact that its guy-ropes are torn, all setting forth the desolation of the land; **my children are gone forth of me, and they are not,** this bereavement being the height of Judah's visitation on the part of the Lord; **there is none to stretch forth my tent any more and to set up my curtains,** the reference being to the pitching of the tent by extending and coupling its individual covers, a further description of the desolation of the land. V. 21. **For the pastors,** the rulers and leaders of the people, **are become brutish,** gone down to the level of irrational beasts, **and have not sought the Lord,** this fact explaining their growing stupidity; **therefore they shall not prosper,** they could not rule or effect any reforms with the proper wisdom, **and all their flocks shall be scattered,** their subjects dispersed in exile. V. 22. **Behold, the noise of the bruit is come,** the report that the threatened invasion is about to begin, **and a great commotion out of the north country,** the tumult of an advancing army, **to make the cities of Judah desolate and a den of dragons,** a habitation of jackals. With this situation facing Judah, the prophet utters a prayer in the name of the congregation. V. 23. **O Lord, I know that the way of man is not in himself,** it is not in the power of any person to determine his way and manner of living nor the trend of his life's vicissitudes; **it is not in man that walketh to direct his steps.** The heart of man plans his way, but the Lord directs it; man proposes, but God disposes. V. 24. **O Lord, correct me, but with judgment,** with a moderation guided by the exact demands of the case, in order to lead the repentant sinner on the way of righteousness; **not in Thine anger,** as in the case of obstinate sinners, **lest Thou bring me to nothing.** V. 25. **Pour out Thy fury upon the heathen that know Thee not,** although they are now God's instruments in the punishment of Israel, **and upon the families that call not on Thy name,** all the nations which have joined hands against Israel; **for they have eaten up Jacob and devoured him and consumed him,** the heaping of synonyms picturing the intense hatred with which they set about to destroy the Lord's people, **and have made his habitation desolate.** Believers will at all times humble themselves under the chastisement of the Lord, trusting firmly that He intends not their destruction, but their salvation.

CHAPTER 11.

The Faithlessness of Judah and Its Consequences.

REMINDER OF THE COVENANT BETWEEN JEHOVAH AND HIS PEOPLE. — V. 1. **The word that came to Jeremiah from the Lord,** an express message from Jehovah, the God of the covenant, **saying,** v. 2. **Hear ye the words of this covenant,** hearkening to them in willing obedience, **and speak unto the men of Judah and to the inhabitants of Jerusalem,** Jeremiah here being reminded of the duty which was incumbent upon all prophets of the Lord, v. 3. **and say unto them,** in calling to remembrance the awful curse found in the books of Moses, in the proclamation of the covenant, **Thus saith the Lord God of Israel, Cursed be the man that obeyeth not the words of this covenant,** Deut. 27, 26, v. 4. **which I commanded your fathers in the day that I brought them forth out of the land of Egypt, from the iron furnace,** Egypt being called thus on account of the severe afflictions which came upon the children of Israel during the last period of their sojourn there, cp. Deut. 4, 20, **saying, Obey My voice and do them,** namely, the words of the covenant, **according to all which I command you; so shall ye be My people, and I will be your God,** cp. Deut. 29, 12; Ex. 6, 7; Lev. 26, 12; Deut. 7, 6, v. 5. **that I may perform the oath which I have sworn unto your fathers,** the special promises given to Abraham, Isaac, and Jacob, Deut. 7, 8, **to give them a land flowing with milk and honey, as it is this day,** this beautiful and rich land being still in the possession of the children of Judah. **Then answered I,** after the manner of the people when they pronounced the will of the Lord antiphonally, Deut. 27, 15—22, **and said, So be it, O Lord,** literally, "Amen, Jehovah." V. 6. **Then the Lord said unto me, Proclaim all these words in the cities of Judah and in the streets of Jerusalem,** on a journey through the entire country, but especially in the capital city, **saying, Hear ye the words of this covenant,** of the Law as it was originally proclaimed and still remained in force, **and do them,** for it is not a mere external hearing of His Word which satisfies the Lord, but only the acceptance of faith and a consequent doing of His will. V. 7. **For I earnestly protested unto your fathers in the day that I brought them up out of the land of Egypt,** when the covenant of Mount Sinai was made, **even unto this day, rising early and protesting,** with all zeal and vehemence, **saying, Obey My voice.** Cp. Deut. 30, 19; Ps. 50, 7. V. 8. **Yet they obeyed not nor inclined their ear,** did not even make an attempt to give heed, **but walked every one in the imagination of their evil heart,** in wicked stubbornness; **therefore I will bring upon them all the words of this covenant,** all the punishments threatened to the transgressors in the special curses pronounced in the proclamation of the Law, **which I commanded them to do, but they did them not.** The Lord is ever ready to show long-suffering and loving-kindness, but in the end He is bound to punish the obstinate transgressors of His holy will.

ISRAEL'S CONSPIRACY AGAINST THE LORD AND ITS PUNISHMENT. — V. 9. **And the Lord said unto me, A conspiracy is found among the men of Judah and among the inhabitants of Jerusalem,** a plot in opposition to Jehovah and to the demands of right and duty, the entire nation being involved in this wickedness. V. 10. **They are turned back to the iniquities of their forefathers,** by which Israelites of the former generations heaped guilt upon themselves, **which refused to hear My words,** deliberately combining to deny Him obedience in His just demands; **and they went after other gods to serve them,** this sin of idolatry being the Lord's chief charge against them; **the house of Israel,** the ten tribes of the northern kingdom, **and the house of Judah,** the southern kingdom, **have broken My covenant which I made with their fathers,** Judah thus being destined to a similar punishment as that which befell Israel. V. 11. **Therefore, thus saith the Lord,** Jehovah, the same God of the covenant who was still seeking His children with the same loving-kindness as of old, **Behold, I will bring evil upon them which they shall not be able to escape,** from which also no deliverance is possible; **and though they shall cry unto Me, I will not hearken unto them,** refusing them assistance and redemption, since their time of grace had now expired. V. 12. **Then shall the cities of Judah,** that is, their people, **and inhabitants of Jerusalem go and cry unto the gods unto whom they offer incense,** the idols whom they have worshiped; **but they,** the false gods in whom they professed to trust, **shall not save them at all in the time of their trouble,** since, of course, they were utterly unable to do so, being but dead images, who could not deliver in any calamity. V. 13. **For according to the number of thy cities were thy gods, O Judah,** pactically a different idol for every city; **and according to the number of the streets of Jerusalem have ye set up altars,** a different one for every open place, **to that shameful thing,** to the idol which is the essence of all that is shameful and will bring confusion upon all who persist in worshiping it, **even altars to burn incense unto Baal,** this idol being the chief abomination of the Canaanite nations since remote times. The Lord, having thus set forth the obstinate wickedness of the people of Judah, turns to His prophet with the command that he should not interfere with His just punishment upon the apostate nation. V. 14. **Therefore pray not thou for this people, neither lift up a cry or prayer for them,** any supplication asking deliverance for them; **for I will not hear them,** He would pay no attention to the prophet's intercession, **in the time that they cry unto Me for their trouble,** on account of the calamity which has befallen them. Moreover, the Lord also resents the hypocritical worship of the people. V. 15. **What hath My beloved to do in Mine house,** the congregation making a pretense at seeking Him in true worship, **seeing she hath wrought lewdness with many,** having become guilty of spiritual adultery in its most revolting form, **and the holy flesh is passed from thee?** The Lord calls their worship an enormity, because it was, in truth, a hollow mockery, with which they deceived none but themselves. **When thou doest evil, then thou rejoicest.** The entire second part of the verse may be rendered: "Will vows and holy flesh take thy calamity from thee? Then mayest thou exult!" All the religious customs upon which they relied could not protect them. If they were sincere in their worship, then there would be reason for congratulating themselves. V. 16. **The Lord called thy name "A green olive-tree," fair and of goodly fruit,** thus He had regarded Israel in the days when He chose it for His own; **with the noise of a great tumult,** amid the rattling of thunder or the noise of battle, **He hath kindled fire upon it,** to destroy the very plant which He formerly cherished so dearly, **and the branches of it are broken,** ten tribes of the original nation having already been taken away into captivity and the tree thus badly crippled. V. 17. **For the Lord of hosts, that planted thee, hath pronounced evil against thee,** being firmly determined upon punishing the apostate nation, **for the evil of the house of Israel and of the house of Judah which they have done against themselves,** to their own hurt, **to provoke Me to anger in offering incense unto Baal.** Jeremiah now notes a proof of the incorrigible nature of the people of his own nation. V. 18. **And the Lord hath given me knowledge of it, and I know it,** their wickedness was revealed to him; **then Thou showedst me their doings.** Even this, however, had not disturbed Jeremiah's trustfulness. V. 19. **But I was like a lamb or an ox that is brought to the slaughter,** with never an inkling of the evil intention of his own familiar friends; **and I knew not that they had devised devices against me, saying, Let us destroy the tree with the fruit thereof and let us cut him off from the land of the living that his name may be no more remembered.** They wanted to bring ruin, if possible, death, to Jeremiah and cause his teaching to be forgotten. Therefore the prophet calls upon the Lord for vengeance in his just cause. V. 20. **But, O Lord of hosts, that judgest righteously, that triest the reins and the heart,** testing the inmost thoughts of man; **let me see Thy vengeance on them,** for it is He whose honor is principally at stake; **for unto Thee have I revealed my cause,** laying the whole matter before Him for adjustment. V. 21. **Therefore, thus saith the Lord of the men of Anathoth,** Jeremiah's own townsmen, **that seek thy life, saying, Prophesy not in the name of the Lord, that thou die not by our hand,** this being the demand which they placed before him; v. 22. **therefore, thus saith the Lord of hosts, Behold, I will punish them,** for daring to threaten the life of His servant; **the young men shall die by the sword,** being cut down by the enemy in battle, **their sons and their daughters shall die by famine,** the result of the unmerciful siege begun by the enemies. V. 23. **And there shall be no remnant of them,** the Lord being determined to carry out His sentence of extermination upon them; **for I will bring evil upon the men of Anathoth, even the year of their visitation.** Thus the punishment of the Lord descends upon the evil-doers in due time, often with terrible effect.

CHAPTER 12.

The Prophet's Complaint and the Lord's Answer.

THE CONSPIRACY IN THE PROPHET'S OWN FAMILY.—V. 1. **Righteous art Thou, O Lord,** maintaining justice, **when I plead with Thee,** when he brings his case to the Lord's attention; **yet let me talk with Thee of Thy judgments,** reasoning with Jehovah concerning a matter which seems incompatible with divine righteousness: **Wherefore doth the way of the wicked prosper?** Why is it that they seem to be fortunate in all their dealings? **Wherefore are all they happy that deal very treacherously?** How may the fact be explained that the very ones who are guilty of the worst perfidy, who practise the basest knavery, live in peace? The same question occasionally rises in the hearts of most children of God, and it is safe to be always armed with the firm conviction that the ways of the Lord are ever right and good. V. 2. **Thou hast planted them, yea, they have taken root,** apparently secure in their places, safe in their happiness; **they grow, yea, they bring forth fruit,** what they undertake is crowned with rich success. **Thou art**

near in their mouth, they are very active in lip-service, **and far from their reins,** their hearts are far from Him. Cp. Is. 29, 13; Matt. 15, 8. V. 3. **But Thou, O Lord, knowest me,** the prophet freely leaving the judgment regarding himself to the Searcher of hearts, secure in the testimony of a good conscience; **Thou hast seen me and tried mine heart toward Thee,** wherefore he freely invites a scrutiny on the part of the Lord. By the same token he can call upon the Lord to bring punishment upon the evil-doers: **Pull them out like sheep for the slaughter,** with violence, as though torn out by the roots, **and prepare them for the day of slaughter,** as animals set apart for sacrifice. V. 4. **How long shall the land mourn and the herbs of every field,** of the entire cultivated plain, **wither? For the wickedness of them that dwell therein the beasts are consumed and the birds,** the very irrational brutes being placed under the ban of Jehovah on account of the hypocrisy of their masters, **because they said, He shall not see our last end,** the wicked Jews trying to persuade themselves that the Lord is blind toward their wickedness, that they may pursue their ungodly ways without interference, safe from the calamity which Jeremiah had threatened. But the Lord answers in such a way as to rebuke the prophet in a gentle manner for the impatience displayed by him, at the same time pointing out that he is due to experience still greater tribulations. V. 5. **If thou hast run with the footmen and they have wearied thee, then how canst thou contend with horses?** If he could not endure the comparatively little trouble which had come upon him till now, he would assuredly never be able to stand the great sufferings which would come to him in the future. **And if in the land of peace, wherein thou trustedst, they wearied thee, then how wilt thou do in the swelling of Jordan?** literally, "And in a land of peace thou wast secure, how wilt thou do along the wooded banks of Jordan?" The comparison is between an inhabited district, with its comparative security, and a country of primitive forests and undergrowth, where wild animals abounded, the application being the same as in the first part of the verse. V. 6. **For even thy brethren and the house of thy father, even they have dealt treacherously with thee,** his very closest relatives practising perfidy against the prophet; **yea, they have called a multitude after thee,** pursuing him after the manner of a pack of dogs. **Believe them not though they speak fair words unto thee.** Thus the Lord warns His servant against hypocrisy and coming tribulation, at the same time intimating that the wickedness of the people had not yet reached its highest stage. But eventually the judgment would strike them.

ISRAEL SPOILED BY THE ENEMIES. — V. 7. **I have forsaken Mine house,** so the Lord tells His prophet, **I have left Mine heritage,** repudiating His chosen people, in the midst of whom He had established, and hoped to maintain, His Church; **I have given the dearly beloved of My soul into the hand of her enemies,** this being said of the exile with which He intended to punish His disobedient people. V. 8. **Mine heritage is unto Me as a lion in the forest,** presuming to rise up against Him like a beast of prey; **it crieth out against Me,** roaring with hatred and rage, **therefore have I hated it,** His former love having departed from it on account of its obstinate opposition to His will. V. 9. **Mine heritage is unto Me as a speckled bird,** a bird of prey with its plumage striped brown and gray, or an albino; **the birds round about are against her,** pouncing upon such a bird in either case with the greatest rage. **Come ye, assemble all the beasts of the field; come to devour!** The whole sentence may also be rendered in the form of a question stating the situation as it actually was found when the heathen nations began their attacks upon Judah. V. 10. **Many pastors,** the very ones who were expected to give the Church the proper spiritual care, **have destroyed My vineyard; they,** together with the heathen kings and their hordes, **have trodden My portion,** His particular property, **under foot; they have made My pleasant portion,** the land and the people of His desire, **a desolate wilderness.** Cp. chap. 3, 19. V. 11. **They have made it desolate,** practically an uninhabited desert, **and being desolate, it mourneth unto Me,** making a lament of sadness over the punishment which had come upon it. **The whole land is made desolate because no man layeth it to heart,** there had been none to turn to the Lord in true repentance. V. 12. **The spoilers are come upon all high places through the wilderness,** appearing on the heights of the steppes throughout the land; **for the sword of the Lord,** the war which the Lord would send upon Judah as a just punishment, **shall devour from the one end of the land even to the other end of the land; no flesh,** in this case the entire sinful population of Judah, **shall have peace,** no section of the country would be excepted in the general affliction. V. 13. **They,** the people of Judah, **have sown wheat,** they have undertaken many things in the pride of their hearts, **but shall reap thorns,** the very opposite of what they expected; **they have put themselves to pain,** exhausting their strength and almost tormenting themselves in the endeavor to gain their proud ends, **but shall not profit,** not getting the results which they had anticipated; **and they shall be ashamed of your revenues,** in the small amounts which they actually produced, **because of the fierce anger of the Lord,** who would not permit their proud plans to mature. God resists the proud, but gives grace to the humble.

THE LORD'S ANSWER. — V. 14. **Thus saith the Lord against all Mine evil neighbors, that touch the inheritance which I have caused My people Israel to inherit,** laying their hands upon the Land of Promise: **Behold, I will pluck them out of their land,** causing them also to be led away into captivity, **and pluck out the house of Judah from among them,** restoring them once more to the land promised to their fathers. V. 15. **And it shall come to pass after that I have plucked them out,** the heathen nations, **I will return and have compassion on them,** showing mercy also to these children of the Gentiles, giving evidence of the fact that He is the Savior of all men, **and will bring them again, every man to his heritage and every man to his land,** the return of the Lord's own people being assumed as a matter of course, preceding that of the heathen to their country. V. 16. **And it shall come to pass, if they will diligently learn the ways of My people,** the true and only religion, **to swear by My name, "The Lord liveth,"** this being one of the chief manifestations of religious life in those days, **as they taught My people to swear by Baal, then shall they be built in the midst of My people,** being added to the Church of the living God. V. 17. **But if they will not obey,** if they refuse to heed God's message of salvation, **I will utterly pluck up and destroy that nation, saith the Lord;** for sin is a reproach to any people and will be treated accordingly by the just God. The passage clearly has a Messianic trend, referring to that period of time when people from every nation would find their way into the Church of Christ.

CHAPTER 13.

The Pride of Judah Rebuked.

THE SYMBOL OF THE GIRDLE. — V. 1. **Thus saith the Lord unto me,** in bidding the prophet perform an act of symbolic significance, **Go and get thee a linen girdle,** a very important article of apparel in those days, since it held the garments together and enabled a person to stride forward without hindrance, **and put it upon thy loins, and put it not in water,** thus using it and taking good care of it. V. 2. **So I got a girdle according to the word of the Lord and put it on my loins,** wearing it for some time. V. 3. **And the word of the Lord came unto me the second time, saying,** v. 4. **Take the girdle that thou hast got, which is upon thy loins,** soiled now on account of the wear to which it was put, **and arise, go to Euphrates,** the great river which had formerly formed the extreme northeastern boundary of the united kingdom and the western boundary of Mesopotamia, **and hide it there in a hole of the rock,** in a cleft of the hills near the riverbank. V. 5. **So I went and hid it by Euphrates, as the Lord commanded me.** V. 6. **And it came to pass after many days,** after a considerable period of time had elapsed, **that the Lord said unto me, Arise, go to Euphrates, and take the girdle from thence which I commanded thee to hide there,** the Lord's purpose concerning it having meanwhile been accomplished. V. 7. **Then I went to Euphrates,** making the long journey a second time, to bring out its significance with greater emphasis, **and digged,** opening up the cleft in the rock, **and took the girdle from the place where I had hid it; and, behold, the girdle was marred,** its soiled condition having hastened the process of rotting, **it was profitable for nothing,** it could no longer be used as an article of apparel. V. 8. **Then the word of the Lord came unto me, saying,** v. 9. **Thus saith the Lord, After this manner will I mar the pride of Judah and the great pride of Jerusalem.** This is in agreement with Lev. 26, 36. 39, where the fate of the unbelievers is pictured as a destruction in the land of the enemies, as a pining away in their iniquity; for although a remnant of Judah returned to the Land of Promise, the nation as such had disintegrated during the period of the Exile and never recovered its ancient standing. V. 10. **This evil people, which refuse to hear My words, which walk in the imagination of their heart,** in deliberate stubbornness, **and walk after other gods, to serve them and to worship them,** in that most reprehensible sin of all, in wilful idolatry, **shall even be as this girdle, which is good for nothing.** V. 11. **For as the girdle cleaveth to the loins of a man, so have I caused to cleave unto Me the whole house of Israel and the whole house of Judah, saith the Lord,** in the wonderful fellowship wherewith Jehovah had joined Israel and Judah to Himself by reason of the covenant of Sinai, **that they might be unto Me for a people,** His own peculiar nation, **and for a name,** an object of glory, **and for a praise, and for a glory,** for a rich ornament to His majesty. **But they would not hear,** wherefore the punishment of the Lord came upon them in the manner here set forth; for His threats will certainly be fufilled, just as His promises are.

AN EXHORTATION WITH REGARD TO THE IMPENDING DESTRUCTION. — V. 12. **Therefore thou shalt speak unto them this word, Thus**

saith the Lord God of Israel, Every bottle shall be filled with wine, the point of comparison in this instance being the fact that the purpose of the pitchers was fulfilled when they were filled with wine, but that they at the same time were very fragile. **And they shall say unto thee, Do we not certainly know that every bottle shall be filled with wine?** This statement, as their surprised tone would suggest, offered no particularly new thing or an unusual phenomenon. V. 13. **Then shalt thou say unto them,** in explaining to them what seemed so absolutely self-evident, **Thus saith the Lord, Behold, I will fill all the inhabitants of this land,** who in this case are regarded as the pitcher, **even the kings that sit upon David's throne, and the priests, and the prophets, and all the inhabitants of Jerusalem,** the careful enumeration serving to increase the emphasis of the Lord's statement, **with drunkenness.** As wine brings on a state of intoxication, so the effect of God's wrath and judgments upon the entire nation would be to reduce all its members to a state of helpless distraction, which would cause them to rush to their own ruin. V. 14. **And I will dash them one against another, like a potter's vessel, even the fathers and the sons together, saith the Lord,** the older generation perishing with the younger, since both are in the same condemnation; **I will not pity, nor spare, nor have mercy,** the synonyms again being heaped in this case to place the greater stress upon the warning of the Lord, since He will not draw back His hand once He has begun to punish, but destroy them. It is a historical fact that the internal disruption of the Jewish nation was an important factor in hastening the destruction of their kingdom. V. 15. **Hear ye and give ear,** paying close attention to the Lord's warning; **be not proud,** chiefly in disregarding the rebuke of Jehovah, **for the Lord hath spoken.** V. 16. **Give glory to the Lord, your God,** to Him who has given abundant evidence of His godhead and of His loving-kindness to Judah, **before He cause darkness,** bringing misfortune upon His people, **and before your feet stumble upon the dark mountains,** literally, "mountains of gloom," where the traveler is in danger of losing his way and coming to grief, **and, while ye look for light, He turn it into the shadow of death and make it gross darkness,** into a cloudy night, with densest gloom, a picture of the most severe affliction. Moreover, the prophet adds: v. 17. **But if ye will not hear it,** refusing him obedience in his appeal, **my soul shall weep in secret places for your pride,** such being the effect which their obstinacy would have upon him who was so sincerely concerned for their welfare; **and mine eye shall weep sore and run down with tears,** in an excess of grief, **because the Lord's flock,** the members of the Church whom Jehovah loved, **is carried away captive;** for even the disobedient people are still considered the Lord's people, since He has hopes of gaining them for the truth once more. V. 18. **Say unto the king and to the queen,** in a prophecy foretelling the fall of the kingdom, **Humble yourselves, sit down,** taking a very low and humble seat instead of occupying a proud throne; **for your principalities shall come down, even the crown of your glory,** literally, "for fallen is the ornament of your head, the diadem of your glory," as a sign of the fact that the king has lost his power and his kingdom. V. 19. **The cities of the South shall be shut up,** all the portals and roads filled with ruins, **and none shall open them,** no one being present to remove the *débris* left after the destruction of the cities. **Judah shall be carried away captive, all of it, it shall be wholly carried away captive,** so that not one inhabitant would be left behind. V. 20. **Lift up your eyes and behold them that come from the North,** the reference being to Nebuchadnezzar and his Chaldean hordes; **where is the flock that was given thee, thy beautiful flock?** the daughter of Zion being held responsible for the flock of Jehovah, which, by virtue of His election, was a flock of glory. V. 21. **What wilt thou say when He shall punish thee? For thou hast taught them,** the heathen rulers whom Zion herself had called as her friends, **to be captains and as chief over thee,** that is, the Lord Himself would punish Zion by giving her into the hands of these strangers. **Shall not sorrows take thee as a woman in travail?** the most severe pangs of affliction. V. 22. **And if thou say in thine heart, Wherefore come these things upon me?** in an attempt to deny the blame and the guilt which attached to Judah's many transgressions, then the Lord's answer is: **For the greatness of thine iniquity are thy skirts discovered and thy heels made bare,** since she would be driven into exile in scanty clothing and with bare feet, a form of the deepest degradation. Furthermore, the Lord tells Judah that it will not escape this lot because wickedness had become a second nature with it, and it seemed practically impossible to effect a change of heart. V. 23. **Can the Ethiopian change his skin,** turning it to a white color, **or the leopard his spots,** characteristic as they have become of him? **Then may ye also do good that are accustomed to do evil.** The one was practically as impossible as the other; they were entirely given over to wickedness. V. 24. **Therefore,** on account of this sad state of affairs, **will I scatter them as the stubble that passeth away by the wind of the wilderness,** the violent east wind which carried away the stubble like chaff. V. 25. **This is**

thy lot, so the Lord says in concluding this message, **the portion of thy measures from Me, saith the Lord,** what Judah may expect from Jehovah, **because thou hast forgotten Me and trusted in falsehood,** in deceitful promises as well as in the help of vain idols. V. 26. **Therefore will I discover thy skirts upon thy face,** from before, covering her with confusion and disgrace, **that thy shame may appear.** V. 27. **I have seen thine adulteries,** in her idolatry and the adulterous customs connected with false worship, **and thy neighings, the lewdness of thy whoredom,** namely, in the enormity of her unchastity in yielding to idolatry, **and thine abominations on the hills in the fields,** where so many heathen altars were erected. **Woe unto thee, O Jerusalem! Wilt thou not be made clean? When shall it once be?** The Lord is still stretching out arms of mercy to an apostate nation, a proof of the greatness of His love for sinners.

CHAPTER 14.

The Rejection of the Prophet's Intercession for Judah.

THE PROPHET INTERCEDES THE FIRST TIME. V. 1. **The word of the Lord that came to Jeremiah concerning the dearth,** the various periods of drouth which Jehovah sent in order to call His people to repentance, this form of punishment being expressly threatened in the curses which the Lord attached to His proclamation of the Law. Cp. Lev. 26, 19. 20; Deut. 11, 17; 28, 23. V. 2. **Judah mourneth,** the entire nation being plunged in grief, **and the gates thereof languish,** the people who usually assembled in this public meeting-place being in trouble; **they are black unto the ground,** as a token of deep sorrow, **and the cry of Jerusalem is gone up,** as the people give expression to their bitterness of heart. V. 3. **And their nobles,** the mighty ones, the rulers of the nation, **have sent their little ones,** either their own servants or the common people generally, **to the waters; they came to the pits,** the cisterns for collecting rain-water, **and found no water; they returned with their vessels empty,** the last drops of the precious fluid having disappeared; **they were ashamed and confounded and covered their heads,** in an excess of sorrow and grief. V. 4. **Because the ground is chapped,** literally, "dismayed," joining the people of Judah in their attitude of horror, **for there was no rain in the earth,** so that apprehension and consternation seized the soil; **the plowmen were ashamed,** because they could not till the land, **they covered their heads,** in the same feeling of humiliation which took hold of every animate and inanimate thing. V. 5. **Yea, the hind also calved in the field and forsook it,** abandoning her offspring, although noted for her affection toward her young, **because there was no grass,** no green thing to sustain life. V. 6. **And the wild asses did stand in the high places,** the bare hills most exposed to the wind, **they snuffed up the wind like dragons,** like jackals, eagerly seeking a breath of cooling air; **their eyes did fail,** unable to find so much as one blade of green grass, **because there was no grass.** V. 7. **O Lord,** so the prophet now makes his appeal for his countrymen, **though our iniquities testify against us,** serving as a most serious obstacle to the assistance and salvation of the Lord, **do Thou it for Thy name's sake,** relieving the distress of the terrible drouth in order to bring honor upon Himself; **for our backslidings are many,** thus preventing His interposing in their behalf so far as they were concerned; **we have sinned against Thee,** whence they must throw themselves entirely upon His mercy. V. 8. **O the Hope of Israel,** He who was properly the One in whom all true children of Israel trusted, since His covenant with them stood secure, **the Savior thereof in time of trouble,** as He had so often proved Himself, **why shouldest Thou be as a stranger in the land,** who has no interest in its welfare, **and as a wayfaring man that turneth aside to tarry for a night?** pitching his tent for only a very short period of time and feeling no sympathy for the inhabitants. Surely the Lord and Owner of Israel would not act in this manner! V. 9. **Why shouldest Thou be as a man astonied,** taken by surprise and therefore unable to lift His hand, stunned by a sudden calamity, **as a mighty man that cannot save?** having become weak and helpless in an unexpected extremity. **Yet Thou, O Lord, art in the midst of us,** namely, in His Sanctuary, which He had established at Jerusalem, **and we are called by Thy name,** bearing the name of Jehovah's people; **leave us not!** Thus Jeremiah turned to the God who had revealed Himself as the God of salvation, pleading in behalf of a people that had become guilty of rebellion against their one Source of help.

THE LORD REFUSES JEREMIAH'S REQUEST. — V. 10. **Thus saith the Lord unto this people, Thus have they loved to wander,** like the wild beasts whose behavior had been described in the previous section, **they have not refrained their feet,** not restraining them from the ways of idolatry, **therefore the Lord doth not accept them,** He confirms them in their idolatrous practises; **He will now remember their iniquity and visit their sins.** Cp. Hos. 8, 13. V. 11. **Then said the Lord unto me, Pray not for this people for their** good, so that any kind of benefit is given them. V. 12. **When they fast,** with a show of devotion toward Jehovah which they were far from feeling, **I will not hear their cry,** pay no attention to their appeals, **and when they offer burnt offering and an oblation,** professing adherence to the God of Israel, **I will not accept them,** because their service was thoroughly hypocritical; **but I will consume them by the sword and by the famine and by the pestilence,** the three great scourges of ancient times. V. 13. **Then said I, Ah, Lord God! Behold, the prophets,** namely, the false prophets who were influencing the people for evil, **say unto them, Ye shall not see the sword, neither shall ye have famine, but I will give you assured peace in this place,** literally, "peace of truth or faithfulness," that is, a sure and lasting peace. By such vain promises the false prophets tried to maintain their leadership among the people and to lead them astray. V. 14. **Then the Lord,** brushing aside this excuse offered on behalf of the people of Judah, **said unto me, The prophets prophesy lies in My name,** insisting that they were proclaiming their messages by authority of Jehovah; **I sent them not, neither have I commanded them, neither spake unto them,** thus stating most emphatically that they were not engaged by authority from Him; **they prophesy unto you a false vision and divination and a thing of naught,** literally, "nothingness," to set forth the utter emptiness of their message, **and the deceit of their heart,** evil plans which they had laid in order to work mischief. V. 15. **Therefore, thus saith the Lord concerning the prophets that prophesy in My name and I sent them not,** who were acting entirely without authority in bringing people a message of their own invention, **yet they say, Sword and famine shall not be in this land: By sword and famine shall these prophets be consumed,** perishing by the very punishments whose existence they had denied. V. 16. **And the people to whom they prophesy shall be cast out in the streets of Jerusalem,** suffering a shameful death, **because of the famine and the sword; and they shall have none to bury them,** thus being deprived of even the last honor usually accorded to men, **them, their wives, nor their sons, nor their daughters,** all of these being in the same guilt and therefore in the same condemnation; **for I will pour their wickedness upon them,** so that its consequences will submerge them. V. 17. **Therefore thou shalt say this word unto them, Let mine eyes run down with tears night and day and let them not cease,** nothing but weeping being left for the prophet; **for the virgin daughter of my people is broken with a great breach,** with a wound which is very dangerous, **with a very grievous blow,** a fact which stirs the love of the prophet to its very depths. V. 18. **If I go forth into the field, then behold the slain with the sword! and if I enter into the city, then behold them that are sick with famine!** no matter where he turns, the prophet's eyes encounter the ravages of war. **Yea, both the prophet and the priest go about into a land that they know not,** the destruction having rendered the country strange in their eyes, as familiar as they were formerly with every feature of the landscape on account of their frequent journeys. Thus had the Lord fulfilled the words of His threats and rebukes upon Judah.

THE PROPHET AGAIN INTERCEDES. — V. 19. **Hast Thou utterly rejected Judah?** so the prophet sorrowfully asks Jehovah. **Hath Thy soul loathed Zion?** feeling nothing but disgust for her. **Why hast Thou smitten us, and there is no healing for us? We looked for peace, and there is no good, and for the time of healing, and behold trouble!** Terror beset them on every hand, and there was no respite in sight. V. 20. **We acknowledge, O Lord, our wickedness, and the iniquity of our fathers,** the guilt which was found in the children also, **for we have sinned against Thee.** It is a confession in the name of those who were still Israelites in truth, since He, in the event of their repenting, had promised them forgiveness. V. 21. **Do not abhor us,** in an utter rejection, **for Thy name's sake,** which guaranteed to them the true covenant relation with all its benefits, **do not disgrace the throne of Thy glory,** namely, by repudiating Jerusalem and the Temple of Jehovah. **Remember, break not, Thy covenant with us,** upholding His promise made to the patriarchs. The prophet finally urges, as a consideration which ought to influence Jehovah, the fact that He alone is able to help in this emergency. V. 22. **Are there any among the vanities of the Gentiles,** their empty idols, **that can cause rain? Or can the heavens give showers?** God, as the only Creator, the one true God, is the only One who can dispense rain and give showers as He sees best. **Art not Thou He, O Lord, our God?** Since He had sent the dreadful drouths under whose hardships the land was groaning, therefore He alone could provide relief. **Therefore we will wait upon Thee, for Thou hast made all these things.** It is this understanding which is required of all men who would stand in the proper relation to Jehovah, the one God of mercy.

CHAPTER 15.

The Lord's Refusal and the Prophet's Complaint.

THE LORD REFUSES HELP THE SECOND TIME. V. 1. **Then said the Lord unto me, Though Moses and Samuel,** who are hereby affirmed to be historical persons, **stood before Me,** the high regard in which He held these His servants tending to have Him look upon them with favor, **yet My mind could not be toward this people,** their intercession could not save the people from the threatened destruction. **Cast them out of My sight and let them go forth,** since Jehovah utterly repudiates His chosen people. V. 2. **And it shall come to pass, if they say unto thee, Whither shall we go forth? then thou shalt tell them,** in a very harsh answer, as befitted the occasion, **Thus saith the Lord, Such as are for death, to death; and such as are for the sword, to the sword; and such as are for the famine, to the famine; and such as are for the captivity, to the captivity.** The Lord's previous sentence, in which He names three scourges, chap. 14, 12, is here strengthened and intensified in order to bring out the inevitable certainty of the impending destruction. V. 3. **And I will appoint over them four kinds saith the Lord,** four varieties of death: **the sword to slay,** so that their carcasses would lie on the ground, **and the dogs to tear, and the fowls of the heaven, and the beasts of the earth, to devour and destroy,** the last three agencies completing the judgment upon the dead bodies. V. 4. **And I will cause them to be removed into all kingdoms of the earth,** cp. Deut. 28, 25, there being a great many countries making up the Babylonian Empire, **because of Manasseh, the son of Hezekiah, king of Judah, for that which he did in Jerusalem,** in introducing and practising the abominations of idolatry. Cp. 2 Kings 21, 11 ff. V. 5. **For who shall have pity upon thee, O Jerusalem, or who shall bemoan thee?** in a feeling of sympathy for the various punishments which were about to strike her. **Or who shall go aside to ask how thou doest?** in a neighborly form of inquiry concerning her welfare. By the dispensation of Jehovah, men were simply ignoring her and her plight, letting her alone in her misery. V. 6. **Thou hast forsaken Me, saith the Lord,** rejecting the God of the covenant, **thou art gone backward,** away from Him and His Word; **therefore will I stretch out My hand against thee and destroy thee,** in one mighty stroke of punishment; **I am weary with repenting,** since His gracious offers had so often been abused and rejected, He would now no longer show mercy. V. 7. **And I will fan them with a fan in the gates of the land;** even as a man at the opening of a threshing-floor makes use of every gust of wind to remove the chaff from the wheat, so the Lord would stand at the entrance of the land and let its inhabitants pass through a sifting process. **I will bereave them of children,** by causing the flower of their youth to fall in battle; **I will destroy My people since they return not from their ways,** persisting in their rejection of Jehovah. V. 8. **Their widows are increased to Me above the sand of the seas,** beyond the possibility of counting them; **I have brought upon them against the mother of the young men,** the wife in the fulness of her strength, **a spoiler at noonday,** the enemy hordes; **I have caused him to fall upon it,** the city with all its inhabitants, **suddenly, and terrors upon the city,** so that she was filled with anguish. V. 9. **She that hath borne seven,** the woman usually in her best years and strength, **languisheth, she hath given up the ghost,** despairing because not one of her sons remained; **her sun is gone down while it was yet day,** her good fortune leaving her just at a time when she should have been at the height of her prosperity; **she hath been ashamed and confounded,** put to shame on account of the disappointment over the loss of her children; **and the residue of them,** those still remaining at the time when Jerusalem was taken, **will I deliver to the sword before their enemies, saith the Lord.** Cp. Micah 6, 14. Thus the fate of the city was determined upon in every respect, as the Lord proceeded to carry out His sentence upon its inhabitants.

THE PROPHET'S LAMENTATION. — V. 10. **Woe is me, my mother, that thou hast borne me a man of strife and a man of contention to the whole earth!** that is, one with whom the whole world, all men with whom he came into contact, were anxious to pick a quarrel. **I have neither lent on usury, nor men have lent to me on usury,** he had neither borrowed nor lent, either practise being a sure way of arousing enmity, **yet every one of them doth curse me,** all of them being his enemies without cause. V. 11. **The Lord said, Verily, it shall be well with thy remnant,** literally, "I confirm thee for good," namely, that his tribulations would finally turn out to his benefit; **verily, I will cause the enemy to entreat thee well in the time of evil and in the time of affliction,** that is, the enemy would, when trouble came upon him, turn to the prophet with an imploring appeal, believing that the intercession of Jeremiah would have much weight in the eyes of Jehovah. V. 12. **Shall iron break the northern iron and the steel?** literally, "Will then iron," that is, the ordinary iron used in Palestine, "break iron from the north and brass?" for the steel of Syria and of various parts of Asia Minor was noted for its excellence. The meaning evidently is that the people of Judah could not withstand the armies of the great northern empire which would soon be sent against them. V. 13. **Thy substance and thy treasures,** all the wealth of Judah, **will I give to the spoil without price,** they will be theirs to take away for nothing, **and that for all thy sins, even in all thy borders,** the material wealth throughout the country would be taken away on account of the sins of the people. V. 14. **And I will make thee to pass with thine enemies into a land which thou knowest not,** literally, "I let them," the treasures, "pass over into a land unknown to thee, as the booty of the enemy"; **for a fire is kindled in Mine anger which shall burn upon you.** Cp. Deut. 32, 22. V. 15. **O Lord, Thou knowest,** thus Jeremiah now presents his appeal to the Lord; **remember me and visit me,** in kindness and mercy, **and revenge me of my persecutors,** carrying out His revenge upon them; **take me not away in Thy long-suffering,** in a sudden calamity while over-patient toward the wicked. **Know that for Thy sake I have suffered rebuke,** the reproach of all the scoffers in Judah. V. 16. **Thy words were found, and I did eat them,** the prophet eagerly laying hold of the words of Jehovah as they were offered; **and Thy Word was unto me the joy and rejoicing of mine heart, for I am called by Thy name, O Lord God of hosts,** it was revealed to Jeremiah, he was called as a minister of His Word. He had, therefore, devoted himself to this calling with all seriousness. V. 17. **I sat not in the assembly of the mockers nor rejoiced,** he had not taken part in any frivolous gatherings; **I sat alone because of Thy hand,** being isolated on account of the fact that the power of the Lord had taken hold of him and urged him to do the work of a prophet; **for Thou hast filled me with indignation,** with a holy wrath over the corruption and obstinacy of Judah. V. 18. **Why is my pain perpetual,** namely, the grief and sorrow which the prophet felt over the judgment of condemnation which he was obliged to proclaim to his people, **and my wound incurable, which refuseth to be healed? Wilt Thou be altogether unto me as a liar,** literally, "as a deceitful brook," whose dry bed disappointed the thirsty traveler, **and as waters that fail?** lacking the qualities of a perennial stream. To this reproachful exclamation the Lord answers. V. 19. **Therefore, thus saith the Lord,** in a gentle reproof of His servant, **If thou return,** turning from his course of discontent with the ways of the Lord, which had almost brought him to the point of doubting the faithfulness of God, **then will I bring thee again, and thou shalt stand before Me,** so that he would once more occupy the right relation to Jehovah and accept His commands at His mouth; **and if thou take forth the precious from the vile,** carefully separating them, as an assayer does, and retaining only that which is good, the reference being to the need of letting the virtues of patience and trust govern all his actions instead of impatience and hastiness, **thou shalt be as My mouth,** the instrument through which the Lord makes known His will to men. **Let them return unto thee,** in yielding to his entreaties and begging him to intercede for them, **but return not thou unto them,** following their profane ways and causing himself to be led astray by them. V. 20. **And I will make thee unto this people a fenced brazen wall,** an impregnable wall against their attacks; **and they shall fight against thee, but they shall not prevail against thee,** not be able to overcome his firm resistance; **for I am with thee to save thee and to deliver thee, saith the Lord.** V. 21. **And I will deliver thee out of the hand of the wicked, and I will redeem thee out of the hand of the terrible,** from the might of the violent, the enemies who would interfere with the message of Jehovah. In a similar way the assurance of the Lord sustains His servants, the true ministers of the Gospel, in our days also.

CHAPTER 16.

The Conduct of the Prophet with Regard to Judah's Destruction.

THE INSTRUCTION OF JEHOVAH. — V. 1. **The word of the Lord came also unto me, saying,** v. 2. **Thou shalt not take thee a wife, neither shalt thou have sons or daughters in this place,** he should not have a family, although this was otherwise self-evident among the Jews. V. 3. **For thus saith the Lord concerning the sons and concerning the daughters that are born in this place, and concerning their mothers that bare them, and concerning their fathers that begat them in this land,** all the persons belonging to the married estate being included in this enumeration: v. 4. **They shall die of grievous deaths,** in a most miserable manner; **they shall not be lamented, neither shall they be buried, but they shall be as dung upon the face of the earth,** cp. chap. 8, 2; 9, 22; **and they shall be consumed by the sword and by famine,** perishing in some of the great scourges of the ancient world; **and their carcasses shall be meat for the fowls of heaven and for the beasts of the earth,** the birds and beasts of prey devouring them where they fell. V. 5. **For thus saith the Lord,** in bidding Jeremiah refrain from every show of sympathy for the fate of the apostate people, **Enter not into the house of mourning**, where some one had died and where people were giving loud expression to their grief, **neither go to lament nor bemoan them; for I have taken away My peace from this people, saith the Lord,** that upon which every blessing and all happiness depend, **even loving-kindness and mercies,** the source of every good and perfect gift. V. 6. **Both the great and the small shall die in this land,** as a result of the withdrawal of His blessing; **they shall not be buried, neither shall men lament for them,** with the usual signs of mourning, **nor cut themselves,** making incisions in the flesh, **nor make themselves bald for them,** by shaving off a part of their hair, a token of excessive sorrow and grief in the Orient; v. 7. **neither shall men tear themselves for them in mourning,** literally, "break bread for them," to comfort them for the dead; **neither shall men give them the cup of consolation to drink for their father or for their mother.** The reference is to the custom of sending bread and wine to the house of such as had been bereaved by death in order to refresh and comfort them. V. 8. **Thou shalt not also go into the house of feasting to sit with them to eat and to drink,** to attend such a mournful feast of survivors in person and to show sympathy in any form whatever. V. 9. **For thus saith the Lord of hosts, the God of Israel,** who here again makes announcement of His intention in a most solemn manner, **Behold, I will cause to cease out of this place in your eyes,** that is, "before your eyes," **and in your days the voice of mirth and the voice of gladness, the voice of the bridegroom and the voice of the bride,** this being the usual formula for announcing the full sweep of the Lord's wrath. Cp. Is. 24, 7. 8; Rev. 18, 23.

REASONS FOR THE CAPTIVITY. — V. 10. **And it shall come to pass, when thou shalt show this people all these words,** declaring to them the judgment of the Lord, **and they shall say unto thee, Wherefore hath the Lord pronounced all this great evil against us?** this being asked with a great show of pretended innocence, **or what is our iniquity? or what is our sin that we have committed against the Lord, our God?** the implied assertion being that they were being threatened without a cause, v. 11. **then shalt thou say unto them, Because your fathers have forsaken Me, saith the Lord, and have walked after other gods,** thus habitually indulging in idolatry, **and have served them, and have worshiped them, and have,** on the other hand, **forsaken Me, and have not kept My Law.** V. 12. **And ye have done worse than your fathers; for, behold, ye walk every one after the imagination of his evil heart,** in deliberate stubbornness, **that they may not hearken unto Me,** or, "that ye hearken not unto Me," obstinately ignoring His Word; v. 13. **therefore will I cast you out of this land into a land that ye know not, neither ye nor your fathers,** a country altogether strange to them, **and there shall ye serve other gods day and night,** without intermission; **where I will not show you favor.** This is a form of holy irony: what they willingly did in their own country, they would be obliged to do in the land of their captivity; because they voluntarily forsook the true God at home, they would be prevented from serving Him elsewhere. At the same time the Lord opens up before the eyes of Judah a way of redemption, the thought of which was intended to keep His people from despair. V. 14. **Therefore, behold, the days come, saith the Lord, that it shall no more be said,** according to the asseveration which had been common in Judah these many centuries, **The Lord liveth that brought up the children of Israel out of the land of Egypt,** this being a very emphatic statement, v. 15. **but, The Lord liveth that brought up the children of Israel from the land of the North,** from Babylon, **and from all the lands whither He had driven them,** from the lands of their exile; **and I will bring them again into their land that I gave unto their fathers,** this promise being like a ray of light in the midst of extreme darkness. This thought is expanded still more in the next paragraph. V. 16. **Behold, I will send for many fishers, saith the Lord,** whose nets would enfold large multitudes to take them captive, **and they shall fish them; and after will I send for many hunters, and they shall hunt them from every mountain and from every hill and out of the holes of the rocks,** this indicating the extent in which the sentence of captivity was carried out. V. 17. **For Mine eyes are upon all their ways,** observing their entire conduct; **they are not hid from My face, neither is their iniquity hid from Mine eyes,** they are unable to conceal it before His omniscient gaze. V. 18. **And first,** that is, to begin with, **I will recompense their iniquity and their sin double,** in twice the measure in which they committed their wicked deeds; **because they have defiled My land,** desecrating the country which was considered hallowed to Him; **they have filled Mine inheritance,** what He had given them to possess as their own, **with the carcasses of their detestable and abominable things,** with their dead and loathsome idols. V. 19. **O Lord,** so the prophet now addresses Jehovah, the God of the covenant, in expressing his own hope and that of all true Israelites concerning the return of the people to the true God, **my Strength and my Fortress,** his Protection against the enemies, **and my Refuge in the**

day of affliction, the Gentiles shall come unto Thee from the ends of the earth, thus joining the believers in Israel in their recognition of the vanity of their own idols, **and shall say, Surely our fathers have inherited lies, vanity, and things wherein there is no profit,** the trouble in which they found themselves bringing them to this realization. This admission on the part of the Gentiles is now substantiated by the prophet. V. 20. **Shall a man make gods unto himself, and they are no gods?** The question has the strength of a most emphatic denial, of a stern rebuke to the men of Judah for their idolatrous ways. Moreover, the Lord expresses His emphatic agreement with this statement of Jeremiah. V. 21. **Therefore, behold, I will this once cause them to know,** in the impending catastrophe, **I will cause them to know Mine hand and My might,** as it descends upon them in anger; **and they shall know that My name is "The Lord,"** that He alone is God in truth. Cp. Ezek. 12, 15; Ex. 3, 14. Many a person has since that time been brought to a realization of the same truth by similar stern measures of the Lord.

CHAPTER 17.

The Jews' Persistent Course in Corruption.

The Reason for Judah's Rejection. — V. 1. **The sin of Judah is written with a pen of iron,** as with a stylus which was used for writing on wax tablets in ancient times, **and with the point of a diamond,** which was used for etching words into metal surfaces; **it is graven upon the table of their heart,** deep and ineradicable, with a lasting impression, **and upon the horns of your altars,** where they wrote the names of their idols, v. 2. **whilst their children,** the entire nation, **remember their altars and their groves by the green trees upon the high hills,** that is, they were so deeply steeped in idolatry that the mere sight of a green tree and of a high hill awoke in them the remembrance of those terrible altars and of the Asherah images which they had erected there. V. 3. **O my mountain in the field,** Jerusalem, and especially Zion and the Temple, **I will give thy substance and all thy treasures to the spoil,** into the possession of **the enemies, and thy high places for sin,** on account of the wickedness of the people, because they had been used for idolatrous sacrifices, **throughout all thy borders.** V. 4. **And thou, even thyself, shalt discontinue from thine heritage that I gave thee,** disowned, cast out of their land; **and I will cause thee to serve thine enemies in the land which thou knowest not; for ye have kindled a fire in Mine anger which shall burn forever.** Thus the Jews would lose their inheritance by their own fault, and those who persisted in their godless ways would be subject to the eternal wrath of a holy God, in the same way in which the idolaters of our days will experience it.

The Depth of the Nation's Corruption. — V. 5. **Thus saith the Lord,** in rebuking the tendency of Judah to rely upon various heathen allies, **Cursed be the man that trusteth in man,** as the Jews did in relying upon Egypt, **and maketh flesh his arm,** in depending upon the strength of men, **and whose heart departeth from the Lord,** this fact explaining the reason for such foolish trust in man. V. 6. **For he shall be like the heath in the desert,** literally, "like a naked one in the wilderness," one destitute of all means of subsistence, **and shall not see when good cometh,** shall never see good fortune, **but shall inhabit the parched places in the wilderness,** where the lack of water prevents the maturing of crops, **in a salt land,** where the soil is impregnated with alkali, **and not inhabited.** Over against such a person the Lord pictures him who conducts himself in agreement with His will. V. 7. **Blessed is the man that trusteth in the Lord,** with the confidence of true faith, **and whose hope the Lord is.** Cp. Ps. 1, 3. 4. V. 8. **For he,** utterly unlike the man whose description has just been given, **shall be as a tree planted by the waters,** where a plentiful supply of moisture insures a luxuriant growth, **and that spreadeth out her roots by the river, and shall not see when heat cometh,** being unaffected by its fiery breath, **but her leaf shall be green,** on account of her perpetual supply of life-giving water; **and shall not be careful in the year of drought,** there being no cause to worry even then, **neither shall cease from yielding fruit,** because the stream at which it is located will never dry up. In order to bring this truth home with particular emphasis, the Lord describes the human heart as it is. V. 9. **The heart is deceitful above all things,** full of perfidy and treachery, **and desperately wicked,** profoundly corrupt; **who can know it?** Who can understand and plumb the depths of its wickedness? This alone is reason enough why no man should place confidence in the ideas of his heart. V. 10. **I, the Lord, search the heart, I try the reins,** the seat of the innermost desires and feelings, **even to give every man according to his ways,** as his conduct deserves, **and according to the fruit of his doings,** in accordance with his deeds, as the expression of his heart's condition. V. 11. **As the partridge sitteth on eggs and hatcheth them not,** or, "a partridge hatching eggs which it has not laid," so **he that getteth riches, and not by right,** accumulating unjust wealth, ill-gotten gain, **shall leave them in the midst of his days, and at his end shall be a fool,** the foolishness of his acts appearing at the end of his life. V. 12. **A glorious high throne from the beginning is the place of our Sanctuary,** or, in the form of an address directed to the seat of God's majesty, "Thou throne of glory, loftiness from the beginning, place of our Sanctuary!" Zion, where God revealed Himself to His people, where His glory was enthroned above the lid of the Ark, is here regarded as a person, in order to heighten the effect of the appeal, which now turns directly to God. V. 13. **O Lord, the Hope of Israel!** the God of the covenant being the only one in whom the Jews might expect redemption, **all that forsake Thee shall be ashamed, and they that depart from Me shall be written in the earth,** their names being traced in loose soil or sand, where the writing would soon be obliterated, **because they have forsaken the Lord, the Fountain of living waters.** Cp. chap. 2, 13. In connection with this the prophet begs the Lord to grant him deliverance from his enemies. V. 14. **Heal me, O Lord, and I shall be healed,** both making him whole in his distress and keeping him so; **save me, and I shall be saved,** delivered from the enemies who were seeking his soul; **for Thou art my Praise,** the object of his confident boasting. Cp. Ps. 71, 6; Deut. 10, 21. V. 15. **Behold, they say unto me, Where is the word of the Lord?** How is it that His threats are not fulfilled? **Let it come now!** The enemies challenge the prophet to produce proofs of the truth which he declared he was proclaiming in the name of the Lord. V. 16. **As for me, I have not hastened from being a pastor to follow Thee,** he had not left his duties as shepherd in his home town in precipitous haste for the sake of being Jehovah's special minister, or, he had not withdrawn himself hastily from the Lord's service; **neither have I desired the woeful day, Thou knowest,** he had not wished that the day of calamity might strike Judah; **that which came out of my lips was right before Thee,** it was not only known to the Lord, but it was uttered by His express command. V. 17. **Be not a terror unto me,** causing consternation to strike him; **Thou art my Hope in the day of evil,** his Refuge in the time of distress. V. 18. **Let them be confounded that persecute me,** so that they will be heaped with disgrace before him, **but let not me be confounded,** with his simple trust in the Lord; **let them be dismayed, but let not me be dismayed. Bring upon them the day of evil,** the promised destruction, **and destroy them with double destruction,** literally, "with a double portion in ruin." This was not a prayer of vindictiveness, but of zeal for the honor of the Lord, which was at stake in the attacks made upon His servant. A prayer that the Lord would avenge His honor in punishing His enemies is altogether in order to this day.

THE HALLOWING OF THE SABBATH. — V. 19. **Thus saith the Lord unto me,** with reference to the flagrant disregard of one of the chief commandments in the form in which it concerned the Jews, **Go and stand in the gate of the children of the people,** probably the main portal of the Temple, **whereby the kings of Judah come in, and by the which they go out,** identified by some as the "Gate of David," or the "Gate of the Fountain," at the foot of Zion, **and in all the gates of Jerusalem,** in order that this word might be observed at all entrances of the city, v. 20. **and say unto them, Hear ye the word of the Lord, ye kings of Judah,** its successive rulers, **and all Judah, and all the inhabitants of Jerusalem that enter in by these gates:** v. 21. **Thus saith the Lord, Take heed to yourselves,** literally, "preserve your souls," guard over your souls, namely, on account of the danger which otherwise threatened their lives, **and bear no burden on the Sabbath-day, nor bring it in by the gates of Jerusalem,** v. 22. **neither carry forth a burden out of your houses on the Sabbath-day, neither do ye any work,** for all of this was forbidden the Jews under the old dispensation, Ex. 12, 16; 20, 10; Deut. 5, 14, **but hallow ye the Sabbath-day, as I commanded your fathers,** the commandment to keep the Sabbath being insisted upon with great severity by the Lord at that time. V. 23. **But they obeyed not, neither inclined their ear,** they did not pay the slightest attention to His precepts, **but made their neck stiff,** in deliberate stubbornness, **that they might not hear nor receive instruction,** their whole history being a series of examples in proof of this statement. V. 24. **And it shall come to pass, if ye diligently hearken unto Me, saith the Lord, to bring in no burden through the gates of this city on the Sabbath-day, but hallow the Sabbath-day to do no work therein,** v. 25. **then shall there enter into the gates of this city kings and princes sitting upon the throne of David, riding in chariots and on horses,** the kingdom being restored to its ancient power and splendor, **they and their princes, the men of Judah, and the inhabitants of Jerusalem,** the entire country participating in the benefits given to its capital; **and this city shall remain forever,** according to the promises made to the patriarchs and kings of old. V. 26. **And they shall come from the cities of Judah,** in the neighborhood of the capital, **and from the places about Jerusalem, and from the land of Benjamin,** the northern district of the kingdom, **and from the plain,** the lowlands toward the Mediterranean Sea, **and from the mountains**, the hill section of the kingdom, **and from the south**, the great steppes west and southwest of the Dead Sea, **bringing burnt offerings, and sacrifices, and meat-offerings, and incense, and bringing sacrifices of praise**, or thank-offerings, the various bloody and bloodless sacrifices of the Jews being thus briefly enumerated, **unto the house of the Lord.** V. 27. **But if ye will not hearken unto Me to hallow the Sabbath-day and not to bear a burden, even entering in at the gates of Jerusalem on the Sabbath-day**, that is, if their deliberate desecration of the Sabbath would continue, **then will I kindle a fire in the gates thereof**, as the attack of the enemies would succeed, **and it shall devour the palaces of Jerusalem, and it shall not be quenched.** Thus the warning of the Lord called the Jews to repentance again and again, for He does not desire the death of sinners, but wants all men to repent of their sins and be saved.

CHAPTER 18.

The Symbol of the Clay and the Potter.

THE PARABLE OF THE POTTER. — V. 1. **The word which came to Jeremiah from the Lord, saying**, v. 2. **Arise and go down to the potter's house**, his workshop being located in the lower part of the city, near the clay-pits, **and there I will cause thee to hear My words**, in a special message intended for the people of Judah. V. 3. **Then I went down to the potter's house, and, behold, he wrought a work on the wheels**, literally, "on the disks," for the potter's lathe consisted of two horizontal wooden plates, the lower one larger than the upper, the clay being molded into shape on the upper disk. V. 4. **And the vessel that he made of clay was marred in the hand of the potter**, it was spoiled in the making, due to some mischance; **so he made it again another vessel**, using the same lump of clay over again, **as seemed good to the potter to make it.** This was the incident which the Lord used as the basis of His parable. V. 5. **Then the word of the Lord came to me, saying**, v. 6. **O house of Israel**, the entire nation being addressed, as including the true Church of God, **cannot I do with you as this potter? saith the Lord**, namely, in discarding a people that had proved unfaithful to His call and choosing others in its stead. **Behold, as the clay is in the potter's hand, so are ye in Mine hand, O house of Israel**, still in a position to be molded if they but heeded His call. V. 7. **At what instant**, namely, in a moment of time, when the nation least expects it, **I shall speak concerning a nation and concerning a kingdom to pluck up, and to pull down, and to destroy it**, threatening extermination: v. 8. **if that nation against whom I have pronounced turn from their evil**, giving heed to His warnings, **I will repent of the evil that I thought to do unto them**, in accordance with His long-suffering and mercy, according to which He does not desire the death of the sinner. V. 9. **And at what instant**, with the same suddenness, **I shall speak concerning a nation and concerning a kingdom to build and to plant it**, having arranged to carry out a plan of blessing upon it, to give it a position of power and authority above others: v. 10. **if it do evil in My sight, that it obey not My voice, then I will repent of the good wherewith I said I would benefit them**, the obstinacy and wickedness of such a people depriving it of the blessings which the Lord would freely have vouchsafed all its members. It is man's own fault if he does not become a partaker of the benefits which God's kindness and mercy would like to bestow upon all men.

THE PARABLE FURTHER APPLIED. — V. 11. **Now, therefore, go to, speak to the men of Judah, and to the inhabitants of Jerusalem**, in announcing the intention of the Lord on the basis of the nation's behavior, **saying, Thus saith the Lord, Behold, I frame evil against you**, shaping it as the potter shapes the clay on his wheel, **and devise a device against you**, a plan to work destruction; **return ye now, every one, from his evil way and make your ways and your doings good**, so that all their doings would bear the inspection of His holy eyes. V. 12. **And they said**, once more stubbornly refusing to heed the warning of the Lord, **There is no hope**, or, "No use!" **But we will walk after our own devices**, following after the wicked designs of their own mind, **and we will every one do the imagination of his evil heart**, abandoning themselves entirely to their sins and to the penalty placed upon them by God. V. 13. **Therefore, thus saith the Lord**, in expressing His horror over such behavior as here exhibited by Judah, **Ask ye now among the heathen who hath heard such things. The virgin of Israel**, the Lord's betrothed, in whose case one would not have believed such shameless indecency possible, **hath done a very horrible thing**, an act which was abominable in His sight. V. 14. **Will a man leave the snow of Lebanon which cometh from the rock of the field?** literally, "Will the snow of Lebanon desert the rock of the mountain range?" the point of comparison being in the fact that the snow of the mountains is perennial. **Or shall the cold flowing waters that come from another place be forsaken?** Will the strange, cold, rippling waters, fed by the glaciers of Hermon, dry up? As the snow covers the summits of Lebanon with a perpetual mantle, so the flow of waters at its foot is perpetual, there is no interruption, the connection between the two is unbroken. All the more reprehensible, then, is the conduct of the people of Judah. V. 15. **Because My people hath forgotten Me, they have burned incense to vanity,** to the idols, which are nothing in the sight of God, **and they have caused them to stumble in their ways from the ancient paths,** thus leaving the way of the conduct prescribed by God in ancient days, **to walk in paths, in a way not cast up,** where proper progress was impossible; v. 16. **to make their land desolate and a perpetual hissing,** an object of eternal derision and loathing; **every one that passeth thereby,** taking note of the desolation which had come upon the former rich land, **shall be astonished,** be rigid with astonishment, **and wag his head,** in a gesture expressing malicious enjoyment of their misfortune. V. 17. **I will scatter them as with an east wind,** a violent wind from the desert, **before the enemy; I will show them the back, and not the face, in the day of their calamity,** this being done in just retribution upon them, for they had turned their backs to Him and refused Him obedience, chap. 2, 27. This threat on the part of God filled the reprobates with fury, which was promptly directed against Jeremiah, His faithful servant. V. 18. **Then said they, Come and let us devise devices against Jeremiah,** planning wicked designs against his person and life; **for the Law shall not perish from the priest, nor counsel from the wise, nor the word from the prophet.** The meaning evidently is this, that they had no need of Jeremiah, the prophet of doom, since they would always have priests to instruct them, wise men to advise them, and prophets to proclaim to them the Word of the Lord, men, moreover, more to their liking, who would not be forever harping on the subject of repentance and judgment. **Come and let us smite him with the tongue,** making life unbearable for him by defamation, shortening his life by the grief caused him by this manner of dealing with him, **and let us not give heed to any of his words,** this being another way in which they intended to show their spite. The prophet, therefore, raises his voice in an earnest appeal to God. V. 19. **Give heed to me, O Lord,** listening attentively to his cry for deliverance and protection, **and hearken to the voice of them that contend with me,** taking note of those who oppose him in his work. V. 20. **Shall evil be recompensed for good?** namely, by the fact that the evil plans of his adversaries would be successful. **For they have digged a pit for my soul,** where they hoped to catch him unawares. **Remember that I stood before Thee to speak good for them,** in an earnest intercession in their behalf, cp. chap. 14, 7 ff., **and to turn away Thy wrath from them,** pleading that the Lord would not visit their iniquity upon them. V. 21. **Therefore,** because they disregarded all attempts to bring them to their senses and increased in wickedness from day to day, **deliver up their children to the famine, and pour out their blood by the force of the sword,** the sword, in the Hebrew, being regarded as possessing hands to perform its murderous work; **and let their wives be bereaved of their children and be widows,** losing also their husbands, with whom they were one in wickedness; **and let their men be put to death; let their young men be slain by the sword in battle.** V. 22. **Let a cry be heard from their houses,** as the attacking forces enter, **when thou shalt bring a troop suddenly upon them,** namely, the murderous hordes of the invaders; **for they have digged a pit to take me and hid snares for my feet,** as the fowler does for the bird. V. 23. **Yet, Lord, Thou knowest all their counsel against me to slay me,** being fully aware of their murderous plans against Jeremiah. **Forgive not their iniquity, neither blot out their sin from Thy sight,** indulgently overlooking their wickedness, **but let them be overthrown before Thee; deal thus with them in the time of Thine anger.** This appeal, altogether in the manner of the imprecatory psalms, was inspired by the zeal of the prophet for the honor of Jehovah, since the opponents stubbornly refused to listen to reason and to the warnings of God which called them to repentance.

CHAPTER 19.

The Symbol of the Broken Vessel.

THE PARABOLIC ACTION AND ITS EXPLANATION. — V. 1. **Thus saith the Lord, Go and get a potter's earthen bottle,** a pitcher with a long neck, **and take of the ancients of the people,** the elders of their chief council, **and of the ancients of the priests,** cp. Is. 36, 2, v. 2. **and go forth unto the Valley of the Son of Hinnom,** or the Valley of Ben-hinnom, south and southwest of the city, **which is by the entry of the East Gate,** or the Potsherd Gate, probably identical with the Dung Gate, Neh. 3, 13—15, near which were the clay-pits or the dumping-grounds of the potters, **and proclaim there the words that I shall tell thee,** the fact of verbal inspiration being brought out again, v. 3. **and say, Hear ye the word of the Lord, O kings of Judah and** inhabitants of **Jerusalem,** both of whom had become guilty together of idolatrous customs such as were practised in this valley, sacrifices to Moloch, the abomination of the Moabites, **Thus saith the Lord of hosts, the God of Israel,** the only one entitled to worship on the part of the people bearing the name of Israel: **Behold, I will bring evil upon this place, the which whosoever heareth, his ears shall tingle,** ringing as after a peal of thunder with the unequaled horror of the news. V. 4. **Because they have forsaken Me and have estranged this place,** devoting it to the worship of strange gods, **and have burned incense in it unto other gods, whom neither they nor their fathers have known, nor the kings of Judah,** idols which should have been utterly foreign to the mind of the nation, **and have filled this place with the blood of innocents,** namely, in the unnatural sacrifice of children offered to Moloch; v. 5. **they have built also the high places of Baal,** the chief idol of the Canaanites, **to burn their sons with fire for burnt offerings unto Baal, which I commanded not nor spake it, neither came it into my mind,** the heaping of synonymous expressions indicating that the very idea of such offerings was utterly loathsome to Him: v. 6. **therefore, behold, the days come, saith the Lord, that this place shall no more be called Tophet,** a name thought by some commentators to have been given to the place because drums (Hebrew, *toph*) were beaten to drown out the cries of the children that were being sacrificed, **nor The Valley of the Son of Hinnom, but The Valley of Slaughter,** where the enemies would descend upon the men of Judah to cut them down unmercifully. V. 7. **And I will make void the counsel of Judah and Jerusalem in this place,** frustrating their plans for the defense of their city, **and I will cause them to fall by the sword before their enemies and by the hands of them that seek their lives,** in a general slaughter, **and their carcasses will I give to be meat for the fowls of the heaven and for the beasts of the earth,** the birds and beasts of prey making a welcome meal of their unburied corpses. V. 8. **And I will make this city desolate and an hissing,** so that people would make noises of surprise and sneering at its downfall, cp. chap. 18, 16; **every one that passeth thereby shall be astonished and hiss because of all the plagues thereof,** because it was so severely smitten by Jehovah. V. 9. **And I will cause them to eat the flesh of their sons and the flesh of their daughters,** in a form of the most abhorrent cannibalism, as threatened in the special curses of the Law, Lev. 26, 29; Deut. 28, 53, **and they shall eat every one the flesh of his friend in the siege and straitness,** in the severity of the famine, **wherewith their enemies and they that seek their lives shall straiten them,** all demands and considerations of friendship and kinship being forgotten. All this was literally fulfilled, as we read in Lam. 4, 10. All this was said in explanation of the clay pitcher which Jeremiah carried. V. 10. **Then shalt thou break the bottle in the sight of the men that go with thee,** thereby calling their attention to the symbolism of his action, v. 11. **and shalt say unto them, Thus saith the Lord of hosts,** the great Commander of the heavenly armies, the Ruler of the universe, **Even so will I break this people and this city as one breaketh a potter's vessel,** whose fragile nature is so obvious, **that cannot be made whole again,** though the same material may be used once more in making another vessel; **and they shall bury them in Tophet,** in an unclean place, the regular burial-places being insufficient to hold them all, **till there be no place to bury.** It is significant that Aceldama, the Field of Blood, Matt. 27, 3 ff.; Acts 1, 18. 19, was located in this neighborhood. V. 12. **Thus will I do unto this place, saith the Lord, and to the inhabitants thereof,** as He had now described in detail, **and even make this city as Tophet,** as an unclean place, full of rubbish and carcasses, v. 13. **and the houses of Jerusalem and the houses of the kings of Judah,** the various buildings comprising their palaces, **shall be defiled as the place of Tophet,** polluted with dead bodies, **because of all the houses upon whose roofs they have burned incense unto all the host of heaven,** offering sacrifices to the sun and to the planets, this form of idolatry having been established or fostered by Manasseh, 2 Kings 21, 3, **and have poured out drink-offerings unto other gods,** the Lord's complaint with regard to these transgressions being repeated time and again. In our days the gross idolatry of ancient days has been replaced by a finer form of false worship, but its guilt is just as bad as in those days.

CHAPTER 20.

(Chapter 19, 14—20, 18.)

Various Experiences of Jeremiah.

PASHUR OPPOSES JEREMIAH. — Chap. 19, 14. **Then came Jeremiah from Tophet,** where his last parable had been proclaimed, **whither the Lord had sent him to prophesy; and he stood in the court of the Lord's house,** the outside court, where the people assembled in the largest numbers, **and said to all the people,** probably after repeating the prophecy pronounced in the Valley of Ben-hinnom, v. 15.

Thus saith the Lord of hosts, the God of Israel, whose majesty and supreme authority is here purposely emphasized, **Behold, I will bring upon this city and upon all her towns,** all the suburban villages, **all the evil that I have pronounced against it,** threatening destruction to the capital and death and captivity to its inhabitants, **because they have hardened their necks,** like a rebellious beast of burden, **that they might not hear My words.** Cp. chap. 16, 12; 18. 10. Chap. 20, 1. **Now, Pashur, the son of Immer, the priest, who was also chief governor in the house of the Lord,** the highest commander of the Temple-watch, who was superior even to the captains of the individual orders in charge of the Temple in the course of their service, **heard that Jeremiah prophesied these things.** V. 2. **Then Pashur,** by virtue of the police- and judicial power vested in him, which he believed he must exercise in this instance, **smote Jeremiah, the prophet,** whose office is here purposely mentioned, **and put him in the stocks,** a five-holed instrument of torture in which the neck, the two hands, and the two feet were thrust, **that were in the high gate of Benjamin,** the northern gate in the inner court of the Temple, **which was in the house of the Lord.** V. 3. **And it came to pass on the morrow,** after Jeremiah had been kept in this crooked posture over night and suffered all its tortures, **that Pashur brought forth Jeremiah out of the stocks. Then said Jeremiah unto him, The Lord hath not called thy name Pashur,** which has been interpreted by linguists as meaning "largeness and security on every side," but **Magor-missabib,** that is, "terror round about," the name, of course, signifying the fate that would befall him for his blasphemous behavior toward the Lord's servant. V. 4. **For thus saith the Lord, Behold, I will make thee a terror to thyself,** so that his evil conscience and the fear of God's wrath would leave him no rest, **and to all thy friends,** who would be dismayed upon discovering the extent to which they had been duped; **and they shall fall by the sword of their enemies,** as a result of their having given heed to Pashur's leading them astray, **and thine eyes shall behold it,** and thus be tortured by anxiety for an indefinite time; **and I will give all Judah into the hand of the king of Babylon, and he shall carry them captive into Babylon and shall slay them with the sword,** captivity and death being the fate which He had determined for them. V. 5. **Moreover, I will deliver all the strength of this city,** the total resources of the capital city, **and all the labors thereof,** what they had gained in the course of time, the uncounted material wealth, **and all the precious things thereof,** whatever treasures had been heaped up there in the course of time, **and all the treasures of the kings of Judah,** their riches as amassed from time to time, **will I give into the hand of their enemies, which shall spoil them and take them and carry them to Babylon.** V. 6. **And thou, Pashur, and all that dwell in thine house,** all the members of his family following him in his wickedness, **shall go into captivity; and thou shalt come to Babylon, and there,** far from the land of his fathers, **thou shalt die and shalt be buried there, thou and all thy friends to whom thou hast prophesied lies,** abusing his office of priest for the purpose of deceiving people. Like Pashur, there are many men in high offices in the Church to-day who abuse their position for the purpose of leading men astray and dragging them down to ruin with themselves.

THE PROPHET'S JOY AND SORROW. — V. 7. **O Lord,** thus Jeremiah now addresses the Lord in bringing his complaint over his persecutions to His attention, **Thou hast deceived me,** rather persuaded, enticed me, **and I was deceived,** he had yielded to the Lord in accepting the office of prophet; **Thou art stronger than I and hast prevailed,** His Spirit having taken hold of Jeremiah and constrained him to make known the Lord's Word and will, just as he had done; **I am in derision daily, every one mocketh me,** sneering and jeering at him when he exercised his office. V. 8. **For since I spake, I cried out, I cried violence and spoil,** or, "For as often as I speak, I must call out, I must cry, I am compelled to cry, concerning violence and desolation," he was obliged to raise his voice in complaint, **because the word of the Lord was made a reproach unto me and a derision daily,** the message which he proclaimed brought nothing but scorn upon him. V. 9. **Then I said,** or, "If I said," **I will not make mention of Him, nor speak any more in His name,** in trying to escape the unpleasant experiences which attached to his fearless testifying, **but His Word was in mine heart as a burning fire shut up in my bones,** which, without an outlet, would surely consume him, for which reason he must reveal what was communicated to him, **and I was weary with forbearing,** with refraining from testifying for the Lord, **and I could not stay.** He now states the reason for not keeping his resolve to hold his peace concerning the message of Jehovah. V. 10. **For I heard the defaming of many,** as they talked about him and his office in a derogatory manner: **Fear on every side,** or, "Terror round about!" an attempt to deride the prophecy against Pashur. **Report, say they, and we will report it,** that is, they want people to bring any sort of accusation against Jeremiah, and they would immediately act upon such information in bringing the matter to the attention of the authorities and having him punished. **All my familiars,** men who enjoyed his confidence, whom he considered his friends, **watched for my halting,** for any indication of stumbling on his part, **saying, Peradventure he will** be enticed, be induced to commit some sin, **and we shall prevail against him,** getting the better of Jeremiah in this situation, **and we shall take our revenge on him.** Over against this behavior of his false friends the prophet states the firm conviction of his heart: v. 11. **But the Lord is with me as a mighty terrible one,** as a mighty hero to defend him; **therefore my persecutors shall stumble,** come to grief in the very way in which they hoped to see the prophet humbled, **and they shall not prevail,** as they had hoped to; **they shall be greatly ashamed, for they shall not prosper,** have no success in their plotting and scheming against him; **their everlasting confusion shall never be forgotten,** they would be heaped with eternal disgrace, the ignominy of which would attach to them forever. This confidence on the part of Jeremiah now finds expression in a fervent appeal to Jehovah to take his part and defend his cause. V. 12. **But, O Lord of hosts, that triest the righteous,** not judging superficially or hastily after the manner of men, **and seest the reins and the heart,** acquainted with the innermost thoughts and desires of men, **let me see Thy vengeance on them,** for, after all, it was the Lord's matter to take up; **for unto Thee have I opened my cause,** placing his own suit or case in the hands of Jehovah. V. 13. **Sing unto the Lord, praise ye the Lord,** this being the attitude of the heart trusting in His promises, **for He hath delivered the soul of the poor,** of the lowly and unfortunate, **from the hand of evil-doers,** the believer thus possessing the gifts of the future by faith. But since Jeremiah, for the present, sees nothing but misfortune and sorrow, he cries out in the bitterness of his soul over his unhappy condition: v. 14. **Cursed be the day wherein I was born; let not the day wherein my mother bare me be blessed,** since life had not brought him blessings, but only afflictions and misery. V. 15. **Cursed be the man who brought tidings to my father, saying, A man-child is born unto thee, making him very glad,** for the birth of a boy was a very happy event. V. 16. **And let that man be as the cities which the Lord overthrew and repented not,** that is, which He destroyed without mercy; **and let him hear the cry in the morning,** namely, that of people besieged and oppressed, **and the shouting at noontide,** the wild battle-cry of the invading army, v. 17. **because he,** the person who brought the news, **slew me not from the womb, or that my mother might have been my grave and her womb to be always great with me,** so that the prophet would never have seen the light of day. V. 18. **Wherefore came I forth out of the womb to see labor and sorrow,** to experience nothing but misery, **that my days should be consumed with shame?** This cry is wrung from his lips because his office was apparently without success, because his prophetical laboring was in vain, since he was unable to save his people from destruction. Cp. Job 3, 3 ff. Similar periods of depression are liable to strike all Christians, wherefore it is necessary that all without exception grow in trust in His mercy.

CHAPTER 21.

Jerusalem to be Taken by the Chaldeans.

ZEDEKIAH'S QUESTION AND ITS ANSWER. — V. 1. **The word which came unto Jeremiah from the Lord, when King Zedekiah sent unto him Pashur, the son of Melchiah,** not the same Pashur who was mentioned in the last chapter, but the man listed with other prominent men of the kingdom in chap. 38, 1, **and Zephaniah, the son of Maaseiah, the priest, saying,** v. 2. **Enquire, I pray thee, of the Lord for us,** to find out what attitude Jehovah would take, and whether they could count on His assistance on the basis of a special revelation; **for Nebuchadrezzar, king of Babylon, maketh war against us,** this incident taking place at the time when the invaders were already near the city or about to enter; **if so be that the Lord will deal with us according to all His wondrous works,** the fact that the true God is almighty coming to their remembrance at the time of this affliction, **that he,** the invading king, **may go up from us,** discontinue his advance or raise the siege which he had even then begun. It has ever been thus, that affliction drove people to seek the Lord and His mercy, much as the same people otherwise ignored Him. V. 3. **Then said Jeremiah unto them, Thus shall ye say to Zedekiah,** v. 4. **Thus saith the Lord God of Israel,** the one true God, of whose existence the people and their king seemed to be aware only as it suited their needs and their fancy, **Behold, I will turn back the weapons of war that are in your hands wherewith ye fight against the king of Babylon and against the Chaldeans which besiege you without the walls,** so that their entire defense would be rendered vain, **and I will assemble them into the midst of this city,** so that its defenders, who were still attempting to repel the invaders outside the walls, would be compelled to take refuge in the city, their weapons having proved powerless against the enemy. V. 5. **And I Myself will fight against you with an outstretched hand and with a strong arm,** exhibiting His almighty power in punishing them, **even in anger and in fury and in great wrath,** the climax presented by the synonyms indicating that He was possessed with the highest degree of indignation, v. 6. **and I will smite the inhabitants of this city, both man and beast,** in a general sentence of punishment; **they shall die of a great pestilence,** this being the first part of the destruction decided upon by the Lord. V. 7. **And afterward, saith the Lord, I will deliver Zedekiah, king of Judah, and his servants, and the people,** the inhabitants in general, **and such as are left in this city from the pestilence, from the sword, and from the famine,** the survivors after the coming of these great scourges, **into the hand of Nebuchadrezzar, king of Babylon, and into the hand of their enemies, and into the hand of those that seek their life,** the inevitable doom being brought out in these expressions, **and he shall smite them with the edge of the sword,** in a relentless slaughter; **he shall not spare them, neither have pity nor have mercy.** Cp. Deut. 29, 29; 2 Kings 25, 6. 7; Ezek. 12, 13. Thus did Zedekiah receive his answer in agreement with his actions and his state of mind, for he did evil in the sight of the Lord.

A MESSAGE TO JUDAH AND ITS KING. — V. 8. **And unto this people thou shalt say, Thus saith the Lord, Behold, I set before you the way of life and the way of death,** putting it up to their own choice and laying the responsibility of their decision upon them. V. 9. **He that abideth in this city shall die by the sword and by the famine and by the pestilence,** the three great scourges of God's punishment which have been mentioned time and again; **but he that goeth out and falleth to the Chaldeans that besiege you,** voluntarily surrendering to them, **he shall live, and his life shall be unto him for a prey,** keeping it safely from the greed of the enemies. V. 10. **For I have set My face against this city for evil and not for good, saith the Lord,** being fully determined to pursue His course of vengeance; **it shall be given into the hand of the king of Babylon, and he shall burn it with fire.** V. 11. **And touching the house of the king of Judah,** addressing himself to the reigning house, **say, Hear ye the word of the Lord:** v. 12. **O house of David,** whose descendants were still occupying the throne of Judah, **thus saith the Lord, Execute judgment in the morning,** with all promptness and eager application, **and deliver him that is spoiled out of the hand of the oppressor,** so that justice would be dispensed in his case, **lest My fury go out like fire and burn that none can quench it, because of the evil of your doings,** which challenged the holiness of the avenging Lord. V. 13. **Behold, I am against thee, O inhabitant of the valley and rock of the plain, saith the Lord,** Jerusalem being considered, on the one hand, as being situated beneath Mount Olivet and its range, and on the other as being exalted above the lowlands toward the south and west, **which say,** in proud self-confidence, **Who shall come down against us? or who shall enter into our habitations?** deeming themselves safe from attack within fortifications which were well-nigh impregnable in those days. V. 14. **But I will punish you according to the fruit of your doings, saith the Lord,** in agreement with her wicked deeds; **and I will kindle a fire in the forest thereof, and it shall devour all things round about it,** the city itself, with all its suburbs, being considered a forest of dwellings. Thus the specific items in the destruction of Jerusalem were ever and again brought to the attention of the apostate Jews, just as the individual incidents of the Last Judgment are set forth at length and with careful attention to details in the New Testament.

CHAPTER 22.

Against the Wicked Kings of Judah.

WARNING AGAINST UNRIGHTEOUSNESS AND OPPRESSION. — V. 1. **Thus saith the Lord, Go down to the house of the king of Judah,** from the Temple to the palace, which was situated at a lower level, **and speak there this word,** not merely in the presence of the king, but as a message to the entire nation, v. 2. **and say, Hear the word of the Lord, O king of Judah, that sittest upon the throne of David,** a fact which committed him to the high standards set by that friend of God, **thou and thy servants,** the members of his court, **and thy people that enter in by these gates,** those of the royal palace: v. 3. **Thus saith the Lord, Execute ye judgment and righteousness,** as the fundamental principle of Jehovah's nation, cp. chap. 7, 6; 21, 12, **and deliver the spoiled out of the hand of the oppressor,** rescuing those who were being systematically plundered by the mightier people of the nation; **and do no wrong, do no violence to the stranger, the fatherless, nor the widow,** in excessive taxation and other unjust exactions, **neither shed innocent blood in this place,** all of these transgressions having freely been committed by the later kings of Judah; for in the same measure as their standing among the nations lost in prestige, they practised tyranny at home. V. 4. **For if ye do this thing indeed, then shall there enter in by the gates of this house kings sitting upon the throne of David,** as his successors in a direct line, **riding in chariots and on horses, he and his servants and his people.** Cp. chap. 17, 25.

V. 5. **But if ye will not hear these words,** disregarding their solemn warning, **I swear by Myself, saith the Lord,** by the highest instance to which appeal can be made at any time, **that this house shall become a desolation,** the splendid royal palace becoming a total ruin. V. 6. **For thus saith the Lord unto the king's house of Judah,** concerning the royal palace with all its inestimable splendor, **Thou art Gilead unto Me and the head of Lebanon,** the point of comparison being the many pillars and ornaments of costly wood derived from the forests of Gilead and of Lebanon, which made the complex of buildings comprising the royal palace a veritable forest of oaks and cedars; **yet surely I will make thee a wilderness,** a treeless wilderness, **and cities which are not inhabited.** V. 7. **And I will prepare destroyers against thee,** consecrated, as it were, to perform His will in bringing destruction upon Jerusalem and the palace of the king, **every one with his weapons; and they shall cut down thy choice cedars and cast them into the fire,** the picture of a forest's destruction being maintained to this point. V. 8. **And many nations shall pass by this city,** the entire capital being destroyed with the Temple and the royal palace, **and they shall say every man to his neighbor,** in wonder and astonishment over such utter desolation, **Wherefore hath the Lord done thus unto this great city?** V. 9. **Then they shall answer, Because they have forsaken the covenant of the Lord, their God, and worshiped other gods, and served them.** Cp. Deut. 29, 23 ff.; 1 Kings 9, 8. 9. Jerusalem is only one of the many cities which, in the course of time, have become spectacles of God's vengeance, as a warning to all men to heed His commands.

PROPHECIES RELATING TO SHALLUM, JEHOIAKIM, AND JEHOIACHIN. — V. 10. **Weep ye not for the dead,** so Jeremiah admonished the people of Judah, **neither bemoan him,** namely, Josiah, the last good king, who had stayed the doom pronounced upon the reprobate people, **but weep sore for him that goeth away,** whose departure in this case is truly an occasion for great sorrowing, **for he shall return no more nor see his native country,** being dragged into a shameful exile, from which there would be no deliverance. V. 11. **For thus saith the Lord touching Shallum,** or Jehoahaz, 2 Kings 23, 30. 31, **the son of Josiah, king of Judah, which reigned instead of Josiah, his father, which went forth out of this place,** having been taken to Egypt by Pharaoh-Nechoh, who placed his older brother Jehoiakim on the throne, much to the dissatisfaction of the people, **He shall not return thither any more,** v. 12. **but he shall die in the place whither they have led him captive, and shall see this land no more.** It happened in just this way, as the sacred narrative informs us, 2 Kings 23, 34. V. 13. **Woe unto him,** so the Lord now proceeds to call out upon Jehoiakim, **that buildeth his house by unrighteousness,** by unjust measures, **and his chambers by wrong,** in impressing people into work without right and compensation, **that useth his neighbor's service without wages and giveth him not for his work;** v. 14. **that saith, I will build me a wide house and large chambers,** roomy, airy upper chambers, **and cutteth him out windows,** with wide and high openings, such as were found in the palaces of the rich; **and it is ceiled with cedar and painted with vermilion,** a costly paint made of sulphur and quicksilver. All this oppressing of poor workmen and the proud show of splendor that went with it was characteristic of the reign of Jehoiakim. V. 15. **Shalt thou reign because thou closest thyself in cedar?** making a show of wealth which he did not in reality possess and had no right to parade. **Did not thy father eat and drink,** enjoying the ordinary comforts of life, **and do judgment and justice?** exercising these two virtues according to the demands of righteousness. **And then it was well with him,** the blessing of the Lord resting upon him for his upright behavior. V. 16. **He judged the cause of the poor and needy; then it was well with him. Was not this to know Me? saith the Lord.** V. 17. **But thine eyes and thine heart are not but for thy covetousness,** being directed only to the gaining of his own advantage, regardless of the rights of other people, **and for to shed innocent blood and for oppression and for violence to do it,** Jehoiakim thus proving himself a tyrant in every sense of the word. V. 18. **Therefore, thus saith the Lord concerning Jehoiakim, the son of Josiah, king of Judah,** the subject of this entire paragraph of denunciation, **They shall not lament for him, saying, Ah, my brother! or, Ah, sister!** none of the mournful cries such as relatives make at the death of those near and dear to them being heard in this instance. **They shall not lament for him, saying, Ah, lord! or, Ah, his glory!** that is, "Alas, His Majesty!" his subjects also declining to show any grief over his end. Unpraised, unhonored, and unsung he would pass away from among the living. V. 19. **He shall be buried with the burial of an ass, drawn and cast forth beyond the gates of Jerusalem,** not interred, but dragged forth and left as carrion to the birds and beasts of prey. V. 20. **Go up to Lebanon,** so the prophet now bids the people, personified as the daughter of Zion, **and cry, and lift up thy voice in Bashan,** that is, the mountains of Bashan, in the country east of Jordan, **and cry from the passages,** rather, "from Abarim," the mountain range east of the Dead Sea, to which Nebo belonged, the three highest points being named, from which one could overlook the entire country; **for all thy lovers are destroyed,** namely, all the kings of the allied nations, upon whom Judah depended for help, together with their people, not only Egypt, but the smaller kingdoms of Syria and of Northern Arabia as well. All of these were brought into subjection by Nebuchadnezzar and his armies. V. 21. **I spake unto thee in thy prosperity,** while the country was enjoying prosperous, secure, peaceful relations; **but thou saidst, I will not hear. This hath been thy manner from thy youth,** from the days that He chose Israel to be His people and led them forth from the land of their bondage, Hos. 2, 17, **that thou obeyedst not My voice,** the Lord being obliged to rebuke them time and again for their rebellious conduct. V. 22. **The wind shall eat up all thy pastors,** all their rulers and leaders, as the hot desert wind singed off the meadows, **and thy lovers shall go into captivity. Surely then shalt thou be ashamed and confounded for all thy wickedness;** for with her rulers in captivity, Judah would be helpless before the invaders. V. 23. **O inhabitant of Lebanon, that makest thy nest in the cedars,** this picture being chosen because, as the birds of Lebanon make their nests in the cedars, so the princes of Judah built their homes of the cedars of Lebanon, **how gracious shalt thou be,** rather, "how shalt thou moan," **when pangs come upon thee, the pain as of a woman in travail!** After this digression with its warning to the people as a whole the prophet turns to the consideration of Jehoiachin's fate. V. 24. **As I live, saith the Lord, though Coniah,** abbreviated from Jeconiah, 1 Chron. 3, 16, **the son of Jehoiakim, king of Judah, were the signet upon My right hand,** a most costly and valued ornament, which one guards with great care, **yet would I pluck thee thence,** this being affirmed with a solemn vow, God's most impressive formula of oath, by His own life! V. 25. **And I will give thee into the hand of them that seek thy life, and into the hand of them whose face thou fearest,** deliberately delivering him into the power of his enemies everywhere, **even into the hand of Nebuchadrezzar, king of Babylon, and into the hand of the Chaldeans.** V. 26. **And I will cast thee out, and thy mother that bare thee,** namely, Nehushta, the daughter of Elnathan, 2 Kings 24, 8, **into another country, where ye were not born,** one utterly strange to them in every way; **and there shall ye die.** V. 27. **But to the land whereunto they,** Coniah and his mother, **desire to return, thither shall they not return.** By the change to the third person these two were put out of sight, as unworthy to be addressed directly any longer. The prophet now addresses the country as such with reference to the fate of this favorite king, whom the people idolized. V. 28. **Is this man Coniah a despised broken idol?** so the people are represented as asking. **Is he a vessel wherein is no pleasure?** with whom neither God nor men were pleased. **Wherefore are they cast out, he and his seed,** the presence of minor children at the time when he was led away into captivity being altogether probable, **and are cast into a land which they know not?** Upon this astonished question the Lord answers with a powerful appeal. V. 29. **O earth, earth, earth,** the threefold repetition serving to lay particular stress upon the contents of this warning, **hear the word of the Lord!** V. 30. **Thus saith the Lord, Write ye this man childless,** bereaved of his children, **a man that shall not prosper in his days; for no man of his seed shall prosper, sitting upon the throne of David,** succeeding to the kingdom, **and ruling any more in Judah.** According to the list given in 1 Chron. 3, 16. 17, the family of Jeconiah became extinct in the second generation. It is to be noted, however, that, although the succession to the throne failed in the line of this king, still the promise of the Lord to David, Ps. 89, 30—37, was revived in Zerubbabel and thus continued to Christ.

CHAPTER 23.

Of the Messiah, the True Shepherd.

THE RESTORATION OF THE SCATTERED FLOCK. V. 1. **Woe be unto the pastors,** the rulers, the spiritual leaders of the people in particular, **that destroy and scatter the sheep of My pasture! saith the Lord,** Israel and Judah, specifically the congregation of the Lord in the midst of the people, are called the flock of Jehovah's pasturage because He attends them with His particular care. All the more reason, therefore, to denounce the leaders who were so wilfully forgetful of their duties. V. 2. **Therefore thus saith the Lord God of Israel against the pastors that feed My people,** to whom this sacred duty was entrusted, **Ye have scattered My flock and driven them away,** instead of holding them together in a compact flock, **and have not visited them,** this being the most reprehensible form of neglect. **Behold, I will visit upon you,** in a visitation of His avenging wrath, **the evil of your doings, saith the Lord.** V. 3. **And I will gather the remnant of My flock,** the true spiritual Israel, **out of all countries whither I have driven them,** for although the people themselves had permitted themselves to be corrupted by their false leaders, yet the burden of the guilt lay on the rulers, this phase of the matter being emphasized in this instance, **and will bring them again to their folds,** as congregations of believers; **and they shall be fruitful and increase,** according to the blessings of the Gospel-promise. V. 4. **And I will set up shepherds over them which shall feed them,** teach them in full agreement with the will of Jehovah; **and they shall fear no more nor be dismayed,** terrified by the coming of the enemies, **neither shall they be lacking, saith the Lord,** they will not be missed, that is, they would no more be lost from the flock, since the Lord's shepherds would take the best care of them. The Messianic import of this passage is unmistakable, but this factor is brought out even more strongly in the next paragraph. V. 5. **Behold, the days come, saith the Lord, that I will raise unto David a righteous Branch, and a King shall reign and prosper,** success attending His wise and prudent dealing, **and shall execute judgment and justice in the earth.** V. 6. **In His days Judah shall be saved and Israel shall dwell safely. And this is His name whereby He shall be called, THE LORD OUR RIGHTEOUSNESS.** Here the Messiah is spoken of by a name, in a figure, which is used also by Isaiah and Zechariah. To David, namely, as a descendant of Judah, as a member of his family, Jehovah will cause to arise a righteous Branch, a shoot characterized by, and distinguished for, righteousness. This Branch will at the same time be a King, who would have royal power and would make use of that power and authority in taking care of the affairs of His kingdom in a prudent manner. The excellency of His rule would be brought out particularly by the fact that He would perform judgment and execute righteousness according to unquestioned standards, although unusual in the eyes of men. For He would show these traits in bringing salvation to Judah and in letting Israel dwell in safety, both expressions referring to the true spiritual Israel, the Church of Christ. No wonder, then, that His name would be called "Jehovah Our Righteousness," since, by virtue of His perfect atonement, all men may become partakers of the righteousness earned by Him for them. V. 7. **Therefore, behold, the days come, saith the Lord, that they shall no more say,** in the form of oath prevalent at that time, **The Lord liveth, which brought up the children of Israel out of the land of Egypt;** v. 8. **but, The Lord liveth, which brought up and which led the seed of the house of Israel,** the stock of the new people of Jehovah, **out of the north country, and from all countries whither I had driven them,** since the Lord had scattered them throughout the countries pertaining to the Babylonian Empire; **and they shall dwell in their own land.** Cp. chap. 16, 14. 15. "Jehovah Our Righteousness" is the one Hope of all mankind; for by faith in His redemption men become partakers of the righteousness earned by Him, which makes them just in the sight of God.

AGAINST THE FALSE PROPHETS. — V. 9. **Mine heart within me is broken because of the prophets,** the inscription of this entire section being "Concerning the Prophets," **all my bones shake,** in deep agitation and horror; **I am like a drunken man and like a man whom wine hath overcome, because of the Lord and because of the words of His holiness,** namely, because he feels in advance the terrors of the judgment which would come upon his countrymen on account of the wickedness of the false prophets. V. 10. **For the land is full of adulterers,** this crime being unusually prevalent at that time, as a natural consequence of the shameless rites introduced in connection with the idolatry practised by the false prophets; **for because of swearing the land mourneth,** that is, on account of the curse following such a grave transgression the land was fading away like a wilting flower, **the pleasant places of the wilderness are dried up,** the very pastures of the steppes no longer yielding sufficient food for the herds of cattle which usually dotted their slopes; **and their course,** that of both prophets and people, in practising adultery, **is evil,** their thought and endeavor in general, their entire behavior, being wicked and guilty, **and their force is not right,** they excel in wrong and wickedness. V. 11. **For both prophet and priest are profane,** void of all true consecration; **yea, in My house have I found their wickedness, saith the Lord,** most likely in their shameless idolatry, which they did not hesitate to practise in the very courts of the Lord's Temple. V. 12. **Wherefore their way shall be unto them as slippery ways in the darkness,** their false doctrine and their sinful life proving their downfall; **they shall be driven on and fall therein,** that is, they would be pushed and thus brought to fall in their own transgressions; **for I will bring evil upon them, even the year of their visitation, saith the Lord,** so that His calamity would strike them at the appointed time, at the time of Jehovah's punishment. In order to emphasize the wickedness of the prophets, they are now compared with the prophets of Samaria, the religion of which was a strange mixture of Jehovah cult and heathen abominations. V. 13. **And I have seen folly in the prophets of Samaria,** perversity and absurdity, the teaching of insipid doctrines; **they prophesied in Baal,** insisting that they were inspired by this idol, **and caused My people Israel to err.** Cp. 1 Kings 18, 19 ff. But the behavior of the prophets of Judah is still more terrible. V. 14. **I have seen also in the prophets of Jerusalem an horrible thing,** an abomination which filled him with loathing: **they commit adultery and walk in lies,** in an utterly immoral and hypocritical life; **they strengthen also the hands of evil-doers,** instead of reproving and converting them, **that none doth return from his wickedness; they are all of them unto Me as Sodom and the inhabitants thereof as Gomorrah,** the essence of all putrid wickedness. V. 15. **Therefore, thus saith the Lord of hosts concerning the prophets,** the leaders in wickedness, the seducers of the people, **Behold, I will feed them with wormwood and make them drink the water of gall,** poison water, cp. chap. 9, 14; **for from the prophets of Jerusalem is profaneness gone forth into all the land,** so that profligacy was practised everywhere; the Holy Land was desecrated and the Word of the Lord blasphemed, even as it is to-day in consequence of similar behavior on the part of men who call themselves ministers of the Word. V. 16. **Thus saith the Lord of hosts,** in warning the true believers against the deception of the false prophets, **Hearken not unto the words of the prophets that prophesy unto you; they make you vain,** deceiving them, seducing them to the vanity of idolatry; **they speak a vision of their own heart,** revelations of their own imagination, **and not out of the mouth of the Lord,** their so-called messages to the people being made without authorization of Jehovah. V. 17. **They say still unto them that despise Me,** to the outspoken enemies of the Lord, **The Lord hath said, Ye shall have peace,** be safe from harm; **and they say unto every one that walketh after the imagination of his own heart,** in the stubbornness of a wilful disobedience to the Lord's will, **No evil shall come upon you,** thus proclaiming a security which the Lord had expressly denied them. V. 18. **For who hath stood in the counsel of the Lord,** when He made His plans concerning the punishment of the wicked, **and hath perceived and heard His Word?** The answer implied is an emphatic *no,* so far as the false prophets are concerned. **Who hath marked His Word and heard it?** The prophet again denies that any of these false, self-appointed prophets can be mouthpieces of Jehovah. Jeremiah, on the contrary, now proclaims a word of the Lord which is entirely different in content from the inventions of the false prophets. V. 19. **Behold, a whirlwind of the Lord is gone forth in fury, even a grievous whirlwind!** or, "Behold a storm from Jehovah! Fury goes forth and a whirling storm"; **it shall fall grievously upon the head of the wicked,** falling upon the ungodly, hurled upon them to their utter destruction. V. 20. **The anger of the Lord shall not return,** not cease from carrying out His judgment, **until He have executed and till He have performed the thoughts of His heart,** everything that He had planned with regard to the destruction of Judah and Jerusalem. **In the latter days,** at the time when His judgment would strike the people, **ye shall consider it perfectly,** becoming fully aware of the truth of His threats. At the same time the Lord denies that He has in any way authorized the deceivers of His people. V. 21. **I have not sent these prophets,** they had not been commissioned as His messengers, **yet they ran,** unnaturally eager to carry out their self-imposed task; **I have not spoken to them, yet they prophesied,** insisting that they possessed the prophetic spirit of the true God. V. 22. **But if they had stood in My counsel and had caused My people to hear My words,** proclaiming them as they were truly revealed, **then they should have turned them from their evil way and from the evil of their doings,** in other words, they would preach repentance from idolatry instead of confirming the people in their false security, which has ever been a trick of such as falsely proclaimed themselves messengers of the Lord. To give weight to these reproofs, the Lord now shows why it is that He is familiar with the hypocritical conduct of the false prophets. V. 23. **Am I a God at hand, saith the Lord,** one whose power is limited to a small circle, **and not a God afar off?** whose power and understanding is unlimited. V. 24. **Can any hide himself in secret places that I shall not see him? saith the Lord.** It was a foolish idea to think that the all-knowing God would not know his whereabouts. **Do not I fill heaven and earth? saith the Lord,** nothing being hidden from His omniscient gaze, from His omnipresence. With these attributes at His disposal, the Lord is naturally familiar with the acts and thoughts of all men everywhere. V. 25. **I have heard what the prophets said that prophesy lies in My name, saying, I have dreamed, I have dreamed,** offering the dross of their own imagination instead of the gold of God's Word. V. 26. **How long shall this be in the heart of the prophets that prophesy lies? Yea, they are prophets of the deceit of their own heart,** with which they lead men astray, v. 27. **which think to cause My people to forget My name by their dreams which they tell every man to his neighbor,** since they substituted them for the truth revealed in the Word of the Lord, **as their fathers have forgotten My name for Baal.** Cp. Judg. 3, 7; 8, 33. 34. The Lord now sets forth the principle which is to guide those who claim for themselves the authority of His messengers. V. 28. **The prophet that hath a dream, let him tell a dream,** frankly relating it as such, without indulging in extravagant assertions; **and he that hath My Word,** being entrusted with its proclamation, **let him speak My Word faithfully,** in sincerity and truth. **What is the chaff to the wheat? saith the Lord.** The dreams of the false prophets are chaff, empty straw; God's Word alone is the grain, the real substance. And still more the Lord asserts in characterizing His Word, the only message that has the right to be proclaimed as the eternal truth. V. 29. **Is not My Word like as a fire? saith the Lord,** devouring and destroying all the philosophy of men which will not stand the test of His eternal truth, **and like a hammer that breaketh the rock in pieces?** its power overcoming even the hardest and the strongest fabric of men's imagination. Cp. Heb. 4, 12. V. 30. **Therefore,** because the false prophets were practising deceit and seducing the people, **behold, I am against the prophets, saith the Lord, that steal My words, every one from his neighbor.** They appropriated the inspired sayings of the true prophets in order to give their own oracles a show of right. V. 31. **Behold, I am against the prophets, saith the Lord, that use their tongues and say, He saith,** literally, "that take their own tongues and utter a divine oracle," asserting that they were proclaiming messages from the true God, when they were setting forth nothing but their own inventions. V. 32. **Behold, I am against them that prophesy false dreams, saith the Lord,** insisting that the fabric of their own thoughts was to be accepted as God's revelation, **and do tell them, and cause My people,** as the Lord still calls them for the sake of the true believers in their midst, **to err by their lies and by their lightness,** by their boastful and wanton inventions; **yet I sent them not nor commanded them; therefore they shall not profit this people at all, saith the Lord,** a most emphatic statement that their activity would result in nothing but injury to the people. V. 33. **And when this people or the prophet or a priest,** either the common people or one of their spiritual leaders, **shall ask thee, saying, What is the burden of the Lord?** according to a custom by which the prophet was asked concerning some probable new revelations, which they purposely designated as an unpleasant burden, **thou shalt then say unto them, What burden?** or, "Thou shalt tell them what the burden of Jehovah is," namely, **I will even forsake you, saith the Lord,** an unloading of the burden, a rejecting of the people. V. 34. **And as for the prophet and the priest and the people that shall say, The burden of the Lord,** in blasphemous mockery of His solemn announcement, **I will even punish that man and his house,** all the members of a man's family who are guilty with him. V. 35. **Thus shall ye say, every one to his neighbor and every one to his brother, What hath the Lord answered? and, What hath the Lord spoken?** thus showing the proper respect for the prophecy of Jehovah. V. 36. **And the burden of the Lord shall ye mention no more,** no more toss this expression about in mockery; **for every man's word shall be his burden,** that is, this expression, if used in such a jeering sense, would become a burden to such a scorner, heavy enough to bear him down to the ground; **for ye have perverted the words of the living God, of the Lord of hosts, our God,** whose majesty is here emphatically declared, to give added weight to His proclamation. V. 37. **Thus shalt thou say to the prophet, What hath the Lord answered thee? and, What hath the Lord spoken?** That alone was the proper way of speaking to Jehovah's messenger. V. 38. **But since ye say, The burden of the Lord,** persisting in their meanness in spite of the Lord's express command, **therefore, thus saith the Lord, Because ye say this word, The burden of the Lord, and I have sent unto you, saying, Ye shall not say, The burden of the Lord,** v. 39. **therefore, behold, I, even I,** spoken with great solemnity and impressiveness, **will utterly forget you,** rather, "I will altogether lift you up and burden you," **and I will forsake you,** thrusting them with great force, **and the city that I gave you and your fathers, and cast you out of My presence;** v. 40. **and I will bring an everlasting reproach upon you and a perpetual shame,** namely, on the part of all her enemies and all the witnesses of her downfall, **which shall not be forgotten.** A similar fate awaits those who in our days purposely follow the lead of the false prophets and join them in jeering and mocking those who confess the truth of God's Word.

CHAPTER 24.

The Two Baskets of Figs.

A TYPE OF JUDAH'S FUTURE. — V. 1. **The Lord showed me, and, behold,** as Jeremiah was vouchsafed this strange vision, **two baskets of figs were set before the Temple of the Lord,** in the place which was set apart for offerings of this kind, cp. Amos 7, 1. 4. 7, **after that Nebuchadrezzar, king of Babylon, had carried away captive Jeconiah, the son of Jehoiakim, king of Judah, and the princes of Judah,** the rulers and nobles, the mighty of the land, **with the carpenters and smiths,** the craftsmen skilled in the making of weapons, **from Jerusalem, and had brought them to Babylon,** an act which so weakened the power of the Jews as to make it practically impossible for them to prepare for war. Cp. 2 Kings 24, 14—17. This incident evidently happened at the beginning of Zedekiah's reign, when the country had been reduced to a condition of vassalage to the Chaldeans. V. 2. **One basket had very good figs,** being full of very fine specimens of this fruit, **even like the figs that are first ripe,** which were considered special delicacies; **and the other basket had very naughty figs,** bad, unwholesome, rotten fruit, **which could not be eaten, they were so bad.** V. 3. **Then said the Lord unto me, What seest thou, Jeremiah? And I said, Figs; the good figs very good and the evil very evil, that cannot be eaten, they are so evil.** The purpose of the question was to impress the lesson upon Jeremiah's mind, to call attention to the objects which were to symbolize the Jews. V. 4. **Again the word of the Lord came unto me, saying,** v. 5. **Thus saith the Lord, the God of Israel,** still the God of the covenant to all who are Israelites in truth, **Like these good figs, so will I acknowledge them that are carried away captive of Judah,** regarding them with favor, extending His pleasure to them, **whom I have sent out of this place into the land of the Chaldeans for their good,** to let them experience His blessings, to have them realize that His method of dealing with them was for their own benefit. V. 6. **For I will set Mine eyes upon them for good,** being most attentive to their wants in this respect, **and I will bring them again to this land; and I will build them and not pull them down,** as a building condemned to be wrecked; **and I will plant them and not pluck them up,** like a poisonous plant or dangerous weed. The removal of these Jews to Babylon saved them from the calamities which befell the rest of the nation, and led them to repentance in the land of their captivity, the result being that their condition was bettered. V. 7. **And I will give them an heart to know Me, that I am the Lord,** the punishment of the Babylonion captivity directing their minds to the one true God, who could thus carry out His threats, so that they likewise looked for mercy to Him alone; **and they shall be My people, and I will be their God,** thus restoring the original relation, which had been so rudely disturbed and made impossible by their idolatry; **for they shall return unto Me with their whole heart,** or, "I will be their God when they return to Me with their whole heart." V. 8. **And as the evil figs, which cannot be eaten they are so evil: surely thus saith the Lord, So will I give Zedekiah, the king of Judah, and his princes,** all the rulers and nobles of the people, **and the residue of Jerusalem that remain in this land, and them that dwell in the land of Egypt,** the obstinate Jews, who refused to heed His warning and accept His advice to yield to the Chaldeans; v. 9. **and I will deliver them to be removed into all the kingdoms of the earth for their hurt,** literally, "I will give them for a shaking-up, for evil to all kingdoms of the earth," so that abuse and misfortune would strike them everywhere, **to be a reproach and a proverb, a taunt and a curse, in all places whither I shall drive them,** they would be the object of blasphemous derision on the part of all those with whom they would come into contact. V. 10. **And I will send the sword, the famine, and the pestilence,** the great scourges of all times, **among them, till they be consumed from off the land,** exterminated, extirpated from the Land of Promise, **that I gave unto them and to their fathers.** Thus the Lord predicts further invasions and repeated sackings of Jerusalem. Thus was His curse, as uttered in the Law, Deut. 28, 37, carried out upon all those who refused Him obedience according to His demand, as a warning to the men of all times.

CHAPTER 25.

The Judgment on Judah and the Kingdoms of the World.

THE JUDGMENT ON JUDAH. — V. 1. **The word that came to Jeremiah concerning all the people of Judah in the fourth year of Jehoiakim, the son of Josiah, king of Judah, that was the first year of Nebuchadrezzar, king of Babylon,** the year 606 B. C., the date being determined so exactly because it marked the final turning-point in the history of Judah as well as for the nations of the entire Orient, since Nebuchadnezzar at that time took charge of the Babylonian armies as king in fact, if not in name, although his aged father, Nabopolassar, was still living, defeated Pharaoh-Nechoh at Carchemish on the Euphrates, overran Canaan, took Jerusalem, and made Jehoiakim his vassal; v. 2. **the which,** namely, the word of prophecy transmitted to him from the Lord, **Jeremiah, the prophet, spake unto all the people of Judah and to all the inhabitants of Jerusalem, saying,** v. 3. **From the thirteenth year of Josiah, the son of Amon, king of Judah,** who reigned from approximately 641 to 610 B. C., **even unto this day, that is, the three and twentieth year,** in other words, for twenty-three years, **the word of the Lord hath come unto me,** his public ministry having begun approximately in the year 629 B. C., **and I have spoken unto you, rising early and speaking,** devoting himself with all zeal and earnestness to his work; **but ye have not hearkened,** the same accusation being made here which he had been obliged to bring against them time and again. V. 4. **And the Lord hath sent unto you all His servants, the prophets,** for Zephaniah and Habakkuk and the prophetess Huldah had also been active during this period, **rising early and sending them,** eagerly concerned about their welfare; **but ye have not hearkened nor inclined your ear to hear,** they had paid not the slightest attention, they had completely ignored His message. V. 5. **They said,** literally, "saying," the word referring either to Jeremiah alone or to all the prophets, **Turn ye again now every one from his evil way,** from his wicked manner of living, **and from the evil of your doings,** their wickedness finding its expression in all the acts of their life, **and dwell in the land that the Lord hath given unto you and to your fathers forever and ever,** with the intention that they should always possess it; v. 6. **and go not after other gods to serve them and to worship them,** in the idolatry which they had practised so flagrantly and shamelessly, **and provoke Me not to anger with the works of your hands,** chiefly their idolatrous sacrifices, **and I will do you no hurt,** for all the prophets had told them time and again that their conduct would bring God's punishment upon them. V. 7. **Yet ye have not hearkened unto Me, saith the Lord; that ye might provoke Me to anger with the works of your hands,** as the natural consequence of their obstinate disobedience, **to your own hurt.** V. 8. **Therefore, thus saith the Lord of hosts,** whose sublime authority is unquestioned, **Because ye have not heard My words,** v. 9. **behold, I will send and take all the families of the North, saith the Lord,** all the nations which were allies to the Chaldeans, **and Nebuchadrezzar, the king of Babylon, My servant,** who is so designated in this case because in this campaign he carried out the plans of the Lord, **and will bring them against this land and against the inhabitants thereof and against all these nations round about,** whom Judah had so often chosen as allies, **and will utterly destroy them and make them an astonishment and an hissing and perpetual desolations,** so that onlookers would be filled with horror, which, however, would quickly be changed to a sneer of satisfaction and malice as the former fruitful fields were gradually converted into a wilderness. V. 10. **Moreover, I will take from them the voice of mirth,** of loud rejoicing, **and the voice of gladness, the voice of the bridegroom and the voice of the bride, the sound of the millstones,** whose incessant grinding noise indicated a happy household in the Orient, **and the light of the candle,** even the poorest house in the East having an open oil-lamp with a linen or cotton wick burning all night. Cp. Is. 24, 7. V. 11. **And this whole land shall be a desolation,** the territory not only of Judah, but of the surrounding nations as well, **and an astonishment,** a source of amazement to all beholders; **and these nations,** Judah and its neighbors, **shall serve the king of Babylon seventy years,** which, beginning with 606 B. C., was the length of the period during which the supremacy of Babylon was unquestioned. The exactness with which every detail of the prophecy is set forth is no more remarkable than the literal fulfilment of the Lord's prediction.

THE JUDGMENT ON THE KINGDOMS. — V. 12. **And it shall come to pass, when seventy years are accomplished,** namely, from the time of the first deportation to Babylon, **that I will punish the king of Babylon and that nation, saith the Lord, for their iniquity,** visiting their guilt upon them **and the land of the Chaldeans, and will make it perpetual desolations,** the enemies thus being punished in turn, even as it happened when the Medes and Persians under the command of Cyrus overthrew the Babylonian empire. V. 13. **And I will bring upon that land all My words which I have pronounced against it,** carrying out His threats upon the entire country, **even all that is written in this book, which Jeremiah hath prophesied against all the nations,** for it was in this year that Jeremiah was, for the first time, told to write all his prophecies against the various foreign nations in a book, so that this remark was inserted when the collection was made. V. 14. **For many nations and great kings shall serve themselves of them also,** that is, the Chaldeans themselves would, in turn, become servants to others, so that their masters would exact the service of vassals from them; **and I will recompense them according to their deeds and according to the works of their own hands.** This is further emphasized by the picture of the Lord's cup of fury. V. 15. **For thus saith the Lord God of Israel unto me, Take the wine-cup of this fury at My hand,** a symbol of stupefying judgments, **and cause all the nations to whom I send thee to drink it,** a symbolical action which could be used to illustrate an important truth. V. 16. **And they shall drink and be moved,** so that they would stagger and reel, **and be mad,** stunned and stupefied with the intoxicating effects of the liquid consumed, **because of the sword that I will send among them,** that is, the war which the Lord intended to bring upon these nations would be so severe, so horrible, that people would be stupefied by its terrors and perish in helpless confusion. V. 17. **Then took I the cup at the Lord's hand,** all this in the vision which was vouchsafed him, **and made all the nations to drink unto whom the Lord had sent me,** namely, by making an open announcement of this intention on the part of Jehovah: v. 18. **to wit, Jerusalem and the cities of Judah,** these two heading the list as the chief offenders against the Lord of the covenant, **and the kings thereof and the princes thereof, to make them a desolation, an astonishment, an hissing, and a curse,** objects of mockery and imprecations,

as it is this day; v. 19. **Pharaoh, king of Egypt,** upon whom the Jews had chiefly relied, **and his servants and his princes and all his people,** v. 20. **and all the mingled people,** small tribes of a mixed population near the borders of Egypt and elsewhere, **and all the kings of the land of Uz,** in Northwestern Arabia, near the borders of Idumea and Egypt, **and all the kings of the land of the Philistines,** of the various Philistine city-states, **and Ashkelon, and Azzah,** or Gazah, **and Ekron, and the remnant of Ashdod,** this city being very much reduced in size and influence on account of the Egyptian oppression, Gath, the fifth of the ancient city-states, not being mentioned, probably because it no longer was a separate capital, v. 21. **Edom,** south of the Dead Sea, **and Moab,** east of the Dead Sea, **and the children of Ammon,** tribes to the northeast of Moab, v. 22. **and all the kings of Tyrus, and all the kings of Zidon,** the representative cities of Phenicia on the Mediterranean Sea, **and the kings of the isles which are beyond the sea,** all the distant countries along the shores of the Mediterranean and the nations on its islands, v. 23. **Dedan,** north of Arabia, **and Tema,** an Arabian city not far from Damascus, **and Buz,** another city and tribe in this neighborhood, **and all that are in the utmost corners,** the entire section of Arabia bordering on Palestine, v. 24. **and all the kings of Arabia, and all the kings of the mingled people that dwell in the desert,** where tribes no longer were of pure blood, v. 25. **and all the kings of Zimri,** probably a country toward the Euphrates, **and all the kings of Elam,** to the east of the Tigris, used for Persia in general, **and all the kings of the Medes,** v. 26. **and all the kings of the North, far and near,** a general expression referring to all the empires in the valleys of the Euphrates and the Tigris and beyond, **one with another, and all the kingdoms of the world, which are upon the face of the earth, and the king of Sheshach, shall drink after them,** Babylon itself being designated by this term and included in the list of those who were to be stunned by the wine of God's avenging fury. V. 27. **Therefore thou shalt say unto them, Thus saith the Lord of hosts,** whose majesty and power would here find expression, **the God of Israel, Drink ye,** namely, the cup of the Lord's fierce anger, **and be drunken, and spue,** vomiting as a result of their excessive drinking, **and fall, and rise no more,** being completely overcome by the powerful potion, **because of the sword which I will send among you.** V. 28. **And it shall be, if they refuse to take the cup at thine hand to drink,** unwilling to let His punishment strike them, **then shalt thou say unto them, Thus saith the Lord of hosts, Ye shall certainly drink,** compelled to endure the destruction which had been resolved upon in their case. V. 29. **For, lo, I begin to bring evil on the city which is called by My name,** revealed in the Word which had been proclaimed by His prophets from the early days, Jerusalem being the center of the true worship, **and should ye be utterly unpunished?** Should the Lord treat the others as innocent and forbear wreaking His vengeance upon them, if He did not spare the city which He had chosen as the place of His Sanctuary? **Ye shall not be unpunished; for I will call for a sword upon all the inhabitants of the earth, saith the Lord of hosts.** His patience was now exhausted, and He intended to include all His enemies in the punishment which was about to go forth.

THE JUDGMENT UPON THE WORLD. — V. 30. **Therefore prophesy thou against them all these words,** all nations being included in this address, **and say unto them, The Lord shall roar from on high,** with an angry voice, **and utter His voice from His holy habitation,** heaven being regarded as His dwelling-place. **He shall mightily roar upon His habitation,** or "against His pasturage," the picture of a lion roaring against the flock in the pasture being continued. **He shall give a shout,** a clear cry of exultation, **as they that tread the grapes,** to the accompaniment of a regular shout enabling them to keep time, **against all the inhabitants of the earth,** that is, of the land of Judah as beginning the judgment upon the whole world. V. 31. **A noise shall come even to the ends of the earth,** that is, the tumult of enormous armies; **for the Lord hath a controversy with the nations,** a cause at issue before the tribunal of His justice; **He will plead with all flesh,** cp. Is. 66, 16; **He will,** as the result of this just trial, **give them that are wicked to the sword, saith the Lord,** to be executed in battle at His command. V. 32. **Thus saith the Lord of hosts,** the Commander of the heavenly armies, **Behold, evil shall go forth from nation to nation,** in a continual progress, **and a great whirlwind shall be raised up from the coasts of the earth,** a storm arising at its extremities, which gradually expands to cover the whole world and to sweep through all nations. V. 33. **And the slain of the Lord,** those who have become the victims of His sword in the war brought upon them, **shall be at that day from one end of the earth even unto the other end of the earth,** their corpses lying everywhere; **they shall not be lamented, neither gathered nor buried,** cp. chap. 16, 4. 6; **they shall be dung upon the ground,** their decaying bodies acting as fertilizer. Since neither rank nor station escapes the fury of the Lord, the prophet now addresses himself to the leaders of the people, bidding them mourn. V. 34. **Howl, ye shep-**

herds, the kings and rulers of the earth, **and cry, and wallow yourselves in the ashes,** as a token of great sorrow, **ye principal of the flock,** the strong ones, the nobles, the wealthy among the people; **for the days of your slaughter and of your dispersion are accomplished,** rather, "And I scatter you, so that one part of the flock is dispersed, the other part slaughtered"; **and ye shall fall like a pleasant vessel,** like a dainty piece of pottery, to be utterly shattered. V. 35. **And the shepherds shall have no way to flee,** literally, "And there vanishes the refuge away from the shepherds," so that they cannot depend upon it, **nor the principal of the flock to escape,** the flock being destroyed together with its leaders. V. 36. **A voice of the cry of the shepherds and an howling of the principal of the flock shall be heard; for the Lord hath spoiled their pasture,** utterly destroying the meadows which they thought inexhaustible by the blast of His burning wrath. V. 37. **And the peaceable habitations are cut down because of the fierce anger of the Lord,** rendered desolate as He gave vent to His fury. The description once more returns to the picture of a lion. V. 38. **He hath forsaken His covert as the lion,** leaving the thicknesses where his den is located; **for their land is desolate because of the fierceness of the oppressor,** before the fury of the destroyer sent by God, **and because of His fierce anger,** the Lord Himself having gone forth to punish His enemies.

CHAPTER 26.

Jeremiah's Conflict with the False Prophets.

THE FIRST PROPHECY AND ITS EFFECT. — V. 1. **In the beginning of the reign of Jehoiakim, the son of Josiah, king of Judah,** about 609 B. C., **came this word from the Lord, saying,** v. 2. **Thus saith the Lord, Stand in the court of the Lord's house,** the large outer court, where the people assembled for worship, **and speak unto all the cities of Judah,** the believers who still were found in the nation and those who made a pretense at serving the Lord, **which come to worship in the Lord's house, all the words that I command thee to speak unto them; diminish not a word,** the threatening prophecy being proclaimed in all its ruthless severity, v. 3. **if so be they will hearken,** His own goodness making another effort in their behalf and leaving them without excuse in the event of their refusing to listen, **and turn every man from his evil way,** for repentance on the part of the people was still the Lord's object, **that I may repent Me of the evil which I purpose to do unto them because of the evil of their doings.** V. 4. **And thou shalt say unto them, Thus saith the Lord, If ye will not hearken to Me to walk in My Law,** in complete agreement with its precepts, **which I have set before you,** v. 5. **to hearken to the words of My servants, the prophets, whom I sent unto you, both rising up early and sending them,** thus showing the earnestness of His interest in them and their welfare, — **but ye have not hearkened,** this having been their regular attitude throughout the centuries, — v. 6. **then will I make this house,** the Temple of Solomon, **like Shiloh,** from which the Tabernacle had been removed and the city itself reduced to ruins, cp. chap. 7, 12. 14, **and will make this city,** the rich and proud capital of Judah, **a curse to all the nations of the earth,** an object of execration. V. 7. **So the priests and the prophets and all the people heard Jeremiah speaking these words in the house of the Lord,** for he brought his message to their attention in accordance with the command of the Lord. V. 8. **Now, it came to pass when Jeremiah had made an end of speaking all that the Lord had commanded him to speak unto all the people, that the priests,** those whose division was on duty at that time, **and the prophets,** the men who assumed the dignity of this office without really being sent by the Lord or commissioned to act as His servants, **and all the people,** the assembly which was gathered in the Temple upon that occasion, **took him, saying, Thou shalt surely die.** V. 9. **Why hast thou prophesied in the name of the Lord, saying, This house shall be like Shiloh, and this city shall be desolate without an inhabitant?** They not only regarded his message as an insult to their capital and country, but they charged him with uttering falsehoods in the name of Jehovah, which was an act punishable by death, Deut. 18, 20. **And all the people were gathered against Jeremiah in the house of the Lord,** an angry mob, carried away by its passions, ready to carry out the death sentence at once. V. 10. **When the princes of Judah,** the rulers, the members of the Great Council, in whose hands alone was the authority to carry out sentences of death, **heard these things, then they came up from the king's house,** the royal palace being situated at a lower level than the Temple court, **unto the house of the Lord and sat down in the entry of the new gate of the Lord's house,** at the entrance to the inner court, 2 Kings 15, 35. Since they were members of the highest judicial tribunal in the nation, they proceeded to investigate the matter which was causing all the disturbance, to try the case. V. 11. **Then spake the priests and the prophets,** whose pride was injured by the message of Jeremiah, who were personally enraged against him, **unto the princes and to all the people, saying, This man is worthy to die,** literally, "A sentence of death upon this man"; **for he hath prophesied against this city, as ye have heard with your ears.** This expediency, that of appealing to a false patriotism, is resorted to by demagogs even in our day, when in reality they are merely trying to give vent to their own personal spite and grudge against the faithful citizens of a country.

JEREMIAH'S DEFENSE AND DELIVERANCE. — V. 12. **Then spake Jeremiah unto all the princes and to all the people, saying, The Lord sent me to prophesy against this house and against this city,** rather, "to" or "concerning this house and this city"; for Jeremiah purposely avoided any expression which might cause irritation, **all the words that ye have heard.** He was not giving his own personal opinion or voicing any spite which he might have felt, but he had only done his duty. V. 13. **Therefore, now amend your ways and your doings,** this appeal showing his disinterested motives, his desire to help his people in this emergency, **and obey the voice of the Lord, your God; and the Lord will repent Him of the evil that He has pronounced against you.** It was the one condition under which he could promise salvation. V. 14. **As for me, behold, I am in your hand,** he was resigned to his fate at their hands; **do with me as seemeth good and meet unto you;** he bowed in humility and submission to the constituted authority. V. 15. **But know ye for certain that, if ye put me to death,** in the hope of thereby getting rid of an unpleasant exhorter and escaping his warnings, **ye shall surely bring innocent blood upon yourselves and upon this city and upon the inhabitants thereof,** thereby increasing their guilt and incurring heavier penalties; **for of a truth the Lord hath sent me unto you to speak all these words in your ears,** Jeremiah feeling it necessary to affirm this truth a second time in order to give emphasis to his warning. V. 16. **Then said the princes and all the people unto the priests and to the prophets,** in giving their verdict in this important matter, convinced of the truth of Jeremiah's statements, **This man is not worthy to die,** he has not deserved to be executed as a blasphemer, **for he hath spoken to us in the name of the Lord, our God.** Although they had, in the beginning, clamored for his death, they had quickly been influenced in the opposite direction, after the manner of fickle mobs the world over. V. 17. **Then rose up certain of the elders of the land,** either the most venerable and experienced of the princes or aged representatives of the people, who were highly respected for their wisdom, **and spake to all the assembly of the people, saying,** v. 18. **Micah, the Morasthite,** called so after a village in the tribe of Judah, **prophesied in the days of Hezekiah, king of Judah, and spake to all the people of Judah, saying, Thus saith the Lord of hosts, Zion shall be plowed like a field,** after being utterly destroyed, **and Jerusalem shall become heaps,** a pile of ruins, **and the mountain of the house,** the hill Moriah, on which the Temple stood, **as the high places of a forest,** so that the trees of the forest would freely get a foothold there. Cp. Micah 3, 12. It was thus a historical fact that Jeremiah was not the first prophet or the only one who had prophesied against Jerusalem and the Temple. V. 19. **Did Hezekiah, king of Judah, and all Judah put him at all to death?** Did they attempt to escape his unpleasant message by putting him to death? **Did he not,** instead of venting a possible personal spite in such a manner, **fear the Lord and besought the Lord,** begging Him to show mercy upon His people, **and the Lord repented Him of the evil which He had pronounced against them? Thus,** namely by killing Jeremiah as had been suggested, **might we procure great evil against our souls,** they might bring upon themselves the swift judgment of God. Moreover, the elders have still another historical example to urge in this case. V. 20. **And there was also a man that prophesied in the name of the Lord, Urijah, the son of Shemaiah, of Kirjath-jearim,** a prophet otherwise unknown, **who prophesied against this city and against this land according to all the words of Jeremiah,** that is, in the same manner, his message having the same content, v. 21. **and when Jehoiakim, the king, with all his mighty men and all the princes,** the most powerful men of the nation, **heard his words, the king sought to put him to death; but when Urijah heard it,** being informed of the king's intention, **he was afraid and fled and went into Egypt,** where he hoped to find security; v. 22. **and Jehoiakim, the king,** who had been placed on the throne by Pharaoh of Egypt, 2 Kings 23, 34, **sent men into Egypt, namely, Elnathan, the son of Achbor, and certain men with him into Egypt.** V. 23. **And they fetched forth Urijah out of Egypt,** whose people readily delivered him to their allies, **and brought him unto Jehoiakim, the king, who slew him with the sword and cast his dead body into the graves of the common people,** in the Valley of the Kidron, instead of giving it the honorable burial of a prophet of the Lord. V. 24. **Nevertheless, the hand of Ahikam, the son of Shaphan,** the worthy son of a noble father, 2 Kings 22, 12. 14, and the father of Gedaliah, who followed in his steps, 2 Kings 25, 22, **was with Jeremiah,** he brought all his influence to bear in his favor, **that they should not give him into the hand of the people to put him to death,** for this course was sometimes followed by rulers in order to remove the stigma of a judicial murder from themselves. Note: Urijah was faithful in delivering his message, but erred in this, that he forsook his post when danger threatened; so God permitted him to lose his life, while that of Jeremiah was spared. God's ministers must firmly believe that He can and will protect them in every emergency, according to His will.

CHAPTER 27.

The Yoke of Babylon.

THE MESSAGE OF THE YOKES. — V. 1. **In the beginning of the reign of Jehoiakim** (rather, of Zedekiah), **the son of Josiah, king of Judah,** about 609 B. C., **came this word unto Jeremiah from the Lord, saying,** v. 2. **Thus saith the Lord to me, Make thee bonds and yokes,** the yokes being held in place on the neck by strong cords or thongs, **and put them upon thy neck,** retaining the one for himself, v. 3. **and send them to the king of Edom, and to the king of Moab, and to the king of the Ammonites, and to the king of Tyrus, and to the king of Zidon,** all the smaller nations round about Palestine, **by the hand of the messengers which come to Jerusalem unto Zedekiah, king of Judah,** ambassadors who were trying to cement the alliance between Judah and their own nations, in order to shake off the yoke of Nebuchadnezzar; v. 4. **and command them to say unto their masters,** the rulers of the nations which they represented, **Thus saith the Lord of hosts, the God of Israel, Thus shall ye say unto your masters:** v. 5. **I have made the earth, the man, and the beast that are upon the ground,** calling them into being by an act of His will, as the King of the universe, **by My great power and by My outstretched arm,** symbol of irresistible might, **and have given it unto whom it seemed meet unto Me,** not on the basis of any one's merits, but according to His good pleasure. V. 6. **And now have I given all these lands,** the various countries enumerated above, **into the hand of Nebuchadnezzar, the king of Babylon, My servant,** who, in this instance, carried out the Lord's will; **and the beasts of the field have I given him also to serve him,** so that his authority and power is practically unlimited. V. 7. **And all nations shall serve him and his son and his son's son,** three generations being represented in the dynasty of Babylonian emperors, in a total of five rulers, **until the very time of his land come,** when Babylon would, in turn, be conquered by another nation; **and then many nations and great kings shall serve themselves of him,** be impressed into service to Nebuchadnezzar and his successors. V. 8. **And it shall come to pass that the nation and kingdom which will not serve the same Nebuchadnezzar, the king of Babylon, and that will not put their neck under the yoke of the king of Babylon,** willingly submitting to his power, accepting his overlordship, **that nation will I punish, saith the Lord, with the sword and with the famine and with the pestilence,** the dreaded exterminators of nations, **until I have consumed them by his hand,** Nebuchadnezzar being the instrument of the Lord in this instance. V. 9. **Therefore hearken not ye to your prophets,** the self-appointed leaders of this class, **nor to your diviners,** those who insisted that they could uncover the future, **nor to your dreamers,** literally, "your dreams," to show the vanity of such a reliance, **nor to your enchanters, nor to your sorcerers,** the last two classes making use of witchcraft to deceive the people, **which speak unto you, saying, Ye shall not serve the king of Babylon,** v. 10. **for they prophesy a lie unto you to remove you far from your land,** that being their object in making deliberate misstatements, **and that I should drive you out,** for refusing to obey His injunction to submit to the Chaldean king, **and ye should perish.** V. 11. **But the nations that bring their neck under the yoke of the king of Babylon and serve him, those will I let remain still in their own land, saith the Lord,** not subjecting them to the disgrace of deportation; **and they shall till it and dwell therein.** The Oriental despots were satisfied if nations would but accept their sovereignty and pay their tribute-money, resorting to sterner measures only when a nation stubbornly refused to submit. It is ever thus that misfortune and destruction comes upon those who follow the guidance of false prophets.

THE SPECIAL MESSAGE TO ZEDEKIAH. — V. 12. **I spake to Zedekiah, king of Judah,** applying the statements of the first part of the chapter to him and Judah in particular, **according to all these words, saying, Bring your necks under the yoke of the king of Babylon and serve him and his people and live,** maintaining their national existence. V. 13. **Why will ye die, thou and thy people, by the sword, by the famine, and by the pestilence,** deliberately inviting these scourges by their disobedience, **as the Lord hath spoken against the nation that will not serve the king of Babylon?** V. 14. **Therefore hearken not unto the words of the prophets,** those that bore this name by their own choice, not by God's appointment,

that speak unto you, saying, Ye shall not serve the king of Babylon; for they prophesy a lie unto you. V. 15. **For I have not sent them, saith the Lord, yet they prophesy a lie in My name,** adorning their false doctrine with the tag of His revelation, **that I might drive you out, and that ye might perish, ye and the prophets that prophesy unto you,** the latter being swept away in the same calamity which their false statements had brought upon Judah. V. 16. **Also I spake to the priests and to all this people, saying, Thus saith the Lord, Hearken not to the words of your prophets that prophesy unto you, saying, Behold, the vessels of the Lord's house,** which had been taken to Babylon at the time of Jehoiakim, 2 Chron. 36, 5—7, and Jeconiah, 2 Kings 24, 13, **shall now shortly be brought again from Babylon,** in the near future; **for they prophesy a lie unto you,** deceiving the people of Judah also in this case. V. 17. **Hearken not unto them; serve the king of Babylon and live,** retaining their homes and maintaining their national existence; **wherefore should this city be laid waste?** Why simply challenge the calamity by their obstinacy? V. 18. **But if they be prophets,** servants of the Lord by His appointment, and **if the Word of the Lord be with them,** as they insisted that it was, **let them now make intercession to the Lord of hosts that the vessels which are left in the house of the Lord,** which the Chaldeans had not yet carried away, **and in the house of the king of Judah and at Jerusalem go not to Babylon,** that the final act of the drama might not be staged. If they were true prophets, their intercession would carry enough weight to influence the Lord, so that He would avert the catastrophe which despoiled the nation entirely. V. 19. **For thus saith the Lord of hosts concerning the pillars,** the two brass or bronze towers known as Jachin and Boaz, 1 Kings 7, 15 ff., **and concerning the sea,** 1 Kings 7, 23 ff., **and concerning the bases,** 1 Kings 7, 27 ff., **and concerning the residue of the vessels that remain in this city,** the vessels and instruments of worship which had not yet been taken away by the conquerors, v. 20. **which Nebuchadnezzar, king of Babylon, took not when he carried away captive Jeconiah, the son of Jehoiakim, king of Judah, from Jerusalem to Babylon, and all the nobles of Judah and Jerusalem,** as related in 2 Kings 25, 13 ff. V. 21. **Yea, thus saith the Lord of hosts, the God of Israel, concerning the vessels that remain in the house of the Lord and in the house of the king of Judah and of Jerusalem,** the repetition serving to increase the impression of inevitable calamity and disaster: v. 22. **They shall be carried to Babylon,** as a welcome booty, **and there shall they be until the day I visit them, saith the Lord,** namely, when Cyrus overthrew the Babylonian power. **Then will I bring them up and restore them to this place.** This prophecy was fulfilled in every detail, although only a minor prediction, whereas the greater prophecies concerning the Messiah found an even more glorious fulfilment.

CHAPTER 28.

Against the False Prophet Hananiah.

HANANIAH'S FALSE PROPHECY. — V. 1. **And it came to pass the same year, in the beginning of the reign of Zedekiah, king of Judah,** that is, in the first half of his reign, after he had become fully established in his position, **in the fourth year and in the fifth month, that Hananiah, the son of Azur, the prophet,** a member of a family of priests, **which was of Gibeon,** a city some eight miles northwest of Jerusalem, **spake unto me in the house of the Lord in the presence of the priests and of all the people, saying,** in a false message modeled after the true revelations given the real prophets, v. 2. **Thus speaketh the Lord of hosts, the God of Israel, saying, I have broken the yoke of the king of Babylon,** which the country had then borne for about ten years. V. 3. **Within two full years,** literally, "years of days," that is, after the years would be completed down to the last day, **will I bring again into this place all the vessels of the Lord's house that Nebuchadnezzar, king of Babylon, took away from this place and carried them to Babylon,** 2 Kings 24, 13; v. 4. **and I will bring again to this place Jeconiah, the son of Jehoiakim, king of Judah, with all the captives of Judah that went into Babylon, saith the Lord,** 2 Kings 24, 14. 15; **for I will break the yoke of the king of Babylon.** This was a bold move on the part of the false prophet, intended to offset and neutralize the clear proclamation which Jeremiah had made concerning the length of the coming captivity. V. 5. **Then the prophet Jeremiah said unto the prophet Hananiah in the presence of the priests and in the presence of all the people that stood in the house of the Lord,** for, having the truth on his side, he possessed the boldness which a true servant of the Lord should always exhibit, v. 6. **even the prophet Jeremiah said, Amen,** that is, So be it! **The Lord do so; the Lord perform thy words which thou hast prophesied to bring again the vessels of the Lord's house, and all that is carried away captive, from Babylon into**

this place! Jeremiah was personally in the heartiest accord with this idea of the early restoration of the captives and of the Temple vessels; nothing would have pleased him better than to have this fortunate turn of events come true. V. 7. **Nevertheless hear thou now this word that I speak in thine ears,** in a most emphatic manner, **and in the ears of all the people:** v. 8. **The prophets that have been before me and before thee of old,** as Isaiah, Joel, Hosea, Amos, and others, **prophesied both against many countries and against great kingdoms, of war and of evil,** of misfortune and calamity of every kind, **and of pestilence.** V. 9. **The prophet which prophesieth of peace, when the word of the prophet shall come to pass, then shall the prophet be known that the Lord hath truly sent him.** That is, the fulfilment of a prophecy such as had been made by Hananiah would be the best proof of his having spoken the truth. But from the start the presumption of truth is in favor of the prophecies of calamity, since they are connected with danger to him who brings the message. Prophecies of good fortune may be flattery and have the object of providing their maker with pleasant conditions; it is necessary, therefore, to wait for results before accepting them. V. 10. **Then Hananiah, the prophet, took the yoke from off the prophet Jeremiah's neck,** which he wore by God's order, chap. 27, 2, **and brake it,** an act of audacity and impertinence with which he intended to strengthen his position over against the people. V. 11. **And Hananiah spake in the presence of all the people, saying,** in another base falsehood, **Thus saith the Lord, Even so will I break the yoke of Nebuchadnezzar, king of Babylon, from the neck of all nations within the space of two full years.** He thought that the bold repetition of his false prophecy, together with the symbolic act which accompanied it, would cause the people to believe him without question. **And the prophet Jeremiah went his way,** leaving the justification of his prophecy to the Lord for the present. In many cases it is the part of true wisdom for believers not to reply to bold statements on the part of the adversaries, but to leave the vindication of the Lord's honor to the Lord Himself.

THE REBUKE GIVEN TO HANANIAH. — V. 12. **Then the word of the Lord came unto Jeremiah, the prophet, after that Hananiah, the prophet, had broken the yoke from off the neck of the prophet Jeremiah,** that is, within a few weeks or a month later, **saying,** v. 13. **Go and tell Hananiah, saying, Thus saith the Lord, Thou hast broken the yokes of wood, but thou shalt make for them,** in their stead, **yokes of iron.** The result of Hananiah's rash and impertinent action was merely to increase the emphasis which the Lord placed upon the fulfilment of His prophecy against Judah. V. 14. **For thus saith the Lord of hosts, the God of Israel,** speaking with the solemnity of His majestic power, **I have put a yoke of iron upon the neck of all these nations,** cp. Deut. 28, 48, **that they may serve Nebuchadnezzar, king of Babylon, and they shall serve him,** the punishment of the Lord being certain to strike them; **and I have given him the beasts of the field also,** a power which was, for the time being, practically unlimited. Cp. chap. 27, 6. V. 15. **Then said the prophet Jeremiah unto Hananiah, the prophet, Hear now, Hananiah: The Lord hath not sent thee,** thus confronting the false prophet with his base deception; **but thou makest this people to trust in a lie,** in getting them to believe the message which he imagined. V. 16. **Therefore, thus saith the Lord, Behold, I will cast thee from off the face of the earth,** the words implying a complete removal, to take away also the effect of his false prophecy; **this year thou shalt die, because thou hast taught rebellion against the Lord,** causing men to forsake Him and the Word of Truth. V. 17. **So Hananiah, the prophet, died the same year in the seventh month,** the quick fulfilment of Jeremiah's prophecy serving to emphasize all the more strongly the seriousness of his offense against Jehovah. The punishment of the Lord upon the false prophets of our day may often seem to be delayed in coming, but He will certainly vindicate His honor against all who assail His Word.

CHAPTER 29.

Jeremiah's Letter to the Exiles and Its Consequences.

THE CONTENTS OF THE LETTER. — Just as certain false prophets in Jerusalem had tried to arouse and maintain false hopes in the inhabitants of the capital, thus also certain men of the same type were active among the exiles who had been taken to Babylon at the time of Jeconiah. The result was that a spirit of discontent and restlessness took hold of the Jews, which not only increased the bitterness of their affliction, but also tended to break down all moral restraint. Jeremiah therefore, by God's command, sent a letter to the exiled Jews, in which he gives them some excellent rules of behavior in the midst of the trying circumstances in which they found themselves. V. 1. **Now, these are the words of the letter that Jeremiah the prophet sent from Jerusalem unto the residue of the elders,** to those who had survived the hardships of the exile up to that time, **which were carried away captives, and to the priests, and to the prophets, and to all the people whom Nebuchadnezzar had carried away captive from Jerusalem to Babylon,** to the congregation of the exiled Jews, disorganized as it was in the conditions of the exile, v. 2. **(after that Jeconiah, the king, and the queen,** Nehushta, the dowager, daughter of Elnathan, 2 Kings 24, 8. 15, **and the eunuchs,** the courtiers or chamberlains, high court officers, **the princes of Judah and Jerusalem, and the carpenters, and the smiths,** all the artisans and craftsmen of the city, 2 Kings 24, 16, **were departed from Jerusalem,)** v. 3. **by the hand of Elasah, the son of Shaphan, and Gemariah, the son of Hilkiah, (whom Zedekiah, king of Judah, sent unto Babylon, to Nebuchadnezzar, king of Babylon,** nothing further being known of the message carried by this embassy, except that Zedekiah ruled only by the pleasure of the Babylonian king and was bound to use the highest diplomacy to hold his position), **saying,** the actual wording of Jeremiah's letter now being given, v. 4. **Thus saith the Lord of hosts, the God of Israel,** His exact words being given in the message, as throughout the book, **unto all that are carried away captives, whom I have caused to be carried away from Jerusalem unto Babylon,** the fact that they were suffering the just punishment of their transgressions being made fundamental in this address, as preparing the way for repentance: v. 5. **Build ye houses and dwell in them,** thereby preparing for a long stay in the land of their captivity, against the advice of the false prophets who were trying to mislead them; **and plant gardens, and eat the fruit of them,** altogether in agreement with the idea that their homes would, for some time, be in the strange country; v. 6. **take ye wives and beget sons and daughters,** thereby establishing families; **and take wives for your sons and give your daughters to husbands,** for the giving in marriage is essentially a function of the parents, a duty which they dared not disregard, **that they may bear sons and daughters, that ye may be increased there and not diminished,** for the nation was not to die out during the period of the Babylonian Exile. V. 7. **And seek the peace,** the welfare, **of the city whither I have caused you to be carried away captives,** striving with all their might to promote its best interests, **and pray unto the Lord for it,** such intercessions being commanded by God even in the case of a heathenish government; for true religion teaches patient submission to the government in all things which are not in conflict with God's Word; **for in the peace thereof shall ye have peace,** the Lord blessing a country for the sake of the believers among its citizens, and they, in turn, being benefited by the blessings which the Lord grants their country. V. 8. **For thus saith the Lord of hosts, the God of Israel, Let not your prophets and your diviners that be in the midst of you,** whose business flourished because of the willing credulity of the people, **deceive you, neither hearken to your dreams which ye cause to be dreamed,** for it was the attitude of the people themselves, in encouraging prophecies of this kind, which gave them false hopes, that was at the bottom of the whole situation. V. 9. **For they prophesy falsely unto you,** with a lie they posed as prophets, **in My name,** adorning their base deceptions with the name of the Lord, insisting that He had sent them; **I have not sent them, saith the Lord,** their claims being utterly unfounded. Over against their deceitful promises, therefore, He tells them the plain truth concerning the length of their captivity. V. 10. **For thus saith the Lord, That after seventy years be accomplished at Babylon,** counting from the time the first exiles were taken to Babylon with their King Jeconiah, **I will visit you,** turn to them in merciful kindness, **and perform My good word toward you,** cause His promise to them to be fulfilled, **in causing you to return to this place,** to Jerusalem and Judah, the home of their fathers. V. 11. **For I know the thoughts that I think toward you,** He would still accomplish His merciful purposes with regard to them, **saith the Lord, thoughts of peace and not of evil, to give you an expected end,** literally, "future and hope," that is, the end which they desired, but which could be theirs only on condition of their showing true repentance. The Lord shows in just what manner the Jews would continue in their course: first, in vain confidence, relying upon the empty promises of the false prophets; then, in deepest despondency, believing that they were doomed to extermination; but finally, in true repentance, when they would be accepted by the Lord. V. 12. **Then shall ye call upon Me,** in a realization of their sinfulness and guilt, **and ye shall go and pray unto Me, and I will hearken unto you,** turning to them in the grace and mercy which He much prefers to exercise. V. 13. **And ye shall seek Me and find Me, when ye shall search for Me with all your heart,** if their repentance proved to be sincere, of the right kind. Cp. Lev. 26, 40—45. V. 14. **And I will be found of you, saith the Lord,** Is. 55, 6; **and I will turn away your captivity, and I will gather you from all the nations and from all the places whither I have driven you, saith the Lord,** for the Jews were finally dispersed throughout the various countries of the world empire; **and I will bring you again into the place whence I caused you to be carried away captive.** Cp. Deut. 4, 29. 30; 30, 3—5. The return from exile was only the beginning of the fulfilment of our prophecy, which clearly has Messianic significance. V. 15.

Because ye have said, The Lord hath raised us up prophets in Babylon, literally, "as far as Babylon," the people of Judah insisting that the ministry of the prophets extended far beyond the confines of the Holy Land, and that therefore the threatening prophecy had no effect upon them, v. 16. **know that thus saith the Lord of the king that sitteth upon the throne of David,** in this case Zedekiah, **and of all the people that dwelleth in this city,** those remaining after the first company of exiles had left, **and of your brethren that are not gone forth with you into captivity:** v. 17. **thus saith the Lord of hosts, Behold, I will send upon them the sword, the famine, and the pestilence,** the dreaded scourges which are the worst punishments of nations, **and will make them like vile figs,** chap. 24, 8, **that cannot be eaten, they are so evil.** V. 18. **And I will persecute them with the sword, with the famine, and with the pestilence and will deliver them to be removed to all the kingdoms of the earth,** scattered throughout the kingdoms which belonged to the great world empire, **to be a curse,** an object of execration, **and an astonishment, and an hissing, and a reproach,** to be jeered at and treated with contempt on every side, **among all the nations whither I have driven them,** v. 19. **because they have not hearkened to My words, saith the Lord, which I sent unto them by My servants, the prophets, rising up early and sending them,** in eager zeal for the welfare of their souls; **but ye would not hear, saith the Lord.** Note that the change from the third to the second person places the exiled Jews into the same class with those who were still in Judah, for all were alike guilty. V. 20. **Hear ye therefore the Word of the Lord, all ye of the captivity whom I have sent from Jerusalem to Babylon,** for the Chaldeans, in this instance, were only the instruments in the hands of the Lord: V. 21. **Thus saith the Lord of hosts, the God of Israel, of Ahab, the son of Kolaiah, and of Zedekiah, the son of Maaseiah,** two men who are otherwise unknown, **which prophesy a lie unto you in My name,** since they were evidently the leaders of the false prophets, **Behold, I will deliver them into the hand of Nebuchadrezzar, king of Babylon, and he shall slay them before your eyes,** this execution evidently taking place because the king feared their exciting and rebellious preaching, v. 22. **and of them shall be taken up a curse by all the captivity of Judah which are in Babylon,** that is, the exiles made this event a proverb, a formula of imprecation, **saying, The Lord make thee like Zedekiah and like Ahab, whom the king of Babylon roasted in the fire,** a Chaldean form of punishment in general use at that time, cp. Dan. 3, 6, v. 23. **because they have committed villainy in Israel,** a deed of shame, a sinful folly, **and have committed adultery with their neighbors' wives,** acts of gross immorality often being associated with false teaching, **and have spoken lying words in My name, which I have not commanded them; even I know and am a Witness, saith the Lord.** Jehovah is not only intimately acquainted with the truth, but also brings it to light and testifies of it before men.

THE DOOM OF SHEMAIAH FORETOLD. — Jeremiah's letter to the men in exile had evidently caused a great stir among the false prophets in Babylon, who had predicted a speedy termination of the exile. Accordingly, one of their number promptly sent letters to Jerusalem, in the endeavor to stir up the inhabitants of the capital against Jeremiah. But the Lord, in turn, gave His servant the command to proclaim His punishment upon the man who interfered with His commands. V. 24. **Thus shalt thou also speak to Shemaiah, the Nehelamite,** a false prophet not mentioned elsewhere, **saying,** v. 25. **Thus speaketh the Lord of hosts, the God of Israel, saying, Because thou hast sent letters in thy name,** without any authority from the Lord, **unto all the people that are at Jerusalem, and to Zephaniah, the son of Maaseiah, the priest,** the so-called "second priest," or substitute for the high priest, **and to all the priests, saying,** v. 26. **The Lord hath made thee priest in the stead of Jehoiada, the priest,** who was then in exile in Babylon, **that ye should be officers in the house of the Lord,** men charged with keeping order throughout the Temple-grounds and buildings, **for every man that is mad,** the inspired prophets often being charged by their enemies with being possessed with a spirit of madness, **and maketh himself a prophet, that thou shouldest put him in prison, and in the stocks,** as Pashur had done with Jeremiah in his day, chap. 20, 2. V. 27. **Now, therefore, why hast thou not reproved Jeremiah of Anathoth, which maketh himself a prophet to you?** He boldly accuses Zephaniah of a gross neglect of duty in not arresting Jeremiah and making it impossible for him to commit further damage. V. 28. **For therefore he sent unto us in Babylon, saying, This captivity is long; build ye houses and dwell in them; and plant gardens and eat the fruit of them.** Cp. v. 5. V. 29. **And Zephaniah, the priest, read this letter in the ears of Jeremiah, the prophet,** probably with the object of making him acquainted with the machinations of the false prophets in Babylon. V. 30. **Then came the word of the Lord unto Jeremiah, saying,** v. 31. **Send to all them of the captivity,** to counteract the activity of Shemaiah, **saying, Thus saith the Lord concerning Shemaiah, the Nehelamite, Because that Shemaiah hath prophesied unto you, and I sent him not, and he caused you to trust in a lie,** his message being a falsehood from beginning to end, without the slightest foundation of divine truth, v. 32. **therefore thus saith the Lord, Behold, I will punish Shemaiah, the Nehelamite, and his seed,** his children. **He shall not have a man to dwell among this people,** his family was to die out very soon, **neither shall he behold the good that I will do for My people, saith the Lord,** namely, when, at His word, they would repent of their wicked ways, **because he hath taught rebellion against the Lord.** False teachers not only bring condemnation upon their own souls by their false teaching, but they also transgress against the honor of the true God, who, therefore, will not let them go unpunished.

CHAPTER 30.

The Redemption of Israel.

THE PROMISE OF DELIVERANCE. — V. 1. **The word that came to Jeremiah from the Lord,** being given him by special and direct inspiration, **saying,** v. 2. **Thus speaketh the Lord God of Israel,** His very words being recorded, **saying, Write thee all the words that I have spoken unto thee in a book,** the prophecy thus inscribed on a roll becoming a part of the sacred record of the Bible. V. 3. **For, lo, the days come, saith the Lord, that I will bring again the captivity of My people Israel and Judah, saith the Lord,** the restoration of all the members of His Church being included here, **and I will cause them to return to the land that I gave to their fathers, and they shall possess it.** This introduction serves as a heading and summary of this entire section of Jeremiah's prophecy, and must be understood in the light of all that follows. V. 4. **And these are the words that the Lord spake concerning Israel and concerning Judah,** His message transporting us with dramatic vividness into the very midst of the future, a future, moreover, which includes more than the history of the two nations as such. V. 5. **For thus saith the Lord, We have heard a voice of trembling, of fear, and not of peace,** or, "A cry of terror have we heard: fear and no deliverance." V. 6. **Ask ye now and see whether a man doth travail with child,** which, of course, is contrary to nature. **Wherefore do I see every man with his hands on his loins as a woman in travail, and all faces are turned into paleness?** It must be an extraordinary terror which could produce such a condition. V. 7. **Alas! for that day,** the Messianic period with its sifting process among the nations, **is great,** Luke 2, 34. 35, **so that none is like it; it is even the time of Jacob's trouble,** a testing of hearts and minds. **But he shall be saved out of it,** all the true children of Jacob, the members of the spiritual Israel, being delivered from the wrath to come. V. 8. **For it shall come to pass in that day, saith the Lord of hosts, that I will break his yoke from off thy neck,** deliver His people from the oppression of all its enemies, **and will burst thy bonds,** those with which the oppressors were trying to keep His children in subjection, **and strangers shall no more serve themselves of him,** keeping Israel in bondage; v. 9. **but they shall serve the Lord, their God, and David, their King,** the great Ruler Messiah, who was of the house and lineage of David, **whom I will raise up unto them,** for it was to Christ that the entire Messianic prophecy of the Old Testament pointed. V. 10. **Therefore fear not thou, O my servant Jacob, saith the Lord, neither be dismayed,** be filled with terror, **O Israel,** the cheering admonition being addressed to all believers; **for, lo, I will save thee from afar and thy seed from the land of their captivity,** the redemption of the world being spoken of under the picture of the deliverance from the Babylonian bondage; **and Jacob shall return and shall be in rest and be quiet, and none shall make him afraid,** the security of the children of God thus being emphasized. Cp. Ps. 46, 5. V. 11. **For I am with thee, saith the Lord, to save thee,** taking the part of those that are His own; **though I make a full end of all nations whither I have scattered thee,** the overthrow of the world empire being a type of the overthrow of all enemies of Jehovah and His Church, **yet will I not make a full end of thee,** the deliverance of His people being always assured in the Gospel-message; **but I will correct thee in measure,** literally, "with judgment," in such moderation as will bring about a change of heart for the better in them, **and will not leave thee altogether unpunished,** for a chastisement of His children such as He exercises is intended to keep them in His ways, for the Lord's thoughts toward them are thoughts of love and of peace. Thus is the culmination of the Messianic period portrayed.

THE TURN OF AFFAIRS AND THE CONSUMMATION OF SALVATION. — V. 12. **For thus saith the Lord, Thy bruise is incurable, and thy wound is grievous,** the stroke delivered to the Jews as a nation is mortal, the hopes which they entertained of having their exile end soon were vain. V. 13. **There is none to plead thy cause,** intercession could no longer be expected by them, **that thou mayest be bound up,** the wounds of their body politic being bandaged; **thou hast no healing medicines,** no remedies of bandages and plasters. Cp. chap. 8, 22. V. 14. **All thy lovers,** the former allied nations that had professed friendship for Judah, **have forgotten thee, they seek thee not,** not being at all concerned about Judah's welfare; **for I have wounded thee with the wound of an enemy,** with a sharp smiting, **with the chastisement of a cruel one, for the multitude of thine iniquity,** or "with cruel chastisement for the greatness of thy guilt," cp. chap. 5, 6; 13, 22, **because thy sins were increased.** Although the Lord in Himself is incapable of enmity and cruelty, yet the grievous sins of the Jews challenged His avenging justice, so that He was obliged to act as though He were indeed cruel. V. 15. **Why criest thou for thine affliction? Thy sorrow is incurable,** or, "that thy pain is malignant?" **For the multitude of thine iniquity, because thy sins were increased, I have done these things unto thee.** Whatever evil was descending upon Judah, its people had no one but themselves to blame; their punishment was strictly according to justice. But just when Israel was submerged in the evils descending upon it, the mercy of the Lord turned to His people, to vindicate His honor over against all the enemies. V. 16. **Therefore all they that devour thee shall be devoured, and all thine adversaries, every one of them, shall go into captivity,** the fate of the oppressed Jews striking them in full measure; **and they that spoil thee shall be a spoil, and all that prey upon thee will I give for a prey,** so that they would be plundered in turn. The enemies were, indeed, the instruments for carrying out the punishment of God upon His people, but at the same time they were guilty before Him and were bound to suffer accordingly. V. 17. **For I will restore health unto thee,** by means of healing plasters, **and I will heal thee of thy wounds, saith the Lord; because they called thee an outcast,** a wife put away by her husband, **saying, This is Zion, whom no man seeketh after,** because the Lord had, for the purposes of His mercy, forsaken His people for the time being. V. 18. **Thus saith the Lord, Behold, I will bring again the captivity of Jacob's tents,** so that the time of oppression and exile would be a thing of the past, **and have mercy on his dwelling-places,** on the places where His holy congregation was wont to assemble; **and the city shall be builded upon her own heap,** to arise anew from its heap of ruins, to be established on the hill of the Lord, **and the palace shall remain after the manner thereof,** to be inhabited as of old. V. 19. **And out of them,** the palaces, the congregations of the Lord, **shall proceed thanksgiving and the voice of them that make merry,** their voices raised in psalms of rejoicing; **and I will multiply them, and they shall not be few,** the number of God's children being increased under His blessing; **I will also glorify them, and they shall not be small,** they will be honored and not despised in His sight. V. 20. **Their children also shall be as aforetime,** at the time when the Lord's Church was in its most flourishing condition, **and their congregation shall be established before Me,** founded upon the Rock of Ages, **and I will punish all that oppress them.** V. 21. **And their nobles shall be of themselves,** their most Glorious One being a member of their own nation, **and their Governor shall proceed from the midst of them,** namely, in the person of the Messiah, under whom the kingdom of David was restored in the best sense of the term; **and I will cause Him to draw near, and He shall approach unto Me,** consecrated to the Lord's service, as the great High Priest, entering in once into the most holy place of heaven, Heb. 9, 12; **for who is this that engaged His heart to approach unto Me? saith the Lord.** No mere man could take his life into his hands in approaching the holy God in the capacity of Redeemer and Mediator, because all ordinary men, being sinful creatures, would be destroyed by His holiness. Only in and through the Messiah is this approach possible. V. 22. **And ye shall be My people,** in and through the Messiah, **and I will be your God.** Cp. 2 Cor. 6, 18. V. 23. **Behold, the whirlwind of the Lord,** a tempest of Jehovah, **goeth forth with fury,** or, "fury goes forth," **a continuing whirlwind,** a rolling and swishing tornado; **it shall fall with pain upon the head of the wicked,** bowling them over like leaves driven before a strong wind. V. 24. **The fierce anger of the Lord shall not return,** not be abated or withdrawn, **until He have done it, and until He have performed the intents of His heart,** so that all His plans are executed, down to the smallest detail; **in the latter days ye shall consider it,** for then they would realize the object of the lesson which the Lord wanted them to learn, at the time when the Messianic period would reach its culmination, the supreme test coming with the Last Judgment.

CHAPTER 31.

Salvation for All Generations of Israel.

THE DECREE OF RESTORATION AND ITS EXECUTION. — V. 1. **At the same time, saith the Lord,** at the time of the Messiah's rule, **will I be the God of all the families of Israel,** of all true Israelites, of His spiritual children, **and they shall be My people.** V. 2. **Thus saith the Lord, The people which were left of the sword found grace in the wilderness,** that is, those who escaped the sword of Pharaoh by the Lord's deliverance were objects of His merciful intervention against all enemies; **even Israel, when I went to cause him to rest,** when He was leading them forward to occupy the peaceful habitations of the Land of Promise. V. 3. **The Lord hath appeared of old unto me,** so His Church sings in grateful acknowledgment of His grace, **saying, Yea, I have loved thee with an everlasting love, therefore with loving-kindness have I drawn thee,** giving them respite, preserving them from extinction. As He had done in delivering His people from the bondage of Egypt, so He intended to continue His mercy upon them. V. 4. **Again I will build thee, and thou shalt be built, O virgin of Israel,** be established for sound prosperity; **thou shalt again be adorned with thy tabrets,** marching in processions with tambourines, or timbrels, **and shalt go forth in the dances of them that make merry,** in agreement with the custom observed upon occasions of public rejoicings, but in holy joy, not in carnal mirth. V. 5. **Thou shalt yet plant vines upon the mountains of Samaria; the planters shall plant and shall eat them as common things,** a reference to the ordinance which commanded the children of Israel not to eat the fruit of the orchard and of the vineyard the first three years after planting, the fourth year's fruit being consecrated to the Lord, and only that of the fifth year being permitted to be profaned, that is, to be used by the owner. Cp. Lev. 19, 23 ff.; Judg. 9, 27; Deut. 20, 6; also 28, 30. V. 6. **For there shall be a day that the watchmen upon the Mount Ephraim,** those who were delegated to observe the time of the new moon, which determined the date of most festivals in the Jewish church-year, **shall cry, Arise ye and let us go up to Zion unto the Lord, our God.** Thus the work of the Gospel-messengers summoning the believers to the worship of Jehovah, the true God, is pictured. V. 7. **For thus saith the Lord, Sing with gladness for Jacob,** shouting over the Church's good fortune in songs of praise, **and shout among the chief of the nations,** exult over the head of the peoples, for the Church is composed of members of all nations; **publish ye, praise ye, and say,** in loud psalms of thanksgiving and intercession, **O Lord, save Thy people, the remnant of Israel,** so that the blessings of redemption would be known to, experienced by, all its members. V. 8. **Behold, I will bring them,** the members of Jehovah's Church, **from the North country and gather them from the coasts of the earth,** from its most remote boundaries, **and with them the blind and the lame,** the poorest and the least important, the very outcasts of society, Matt. 22, 9; Luke 14, 21—23, **the woman with child and her that travaileth with child together,** even the weak and frail of every kind; **a great company shall return thither,** being welcomed into the Church of Jehovah. V. 9. **They shall come with weeping, and with supplications will I lead them,** with tears of mingled joy and penitence, on account of the unmerited grace of God in accepting them into His kingdom. **I will cause them to walk by the rivers of waters in a straight way, wherein they shall not stumble,** on paths of righteousness; **for I am a Father to Israel, and Ephraim is My first-born,** all His spiritual children being included in these terms. V. 10. **Hear the Word of the Lord, O ye nations, and declare it in the isles afar off,** the Gospel-message being proclaimed in the most remote regions of the earth, **and say, He that scattered Israel will gather him and keep him as a shepherd doth his flock,** one of the Lord's favorite pictures to describe His loving care for His people. V. 11. **For the Lord hath redeemed Jacob and ransomed him from the hand of him that was stronger than he,** liberating His people from the hands of all tyrants. V. 12. **Therefore they shall come and sing in the height of Zion,** on its summit, that is, in the Temple of the Lord, **and shall flow together,** in a mighty stream of humanity, **to the goodness of the Lord,** to receive the blessing of Jehovah, **for wheat and for wine and for oil,** the greatest riches of His mercy, **and for the young of the flock and of the herd,** all these being types of the richest and fullest strength of life; **and their soul shall be as a watered garden,** Is. 58, 11, **and they shall not sorrow any more at all,** enjoying, rather, all the riches of God's grace. V. 13. **Then shall the virgin rejoice in the dance,** for the young women went out in processions with rhythmic movements, **both young men and old together,** that is, they would give expression to their joy; **for I will turn their mourning into joy, and will comfort them, and make them rejoice from their sorrow,** so that they would be abundantly comforted. V. 14. **And I will satiate the soul of the priests with fatness,** namely, by the great number of the fat pieces of thank-offerings, **and My people shall be satisfied with My goodness, saith the Lord.** Thus the Messianic promise concerning rest and peace, Matt. 11, 28, was brought out even in the Old Testament, for He gave His blessings in rich measure even at that time.

SORROW TURNED INTO JOY. — V. 15. **Thus saith the Lord, A voice was heard in Ramah,** a city some nine or ten miles north of Jerusalem, on the boundary between the former kingdoms of Israel and Judah, **lamentation and bitter weeping: Rahel,** the beloved wife of Jacob, as the ancestress of Ephraim, Manasseh, and Benjamin, **weeping for her children,** the members of the northern kingdom, **refused to be comforted for her children because they were not.** This verse is quoted by Matthew, chap. 2, 18, with reference to the slaughter of the innocents of Bethlehem, because the extermination of Israel through the Assyrian power was a type of the murder of the children at Bethlehem, and because Rachel was regarded as the mother of Bethlehem and its environs. V. 16. **Thus saith the Lord, Refrain thy voice from weeping and thine eyes from tears,** bidding all sorrow be far removed; **for thy work shall be rewarded,** namely, that of bearing and bringing up her children, **saith the Lord, and they shall come again from the land of the enemy,** those whom the Lord had chosen as His own being assembled once more, namely, in His congregation, in the communion of His saints. V. 17. **And there is hope in thine end, saith the Lord,** that is, for the future, **that thy children shall come again to their own border,** on the basis of a sincere repentance. V. 18. **I have surely heard Ephraim bemoaning himself thus,** so the Lord now declares: **Thou hast chastised me, and I was chastised,** being obliged to accept the Lord's punishment, **as a bullock unaccustomed to the yoke,** unused to the restraint of the yoke and of harness; cp. Hos. 10, 11. **Turn Thou me,** back from the path of wickedness and sin, **and I shall be turned,** the change of repentance in the heart of any man being possible only through the merciful power of God; **for Thou art the Lord, my God,** and it is the confidence in His grace as the God of the covenant that brings His blessings to the repentant heart. V. 19. **Surely after that I was turned, I repented,** or, "For after my apostasy I felt sorrow," since God wrought repentance in the heart of the true Israelites among the children of Ephraim; **and after that I was instructed,** coming to a right understanding through the Lord's chastisement, **I smote upon my thigh,** in token of deep grief; **I was ashamed, yea, even confounded,** fully conscious of the disgrace attaching to the former behavior, **because I did bear the reproach of my youth,** that attending the idolatry which had been practised in the northern kingdom since the time when Jeroboam set up the golden calves at Bethel and Dan. Upon this cry the Lord answers in a strain of coaxing appeal. V. 20. **Is Ephraim My dear son?** literally, "a son of My favor." **Is he a pleasant child?** literally, "a child of delights." The question implies a decided negative answer if the actual condition of Ephraim's mind is taken into consideration, but an equally decided positive statement when one takes note of Jehovah's mercy. **For since I spake against him,** in words of stern reproof, **I do earnestly remember him still,** the Lord being astonished at Himself, as it were, on account of such tender feelings toward this reprobate child; **therefore My bowels are troubled for him,** His inmost feelings being touched. **I will surely have mercy upon him, saith the Lord,** like a father who still regards his wayward son with tender love. V. 21. **Set thee up way-marks,** finger-posts directing him back to his Father's home; **make thee high heaps,** wooden posts or pillars of stone showing the way; **set thine heart toward the highway, even the way which thou wentest,** the road which would lead him back home. **Turn again, O virgin of Israel,** for the believers of Ephraim and the congregation of the Lord are identical, **turn again to these thy cities,** returning to the Lord in true repentance. V. 22. **How long wilt thou go about,** turning first one way and then the other, like a dissolute and wanton woman, **O thou backsliding daughter?** the congregation which had so often proved apostate. **For the Lord hath created a new thing in the earth, A woman shall compass a man,** the weak and tender woman clinging to the stronger with yielding affection, the repentant congregation once more turning to the Lord in the relation of love which should characterize the believers at all times. V. 23. **Thus saith the Lord of hosts, the God of Israel,** whose majesty and power are here emphasized, **As yet they shall use this speech in the land of Judah and in the cities thereof when I shall bring again their captivity,** when His Church would once more be established, **The Lord bless thee, O habitation of justice,** where true righteousness would once more find its dwelling-place, **and mountain of holiness,** Mount Zion, of course, representing the Church of Jehovah. V. 24. **And there shall dwell in Judah itself, and in all the cities thereof together, husbandmen,** such as till the ground, **and they that go forth with flocks,** this picture being descriptive of the blessings which the Lord would pour out upon His people. V. 25. **For I have satiated the weary soul,** refreshing the soul which panted after relief, **and I have replenished every sorrowful soul,** satisfying the soul that was languishing for relief. Cp. Matt. 11, 28. The prophet closes this section with the remark: v. 26. **Upon this I awaked,** namely, from the vision, or ecstasy, in which he had received the revelation of the Lord, **and beheld; and my sleep was sweet unto me.** The glance into the future which had been vouchsafed him was so glorious that he kept it in his memory as a pleasant picture. To all true ministers of the Word it is a source of great satisfaction to find the Church returning to a condition of repentance and zeal for the Lord.

THE NEW LIFE AND THE NEW COVENANT. — V. 27. **Behold, the days come, saith the Lord, that I will sow the house of Israel and the house of Judah,** the congregation of true believers in Him, **with the seed of man and with the seed of beast,** with great spiritual blessings, as a field of exceeding fruitfulness. V. 28. **And it shall come to pass that like as I have watched over them,** regarding them with wakeful attention, **to pluck up, and to break down,** or "to root out," **and to throw down, and to destroy,**

and to afflict, the heaping of the synonyms emphasizing the thoroughness of the Lord's punishment upon His apostate people, **so will I watch over them**, namely, in the promised restoration, **to build and to plant, saith the Lord.** V. 29. **In those days they shall say no more**, according to a proverb which had been coined during the years of tribulation in Israel, **The fathers have eaten a sour grape, and the children's teeth are set on edge**, the meaning being, of course, that the transgressions of the fathers were visited upon the innocent children, a statement intended to express that they suffered the evil consequences of their fathers' sins rather than of their own. V. 30. **But every one shall die for his own iniquity; every man that eateth the sour grape, his teeth shall be set on edge.** Cp. Lam. 5, 7; Ezek. 18, 2. 3. V. 31. **Behold, the days come, saith the Lord, that I will make a new covenant with the house of Israel and with the house of Judah**, a covenant concerning all those who were His children in truth, v. 32. **not according to the covenant that I made with their fathers in the day that I took them by the hand to bring them out of the land of Egypt, which My covenant they brake, although I was an Husband unto them, saith the Lord**, surrounding His bride, the Church represented in the children of Israel, with the fulness of His loving care; v. 33. **but this shall be the covenant that I will make with the house of Israel**, when in the realization of His mercy the justice of His judgments will freely be acknowledged, **After those days, saith the Lord**, in the Messianic era, **I will put My Law**, the glorious message of His eternal Gospel, **in their inward parts and write it in their hearts**, so that it would become the inmost possession of all believers, **and will be their God, and they shall be My people.** The Word of the Gospel, implanted into the hearts of men by faith, is the fundamental principle, the guiding and driving power in their lives, by and through which the relation of the believer to the God of his salvation is established and maintained. Cp. 2 Cor. 6, 18; 1 Pet. 2, 9. V. 34. **And they shall teach no more every man his neighbor and every man his brother, saying, Know the Lord**, such admonitory instruction in the knowledge of Jehovah being no longer required; **for they shall all know Me, from the least of them unto the greatest of them, saith the Lord**, the Spirit of God Himself having enlightened and instructed them, Is. 54, 13; **for I will forgive their iniquity, and I will remember their sin no more**, the remission of sins through the merits of the Messiah being the central thought of all New Testament instruction. It is clear, of course, that this knowledge and experience of the grace of God does not exclude, but rather presupposes, the proclamation of God's gracious will in Christ Jesus. V. 35. **Thus saith the Lord, which giveth the sun for a light by day and the ordinances of the moon and of the stars for a light by night**, who established the laws of nature to endure as long as the earth stands, **which divideth the sea when the waves thereof roar**, exciting its billows and lashing them into a fury as His almighty power chooses; **The Lord of hosts is His name**, the almighty Ruler of the universe: v. 36. **If those ordinances depart from before Me, saith the Lord**, if the entire order of nature will be overthrown, **then the seed of Israel also shall cease from being a nation before Me forever**, that is, His Church would be maintained so that the very portals of hell will not be able to overcome it, Matt. 16, 18. V. 37. **Thus saith the Lord**, in another solemn affirmation of His unchanging mercy toward His spiritual children, **If heaven above can be measured and the foundations of the earth searched out beneath**, the heavens being immeasurable and the profoundest depths of the earth unsearchable to this day, **I will also cast off all the seed of Israel for all that they have done, saith the Lord.** In spite of the fact that the justice of God compels Him to reject the wilful transgressors, His mercy will always find some whom He will save from the general fate, for He does not desire the death of the sinner. V. 38. **Behold, the days come, saith the Lord, that the city shall be built to the Lord**, for the honor of His holy name, **from the tower of Hananeel**, in the northeastern corner of the city wall, **unto the gate of the corner**, on the north or northwest, near the present Jaffa Gate, the entire northern wall of the city being included in this description. V. 39. **And the measuring-line shall yet go forth over against it upon the hill Gareb**, probably the hill of the lepers, to the northwest of the city, **and shall compass about to Goath**, a hill with a sharp ascent to the southwest of Jerusalem. V. 40. **And the whole valley of the dead bodies, and of the ashes**, where the ashes of the sacrificial fires were dumped, **and all the fields unto the brook of Kidron**, on the east side, **unto the corner of the Horse Gate toward the east, shall be holy unto the Lord**, consecrated to His service; **it shall not be plucked up nor thrown down any more forever**, never suffer destruction. The entire passage is evidently figurative, the purpose being to set forth the increase and the glory of the New Testament Church, especially in its final perfection. It is proper that this description of Jehovah's Church should form the conclusion of the prophecy concerning the restoration of the Lord's people, since it includes both the redemption through the Messiah and the establishment of the holy Christian Church in its beginning here on earth and in its glorification in heaven.

CHAPTER 32.

The Purchase of a Field as a Type of the Restoration.

THE TRANSACTION ITSELF. —V. 1. **The word that came to Jeremiah from the Lord,** by direct inspiration, **in the tenth year of Zedekiah, king of Judah, which was the eighteenth year of Nebuchadrezzar.** V. 2. **For then the king of Babylon's army besieged Jerusalem,** the siege having begun in the tenth month of the ninth year of Zedekiah, chap. 39, 1; **and Jeremiah, the prophet, was shut up in the court of the prison,** kept in ward in the guard-room, **which was in the king of Judah's house.** V. 3. **For Zedekiah, king of Judah, had shut him up, saying, Wherefore dost thou prophesy and say, Thus saith the Lord, Behold, I will give this city into the hand of the king of Babylon, and he shall take it,** v. 4. **and Zedekiah, king of Judah, shall not escape out of the hand of the Chaldeans, but shall surely be delivered into the hand of the king of Babylon and shall speak with him mouth to mouth,** or, as we should say, face to face, **and his eyes shall behold his eyes;** v. 5. **and he shall lead Zedekiah to Babylon, and there shall he be until I visit him, saith the Lord,** turning once more to him in mercy; **though ye fight with the Chaldeans, ye shall not prosper?** The circumstances here referred to occurred at the beginning of the siege, when Jeremiah foretold the capture of the city. Cp. chap. 34, 1—7. The prophet had at that time been placed in custody by Zedekiah, but had regained his liberty when Pharaoh-hophrah caused the Chaldeans to raise the siege of the city. He had then been cast into the dungeon once more, but obtained leave to be removed to the court of the prison. Cp. chap. 34, 12—21. V. 6. **And Jeremiah said,** this being the continuation of verse 1, the thought of which was interrupted by the long parenthesis following, **The word of the Lord came unto me, saying,** v. 7. **Behold, Hanameel, the son of Shallum, thine uncle,** that is, the cousin of Jeremiah, **shall come unto thee, saying, Buy thee my field that is in Anathoth,** Jeremiah's home town; **for the right of redemption is thine to buy it.** This right consisted in the privilege or duty of the nearest blood relative of one who wished to sell to buy the land concerned, in order that possession of the property might continue to be vested in the family of the original owners. V. 8. **So Hanameel, mine uncle's son, came to me in the court of the prison according to the word of the Lord,** that is, just as the Lord had prophesied, **and said unto me, Buy my field, I pray thee, that is in Anathoth, which is in the country of Benjamin,** within the boundaries of this tribe; **for the right of inheritance is thine, and the redemption is thine; buy it for thyself. Then I knew that this was the word of the Lord,** that is, Jeremiah was confirmed in his knowledge by this outward proof of the Lord's prophecy. V. 9. **And I bought the field of Hanameel, my uncle's son, that was in Anathoth, and weighed him the money,** after the manner of payment then in use, **even seventeen shekels of silver** (somewhat less than eleven dollars), a comparatively small price, for in reality only the harvest until the next year of the jubilee was sold. V. 10. **And I subscribed the evidence,** the purchase being completed in agreement with all the demands of the law, **and sealed it,** folding it up and covering the flap with the public seal, the signature to the deed thus being established beyond a doubt, **and took witnesses and weighed him the money in the balances.** V. 11. **So I took the evidence of the purchase,** the contract of sale, **both that which was sealed according to the law and custom,** which had the validity of a registered warranty deed in our days, **and that which was open,** apparently only a copy of the deed, v. 12. **and I gave the evidence of the purchase unto Baruch, the son of Neriah, the son of Maaseiah,** who was Jeremiah's secretary and assistant, **in the sight of Hanameel, mine uncle's son, and in the presence of the witnesses that subscribed the book of the purchase,** who had placed their names under the document as witnesses of the transaction, **before all the Jews that sat in the court of the prison,** who were present at the time, although not as formal witnesses of the sale. V. 13. **And I charged Baruch before them, saying,** v. 14. **Thus saith the Lord of hosts, the God of Israel,** a special command of the Lord being issued in this instance on account of the significance attaching to the act, **Take these evidences, this evidence of the purchase, both which is sealed and this evidence which is open,** the documents as now made out, **and put them in an earthen vessel that they may continue many days,** being protected against mold and decay. V. 15. **For thus saith the Lord of hosts, the God of Israel, Houses and fields and vineyards shall be possessed again in this land.** The desolation of the land of Judah would last only for the length of time which God had determined, after which He intended to restore His people to their homes. For this reason the careful keeping of the deed transferring the land from Hanameel to Jeremiah was important as a record for the use of his family. The Lord was even then thinking of the return of Judah from Babylon and of the restoration of the true worship in Jerusalem. His thoughts are always upon the blessings which He wishes to bestow upon His people rather than upon the punishments which He must occasionally dispense.

JEREMIAH'S PRAYER AND JEHOVAH'S ANSWER. V. 16. **Now, when I had delivered the evidence of the purchase unto Baruch, the son of Neriah, I prayed unto the Lord, saying,** v. 17. **Ah, Lord God!** his perplexity on account of the strange proceeding in which he had just taken part at God's command causing him to take recourse to prayer, **behold, thou hast made the heaven and the earth by Thy great power and stretched-out arm,** the entire creation being evidence of Jehovah's omnipotence, **and there is nothing too hard for Thee,** literally, "not is too difficult or miraculous beyond Thee anything." V. 18. **Thou showest loving-kindness unto thousands and recompensest the iniquity of the fathers into the bosom of their children after them,** so that they are obliged to accept and bear it, since they follow their parents in their wicked ways, Ex. 20, 5. 6; 34, 7; **the Great, the Mighty God, the Lord of hosts, is His name,** Jehovah Sabaoth, the Commander of all the heavenly armies, v. 19. **great in counsel and mighty in work,** His almighty power being directed by His boundless wisdom, both in devising and in executing His plans for the benefit of man; **for Thine eyes are open upon all the ways of the sons of men,** Prov. 5, 21, **to give every one according to his ways and according to the fruit of his doings;** cp. chap. 17, 10; v. 20. **which hast set signs and wonders,** miraculous deeds, which served to bring out the majesty of His essence, **in the land of Egypt, even unto this day,** for the wonder-working power of Jehovah, set in operation at that time, had continued to exert its might through the centuries, **and in Israel, and among other men, and hast made Thee a name, as at this day,** so that the honor of the Lord was extolled wherever men heard of His deeds; v. 21. **and hast brought forth Thy people Israel out of the land of Egypt with signs, and with wonders, and with a strong hand, and with a stretched-out arm, and with great terror,** cp. Deut. 26, 8; v. 22. **and hast given them this land, which Thou didst swear to their fathers,** beginning with Abraham, **to give them, a land flowing with milk and honey,** unusually rich in resources; v. 23. **and they came in and possessed it,** willing enough to receive rich benefits from the hand of Jehovah. **But they obeyed not Thy voice, neither walked in Thy Law,** rewarding the goodness of the Lord with base ingratitude; **they have done nothing of all that Thou commandedst them to do,** the complaint which the Lord had been obliged to voice time and again. **Therefore Thou hast caused all this evil to come upon them,** their punishment thus striking them in a measure agreeing with their transgression. V. 24. **Behold the mounts,** the ramparts of the besieging army as it prepared to take the city, **they are come unto the city to take it, and the city is given into the hand of the Chaldeans that fight against it because of,** or "in the presence of, as a consequence of," **the sword and of the famine and of the pestilence. And what Thou hast spoken is come to pass, and, behold, Thou seest it,** for the siege was then going on. V. 25. **And Thou hast said unto me, O Lord God,** the prophet's perplexity here finding expression, **Buy thee a field for money and take witnesses; for,** or "and yet," **the city is given into the hand of the Chaldeans.** Although the city, by the word of the Lord and according to the evidence visible in the presence of the besieging army, was doomed to destruction, yet Jeremiah had received the command which, in view of the situation, seemed very strange to him. So he looks to the Lord for an explanation regarding the future. V. 26. **Then came the word of the Lord unto Jeremiah,** in answer to his prayer, **saying,** v. 27. **Behold, I am the Lord, the God of all flesh,** of all men, weak and mortal as they are; **is there anything too hard for Me?** as Jeremiah himself had stated, v. 17. V. 28. **Therefore, thus saith the Lord, Behold, I will give this city into the hand of the Chaldeans and into the hand of Nebuchadrezzar, king of Babylon, and he shall take it;** v. 29. **and the Chaldeans that fight against this city shall come and set fire on this city and burn it with the houses upon whose roofs they have offered incense unto Baal,** in the flagrant form of idolatry which the Lord had taken occasion to reprove so often, **and poured out drink-offerings unto other gods to provoke Me to anger.** V. 30. **For the children of Israel,** upon whom the Lord's punishment had already descended, **and the children of Judah,** who had not profited by their example, **have only done evil before Me from their youth; for the children of Israel have only provoked Me to anger with the work of their hands, saith the Lord,** they indulged only in such things as were displeasing to Jehovah, the God of the covenant. V. 31. **For this city hath been to Me as a provocation of Mine anger and of My fury,** an object calling forth His indignation, challenging His wrath and punishment, **from the day that they built it even unto this day, that I should remove it from before My face,** this, as it were, being the object which its inhabitants had in mind with their idolatrous behavior, v. 32. **because of all the evil of the children of Israel and of the children of Judah which they have done to provoke Me to anger, they, their kings, their princes, their priests, and their prophets, and the men of Judah, and the inhabitants of Jerusalem,** practically the entire nation indulging in the same transgressions. V. 33. **And they have turned unto Me the back and not the face,** a complaint which the Lord had repeatedly voiced, cp. chap. 2, 27, **though I taught them, rising up**

early and teaching them, with eager and merciful zeal, **yet they have not hearkened to receive instruction.** V. 34. **But they set their abominations in the house which is called by My name to defile it,** all pictures of idols being abhorred in the sight of the Lord, especially since the glory of His own name was besmirched by such acts. V. 35. **And they built the high places of Baal,** the supreme idol of the Canaanitish nations, **which are in the Valley of the Son of Hinnom,** or of Ben-hinnom, **to cause their sons and their daughters to pass through the fire unto Molech,** in the loathsome sacrifice made to this chief idol of the Moabites, **which I commanded them not, neither came it into My mind that they should do this abomination to cause Judah to sin,** to bring transgression and guilt upon the entire nation. Cp. chap. 7, 30. 31. V. 36. **And now, therefore, thus saith the Lord, the God of Israel, concerning this city, whereof ye say,** having passed from the extreme of self-confidence to the very depths of despair, **It shall be delivered into the hand of the king of Babylon by the sword and by the famine and by the pestilence,** the Lord now, in spite of the fact that the great majority of the people had richly deserved their fate, giving them a gracious promise of deliverance. V. 37. **Behold, I will gather them out of all countries whither I have driven them in Mine anger and in My fury and in great wrath,** the use of the synonyms serving to bring out the extremity of God's indignation; **and I will bring them again unto this place, and I will cause them to dwell in safety,** all this stated of the future security of the Church. V. 38. **And they shall be My people, and I will be their God,** cp. chap. 30, 22; 24, 7. V. 39. **And I will give them one heart and one way,** directing them to the one road which was well-pleasing to Him, **that they may fear Me forever, for the good of them and of their children after them,** since this course would keep them from the various evil ways of the heathen. V. 40. **And I will make an everlasting covenant with them,** so that they would once more enter into the relation with Him which He desired, **that I will not turn away from them to do them good,** that is, not refrain from doing them good; **but I will put My fear in their hearts that they shall not depart from Me.** The Lord here represents Himself as an eager and diligent Educator, a faithful Pedagog, who follows His pupils everywhere in order to impart to them the instruction which they needed for the proper way of living. V. 41. **Yea, I will rejoice over them to do them good,** it being His greatest delight to shower benefits upon them; **and I will plant them in this land assuredly with My whole heart and with My whole soul,** so that His faithfulness toward them would find its most emphatic expression in His treatment of them. V. 42. **For thus saith the Lord, Like as I have brought all this great evil upon this people,** in having them led away into captivity, **so will I bring upon them all the good that I have promised them.** Cp. chap. 31, 28. From this fact the Lord now draws a conclusion which serves as an answer to the question of Jeremiah. V. 43. **And fields shall be bought in this land, whereof ye say, It is desolate, without man or beast,** such statements expressing their despair of ever seeing the land restored to a habitable state; **it is given into the hand of the Chaldeans.** Over against this fact stands the promise of Jehovah, v. 44. **Men shall buy fields for money,** conducting their purchases in accordance with the forms required by law, **and subscribe evidences,** deeds of conveyance, **and seal them, and take witnesses in the land of Benjamin,** where Jeremiah had made his symbolical purchase, **and in the places about Jerusalem,** which would again occupy the position of capital, **and in the cities of Judah, and in the cities of the mountains,** in the northern and eastern part of Judea, **and in the cities of the valley,** the lowlands toward the west, **and in the cities of the South,** the semiarid plains bordering the Arabian Desert; **for I will cause their captivity to return, saith the Lord.** Although the expressions refer to the restoration of Judah, the description clearly includes the Church of Jehovah as such; for only the believers are in truth members of the people of God.

CHAPTER 33.

A Further Promise Concerning the Restoration and Glorification of God's People.

THE CONTRAST BETWEEN DESTRUCTION AND RESTORATION. — V. 1. **Moreover, the word of the Lord came unto Jeremiah the second time, while he was yet shut up in the court of the prison,** during the shameful imprisonment inflicted upon him by Zedekiah, **saying,** v. 2. **Thus saith the Lord, the Maker thereof,** literally, "the Doer," He who performs what He promises and threatens, **the Lord that formed it, to establish it,** or, "He who prepares it to complete it," carrying out His plans without fail; **the Lord is His name,** Jehovah, the God of the covenant: v. 3. **Call unto Me,** namely, in making a plea for the restoration of Judah, **and I will answer thee and show thee great and mighty things,** proclaiming or announcing great and inaccessible things, **which thou knowest not,** which are beyond human understanding and comprehension, which human knowledge would never expect. V. 4. **For thus saith the Lord, the God of Israel, concerning the houses of this city and concerning the houses of the kings of Judah,** the various buildings making up the royal palace, **which are thrown down by the mounts and by the sword,** literally, "against the ramparts and against the sword," for the buildings of Jerusalem were wrecked in order to get a sufficient amount of stones to strengthen the walls against the advancing army of the invaders; v. 5. **they come to fight with the Chaldeans,** the people of Judah being determined to resist the hostile army, **but it is to fill them,** namely, the houses of the city, **with the dead bodies of men, whom I have slain in Mine anger and in My fury, and for all whose wickedness I have hid My face from this city,** this last verse being inserted by way of parenthesis: v. 6. **Behold, I will bring it,** the city of Jerusalem, **health and cure,** by binding up the wounds of the war, **and I will cure them,** healing the wounds inflicted by the enemies, **and will reveal unto them,** His people, **the abundance of peace and truth,** that is, genuine, lasting prosperity. V. 7. **And I will cause the captivity of Judah and the captivity of Israel,** of all those who are His children in truth, **to return, and will build them, as at the first,** when He first made them His people, at the time of the exodus from Egypt. V. 8. **And I will cleanse them from all their iniquity whereby they have sinned against Me,** their guilt being removed by His forgiveness; **and I will pardon all their iniquities whereby they have sinned, and whereby they have transgressed against Me.** This is the basis of the lasting covenant of salvation, the Lord's pardoning grace over against all poor sinners. V. 9. **And it shall be to Me a name of joy, a praise, and an honor before all the nations of the earth,** Jerusalem itself, with its congregation of believers, becoming a city the very mention of whose name would cause Jehovah to rejoice, while nations in every part of the world would praise her, **which shall hear all the good that I do unto them; and they shall fear and tremble,** with the fear of repentant sinners, **for all the goodness and for all the prosperity that I procure unto it,** on account of the miraculous power of God displayed in behalf of the Jews. Even thus men everywhere, in coming to the knowledge of the true God, serve Him with fear and rejoice with trembling, walking before Him and increasing daily in holiness.

THE GLORY OF THE FUTURE. — V. 10. **Thus saith the Lord, Again there shall be heard in this place, which, ye say, shall be desolate without man and without beast,** chap. 32, 43, **even in the cities of Judah and in the streets of Jerusalem, that are desolate, without man and without inhabitant and without beast,** the invaders having already spread ruin along their entire line of march, v. 11. **the voice of joy and the voice of gladness, the voice of the bridegroom and the voice of the bride,** expressions setting forth the happiness of a people living in peace and security, **the voice of them that shall say, Praise the Lord of hosts, for the Lord is good, for His mercy endureth forever,** the words of Ps. 136, 1, which were actually used by the Jews at the time of the restoration, Ezra 3, 11; **and of them that shall bring the sacrifice of praise into the house of the Lord. For I will cause to return the captivity of the land,** reversing it, so that it no longer exists, **as at the first, saith the Lord,** so that the people of Judah would again be His free people, as He had intended it from the beginning. V. 12. **Thus saith the Lord of hosts, Again in this place, which is desolate without man and without beast, and in all the cities thereof,** many of which were, or were to be, heaps of ruins, **shall be an habitation of shepherds causing their flocks to lie down,** as under conditions of the utmost peace and security. V. 13. **In the cities of the mountains,** the mountainous region of Judah, toward the north and northeast, **in the cities of the vale,** the plains or lowlands toward the Mediterranean Sea, **and in the cities of the south,** the semiarid region bordering on Arabia and the Sinaitic Peninsula, **and in the land of Benjamin, and in the places about Jerusalem, and in the cities of Judah,** the very detailed enumeration serving to lay stress on the completeness of the fulfilment, **shall the flocks pass again under the hands of him that telleth them, saith the Lord,** for faithful shepherds kept a very careful count of the sheep entrusted to them. The words thus imply that a most watchful and provident care would again be exercised with regard to the believers. V. 14. **Behold, the days come, saith the Lord,** this being the standing formula for introducing statements pertaining to Messianic conditions, **that I will perform that good thing which I have promised unto the house of Israel and to the house of Judah,** to those who were members of His people in truth, for His Church in the Old Testament is continued in the congregation or communion of saints in the New. V. 15. **In those days and at that time,** in the Messianic era, **will I cause the Branch of Righteousness,** the name applied to the Messiah also by Isaiah and Zechariah, **to grow up unto David,** for Christ was born of the seed of David, and it was He who earned, and is the representative of, the true righteousness, that which is valid in the sight of God; **and He shall execute judgment and righteousness in the land,** as the true King of His people. V. 16. **In those days shall Judah be saved, and Jerusalem shall dwell safely,** the name in either case designating the Church of the Lord, His chosen people in the true sense of the term; **and this is the name wherewith she shall be called, The Lord our Righteousness,** the city, as representing the congregation of the Lord, being united with Him by virtue of the mystical union, so that, whatsoever belongs to the Head, belongs also to the members. The Church draws all her righteousness from Christ and is a representative of His righteousness, hence His attributes may be transferred to her. V. 17. **For thus saith the Lord, David shall never want a man,** his family would never lack a representative, **to sit upon the throne of the house of Israel.** In other words, the kingdom of Christ was to be an eternal kingdom. V. 18. **Neither shall the priests, the Levites,** the members of the tribe of Levi, **want a man before Me,** there would never be a time when there would be no priest, namely, in the highest sense, spoken of the person of the Messiah, **to offer burnt offerings and to kindle meat-offerings and to do sacrifice continually.** Christ's one sacrifice has an eternal effect, and all external forms of worship are but types of His perfect offering. V. 19. **And the word of the Lord came unto Jeremiah, saying,** v. 20. **Thus saith the Lord, If ye can break My covenant of the day and My covenant of the night, and that there should not be day and night in their season,** that the order of nature, as established by Him, would be overthrown, v. 21. **then may also My covenant be broken with David, My servant, that he should not have a son to reign upon his throne,** 2 Sam. 7, 12—29, **and with the Levites the priests, My ministers.** The Lord would break His promise neither to David nor to His servants in the office of the ministry. He would give them all the blessings of the Messianic era in full. V. 22. **As the host of heaven cannot be numbered, neither the sand of the sea measured, so will I multiply the seed of David, My servant, and the Levites that minister unto Me,** in either case their spiritual children, the believers of all times, for of them it is rightly said that Christ has made them to be kings and priests before God and His Father. V. 23. **Moreover, the word of the Lord came to Jeremiah, saying,** v. 24. **Considerest thou not what this people have spoken, saying, The two families which the Lord hath chosen,** namely, Israel and Judah, as representing His Church of all times, **He hath even cast them off?** This was the statement made by some of the reprobate Jews in order to ridicule the true believers. **Thus they have despised My people that they should be no more a nation before them,** that is, before their eyes, according to their opinion. The Lord reproves this notion with great sternness. V. 25. **Thus saith the Lord, If My covenant be not with day and night,** Gen. 8, 22, **and if I have not appointed the ordinances of heaven and earth,** if He has not established the laws of nature, v. 26. **then will I cast away the seed of Jacob,** His spiritual children, **and David, My servant, so that I will not take any of his seed to be rulers over the seed of Abraham, Isaac, and Jacob,** namely, those who are their children and descendants in spirit; **for I will cause their captivity to return, and have mercy on them.** All this was fulfilled and is being fulfilled in the kingdom of Christ, where those who have been redeemed from the bondage of Satan rejoice in the fulness of the grace given them by virtue of the Messiah's vicarious sacrifice.

CHAPTER 34.

Prophecies Concerning Conditions at Zedekiah's Time.

OF THE CAPTIVITY OF ZEDEKIAH.—V. 1. **The word which came unto Jeremiah from the Lord, when Nebuchadnezzar, king of Babylon, and all his army, and all the kingdoms of the earth of his dominion,** literally, "all the kingdoms of the country of the rule of his hand," **and all the people,** the heaping of these expressions denoting the overwhelming power of His army, against which all resistance was useless, **fought against Jerusalem and against all the cities thereof,** the cities of Judah, which were considered tributary to the capital, **saying,** v. 2. **Thus saith the Lord, the God of Israel, Go and speak to Zedekiah, king of Judah, and tell him, Thus saith the Lord, Behold, I will give this city into the hand of the king of Babylon,** delivering it according to His supreme will and purpose, **and he shall burn it with fire;** v. 3. **and thou shalt not escape out of his hand,** as he afterwards attempted to do, 2 Kings 25, 4—6, **but shalt surely be taken and delivered into his hand; and thine eyes shall behold the eyes of the king of Babylon, and he shall speak with thee mouth to mouth, and thou shalt go to Babylon.** Cp. chap. 32, 3—5. V. 4. **Yet hear the word of the Lord,** who was ever ready to show mercy even in the midst of His punishments, **O Zedekiah, king of Judah, Thus saith the Lord of thee, Thou shalt not die by the sword,** not be subject to a violent death, v. 5. **but thou shalt die in peace,** depart this life by a natural death; **and with the burnings of thy fathers, the former kings which were before thee, so shall they burn odors for thee,** after the custom of burning aromatic spices, which was observed for the kings and the members of the royal family; **and they will lament thee,** saying, **Ah, lord;** or, Alas, master; **for I have pronounced the word, saith the Lord.** So it was not to be his fate to die in battle like Jehoiakim and to remain unlamented and unburied. Cp. chap. 22, 18. 19. V. 6. **Then Jeremiah, the prophet, spake all these words unto Zedekiah, king of Judah, in Jerusalem,** v. 7. **when the king of Babylon's army fought against Jerusalem and against all the cities of Judah that were left,** which had not been reduced in previous campaigns, **against Lachish and against Azekah,** two cities in the lowlands toward the southwest, on the border of the Philistine territory; **for these defensed cities remained of the cities of Judah.** As the Lord here showed mercy to Zedekiah, so He is ever full of compassion toward His children, for He remembers that they are dust.

OF THE EVIL TREATMENT OF BOND-SERVANTS. V. 8. **This is the word that came unto Jeremiah from the Lord,** which he recorded as faithfully as he had received it, **after that the King Zedekiah had made a covenant with all the people which were at Jerusalem,** entering into a solemn agreement with them, **to proclaim liberty unto them,** according to the Lord's ordinance which permitted the Hebrews to keep the members of their own nation as bond-servants for only six years, since in the seventh year they must all be given their liberty, Ex. 21, 22; Deut. 15, 12, v. 9. **that every man should let his man-servant and every man his maid-servant being an Hebrew or an Hebrewess go free, that none should serve himself of them,** cause or compel them to be bond-servants, **to wit, of a Jew, his brother,** for the Law concerned these only, not the slaves of another nationality. V. 10. **Now, when all the princes and all the people which had entered into the covenant,** with due solemnity, including the bringing of sacrifices, **heard that every one should let his man-servant and every one his maid-servant go free that none should serve themselves of them any more, then they obeyed and let them go.** They were momentarily impressed by the Lord's command and acted in agreement with it. V. 11. **But afterward they turned,** they changed their minds, **and caused the servants and the handmaids whom they had let go free to return and brought them into subjection for servants and for handmaids.** When the Chaldean invasion was upon them, they pretended a meek submission under the will of the Lord, but when the danger seemed to be past, at the temporary withdrawal of the invading army, they once more brought their servants under the yoke, thus proving that their conversion was not sincere. Like the hypocrites of our day they feigned submission in order to gain their end. V. 12. **Therefore the word of the Lord came to Jeremiah from the Lord, saying,** v. 13. **Thus saith the Lord, the God of Israel,** in reproving the hypocritical behavior of the Jewish nobles, **I made a covenant with your fathers in the day that I brought them forth out of the land of Egypt, out of the house of bondmen,** this ordinance being included in the laws given during the wilderness journey, **saying,** v. 14. **At the end of seven years,** in the so-called Sabbatical Year, **let ye go every man his brother, an Hebrew, which hath been sold unto thee,** rather, "who hath sold himself to thee"; **and when he hath served thee six years, thou shalt let him go free from thee;** cp. Ex. 21, 2; Deut. 15, 12. **But your fathers hearkened not unto Me, neither inclined their ear,** they paid not the slightest attention to His command. V. 15. **And ye were now turned,** in a change which seemed sincere enough, **and had done right in My sight, in proclaiming liberty every man to his neighbor,** v. 10. **and ye had made a covenant before Me in the house which is called by My name,** in a solemn service in the Temple; v. 16. **but ye turned and polluted My name,** by violating the oath made in the name of Jehovah, **and caused every man his servant and every man his handmaid whom he had set at liberty at their pleasure,** as the bond-servants themselves chose, **to return and brought them into subjection, to be unto you for servants and for handmaids,** in the same state of peonage and even of slavery as before. V. 17. **Therefore, thus saith the Lord, Ye have not hearkened unto Me, in proclaiming liberty, every one to his brother and every man to his neighbor,** for the ceremony in which they had taken part in the Temple had been nothing but sham and hypocrisy and had no value in the sight of the Lord. **Behold, I proclaim a liberty for you, saith the Lord,** He would now, in just retribution, dismiss them from being His servants, He would sever the relation of which they had been so proud, delivering them, instead, **to the sword, to the pestilence, and to the famine,** the three dreaded scourges of nations; **and I will make you to be removed into all the kingdoms of the earth,** as exiles among strangers. V. 18. **And I will give the men that have transgressed My covenant, which have not performed the words of the covenant which they had made before Me, when they cut the calf in twain and passed between the parts thereof,** a solemn rite in which the contracting parties walked through between the halves of a slaughtered animal. As such a slain beast the Lord intended to deliver the nobles of Judah, as He now expressly states. V. 19. **The princes of Judah and the princes of Jerusalem, the eunuchs,** the chamberlains or officers of the court, **and the priests, and all the people of the land, which passed between the parts of the calf,** v. 20. **I will even give them into the hand of their**

enemies and into the hand of them that seek their life, to be slain without mercy; **and their dead bodies shall be for meat unto the fowls of the heaven and to the beasts of the earth,** so that the birds and beasts of prey would feast on their carcasses — a gruesome meal. V. 21. **And Zedekiah, king of Judah, and his princes will I give into the hand of their enemies and into the hand of them that seek their life, and into the hand of the king of Babylon's army, which are gone up from you,** having temporarily abandoned the siege of Jerusalem on account of the approach of Pharaoh-hophrah. V. 22. **Behold, I will command, saith the Lord, and cause them to return to this city,** acting in this case as the Lord's servants; **and they shall fight against it and take it and burn it with fire; and I will make the cities of Judah a desolation without an inhabitant.** The punishment of the Lord is sure to find the offenders against His holy Law, and hypocrites particularly are an abomination in His sight.

CHAPTER 35.

The Example of the Rechabites.

THE FACT. — V. 1. **The word which came unto Jeremiah from the Lord in the days of Jehoiakim, the son of Josiah, king of Judah,** about in the summer of the year 606 B. C., **saying,** v. 2. **Go unto the house of the Rechabites,** a family descending from the tribe of the Kenites, with some prominent members, 2 Kings 10, 15. 23, **and speak unto them, and bring them into the house of the Lord, into one of the chambers,** the small cells built on the outside of the walls, used chiefly for storage purposes, 1 Kings 6, 5, **and give them wine to drink,** offering them this intoxicant to put them to a test. Rechab, the father of Jonadab and the ancestor of the tribe, had given his children the command to abstain from wine in order to keep them in the simplicity of their forefathers and to protect them from moral decay. V. 3. **Then I took Jaazaniah, the son of Jeremiah, the son of Habaziniah, and his brethren, and all his sons, and the whole house of the Rechabites,** all the members of the family that could be found, v. 4. **and I brought them into the house of the Lord, into the chamber of the sons of Hanan, the son of Igdaliah, a man of God,** that is, a prophet who occupied this cell, **which was by the chamber of the princes,** where the rulers of the people assembled at that time for the sessions of the great council, **which was above the chamber of Maaseiah, the son of Shallum,** probably the same man that occupied the position of second priest in the nation, cp. chap. 29, 25 and 21, 1, **the keeper of the door,** the chief officer of the Temple-guard or of that section which was entrusted with watching the Temple-gates; v. 5. **and I set before the sons of the house of the Rechabites pots full of wine and cups, and I said unto them, Drink ye wine.** This invitation was included in the plan of the Lord, for their passing the test successfully was to be made the theme of a discourse to the people. V. 6. **But they said, We will drink no wine; for Jonadab, the son of Rechab, our father, commanded us, saying, Ye shall drink no wine, neither ye nor your sons, forever,** not merely a wise temperance, but a total abstinence being required of them; v. 7. **neither shall ye build house, nor sow seed, nor plant vineyard, nor have any,** in following any agricultural or horticultural pursuit, on account of which they might become settled in any one place; **but all your days ye shall dwell in tents,** leading a more or less nomadic life, like their forefathers before them, **that ye,** in obedience to their ancestor's command, **may live many days in the land where ye be strangers;** for, although living in the midst of Israel and Judah and having accepted the true God, the Rechabites maintained their own nationality. V. 8. **Thus have we obeyed the voice of Jonadab, the son of Rechab, our father, in all that he hath charged us,** thereby setting a splendid example of obedience, **to drink no wine all our days, we, our wives, our sons, nor our daughters,** v. 9. **nor to build houses for us to dwell in; neither have we vineyard, nor field, nor seed;** v. 10. **but we have dwelt in tents and have obeyed and done according to all that Jonadab, our father, commanded us.** V. 11. **But it came to pass, when Nebuchadrezzar, king of Babylon, came up into the land,** his invading army threatening the ancient dwelling-places of the Kenites first, **that we said, Come and let us go to Jerusalem for fear of the army of the Chaldeans and for fear of the army of the Syrians,** for marauding bands of Syrian tribes took every opportunity to plunder exposed parts of Palestine, 2 Kings 24, 2. **So we dwell at Jerusalem,** making use of the city as a temporary refuge, until they might return to their home-land. The Rechabites thus offered a fine example of willing obedience to the command of their tribal head.

THE APPLICATION. — V. 12. **Then came the word of the Lord unto Jeremiah, saying,** v. 13. **Thus saith the Lord of hosts, the God of Israel, Go and tell the men of Judah and the inhabitants of Jerusalem, Will ye not receive instruction** by which they might be trained properly, **to hearken to My words? saith the Lord.** V. 14. **The words of Jona-**

dab, the son of Rechab, that he commanded his sons not to drink wine are performed, the commands of a mere man having so much weight; **for unto this day they drink none, but obey their father's commandment,** in unwavering faithfulness and obedience; **notwithstanding I have spoken unto you, rising early and speaking, but ye hearkened not unto Me.** The Rechabites had received only one ordinance, and they had clung to its observance for almost three hundred years, although it was transmitted by oral tradition from father to son only; but the Lord's people took no interest in His admonitions, although they were repeated continually. V. 15. **I have sent also unto you all My servants, the prophets, rising up early and sending them, saying, Return ye now every man from his evil way and amend your doings and go not after other gods to serve them,** a warning which we find time and again, **and ye shall dwell in the land which I have given to you and to your fathers; but ye have not inclined your ear nor hearkened unto Me.** He had commanded nothing unreasonable, but simply to serve Him, and he had attached to His command a most gracious promise, but all in vain. V. 16. **Because the sons of Jonadab, the son of Rechab, have performed the commandment of their father which he commanded them, but this people hath not hearkened unto Me,** v. 17. **therefore thus saith the Lord God of hosts, the God of Israel, Behold, I will bring upon Judah and upon all the inhabitants of Jerusalem all the evil that I have pronounced against them, because I have spoken unto them, but they have not heard, and I have called unto them, but they have not answered.** The connection of thought is this: Just as faithfulness in keeping a father's commands has a promise of blessings, so, and much more so, disobedience to the Lord's commands will, on the other hand, bring a most severe punishment. The emphasis of the passage lies in the contrast. V. 18. **And Jeremiah said unto the house of the Rechabites, Thus saith the Lord of hosts, the God of Israel, Because ye have obeyed the commandment of Jonadab, your father, and kept all his precepts and done according unto all that he hath commanded you,** their obedience being brought out very strongly by the synonymous expressions, v. 19. **therefore thus saith the Lord of hosts, the God of Israel, Jonadab, the son of Rechab, shall not want a man to stand before Me forever,** that is, the family of the Rechabites would not die out, and it would continue in the worship of Jehovah without interruption. According to the accounts of trustworthy travelers, the descendants of Rechab are still living in the desert of Yemen, near Senaar, on the border of Mesopotamia and Arabia. Thus the Lord rewards the careful observance of the Fourth Commandment by blessings continuing through many generations.

CHAPTER 36.

The Prophecies of Jeremiah Preserved.

THE PROPHECIES RECORDED AND READ. — V. 1. **And it came to pass in the fourth year of Jehoiakim, the son of Josiah, king of Judah,** about in the year 607 B. C., **that this word came unto Jeremiah from the Lord, saying,** v. 2. **Take thee a roll of a book,** a long strip of parchment such as was used for manuscripts at that time, **and write therein all the words that I have spoken unto thee against Israel and against Judah and against all the nations, from the day I spake unto thee, from the days of Josiah,** chap. 25, 3, **even unto this day,** a period of twenty-three years. The command was given at that time, but the public reading of the prophecies did not take place until the next year, in the ninth month of the fifth year of Jehoiakim. Meanwhile Nebuchadnezzar had gathered his army and took the city at the end of the fifth or the beginning of the sixth year of Jehoiakim. Jehoiakim was taken captive and brought to Babylon, but upon his promising allegiance was returned to Jerusalem. When he withheld the stipulated tribute, however, he was again carried off and died before the campaign was brought to an end. The prophecies which were here recorded may have been written down before, but they were now brought together in one roll, to be read to the Jews. V. 3. **It may be that the house of Judah will hear all the evil which I purpose to do unto them, that they may return every man from his evil way,** this being the gracious purpose of the Lord in preaching repentance, **that I may forgive their iniquity and their sin,** for a return to the Lord in true sorrow for sins committed, such grief having been wrought by the power of His Word, will find Him more than ready to dispense forgiveness. V. 4. **Then Jeremiah called Baruch, the son of Neriah,** who acted as his clerk or secretary; **and Baruch wrote from the mouth of Jeremiah,** by exact dictation, **all the words of the Lord which He had spoken unto him upon a roll of a book,** a process which evidently took some time. V. 5. **And Jeremiah commanded Baruch, saying, I am shut up,** he was prevented at that time from attending to this matter in person; **I cannot go into the house of the Lord;** v. 6. **therefore go thou and read in**

the roll which thou hast written from my mouth the words of the Lord in the ears of the people in the Lord's house, before the entire congregation assembled for worship, **upon the fasting-day,** a day specially set apart for this purpose by the king, probably in commemoration of the first capture of the city by Nebuchadnezzar; **and also thou shalt read them in the ears of all Judah that come out of their cities,** so that the message would be brought to the attention of as many people as possible. V. 7. **It may be they will present their supplication before the Lord,** literally, "Possibly will fall down their pleadings before the face of Jehovah," as though kneeling before Him in an attitude of begging, **and will return every one from his evil way; for great is the anger and the fury that the Lord hath pronounced against this people,** because He had threatened a very severe punishment. V. 8. **And Baruch, the son of Neriah, did according to all that Jeremiah, the prophet, commanded him, reading in the book the words of the Lord in the Lord's house,** before the entire congregation assembled in the courts. V. 9. **And it came to pass in the fifth year of Jehoiakim, the son of Josiah, king of Judah, in the ninth month, that they proclaimed a fast before the Lord to all the people in Jerusalem and to all the people that came from the cities of Judah unto Jerusalem,** the celebration being ordered by those in authority and proclaimed throughout the country for the specified day, the object probably being to arouse the national consciousness against the Babylonian invasion and oppression by combining the religious features of a fast with a public assembly of this magnitude. Jeremiah very likely had Baruch read the words of Jehovah in order to counteract the plans of the king and his counselors. V. 10. **Then read Baruch in the book,** from the roll, **the words of Jeremiah in the house of the Lord, in the chamber of Gemariah, the son of Shaphan, the scribe, in the higher court,** the Court of the Priests, **at the entry of the new gate of the Lord's house, in the ears of all the people.** The cell of Gemariah was evidently located at or near the outer wall of the Court of the Priests, so that it overlooked the Court of Israel, where the people were assembled. V. 11. **When Michaiah, the son of Gemariah, the son of Shaphan, had heard out of the book all the words of the Lord,** as Baruch declaimed with a loud voice, v. 12. **then he went down into the king's house, into the scribe's chamber,** into the office of the chancellor in the royal palace; **and, lo, all the princes sat there,** the king's counselors sitting in the office of the Secretary of State, **even Elishama, the scribe,** a political officer of very high standing, **and Delaiah, the son of Shemaiah, and Elnathan, the son of Achbor, and Gemariah, the son of Shaphan, and Zedekiah, the son of Hananiah, and all the princes.** V. 13. **Then Michaiah declared unto them all the words that he had heard when Baruch read the book in the ears of the people.** He rendered a complete report of the message which had been read in the Temple. V. 14. **Therefore all the princes,** aroused by the report given them by Michaiah, **sent Jehudi, the son of Nethaniah, the son of Shelamiah, the son of Cushi, unto Baruch, saying, Take in thine hand the roll wherein thou hast read in the ears of the people and come. So Baruch, the son of Neriah, took the roll in his hand and came unto them.** V. 15. **And they said unto him, Sit down now and read it in our ears. So Baruch read it in their ears.** V. 16. **Now it came to pass, when they had heard all the words, they were afraid both one and other,** that is, their faces and bearing showed the terror which they felt on account of this proclamation with its horrible threats, a message which was, at the same time, so utterly at variance with the wishes and hopes of the king, **and said unto Baruch, We will surely tell the king of all these words.** They felt that it was their duty as officers of the kingdom to make known what they had now heard, since it affected the whole country. V. 17. **And they asked Baruch, saying, Tell us now, How didst thou write all these words at his mouth?** They wanted exact information before proceeding any farther in the matter. V. 18. **Then Baruch answered them, He,** Jeremiah, **pronounced all these words unto me with his mouth, and I wrote them with ink in the book.** He was very frank in his report, as believers may readily be at all times, knowing that they have the truth on their side.

THE ROLL DESTROYED AND REWRITTEN. — V. 19. **Then said the princes unto Baruch, Go, hide thee, thou and Jeremiah; and let no man know where ye be.** The reading had made a deep impression upon them, but they had an instinctive feeling that Jeremiah and Baruch were in danger of their lives on account of the message which they proclaimed, especially since a report of the happening had to be made to the king. V. 20. **And they went in to the king, into the court,** the great hall or throne-room, **but they laid up the roll in the chamber of Elishama, the scribe,** leaving it in his office for safe-keeping, **and told all the words in the ears of the king.** V. 21. **So the king sent Jehudi,** who seems to have been the court messenger, **to fetch the roll; and he took it out of Elishama the scribe's chamber. And Jehudi read it in the ears of the king and in the ears of all the princes which stood beside the king,** literally, "over the king"; for, since they were standing in his presence, their heads were higher than his. V. 22. **Now, the king sat in the winter-house,** in one of the inner and sheltered rooms of the palace, where also the great hall was situated, **in the ninth month,** corresponding roughly to our December; **and there was a fire on the hearth burning before him,** a brazen vessel with glowing charcoal such as are used in the Orient. V. 23. **And it came to pass that, when Jehudi had read three or four leaves, he cut it with the penknife,** the writer's knife with which the reed or style used for writing was pointed from time to time, **and cast it into the fire that was on the hearth, until all the roll was consumed in the fire that was on the hearth.** The king had become so enraged on account of the passage which he had heard that he could not contain himself, but laid blasphemous hands upon the sacred roll, slashing it right and left and destroying it completely. V. 24. **Yet they were not afraid,** they were not terrified by the Lord's threats, **nor rent their garments,** as they should have done in grief and mourning over their sins and the Lord's impending punishment upon them, **neither the king, nor any of his servants that heard all these words.** V. 25. **Nevertheless, Elnathan and Delaiah and Gemariah,** three, at least, of the king's counselors, **had made intercession to the king that he would not burn the roll, but he would not hear them,** he was deaf to all remonstrances. V. 26. **But the king commanded Jerahmeel, the son of Hammelech, and Seraiah, the son of Azriel, and Shelemiah, the son of Abdeel, to take Baruch, the scribe, and Jeremiah, the prophet,** that is, to arrest them; **but the Lord hid them,** He did not permit the searchers to find their hiding-place. V. 27. **Then the word of the Lord came to Jeremiah, after that the king had burned the roll and the words which Baruch wrote at the mouth of Jeremiah, saying,** v. 28. **Take thee again another roll,** a new strip of parchment, **and write in it all the former words that were in the first roll, which Jehoiakim, the king of Judah, hath burned.** V. 29. **And thou shalt say to Jehoiakim, king of Judah, Thus saith the Lord, Thou hast burned this roll, saying, Why hast thou written therein, saying, The king of Babylon shall certainly come and destroy this land and shall cause to cease from thence man and beast?** The king had evidently given vent to his anger in exclamations of this kind when he destroyed the roll. V. 30. **Therefore, thus saith the Lord of Jehoiakim, king of Judah, He shall have none to sit upon the throne of David,** for his son Jehoiachin was nothing but a vassal of the foreign emperor and could in no sense call the kingdom his own; **and his dead body shall be cast out in the day to the heat and in the night to the frost,** namely, in the hardships attending his exile. V. 31. **And I will punish him and his seed and his servants for their iniquity,** for by following the king they placed themselves in the same condemnation with him; **and I will bring upon them and upon the inhabitants of Jerusalem and upon the men of Judah all the evil that I have pronounced against them; but they hearkened not.** V. 32. **Then took Jeremiah another roll and gave it to Baruch, the scribe, the son of Neriah, who wrote therein from the mouth of Jeremiah all the words of the book which Jehoiakim, king of Judah, had burned in the fire; and there were added besides unto them many like words;** for Jeremiah had received other inspired messages, and the Lord took this opportunity of embodying them all in the book which was to be preserved as a testimony against the disobedient nation and its king.

CHAPTER 37.

Jeremiah's Faithful Testimony Rewarded with Imprisonment.

A PROPHECY CONCERNING THE OUTCOME OF THE SIEGE. — V. 1. **And King Zedekiah, the son of Josiah,** whose original name had been Mattaniah, a brother of Jehoiakim, 2 Kings 24, 17, **reigned instead of Coniah,** or Jeconiah, **the son of Jehoiakim, whom Nebuchadrezzar, king of Babylon, made king in the land of Judah,** a mere vassal of the mighty Eastern ruler. V. 2. **But neither he nor his servants, nor the people of the land did hearken unto the words of the Lord which He spake by the prophet Jeremiah.** Cp. chap. 36, 31. V. 3. **And Zedekiah, the king, sent Jehucal, the son of Shelemiah,** one of his high officers, **and Zephaniah, the son of Maaseiah, the priest,** the highest church dignitary of the land at that time, chap. 21, 1; 29, 25, **to the prophet Jeremiah, saying, Pray now unto the Lord, our God, for us.** This was, in the first place, an act of amazing stupidity in view of the king's deliberate disobedience, but also one of revolting hypocrisy, since Zedekiah feigned an allegiance to Jehovah which he was far from possessing. Zedekiah, moreover, did not seem to notice that his act was a further insult to Jeremiah, after the manner in which his messages had been received by the men in high places. V. 4. **Now, Jeremiah came in and went out among the people,** he was at that time unhampered in his movements; **for they had not put him into prison,** he was not in ward in the prison court, where he had been compelled to spend so much time before. V. 5. **Then Pharaoh's army was come forth out of Egypt,** Pharaoh-hophrah having undertaken to make war on the mighty Eastern ruler, probably as a result of a message sent by Zedekiah, Ezek. 17, 15; **and when the Chaldeans that besieged Jerusalem heard tidings of them,** received news of their approach, **they departed from Jerusalem,** they discontinued the siege in order to meet this new danger. Such were the circumstances at the time when Zedekiah sent his men to Jeremiah. V. 6. **Then came the word of the Lord unto the prophet Jeremiah, saying,** v. 7. **Thus saith the Lord, the God of Israel,** the name expressing His majesty and power, **Thus shall ye say to the king of Judah that sent you unto Me to inquire of Me: Behold, Pharaoh's army, which is come forth to help you,** with the object, however, of trying to gain the world-power, **shall return to Egypt, into their own land.** It was foolish, therefore, for the people of Judah to attach too much importance to this temporary relief. V. 8. **And the Chaldeans shall come again, and fight against this city, and take it, and burn it with fire.** V. 9. **Thus saith the Lord, Deceive not yourselves,** by entertaining vain hopes, **saying, The Chaldeans shall surely depart from us; for they shall not depart,** they would not permanently discontinue their siege. V. 10. **For though ye had smitten the whole army of the Chaldeans that fight against you, and there remained but wounded men among them,** according to the Hebrew, "such as had been severely wounded," **yet should they rise up every man in his tent and burn this city with fire.** As the disobedient Jews in this instance, so the unbelievers ever depend upon false conclusions and vain delusions in order to have some basis for their opposition to the Lord and His Word. But they merely deceive themselves.

JEREMIAH'S ARREST AND IMPRISONMENT. — V. 11. **And it came to pass that when the army of the Chaldeans was broken up from Jerusalem,** withdrawing for the time being in order to await developments or call for reenforcements, **for fear of Pharaoh's army,** so that the land, for a little while, was clear of enemies, v. 12. **then Jeremiah went forth out of Jerusalem to go into the land of Benjamin,** the country of his own tribe, **to separate himself thence in the midst of the people,** literally, "to make a division of inheritance," his business probably consisting in his taking away the personal property which he had inherited. V. 13. **And when he was in the Gate of Benjamin,** the northern gate of Jerusalem, which led to the country of Benjamin and the northern province, **a captain of the ward was there,** one of the watchmen of the city of Jerusalem, **whose name was Irijah, the son of Shelemiah, the son of Hananiah; and he took Jeremiah, the prophet,** placing him under arrest, **saying, Thou fallest away to the Chaldeans.** Since the Chaldeans had undoubtedly retired in a northerly direction, the accusation of Irijah had a semblance of right, although it was, as a matter of fact, nothing but base slander. V. 14. **Then said Jeremiah,** feeling a just resentment on account of the unjust accusation which was brought against him, **It is false; I fall not away to the Chaldeans. But he hearkened not to him; so Irijah took Jeremiah and brought him to the princes,** to the king's counselors, who sat in judgment with him. V. 15. **Wherefore the princes,** evidently of a different type from those who had taken his part under Jehoiakim, **were wroth with Jeremiah and smote him,** apparently without so much as a hearing, **and put him in prison in the house of Jonathan, the scribe,** the chancellor, or secretary of state, **for they had made that the prison,** very likely because it contained subterranean cells, or cellars, which could readily be used for that purpose. V. 16. **When Jeremiah was entered into the dungeon and into the cabins,** or underground vaults, **and Jeremiah had remained there many days,** in this unjust imprisonment, v. 17. **then Zedekiah, the king, sent and took him out; and the king asked him secretly in his house,** probably because he was ashamed to be seen by his courtiers, **and said, Is there any word from the Lord?** any revelation from Jehovah favorable to his cause. **And Jeremiah said, There is,** but not in the sense which Zedekiah had in mind; **for, said he, thou shalt be delivered into the hand of the king of Babylon.** V. 18. **Moreover, Jeremiah said unto King Zedekiah, What have I offended against thee or against thy servants or against this people that ye have put me in prison?** He protested against the injustice of an imprisonment without so much as an attempt at a trial. V. 19. **Where are now your prophets which prophesied unto you, saying, The king of Babylon shall not come against you nor against this land?** Since the predictions of the false prophets had been found to be falsehoods, and since, on the other hand, the event prophesied by Jeremiah had come to pass, this, therefore, was a further argument for the fact that his arrest and imprisonment were acts of injustice. V. 20. **Therefore hear now, I pray thee, O my lord the king, let my supplication, I pray thee, be accepted before thee,** his plea, according to the strongly figurative language of the Orient, being represented as falling down in supplication, **that thou cause me not to return to the house of Jonathan, the scribe, lest I die there,** for the cells of the dungeon were anything but healthful places to live in for any length of time. V. 21. **Then Zedekiah, the king**, yielding at least to this extent, **commanded that they should commit Jeremiah into the court of the prison**, where he at least had the advantages of light and air, **and that they should give him daily a piece of bread out of the bakers' street**, for in the Orient persons of the same trade or business often occupied their own streets and even their own quarters, **until all the bread in the city were spent.** Zedekiah either continued to feel resentful against Jeremiah for his prophetic sayings, or he, at least, did not have the courage of his convictions in setting him at liberty. **Thus Jeremiah remained in the court of the prison.** As in the case of Jeremiah, so to-day fearless testifying for and of the truth of the Lord is demanded of all who bear the name of His servants.

CHAPTER 38.

Jeremiah Subjected to Further Indignities.

JEREMIAH CAST INTO A PIT. — V. 1. **Then Shephatiah, the son of Mattan, and Gedaliah, the son of Pashur**, the latter being of priestly descent, but full of enmity toward the prophet, **and Jucal, the son of Shelemiah, and Pashur, the son of Malchiah**, chap. 21, 1, **heard the words that Jeremiah had spoken unto all the people, saying**, v. 2. **Thus saith the Lord, He that remaineth in this city shall die by the sword, by the famine, and by the pestilence**, chap. 21, 9; **but he that goeth forth to the Chaldeans shall live**, since Jehovah had now definitely decided that they should possess the land of Judah; **for he shall have his life for a prey and shall live.** Though all his goods might perish, the life of every such person would be spared. V. 3. **Thus saith the Lord, This city shall surely be given into the hand of the king of Babylon's army, which shall take it.** Sayings of this kind were the gist of Jeremiah's proclamation to the soldiers and to all members of the nation who happened to come into the court of the prison. Although he was under suspicion as favoring the enemy's cause and even of playing traitor to his own nation, Jeremiah was not deterred from his course of action as the Lord's messenger. This fact, however, filled the leaders of the people with the greatest bitterness. V. 4. **Therefore the princes said unto the king, We beseech thee, let this man be put to death; for thus he weakeneth the hands of the men of war that remain in this city, and the hands of all the people, in speaking such words unto them**, he caused their hands to hang down helplessly, he discouraged them utterly; **for this man seeketh not the welfare of this people, but the hurt.** So far as outward appearances were concerned, there was some foundation for the complaint of the rulers, for the words of Jeremiah certainly tended to discourage any attempts at defending the city. At the same time, Jeremiah was the best of patriots, having the true welfare of his people in view, for the spirit exhibited by the rulers was not a confidence founded on the divine will, but a carnal obstinacy, which was bound to lead to destruction. V. 5. **Then Zedekiah, the king**, weakly yielding to the demand of his counselors, especially since he seems to have harbored a secret grudge against the prophet on his own account, **said, Behold, he is in your hand; for the king is not he that can do anything against you.** It was a complimentary speech, but at the same time a confession both of weakness of character and of weakness of authority. V. 6. **Then took they Jeremiah and cast him into the dungeon**, a pit formerly used as a cistern, **of Malchiah, the son of Hammelech, that was in the court of the prison; and they let down Jeremiah with cords**, there being no direct way of access to the bottom of the pit. **And in the dungeon there was no water, but mire**, the mud and settlings that remained after the water had been drawn out; **so Jeremiah sunk in the mire.** The act shows the hatred of the princes. They did not have Jeremiah executed with the sword, as they might have done; but they deliberately chose this method of letting the prophet die under the most distressing circumstances, while they, at the same time, could quiet the voice of their conscience by declaring that they had not shed Jeremiah's blood. V. 7. **Now, when Ebed-melech, the Ethiopian, one of the eunuchs which was in the king's house**, probably the chief officer of the king's harem, **heard that they had put Jeremiah in the dungeon, the king then sitting in the Gate of Benjamin**, one of the northern gates of the city, where he may have been superintending some work connected with the defense of the city, v. 8. **Ebed-melech went forth out of the king's house and spake to the king**, not secretly, but openly, fearlessly championing the cause of the persecuted prophet and risking the displeasure of the capricious king, **saying**, v. 9. **My lord the king, these men**, who had ordered this cruelty to be performed against Jeremiah, **have done evil in all that they have done to Jeremiah, the prophet, whom they have cast into the dungeon; and he is like to die for hunger in the place where he is**, where he would be most likely to be overlooked; **for there is no more bread in the city.** Jeremiah had formerly received a daily allowance of bread, chap. 37, 21, but now either the public store of bread was exhausted, or there was practically no bread left anywhere. V. 10. **Then the king commanded Ebed-melech, the Ethiopian, saying, Take from hence thirty men with thee,** a sufficiently large squad under his command to protect Jeremiah in case some of the princes or their retainers should attempt to interfere with the work of rescuing the prophet, **and take up Jeremiah, the prophet, out of the dungeon before he die.** The remonstrance of Ebed-melech had had at least this much effect upon Zedekiah, that he determined to prevent outright murder. V. 11. **So Ebed-melech took the men with him and went into the house of the king under the treasury,** to a room which was evidently used for storage purposes, **and took thence old cast clouts and old rotten rags,** remnants of cast-off and worn-out garments of every description, **and let them down by cords into the dungeon to Jeremiah.** Ebed-melech evidently possessed both presence of mind and resourcefulness, for he lost no time in beginning his work of rescuing the prophet. V. 12. **And Ebed-melech, the Ethiopian,** whose nationality is clearly mentioned time and again with the object of making his behavior stand out favorably by way of contrast with that of the Jews, **said unto Jeremiah, Put now these old cast clouts and rotten rags under thine armholes under the cords,** to prevent them from cutting into the flesh as they drew him out of the pit. **And Jeremiah did so.** V. 13. **So they drew up Jeremiah with cords and took him up out of the dungeon; and Jeremiah remained in the court of the prison,** still under arrest, but no longer in danger of slow death by starvation. God makes use even of the poor and lowly as instruments of His goodness in protecting His children.

JEREMIAH'S ADVICE TO THE KING. — V. 14. **Then Zedekiah, the king, sent and took Jeremiah, the prophet, unto him into the third entry that is in the house of the Lord,** very likely the vaulted north gate of the Temple court, which faced the palace; **and the king said unto Jeremiah, I will ask thee a thing; hide nothing from me.** The very attitude of the prophet, together with the definiteness of his message, filled the king with apprehension and a foreboding of evil for himself. V. 15. **Then Jeremiah said unto Zedekiah, If I declare it unto thee,** telling him the plain truth as it had been revealed by the Lord, **wilt thou not surely put me to death? And if I give thee counsel,** namely, concerning the manner in which he was to proceed in this emergency, **wilt thou not hearken unto me?** It is plain that Jeremiah trusted the king neither with regard to the safety of his own person nor concerning the acceptance of any advice which he might give. V. 16. **So Zedekiah, the king, sware secretly unto Jeremiah, saying, As the Lord liveth, that made us this soul,** a most solemn oath by the God of life and by his own life, **I will not put thee to death, neither will I give thee into the hand of these men that seek thy life.** It was a most emphatic assurance that he would safeguard the prophet's life. V. 17. **Then said Jeremiah unto Zedekiah,** in reliance upon the king's promise, **Thus saith the Lord, the God of hosts, the God of Israel: If thou wilt assuredly go forth unto the king of Babylon's princes,** voluntarily surrendering to the Chaldean generals in charge of the siege, **then thy soul shall live, and this city shall not be burned with fire; and thou shalt live and thine house,** their lives would be spared; v. 18. **but if thou wilt not go forth to the king of Babylon's princes, then shall this city be given into the hand of the Chaldeans, and they shall burn it with fire, and thou shalt not escape out of their hand,** an emphatic way of saying that he would be taken captive. Cp. chap. 34, 2—5; 32, 4; 21, 4—10. V. 19. **And Zedekiah, the king,** whose weakness of character appears here once more, **said unto Jeremiah, I am afraid of the Jews that are fallen to the Chaldeans,** he dreaded the insults of his fugitive subjects, **lest they deliver me into their hand and they mock me.** It was not merely ridicule that he feared, but actual physical abuse as well. V. 20. **But Jeremiah said, They shall not deliver thee. Obey, I beseech thee, the voice of the Lord, which I speak unto thee; so it shall be well unto thee, and thy soul shall live.** V. 21. **But if thou refuse to go forth, this is the word that the Lord hath showed me,** the alternative to the mockery of the fugitive Jews: v. 22. **and, behold, all the women that are left in the king of Judah's house,** all the members of his harem, including also the wives of former kings who remained in his care, **shall be brought forth to the king of Babylon's princes,** as captives of the Chaldean generals, **and those women shall say,** in a satirical song of mockery upon Zedekiah, **Thy friends have set thee on,** the king's ministers and his false prophets had misled him, **and have prevailed against thee,** getting the better of him with their evil counsel; **thy feet are sunk in the mire, and they are turned away back,** slipping in the uncertain footing of the mud into which he had been led by his alleged advisers. V. 23. **So they shall bring out all thy wives and thy children to the Chaldeans; and thou shalt not escape out of their hand, but shalt be taken by the hand of the king of Babylon, and thou shalt cause this city to be burned with fire,** that is, Zedekiah's weakness, vacillation, and disobedience would bring the guilt of its destruction upon his head. V. 24. **Then said Zedekiah unto Jeremiah,** still with the same lack of firmness and decision which was characteristic of him throughout, **Let no man know of these words, and thou shalt not die,** he should feel sure of the king's protection. V. 25. **But if the princes hear that I have talked with thee, and they come unto thee and say unto thee, Declare unto us now what thou hast said unto the king, hide it not from us, and we will not put thee to death,** the words which the princes would probably use in threatening him, **also what the king said unto thee,** v. 26. **then thou shalt say unto them, I presented my supplication before the king that he would not cause me to return to Jonathan's house,** chap. 37, 15, **to die there.** V. 27. **Then came all the princes unto Jeremiah,** just as the king had expected that they would, **and asked him; and he told them according to all these words that the king had commanded. So they left off speaking with him,** literally, "they kept their silence away from him," that is, they went away in silence and ceased to bother him; **for the matter was not perceived,** the explanation given by Jeremiah seemed altogether plausible. V. 28. **So Jeremiah abode in the court of the prison until the day that Jerusalem was taken; and he was there when Jerusalem was taken.** The Lord has ways and means of protecting and delivering His children from all evil, even when there seems to be no way of escape.

CHAPTER 39.

The Capture and Plunder of Jerusalem.

JERUSALEM TAKEN. — V. 1. **In the ninth year of Zedekiah, king of Judah, in the tenth month,** the day of the month being the tenth, chap. 52, 4; 2 Kings 25, 1—4, **came Nebuchadrezzar, king of Babylon, and all his army against Jerusalem, and they besieged it.** V. 2. **And in the eleventh year of Zedekiah, in the fourth month, the ninth day of the month, the city was broken up,** the enemies gained an entry into the city by battering down a part of the wall. The siege thus lasted eighteen months, if we except the suspension of it caused by the coming of Pharaoh-hophrah. Nebuchadnezzar was present at the beginning of the siege, but was in Riblah at its close. V. 3. **And all the princes of the king of Babylon came in,** the generals entering through the breach in the wall, **and sat in the middle gate,** they occupied that part of the city by encamping in a gate of Zion, in the wall which separated the upper city from the lower, a position which gave them control of the capital, **even Nergal-sharezer, Samgar-nebo, Sarsechim, Rab-saris, Nergal-sharezer, Rab-mag,** Rab-saris being chief of the chamberlains and the second Nergal-sharezer chief of the magi, **with all the residue of the princes of the king of Babylon,** an imposing array of mighty men. V. 4. **And it came to pass that, when Zedekiah, the king of Judah, saw them, and all the men of war,** that is, when Zedekiah and his soldiers noted the pomp and the warlike appearance of the Chaldean generals at close range, **then they fled and went forth out of the city,** the upper city, where the royal palace was situated, **by night, by the way of the king's garden, by the gate betwixt the two walls,** those on the western edge of Ophel and on the eastern edge of Zion, for the royal gardens were situated southeast of the city, on the slopes of the Kidron Valley; **and he went out the way of the plain,** the meadows of the Jordan near Jericho. There may have been a gap in the lines of the besieging army at this point, since the upper city was almost impregnable from the east and southeast; so this plan was the only one which promised success. V. 5. **But the Chaldeans' army pursued after them,** the attempt of Zedekiah and his soldiers to escape being noticed very soon and the alarm accordingly given, **and overtook Zedekiah in the plains of Jericho,** for his intention evidently was to escape into the country of the Moabites beyond the river; **and when they had taken him, they brought him up to Nebuchadnezzar, king of Babylon, to Riblah, in the land of Hamath,** beyond the northern border of Canaan, where the headquarters of the Chaldean king had been established during his campaign of conquest of the countries along the Mediterranean, **where he gave judgment upon him,** Zedekiah now receiving evidence of the truth of Jeremiah's prophecy. V. 6. **Then the king of Babylon slew the sons of Zedekiah in Riblah before his eyes,** for they were guilty, with their father, of the revolt against the Babylonian supremacy; **also, the king of Babylon slew all the nobles of Judah,** who really had been the chief rebels against his authority. V. 7. **Moreover, he put out Zedekiah's eyes,** commanding that he be blinded, probably by passing a heated metal rod before his open eyes, **and bound him with chains,** doubly fettered hand and foot, **to carry him to Babylon,** in a most shameful captivity. V. 8. **And the Chaldeans burned the king's house,** the beautiful royal palace, **and the houses of the people, with fire,** destroying all the finer residences of the city, **and brake down the walls of Jerusalem,** the fortifications of the city, which, in the past, had rendered it almost impregnable. V. 9. **Then Nebuzar-adan, the captain of the guard,** the commander of the royal Chaldean body-guard, one of the chief officers of Nebuchadnezzar, **carried away cap-**

tive into Babylon the remnant of the people that remained in the city, the few who had escaped the ravages of the sword and of famine, **and those that fell away, that fell to him,** those who had deserted and come over into the camp of the enemy during the siege, **with the rest of the people that remained,** those of any importance who had not yet been led away into exile. V. 10. **But Nebuzar-adan, the captain of the guard, left of the poor of the people, which had nothing in the land of Judah,** no landed possessions, **and gave them vineyards and fields at the same time,** at that time, namely, when he led the others captive. They received orders to cultivate the vineyards and fields, lest the country revert to its wild state and yield no revenue. Thus the threatening words of the Lord concerning the fate of the disobedient Jews were fulfilled in every detail, as an example of warning to the unbelievers of all times.

CONCERNING THE FATE OF JEREMIAH AND OF EBED-MELECH. — V. 11. **Now Nebuchadrezzar, king of Babylon, gave charge concerning Jeremiah,** whose prophecies and warning were known to him through deserters and through Jews carried to Babylon with Jeconiah, **to Nebuzar-adan, the captain of the guard, saying,** v. 12. **Take him and look well to him,** literally, "thine eyes set upon him," in providing for, and watching over, his well-being, **and do him no harm,** the protection against the wiles of others being included in this care; **but do unto him even as he shall say unto thee,** as he might request to safeguard his person. V. 13. **So Nebuzar-adan, the captain of the guard, sent, and Nebushasban, Rab-saris, and Nergal-sharezer, Rab-mag,** that is, the chief of the magi, **and all the king of Babylon's princes,** all the commanders of the army which made the campaign against Judah; v. 14. **even they sent and took Jeremiah out of the court of the prison,** gave him his liberty after the shameful imprisonment which he had suffered, **and committed him unto Gedaliah, the son of Ahikam, the son of Shaphan,** Ahikam being the man who had protected him on a former occasion, chap. 26, 24, **that he should carry him home; so he dwelt among the people,** as a free man, not as a captive under restraint. The apparent contradiction between this statement and that of chap. 40, 1 is very easily adjusted if we remember that Jeremiah, although transported to Ramah with the prisoners among his own countrymen, was still technically their prisoner, for he had not been released from his place in the court of the prison in Jerusalem. Nebuzar-adan separated Jeremiah from the other captives and gave him his choice of places to dwell. V. 15. **Now the word of the Lord came unto Jeremiah, while he was shut up in the court of the prison,** before the Jews of the city were taken down to Ramah and the prophet was given his liberty, **saying,** v. 16. **Go and speak to Ebed-melech, the Ethiopian,** who had befriended Jeremiah when his life was in the greatest danger, chap. 38, 7—14, **saying, Thus saith the Lord of hosts, the God of Israel: Behold, I will bring My words upon this city for evil and not for good,** cp. Dan. 9, 12; **and they shall be accomplished in that day before thee,** so that the threatened misfortune would strike the city in its full force, Ebed-melech being a witness of this calamity. V. 17. **But I will deliver thee in that day, saith the Lord,** as a reward of his goodness in rescuing the Lord's prophet; **and thou shalt not be given into the hand of the men of whom thou art afraid,** for the Ethiopian shared the fear of the other inhabitants of the city. V. 18. **For I will surely deliver thee, and thou shalt not fall by the sword, but thy life shall be for a prey unto thee,** a precious treasure to be carried away and safely hidden, **because thou hast put thy trust in Me, saith the Lord.** Jehovah, the true God, is the Hope and Refuge of all those who put their trust in Him, and He delivers them from all the evil which may threaten and overwhelm them.

CHAPTER 40.

Jeremiah Released. Gedaliah's Life Threatened.

JEREMIAH SET FREE. — V. 1. **The word that came to Jeremiah from the Lord,** this being the heading or superscription of the entire next section of Jeremiah's book of prophecies, of which chapters 40 and 41 are the historical introduction, **after that Nebuzar-adan, the captain of the guard, had let him go from Ramah, when he had taken him, being bound in chains,** fetters for the hands or arms such as were used to tie captives together on the march, **among all that were carried away captive of Jerusalem and Judah, which were carried away captive unto Babylon.** The command to release Jeremiah seems to have been given while he was still in the court of the prison in Jerusalem, but He was not actually set at liberty until the company of captives reached the city of Ramah. V. 2. **And the captain of the guard took Jeremiah and said unto him, The Lord, thy God, hath pronounced this evil upon this place,** for the Chaldean general was evidently familiar with the prophecies concerning the destruction of the Jewish capital. V. 3. **Now, the Lord hath brought it,** let the calamity come upon Judah, **and done accord-**

ing as He hath said; because ye have sinned against the Lord and have not obeyed His voice, therefore this thing is come upon you. The Chaldean general expressed it as his conviction that the evil which had come upon the Jews was the result of their disobeying the command of the Lord. V. 4. **And now, behold, I loose thee this day from the chains which were upon thine hand,** those of the Jews which had been placed upon him in malicious persecution as well as those of the Chaldeans which he had carried along on account of the negligence or ignorance of his Chaldean captors. **If it seem good unto thee to come with me unto Babylon, come, and I will look well unto thee,** taking good care of him; **but if it seem ill unto thee to come with me into Babylon,** that is, if it did not please Jeremiah for any reason whatever, **forbear.** The matter was entirely for the prophet to decide, and no one would interfere with his choice. **Behold, all the land is before thee; whither it seemeth good and convenient for thee to go, thither go.** Thus Nebuzar-adan carried out the command of Nebuchadnezzar concerning Jeremiah, chap. 39, 12. V. 5. **Now, while he was not yet gone back,** that is, when Jeremiah hesitated about making up his mind, while he was trying to reach a decision, **he said,** in suggesting a solution, **Go back also to Gedaliah, the son of Ahikam, the son of Shaphan, whom the king of Babylon hath made governor over the cities of Judah,** as the victor's representative in a province now entirely in his hand, **and dwell with him among the people; or go wheresoever it seemeth convenient unto thee to go. So the captain of the guard gave him victuals,** a supply of food for the return journey, **and a reward and let him go.** V. 6. **Then went Jeremiah unto Gedaliah, the son of Ahikam, to Mizpah,** the city in Benjamin known from the history of Samuel and Saul, 1 Sam. 7, 15 ff.; 10, 17, **and dwelt with him,** Gedaliah, **among the people that were left in the land.** Jeremiah showed himself a true patriot in choosing to remain in his own country in the midst of adverse conditions and in spite of the ingratitude of the Jews, rather than to enjoy honors and pleasures at a heathen court. Christian patriotism is properly patterned after this behavior of the prophet.

GEDALIAH MADE GOVERNOR AND THREATENED BY THE JEWS. — V. 7. **Now, when all the captains of the forces which were in the fields,** the leaders of the Jewish army who had fled to hide themselves in remote and inaccessible places of the land, **even they and their men, heard that the king of Babylon had made Gedaliah, the son of Ahikam, governor in the land and had committed unto him men and women and children and of the poor of the land, of them that were not carried away captive to Babylon,** chap. 39, 10, the lowliest of the whole country, those who had formerly been treated with contempt by the wealthy and noble, v. 8. **then they came to Gedaliah to Mizpah, even Ishmael, the son of Nethaniah,** of royal lineage, chap. 41, 1, **and Johanan and Jonathan, the sons of Kareah, and Seraiah, the son of Tanhumeth, and the sons of Ephai, the Netophathite,** of a town in Judah not far from Bethlehem, **and Jezaniah, the son of a Maachathite,** Maachah being a province of Syria on the northern border of Palestine, **they and their men.** V. 9. **And Gedaliah, the son of Ahikam, the son of Shaphan, sware unto them and to their men, saying, Fear not to serve the Chaldeans,** or, as 2 Kings 25, 24 has it, to be the servants of the Chaldeans; **dwell in the land and serve the king of Babylon,** readily acknowledging his overlordship, **and it shall be well with you.** V. 10. **As for me, behold, I will dwell at Mizpah, to serve the Chaldeans which will come unto us,** cheerfully recognizing the authority of the governors, or satraps, representing the Babylonian government, and governing his actions accordingly; **but ye, gather ye wine and summer-fruits and oil,** for it was now about midsummer and therefore time for the fruits to ripen, **and put them in your vessels, and dwell in your cities that ye have taken.** He skilfully put it so as if they were to enjoy the fruits of the land for themselves alone, in order to reduce the resentful attitude of the Jews, lest the idea of tribute-money make them rebellious at once. V. 11. **Likewise, when all the Jews that were in Moab and among the Ammonites and in Edom, and that were in all the countries,** wherever they had found refuge at the approach of the Chaldean army, **heard that the king of Babylon had left a remnant of Judah, and that he had set over them Gedaliah, the son of Ahikam, the son of Shaphan,** v. 12. **even all the Jews returned out of all places whither they were driven and came to the land of Judah, to Gedaliah,** who was charged with taking care of them and providing dwelling-places for them, **unto Mizpah, and gathered wine and summer-fruits very much,** the harvest being all the more plentiful since there were comparatively few people left in the land. V. 13. **Moreover, Johanan, the son of Kareah, and all the captains of the forces that were in the fields,** those who had managed to escape the vigilance of the Chaldean invaders in remote parts of the land, **came to Gedaliah to Mizpah** v. 14. **and said unto him, Dost thou certainly know that Baalis, the king of the Ammonites,** who may have harbored plans to put himself into possession of the entire country by one bold stroke, **hath sent Ishmael, the son of Nethaniah, to slay thee? But Gedaliah,**

the son of Ahikam, believed him not. He was generous and unsuspecting, but not wise. V. 15. **Then Johanan, the son of Kareah, spake to Gedaliah in Mizpah secretly, saying, Let me go, I pray thee, and I will slay Ishmael, the son of Nethaniah, and no man shall know it,** the jealous and ambitious rival, who envied Gedaliah his position of governor, would thus have been removed without tumult. **Wherefore should he slay thee, that all the Jews which are gathered unto thee,** with some semblance of order, **should be scattered and the remnant in Judah perish?** The confusion which was bound to follow the removal of Gedaliah was sure to result in great harm to the country, possibly to the undoing of all the labor bestowed upon its restoration by Gedaliah. V. 16. **But Gedaliah, the son of Ahikam, said unto Johanan, the son of Kareah, Thou shalt not do this thing,** remove Ishmael by assassination; **for thou speakest falsely of Ishmael,** which does not mean that he accused Johanan of lying, but that he declared the rumor concerning his intentions to be false. It is one of the mysteries of providence that the Lord sometimes permits the righteous, in spite of warning, to rush to their destruction.

CHAPTER 41.

The Murder of Gedaliah and Its Consequences.

ISHMAEL SLAYS GEDALIAH. — V. 1. **Now it came to pass in the seventh month,** only about two months after the destruction of Jerusalem and the appointment of Gedaliah as governor, **that Ishmael, the son of Nethaniah, the son of Elishama, of the seed royal and the princes of the king,** he belonged to a side-line of the house of David and therefore of the mighty ones of the land, **even ten men with him, came unto Gedaliah, the son of Ahikam, to Mizpah; and there they did eat bread together in Mizpah,** as the guests of Gedaliah, who received them apparently without a show of suspicion and without any attempt at safeguarding himself against any wickedness on their part. V. 2. **Then arose Ishmael, the son of Nethaniah,** while he and his men were partaking of this hospitality, **and the ten men that were with him, and smote Gedaliah, the son of Ahikam, the son of Shaphan, with the sword and slew him,** or, literally, "so he slew him," **whom the king of Babylon had made governor over the land.** The men with Ishmael were all of them guilty of his murder, but the heaviest burden of guilt rested upon him who had planned the foul deed. V. 3. **Ishmael also slew all the Jews that were with him, even with Gedaliah, at Mizpah,** the armed men who had placed themselves at the disposal of the governor, **and the Chaldeans that were found there,** various officials of the Babylonian government, **and the men of war,** who were evidently unprepared for such an unexpected attack on the part of the governor's guest. V. 4. **And it came to pass the second day after he had slain Gedaliah, and no man knew it,** news of the murder not having reached any other part of the country as yet, v. 5. **that there came certain from Shechem, from Shiloh, and from Samaria,** three cities farther north in the province, **even fourscore men, having their beards shaven,** as a sign of deep mourning, **and their clothes rent, and having cut themselves,** such incisions into the skin being forbidden to the children of Israel, as a heathen custom, Lev. 19, 27. 28; Deut. 14, 1, **with offerings and incense in their hand, to bring them to the house of the Lord.** These men mourned the destruction of the Temple, but continued their acts of worship even upon its site, covered with ruins as it was. Their road naturally led past the city of Mizpah, and they traveled along without the slightest apprehension of danger. V. 6. **And Ishmael, the son of Nethaniah,** whose scouts had undoubtedly informed him of their coming, **went forth from Mizpah to meet them, weeping all along as he went,** pretending to weep, as they did, over the ruin of the Temple; **and it came to pass, as he met them, he said unto them, Come to Gedaliah, the son of Ahikam,** thus assuming the rôle of the governor's messenger. V. 7. **And it was so, when they came into the midst of the city,** still without the slightest suspicion regarding the ruse employed by Ishmael, **that Ishmael, the son of Nethaniah, slew them,** murdered them in cold blood, **and cast them into the midst of the pit,** which was either the trench about the city or a large cistern used for storing water in the event of a siege, **he and the men that were with him,** for he could hardly have committed this wholesale murder single-handed. V. 8. **But ten men were found among them,** the eighty who fell into Ishmael's trap, **that said unto Ishmael, Slay us not, for we have treasures in the field, of wheat, and of barley, and of oil, and of honey,** for it was customary for men to hide their stores of grain and fruit in underground bins during troublous times in order to prevent their being taken by invading hordes. **So he forbare and slew them not among their brethren,** very likely taking their goods as a ransom for their lives, for the motive for Ishmael's crime seems to have been plain robbery, since he was evidently a wild and lawless man. V. 9. **Now, the pit wherein Ishmael had cast all the dead bodies of the men whom he had slain be-**

cause of Gedaliah, literally, "at the hand of Gedaliah," that is, next to Gedaliah, whom he had first cast into this trench or cistern, was it which Asa, the king, had made for fear of Baasha, king of Israel, cp. 1 Kings 15, 16—22; and Ishmael, the son of Nethaniah, filled it with them that were slain, a gruesome heap of his victims. V. 10. Then Ishmael carried away captive all the residue of the people that were in Mizpah, even the king's daughters, all the princesses of the royal household, including the daughters of Zedekiah, and all the people that remained in Mizpah, whom Nebuzar-adan, the captain of the guard, had committed to Gedaliah, the son of Ahikam, putting them into his care as people who had professed their loyalty to the Babylonian rule; and Ishmael, the son of Nethaniah, carried them away captive and departed to go over to the Ammonites, his intention being either to have his captives settle in the territory of the Ammonites, in the service of whose king he seems to have placed himself, or to sell them outright as slaves. Such is the way of men who yield to a life of sin: one crime leads to another, until they are fairly steeped in sins.

THE PREPARATIONS TO EMIGRATE TO EGYPT. V. 11. But when Johanan, the son of Kareah, and all the captains of the forces that were with him, who had warned Gedaliah against Ishmael, heard of all the evil that Ishmael, the son of Nethaniah, had done, v. 12. then they took all the men, quickly summoning them upon receiving the sad news, and went to fight with Ishmael, the son of Nethaniah, and found him by the great waters that are in Gibeon, only a few miles northeast of Mizpah. The disposing of the seventy slain men and the gathering of the people of the city to be deported had clearly delayed Ishmael to such an extent that he could not get away in time. V. 13. Now it came to pass that, when all the people which were with Ishmael saw Johanan, the son of Kareah, and all the captains of the forces that were with him, then they were glad, for the prospect of being sold into slavery was not pleasant. V. 14. So all the people that Ishmael had carried away captive from Mizpah cast about, they came around, they circled back, and returned and went unto Johanan, the son of Kareah, they took this opportunity of joining the forces of their deliverer, since Ishmael was now engaged in defending himself against Johanan's attack. V. 15. But Ishmael, the son of Nethaniah, escaped from Johanan, upon the latter's determined attack, with eight men and went to the Ammonites, two of his men evidently having fallen in the fight. V. 16. Then took Johanan, the son of Kareah, and all the captains of the forces that were with him all the remnant of the people whom he had recovered from Ishmael, the son of Nethaniah, rescuing them out of his hand, from Mizpah, after that he had slain Gedaliah, the son of Ahikam, even mighty men of war, and the women, and the children, and the eunuchs, the special servants of the harem, whom he had brought again from Gibeon; v. 17. and they departed and dwelt in the habitation of Chimham, a khan or caravansary, where large companies of travelers stopped for the night, which is by Bethlehem, to go to enter into Egypt, v. 18. because of the Chaldeans; for they were afraid of them because Ishmael, the son of Nethaniah, had slain Gedaliah, the son of Ahikam, whom the king of Babylon made governor in the land, they feared that they would be implicated in Ishmael's treason or in some way be held responsible for it. It would have been far better, since they had a good conscience in the matter, had they laid the facts in the case before the Chaldean authorities and cleared themselves. As it was, their removal from Judea placed them under the suspicion of the Babylonians. Fear often dictates a wrong course, even where people are altogether innocent.

CHAPTER 42.

The Word of the Lord Concerning the Removal to Egypt.

THE HYPOCRITICAL INQUIRY. — V. 1. Then, while the caravan of refugees was encamped at the khan near Bethlehem, all the captains of the forces and Johanan, the son of Kareah, and Jezaniah, the son of Hoshaiah, who was a native of Maachah, chap. 40, 8, and all the people, from the least even unto the greatest, came near v. 2. and said unto Jeremiah, the prophet, who had been taken along from Mizpah together with the other inhabitants of the city, Let, we beseech thee, our supplication be accepted before thee, literally, "fall before thy face," as a petitioner on bended knee, and pray for us unto the Lord, thy God, even for all this remnant, the small band of refugees who remained of the former great and mighty nation, (for we are left but a few of many, as thine eyes do behold us,) v. 3. that the Lord, thy God, may show us the way wherein we may walk, and the thing that we may do, that is, what they should do now, where they should turn in this emergency, in order to escape the certain vengeance of the Chaldeans. The expression "thy God" in this connection emphasizes the peculiar, intimate relation in which Jeremiah stood over against Jehovah, as His servant and prophet. V. 4. **Then Jeremiah, the prophet, said unto them, I have heard you,** he was ready to do as they requested; **behold, I will pray unto the Lord, your God, according to your words, and it shall come to pass that whatsoever thing the Lord shall answer you, I will declare it unto you; I will keep nothing back from you.** His words implied that, whether Jehovah's answer were favorable or unfavorable to their plans, he would in any event proclaim it. It seems clear from the first that the leaders of the refugees had already decided not to remain in Judea, but to go to some neighboring country. They acted just as many people do in our days, who call upon the Lord to direct them, but only along the lines which they themselves have chosen. V. 5. **Then they said to Jeremiah, The Lord be a true and faithful Witness between us if we do not even according to all things for the which the Lord, thy God, shall send thee to us,** apparently an unconditional yielding to the guidance of God, whether they were at this time aware of their insincerity or not. V. 6. **Whether it be good, or whether it be evil, we will obey the voice of the Lord, our God, to whom we send thee, that it may be well with us when we obey the voice of the Lord, our God,** their obedience being the reason for the Lord's good pleasure upon them. In every true prayer it is essential that both doubt and hypocrisy be absent, lest the supplication made defeat its own ends.

THE LORD'S WARNING ANSWER. — V. 7. **And it came to pass after ten days,** during which the caravan remained encamped in the same place, since Jeremiah did not presume to speak of himself, but awaited the inspiration of the Lord, **that the word of the Lord came unto Jeremiah,** by special revelation or in a vision. V. 8. **Then called he Johanan, the son of Kareah, and all the captains of the forces which were with him, and all the people, from the least even to the greatest,** the same ones who had presented their petition to him, v. 1, v. 9. **and said unto them, Thus saith the Lord, the God of Israel,** the fact that He is the Lord of His people, of His Church, being brought out here, **unto whom ye sent me to present your supplications before Him:** v. 10. **If ye will still abide in this land,** continuing to make their home in the country of their fathers, **then will I build you and not pull you down,** a figure taken from the erection of buildings, **and I will plant you and not pluck you up,** a figure taken from the work of a gardener; **for I repent Me of the evil that I have done unto you,** their repentance would cause His good will to return upon them. V. 11. **Be not afraid of the king of Babylon, of whom ye are afraid,** the fear of whose vengeance had caused them to prepare for flight; **be not afraid of him, saith the Lord, for I am with you to save you and to deliver you from his hand,** an assurance of safety which should have quieted all their fears. V. 12. **And I will show mercies unto you,** literally, "I will give you to experience mercies," **that he,** the king of Babylon, **may have mercy upon you and cause you to return to your own land,** which they were now leaving in abject flight. V. 13. **But if ye say, We will not dwell in this land, neither obey the voice of the Lord, your God,** thereby once more becoming guilty of open rebellion against God, v. 14. **saying, No, but we will go into the land of Egypt,** a plan which they had at least been discussing, if they had not yet decided upon it, **where we will see no war nor hear the sound of the trumpet,** as it called the soldiers to the battle, **nor have hunger of bread,** in the various unfortunate conditions accompanying war with which they had become so familiar in the last year, **and there will we dwell;** v. 15. **and now, therefore,** the direct prophecy resumed after the parenthetical remark concerning the possibility of their resuming their rebellious ways, **hear the word of the Lord, ye remnant of Judah, Thus saith the Lord of hosts, the God of Israel, If ye wholly set your faces to enter into Egypt,** determined upon their course, no matter what the consequences would be, **and go to sojourn there,** to make it a place of refuge at least for the time being, v. 16. **then it shall come to pass that the sword which ye feared,** contrary to the assurance of Jehovah, **shall overtake you there in the land of Egypt, and the famine whereof ye were afraid shall follow close after you there in Egypt,** pursuing them with unrelenting fierceness; **and there ye shall die.** V. 17. **So shall it be with all the men that set their faces to go into Egypt to sojourn there,** having definitely made up their mind to that effect: **they shall die by the sword, by the famine, and by the pestilence,** which, by God's punishment, could strike them in Egypt as well as in Judea; **and none of them shall remain or escape from the evil that I will bring upon them.** V. 18. **For thus saith the Lord of hosts, the God of Israel, As Mine anger and My fury hath been poured forth upon the inhabitants of Jerusalem,** resulting in the destruction which they had witnessed, **so shall My fury be poured forth upon you when ye shall enter into Egypt; and ye shall be an execration,** an object of cursing, **and an astonishment,** an object of horror, **and a curse, and a reproach,** an object of derision; **and ye shall see this place no more.** V. 19. **The Lord hath said concerning you, O ye** remnant of Judah, so the prophet now elaborates upon the direct prophecy of Jehovah, **Go ye not into Egypt; know certainly that I have admonished you this day**, testifying against them and warning them. V. 20. **For ye dissembled in your hearts**, literally, "ye have used deceit upon your own souls," **when ye sent me unto the Lord, your God, saying, Pray for us unto the Lord, our God, and according unto all that the Lord, our God, shall say, so declare unto us, and we will do it.** Cp. vv. 5. 6. V. 21. **And now I have this day declared it to you; but ye have not obeyed the voice of the Lord, your God, nor anything for the which He hath sent me unto you**, their very attitudes expressing their dissatisfaction with the directions transmitted to them. V. 22. **Now, therefore, know certainly that ye shall die by the sword, by the famine, and by the pestilence, in the place whither ye desire to go and to sojourn.** It was a last solemn warning, which, however, was bound to be disregarded by the obstinate Jews, just as so many similar warnings since have been neglected to the unbelievers' hurt.

CHAPTER 43.

The Jews Carry Out Their Plan.

THE FLIGHT INTO EGYPT. — V. 1. **And it came to pass that, when Jeremiah had made an end of speaking unto all the people all the words of the Lord, their God, for which the Lord, their God**, who was still ready to be considered as such by them, **had sent him to them, even all these words**, the full message, just as it had been transmitted to Jeremiah by inspiration of the Lord, v. 2. **then spake Azariah**, or Jezaniah, **the son of Hoshaiah, and Johanan, the son of Kareah, and all the proud men**, the pride of their heart showing in the insolence of their behavior at this juncture, **saying unto Jeremiah, Thou speakest falsely; the Lord, our God, hath not sent thee to say, Go not into Egypt to sojourn there**, they saucily discredited his entire message; v. 3. **but Baruch, the son of Neriah**, whom they suspected of sympathizing with the Chaldeans, **setteth thee against us for to deliver us into the hand of the Chaldeans that they might put us to death and carry us away captives into Babylon.** Upon this suspicion and accusation, which was wholly unfounded, these men based their opposition to Jeremiah's counsel which conveyed to them the warnings of the Lord. V. 4. **So Johanan, the son of Kareah, and all the captains of the forces and all the people**, in accordance with the idea which they had had in mind practically all this while, **obeyed not the voice of the Lord to dwell in the land of Judah.** V. 5. **But Johanan, the son of Kareah, and all the captains of the forces took all the remnant of Judah that were returned from all nations whither they had been driven**, the various smaller countries round about, **to dwell in the land of Judah**, v. 6. **even men, and women, and children, and the king's daughters**, the princesses of the royal household, chap. 41, 10, **and every person that Nebuzar-adan, the captain of the guard, had left with Gedaliah, the son of Ahikam, the son of Shaphan, and Jeremiah, the prophet, and Baruch, the son of Neriah.** All of these people were obliged to join the caravan of the refugees, whether they protested or not, for in this case also might made right. V. 7. **So they came into the land of Egypt, for they obeyed not the voice of the Lord**, as made known by the mouth of Jeremiah; **thus came they even to Tahpanhes**, the city of Daphne on one of the eastern delta-arms of the Nile, one of the cities nearest to the border of Palestine. Here they halted for a time, in order to consider ways and means of making their sojourn in the strange country safe and profitable. When men deliberately set aside the commands of the Lord and choose their own way of doing things, they invite destruction and ruin upon themselves.

JEREMIAH IN TAHPANHES.—V. 8. **Then came the word of the Lord unto Jeremiah in Tahpanhes, saying**, v. 9. **Take great stones in thine hand and hide them in the clay in the brick-kiln which is at the entry of Pharaoh's house in Tahpanhes, in the sight of the men of Judah**, so that he would have trustworthy witnesses of his act. The palace of Pharaoh included not only the buildings proper, but their entire enclosure as well, which usually was surrounded by a high wall. Opposite the entrance of this enclosure the bricks for the building or for the repairing of the royal palace were made, and it was in the clay of this kiln that the stones carried by Jeremiah were to be hid. V. 10. **And say unto them**, the witnesses of his symbolical act, **Thus saith the Lord of hosts, the God of Israel, Behold, I will send and take Nebuchadrezzar, the king of Babylon, My servant**, for as such he acted in this instance, in carrying out the Lord's purpose upon Egypt, **and will set his throne upon these stones that I have hid; and he shall spread his royal pavilion over them**, namely, the rich tapestry which formed the curtains of the throne. V. 11. **And when he cometh**, in extending his campaign of conquest to Africa, **he shall smite the land of Egypt and deliver such as are for death**, principally by famine and pestilence, **to death, and such as**

are for captivity to captivity, and such as are for the sword, that is, death in battle, **to the sword.** In this way, as the scourge of the Lord, he would also act as the servant of Jehovah. Both the act of laying the stones and the material spoken of are significant; for the stones of the throne's foundation are symbolical of the power and firmness of Nebuchadnezzar's rule, while the clay of Pharaoh's palace signifies the weakness of his power. V. 12. **And I will kindle a fire in the houses of the gods of Egypt,** to show the helplessness of the idols in the country whose security the Jews were seeking; **and he shall burn them and carry them away captives,** the very gods of Egypt being in his power; **and he shall array himself with the land of Egypt as a shepherd putteth on his garment, and he shall go forth from thence in peace.** The point of camparison is the freedom and the ease of the act; for just as easily and quickly as a shepherd takes up his mantle, practically his only garment, and wraps it about him, so easily will Nebuchadnezzar take hold upon Egypt and, with the whole country in his power, leave without hindrance, with no one opposing him. V. 13. **He shall break also the images of Beth-shemesh that is in the land of Egypt,** the renowned Temple of the Sun at Heliopolis, one of the greatest sanctuaries of the country; **and the houses of the gods of the Egyptians shall he burn with fire.** "The images of Beth-shemesh are, above all, the obelisks, of which there was an unlimited number in the city. Of the oldest, which, however, were not the largest, one still remains in its place." In this manner would all the representatives of Egyptian idol-worship fall before the power of Nebuchadnezzar, and the hope and trust of the Jews who fled to Egypt would be found to be vain. Thus all the plans of the wicked according to which they leave the command of God are frustrated to their own confusion.

CHAPTER 44.

Jeremiah Reproves the Idolatry of the Jews.

JEREMIAH'S FIRST WARNING. — V. 1. **The word that came to Jeremiah concerning all the Jews which dwell in the land of Egypt,** where they had settled in spite of the earnest remonstrances of Jeremiah, **which dwell at Migdol,** on the northeastern boundary of Egypt, **and at Tahpanhes,** in the delta of the Nile, **and at Noph,** or Memphis, the capital of Lower Egypt, **and in the country of Pathros,** that is, Upper Egypt, — for in the intervening years the Jews had selected different parts of Egypt for temporary homes, but Jeremiah was still the faithful messenger of God and here addressed them in a large assembly, possibly upon the occasion of some great festival, — **saying,** v. 2. **Thus saith the Lord of hosts, the God of Israel, Ye have seen all the evil that I have brought upon Jerusalem and upon all the cities of Judah,** most of the Jews addressed having been witnesses of the terrible catastrophe which brought destruction to the southern kingdom; **and, behold, this day they are a desolation, and no man dwelleth therein,** the entire land, formerly so rich, fruitful, and populous, had become an uninhabited desert, v. 3. **because of their wickedness which they have committed to provoke Me to anger, in that they went,** leaving the path of right and duty set before them by the Word of God, **to burn incense and to serve other gods,** by such act of worship, **whom they knew not, neither they, ye, nor your fathers.** That was the first cause of the calamity which came upon Jerusalem. V. 4. **Howbeit, I sent unto you all My servants, the prophets, rising early and sending them,** full of merciful eagerness to prevent the threatened catastrophe, **saying, Oh, do not this abominable thing that I hate,** which filled Him with loathing. V. 5. **But they hearkened not nor inclined their ear to turn from their wickedness,** they paid not the slightest attention to Jehovah's admonitions and warnings, **to burn no incense unto other gods.** V. 6. **Wherefore My fury and Mine anger was poured forth,** like an overturned vessel spilling all its contents at once, **and was kindled in the cities of Judah and in the streets of Jerusalem,** for the fire of destruction was a manifestation of the divine anger; **and they are wasted and desolate, as at this day,** their ruin being entirely the fault of the stubbornness of the rebellious Jews, and the consequences were still evident. V. 7. **Therefore, now, thus saith the Lord, the God of hosts, the God of Israel, Wherefore commit ye this great evil against your souls,** to the destruction of their own lives, for they were not injuring the Lord, but merely themselves, **to cut off from you man and woman, child and suckling, out of Judah,** in a judgment of complete extermination, **to leave you none to remain,** v. 8. **in that ye provoke Me unto wrath with the works of your hands, burning incense unto other gods in the land of Egypt, whither ye be gone to dwell,** having profited nothing by the example of Jerusalem's destruction, **that ye might cut yourselves off, and that ye might be a curse and a reproach among all the nations of the earth?** V. 9. **Have ye forgotten the wickedness of your fathers,** their manifold evil doings, **and the wicked-**

ness of the kings of Judah, and the wickedness of their wives, and your own wickedness, and the wickedness of your wives, which they have committed in the land of Judah and in the streets of Jerusalem? The queens of Judah, together with the women throughout the country, had been the chief promoters of idolatry; for just as women may be the chief upholders of virtue, they may also be the chief agents for the spreading of wickedness. V. 10. **They are not humbled, even unto this day,** they had not yet learned to turn to the Lord with contrite hearts, **neither have they feared, nor walked in, My Law nor in My statutes that I set before you and before your fathers.** They had deliberately ignored the norm and rule which the Lord had given them to follow, and the Lord speaks of them partly in the third person to give expression to the supreme disgust which filled His heart at their behavior. V. 11. **Therefore, thus saith the Lord of hosts, the God of Israel, Behold, I will set My face against you for evil and to cut off all Judah,** namely, those who had gone to Egypt against His will. The Lord was absolutely determined to carry out His plans in this instance, to exterminate the rebels who had been so flagrantly disobedient to His will. V. 12. **And I will take the remnant of Judah, that have set their faces to go into the land of Egypt to sojourn there, and they shall all be consumed and fall in the land of Egypt,** in a total destruction; **they shall even be consumed by the sword and by the famine, they shall die, from the least even unto the greatest, by the sword and by the famine, and they shall be an execration,** an object of cursing, **and an astonishment,** an object of surprise, **and a curse, and a reproach.** V. 13. **For I will punish them that dwell in the land of Egypt, as I have punished Jerusalem, by the sword, by the famine, and by the pestilence,** v. 14. **so that none of the remnant of Judah which are gone into the land of Egypt to sojourn there shall escape or remain that they should return into the land of Judah, to the which they have a desire to return to dwell there,** they were literally, "lifting up their souls with eagerness" and hoped to make Judea their home once more; **for none shall return but such as shall escape.** Since the Lord was speaking in general terms, He pictured the destruction as so universal that practically no one would escape, and the heaping of similar expressions heightens the impression of grim determination on His part. He is a jealous God, who visits the iniquity of sinners upon them with all the sternness which His justice demands.

THE ANSWER OF THE JEWS AND THE LORD'S PROPHECY OF PUNISHMENT. — V. 15. **Then all the men which knew that their wives had burned incense unto other gods and all the women that stood by, a great multitude,** the female contingent apparently being in the majority, from which many have concluded that the festival was one in honor of the Queen of Heaven herself, in whose service the women were very zealous, **even all the people that dwelt in the land of Egypt, in Pathros,** where this meeting was held, **answered Jeremiah, saying,** v. 16. **As for the word that thou hast spoken unto us in the name of the Lord, we will not hearken unto thee,** they flatly refused to obey. V. 17. **But we will certainly do whatsoever thing goeth forth out of our own mouth,** the vows which they had made when they embraced idolatry, **to burn incense unto the Queen of Heaven,** that is, Ashtaroth, or Astarte, **and to pour out drink-offerings unto her, as we have done, we and our fathers, our kings and our princes, in the cities of Judah and in the streets of Jerusalem,** this statement amounting to the worst form of self-accusation, with a tinge of revolting boastfulness; **for then had we plenty of victuals,** literally, "we were satisfied with bread," having food of every kind in sufficient amounts, **and were well and saw no evil,** they enjoyed good fortune and happiness, as they believed. Fools attribute what they consider prosperity to the fact that God connives at their sin, so that they finally deny His very existence. V. 18. **But since we left off to burn incense to the Queen of Heaven and to pour out drink-offerings unto her,** very likely due to the reformation under Josiah, 2 Kings 23, 4—20, **we have wanted all things,** they had lacked those things which they had enumerated, **and have been consumed by the sword and by the famine.** V. 19. **And when we burned incense to the Queen of Heaven and poured out drink-offerings unto her, did we make her cakes,** the customary cakes used with sacrifices, chap. 7, 18, **to worship her and pour out drink-offerings unto her without our men?** So the women, who made up the majority of the assembly, boldly stated that their husbands had not only connived at their idolatry, cp. Num. 30, 9 ff., but had even become guilty with them. The reference seems to be to the custom of giving their sacrificial cakes the form of a half-moon or even of the full moon, after the manner of other heathen cults. In this manner the demands of the Lord were met by a flat refusal on the part of the Jews. V. 20. **Then Jeremiah said unto all the people, to the men, and to the women, and to all the people which had given him that answer, saying,** v. 21. **The incense that ye burned in the cities of Judah and in the streets of Jerusalem, ye and your fathers, your kings and your princes, and the people of the land,** of which they, in their wickedness, now presumed to boast, **did not the Lord remember them, and came it not into His** mind? Did not the present desolation of their homeland testify to the fact that the Lord was very well aware of their wickedness, and that He had repaid their evil-doing? V. 22. **So that the Lord could no longer bear because of the evil of your doings and because of the abominations which ye have committed,** with all His long-suffering He could no longer endure it; **therefore is your land a desolation and an astonishment and a curse, without an inhabitant, as at this day.** The evidences of His wrath upon the Land of Promise were still evident, and all on account of their idolatry, as the prophet now repeats once more, for the sake of emphasis. V. 23. **Because ye have burned incense, and because ye have sinned against the Lord,** chiefly in the customs connected with their idolatry, **and have not obeyed the voice of the Lord nor walked in His Law,** in following the precepts of the Moral Law, **nor in His statutes,** the ordinances of the Ceremonial Law, **nor in His testimonies,** the judicial sayings of the Lord throughout His Word, **therefore this evil is happened unto you as at this day.** V. 24. **Moreover, Jeremiah said unto all the people and to all the women, Hear the word of the Lord, all Judah that are in the land of Egypt,** whom he now proceeds to admonish in a most solemn manner, v. 25. **Thus saith the Lord of hosts, the God of Israel, saying, Ye and your wives have both spoken with your mouths and fulfilled with your hand, saying, We will surely perform our vows that we have vowed to burn incense to the Queen of Heaven, and to pour out drink-offerings unto her; ye will surely accomplish your vows and surely perform your vows.** Here is a bit of holy irony; for, as Jeremiah states, no one could accuse them of unsteadiness in keeping their idolatrous promises. If they had only been as steadfast toward Jehovah, the God of the covenant! V. 26. **Therefore hear ye the word of the Lord, all Judah that dwell in the land of Egypt, Behold, I have sworn by My great name, saith the Lord,** by Himself as He has revealed Himself in His great and mighty acts, the most solemn oath which He could swear, **that My name shall no more be named in the mouth of any man of Judah in all the land of Egypt, saying, The Lord God liveth.** Since they had rejected Him, He would also reject them, He would bring about their destruction. V. 27. **Behold, I will watch over them for evil and not for good,** the same God whose tender solicitude watches over His children to do them good would in this instance just as solicitously bring evil upon the rebellious Jews; **and all the men of Judah that are in the land of Egypt shall be consumed by the sword and by the famine until there be an end of them.** This is true in general; it presents the fulfilment of His threat. V. 28. **Yet a small number that escape the sword shall return out of the land of Egypt into the land of Judah,** a band readily counted on account of its smallness, whereas the entire contingent had planned to return to their former homeland; **and all the remnant of Judah that are gone into the land of Egypt to sojourn there shall know whose words shall stand, Mine or theirs,** literally, "the word from Me or that from them," that by which the Lord had predicted ruin to them or that by which they had predicted good fortune to themselves. V. 29. **And this shall be a sign unto you, saith the Lord, that I will punish you in this place, that ye may know that My words shall surely stand against you for evil:** v. 30. **thus saith the Lord, Behold, I will give Pharaoh-hophra, king of Egypt, into the hand of his enemies and into the hand of them that seek his life, as I gave Zedekiah, king of Judah, into the hand of Nebuchadrezzar, king of Babylon, his enemy, and that sought his life.** Pharaoh-hophra lost his life in consequence of a revolt of the Egyptians, who caused him to be executed by strangulation about 570 B. C. If people persist in their opposition to God, He gives them up to the powers of evil to their complete destruction.

CHAPTER 45.

Jeremiah Comforts Baruch.

V. 1. **The word that Jeremiah, the prophet, spake unto Baruch, the son of Neriah,** his secretary and, in a sense, his fellow-worker, **when he had written these words in a book at the mouth of Jeremiah,** as the latter dictated his prophecies from the thirteenth year of Josiah to the fourth of Jehoiakim, **in the fourth year of Jehoiakim, the son of Josiah, king of Judah, saying,** v. 2. **Thus saith the Lord, the God of Israel, unto thee, O Baruch,** for even the disciple of the prophet was not spared by the Lord as far as reproving the faults of those whose welfare He sought was concerned, v. 3. **Thou didst say, Woe is me now!** namely, on account of the hatred of his enemies, **for the Lord hath added grief to my sorrow,** that which he felt on account of the depravity of his people. **I fainted in my sighing, and I find no rest.** The grief which Baruch felt was intensified by fear for his own life on account of the suspicions of his own countrymen, chap. 43, 3. All of this seemed to him to amount to a very harsh treatment on the part of God. V. 4. **Thus shalt thou say unto**

him, The Lord saith thus, Behold, that which I have built will I break down, and that which I have planted I will pluck up, even this whole land. Cp. chap. 31, 28; Is. 5, 5. V. 5. **And seekest thou great things for thyself?** as the one solitary human being that thought to find himself an exception in the general destruction. **Seek them not; for, behold, I will bring evil upon all flesh, saith the Lord,** in a universal punishment; **but thy life will I give unto thee for a prey in all places whither thou goest.** Baruch was not to claim exemption in the general overthrow, but he had the consolation of knowing that his life would be spared, no matter what else he might have to endure. "This is part of God's design in suffering His servants to be tempted, that their temptations may adapt them for ministering to their fellow-servants when tempted."

CHAPTER 46.

Prophecies against Egypt.

THE FIRST PROPHECY AGAINST EGYPT. — V. 1. **The word of the Lord which came to Jeremiah, the prophet,** by direct inspiration, **against the Gentiles,** this verse serving as a superscription of a series of prophecies directed against various foreign peoples. V. 2. **Against Egypt, against the army of Pharaoh-necho, king of Egypt, which was by the river Euphrates in Carchemish,** a strongly fortified commercial center, on a peninsula between the Khaboor and the Euphrates, **which,** or whom, **Nebuchadrezzar, king of Babylon, smote in the fourth year of Jehoiakim, the son of Josiah, king of Judah.** This serves as a historical introduction to the prophecy which follows. Pharaoh-necho had landed in the Bay of Acco, his intention being to conquer all the countries between the Mediterranean Sea and the Euphrates. When Josiah, king of Judah, dared to interfere with his progress, meeting him in battle at Megiddo, the army of the Jews was beaten and Josiah himself mortally wounded. Pharaoh then subjugated Phenicia and Syria and moved onward to Carchemish (Cercusium), where he was probably encamped at the time when this prophecy was first made, about in the year 606 B. C., before the forces of Nebuchadnezzar had entered upon their campaign against the Egyptian army. V. 3. **Order ye the buckler,** the smaller protecting shield, **and shield,** the large shield, behind which the entire body could be hidden, **and draw near to battle!** It is a description picturing the preparations for battle, with a call to battle which enlivens the narrative. V. 4. **Harness the horses,** a call addressed to the charioteers; **and get up, ye horsemen,** the cavalry mounting their steeds for the attack, **and stand forth with your helmets,** this being directed to the infantry; **furbish the spears,** sharpening them for offensive work, **and put on the brigandines,** the coats of mail which were essential in ancient warfare. But now the prophet sees the army, which was so eager for the attack, most miserably defeated. V. 5. **Wherefore have I seen them dismayed and turned away back?** the soldiers who set out so confidently for the attack being overcome with terror at their defeat. **And their mighty ones are beaten down,** broken to pieces, scattered and wounded, **and are fled apace,** literally, "fled a flight," that is, with the greatest haste, **and look not back; for fear was round about, saith the Lord,** this being the explanation for the precipitate flight of the Egyptians. V. 6. **Let not the swift flee away, nor the mighty man escape,** such attempts would be utterly useless, all efforts along that line would avail them nothing; **they shall stumble and fall toward the north by the river Euphrates.** The prophet sees their defeat so vividly that the tottering and falling are accomplished facts before his eyes. A second scene of battle is now painted, more detailed, more concrete than the first. V. 7. **Who is this that cometh up as a flood,** like the Nile overflowing its banks, **whose waters are moved as the rivers?** surging to and fro with irresistible force. V. 8. **Egypt riseth up like a flood,** like the mighty Nile itself, **and his waters are moved like the rivers,** like the rush of water near its mouths; **and he saith, I will go up and will cover the earth; I will destroy the city,** that is, every city, **and the inhabitants thereof.** Such was the proud boast of Egypt in relying on its own strength. V. 9. **Come up, ye horses,** rearing back with impatience; **and rage, ye chariots,** as in uncontrollable anger, **and let the mighty men come forth,** moving forward to battle; **the Ethiopians and the Libyans, that handle the shield,** these mercenary troops being chosen for their skill in using this weapon of defense in battle, **and the Lydians,** those of northern Africa, descendants of the Egyptians, **that handle and bend the bow.** Cp. Gen. 10, 13; Ezek. 30, 5. The Egyptians had made all preparations for a victorious campaign; they went forth confident of an early and complete victory. But they were soon to learn their mistake. V. 10. **For this is the day of the Lord God of hosts,** the great Commander of the heavenly armies, **a day of vengeance, that He may avenge Him of His adversaries,** the Egyptians belonging to this class, not only for the killing of Josiah and the subsequent humiliation of Judah, but since ancient times; **and the sword shall devour, and it shall be satiate,** filled to the point of being surfeited, and made drunk with their blood; for the Lord God of hosts hath a sacrifice in the North country by the river Euphrates, for the slaughter of the Egyptians at Carchemish would be like an offering made to satisfy His righteous anger. Therefore the Lord addresses Egypt in a final emphatic prediction of evil. V. 11. Go up into Gilead and take balm, O virgin, the daughter of Egypt, hitherto not having been subject to any other power; in vain shalt thou use many medicines, for thou shalt not be cured, the wound inflicted upon her at this time would be beyond medical skill. V. 12. The nations have heard of thy shame, the humiliation which would come upon her by this defeat, and thy cry hath filled the land, as the stricken ones made known their misery; for the mighty man hath stumbled against the mighty, in the confusion of headless flight, and they are fallen both together. It is a most vivid description of the utter defeat which would strike the Egyptians by God's counsel, for His judgment invariably finds His enemies.

THE SECOND PROPHECY AGAINST EGYPT. — V. 13. The word that the Lord spake to Jeremiah, the prophet, how Nebuchadrezzar, king of Babylon, should come and smite the land of Egypt, this prophecy belonging to a later period than that of the first part of the chapter. V. 14. Declare ye in Egypt, in a formal proclamation throughout the country, and publish in Migdol and publish in Noph and in Tahpanhes, that is, in the regions along the northeastern boundary and in Memphis, the capital of the northern part of the country; say ye, Stand fast and prepare thee, for the sword shall devour round about thee, the prophet even then seeing the surrounding nations devastated by the advancing Chaldeans. V. 15. Why are thy valiant men swept away? Why this complete overthrow of Egypt's ruler? They stood not because the Lord did drive them, the king with all his mighty men was powerless against the attack of the Lord, against the punishment meted out by Him through the Chaldean king. V. 16. He made many to fall, yea, one fell upon another, Jehovah Himself causing them to stumble and to sink to the ground; and they said, Arise and let us go again to our own people, since they were but visitors and strangers in Egypt, and to the land of our nativity, from the oppressing sword, to escape its murderous fierceness. Thus the confederates and mercenaries of Egypt would make ready to save their own lives in the general destruction. V. 17. They did cry there, namely, the people who were in Egypt at the time of this great calamity, Pharaoh, king of Egypt, is but a noise, or "is destruction, ruin," since his overthrow was evidently a matter of only a short time; he hath passed the time appointed, it was now too late to avert the Lord's judgment. V. 18. As I live, saith the King, whose name is the Lord of hosts, the supreme Ruler of the universe, in a most solemn oath by His own life, Surely as Tabor is among the mountains, looking down upon all the lower hills, and as Carmel by the sea, standing out as a bold promontory, so shall he come, namely, the destroyer of Egypt, the Chaldean conqueror. V. 19. O thou daughter dwelling in Egypt, the entire Egyptian people, furnish thyself to go into captivity, by getting ready vessels and containers for food on the journey into exile; for Noph shall be waste and desolate without an inhabitant, such being the fate of the proud capital according to the judgment of God upon it. V. 20. Egypt is like a very fair heifer, occupying a fine and fertile land and therefore well nourished, but destruction cometh; it cometh out of the North, the direction from which the Chaldeans would approach, like stinging gad-flies. V. 21. Also her hired men, the mercenaries in her employ, are in the midst of her like fatted bullocks, provided with the best of everything, in order to keep them favorably inclined; for they also are turned back, even they lost all their former courage, and are fled away together; they did not stand because the day of their calamity was come upon them and the time of their visitation, when God would visit His anger upon them. V. 22. The voice thereof, of the daughter of Egypt, shall go like a serpent, hissing from her thicket as she hears some one approaching; for they shall march with an army and come against her with axes, as hewers of wood. As the human forest of Egypt would be hewn down, she would flee with a noise as that of rustling leaves, weakly hissing out her protest, but without power effectually to resent it. V. 23. They shall cut down her forest, saith the Lord, though it cannot be searched, it was impossible to estimate the number of the enemy; because they are more than the grasshoppers, whose swarms contain countless insects, and are innumerable. The gist of the prophecy is now given without pictures. V. 24. The daughter of Egypt shall be confounded; she shall be delivered into the hand of the people of the North, of the Chaldean hordes. V. 25. The Lord of hosts, the God of Israel, saith, Behold, I will punish the multitude of No, literally, "the Amon of No," the chief idol of Egypt, and Pharaoh, and Egypt with their gods and their kings, all the people of the country, great and small, together with their idols; even Pharaoh and all them that trust in him; v. 26. and I will deliver them into the hand of those that seek their lives and into the hand of Nebuchadrezzar, king of Babylon, and into the hand of his servants; and afterward, when its power would be broken and its ambition for world influence would no longer be in evidence, it shall be inhabited as in the days of old, saith the Lord, the Messianic idea finding its expression at this point. This is evident especially from the concluding verses of the chapter, which are addressed to the spiritual Israel. V. 27. **But fear not thou, O My servant Jacob, and be not dismayed, O Israel,** both expressions referring to the Lord's people in the highest and best sense of the term; **for, behold, I will save thee from afar off,** bringing back His own children from the far distances to which they had been carried, **and thy seed from the land of their captivity,** this word finding its application particularly in the spiritual sense; **and Jacob shall return and be in rest and at ease, and none shall make him afraid,** since he would be entirely in the care and under the protection of Jehovah. V. 28. **Fear thou not, O Jacob, My servant, saith the Lord, for I am with thee; for I will make a full end of all the nations whither I have driven thee,** the world-powers of that day being symbolical of the powers of evil which beset the believers of all times **But I will not make a full end of thee, but correct thee in measure,** with a chastisement of mercy, not tempting His children above that they are able; **yet will I not leave thee wholly unpunished,** for the visitation of the Lord is intended to lead men to repentance. All this is figurative of the one great deliverance by which the Lord saved His people from all their enemies and established His Church of the New Testament.

CHAPTER 47.

Prophecy against the Philistines.

V. 1. **The word of the Lord that came to Jeremiah, the prophet, against the Philistines,** the ancient enemies of the people of Israel on the west, along the shores of the Mediterranean, **before that Pharaoh smote Gaza.** The exact occasion of this conquest is a matter of conjecture. It may be that Pharaoh-necho took the city after the battle of Megiddo, or that Pharaoh-hophra smote the city after his vain attempt to drive the Chaldeans out of the country. At any rate, Gaza was strong enough after its conquest by Pharaoh to be an object of anxious concern and to demand stern measures on account of its opposition to Jehovah. V. 2. **Thus saith the Lord, Behold, waters rise up out of the North,** namely, the Chaldean armies, **and shall be an overflowing flood and shall overflow the land and all that is therein, the city and them that dwell therein,** like a winter torrent, carrying everything before it. **Then the men shall cry, and all the inhabitants of the land shall howl,** for terror at the impending calamity. The figurative description is now explained. V. 3. **At the noise of the stamping of the hoofs of his strong horses, at the rushing of his chariots, and at the rumbling of his wheels,** all expressive of the Chaldean power, **the fathers shall not look back to their children,** thereby denying even the natural affections, **for feebleness of hands,** a general powerlessness having taken hold of them, making it impossible for them even to think of defending themselves, v. 4. **because of the day that cometh to spoil all the Philistines and to cut off from Tyrus and Zidon every helper that remaineth,** so that all the allies would withdraw their assistance; **for the Lord will spoil the Philistines, the remnant of the country of Caphtor,** most likely Crete; for it was from this island that the Philistines, although descended from the Mizraim, Gen. 10, 13. 14, originally emigrated to the shores of the Mediterranean. Cp. Amos 9, 7; Deut. 2, 23. V. 5. **Baldness is come upon Gaza,** one of the city-states of Philistia, due to tearing out the hair because of great grief; **Ashkelon,** another of the Philistine cities, **is cut off with the remnant of their valley,** the long coastal plain which was the territory of Philistia. **How long wilt thou cut thyself?** with incisions in the flesh, after the manner in which the heathen expressed the height of sorrow and mourning. V. 6. **O thou sword of the Lord,** so the prophet apostrophizes Jehovah's weapon of punishment, **how long will it be ere thou be quiet?** desisting from further slaughter. **Put up thyself into thy scabbard, rest, and be still.** But the prophet, after addressing the sword in the second person, turns to his hearers and explains in the third person why this deliverance is impossible, why God cannot rest, desist from punishing. V. 7. **How can it be quiet, seeing the Lord hath given it a charge against Ashkelon and against the seashore?** Not only Philistia, but also Phenecia was included in the Lord's punishment. **There hath He appointed it,** ordering the sword of His anger to work havoc against these obstinate enemies of His plans; for those who rebel against His authority make themselves subject to His condemnation.

CHAPTER 48.

Prophecy against Moab.

THE COMING DEVASTATION OF MOAB DESCRIBED. — V. 1. **Against Moab. Thus saith the Lord of hosts, the God of Israel, Woe unto Nebo!** an important city in Southwestern Moabitis. **For it is spoiled,** laid waste by the enemies; **Kiriathaim,** another ancient city of the country, **is confounded and taken; Misgab,** literally, "the citadel," probably Kir-Moab, the strongest fort of the Moabites, or a general expression denoting the overthrow of Moab's power, **is confounded and dismayed.** V. 2. **There shall be no more praise of Moab,** literally, "Not is there any more boasting of Moab," that is, Moab no longer has cause for praising herself; **in Heshbon they have devised evil against it,** this ancient capital of the Amorites, almost directly opposite Jericho, being in the hands of the invaders, who were there making plans for further humiliating Moab, **Come and let us cut it off from being a nation!** Moab, although repeatedly tributary to the kingdom of Israel, especially under David and Solomon, nevertheless retained its national organization and finally regained its independence, even to the extent of joining in an attack on Judah. But this glory would now be definitely ended. **Also thou shalt be cut down, O Madmen,** another city of Moab; **the sword shall pursue thee,** to bring slaughter and destruction to its inhabitants. V. 3. **A voice of crying shall be from Horonaim,** a village east of the Dead Sea, **spoiling and great destruction,** the town sinking into ruins. V. 4. **Moab,** that is, Ar-Moab, the ancient capital of the land, **is destroyed; her little ones have caused a cry to be heard,** her citizens giving voice to the distress which they felt. V. 5. **For in the going up of Luhith,** a town in the hilly section south of the Arnon, **continual weeping shall go up; for in the going down of Horonaim,** which lay in the plain, **the enemies have heard a cry of destruction.** As the enemy advances from the north, the inhabitants of Moab, weeping bitterly over the devastation of their cities, flee over the heights of Luhith and down the long incline toward Horonaim to save their lives if possible. V. 6. **Flee!** so the cry goes forth to them, **save your lives and be like the heath in the wilderness,** like forsaken ones, like those stripped of everything out in the desert, that being Moab's eventual lot. V. 7. **For because thou hast trusted in thy works and in thy treasures,** in her successful undertakings and the wealth which she had thereby amassed, **thou shalt also be taken,** the land subdued and its inhabitants led away into captivity; **and Chemosh,** the chief idol of the Moabites, worshiped chiefly as the god of war, **shall go forth into captivity with his priests and his princes together,** both the spiritual and the temporal rulers of the country included in the judgment of Jehovah. V. 8. **And the spoiler shall come upon every city, and no city shall escape,** all of them being doomed to ruin and their inhabitants to slaughter and captivity; **the valley also shall perish,** that is, the inhabitants of the lowlands near the Jordan, **and the plain shall be destroyed,** the plateau which extended from the Arnon toward the north and northeast beyond what had been Rabbath-Ammon, **as the Lord hath spoken.** V. 9. **Give wings unto Moab that it may flee and get away,** on account of the suddenness of the calamity which was threatening; **for the cities thereof shall be desolate, without any to dwell therein.** V. 10. **Cursed be he that doeth the work of the Lord deceitfully,** being negligent in carrying out the judgment of God upon Moab, **and cursed be he that keepeth back his sword from blood,** the invader charged with the slaughter of Moab. V. 11. **Moab hath been at ease from his youth,** never really having suffered the reverses which fell to the lot of some other nations, **and he hath settled on his lees,** like poor wine which turns to vinegar after long standing, **and hath not been emptied from vessel to vessel, neither hath he gone into captivity.** Because the people of Moab had not suffered the calamities which befell some other nations because they had not been tried out by repeated exiles, their character had become harsh and supercilious. **Therefore his taste remained in him, and his scent is not changed,** his bearing toward other nations, and particularly against the children of Israel, had remained the same throughout the centuries. V. 12. **Therefore, behold, the days come, saith the Lord, that I will send unto him wanderers,** literally, "pourers-out," the Hebrew word being used of men who handled wine-kegs and skins, especially in transferring or transfusing wine from one vessel to another and thereby separating it from the lees, **that shall cause him to wander,** tilting him up and pouring him out, **and shall empty his vessels and break their bottles,** dash his dishes in pieces. The conquerors would not only lead the Moabites away into exile, but would also destroy their national organization. V. 13. **And Moab shall be ashamed of Chemosh,** getting evidence of the powerlessness and utter vanity of their chief idol, **as the house of Israel was ashamed of Bethel, their confidence,** finding out to their sorrow that the golden calf was a vain idol. V. 14. **How say ye, We are mighty and strong men for the war?** Moab would no longer boast of its courage and strength, because terror would possess every heart. V. 15. **Moab,** as a result of this attitude, **is spoiled and gone up out of her cities,** or, "men go up," that is, they take her cities, and his chosen young men, the soldiers of the country, are gone down to the slaughter, saith the King, whose name is the Lord of hosts, the one supreme Ruler of the whole world. Before Him all nations must finally bow, either in meek submission, which accepts His rule, or in the subjection of terror, which fawns before the Victor.

MOAB'S GLORY FOLLOWED BY ITS DEEP FALL. V. 16. **The calamity of Moab is near to come,** so that destruction will soon overtake him, **and his affliction hasteth fast,** his misfortune coming on apace, with great speed. V. 17. **All ye that are about him,** all his neighbors, **bemoan him, and all ye that know his name,** those living at a distance and knowing only the fame of Moab, **say, How is the strong staff broken and the beautiful rod!** The breaking of Moab's scepter of beauty and splendor signifies the total overthrow of his government and rule. The admonition is addressed in a general way, to emphasize the total ruin of the former mighty people. V. 18. **Thou daughter that dost inhabit Dibon,** a city some four miles north of the Arnon, **come down from thy glory and sit in thirst,** her surroundings becoming an arid wilderness; **for the spoiler of Moab shall come upon thee, and he shall destroy thy strongholds,** leveling all her proud fortifications in which she trusted. V. 19. **O inhabitant of Aroer,** a city on the northern bank of the Arnon, originally belonging to Ammon, Deut. 2, 36; 3, 12, **stand by the way and espy,** watching, as it were, for the fugitive Moabites coming down from the north to escape the Chaldean invaders; **ask him that fleeth and her that escapeth,** for both men and women were seeking to save their lives by a hurried flight, **and say, What is done?** The answer to this question is given in the next verse. V. 20. **Moab is confounded,** put to shame and confusion; **for it is broken down; howl and cry! Tell ye it in Arnon,** the former northern boundary between Moab and Ammon, **that Moab is spoiled,** the news of its destruction traveling southward with the fugitives. V. 21. **And judgment is come upon the plain country,** upon the plateau north of the Arnon, cities which had been in the possession of the tribe of Reuben for some centuries after the conquest, **upon Holon, and upon Jahazah, and upon Mephaath,** v. 22. **and upon Dibon, and upon Nebo, and upon Beth-diblathaim,** v. 23. **and upon Kiriathaim, and upon Beth-gamul, and upon Beth-meon,** v. 24. **and upon Kerioth,** probably another name for the capital of the country, **and upon Bozrah, and upon all the cities of the land of Moab, far and near,** most of these being situated in the region east of the Dead Sea. The fact that the judgment has struck Moab is made more specific by the enumeration of the individual cities that have been destroyed. V. 25. **The horn of Moab,** emblem of strength and sovereignty, **is cut off, and his arm is broken, saith the Lord,** he has lost all his former great power, his mighty position is shattered. All this, as the prophet now points out, is the result of Moab's pride. V. 26. **Make ye him drunken,** so the prophet addresses all those whom the Lord has made executors of His punishment, **for he magnified himself against the Lord,** wherefore he must drink the cup of Jehovah's avenging fury; **Moab also shall wallow in his vomit,** the consequence of his intoxication, **and he also shall be in derision,** an object of mockery on the part of all men. This is retribution in kind. V. 27. **For was not Israel a derision unto thee?** Did Moab not make a mockery of the people of God? **Was he found among thieves? for since thou spakest of him, thou skippedst for joy,** or, "Had he been found among thieves that thou, as often as thou spakest of him, shookest thy head?" Moab had given every exhibition of derision and mockery over Israel, while, in truth, this nation, together with other heathen nations near by, had been the cause of Israel's criminal conduct. V. 28. **O ye that dwell in Moab, leave the cities,** dwellings which no longer offered a sufficient shelter, **and dwell in the rock,** in caves of inaccessible mountain fastnesses, **and be like the dove that maketh her nest in the sides of the hole's mouth,** on the walls of the yawning ravine. V. 29. **We have heard the pride of Moab (he is exceeding proud), his loftiness, and his arrogancy, and his pride, and the haughtiness of his heart,** the synonymous terms being heaped to express, in a way, the unusual hatefulness of Moab's sin. V. 30. **I know his wrath,** his furious insolence, **saith the Lord; but it shall not be so,** his boastings are nothingness, idle talk, vain vauntings; **his lies shall not so effect it,** his deeds being just as vain as his words. All this causes the prophet to give expression to his sympathy for Moab, well as it had deserved its fate. V. 31. **Therefore will I howl for Moab,** raise his voice in lamentation, **and I will cry out for all Moab; mine heart shall mourn for the men of Kir-heres,** the strongest citadel of the country, probably identical with Kir-Moab. V. 32. **O vine of Sibmah, I will weep for thee with the weeping of Jazer,** or, "more than Jazer," since, because the vines of Sibmah excelled in grapes which they produced, their destruction by the enemy was a calamity; **thy plants are gone over the sea, they reach even to the Sea of Jazer,** to the Dead Sea and beyond, and northward to the pools of Jazer, considerably beyond Heshbon. **The spoiler is fallen upon thy summer-fruits and upon thy vintage,** so that this entire industry was ruined. V. 33. **And joy and gladness is taken from the plentiful field,** from the fertile farm- and garden-land which has just been described, **and from the land of Moab,** from the entire country; **and I have caused wine to fail from the wine-presses,** there being no longer a supply of grapes for them; **none shall tread with shouting**, with the usual cry of "Hedad!" heard in the fields; **their shouting shall be no shouting**. Cp. Is. 16, 7—10. V. 34. **From the cry of Heshbon even unto Elealeh, and even unto Jahaz, have they uttered their voice**, that is, throughout the entire country inhabited by the Moabites, from the northern part to the southern end of their land, the cry of distress was heard, **from Zoar**, in the southwest, **even unto Horonaim, as an heifer of three years old**, or, "to the third Eglat," one of three villages bearing the same name; **for the waters also of Nimrim**, copious springs with the meadow-lands belonging to them, near the southern end of the Dead Sea, **shall be desolate**, dried up as a result of God's punishment. V. 35. **Moreover, I will cause to cease in Moab, saith the Lord, him that offereth in the high places and him that burneth incense to his gods**, making an end of all idolaters, as He would break down their places of worship. The same fate eventually awaits all idolaters, also those who indulge in the finer forms of the sin only and consider themselves safe in their insolent behavior.

LAMENTATION OVER MOAB. — V. 36. **Therefore mine heart shall sound for Moab like pipes**, sighing with the wailing sound of the flute, **and mine heart shall sound like pipes for the men of Kir-heres**, the chief stronghold of Moab, **because the riches that he hath gotten are perished**, literally, "because the remnant that they had gained, perished." Because the judgment of destruction had struck Moab, therefore his heart was wailing so bitterly, and therefore also the wealth of Moab was lost. V. 37. **For every head shall be bald**, shaved as a sign of deep grief, **and every beard clipped**, another evidence of mourning; **upon all the hands shall be cuttings**, incisions such as the heathen made in deep sorrow, **and upon the loins sackcloth**, the whole nation lamenting on account of the great losses which had come upon the entire land. V. 38. **There shall be lamentation generally**, nothing but wailing, **upon all the housetops of Moab, and in the streets thereof**, both at home and abroad; **for I have broken Moab like a vessel wherein is no pleasure, saith the Lord**, like a worthless vase which is cast aside without so much as a backward glance. V. 39. **They shall howl**, literally, "How is it broken!" saying, **How is it broken down! How hath Moab turned the back with shame!** no longer proud and insolent, but utterly broken in spirit. **So shall Moab be a derision and a dismaying to all them about him**, an object of scorn, mockery, and horror. V. 40. **For thus saith the Lord, Behold, he**, namely, Nebuzar-adan, the captain of Nebuchadnezzar, **shall fly as an eagle and shall spread his wings over Moab**, to pounce upon them as a welcome prey, to tear them to pieces. V. 41. **Kerioth**, cp. v. 24, **is taken, and the strongholds are surprised, and the mighty men's hearts in Moab at that day shall be as the heart of a woman in her pangs**, full of fear and terror. V. 42. **And Moab shall be destroyed from being a people**, losing its identity among the nations, **because he hath magnified himself against the Lord**, and Jehovah resisteth the proud. V. 43. **Fear and the pit**, used by the hunter of big game, **and the snare**, used by the fowler, **shall be upon thee, O inhabitant of Moab, saith the Lord**, some sort of catastrophe being sure to strike the proud and defiant people. V. 44. **He that fleeth from the fear**, trying to escape the general horror, **shall fall into the pit, and he that getteth up out of the pit shall be taken in the snare**, one or the other of the calamities will be sure to catch him; **for I will bring upon it, even upon Moab, the year of their visitation, saith the Lord.** V. 45. **They that fled**, the fugitives who escaped the slaughter, **stood under the shadow of Heshbon because of the force**, powerless in the face of the danger confronting them; **but a fire shall come forth out of Heshbon**, the city in which they hoped to find refuge, **and a flame from the midst of Sihon**, the ancient king of the Amorites, **and shall devour the corner of Moab**, so that it would be totally destroyed, **and the crown of the head of the tumultuous ones**, of the sons of warlike confusion. The prophet here applies the ancient hymn, Num. 21, 27. 28, to the circumstances before him; for as in ancient times Sihon, king of the Amorites, came forth from his city, Heshbon, like a devouring flame, which consumed Moab, so the Chaldeans, starting from Heshbon, would descend upon the country of the Moabites and destroy their power. V. 46. **Woe be unto thee, O Moab! The people of Chemosh perisheth**, the idolaters with their false god; **for thy sons are taken captives**, led away into prison, **and thy daughters captives**, dragged into exile. V. 47. **Yet will I bring again the captivity of Moab in the latter days, saith the Lord**, the Messianic idea becoming evident in this promise of restoration. **Thus far is the judgment of Moab.** The Lord has His children even in the midst of a people which has rejected Him, which, for this reason, He is bound to punish according to His holiness. The Gospel-message has reached many Gentiles, and the Gospel-blessings have descended upon many persons outside of Israel according to the flesh.

CHAPTER 49.

Prophecies against Ammon, Idumea, Damascus, and Other Nations.

AGAINST AMMON. — V. 1. **Concerning the Ammonites,** literally, "Against the children of Ammon," **thus saith the Lord, Hath Israel no sons? Hath he no heir?** some one who may legitimately take possession of the land which was now left vacant, since Israel had been led away into exile. **Why, then, doth their king,** the ruler of the Ammonites, **inherit Gad,** the territory of this tribe, east of the Jordan, **and his people dwell in his cities?** "Judah was by right of kindred the heir, not Ammon; but Ammon joined with Nebuchadnezzar against Judah and Jerusalem, 2 Kings 24, 2, and exulted over its fall, Ps. 83, 4—7. 8; Zeph. 2, 8. 9. It had already in the days of Jeroboam, in Israel's affliction, tried to enlarge its border, 2 Kings 14, 26; Amos 1, 1." V. 2. **Therefore, behold, the days come, saith the Lord, that I will cause an alarm of war to be heard in Rabbah of the Ammonites,** their capital; **and it shall be a desolate heap,** literally, "a hill of desolation," a pile of ruins; **and her daughters,** her suburbs, the smaller cities and towns within her sphere of influence, **shall be burned with fire; then shall Israel be heir unto them that were his heirs, saith the Lord,** be in a position once more to occupy the land which the Ammonites had gotten by unfair means. On account of this misfortune, wailing and lamenting would be in order in the land of the Ammonites. V. 3. **Howl, O Heshbon,** at that time occupied by the Ammonites, **for Ai is spoiled,** had already been subdued by the invaders; **cry, ye daughters of Rabbah,** the towns and villages near the capital, **gird you with sackcloth,** in token of deep mourning; **lament and run to and fro by the hedges,** in the fenced encampment, such as were quickly erected out in the open fields, since the cities no longer offered any protection; **for their king shall go into captivity,** in this case their idol Melchom, with whom the heathen king was pleased to identify himself, **and his priests and his princes together.** Cp. Amos 1, 15. The reason for the Lord's punishment upon Ammon is now set forth, as the prophet pictures the pride, the stubbornness, and the security of its inhabitants. V. 4. **Wherefore gloriest thou in the valleys, thy flowing valley,** flowing with abundance, with milk and honey, **O backsliding daughter?** so called because the children of Ammon had denied their descent from Lot and had turned to idolatry, **that trusted in her treasures,** in her wealth of resources and goods, **saying, Who shall come unto me?** namely, in a hostile attack. The Ammonites boasted that no enemy could successfully launch a campaign against their land. V. 5. **Behold, I will bring a fear upon thee, saith the Lord God of hosts, from all those that be about thee,** whose misfortune and overthrow would bring terror upon them; **and ye shall be driven out, every man, right forth,** straight ahead, without turning; **and none shall gather up him that wandereth,** make any attempt to bring about so much as a semblance of order among the scattered fugitives. According to secular accounts the overthrow of Ammon took place in the fifth year after the destruction of Jerusalem, after King Baalis had executed the murder of Gedaliah, chap. 40, 14. V. 6. **And afterward I will bring again the captivity of the children of Ammon, saith the Lord,** for in their case also the Messianic promises were held out to all those who would return to the Lord in true repentance.

AGAINST EDOM. — V. 7. **Concerning Edom, thus saith the Lord of hosts, Is wisdom no more in Teman?** a city on the boundary of Idumea and Arabia, the home of Eliphaz, Job 2, 11. **Is counsel perished from the prudent?** from those who formerly showed intelligence. **Is their wisdom vanished?** The rhetorical question has, of course, a strong negative significance: Wisdom and common sense seem to have disappeared entirely. V. 8. **Flee ye, turn back, dwell deep,** hiding in caves and remote places, **O inhabitants of Dedan,** a nomad tribe tributary to Edom; **for I will bring the calamity of Esau upon him, the time that I will visit him,** that is, the misfortune which would strike Edom would come upon Dedan as well. Cp. Obad. 1—9. V. 9. **If grape-gatherers,** the usual vintagers, **come to thee, would they not leave some gleaning grapes?** according to the custom of the Orient to leave a few berries for the poor; **if thieves by night, they will destroy till they have enough,** leaving the rest behind. The Chaldeans, however, would be less considerate in their treatment of Idumea. V. 10. **But I,** so Jehovah says, **have made Esau bare,** by using the Chaldeans as instruments in carrying out His punishment, **I have uncovered his secret places,** where his treasures were hidden, **and he shall not be able to hide himself; his seed is spoiled,** his direct descendants ceased from being a nation, **and his brethren,** the nations related to him, **and his neighbors,** the nations tributary to him, **and he is not.** Edom ceased to be a factor politically at the time of the Romans. V. 11. **Leave thy fatherless children, I will preserve them alive; and let thy widows trust in Me;** for Jehovah, whom Edom had forsaken for false gods, would be the Help of the orphans and widows after the men would have fallen in battle. The words imply an exhibition of mercy on the part of the Lord toward all those who, in true sorrow over their sins, turn to Him for help. V. 12. **For thus saith the Lord, Behold, they whose judgment was not to drink of the cup,** the children of Israel, in whose case it was an abnormal thing to be obliged to drink the cup of God's wrath, since they were Jehovah's own people, have assuredly drunken; and art thou he that shall altogether go unpunished? Even the fact that Israel had been chosen as God's people did not give them exemption and deliverance from God's punishment if they took part in the idolatry of the heathen; how much more, then, would the heathen be subject to the judgment of Jehovah! **Thou shalt not go unpunished, but thou shalt surely drink of it;** the punishment had fully been determined upon by God. V. 13. **For I have sworn by Myself, saith the Lord,** in His most solemn oath, **that Bozrah,** at that time the capital of Idumea, **shall become a desolation, a reproach, a waste, and a curse,** an object of execration; **and all the cities thereof,** the other towns of Edom, **shall be perpetual wastes.** V. 14. **I have heard a rumor from the Lord,** a report from Jehovah, **and an ambassador is sent unto the heathen, saying, Gather ye together,** assembling in armies, **and come against her, and rise up to the battle,** ready for war against Edom. V. 15. **For, lo,** so the Lord takes up the message in person, **I will make thee small among the heathen and despised among men,** in just retribution for Edom's pride. V. 16. **Thy terribleness hath deceived thee,** the fact that other nations seemed to stand in awe of Edom had caused him to think that he was really formidable, **and the pride of thine heart,** insolence usually having this influence upon the heart of the proud, to deceive them, wherefore the Lord now calls out, **O thou that dwellest in the clefts of the rock, that holdest the height of the hill,** some of the forts of Idumea being situated on almost inaccessible cliffs, **though thou shouldest make thy nest as high as the eagle, I will bring thee down from thence, saith the Lord,** showing that before Him no stronghold is impregnable. V. 17. **Also Edom shall be a desolation; every one that goeth by it shall be astonished,** filled with horrified surprise at the total overthrow of the country, **and shall hiss at all the plagues thereof,** with a sound expressing derision and mockery. V. 18. **As in the overthrow of Sodom and Gomorrah and the neighbor cities thereof,** namely, Admah and Zeboim, **saith the Lord, no man shall abide there, neither shall a son of man dwell in it,** it would be an uninhabited desert. V. 19. **Behold, he,** the conqueror sent by Jehovah, **shall come up like a lion from the swelling of Jordan,** from his den in the thickets of the river, **against the habitation of the strong,** into the meadow of the rocks, where Idumea was situated; **but I will suddenly make him,** Edom, **run away from her,** from the fine meadow which is his home; **and who is a chosen man that I may appoint over her?** The Lord would make the man of His choice ruler of Idumea. **For who is like Me? And who will appoint Me the time?** Who will dare to call Him to account for it? **And who is that shepherd that will stand before Me?** attempting to protect his flock against the wrath of Jehovah. V. 20. **Therefore hear the counsel of the Lord that He hath taken against Edom,** a decree which is already firmly resolved upon, **and His purposes that He hath purposed against the inhabitants of Teman,** v. 7: **Surely the least of the flock shall draw them out,** literally, "Most certainly they will be dragged away, the feeble of the flock," the Edomites being helpless before the attack of the invaders; **surely he shall make their habitations desolate with them,** or, "Certainly their pasturage will be astounded at them," their own land being horrified at the misfortune which had befallen them. V. 21. **The earth is moved at the noise of their fall,** quaking with its intensity, **at the cry the noise thereof was heard in the Red Sea,** or, "a crying — the noise of it is heard at the Red Sea." V. 22. **Behold, he,** the conqueror, **shall come up and fly as the eagle and spread his wings over Bozrah,** to pounce down upon the whole country; **and at that day shall the heart of the mighty men of Edom be as the heart of a woman in her pangs.** No matter how impregnable the position of God's enemies may seem in the eyes of human beings, they will quickly fall before the attack of the Lord.

AGAINST DAMASCUS, HAZOR, AND ELAM. — V. 23. **Concerning Damascus. Hamath,** a powerful city on the Orontes and formerly the capital of a country of the same name, **is confounded, and Arpad,** another mighty city, both of them now within the confines of Syria, **for they have heard evil tidings; they are faint-hearted,** full of concern on account of the reports which they have heard; **there is sorrow on the sea,** terror among the inhabitants along its shores; **it cannot be quiet,** there is no rest for worry over the outlook. **V. 24. Damascus is waxed feeble,** utterly discouraged and enfeebled, **and turneth herself to flee, and fear hath seized on her, anguish and sorrows have taken her, as a woman in travail,** the terror of utter despair. V. 25. **How is the city of praise not left, the city of my joy?** How was it that the place of delight, as Damascus was called of old, was not abandoned by its inhabitants, so that they might have saved their lives by a speedy flight? V. 26. **Therefore her young men shall fall in her streets, and all the men of war shall be cut off in that day, saith the Lord of hosts.** So great had been their terror at the approach of the enemy that they had not even had recourse to flight and so were cut down in the very streets of their city. V. 27. **And I will kindle a fire in the wall of Damascus,** inside the walls, **and it shall consume the palaces of Benhadad,** the royal dwellings, and therewith at least a part, if not all, of the city. V. 28. **Concerning Kedar**, a tribe of Bedouins, descendants of Ishmael found in Northern Arabia, **and concerning the kingdoms of Hazor**, a district in Northeastern Arabia, **which Nebuchadrezzar, king of Babylon, shall smite, thus saith the Lord, Arise ye, go up to Kedar, and spoil the men of the East**, as the people of Canaan designated all the wilderness dwellers of Arabia. V. 29. **Their tents and their flocks**, the chief possessions of nomads, **shall they take away; they shall take to themselves their curtains**, the costly woven goods and the hangings of their tents, **and all their vessels**, household utensils as well as such pieces of furniture and adornment as comprised their wealth, **and their camels; and they**, the invading forces, **shall cry unto them**, in a shout of war, **Fear is on every side.** V. 30. **Flee, get you far off**, run apace, **dwell deep**, hiding themselves in remote places, **O ye inhabitants of Hazor! saith the Lord; for Nebuchadrezzar, king of Babylon, hath taken counsel against you**, devised a plan to subdue them, **and hath conceived a purpose against you.** This warning is addressed to the wilderness dwellers, since no conqueror would venture to follow them into the trackless wastes of the desert. In the next words the Lord once more turns to the enemies, bidding them continue their work of destruction. V. 31. **Arise, get you up unto the wealthy nation**, a tranquil tribe, having no presentiment of evil, **that dwelleth without care**, in calm security, **saith the Lord, which have neither gates nor bars**, not dwelling in fenced and fortified cities, **which dwell alone**, with little or no intercourse with other nations or tribes, from which they might expect assistance in case of an attack. V. 32. **And their camels shall be a booty and the multitude of their cattle a spoil**, a welcome bit of plunder for the enemies; **and I will scatter into all winds them that are in the utmost corners**, those who have the edges of their hair trimmed; for these tribes had the custom of clipping the hair of head and beard in a peculiar angle; **and I will bring their calamity from all sides thereof, saith the Lord.** V. 33. **And Hazor shall be a dwelling for dragons**, the habitation of jackals, **and a desolation forever; there shall no man abide there, nor any son of man dwell in it.** This prophecy was fulfilled when the Chaldeans, on their way to the West and South, sent detachments of troops to bring these nomadic tribes into subjection. V. 34. **The word of the Lord that came to Jeremiah, the prophet, against Elam**, a Semitic tribe in the Persian province of Susiana, especially that section nearest to Palestine, **in the beginning of the reign of Zedekiah, king of Judah**, at the beginning of the sixth century B. C., **saying**, v. 35. **Thus saith the Lord of hosts, Behold, I will break the bow of Elam**, for the skilful use of which the Elamites were known, **the chief of their might**, thus rendering them helpless before their enemies. V. 36. **And upon Elam will I bring the four winds from the four quarters of heaven and will scatter them toward all those winds**, so that their power would be definitely and finally broken; **and there shall be no nation whither the outcasts of Elam shall not come.** V. 37. **For I will cause Elam to be dismayed before their enemies and before them that seek their life**, no specific enemy being named, but all of them included; **and I will bring evil upon them, even My fierce anger, saith the Lord; and I will send the sword after them till I have consumed them**, so that their identity as a separate nation would be lost; v. 38. **and I will set My throne in Elam**, Jehovah showing Himself as King by His judgments there, **and will destroy from thence the king and the princes, saith the Lord.** V. 39. **But it shall come to pass in the latter days**, an expression used invariably of the Messianic era, **that I will bring again the captivity of Elam, saith the Lord**, so that from this country also there were some who accepted the Messiah as their Lord and Savior. It is interesting to note that among the strangers present on the great day of Pentecost to hear the sermon of Peter there were also people of Elam. Cp. Acts 2, 9.

CHAPTER 50.

Babylon's Downfall. Israel's Redemption.

CHALDEA PUNISHED; ISRAEL REDEEMED. — V. 1. **The word that the Lord spake against Babylon and against the land of the Chaldeans by Jeremiah, the prophet**, when Seraiah, to whom it was committed, was sent to Babylon, chap. 51, 59. 60. It seems that the various prophecies against Babylon were collected at this time, to be sent as one message, partly to pronounce the doom of the oppressor, chap. 25, 12, partly to console the captive Jews and to remind them of the eventual end of their captivity. V. 2. **Declare ye among the nations and publish and set up a standard**, to call the attention of all men to the importance and the significance of this announcement; **publish, and conceal not; say, Babylon is taken; Bel**, the chief deity of the Chaldeans, **is confounded; Merodach**, another name for the same idol, **is broken in pieces. Her idols are confounded**, covered with shame and confusion, **her images are broken in pieces**, powerless before the almighty power of Jehovah. V. 3. **For out of the North,** whence the army of the Medes approached some sixty years later, **there cometh up a nation against her which shall make her land desolate, and none shall dwell therein; they shall remove, they shall depart, both man and beast,** making the former populous land a desolate waste. V. 4. **In those days and in that time,** when the punishment would strike Babylon, **saith the Lord, the children of Israel shall come,** the members of the Lord's Church of believers among His chosen people, **they and the children of Judah together, going and weeping,** with tears of joy over the restoration which had been almost beyond their hopes; **they shall go and seek the Lord, their God,** with a repentant heart. V. 5. **They shall ask the way to Zion,** the habitation of Jehovah, **with their faces thitherward,** set with steadfast purpose not to be daunted or to be turned aside by difficulties along the way, **saying, Come and let us join ourselves to the Lord in a perpetual covenant that shall not be forgotten,** as the first covenant had been set aside by an apostate nation. V. 6. **My people hath been lost sheep; their shepherds have caused them to go astray,** the very men who were entrusted with their care being guilty of this gross neglect, **they have turned them away on the mountains,** the places of idolatry; **they have gone from mountain to hill,** from one altar of idolatrous worship to the next; **they have forgotten their resting-place,** in the care of Jehovah, where they could lie down in safety. V. 7. **All that found them have devoured them,** the enemies everywhere making a practise of preying on the Lord's people; **and their adversaries said, We offend not, because they have sinned against the Lord, the Habitation of justice,** He who is the essence of righteousness, the Fountain of Israel's salvation, **even the Lord, the Hope of their fathers,** in whom the true believers had ever trusted for help. Their adversaries felt that they incurred no guilt, that they were, in fact, justified in taking advantage of the children of Israel. V. 8. **Remove out of the midst of Babylon,** so all Israelites in truth are now warned, **and go forth out of the land of the Chaldeans,** where they were as yet held in captivity, **and be as the he-goats before the flocks,** the leaders of all oppressed nations, as they now turned to flee. V. 9. **For, lo, I will raise, and cause to come up, against Babylon an assembly of great nations from the North country,** an army composed of representatives of many nations; **and they shall set themselves in array against her,** with full equipment for warfare; **from thence,** or "there," **she shall be taken,** namely, where the hostile nations have assembled themselves; **their arrows shall be as of a mighty expert man,** one well versed in the art of warfare; **none shall return in vain,** none of them would fail to perform its deadly work. V. 10. **And Chaldea shall be a spoil,** a prey ready for the invaders; **all that spoil her shall be satisfied, saith the Lord,** since they were getting all that their heart desired in the way of rich booty. In this sense the Lord now turns directly to Babylon in pronouncing sentence upon the Chaldean Empire. V. 11. **Because ye were glad, because ye rejoiced, O ye destroyers of Mine heritage,** the Chaldeans called so on account of the pillage committed by them in destroying Judah, **because ye are grown fat as the heifer at grass,** skipping like a threshing calf or heifer, with proud insolence, **and bellow as bulls,** or, "neigh as steeds," in overweening, challenging pride, v. 12. **your mother shall be sore confounded,** the nation as such being heaped with disgrace; **she that bare you shall be ashamed,** blushing with the shame of it all. **Behold, the hindermost of the nations,** for this was the station to which Babylon had now been reduced, **shall be a wilderness, a dry land, and a desert,** the nation itself, of course, having been destroyed. V. 13. **Because of the wrath of the Lord it shall not be inhabited, but it shall be wholly desolate,** since His anger had caused the inhabitants to be driven away or slaughtered; **every one that goeth by Babylon shall be astonished and hiss at all her plagues,** in sneering derision. In order to carry out this judgment upon Babylon, the nations everywhere are now called upon to take the city. V. 14. **Put yourselves in array against Babylon round about,** to surround the city and to attack her from all sides simultaneously; **all ye that bend the bow,** the archers representing the entire army of the enemy, **shoot at her, spare no arrows; for she hath sinned against the Lord,** she has fully deserved the punishment being meted out to her. V. 15. **Shout against her round about,** encouraging one another with loud and fierce battle-cries; **she hath given her hand,** thereby submitting to the conquerors; **her foundations are fallen,** the fortifications in which she trusted for safety, **her walls are thrown down,** so that she is now helpless before the invaders; **for it is the vengeance of the Lord,** the destruction of Babylon was a punishment determined by Him; **take vengeance upon her,** retaliation being permitted in this instance; **as she hath done, do unto her.** V. 16. **Cut off the sower from Babylon and him that handleth the sickle,** or scythe, **in the time of harvest,** so that both sowers and reapers would be destroyed, and there could be no harvesting in the entire country; **for fear of the oppressing sword they shall turn every one to his people, and they shall flee every one to his own land,** the strangers in the country getting ready to preserve their lives before the threatening catastrophe comes. Over against this fate of Babylon is placed the deliverance of Judah from oppression and exile. V. 17. **Israel is a scattered sheep,** like a lonely sheep driven away from its flock, **the lions have driven him away,** the enemies chasing him far from his homeland; **first, the king of Assyria hath devoured him,** especially in the campaigns at the time of Hezekiah; **and last, this Nebuchadrezzar, king of Babylon, hath broken his bones,** like a beast of prey striking down his victim. V. 18. **Therefore, thus saith the Lord of hosts, the God of Israel, Behold, I will punish the king of Babylon and his land as I have punished the king of Assyria,** whose judgment had already been brought about. V. 19. **And I will bring Israel,** His own congregation, **again to his habitation, and he shall feed on Carmel and Bashan,** occupying the richest sections of his fertile land, **and his soul shall be satisfied upon Mount Ephraim and Gilead,** the northern part of Canaan, which included the rich Valley of Jezreel. V. 20. **In those days and in that time, saith the Lord,** the prophecy now again turning to the Messianic trend, **the iniquity of Israel shall be sought for, and there shall be none,** no longer any guilt would be charged against it; **and the sins of Judah, and they shall not be found; for I will pardon them whom I reserve,** granting them forgiveness and pardon by virtue of the Messiah's merits. If enemies of the Lord, whom He, for any reason whatever, has used as His instruments to carry out His plans, become overbearing and insolent as a consequence, He readily plunges them from the height of their pride to the depths of humiliation and confusion.

THE ENEMIES OF BABYLON SUMMONED TO THE ATTACK. — V. 21. **Go up against the land of Merathaim,** "of double defiance," a name applied to Babylon on account of its rebellion against Jehovah and His commandments, **even against it and against the inhabitants of Pekod,** "of visitation," since Babylon was now to be visited by the punishment of God; **waste and utterly destroy after them, saith the Lord,** to the point of total extermination, **and do according to all that I have commanded thee,** the heathen power here being regarded as the servant of Jehovah in carrying out His counsel of destruction upon Babylon. V. 22. **A sound of battle is in the land,** the din of war, **and of great destruction.** V. 23. **How is the hammer of the whole earth,** as Babylon is called on account of the fact that the Lord used it to strike and destroy many nations, **cut asunder and broken!** itself subject to crushing blows. **How is Babylon become a desolation among the nations!** so that men stand aghast at the horror of her downfall. V. 24. **I have laid a snare for thee, and thou art also taken, O Babylon, and thou wast not aware,** the calamity overtaking her before she realized it; **thou art found and also caught because thou hast striven against the Lord.** When Cyrus took the city, his stratagem in diverting the waters of the Euphrates caught the inhabitants by surprise to such an extent that parts of the city were in the hands of his soldiers before those living in its center were aware of it. V. 25. **The Lord hath opened His armory and hath brought forth the weapons of His indignation,** Jehovah Himself going forth to battle; **for this is the work of the Lord God of hosts in the land of the Chaldeans,** His business being to punish them for their obstinacy. V. 26. **Come against her from the utmost border,** from the most remote corner of the earth, or, "all men, down to the very last," **open her storehouses; cast her up as heaps,** that is, all the plunder of the city, **and destroy her utterly; let nothing of her be left,** the city with all its possessions and treasures was to be burned with fire. V. 27. **Slay all her bullocks,** her entire population; **let them go down to the slaughter. Woe unto them! for their day is come, the time of their visitation,** their punishment at the hands of Jehovah. V. 28. **The voice of them that flee and escape out of the land of Babylon,** the fugitives saving their lives in the midst of the general destruction, **to declare in Zion the vengeance of the Lord, our God, the vengeance of His Temple,** for by the destruction of Babylon the Lord punished the Chaldeans for their profanation of His Sanctuary on Zion. Once more the call to carry out the judgment of the Lord upon Babylon goes forth. V. 29. **Call together the archers against Babylon,** for the siege of the city; **all ye that bend the bow, camp against it round about,** leaving no loophole for escape; **let none thereof escape. Recompense her according to her work,** cp. v. 15; **according to all that she hath done, do unto her,** paying her back in her own coin; **for she hath been proud against the Lord, against the Holy One of Israel,** this pride being the fundamental transgression and fault of Babylon, a form of blasphemy challenging the Lord's honor. V. 30. **Therefore shall her young men fall in the streets, and all her men of war shall be cut off in that day, saith the Lord.** Cp. chap. 49, 26. V. 31. **Behold, I am against thee, O thou most proud, saith the Lord God of hosts,** coming to teach her humility; **for thy day is come, the time that I will visit thee,** to bring His punishment upon her in full measure. V. 32. **And the most proud shall stumble and fall,** literally, "Then pride totters and falls," the abstract being used to emphasize Babylon's guilt, **and none shall raise him up; and I will kindle a fire in his cities, and it shall devour all round about him,** the smaller cities sharing the fate of the metropolis. V. 33. **Thus saith the Lord of hosts, The children of Israel and the children of Judah were oppressed together,** in the captivity of the exile, and all that took them captives held them fast, were still holding them at the time when this prophecy was given; they refused to let them go, so that it might seem as though deliverance were a matter far beyond any possibility. Over against this, however, stands the strong assurance of Jehovah. V. 34. **Their Redeemer is strong, the Lord of hosts is His name,** the Commander of all the heavenly armies; **He shall throughly plead their cause,** taking their part with all needed energy, **that He may give rest to the land,** so that Judah would once more enjoy peace and security, **and, on the contrary, disquiet the inhabitants of Babylon,** who thought that they were altogether secure against all enemies. In order to take the part of His people with the proper zeal, the Lord now calls upon the sword to perform its work against the Chaldeans. V. 35. **A sword is upon the Chaldeans, saith the Lord, and upon the inhabitants of Babylon and upon her princes and upon her wise men,** for whom Chaldea was noted. The sentence is really in the form of an exclamation, a call, bidding the sword do its work of slaughtering. V. 36. **A sword is upon the liars,** the idle talkers, the astrologers of Babylon, **and they shall dote,** become fools with their empty and deceitful statements; **a sword is upon her mighty men,** the Chaldean champions, **and they shall be dismayed.** V. 37. **A sword is upon their horses and upon their chariots,** which were her boast in warfare, **and upon all the mingled people that are in the midst of her,** her mercenaries and allies, **and they shall become as women,** weak and utterly unable for effective resistance; **a sword is upon her treasures,** the wealth which she had accumulated in the course of her campaigns, **and they shall be robbed.** V. 38. **A drought is upon her waters, and they shall be dried up,** the dams and irrigation canals being destroyed by the invading army; **for it is the land of graven images, and they are mad upon their idols,** literally, "their objects of horror or terror," for the images which are usually found in heathen sanctuaries are really more likely to frighten than to attract. They have indulged in gross and revolting idolatry and must therefore bear their iniquity. V. 39. **Therefore the wild beasts of the desert with the wild beasts of the islands,** the jackals, **shall dwell there, and the owls,** literally, "daughters of crying," that is, the female ostriches, **shall dwell therein, and it shall be no more inhabited forever, neither shall it be dwelt in from generation to generation.** Cp. Is. 13, 20—22; 34, 14. V. 40. **As God overthrew Sodom and Gomorrah and the neighbor cities thereof,** the smaller towns of Admah and Zeboim, **saith the Lord, so shall no man abide there,** in Babylon, **neither shall any son of man dwell therein.** V. 41. **Behold, a people shall come from the North,** the armies of the Medes and Persians, **and a great nation and many kings shall be raised up from the coasts of the earth,** from the remote parts of Asia. V. 42. **They shall hold the bow and the lance,** weapons of attack; **they are cruel and will not show mercy,** give no quarter in battle; **their voice shall roar like the sea,** in their fierce battle-cry, **and they shall ride upon horses, every one put in array like a man to the battle,** all of them a unit in their desire to work mischief, **against thee, O daughter of Babylon.** The very words the prophet used to describe the calamity which would come upon Judah, chap. 6, 22—24, are here used to picture the destruction which would strike the Chaldeans. V. 43. **The king of Babylon hath heard the report of them,** of their victorious advance, **and his hands waxed feeble,** terror so overwhelmed him that he did not even attempt resistance; **anguish took hold of him and pangs as of a woman in travail.** V. 44. **Behold,** he, the invader, **shall come up like a lion from the swelling of Jordan,** from his den in its thickets, **unto the habitation of the strong,** chap. 49, 19; **but I will make them,** the Babylonians, **suddenly run away from her,** from the dwelling where they felt so secure; **and who is a chosen man that I may appoint over her?** to carry out the Lord's counsel. **For who is like Me? And who will appoint Me the time? And who is that shepherd that will stand before Me?** V. 45. **Therefore hear ye the counsel of the Lord that He hath taken against Babylon, and His purposes that He hath purposed against the land of the Chaldeans, Surely the least of the flock shall draw them out,** or, "verily, they will be dragged along," the feeble little sheep, **surely he shall make their habitation desolate with them,** their pasturage, their own homeland, being amazed concerning them. V. 46. **At the noise of the taking of Babylon the earth is moved,** that is, when that cry, "Babylon is taken," goes forth, the earth trembles, **and the cry is heard among the nations.** Cp. chap. 49, 19—21. In the history of nations, as well as in that of individual people, it is true that God resisteth the proud and giveth grace to the humble.

CHAPTER 51.

Continuation of the Prophecy against Babylon.

THE THREAT OF JEHOVAH IN ITS VARIOUS FORMS. — V. 1. **Thus saith the Lord, Behold, I will raise up against Babylon and against them that dwell in the midst,** literally, "in the heart," **of them that rise up against Me,** the inhabitants of the insurgent country, **a destroying wind,** or "the spirit of destruction," v. 2. **and will send unto Babylon fanners,** whose work it was to separate the wheat from the chaff by casting up and scattering the threshed grain, **that shall fan her and shall empty her land,** sweeping away the guilty like chaff before the wind; **for in the day of trouble they shall be against her round about,** attacking from all sides. V. 3. **Against him that bendeth let the archer bend his bow,** sure to put to death every one who attempts resistance, **and against him that lifteth himself up in his brigandine,** having put on his armor for battle; **and spare ye not her young men,** the ablest warriors, **destroy ye utterly all her host.** V. 4. **Thus the slain shall fall in the land of the Chaldeans, and they that are thrust through,** pierced by arrow or lance, **in her streets.** All this would happen on account of Israel's just cause against the Chaldeans. V. 5. **For Israel hath not been forsaken nor Judah of his God, of the Lord of hosts,** the chosen people of Jehovah being still in His care, under His gracious protection; **though their land was filled with sin against the Holy One of Israel,** rather, "but the land of the Chaldeans is filled with guilt," because they refused to accept the true God in spite of the many manifestations of His power and glory in their midst as brought to their attention, for instance, through Daniel and his friends. Therefore the Lord addresses Himself to the members of His chosen people living in Babylon, urging the proper behavior at the time of Babylon's downfall. V. 6. **Flee out of the midst of Babylon, and deliver every man his soul,** not only his physical life, but his spiritual life as well; **be not cut off in her iniquity,** by taking part in the idolatry which brought destruction upon her; **for this is the time of the Lord's vengeance; He will render unto her a recompense.** Note the contrast between human transgression, on the one hand, and the righteous punishment of the Lord, on the other. This is brought out most strongly by the picture of the golden cup. V. 7. **Babylon hath been a golden cup in the Lord's hand,** a nation noted for power and glory, all this due to the Lord's blessing, **that made all the earth drunken,** namely, in pouring out the wine of His wrath upon all whom He desired to punish; **the nations have drunken of her wine; therefore the nations are mad,** intoxicated, bereft of reason, bound for destruction. V. 8. **Babylon is suddenly fallen and destroyed,** no longer a golden cup, but a fragile glass; **howl for her,** make a lamentation for her; **take balm for her pain,** a balsam to heal her bruises, **if so be she may be healed,** if there is still a possibility of effecting a cure. But the representatives of the various nations assembled in Babylon state that their attempts are vain. V. 9. **We would have healed Babylon, but she is not healed,** it is impossible to mend her hurt. **Forsake her,** so they now admonish one another, **and let us go every one into his own country; for her judgment reacheth unto heaven,** her guilt crying to the Lord to be avenged, **and is lifted up even to the skies,** it towers up to the clouds. V. 10. **The Lord hath brought forth our righteousness,** the just cause of the captives, so the Israelites in their midst declare. **Come and let us declare in Zion the work of the Lord, our God.** Cp. Ps. 102, 13—21. The Lord now calls upon the northern nations to make their attack upon Babylon. V. 11. **Make bright the arrows,** polishing and sharpening them; **gather the shields,** literally, "fill the shields," slipping their straps over their arms for immediate use. **The Lord hath raised up the spirit of the kings of the Medes,** the conquerors of Babylon; **for His device is against Babylon to destroy it,** He has definitely made up His mind to that effect; **because it is the vengeance of the Lord, the vengeance of His Temple,** whose profanation at the hands of the Chaldeans must be punished. V. 12. **Set up the standard upon the walls of Babylon,** raising a flag or emblem to indicate a particular point of attack, **make the watch strong,** so that the siege would be equally effective along the whole line, **set up the watchmen,** against the city, so that there would be no loophole of escape for the besieged, **prepare the ambushes,** in order to take the first opportunity of entering into the city; **for the Lord hath both devised and done that which He spake against the inhabitants of Babylon,** that is, what He had determined upon He would most certainly carry out against the wicked city. V. 13. **O thou that dwellest upon many waters,** the Euphrates with all its tributary canals, irrigation ditches, and swamps being included here, **abundant in treasures,** both on account of its natural resources and on account of the plunder which had been amassed in the city, **thine end is come and the measure of thy covetousness,** for there would be no more unjust enrichment through robbery and plunder after the fall of the city. V. 14. **The Lord of hosts hath sworn by Himself,** by His own soul or life, **saying, Surely I will fill thee with men as with caterpillars,** rather, "Have I filled thee with men as with locusts?" **and they shall**

lift up a shout against thee, that is, numerous as the people of Babylon were, the invaders would be more numerous and would sing a "Hedad," the shout of the vine-dressers, the song of slaughter, upon the city. V. 15. **He hath made the earth by His power, He hath established the world by His wisdom, and hath stretched out the heaven by His understanding.** V. 16. **When He uttereth His voice, there is a multitude of waters in the heavens, and He causeth the vapors to ascend from the ends of the earth; He maketh lightnings with rain and bringeth forth the wind out of His treasures.** V. 17. **Every man is brutish by his knowledge; every founder is confounded by the graven image; for his molten image is falsehood, and there is no breath in them.** V. 18. **They are vanity, the work of errors; in the time of their visitation they shall perish.** V. 19. **The Portion of Jacob is not like them; for He is the Former of all things, and Israel is the rod of His inheritance; the Lord of hosts is His name.** This paragraph is repeated from chapter 10, 12—16, where the prophet described the almighty power of the living God and pointed to the destruction of the idols at the time of the great judgment. In chapter 10 he intended to combat the fear of the idolatrous people concerning the power of the heathen gods; here he wants to overthrow the confidence of the Chaldeans in their idols, telling them that their gods are powerless before the omnipotence of Jehovah, and that Israel would realize this fact when the judgment would be brought about. By the overthrow of Babylon, Jehovah proved Himself to be the Creator of Israel, the Former of the universe, the one true God. The next paragraph is addressed to Babylon, as the "hammer of nations," chap. 50, 23, and the narrative ought to be given in the present or in the past tense, as a prophetic statement. V. 20. **Thou art My battle-ax,** a hammer, a club used for total destruction, **and weapons of war,** all instruments of warfare being comprehended in this term; **for with thee will I break in pieces the nations, and with thee will I destroy kingdoms,** Jehovah had, in fact, used Babylon to overthrow nations; v. 21. **and with thee will I break in pieces the horse and his rider, and with thee will I break in pieces the chariot and his rider,** the armies of the enemies with all their divisions; v. 22. **with thee also will I break in pieces man and woman, and with thee will I break in pieces old and young, and with thee will I break in pieces the young man and the maid,** every age and every station; v. 23. **I will also break in pieces with thee the shepherd and his flock; and with thee will I break in pieces the husbandman and his yoke of oxen,** all the laboring classes; **and with thee will I break in pieces captains and rulers,** the highest dignitaries of the realm. But at the same time the hammer would itself be overthrown, both actions taking place at the same time in the sight of the eternal God. V. 24. **And I will render unto Babylon and to all the inhabitants of Chaldea all their evil that they have done in Zion in your sight,** before the eyes of the Jews, when they defiled the Lord's Sanctuary, **saith the Lord.** V. 25. **Behold, I am against thee, O destroying mountain, saith the Lord,** Babylon called thus on account of the physical and moral destruction which it brought upon the nations by a false use of its great power, **which destroyest all the earth; and I will stretch out Mine hand upon thee and roll thee down from the rocks,** which it occupied, as it were, in its position on the summit of the mountains above all nations, **and will make thee a burnt mountain,** a volcano extinct on account of having its substance devoured by fire, so that it could no more serve as a rock-foundation for further kingdoms of destruction. V. 26. **And they shall not take of thee a stone for a corner nor a stone for foundations; but thou shalt be desolate forever, saith the Lord,** perpetual ruins. The great mass of materials of which Babylon was built to this day are lying more or less decomposed in the mountains of rubbish which mark the site of the once magnificent city. Thus the word of the Lord was fulfilled with its usual exactness.

THE WORK OF THE SPOILERS. — V. 27. **Set ye up a standard in the land,** around which the attacking forces might rally in order to proceed against Babylon, **blow the trumpet among the nations,** summoning them to be mustered for war, **prepare the nations against her, call together against her the kingdoms of Ararat,** Upper Armenia, **Minni,** Lower Armenia, and **Ashchenaz,** a country bordering on Armenia; **appoint a captain against her,** so that there would be efficient leadership; **cause the horses to come up as the rough caterpillars,** like hairy-crested grasshoppers. V. 28. **Prepare against her the nations with the kings of the Medes,** the satraps, or princes, of the empire, **the captains thereof,** the governors of the smaller provinces, **and all the rulers thereof, and all the land of his dominion.** This detailed enumeration is made for the purpose of increasing the impression of great and irresistible power. V. 29. **And the land shall tremble and sorrow,** as with a great earthquake; **for every purpose of the Lord shall be performed against Babylon,** every plan that He had decided upon, **to make the land of Babylon a desolation without an inhabitant.** V. 30. **The mighty men of Babylon have forborne to fight,** they gave up resistance, they no longer waged offensive warfare, **they have remained in their holds,** what they believed to be impregnable fortresses; **their might hath failed, they became as women,** altogether discouraged, not daring to offer active opposition; **they,** the enemies, **have burned her dwelling-places, her bars are broken.** When the stratagem of Cyrus in diverting the stream of the Euphrates succeeded and his soldiers entered the city through its empty bed, they found little or no opposition and could easily open the city gates from within. V. 31. **One post,** or courier, **shall run to meet another, and one messenger to meet another,** coming from all parts of the city with their information concerning the taking of the city, **to show the king of Babylon,** to bring him the news, **that his city is taken at one end,** that is, to its utmost end, every part in the hands of the enemies, v. 32. **and that the passages are stopped,** the places where the river was usually crossed being occupied by the enemy's forces, **and the reeds they have burned with fire,** taking away even the last means of defense, **and the men of war are affrighted.** Such was the message which the couriers would bring from every side. V. 33. **For thus saith the Lord of hosts, the God of Israel, The daughter of Babylon is like a threshing-floor,** the whole empire being included in this figure; **it is time to thresh her,** by the customary treading or stamping by means of which the kernels of grain were separated from their hulls; **yet a little while, and the time of her harvest shall come,** when she would be trodden under foot. The inhabitants of Israel and Judah are now introduced with a lament showing the reason for the Lord's punishment upon Babylon. V. 34. **Nebuchadrezzar, the king of Babylon, hath devoured me, he hath crushed me, he hath made me an empty vessel,** discarding them like a useless dish, **he hath swallowed me up like a dragon,** like some monster of the deep, **he hath filled his belly with my delicates,** with all the finest foods, **he hath cast me out.** The heaping of similar expressions brings out the greatness of the ruin which had come upon Judah. V. 35. **The violence done to me and to my flesh be upon Babylon, shall the inhabitant of Zion say,** in pleading for justice against the oppressor; **and my blood upon the inhabitants of Chaldea, shall Jerusalem say.** V. 36. **Therefore, thus saith the Lord,** in answering this cry of His children, **Behold, I will plead thy cause and take vengeance for thee,** acting as the Advocate in defending the rights of His people; **and I will dry up her sea,** the Euphrates with all its channels, canals, and swamps, **and make her springs dry,** so that she would no longer have a rich supply of water to give fertility to her land. V. 37. **And Babylon shall become heaps,** abandoned ruins, **a dwelling-place for dragons,** of jackals, **an astonishment, and an hissing, without an inhabitant.** V. 38. **They shall roar together like lions,** shouting in drunken revelry; **they shall yell as lions' whelps,** growling over their food. This probably is a reference to the fact that Babylon was taken on a night when its rulers and leading citizens were attending a drunken debauch. V. 39. **In their heat I will make their feasts,** or, "For their intoxication I prepare them a drinking-bout," **and I will make them drunken that they may rejoice and sleep a perpetual sleep,** being overcome by death, **and not wake, saith the Lord.** V. 40. **I will bring them down like lambs to the slaughter, like rams with he-goats,** all the classes of Babylon's population being included. And here the prophet inserts a word of astonishment over the downfall of Babylon. V. 41. **How is Sheshach taken!** cp. chap. 25, 26. **And how is the praise of the whole earth surprised!** namely, Babylon, which was an object of envy and praise throughout the world. **How is Babylon become an astonishment among the nations!** an object of surprised horror. V. 42. **The sea is come up upon Babylon,** namely, in the hostile armies which would flood the land; **she is covered with the multitude of the waves thereof.** The image is based upon the action of the Euphrates, which, without the restraint of dikes and irrigation canals, would sometimes rise so high as to overflow the entire valley. V. 43. **Her cities are a desolation,** reverting back to the desert stage, **a dry land and a wilderness,** where arid steppes stretched interminably, **a land wherein no man dwelleth, neither doth any son of man pass thereby.** V. 44. **And I will punish Bel in Babylon,** the chief deity of the Babylonians, **and I will bring forth out of his mouth that which he hath swallowed up,** taking away from him what he had robbed and devoured through the hands of those who worshiped him; **and the nations shall not flow together any more unto him,** flocking to Babylon in streams to consecrate their treasures to him; **yea, the wall of Babylon shall fall,** so that the city would be open to all enemies. The destruction of Babylon thus being decided, the people of God are admonished to leave its confines. V. 45. **My people, go ye out of the midst of her,** fleeing out of the city appointed to ruin, **and deliver ye every man his soul from the fierce anger of the Lord,** which would be poured out upon Babylon. V. 46. **And lest your heart faint and ye fear for the rumor that shall be heard in the land,** namely, tales of war and of acts of violence, which should not daunt the people of Jehovah: **a rumor shall both come one year, and after that, in another year, shall come a rumor and violence in the land, ruler against ruler,** so that rebellion and revolution preceded the fall of the empire. Some commentators find here a sequence of events for the guidance of the Jews; for the first rumor spoke of the uprising of the Medes, the second of the approach of Cyrus, while this event fixed the time when the Jews should prepare to leave the city of Babylon. V. 47. **Therefore, behold, the days come that I will do judgment upon the graven images of Babylon,** executing His sentence of destruction upon them; **and her whole land shall be confounded,** be put to shame by His punishment, **and all her slain shall fall in the midst of her,** practically all her inhabitants being included in the slaughter. V. 48. **Then the heaven and the earth and all that is therein shall sing for Babylon,** rejoicing over her fall; **for the spoilers shall come unto her from the North, saith the Lord,** and the sentence executed by him is the cause of their jubilation. V. 49. **As Babylon hath caused the slain of Israel to fall,** being engaged in their slaughter, **so at Babylon,** by a just recompense, **shall fall the slain of all the earth,** for representatives of the various nations of the earth were at Babylon at the time of her overthrow. The prophet now summarizes the guilt and the punishment of Babylon. V. 50. **Ye that have escaped the sword,** at or before the taking of the city, **go away, stand not still,** in order not to share the fate of Babylon. **Remember the Lord afar off,** Jehovah, the God of the covenant, **and let Jerusalem come into your mind,** so that the thought of the return to their home country and its capital would immediately occur to them. But the prophet now, in the name of the congregation, gives utterance to an objection on their part, with the purpose of removing it. V. 51. **We are confounded,** so the Jews might say, **because we have heard reproach,** they had recollections only of the deepest shame and humiliation in connection with Jerusalem and the Temple; **shame hath covered our faces, for strangers are come into the sanctuaries of the Lord's house,** even into those parts which were forbidden to the heathen. But the prophet anticipates and removes these objections. V. 52. **Wherefore, behold, the days come, saith the Lord, that I will do judgment upon her graven images,** the idols of Babylon, this being Jehovah's answer upon their taunt in burning His Temple as though He were powerless to avenge Himself; **and through all her land the wounded shall groan,** stricken down by the Lord's mighty hand. V. 53. **Though Babylon should mount up to heaven,** in an attempt to storm the stronghold of the Lord itself, **and though she should fortify the height of her strength,** literally, "make inaccessible the height of her firmness," so that her walls would rise up to a precipitous height, apparently impregnable, **yet from Me shall spoilers come unto her, saith the Lord,** so that she would be overthrown and destroyed. V. 54. **A sound of a cry cometh from Babylon,** as the invading enemies begin their work of destruction, **and great destruction from the land of the Chaldeans,** v. 55. **because the Lord hath spoiled Babylon, and destroyed out of her the great voice,** the deafening din of the boastful revelers; **when her waves,** the surging streams of her inhabitants, **do roar like great waters, a noise of their voice is uttered,** it sounds far and wide, in a mighty commotion. V. 56. **Because the spoiler is come upon her, even upon Babylon, and her mighty men are taken,** her greatest champions and heroes being obliged to submit without a struggle, since resistance was impossible, **every one of their bows is broken,** all their weapons rendered useless, **for the Lord God of recompenses shall surely requite,** rewarding them the evil which they had committed, paying back their wickedness as they deserved. V. 57. **And I will make drunk her princes and her wise men,** the counselors of the kingdom, **her captains and her rulers and her mighty men,** all those who were at the head of the nation, both in peace and in war; **and they shall sleep a perpetual sleep, and not wake,** namely, the sleep of death, **saith the King, whose name is the Lord of hosts.** V. 58. **Thus saith the Lord of hosts,** in a final summary of His warning and threat against Babylon, **The broad walls of Babylon,** which, according to some accounts, were so broad that two four-horse chariots could pass anywhere, **shall be utterly broken,** demolished completely; **and her high gates,** the one hundred magnificent gates of brass, **shall be burned with fire; and the people shall labor in vain,** in erecting the mighty wall which was their pride, **and the folk in the fire,** rather, "for the fire," their handiwork being consumed in the general destruction, **and they shall be weary.** Cp. Hab. 2, 13. The prophecy thus having been stated, the chapter closes with a historical conclusion concerning the manner in which the prophecy was delivered. V. 59. **The word which Jeremiah, the prophet, commanded Seraiah, the son of Neriah, the son of Maaseiah,** evidently a brother of Baruch, **when he went with Zedekiah, the king of Judah,** rather, "in behalf of Zedekiah," on an embassy for him, **into Babylon in the fourth year of his reign,** six years before Jerusalem was destroyed by the Babylonians. **And this Seraiah was a quiet prince,** literally, "prince of the resting-place," that is, marshal of the caravan, he who had charge of the journey. V. 60. **So Jeremiah wrote in a book all the evil that should come upon Babylon, even all these words that are written against Babylon,** as contained in the last two chapters. V. 61. **And Jeremiah said to Seraiah, When thou comest to Babylon and shalt see,** rather, "then observe very carefully," **and shalt read all these words,** v. 62. **then shalt**

thou say, O Lord, Thou hast spoken against this place to cut it off that none shall remain in it, neither man nor beast, but that it shall be desolate forever, reminding the Lord, as it were, that the threats of His prophecy must be fulfilled. V. 63. **And it shall be, when thou hast made an end of reading this book,** the communication contained on this roll, **that thou shalt bind a stone to it and cast it into the midst of Euphrates,** in a symbolical act expressing the fulfilment of the prophecy upon Babylon, v. 64. **and thou shalt say, Thus shall Babylon sink and shall not rise from the evil that I will bring upon her; and they,** the Babylonians, **shall be weary,** they shall be so overcome that it would be impossible for them to recover their strength. **Thus far are the words of Jeremiah,** the last chapter being in the nature of a historical epilog added by some other inspired writer. To proclaim the Word of God to friend and foe alike, regardless of consequences, that is a characteristic of the true servant of the Lord.

CHAPTER 52.

Historical Conclusion of the Book of Jeremiah's Prophecies.

CIRCUMSTANCES ATTENDING THE CAPTURE OF JERUSALEM. — V. 1. **Zedekiah was one and twenty years old when he began to reign,** when Nebuchadnezzar made him a tributary ruler over Judah, **and he reigned eleven years in Jerusalem. And his mother's name was Hamutal, the daughter of Jeremiah of Libnah.** Note that the entire account of the chapter is parallel and, in part, supplementary to the narrative of 2 Kings 24, 18—25, 7 and Jer. 39, 1—7. V. 2. **And he did that which was evil in the eyes of the Lord, according to all that Jehoiakim had done.** Cp. 2 Chron. 36, 11—13. V. 3. **For through the anger of the Lord it came to pass in Jerusalem and Judah,** His wrath over their idolatry causing Him to cast them from His presence and to permit the rebellion of Zedekiah, which resulted in the final overthrow of the southern kingdom, **till He had cast them out from His presence, that Zedekiah rebelled against the king of Babylon.** V. 4. **And it came to pass in the ninth year of his reign, in the tenth month, in the tenth day of the month, that Nebuchadrezzar, king of Babylon, came, he and all his army, against Jerusalem and pitched against it,** establishing the camp of the besieging army, **and built forts against it round about,** very likely towers of wood used for purposes of observation and as foundations for casting missiles into the city. V. 5. **So the city was besieged unto the eleventh year of King Zedekiah.** V. 6. **And in the fourth month, in the ninth day of the month, the famine was sore in the city,** reaching a height which made conditions very serious, **so that there was no bread for the people of the land.** V. 7. **Then the city was broken up,** the enemies penetrating through the outer line of defenses, **and all the men of war fled and went forth out of the city by night, by the way of the gate between the two walls, which was by the king's garden; (now, the Chaldeans were by the city round about;) and they went by the way of the plain,** down toward the lowlands of the Jordan, near Jericho. Cp. chap. 39, 4—7. V. 8. **But the army of the Chaldeans pursued after the king and overtook Zedekiah in the plains of Jericho; and all his army was scattered from him,** for in a panic, as they were, there was no thought of real resistance. V. 9. **Then they took the king and carried him up unto the king of Babylon, to Riblah, in the land of Hamath,** where Nebuchadnezzar had meanwhile established his headquarters, leaving the taking of Jerusalem to one of his generals, Nebuzar-adan, **where he gave judgment upon him,** for perjury and rebellion. V. 10. **And the king of Babylon slew the sons of Zedekiah before his eyes; he slew also all the princes of Judah in Riblah,** because they had agreed to, and promoted, the rebellion of Zedekiah. V. 11. **Then he put out the eyes of Zedekiah; and the king of Babylon bound him in chains,** which meant the extremity of humiliation, **and carried him to Babylon, and put him in prison till the day of his death,** literally, "in the house of visitations," in penal servitude, which may have been a little less dishonorable than incarceration, for which reason he may also have had an honorable burial. Cp. chap. 34, 1—5. V. 12. **Now, in the fifth month, in the tenth day of the month, which was the nineteenth year of Nebuchadrezzar, king of Babylon, came Nebuzar-adan, captain of the guard,** one of the chief officers of the Chaldean king, **which served the king of Babylon, into Jerusalem,** or, having started from Riblah on the seventh, he actually reached Jerusalem on the tenth, 2 Kings 25, 8, v. 13. **and burned the house of the Lord,** the magnificent Temple of Solomon, **and the king's house; and all the houses of Jerusalem and all the houses of the great men,** all the prominent buildings of the city, **burned he with fire;** v. 14. **and all the army of the Chaldeans that were with the captain of the guard brake down all the walls of Jerusalem round about,** so that all its fortifications were demolished down to the very foundations. V. 15. **Then Nebuzar-adan, the captain of the guard, carried** away captive certain of the poor of the people and the residue of the people that remained in the city, and those that fell away, that fell to the king of Babylon, and the rest of the multitude. Cp. chap. 39, 9. Thus the capture of the city was effected in exact agreement with the prophecy of the Lord against Jerusalem.

DISPOSITION OF THE SPOIL AND OF THE CAPTIVES. — V. 16. **But Nebuzar-adan, the captain of the guard, left certain of the poor of the land,** of those who had no possessions in money or goods, **for vine-dressers and for husbandmen,** so that the country would not revert to a wilderness on account of total neglect. V. 17. **Also the pillars of brass that were in the house of the Lord,** on either side of the main entrance of the Sanctuary, 1 Kings 7, 15, **and the bases, and the brazen sea that was in the house of the Lord, the Chaldeans brake,** in order to make all these pieces fit for transportation, **and carried all the brass of them to Babylon.** V. 18. **The caldrons also,** large pots used for sacrificial worship, **and the shovels, and the snuffers, and the bowls, and the spoons,** vessels for incense, **and all the vessels of brass wherewith they ministered, took they away,** all those used for the altar of burnt offerings in the Court of the Priests. V. 19. **And the basins, and the fire-pans, and the bowls, and the caldrons, and the candlesticks, and the spoons, and the cups,** all these used chiefly in the ministrations of the Holy Place; **that which was of gold in gold, and that which was of silver in silver,** in either case of solid metal, not of some cheap alloy or merely plated, **took the captain of the guard away.** V. 20. **The two pillars, one sea, and twelve brazen bulls that were under the bases,** 1 Kings 7, 23—26, **which King Solomon had made in the house of the Lord. The brass of all these vessels was without weight,** its mass beyond calculation. V. 21. **And concerning the pillars, the height of one pillar was eighteen cubits, and a fillet of twelve cubits did compass it,** that, in round numbers, being the circumference of either of the pillars; **and the thickness thereof was four fingers; it was hollow.** The thirty-five cubits of 2 Chron. 3, 15 either refer to a different cubit, or they give the sum total of both pillars less the bases. V. 22. **And a chapiter,** or capital, **of brass was upon it, and the height of one chapiter,** that is, of its upper part, where it curved away from the shaft, **was five cubits, with network and pomegranates upon the chapiters round about, all of brass,** in the nature of ornaments in chains or festoons. **The second pillar also and the pomegranates were like unto these.** V. 23. **And there were ninety and six pomegranates on a side,** set towards the four winds or sides; **and all the pomegranates upon the network were an hundred round about,** including those on the corners of the capitals. V. 24. **And the captain of the guard took Seraiah, the chief priest,** not identical w[ith] the man named chap. 51, 59, **and Zephaniah, the second priest,** a very important member of the hierarchy, **and the three keepers of the door,** officers of the Temple-guard. V. 25. **He took also out of the city an eunuch, which had the charge of the men of war,** the commander of the city forces, **and seven men of them that were near the king's person,** of the king's intimate counselors, **which were found in the city; and the principal scribe of the host,** an officer in the direct service of the commander-in-chief, **who mustered the people of the land,** enrolling them for military service; **and threescore men of the people of the land that were found in the midst of the city,** either leaders in the rebellion or such as had distinguished themselves in the defense of the city. V. 26. **So Nebuzar-adan, the captain of the guard, took them and brought them to the king of Babylon to Riblah.** V. 27. **And the king of Babylon smote them,** for the part they had taken in the rebellion of Judah, **and put them to death in Riblah, in the land of Hamath,** the Syrian province in the extreme northern part of Palestine. **Thus Judah was carried away captive out of his own land.** There follows a summary or enumeration of the prominent captives. V. 28. **This is the people whom Nebuchadrezzar carried away captive: in the seventh year,** at the first captivity under Jehoiachin, **three thousand Jews and three and twenty,** these being of the tribe of Judah only, those from other tribes being more than twice as many; v. 29. **in the eighteenth year of Nebuchadrezzar,** after his actual accession to the throne, but nineteen years after he had gotten into power, 2 Kings 25, 8, **he carried away captive from Jerusalem eight hundred thirty and two persons;** v. 30. **in the three and twentieth year of Nebuchadrezzar, Nebuzar-adan, the captain of the guard, carried away captive of the Jews seven hundred forty and five persons; all the persons,** evidently of the tribe of Judah alone, not including any of the other tribes who had sought and found refuge in Jerusalem since the fall of the northern kingdom, **were four thousand and six hundred,** not including the general multitude, and the women and children. V. 31. **And it came to pass in the seven-and-thirtieth year of the captivity of Jehoiachin, king of Judah, in the twelfth month, in the five and twentieth day of the month,** the decree being issued on that day, although it was not carried out till two days later, 2 Kings 25, 27, **that Evil-merodach, king of Babylon,** son and successor of Nebuchadrezzar, **in the first year of his reign, lifted up the head of Jehoia-**

chin, king of Judah, and brought him forth out of prison, delivering him from the special bondage in which he had been held all these years, v. 32. **and spake kindly unto him and set his throne above the throne of the kings that were with him in Babylon,** captive monarchs of other conquered nations, v. 33. **and changed his prison-garments,** witnesses of his deep humiliation; **and he did continually eat bread before him all the days of his life.** V. 34. **And for his diet there was a continual diet given him of the king of Babylon, every day a portion, until the day of his death, all the days of his life.** Cp. 2 Kings 25, 27—30. The same Lord who humbles the proud transgressors is able also to exalt those who turn to Him in true repentance.

THE LAMENTATIONS OF JEREMIAH.

INTRODUCTION.

The Jews had the custom of singing songs of lamentation after the death of some beloved person, some of these elegies being of unusual beauty and power. Cp. 2 Sam. 1, 17; 3, 33. In a similar way they mourned over the destruction of cities and countries. Cp. Amos 7, 1; Ezek. 26, 17.

It is no matter for surprise, then, that we find an entire group of such songs concerning the destruction of Jerusalem and the devastation of Judah, the poems contained in the Lamentations of Jeremiah. These elegies were evidently composed while Jerusalem lay in ruins, some time between 587 and 536. And since the author appears as an eye-witness of the catastrophe, a fact which is brought out also by the vividness of his presentation, it seems plausible to place the date of the poems in the early decades of the sixth century before Christ.

Both the Jewish Synagog and the Christian Church state that Jeremiah is the author of Lamentations, this statement being made expressly in the introduction to the book which was added by the Greek translators in the version known as the Septuagint. The language of the book is characterized by the same emphasis upon the guilt of the Jews, the frequent repetition of the same expressions and figures of speech, the reference to words of the Law, and a certain broadness and monotony of narration which is so obvious in the Book of Jeremiah. It was natural, therefore, that the various Bible versions placed Lamentations immediately after the book of Jeremiah's prophecy, although they are strictly poetical in character and for this reason might be grouped with Job, the Psalms, and the poetical books of Solomon.

We have five chapters, that is, five poems in the Book of Lamentations, all of them, with the exception of the last, in the form of an alphabetical acrostic, chapter 3 having three verses for every letter of the Hebrew alphabet. Chapter 1 is a lamentation over the exile of the Jews and the misery of the ruined city, chapter 2 a song of Jerusalem's destruction and the mockery of the enemies, chapter 3 an elegy picturing the grievous sufferings of the pious, but also the hope of eventual deliverance, chapter 4 a discourse on the fact that the destruction of the Temple and the distress of the city were well deserved, and chapter 5 a prayer to God that He would not forget the pitiful condition of His stricken people, but give them speedy help.1)

1) Cp. Fuerbringer, *Einleitung in das Alte Testament*, 70—72; *Concordia Bible Class*, May, 1919, 71. 72.

CHAPTER 1.

Lamentation over the Destruction of the City, the Nation, and the Temple.

DESCRIPTION OF THE SHAMEFUL LOT WHICH HAS COME UPON JERUSALEM.—V. 1. **How doth the city sit solitary that was full of people!** It is a strong expression of horrified astonishment over the fact that the formerly populous city is now lonely and deserted, sitting alone in deep mourning. **How is she become as a widow!** She no longer enjoys the fellowship of Jehovah, her Husband, and she has lost her children, who have been killed in battle and carried away into exile. **She that was great among the nations and princess among the provinces,** her rule being accepted more or less continuously in the surrounding provinces from the Brook of Egypt to the Euphrates, **how is she become tributary!** herself condemned to servitude and to the payment of tribute-money. V. 2. **She weepeth sore in the night,** the slumber being driven away from her eyelids by the greatness of her sorrow, **and her tears are on her cheeks,** since they flow without stopping and have no chance to dry; **among all her lovers**, who formerly professed affection for her, **she hath none to comfort her; all her friends**, upon whom she depended for assistance, **have dealt treacherously with her**, deserting her in the midst of the dangers which came upon her; **they are become her enemies**, their former profession of loyalty changing to open hostility. V. 3. **Judah is gone into captivity**, led away into exile, **because of affliction**, the misery upon the country on account of the occupation of the land by the Chaldeans, **and because of great servitude**, the servile work which was included in the tributary service exacted by the conquerors; **she dwelleth among the heathen**, sojourning among them, as it were, in the hope of finding some measure of security; **she findeth no rest**, being disappointed also in this respect; **all her persecutors overtook her between the straits**, so that there was no outlet for her, no chance to escape. V. 4. **The ways of Zion do mourn**, all the roads leading to the capital lying desolate, **because** there are no pilgrims found there, **because none come to the solemn feasts**, the great festivals of the Jewish year; **all her gates are desolate**, for there is no longer the happy traffic of former years; **her priests sigh**, under the heavy oppression which they suffer and because the Temple and its worship are no longer in existence, **her virgins are afflicted**, since their joyful singing no longer enlivened the great festivals, **and she is in bitterness**, she feels her misfortunes with poignant grief. V. 5. **Her adversaries are the chief**, that is, the head, the rulers of Judah, **her enemies prosper**, their good fortune intensifying the darkness of her own calamity; **for the Lord hath afflicted her for the multitude of her transgressions**, the punishment which she was suffering being fully deserved; **her children are gone into captivity before the enemy**, literally, "her infants in absence of strength before the pursuer." V. 6. **And from the daughter of Zion all her beauty is departed**, the presence of Jehovah and His glory in her midst; **her princes are become like harts that find no pasture**, so that they have no strength to flee and escape from the enemy, **and they are gone without strength before the pursuer.** Cp. 2 Kings 25, 3. 4. V. 7. **Jerusalem remembered in the days of her affliction and of her miseries all her pleasant things that she had in the days of old**, the members of the Jewish Church recalling with eager remembrance the glorious evidences of God's blessing which had been theirs, **when her people fell into the hand of the enemy, and none did help her**, the days of her calamity contrasting very strikingly with her former state of blessedness; **the adversaries saw her and did mock at her Sabbaths.** As the Jewish day of rest was a favorite object of mockery on the part of the enemies, so they now thought it a huge joke that a general and lasting Sabbath had come upon their country. V. 8. **Jerusalem hath grievously sinned**, chiefly by joining in the idolatry of Israel and the heathen nations, **therefore she is removed**, as one separated from the congregation on account of legal impurity; **all that honored her despise her because they have seen her nakedness**, her sins and vices having now become known; **yea, she sigheth**, since now at last she has, in a measure, come to the realization of her transgressions, **and turneth backward**, withdrawing from men, so that her shame may no longer be witnessed. V. 9. **Her filthiness is in her skirts**, as of a woman Levitically unclean; **she remembereth not her last end**, she did not consider the result of her persistent iniquity, **therefore she came down wonderfully**, the greatness of her fall being such as to cause men to marvel; **she had no comforter**, no one to take her part with so much as a word of consolation. It is for this reason that her sighing is heard: **O Lord, behold my affliction; for the enemy hath magnified himself**, increasing his insolence and violence. The prophet now continues his description of Jerusalem's misery. V. 10. **The adversary hath spread out his hand upon all her pleasant things**, blasphemously robbing even the precious vessels and appointments of the Temple; **for she hath seen that the heathen entered into her Sanctuary, whom thou didst command that they should not enter into thy congregation**, the heathen as such being excluded from the Temple, except where they were proselytes of righteousness. They had been excluded from the Sanctuary, but here they entered with blasphemous intent, ruthlessly trampling down and robbing just as they chose. V. 11. **All her people sigh**, with the calamity of the severe famine as a further cause for groaning, **they seek bread; they have given their pleasant things for meat to relieve the soul**, no valuables being too precious, in this emergency, where the question is to save lives. Their groaning arises in a fervent appeal: **See, O Lord, and consider, for I am become vile**, an object of wretchedness. The first step of true repentance is a full and unequivocal acknowledgment of one's own sinfulness and a corresponding free confession of it to the Lord.

THE LAMENT OF THE CITY AND THE ANSWER OF THE LORD. — V. 12. **Is it nothing to you, all ye that pass by?** Will none of those who are witnesses of her misery and shame take the proper notice of her calamity? **Behold and see if there be any sorrow like unto my sorrow which is done unto me, wherewith the Lord hath afflicted me in the day of His fierce anger.** The greatness of Jerusalem's misery was so unusual that men seeing it were bound to conclude that there was a special hand and work of God in it. The picture is that of an outcast by the wayside begging the passers-by for at least some show of sympathy. And it may be said that Jerusalem, in this instance, prefigures Christ, whom the language is prophetically made to suit. V. 13. **From above hath He sent fire into my bones,** which are here thought of as organs of the body that are first to feel a racking pain, **and it prevaileth against them,** so that the very vital powers are affected; **He hath spread a net for my feet,** to entangle her in His judgments; **He hath turned me back,** making it impossible to become free from the meshes of the net; **He hath made me desolate and faint all the day.** The city is thus pictured as a person whose happiness is destroyed and whose health is broken. V. 14. **The yoke of my transgressions is bound by His hand,** sin being not only a taskmaster, but a yoke pressing the sinner down, with God Himself, as it were, holding the reins firmly twisted round His hand, so that escape is impossible; **they are wreathed,** the many cords of sin being woven together increasing the load, **and come up upon my neck,** binding the sinners to their wilful transgressions; **He hath made my strength to fall,** so that it is entirely broken; **the Lord hath delivered me into their hands from whom I am not able to rise up,** whom she did not have the strength to resist. V. 15. **The Lord hath trodden under foot all my mighty men in the midst of me,** slaying them while they were engaged in the defense of the city; **He hath called an assembly against me to crush my young men,** the very expression setting forth the strange contrast and the severity of the punishment; **the Lord hath trodden the virgin, the daughter of Judah, as in a wine-press.** Cp. Joel 4, 13; Is. 63, 2. 3. V. 16. **For these things I weep,** giving free rein to her tears, **mine eye, mine eye, runneth down with water, because the comforter that should relieve my soul is far from me,** the friends to whom she might have looked for words and deeds which would restore her soul having forsaken her; **my children are desolate because the enemy prevailed,** the enemy being still in power, with the result that the inhabitants of Jerusalem were destroyed, that they perished most miserably. V. 17. **Zion spreadeth forth her hands,** in a gesture imploring help, **and there is none to comfort her; the Lord hath commanded concerning Jacob that his adversaries should be round about him,** his very neighbors being his enemies and seeking his destruction. **Jerusalem is as a menstruous woman among them,** shut out from intercourse with people and from attendance at the Temple-worship. These facts impress Jerusalem as being important and true; she must admit their justice. V. 18. **The Lord is righteous,** just in His treatment of the rebellious city; **for I have rebelled against His commandment. Hear, I pray you, all people, and behold my sorrow,** since she feels the need of sympathy; **my virgins and my young men are gone into captivity,** this fact showing the very climax of her afflictions. V. 19. **I called for my lovers,** the nations which had professed an interest of true affection, **but they deceived me; my priests and mine elders gave up the ghost in the city,** both the spiritual and the temporal rulers expiring in the neighborhood of the Sanctuary of Jehovah, **while they sought their meat to relieve their souls,** the very nobles of the people being obliged to seek food of any kind whatsoever, if it only would suffice to preserve their lives. V. 20. **Behold, O Lord, for I am in distress,** she implored Him to observe how badly she fared. **My bowels are troubled,** being violently excited with excessive grief; **mine heart is turned within me, for I have grievously rebelled,** the punishment being altogether deserved, in the full measure in which it struck her. **Abroad the sword bereaveth,** as the battle demanded its victims; **at home there is as death,** namely, by famine and pestilence. V. 21. **They have heard that I sigh,** the former friends and allies being fully aware of her groaning; **there is none to comfort me,** for they all ignore her trouble. **All mine enemies have heard of my trouble; they are glad that Thou hast done it,** rejoicing over the Lord's punishment upon Zion. **Thou wilt bring the day that Thou hast called,** the day of wrath with whose coming the Lord had threatened for many years, **and they shall be like unto me,** for the Lord would visit her enemies as He had punished her. V. 22. **Let all their wickedness come before Thee,** for a just punishment, **and do unto them as Thou hast done unto me for all my transgressions,** according to the same righteous judgment; **for my sighs are many, and my heart is faint.** This is not a vindictive prayer, but a plea for justice, which repentant believers of all times may well send up to the throne of God. The very punishment of God upon rebellious children is intended to change into a blessed experience of good.

CHAPTER 2.

Lamentation over the Destruction of Zion and the Desolation of Judah.

A Description of Jehovah's Judgment. — V. 1. **How hath the Lord covered the daughter of Zion,** His own city, formerly the seat of His Church, **with a cloud in His anger,** with the chilly darkness of ignominy and shame, **and cast down from heaven unto the earth the beauty of Israel,** the glory of the capital itself, chosen by God, as it had been, for the seat of His glory and power in the midst of His people had been established there, and **remembered not His footstool in the day of His anger!** so that the very Ark of the Covenant, 1 Chron. 28, 2, where Jehovah was enthroned between the wings of the cherubim, was removed and destroyed. V. 2. **The Lord hath swallowed up all the habitations of Jacob,** the entire country being included in the ruin, **and hath not pitied,** carrying out His judgment with merciless severity; **He hath thrown down in His wrath the strongholds of the daughter of Judah,** the fortified places sharing the fate of the hamlets in the open country; **He hath brought them down to the ground,** in a total destruction; **He hath polluted the kingdom and the princes thereof,** by delivering the country together with its rulers into the hands of the heathen conquerors. V. 3. **He hath cut off in His fierce anger all the horn of Israel,** symbol of strength and majesty, breaking it in the heat of His indignation; **He hath drawn back His right hand from before the enemy,** withdrawing His assistance from His people and thus delivering them into the power of the invaders, **and He burned against Jacob like a flaming fire which devoureth round about,** the Lord thus being directly active in its destruction. V. 4. **He hath bent His bow like an enemy,** attacking them with a deadly weapon; **He stood with His right hand as an adversary,** wielding a ruthless sword, **and slew all that were pleasant to the eye,** all that charmed and delighted the eye, both in children and in goods, **in the tabernacle of the daughter of Zion,** in the entire city of Jerusalem; **He poured out His fury like fire,** in the capture and destruction of the city. V. 5. **The Lord was as an enemy; He hath swallowed up Israel,** or, "The Lord became — as a hero He hath destroyed"; **He hath swallowed up all her palaces,** the fine dwellings of the rich and mighty; **He hath destroyed His strongholds,** all the fortified places throughout the country, **and hath increased in the daughter of Judah mourning and lamentation,** or "sorrow and sadness, mourning and misery," as we might translate in following the play of similar sounds in the original. V. 6. **And He hath violently taken away His Tabernacle as if it were of a garden,** the Temple being subjected to ruin like a garden which the owner converts into some other kind of plot if it no longer suits his purposes; **He hath destroyed His places of the assembly,** where He met with His people in the communion of the covenant, in the Sanctuary protected by His holy Law. **The Lord hath caused the solemn feasts and Sabbaths to be forgotten in Zion,** this being the natural result of the city's destruction, **and hath despised, in the indignation of His anger, the king and the priest;** for He no longer desired these mediators of His covenant, and the service of the priests was no longer required when the Temple-worship ceased. V. 7. **The Lord hath cast off His altar,** rejecting it with disdain, chiefly on account of the hypocritical worship connected with it; **He hath abhorred His Sanctuary,** the Holy Place and the Holy of Holies, the center of the Jewish cultus; **He hath given up into the hand of the enemy the walls of her palaces,** the proud buildings of the Temple, which reared their columns high above the surrounding city and country. **They have made a noise in the house of the Lord,** the enemies breaking forth into loud shouts of rejoicing over their victory, **as in the day of a solemn feast,** in a noisy celebration. V. 8. **The Lord hath purposed to destroy the wall of the daughter of Zion,** the destruction of Jerusalem setting into execution the judgment of God, 2 Kings 25, 10; **He hath stretched out a line,** in taking measures to level the city in unsparing rigidity of punishment; **He hath not withdrawn His hand from destroying,** from bringing total ruin upon the city; **therefore He made the rampart and the wall to lament, they languished together,** overcome by the shame which was done to them. V. 9. **Her gates are sunk into the ground,** buried under a mass of rubbish and earth, which the destruction of the city has scattered over them; **He hath destroyed and broken her bars,** with which the gates were bolted against the attack of the enemies. **Her king and her princes are among the Gentiles,** in shameful captivity; **the Law is no more,** its ordinances and provisions no longer being in force; **her prophets also find no vision from the Lord,** the Lord withholding His ordinary revelations and communications, as at the time of the Judges, 1 Sam. 3, 1. V. 10. **The elders of the daughter of Zion,** the leaders of the Jewish Church, **sit upon the ground and keep silence,** they have no counsel to give, chiefly because they are dumb with grief; **they have cast up dust upon their heads, they have girded themselves with sackcloth,** in token of the greatness of their mourning; **the virgins of Jerusalem,** ordinarily care-free and happy, **hang down their heads to the ground,** in an excess of grief. Such is the effect when the Lord carries out His sentence of judgment upon nations and upon individuals who oppose His will.

THE VANITY OF HUMAN CONSOLATION TOGETHER WITH A PLEA FOR HELP. — V. 11. **Mine eyes do fail with tears,** being spent, worn out, with weeping, **my bowels are troubled,** his heart being most deeply affected, **my liver is poured upon the earth,** that is, — since the liver was considered the seat of the passions, — all my feelings are dissolved with pain, **for the destruction of the daughter of my people, because the children and the sucklings swoon in the streets of the city,** the fainting away of these innocent victims of the calamity being the very climax of its severity. V. 12. **They say to their mothers,** as they are tortured with the pangs of hunger, **Where is corn and wine?** anything to eat, **when they swooned as the wounded in the streets of the city,** faint with weakness for lack of food, **when their soul was poured out into their mothers' bosom,** breathing out their lives while lying on their mothers' laps, the latter being compelled to look on in helpless misery. V. 13. **What thing shall I take to witness for thee?** to bring some measure of comfort from the experience of others. **What thing shall I liken to thee, O daughter of Jerusalem?** in making some comparison which would tend to arouse her drooping spirits. **What shall I equal to thee that I may comfort thee, O virgin daughter of Zion?** Any attempt of this kind is bound to fail in this instance, since no real comparison can be made. **For thy breach is great like the sea,** immeasurably boundless in extent and depth; **who can heal thee?** As the conditions are, Jerusalem can expect neither comfort nor healing from her prophets. V. 14. **Thy prophets have seen vain and foolish things for thee,** namely, the false prophets, to whom the people of Jerusalem listened, much against Jeremiah's advice; **and they have not discovered thine iniquity,** pointing out the real cause of all this misery, **to turn away thy captivity,** namely, by leading the people to repentance, **but have seen for thee false burdens and causes of banishment,** that is, the contents of their prophecies, while apparently directed against the enemies, are such as to bring ruin upon Judah. V. 15. **All that pass by clap their hands at thee,** in scorn and mockery; **they hiss and wag their head at the daughter of Jerusalem, saying,** in expressing the derision which they felt, **Is this the city that men call The perfection of beauty, The joy of the whole earth?** It is a question of scornful wonderment, denying Jerusalem's right ever to have borne such designations. To this behavior of strangers is added the mocking triumph of enemies. V. 16. **All thine enemies have opened their mouth against thee,** in a gesture of mockery and derision; **they hiss and gnash the teeth,** as an expression of satisfied rage, of vindictive malice. **They say, We have swallowed her up,** thus effecting a complete destruction; **certainly this is the day that we looked for,** which they had so eagerly awaited; **we have found, we have seen it,** and they feel a corresponding satisfaction and pleasure. But the destruction of Jerusalem was not a chance happening, nor was it alone the culmination of men's hateful plans. V. 17. **The Lord hath done that which He had devised,** what He had resolved upon; **He hath fulfilled His word that He had commanded in the days of old,** for the holiness of the Lord demands the punishment of every act of rebellion against His holy Law; **He hath thrown down and hath not pitied,** carrying out His threat with merciless severity; **and He hath caused thine enemy to rejoice over thee; He hath set up the horn of thine adversaries,** so that they were given power, authority, and victory. V. 18. **Their heart,** that of the Jews suffering such great afflictions, **cried unto the Lord,** even while they addressed the fortifications of their city, **O wall of the daughter of Zion,** the city with all its inhabitants, **let tears run down like a river day and night,** in the intensity of grief over the present conditions; **give thyself no rest,** no surcease from sorrow; **let not the apple of thine eye cease,** in desisting from shedding tears. V. 19. **Arise, cry out in the night,** throughout all the watches of the night; **in the beginning of the watches,** with the desire and strength for weeping renewed again and again, **pour out thine heart like water before the face of the Lord,** the very heart dissolving in tears, as it were, in the excess of the sorrow caused by the great calamity; **lift up thy hands toward Him,** in a gesture of fervent supplication, **for the life of thy young children that faint for hunger in the top,** at the head, **of every street.** V. 20. **Behold, O Lord, and consider to whom Thou hast done this,** so the prayer of the city's inhabitants now arises. **Shall the women eat their fruit, and children of a span long?** in revolting cannibalism caused by excessive hunger. Cp. Lev. 26, 29; Deut. 28, 53; Jer. 19, 9. **Shall the priest and the prophet be slain in the Sanctuary of the Lord?** The one was against God's moral order governing the universe, the other conflicted with His covenant and the worship connected with it. V. 21. **The young and the old lie on the ground in the streets,** being slaughtered without mercy; **my virgins and my young men are fallen by the sword,** neither age nor sex being spared. **Thou hast slain them in the day of Thine anger; Thou hast killed and not pitied.** V. 22. **Thou hast called as in a solemn day,** as for a festival prepared for the enemies, **my terrors round about,** from every direction, so that Jerusalem was surrounded by them, so that **in the day of the Lord's anger none escaped nor remained,** all being involved in the common ruin; **those that I have swaddled and brought up,** with the fondest love of a parent, **hath mine enemy consumed.** Fortunate is the person who, when experiencing the Lord's punishment, cries out thus in true repentance!

CHAPTER 3.

The Suffering and Comfort of the Pious.

A LAMENT OVER GRIEVOUS SUFFERINGS. — V. 1. **I am the man that hath seen affliction by the rod of His wrath,** so Jeremiah writes in setting forth his own experiences as characteristic of the misery which is often the lot of God's children in the world, as He Himself chastises those whom He loves. V. 2. **He hath led me and brought me into darkness,** into various calamities, **but not into light,** this being the manner in which the pious of all times have regarded adversity, as though they had been shut out from the rays of God's mercy. V. 3. **Surely against me is He turned,** in continual and severe chastisements; **He turneth His hand against me all the day,** smiting without ceasing. V. 4. **My flesh and my skin hath He made old,** so that they were wasting away with sickness and premature old age; **He hath broken my bones.** Cp. Is. 38, 13. V. 5. **He hath builded against me,** like a besieging army, **and compassed me with gall and travel** (travail), that is, with poison and heavy afflictions. V. 6. **He hath set me in dark places,** literally, "He caused me to dwell in darkness," **as they that be dead of old,** those encompassed by the long night of death. Cp. Ps. 143, 3. V. 7. **He hath hedged me about,** surrounding him with a solid enclosure, **that I cannot get out,** that there is no escape; **He hath made my chain heavy,** so that he was absolutely hemmed in. V. 8. **Also when I cry and shout,** begging for deliverance, **He shutteth out my prayer,** this refusal to hear making the afflictions all the harder to bear. V. 9. **He hath enclosed my ways with hewn stone,** with a strong wall, placing insurmountable obstacles in his way; **He hath made my paths crooked,** so that he could not proceed on his way. V. 10. **He was unto me as a bear lying in wait,** lurking to pounce upon his prey, **and as a lion in secret places,** crouched in ambush, ready to spring upon the unsuspecting traveler. V. 11. **He hath turned aside my ways,** so that he went astray, **and pulled me in pieces,** so that his members were as severed from his body; **He hath made me desolate,** casting him away, lonely and miserable. V. 12. **He hath bent His bow,** taking deliberate aim at His target, **and set me as a mark for the arrow.** Cp. Job 16, 12. V. 13. **He hath caused the arrows of His quiver,** the darts of affliction, **to enter into my reins,** the vital organs of the body, as we now speak of the heart. V. 14. **I was a derision to all my people,** as when they mockingly set aside his advice not to go down to Egypt, **and their song all the day,** so that they made him their laughing-stock. V. 15. **He hath filled me with bitterness,** Job 9, 18; **He hath made me drunken with wormwood,** with the nauseous cup which He caused him to drink, instead of the strengthening medicine which his condition seemed to require. V. 16. **He hath also broken my teeth with gravel-stones,** feeding him stones instead of bread; **He hath covered me with ashes,** in shameful humiliation. V. 17. **And Thou hast removed my soul far off from peace,** thrusting it back from happiness; **I forgat prosperity,** the very recollection of it no longer being present with him. V. 18. **And I said, My strength and my hope is perished from the Lord.** His vitality was sapped by his afflictions, and his hope and trust in Jehovah had left him. Thus even children of the Lord are at times so deeply affected by the griefs which they must bear that they come very near to despair.

GOD'S MERCY AND POWER REVEALED. — V. 19. **Remembering,** or, "Remember," **mine affliction and my misery, the wormwood and the gall,** the sufferings about which he has just complained so bitterly. V. 20. **My soul hath them still in remembrance and is humbled in me,** still bowed down, as under a heavy weight. V. 21. **This,** namely, the fact that his soul is deeply afflicted by the mere remembrance of his sufferings, **I recall to my mind,** taking it to heart, **therefore have I hope.** Throwing off the feeling of despair which threatened him, he thinks of the fact that God alone can help him, and upon this fact he places his hope. A consideration of the boundless mercy of the Lord strengthens his hope. V. 22. **It is of the Lord's mercies,** on account of the fact that He delights in making known His fatherly kindness and grace toward us, **that we are not consumed, because His compassions fail not,** they have no end. V. 23. **They are new every morning,** namely, the evidences of His love and mercy; **great is Thy faithfulness,** the outflow of His compassionate love in fulfilling His promises. These wonderful facts the sacred writer now applies to himself. V. 24. **The Lord is my Portion, saith my soul,** cp. Ps. 16, 5; 73, 26; 142, 6; **therefore will I hope in Him,** resting his trust in Him in the certainty of faith. V. 25. **The Lord is good unto them that wait for Him,** in this steadfast trust, **to the soul that seeketh Him,** looking to Him alone for help and deliverance. The thoughts of Jehovah are always good and kind, even when He causes pain. Though man be in trouble, he should yet perceive the goodness of the Lord, so that he cannot defiantly murmur or faint-heartedly despair. V. 26. **It is good that a man should both hope and quietly wait for the salvation of the Lord,** in the calm certainty that He will send His deliverance in due time. It is a wonderful achievement to be humbly patient and quiet under all circumstances, no matter what tribulations may come, ever resting in the will of God. V. 27. **It is good for a man that he bear the yoke in his youth,** so that the disciplinary value of various sufferings may have an opportunity to work patience in his heart and enable him to bear the burdens of age with greater fortitude and trust in the Lord. He who has learned to take up his cross in patient resignation while he was still young will have no trouble in exercising the proper submissiveness when he is old. V. 28. **He sitteth alone and keepeth silence,** practising patience in a solitude which enables him to value the divine chastisements, **because He hath borne it upon him,** because and when Jehovah has laid the burden upon him. V. 29. **He putteth his mouth in the dust,** in the position of most humble submission, restraining himself from murmuring, **if so be there may be hope,** or, "perhaps there is still hope," namely, that God will have compassion and withdraw His chastening hand. V. 30. **He giveth his cheek to him that smiteth him,** submitting even to injustice if it serves the cause of the Lord, cp. Matt. 5, 39—41; **he is filled full with reproach,** enduring also the scorn which men heap upon him for his trust in God. Note the climax beginning with the easiest matter and ending with the most difficult, the patient bearing of insults, if it serves the glory of the Lord. V. 31. **For the Lord will not cast off forever,** cp. Ps. 77, 8; v. 32; **but though He cause grief, yet will He have compassion according to the multitude of His mercies,** so that His grace and love outweigh the burden of even the severest affliction. V. 33. **For He doth not afflict willingly,** literally, "from His heart," **nor grieve the children of men.** It is not because the Lord takes a vindictive delight in punishing men that He lays afflictions upon them, but because His chastisement is necessary for sinful men, for the furtherance of their soul's salvation. Cp. Heb. 12, 5—11. V. 34. **To crush under his feet all the prisoners of the earth,** as in the cruel treatment accorded the Jews by the Chaldeans, v. 35. **to turn aside the right of a man before the face of the Most High,** as when a judge perverts justice before the very eyes of God, who sees and hears it all, v. 36. **to subvert in his cause,** so that justice cannot be done, **the Lord approveth not,** He very decidedly does not favor such injustice. The thoughts naturally arise at this point whether the Lord, then, has nothing to do with all such happenings. V. 37. **Who is he that saith, and it cometh to pass, when the Lord commandeth it not?** There is nothing happening on the earth which is not in accordance with the Lord's intention or not happening with His permission. While no one may injure his neighbor with the approbation of the Lord, yet the injury he does serves the purposes of God's providential chastisement of transgressors. V. 38. **Out of the mouth of the Most High proceedeth not evil and good?** so that the one as well as the other is done by His command or permission. V. 39. **Wherefore doth a living man complain?** with sighs and groans over his afflictions, **a man for the punishment of his sins?** That is, to rectify the evil in the world, let each one lament over his sins. It is only by daily contrition and repentance that we make any headway in combating the evils of this present world. If we grow weary of this lifelong battle, acts of wickedness are bound to multiply.

CONFESSION OF SIN AND COMPLAINT OVER THE CRUELTY OF THE ENEMIES. — V. 40. **Let us search and try our ways,** in true contrition, to find the reason for God's displeasure, **and turn again to the Lord,** returning all the way, in sincere repentance. V. 41. **Let us lift up our heart with our hands unto God in the heavens,** with the last shred of hypocrisy banished. V. 42. **We have transgressed and have rebelled,** the emphasis being on the pronoun, as in every sincere confession of sin; **Thou hast not pardoned,** that is, He had not, like a weak earthly father, overlooked and condoned the transgression, but had meted out the punishment which it deserved. V. 43. **Thou hast covered with anger,** shutting Himself off so as not to see them, **and persecuted us.** The veil of His wrath kept Him, as it were, from feeling a weak sympathy. **Thou hast slain, Thou hast not pitied.** Cp. Jer. 29, 18. V. 44. **Thou hast covered Thyself with a cloud,** an impenetrable covering, **that our prayer should not pass through,** and help, therefore, was not forthcoming. V. 45. **Thou hast made us,** by refusing His assistance, **as the offscouring and refuse in the midst of the people.** Israel, ground down to the dust, had become an object of contempt among the heathen nations. V. 46. **All our enemies have opened their mouths against us,** gaping at them in a gesture of scorn and derision. V. 47. **Fear and a snare is come upon us, desolation and destruction.** The picture is taken from the hunting of wild beasts, which, filled with terror by the cries of the hunters, fall into the pits that have been prepared for their capture. This situation fills the heart of the inspired poet with deep anguish. V. 48. **Mine eye runneth down with rivers of water** in an excess of sorrow, **for the destruction of the daughter of my people.** Cp. Ps. 119, 136. V. 49. **Mine eye trickleth down,** in a steady flow of tears, **and ceaseth not, without any intermission,** there being no abatement of the feeling of grief and therefore also no cessation of tears, v. 50. **till the Lord look down and behold from heaven,** namely, to make an end of His people's misery, to have mercy upon them. V. 51. **Mine eye affecteth mine heart,** literally, "my eye puts an ache upon my soul," the pain of the eye from its ceaseless weeping affecting the soul as well, **because of all the daughters of my city,** whose fate was most deeply to be deplored. V. 52. **Mine enemies chased me sore,** hunting him down like fowlers, **like a bird, without cause.** Cp. Prov. 1, 17. V. 53. **They have cut off my life in the dungeon,** desiring to destroy it by taking such extreme measures, **and cast a stone upon me,** heaping this further indignity upon him as he was helpless in their power. V. 54. **Waters flowed over mine head,** the picture of a flood of waters being used to give some idea of the greatness and intensity of his suffering; **then I said, I am cut off,** abandoned by God, removed from the comfort of His fatherly eye and hand. To such heights does the feeling of being forsaken by the Lord sometimes rise that the believers consider themselves shut out entirely from His mercy.

PRAYER FOR DELIVERANCE. — V. 55. **I called upon Thy name, O Lord,** thus overcoming the despair which was trying to paralyze his faith, **out of the low dungeon,** out of the pit which threatened to become his grave. V. 56. **Thou hast heard my voice,** so he cries out in the triumphant confidence of his faith; **hide not Thy ear at my breathing, at my cry,** as he recovered his breath sufficiently to lay his case before Jehovah once more. V. 57. **Thou drewest near in the day that I called upon Thee. Thou saidst, Fear not,** thus assuring the believer of His merciful interest and assistance. Cp. Ps. 145, 18. V. 58. **O Lord, Thou hast pleaded the causes of my soul,** being active in all matters pertaining to the believer's welfare; **Thou hast redeemed my life,** rescuing him from what seemed to be certain destruction. V. 59. **O Lord, Thou hast seen my wrong,** how his rights were violated by the enemies; **judge Thou my cause,** securing for him the right which he knew was on his side. V. 60. **Thou hast seen all their vengeance and all their imaginations against me,** all their vindictive, malicious devices. V. 61. **Thou hast heard their reproach, O Lord, and all their imaginations against me,** v. 62. **the lips of those that rose up against me,** with scornful mockery, **and their device against me all the day,** as they meditated evil. V. 63. **Behold their sitting down and their rising up,** observing all the conduct and doing of the enemies; **I am their music,** the object of their derisive songs. V. 64. **Render unto them a recompense, O Lord, according to the work of their hands,** as they had so plentifully deserved it. V. 65. **Give them sorrow of heart,** literally, "blindness or covering of heart," a stupidity which shut them out from spiritual understanding, **Thy curse unto them!** V. 66. **Persecute and destroy them in anger from under the heavens of the Lord,** so that they would be forever removed from the sphere of Jehovah's kingdom of the world, thereby losing all their opportunity to do any more harm. Christians may well pray that God would foil all attempts of the enemies to take away His honor and to harm the cause of His kingdom in the world.

CHAPTER 4.

Submission under God's Judgment and Hope for the Future.

JERUSALEM'S AFFLICTION A PUNISHMENT FOR HER GUILT. — V. 1. **How is the gold become dim! How is the most fine gold changed!** losing its splendor and color. **The stones of the Sanctuary are poured out in the top of every street,** or, "The hallowed stones are cast forth at all street corners," with utter disregard of their costliness. The two expressions together are a picture of the holy people of the Lord, consecrated to be a kingdom of priests unto the Lord. V. 2. **The precious sons of Zion,** all its inhabitants, noble by virtue of the Lord's selection, **comparable to fine gold, how are they esteemed as earthen pitchers,** of little or no value, **the work of the hands of the potter!** readily shattered in pieces for their sins. V. 3. **Even the sea monsters,** the great mammalian animals of the ocean, or "the jackals of the desert," **draw out the breast, they give suck to their young ones,** thereby giving some evidence of motherly feeling; **the daughter of my people is become cruel, like the ostriches in the wilderness,** whose want of affection for their young is referred to also Job 39, 16. This point of cruelty has been reached also by the Jewish mothers, so that they have abandoned the natural feelings of motherhood. V. 4. **The tongue of the sucking child cleaveth to the roof of his mouth for thirst,** there being no nourishment for infants; **the young children ask bread, and no man breaketh it unto them,** since no one was left to distribute food, even if the supply had not been exhausted. V. 5. **They that did feed delicately,** being very choicy in the selection of the viands which loaded down their tables, **are desolate in the streets,** without homes and without food as well; **they that were brought up in scarlet,** borne on couches of the finest crimson material, **embrace dunghills,** fortunate in finding so much as a rubbish-heap for their weary limbs. V. 6. **For the punishment of the iniquity of the daughter of my people is greater than the punishment of the sin of Sodom, that was overthrown as in a moment,** the catastrophe coming upon the city with great suddenness, and no hands stayed on her, it was not necessary for any human hands to be active in her destruction, since the Lord Himself brought the calamity upon her. The fate of Jerusalem was more terrible than that of Sodom because her guilt was greater. Thus Sodom, for instance, was spared the slow tortures of hunger and pestilence by the suddenness of the punishment which ended her existence. V. 7. **Her Nazarites,** her princes or rulers, separated from the rest of the people by virtue of the dignity of their office, **were purer than snow, they were whiter than milk, they were more ruddy in body than rubies,** or "corals"; **their polishing was of sapphire,** beautiful in form. V. 8. **Their visage,** now that the calamity has come upon them, **is blacker than a coal,** than blackness, or soot; **they are not known in the streets,** because their appearance is so dreadfully altered; **their skin cleaveth to their bones,** on account of the excessive loss of flesh which they had suffered; **it is withered,** dry and yellow; **it is become like a stick,** without sap and vigor. V. 9. **They that be slain with the sword are better,** more fortunate, **than they that be slain with hunger,** because they were not obliged to suffer the agonies of a slow death; **for these pine away, stricken through for want of the fruits of the field.** Such was the fate of the men, of the nobles of Judah and Jerusalem; far more pitiful was that of the women. V. 10. **The hands of the pitiful women,** of those who were tender-hearted and merciful, from whom one might have expected a different behavior, **have sodden their own children,** in an abhorrent and almost unexplainable form of cannibalism; **they were their meat in the destruction of the daughter of my people,** during the siege of Jerusalem. Cp. Deut. 28, 57. Thus the extremity of the case influenced even delicate and kind-hearted women to commit such horrible crimes. V. 11. **The Lord hath accomplished His fury,** fulfilling the designs of His wrath; **He hath poured out His fierce anger and hath kindled a fire in Zion, and it hath devoured the foundations thereof,** the reference being to the total destruction of the city by the punishment of Jehovah. Thus the Lord proved Himself a holy and a jealous God, who was bound to visit the iniquity of the sinners upon them.

GOD'S JUDGMENT A CONSEQUENCE OF THE SINS OF THE PROPHETS AND PRIESTS. — V. 12. **The kings of the earth and all the inhabitants of the world would not have believed that the adversary and the enemy should have entered into the gates of Jerusalem.** It had indeed been taken in the earlier years, by Shishak of Egypt and by Joash of Israel, 1 Kings 14; 2 Kings 14, but it had since been fortified to such an extent that it was regarded as impregnable; moreover, there was an idea prevailing among the surrounding nations that it was under the special protection of Jehovah. But the unheard-of had come to pass. V. 13. **For the sins of her prophets and the iniquities of her priests,** cp. Jer. 23, 11. 21; 26, 7—16, **that have shed the blood of the just in the midst of her,** practising even in those days what the Lord accused them of six centuries later, Matt. 23, 31. 37. Because the leaders and spiritual rulers of the people had been guilty of such sins, therefore the punishment of the Lord had come upon the city. V. 14. **They have wandered as blind men in the streets, they have polluted themselves with blood,** or, "they," the priests and prophets, "reeled through the streets, defiled with the blood which they had shed," **so that men could not touch their garments,** for fear of contamination, of Levitical uncleanness. V. 15. **They,** namely, the people of the city meeting them, **cried unto them, Depart ye! It is unclean; depart, depart, touch not!** thereby applying to them the call of warning used in the case of lepers, Lev. 13, 45, lest their blood-stained garments bring defilement. **When they fled away and wandered,** or when they had fled away and continued as fugitives in strange lands, **they said among the heathen, They shall no more sojourn there,** the heathen themselves being afraid of pollution and denying the exiled and fugitive priests a retreat in their midst. V. 16. **The anger of the Lord hath divided them,** literally, "the countenance of Jehovah has scattered them"; **He will no more regard them,** no longer look upon them in mercy; **they,** the enemies, **respected not the persons of the priests, they favored not the elders,** had no compassion on them. The rank, station, and age of the priests no longer shielded them from humiliation and degradation. V. 17. **As for us, our eyes as yet failed for our vain help,** that is, the Jews, still hoping for the assistance of Egypt and other allied nations, were deeply disappointed; **in our watching we have watched for a nation that could not save us,** as was shown also by the fact that the small band of people remaining after the murder of Gedaliah fled to Egypt. But all their hopes were in vain; they found that their trust had been misplaced. V. 18. **They hunt our steps that we cannot go in our streets,** that is, the Chaldeans were so vigilant in their siege that there was no chance to escape. **Our end is near, our days are fulfilled; for our end is come,** it seemed that their very existence as a nation was at an end. The city was taken, the bulk of its population transported to Babylon or put to the sword, and the remaining fugitives scattered among the nations. V. 19. **Our persecutors are swifter than the eagles of the heaven,** their pursuit having begun instantly and having been carried forward with the greatest energy; **they pursued us upon the mountains, they laid wait for us in the** wilderness, everywhere, even in the most inaccessible places. V. 20. **The breath of our nostrils,** namely, the king, who was needed for the life of the nation, **the anointed of the Lord, was taken in their pits,** caught by the enemies, **of whom we said, Under his shadow we shall live among the heathen;** they had hoped to live safe under his protection. But in spite of the gloomy picture there is still some hope for the future. V. 21. **Rejoice and be glad, O daughter of Edom, that dwellest in the land of Uz,** on the border of the great Arabian Plain; that is, no matter if the Edomites were now exulting, **the cup,** namely, that of God's punishment, **also shall pass through unto thee; thou shalt be drunken,** with the contents of this cup, **and shalt make thyself naked,** be heaped with shame as a result of the Chaldean conquest. On the other hand, there is comfort for the children of the Lord. V. 22. **The punishment of thine iniquity is accomplished, O daughter of Zion,** her guilt being removed by the mercy of Jehovah; **He will no more carry thee away into captivity,** not cause another sentence of banishment to be executed; **He will visit thine iniquity, O daughter of Edom; He will discover thy sins,** that is, uncover them for the purpose of meting out His punishment. Thus the Messianic idea is brought out, even in the midst of misery and affliction, with the same comfort of the Gospel which is ours to-day.

CHAPTER 5.

Prayer of the Congregation for the Restoration of the Covenant Relation.

DESCRIPTION OF THE PRESENT MISERY. — V. 1. **Remember, O Lord, what is come upon us,** the evils which had befallen the Lord's congregation in the ruin of the entire nation; **consider and behold our reproach,** turning to their pitiable condition with merciful attention. The misery of Jerusalem and Judah, the home of the true Church, is now depicted. V. 2. **Our inheritance is turned to strangers, our houses to aliens,** since the invading Chaldeans had taken possession of the entire land. V. 3. **We are orphans and fatherless,** like those that have been deprived of their natural protectors; **our mothers are as widows,** this statement bringing out the fact that large numbers of men, the defenders of the city and country, had either fallen in battle or been led away into captivity. V. 4. **We have drunken our water for money,** namely, that which was rightfully their own; **our wood is sold unto us,** they were obliged to buy the very necessaries of life from the conquerors or pay exorbitant taxes. V. 5. **Our necks are under persecution,** their pursuers and tormentors being continually upon them, driving them headlong; **we labor and have no rest,** no matter how tired they were, rest was denied them. V. 6. **We have given the hand,** stretching it out in humble supplication, **to the Egyptians and to the Assyrians, to be satisfied with bread,** since the nation as such was reduced to absolute beggary. V. 7. **Our fathers have sinned and are not, and we have borne their iniquities,** the generation of Jews at the time of the destruction of the city being obliged to bear not only its own guilt, but that of the previous generations as well, placing them under a double misfortune. God punished the iniquities of the fathers upon the children who followed their fathers on their ways of wickedness. V. 8. **Servants have ruled over us,** many of the Chaldean overseers and petty officers actually being slaves; **there is none that doth deliver us out of their hand,** the former kingdom of priests having become a servant of servants. V. 9. **We gat our bread with the peril of our lives because of the sword of the wilderness,** for the country, sparsely populated as it was after the deportation of the exiles, was open to the ravages of nomad hordes, whose raids were a constant menace. V. 10. **Our skin was black like an oven because of the terrible famine,** glowing with the heat of fever brought on by their condition. V. 11. **They,** the invading armies and the raiding hordes, **ravished the women in Zion and the maids in the cities of Judah,** the usual accompaniment of barbarous warfare. V. 12. **Princes are hanged up by their hand,** the disgrace of their slaughter thus being intensified by their suspension from the accursed tree; **the faces of elders were not honored,** the enemies showing no respect for dignity or age. V. 13. **They took the young men to grind,** compelling them to perform the work of slaves, **and the children fell under the wood,** as they dragged the heavy mill-stones with which the grinding was done. The Jewish young men and boys were required to do the lowest and most menial services. V. 14. **The elders have ceased from the gate,** no longer assembling at the customary place for deliberations and judgments, **the young men from their music,** for the joyful meetings were also held in the open space at the gates of the cities. V. 15. **The joy of our heart is ceased; our dance is turned into mourning,** all mirth and cheer being things of the past. V. 16. **The crown is fallen from our head,** their former position of glory and honor and influence apparently being put from them forever. **Woe unto us that we have sinned!** The realization of sinfulness and the acknowledgment of guilt, as in a confession of this kind, is the first step toward true repentance.

PLEA FOR THE RENEWAL OF JEHOVAH'S LOVE. V. 17. **For this,** on account of the great afflictions, well deserved as they were, **our heart is faint,** with the bitterness of the soul's pain; **for these things are our eyes dim,** the sorrow of the heart finding its expression in tears. V. 18. **Because of the mountain of Zion,** where the Temple had formerly stood, **which is desolate, the foxes walk upon it,** jackals making their dens in its ruins. In the midst of all this sorrow, however, the hearts of the believers turn to the true source of comfort and consolation. V. 19. **Thou, O Lord, remainest forever,** sitting as the one true Monarch ruling the entire world; **Thy throne from generation to generation,** through all eternity. V. 20. **Wherefore dost Thou forget us forever and forsake us so long time?** That Jehovah should be so inclined is beyond the conception of the inspired poet; he firmly believes that the Lord will yet remember His mercy. V. 21. **Turn Thou us unto Thee, O Lord,** by a true conversion, which is the work of the Lord alone, and **we shall be turned; renew our days as of old,** restoring them to their position as His children, as His Church, as in former times. V. 22. **But,** or "Unless," **Thou hast utterly rejected us; Thou art very wroth against us.** It is hardly plausible that God's anger is so excessively great as to cause Him to shut out His repentant children forever. Thus the song of supplication, the prayer for mercy, ends with a statement of assurance, which hopes for a speedy fulfilment of its desire. Herein it is a model prayer for all times; for in the very midst of misery and affliction the believers are bound still to trust in the compassion of their heavenly Father.

THE BOOK OF THE PROPHET EZEKIEL.

INTRODUCTION.

This book, as the introductory paragraph clearly states, was written by Ezekiel, the son of Buzi, a priest of Jerusalem. He belonged to that company of Jews which had been carried into captivity from Jerusalem to Babylon about 597 B. C., some ten years before the destruction of the city. In the fifth year of his captivity he was called by God in a majestic vision to be His prophet. In this capacity he labored for at least twenty-two years among the captive Jews. He lived in the northern part of Mesopotamia, at Tel-a-bib, by the river Chebar. He owned a house there and was married. He apparently enjoyed the confidence of his fellow-exiles, for their elders frequently sought his advice and guidance; yet he shared the lot of other true prophets inasmuch as most of his hearers did not hearken to him nor do his words. The fall of Jerusalem served to give his words more emphasis and established his standing in a fair measure. The last date given in his book is the twenty-seventh year of the captivity; but we do not know how long he lived after that.

The special problem of Ezekiel was to testify to the Babylonian Jews, who were, for the most part, in comfortable circumstances and had built up a lively commerce with the Jews still remaining in Judea, but were still hard-hearted and idolatrous, showing them that the destruction of Jerusalem was not only inevitable, but also well deserved under the circumstances, lest they harden their hearts by a false comfort and refuse to be brought to repentance. It was necessary, moreover, to dissipate the false and foolish hopes which had been raised in the hearts of the exiled Jews by the alleged visions of false prophets and prophetesses. Ezekiel was eminently fitted for this task, for he possessed an unusual measure of mental and spiritual gifts; he had a good education; he had the priestly attitude and viewpoint; he was endowed with a wonderful imagination and a powerful gift of oratory; and he had received the firmness and courage for his difficult calling in an unusual degree. His activity, therefore, had a decisive influence on the development of the Jewish people during the Exile. Nor is it to be overlooked that one of the objects of Ezekiel's ministry was to comfort the true believers among the people, the faithful few who felt the loss of the Temple and its cult very deeply and longed for the salvation which was to come out of Zion.

The style of Ezekiel's book is in accordance with the energetic, fiery character of the prophet. While a part of his prophecy is in the didactic form and teaches in the usual manner of parables and proverbs, the general trend of his writing is toward symbolism and allegory, a fact which makes some parts of his book somewhat difficult to explain satisfactorily. But his object is always clearly presented, especially in the Messianic prophecies which we have in this book. Mingled with the messages of divine wrath and punishment we find sweet promises to the effect that God will not utterly destroy the entire nation, but will preserve a remnant of His people and at the end of seventy years bring them back to

Palestine and pour out upon them the blessings of His mercy. But the climax of the book is reached in the passages describing the Shepherd whom the Lord has promised to set up over His redeemed people, and in those speaking of the promised King.

The outline of the Book of Ezekiel may easily be discerned. The introductory section, chap. 1, 1—3, 21, speaks of the call and commission of the prophet. Then follow prophecies concerning the destruction of Jerusalem, up to and including chapter 24. We next find prophecies regarding the heathen nations, the enemies of God's people, chaps. 25—39. The last part is a prophetical description of the future glory of God's kingdom under the picture of the division of Canaan and of the New Jerusalem, chaps. 40—48.1)

1) Cp. Fuerbringer, *Einleitung in das Alte Testament*, 72—74; *Concordia Bible Class*, May, 1919, 72—75.

CHAPTER 1.

Ezekiel's Vision of God's Glory.

THE FOUR LIVING CREATURES. — V. 1. **Now it came to pass in the thirtieth year,** either of the prophet's life or of some period or era which can no longer be definitely determined, **in the fourth month, in the fifth day of the month, as I was among the captives by the river of Chebar,** for, having been led into captivity with Jehoiachin, he settled near this stream, which may have been one of the large irrigation ditches of the Euphrates Valley, **that the heavens were opened, and I saw visions of God,** the very first sentence of his book thus emphasizing Ezekiel's divine authorization. He was in a state of ecstasy, during which divine revelations were vouchsafed him, as opposed to any visions of his own heart, the empty fancies of false prophets. Note that Ezekiel names the thirtieth year, this being the one in which the priests entered upon the duties of their office. So God here prepared His servant, not by an unreal hallucination, but by an actual manifestation, for the ministry in which he was to testify of the Word made known to him. The time is now further specified with reference to a well-known date. V. 2. **In the fifth day of the month, which was the fifth year of King Jehoiachin's captivity,** with whom the second company of exiles had been brought to Babylon, v. 3. **the word of the Lord came expressly,** or "verily, truly," so that there can be no doubt of the fact, **unto Ezekiel, the priest, the son of Buzi, in the land of the Chaldeans, by the river Chebar; and the hand of the Lord was there upon him,** so that, by this divine manifestation of power, he was endowed with the faculty of seeing and proclaiming heavenly truths. The prophet now immediately launches forth in a description of the heavenly vision. V. 4. **And I looked, and, behold, a whirlwind came out of the north,** an emblem of God's mighty judgments, **a great cloud, and a fire infolding itself,** literally, "taking itself within itself," which does not merely mean, formed into a ball or lump of fire, but at the same time flashing as if there was a continual kindling of flame within the fiery mass forming the center of the cloud, **and a brightness was about it,** so that it glowed like gold being refined in the assayer's furnace, **and out of the midst thereof as the color of amber,** metal glowing in the melting-pot, **out of the midst of the fire,** as though the heart of it were made of polished brass. V. 5. **Also out of the midst thereof came the likeness of four living creatures. And this was their appearance: they had the likeness of a man,** possessing the general structure of a human body. V. 6. **And every one had four faces, and every one had four wings,** similarly as the seraphim in Is. 6, 2 had six wings apiece. V. 7. **And their feet,** evidently only two in number, **were straight feet,** literally, "a foot of straightness," not only firm, but without a bend at the knee, altogether upright and symmetrical; **and the sole of their feet was like the sole of a calf's foot,** standing vertically, not horizontally; **and they sparkled like the color of burnished brass,** thereby indicating the purity of God's essence and the glory of His avenging justice. V. 8. **And they had the hands of a man under their wings on their four sides,** the wings thus being fastened at the shoulders, whence the hands proceeded likewise; **and they four had their faces and their wings,** one each on every one of the four sides. V. 9. **Their wings were joined one to another,** connected or interlaced with one another. **They turned not when they went,** namely, in twisted maneuvers; **they went every one straight forward,** due to the fact that their wings were thus joined. V. 10. **As for the likeness of their faces, they four had the face of a man and the face of a lion on the right side,** namely, of one beholding them; **and they four had the face of an ox on the left side; they four also had the face of an eagle,** evidently on the side turned away from the beholder. The meaning of these four faces may have been to symbolize the strength, the power, the wisdom, and the nearness of God. V. 11. **Thus were their faces; and their wings were stretched upward,** literally, "parted from above," the heads being set on four separate necks; **two wings of every one were joined one to another,** the ends of the outstretched pinions being thus interlaced, and two covered their bodies, as in holy fear and reverence in the presence of God. V. 12. **And they went every one straight forward**, keeping their direction with unswerving directness; **whither the spirit**, the life-breath of God in them, **was to go, they went**, the four acting always in perfect unison; **and they turned not when they went**, in confusing maneuvers. V. 13. **As for the likeness of the living creatures**, the impression made by their appearance in general, **their appearance was like burning coals of fire**, like kindled coals, **and like the appearance of lamps**, in a quick and flickering motion, like the play of lightning; **it went up and down among the living creatures**, moving back and forth between them; **and the fire was bright, and out of the fire went forth lightning**, in a threatening effect toward the outside. V. 14. **And the living creatures ran and returned**, always straight before them, **as the appearance of a flash of lightning**, with the suddenness of an electric flash. The Lord, if He so chooses, is able to reveal His will in a most startling and majestic manner, as also some phenomena of nature show to this day.

THE FOUR-FACED WHEELS AND THE FOUR CREATURES. — V. 15. **Now, as I beheld the living creatures**, which were associated with the menacing cloud and must therefore be thought of as being elevated above the earth, **behold one wheel upon the earth**, that is, a unit of four wheels in one, **by the living creatures, with his four faces**, toward their four fronts. V. 16. **The appearance of the wheels and their work**, their make-up, their workmanship and shape, **was like unto the color of a beryl**, of the chrysolite, which had a yellow color, as of clear fire; **and they four had one likeness, and their appearance and their work**, their shape as seen by the prophet, **was as it were a wheel in the middle of a wheel**, the one set crosswise within the other, as in a gyroscope. V. 17. **When they went, they went upon their four sides**, they could go in four directions, due to that double construction; **and they turned not when they went**, just like the four creatures. V. 18. **As for their rings**, the felloes of the wheels, **they were so high that they were dreadful**, on account of the effect of sublimity; **and their rings were full of eyes round about them four**, this fact introducing the element of life. V. 19. **And when the living creatures went, the wheels went by them**, being always in the closest relation to them; **and when the living creatures were lifted up from the earth, the wheels were lifted up**, the impulse being transmitted to them in some unexplained manner. V. 20. **Whithersoever the spirit was to go, they went, thither was their spirit to go**, following the direction taken by the creatures; **and the wheels were lifted up over against them; for the spirit of the living creature was in the wheels.** V. 21. **When those went, these went; and when those stood, these stood; and when those were lifted up from the earth**, as the cloud lifted up in its onward course, **the wheels were lifted up over against them; for the spirit of the living creature was in the wheels.** The wheels thus, both when moving and when standing still, were governed by the motion and the rest of the living creatures because the same spirit of life animated them both. This scene is now brought in relation to the description of Jehovah's throne. V. 22. **And the likeness of the firmament upon the heads of the living creature was as the color of the terrible crystal**, literally, "a likeness over the head of the living creature, like unto the appearance of crystal, of the fearful," **stretched forth over their heads above.** The dazzling clearness and purity of the glittering crystal caused the spectator to feel awe, as from the reflection of the Creator's splendor. V. 23. **And under the firmament were their wings straight**, raised aloft as they moved forward in an erect position, **the one toward the other; every one had two, which covered on this side**, when let down, **and every one had two, which covered on that side, their bodies.** "The tips of the wings (of the pair of wings serving for flight) reach along to the vault. For support they are not adapted, and particularly for this reason that the wings, v. 24, make a loud noise and are therefore in free motion; and further, because upon occasion they are let down. The wheels also do not support the chariot. The local proximity seems only to indicate the connection between the several provinces of creation; it is meant to represent the creation as a united whole." (Hengstenberg.) V. 24. **And when they went, I heard the noise of their wings like the noise of great waters**, of the surging and roaring of the ocean, **as the voice of the Almighty**, in the thunder of His power, **the voice of speech**, a dull, confused noise **as of a tumult, as the noise of an host; when they stood, they let down their wings**, in reverential rest before the only living God, who now puts a restraint on the fierceness of the creatures in carrying out the divine wrath. V. 25. **And there was a voice from the firmament that was over their heads**, a command from Jehovah Himself, **when they stood and had let down their wings**, in full and submissive silence, awaiting the commands of Him who has power over all created beings. V. 26. **And above the firmament that was over their heads was the likeness of a throne**, that being the highest object in the prophet's vision, **as the appearance of a sapphire stone**, a sky-blue, or violet-colored stone; **and upon the likeness of the throne was the likeness as the appearance of a man above upon it**, the Godhead thus appearing in the likeness of enthroned humanity. Cp. Ex. 24, 10. V. 27. **And I saw as the color of amber,** like metal glowing in the refiner's furnace, **as the appearance of fire round about within it, from the appearance of his loins even upward and from the appearance of his loins even downward, I saw as it were the appearance of fire, and it had brightness round about,** the glow apparently enclosed within a definite space. V. 28. **As the appearance of the bow that is in the cloud in the day of rain,** the rainbow occupying a well-defined area of brilliancy, **so was the appearance of the brightness round about.** Cp. Rev. 4, 3. **This was the appearance of the likeness of the glory of the Lord,** in this way Ezekiel received some impression of the exalted majesty of the Lord of the covenant, of the true God. A similar experience was accorded the prophet upon three subsequent occasions. Cp. chap. 3, 22 ff.; 8, 4 ff.; 43, 1 ff. **And when I saw it, I fell upon my face,** a sinful man overcome by the glorious majesty of the holy God, **and I heard the voice of one that spake.** The purpose of God in granting this vision to Ezekiel was to reveal His almighty and merciful presence as the Lord and King whose power extends over the whole world, who has the strength to judge the heathen and to deliver His people, now held in shameful captivity, and let them once more enjoy the beauty of His grace. Would that the believers of all times, yea, all men, might receive the Word of the Lord with the same humility here shown by the prophet.

CHAPTER 2.

The Commission of Ezekiel to Be the Lord's Prophet.

The Lord, having revealed Himself to His servant in the fulness of His divine power and majesty, now issued to him the formal call, extended to him the formal commission to be His prophet to the rebellious Jews. V. 1. **And He said unto me, Son of man,** the name reminding him of the frailty of the human race, but also of the fact that the Lord here addressed him as a man speaks to his friends, **stand upon thy feet, and I will speak unto thee.** V. 2. **And the spirit entered into me when He spake unto me,** with divine power enabling him to stand before the face of God and to receive his commission, **and set me upon my feet, that I heard Him that spake unto me,** ready to heed and to carry out His commands. V. 3. **And He said unto me, Son of man, I send thee to the children of Israel,** the expression here referring to Israel as a nation, not as the Lord's people, **to a rebellious nation,** on a level with the heathen nations, **that hath rebelled against Me; they and their fathers have transgressed against Me, even unto this very day.** Those who should have been true sons of him who wrestled and prevailed in faith with God and man had sunk to the level of the heathen world, with its rebellious attitude over against all that was right and good. V. 4. **For they are impudent children,** with hard faces, devoid of all shame, **and stiff-hearted,** without the slightest inclination toward repentance. **I do send thee unto them,** in spite of this condition of their understanding and of their heart; **and thou shalt say unto them, Thus saith the Lord God,** Jehovah, the God of the covenant, who here delegated and commissioned Ezekiel to be His personal representative, giving him the very words of the message to the rebellious people. V. 5. **And they, whether they will hear, or whether they will forbear,** no matter what their attitude toward the Lord's proclamation would be, **(for they are a rebellious house,) yet shall know that there hath been a prophet among them,** this admission being forced from them in spite of their rebellious and insolent behavior. V. 6. **And thou, son of man,** a minister of the Lord in spite of his natural frailty, **be not afraid of them,** with a timidity caused by the insulting impudence of his hearers, **neither be afraid of their words,** with which they would challenge his authority and ridicule his testimony, **though briers and thorns be with thee,** namely, in the persons of these refractory, hostile people, **and thou dost dwell among scorpions,** arachnids, with poisonous stings in their tails, this name being fitly applied to such dangerous persons as would oppose the prophet's labors; **be not afraid of their words, nor be dismayed at their looks, though they be a rebellious house.** The proof of Ezekiel's divine commission would be exhibited in the fulfilment of his prophecies, and the enemies would thereby be confounded. V. 7. **And thou shalt speak My words unto them,** the fact of the divine inspiration of Ezekiel's prophecies being repeated thus with special emphasis, **whether they will hear, or whether they will forbear; for they are most rebellious.** V. 8. **But thou, son of man,** by birth and descent a member of this rebellious nation, **hear what I say unto thee, Be not thou rebellious like that rebellious house,** thereby to become guilty of the same insolent behavior; **open thy mouth and eat that I give thee,** in a symbolical action which explains itself. V. 9. **And when I looked, behold, an hand was sent unto me,** extended toward the prophet; **and, lo, a roll of a book was therein,** as books were written in those days, the characters inscribed on long strips of parchment, which were then usually rolled up; v. 10. **and**

He spread it before me, unrolling the parchment strip before his astonished eyes; **and it was written within and without,** on both sides of the parchment, indicating also a writing of great size; **and there was written therein lamentations and mourning and woe,** this being the message which the prophet was to set forth, as included in this his book of prophecy. It is doubly hard for a believer to maintain his faith if in the very church-body of which he is a member things occur which have a tendency to offend him deeply; but it is in just such circumstances that faith will be tested.

CHAPTER 3.

The Prophet's Further Commission.

DIVINE STRENGTH IN THE FACE OF CERTAIN OPPOSITION. — V. 1. **Moreover, He said unto me, Son of man, eat that thou findest,** the book being something that he did not seek, but which was placed before him; **eat this roll and go speak unto the house of Israel,** to whom the first part of Ezekiel's prophecy is addressed. V. 2. **So I opened my mouth, and He caused me to eat that roll,** the prophet's eating signifying his acceptance of the Lord's commission. V. 3. **And He said unto me, Son of man, cause thy belly to eat and fill thy bowels with this roll that I give thee,** so that the Word of God contained in the roll would, as it were, become the very substance of his being. **Then did I eat it; and it was in my mouth as honey for sweetness,** for, because its contents were the Word of God, expressed the will of Jehovah, Ezekiel delighted in them, painful though their import was with regard to his fellow-countrymen. Cp. Ps. 19, 10; 119, 103. The taste of the roll in his mouth filled him with a cheerful alacrity. Cp. 1 Sam. 14, 29. V. 4. **And He said unto me, Son of man, go, get thee unto the house of Israel,** the members of the prophet's own nation, **and speak with My words unto them,** the entire message being given by inspiration of God. V. 5. **For thou art not sent to a people of a strange speech and of an hard language,** literally, "obscure of lip and difficult of tongue," that is, a nation whose language was unknown to him, whose entire trend of thought was obscure, whose interpretation would offer unusual difficulties, **but to the house of Israel,** in whose case the language, at least, would offer no insurmountable obstacle; v. 6. **not to many people of a strange speech and of an hard language,** so that the learning of a number of languages and dialects would increase the difficulties of communication and therefore of proclaiming the Lord's will, **whose words thou canst not understand. Surely, had I sent thee to them, they,** in spite of all the obstacles and hindrances just enumerated, **would have hearkened unto thee,** showing less obstinacy and thus a corresponding greater interest in the prophet's message than the members of his own people. V. 7. **But the house of Israel will not hearken unto thee,** will show no interest in the prophet's message, will refuse to be obedient; **for they will not hearken unto Me,** as the history of the last centuries had shown; **for all the house of Israel are impudent and hard-hearted,** literally, "hard of forehead and stiff of heart are they," thoroughly obstinate and rebellious. There was need of unusual firmness in dealing with this situation, and this the Lord provided for His servant. V. 8. **Behold, I have made thy face strong against their faces,** filling him with indomitable courage, **and thy forehead strong against their foreheads,** in unshakable determination. V. 9. **As an adamant,** the diamond, hardest of precious stones, **harder than flint have I made thy forehead; fear them not, neither be dismayed at their looks,** blasphemous and hostile though they were, **though they be a rebellious house.** Cp. chap. 2, 4—6. V. 10. **Moreover, He said unto me,** in further preparation for the work of his peculiar ministry, **Son of man, all My words that I shall speak unto thee receive in thine heart and hear with thine ears,** in perfect obedience, in ready acceptance, with a willing understanding, so that they would be translated into right action. V. 11. **And go, get thee to them of the captivity, unto the children of thy people,** with whom the first part of his message was concerned, **and speak unto them and tell them, Thus saith the Lord God; whether they will hear, or whether they will forbear.** This is the attitude which ought to characterize the Lord's servants at all times: to preach the Word regardless of consequences. The plea of the need of pastoral tact which is often made by opportunists tends to make this a cloak to shield moral cowardice.

EZEKIEL AS WATCHMAN. — V. 12. **Then the Spirit took me up,** so that he would at once be placed into a position where he might perform the work of his calling, **and I heard behind me a voice of a great rushing,** a tumultuous noise, **saying, Blessed be the glory of the Lord from His place,** going forth, from His throne, into all the world, manifested even in the great disasters which would strike the rebellious Jews. V. 13. **I heard also the noise of the wings of the living creatures that touched one another,** literally, "kissed each other," the one toward her sister, said of the gentle touch of the ends of the wings, **and the noise of the wheels over against them and a noise of a great rushing,** the vision of chapter 1 thus being brought into the closest relation to the commission of Ezekiel. V. 14. **So the Spirit lifted me up,** placing him into a state of ecstasy, **and took me away; and I went in bitterness, in the heat of my spirit,** in deep sadness on account of the calamities of which he was required to be the unwelcome messenger; **but the hand of the Lord was strong upon me,** holding him firmly in this strange conflict within him. V. 15. **Then I came to them of the captivity,** the main colony of the Jewish exiles, **at Tel-abib, that dwelt by the river of Chebar, and I sat where they sat,** joining them in their misery, **and remained there astonished among them seven days,** almost motionless, staring down before him, as one almost paralyzed with grief and horror. V. 16. **And it came to pass at the end of seven days,** the usual period of preparation for acts of special worship, **that the word of the Lord came unto me, saying,** v. 17. **Son of man, I have made thee a watchman unto the house of Israel,** the seer on the watch-tower applying the revelations which are made to him for the weal and woe of the people entrusted to him. **Therefore hear the word at My mouth,** the message of commandment and threatened judgment, **and give them warning from Me,** by a continual appeal to the divine instructions received. V. 18. **When I say unto the wicked, Thou shalt surely die,** namely, paying the penalty for open transgressions of the holy will of God, **and thou givest him not warning nor speakest to warn the wicked from his wicked way,** in an urgent attempt to save him from his wickedness and its results, **to save his life,** which would otherwise be threatened with eternal perdition, **the same wicked man shall die in his iniquity,** being obliged, indeed, to pay the penalty of his sins; **but his blood will I require at thine hand,** as having caused the slaughter of an immortal soul by his negligence. V. 19. **Yet if thou warn the wicked,** performing the solemn duty laid upon him as watchman, unpleasant though this may be, **and he turn not from his wickedness,** the inner evil condition of his heart, **nor from his wicked way,** the outward manifestation of his evil heart, **he shall die in his iniquity,** on account of his deliberate, habitual wickedness, **but thou hast delivered thy soul,** having done his duty in sounding the warning in time. V. 20. **Again, when a righteous man,** one who has always lived an upright and honest life, **doth turn from his righteousness and commit iniquity, and I lay a stumbling-block before him, he shall die,** for he has sunk to the level of the wicked; **because thou hast not given him warning,** to keep him from the path of sin, **he shall die in his sin,** whose guilt will certainly be charged to him, **and his righteousness which he hath done shall not be remembered,** will no longer count in his favor; **but his blood will I require at thine hand,** the watchman again being charged with negligence for failing to prevent the apostasy. V. 21. **Nevertheless, if thou warn the righteous man that the righteous sin not,** not yielding to any temptation which might come in his way, **and he doth not sin, he shall surely live because he is warned,** he has heeded the warning in time; **also thou hast delivered thy soul,** in performing the solemn duty included in his prophetical commission. God, indeed, tempts no one to sin, Jas. 1, 13, but He permits even the believers to be surrounded with conditions which put their faith to a test, as in the case of Job. Thus was the great and solemn commission transmitted to Ezekiel. V. 22. **And the hand of the Lord was there upon me,** symbolizing the fact that His power and authority was transferred to the prophet for his special sphere of labor; **and He said unto me, Arise, go forth into the plain,** down from the height on which Tel-abib was situated to the valley below, **and I will there talk with thee.** V. 23. **Then I arose and went forth into the plain,** whose solitude was favorable to the Lord's plan; **and, behold, the glory of the Lord stood there, as the glory which I saw by the river of Chebar,** chap. 1, 1; **and I fell on my face,** once more overcome by the majesty of the vision. V. 24. **Then the Spirit,** as in the other instance, **entered into me, and set me upon my feet, and spake with me, and said unto me, Go, shut thyself within thine house,** the purpose of this seclusion becoming evident from the connection, shut out from social intercourse, but not as if imprisoned. V. 25. **But thou, O son of man, behold, they shall put bands upon thee,** the Lord Himself putting the restraint of a strange ecstasy upon him, **and shall bind thee with them, and thou shalt not go out among them,** this very fact being intended to arrest their attention, v. 26. **and I will make thy tongue cleave to the roof of thy mouth,** before the very eyes of the rebellious people, **that thou shalt be dumb and shalt not be to them a reprover,** lest the words of his reproof might win the self-hardened sinners back; **for they are a rebellious house,** confirming themselves in their apostasy and obstinacy. V. 27. **But when I speak with thee, I will open thy mouth,** in revealing the judgment of God upon his countrymen, **and thou shalt say unto them, Thus saith the Lord God, He that heareth, let him hear, and he that forbeareth, let him forbear; for they are a rebellious house,** and therefore would have only themselves to blame for the calamity which would surely strike them. Every pastor, as the Lord's watchman in the midst of his congregation, has a tremendous responsibility resting upon him, both in calling sinners to repentance and in warning the believers against the ways of unrighteousness. One negligent in this duty is a murderer of souls.

CHAPTER 4.

The Four Signs and Their Interpretation.

THE SYMBOL OF THE SIEGE. — V. 1. **Thou also, son of man, take thee a tile,** very likely a Babylonian brick, a foot square and about five inches thick, **and lay it before thee,** while the clay was still soft, **and portray upon it the city, even Jerusalem,** drawing the map of the Jewish capital with the usual pencil, or style, v. 2. **and lay siege against it, and build a fort against it,** very likely a watch-tower or bulwark, which permitted the invading army to observe every movement of the besieged, **and cast a mount against it,** the usual earthworks with their trenches; **set the camp also against it,** to surround the city on all sides, **and set battering-rams against it round about,** the latter being logs of hard wood, with heads of wrought iron. All this was to be shown in the sketch prepared by the prophet, the map thus emphasizing the fact that Jerusalem would be besieged. V. 3. **Moreover, take thou unto thee an iron pan,** such as were used in Jewish households, as well as in the Temple, **and set it for a wall of iron between thee and the city,** as representing the divine decree regarding the Chaldean invasion; **and set thy face against it,** in stern opposition, **and it shall be besieged, and thou shalt lay siege against it. This shall be a sign to the house of Israel,** to the people of God, formerly identical with the covenant nation. V. 4. **Lie thou also upon thy left side,** in another symbolical act, **and lay the iniquity of the house of Israel upon it,** like a sickness which causes the diseased person to lie in one position without shifting; **according to the number of the days that thou shalt lie upon it thou shalt bear their iniquity,** not in a vicarious, but in a symbolical act. V. 5. **For I have laid upon thee the years of their iniquity,** that Ezekiel was, figuratively, bearing their guilt, **according to the number of the days, three hundred and ninety days,** a number of years which may refer to the time of the Egyptian bondage, or as simply strokes of divine chastisement; **so shalt thou bear the iniquity of the house of Israel.** V. 6. **And when thou hast accomplished them,** having fulfilled the three hundred and ninety days typical of the bearing of Israel's burden, **lie again on thy right side, and thou shalt bear the iniquity of the house of Judah forty days,** a number which may refer to various periods in the history of the people or, as some think, to the last forty years of the Egyptian bondage, which were at the same time the years which gave Moses his test for leadership; **I have appointed thee each day for a year,** that is, one day of the symbolical act stood for a whole year in the actual history to which it referred. V. 7. **Therefore thou shalt set thy face toward the siege of Jerusalem,** which was always before the prophet in the sketch which he had drawn, **and thine arm,** namely, the free arm in either case, **shall be uncovered,** bare to the shoulder, to have free use of it at all times, **and thou shalt prophesy against it,** both by his symbolical acting and by proclaiming the Lord's message. V. 8. **And, behold, I will lay bands upon thee,** holding him down, causing him to hold out with patience in the difficult feat proposed, **and thou shalt not turn thee from one side to another,** to relieve the tediousness of lying on one side alone, **till thou hast ended the days of thy siege,** the fulfilling of the time indicating the conquest of the city. No matter in what way God makes known His will, the outstanding fact is that it will certainly be fulfilled, for not one of His words may fail.

THE SYMBOLS OF THE FAMINE. — V. 9. **Take thou also unto thee wheat, and barley,** these grains usually being eaten in the form of roasted kernels, **and beans, and lentils, and millet, and fitches,** or spelt, **and put them in one vessel,** as signifying the last of provisions to be had, gathered for the extremity of the siege, **and make thee bread thereof,** food in the customary roasted form, **according to the number of the days that thou shalt lie upon thy side; three hundred and ninety days shalt thou eat thereof,** the number of Israel's years of oppression being named as sufficient to emphasize the difficulty of the situation. V. 10. **And thy meat which thou shalt eat,** the food which he should consume according to this strict rationing, **shall be by weight, twenty shekels a day,** estimated at some twenty ounces avoirdupois, about half as much as the average man needs for his daily sustenance; **from time to time shalt thou eat it,** not according to the demands of hunger, but according to the rations provided for, that is, at long intervals, very sparingly. V. 11. **Thou shalt drink also water by measure,** instead of according to desire and ordinary need, **the sixth part of an hin,** approximately a pint and a half; **from time to time shalt thou drink.** V. 12. **And thou shalt eat it,** the food provided for, **as barley cakes,** baked or roasted in the ashes of his fire, or on stones heated by this fire; **and thou shalt bake it with dung that cometh out of man,** whose use as fuel must have been exceedingly repulsive, **in their sight.** The situation, then, was this, that filth and misery surrounded the prophet on every side — a very vivid picture, in order to emphasize his message before his countrymen. V. 13. **And the Lord said, Even thus shall the children of Israel eat their defiled bread,** polluted with the odor of the unspeakable fuel used, **among the Gentiles,**

whither I will drive them, where they would be obliged to sojourn and come in contact with the abominations of the heathen. The uncleanness was not so much a Levitical defilement as a pollution outraging the universal feeling of human beings concerning decency. V. 14. **Then said I,** in voicing an objection to the loathsome fuel proposed by the Lord, **Ah, Lord God! Behold, my soul hath not been polluted,** for so he might interpret Lev. 5, 3; 7, 21 as pertaining to this present case; **for from my youth up even till now have I not eaten of that which dieth of itself or is torn in pieces,** cp. Ex. 22, 30; Deut. 14, 21, **neither came there abominable flesh into my mouth.** Cp. Deut. 14, 3. Note the emphasis of the prophet's expression in setting forth his consciousness of the loathsomeness of the method suggested to him. V. 15. **Then He said unto me,** in yielding the point for the sake of the prophet's scruples, **Lo, I have given thee cow's dung for man's dung,** a fuel still used very extensively in the Orient, **and thou shalt prepare thy bread therewith.** V. 16. **Moreover, He said unto me, Son of man, behold, I will break the staff of bread in Jerusalem,** bread being one of the chief articles of food, one of man's main articles of nourishment; **and they shall eat bread by weight,** in careful rations, as demonstrated by the prophet, **and with care,** in worried anxiety about the means of subsistence; **and they shall drink water by measure and with astonishment,** in dull grief, in speechless pain, v. 17. **that they may want bread and water,** be in dire need of the food barely sufficing for their daily needs, **and be astonied one with another,** with the stupefied look of total despair, **and consume away for their iniquity.** Thus the Lord, by these various signs, set forth the early destruction of Jerusalem and the sufferings which would come upon its inhabitants in connection with the Chaldean conquest.

CHAPTER 5.

The Vision of the Cutting of Hair.

THE SIGN ITSELF. — V. 1. **And thou, son of man, take thee a sharp knife,** a sword such as was used in war, **take thee a barber's razor,** the sword itself being used like the razor of a barber, **and cause it to pass upon thine head and upon thy beard,** Ezekiel here representing Jerusalem besieged and his shaving the severe straits in which the capital would find itself shortly; **then take the balances to weigh,** as symbolizing the divine justice, **and divide the hair.** V. 2. **Thou shalt burn with fire a third part,** namely, of the hair thus set apart by his careful division, **in the midst of the city, when the days of the siege are fulfilled,** when the city is taken by the Chaldeans; **and thou shalt take a third part and smite about it with a knife,** striking and felling it with a sword; **and a third part thou shalt scatter in the wind,** so as to leave no two hairs together, **and I will draw out a sword after them.** V. 3. **Thou shalt also take thereof,** of the last third of the mass of hair, **a few in number and bind them in thy skirts,** thus preserving a few in the midst of the general calamity. V. 4. **Then take of them again,** of the few thus saved, **and cast them into the midst of the fire and burn them in the fire,** the fire being considered a purifying agent; **for thereof shall a fire come forth into all the house of Israel.** The thought underlying this last statement is that of the refiner's fire, for it was this phase of the matter which was brought to bear upon Israel, so that a remnant at least was saved. Cp. Is. 6, 12. 13; Luke 12, 49. God poured out His loving-kindness upon the Jews in an ever-increasing measure.

THE INTERPRETATION OF THE SIGN. — V. 5. **Thus saith the Lord God, This is Jerusalem,** the exalted city of the Lord's habitation; **I have set it in the midst of the nations and countries that are round about her,** the center of the true worship, from which rays go forth to all the world. V. 6. **And she hath changed My judgments,** the decrees of the Lord concerning justice and righteousness, **into wickedness more than the nations,** the people heaping upon themselves a greater guilt than the very heathen, **and My statutes more than the countries that are round about her,** in an utter disregard of the Lord's will; **for they have refused My judgments and My statutes, they have not walked in them.** Israel, hating and rejecting the way of justice and righteousness pointed out by the Lord, preferred to follow the evil, sinful customs of the heathen. Cp. chap. 11, 12. V. 7. **Therefore, thus saith the Lord God, Because ye multiplied more than the nations that are round about you,** raving and raging in their transgressions of His holy will, **and have not walked in My statutes,** in bringing their whole life into agreement with their demands, **neither have kept My judgments, neither have done according to the judgments of the nations that are round about you,** who, at least in a measure, tried to follow the dictates of the Moral Law in the faint impressions still remaining in their hearts, Rom. 2, 14—16, v. 8. **therefore thus saith the Lord God, Behold, I, even I, am against thee,** setting Himself against the Jewish nation in stern opposition, **and will execute judgments in the midst of thee in the sight of the nations,** as a spectacle of His avenging justice. V. 9. **And I will do in thee that which I have not done,** punishing in a degree heretofore unheard of, **and whereunto I will not do any more the like,** never repeating a like punishment upon men, **because of all thine abominations,** because Israel had exceeded the heathen in every form of wickedness. V. 10. **Therefore the fathers shall eat the sons in the midst of thee,** in a most revolting form of cannibalism, **and the sons shall eat their fathers,** utterly forgetful, like them, of the fundamental demands of nature, cp. Lev. 26, 29; Deut. 28, 53; **and I will execute judgments in thee,** as shown by the symbolism of the hair, **and the whole remnant of thee will I scatter into all the winds,** into all parts of the world. V. 11. **Wherefore, as I live, saith the Lord God,** in a most solemn form of oath, by His own life and being, **Surely, because thou hast defiled My Sanctuary with all thy detestable things,** with the various idolatrous customs and the false worship introduced from time to time, **and with all thine abominations,** cp. 2 Chron. 36, 14, **therefore will I also diminish thee, neither shall Mine eye spare,** literally, "and also I shall withdraw — and not have mercy — Mine eye," **neither will I have any pity.** V. 12. **A third part of thee,** corresponding to the first third of the hair of the prophet, **shall die with the pestilence, and with famine shall they be consumed in the midst of thee,** during the course of the siege of the city and when it was taken; **and a third part shall fall by the sword round about thee,** as indicated in the second part of the symbolical action; **and I will scatter a third part into all the winds,** among various provinces and nations; **and I will draw out a sword after them,** to complete His vengeance upon them. V. 13. **Thus shall Mine anger be accomplished,** the full measure of His wrath be exhausted upon the Jewish nation, **and I will cause My fury to rest upon them,** so that it would be satisfied in the punishment meted out, **and I will be comforted,** feeling this satisfaction; **and they shall know that I, the Lord, have spoken it in My zeal,** as a guarantee of His sincerity in making His threats, **when I have accomplished My fury in them,** carrying out His punishment upon them in full. V. 14. **Moreover, I will make thee waste,** so that the city would be changed to a heap of ruins, **and a reproach among the nations that are round about thee,** so that people everywhere would mock and deride her, cp. Deut. 29, 23. 24, **in the sight of all that pass by.** V. 15. **So it,** Jerusalem, the former proud capital city, **shall be a reproach and a taunt, an instruction,** an example of warning to teach people a lesson, **and an astonishment unto the nations that are round about thee when I shall execute judgments in thee in anger and in fury and in furious rebukes,** in chastisements of His divine indignation. **I, the Lord, have spoken it.** V. 16. **When I shall send upon them the evil arrows of famine,** such as hail, rain, mice, locusts, mildew, Deut. 32, 23. 24, **which shall be for their destruction, and which I will send to destroy you; and I will increase the famine upon you,** gathering its forces like those of an invading army, to work havoc on every hand, **and will break your staff of bread,** upon which men ordinarily lean for support and sustenance of life; v. 17. **so will I send upon you famine and evil beasts,** Lev. 26, 22, **and they shall bereave thee; and pestilence,** in various severe epidemics, **and blood shall pass through thee,** in slaughter by the Chaldean invaders; **and I will bring the sword upon thee,** here chiefly in civil war. **I, the Lord, have spoken it.** There is special emphasis in the repetition of this statement and in the heaping of terms denoting the severity of the Lord's punishment, also in the change from the second to the third person, as though the Lord were becoming increasingly estranged from His own people. His avenging fury strikes men with deadly effect, no matter in what form He sends it.

CHAPTER 6.

The Judgment of God upon the Places and the Servants of Idolatry.

THE DESOLATION OF THE LAND AND THE SLAUGHTER OF THE IDOLATERS.—V. 1. **And the word of the Lord came unto me,** again in direct verbal inspiration, **saying,** v. 2. **Son of man, set thy face toward the mountains of Israel,** in a prophecy of condemnation, **and prophesy against them,** v. 3. **and say, Ye mountains of Israel,** the special places of idolatrous cults, here representing the entire country formerly occupied by the Lord's people, **hear the word of the Lord God,** of the sovereign Ruler of the universe: **Thus saith the Lord God to the mountains and to the hills,** the high places of heathen worship, **to the rivers and to the valleys,** where the idolaters lived, **Behold, I, even I, will bring a sword upon you,** the murderous sword of the invading foes, **and I will destroy your high places,** where the altars and sanctuaries erected to idols were commonly found. V. 4. **And your altars,** namely, those devoted to the service of idols, **shall be desolate, and your images shall be broken,** the sun-pillars erected in honor of the Phenician god Baal; **and I will cast down your slain men before your idols.** In the original the word here used has a contemptuous flavor, so that it means either stone monuments, loose stones, dead masses of stone, or — dung-idols. In the presence of the very logs or pillars in which they trusted these men would be slaughtered, for their idols were powerless to help them. V. 5. **And I will lay the dead carcasses of the children of Israel before their idols,** as a proper votive offering; **and I will scatter your bones round about your altars,** a fitting mockery of their idolatrous trust. V. 6. **In all your dwelling-places,** that is, throughout the country occupied by them, **the cities shall be laid waste, and the high places shall be desolate,** heaps of ruins, **that your altars may be laid waste and made desolate and your idols may be broken and cease,** totally exterminated, **and your images may be cut down,** the sun-pillars being destroyed utterly, **and your works may be abolished,** all the buildings and vessels of idolatry which they had erected or made. V. 7. **And the slain shall fall in the midst of you,** so that some, indeed, would still be delivered, **and ye shall know that I am the Lord,** the one and only true God, as contrasted with the idols, which have no true existence and pass away under the blows of the enemy's hammer. The falling of the slain, of the idolaters with their idols, leads to the knowledge of Jehovah as the almighty Lord.

THE FATE OF THOSE WHO REMAIN. — V. 8. **Yet will I leave a remnant,** in the general destruction spoken of in the first part of the chapter, **that ye may have some that shall escape the sword among the nations when ye shall be scattered through the countries,** in the exile which had been threatened by various prophets. V. 9. **And they that escape of you shall remember Me among the nations whither they shall be carried captives,** realizing that He who brought this calamity upon them was Jehovah, the God of Israel, and that His Word is the eternal truth, also in the threats uttered against their idolatry, **because I am broken with their whorish heart,** or, "when I have broken their whorish heart," **which hath departed from Me,** in the spiritual adultery so often reproved in the Old Testament, **and with their eyes, which go a-whoring after their idols,** instead of being faithful to the God of the covenant; **and they shall loathe themselves for the evils which they have committed in all their abominations,** they will have a feeling of revulsion against themselves for ever having yielded to the idolatry of the heathen nations. Thus the first part of a true repentance would be wrought in them, the feeling of disgust over their unfaithfulness to the true Lord. V. 10. **And they shall know that I am the Lord,** being brought to this realization by the lessons of a bitter experience, **and that I have not said in vain,** with an empty threat, **that I would do this evil unto them.** Since they would not listen before, they would be obliged to heed when the proof of the Lord's faithfulness in keeping His word would bring them to their senses. V. 11. **Thus saith the Lord God, Smite with thine hand,** either in clapping or in striking the thigh, **and stamp with thy foot,** in indignant impatience with Israel's hard-heartedness, **and say, Alas for all the evil abominations of the house of Israel!** that it should have been necessary to go to such extremes in bringing them to their senses. **For they shall fall by the sword, by the famine, and by the pestilence,** the great scourges of the Lord's wrath. V. 12. **He that is far off,** out of the enemies' reach, **shall die of the pestilence,** being unable to escape the avenging anger of the Lord; **and he that is near,** within reach of the invaders, **shall fall by the sword; and he that remaineth and is besieged shall die by the famine,** having escaped the sword in the siege, he nevertheless becomes a victim. **Thus will I accomplish,** fully carry out, **My fury upon them.** V. 13. **Then shall ye know that I am the Lord, when their slain men shall be among their idols round about their altars,** v. 5, **upon every high hill, in all the tops of the mountains,** where the idolatrous sanctuaries to the heavenly powers were usually erected, **and under every green tree, and under every thick oak,** the terebinth-oak of Palestine, found either in groves or as individual trees in the brook-channels and ravines, **the place where they did offer sweet savor to all their idols,** namely, in sacrificing incense to Baal and Astarte. V. 14. **So will I stretch out My hand upon them,** in sending His punishment, **and make the land desolate, yea, more desolate than the wilderness toward Diblath,** a desert otherwise unknown, but probably located in Arabia, **in all their habitations; and they shall know that I am the Lord.** In one form or other, but with constantly increasing emphasis, the Lord brings out His lesson: "Be not deceived; God is not mocked!"

CHAPTER 7.

The Final Destruction of Israel.

THE APPROACHING RUIN. — V. 1. **Moreover, the word of the Lord came unto me, saying,** v. 2. **Also, thou son of man,** the direct address distinguishing this communication from those intended for the people in general, **thus saith the Lord God unto the land of Israel,** the home of the covenant people, **An end,** that which terminates the long-suffering of God toward the whole of Judea, **the end,** that now definitely fixed, **is come upon the four corners of the land,** to its extreme boundaries, throughout its borders. V. 3. **Now is the end come upon thee,** the entire land of the covenant nation, **and I will send Mine anger upon thee and will judge thee according to thy ways,** the manner of conduct in all its forms, **and will recompense upon thee all thine abominations,** so that they would be duly repaid upon their heads. V. 4. **And Mine eye shall not spare thee,** in any form of compassion, **neither will I have pity,** such as an indulgent father might have been tempted to show; **but I will recompense thy ways upon thee, and thine abominations shall be in the midst of thee,** manifest to all in their consequences, the divine punishments; **and ye shall know,** as the punishment struck them in strict accordance with the Lord's prophecy, **that I am the Lord,** the evidence offered being sufficient and conclusive. V. 5. **Thus saith the Lord God, An evil, an only evil, behold, is come,** a peculiar calamity such as had never been heard of before, unparalleled in the history of the world. V. 6. **An end is come, the end is come,** literally, "An end cometh, there cometh the end," its absolute certainty thus being brought out; **it watcheth for thee,** awaking from its slumber, as it were, to pounce upon its victim; **behold, it is come.** V. 7. **The morning is come unto thee,** the turn of events, the destiny, the fate allotted them, **O thou that dwellest in the land,** all its inhabitants. **The time is come,** the period which completes the time set by God; **the day of trouble is near and not the sounding again of the mountains,** literally, "tumult and not joyous shouting on the mountains," such as was the rule when the harvest was gathered in the vineyards. The time of such untroubled happiness was past. V. 8. **Now will I shortly pour out My fury upon thee,** as from an overturned vessel, **and accomplish Mine anger upon thee,** in the fierceness of His punishment; **and I will judge thee according to thy ways and will recompense thee for all thine abominations,** the repetition of this statement making it the more emphatic. V. 9. **And mine eye shall not spare, neither will I have pity; I will recompense thee according to thy ways and thine abominations that are in the midst of thee; and ye shall know that I am the Lord that smiteth.** The true God is a jealous God, visiting the iniquity of the sinners upon them with a sharp reckoning.

THE RUIN ACCOMPLISHED. — V. 10. **Behold the day,** that of the final reckoning, **behold, it is come; the morning is gone forth,** the destined calamity has arisen; **the rod hath blossomed, pride hath budded,** the powers of vengeance maturing for the purpose of performing the Lord's punishment upon the covenant people. V. 11. **Violence,** namely, that of the conquering Chaldeans, **is risen up into a rod of wickedness,** namely, to carry out the punishment upon the wicked; **none of them shall remain,** the inhabitants being either slaughtered or carried into captivity, **nor of their multitude,** noisy and boisterous though they formerly were, **nor of any of theirs,** of their riches or possessions; **neither shall there be wailing for them,** literally, "neither is there anything glorious among them," anything of which they might feel justly proud. V. 12. **The time is come, the day draweth near. Let not the buyer rejoice,** on account of a bargain which he made, **nor the seller mourn,** over the loss of property which he would gladly have retained; **for wrath is upon all the multitude thereof,** the Lord's judgment striking them all in the same manner. V. 13. **For the seller shall not return to that which is sold,** since all laws regarding the return of property would be annulled by Israel's removal from the land, **although they were yet alive,** literally, "even were their life still among the living," at the time when, according to ancient regulations, the seller might regain possession of his property; **for the vision is touching the whole multitude thereof, which shall not return,** that is, the vision vouchsafed by the Lord to His prophet is against the entire mass of the people and will not be changed, **neither shall any strengthen himself in the iniquity of his life,** that is, possession should be withdrawn from the whole nation, because no evil person should, by committing wickedness, be strengthened in his life and thus be enabled to withstand the enemy. V. 14. **They,** the Jews, the people of the covenant nation, **have blown the trumpet,** as though preparing for battle, **even to make all ready; but none goeth to the battle,** their courage having been taken from them by the Lord's judgment; **for My wrath is upon all the multitude thereof,** and their timidity is the consequence of His anger. V. 15. **The sword is without,** in the persons of the invaders, **and the pestilence and the famine within,** so that the attack of the Lord comes from both sides; **he that is in the field,** out in the line of battle, **shall die with the sword, and he that is in the city, famine and pestilence shall devour him,** so that no one may escape the punishment of the Lord. V. 16. **But they that escape of them shall escape and shall be on the montains like doves of the valleys,** driven from their natural habitat, far removed from their nests, **all of them mourning,** making known their sorrow, their feeling of pain and grief, **every one for his iniquity.** The mournful cry of the dove is a fitting comparison at this point, the mixing of figure and reality tending to increase the emphasis. V. 17. **All hands shall be feeble,** on account of the weakness brought about by terror and the feeling of disgrace,

and all knees shall be weak as water, their strength being taken from them, so that they refuse to stand up and remain firm. V. 18. **They shall also gird themselves with sackcloth,** as a sign of deep mourning, **and horror shall cover them,** surrounding them like a garment; **and shame shall be upon all faces,** as a result of their finally realizing their iniquity, **and baldness upon all their heads,** as they pluck out their hair in the depth of their mourning. V. 19. **They shall cast their silver in the streets, and their gold shall be removed,** they themselves discarding the precious metals which they possessed as having now lost all their value, as being loathsome, in fact, in view of the abuses to which they had been put; **their silver and their gold shall not be able to deliver them in the day of the wrath of the Lord;** cp. 1 Pet. 1, 18. **They shall not satisfy their souls,** so that their lives would be spared, **neither fill their bowels,** in providing the necessaries of life, their money being unable to procure for them either deliverance from the sword or deliverance from a death by hunger, **because it,** their wealth, **is the stumbling-block of their iniquity,** the cause of many of their transgressions. V. 20. **As for the beauty of his ornament,** the riches with which Israel was endowed, with which he might adorn himself, **he set it in majesty,** he turned it to the service of pride; **but they made the images of their abominations and of their detestable things therein,** that is, out of the gold and silver given them by God the children of Israel made idols, loathsome things in the sight of Jehovah; **therefore have I set it far from them,** He had removed their wealth, their gold and silver, and also their Temple, from them, so that they could no longer defile it with their abominations. V. 21. **And I will give it into the hands of the strangers for a prey,** to the invaders, to use as they saw fit, **and to the wicked of the earth for a spoil,** the Babylonians, of course, taking advantage of their victory to the full, **and they shall pollute it,** both the Temple and all the wealth captured by them. V. 22. **My face will I turn also from them,** from the inhabitants of Jerusalem, **and they,** the invaders, **shall pollute My secret place,** namely, the treasury of the Sanctuary, which was profaned by the Chaldeans as they took it to Babylon; **for the robbers shall enter into it and defile it.** V. 23. **Make a chain,** forging fetters for the inhabitants of the land; **for the land is full of bloody crimes,** of blood-guiltiness, **and the city,** namely, Jerusalem, **is full of violence.** V. 24. **Wherefore I will bring the worst of the heathen,** those who excelled in transgressions as they invaded the land of Israel, **and they shall possess their houses,** occupying them for themselves; **I will also make the pomp of the strong,** the might of Israel wherein they trusted, **to cease, and their holy places,** which the Lord will no longer accept as consecrated to Him, **shall be defiled.** V. 25. **Destruction cometh,** literally, "contraction," to emphasize the force of the blow to be delivered; **and they shall seek peace,** making every attempt to find deliverance from the impending calamities, **and there shall be none.** V. 26. **Mischief shall come upon mischief, and rumor shall be upon rumor,** one blow following the other; cp. Matt. 24, 6. **Then,** when it is really too late, **shall they seek a vision of the prophet; but the Law shall perish from the priest and counsel from the ancients,** that is, they would seek advice in vain, their very leaders having their understanding dulled. V. 27. **The king shall mourn,** as the ruler of the nation, **and the prince,** the heads of the smaller divisions in the nation, **shall be clothed with desolation, and the hands of the people of the land,** that is, of the nation as such, **shall be troubled,** trembling with terror. **I will do unto them after their way,** according to their behavior, **and according to their deserts will I judge them,** as they deserved by their misdeeds; **and they shall know that I am the Lord,** this fact being impressed upon them with special force by the Lord's punishment upon the whole nation. If people will not heed the Lord's Word and will with ready obedience, His punishment will call their attention to the fact of His sovereignty.

CHAPTER 8.

Israel's Abomination of Idolatry.

THE TIME AND PLACE OF THE VISION. — V. 1. **And it came to pass in the sixth year,** the year after the captivity of King Jehoiachin, **in the sixth month, in the fifth day of the month, as I sat in mine house,** where Ezekiel had shut himself up in agreement with the Lord's command, chap. 3, 24, **and the elders of Judah sat before me,** those of the captivity having come to consult with him on some question, **that the hand of the Lord God fell there upon me,** transmitting an unusual measure of power to him for the purpose of a special manifestation. V. 2. **Then I beheld,** while in the state of peculiar ecstasy brought on by the Lord's influence upon him, **and, lo! a likeness as the appearance of fire,** the form of a person shining with fire or emitting a fiery glow; **from the appearance of His loins even downward, fire,** as though kindled or burning; **and from His loins even upward as the** appearance of brightness, of a wonderful splendor, as the color of amber, the glitter of polished brass. This shining person has been identified, and probably correctly, with the Angel of Jehovah, with the Son of God, as He revealed Himself in the Old Testament. V. 3. **And He put forth the form of an hand,** which may have represented the Spirit of the Lord, **and took me by a lock of mine head; and the Spirit lifted me up between the earth and the heaven,** in ecstasy, not in an actual physical removal, **and brought me in the visions of God,** in the state brought about by the Lord's direct influence, **to Jerusalem, to the door of the inner gate,** that leading from the court of the priests, **that looketh toward the north,** the prophet thus occupying a position as one summoning the avenging hosts from the north; **where was the seat of the image of jealousy,** some sort of idol-image, **which provoketh to jealousy,** challenging the jealous wrath of Jehovah. The image may have been one of Baal or of Astarte, such as Manasseh had erected in the Sanctuary; cp. 2 Kings 21, 7. V. 4. **And, behold, the glory of the God of Israel,** so called on account of the contrast inferred over against the idols of the heathen, **was there, according to the vision that I saw in the plain,** chap. 3, 22. 23, where He appeared on His throne accompanied by cherubs and wheels, an awe-inspiring spectacle. The Lord purposely revealed Himself in all His glory, in order to make the idolatrous practises of the apostate Jews appear all the more repulsive by way of contrast.

VARIOUS ABOMINATIONS. — V. 5. **Then said He unto me, Son of man, lift up thine eyes now the way toward the north,** to the left of the direction in which the Temple faced. **So I lifted up mine eyes the way toward the north and behold northward, at the Gate of the Altar,** probably just outside the entrance, **this image of jealousy in the entry,** the idol which filled the Lord with such deep resentment and anger. V. 6. **He said furthermore unto me, Son of man, seest thou what they do?** namely, the members of the house of Israel in erecting and worshiping a picture devoted to idolatry. **Even the great abominations that the house of Israel,** the members of the covenant nation, **committeth here, that I should go far off from My Sanctuary?** being obliged to forsake His own seat of worship on account of the fact that it was now entirely devoted to idolatrous practises. The north gate of the Temple was called the Gate of the Altar probably because the sacrificial animals were brought in there, to be slaughtered near this entrance. **But turn thee yet again, and thou shalt see greater abominations.** V. 7. **And He brought me to the door of the court,** very likely the northern entrance to the outer court; **and when I looked, behold a hole in the wall,** in that portion of the wall which divided the courts. V. 8. **Then said He unto me, Son of man, dig now in the wall,** enlarging the hole which he saw before him; **and when I had digged in the wall, behold a door.** Some commentators think that the text speaks of an opening which had been made contrary to the Law to admit such people to the inner court as had no right to enter, and that this opening had been blocked up during Josiah's reformation. V. 9. **And He said unto me, Go in and behold the wicked abominations that they do here,** the idolatrous customs which they practised. V. 10. **So I went in and saw; and behold every form of creeping things,** of reptiles, worms, and similar animals, Lev. 11, 29—32, **and abominable beasts,** such as were regarded as Levitically unclean, **and all the idols of the house of Israel, portrayed upon the wall round about,** after the manner of decorative painting indulged in by heathen, especially by Egyptians. V. 11. **And there stood before them seventy men of the ancients of the house of Israel,** a number which is found also elsewhere for representative bodies among the people of the covenant, **and in the midst of them stood Jaazaniah, the son of Shaphan, with every man his censer in his hand; and a thick cloud of incense went up,** as all these men were deeply engrossed with their idolatrous worship. The picture was a representation of what was done throughout the nation, in the form of secret idolatry, in various abominable cults which had gained a foothold in the country. V. 12. **Then said He unto me, Son of man, hast thou seen what the ancients of the house of Israel do in the dark,** in the secrecy of these hidden cells, **every man in the chambers of his imagery?** where idolatrous pictures were painted on the walls and other evidences of idolatrous abominations were freely exposed. **For they say, The Lord seeth us not,** not being aware of their transgression; **the Lord hath forsaken the earth,** having withdrawn His merciful presence from His people. Thus they denied both the omniscience and the omnipresence of God. V. 13. **He said also unto me, Turn thee yet again, and thou shalt see greater abominations that they do.** V. 14. **Then He brought me to the door of the gate of the Lord's house which was toward the north,** where the outer court of the Temple opened toward the outside, **and, behold, there sat women weeping for Tammuz,** an idol identified with the Adonis of the Greeks, whose festival, celebrated in June, was celebrated with immoral excesses. This public weeping for a heathen idol of this kind characterizes the state of affairs among the women of Israel at that time. V. 15. **Then said He unto me, Hast thou seen this, O son of man?** being duly impressed with the heinousness of the abominations practised by people who would be regarded the nation of the Lord. **Turn thee yet again, and thou shalt see greater abominations than these,** some which challenged the Lord's punishment in a still greater degree. V. 16. **And He brought me into the inner court of the Lord's house,** to the Court of the Priests, immediately before the sanctuary of the Temple, **and, behold, at the door of the Temple of the Lord, between the porch and the altar,** the most sacred part of the inner court, forbidden to all but the priests, **were about five and twenty men, with their backs toward the Temple of the Lord,** as though ignoring or despising the Sanctuary altogether, **and their faces toward the east,** away from the Holy Place and from the altar of burnt offerings; **and they worship the sun toward the east,** in the idolatrous worship practised by many heathen, as they gave divine honor to the lights of the heavens. V. 17. **Then He said unto me, Hast thou seen this, O son of man?** this open denial of the one true God. **Is it a light thing to the house of Judah that they commit the abominations which they commit here? For they have filled the land with violence,** in thus heaping guilt upon guilt by utterly disregarding the rights of their neighbors, **and have returned to provoke Me to anger; and, lo, they put the branch to their nose,** apparently in a gesture or act expressing their utter contempt for the true worship of Jehovah, and that in the very Temple dedicated to Him. V. 18. **Therefore will I also deal in fury; Mine eye shall not spare,** in showing them any measure of mercy, **neither will I have pity; and though they cry in Mine ears with a loud voice,** in an attempt to influence the Lord to show them a favor, **yet will I not hear them.** Open and vicious sinners will finally place themselves in a position where they are outside the pale of God's mercy, when even repentance comes too late.

CHAPTER 9.

The Lord's Judgment upon the Guilty.

The wickedness of the people described in chapter 8 is now followed by its proper punishment at the hand of the Lord, in full agreement with the certain fulfilment of all His threats upon the wicked. V. 1. **He cried also in mine ears, with a loud voice,** the Lord thus emphasizing the importance of His command, **saying, Cause them that have charge over the city,** the heavenly watchmen, the angels through whom the Lord intended to carry out His punishment, **to draw near, even every man with his destroying weapon in his hand,** in order to punish the wicked. V. 2. **And, behold, six men came from the way of the higher gate,** the angels assuming the shape of men and coming down from the upper entrance of the Temple, **which lieth toward the north, and every man a slaughter-weapon in his hand,** literally, "his weapon for shattering," for in this manner the judgment was to be executed; **and one man among them was clothed with linen, with a writer's inkhorn by his side,** literally, "on his loins," that is, suspended from his girdle; **and they went in and stood beside the brazen altar,** the altar of burnt offerings, their attitude showing a deferential waiting for the commands of the Lord. The white linen color of the writer in their midst was symbolical of the divine holiness and glory. V. 3. **And the glory of the God of Israel,** which is evidently thought of as the cloud in which He revealed Himself in His Temple, **was gone up from the cherub, whereupon He was, to the threshold of the house,** to the entrance of the Holy Place, whence the Lord intended to issue His commands concerning the destruction of the apostate people. **And He called to the man clothed with linen, which had the writer's inkhorn by his side,** v. 4. **and the Lord said unto him, Go through the midst of the city, through the midst of Jerusalem,** the repetition of this expression indicating the thoroughness with which the work was to be done, every part of the city was to be reached, **and set a mark upon the foreheads of the men that sigh and that cry for all the abominations that be done in the midst thereof.** This mark, which some of the old Church Fathers like to identify with that of the cross, since it was the Hebrew letter *tau*, was a seal by which the wearers were to be securely guarded against special calamities about to be sent. They were the ones who were as yet deeply concerned about the increasing godlessness and were therefore to receive this consideration at the hand of the destroyers. V. 5. **And to the others He said in mine hearing, Go ye after him through the city and smite,** in a terrible judgment of extermination; **let not your eye spare,** as it might when seeing pitiful sights or hands raised in supplication, **neither have ye pity;** v. 6. **slay utterly,** to a complete destruction, with the purpose of working an utter extermination, **old and young, both maids and little children,** the very infants, **and women,** neither age nor sex being spared; **but come not near any man upon whom is the mark,** who was safeguarded by the Lord's seal upon his forehead, where it could most easily be seen; **and begin at My Sanctuary,** for it was there that the greatest abominations had been committed, and that by the priests themselves. **Then they began at the ancient men which were before the house,** who were guilty of sinful sacrifices. V. 7. **And He said unto them, Defile the house,** namely, by this slaughter, **and fill the courts with the slain; go ye forth. And they went forth,** after having performed their gruesome task in the entire Temple area, **and slew in the city.** V. 8. **And it came to pass while they were slaying them and I was left,** he being the first one to be spared, and possibly the only one in the Temple area, **that I fell upon my face,** in the attitude of most urgent supplication, **and cried and said, Ah, Lord God, wilt Thou destroy all the residue of Israel in Thy pouring out of Thy fury upon Jerusalem?** He showed the same feeling of compassion as was exhibited by Abraham in making intercession for Sodom and Gomorrha. V. 9. **Then said He unto me, The iniquity of the house of Israel and Judah,** of the entire covenant people, **is exceeding great, and the land is full of blood,** on account of the murders and similar crimes which had been committed, **and the city full of perverseness,** not only of lawless conduct, but also of wresting of judgment; **for they say,** cp. chap. 8, 12, **The Lord hath forsaken the earth, and the Lord seeth not,** thus denying both His interest in His people and His providence. To this the Lord gives His answer. V. 10. **And as for Me also, Mine eye shall not spare, neither will I have pity, but I will recompense their way upon their head,** fully repaying them for all their wickedness. The time for mercy was past, and nothing but punishment remained. V. 11. **And, behold, the man clothed with linen, which had the inkhorn by his side,** the more easily to keep record of all his works, **reported the matter,** announcing the accomplished fact, **saying, I have done as thou hast commanded me.** Thus the first act of the judgment was accomplished. In the midst of this general punishment it is a consoling thought that God renders His people secure against the common ruin, though all things else on earth are confounded.

CHAPTER 10.

God's Act of Judgment upon Jerusalem.

THE BURNING OF THE CITY. — V. 1. **Then I looked, and, behold, in the firmament,** the vaulted expanse above, **that was above the head of the cherubim,** the living creatures of the first vision, **there appeared over them as it were a sapphire stone, as the appearance of the likeness of a throne.** In the previous chapter the Lord had left this throne and occupied a position at the threshold of the Holy Place. Here He is again on His throne above the cherubim, as the majestic Sovereign of the universe. V. 2. **And He spake unto the man clothed with linen,** the chief of the six avenging angels, **and said, Go in between the wheels, even under the cherub,** here spoken of as collective, on account of the unity of the vision, **and fill thine hand with coals of fire from between the cherubim,** chap. 1, 13, **and scatter them over the city,** to bring about its destruction by fire. **And he went in in my sight,** performing the work which he was commanded to do while Ezekiel was witness of his act. V. 3. **Now, the cherubim stood on the right side of the house,** that is, on the south side, **when the man went in; and the cloud filled the inner court,** the Court of the Priests. V. 4. **Then the glory of the Lord,** once more leaving its position on the throne above the cherubim, **went up from the cherub,** literally, "was raised up high from off the cherub," **and stood over the threshold of the house,** removing to this place as before; **and the house,** the Sanctuary proper, **was filled with the cloud, and the court,** the inner court, **was full of the brightness of the Lord's glory,** as reflected from the cloud which filled the Holy Place. V. 5. **And the sound of the cherubim's wings,** chap. 1, 24, **was heard even to the outer court, as the voice of the almighty God when He speaketh.** V. 6. **And it came to pass that, when He had commanded the man clothed with linen, saying, Take fire from between the wheels, from between the cherubim; then he went in and stood beside the wheels,** beneath the cherubim, who were now changed from ministers of God's grace to ministers of God's vengeance. V. 7. **And one cherub stretched forth his hand from between the cherubim,** as they stood in close array, **unto the fire that was between the cherubim and took thereof and put it into the hands of him that was clothed with linen,** who had received his command directly from the Lord, **who took it and went out,** in order to carry out the punishment of burning upon the city. V. 8. **And there appeared in the cherubim the form of a man's hand under their wings,** this hand performing the office of handing out the fiery coals for the destruction of Jerusalem. The attention to details increases the effect of the entire passage: the idea of deliberate preparation for the ruin of the city.

THE REMOVAL OF JEHOVAH FROM HIS TEMPLE. — V. 9. **And when I looked, behold the four wheels by the cherubim, one wheel by one cherub and another wheel by another cherub; and the appearance of the wheels was as the color of a beryl stone,** as in the first vision, chapter 1. V. 10. **And** as for their appearances, they four had one likeness, as if a wheel had been in the midst of a wheel, at right angles, as in the case of a gyroscope. V. 11. **When they went, they went upon their four sides; they turned not as they went,** for their structure made it unnecessary for them to change their direction, **but to the place whither the head looked they followed it; they turned not as they went.** Cp. chap. 1, 17. 19. V. 12. **And their whole body,** literally, "all their flesh," **and their backs, and their hands, and their wings, and the wheels,** serving as a sort of conveyance to the cherubim, **were full of eyes round about, even the wheels that they four had.** V. 13. **As for the wheels, it was cried unto them in my hearing,** in a mighty command by the mouth of the Lord, **O wheel!** this call preparing for the further commands which were given. V. 14. **And every one had four faces,** as in chap. 1, 10, the prophet here naming the face of each which was turned in his direction; **the first face was the face of a cherub, and the second face was the face of a man and the third the face of a lion and the fourth the face of an eagle.** Cp. Rev. 4, 7. V. 15. **And the cherubim were lifted up,** to be removed from the place which they then occupied. **This is the living creature that I saw by the river of Chebar.** V. 16. **And when the cherubim went, the wheels went by them; and when the cherubim lifted up their wings to mount up from the earth, the same wheels also turned not from beside them,** so that the movement of the two was absolutely harmonious. V. 17. **When they stood, these stood; and when they were lifted up, these lifted up themselves also; for the spirit of the living creature was in them,** the expression here used collectively, as in many instances. V. 18. **Then the glory of the Lord departed from off the threshold of the house,** from the entrance to the Holy Place, **and stood over the cherubim,** on the throne which it had occupied at the beginning of the vision. V. 19. **And the cherubim lifted up their wings and mounted up from the earth in my sight,** the Lord thus removing His gracious presence from His people; **when they went out, the wheels also were beside them, and every one,** that is, the vision with the throne, **stood at the door of the East Gate of the Lord's house,** that is, the eastern entrance of the outer court; **and the glory of the God of Israel was over them above.** V. 20. **This is the living creature that I saw under the God of Israel by the river of Chebar; and I knew that they were the cherubim,** and their leaving completed the abandonment of the Temple as a whole. V. 21. **Every one had four faces apiece and every one four wings; and the likeness of the hands of a man was under their wings.** Cp. chap. 1, 6. V. 22. **And the likeness of their faces was the same faces which I saw by the river of Chebar, their appearances and themselves; they went every one straight forward,** always under the direction of the Spirit of the Lord, whose power moved them.

CHAPTER 11.

A Warning and a Promise.

THE JUDGMENT UPON THE RULERS. — V. 1. **Moreover, the Spirit lifted me up and brought me unto the East Gate of the Lord's house, which looketh eastward,** where the entire vision had been placed, chap. 10, 19; **and behold at the door of the gate,** the large portal of the Temple, **five and twenty men,** most likely not identical with those of chap. 8, 16; **among whom I saw Jaazaniah, the son of Azur, and Pelatiah, the son of Benaiah, princes of the people,** men of influence in guiding the destinies of the people, if not members of the civil authorities. V. 2. **Then said He unto me, Son of man, these are the men that devise mischief and give wicked counsel in this city,** such as turns out ill and causes injustice to be done; v. 3. **which say, It is not near; let us build houses,** literally, "not in near proximity building of houses," that is, the threatened ruin of the city is entirely out of the question, wherefore it is not necessary to worry about the building or the rebuilding of Jerusalem; **this city is the caldron, and we be the flesh,** that is, they considered themselves as safe and as protected in their city as the flesh is in the pot. V. 4. **Therefore prophesy against them, prophesy, O son of man,** the repetition giving added emphasis to the Lord's command. V. 5. **And the Spirit of the Lord fell upon me and said unto me, Speak, Thus saith the Lord,** His very words being quoted, as throughout the inspired Scripture: **Thus have ye said, O house of Israel, for I know the things that come into your mind, every one of them,** the omniscient God reading their hearts and minds like an open book. V. 6. **Ye have multiplied your slain in this city,** in the execution of innocent people as a result of their wicked judgments, **and ye have filled the streets thereof with the slain,** by their unjust oppression of those unable to defend themselves against tyranny. V. 7. **Therefore, thus saith the Lord God, Your slain whom ye have laid in the midst of it, they are the flesh, and this city is the caldron,** their blasphemous boast thus being interpreted in the Lord's way and Jerusalem being called the flesh-pot of those whom they caused to be slain; **but I will bring you forth out of the midst of it,** the wicked transgressors themselves were to be dragged forth and cut in pieces elsewhere. V. 8. **Ye have feared the sword,** for they had refused to follow the advice of Jeremiah to give themselves up to the Babylonians, since they were afraid of being put to death by them; **and I will bring a sword upon you, saith the Lord God,** to punish them in the very manner which they feared. V. 9. **And I will bring you out of the midst thereof,** out of the city where they boastfully declared themselves safe, **and deliver you into the hands of strangers, and will execute judgments among you,** in bringing upon them the punishment which they deserved. V. 10. **Ye shall fall by the sword,** put to death by the invaders; **I will judge you in the border of Israel,** on the frontier, at Riblah, in the land of Hamath, Jer. 52, 24—27; **and ye shall know that I am the Lord,** convinced by this evidence of His avenging fury. V. 11. **The city shall not be your caldron,** namely, in the sense in which they had spoken of it, v. 5, **neither shall ye be the flesh in the midst thereof,** to be safe from destruction; **but I will judge you in the border of Israel,** far from the protection of the walls of the capital, v. 12. **and ye shall know that I am the Lord,** by the judgments inflicted by Him; **for ye have not walked in My statutes,** or, "in whose statutes," in their special application to Israel's case, "ye have not walked," **neither executed My judgments,** to lead their lives in agreement with His righteousness, **but have done after the manners of the heathen that are round about you,** in becoming guilty of the idolatry which was practised by the Gentile nations. Cp. chap. 5, 7. The truth and power of this word was now brought out in a most impressive manner. V. 13. **And it came to pass, when I prophesied, that Pelatiah, the son of Benaiah, died,** this occurrence substantiating the threatening prophecy uttered by inspiration of the Lord. **Then fell I down upon my face,** overcome by this evidence of the Lord's avenging justice, **and cried with a loud voice and said, Ah, Lord God! Wilt Thou make a full end of the remnant of Israel?** The Lord's children will intercede even for their enemies, hoping that there will always be some who will be saved from the general destruction. In this respect Abraham, who begged the Lord to desist from destroying Sodom and Gomorrah, is an outstanding example.

The Promise to Save a Remnant. — V. 14. **Again the word of the Lord came unto me, saying,** v. 15. **Son of man, thy brethren, even thy brethren, the men of thy kindred,** a very close relationship being implied, more than that of the flesh only, as the repetition shows, **and all the house of Israel wholly,** or "the whole house of Israel," it wholly, those who are Israelites in truth, **are they unto whom the inhabitants of Jerusalem have said, Get you far from the Lord; unto us is this land given in possession.** These were the contemptuous words spoken by the inhabitants of Jerusalem at the time the exiles were carried away with Jeconiah. They believed themselves to be secure in the possession of the land and despised the men whom they considered outcasts of Jehovah. V. 16. **Therefore say, Thus saith the Lord God, Although I have cast them far off among the heathen, and although I have scattered them among the countries,** this punishment being indeed administered by the hand of Jehovah, **yet will I be to them as a little sanctuary in the countries where they shall come,** so that, in the midst of the dispersion, He would be the refuge of them who trusted in Him. V. 17. **Therefore say, Thus saith the Lord God, I will even gather you from the people and assemble you out of the countries where ye have been scattered, and I will give you the land of Israel.** This is spoken in the Messianic vein of the gathering of the Church of God from the dispersion everywhere, just as we find it in the other prophets. The believing Jews who returned from the exile became the nucleus of the band of believers, many of whose descendants afterwards accepted the Messiah in simple faith, while also the heathen, among whom they spread the knowledge of the living God, retained some knowledge of Him, many of whose descendants were afterward gathered into Christian congregations. V. 18. **And they shall come thither,** back to the land of Israel, **and they shall take away all the detestable things thereof and all the abominations thereof from thence,** all the evidences of idolatrous worship and customs, making ready for the worship in spirit and in truth which was taught by Jesus Christ. V. 19. **And I will give them one heart,** one united in His fear, **and I will put a new spirit within you,** by a conversion in truth; **and I will take the stony heart out of their flesh,** their obstinate and perverse spirit, **and will give them an heart of flesh,** one filled with the true fear of the Lord, pliable and yielding with respect to His will, v. 20. **that they may walk in My statutes,** to fashion their behavior in accordance with the manner pleasing to Him, **and keep Mine ordinances and do them; and they shall be My people, and I will be their God,** true regeneration thus restoring the right relation between God and man. V. 21. **But as for them whose heart walketh after the heart of their detestable things and their abominations, I will recompense their way upon their**

own heads, saith the Lord God, thereby pronouncing sentence upon the wilful idolaters and all those who persist in their enmity against God. V. 22. **Then did the cherubim lift up their wings and the wheels beside them; and the glory of the God of Israel was over them above,** occupying the magnificent throne above, as described before. V. 23. **And the glory of the Lord went up from the midst of the city,** where it had been stationed at the East Gate of the Temple, **and stood upon the mountain which is on the east side of the city,** that is, the Mount of Olives. Thus the Lord had entirely abandoned His city, thereby definitely designating it as ripe for destruction. V. 24. **Afterwards the spirit took me up and brought me in a vision by the Spirit of God,** under whose influence the entire happening was engineered, **into Chaldea, to them of the captivity. So the vision that I had seen went up from me,** this being the end of the present revelation. V. 25. **Then I spake unto them of the captivity,** for whom this message was really intended, **all the things that the Lord had showed me.** It was in itself no easy task to proclaim these facts to the exiles, but the true servant of the Lord is not influenced by considerations of weak expediency, his sole object being to make known the will of the Lord.

CHAPTER 12.

Two Impressive Signs to the House of Israel.

The Sign of the King's Departure. — V. 1. **The word of the Lord also came unto me, saying,** v. 2. **Son of man, thou dwellest in the midst of a rebellious house,** literally, "in the midst of a house of rebelliousness art thou living," **which have eyes to see and see not; they have ears to hear and hear not,** thus proving themselves to be deliberately perverse and wilfully obstinate; **for they are a rebellious house.** V. 3. **Therefore, thou son of man, prepare thee stuff for removing,** an exile's outfit, utensils needed to sustain life during a journey of some length, **and remove by day in their sight,** in broad daylight, thereby drawing the attention of men to his actions; **and thou shalt remove from thy place,** where he was then living, **to another place in their sight; it may be they will consider,** contemplate the prophet's action and make the proper application, **though they be a rebellious house.** V. 4. **Then shalt thou bring forth thy stuff,** such as his staff, his dunnage sack, his cooking utensils, **by day in their sight, as stuff for removing; and thou shalt go forth at even,** after the coming of twilight, **in their sight, as they that go forth into captivity,** not emigrants of their own free will, but under restraint. V. 5. **Dig thou through the wall in their sight,** the mud walls of most Oriental houses being easily broken down, **and carry out thereby,** through the hole thus produced. V. 6. **In their sight shalt thou bear it upon thy shoulders,** loading himself with the utensils which he had gotten ready, **and carry it forth in the twilight,** as the darkness of night was falling; **thou shalt cover thy face, that thou see not the ground,** muffling his face, as one afraid of being recognized by any one meeting him, as one heaped with shame and sorrow; **for I have set thee for a sign unto the house of Israel,** a type which they should recognize and whose lesson they should heed. V. 7. **And I did so as I was commanded; I brought forth my stuff by day, as stuff for captivity,** as the outfit of an exile, **and in the even I digged through the wall with mine hand,** performing the work in person, all the more strongly to convey the lesson of his action; **I brought it forth in the twilight,** at nightfall, **and I bare it upon my shoulder in their sight,** as one emigrating under the stress of adverse circumstances, as one going into captivity. Thus the sign, the portent of evil, was set before the eyes of Ezekiel's countrymen. V. 8. **And in the morning came the word of the Lord unto me, saying,** v. 9, **Son of man, hath not the house of Israel, the rebellious house,** that is, all those who were witnesses of his symbolical act, **said unto thee,** in a natural curiosity concerning the meaning of his act, **What doest thou?** V. 10. **Say thou unto them, Thus saith the Lord God,** in explaining the act and reproving the spirit of blasphemous jesting which possessed them. **This burden concerneth the prince in Jerusalem and all the house of Israel that are among them.** V. 11. **Say, I am your sign,** Ezekiel himself serving as a type; **like as I have done, so shall it be done unto them; they shall remove and go into captivity,** literally, "into banishment, into captivity, they shall go." V. 12. **And the prince that is among them,** the king of Judah at that time, **shall bear upon his shoulder in the twilight,** trying to make his escape at nightfall, **and shall go forth; they shall dig through the wall,** hurrying away by the speediest available route, **to carry out thereby,** to bring forth whatever he hoped to save in flight; **he shall cover his face that he see not the ground with his eyes,** taking all precautions lest he be recognized. V. 13. **My net also will I spread upon him,** in this case the Chaldean army, **and he shall be taken in My snare,** for the host of the invaders, even without knowing and intending it, were God's instruments of punishment; and **I will bring him to Babylon, to the land of the Chaldeans; yet shall he not see it,** having been blinded at Riblah, **though he shall die there.** All this was fulfilled at the time of Zedekiah, when he tried to escape from the doomed city, but was ignominiously caught by the Chaldean army and met the fate which the Lord had determined for him. Cp. Jer. 39; 52; 2 Kings 25. V. 14. **And I will scatter toward every wind,** to all parts of the world, **all that are about him to help him,** his counselors and his body-guard, **and all his bands,** literally, "all his wings of an army," the military forces under his command; **and I will draw out the sword after them.** V. 15. **And they shall know that I am the Lord,** the argument of His sentence carried out upon them being sufficiently emphatic to make this fact clear, **when I shall scatter them among the nations and disperse them in the countries.** V. 16. **But I will leave a few men of them,** the prophecy thus merging into the usual Messianic promise, **from the sword, from the famine, and from the pestilence,** these people representing the Church of God on earth, **that they may declare all their abominations among the heathen whither they come,** frankly confessing their transgressions and vindicating the punishment of God upon their sins; **and they shall know that I am the Lord.** It was the Israelites in truth who were led to repentance by God's punishment; and they were also the ones to perpetuate the knowledge of Jehovah, the God of the covenant, to their children after them. The Lord has always had His children on earth, at times even in the midst of heathen nations.

THE SIGN OF BREAD AND WATER. — V. 17. **Moreover, the word of the Lord came to me, saying,** v. 18. **Son of man, eat thy bread with quaking and drink thy water with trembling and with carefulness,** his entire bearing, as he partook of his scanty meal, of the barest necessaries of life, being one of anxiety in the presence of an impending calamity; v. 19. **and say unto the people of the land,** the Jews among the captives of Chaldea, **Thus saith the Lord God of the inhabitants of Jerusalem and of the land of Israel,** of all the people who were still left in their native country, **They shall eat their bread with carefulness,** with anxiety, **and drink their water with astonishment,** with worry and pain, **that her land may be desolate from all that is therein,** stripped of both its inhabitants and the abundance of all its products, **because of the violence of all them that dwell therein,** since they had become guilty of wickedness in such an unusual degree. V. 20. **And the cities that are inhabited shall be laid waste, and the land shall be desolate,** the entire country sharing the fate of the capital city; **and ye shall know that I am the Lord,** whose words are not spoken in vain. V. 21. **And the word of the Lord came unto me, saying,** v. 22. **Son of man, what is that proverb that ye have in the land of Israel, saying, The days are prolonged,** more and more time is passing, **and every vision faileth?** that is, the prophecy threatening destruction is not fulfilled. Cp. 2 Pet. 3, 3. 4. That is a common saying of mocking blasphemers, that none of the divine threats come true, that they are spoken merely to frighten men into submission. V. 23. **Tell them therefore, Thus saith the Lord God, I will make this proverb to cease,** making an end of its blasphemous mockery, **and they shall no more use it as a proverb in Israel; but say unto them, The days are at hand,** the time of the fulfilment of the Lord's words, **and the effect of every vision,** so that every predicted word would be realized. V. 24. **For there shall be no more any vain vision,** the false prophets being confounded by the fulfilment of the true prediction, **nor flattering divination within the house of Israel,** for the false prophets tried to gain credence for their falsehoods by predictions and statements of smooth flattery. V. 25. **For I am the Lord; I will speak, and the word that I shall speak shall come to pass, it shall be no more prolonged,** literally, "For I, Jehovah, will speak that which I will speak, and it shall come to pass, it shall be no more drawn out"; **for in your days,** during their lifetime, **O rebellious house, will I say the word and will perform it, saith the Lord God.** He has uncontrolled power to speak, and He possesses almighty power to carry out His threats. V. 26. **Again the word of the Lord came to me, saying,** v. 27. **Son of man, behold, they of the house of Israel,** again those dwelling in exile in Chaldea, **say, The vision that he seeth is for many days to come, and he prophesieth of the times that are far off,** thus refusing to believe that the catastrophe was near at hand. V. 28. **Therefore say unto them, Thus saith the Lord God, There shall none of My words be prolonged any more,** that is, their fulfilment put off indefinitely, **but the word which I have spoken shall be done, saith the Lord God,** the sovereign God of the covenant. It is true also in our days that the Lord may delay the fulfilment of some word, but He will eventually bring every one of His predictions to pass.

CHAPTER 13.

Denunciation of False Teachers and Teachings.

AGAINST THE FALSE PROPHETS. — V. 1. **And the word of the Lord came unto me, saying, v. 2. Son of man, prophesy against the prophets of Israel,** self-styled teachers and leaders as they were, **that prophesy, and say thou unto them that prophesy out of their own hearts,** without a call from the Lord, speaking of a speedy return to Jerusalem without any warrant on His part, **Hear ye the word of the Lord,** whose proclamation of truth was opposed to all such deception, v. 3. **Thus saith the Lord God,** the sovereign Ruler of the universe, **Woe unto the foolish prophets,** vaunting themselves with a wisdom which was nothing but foolishness in the sight of God, **that follow their own spirit,** the imagination of their own hearts, **and have seen nothing!** have had no vision given them by God, teaching only what they themselves have thought out. V. 4. **O Israel, thy prophets are like the foxes in the deserts,** in the ruins, for the self-appointed leaders and teachers of the people were wily destroyers, who worked stealthily, but none the less surely, at the ruin of the nation. The Lord now once more turns to the false prophets themselves. V. 5. **Ye have not gone up into the gaps,** by placing themselves in the breaches to resist the attacks of the enemies directed against such weak spots, **neither made up the hedge for the house of Israel,** literally, "neither built a wall about Israel," **to stand in the battle in the day of the Lord,** in the war which all believers must wage for the honor of Jehovah. The false prophets did not try to repair the evil with which the nation was suffering; they made no attempt to bring back the people to the Law of God with good counsels, nor by withstanding the efforts of the wicked with proper rebukes. V. 6. **They have seen vanity,** nothingness, empty imaginations, **and lying divination,** so that they even believed their own lies, **saying, The Lord saith,** insisting that their message was the inspired Word of God, **and the Lord hath not sent them; and they have made others to hope that they would confirm the word,** literally, "and hope for confirmation of a word," that is, they foolishly trusted that their false prophecy, in spite of all evidences to the contrary, would yet be fulfilled. V. 7. **Have ye not seen a vain vision, and have ye not spoken a lying divination, whereas ye say, The Lord saith it, albeit I have not spoken?** They should deceive neither themselves nor others, for there was not the slightest foundation for their claim. V. 8. **Therefore, thus saith the Lord God,** Jehovah, the sovereign Ruler of the universe, **Because ye have spoken vanity and seen lies,** publishing them as the truth of the Lord, **therefore, behold, I am against you,** coming against them with a severe punishment, **saith the Lord God.** V. 9. **And Mine hand shall be upon the prophets that see vanity and that divine lies,** namely, for the purpose of severely punishing them; **they shall not be in the assembly of My people,** in the roll of the citizens belonging to the Lord, to the people of God, **neither shall they be written in the writing of the house of Israel,** excluded from those whom the Lord had chosen as His own, **neither shall they enter into the land of Israel,** namely, as members entitled to possess the Lord's heritage; **and ye shall know that I am the Lord God.** The false prophets should lose all the rights and privileges which the members of God's nation had, being denied all the special blessings which are the portion of His children. V. 10. **Because, even because they have seduced My people,** the introduction to His sentence being made in a most solemn and formal manner in order to heighten the effect of its condemnation, **saying, Peace, and there was no peace,** speaking of deliverance and salvation in spite of God's threats to the contrary; **and one built up a wall,** by proclaiming false hopes, **and, lo, others,** members of the same class of false teachers, **daubed it with untempered mortar,** with worthless building material, with a cheap grade of whitewash. Thus the unsoundness of the wall from the absence of true binding cement is brought out. V. 11. **Say unto them which daub it with untempered mortar that it shall fall,** this being the consequence of building so unsafely, even if it was not the intention. **There shall be an overflowing shower,** a very severe shower of rain, a rainstorm; **and ye, O great hailstones, shall fall, and a stormy wind shall rend it,** so that the weak wall with its many breaches would not be able to stand up under the impact of the forces of nature summoned against it by God. Thus the deceitful, hypocritical covering over of the inner corruption would become evident. V. 12. **Lo, when the wall is fallen, shall it not be said unto you, Where is the daubing wherewith ye have daubed it?** The hypocrisy and falsehood of the false prophets' ministry would become evident in the course of time, so that they would be exposed before all men. V. 13. **Therefore, thus saith the Lord God, I will even rend it with a stormy wind in My fury,** or, "I cause a windstorm to break forth in My fury"; **and there shall be an overflowing shower in Mine anger and great hailstones in My fury to consume it,** unto utter destruction. V. 14. **So will I break down the wall that ye have daubed with untempered mortar and bring it down to the ground, so that the foundation thereof shall be discovered,** laid bare, **and it shall**

fall, and ye shall be consumed in the midst thereof, perishing in the midst of Jerusalem, as the center of the theocracy; **and ye shall know that I am the Lord. V. 15. Thus will I accomplish My wrath upon the wall and upon them that have daubed it with untempered mortar,** with the coating of hypocritical whitewash which lacked all the qualities of a binding cement, **and will say unto you, The wall is no more, neither they that daubed it, v. 16. to wit, the prophets of Israel which prophesy concerning Jerusalem,** setting forth their own false predictions, **and which see visions of peace for her,** of salvation and deliverance in spite of her idolatrous ways, **and there is no peace, saith the Lord God.** It is true of all false prophets that their hypocrisy and deceit will eventually be uncovered, if not before, then on the day of the Lord's great reckoning with the whole world.

AGAINST THE FALSE PROPHETESSES. — V. 17. **Likewise, thou son of man, set thy face against the daughters of thy people,** the very expression signifying that these false prophetesses had cut themselves off from any true fellowship with the true God, **which prophesy out of their own heart,** pretending an inspiration which had not been vouchsafed them; **and prophesy thou against them, v. 18. and say, Thus saith the Lord God, Woe to the women that sew pillows to all armholes, and make kerchiefs upon the head of every stature to hunt souls,** literally, "who sew together for themselves coverings for all joints of My hands and make caps for the head of every size to catch souls!" that is, their false prophecies served to cover the joints of the Lord, so that He was hindered in carrying out His intentions against them; and they provide veils, or caps, thick coverings, for the heads of all men, no matter what their status and stature, so that they fit each individual case and keep the persons concerned from hearing and seeing the truth and the effect of the truth upon others. **Will ye hunt the souls of My people,** coaxing them to their destruction, **and will ye save the souls alive that come unto you?** or, "ye will hunt the souls among My people, and ye will save souls alive among you!" that is, they would cause the souls of others to perish, while making every attempt to save their own. V. 19. **And will ye pollute Me among My people for handfuls of barley and for pieces of bread,** the reward of unrighteousness, the price which they demanded for their false messages proclaimed by them, **to slay the souls that should not die,** to barter away immortal souls for paltry gain, **and to save the souls alive that should not live,** by promising safety to those on the broad way to ruin, **by your lying to My people that hear your lies,** accepting their false statements as divine truth. V. 20. **Wherefore, thus saith the Lord God, Behold, I am against your pillows wherewith ye there hunt the souls to make them fly,** that is, Jehovah, the God of the covenant, intended to take away the covers which the false prophetesses used, and to liberate the souls which they had enmeshed by their fine speeches; **and I will tear them from your arms and will let the souls go, even the souls that ye hunt to make them fly,** so that they might escape like birds from the net of a fowler. V. 21. **Your kerchiefs also,** the caps which they used for such evil purposes, **will I tear and deliver My people out of your hand, and they shall be no more in your hand to be hunted,** to be the prey of their wicked designs; **and ye shall know that I am the Lord,** His righteous judgments, carried out in this manner, being a proof of His true godhead. V. 22. **Because with lies ye have made the heart of the righteous sad,** since their false messages threw suspicion upon the true believers among the exiles, **whom I have not made sad, and strengthened the hands of the wicked,** who relied upon their false representations, **that he should not return from his wicked way, by promising him life, v. 23. therefore ye shall see no more vanity,** have visions of things which were without foundation, which were invented by them for their own evil purposes, **nor divine divinations,** in false predictions of the future; **for I will deliver My people out of your hand,** namely, those who are Israelites in truth; **and ye shall know that I am the Lord.** As false teachers, imitating the ways of the Lord's true servants, deceive souls and cause them to perish, so, on the other hand, the true ministers of God plainly tell the unrighteous that they are doomed to destruction, while they promise safety and deliverance to those who place their trust in the grace of Jehovah.

CHAPTER 14.

Testimony against the Idolaters.

JEHOVAH REFUSES TO ANSWER THE IDOLATERS. V. 1. **Then came certain of the elders of Israel unto me,** namely, of the exiles in Chaldea, **and sat before me,** evidently for the purpose of obtaining some information concerning the fate of Jerusalem and of the Jewish people, their bearing expressive of the anxiety which they felt. V. 2. **And the word of the Lord came unto me, saying, v. 3. Son of man, these men have set up their idols in their heart,** literally, "have caused their filthy gods to go up upon their heart," for the corruption of man begins in his heart, **and put the stum-**

bling-block of their iniquity before their face, for the iniquity of their heart became manifest in their outward actions, their evil thoughts causing them to stumble, Prov. 3, 21. 23; **should I be enquired of at all by them?** Were such transgressors, who were here acting the hypocrites, at all worthy of an answer? The emphatic question of the Lord denies this fact with unmistakable vehemence. V. 4. **Therefore speak unto them and say unto them,** in a message every word of which was divinely inspired, as the entire book of prophecies is, **Thus saith the Lord God, Every man of the house of Israel,** each individual being held responsible for his every act, **that setteth up his idols,** his filthy gods, **in his heart and putteth the stumbling-block of his iniquity before his face and cometh to the prophet,** increasing the guilt of his idolatry by his insolent oracle-seeking: **I, the Lord, will answer him that cometh according to the multitude of his idols,** in proportion to the idolatry practised by him, v. 5. **that I may take the house of Israel in their own heart,** to bend and mold their hearts by means of His judgments, **because they are all estranged from Me through their idols.** If the present judgments did not succeed in bringing the people to their senses, they would act as fitting punishments for their idolatry. V. 6. **Therefore say unto the house of Israel, Thus saith the Lord God, Repent and turn yourselves from your idols,** from the filthy gods which they had chosen for themselves, **and turn away your faces from all your abominations,** with the proper revulsion and loathing. V. 7. **For every one of the house of Israel, or of the stranger that sojourneth in Israel,** associated with the people of God either by birth or by accession in later life, **which separateth himself from Me,** through idolatry becoming estranged from the true God, whom he once confessed, **and setteth up his idols in his heart, and putteth the stumbling-block of his iniquity before his face,** as described above, **and cometh to a prophet to enquire of him concerning Me,** regarding God's will and intentions over against himself and others: **I, the Lord, will answer him by Myself,** giving him the answer which his apostasy and hypocrisy deserve, v. 8. **and I will set My face against that man,** as an implacable enemy, **and will make him a sign and a proverb,** so that his case would serve as a standing example of warning to men everywhere, **and I will cut him off from the midst of My people,** cp. Num. 26, 10; Deut. 28, 37; **and ye shall know that I am the Lord.** Nor should the message of any prophet differ from that proclaimed by the Lord. V. 9. **And if the prophet,** one who really considers himself a minister of Jehovah, **be deceived when he hath spoken a thing,** permitting himself, for any reason whatever, to be led astray and to deviate from the clearly expressed will of the Lord, so that his message confirms sinners in their obstinacy, **I, the Lord, have deceived that prophet,** permitting a spirit of falsehood to convey to him a message in agreement with the obstinacy of the people; **and I will stretch out My hand upon him and will destroy him from the midst of My people Israel.** One of God's reasons for letting false prophecy gain such headway in the latter years of Judah's existence was to have the process of separation between the true and the false Israelites go forward with the proper vigor and speed. V. 10. **And they shall bear the punishment of their iniquity,** that which they deserved for their wilful transgressions; **the punishment of the prophet shall be even as the punishment of him that seeketh unto him,** thereby supporting hypocrisy and deceit, v. 11. **that the house of Israel may go no more astray from Me, neither be polluted any more with all their transgressions,** for the effect of sin is to bring corruption and pollution upon every one that sins, **but that they may be My people, and I may be their God, saith the Lord God.** The purpose of the Lord, even in His severest chastisements, is to gain the sinner, if possible, and to preserve his soul from eternal destruction. Well-deserved as every chastening is, it is still an instrument of mercy in the hands of God, unless the sinner hardens his heart against every influence for good and deliberately invites perdition.

GOD'S IRREVOCABLE SENTENCE. — V. 12. **The word of the Lord came again to me, saying,** v. 13. **Son of man, when the land sinneth against Me by trespassing grievously,** in unfaithfulness and treachery, **then will I stretch out Mine hand upon it,** to mete out the well-deserved punishment upon its idolatrous inhabitants, **and will break the staff of the bread thereof,** taking away that upon which man chiefly relies for food, **and will send famine upon it and will cut off man and beast from it,** cp. chap. 4, 16; 5, 16. V. 14. **Though these three men, Noah, Daniel, and Job, were in it,** the fact of whose historical existence, together with the piety of their lives, is thus established, **they should deliver but their own souls by their righteousness, saith the Lord God.** Each of these three men not only saved his own life by his fear of the Lord, but was instrumental also in delivering others from danger and death. But in this case even their presence in the doomed city would avail nothing, since the guilt of idolatry weighed down too heavily in challenging the wrath of God. V. 15. **If I cause noisome beasts,** various reptiles and beasts of prey, **to pass through the land,** causing them to multiply and increase in an unusual degree, **and they spoil it,** by making men and beasts their prey, **so that it be desolate, that no man may pass through because of the beasts:** v. 16. **though these three men were in it,** paragons of virtue though they were, **as I live, saith the Lord God,** the sovereign Ruler of the world, using the most solemn oath possible for Him, **they shall deliver neither sons nor daughters,** it would be impossible for them to ward off the punishment from the land doomed by its own guilt; **they only shall be delivered, but the land shall be desolate.** V. 17. **Or if I bring a sword upon that land,** in a third scourge, **and say, Sword, go through the land,** the figure being purposely strong in order to emphasize the severity of the Lord's punishment through the slaughter of the battle, **so that I cut off man and beast from it:** v. 18. **though these three men were in it, as I live, saith the Lord God, they shall deliver neither sons nor daughters, but they only shall be delivered themselves.** V. 19. **Or if I send a pestilence into that land,** the usual companion of devastating wars, **and pour out My fury upon it in blood, to cut off from it man and beast:** v. 20. **though Noah, Daniel, and Job were in it, as I live, saith the Lord God, they shall deliver neither son nor daughter,** not so much as one child; **they shall but deliver their own souls by their righteousness.** These facts, the prophet says, are generally true; they would be maintained under all conditions. V. 21. **For thus saith the Lord God, How much more when I send my four sore judgments upon Jerusalem,** the four principal scourges of His wrath, **the sword, and the famine, and the noisome beast, and the pestilence, to cut off from it man and beast?** The people of God were like the servant who knew his Lord's will and still persisted in going contrary to it; wherefore he was punished with more stripes than another, all four scourges being used at once in this case. "War brings famine into the cities, corpses outside, which attract the beasts; and from all there follows the pestilence." Note: If Noah, Daniel, and Job, noted for the piety of their lives, could not deliver the land when deserving but one judgment, how much more when all four judgments combined are justly laid upon the land for its sin! V. 22. **Yet, behold, therein shall be left a remnant,** an escaped portion, **that shall be brought forth, both sons and daughters,** whom the mercy of the Lord would spare in the general destruction, although the punishment of the exile would strike them; **behold, they shall come forth unto you,** namely, the exiles of Judea in Chebar, **and ye shall see their way and their doings,** thereby obtaining the knowledge that corruption of this magnitude fully deserved such destruction; **and ye shall be comforted concerning the evil that I have brought upon Jerusalem,** realizing the justice of the Lord's punishments, **even concerning all that I have brought upon it.** V. 23. **And they shall comfort you,** by offering proof for the righteousness of God's acts, **when ye see their ways and their doings; and ye shall know that I have not done without cause,** in arbitrary cruelty, **all that I have done in it, saith the Lord God.** This will eventually be true in the case of all those who feel the heavy hand of God upon them for their transgressions; they and others with them will be obliged to acknowledge the justice of God's punishment, as Abraham also reminded the rich man. Cp. Luke 16, 25.

CHAPTER 15.

The Vine-Tree Fit for Burning Only.

As little as the Lord, for the sake of a handful of righteous people, will spare Jerusalem, so little can a preference of Israel before other nations be alleged, as placing the Jews in a position of safety. As the preceding prophecy is directed against any false confidence on the part of the righteous, so the present message takes away the illusion held by some as though the people of Israel on account of their position as the children of God were safe from destruction. V. 1. **And the word of the Lord came unto me, saying,** v. 2. **Son of man, what is the vine-tree more than any tree,** what advantage has it above other trees, **or than a branch which is among the trees of the forest?** The wild vine has nothing that would make it particularly acceptable above other trees; on the contrary, it is less useful even than the ordinary forest-tree. V. 3. **Shall wood be taken thereof to do any work?** in building or manufacture. **Or will men take a pin of it to hang any vessel thereon?** to suspend vessels used in the household. V. 4. **Behold, it is cast into the fire for fuel,** that being about the only purpose which it serves; **the fire devoureth both the ends of it,** consuming them entirely, **and the midst of it is burned,** scorched, the aim even here not being realized entirely. **Is it meet for any work?** After the long exposition, the question is brought out with great emphasis, thus preparing the way for the answer. V. 5. **Behold, when it was whole,** uninjured, when it was still growing, or immediately after it had been cut off, **it was meet for no work,** unfit for any purpose which would be of real benefit; **how much less shall it be meet yet for any work when the fire hath devoured it and it is burned!** that is, scorched, set afire. The two ends that had been consumed were evidently Israel and the bulk of Judah; what still remained was but a small remnant, and that subject to swift destruction. V. 6. **Therefore, thus saith the Lord God, As the vine-tree among the trees of the forest which I have given to the fire for fuel, so will I give the inhabitants of Jerusalem,** of whom the vine-tree of the parable was a type. V. 7. **And I will set My face against them,** determined upon their destruction; **they shall go out from one fire,** as from the calamities which had even now partly consumed them, **and another fire,** a final catastrophe, **shall devour them; and ye shall know that I am the Lord when I set My face against them.** V. 8. **And I will make the land desolate, because they have committed a trespass, saith the Lord God,** their treachery being that of their shameless idolatry. As in the case of the Jews their guilt was increased by their deliberate revolt and apostasy, so all those who fall away from the truth in our days will make themselves liable to a much severer punishment than the people who have never known the way of God's mercy.

CHAPTER 16.

Jerusalem's Ingratitude and Unfaithfulness; Her Punishment and Exposure.

GOD'S EARLY GRACE UPON HIS PEOPLE. — V. 1. **Again the word of the Lord came unto me, saying,** v. 2. **Son of man, cause Jerusalem,** where the remnant of the Lord's people were now concentrated, **to know her abominations,** an open exposure of Jerusalem and a frank discussion of her guilt being intended to bring her to repentance, v. 3. **and say, Thus saith the Lord God unto Jerusalem, Thy birth and thy nativity,** namely, in the spiritual sense, **is of the land of Canaan,** for the inhabitants of Jerusalem had followed the idolatrous Canaanites in their wicked ways. **Thy father was an Amorite and thy mother an Hittite,** from both of which heathen nations the children of Israel had accepted much that was loathsome in the eyes of the Lord. They had become so heathenish in their customs and in their morals that the only explanation of their conduct was the assumption of a heathen parentage. V. 4. **And as for thy nativity,** concerning the manner of Jerusalem's birth: **in the day that thou wast born thy navel was not cut, neither wast thou washed in water to supple thee,** for the purpose of a thorough cleansing; **thou wast not salted at all,** as was customary in order to harden the tender skin, **nor swaddled at all.** Jerusalem is pictured as a neglected and forsaken infant. V. 5. **None eye pitied thee to do any of these unto thee,** the acts customary in the case of a new-born infant, **to have compassion upon thee; but thou was cast out in the open field,** the exposure of infants being common in many ancient nations, **to the loathing of thy person,** as an object of loathing, **in the day that thou wast born.** Such, figuratively speaking, is the pitiful condition of all men by nature, objects of revulsion in the sight of the holy God. V. 6. **And when I passed by thee and saw thee polluted in thine own blood,** altogether abandoned and wallowing in its own blood, as though stamping it down, **I said unto thee when thou wast in thy blood,** in the very depths of degradation and misery, **Live; yea, I said unto thee when thou wast in thy blood, Live,** the repetition of the reassuring words serving to place the utmost emphasis upon the mercy of Jehovah. V. 7. **I have caused thee to multiply as the bud of the field,** like the flowers that spring up at the beginning of the rainy season, **and thou hast increased and waxen great, and thou art come to excellent ornaments,** in the highest charm of youthful beauty; **thy breasts are fashioned, and thine hair is grown,** as in the fulness of puberty, **whereas thou wast naked and bare.** All this was indicative of the marriageable age, which is the point of comparison. The description refers to the marvelous preservation and multiplication of the children of Israel in Egypt, before the Lord formally chose them as His people. V. 8. **Now, when I passed by thee,** at that stage of her history, **and looked upon thee, behold, thy times was the time of love,** that is, when marriage should have taken place, when some one should have taken her to wife; **and I spread My skirt over thee,** in the gesture signifying a man's willingness to marry a woman, Ruth 3, 9, **and covered thy nakedness; yea, I sware unto thee,** promising the faithfulness of the bridegroom, **and entered into a covenant with thee, saith the Lord God, and thou becamest Mine,** the formal espousal being held, by which the Lord entered into the wedded state with Israel, His chosen people. V. 9. **Then washed I thee with water,** to take away the filth of her nakedness and sinfulness and to prepare her for the wedding; **yea, I throughly washed away thy blood from thee, and I anointed thee with oil,** thus imparting the power and grace of His Spirit. V. 10. **I clothed thee also with broidered work,** with princely magnificence, **and shod thee with badgers' skin,** sandals made of the leather of the sea-cow, **and I girded thee about with fine linen, and I covered thee with silk,** all of which indicates that the Lord gave Israel rich gifts, also in the blessings pertaining to this life. V. 11. **I decked thee also with ornaments, and I put bracelets upon thy hands and a chain on thy neck.** All this seems to point quite definitely to the era of Solomon, when the outward splendor of the kingdom reached its highest stage. V. 12. **And I put a jewel on thy forehead,** the nose-ring which Oriental women wore, **and earrings in thine ears, and a beautiful crown upon thine head.** Thus Jerusalem was elevated to the rank of a princess among the nations. V. 13. **Thus wast thou decked with gold and silver,** with great and outstanding wealth; **and thy raiment was of fine linen and silk and broidered work; thou didst eat fine flour and honey and oil,** being given the richest nourishment; **and thou wast exceeding beautiful, and thou didst prosper into a kingdom,** into such dignity and standing among the nations of the world. V. 14. **And thy renown went forth among the heathen for thy beauty,** the glory of Israel being spoken of in wondering terms by heathen nations everywhere; **for it was perfect through My comeliness which I had put upon thee, saith the Lord God.** Just as Israel's position, both outward and spiritual, was in every way the gift of God's mercy, so it is due to His grace alone if individuals as well as nations become prosperous in the things pertaining to this life or to the life beyond.

THE HORRIBLE UNFAITHFULNESS OF THE LORD'S PEOPLE. — V. 15. **But thou,** namely, Jerusalem, as representing the people who were the chosen of the Lord, **didst trust in thine own beauty,** as she gained in power, influence, and the respect of other nations, **and playedst the harlot,** in spiritual adultery and in seeking the friendship of heathen nations, **because of thy renown,** by allowing the name which she had among other nations to lead her into idolatry and into leagues with idolaters, **and pouredst out thy fornications on every one that passed by,** inviting heathen abominations; **his it was,** namely, the beauty which she yielded up to every passer-by. This is significant in describing what actually amounted to an anxiety on the part of Israel to participate in heathen worship. V. 16. **And of thy garments,** the material wealth which was the Lord's gift to His people, **thou didst take and deckedst thy high places,** the summits of hills and mountains where the heathen altars were usually erected, **with divers colors,** literally, "high places, spotted," or "patched ones," for the tabernacles near the heathen altars were usually woven or sewed of various colors and pieces, **and playedst the harlot thereupon,** on the carpets and tapestries of the heathen temples. **The like things shall not come, neither shall it be so,** for all such acts are utterly abominable in the sight of God. V. 17. **Thou hast also taken thy fair jewels of My gold and of My silver which I had given thee,** for all of this was still the Lord's, all the wealth given to men being entrusted to them only as His stewards, **and madest to thyself images of men,** male idols being mentioned especially, since Jerusalem is represented as a woman and a harlot, **and didst commit whoredom with them.** V. 18. **And tookest thy broidered garments and coveredst them,** the idols often being decked with the richest draperies; **and thou hast set Mine oil and Mine incense,** which should have been used in His worship alone, **before them.** V. 19. **My meat also which I gave thee, fine flour and oil and honey, wherewith I fed thee,** the rich fruit of the soil which the Lord provided for His people in the Promised Land, **thou hast even set it before them for a sweet savor,** in various meat-offerings; **and thus it was, saith the Lord God,** this abomination actually took place, flagrantly, continuously. V. 20. **Moreover, thou hast taken thy sons and thy daughters, whom thou hast borne unto Me,** for children are ever a gift of God, **and these hast thou sacrificed unto them to be devoured,** this being done chiefly in the worship of Molech, or Moloch, the idol of the Moabites. **Is this of thy whoredoms a small matter?** literally, "Was it less than thy whoredoms?" that is, Was it not enough that Jerusalem had committed spiritual adultery in such great measure? Must she, in addition, also sacrifice her children to such abominations? V. 21. **That thou hast slain My children and delivered them to cause them to pass through the fire for them?** namely, for the idols. V. 22. **And in all thine abominations and thy whoredoms,** in all the wilful apostasy practised by the children of Israel, **thou hast not remembered the days of thy youth, when thou wast naked and bare and wast polluted in thy blood,** as described in the opening verses of the chapter. But the Lord's accusation gains in fierceness as He proceeds. V. 23. **And it came to pass after all thy wickedness,** after such a heap of guilt had accumulated, **(woe, woe unto thee, saith the Lord God,)** v. 24. **that thou hast also built unto thee an eminent place,** a vault or vaulted chamber, such as were used for immoral purposes in connection with idolatrous customs, **and hast made thee an high place in every street,** the temples of idolatry finally being erected anywhere, without the slightest feeling of shame. V. 25. **Thou hast built thy high place at every head of the way,** at every crossroads, **and hast made thy beauty to be abhorred,** familiarity and a too willing yielding breeding contempt also in this instance, **and hast opened thy feet,** in shameless invitation, **to every one that passed by and multiplied thy whoredoms.** This is said chiefly in reference to the fact that all the heathen nations whose trade-routes passed through Canaan found Israel willing to accept their idols. V. 26. **Thou hast also committed fornication with the Egyptians, thy neighbors,** political aspirations, in this case, leading to idolatry, **great of flesh,** of brutal lowness, **and hast increased thy whoredoms to** provoke Me to anger. V. 27. **Behold, therefore I have stretched out My hand over thee,** in a gesture threatening quick punishment, **and have diminished thine ordinary food,** the allowance which she, as a faithful wife, had originally received, **and delivered thee unto the will of them that hate thee, the daughters of the Philistines, which are ashamed of thy lewd way.** They were haters from the beginning, and Moses had good reasons for choosing the longer way to journey to the Land of Promise, Ex. 13, 17. But they became despisers as well. It was on account of the rebellious, idolatrous attitude of the children of Israel almost from the very start that the Lord did not permit them to occupy the peak of magnificence and glory which might have been theirs, and did not give them the full and undisturbed possession of the land of Canaan, but let the Philistines be one of the nations which served as scourges to chastise Israel. V. 28. **Thou hast played the whore also with the Assyrians,** to whom Israel as well as Judah made overtures at a later date, **because thou wast unsatiable,** not satisfied with the chaste intercourse of an honorable marriage, nor even with the whoredoms with neighboring nations; **yea, thou hast played the harlot with them and yet couldest not be satisfied,** seeking leagues with them, in direct defiance of God's prohibition. V. 29. **Thou hast, moreover, multiplied thy fornication,** still with her lust for idolatry unsatisfied, **in the land of Canaan unto Chaldea,** the land of Chaldea known for its Canaanitish abominations and immoralities; **and yet thou wast not satisfied herewith.** Thus the wickedness of the people of Israel and Judah, represented by the city of Jerusalem, had reached a stage which was without example even in those days of loose morality. V. 30. **How weak is thine heart,** withered and languishing with idolatrous love, **saith the Lord God,** speaking in a holy, but bitter sarcasm, **seeing thou doest all these things, the work of an imperious whorish woman,** one whose wealth and power causes her to put aside all restrictions, v. 31. **in that thou buildest thine eminent place,** the vault or chamber of immorality, **in the head of every way and makest thine high place in every street,** cp. v. 25; **and hast not been as an harlot in that thou scornest hire,** prostituting her person merely to satisfy her idolatrous lust, v. 32. **but as a wife that committeth adultery, which taketh strangers instead of her husband,** for so Israel had acted in forsaking Jehovah, the God of the covenant. V. 33. **They give gifts to all whores,** this being the rule generally observed, **but thou givest thy gifts to all thy lovers,** drawing upon the resources with which the goodness of the Lord provided her, **and hirest them,** thereby reversing the process, **that they may come unto thee on every side for thy whoredom.** Thus Israel hired her lovers instead of being, like other harlots, hired by them. V. 34. **And the contrary is in thee from other women in thy whoredoms, whereas none followeth thee to commit whoredoms,** for she was no longer sought by them, **and in that thou givest a reward, and no reward is given unto thee, therefore thou art contrary.** It is the manner of sin, especially of idolatry, that it so enmeshes the sinner as to harden him to the point of utter shamelessness, no matter in which particular field his transgression may lie.

THE PUNISHMENT OF THE LORD ANNOUNCED. V. 35. **Wherefore, O harlot, hear the word of the Lord:** v. 36. **Thus saith the Lord God,** the sovereign Ruler of the universe, **Because thy filthiness was poured out,** literally, "thy brass was emptied out," figurative of a free abandonment to filthy lewdness in spiritual adultery, **and thy nakedness discovered,** that is, uncovered, made known, **through thy whoredoms with thy lovers,** the various heathen nations with which she had allied herself, **and with all the idols of thy abominations, and by the blood of the children which thou didst give unto them,** v. 20: v. 37. **behold, therefore I will gather all thy lovers with whom thou hast taken pleasure,** the very ones whom she had sought with shameless overtures, **and all them that thou hast loved, with all them that thou hast hated,** who would, of course, also gloat over her downfall; **I will even gather them round about against thee,** as witnesses, **and will discover thy nakedness unto them that they may see all thy nakedness.** By the punishment of God Israel became an object of loathing to its former allies and an object of mockery to its enemies. V. 38. **And I will judge thee as women that break wedlock,** the sentence pronounced upon adulteresses being carried out in her case, Lev. 20, 10; Deut. 22, 22 **and** [as those who] **shed blood are judged,** the latter sin being charged against Israel on account of the sacrifices to Moloch; **and I will give thee blood in fury and jealousy,** to be dissolved into blood as a consequence of such fury and jealousy. V. 39. **And I will also give thee into their hand,** so that the former witnesses would be executors of the Lord's sentence, **and they shall throw down thine eminent place and shall break down thy high places,** the temples and the objects of idolatry; **they shall strip thee also of thy clothes and shall take thy fair jewels,** the articles of splendor with which she bedecked herself, **and leave thee naked and bare,** deprived of the honor and dignity which belonged to the people of God by virtue of their election to this position. V. 40. **They shall also bring up a company against thee,** both witnesses and executioners, **and they shall stone thee with stones,** in keeping with the picture of the execution of an adulteress, **and thrust thee through with** their swords. V. 41. **And they shall burn thine houses with fire and execute judgments upon thee in the sight of many women; and I will cause thee to cease from playing the harlot, and thou also shalt give no hire any more.** V. 42. **So will I make My fury toward thee to rest,** being satisfied with the punishment meted out, and **My jealousy,** the jealous rage of a wronged husband, **shall depart from thee, and I will be quiet and will be no more angry.** Since His justice had exacted the full penalty in keeping with the measure of her guilt, He would rest in anticipation of its beneficial effects. V. 43. **Because thou hast not remembered the days of thy youth,** with the blessings which the Lord poured out upon her at that time, **but hast fretted Me in all these things,** raging against Jehovah with her idolatrous behavior, **behold, therefore I also will recompense thy way upon thine head,** so that His punishment would bear down upon her like a heavy load, **saith the Lord God; and thou shalt not commit this lewdness above all thine abominations,** literally, "lest I commit the misdeed above all thy abominations," that is, if the Lord should permit the wickedness of Israel to continue unpunished, He Himself would add an abominable deed, since, by a false leniency, He would become guilty of the same wickedness, become a partaker in the idolatry of Israel. V. 44. **Behold, every one that useth proverbs shall use this proverb against thee,** rightly applying it to the children of Israel, **saying, As is the mother, so is her daughter,** Jerusalem being considered here as the daughter of ancient heathenish Canaan. V. 45. **Thou art the mother's daughter, that loatheth her husband and her children,** rejecting the knowledge of the true God, just as the nations of Canaan had done, although He had still been known in their midst, as the example of Melchizedek shows; **and thou art the sister of thy sisters,** akin in guilt to Samaria and Sodom, **which loathed their husbands and their children. Your mother was an Hittite and your father an Amorite,** and they had all inherited the spiritual make-up of these heathen nations, partly due to the fact that they did not exterminate the heathen as the Lord had bidden them do. V. 46. **And thine elder sister is Samaria,** so called because she was in a moral respect more nearly related to Judah, **she and her daughters that dwell at thy left hand,** to the north; **and thy younger sister,** the smaller and in many respects not so nearly related to Judah, **that dwelleth at thy right hand,** toward the south, **is Sodom and her daughters,** that is, Ammon and Moab with their towns. V. 47. **Yet hast thou not walked after their ways nor done after their abominations,** not even being satisfied with the deeds of wickedness for which these cities were known; **but, as if that were a very little thing,** as if their idolatrous conduct were not sufficiently wicked, **thou wast corrupted more than they in all thy ways,** exceeding even the heathen in the measure of idolatry and the evils connected with idolatrous worship. V. 48. **As I live, saith the Lord God,** in the most solemn oath which He could swear, **Sodom, thy sister, hath not done, she nor her daughters,** any of the smaller cities belonging to her city-state, **as thou hast done, thou and thy daughters,** the guilt of the heathen cities being less great than that of Jerusalem. V. 49. **Behold, this was the iniquity of thy sister Sodom,** in these forms of transgression she excelled: **pride,** cp. Gen. 18, 21, **fulness of bread,** that is, more than an abundance of material wealth, **and abundance of idleness,** a security far removed from all anxiety, **was in her and in her daughters,** the result being a haughty arrogance; **neither did she strengthen the hand of the poor and needy,** for that is the way of such as are puffed up with their prosperity. V. 50. **And they were haughty and committed abomination before Me,** their transgression being so heinous as to call out to the Lord for punishment; **therefore I took them away as I saw good,** by the terrible catastrophe of the overthrow of their city. Yet Sodom was not as wicked as Jerusalem had now become. V. 51. **Neither hath Samaria committed half of thy sins,** it was, in fact, not particularly conspicuous in its heathenism after the time of Ahab; **but thou hast multiplied thine abominations more than they and hast justified thy sisters in all thine abominations which thou hast done,** making them actually appear righteous by comparison with her own wickedness. V. 52. **Thou also, which hast judged thy sisters,** condemning them for their transgressions and, with hypocritical demeanor, considering herself better than they, **bear thine own shame for thy sins that thou hast committed more abominable than they,** being committed in spite of Jerusalem's possession of the Law of God; **they are more righteous than thou,** namely, by way of comparison; **yea, be thou confounded also and bear thy shame in that thou hast justified thy sisters,** making them appear almost innocent in comparison with her own guilt. It is always a greater and deeper fall if people who have been in possession of the truth, who have enjoyed unusual advantages in the matter of God's mercy, fall away from the path of righteousness than if those unacquainted with God's holy will live in the sins which they have always followed, with little or no idea of the better way.

MERCY PROMISED FOR THE LATTER END. — V. 53. **When I shall bring again their captivity, the captivity of Sodom and her daughters, and the captivity of Samaria and her daughters,** restoring sinners of even the worst type to the enjoyment of His grace, **then will I bring again the captivity of thy captives in the midst of them,** rather, "and the captivity of thy captivity in their midst," Israel being placed on the same level with the greatest sinner from among the heathen, also in her relation to the grace of God, v. 54. **that thou mayest bear thine own shame,** suffer the well-deserved punishment, **and mayest be confounded in all that thou hast done, in that thou art a comfort unto them,** her own eventual restoration serving as an encouragement to other sinners, that they also may find mercy. V. 55. **When thy sisters, Sodom and her daughters, shall return to their former estate, and Samaria and her daughters shall return to their former estate,** the position which they held before they yielded to the godless behavior which brought the decline upon them, **then thou and thy daughters shall return to your former estate.** This is said only by way of comparison, to bring home the fact that the mercy of the Lord is able to lift up men from the very abysses of degradation and give them the privileges and blessings of His children for the sake of His mercy. V. 56. **For thy sister Sodom was not mentioned by thy mouth in the day of thy pride,** her fate was not made the subject of discussion, with the purpose of letting it serve as a warning; Israel did not profit by the example of Sodom's destruction, v. 57. **before thy wickedness was discovered,** when Judah still stood proud and haughty, **as at the time of thy reproach of the daughters of Syria, and all that are round about her, the daughters of the Philistines, which despise thee round about.** By the judgment which was carried out upon Jerusalem on the part of the Chaldeans her wickedness was uncovered, to her great shame, as at the time when the Syrians on the east and the Philistines on the west took every opportunity to humiliate her. V. 58. **Thou hast borne thy lewdness and thine abominations, saith the Lord,** suffering the well-deserved punishment of her sins, especially of her pride. V. 59. **For thus saith the Lord God, I will even deal with thee as thou hast done,** in forgetting the oath of faithfulness and in forsaking the covenant relation, **which hast despised the oath in breaking the covenant.** Cp. Deut. 29, 11. 12. But although Israel has been guilty of treachery and must bear the punishment of her sins, yet all faithlessness on the part of men cannot change the eternal faithfulness of Jehovah. V. 60. **Nevertheless I will remember My covenant with thee in the days of thy youth,** being ready once more to show mercy to a repentant people, **and I will establish unto thee an everlasting covenant,** the Messianic idea being brought out at this point. V. 61. **Then thou shalt remember thy ways,** the goodness of God leading at least a few to repentance, **and be ashamed, when thou shalt receive thy sisters, thine elder and thy younger,** representatives from various parts of the heathen world becoming partakers of the privileges formerly accorded to Israel alone; **and I will give them unto thee for daughters, but not by the covenant,** that is, not by that of the Old Testament, under which Israel had been chosen. V. 62. **And I will establish My covenant with thee,** namely, that of the new dispensation, **and thou shalt know that I am the Lord,** realizing the new covenant relation and making use of it in the proper way, v. 63. **that thou mayest remember and be confounded and never open thy mouth any more because of thy shame,** all boasting on the part of man being excluded by the obvious deliverance by grace alone, **when I am pacified toward thee for all that thou hast done, saith the Lord God.** Thus the grace of God which has pardoned so many and so great sins is the one great subject of Gospel-preaching at all times. Nothing is so conducive to love and humility as the sense of the riches of God's pardoning grace.

CHAPTER 17.

The Parable of the Royal House of David.

THE RIDDLE ITSELF. — V. 1. **And the word of the Lord came unto me, saying,** v. 2. **Son of man, put forth a riddle,** a continued allegory with a hidden deeper meaning, **and speak a parable unto the house of Israel,** a story of a comparison based upon facts, showing the likeness of the figure to the thing compared, v. 3. **and say, Thus saith the Lord God, A great eagle, with great wings,** pointing to a very extensive dominion, **long-winged,** symbolical of great energy, **full of feathers,** with many subjects and a large army, **which had divers colors,** a reference to the various nationalities combined in one empire, **came unto Lebanon,** representative of Jerusalem with its palaces and Temple built of cedar-wood from Lebanon, **and took the highest branch of the cedar,** the topmost of its shoots; v. 4. **he cropped off the top of his young twigs,** the uppermost one, **and carried it into a land of traffic,** literally, "to the land of Canaan," that is, to a land which, in both its commercial ambitions and in its idolatry, was just like the heathen Canaan of old; **he set it in a city of merchants.** It is evident at once that the great eagle is Nebuchadnezzar, that the city is Babylon, and the shoot taken from the cedar of Jerusalem is Jehoiachin. V. 5. **He took also of the seed of the land,** one of the native royal family of Judah, in this case undoubtedly Zedekiah, **and planted it in a fruitful field,** in very productive soil; **he placed it by great waters,** in a most fertile situation, **and set it as a willow-tree,** the well-watered location being such as the willow loves. V. 6. **And it grew and became a spreading vine,** though no longer the cedar of David, **of low stature, whose branches turned toward him,** namely, they were intended to turn toward the eagle in humble submission, **and the roots thereof were under him,** deriving their strength from Babylon's practically exhaustless store; **so it became a vine and brought forth branches and shot forth sprigs,** always deriving its existence and vigor from Babylon, upon which it was dependent. If Zedekiah, so the text implies, had maintained his connection with the emperor of Babylon, his dependent position, then his kingdom might have had a steady growth. But here is where he made his mistake. V. 7. **There was also another great eagle with great wings,** namely, the king of Egypt, **and many feathers,** with a large population and a mighty army; **and, behold, this vine,** although tributary to Babylon, **did bend her roots toward him and shot forth her branches toward him, that he might water it by the furrows of her plantation,** from the beds of its planting, with the assistance which Zedekiah hoped to get from the land of the Nile. V. 8. **It was planted in a good soil,** in a well-cultivated and well-watered field, **by great waters that it might bring forth branches, and that it might bear fruit, that it might be a goodly vine.** The thought is the same as that urged so often by Jeremiah when he admonished his countrymen and their ruler to submit to the rule of Nebuchadnezzar. It was not tyrannical oppression on the part of the Babylonian ruler which caused Zedekiah to revolt, but inordinate ambition, pride, and ingratitude. V. 9. **Say thou,** namely, Ezekiel, in rebuking this spirit, **Thus saith the Lord God, Shall it prosper? Shall he,** the great eagle, Nebuchadnezzar, **not pull up the roots thereof and cut off the fruit thereof that it wither?** He would certainly punish rebellion in this manner. **It shall wither in all the leaves of her spring,** with its entire productive energy and vital force, **even without great power or many people to pluck it up by the roots thereof,** that is, the Chaldean king would not have to employ his whole military forces in bringing about the downfall of Judah. V. 10. **Yea, behold, being planted, shall it prosper?** Will the southern kingdom be able to maintain itself against the Chaldean power? **Shall it not utterly wither when the east wind toucheth it?** very appropriately said of the Babylonians, who dwelt to the northeast of Canaan. **It shall whither in the furrows where it grew,** on the very spot of its ungrateful pride, in spite of the apparent chance which it had to continue its existence. It is usually the pride of the sinner which hastens his downfall, on account of his deliberately setting aside the Lord's will.

THE DOUBLE APPLICATION OF THE PARABLE. V. 11. **Moreover, the word of the Lord came unto me, saying,** v. 12. **Say now to the rebellious house,** literally, "the house of rebelliousness," the children of Israel, to whom this parable had been told as a warning, **Know ye not what these things mean?** Were they intellectually as well as morally stupid? **Tell them, Behold, the king of Babylon is come to Jerusalem,** 2 Kings 24, 11 ff.; Jer. 24, 1; 29, 2, **and hath taken the king thereof,** namely, Jehoiachin, **and the princes thereof and led them with him to Babylon,** theirs being the first company of exiles from Jerusalem; v. 13. **and hath taken of the king's seed,** of the royal family, **and made a covenant with him and hath taken an oath of him,** the oath of allegiance as a tributary ruler, this man being Zedekiah himself; **he hath also taken the mighty of the land,** all the representatives of the wealthier class, the landowners and the artisans, v. 14. **that the kingdom might be base,** of a low condition, of a very secondary rank, **that it might not lift itself up,** not develop enough strength to regain its independence, **but that by keeping of his covenant it might stand.** V. 15. **But he,** the king of Judah, **rebelled against him,** namely, Nebuchadnezzar, king of Babylon, **in sending his ambassadors into Egypt,** 2 Kings 24, 20, **that they might give him horses and much people,** come to his assistance with a strong army. **Shall he prosper? Shall he escape that doeth such things? Or shall he break the covenant,** his oath of fealty, **and be delivered?** V. 16. **As I live, saith the Lord God,** the sovereign Ruler of the universe swearing His most solemn oath, **surely, in the place where the king dwelleth that made him king, whose oath he despised,** rejecting the obligation which it laid upon him, **and whose covenant he brake, even with him in the midst of Babylon he shall die.** Zedekiah's revolt was an act of treachery, and was to be punished as it well deserved. V. 17. **Neither shall Pharaoh,** upon whom Zedekiah depended, **with his mighty army and great company, make for him in the war,** as Zedekiah's ally in battle, **by casting up mounts and building forts, to cut off many persons,** in an effort to relieve the besieged city; v. 18. **seeing he despised the oath,** valid and sacred as it was, **by breaking the covenant, when, lo, he had given his hand,** in a solemn pledge, **and hath done all these things, he shall not escape,** he was to pay the penalty of his perjury. V. 19. **Therefore, thus saith the Lord God, As I live, surely Mine oath that he hath despised,** for it was made in the name of Jehovah, **and My covenant that he hath**

broken, even it will I recompense upon his own head, in His punishment upon the perjurer. V. 20. **And I will spread My net upon him,** like a fowler setting his traps for birds, **and he shall be taken in My snare, and I will bring him to Babylon,** these words coming true a few years later, **and will plead with him there,** contending with him as when a case is argued in court, **for his trespass that he hath trespassed against Me,** the accusation here involving also the punishment. V. 21. **And all his fugitives with all his bands,** even the picked ones of his military forces, **shall fall by the sword, and they that remain shall be scattered toward all winds,** doomed to death though they escape the first onslaught; **and ye shall know that I, the Lord, have spoken it,** bitter experience teaching them what all the admonitions of the Lord's prophets had not been able to accomplish. V. 22. **Thus saith the Lord God, I will also take of the highest branch of the high cedar,** a shoot of the royal house of David, **and will set it,** give it a place where it might grow; **I will crop off from the top of his young twigs a tender one,** tender both in age and in character, **and will plant it upon an high mountain and eminent,** in a position of power and magnificence; v. 23. **in the mountain of the height of Israel will I plant it,** figurative for the exalted position of the Kingdom of Grace; **and it shall bring forth boughs and bear fruit and be a goodly cedar,** a glorious and beautiful tree; **and under it shall dwell all fowl of every wing,** representative of all nations; **in the shadow of the branches thereof shall they dwell.** Cp. Matt. 13, 32. V. 24. **And all the trees of the field,** men throughout the world, **shall know that I, the Lord, have brought down the high tree,** the proud Zedekiah, **have exalted the low tree,** the lowly Messiah, **have dried up the green tree,** which the last king of Judah considered himself to be, **and have made the dry tree to flourish,** cp. Is. 53, 2. **I, the Lord, have spoken and have done it.** The passage sets forth, in a most unmistakable fashion, the rise of the Messiah from His lowly origin, as a branch of the impoverished family of David, to be the King of His Church, which, under His benign and powerful rule, extends throughout the world and gathers into its communion men from every race and nation.

CHAPTER 18.

The Avenging Justice of God.

THE PARABLE OF THE SOUR GRAPES. — V. 1. **The word of the Lord came unto me again, saying,** v. 2. **What mean ye, that ye use this proverb concerning the land of Israel,** literally, "upon the land of Israel," in the sense of something that is harmful and wrong, **saying, The fathers have eaten sour grapes, and the children's teeth are set on edge?** This proverbial saying in the land of Judah reflected the self-righteousness of its inhabitants, for they meant to say that the sins of their fathers, of which they considered themselves innocent, were unjustly visited upon them. It is the tendency of natural man to place the blame for his troubles upon others; but although others may be guilty, yet it is the nature of true contrition to disregard the transgressions of every one else and to see nothing but one's own guilt and proneness to punishment. For that reason this false understanding of Ex. 20, 5 was combated also by Jeremiah, chap. 31, 29; 32, 18. The sins of the fathers are visited upon the children only in the case of those who hate Him, who follow their fathers in the enmity against the Lord. V. 3. **As I live, saith the Lord God,** the sovereign Ruler of the universe making this declaration with a solemn oath, **ye shall not have occasion any more to use this proverb in Israel.** His intention was, by means of His righteous punishments, so to emphasize the justice of His acts that the people would no longer seek excuses of this kind. V. 4. **Behold,** so the Lord says in stating the theme for His further discussion of the principle of His righteousness, **all souls are Mine,** they are all equally His, as Creator of the universe, as Father of all mankind; **as the soul of the father, so also the soul of the son is Mine,** each one standing before the Lord for himself alone, responsible only for his act; **the soul that sinneth, it shall die,** becoming subject to the final summary and climax of all sufferings which are the consequence of sin, temporal death, in this instance, becoming the portal to everlasting death and damnation. For a sinner to put the blame for his sufferings upon others, whereas he alone is guilty, is both foolish and unjust. True repentance puts aside all excuses and humbly says with the publican, "God be merciful to me, a sinner." Cp. 1 Tim. 1, 15.

THE PRINCIPLE OF GOD'S AVENGING JUSTICE. V. 5. **But if a man be just,** righteous in all his doing, **and do that which is lawful and right,** literally, "judgment and righteousness," exercising himself in the demands of the Law of God, v. 6. **and hath not eaten upon the mountains,** in sacrificial meals consecrated to idols, **neither hath lifted up his eyes to the idols of the house of Israel,** in order to make them objects of confidence, of worshipful supplication, **neither hath defiled his neighbor's wife,** in the sin of adultery, Ex. 20, 14; Lev. 20, 10, **neither hath come near to a menstruous woman, Lev. 18, 19;** 20, 18,

v. 7. **and hath not oppressed any,** no matter with what degree of violence this was done, Ex. 22, 28; Lev. 25, 14. 17, **but hath restored to the debtor his pledge,** the Law requiring that this raiment be restored before sunset, Ex. 22, 26. 27, **hath spoiled none by violence,** not gaining the property of another by false ware or dealing, **hath given his bread to the hungry,** Is. 58, 7, **and hath covered the naked with a garment,** Matt. 25, 26; v. 8. **he that hath not given forth upon usury, neither hath taken any increase,** in exacting interest from a poor neighbor, contrary to the law of love, Deut. 23, 20; Lev. 25, 36. 37, **that hath withdrawn his hand from iniquity,** from the injustice or wickedness which selfishness prompts, in promoting one's own gain at the expense of one's neighbor, **hath executed true judgment between man and man,** literally, "the judgment of truth," namely, in a manner in full agreement with the facts and conditions of every case presented, v. 9. **hath walked in My statutes and hath kept My judgments,** in all ordinances, whether pertaining to Israel only or to all men, **to deal truly,** with sound integrity: **he is just, he shall surely live, saith the Lord God.** It is not that the righteousness of a man's life earns for him the fulness of life, including the blessings of eternal life, but that God rewards such evidences of true faith by bestowing His mercy upon the believers. Such a man, then, stands before the Lord for his own person, responsible for himself, the Lord dealing with his case on its own merits, regardless of his children or other relatives. V. 10. **If he beget a son that is a robber,** one addicted to violence, **a shedder of blood, and that doeth the like to any one of these things,** becoming guilty of any of the sins mentioned in the next verses, v. 11. **and that doeth not any of those duties,** or, "whereas the father was not guilty of such wickedness," **but even hath eaten upon the mountains and defiled his neighbor's wife,** v. 12. **hath oppressed the poor and needy,** those unable to defend themselves against violence in any form, **hath spoiled by violence, hath not restored the pledge, and hath lifted up his eyes to the idols, hath committed abomination,** such as is mentioned at the end of v. 6, v. 13. **hath given forth upon usury, and hath taken increase: shall he then live?** Is it possible for him to become a partaker of that fulness of life which God has intended for His children? **He shall not live; he hath done all these abominations; he shall surely die,** be condemned to eternal death if he persists in his wickedness; **his blood shall be upon him,** he will have but himself to blame for the terrible fate which will surely strike him. The thought of this paragraph, then, is this: If the wicked son of a righteous man will be punished if he commits even so much as a single sin of those which his father abhorred, how much more if he become guilty of the entire catalog of sins which are enumerated! So much for the second generation and its wickedness. V. 14. **Now, lo, if he beget a son,** thereby establishing the third generation of the family whose example is cited for the sake of the lesson the entire parable teaches, **that seeth all his father's sins which he hath done, and considereth,** carefully observing the wickedness of his doings, **and doeth not such like,** not following in his father's footsteps, v. 15. **that hath not eaten upon the mountains, neither hath lifted up his eyes to the idols of the house of Israel, hath not defiled his neighbor's wife,** v. 16. **neither hath oppressed any, hath not withholden the pledge,** literally, "and the pledge not hath he pledged," **neither hath spoiled by violence, but hath given his bread to the hungry and hath covered the naked with a garment,** v. 17. **that hath taken off his hand from the poor,** abstaining from doing him harm, even if he might have done so with impunity, **that hath not received usury nor increase, hath executed My judgments, hath walked in My statutes,** thus refusing to partake of the guilt of his father: **he shall not die for the iniquity of his father,** the father's guilt not being imputed to him; **he shall surely live.** V. 18. **As for his father, because he cruelly oppressed, spoiled his brother by violence, and did that which is not good among his people,** as stated in detail above, **lo, even he shall die in his iniquity,** being punished for the guilt which he loaded upon himself. V. 19. **Yet say ye,** in accordance with the ancient false proverb which had been in circulation, **Why? Doth not the son bear the iniquity of the father?** That is, Would not that be the right and the just thing? God's answer is, **When the son hath done that which is lawful and right and hath kept all My statutes and hath done them, he shall surely live.** On the basis of all the arguments offered thus far the Lord now states His conclusion. V. 20. **The soul that sinneth, it shall die,** every person in the world being held responsible for his own acts. **The son shall not bear the iniquity of the father,** so that his father's guilt would be imputed to him, **neither shall the father bear the iniquity of the son; the righteousness of the righteous shall be upon him,** so that he who is righteous, even if only by virtue of the righteousness of Christ imputed to him, will receive the reward of righteousness, **and the wickedness of the wicked shall be upon him,** so that he is compelled to endure its punishment. In this way the Lord stated the principle of His avenging justice, a principle which He has ever followed in all His dealings with men.

GOD'S MERCIFUL CALL TO REPENTANCE. — V. 21. **But if the wicked,** no matter where or what he may be, or in what relation he may stand to others, **will turn from all his sins that he hath committed,** by an act of true repentance, **and keep all My statutes,** in particular those given to the children of Israel, **and do that which is lawful and right,** what God expects all men to observe, as evidence and proof of the faith of his heart: **he shall surely live, he shall not die.** God, in His great mercy, is ready to deal with him according to his new obedience, not according to his former sins. V. 22. **All his transgressions that he hath committed,** by which he brought guilt upon himself, **they shall not be mentioned unto him,** the Lord's forgiveness being essentially a complete forgetting of the former sins; **in his righteousness that he hath done,** by virtue of the new life which followed his repentance, **he shall live.** V. 23. **Have I any pleasure at all that the wicked should die? saith the Lord God,** an inherent delight, as it were, in cruel punishment of the wicked, **and not that he should return from his ways and live?** this being much preferable in the sight of the Lord, since He delights in showing mercy. This is the one side of the question, by which the Lord intends to call the wicked to repentance. On the other hand, however, He just as earnestly warns against backsliding and apostasy. V. 24. **But when the righteous turneth away from his righteousness and committeth iniquity,** in the foolish notion that he may do so with impunity, since his good record will serve to excuse him, **and doeth according to all the abominations that the wicked man doeth, shall he live?** Will he be able to escape from the punishment which threatens sinners? The Lord's answer is: **All his righteousness that he hath done shall not be mentioned,** not be taken into account so as to save him; **in his trespass that he hath trespassed and in his sin that he hath sinned,** by which he nullified all his former good conduct, **in them shall he die.** Thus the justice of the Lord weighed the acts of men, as expressive of their inner life, and dealt with them accordingly. V. 25. **Yet ye say,** in a statement which lacked all foundation, **The way of the Lord is not equal,** not in agreement with true equity. **Hear now, O house of Israel, Is not My way equal?** Did He really treat different classes of men in a different way? **Are not your ways unequal?** since they, although living in sin, expected the Lord to treat them as if they were righteous. That surely was not fair and just. The Lord therefore states the two cases once more, in inverse order, to impress their significance upon His hearers. V. 26. **When a righteous man turneth away from his righteousness and committeth iniquity and dieth in them,** or "on account of this wickedness"; **for his iniquity that he hath done shall he die.** V. 27. **Again, when the wicked man turneth away from his wickedness that he hath committed,** by a true repentance, not from a mere aesthetic loathing, **and doeth that which is lawful and right,** in agreement with God's holy will, **he shall save his soul alive,** the mercy of God being put into operation in his case. V. 28. **Because he considereth,** observing carefully and thereby, under the guidance of the Lord, obtaining the right understanding, **and turneth away from all his transgressions that he hath committed, he shall surely live, he shall not die.** Thus the divine procedure was justified, and the complaint of the people proved to be unfounded. But since the object of the Lord was to effect the deliverance of His people from corruption and perdition, He closes this section of the prophecy with an earnest appeal. V. 29. **Yet saith the house of Israel, The way of the Lord is not equal,** right and just. **O house of Israel, are not My ways equal? Are not your ways unequal?** V. 30. **Therefore I will judge you, O house of Israel,** thereby bringing their whining and caviling to an end, **every one according to his ways,** according to his manner of living and acting, **saith the Lord God.** The Lord's way was right and good, and those who were not in agreement with His way and order would be unfortunate indeed. **Repent and turn yourselves from all your transgressions; so iniquity shall not be your ruin,** the cause of their damnation. This admonition is now repeated in a still more emphatic vein. V. 31. **Cast away from you all your transgressions whereby ye have transgressed,** the expression referring especially to the utter removal of all idols and idolatrous ways, **and make you a new heart and a new spirit,** not in their own strength, indeed, but by the gracious gift of God; **for why will ye die, O house of Israel?** The way of death and damnation is ever a matter of man's deliberate choice, and he has no one but himself to blame in that event. V. 32. **For I have no pleasure in the death of him that dieth,** a victim of perdition by his own fault, **saith the Lord God; wherefore turn yourselves and live ye.** Every sinner is a victim of spiritual death, and this will eventually lead to eternal death, unless the way of repentance is followed at the Lord's urgent invitation. The readiness of the divine grace is the outstanding feature of the Gospel-message.

CHAPTER 19.

Lament over the Rulers of Israel.

OVER THE KINGS. — V. 1. **Moreover, take thou up a lamentation,** an elegy, **for the princes of Israel,** evidently the kings then living, namely, Jehoahaz and Jehoiachin, v. 2. **and say, What is thy mother?** the address here referring to the house of David in general, specifically to Jerusalem, as capital of the nation. **A lioness,** royal, powerful, with the nature of a lion; **she lay down among lions,** as the equal of all the mighty nations round about; **she nourished her whelps among young lions,** instilling into them all the cruelty of a beast of prey. V. 3. **And she brought up one of her whelps,** namely, Jehoahaz, son of Josiah; **it became a young lion, and it learned to catch the prey; it devoured men,** having developed in kingly power until he abused it to the detriment of his people. V. 4. **The nations also heard of him,** their attention being called to him by his increasing daring and by his depredations; **he was taken in their pit,** in this case in that of Egypt, **and they brought him with chains unto the land of Egypt,** for Pharaoh deposed him and led him into captivity in Egypt, where he died. Cp. 2 Kings 23, 33. 34. V. 5. **Now, when she saw that she had waited and her hope was lost,** that is, "while she waited, her hope had perished," so far as this one whelp was concerned, **then she took another of her whelps and made him a young lion,** in this instance Jehoiachin, for Jehoiakim hardly comes into consideration. V. 6. **And he went up and down among the lions,** trying to imitate the recklessness and the tyranny of the surrounding kings; **he became a young lion and learned to catch the prey and devoured men,** thus following in the footsteps of other rulers of Judah who chose their own way. V. 7. **And he knew their desolate palaces,** or, "he defiled their widows," taking advantage of their helplessness, **and he laid waste their cities,** so that his tyrannical behavior ruined his own country; **and the land was desolate and the fulness thereof,** that is, all it contained, **by the noise of his roaring,** as he pursued his cruel course. V. 8. **Then the nations set against him on every side,** chiefly the Chaldeans, Syrians, Moab, and Ammon, 2 Kings 24, 2, **from the provinces,** marching up against Judah with their armies, **and spread their net over him,** like a hunter capturing an animal; **he was taken in their pit.** V. 9. **And they put him in ward in chains,** 2 Chron. 36, 10, **and brought him to the king of Babylon; they brought him into holds,** into one of the fortresses or strongholds of the country, **that his voice should no more be heard upon the mountains of Israel,** so that he could not continue his insolent and cruel tactics. The Lord has ways by which He curbs the pride of man's heart, if necessary, by measures of the most strenuous kind.

CONCERNING THE MOTHER OF KINGS. — V. 10. **Thy mother,** that of the royal family and of Israel and Jerusalem in general, **is like a vine in thy blood, planted by the waters,** or "planted in peaceful security"; for this was originally Israel's condition. **She was fruitful and full of branches by reason of many waters,** in a position where the richest and strongest growth was possible, for Canaan was a land flowing with milk and honey, and Israel had the Lord's promise of blessings. V. 11. **And she had strong rods,** powerful branches, **for the scepters of them that bare rule,** assuring all members of the royal race a safe position as long as they adhered to the Word of the Lord; **and her stature was exalted among the thick branches,** or "to the heavy clouds above," **and she appeared in her height with the multitude of her branches,** occupying a mighty position among the nations. V. 12. **But she was plucked up in fury,** the prophecy representing the punishment as having been accomplished, **she was cast down to the ground, and the east wind dried up her fruit,** the figure, of course, referring to the overthrow of Judah by the power of Babylon; **her strong rods were broken and withered,** namely, when her best citizens were carried into captivity; **the fire consumed them,** in the Lord's judgment of condemnation. V. 13. **And now,** when the exile has begun, **she is planted in the wilderness,** in a condition in which Israel would not be able to prosper, **in a dry and thirsty ground,** far from the blessings of the mother country. V. 14. **And fire is gone out of a rod of her branches,** literally, "of its boughs," the destruction proceeding from within, **which hath devoured her fruit,** ruining all the blessings which had been vouchsafed to Israel and Judah by the Lord, **so that she hath no strong rod to be a scepter to rule,** no more kings of the house of David were now to rule the nation. **This is a lamentation,** the elegy presenting the conditions as they now produced sorrow in the heart of the prophet, **and shall be for a lamentation,** namely, by the further fulfilment of the Lord's threats. It is a matter of true wisdom to heed the Lord's warnings in time, lest the proper appreciation of His seriousness come too late.

CHAPTER 20.

A Survey of Israel's History.

IN THE EARLY DAYS. — V. 1. **And it came to pass in the seventh year, in the fifth month, the tenth day of the month,** about in the middle of the first period of Ezekiel's prophetic activity, **that certain of the elders of Israel,** who were their spiritual leaders also in the captivity, **came to enquire of the Lord,** as on a former occasion, seeking a special revelation, very likely concerning the speedy termination of their captivity, **and sat before me,** according to the custom of such delegations. V. 2. **Then came the word of the Lord unto me, saying,** v. 3. **Son of man, speak unto the elders of Israel,** giving them information which was verbally the expression of the will of God, **and say unto them, Thus saith the Lord God,** the supreme Ruler of the universe, at the same time the God of the covenant, **Are ye come to enquire of Me?** Was their impudence such as to cause them to appear before Jehovah without previous change of heart, in an excess of bold hypocrisy? **As I live, saith the Lord God, I will not be enquired of by you,** this emphatic declaration being made chiefly on account of their inability, in their present moral state, to understand the will of the Lord. In connection with this inquiry, therefore, the Lord takes occasion to charge His servant with a message of earnest rebuke addressed to the disobedient and hard-hearted Jews. V. 4. **Wilt thou judge them, son of man, wilt thou judge them?** the question showing the impatience of the Lord in pronouncing sentence upon the unrepentant sinners. **Cause them to know the abominations of their fathers,** this rehearsal having the purpose not only of presenting the greatness of Israel's guilt, but also of emphasizing the patience which the Lord had till now exhibited in dealing with His people. V. 5. **And say unto them, Thus saith the Lord God, In the day when I chose Israel,** selecting them, on the basis of His grace and mercy, from among the nations of the world, **and lifted up Mine hand unto the seed of the house of Jacob,** in the gesture of a solemn oath to the children of His servant Israel, **and made Myself known unto them in the land of Egypt,** under the name of Jehovah, the God of the covenant, Ex. 6, 3, **when I lifted up Mine hand unto them, saying, I am the Lord, your God,** Ex. 6, 8; v. 6. **in the day that I lifted up Mine hand unto them to bring them forth of the land of Egypt into a land that I had espied for them,** seeking it out and choosing it for them as the best of all lands for His special purpose, Deut. 8, 7. 8, **flowing with milk and honey, which is the glory of all lands,** the most lovely and delightful of all lands, Dan. 8, 9, v. 7. **then said I unto them,** this being the gist of the entire message of Moses, **Cast ye away every man the abominations of his eyes,** that which was loathsome in God's eyes and should have been so in theirs, **and defile not yourselves with the idols of Egypt,** for such idolatry was still carried on in secret, cp. Lev. 17, 7; Josh. 24, 14. **I am the Lord, your God.** V. 8. **But they rebelled against Me and would not hearken unto Me,** being filled even in those days with the obstinacy which proved their undoing; **they did not every man cast away the abominations of their eyes, neither did they forsake the idols of Egypt,** cp. Ex. 32. **Then I said, I will pour out My fury upon them,** having reached this conclusion concerning them even before they left Egypt, **to accomplish My anger against them in the midst of the land of Egypt,** to punish them even at that time. V. 9. **But I wrought for My name's sake,** He refrained from executing His wrath for the sake of His own honor, **that it should not be polluted before the heathen,** who would have taken occasion to blaspheme if Israel had been severely punished by the Lord at that time, while the Egyptians were witnesses, **among whom they were, in whose sight I made Myself known unto them,** as by the ten great plagues, **in bringing them forth out of the land of Egypt.** That was the first stage of Israel's national existence, or rather the preparation for this stage. Even in those days the children of Israel had been so stubborn and wilful that the Lord felt constrained to punish them severely, and only His great mercy had saved them from the well-merited punishment.

IN THE WILDERNESS. — V. 10. **Wherefore I caused them to go forth out of the land of Egypt,** in agreement with His merciful intention, **and brought them into the wilderness,** delivering them from oppression and preparing them for entry into the Land of Promise. V. 11. **And I gave them My statutes and showed them My judgments,** namely, in the giving of the Law on Mount Sinai, **which if a man do, he shall even live in them,** for a perfect keeping of the Law would indeed merit eternal life. Cp. Rom. 10, 5; Gal. 3, 12; Luke 10, 28. V. 12. **Moreover, also, I gave them My Sabbaths,** whose special observance was a distinction to the Jews, **to be a sign between Me and them,** in their ever-recurring celebration, **that they might know that I am the Lord that sanctify them,** by separating them from the other nations of the world and by reminding them of the fact that the rest and contemplation of the Sabbath was a type of the greater and more wonderful rest prepared for the people of God. Cp. Heb. 4, 9. V. 13. **But the house of Israel rebelled against Me in the wilderness,** repeating the former performance; **they walked not in My statutes, and they despised My judgments,** the general ordinances as well as the specific commands, **which if a man do, he shall even live in them; and My Sabbaths they greatly polluted,** by disregarding their proper observance, cp. Ex. 32, 1—6; Num. 25, 1—3; Ex. 16, 27; Num. 15, 32. **Then I said I would pour out My fury upon them in the wilderness to consume them,** as He repeatedly stated. Cp. Ex. 32, 10; Num. 14, 11. 12. V. 14. **But I wrought for My name's sake,** again working deliverance and refraining from striking in His wrath, **that it should not be polluted before the heathen, in whose sight I brought them out,** the Lord's explanation here agreeing exactly with the plea by which Moses effected the deliverance of the people whom he loved. V. 15. **Yet also I lifted up My hand unto them in the wilderness,** in another solemn oath, Num. 14, 28, **that I would not bring them into the land which I had given them, flowing with milk and honey, which is the glory of all lands,** v. 16. **because they despised My judgments and walked not in My statutes, but polluted My Sabbaths; for their heart went after their idols,** as their fierce longing for the flesh-pots of Egypt indicated. Cp. Num. 15, 39; Ps. 78, 37; Amos 5, 25; Acts 7, 42. 43. V. 17. **Nevertheless Mine eye spared them from destroying them,** although all adults who had left the land of Egypt died in the wilderness, with the exception of Joshua and Caleb, **neither did I make an end of them in the wilderness,** namely, by a sentence of total extermination, as He had threatened. V. 18. **But I said unto their children in the wilderness,** whom He spared by a special act of His mercy, **Walk ye not in the statutes,** the idolatrous customs and usages, **of your fathers, neither observe their judgments,** the manner in which they pretended to do justice and practise righteousness, **nor defile yourselves with their idols.** V. 19. **I am the Lord, your God; walk in My statutes,** as opposed to the self-appointed ordinances of men, **and keep My judgments,** the manner in which He chose to exercise righteousness, **and do them;** v. 20. **and hallow My Sabbaths,** by knowing them according to their spirit, not only in outward form; **and they shall be a sign between Me and you that ye may know that I am the Lord, your God.** V. 21. **Notwithstanding the children,** the younger generation, whom His mercy had spared, **rebelled against Me; they walked not in My statutes, neither kept My judgments to do them, which if a man do, he shall even live in them; they polluted My Sabbaths,** showing that in every way they followed the stubbornness and wickedness of their fathers. **Then I said I would pour out My fury upon them to accomplish My anger against them in the wilderness.** Some of this is shown in the story of Israel's sojourn in the Plains of Moab, when they yielded to the wiles of the Midianitish women. V. 22. **Nevertheless I withdrew Mine hand,** in sparing the sinners even then, **and wrought for My name's sake that it should not be polluted in the sight of the heathen, in whose sight I brought them forth,** who were watching the progress of Israel with a great deal of interest. V. 23. **I lifted up Mine hand unto them also in the wilderness,** in a solemn oath concerning also this generation, **that I would scatter them among the heathen and disperse them through the countries,** cp. Jer. 15, 4, v. 24. **because they had not executed My judgments,** the decrees of His righteousness, **but had despised My statutes and had polluted My Sabbaths, and their eyes were after their fathers' idols,** in a continual desire to commit idolatry, in a strange eagerness to transgress the First Commandment. V. 25. **Wherefore I gave them also,** in just retribution upon them, **statutes that were not good,** which brought them no deliverance, no blessings, **and judgments whereby they should not live,** which would, on account of their stubbornness, become stumbling-blocks to them; v. 26. **and I polluted them in their own gifts, in that they caused to pass through the fire all that openeth the womb,** thereby consecrating their first-born children to Molech, the abomination of the Moabites, instead of offering them to Jehovah according to the manner prescribed by Him, Ex. 13, 12, **that I might make them desolate,** visiting their obstinacy upon them in just this way, by letting the loathsome and revolting custom continue, since He had so emphatically forbidden it, Lev. 18, 21; Deut. 18, 10, **to the end that they might know that I am the Lord.** It was God's judgment upon the stubborn Jews that He permitted them to be dominated by the spirit of idolatry to such an extent that they were helpless in its power. At the same time His intention was, if possible, so to shock the Jews by the reflection of their loathsome customs that they might feel the unnaturalness of their conduct and turn to the Lord in true repentance.

ISRAEL'S BEHAVIOR IN CANAAN AND THE LORD'S SENTENCE. — V. 27. **Therefore, son of man, speak unto the house of Israel,** represented by the elders who had come to inquire of the Lord, **and say unto them, Thus saith the Lord God, Yet in this,** or, "In this again," **your fathers have blasphemed Me,** holding Him up to mockery and derision, **in that they have committed a trespass against Me,** becoming guilty of faithlessness and treachery. V. 28. **For when I had brought them into the land, for the which I lifted up Mine hand to give it to them,** promising it to them by a solemn oath, **then they saw every high hill and all the thick trees,** places which were commonly devoted to idolatrous worship by the heathen, **and they offered there their sacrifices, and there they presented the provocation of**

their offering, for their sacrifices continually provoked the Lord to anger, since they were made contrary to His command and will; **there also they made their sweet savor,** said here of all burnt offerings, **and poured out there their drink-offerings,** thus including all bloody and unbloody sacrifices in their heathenish worship. This was the principal transgression of the entire people of Israel after they had reached the Land of Promise. V. 29. **Then I said unto them, What is the high place whereunto ye go? And the name thereof is called Bamah,** that is, height, **unto this day.** In spite of the Lord's remonstrance, Israel and Judah continued to regard the high places as places of worship, persisting in their idolatrous treachery to the very last. V. 30. **Wherefore say unto the house of Israel,** namely, the generation then living, **Thus saith the Lord God, Are ye polluted after the manner of your fathers?** in being guilty of the same idolatry as that which brought God's wrath upon Israel in the first centuries of its national existence. **And commit ye whoredom,** spiritual adultery, **after their abominations?** V. 31. **For when ye offer your gifts,** as described above, **when ye make your sons to pass through the fire, ye pollute yourselves with all your idols, even unto this day; and shall I be enquired of by you, O house of Israel?** whose representatives were even then sitting before the prophet. **As I live, saith the Lord God, I will not be enquired of by you,** he would give them no hearing until they had done away with the wickedness which was now charged against them. V. 32. **And that which cometh into your mind,** what they were now deliberately planning to do, **shall not be at all,** shall not come to pass, **that ye say, We will be as the heathen, as the families of the countries,** amalgamating with them in every respect, losing their identity as a separate people altogether, **to serve wood and stone,** and thus become the equal of the heathen also in this respect. It was an exclamation, partly of stubbornness, partly of despair, which they here uttered. Therefore the Lord gives them a fitting answer. V. 33. **As I live, saith the Lord God, surely with a mighty hand and with a stretched-out arm,** by applying His almighty power, **and with fury poured out will I rule over you,** asserting His sovereign right over them in spite of their resistance; v. 34. **and I will bring you out from the people and will gather you out of the countries wherein ye are scattered, with a mighty hand and with a stretched-out arm and with fury poured out,** so that they would have to acknowledge the rule of God, unwilling though they were. V. 35. **And I will bring you into the wilderness of the people,** the spiritual wilderness which characterizes the great mass of the world, with its heathenism and wickedness, **and there will I plead with you face to face,** bringing the matter to an issue as in a court of law. V. 36. **Like as I pleaded with your fathers in the wilderness of the land of Egypt,** upon the occasion of the giving of the Law, Deut. 5, 4, **so will I plead with you, saith the Lord God.** Cp. Num. 17, 5. 6. 10. V. 37. **And I will cause you to pass under the rod,** as a shepherd does with his sheep, in order to determine their number and thus to prepare their benefits, **and I will bring you into the bond of the covenant,** His chastizing having prepared the way to a true sorrow; v. 38. **and I will purge out from among you the rebels,** those who persisted in their opposition to His guidance and rule, **and them that transgress against Me,** those who were guilty of apostasy and treachery; **I will bring them forth out of the country where they sojourn,** the land of their exile, **and they shall not enter into the land of Israel,** not partake of the blessings of the Lord's covenant; **and ye shall know that I am the Lord,** in His summary judgment upon the apostates. But now comes the Messianic promise to shed light into the intense darkness of faithlessness, rebellion, and idolatry. V. 39. **As for you, O house of Israel,** those whom the Lord desires once more to gather as His Church, **thus saith the Lord God,** in an admonition calling them to repentance, not without a mixture of holy irony, **Go ye, serve ye every one his idols,** for open idolatry is better than hypocrisy, **and hereafter also, if ye will not hearken unto Me,** since it is easier to deal with downright opponents of the truth than with such as are enmeshed in dead orthodoxy; **but pollute ye My holy name no more with your gifts and with your idols,** with hypocritical worship, with abominable sacrifices which they brought under the guise of true worship. V. 40. **For in Mine holy mountain, in the mountain of the height of Israel, saith the Lord God,** in the Zion of the New Testament, **there shall all the house of Israel,** all those who belonged to the true, the spiritual Israel, **all of them in the land, serve Me; there will I accept them,** as His children by faith, **and there will I require your offerings and the first-fruits of your oblations with all your holy things,** that is, the worship which is done in spirit and in truth. V. 41. **I will accept you with your sweet savor,** the believers themselves being a sweet odor in the nostrils of Jehovah with the incense of their faith, **when I bring you out from the people and gather you out of the countries wherein ye have been scattered,** this being used in general for the separation of the believers from the great mass of those who are enemies of God; **and I will be sanctified in you before the heathen,** for the very existence of the Church of Christ serves to spread the glory of God's holy name. V. 42. **And ye shall know that I am the Lord,** Jehovah, the everlasting God of the covenant, **when I shall bring you into the land of Israel, into the country for the which I lifted up Mine hand to give it to your fathers.** The return of Israel to the Land of Promise after the Babylonian Exile was a guarantee of the greater and more wonderful restoration of God's kingdom through the Messiah. V. 43. **And there shall ye remember your ways and all your doings wherein ye have been defiled,** in true sorrow over their past wickedness; **and ye shall loathe yourselves in your own sight for all your evils that ye have committed;** for such is the nature of true repentance. V. 44. **And ye shall know that I am the Lord,** the one and only true God, **when I have wrought with you,** in effecting their deliverance, **for My name's sake, not according to your wicked ways, nor according to your corrupt doings, O ye house of Israel, saith the Lord God.** That is the remarkable, the marvelous thing about the dealings of God with men, that He does not deal with us according as we have deserved, but according to His grace and mercy in Jesus Christ.

CHAPTER 21.

(Chapter 20, 45—21, 32.)

The Approaching Judgment.

THE PICTURE OF THE FOREST FIRE. — V. 45. **Moreover, the word of the Lord came unto me,** in a message of verbal inspiration, as always, **saying,** v. 46. **Son of man, set thy face toward the South,** literally, toward the right hand, for the Jew always considered himself facing east, **and drop thy word toward the South,** in a constant dripping, more or less violently, **and prophesy against the forest of the south field,** where dryness and heat prevailed, namely, the southern part of Palestine, specifically of Judah, v. 47. **and say to the forest of the South,** the densely populated districts of that section of the country, **Hear the word of the Lord, Thus saith the Lord God,** whose power and sovereignty is unquestioned, **Behold, I will kindle a fire in thee,** in the form of the various judgments which He would send upon them, **and it shall devour every green tree in thee and every dry tree,** fit and unfit, righteous and wicked alike, in an unsparing punishment; **the flaming flame,** the burst of fire kindled by His anger, **shall not be quenched and all faces from the South to the North,** all the inhabitants of the entire country included, **shall be burned therein,** struck by the punishment of the Lord in some manner. V. 48. **And all flesh shall see that I, the Lord, have kindled it; it shall not be quenched;** no earthly power could stop the vengeance of the Lord, it would endure until it had acccomplished His purpose. V. 49. **Then said I, Ah, Lord God! They say of me, Doth he not speak parables?** Ezekiel thus complaining that his countrymen could not understand this form of message and therefore despised and rejected his warnings. When men do not want to understand the message of the Lord, they manage to find excuses of various kinds or, failing in this, ridicule His servants and their preaching.

THE SWORD OF THE LORD. — Chap. 21, 1. **And the word of the Lord came unto me,** evidently in answer to his complaint, **saying,** v. 2. **Son of man, set thy face,** in firm determination, **toward Jerusalem,** the capital of this same south country of which the Lord had just spoken in figurative language, **and drop thy word,** in a stream of denunciation and threatening, **toward the holy places,** the various parts of the Temple, **and prophesy against the land of Israel,** v. 3. **and say to the land of Israel, Thus saith the Lord, Behold, I am against thee,** in stern opposition, **and will draw forth My sword out of his sheath,** in sending war with bloodshed and devastation, **and will cut off from thee the righteous and the wicked,** all of them being included alike in the outward form of the punishment. V. 4. **Seeing, then, that I will cut off from thee the righteous and the wicked,** the Lord having the external aspect of His visitation upon Judah in mind, **therefore,** in fulfilment of this object, **shall My sword go forth out of his sheath against all flesh from the South to the North,** against all the inhabitants of the country, v. 5. **that all flesh may know that I, the Lord, have drawn forth My sword out of his sheath,** to accomplish this sweeping overthrow, this fearful catastrophe; **it shall not return any more,** it must perform its mission of carnage and distress. V. 6. **Sigh, therefore, thou son of man, with the breaking of thy loins,** as though the very seat of strength would burst; **and with bitterness sigh before their eyes,** in bitter sorrow and pain over the coming calamity. V. 7. **And it shall be when they say unto thee, Wherefore sighest thou? that thou shalt answer, For the tiding, because it cometh,** because the message contained in the evil tidings would be fulfilled; **and every heart shall melt,** in utter discouragement and despair, **and all hands shall be feeble,** hanging down in a disheartened manner, **and every spirit shall faint,** be dull with apprehension and fear, **and all knees shall be** weak as water, in utter weakness; **behold, it cometh and shall be brought to pass, saith the Lord God,** for He was fully determined to carry out His punishment upon His rebellious children. This thought is now set forth in greater detail. V. 8. **Again the word of the Lord came unto me, saying,** v. 9. **Son of man, prophesy and say, Thus saith the Lord, Say, A sword, a sword, is sharpened,** the repetition increasing the emphasis upon the deadliness of the weapon, and **also furbished,** ready for immediate use, for terrifying bloodshed; v. 10. **it is sharpened to make a sore slaughter,** literally, "that, killing, it may kill"; **it is furbished that it may glitter,** the flash of its wielding striking terror to the hearts of all beholders. **Should we, then, make mirth? It contemneth the rod of my son, as every tree,** literally, "Shall we rejoice over the staff of my son, despising every tree?" or, "Shall we rejoice, saying, The scepter of my son despises every tree?" that is, the kingly power and authority of Judah could afford to despise every other power as inferior, on account of the Messianic promise to Judah. V. 11. **And he hath given it to be furbished that it may be handled,** Judah himself causing the preparations for the slaughter of his own people; **this sword is sharpened, and it is furbished, to give it into the hand of the slayer,** so that the judgment upon Judah might take its course. V. 12. **Cry and howl, son of man,** namely, from fear and grief; **for it shall be upon My people, it shall be upon all the princes of Israel; terrors by reason of the sword shall be upon My people,** the sword of slaughter being sure to accomplish its purpose. **Smite therefore upon thy thigh,** as a mark of extreme terror and pain. V. 13. **Because it is a trial,** literally, "for a testing-out it is," **and what if the sword contemn even the rod?** What if the despising scepter shall not be? the power of Judah coming to an end before the advance of the Chaldean host; **It shall be no more, saith the Lord God.** V. 14. **Thou therefore, son of man, prophesy and smite thine hands together,** in extreme agitation, **and let the sword be doubled, the third time, the sword of the slain,** so that its sharpness and strength will be increased in their terrible effects. **It is the sword of the great men that are slain,** for rank and standing shielded no man against the Chaldean attack and slaughter, **which entereth into their privy chambers,** literally, "which encircles them, which circulates about them," giving them no chance to escape. V. 15. **I have set the point of the sword against all their gates that their heart may faint and their ruins,** literally, "their stumbling-blocks," that is, the occasions for them to fall by the sword, **be multiplied. Ah! it,** the sword, **is made bright, it is wrapped up for the slaughter,** sharpened and drawn for the fray, for the bloodshed. With this in mind, the sword is directly addressed. V. 16. **Go thee one way or other,** literally, "gather thy strength," **either on the right hand or on the left,** striking wherever an opportunity offers, **whithersoever thy face is set,** the activity and rapidity of the sword-strokes thus being pictured. V. 17. **I will also smite Mine hands together,** so Jehovah states, **and I will cause My fury to rest,** to find satisfaction in carrying out His vengeance. **I, the Lord, have said it.** Jehovah excels in long-suffering, but when His hour for punishing comes, He gives vent to His fury in a manner which is not readily forgotten. It is a terrible thing to fall into the hands of the living God.

THE SWORD OF BABYLON UPON JUDAH AND UPON AMMON. — V. 18. **The word of the Lord came unto me again, saying,** v. 19. **Also, thou son of man, appoint thee two ways,** by means of a drawing or map showing a road branching off in two directions, **that the sword of the king of Babylon may come,** as his armies advanced to the conquest, — **both twain shall come forth out of one land, — and choose thou a place,** a finger-post, or pointer, to guide men aright; **choose it at the head of the way to the city,** placing it at the parting of the ways, so that no mistake as to directions would be possible. V. 20. **Appoint a way,** pointing out the road, **that the sword may come to Rabbath of the Ammonites,** to destroy the capital with the nation, **and to Judah in Jerusalem, the defensed,** for the capital practically represented and included the entire nation. V. 21. **For the king of Babylon stood at the parting of the way,** literally, "at the mother of the way," undecided, for the moment, which way to take, **at the head of the two ways, to use divination,** to determine by supernatural means which road he should take first. **He made his arrows bright, he consulted with images, he looked in the liver.** These are the three ways in which he practised divination, by shaking arrows together in a vessel and then making a drawing at random, by asking the teraphim, or household gods, whose will was made known in some strange manner, by inspecting the liver of certain sacrificial animals, the appearance or the position of the lobes determining the matter. We have here a graphic bit of description, which must have impressed all hearers with the certainty of the approaching doom. V. 22. **At his right hand was the divination for Jerusalem,** that is, Nebuchadnezzar held up in his right hand the arrow marked "Jerusalem," to indicate that this was their goal, **to appoint captains,** rather, to place battering-rams against the city, **to open the mouth in the slaughter,** in murderous shouting, **to lift up the voice with shouting,** in a loud battle-cry, **to appoint battering-rams against the gates,** the taking of which would mean the taking of the city, **to cast a mount, to build** trenches, **and to build a fort,** siege-towers. V. 23. **And it shall be unto them,** namely, to the Jews, who were prone to yield to false hopes, **as a false divination in their sight,** they refused to believe that matters would come to such a pass, **to them that have sworn oaths,** literally, "oaths of oaths are to them," that is, they relied either upon the solemn promises of the Lord which He had made to their fathers, or they depended upon the oaths of allegiance sworn by them to the Chaldean king, forgetting that these oaths had been violated on their part; **but He,** either God or Nebuchadnezzar, **will call to remembrance the iniquity,** the violation of their oath of allegiance, **that they may be taken,** that their conquest may be accomplished. V. 24. **Therefore, thus saith the Lord God, Because ye have made your iniquity to be remembered,** their chief transgression being their unfaithfulnes to the covenant God, **in that your transgressions are discovered,** laid bare before the eyes of all men, **so that in all your doings your sins do appear; because, I say, that ye are come to remembrance,** the Lord's attention being directed to them time and again, **ye shall be taken with the hand,** namely, that of the king of Babylon. V. 25. **And thou, profane wicked prince of Israel,** Zedekiah, who had desecrated his office as the Lord's anointed by idolatry and perjury, **whose day is come,** the day of his punishment, **when iniquity shall have an end,** or, "at the time of the iniquity of the end." V. 26. **Thus saith the Lord God, Remove the diadem,** the high-priestly miter, with which Zedekiah was associated as the representative of a priestly people, **and take off the crown,** the symbol of kingly power; **this shall not be the same,** they will not remain as heretofore, Judah having lost its ancient position. **Exalt him that is low, and abase him that is high,** there will be a complete overthrow of conditions, particularly in the Messianic era. V. 27. **I will overturn, overturn, overturn it, and it shall be no more,** the threefold repetition denoting the awful certainty of the event, **until He come whose right it is,** until the rightful Heir, the Messiah, would make His appearance; **and I will give it Him,** so that He would perform the functions both of priest and of king in the highest and truest sense of the terms. Until the time of His coming everything was preparatory and imperfect. V. 28. **And thou, son of man, prophesy and say, Thus saith the Lord God concerning the Ammonites and concerning their reproach,** who were allied with Israel against the Babylonians, but continued in their enmity toward Judah throughout, **even say thou, The sword, the sword is drawn,** ready to descend in punishment; **for the slaughter it is furbished, to consume because of the glittering,** as it falls with lightninglike flashes; v. 29. **whiles they see vanity unto thee, whiles they divine a lie unto thee,** that is, while the false prophets were prophesying deception and falsehood to the Ammonites eager for such support, **to bring thee upon the necks of them that are slain, of the wicked,** that is, the sword would lay them low with the wicked already slaughtered, **whose day is come when their iniquity shall have an end,** "at the time of the iniquity of the end," that just preceding the final punishment. V. 30. **Shall I cause it to return into his sheath?** namely, without having performed this work of vengeance; or, "Cause it to return to its sheath," the punishment being carried out with great rapidity, so that the very idea of defense is futile. **I will judge thee in the place where thou wast created, in the land of thy nativity,** so that Ammon would be destroyed in its own country, without being carried into exile. V. 31. **And I will pour out Mine indignation upon thee,** as from an overturned vessel; **I will blow against thee in the fire of My wrath,** so that this fire would consume the children of Ammon, **and deliver thee into the hand of brutish men,** such as are fierce and cruel in warfare, **and skilful to destroy.** V. 32. **Thou shalt be for fuel to the fire,** the land to be consumed by fire; **thy blood shall be in the midst of the land,** in their own homes, all weapons of defense being of no avail; **thou shalt be no more remembered,** be consigned to oblivion as a nation; **for I, the Lord, have spoken it.** Thus the Lord carries out His sentence of destruction upon the enemies of His people, even if He, at the same time, finds it necessary to punish His children severely.

CHAPTER 22.

Jerusalem Ripe for the Judgment.

THE WEIGHT OF JERUSALEM'S GUILT. — V. 1. **Moreover, the word of the Lord came unto me, saying,** v. 2. **Now, thou son of man, wilt thou judge, wilt thou judge, the bloody city?** so called on account of the murders committed in her and the sacrifices of children to Molech. **Yea, thou shalt show her all her abominations,** so that she was bound to acknowledge them, even if she was lacking in repentance. V. 3. **Then say thou, Thus saith the Lord God,** who excels in the might of His sovereignty, **The city sheddeth blood in the midst of it,** in bloody sacrifices to idols, in judicial murders, and in civil war, **that her time may come,** namely, the time of her punishment, **and maketh idols against herself**, literally, "over herself," that is, throughout her boundaries, **to defile herself**, the burden and debt of idolatry bringing defilement. V. 4. **Thou art become guilty in thy blood that thou hast shed**, which placed the stamp of murder upon the entire city, **and hast defiled thyself in thine idols which thou hast made**, the one growing forth out of the other, the defilement out of the abomination; **and thou**, by such transgressions, **hast caused thy days to draw near**, the time when sentence would be executed upon her, **and art come even unto thy years**, the measure of her guilt being full; **therefore have I made thee a reproach unto the heathen and a mocking to all countries**, namely, by the overthrow of Jerusalem and the captivity of Judah. V. 5. **Those that be near and those that be far from thee**, the neighboring nations as well as those at a distance, **shall mock thee, which art infamous and much vexed**, literally, "polluted in name and full of confusion," an object of derision and loathing. V. 6. **Behold, the princes of Israel, every one, were in thee to their power**, literally, "every one according to his arm," that is, to the best of his ability, **to shed blood**, this being their object and the end of their desire. V. 7. **In thee have they set light by father and mother**, a transgression which was most sharply reproved and punished at that time; **in the midst of thee have they dealt by oppression with the stranger**, treating him with injustice and deceit; **in thee have they vexed the fatherless and the widow**, although both, as helpless and depending upon others for support and protection, should have had special consideration. V. 8. **Thou hast despised Mine holy things**, treating matters of which the Lord thought highly, which He had set apart to be revered properly, with contempt, **and hast profaned My Sabbaths**, by refusing to hallow them according to Old Testament regulations. Cp. Ex. 22, 20 ff.; Lev. 19, 13; Deut. 24, 14 ff. V. 9. **In thee are men that carry tales to shed blood**, slanderers, whose object is to bring harm upon others, preferably death; **and in thee they eat upon the mountains**, some of her inhabitants having become guilty of partaking of meals consecrated to idols; **in the midst of thee they commit lewdness**, immorality of every kind and description. V. 10. **In thee have they discovered their fathers' nakedness**, in sins of incest, Lev. 18 and 19; **in thee have they humbled her that was set apart for pollution**, forcing a woman at the time of her uncleanness, Lev. 18, 19. V. 11. **And one hath committed abomination with his neighbor's wife**, in base adultery, **and another hath lewdly defiled his daughter-in-law**, another instance of revolting immorality; **and another in thee hath humbled his sister, his father's daughter**, his step-sister, who was within the prohibited degrees, Lev. 18, 9. V. 12. **In thee have they taken gifts to shed blood**, accepting bribes to commit murder; **thou hast taken usury and increase**, the enriching of men at the cost of their neighbors being the usual thing, a form of graft in which the great majority indulged, **and thou hast greedily gained of thy neighbors by extortion**, overreaching them in business dealings and at all other times, **and hast forgotten Me, saith the Lord God.** There was evidence indeed of this fact, for men sound in faith and love toward God cannot become guilty of such terrible trespasses. V. 13. **Behold, therefore I have smitten Mine hand**, striking them both together in dismay and horror at such manifestations of wickedness, **at thy dishonest gain which thou hast made, and at thy blood which hath been in the midst of thee**, the guilt of the shedding of blood which rested upon the whole city and country. V. 14. **Can thine heart endure**, be steadfast, **or can thine hands be strong, in the days that I shall deal with thee?** when God's sentence of punishment would go into effect. It is a last warning against false security. **I, the Lord, have spoken it and will do it**, there being no doubt either as to His determination or to His ability to perform His sentence of punishment. V. 15. **And I will scatter thee among the heathen**, cp. chap. 12, 15; 20, 23, **and disperse thee in the countries**, in captivity and exile, **and will consume thy filthiness out of thee**, namely, by the purging power of this sentence of punishment. V. 16. **And thou shalt take thine inheritance in thyself in the sight of the heathen**, literally, "thou shalt be profaned in thyself before the eyes of the heathen," all of them being witnesses of the shameful plight and degradation of Judah on account of her sins, **and thou shalt know that I am the Lord.** The shame and disgrace which are heaped upon the sinner in the eyes of the witnesses of his downfall should at least be one point which he ought to keep in mind to deter him from further sinning.

THE CORRUPTION OF JUDAH INVITING DESTRUCTION. — V. 17. **And the word of the Lord came unto me, saying**, v. 18. **Son of man, the house of Israel is to Me become dross**, the refuse of the purer metals, thrown out as unfit for fine use; **all they are brass, and tin, and iron, and lead in the midst of the furnace**, all the baser metals, unfit for the divine Refiner's purpose; **they are even the dross of silver**, full of impurity. V. 19. **Therefore, thus saith the Lord God, Because ye are all become dross**, impure with idolatry and other wickedness, **behold, therefore I will gather you into the midst of Jerusalem**, heaped together like quartz in a furnace. V. 20. **As they gather silver, and brass, and iron, and lead, and tin into the midst of the furnace**, the baser metals being mixed with the precious and the object being to separate them, **to blow the fire upon it, to melt it,** the process resulting in an almost pure extraction of the nobler metal, **so will I gather you in Mine anger and in My fury,** in carrying out the contemplated judgment upon Jerusalem and Judah, **and I will leave you there and melt you.** Note that the process of refining is not used in the figure, the smelting as such being a picture of the avenging wrath of God. V. 21. **Yea, I will gather you and blow upon you in the fire of My wrath,** as silver alloyed with baser metals is submitted to a blast of air in the so-called cupeling process, **and ye shall be melted in the midst thereof.** V. 22. **As silver is melted in the midst of the furnace, so shall ye be melted in the midst thereof,** Judah experiencing this operation during the last siege of the city; **and ye shall know that I, the Lord, have poured out My fury upon you.** Having thus set forth the punishment upon Jerusalem, the Lord proceeds to show the corruptness of all classes of people in Judah. V. 23. **And the word of the Lord came unto me, saying,** v. 24. **Son of man, say unto her,** namely, to Jerusalem and Judah, **Thou art the land that is not cleansed,** namely, from the weeds, briars, and thorns with which it is overgrown, or upon which the sun does not shine in due season, **nor rained upon in the day of indignation,** that is, from which the Lord withholds fruitfulness on account of its wickedness. V. 25. **There is a conspiracy of her prophets in the midst thereof,** self-appointed teachers and leaders as these false prophets were, **like a roaring lion ravening the prey they have devoured souls,** the fierceness and cruelty of their actions being in evidence throughout; **they have taken the treasure and precious things,** property and jewels in possession of the people; **they have made her many widows in the midst thereof,** for pious men were put to death by them. V. 26. **Her priests,** who held the office of keepers and protectors of the Law, **have violated My Law,** since they did the very things from which they were supposed to keep the people by their warnings, **and have profaned Mine holy things,** by not observing them with the proper respect, cp. Zeph. 3, 4; **they have put no difference between the holy and profane, neither have they showed difference between the unclean and the clean,** Lev. 10, 10. 11, that is, they calmly disregarded the ordinances of the Lord concerning these distinctions, **and have hid their eyes from My Sabbaths,** by neglecting the law of the Sabbath, **and I am profaned among them,** for all these acts detracted from the Lord's glory. V. 27. **Her princes in the midst thereof,** the leaders and chief protectors of the people, **are like wolves ravening the prey, to shed blood, and to destroy souls, to get dishonest gain,** the civil rulers thus siding with the church powers in performing deeds of wickedness. V. 28. **And her prophets have daubed them with untempered mortar,** cp. chap. 13, 10, by flattering the people with false assurances of peace and safety, **seeing vanity,** unfounded promises of good, **and divining lies unto them, saying, Thus saith the Lord God, when the Lord hath not spoken.** V. 29. **The people of the land,** following the bad example of their leaders, **have used oppression,** practising extortion and violence in every form, **and exercised robbery,** either open or hidden, **and have vexed the poor and needy,** cp. chap. 18, 7. 12. 18; **yea, they have oppressed the stranger wrongfully,** in spite of the earnest warnings of the Lord concerning this practise, Ex. 22, 20. 21; Deut. 24, 17. V. 30. **And I sought for a man among them that should make up the hedge,** building up a wall against these various acts of wickedness, **and stand in the gap before Me for the land,** to close up the breach and make intercession for Judah, **that I should not destroy it; but I found none,** the moral degeneration was such as to leave even the few righteous without the power to do anything. V. 31. **Therefore have I poured out Mine indignation upon them,** as explained above; **I have consumed them with the fire of My wrath,** in melting them in the furnace of His punishment; **their own way have I recompensed upon their heads, saith the Lord God,** punishing them in exact agreement with their wicked deeds. It is this fact, that they themselves have brought the evil fate upon them, which will cause many wicked the greatest torment in the last great punishment.

CHAPTER 23.

The Sin and Punishment of Samaria and Judah.

THE SPIRITUAL ADULTERY OF THE TWO KINGDOMS. — V. 1. **The word of the Lord came again unto me, saying,** in an inspired allegory setting forth the fact that both kingdoms were ripe for God's judgment, v. 2. **Son of man, there were two women, the daughters of one mother,** namely, Israel and Judah, one nation by descent; v. 3. **and they committed whoredoms in Egypt,** being guilty of idolatry even at that time; **they committed whoredoms,** spiritual adultery, **in their youth; there were their breasts pressed, and there they,** the people with whom they sinned, **bruised the teats of their virginity,** both being immoral acts and a species of adultery. V. 4. **And the names of**

them were Aholah, the elder, the meaning, "Her tent," referring to the fact that the first worship of God in Israel was in a tent, or tabernacle, **and Aholibah, her sister,** this name for Judah, meaning, "My tent in her," indicating that God appointed His worship in the midst of Judah. **And they were Mine,** they belonged to the Lord in the most peculiar sense before the apostasy under Jeroboam; **and they bare sons and daughters,** for they were at that time still considered the Lord's brides. **Thus were their names: Samaria is Aholah,** called the elder, or rather, greater, on account of the larger size of her territory, **and Jerusalem Aholibah.** V. 5. **And Aholah played the harlot when she was Mine,** forsaking the Lord in her idolatry; **and she doted on her lovers,** inflamed with her evil passion, **on the Assyrians, her neighbors,** with whom the people of the northern kingdom sought alliance and whose heathenish customs they aped, v. 6. **which were clothed with blue,** the royal purple of ancient times, Israel being seduced by the splendor and pomp of Assyria, **captains and rulers, all of them desirable young men, horsemen riding upon horses,** making a bold show intended to impress passionate Samaria. V. 7. **Thus she committed her whoredoms with them,** bestowing her wantonness upon them, **with all them that were the chosen men of Assyria and with all on whom she doted,** with the same passion for spiritual adultery; **with all their idols she defiled herself,** this being the essence of her transgression, shameless idolatry. V. 8. **Neither,** in addition to this new transgression, **left she her whoredoms brought from Egypt,** since the calves set up by Jeroboam at Dan and Bethel were copies of Egyptian idols, of the Apis statues; **for in her youth they lay with her, and they bruised the breasts of her virginity, and poured their whoredom upon her,** the full measure of their idolatrous wickedness. V. 9. **Wherefore,** in just punishment, **I have delivered her into the hand of her lovers,** who professed an affection for her which they were far from feeling, **into the hand of the Assyrians, upon whom she doted,** with such foolishly passionate desire. V. 10. **These,** in making sport of her wantonness, **discovered her nakedness; they took her sons and her daughters,** leading them into exile, **and slew her with the sword,** destroying the kingdom of which Samaria was the capital; **and she became famous among women,** the object of jeering speech and mockery; **for they had executed judgment upon her,** her shameful overthrow was notorious throughout the known world. V. 11. **And when her sister Aholibah saw this,** having the evil example of Samaria before her eyes always, **she was more corrupt in her inordinate love than she,** Judah going even beyond Samaria in the extent of her idolatry, **and in her whoredoms more than her sister in her whoredoms,** outranking the northern kingdom in the spiritual adultery practised in Jerusalem. V. 12. **She doted upon the Assyrians, her neighbors,** having conceived a sinful affection for the heathenish neighbors and seeking an alliance with them, **captains and rulers clothed most gorgeously, horsemen riding upon horses, all of them desirable young men,** whose pomp and political splendor dazzled the Jews. V. 13. **Then I saw,** the Lord says in a statement of the true situation, **that she was defiled, that they,** Samaria and Jerusalem, **took both one way,** the way of transgression and wickedness, v. 14. **and that she increased her whoredoms,** becoming, with the passing of time, ever more shameless in her idolatry; **for when she saw men portrayed upon the wall, the images of the Chaldeans portrayed with vermilion,** probably in basreliefs colored in ocher, v. 15. **girded with girdles upon their loins, exceeding in dyed attire upon their heads,** with the flowing turbans which are so familiar from Assyrian sculpture, **all of them princes to look to,** appearing majestic and imposing, **after the manner of the Babylonians of Chaldea, the land of their nativity,** between the Black and the Caspian Sea; v. 16. **and as soon as she saw them with her eyes,** probably when her merchants went to the East on business trips, or when Assyrian sculpture was brought to Jerusalem to adorn the palaces of the wealthy, **she doted upon them,** desiring entangling alliances which God had expressly forbidden, **and sent messengers unto them into Chaldea,** soliciting the friendship of the mightier empire. V. 17. **And the Babylonians,** gladly availing themselves of this opportunity, **came to her into the bed of love,** in the unholy alliance forbidden by the Lord, **and they defiled her with their whoredom,** with the excess of their idolatry, **and she was polluted with them,** as committing spiritual adultery, **and her mind was alienated from them,** for now the fickle Jews turned once more to the Egyptians. V. 18. **So she discovered her whoredoms,** openly parading them before the whole world, **and discovered her nakedness,** her most shameful condition. **Then My mind was alienated from her,** so that He turned from her in disgust and loathing, **like as My mind was alienated from her sister.** V. 19. **Yet,** in spite of this experience, which should have sobered her, **she multiplied her whoredoms, in calling to remembrance the days of her youth,** the lusts she had then practised, **wherein she had played the harlot in the land of Egypt,** practising idolatry even before the Exodus. V. 20. **For she doted upon their paramours,** upon her lovers, the eunuchs, princes, and courtiers who were instrumental in bringing about the alliance, **whose flesh,** the member concerned, **is as the flesh of asses,** said in bitter irony, **and whose issue**

is like the issue of horses, said of carnal desire. V. 21. **Thus thou calledst to remembrance the lewdness of thy youth, in bruising the teats by the Egyptians for the paps of thy youth,** literally, "on account of thy youthful breasts." In the early history there had at least been an explanation of Judah's conduct, namely, the inexperienced sensuousness and carnality of the people. But here, in their later history, they were acting against better knowledge, wilfully prostituting themselves and their sacred honor upon the altar of idolatry.

THE LORD'S PUNISHMENT UPON THE TWO KINGDOMS. — V. 22. **Therefore, O Aholibah, thus saith the Lord God,** the sovereign Ruler of the universe, **Behold, I will raise up thy lovers against thee,** the very allies upon whose constancy Jerusalem thought she could depend, **from whom thy mind is alienated,** as she turned from Assyria to Egypt, **and I will bring them against thee on every side,** in manifest enmity, with a desire to wreak their vengeance upon the fickle wanton: v. 23. **the Babylonians and all the Chaldeans,** at that time representing the world empire, **Pekod, and Shoa, and Koa,** words signifying leadership or supremacy, and probably standing for the leaders of the three branches of military forces in the Chaldean army, **and all the Assyrians with them, all of them desirable young men, captains and rulers, great lords and renowned, all of them riding upon horses.** The latter is said in bitter irony, for the same most desirable allies upon whom Judah had doted in foolish passion now became the instruments of God's wrath to chastise her. V. 24. **And they shall come against thee with chariots, wagons, and wheels,** scythe-armed battle-chariots, the size of whose wheels made them doubly formidable, **and with an assembly of people,** troops of the various provinces and countries under the Babylonian dominion, **which shall set against thee buckler and shield and helmet round about,** using all the weapons of war to gain their ends; **and I will set judgment before them,** appointing them to carry out His sentence of punishment, **and they shall judge thee according to their judgments,** which, in agreement with their heathenish ideas, were barbarously severe. V. 25. **And I will set My jealousy against thee,** which in this case took on the nature of a zeal for destruction, **and they shall deal furiously with thee,** with unbridled wrath; **they shall take away thy nose and thine ears,** an allusion to the Oriental custom of mutilating adulteresses, **and thy remnant shall fall by the sword,** the destruction of Judah thus being consummated; **they shall take thy sons and thy daughters; and thy residue,** with reference to rich dresses and costly jewels by means of which lewd women seek to attract, **shall be devoured by the fire.** V. 26. **They shall also strip thee out of thy clothes,** instruments of luxury and lewdness as they were, **and take away thy fair jewels,** the gaudy ornaments with which the spiritual adulteress bedecked herself. V. 27. **Thus will I make thy lewdness to cease from thee,** so that the Jews would learn to abhor idolatry, **and thy whoredom brought from the land of Egypt,** which had persisted through all these centuries, **so that thou shalt not lift up thine eyes unto them,** namely, in reverence and adoration, **nor remember Egypt any more.** V. 28. **For thus saith the Lord God, Behold, I will deliver thee into the hand of them whom thou,** after her recent transfer of affection, **hatest, into the hand of them from whom thy mind is alienated;** v. 29. **and they shall deal with thee hatefully,** with the hatred of those who feel themselves spurned, **and shall take away all thy labor,** all that she had worked so hard to accumulate, **and shall leave thee naked and bare,** stripped of all her possessions; **and the nakedness of thy whoredoms shall be discovered,** laid bare before the eyes of the whole world, **both thy lewdness and thy whoredoms,** so that men would speak of her spiritual adultery with loathing. V. 30. **I will do these things unto thee because thou hast gone a-whoring after the heathen,** becoming partaker of their idolatrous wickedness, **and because thou art polluted with their idols.** V. 31. **Thou hast walked in the way of thy sister,** following the wicked example of Samaria; **therefore will I give her cup into thine hand,** namely, the cup of her punishment. V. 32. **Thus saith the Lord God, Thou shalt drink of thy sister's cup deep and large,** in full draughts; **thou shalt be laughed to scorn and had in derision,** an object of mockery and contempt on every hand; **it containeth much,** for God is not lax and lenient in His punishment upon idolaters. V. 33. **Thou shalt be filled with drunkenness and sorrow,** her intoxication being caused by the Lord and followed by extreme misery, **with the cup of astonishment and desolation, with the cup of thy sister Samaria,** rather, "a cup of wasting and desolation is the cup of thy sister Samaria." V. 34. **Thou shalt even drink it and suck it out,** so that she would feel the full effect of its bitterness, **and thou shalt break the sherds thereof,** gnawing them in a sort of passion to feel the fulness of God's anger, **and pluck off thine own breasts,** wilfully mutilating them as the instruments of lewdness; **for I have spoken it, saith the Lord God.** V. 35. **therefore, thus saith the Lord God,** in once more summarizing His sentence upon Judah, **Because thou hast forgotten Me,** the Lord and Master of her youth, **and cast Me behind thy back,** in the height of contempt, **therefore,** in just retribution, **bear thou also thy lewdness and thy whoredoms,** namely, in their guilt and damnableness. V. 36. **The Lord said moreover unto me, Son of man, wilt thou judge,** namely, in pronouncing judgment upon, **Aholah and Aholibah? Yea, declare unto them their abominations,** setting forth the individual acts of wickedness with which they are charged, v. 37. **that they have committed adultery, and blood is in their hands,** the blood of unlawful sacrifices; **and with their idols have they committed adultery,** for the spiritual adultery of idol-worship was often connected with physical adultery and immorality of the worst kind, **and have also caused their sons, whom they bare unto Me, to pass for them through the fire, to devour them,** in the hideous and repulsive Molech cult. V. 38. **Moreover, this they have done unto Me: they have defiled My Sanctuary in the same day,** in the very day that they committed such shocking abominations, **and have profaned My Sabbaths.** Cp. chap. 20, 13. 16. V. 39. **For when they had slain their children to their idols,** sacrificing them to Molech, the abomination of the Moabites, **then they came the same day,** while the guilt of their wickedness was still on their hands, **into My Sanctuary to profane it; and, lo, thus have they done in the midst of Mine house,** without the slightest regard for the sanctity of the Lord's Temple. V. 40. **And furthermore,** another point to be urged against the Jews in their apostasy, **that ye have sent for men to come from far, unto whom a messenger was sent,** the Jews going to much trouble in carrying out their purpose; **and, lo, they came, for whom thou,** like a lewd woman, **didst wash thyself, paintedst thine eyes,** staining the eyelashes to make the glance of the eye more brilliant, for that is the object of women of this type, who barter their soul by such means, **and deckedst thyself with ornaments,** all to make herself more attractive to men, v. 41. **and satest upon a stately bed,** on an elaborately cushioned couch, **and a table prepared before it, whereupon thou hast set Mine incense and Mine oil,** gifts of the Lord and properly made as sacrifices to Him alone. V. 42. **And a voice of a multitude being at ease was with her,** a loose and boisterous crowd taking advantage of the invitation of Jerusalem; **and with the men of the common sort,** the members of the mobs surging through the streets, **were brought Sabeans from the wilderness,** drunken revelers, **which put bracelets upon their hands and beautiful crowns upon their heads,** both of the lewd women being thus bedecked by their wicked lovers. V. 43. **Then said I unto her that was old in adulteries,** well versed in adulteries, worn out by adulteries, **Will they now commit whoredoms with her and she with them?** Was their sense of shame so far gone as to cause them to desecrate the very city of God's holiness? V. 44. **Yet they went in unto her; as they go in unto a woman that playeth the harlot, so went they in unto Aholah and unto Aholibah, the lewd women.** In spite of all the warnings of God they became guilty of gross idolatry, calmly ignoring the very sense of decency and shame. V. 45. **And the righteous men,** in this case the Chaldeans, as the executioners of God's sentence of judgment, **they shall judge them after the manner of adulteresses and after the manner of women that shed blood,** such as are guilty of murder, **because they are adulteresses, and blood is in their hands,** they have been found guilty of the most flagrant crimes. V. 46. **For thus saith the Lord God, I will bring up a company upon them,** a council of judges to pass sentence upon the criminals, **and will give them to be removed and spoiled,** to be exiled and plundered. V. 47. **And the company shall stone them with stones,** the usual mode of execution in the case of adulteresses, **and dispatch them with their swords,** as though removing them out of their misery; **they shall slay their sons and their daughters,** the inhabitants of Jerusalem and Judah, **and burn up their houses with fire.** V. 48. **Thus will I cause lewdness,** every form of idolatry, **to cease out of the land, that all women,** in this case all nations, **may be taught not to do after your lewdness.** V. 49. **And they shall recompense your lewdness upon you,** paying them back in the proper coin, as they had deserved, **and ye shall bear the sins of your idols,** those committed with them, by means of them; **and ye shall know that I am the Lord God.** The very horror of the description makes the sin of Judah stand out all the more strongly, the effect intended by the Lord being that of making all men look upon similar transgressions with shuddering revulsion.

CHAPTER 24.

The Destruction of Jerusalem Typified by Parable and Sign.

VISION OF THE BOILING CALDRON. — V. 1. **Again, in the ninth year, in the tenth month,** namely, after the deportation of Jehoiachin and the accession of Zedekiah, **in the tenth day of the month,** the exact fixing of the day emphasizing the divinity of Ezekiel's mission, **the word of the Lord came unto me, saying,** v. 2. **Son of man, write thee the name of the day,** as a significant date, one prominent in the history of the Jewish race, **even of this same day; the king of Babylon set himself against Jerusalem**

this same day, the siege of the Jewish capital thus being begun and Ezekiel being informed of this fact by revelation of God. V. 3. **And utter a parable unto the rebellious house,** literally, "the house of rebelliousness," for the exiled Jews were, on the whole, still filled with stubborn resentment, **and say unto them, Thus saith the Lord God, Set on a pot,** a large caldron for cooking over an open fire, **set it on and also pour water into it,** their own proverb, chap. 11, 3, thereby proving awfully true, but in an entirely different sense from that intended by them; v. 4. **gather the pieces thereof into it,** those which properly belong into such a caldron for specified purposes, **even every good piece, the thigh, and the shoulder; fill it with the choice bones,** those having a good amount of flesh adhering to them. V. 5. **Take the choice of the flock,** of all small cattle, **and burn also the bones under it,** literally, "a rounded heap of kindling-wood under it for the bones," which may indicate that dry bones were mingled with the pieces of wood beneath the caldron, **and make it boil well and let them seethe the bones of it therein.** Thus Jerusalem, as the caldron, was placed over the fire of a fierce war and siege, by which the inhabitants of the city would be sodden to pieces, the poorest suffering first, but the wealthier inhabitants likewise enduring destruction, though by a slower process. These facts are now stated in explicit terms. V. 6. **Wherefore, thus saith the Lord God, Woe to the bloody city,** to the city whose blood-guiltiness is so great, **to the pot whose scum is therein,** like spots of rust that cannot be removed, **and whose scum is not gone out of it,** the reference being to the people's all-pervading wickedness. **Bring it out piece by piece,** in a slow judgment and process of destruction; **let no lot fall upon it,** or, "not has fallen upon it the lot," in which case there might be some chance of deliverance and salvation. V. 7. **For her blood,** that shed in the wickedness of her murderous actions, **is in the midst of her; she set it upon the top of a rock,** on the bare rock, shamelessly exposing her wickedness before the eyes of all men; **she poured it not upon the ground to cover it with dust,** thereby openly challenging the wrath and vengeance of God, v. 8. **that it might,** in bringing near the judgment of God, **cause fury to come up to take vengeance,** or, "to make fury to ascend, to execute vengeance." **I have set her blood upon the top of a rock,** on the bare, exposed rock, so as to make it conspicuous before the eyes of all men, **that it should not be covered.** V. 9. **Therefore, thus saith the Lord God,** in introducing another element pertaining to the execution of His wrath, **Woe to the bloody city! I will even make the pile for fire great,** so as to consume Jerusalem with siege and destruction. V. 10. **Heap on wood,** so the prophet is bidden, **kindle the fire,** in a mighty heaping of materials for the city's destruction, **consume the flesh,** so that it would be cooked to pieces, **and spice it well,** literally, "let the mixture seethe," **and let the bones be burned,** so that they would be softened into one mass with the flesh, a heavy broth or thick mixture, which could then be dumped out. V. 11. **Then set it empty upon the coals thereof that the brass of it may be hot and may burn,** glowing in white heat, **and that the filthiness of it,** the remnants of the broth clinging to its sides, **may be molten in it, that the scum of it,** the rust of the people's wickedness, **may be consumed,** burned away by the heat of the fire. V. 12. **She,** that is, Jerusalem, **hath wearied herself with lies,** literally, "it has caused labors to grow weary," that is, all the Lord's efforts in the interest of the city had been in vain, **and her great scum went not forth out of her,** the wickedness being ingrained, as it were; **her scum shall be in the fire,** or, "Into the fire with her scum!" Everything else having failed, the wrath of the Lord would now burn, with nothing to hold back. V. 13. **In thy filthiness is lewdness,** an abomination in the sight of the Lord. **Because I have purged thee,** making the most earnest efforts to cleanse the people from their wickedness, **and thou wast not purged,** resisting every effort of the Lord's mercy, **thou shalt not be purged from thy filthiness any more till I have caused My fury to rest upon thee,** in the punishment which Jerusalem so richly deserved. V. 14. **I, the Lord, have spoken it; it shall come to pass, and I will do it; I will not go back,** not show a weak lenience, **neither will I spare, neither will I repent,** as an over-indulgent father might be inclined to do; **according to thy ways and according to thy doings,** in exact agreement with her behavior and deeds, **shall they judge thee, saith the Lord God.** Note the heaping of synonymous expressions to emphasize the certainty of the approaching judgment. If men persist in wickedness in spite of better knowledge and warning, the Lord punishes them by letting their hearts be hardened in this wickedness and then bringing destruction upon them.

THE DEATH OF EZEKIEL'S WIFE AND ITS SIGNIFICANCE. — V. 15. **Also the word of the Lord came unto me, saying,** v. 16. **Son of man, behold, I take from thee the desire of thine eyes,** his very beloved wife, **with a stroke,** by a sudden death; **yet neither shalt thou mourn nor weep, neither shall thy tears run down,** that is, Ezekiel was to abstain from every show of mourning or sorrow over the deep loss which he would sustain. V. 17. **Forbear to cry,** violently repressing the natural show of grief, **make no mourning for the dead,** as was customary in the Orient, **bind the tire of thine head,** the head-ornament which was laid aside during times of mourning, **upon thee and put on**

thy shoes upon thy feet, instead of going barefoot in token of a deep sorrow, **and cover not thy lips,** as custom decreed in such a case, **and eat not the bread of men,** as people sent food in case of a death and relieved the survivors of the burden of preparing food for themselves. In everything Ezekiel was to act contrary to the established custom in the case of a death in the family. V. 18. **So I spake unto the people in the morning,** bringing them the message of the first part of the chapter; **and at even my wife died,** being torn suddenly from his side; **and I did in the morning as I was commanded,** acting in the unusual manner commanded him by the Lord. V. 19. **And the people,** noticing his strange behavior and surmising a special reason for it, **said unto me, Wilt thou not tell us what these things are to us,** what meaning his behavior was to convey to them, **that thou doest so?** This would give Ezekiel the opening which the Lord intended him to have in speaking to the people. V. 20. **Then I answered them, The word of the Lord came unto me, saying,** v. 21. **Speak unto the house of Israel, Thus saith the Lord God, Behold, I will profane My Sanctuary,** namely, the Temple at Jerusalem, **the excellency of your strength,** in which they took such great pride, **the desire of your eyes,** held as dearly by them as a man holds his beloved wife, **and that which your soul pitieth,** what they desired with a deep and abiding affection; **and your sons and your daughters whom ye have left,** those remaining in Jerusalem when the first exiles were taken to Babylon, **shall fall by the sword.** V. 22. **And ye shall do as I have done,** in restraining every show of grief in a similar manner: **ye shall not cover your lips nor eat the bread of men.** V. 23. **And your tires,** their turbans or head ornaments, **shall be upon your heads and your shoes upon your feet; ye shall not mourn nor weep,** in an outward demonstration of sorrow; **but ye shall pine away for your iniquities,** in an overwhelming measure of grief and pain, **and mourn one toward another,** all the more deeply affected since their sorrow was beyond the ordinary means of expression. V. 24. **Thus Ezekiel is unto you a sign,** so the Lord tells the people of Jerusalem in addressing them directly; **according to all that he hath done shall ye do; and when this cometh,** namely, this calamity or catastrophe, **ye shall know that I am the Lord God.** But the Lord intended that the token of the prophet should have another consequence as well. V. 25. **Also, thou son of man, shall it not be in the day when I take from them their strength, the joy of their glory, the desire of their eyes,** the Temple, as the center of their entire religious cult, **and that whereupon they set their minds,** with natural parental affection, **their sons and their daughters,** v. 26. **that he that escapeth in that day,** any one not taken away in the general destruction, **shall come unto thee to cause thee to hear it with thine ears,** to make known the awful greatness of the catastrophe? V. 27. **In that day shall thy mouth be opened to him which is escaped,** that is, at the same time with that of the escaped fugitive, so that he would no longer be compelled to hold back his grief, **and thou shalt speak and be no more dumb; and thou shalt be a sign unto them,** once more typically representative in his own person of the things which would befall them; **and they shall know that I am the Lord.** In all ages of the world the believers have been a sign to the enemies of the Lord in one way or the other, always as a living testimony before their eyes, if possibly they might be induced to see the error of their ways and turn to the Lord in true repentance.

CHAPTER 25.

Prophecies against Ammon, Moab, Edom, and the Philistines.

In the eight chapters now following there are contained some of the mightiest prophecies of the Old Testament against the chief heathen nations of the time, all of whom had, at one time or another, opposed the people of God and hindered His good and gracious will concerning them.

AGAINST AMMON AND MOAB. — V. 1. **The word of the Lord,** now withheld from the Jews for a time, **came again unto me, saying,** v. 2. **Son of man, set thy face against the Ammonites,** the descendants of Lot's younger daughter and therefore related to Israel, whose God they had originally known, Gen. 19, 38, **and prophesy against them,** v. 3. **and say unto the Ammonites,** in a formal declaration of God's attitude toward them, **Hear the word of the Lord God,** of the sovereign Ruler of the universe, who is at the same time the God of the covenant, **Thus saith the Lord God, Because thou saidst, Aha!** an expression of malignant joy, **against My Sanctuary when it was profaned,** exulting over the triumph which heathenism desired to celebrate over the supposed downfall of Israel's religion, **and against the land of Israel when it was desolate,** cp. Ps. 83, 4. 7. 8. 12, **and against the house of Judah when they went into captivity,** from the time when the first companies of Jews were driven away into exile, for the Ammonites had been the auxiliaries of the Chaldeans at that time, 2 Kings 24, 2: v. 4. **behold, therefore I will deliver thee to the men of the East,** that is, the Bedouin tribes of the Arabian deserts, **for a possession, and they shall set their palaces in thee**, that is, their corrals and enclosures for their cattle, **and make their dwellings in thee**, pitching their tents wherever they chose; **they shall eat thy fruit**, all the products of the land, **and they shall drink thy milk**, for that, in a stock-raising country, was a staple product. V. 5. **And I will make Rabbah**, the capital of Ammonitis, Deut. 3, 11, **a stable for camels**, the nomad tribes using it for this very purpose, **and the Ammonites**, the inhabitants of the country here standing for the entire province, **a couching-place for flocks**, the Arabs choosing any place they liked for the purpose, to bed down their flocks for the night; **and ye shall know that I am the Lord**, being fully convinced by the evidence of righteous anger and punishment. V. 6. **For thus saith the Lord God, Because thou hast clasped thine hands**, in malignant glee, **and stamped with the feet**, as if dancing for joy, **and rejoiced in heart**, with a malicious delight of the innermost soul, **with all thy despite against the land of Israel**, with all the contempt of which the Ammonites were able, v. 7. **behold, therefore I will stretch out Mine hand upon thee**, in the gesture and act of a stern punishment, **and will deliver thee for a spoil to the heathen**, the nation which eventually brought about the complete destruction of Ammon; **and I will cut thee off from the people, and I will cause thee to perish out of the countries**, in its position among the nations; **I will destroy thee**, thereby causing their identity as a state to be lost and bringing about an almost total annihilation of them as a people; **and thou shalt know that I am the Lord.** Cp. Amos 1, 13—15; Jer. 49, 1—5. V. 8. **Thus saith the Lord God, Because that Moab and Seir**, Idumea joining Moab in its hatred of the Lord's people, **do say, Behold, the house of Judah is like unto all the heathen**, that is, without advantage over them, subject to the same in life, without the protection of God, v. 9. **therefore, behold, I will open the side of Moab**, literally, "the shoulder of Moab," the Moabites being descendants of the older daughter of Lot, Gen. 19, 37, **from the cities**, so that the entire country would be included in this sentence of punishment, **from his cities which are on his frontiers**, from the greatest to the least, **the glory of the country**, distinguished for their fine location and architectural beauty, **Beth-jeshimoth, Baal-meon, and Kiriathaim**, the most important cities of the entire province, v. 10. **unto the men of the East**, the Bedouin tribes, **with the Ammonites**, whose fate they would be obliged to share, **and will give them in possession, that the Ammonites may not be remembered among the nations**, Moab thus sharing the fate of her sister state toward the north. V. 11. **And I will execute judgments upon Moab; and they shall know that I am the Lord.** Cp. Is. 16, 6—8; Jer. 48. While the Moabites are indeed still mentioned after the exile, they were no longer of importance as a nation and soon disappeared entirely from historical accounts, the word of the Lord thus being fulfilled in every detail.

AGAINST IDUMEA AND PHILISTIA. — V. 12. **Thus saith the Lord God, Because that Edom**, whose people were direct descendants of Jacob's brother Esau, **hath dealt against the house of Judah by taking vengeance**, or, "by exercising vindictive revenge," **and hath greatly offended**, heaping guilt upon itself, **and revenged himself upon them**, still smarting under the feeling of having been cheated of the right of the first-born, cp. Gen. 27, 41, v. 13. **therefore thus saith the Lord God, I will also stretch out Mine hand upon Edom**, in a stern and comprehensive punishment, **and will cut off man and beast from it**, in a general destruction; **and I will make it desolate from Teman**, the southernmost part of the country; **and they of Dedan**, of the northern section of the country, **shall fall by the sword**, that is, the entire land would become subject to the punishment of the Lord. V. 14. **And I will lay My vengeance upon Edom by the hand of My people Israel**, not only in a physical subjection brought about at the time of the Maccabees, but also in the more complete conquest in the Messianic times, when at least some of the inhabitants of this country bowed down before the true God; **and they shall do in Edom**, in its physical subjection, **according to Mine anger and according to My fury; and they shall know My vengeance, saith the Lord God**, the manner in which He takes revenge upon such as will not bow down to His rule. V. 15. **Thus saith the Lord God, Because the Philistines**, Judah's neighbors to the southwest, along the shores of the Mediterranean Sea, **have dealt by revenge**, in vindictive malice, **and have taken vengeance with a despiteful heart**, in a perpetual war of spite, **to destroy it for the old hatred**, on account of the enmity which reached back into the earliest history of the relations between the two nations, v. 16. **therefore thus saith the Lord God, Behold, I will stretch out Mine hand upon the Philistines, and I will cut off the Cherethims**, another name for the Philistines on account of their Cretan descent, **and destroy the remnant of the seacoast.** Cp. Amos 1, 8; Is. 14, 30; Jer. 47, 4. V. 17. **And I will execute great vengeance upon them with furious rebukes**, or, "in punishments of fury"; **and they shall know that I am the Lord when I shall lay My vengeance upon them**, forcing them to concede the unlimited range of His power, so that they would have to confess, even though most unwillingly, that He alone is the true God.

CHAPTER 26.

The Judgment upon Tyre.

A General Outline of the Judgment. — V. 1. **And it came to pass in the eleventh year,** namely, after the deportation of Jehoiachin, **in the first day of the month,** the month of the year not being mentioned, **that the word of the Lord came unto me, saying,** v. 2. **Son of man, because that Tyrus hath said against Jerusalem,** in the same malicious joy which had been found in the Ammonites, chap. 25, 3, **Aha! she is broken that was the gates of the people,** Jerusalem being the chief commercial rival of Tyrus, the great mart of trade on the Mediterranean; **she is turned unto me,** that is, good fortune had begun to favor Tyre, as she now thought; **I shall be replenished,** literally, "I will become full," that is, gain all the trade formerly held by her hated rival, **now she is laid waste,** for it seemed that Jerusalem was now definitely disposed of and could no longer come into consideration as a rival: v. 3. **therefore, thus saith the Lord God, Behold, I am against thee, O Tyrus,** the Lord setting Himself in stern opposition to her ambitions, and **will cause many nations to come up against thee,** namely, in the armies mustered for the conquest of the proud city, **as the sea causeth his waves to come up,** especially in the form of an immense tidal wave, which overwhelms all that comes in its way. V. 4. **And they shall destroy the walls of Tyrus,** whose business section was built on an island and was strongly fortified, **and break down her towers; I will also scrape her dust from her,** as it were, the last bit of fruitful soil, **and make her like the top of a rock,** absolutely bare and without even the ruins of buildings to indicate the former proud metropolis. V. 5. **It shall be a place for the spreading of nets in the midst of the sea,** this very point of the fulfilment of the prophecy standing out plainly, as travelers relate; **for I have spoken it, saith the Lord God,** whose word cannot fall to the ground; **and it shall become a spoil to the nations,** instead of amassing further fortunes, as she had hoped to do. V. 6. **And her daughters which are in the field,** the cities and towns tributary to Tyrus on the mainland, **shall be slain by the sword,** overthrown by the conquering invaders; **and they shall know that I am the Lord.** Men who refuse to acknowledge the Lord willingly are often obliged to do so under the stress of the convincing power of His judgments.

The Prophecy concerning Nebuchadnezzar's Coming. — V. 7. **For thus saith the Lord God, Behold, I will bring upon Tyrus Nebuchadrezzar, king of Babylon, a king of kings,** a ruler excelling in power, **from the north,** for it was from that side that the attack would naturally be made, **with horses, and with chariots, and with horsemen, and companies, and much people,** both infantry and cavalry being strongly represented in his armies of conquest. V. 8. **He shall slay with the sword thy daughters in the field,** quickly subduing the smaller cities tributary to Tyre; **and he shall make a fort against thee,** battering-towers from which the attacking troops could throw missiles into a besieged city, **and cast a mount against thee,** breastworks behind which trenches could be constructed, **and lift up the buckler against thee,** setting the infantry in array for an attack upon the city, one section of which was built on the mainland. V. 9. **And he shall set engines of war against thy walls,** literally, "wall-breakers," that is, battering-rams. **and with his axes he shall break down thy towers,** the swords of the invaders killing the soldiers on the towers and leaving the towers of the walls unmanned, so that they could easily be torn down by the enemy. V. 10. **By reason of the abundance of his horses their dust shall cover thee,** a strong picture to emphasize the immense mass of horses in the invader's army; **thy walls shall shake at the noise of the horsemen,** as they move forward, galloping to the attack, **and of the wheels and of the chariots when he shall enter into thy gates,** after a victorious onslaught, **as men enter into a city wherein is made a breach,** which can no longer hold out in the siege. V. 11. **With the hoofs of his horses shall he tread down all thy streets,** tramping the pavement to pieces; **he shall slay thy people by the sword, and thy strong garrisons shall go down to the ground,** literally, "and the pillars of thy strength shall sink to the ground," probably a reference to two monuments in the temple of Hercules and expressing the proud boast of the citizens that they could not be conquered. V. 12. **And they shall make a spoil of thy riches,** the great treasures stored up in this great commercial city, **and make a prey of thy merchandise,** taking it away as a welcome booty; **and they shall break down thy walls and destroy thy pleasant houses,** the proud palaces of the merchants, cp. Is. 23, 13; **and they shall lay thy stones and thy timber and thy dust in the midst of the water,** thus razing the city down to the very rock on which it was built. V. 13. **And I will cause the noise of thy songs,** shouted in the proud consciousness of prosperity, **to cease; and the sound of thy harps,** as expressing the joyousness of the inhabitants, **shall be no more heard,** for all joy would give way to sorrow and grief. V. 14. **And I will make thee like the top of a rock,** utterly bare, with not even a heap of ruins to mark the spot; **thou shalt be a place to spread nets upon,** the draw-nets of fishermen being stretched out there to dry. **Thou shalt be built no more; for I, the Lord, have spoken it, saith the Lord God.** Throughout the entire passage the overwhelming strength of the invading host is vividly pictured; for, as the instruments of Jehovah in carrying out His punishment, no one was able to withstand them.

THE EFFECT OF THE FALL OF TYRE. — V. 15. **Thus saith the Lord God of Tyrus, Shall not the isles,** including the colonies located along the shores of the Mediterranean, **shake at the sound of thy fall,** being filled with agitation and terror when the report of Tyre's fall reaches them, **when the wounded cry,** groaning in their pain, **when the slaughter is made in the midst of thee?** namely, at the taking of the city, when the sword mowed down with unrestrained fierceness. V. 16. **Then all the princes of the sea,** the rich merchant princes who were at the head of Tyre's rich colonies, **shall come down from their thrones,** losing all their power, obliged to give up their princely might and pomp, **and lay away their robes,** their outer garments, **and put off their broidered garments,** their rich dresses of state, all this indicating the depth of their mourning; **they shall clothe themselves with trembling,** with terrors, the strong figure indicating the extremity of their position; **they shall sit upon the ground,** instead of the thrones formerly occupied by them, **and shall tremble at every moment,** with fear shaking them again and again, **and be astonished at thee,** horrified at the catastrophe which had come upon the great metropolis. V. 17. **And they shall take up a lamentation for thee,** a song of mourning, **and say to thee, How art thou destroyed,** being overthrown in such a great calamity, **that wast inhabited of seafaring men,** literally, "inhabited from out of the seas," for Tyre had, as it were, arisen out of the seas as a mighty metropolis, **the renowned city,** spoken of in words of praise by men everywhere, **which wast strong in the sea,** not only impregnable in her location, but also dominating the seas with her marine, **she and her inhabitants, which cause their terror to be on all that haunt it,** for the city with all its inhabitants spread a fear of itself wherever its name was heard. V. 18. **Now shall the isles,** the colonies imbued with this spirit, **tremble in the day of thy fall,** frightened at the fall of the metropolis upon which they depended; **yea, the isles that are in the sea shall be troubled at thy departure,** at the horrible end of their proud mistress. V. 19. **For thus saith the Lord God, When I shall make thee a desolate city,** in exact accordance with these and other prophecies, **like the cities that are not inhabited,** which have already been turned into desert wastes; **when I shall bring up the deep upon thee, and great waters shall cover thee,** as by the inundation of an immense tidal wave; v. 20. **when I shall bring thee down with them that descend into the pit,** to all those destroyed in former times, by similar catastrophes, **with the people of old time,** particularly those swept away in the Deluge, **and shall set thee in the low parts of the earth,** in the abode of the dead, **in places desolate of old,** amidst the ruins of ancient civilizations, **with them that go down to the pit,** to share the fate of the godless generation before the Flood, **that thou be not inhabited; and I shall set glory in the land of the living,** by once more establishing His people in power; v. 21. **I will make thee a terror,** an object of horror and aversion, **and thou shalt be no more,** destroyed completely by a sudden calamity; **though thou be sought for, yet shalt thou never be found again, saith the Lord God.** In the case of Old Tyre, this prophecy was literally fulfilled, not a vestige of the former proud city being left.

CHAPTER 27.

A Lament over the Fall of Tyre.

DESCRIPTION OF THE GLORY AND MIGHT OF TYRE. — V. 1. **The word of the Lord came again unto me, saying,** v. 2. **Now, thou son of man, take up a lamentation,** a song of mourning or a funeral dirge, **for Tyrus** v. 3. **and say unto Tyrus,** the direct address intensifying the force of the lament, **O thou that art situate at the entry of the sea,** its double harbor giving it ready access to the Mediterranean Sea and to all the waters of the world, **which art a merchant of the people for many isles,** her commercial relations bringing her to the shores of many islands and of many countries along the Mediterranean and beyond, **Thus saith the Lord God, O Tyrus, thou hast said,** in self-satisfied pride, **I am of perfect beauty,** partly on account of her impregnable location, partly on account of her beautiful buildings. V. 4. **Thy borders are in the midst of the seas,** literally, "in the heart of the sea," for it was this which surrounded the island metropolis; **thy builders have perfected thy beauty.** The picture gradually changes to that describing a beautiful vessel, since the city, surrounded by a sea of masts, had the appearance of a great seagoing vessel. V. 5. **They have made all thy ship-boards,** the timber used in its construction, **of fir-trees of Senir,** the cypress from the Anti-Lebanon being known for its ability to withstand the influence of the elements; **they have taken cedars from Lebanon,** long, slender, and durable, to make masts for thee. V. 6. **Of the oaks of Bashan,** on the eastern side of Jordan, from Jabbok to Hermon, **have they made thine oars,** for oak-wood is strong and tough; **the company of the Ashurites,** skilful workmen summoned from Assyria, **have made thy benches,** those on which the rowers sat, or those on the decks, **of ivory, brought out of the isles of Chittim,** literally, "inlaid in larch or boxwood," from the isles of Chittim, that is, from Cyprus, which was famous for its excellent ship-building materials. V. 7. **Fine linen with broidered work from Egypt,** byssus in various embroidered designs, **was that which thou spreadest forth to be thy sail; blue and purple from the isles of Elishah,** those of the Ionian Sea or those off the coast of Greece, **was that which covered thee,** serving as an awning over the deck, while pennants or emblems floated from the masts. V. 8. **The inhabitants of Zidon,** the oldest city and the other large commercial center of Phenicia, **and Arvad,** a rocky island north of Tripolis, **were thy mariners,** the sailors manning the Tyrian vessels; **thy wise men, O Tyrus, that were in thee,** skilled in the lore of the sea, **were thy pilots,** occupying the responsible positions. V. 9. **The ancients of Gebal,** a Phenician city between Beirut and Tripolis, **and the wise men thereof,** skilful artisans or mechanics, **were in thee thy calkers,** the workmen employed to stop the holes and chinks in a vessel; **all the ships of the sea with their mariners were in thee to occupy thy merchandise,** to carry on trade with this foremost maritime metropolis. V. 10. **They of Persia,** the great Asiatic empire, **and of Lud and of Phut,** of two powerful African states, **were in thine army, thy men of war,** as a mercenary army; **they hanged the shield and helmet in thee,** exercising all the rights of a native army; **they set forth thy comeliness,** emphasizing it before all the world. V. 11. **The men of Arvad,** also a hired band, **with thine army were upon thy walls round about,** the greater part of the garrison proper thus consisting of native troops, **and the Gammadims were in thy towers,** courageous, valiant troops; **they hanged their shields upon thy walls round about; they have made thy beauty perfect,** completing the beauty of her military array. The entire description of Tyre's might and glory serves to enhance the effect of the threatened downfall.

DESCRIPTION OF THE COMMERCE OF TYRE. — V. 12. **Tarshish,** or Tartessus in Spain, known for the wealth of its silver and other metals, **was thy merchant by reason of the multitude of all kind of riches,** for which they exchanged their wealth; **with silver, iron, tin, and lead they traded in thy fairs,** for the wares which Tyre had to offer. V. 13. **Javan,** the Ionians of Asia Minor, **Tubal, and Meshech,** the latter two being countries or states between the Black and the Caspian Sea, **they were thy merchants; they traded the persons of men,** in the traffic in slaves then practised, **and vessels of brass in thy market,** for the copper-mines of eastern Asia Minor were renowned. V. 14. **They of the house of Togarmah,** namely, Armenia, **traded in thy fairs,** in exchanging wares, **with horses and horsemen and mules,** for Armenia was known in ancient times for its wealth in these products. V. 15. **The men of Dedan,** near the Persian Sea, Is. 21, 13, **were thy merchants,** for the location of their country placed them on the great highway between the East and the West; **many isles were the merchandise of thine hand,** acting as agents in promoting the commerce of Tyre; **they brought thee for a present,** literally, "to thee as exchange in value," that is, in payment by barter or trade, **horns of ivory and ebony.** V. 16. **Syria was thy merchant by reason of the multitude of the wares of thy making,** the manufacturing industry of Tyre being a very important item in its wealth; **they occupied in thy fairs,** paying for the wares which they bought in the markets of Tyre, **with emeralds, purple, and broidered work, and fine linen,** the rich byssus fabric of the Orient, **and coral, and agate,** or rubies, for Syria was rich in precious stones. V. 17. **Judah and the land of Israel,** the entire country of Palestine, **they were thy merchants; they traded in thy market wheat of Minnith,** a city in the Ammonitish district east of Jordan, **and Pannag,** which has been defined as a balsam or honey-product, **and honey, and oil, and balm,** for all of which the country of the Jews was famed. V. 18. **Damascus,** the metropolis of Northern Syria, **was thy merchant in the multitude of the wares of thy making,** that is, also an important customer in buying Tyrian manufactures, **for the multitude of all riches,** on account of the abundance of the wealth offered, **in the wine of Helbon,** of Aleppo, famed for its wines, **and white wool,** of the richest and finest kind. V. 19. **Dan also,** or Wedan, probably a district in Arabia, **and Javan,** in this instance a settlement in Arabia, **going to and fro occupied in thy fairs,** taking part likewise in the Tyrian trade; **bright iron,** wrought iron used for sword blades, **cassia,** a kind of cinnamon, **and calamus,** likewise an Arabian spice, **were in thy market.** V. 20. **Dedan,** a district in Northern Arabia, **was thy merchant in precious clothes for chariots,** either the fine tapestries or other ornamental accouterments used on riding-horses and on battle-wagons. V. 21. **Arabia,** the entire country as such, **and all the princes of Kedar,** the sheiks of the interior of Arabia, **they occupied with thee,** being engaged in trade with Tyre, **in lambs and rams and goats; in these were they thy merchants,** for as nomadic tribes they depended upon the products of their herds and flocks. V. 22. **The merchants of**

Sheba, in Arabia Felix, **and Raamah,** on the Persian Gulf, **they were thy merchants; they occupied in thy fairs,** in exchanging wares, **with chief of all spices,** with most excellent perfumes, **and with all precious stones and gold,** for which the mountains of Yemen were known. V. 23. **Haran,** in Mesopotamia, **and Canneh,** the later Ctesiphon, a commercial center on the Tigris, **and Eden,** in Mesopotamia, **the merchants of Sheba, Asshur,** or Assyria, **and Chilmad,** west of the Euphrates, **were thy merchants.** V. 24. **These,** namely, the entire list as enumerated, **were thy merchants in all sorts of things, in blue clothes,** fine wrappings or mantles, **and broidered work, and in chests of rich apparel,** used for storing, **bound with cords and made of cedar, among thy merchandise,** the value of cedar for this purpose having been known since early days. V. 25. **The ships of Tarshish did sing of thee in thy market,** literally, "were thy caravans," thy traffic, for they performed on the sea what caravans did on land in conveying goods; **and thou wast replenished,** always richly stocked with goods, **and made very glorious in the midst of the seas.** Note how vivid the prophet's description of the commerce of Tyre is, how it presents a full, concrete picture of the great trade routes and of the chief articles of manufacture in those days. The description of Tyre's grandeur, however, serves but as a foil in making her fall stand out all the more glaringly.

THE FALL OF TYRE. — V. 26. **Thy rowers have brought thee into great waters,** Tyre being once more represented as a stately vessel of the galley variety, driven by one or more rows of oars in the hands of powerful oarsmen. **The east wind,** which often blows in sudden, furious gusts, **hath broken thee in the midst of the seas,** in a shipwreck which meant the death-blow of Tyre in the midst of her glory. V. 27. **Thy riches,** all the marvelous wealth heaped up in her banks and storehouses, **and thy fairs,** the wares with which she traded, **thy merchandise, thy mariners, and thy pilots, thy calkers, and the occupiers of thy merchandise,** those who actually handled and sold the goods, **and all thy men of war that are in thee, and in all thy company which is in the midst of thee,** that is, all the inhabitants of the city, **shall fall into the midst of the seas in the day of thy ruin,** the destruction being complete, as in the case of a foundered ship, which sinks with all those on board. V. 28. **The suburbs,** the smaller towns immediately dependent upon Tyre, **shall shake at the sound of the cry of thy pilots,** as they, the very ones upon whom the ship of state depended, found themselves facing annihilation. V. 29. **And all that handle the oar, the mariners, and all the pilots of the sea,** namely, those of other ships and nations, **shall come down from their ships,** disembarking on account of the intensity of the horror which they felt, **they shall stand upon the land,** v. 30. **and shall cause their voice to be heard against thee,** in loud lamentation, **and shall cry bitterly and shall cast up dust upon their heads,** cp. Job 2, 12; **they shall wallow themselves in the ashes,** cp. Jer. 6, 26, these latter acts being tokens of deep and uncontrollable grief; v. 31. **and they shall make themselves utterly bald for thee,** shaving their heads as another sign of deep mourning, **and gird them with sackcloth,** as mourners were in the habit of doing, **and they shall weep for thee with bitterness of heart,** in an excess of grief, **and bitter wailing.** V. 32. **And in their wailing they shall take up a lamentation for thee and lament over thee,** in a mournful dirge, saying, **What city is like Tyrus, like the destroyed in the midst of the sea!** now so silent after the former noisy bustle which characterized her. V. 33. **When thy wares went forth out of the seas,** like plants and fruits out of the ground, namely, by virtue of the fact that the many vessels of her commercial pursuits brought in the goods, **thou filledst many people,** meeting their demand for goods of every description; **thou didst enrich the kings of the earth with the multitude of thy riches and of thy merchandise,** for Tyre had included in her trade the richest and most costly goods of the earth. V. 34. **In the time when thou shalt be broken by the seas,** or, "now that thou hast been shattered," or, "hast foundered," **in the depths of the waters thy merchandise and all thy company in the midst of thee shall fall,** all her inhabitants being included in the judgment of destruction upon her. V. 35. **All the inhabitants of the isles shall be astonished at thee,** all those who had the benefit of Tyre's commerce standing aghast at her downfall, **and their kings,** their merchant rulers, **shall be sore afraid, they shall be troubled in their countenance,** trembling lest they share her fate. V. 36. **The merchants among the people shall hiss at thee,** for envy is apt ever to produce a malicious joy when a rival is overthrown; **thou shalt be a terror,** an object of horror, **and never shalt be any more.** Cp. chap. 26, 21. It is a vividly impressive passage, which concludes this section of the prophecy against Tyrus, one setting forth the just wrath of a holy God.

CHAPTER 28.

Against the Ruler of Tyre.

GOD'S JUDGMENT UPON THE PRINCE OF TYRE. V. 1. **The word of the Lord came again unto me, saying,** v. 2. **Son of man, say unto the prince of Tyrus,** the ruler of the great commercial capital and metropolis, **Thus saith the Lord God,** He who holds in His hand the fate of empires as well as of individuals, **Because thine heart is lifted up,** in sinful, blasphemous pride, **and thou hast said, I am a God,** a claim advanced by many heathen rulers who demanded for themselves divine veneration, **I sit in the seat of God,** on the throne of the one heavenly Ruler Himself, **in the midst of the seas,** considering the stronghold of his capital impregnable as far as men and the forces of nature were concerned; **yet thou art a man,** merely a lowly and mortal human being, **and not God, though thou set thine heart as the heart of God,** not only imagining himself to hold the position of God, but also thinking of himself as possessing, and able to use, the almighty power of God; v. 3. **behold, thou art wiser than Daniel,** that is, the Tyrian ruler held this opinion concerning himself, he placed his knowledge and understanding above that of the wisest man of his time; **there is no secret that they can hide from thee,** this assertion on the part of the heathen prince again placing him on the level of Daniel with his revelations concerning the future; v. 4. **with thy wisdom and with thine understanding,** particularly his business acumen, **thou hast gotten thee riches,** his business sagacity having brought its own reward, **and hast gotten gold and silver into thy treasures,** so that the wealth of this commercial metropolis of the world, as later that of Venice, was almost unbelievably great; v. 5. **by thy great wisdom,** with which he credited himself, **and by thy traffic,** the trade which had been established in the course of the centuries, **hast thou increased thy riches, and thine heart is lifted up because of thy riches,** this being the effect which the possession of wealth has in the majority of cases: v. 6. **therefore thus saith the Lord God,** taking up the thought of verse 2 once more, for the intervening statements are intended, of course, only as an ironical concession, picturing the empty boastfulness of the heathen ruler, in his overweening opinion of himself, **Because thou hast set thine heart as the heart of God,** ascribing an honor to himself which only the one true God possesses: v. 7. **behold, therefore I will bring strangers upon thee,** invaders from foreign lands, **the terrible of the nations,** for the Chaldeans were known for the fierceness of their natures; **and they shall draw their swords against the beauty of thy wisdom,** for the showiness of the trade and commerce of Tyre was the offspring of the business acumen with which the king prided himself, **and they shall defile thy brightness,** literally, "profane thy shining beauty," treating it with mocking disrespect, destroying it with rough ruthlessness. V. 8. **They shall bring thee,** namely, the ruler himself, **down to the pit, and thou shalt die the deaths of them that are slain in the midst of the seas,** the expression denoting that the prince, as it were, died the death of every inhabitant of Tyre who was slain, his fate overtaking him as in a mighty shipwreck. V. 9. **Wilt thou yet say before Him that slayeth thee, I am God?** Would the Tyrian prince, after the sentence of God had gone into effect, still make such extravagant claims for himself and his power and wisdom? **But thou shalt be a man and no God,** that is, he would be given proof positive to that effect, **in the hand of Him that slayeth thee,** namely, completely at the mercy of the one and only Ruler of the universe. V. 10. **Thou shalt die the deaths of the uncircumcised,** such as the godless heathen deserve by their blasphemous pride, **by the hand of strangers,** in further humiliation upon him and in just retribution upon him who had probably often scoffed at the Jews; **for I have spoken it, saith the Lord God.** Though the unbelievers jeer at the fact, yet it remains true that the Lord resents every insult offered His saints and will in due time take His revenge upon His enemies.

LAMENTATION OVER THE KING OF TYRE. — V. 11. **Moreover, the word of the Lord,** of Jehovah, the Lord of the covenant, **came unto me, saying,** v. 12. **Son of man, take up a lamentation,** raising a mournful song, **upon the king of Tyrus and say unto him, Thus saith the Lord God, Thou sealest up the sum,** literally, "Thou sealer-up of the measure of perfection," **full of wisdom and perfect in beauty.** The prince of Tyre had erected the building of Tyre's wealth and beauty in perfection of symmetry and exactness of detail and, as it were, placed his seal upon the finished product, which was certainly wonderful in the eyes of men. V. 13. **Thou hast been in Eden, the garden of God,** the outward aspect of Tyre being that of ideal loveliness, of the greatest earthly advantages, as a garden of God; **every precious stone was thy covering,** all possible magnificence was exhibited in the adornment of the city and particularly of the king's person, **the sardius, topaz, and the diamond, the beryl,** or chrysolite, **the onyx and the jasper, the sapphire, the emerald,** or the chrysoprase, **and the carbuncle,** stones of varying degrees of hardness and of the most beautiful colors, **and gold,** for it was this metal in which the precious stones were set; **the workmanship of thy**

tabrets and of thy pipes was prepared in thee in the day that thou wast created, literally, "the service of thy kettledrums and of thy women was ready for thee on the day of thy creation," that is, the prince of Tyre was born to the luxury of music and costly amusements, or he entered upon them on the day of his accession, he was accustomed to them from his earliest days. V. 14. **Thou art the anointed cherub that covereth,** because he, as an anointed king, had the duty of protecting a nation of people, like a sanctuary in God's care; **and I have set thee so; thou wast upon the holy mountain of God,** for he was God's representative in governing the Tyrian state; **thou hast walked up and down in the midst of the stones of fire,** which, like a fiery wall erected by God, protected the king in his office. Note that the pictures throughout are taken from the true Temple-worship and from the functions of kings of Judah, with which Ezekiel was familiar. V. 15. **Thou wast perfect in thy ways,** and therefore, in outer civic righteousness, acceptable to the Lord, **from the day that thou wast created,** which most likely means the day of his accession to the throne, **till iniquity was found in thee,** namely, when he made himself unworthy of his position on account of rebelliousness and perverseness. V. 16. **By the multitude of thy merchandise,** that is, on account of the fact that the commerce of Tyre gave the state great power among the nations, **they have filled the midst of thee with violence,** the unrighteous mammon held in the city having this influence upon those in power, that it caused them to violate the rights of the poor and needy, **and thou hast sinned,** the prince with his people; **therefore I will cast thee as profane out of the mountain of God,** deposing him from his position as leader of the people; **and I will destroy thee, O covering cherub, from the midst of the stones of fire.** Cp. v. 14. V. 17. **Thine heart was lifted up,** in blasphemous self-elation, **because of thy beauty,** of which the ruler of Tyre was so inordinately proud, **thou hast corrupted thy wisdom by reason of thy brightness,** thinking that Tyre's splendor would serve as an excuse for every form of sin and guilt; **I will cast thee to the ground,** dashing him to utter destruction, **I will lay thee before kings that they may behold thee,** as an example of God's wrath upon such as are lifted up in sinful pride. V. 18. **Thou hast defiled thy sanctuaries,** the special holy privileges which are given by the Lord to governments, **by the multitude of thine iniquities, by the iniquity,** the deep corruptness, **of thy traffic; therefore will I bring forth a fire from the midst of thee,** the prince's iniquity itself becoming such a consuming fire; **it shall devour thee, and I will bring thee to ashes upon the earth,** thus completely consumed, **in the sight of all them that behold thee,** the surrounding nations being witnesses of Tyre's complete overthrow. V. 19. **All they that know thee among the people,** being acquainted with Tyre's former position and wealth, **shall be astonished at thee; thou shalt be a terror,** an object of horror to others, **and never shalt thou be any more.** This prophecy, together with the entire cycle of prophecies, was fulfilled partly in the days of Nebuchadnezzar, but still more completely at the time of Alexander the Great. If rightly interpreted and on the basis of all available data, secular history invariably supports the historical descriptions given in the Bible.

PROPHECY AGAINST ZIDON. — V. 20. **Again the word of the Lord came unto me, saying,** v. 21. **Son of man, set thy face against Zidon,** the other large city of Phenicia and formerly its capital, **and prophesy against it** v. 22. **and say, Thus saith the Lord God,** whose powerful rule extends over all the earth, **Behold, I am against thee, O Zidon; and I will be glorified in the midst of thee,** namely, by carrying out His sentence of judgment upon her; **and they shall know that I am the Lord,** the one true God, **when I shall have executed judgments in her and shall be sanctified in her,** her overthrow redounding to the setting forth of His holiness. V. 23. **For I will send into her pestilence and blood into her streets,** two of the three great scourges of war; **and the wounded shall be judged in the midst of her,** the slain falling everywhere, **by the sword upon her on every side; and they shall know that I am the Lord.** V. 24. **And there shall be no more a pricking brier unto the house of Israel,** namely, by the continual temptation and offense which the people of Zidon gave to the Jews, **nor any grieving thorn of all that are round about them,** all the surrounding heathen nations, cp. Josh. 23, 13, **that despised them,** for it was on account of this contempt that the heathen first ensnared Israel in sin and then became the instrument of punishing them; **and they shall know that I am the Lord God.** V. 25. **Thus saith the Lord God,** in rounding out this section of His prophecy, **When I shall have gathered the house of Israel from the people among whom they are scattered,** in the Babylonian captivity, **and shall be sanctified in them in the sight of the heathen,** namely, by their repentant return to the true worship, **then shall they dwell in their land that I have given to My servant Jacob.** V. 26. **And they shall dwell safely therein,** in peace and security, **and shall build houses and plant vineyards,** as in times of perfect peace; **yea, they shall dwell with confidence,** in firm trust in the God of their salvation, **when I have exe-**

cuted judgments upon all those that despise them round about them, by taking every advantage of them; **and they shall know that I am the Lord, their God.** The Messianic era was prepared, in a measure, by the return of the repentant Jews to the home of their fathers, and the Lord had His congregation in their midst from that time on; but the full realization of the tenor of these words did not come until the kingdom of the Messiah was established by the preaching of the Gospel of God's mercy by Jesus and by His apostles.

CHAPTER 29.

The Judgment upon Pharaoh and Egypt.

THE DESTRUCTION OF PHARAOH'S POWER AND THE SUBSEQUENT RESTORATION OF EGYPT. — V. 1. **In the tenth year,** namely, after Jehoiachin had been deposed and led away into captivity, **in the tenth month, in the twelfth day of the month, the word of the Lord came unto me, saying,** v. 2. **Son of man, set thy face against Pharaoh, king of Egypt,** in a gesture which signified stern reproof and opposition on the part of the Lord, **and prophesy against him and against all Egypt,** the country being guilty with its ruler. V. 3. **Speak and say,** in a message which was, in every word, the message of Jehovah against a heathen ruler who was guilty of so much wickedness over against the Lord's people, **Thus saith the Lord God, Behold, I am against thee, Pharaoh, king of Egypt,** this special prophecy referring to Pharaoh-hophra, who then occupied the throne, **the great dragon,** the crocodile, type of the land of Egypt, **that lieth in the midst of his rivers,** the Nile with all its canals and the network of streams which compose its delta, **which hath said,** with the pride which sets aside the blessings of the one true God, **My river is mine own, and I have made it for myself,** the Pharaohs from olden times considering themselves gods of the land and thereby heaping blasphemy upon the name of the one true God. V. 4. **But I will put hooks in thy jaws,** as men did in the case of crocodiles, such rings effectually restraining the fierce reptiles, **and I will cause the fish of thy rivers to stick unto thy scales,** namely, the inhabitants of Egypt, who would, for the most part, share his fate, **and I will bring thee up out of the midst of thy rivers,** like a captured crocodile, **and all the fish of thy rivers shall stick unto thy scales,** and thus share the fate of their ruler. V. 5. **And I will leave thee thrown into the wilderness,** far from food and water, the life-giving element in the case of these animals, **thee and all the fish of thy rivers; thou shalt fall upon the open fields,** literally, "upon the plains of the fields," far from food and nourishment; **thou shalt not be brought together nor gathered,** no one taking the trouble of picking up what was so deliberately cast aside. **I have given thee for meat,** that is, for food, **to the beasts of the field and to the fowls of the heaven.** Thus the prophet draws a very vivid picture of the destruction which would come upon the land of Egypt and its ruler. V. 6. **And all the inhabitants of Egypt shall know that I am the Lord,** the one God who directs the destinies of nations, **because they have been a staff of reed to the house of Israel,** the latter's dependence upon Egypt as a trusted ally proving hurtful to the Lord's people instead of beneficial; for not only was the might of Egypt unequal to the task of protecting Judah against the mighty Eastern empires, but the idolatry spread by the Egyptians was a downright curse to the people of the Lord. V. 7. **When they took hold of thee by thy hand,** in seeking the assistance of Egypt, **thou didst break and rend all their shoulder,** the broken pieces of the staff piercing through the hand and arm, up even to the shoulder; **and when they leaned upon thee,** in relying upon Egypt's help, **thou brakest and madest all their loins to be at a stand,** that is, the firmness of Israel's loins was so badly shaken that the power to stand upright was taken away. Egypt was not only an unreliable ally, but a menace of the worst kind. V. 8. **Therefore, thus saith the Lord God, Behold, I will bring a sword upon thee,** in conquering and devastating warfare, **and cut off man and beast out of thee,** in a universal destruction. V. 9. **And the land of Egypt shall be desolate and waste,** literally, "shall be for a desolation and a waste," **and they shall know that I am the Lord,** by the evidence furnished by His severe punishment upon them, **because he,** the ruler of Egypt, **hath said, The river is mine, and I have made it,** the Lord once more calling attention to this blasphemous statement. V. 10. **Behold, therefore I am against thee and against thy rivers,** the chief source of Egypt's wealth, **and I will make the land of Egypt utterly waste and desolate,** literally, "I will give the land of Egypt to desolations of desolation," **from the tower of Syene,** rather, "from Migdol," the northernmost point of Egypt, "to Syene," on its extreme southern border, **even unto the border of Ethiopia,** the country which extended to the south of Egypt. V. 11. **No foot of man shall pass through it, nor foot of beast shall pass through it, neither shall it be inhabited forty years,** during which time the power of Egypt would be utterly broken, and there would be neither traffic, travel, nor industry. V. 12 **And I will make the land of Egypt desolate in the midst of the countries that**

are desolate, in the general punishment which struck the lands at this end of the Mediterranean Sea in the Chaldean conquest, **and her cities among the cities that are laid waste shall be desolate forty years,** for the time determined upon by the Lord; **and I will scatter the Egyptians among the nations,** so that they also would suffer the evils of an exile, **and will disperse them through the countries,** Egypt thus, as one commentator has it, being the caricature of Israel. Yet the mercy and long-suffering of the Lord becomes apparent also in this connection, and the prophecy takes a more cheerful turn. V. 13. **Yet thus saith the Lord God, At the end of forty years,** the period determined by Him for the carrying out of His judgment, **will I gather the Egyptians from the people whither they were scattered,** in the misery of their subjugation and captivity, v. 14. **and I will bring again the captivity of Egypt and will cause them to return into the land of Pathros,** that is, South or Upper Egypt, with Thebes as its capital, **into the land of their habitation,** literally, "the land of their birth," for the nation of the Egyptians had their origin in this part of Egypt; **and they shall be there a base kingdom,** no longer a power of the first rank, but altogether subordinate to other nations. V. 15. **It shall be the basest of the kingdoms,** instead of occupying the first position, to which it aspired; **neither shall it exalt itself any more above the nations, for I will diminish them that they shall no more rule over the nations,** never again occupy a position which would cause others to look to it for assistance. V. 16. **And it shall be no more the confidence of the house of Israel,** the fact by which the downfall of Judah was brought about, **which bringeth their iniquity to remembrance, when they shall look after them,** that is, the fact that the Jews turned to Egypt for help and sought deliverance with an idolatrous nation causes the Lord to remember that He was bound to punish them; **but they shall know that I am the Lord God.** It is always foolish, and usually disastrous as well, for believers to turn to the enemies of God for help and deliverance in any emergency.

THE CONQUEST AND SPOIL OF EGYPT. —V. 17. **And it came to pass in the seven and twentieth year,** after the accession of Zedekiah, and seventeen years after the message contained in the first part of this chapter was delivered, this section thus being the last prophecy of Ezekiel, in point of time, **in the first month, in the first day of the month, the word of the Lord came unto me, saying,** v. 18. **Son of man, Nebuchadrezzar, king of Babylon, caused his army to serve a great service against Tyrus,** namely, in laying siege to this city, the task, according to secular accounts, taking him thirteen years; **every head was made bald, and every shoulder was peeled,** on account of the difficult labor connected with transporting material to fill up the arm of the sea between the mainland and the island on which Tyre was located; **yet had he no wages, nor his army, for Tyrus,** very likely because the rich spoil which he had hoped to make had meanwhile been removed on the Tyrian ships and stored in safe places in her colonies, **for the service that he had served against it,** he had not found enough to reimburse him for the campaign. V. 19. **Therefore, thus saith the Lord God, Behold, I will give the land of Egypt unto Nebuchadrezzar, king of Babylon,** so that he would bring the country into subjection to Chaldea; **and he shall take her multitude,** a great number of captives, **and take her spoil,** her wealth and stores making a welcome booty, **and take her prey,** so that the country would be stripped of its riches in every form; **and it shall be the wages for his army,** a well-merited reward or recompense, since his army, unknown to the heathen ruler himself, had been the instrument of God in carrying out His will. V. 20. **I have given him the land of Egypt for his labor wherewith he served against it,** namely, against Tyre, **because they,** the Chaldean king and his army, **wrought for Me, saith the Lord God.** V. 21. **In that day,** namely, at the time which was generally included in this section, **will I cause the horn of the house of Israel to bud forth,** the horn being the symbol of power and authority, and the expression pointing forward to a revival of Judah's might, **and I will give thee the opening of the mouth in the midst of them,** so that Ezekiel and every true prophet of the Lord would have willing hearers among the chastened congregation; **and they shall know that I am the Lord.** The words do not promise that the ancient glory of Israel as a political state would be revived, but they contain an earnest of the spiritual growth of the true Israel and of its eventual full glory under the Messiah, the Son of David.

CHAPTER 30.

The Day of Judgment upon Egypt.

ANNOUNCING THE DOOM UPON EGYPT AND ITS ALLIES. —V. 1. **The word of the Lord came again unto me,** the time, in this instance, not being indicated, **saying,** v. 2. **Son of man, prophesy and say,** in another message directed against Egypt, **Thus saith the Lord God, Howl ye! Woe worth the day!** or, "Alas for the day!" V 3. **For the day is near, even the day of the Lord is near, the** day of doom decided upon by Him, **a cloudy day**, the clouds well representative of the storm of His wrath which would break upon the entire country; **it shall be the time of the heathen**, when they would experience His judgment as His vengeance went forth upon them. V. 4. **And the sword shall come upon Egypt**, in bloody uproar and slaughter, **and great pain**, the most severe anguish, **shall be in Ethiopia, when the slain shall fall in Egypt, and they shall take away her multitude**, the wealth amassed within her borders, **and her foundations shall be broken down**, her very existence as state being undermined. V. 5. **Ethiopia**, the country bounding upon Egypt on the south, **and Libya**, a nation toward the west, **and Lydia**, another African desert state, **and all the mingled people**, literally, "the strange people," those allied with the Egyptians and serving together with their soldiers, **and Chub**, probably Nubia, **and the men of the land that is in league**, literally, "the sons of the land of the covenant," an expression taken by some commentators to refer to the Jews who migrated to Egypt, carrying Jeremiah with them, Jer. 42—44, **shall fall with them by the sword**, sharing the fate of the entire country. V. 6. **Thus saith the Lord, They also that uphold Egypt**, chiefly the rulers and the idols upon whom the Egyptians depended, **shall fall, and the pride of her power**, her proud might, **shall come down; from the tower of Syene**, rather, "from Migdol to Syene," chap. 29, 10, **shall they fall in it by the sword, saith the Lord God.** V. 7. **And they shall be desolate in the midst of the countries that are desolate, and her cities shall be in the midst of the cities that are wasted.** Cp. chap. 29, 12. V. 8. **And they shall know that I am the Lord when I have set a fire in Egypt**, the fire of bitter warfare, carried on by a fierce people and with relentless cruelty, **and when all her helpers**, allies and all others upon whom Egypt depended, **shall be destroyed.** V. 9. **In that day shall messengers go forth from Me in ships**, namely, Egyptians fleeing before the calamity threatening their country and now acting as messengers of the Lord in the sense that they could now speak from their own experience concerning the Lord's judgments, **to make the careless Ethiopians afraid**, to fill them with a wholesome dread of the punishment threatening them, **and great pain shall come upon them**, a severe anguish, **as in the day of Egypt**, when the doom struck the mightier nation; **for, lo, it cometh**, it was inevitable, because announced by the Lord, whose word is ever fulfilled just as He has planned His punishments upon all disobedient people, to come at the time determined upon by Him.

THE SENTENCE CARRIED OUT. — V. 10. **Thus saith the Lord God, I will also make the multitude of Egypt**, the large population of the country, with all the wealth possessed by them, **to cease by the hand of Nebuchadrezzar, king of Babylon**, who would, in every way, put an end to the prosperity of the country. V. 11. **He and his people with him, the terrible of the nations**, for the Chaldean soldiers were known for the fierceness of their fighting, **shall be brought to destroy the land**, that being the expressed object of their campaign; **and they shall draw their swords against Egypt and fill the land with the slain**, those pierced through in the ruthless slaughter. V. 12. **And I will make the rivers dry**, thereby taking away from the land some of its natural means of defense and the sources of its prosperity, Deut. 32, 30, **and sell the land into the hand of the wicked**, like a slave sold into the power of a strange master; **and I will make the land waste, and all that is therein, by the hand of strangers**, so that everything would be beaten down and ruined; **I, the Lord, have spoken it.** The description is given from the standpoint of the Egyptians, for according to their conception the Chaldeans were not only strangers, but wicked as well. V. 13. **Thus saith the Lord God, I will also destroy the idols**, Is. 19, 1, **and I will cause their images to cease out of Noph**, that is, Memphis, the ancient capital of Lower Egypt; **and there shall be no more a prince of the land of Egypt**, namely, with the glory of the ancient Pharaohs, who were, at the same time, clothed with divine honor; **and I will put a fear in the land of Egypt**, so that they would be continually under its burden, without a native prince to assist them. Cp. Jer. 46, 25. V. 14. **And I will make Pathros**, that is, Upper Egypt, **desolate and will set fire in Zoan**, the old Tanis, on a branch of the Nile in Lower Egypt, **and will execute judgments in No**, or No-Amon, that is, Thebes, the very ancient metropolis of Upper Egypt. V. 15. **And I will pour my fury upon Sin**, that is, Pelusium, on one of the branches of the Nile in its delta, **the strength of Egypt**, for, being surrounded with swamps, it was hard to attack, and thus kept many an enemy back from the northeastern frontier; **and I will cut off the multitude of No.** V. 16. **And I will set fire in Egypt**, bitter and destructive warfare: **Sin shall have great pain, and No shall be rent asunder**, overthrown as if by highway robbers, **and Noph shall have distresses daily**, literally, "and Noph — besiegers by day," overrunning the city with an utter disregard of any defense. Note the continual change from Upper to Lower Egypt, to emphasize the fact that every part of Egypt would be included in the punishment meted out by the Lord. V. 17. **The young men of Aven**, of Heliopolis, the great city of idols in Lower Egypt, **and of Pi-beseth**, of Boubastis, on a canal in the delta of the Nile, the center of cat-worship in Egypt, **shall fall by the sword**, although both of them were known on account of their valiant garrisons; **and these cities shall go into captivity,** that is, the inhabitants, those not belonging to the warrior caste. V. 18. **At Tehaphnehes,** that is, Taphne, a border city near Pelusium, **also the day shall be darkened,** with the shadow of the approaching calamity, **when I shall break there the yokes of Egypt,** cp. Lev. 26, 13, so that Egypt would never again be a mistress of nations, keeping them in slavery. It was in the last-named city that the band of Jews under the leadership of Johanan had dragged the unwilling Jeremiah, and so they were also included in the Lord's punishment upon Egypt. **And the pomp of her strength,** of which Egypt had boasted throughout the centuries, **shall cease in her; as for her, a cloud shall cover her,** namely, that of this catastrophe, **and her daughters,** her cities with their inhabitants, **shall go into captivity.** V. 19. **Thus will I execute judgments in Egypt,** according to the entire description of the paragraph; **and they shall know that I am the Lord,** this knowledge being forced upon their unwilling minds by the almighty evidences of God's wrath.

THE POWER OF PHARAOH DESTROYED. — V. 20. **And it came to pass in the eleventh year,** this vision thus being placed about three months before the capture of Jerusalem, **in the first month, in the seventh day of the month, that the word of the Lord came unto me, saying,** v. 21. **Son of man, I have broken the arm of Pharaoh, king of Egypt,** and therewith all the strength of his army, upon which he depended; **and, lo, it shall not be bound up to be healed,** not return to its former power, **to put a roller,** that is, a fillet, or splints, **to bind it, to make it strong to hold the sword,** so that he would at all recover his former position. V. 22. **Therefore, thus saith the Lord God, Behold, I am against Pharaoh, king of Egypt, and will break his arms, the strong, and that which was broken,** the power which he had tried and would try to mend in order to regain his lost prestige; **and I will cause the sword to fall out of his hand.** V. 23. **And I will scatter the Egyptians among the nations,** in an exile like that of Israel, **and will disperse them through the countries.** V. 24. **And I will strengthen the arms of the king of Babylon,** who with his army was God's weapon of punishment upon Egypt, **and put my sword in his hand; but I will break Pharaoh's arms,** rendering him helpless before the invaders, **and he shall groan before him,** moaning before the conquering host, **with the groanings of a deadly wounded man.** V. 25. **But I will strengthen the arms of the king of Babylon,** the same statement being repeated in various forms, in order to strengthen the effect of the inevitable disaster, **and the arms of Pharaoh shall fall down,** in helpless weakness; **and they shall know that I am the Lord when I shall put My sword into the hand of the king of Babylon, and he shall stretch it out upon the land of Egypt,** in token of the destruction to be brought upon the whole land. V. 26. **And I will scatter the Egyptians among the nations and disperse them among the countries; and they shall know that I am the Lord.** The entire passage impresses the reader with the sense of the mighty majesty of God in dealing with those who have refused to heed His warnings.

CHAPTER 31.

The Fall of Assyria an Example of Warning.

COMPARISON BETWEEN PHARAOH'S POWER AND THAT OF ASSYRIA. — V. 1. **And it came to pass in the eleventh year,** after the captivity of Jehoiachin, **in the third month, in the first day of the month,** just two months later than the prophecy delivered in chapter 30, **that the word of the Lord came unto me, saying,** v. 2. **Son of man, speak unto Pharaoh, king of Egypt,** by sending him the message here transmitted to the Lord's prophet, **and to his multitude,** the people of Egypt with all their wealth, for the country was then teeming with prosperity, **Whom art thou like in thy greatness?** The Lord intentionally prepares to make a full and detailed comparison, in order to bring out the lesson which He wished to convey. V. 3. **Behold, the Assyrian,** emperor and people, the entire nation, **was a cedar in Lebanon,** distinguished for beauty and excellence, **with fair branches,** that is, beautiful and thick of foliage, **and with a shadowing shroud,** with a thicket of branches which cast a solid shadow, **and of an high stature; and his top was among the thick boughs,** it reached up into the very clouds of the sky. V. 4. **The waters,** the fact that he grew in a well-watered spot, **made him great, the deep set him up on high with her rivers running round about his plants,** literally, "concerning the streams of the flood, she was going round about her planting," that is, about the place where the cedar was situated, **and sent out her little rivers,** the smaller irrigation streams, **unto all the trees of the field.** The Assyrian cedar thus received the first and full benefit of the stream's fertilizing strength, other trees being obliged to be satisfied with smaller canals. Assyria was blessed far above all nations in material prosperity of every kind. V. 5. **Therefore his height was exalted above all the trees of the field,** he excelled in luxuriousness of growth, **and his boughs were multiplied,** so that sturdy branches were sent out in all directions, **and his branches became long because of the multitude of waters when he shot forth,** on account of the abundant moisture which enabled him to send forth new branches in every direction. Assyria, enjoying an almost incomparable prosperity, was able to found colonies as well as to bring smaller kingdoms into subjection, and all these tributary states contributed to the empire's further greatness. V. 6. **All the fowls of heaven made their nests in his boughs, and under his branches did all the beasts of the field bring forth their young, and under his shadow dwelt all great nations,** that is, all the people of the nation and all the dependent states enjoyed a wonderful prosperity during the era of Assyria's greatness. V. 7. **Thus was he fair in his greatness,** on account of the greatness which had been given him, **in the length of his branches,** because the tributary states contributed so much to his stature and strength; **for his root was by great waters.** V. 8. **The cedars in the garden of God could not hide him,** could not outtop him, that is, all other nations and states of the world were outranked by Assyria in greatness and glory; **the fir-trees,** or cypresses, **were not like his boughs, and the chestnut-trees,** the plane-trees, noted for the thickness of their foliage, **were not like his branches, nor any tree in the garden of God,** in this case all the wide world, **was like unto him in his beauty.** V. 9. **I have made him fair by the multitude of his branches,** as described in detail above, **so that all the trees of Eden that were in the garden of God envied him,** he was an object of envy throughout the world. Although the description is confined to Assyria, the object of the message directed to Pharaoh of Egypt is apparent at once, namely, to serve as a warning from the Lord, the Giver of all earthly prosperity, who is able both to grant and to withhold what men prize most highly on earth.

THE LESSON OF ASSYRIA'S FALL. — V. 10. **Therefore, thus saith the Lord God,** here addressing the king of Assyria directly, although the object, bringing home the lesson to Pharaoh by means of the message, is unmistakable, **because thou hast lifted up thyself in height,** in blasphemous high-mindedness on account of a prosperity which was nothing but a gift from above, **and he,** the address here turning to the third person, **hath shot up his top among the thick boughs,** up into the very clouds, **and his heart is lifted up in his height,** in sinful and insulting pride, v. 11. **I have therefore delivered him into the hand of the mighty one of the heathen,** namely, Nebuchadnezzar of Babylon; **he shall surely deal with him,** literally, "he will do, do to him," or, in modern form, he will surely do away with him; **I have driven him out for his wickedness,** the Lord rejecting Assyria from before His face. V. 12. **And strangers,** foreign invaders, **the terrible of the nations,** the Chaldean soldiers, known for their fierceness, **have cut him off and have left him,** the picture of a tree that is felled being retained here; **upon the mountains and in all the valleys his branches are fallen,** all the tributary nations and provinces being lopped off, **and his boughs,** all the colonies and dependent cities, **are broken by all the rivers of the land,** as when a mighty tree, in falling down the mountainside, is shattered into little pieces; **and all the people of the earth,** formerly in dependence upon Assyria, **are gone down from his shadow and have left him.** V. 13. **Upon his ruin,** as he has fallen headlong, thus presenting the picture of a carcass, **shall all the fowls of the heaven remain, and all the beasts of the field shall be upon his branches,** the very ones that had formerly been under his dominion now turning to birds and beasts of prey in tearing the carcass to pieces, that is, in deriving life from Assyria's downfall, in building themselves up on its ruins: v. 14. **to the end,** with this final object in mind, **that none of all the trees by the waters exalt themselves for their height,** all other nations profiting by the example of Assyria, **neither shoot up their top among the thick boughs,** between the very clouds of the sky, **neither their trees stand up in their height,** in the same sinful pride, **all that drink water,** while they are deriving their strength from the Lord alone; **for they are all delivered unto death, to the nether parts of the earth,** to the underground kingdom of death, **in the midst of the children of men, with them that go down to the pit.** How foolish for the mighty of the earth to lift themselves up in sinful pride, when, after all, they are all weak and mortal men, entirely dependent upon the goodness of the God whose providence alone upholds them! V. 15. **Thus saith the Lord God,** in describing the impression which the fall of Assyria made upon other nations and making the application to the case of Pharaoh, **In the day when he went down to the grave,** when the Assyrian world-power was destroyed, **I caused a mourning,** men stopping for a time to consider the calamity in horror and grief; **I covered the deep for him,** literally, "I veiled, on his account, the flood," that which had given him his life-giving power, **and I restrained the floods thereof,** holding back the various streams spoken of in verse 4, **and the great waters were stayed; and I caused Lebanon to mourn for him,** literally, "to become dark over him, in mourning over the fall of the mighty cedar Assyria," **and all the trees of the field fainted for him.** On account of the overthrow of Assyria the entire world was drawn into suffering, so that all sources of wealth and power were cut off. V. 16. **I made the nations to shake at the sound of his fall,** foreseeing in his overthrow a similar calamity for themselves, **when I cast him down to hell with them that descend into the pit,** to the kingdom of death; **and all the trees of Eden, the choice and best of Lebanon,** spoken of in verses 8 and 9, **all that drink water, shall be comforted in the nether parts of the earth,** since mighty Assyria was obliged to share their fate in the realm of those destroyed from off the face of the earth. V. 17. **They also went down into hell with him,** sharing the fate of Assyria, **unto them that be slain with the sword; and they that were his arm,** his auxiliaries, or allies, **that dwelt under his shadow in the midst of the heathen,** depending upon his military power. In concluding this paragraph and chapter, the application is made to Pharaoh, who is here once more directly addressed. V. 18. **To whom art thou thus like in glory and in greatness among the trees of Eden?** among the various nations of the world, blessed by God, as they are, with many and great gifts of His goodness. **Yet shalt thou be brought down with the trees of Eden,** just as Assyria had been, **unto the nether parts of the earth; thou shalt lie in the midst of the uncircumcised,** the godless heathen, **with them that be slain by the sword.** Thus would the fate of Egypt be like that of Assyria. **This is Pharaoh and all his multitude,** so would it happen to him and all his people with their proud wealth and their boastful behavior, **saith the Lord God.** It is an easy matter for God to make an example and a spectacle of all His enemies.

CHAPTER 32.

Two Elegies over Egypt and Its King.

LAMENT OVER THE KING OF EGYPT. — V. 1. **And it came to pass in the twelfth year,** after the carrying away of Jehoiachin, **in the twelfth month, in the first day of the month, that the word of the Lord came unto me, saying,** v. 2. **Son of man,** a weak human being, and yet the mesenger of the almighty God, **take up a lamentation for Pharaoh, king of Egypt,** very likely Pharaoh-hophra, **and say unto him, Thou art like a young lion of the nations,** in his behavior over against them, in the terror which he inspired, **and thou art as a whale in the seas,** rather, a dragon or crocodile, an object of fear wherever he was known; **and thou camest forth with thy rivers,** as a mighty stream from its underground bed, **and troubledst the waters with thy feet,** deliberately dirtying it, **and fouledst their rivers.** Egypt had gone forth to vanquish and subdue other nations, taking away their independence and troubling them in various other ways. V. 3. **Thus saith the Lord God, I will therefore spread out My net over thee,** the invading armies being His instruments, **with a company of many people,** all associated in the work of carrying out the Lord's vengeance upon Pharaoh; **and they shall bring thee up in My net,** the picture being that of the capture of a crocodile. V. 4. **Then will I leave thee upon the land, I will cast thee forth upon the open field,** cp. chap. 29, 5, **and will cause all the fowls of the heaven,** scavengers and birds of prey, **to remain upon thee, and I will fill the beasts of the whole earth with thee,** the thought thus being the same as in chapter 31, 13. V. 5. **And I will lay thy flesh upon the mountains,** like a huge corpse in the process of decay, **and fill the valleys with thy height,** with great heaps of his followers, or in utter humiliation of his boundless pride. V. 6. **I will also water with thy blood,** in great streams of blood shed in the great slaughter, **the land wherein thou swimmest,** in which he had till now disported himself as he chose, **even to the mountains,** the entire lowland thus being filled with the outflowing of Pharaoh's strength; **and the rivers shall be full of thee.** Thus the destruction of Pharaoh was to bring death and destruction upon the entire land of Egypt, while other nations would derive benefit therefrom. V. 7. **And when I shall put thee out,** as when one extinguishes the light of a candle, **I will cover the heaven and make the stars thereof dark,** to express mourning and condolence; **I will cover the sun with a cloud, and the moon shall not give her light,** the underlying thought being that of the great Day of Judgment, for every judgment upon the nations of the world is a type and precursor of the Last Judgment. V. 8. **All the bright lights of heaven,** otherwise given as lights for men, and for the delight of their eyes, **will I make dark over thee,** on account of the judgment upon godless Egypt, **and set darkness upon thy land, saith the Lord God.** V. 9. **I will also vex the hearts of many people,** filling them with extreme fear and terror, their sympathy with fallen Egypt taking this form, **when I shall bring thy destruction among the nations,** when the information concerning the manner and extent of its destruction would be spread, **into the countries which thou hast not known,** as the tidings were carried by captive and dispersed Egyptians. V. 10. **Yea, I will make many people amazed at thee,** in horrified astonishment over the fall of Egypt, **and their kings shall be horribly afraid for thee,** literally, "shudder over thee shudderings," strong enough to make their hair stand on end, **when I shall brandish My sword before them,** swinging it back and forth before their faces in a menacing attitude; **and they shall tremble at every moment, every man for his own life,** fearing that the fate of Egypt would strike them next, **in the day of thy fall.** All this is now more specifically set forth. V. 11. **For thus saith the Lord God, The sword of the king of Babylon,** in this case in the service of the one almighty God, **shall come upon thee.** V. 12. **By the swords of the mighty will I cause thy multitude,** the inhabitants of Egypt with all their wealth and pomp, **to fall, the terrible of the nations,** the fierce and violent Chaldean soldiers, **all of them; and they shall spoil the pomp of Egypt,** that of which Egypt boasted in her pride, **and all the multitude thereof shall be destroyed,** all that had caused them to boast of their numbers and of their wealth. V. 13. **I will destroy also all the beasts thereof,** one of the chief sources of Egypt's wealth being the immense herds of cattle in the delta of the Nile, **from beside the great waters; neither shall the foot of man trouble them any more,** the depopulation being so great that it would happen but seldom that a man would touch the waters of any canal of the Nile, **nor the hoofs of beasts trouble them.** "Foreign dominion, inflicting mischief, causing man and beast to disappear, should bring to a stand the native pernicious rule of Pharaoh." V. 14. **Then will I make their waters deep,** causing the muddiness to sink to the bottom and the water to be clarified, **and cause their rivers to run like oil,** or "with oil," a strong figure to express the blessing of the Lord upon a nation, **saith the Lord God.** While Pharaoh had muddied and spoiled the waters of Egypt, the Lord, after the overthrow of the king, intended to clarify its waters once more and to impart to the land the riches of His blessings. The reference is undoubtedly to the living power of God's Word and Spirit, which could be given to Egypt only after its natural power was destroyed, after its boastful pride had been taken away. V. 15. **When I shall make the land of Egypt desolate,** by the destruction now threatened upon it, **and the country shall be destitute of that whereof it was full,** literally, "is wasted away from its fulness," **when I shall smite all them that dwell therein, then shall they know that I am the Lord,** thus gaining the knowledge which may be the beginning of a new life. V. 16. **This is the lamentation wherewith they shall lament her, the daughters of the nations,** who were usually the professional or principal mourners, **shall lament her; they shall lament for her, even for Egypt, and for all her multitude, saith the Lord God.** The punishments of the Lord, also in our days, have one chief purpose, namely, that of bringing men to the realization of His holiness and righteousness and of their own sin, for with this much done by way of preparing the heart in true repentance, the path is opened for the understanding of the grace and mercy of God in Christ Jesus, the Savior.

DIRGE OVER THE DESTRUCTION OF THE EGYPTIAN POWER. — V. 17. **It came to pass also in the twelfth year, in the fifteenth day of the month,** most likely of the twelfth month and therefore only fourteen days after the previous message of lamentation, **that the word of the Lord came unto me, saying,** v. 18. **Son of man, wail,** in a gloomy, sorrowful grave-song, **for the multitude of Egypt,** the inhabitants of the country with all their pomp, pride, and tumult, **and cast them down, even her, and the daughters of the famous nations,** the various glorious heathen peoples of former times, whose evil fate had already overtaken them, **unto the nether parts of the earth, with them that go down into the pit,** those who were even then in the realm of the dead. V. 19. **Whom dost thou,** namely, Egypt with its king, **pass in beauty?** Where was a heathen people lovelier or more excellent than Egypt? Yet the command here goes forth, **Go down and be thou laid with the uncircumcised,** to share the fate of other heathen nations; for Egypt, after all, could not demand a preference for itself and expect exemption when other great and glorious nations had been overthrown. V. 20. **They,** namely, Pharaoh and his tumultuous and boastful multitude, **shall fall in the midst of them that are slain by the sword,** pierced through in the same slaughter; **she is delivered to the sword,** as one upon whom sentence has been passed; **draw her and all her multitudes,** dragging them down to the realm of the underworld. V. 21. **The strong among the mighty,** the allies and associates of Pharaoh that have preceded him into the realm of the dead, **shall speak to him out of the midst of hell with them that help him,** for so certain is his overthrow; **they are gone down, they lie uncircumcised, slain by the sword,** so that he joins them with the other dead. V. 22. **Asshur is there and all her company,** having been overthrown some time before; **his graves are about him,** all holding their dead, **all of them slain, fallen by the sword,** v. 23. **whose graves are set in the sides of the pit,** according to the custom in the Orient of hollowing out the rock and laying the dead in niches thus hewn out, **and her company is round about her grave, all of them slain, fallen by the sword, which caused terror in the land of the living.** V. 24. **There is Elam,** whose territory lay in what is now Persia, adjoining that of Assyria, **and all her multitude round about her grave,** sharing the fate of Assyria in every particular, **all of them slain, fallen by the sword, which are gone down uncircum-**

cised, perishing in their godlessness, **into the nether parts of the earth, which caused their terror in the land of the living**, also known for the ruthlessness of their conduct over against others; **yet have they borne their shame with them that go down to the pit**, that is, they properly bear this disgrace of being overcome by death. V. 25. **They have set her**, the land of Elam, **a bed in the midst of the slain with all her multitude**, so that there is no question of her being entirely in the power of death and destruction; **her graves are round about him**, those destined to hold the slain of Elam; **all of them uncircumcised, slain by the sword; though their terror was caused in the land of the living**, rather, "because terror was spread before them," **yet have they borne their shame with them that go down to the pit**, properly being loaded down with this disgrace; **he is put in the midst of them that be slain.** V. 26. **There is Meshech**, most likely the Scythians north of the Black Sea, **Tubal**, a northern power, apparently between the Black and the Caspian Sea, **and all her multitude**, the people with all their wealth and tumult; **her graves are round about him**, as in the case of the other heathen powers; **all of them uncircumcised, slain by the sword; though they caused their terror in the land of the living**, they also spread fear before them wherever they went. Yet there is a difference between these nations and those mentioned before. V. 27. **And they shall not lie with the mighty that are fallen of the uncircumcised**, not even be accorded the honor which the other godless nations enjoyed, **which are gone down to hell with their weapons of war**, the burial with weapons being one of the ways in which soldiers fallen in battle were distinguished, **and they have laid their swords under their heads**, the survivors honoring their heroes in this manner; **but their iniquity shall be upon their bones**, namely, by their being obliged to bear the consequences of their guilt, **though they were the terror of the mighty in the land of the living**, so that even those who excelled by virtue of their fierceness were not excluded from the Lord's punishment, for all human accomplishments and excellencies cannot redeem from His wrath. V. 28. **Yea, thou**, namely, Meshech-Tubal, **shalt be broken in the midst of the uncircumcised**, sharing the fate of the godless in every way, **and shalt lie with them that are slain with the sword.** V. 29. **There is Edom**, or Idumea, the country south of the Dead Sea, extending to the Elanitic Gulf, **her kings and all her princes, which with their might**, in spite of all their courage and fearlessness, **are laid by them that were slain by the sword**, also included in the Lord's punishment upon all the godless nations; **they shall lie with the uncircumcised and with them that go down to the pit.** V. 30. **There be the princes of the North, all of them**, very likely all those of ancient Syria and its tributary states, **and all the Zidonians**, the people of Phenicia, **which are gone down with the slain; with their terror they are ashamed of their might**, that is, in spite of their fierce courage which inspired such abject terror in the hearts of their enemies, they have been brought to shame, covered with disgrace; **and they lie uncircumcised with them that be slain by the sword and bear their shame with them that go down to the pit.** V. 31. **Pharaoh**, when entering into the realm of the dead, **shall see them and shall be comforted over all his multitude**, deriving at least some measure of satisfaction over the fact that others, even before him, have had the same fate which now strikes him, **even Pharaoh and all his army slain by the sword, saith the Lord God.** V. 32. **For I have caused My terror in the land of the living**, that is, God permitted him to spread terror on earth, he was, in some instances, the scourge of the Lord; **and he**, having become guilty as set forth throughout these chapters, **shall be laid in the midst of the uncircumcised with them that are slain with the sword, even Pharaoh and all his multitude, saith the Lord God.** It is a somewhat fanciful picture which is drawn in this dirge, in having nations represented in this manner after they have entered into the kingdom of death, but the form is most effective in bringing out the just punishments of the Lord upon all godless people.

CHAPTER 33.

Ezekiel's Divine Mission Renewed and Confirmed.

THE PROPHET AS A WATCHMAN. — V. 1. **Again the word of the Lord came unto me, saying**, in a message which was directly and verbally inspired, v. 2. **Son of man, speak to the children of thy people**, once more turning to the members of his own nation, after having addressed various foreign nations in announcing to them the judgments of the Lord, **and say unto them, When I bring the sword upon a land**, in the punishment of war, **if the people of the land take a man of their coasts**, from their borders, a member of their own nation, **and set him for their watchman;** v. 3. **if, when he seeth the sword come upon the land**, as the invaders advanced to the attack, **he blow the trumpet,** in giving the alarm of their approach, **and warn the people,** for the signal did not merely serve for an announcement, but called upon the people and urged them to save themselves and their property, v. 4. **then, whosoever heareth the sound of the trumpet,** being aware of the signal and its meaning, **and taketh not warning,** refusing and neglecting to heed its admonition, **if the sword come and take him away, his blood shall be upon his own head,** the guilt would rest upon him alone, he would have no one but himself to blame. V. 5. **He heard the sound of the trumpet and took not warning; his blood shall be upon him.** The picture is taken from the sacrificial rites of the Jews, who transferred their own guilt to the head of animals used in sacrificing, by the laying on of hands with prayer. **But he that taketh warning shall deliver his soul,** or, "since, by taking warning, he would cause his life to escape." V. 6. **But if the watchman see the sword come,** as the host of invaders approaches, **and blow not the trumpet,** deliberately neglecting this solemn duty, **and the people be not warned,** since they relied upon his giving the signal: **if the sword come and take any person from among them, he is taken away in his iniquity,** being guilty of negligence in not maintaining constant watchfulness, as those surrounded by enemies ought to do, **but his blood will I require at the watchman's hand,** he would be held responsible for his neglect in warning the people who relied upon him. Note that the meaning of the picture is here already intimated. V. 7. **So thou, O son of man, I have set thee a watchman unto the house of Israel,** the Lord here applying the picture with the one change that the installation of the watchman is taken out of human hands; **therefore thou shalt hear the word at My mouth,** so that it is entirely and in every way a divine warning, not the prophet's own idea, **and warn them from Me,** for so the admonition must be understood. V. 8. **When I say unto the wicked, O wicked man, thou shalt surely die,** namely, in the absence of a true repentance, becoming subject to a certain death, the earnest of everlasting death; **if thou,** namely, the prophet, **dost not speak to warn the wicked from his way,** causing him to forsake his path of iniquity by announcing to him the Lord's warning, **that wicked man shall die in his iniquity,** for the failure to receive the warning would not take away his guilt, **but his blood will I require at thine hand,** thus making the prophet directly responsible, on account of his neglect, for the soul of the wicked. V. 9. **Nevertheless, if thou warn the wicked of his way to turn from it,** not to persist in his iniquity; **if he do not turn from his way,** refusing to give heed to admonition and warning, **he shall die in his iniquity, but thou hast delivered thy soul,** so that no blame could attach to him for the calamity which had befallen the wicked person. Cp. chap. 3, 17—19. V. 10. **Therefore, O thou son of man,** in agreement with the principles thus set forth, **speak unto the house of Israel, Thus ye speak,** in trying to find some excuse for the position in which they found themselves, **saying, If our transgressions and our sins be upon us and we pine away in them,** on account of the load which they represented, **how should we then live?** The penalty of their guilt stared them in the face on every hand, and so they saw only despair or a deliberate continuance in sin before their eyes. V. 11. **Say unto them, As I live, saith the Lord God,** than which there is no more solemn oath, **I have no pleasure in the death of the wicked,** much less is it His intention to have the wicked punished in this manner, **but that the wicked turn from his way and live,** that alone being His gracious purpose. **Turn ye, turn ye, from your evil ways; for why will ye die, O house of Israel?** Surely there can be no more emphatic way of declaring that God wants all men to be saved and to come to the knowledge of the truth. V. 12. **Therefore, thou son of man, say unto the children of thy people,** the Lord thus, in a way, disclaiming any relation with them as His own people in the very peculiar sense in which He had originally acknowledged them, **The righteousness of the righteous shall not deliver him in the day of his transgression,** that is, if he leaves his righteousness for a life of wickedness, his former good life will avail him nothing; **as for the wickedness of the wicked, he shall,** if he duly repents of his sins and lives a life in accordance with God's will, **not fall thereby in the day that he turneth from his wickedness,** since the Lord's forgiveness is of such a nature as to set aside all former guilt, so that it is no more remembered forever; **neither shall the righteous be able to live for his righteousness,** by virtue of the fact that he once was a righteous man, **in the day that he sinneth.** Every one who forsakes the path of righteousness and deliberately chooses the way of sin can no longer expect any consideration when he leaves the path of virtue. V. 13. **When I shall say to the righteous that he shall surely live,** as a reward of mercy in acknowledgment of a life of faith; **if he trust to his own righteousness,** in a false reliance upon his own sanctity of life, **and commit iniquity,** freely risking a transgression with the idea that it would not be charged to him, **all his righteousnesses shall not be remembered,** no longer being counted in his favor; **but for his iniquity that he hath committed, he shall die for it.** Cp. chap. 18, 24—28. V. 14. **Again, when I say unto the wicked,** in pronouncing the sentence of punishment upon him, **Thou shalt surely** die, temporal death being, in his case, the wages of sin and the earnest of eternal damnation; **if he turn from his sin and do that which is lawful and right,** thereby showing the sincerity of his repentance; v. 15. **if the wicked restore the pledge,** the reference being to a form of oppression by which the garment of the poor man was taken as a pledge, Ex. 22, 26, **give again that he hath robbed,** Ex. 22, 1—4, **walk in the statutes of life, without committing iniquity,** that is, follow strictly the commandments, the keeping of which had the promise of life, Lev. 18, 5: **he shall surely live, he shall not die,** for his works gave evidence of the sincerity of his repentance and of the reality of his faith. V. 16. **None of his sins that he hath committed shall be mentioned unto him,** for such is the nature of God's forgiveness; **he hath done that which is lawful and right; he shall surely live.** Cp. chap. 18, 22. V. 17. **Yet the children of thy people say,** as the Lord had complained once before, chap. 18, 25. 29, **The way of the Lord is not equal,** that is, not according to equity, they accused Him of not being fair in His dealings with them; **but as for them, their way is not equal,** it was He who had the right to bring this accusation. Therefore He repeats His guiding principle which He follows in dealing with them. V. 18. **When the righteous turneth from his righteousness and committeth iniquity, he shall even die thereby,** as a result of his deliberate wickedness. V. 19. **But if the wicked turn from his wickedness,** having been brought to the realization of the heinousness of his sins, **and do that which is lawful and right, he shall live thereby,** in possession of the forgiveness of the Lord and of His merciful gift of life. V. 20. **Yet ye say, The way of the Lord is not equal,** thereby heaping blasphemy upon the holiness and righteousness of the Lord. **O ye house of Israel, I will judge you every one after his ways,** thereby giving definite proof of the justice of all His dealings, also in His punishment upon blasphemers. It is the same method which the Lord follows in our days, as many a godless person has found out to his great sorrow.

THE RELATION OF THE PEOPLE TO EZEKIEL. — V. 21. **And it came to pass in the twelfth year of our captivity, in the tenth month, in the fifth day of the month,** that is, a year and a half after the capture of Jerusalem, since Ezekiel was living in a very remote part of Babylon, **that one that had escaped out of Jerusalem came unto me, saying, The city is smitten,** the appalling news of the overthrow of Jerusalem thus being brought to the prophet's attention in a most abrupt manner. V. 22. **Now, the hand of the Lord was upon me in the evening,** causing a kind of ecstasy to fall upon him, **afore he that was escaped came and had opened my mouth,** which had formerly been closed, **until he came to me in the morning,** that is, this opening happened during the night, before the arrival of the messenger; **and my mouth was opened, and I was no more dumb.** Cp. chap. 24, 26. 27. V. 23. **Then the word of the Lord came unto me, saying,** v. 24. **Son of man, they that inhabit those wastes of the land of Israel,** the few dwellers in the ruins of the cities of Israel, **speak, saying, Abraham was one, and he inherited the land; but we are many; the land is given us for inheritance.** Their argument was: If Abraham as an individual person received the land of Canaan for his possession, then surely the same God will not deny to us, the many rightful heirs of Abraham, the possession thus solemnly transmitted to him. V. 25. **Wherefore say unto them, Thus saith the Lord God, Ye eat with the blood,** that is, without letting the blood drain out on the ground, as the ordinance of the Lord prescribed, Lev. 3, 17, **and lift up your eyes toward your idols,** in gross idolatry, **and shed blood,** by freely committing deeds of violence; **and shall ye possess the land?** Did they think that the Lord would permit them to retain possession of the heritage of their fathers with such transgressions found in their midst? V. 26. **Ye stand upon your sword,** depending upon the forceful application of what they desired, **ye work abomination,** by committing base crimes without a show of regard for God's will, **and ye defile every one his neighbor's wife,** sins against the Sixth Commandment being unusually prevalent at that time; **and shall ye possess the land?** The rhetorical question places a double emphasis upon the Lord's horror at their transgressions and the demand of His holiness for the proper punishment of the transgressors. V. 27. **Say thou thus unto them, Thus saith the Lord God,** the God of the covenant, who is at the same time the Ruler of the universe, **As I live,** the most solemn oath which He is able to swear, **surely they that are in the wastes,** having sought refuge in the ruined cities and towns, **shall fall by the sword, and him that is in the open field will I give to the beasts to be devoured,** for the beasts of prey multiplied rapidly in the devastated country, **and they that be in the forts,** in mountain fastnesses, **and in the caves,** many of which, according to the account of Josephus, were inaccessible, **shall die of the pestilence,** unable to escape the punishment of the Lord. V. 28. **For I will lay the land most desolate,** making it an utter waste, Jer. 4, 27; 12, 11, **and the pomp of her strength,** upon which she depended and of which she boasted, **shall cease; and the mountains of Israel shall be desolate that none shall pass through,** all the regular routes of travel through the land being abandoned and only an occasional horde of nomads being seen. V. 29. **Then shall they know that I am the Lord,** this conviction being forced upon them in spite of all their efforts to deny His power, **when I have laid the land most desolate because of all their abominations which they have committed.** Note the force of the description in setting forth the continued state of desolation, on account of which some commentators think of the ruined state of the country, not only during the Exile, but also after the destruction of Jerusalem by the Romans. V. 30. **Also, thou son of man, the children of thy people,** namely, those among the exiles in Babylon, **still are talking against thee by the walls and in the doors of the houses,** both when they met in public and when they felt secure in the privacy of their own homes, **and speak one to another, every one to his brother,** with a show of interest which was far from proceeding from a willing obedience to the Lord's commands, **saying, Come, I pray you, and hear what is the word that cometh forth from the Lord.** Their sole motive was an obstinate curiosity, for they were not really concerned about keeping the will of the Lord; therefore Ezekiel was not to be deceived by this hollow mockery. V. 31. **And they come unto thee as the people cometh,** in an assembly or crowd, as students flock to a teacher, **and they sit before thee as My people,** pretending to be the people of the Lord, **and they hear thy words,** in a respectful attitude, apparently earnest and willing, **but they will not do them,** cp. Matt. 13, 20. 21; Jas. 1, 23. 24; **for with their mouth they show much love,** literally, "for the pleasant things in their mouth they are doing," that is, they follow after, and perform, only such things as please them for the time being, **but their heart goeth after their covetousness,** they have their minds set on advantages which they hope to get. V. 32. **And, lo, thou art unto them as a very lovely song of one that hath a pleasant voice,** like a singer who charms with the sound of his voice, **and can play well on an instrument,** in accompanying his singing; **for they hear thy words, but they do them not,** giving no heed to their import nor obeying their admonition. V. 33. **And when this cometh to pass,** namely, the prophecy concerning the desolation of the entire land of Israel, (**lo, it will come,** this emphatic declaration being inserted as a final warning,) **then shall they know that a prophet hath been among them,** that it was God's message which Ezekiel proclaimed to them. As in those days, thus, too, many people of modern times are still willing enough to listen to a good speaker and even praise his eloquence, but they are altogether unwilling to follow his words, to apply the lessons of God's Word in their own lives. It is a form of hypocrisy which is bound to bring God's punishment upon those who are guilty of such sham.

CHAPTER 34.

Concerning the Shepherds of Israel and the True Shepherd.

WOE UPON THE SHEPHERDS OF ISRAEL. — V. 1. **And the word of the Lord came unto me, saying,** v. 2. **Son of man, prophesy against the shepherds of Israel,** the spiritual leaders of the people, but especially their civil governors, the men responsible for their welfare, set to guard the interests and provide for the good of their subjects, **prophesy and say unto them,** in rebuking them for the selfishness with which they sought their own ends in all their dealings, **Thus saith the Lord God unto the shepherds, Woe be to the shepherds of Israel that do feed themselves!** looking out for their own interests only. **Should not the shepherds feed the flocks?** This emphasizes the reprehensible character of the shepherds' behavior, the fact that they do just the opposite of what is rightly expected of good magistrates. V. 3. **Ye eat the fat,** taking the best part for themselves, **and ye clothe you with the wool,** in the sense in which the term "fleecing the flock" is used even in our days, **ye kill them that are fed,** the most excellent of the flock; **but ye feed not the flock.** The action of the rulers was thus to be condemned as in every way opposed to the attitude which might justly be expected of men of their position. V. 4. **The diseased have ye not strengthened,** though they were weak with the effects of illness, **neither have ye healed that which was sick, neither have ye bound up that which was broken,** such as were crippled by the fracture of some member, **neither have ye brought again that which was driven away,** namely, by the harsh treatment accorded them, **neither have ye sought that which was lost; but with force and with cruelty have ye ruled them,** with acts of oppression like those suffered by their ancestors during the Egyptian bondage. Cp. Lev. 25, 43. The picture is that of a people living under the harsh treatment of severe taskmasters and driven away from their country by punishments inflicted upon rulers and people alike. V. 5. **And they were scattered because there is no shepherd,** none who really performed the true ruler's function in keeping his subjects together in peace and safety; **and they became meat to all the beasts of the field, when they were scattered,** the children of Israel being harassed and robbed by all the surrounding nations, even before they were taken away into exile. V. 6. **My sheep,** as the Lord still desired to regard and treat them, **wandered through all the mountains and upon every high hill,** as their captors scattered them throughout the nations of the world; **yea, My flock was scattered upon all the face of the earth, and none did search or seek after them,** no one being concerned about their welfare nor making any effort to find out about their condition. The rulers were, in short, altogether deficient in the sense of duty which should have characterized them in their relation to their people. V. 7. **Therefore, ye shepherds, hear the word of the Lord,** in His rebuke upon the unfaithfulness of these rulers, v. 8. **As I live, saith the Lord God,** the sovereign Ruler of the world, **surely because My flock became a prey, and My flock became meat to every beast of the field,** as a result of the shepherds' neglect, **because there was no shepherd,** none who really performed the work of a true shepherd, **neither did My shepherds,** men who purported to hold this position, **search for My flock, but the shepherds fed themselves,** concerned about their own welfare only, **and fed not My flock,** v. 9. **therefore, O ye shepherds, hear the word of the Lord,** the sentence pronounced upon them by the supreme Ruler: v. 10. **Thus saith the Lord God, Behold, I am against the shepherds,** sternly opposed to them, **and I will require My flock at their hand,** demanding an accounting from them, **and cause them to cease from feeding the flock,** take away their position of rulers by which they had enriched themselves; **neither shall the shepherds feed themselves any more,** their source of unjust revenue being taken from them; **for I will deliver My flock from their mouth that they may not be meat for them.** We have here a picture of the manner in which the Lord often delivers such as are His children from the injustice and robbery of men who exploit them in their own interest.

JEHOVAH AS ISRAEL'S TRUE SHEPHERD. — V. 11. **For thus saith the Lord God, Behold, I, even I, will both search My sheep and seek them out,** giving them the solicitous attention which their condition demanded and which their earthly rulers failed to give them. V. 12. **As a shepherd seeketh out his flock,** inspecting them with careful solicitude, **in the day that he is among his sheep that are scattered,** earnestly concerned about ways and means to bring them together again after a severe storm or after a raid by wild beasts, **so will I seek out My sheep,** going after them with His divine care, **and will deliver them out of all places where they have been scattered in the cloudy and dark day,** at the time when Judah was led away into captivity. V. 13. **And I will bring them out from the people,** from the nations into whose lands they had been deported, **and gather them from the countries, and will bring them to their own land, and feed them upon the mountains of Israel by the rivers,** in full abundance, **and in all the inhabited places of the country,** the land of Israel here representing the spiritual country of the Church of God. V. 14. **I will feed them in a good pasture,** Ps. 23, 2, **and upon the high mountains of Israel shall their fold be,** where the rich meadows of the uplands offered food in luscious abundance; **there shall they lie in a good fold,** in safe dwelling-places, **and in a fat pasture shall they feed upon the mountains of Israel,** where the Lord Himself provided the richest of food. V. 15. **I will feed My flock,** taking charge of this important function Himself, **and I will cause them to lie down, saith the Lord God,** so that they will be secure under His protection. V. 16. **I will,** by way of contrast to the selfish behavior of the false shepherds, **seek that which was lost, and bring again that which was driven away, and will bind up that which was broken,** crippled by some misfortune or accident, **and will strengthen that which was sick,** thereby faithfully discharging the several duties neglected by the rulers of Israel; **but I will destroy the fat and the strong,** the wealthy and mighty oppressors of the poor; **I will feed them with judgment,** with justice and equity instead of the arbitrary manner and cruel selfishness of the false shepherds. V. 17. **And as for you, O My flock, thus saith the Lord God,** in announcing His policy over against the entire nation, **Behold, I judge between cattle and cattle,** literally, "between sheep and sheep," or the small cattle, lamb and kids, **between the rams and the he-goats,** so that the fat sheep with the rams and he-goats would occupy a place for themselves, where the Lord could readily judge them. V. 18. **Seemeth it a small thing unto you to have eaten up the good pasture,** as the rich and powerful did in oppressing the poor, **but ye must tread down with your feet the residue of your pastures?** thereby preventing the poorer members of the nation from obtaining what the rich and mighty, for some cause or other, could not use at just that moment, **and to have drunk of the deep waters,** getting their fill, **but ye must foul the residue with your feet?** spoiling it so that others would have no benefit from its use. V. 19. **And as for My flock,** consisting of the poor, weak, and helpless, **they eat that which ye have trodden with your feet,** being compelled to be satisfied with the food discarded and spoiled by the mighty; **and they drink that which ye have fouled with your feet,** for want of anything cleaner. V. 20. **Therefore, thus saith the Lord God unto them, Behold, I, even I, will judge**

between the fat cattle and between the lean cattle, between the powerful with their presumption and pride and the weak and oppressed, who were practically at the mercy of the former. V. 21. **Because ye have thrust with side and with shoulder,** like cattle fighting their way to the trough or feeding-rack, **and pushed all the diseased with your horns till ye have scattered them abroad,** v. 22. **therefore will I save My flock,** delivering the poor and helpless from the power of the oppressors, **and they shall no more be a prey,** at the mercy of unscrupulous rulers, **and I will judge between cattle and cattle,** so that justice would be done. The Virgin Mary was right in saying that God hath put down the mighty from their seats and exalted them of low degree. Luke 1, 52.

THE MESSIAH AS THE TRUE SHEPHERD. — V. 23. **And I will set up one Shepherd over them, and He shall feed them,** a singular and preeminent one, the Messiah, who claims this honor for Himself, John 10, 14, **even My Servant David,** the king who was often named as the antitype of Jesus Christ; **He shall feed them, and He shall be their Shepherd,** the one truly fit to be the Ruler and Protector of His people. V. 24. **And I, the Lord, will be their God,** once more occupying this position over against them, **and My Servant David,** the great Son of David, **a Prince among them,** as a Ruler in the best sense of the word; **I, the Lord, have spoken it.** V. 25. **And I will make with them a covenant of peace,** namely, by virtue of the atonement of the Savior, Rom. 5, 1, **and will cause the evil beasts,** the various enemies who tried to hinder the course of the Gospel, **to cease out of the land; and they shall dwell safely in the wilderness,** secure in the very midst of the heathen world, as in the case of missionaries, **and sleep in the woods,** in places where they would ordinarily be in the greatest danger of their lives. V. 26. **And I will make them and the places round about My hill a blessing,** literally, "I give them [the people of God] and the environments of My hill as a blessing"; for this is the function of the Church of God in all its congregations, the visible exponents of the invisible communion of saints; **and I will cause the shower to come down in his season, there shall be showers of blessing,** namely, through the Gospel-message proclaimed in the Church. V. 27. **And the tree of the field shall yield her fruit, and the earth shall yield her increase,** the believers being rich in good works as the outgrowth of faith, **and they shall be safe in their land,** leading a quiet and peaceable life in all godliness and honesty, **and shall know that I am the Lord when I have broken the bands of their yoke,** that of their spiritual oppression as He broke the yoke of Egypt, Lev. 26, 13, **and delivered them out of the hand of those that served themselves of them,** the oppressors who exploited them, including the false teachers of all times. V. 28. **And they shall no more be a prey to the heathen,** to the enemies of God everywhere, **neither shall the beast of the land devour them,** said of the various dangers threatening the existence of the Lord's Church; **but they shall dwell safely,** in the security afforded by God's almighty hand, **and none shall make them afraid,** causing trepidation and terror within the Church. V. 29. **And I will raise up for them a plant of renown,** literally, "a plantation for a name," the expression evidently including both the Messiah Himself, as the Branch of the Lord, Is. 11, 1; Jer. 23, 6, and the Church founded by Him as a garden of the Lord, Is. 60, 21; 61, 3, **and they shall be no more consumed with hunger in the land,** namely, with the spiritual hunger which can be satisfied only with the Gospel of God's grace and mercy, **neither bear the shame of the heathen any more,** for the mockery of the enemies would finally cease. V. 30. **Thus shall they know that I, the Lord, their God, am with them, and that they, even the house of Israel,** those who are Israelites in truth, by faith in the one Redeemer, **are My people, saith the Lord God.** V. 31. **And ye My flock, the flock of My pasture,** who have derived all their spiritual food and strength from the Lord alone, **are men,** enrolled under His banner and standing up for the truth of His Gospel, **and I am your God, saith the Lord God.** This is the preliminary restoration of the Garden of Eden, in the Church of Christ here on earth, the full consummation and glory being reserved for the Church Triumphant.

CHAPTER 35.

The Judgment upon Edom.

AGAINST THE ENMITY OF EDOM. — V. 1. **Moreover, the word of the Lord came unto me, saying,** v. 2. **Son of man, set thy face against Mount Seir,** this mountain range with its valleys, extending southward from the Dead Sea, being the home of the descendants of Esau, or Edom, **and prophesy against it,** v. 3. **and say unto it, Thus saith the Lord God, Behold, O Mount Seir,** the entire country of Idumea, Gen. 36, 9, **I am against thee, and I will stretch out Mine hand against thee,** in an act of punishment, **and I will make thee most desolate,** literally, "desolation and desolation," that is, an utter waste. V. 4. **I will lay thy cities waste, so** that they would be heaps of ruins, **and thou shalt be desolate**, a dreary desert waste, **and thou shalt know**, by the evidence thus given, **that I am the Lord.** V. 5. **Because thou hast had a perpetual hatred**, a lasting enmity, even from the time of Esau, Gen. 25, 22 ff.; 27, 37, **and hast shed the blood of the children of Israel by the force of the sword in the time of their calamity**, literally, "and hast delivered the sons of Israel to the hands of the sword at the time of trouble," **in the time that their iniquity had an end**, literally, "at the time of the guilt of the end," namely, at the time of the Chaldean conquest of Judah, when the Edomites gave particular evidence of the fact that their hostility was as severe as ever: v. 6. **therefore, as I live, saith the Lord God, I will prepare thee unto blood**, so that Edom, as it were, would be dissolved in blood, **and blood shall pursue thee**, slaughter following after the inhabitants of Idumea, no matter where they would go; **sith** (since) **thou hast not hated blood**, had not been found shrinking back from bloodshed upon all occasions, **even blood shall pursue thee.** The measure which Edom had meted unto others would be meted to his own country. V. 7. **Thus will I make Mount Seir most desolate**, an utter waste and desert, **and cut off from it him that passeth out and him that returneth**, so that traffic would no longer be carried on, no caravans passing across the country from Southern Arabia to Egypt. V. 8. **And I will fill his mountains with his slain men**, in an act of slaughter which would wipe out the nation; **in thy hills and in thy valleys and in all thy rivers shall they fall that are slain with the sword**, the war consuming them without mercy. V. 9. **I will make thee perpetual desolations**, a permanent desert waste, **and thy cities shall not return**, not be restored to their former power and be inhabited again; **and ye shall know that I am the Lord.** Idumea lies prostrate and deserted to this day, a lasting memorial of the Lord's punitive anger when He carries out His judgments in righteousness.

AGAINST THE COVETOUSNESS OF EDOM. — V. 10. **Because thou hast said, These two nations and these two countries shall be mine**, namely, Israel and Judah, **and we will possess it**, although the inhabitants of Edom knew that Canaan was given for a possession to the children of Israel, **whereas the Lord was there**, Jehovah was the real Owner of the Land of Promise and held it in trust for His own children, v. 11. **therefore, as I live, saith the Lord God, I will even do according to thine anger**, rewarding it with the injury which it deserved, **and according to thine envy which thou hast used out of thy hatred against them**, for anger and envy grow out of hatred and show themselves in word and deed; **and I will make myself known among them when I have judged thee**, that is, by punishing Edom for his pride and the crimes of his hatred, the Lord would bear witness of Himself that He would not permit His people and their land to be attacked and devastated without taking revenge upon the enemies. V. 12. **And thou shalt know that I am the Lord, and that I have heard all thy blasphemies which thou hast spoken against the mountains of Israel**, for a mockery of the Lord's people amounted to blasphemy of the name of the Lord Himself, **saying, They are laid desolate, they are given us to consume.** The fact that the Lord chose to punish His people did not give the enemies the right to take advantage of Judah's plight and to put themselves in possession of their land. V. 13. **Thus with your mouth ye have boasted against Me**, magnifying themselves to the detriment of the Lord, **and have multiplied your words against Me**, in an excess of blasphemous exultation; **I have heard them.** V. 14. **Thus saith the Lord God, When the whole earth rejoiceth**, when all those who hear and heed the gracious call of Jehovah, men from the great majority of nations acknowledging Him as the one true God, **I will make thee desolate**, as the one exception in the midst of general rejoicing. V. 15. **As thou didst rejoice at the inheritance of the house of Israel because it was desolate**, in vindictive meanness over its downfall, **so will I do unto thee**, in executing the punishment of His vengeance upon them; **thou shalt be desolate, O Mount Seir, and all Idumea, even all of it; and they shall know that I am the Lord.** All those who are guilty of blasphemous mockery against the Lord may expect to share the fate of Edom, as it was here prophesied and as it later came to pass.

CHAPTER 36.

The Restoration of the Lord's People.

THE MOUNTAINS OF ISRAEL COMFORTED. — V. 1. **Also, thou son of man, prophesy unto the mountains of Israel**, here representing the entire country, as Mount Seir stood for Idumea in the foregoing section, **and say, Ye mountains of Israel**, formerly the places of idol worship and as such made prominent in this connection, **hear the word of the Lord:** v. 2. **Thus saith the Lord God, Because the enemy hath said against you**, Edom, as the representative of all God's foes, **Aha! even the ancient high places are ours in possession**, believing that they would surely be masters of the land if they held the places of worship, v. 3. **therefore prophesy and say,**

Thus saith the Lord God, Because they have made you desolate, all the enemies round about having combined to make the Land of Promise a desert waste, **and swallowed you up on every side,** literally, "panted after you," like a beast trying to reach its prey, snorting and snapping in its eagerness, **that ye might be a possession unto the residue of the heathen,** those remaining after their own countries had felt the devastating might of the conquerors, **and ye are taken up in the lips of talkers,** to be bandied about in blasphemous jest and slander, **and are an infamy of the people,** objects of calumny and derision, v. 4. **therefore, ye mountains of Israel, hear the word of the Lord God,** who is ever the Defender of His people, **Thus saith the Lord God to the mountains and to the hills, to the rivers,** or ravines, **and to the valleys, to the desolate wastes,** the ruins scattered throughout the country, **and to the cities that are forsaken,** as a result of the Chaldean conquest, **which became a prey and derision to the residue of the heathen that are round about,** the inanimate objects throughout the country being representative, with great emphasis, of the former inhabitants and of those who would dwell there in the future; v. 5. **therefore thus saith the Lord God, Surely in the fire of My jealousy,** burning with a jealous anger, **have I spoken against the residue of the heathen and against all Idumea,** which was particularly prominent in its covetous jealousy of Israel, chap. 35, 10—15, **which have appointed My land into their possession,** calmly claiming it for themselves, **with the joy of all their heart,** with vindictive gladness, **with despiteful minds, to cast it out for a prey,** emptying it of all its wealth and thereby making it a prey, or tossing it away like a morsel left for the beasts of the desert. V. 6. **Prophesy therefore concerning the land of Israel and say unto the mountains and to the hills, to the rivers,** or ravines, **and to the valleys, Thus saith the Lord God, Behold, I have spoken in My jealousy and in My fury,** in the fierce anger caused by His jealousy, **because ye have borne the shame of the heathen,** that which the heathen poured out upon Israel, v. 7. **therefore thus saith the Lord God, I have lifted up Mine hand,** in token of the solemn oath which He was swearing, **Surely the heathen that are about you, they shall bear their shame,** a perpetual load of disgrace, forever under the curse of Jehovah. V. 8. **But ye, O mountains of Israel, ye shall shoot forth your branches,** like a fruitful tree bringing forth leaves and bearing food in abundance, **and yield your fruit to My people of Israel,** Is. 56, 1; **for they are at hand to come,** that is, this maturing of fruit might be expected very soon. V. 9. **For, behold, I am for you,** the Lord still addressing the mountains of Israel, **and I will turn unto you, and ye shall be tilled and sown,** the return of the inhabitants thus being indicated, v. 10. **and I will multiply men upon you, all the house of Israel, even all of it,** that is, the entire spiritual people of the Lord, for the spiritual significance of the entire passage is obvious; **and the cities shall be inhabited,** after being forsaken for so many years, **and the wastes shall be builded,** the ruins once more being cleared away and houses erected in their stead, v. 11. **and I will multiply upon you man and beast,** the cultivated land thus being strongly populated, **and they shall increase and bring fruit,** both of them multiplying under the blessing of the Lord; **and I will settle you after your old estates,** not only in ancient times, but according to the ancient promises, **and will do better unto you than at your beginnings, and ye shall know that I am the Lord.** Although the description is entirely on the physical plane and the picture is that of Israel's glory, yet the context requires its application to the spiritual blessings of the Messianic period. V. 12. **Yea, I will cause men to walk upon you,** on the mountains of Israel, **even My people Israel,** the elect nation of the Lord in the fullest and highest sense of the term; **and they shall possess thee, and thou shalt be their inheritance,** whose blessings they should enjoy, **and thou shalt no more henceforth bereave them of men,** namely, on account of the fact that famine, pestilence, and war would be brought on by the apostasy of the inhabitants of the land. V. 13. **Thus saith the Lord God, Because they say unto you, Thou, land, devourest up men and hast bereaved thy nations,** literally, "A devourer of men art thou and hast made thy people childless," the land being personified as an unnatural mother and charged with the sins committed in it, with their consequences, v. 14. **therefore thou shalt devour men no more, neither bereave thy nations any more, saith the Lord God,** the explanation in this case being contained in the Hebrew term, which means to cause to stumble and fall. V. 15. **Neither will I cause men to hear in thee the shame of the heathen any more,** namely, the scorn which other nations heaped upon the Lord's people, **neither shalt thou bear the reproach of the people any more,** all the reasons for mockery on the part of the enemies being removed, **neither shalt thou cause thy nations,** the people inhabiting the land, **to fall any more, saith the Lord God.** This change is represented as having been brought about entirely by the Lord, and it is impossible to confine its consequences to the children of Israel according to the flesh, for the returned exiles continued under the rule of the heathen and were obliged to bear their scorn and mockery. The fulfilment of this prophecy is therefore properly to be found only in the establishment of the Messianic kingdom.

ISRAEL RESTORED FOR THE SAKE OF JEHOVAH'S NAME. — V. 16. **Moreover, the word of the Lord came unto me, saying,** v. 17. **Son of man, when the house of Israel dwelt in their own land,** before the time of the Babylonian captivity, **they defiled it by their own way,** their behavior, their manner of acting, **and by their doings,** the sinfulness of their works being brought out even in the terms used; **their way was before Me as the uncleanness of a removed woman,** the monthly purification of a woman by separation, Lev. 15. Cp. Is. 64, 5. V. 18. **Wherefore I poured My fury upon them,** in most severe punishments, **for the blood that they had shed upon the land,** in open bloodshed and murder, **and for their idols wherewith they had polluted it,** this shameless idolatry being the second reason why the Lord was obliged to visit His wrath upon Israel. V. 19. **And I scattered them among the heathen, and they were dispersed through the countries,** in the great Babylonian exile; **according to their way and according to their doings I judged them,** as they had deserved by their manifold transgressions. V. 20. **And when they entered unto the heathen whither they went,** when they were taken away into captivity, **they profaned My holy name,** by the open manner of sinning which was found in their midst, **when they,** namely, the heathen, **said to them, These are the people of the Lord and are gone forth out of His land.** The sinful behavior of the Jews in the various lands of their captivity caused the heathen who witnessed this behavior to blaspheme the name of Jehovah as being responsible for the trespasses. Cp. Rom. 2, 24. There is a great responsibility resting upon believers everywhere, that they make use of tact and care at all times, lest on their account the enemies of the Lord be made to mock the name of the one true God. V. 21. **But I had pity for Mine holy name,** He felt a pitiful concern for His holy name, because it was being so shamefully abused, **which the house of Israel had profaned among the heathen whither they went.** He felt that something must be done to restore the regard in which men had held His honor. V. 22. **Therefore say unto the house of Israel,** in explaining His divine pity and in announcing the application of His mercy in their case, **Thus saith the Lord God, I do not this for your sakes, O house of Israel, but for Mine holy name's sake,** whose honor was at stake on account of their sins, **which ye have profaned among the heathen whither ye went.** V. 23. **And I will sanctify My great name,** so that it would once more be kept holy, **which was profaned among the heathen,** as they heaped reproaches and mockery upon it, **which ye have profaned in the midst of them,** the Jews themselves being the reason why God felt obliged to vindicate His glory and to manifest Himself as holy; **and the heathen shall know that I am the Lord, saith the Lord God,** overcome by the evidence before their eyes, **when I shall be sanctified in you before their eyes,** when the Lord proves that He is holy and righteous and compels the admission of this fact on the part of the heathen. V. 24. **For I will take you from among the heathen and gather you out of all countries and will bring you into your own land,** this act of His power and holiness putting an effectual stop to the blasphemy and mockery in which the heathen had been indulging. V. 25. **Then will I sprinkle clean water upon you,** as in the rite prescribed by Jewish Law, Num. 19, 9—18, **and ye shall be clean; from all your filthiness and from all your idols will I cleanse you,** for their idolatry was a filthy stain upon the whole nation. This is a beautiful description of the forgiveness of sins, of the justification of sinners by the merciful and gracious act of God. V. 26. **A new heart also will I give you,** so that mind and will would be regenerated, **and a new spirit will I put within you,** so that their entire motives and principles of action would be changed in conformity with God's will, Ps. 51, 10; **and I will take away the stony heart out of your flesh,** the natural enmity against God, **and I will give you an heart of flesh,** one that will readily receive the impressions of God's Holy Spirit and be guided by His power in all good works. V. 27. **And I will put My Spirit within you,** for it is He who is the true power in regeneration, and conversion is in every way an act of the grace of God and not of man's reason and strength, **and cause you to walk in My statutes, and ye shall keep My judgments and do them.** It is clear, then, that not only the work of regeneration, but that of sanctification as well is an act of God performed upon the heart of man, that we are His workmanship, created in Christ Jesus unto good works, which God has prepared before, that we should walk in them, Eph. 2, 10. V. 28. **And ye shall dwell in the land that I gave to your fathers,** in the spiritual possessions which were promised to Abraham and his true children; **and ye shall be My people, and I will be your God,** the relation of Messianic times thus being announced. V. 29. **I will also save you from all your uncleannesses,** namely, those which are found even in the regenerated children of God; **and I will call for the corn and will increase it and lay no famine upon you,** the spiritual blessings of the Gospel being given to the believers in full measure, as Psalm 72 also states. V. 30. **And I will multiply the fruit of the tree,** that is, of all the trees in God's spiritual garden, **and the increase of the field,** of everything that grows in the tilled ground of His Church, **that ye shall receive no more reproach of famine among the heathen,** so that all reason for mockery on the part of the unbelievers would be removed as they saw the riches of God's blessings upon His people. V. 31. **Then shall ye remember your own evil ways and your doings that were not good,** for the mercy and grace of God, like His goodness, bring men to an ever greater realization of their unworthiness, **and shall loathe yourselves in your own sight for your iniquities and for your abominations.** That is ever the result of conversion, as we see also in the case of the Apostle Paul, 1 Tim. 1, 13—15. V. 32. **Not for your sakes do I this, saith the Lord God, be it known unto you,** for it is never anything in man which causes the Lord to extend to him His loving-kindness and tender mercies, to work faith in his heart; **be ashamed and confounded for your own ways, O house of Israel!** That is ever all that a repentant sinner sees on his side, namely, reasons to be ashamed, to hide his head on account of the disgrace of sins and transgressions. The salvation of a sinner is altogether and alone the work of our gracious Father in heaven, for the sake of Christ, the Redeemer. V. 33. **Thus saith the Lord God, In the day that I shall have cleansed you from all your iniquities,** at the time when the Messianic redemption would be a fact, **I will also cause you to dwell in the cities, and the wastes shall be builded,** the ruins once more repaired. This is evidently a reference to the gathering of the New Testament Church. V. 34. **And the desolate land shall be tilled, whereas it lay desolate in the sight of all that passed by,** the wasted lands of the Holy Land being a picture of the Lord's Church as it had been devastated by idolatry and other transgressions of His Law. V. 35. **And they shall say, This land that was desolate is become like the Garden of Eden,** a type of the most splendid beauty and glory on earth and a fine picture of the Lord's Church; **and the waste and desolate and ruined cities are become fenced and are inhabited,** so that their inhabitants are secure against all attacks of the enemies. Cp. Ps. 46. V. 36. **Then the heathen that are left round about you shall know that I, the Lord, build the ruined places,** making restitution wherever He chooses, while His punishment strikes down the heathen, **and plant that that was desolate,** as the history of His Church throughout the ages abundantly illustrates. **I, the Lord, have spoken it, and I will do it,** His determination being brought out with great emphasis. V. 37. **Thus saith the Lord God, I will yet for this,** with regard to the restoration of Israel, of His Church, **be enquired of by the house of Israel,** hearing their appeal with gracious willingness, **to do it for them; I will increase them with men like a flock,** known for the rapidity with which they multiply. V. 38. **As the holy flock,** literally, "as a flock of holy things," of animals intended for sacrifices on the festival days, cp. 2 Chron. 35, 7, **as the flock of Jerusalem in her solemn feasts,** which was always very large, as the ordinances pertaining to the festivals show, **so shall the waste cities be filled with flocks of men,** so would the Church of God be increased in numbers; **and they shall know that I am the Lord,** whose glory is established by every act of His merciful power at all times.

CHAPTER 37.

Further Evidences of Israel's Restoration.

THE VISION OF THE RESURRECTION. — V. 1. **The hand of the Lord was upon me and carried me out in the Spirit of the Lord,** in a state of ecstasy in which the prophet was inwardly transported from the things around him, **and set me down in the midst of the valley, which was full of bones,** one representing a huge grave, in which, however, the corpses had not been covered, v. 2. **and caused me to pass by them round about,** so that Ezekiel received a very close view of them, observed them most carefully; **and, behold, there were very many in the open valley,** not in heaps, but scattered over the ground, **and, lo, they were very dry,** bleached by long exposure to the elements, without sap and vitality. V. 3. **And He said unto me, Son of man, can these bones live?** Did it seem possible to human eyes that these dry bones would be restored to life again? **And I answered,** properly leaving the answer of the question to the Lord's almighty power, **O Lord God, Thou knowest.** With God nothing is impossible, and therefore the believers trust in Him to perform His mighty deeds at His own time. V. 4. **Again He said unto me, Prophesy upon these bones,** that is, over or concerning them, **and say unto them, O ye dry bones, hear the word of the Lord,** which is the bearer of life, the mediator of the salvation of Jehovah. V. 5. **Thus saith the Lord God unto these bones, Behold, I will cause breath to enter into you,** His creative divine power, as in the beginning, **and ye shall live;** v. 6. **and I will lay sinews upon you,** literally, "binding matter," for the tendons and sinews hold the bones together and serve as a foundation for the flesh, **and will bring up flesh upon you,** causing it to fill out the human forms, **and cover you with skin and put breath in you, and ye shall live,** cp.

Is. 26, 19; **and ye shall know that I am the Lord,** by this proof of His almighty power. V. 7. **So I prophesied as I was commanded,** without consulting with flesh and blood, simply at the command of the Lord; **and as I prophesied, there was a noise,** a voice, or sound, **and behold a shaking,** a louder rustling from the field of bones, **and the bones came together, bone to his bone,** those of the individual skeletons being assembled in their proper relation. V. 8. **And when I beheld, lo, the sinews and the flesh came up upon them, and the skin covered them above,** so that they were like corpses from which life had but recently fled; **but there was no breath in them,** there was no life in the members. V. 9. **Then said He unto me, Prophesy unto the wind,** announcing to it the command of the Lord, **prophesy, son of man, and say to the wind, Thus saith the Lord God,** the sovereign Ruler of the universe, **Come from the four winds, O breath,** the spirit or power of life, **and breathe upon these slain,** the victims of bloody warfare, **that they may live.** V. 10. **So I prophesied as He commanded me, and the breath came into them,** just as in the beginning of creation, Gen. 2; **and they lived and stood up upon their feet, an exceeding great army.** The vision, therefore, evidently does not concern the resurrection of the dead in general, but only a restoration of the Lord's people in the ideal sense. The Jews who returned from the four winds of the earth, in so far as they were believers, again formed the nucleus of the Church of God, which later included the believers from all over the world. V. 11. **Then He said unto me, Son of man, these bones are the whole house of Israel,** those who were properly included in the Lord's people, the spiritual Israel. **Behold, they say,** on account of the tribulations of the exile, **Our bones are dried, and our hope is lost; we are cut off for our parts,** they were undone. The condition of Israel was such that the believers in its midst felt that there was as little hope of restoration as there was a chance for marrowless bones to regain their vigor and to be surrounded once more with flesh and blood. V. 12. **Therefore prophesy and say unto them, Thus saith the Lord God, Behold, O My people, I will open your graves,** the countries in which they were, in a manner of speaking, buried, **and cause you to come up out of your graves and bring you into the land of Israel,** to the place where His people could once more enjoy the fulness of His spiritual blessings. V. 13. **And ye shall know that I am the Lord,** be established and strengthened in their conviction that Jehovah was truly the God of the covenant, **when I have opened your graves, O My people, and brought you up out of your graves,** v. 14. **and shall put My Spirit in you,** the breath of life with the power of the Holy Ghost, **and ye shall live, and I shall place you in your own land,** once more establishing them as His people; **then shall ye know that I, the Lord, have spoken it,** promised to do it, **and performed it, saith the Lord.** While this passage is not a direct proof-text teaching the resurrection of the dead, it furnishes a very vivid picture of the method in which God will call all men back to life on the Last Day.

THE SYMBOLICAL ACTION WITH THE STICKS. V. 15. **The word of the Lord came again unto me, saying,** v. 16. **Moreover, thou son of man, take thee one stick,** literally, "a wood," that is, a piece of wood or rod, probably in allusion to Num. 17, 2, **and write upon it, "For Judah,"** or "Judah's, pertaining to Judah," **"and for the children of Israel, his companions,"** the reference being to the members of the northern tribes who had joined their cause with that of Judah after the Assyrian conquest, 2 Chron. 30, 5—11. **Then take another stick and write upon it, "For Joseph, the stick of Ephraim,"** the most powerful tribe of the northern kingdom, **"and for all the house of Israel, his companions,"** all those who had adhered to the kingdom of Jeroboam till the end, v. 17. **and join them,** the two pieces, **one to another into one stick; and they shall become one in thine hand,** very likely by a miraculous act of God. The Lord did not explain the meaning of this symbolical action at once, His intention being to have the Jews consult the prophet about its significance. V. 18. **And when the children of thy people,** with whom the Lord, at this point, does not identify Himself, **shall speak unto thee, saying, Wilt thou not show us what thou meanest by these?** for the joining of the sticks would actually be performed before their eyes. V. 19. **Say unto them, Thus saith the Lord God, Behold, I will take the stick of Joseph,** as representing the northern kingdom, Gen. 48, 19; 1 Chron. 5, 1, **which is in the hand of Ephraim,** for Ephraim, though the younger, was given the leading position, **and the tribes of Israel, his fellows, and will put them with him, even with the stick of Judah, and make them one stick, and they shall be one in Mine hand.** In other words, the Lord intended to gather all those who still clung to Him in simple faith, or those who would accept Him in the same spirit, in the great Church of the New Testament. V. 20. **And the sticks whereon thou writest shall be in thine hand before their eyes,** to heighten the effect of the lesson to be conveyed. V. 21. **And say unto them, Thus saith the Lord God, Behold, I will take the children of Israel from among the heathen whither they be gone,** where they were held in captivity, **and will gather them on every side,** from all the nations round about, **and bring them into their own land,** v. 22. **and I will make them one nation,** united under the rule of the one great King, the Messiah, **in the land upon the mountains of Israel,** in the land of the Lord's heritage, **and one king shall be king to them all; and they shall be no more two nations, neither shall they be divided into two kingdoms any more at all;** v. 23. **neither shall they,** now that they have been brought to a full realization of their transgression, **defile themselves any more with their idols nor with their detestable things,** with any of the abominations which accompanied the practise of idolatry, **nor with any of their transgessions,** the many wicked acts which had caused the Lord to reject them from being His people; **but I will save them out of all their dwelling-places wherein they have sinned,** the scene of their idolatries and abominations, **and will cleanse them,** this statement including all the Gospel-promises; **so shall they be My people, and I will be their God,** their gracious Lord through the mediation of the Messiah. As often in the Old Testament, the restoration of Judah as the people of the Lord is typical of the gathering of Jehovah's children, of the believers, from all the nations of the world. V. 24. **And David, My Servant,** He who is both David's Son and David's Lord, **shall be King over them,** over His own spiritual Israel, assembled from Jews and Gentiles, **and they all shall have one Shepherd,** chap. 34, 23; **they shall also walk in My judgments and observe My statutes and do them,** making the will of God, as contained in His holy Word, their one guide and rule in all matters of doctrine and life. V. 25. **And they shall dwell in the land that I have given unto Jacob, My servant, wherein your fathers have dwelt,** the text looking forward to the true spiritual Canaan, of which the earthly was but a faint picture and symbol, cp. Heb. 11, 10; **and they shall dwell therein, even they and their children and their children's children, forever,** the land with the eternal foundations thus being clearly indicated; **and My Servant David shall be their Prince forever,** namely, Christ, the promised Messiah. V. 26. **Moreover, I will make a covenant of peace with them,** that based upon His grace through the redemption of the Savior, Rom. 5, 1; **it shall be an everlasting covenant with them,** not, like that of the Old Testament, of temporary duration; **and I will place them,** setting the Church in an established position, where it could not be assailed by the enemies, **and multiply them,** a great number of believers being gained through the Gospel proclamation, **and will set My sanctuary,** His true spiritual temple, erected in the hearts of all believers, **in the midst of them forevermore.** V. 27. **My tabernacle also shall be with them,** the dwelling-place of the Triune God, the abode of the Redeemer, John 14, 23, to be manifested later in glory, Rev. 21, 3; **yea, I will be their God, and they shall be My people,** a true communion of saints united in the fellowship of the heavenly Father. V. 28. **And the heathen shall know that I, the Lord, do sanctify Israel,** setting it apart as holy to Himself and abounding in holy works, **when My sanctuary shall be in the midst of them forevermore.** The prophet Ezekiel clearly has the same union and communion of the believers with God in mind which Jesus describes in such beautiful terms in the discourses held on the evening before His death. Cp. John 13 to 17.

CHAPTER 38.

The Destruction of Gog and His Host.

GOG PREPARES FOR WARFARE. — V. 1. **And the word of the Lord came unto me, saying,** v. 2. **Son of man, set thy face against Gog, the land of Magog,** names which originally designated the hosts of heathen tribes toward the north, in Scythia and the neighboring countries, but applying, in general, to all enemies of the Church of God, **the chief prince of Meshech and Tubal,** literally, "the ruler of Rosh, Meshech, and Tubal," countries in Asia Minor, south of the Black Sea, with fierce and warlike tribes, greatly feared by the inhabitants of Syria and Palestine, **and prophesy against him** v. 3. **and say, Thus saith the Lord God, Behold, I am against thee, O Gog, the chief prince of Meshech and Tubal,** rather, "the prince of Rosh, Meshech, and Tubal," v. 4. **and I will turn thee back,** causing him to return from the expedition whose magnitude is set forth in the entire paragraph, **and put hooks into thy jaws,** as men put wild beasts into chains and force them to follow their guidance, **and I will bring thee forth and all thine army, horses, and horsemen,** for these tribes were known for their cavalry, **all of them clothed with all sorts of armor,** perfectly equipped for every form of warfare, **even a great company with bucklers and shields,** as weapons of defense, **all of them handling swords,** as weapons of offense: v. 5. **Persia,** representing the far East, **Ethiopia,** representing the remote South, **and Libya with them,** standing for the enemies of the Southwest, along the northern coast of Africa, **all of them with shield and helmet,** fitted out for warfare against the Lord's people, v. 6. **Gomer,** the Celtic Cimmerians of the

North, and all his bands, the house of Togarmah of the north quarters, the Armenians of the Caucasus, and all his bands, and many people with thee. We have here a pictorial, symbolical grouping of nations as representatives of the heathen world, assembled against the Church of God. V. 7. **Be thou prepared,** so the Lord shouts in holy irony, in a challenge to the forces of darkness, **and prepare for thyself, thou and all thy company that are assembled unto thee, and be thou a guard unto them,** their ensign, their leader and guide. Cp. Is. 8, 9. 10. V. 8. **After many days thou shalt be visited,** sought out by the Lord for carrying out His judgment; **in the latter years thou shalt come into the land that is brought back from the sword,** delivered from warfare and destruction, **and is gathered out of many people,** brought back out of exile, **against the mountains of Israel, which have been always waste,** which were for a perpetual devastation; **but it is brought forth out of the nations, and they shall dwell safely, all of them.** This statement clearly points forward beyond the Babylonian exile and even beyond the destruction of Jerusalem by the Romans: the gathering of Israel is that of the Lord's spiritual children, and the hosts assembled against them are the enemies of the Church's latter days on earth, in whose very midst the believers will be safe and secure. V. 9. **Thou shalt ascend and come like a storm,** in an effort to wreck the ship of the Church; **thou shalt be like a cloud to cover the land,** with the multitude of hostile forces summoned together, **thou and all thy bands, and many people with thee.** It is truly a formidable army that is assembled with the avowed intention of destroying the Church of God, and it would be foolish for the believers to deceive themselves by a false security and by trusting in their own powers.

THE SENTENCE OF DESTRUCTION UPON GOG. V. 10. **Thus saith the Lord God, It shall also come to pass that at the same time shall things come into thy mind,** wicked counsels aganist the people of God, **and thou shalt think an evil thought,** proposing a plan to attack the children of the Lord in their apparently defenseless state, v. 11. **and thou shalt say, I will go up to the land of unwalled villages,** for the people of God seem to the enemies to be occupying dwelling-places that are not fortified; **I will go to them that are at rest,** quietly, seemingly without apprehending any danger, **that dwell safely,** as though secure from every enemy, **all of them dwelling without walls and having neither bars nor gates,** depending upon the fact that the Lord Himself is their Tower of defense, v. 12. **to take a spoil and to take a prey,** the Hebrew text, at this point, showing a fine play on words which emphasize the grasping nature of the enemies, **to turn thine hand upon the desolate places that are now inhabited,** the many congregations that would be assembled in Messianic times, **and upon the people that are gathered out of the nations,** the picture of the restoration being still employed, **which have gotten cattle and goods and dwell in the midst of the land,** literally, "upon the navel of the earth," in an elevated and fruitful country. V. 13. **Sheba,** or Arabia Felix, **and Dedan,** Arabian merchant tribes, **and the merchants of Tarshish,** of Tartessus in Spain, **with all the young lions therof,** the trading nations known for their covetousness, **shall say unto thee, Art thou come to take a spoil? Hast thou gathered thy company to take a prey? to carry away silver and gold, to take away cattle and goods, to take a great spoil?** That is what the enemies of the Lord constantly have in mind: to bring harm and destruction upon the congregations of the Lord's Church, to deprive them of the blessings which the Lord gave them. V. 14. **Therefore, son of man, prophesy and say unto Gog,** to the aggregation of all the enemies of the Lord and of His holy Church, **Thus saith the Lord God,** the supreme Ruler of the universe, **In that day when My people of Israel dwelleth safely, shalt thou not know it?** The enemies would indeed find out that the merchant nations had spoken truly, that the spiritual Israel was open to spoil and robbery. V. 15. **And thou shalt come from thy place out of the north parts, thou and many people with thee,** as described in the first part of the chapter, **all of them riding upon horses, a great company and a mighty army;** v. 16. **and thou shalt come up against My people of Israel,** in an attack intended to overthrow the power of the Church, **as a cloud to cover the land,** v. 9; **it shall be in the latter days,** in the Messianic era and in that particular period preceding the Last Judgment, **and I will bring thee against My land,** the Lord expressly permitting this attack upon His children, **that the heathen may know Me when I shall be sanctified in thee, O Gog, before their eyes,** for the judgment of the Lord in the overthrow of the enemies of His Church will reveal His almighty power to all men, as He also said to Pharaoh. Cp. Ex. 9, 16. V. 17. **Thus saith the Lord God, Art thou he of whom I have spoken in old time by My servants, the prophets of Israel, which prophesied in those days many years that I would bring thee against them?** It is a most emphatic way of affirming that the attack of the forces of unbelief was not unexpected, but was altogether in line with various statements of earlier prophets concerning the day of Jehovah's judgment upon the heathen. Cp. Joel 4, 2. 11 ff.; Is. 25, 5. 10 ff.; 26, 21; Jer. 30, 23—25. V. 18. **And it shall come to pass at the same time when Gog shall come against the** land of Israel, at the time of the last great apostasy, saith the **Lord God, that My fury shall come up in My face,** as in the heavy breathing of an angry person. V. 19. **For in My jealousy and in the fire of My wrath have I spoken, Surely in that day there shall be a great shaking,** a mighty quaking, **in the land of Israel,** wherever His spiritual children are living in the assembly of the saints, v. 20. **so that the fishes of the sea, and the fowls of the heaven, and the beasts of the field, and all creeping things that creep upon the earth, and all the men that are upon the face of the earth shall shake at My presence,** as He appears for His great Judgment, **and the mountains shall be thrown down, and the steep places,** the cliffs, **shall fall, and every wall shall fall to the ground,** everything that rose up in opposition to the Lord, v. 21. **And I will call for a sword against him throughout all My mountains, saith the Lord God,** so that the enemy would be overthrown in the Lord's specific domain, in the Church into which he has presumed to penetrate; **every man's sword shall be against his brother,** so that the enemies would really conquer themselves. V. 22. **And I will plead against him with pestilence,** the second great scourge of war, **and with blood,** the description in this verse being reminiscent of the plagues of Egypt; **and I will rain upon him and upon his bands and upon the many people that are with him, an overflowing rain,** as in a mighty cloudburst, sweeping everything before it, **and great hailstones, fire, and brimstone,** as in the destruction of Sodom and Gomorrah. V. 23. **Thus will I magnify Myself,** proving His greatness and His power, **and sanctify Myself,** for in the final analysis all this would redound to the glory of His holy name; **and I will be known in the eyes of many nations, and they shall know that I am the Lord.** While it is true that the enemies of the Church are mighty and terrible, it remains true, on the other hand, that the Lord of the Church is far mightier and will eventually overthrow all the hosts that try to break and hinder His gracious and good will on earth.

CHAPTER 39.

The Judgment upon Gog.

THE DESTRUCTION OF GOG AND HIS HOSTS. V. 1. **Therefore, thou son of man, prophesy against Gog,** in a further statement concerning the Lord's vengeance upon him, **and say, Thus saith the Lord God, Behold, I am against thee, O Gog, the chief prince of Meshech and Tubal,** rather, "the prince of Rosh, Meshech, and Tubal," chap. 38, 2. 3, v. 2. **and I will turn thee back,** leading him back from his projected attack on the children of the Lord, **and leave but the sixth part of thee,** literally, "lead thee about," or "drive thee on," **and will cause thee to come up from the north parts,** to the attack against the people of God which led to Gog's destruction, **and will bring thee upon the mountains of Israel,** apparently for a successful assault upon the Church of the Lord, an expectation, however, in which he would be sorely disappointed; v. 3. **and I will smite thy bow out of thy left hand,** which held the bow, while the right hand bent it, **and will cause thine arrows to fall out of thy right hand,** as they were fitted in place to be sent to their mark. V. 4. **Thou shalt fall upon the mountains of Israel,** in the very place where the enemy hoped to gain a victory, **thou and all thy bands,** the hosts which had joined him for the attack upon the Lord's people, **and the people that is with thee. I will give thee unto the ravenous birds of every sort,** the feathered or winged beasts of prey, from the great vultures down to the tiny parasite, **and to the beasts of the field to be devoured,** in a most ignominious death. V. 5. **Thou shalt fall upon the open field,** literally, "the face of the field"; **for I have spoken it, saith the Lord God,** who carries out His threats, like His promises, with unfailing accuracy and telling effect. V. 6. **And I will send a fire on Magog,** that of warfare and of divine destruction, **and among them that dwell carelessly,** in a self-confident, fancied security, **in the isles; and they shall know that I am the Lord.** V. 7. **So will I make My holy name known in the midst of My people Israel,** for the destruction of the enemies would be to the people of God a proof of His almighty power and would therefore serve to enhance the glory of His name; **and I will not let them pollute My holy name any more,** literally, "I will not permit the name of My holiness to be polluted any more," namely, by such blasphemous attacks on the part of the heathen, **and the heathen shall know that I am the Lord, the Holy One in Israel,** set apart for exclusive veneration on the part of all men, whether by willing reverence or by cringing deference. V. 8. **Behold, it is come, and it is done, saith the Lord God,** the fulfilment being assured with a definiteness of an accomplished fact; **this is the day whereof I have spoken,** the final overthrow of the enemy signifying the definite deliverance of the Lord's people. V. 9. **And they that dwell in the cities of Israel shall go forth,** the Lord's children taking a walk, as it were, to take a look at the fallen enemies, **and shall set on fire and burn the weapons**, the armor of the enemies, **both the shields and the bucklers**, the enemies' weapons of defense, **the bows and the arrows**, the weapons of offense, **and the handstaves**, which some commentators think were the riding-switches of the invaders, **and the spears, and they shall burn them with fire seven years**, this number being used as the holy number of the Bible, v. 10. **so that they shall take no wood out of the field, neither cut down any out of the forests**, that is, there was no need for them to get fuel in the usual way and from the usual places; **for they shall burn the weapons with fire**, this being sufficient for all their needs; **and they shall spoil those that spoiled them, and rob those that robbed them**, the wealth of the enemies, all the treasures in which they trusted, thus becoming the property of the children of God, **saith the Lord God.** V. 11. **And it shall come to pass in that day**, the time of the great Judgment at the latter end, **that I will give unto Gog a place there of graves in Israel**, where this arch-enemy could be buried, **the valley of the passengers on the east of the sea**, literally, "the valley of the passers-through," a place which was much frequented, the picture being that of a valley extending toward the Dead Sea; **and it shall stop the noses of the passengers**, literally, "it stops the passers-through," arresting their attention, almost compelling them to take notice of this instance of God's judgment; **and there shall they bury Gog and all his multitude**, the enemy fallen in the very sight of the Lord's city which he had intended to take by storm; **and they shall call it The Valley of Hamon-gog**, of the great multitude of Gog. V. 12. **And seven months shall the house of Israel be burying of them**, engaged in this task of disposing of the corpses of the enemies, **that they may cleanse the land**, for the presence of dead bodies polluted the land. V. 13. **Yea, all the people of the land shall bury them**, in willing zeal to cleanse the land of corruption; **and it shall be to them a renown**, it will give them a name before men, as being anxious to appear as a people consecrated to the Lord, **the day that I shall be glorified**, by the overthrow of the enemies, **saith the Lord God.** V. 14. **And they shall sever out men of continual employment**, delegating them for just this task, **passing through the land to bury with the passengers those that remain upon the face of the earth**, some of the men making the search for dead bodies and others attending to their burial, **to cleanse it**, so that the land would no longer be polluted; **after the end of seven months shall they search**, to complete the work begun by the entire multitude of people. V. 15. **And the passengers that pass through the land**, those delegated to search for dead bodies, **when any seeth a man's bone**, the skeleton of one of the slain enemies, **then shall he set up a sign by it**, a mark or guide-post of stone, **till the buriers have buried it in the Valley of Hamon-gog.** V. 16. **And also the name of the city shall be Hamonah**, that is, "great multitude," or "tumult." **Thus shall they cleanse the land.** All these descriptive details are added in order to bring out the complete defeat of the Lord's enemies in a most vivid manner. V. 17. **And, thou son of man, thus saith the Lord God, Speak unto every feathered fowl**, cp. v. 4, **and to every beast of the field**, the beasts of prey that follow armies on their campaigns, **Assemble yourselves and come; gather yourselves on every side to My sacrifice that I do sacrifice for you**, in slaughtering the enemies by this shameful defeat and overthrow, **even a great sacrifice upon the mountains of Israel**, the rapacious birds and beasts being invited to the gruesome sacrificial feast, **that ye may eat flesh and drink blood.** V. 18. **Ye shall eat the flesh of the mighty and drink the blood of the princes of the earth**, for it is in this class of people that the Lord's enemies are most numerous, **of rams, of lambs, and of goats**, literally, "great goats," or "he-goats," **of bullocks, all of them fatlings of Bashan**, this name being applied to the ungodly men of might because the province of Bashan, beyond Jordan, was famed for its fat and strong cattle. Cp. Ps. 22, 12. It is evident that the various animals named represent the various ranks among the hosts of the Lord's enemies, rulers, leaders of men, as well as common soldiers, those of a lower station in life. V. 19. **And ye shall eat fat till ye be full and drink blood till ye be drunken, of My sacrifice which I have sacrificed for you**, the sacrificial feast of God's fury prepared by the overthrow of His enemies. V. 20. **Thus ye shall be filled at My table with horses and chariots, with mighty men, and with all men of war, saith the Lord God.** No matter what means the enemies use in trying to overcome the Church of God, no matter what form their hostility takes, they are powerless before His almighty arm. The vividness of the presentation and the detailed manner of description serve to emphasize the complete overthrow of all those who presume to attack the City of God.

THE EFFECT OF GOD'S JUDGMENT. — V. 21. **And I will set My glory among the heathen**, by carrying out this judgment upon Gog, representative of all the hostile forces of the earth, **and all the heathen shall see My judgment that I have executed, and My hand that I have laid upon them**, they are bound to see the heavy hand of God's punishment, unable to deny His sovereign interference. V. 22. **So the house of Israel**, as a second result of the Lord's judgment upon the enemies of His spiritual Israel, **shall know that I am the Lord, their God, from that day and forward,** the interposition of the Lord in their interest strengthening their confidence in Him. V. 23. **And the heathen shall know that the house of Israel,** here chiefly representative of the Church of God in the Old Testament, **went into captivity for their iniquity,** not because the enemies, in their own power, overcame them; **because they trespassed against Me, therefore hid I My face from them,** withdrawing His merciful and almighty presence from them, **and gave them into the hand of their enemies,** so that their captivity at that time, and all the evils which befall them at any time, are the punishments of the Lord; **so fell they all by the sword.** V. 24. **According to their uncleanness,** that of their idolatry, of their rebellion against the God of the covenant, **and according to their transgressions,** the wickedness of their perfidious acts, **have I done unto them,** treating them as they deserved, **and hid My face from them.** It was not Israel's helplessness that delivered Israel into the hands of the enemies, but the judgment of God upon a disloyal people. The enemies, therefore, were not to take the credit for the present situation for themselves; for God had brought it about in order to carry out His plans regarding those who belonged to His people in truth. V. 25. **Therefore, thus saith the Lord God, Now will I bring again the captivity of Jacob,** in restoring His people from the calamity of the exile, **and have mercy upon the whole house of Israel,** to all those who truly were members of His own people, who in simple faith placed their confidence in Him, **and will be jealous for My holy name,** which, as a result of the misfortunes that had come upon His people, was in danger of being blasphemed, v. 26. **after that they have borne their shame and all their trespasses whereby they have trespassed against Me,** namely, by being thoroughly ashamed of their former unfaithfulness and idolatry, by loathing themselves for their perfidiousness, **when they dwelt safely in their land and none made them afraid.** Cp. chap. 16, 54. 61. That is the effect which the realization of God's unmerited goodness has upon the repentant sinner: it causes him to be all the more conscious of his own unworthiness. V. 27. **When I have brought them again from the people,** from the countries where they were living in exile, **and gathered them out of their enemies' lands, and am sanctified in them in the sight of many nations,** who would be bound to acknowledge the power of the one true God and yield Him the respect due Him, v. 28. **then shall they know that I am the Lord, their God,** the true Israelites once more accepting Him as the God of the covenant, as the God of their salvation, **which caused them to be led into captivity among the heathen,** namely, with the express intention of bringing them to a realization of their foolishness and of their helplessness when they forsook Him; **but I have gathered them unto their own land and have left none of them any more there.** This applies to all those who were Israelites in truth, not only to those who actually returned to Canaan and took an active part in establishing the true worship, but also to those who remained in foreign lands, but were believers in the true God; for the latter had free access to their native land and to the Temple at Jerusalem as their spiritual dwelling-place. V. 29. **Neither will I hide My face any more from them,** from those who are His children by faith in the Redeemer; **for I have poured out My Spirit upon the house of Israel, saith the Lord God.** It is the Spirit of God who works conversion in the Old Testament as well as in the New. Without His illumination no member of Israel could believe in the coming Messiah; and without His power no person at the present time can believe in the Redeemer. Cp. 2 Cor. 1, 23; Eph. 1, 14; Phil. 1, 6.

CHAPTER 40.

The Vision of the Temple-Building.

The remaining chapters of Ezekiel's prophecy give an ideal picture of the spiritual temple of the Lord, of His Church of the New Testament, of His glorious kingdom. It was a wonderful vision which was vouchsafed to the prophet, its beauty being enhanced by the descriptive details. As in the case of every parable, however, it would manifestly be a mistake to stress every point of the parallelism. The exposition, therefore, deals with the larger outlines of the picture only. The ideal temple as here pictured exhibits, under Old Testament forms, which are used as being familiar to the men whom Ezekiel was addressing, the essential character of the Church of Christ and of the worship of Messiah as it would be when He would exercise His rule among His own people, among the believers in every part of the earth.

THE WALLS AND THE OUTER GATES. — V. 1. **In the five and twentieth year of our captivity,** very likely the year 575 B. C., **in the beginning of the year,** which began in spring, in the month Abib, or Nisan, **in the tenth day of the month, in the fourteenth year after that the city was smitten,** that is, after it was taken by the Chaldean invaders, **in the selfsame day the hand of the Lord was upon me and brought me thither,** so that he was, in a state of ecstasy, transported to Jerusalem. V. 2. **In the visions of God,** in which his mind was entirely detached from his body, **brought He me into the land of Israel and set me upon a very high mountain,** figurative for the mountain of God's holiness, on which His Church is founded, **by which was as the frame of a city on the south,** the citylike building of the Temple which is described in the following sections, and which the prophet saw as coming from the north. V. 3. **And He brought me thither, and, behold, there was a man,** a heavenly being in the form and appearance of a man, **whose appearance was like the appearance of brass,** bright, shining, resplendent, as befitted this singular Angel of Jehovah, Rev. 1, 15, **with a line of flax in His hand,** used for the purpose of measuring the site, **and a measuring-reed,** more particularly for the masonry; **and He stood in the gate,** as though awaiting the newcomer. V. 4. **And the Man said unto me,** by virtue of His own authority, which is equal to that of God Himself, **Son of man, behold with thine eyes and hear with thine ears,** observing most carefully with all the senses, **and set thine heart,** in close attention, **upon all that I shall show thee; for to the intent that I might show them unto thee art thou brought hither.** It was the purpose of God that Ezekiel should see with his own eyes and take note of the explanation pertaining to every part of the building, so that his own statements concerning it might be accurate and sufficient. **Declare all that thou seest to the house of Israel,** to the men of all times who professed membership in the spiritual Israel. V. 5. **And behold a wall on the outside of the house round about,** enclosing the entire complex of buildings, **and in the Man's hand a measuring-reed of six cubits long by the cubit and an hand breadth,** or about one rod, the length of the measuring-rod thus being greater than the one usually employed; **so He measured the breadth of the building,** that of the masonwork of the wall, **one reed,** or rod, **and the height, one reed,** a very strong piece of masonry. V. 6. **Then came He,** apparently having started from the north gate, **unto the gate which looketh toward the east,** for that was the direction in which the Temple faced, **and went up the stairs thereof and measured the threshold of the gate,** of this main entrance, **which was one reed broad; and the other threshold of the gate, which was one reed broad,** rather, one rod broad, "even one threshold one rod broad," this point being emphasized for the sake of remembering it. V. 7. **And every little chamber,** the guard-room for the gate-watch, **was one reed long and one reed broad, and between the little chambers,** of which there seem to have been at least two, **were five cubits; and the threshold of the gate by the porch of the gate within,** where there was an entrance portico, **was one reed.** V. 8. **He measured also the porch of the gate within,** the pillared archway itself, **one reed.** V. 9. **Then measured He the porch of the gate,** the length of the portico, **eight cubits, and the posts thereof,** the pillars supporting its roof, **two cubits; and the porch of the gate was inward,** literally, "away from the house," serving as an approach to the Temple. V. 10. **And the little chambers of the gate eastward,** in addition to those flanking the entrance, **were three on this side and three on that side; they three were of one measure,** the same size as those mentioned in verse 7, **and the posts,** the pillars or half-columns supporting the pediments or the portico, **had one measure on this side and on that side.** V. 11. **And He measured the breadth of the entry of the gate,** the entire width of the eastern entrance, **ten cubits, and the length of the gate,** either the height or, more likely, the depth of the gateway, **thirteen cubits.** V. 12. **The space also,** literally, "the limit or boundary," apparently a low barrier wall, **before the little chambers,** where they flanked the entrance portico, **was one cubit on this side, and the space was one cubit on that side,** the barrier thus serving to keep those who entered in the center of the passage and preventing their crowding into the nichelike cells of the guard-rooms; **and the little chambers were six cubits on this side and six cubits on that side.** V. 13. **He measured then the gate,** the entire width of the gate-buildings or entrance porticoes, **from the roof of one little chamber to the roof of another,** the entire distance between the outside walls; **the breadth was five and twenty cubits, door against door,** literally, "opening against opening," that is, the measuring was done straight through the interior, the passage being ten cubits, the total depth of the guard-rooms twelve cubits, and the two outer walls, three cubits. V. 14. **He made also posts of threescore cubits,** that is, sixty cubits high, these being the gate-pillars, **even unto the post of the court round about the gate,** literally, "and at the pillar was the court round and round the gate," that is, the outer court of the Temple. V. 15. **And from the face of the gate of the entrance,** where the steps led up into the Temple, **unto the face of the porch of the inner gate,** which led to the Sanctuary proper, **were fifty cubits,** through the entire length of the entrance portico. V. 16. **And there were narrow windows to the little chambers,** small latticed openings for light, slanting inward from the outside of the wall, so as to offer as much light as possible, **and to their posts within the gate round about,** pillars projecting from the walls enclosing these windows, **and likewise to the arches,** or galleries; **and windows**

were round about inward, on the walls of the passage and in the cells, so that they could be seen, no matter which way a person turned; **and upon each post were palm-trees,** ornaments having the shape of palm-trees. V. 17. **Then brought He me into the outward court,** that before and around the outer pillars, **and, lo, there were chambers,** cells or small apartments, **and a pavement,** a floor of tesselated mosaic, **made for the court round about,** on the three open sides; **thirty chambers were upon the pavement,** thus enclosing the court on these three sides. V. 18. **And the pavement by the side of the gates,** it was constructed there, **over against the length of the gates,** exactly the length of the gates, **was the lower pavement,** thereby distinguished from the upper or inner court. V. 19. **Then He measured the breadth from the forefront of the lower gate,** from that of the lower pavement, or court, **unto the forefront of the inner court without,** that is, to the entrance of the inner court, as measured from outside, **an hundred cubits eastward and northward,** the same dimensions being true of the north side as of the east side. V. 20. **And the gate of the outward court that looked toward the north, He measured the length thereof and the breadth thereof,** just as He had done on the east entrance, the description of this section, therefore, being very brief. V. 21. **And the little chambers thereof,** the guard-rooms, **were three on this side and three on that side; and the posts,** or pillars, **thereof, and the arches thereof,** the galleries, or porticoes, **were after the measure of the first gate; the length thereof was fifty cubits,** measuring from the outer entrance, **and the breadth five and twenty cubits,** from outer wall to outer wall of the niches. V. 22. **And their windows and their arches and their palm-trees were after the measure of the gate that looketh toward the east, and they went up unto it by seven steps; and the arches thereof,** the porches, or pediments, **were before them,** projecting over against them. V. 23. **And the gate of the inner court was over against the gate toward the north and toward the east,** so that the gates of the outer and of the inner court were exactly in line with each other; **and He measured from gate to gate an hundred cubits.** V. 24. **After that He brought me toward the south,** the entrance portico of which is described just as briefly, **and behold a gate toward the south; and He measured the posts thereof and the arches thereof,** the pillars and the porches, **according to these measures,** their dimensions being identical with those of the other entrances. V. 25. **And there were windows in it and in the arches thereof round about, like those windows,** the same kind of latticed openings as on the east side; **the length was fifty cubits and the breadth five and twenty cubits.** V. 26. **And there were seven steps to go up to it, and the arches thereof were before them; and it had palm-trees, one on this side and another on that side, upon the posts thereof.** V. 27. **And there was a gate in the inner court toward the south; and He measured from gate to gate toward the south an hundred cubits.** The symmetry and beauty of this figurative Temple are but a faint picture of the greater perfection of the Lord's temple, of His Church.

THE INNER COURT WITH ITS GATES, CELLS, AND SACRIFICIAL TABLES. — V. 28. **And He brought me to the inner court by the south gate,** that is, through this gate, so that they were now within the holy court; **and He measured the south gate according to these measures,** those used for the other parts of the building, v. 29. **and the little chambers thereof,** the guard-rooms, **and the posts thereof and the arches thereof, according to these measures; and there were windows in it and in the arches thereof round about; it was fifty cubits long and five and twenty cubits broad.** V. 30. **And the arches round about,** the pediments, or galleries, **were five and twenty cubits long and five cubits broad.** V. 31. **And the arches thereof were toward the utter court,** the wall projections extending into the outer court, **and palm-trees were upon the posts thereof,** as ornaments sculptured in relief, **and the going up to it had eight steps,** for the inner court rose higher above the outer court than the latter did above the exterior. V. 32. **And He brought me,** as they continued their walk throughout the complex of Temple-buildings, **into the inner court toward the east; and He measured the gate according to these measures,** those employed in the other parts of the building. V. 33. **And the little chambers thereof and the posts thereof and the arches thereof were according to these measures; and there were windows therein and in the arches thereof round about; it was fifty cubits long and five and twenty cubits broad,** the same dimensions as the other approaches. V. 34. **And the arches thereof were toward the outward court; and palm-trees were upon the posts thereof on this side and on that side; and the going up to it had eight steps,** the symmetry of the entire structure thus being shown once more. V. 35. **And He brought me to the north gate and measured it according to these measures:** v. 36. **the little chambers thereof, the posts thereof, and the arches thereof, and the windows to it round about; the length was fifty cubits and the breadth five and twenty cubits.** V. 37. **And the posts thereof,** the pillars bearing the special pediments, **were toward the**

utter court; and palm-trees were upon the posts thereof on this side and on that side; and the going up to it had eight steps. V. 38. **And the chambers and the entries thereof were by the posts of the gates,** literally, "And a cell with its entry was at either pillar at the gates," or at pillars at the gates, for the cell seems to have had a door leading to each of the three interior gates, **where they washed the burnt offering,** a rite which, in the old Temple, had been performed in the Priests' Court only. V. 39. **And in the porch of the gate were two tables on this side and two tables on that side to slay thereon the burnt offering and the sin-offering and the trespass-offering,** that is, to cut up the carcasses of the slain animals according to the rules observed by the priests from olden times. V. 40. **And at the side without, as one goeth up to the entry of the north gate,** on the outside of the Temple-hall, **were two tables; and on the other side, which was at the porch of the gate,** against the wall of the left side, **were two tables.** V. 41. **Four tables were on this side and four tables on that side, by the side of the gate,** on either side of the approach to the inner hall; **eight tables whereupon they slew their sacrifices,** cutting them up according to the prescribed formulas. These tables were evidently of wood, as the next sentence indicates. V. 42. **And the four tables were of hewn stone for the burnt offering,** rather, "and four tables at the ascent," the stairway, "of hewn stone," **of a cubit and an half long and a cubit and an half broad and one cubit high,** apparently lower than the wooden tables, **whereupon also they laid the instruments wherewith they slew the burnt offering and the sacrifice,** the knives and cleavers which they used for dividing the carcasses. V. 43. **And within were hooks,** double staples or forked hooks, **an hand broad, fastened round about,** for the purpose of suspending the slain animals; **and upon the tables was the flesh of the offering,** placed upon them for the purpose indicated. V. 44. **And without the inner gate were the chambers of the singers in the inner court,** these two cells being immediately at the entrance of the court, **which was at the side of the north gate, and their prospect was toward the south,** that is, the one faced in that direction; **one at the side of the east gate having the prospect toward the north,** so that the two faced each other. V. 45. **And He said unto me, This chamber, whose prospect is toward the south, is for the priests, the keepers of the charge of the house,** that is, in charge of the Temple-buildings, superintendents of the entire Temple area. "That the singers are here so prominent is explained by the fact that in the state of exaltation of the community of God more ample material will be given them for new songs, so that in the worship of the new Temple the singing must play a chief part." (Hengstenberg.) V. 46. **And the chamber whose prospect is toward the north is for the priests, the keepers of the charge of the altar,** the superintendents of the sacrificial part of the Temple-worship; **these are the sons of Zadok among the sons of Levi,** for in this line the priesthood was to continue, 1 Kings 2, 35, **which come near to the Lord to minister unto Him,** and the priests were also active in the liturgical part of the Temple-worship. V. 47. **So He measured the court, an hundred cubits long and an hundred cubits broad, four-square, and the altar,** namely, that of burnt offering, **that was before the house,** out before the entrance of the Holy Place. V. 48. **And He brought me to the porch of the house,** the large portico which was before the Sanctuary proper, **and measured each post,** or pillar, of the porch, **five cubits on this side and five cubits on that side; and the breadth of the gate was three cubits on this side and three cubits on that side.** V. 49. **The length of the porch was twenty cubits and the breadth eleven cubits; and He brought me by the steps whereby they went up to it,** ten in number; **and there were pillars by the posts, one on this side and another on that side,** like the towers Jachin and Boaz in the Temple of Solomon. Cp. 1 Kings 7. The effort of some commentators to find exact parallels and to draw minute pictures of the new Temple according to this description are bound to be futile. It is evident throughout that an ideal structure is here pictured, one whose exact dimensions may be expounded only with a perfect understanding of the essence of the Church.

CHAPTER 41.

Dimensions, Parts, and Ornaments of the Temple.

THE SANCTUARY PROPER AND ITS SIDE BUILDING. — V. 1. **Afterward He brought me to the Temple,** literally, "to the palace," the inner edifice, "of the Temple," **and measured the posts,** evidently immense half-pillars, **six cubits broad on the one side and six cubits broad on the other side, which was the breadth of the tabernacle,** or, "the width of the tent was that." This reference indicates that the Old Testament sanctuaries, from the time of the first Tabernacle, were only types of the one great spiritual Temple of the Lord, of His holy Christian Church. V. 2. **And the breadth of the** door was ten cubits; and the sides, literally, "the shoulders," of the door were five cubits on the one side and five cubits on the other side, as measured on the inside of the building. And He measured the length thereof, forty cubits, and the breadth, twenty cubits, the inside dimensions thus being the same as those of Solomon's Temple. Cp. 1 Kings 6, 2. 17. V. 3. Then went He inward and measured the posts of the door, the wall-pillar of the entrance, two cubits, this evidently being the width of these pillars; and the door, six cubits, in height; and the breadth of the door, with its two leaves, seven cubits. V. 4. So He measured the length thereof, inside dimensions, twenty cubits, and the breadth, twenty cubits, before the Temple, in front, where the Temple appeared as a whole, as the palace of holiness. And He said unto me, This is the Most Holy Place, the dimensions again being the same as those of Solomon's Temple. Cp. 1 Kings 6, 20. V. 5. After, that is, afterwards, He measured the wall of the house, beginning with the pillars, six cubits, and the breadth of every side chamber, of the side building of the Temple, four cubits, round about the house on every side, on the east, north, and west sides. V. 6. And the side-chambers were three, an addition to the Temple in three stories, one over another and thirty in order, in each row or story, ninety all told; and they entered into the wall which was of the house for the side-chambers round about, so that their joists rested upon the wall of the Sanctuary proper, that they might have hold, resting upon this solid wall, but they had not hold in the wall of the house, they were not sunk into the masonry. V. 7. And there was an enlarging and a winding about still upward to the side chambers, literally, "And it became broader and was surrounded ever upward with reference to the side-chambers," for with every succeeding story the width of the Temple wall was reduced; for the winding about of the house went still upward round about the house, the depth of the cells increasing with each succeeding story; therefore the breadth of the house was still upward and so increased from the lowest chamber to the highest by the midst. We here supply from 1 Kings 6, 8 the winding stair, for which room was made by increasing the breadth of the side-building upwards, the stairway being on the interior. V. 8. I saw also the height of the house round about, the substructure, on which the foundations rested; the foundations of the side chambers were a full reed of six great cubits. V. 9. The thickness of the wall, which was for the side-chamber without, as high as the first story of this side-building, was five cubits; and that which was left was the place of the side-chambers that were within, or, "and five cubits the space that was left with regard to the house of the side-chambers," which was annexed to the house, apparently an open space between the building proper and the addition. V. 10. And between the chambers was the wideness of twenty cubits round about the house on every side, between the Temple-building and the cells along the wall of the inner court. V. 11. And the doors of the side-chambers were toward the place that was left, facing the open space, one door toward the north and another door toward the south; and the breadth of the place that was left was five cubits round about, on the north, east, and west sides. The entire arrangement was intended to facilitate the proper worship of the Lord.

A FURTHER DESCRIPTION OF THE TEMPLE. — V. 12. Now, the building that was before the separate place, literally, "the off-place," apparently a building where the refuse and offal of the Temple-worship were deposited, at the end, toward the west, was seventy cubits broad; and the wall was seventy cubits broad, for at the great festival seasons the amount of waste material was very great; and the wall of the building was five cubits thick round about, or of the same thickness as the wall farther toward the front, and the length thereof ninety cubits. V. 13. So He measured the house, an hundred cubits long, that is, the entire Temple edifice, and the separate place and the building, with the walls thereof, an hundred cubits long, so that there was a passage of ten cubits each on both the north and the south sides of the Temple-building; v. 14. also the breadth of the face of the house and of the separate place toward the east, another place for refuse, an hundred cubits. V. 15. And He measured the length of the building over against the separate place which was behind it, and the galleries thereof, evidently cloistered walks, on the one side and on the other side, an hundred cubits, with the inner temple and the porches of the court, the pediments projecting into the court; v. 16. the door-posts and the narrow windows and the galleries round about on their three stories, rather, "round about on all three," — over against the door, ceiled with wood round about, literally, "over against the threshold a boarding of wood round and round," and from the ground up to the windows, and the windows were covered, — v. 17. to that above the door, even unto the inner house, and without, and by all the wall round about within and without, by measure, all the dimensions were carefully worked out and observed in the building. V. 18. And it was made with cherubim and palm-trees, these serving as ornaments in the various parts of the structure, so that a palm-tree was between a cherub and a cherub, in artistic alternation; **and every cherub had two faces,** v. 19. **so that the face of a man,** the one face of a cherub, **was toward the palm-tree on the one side and the face of a young lion,** the other face of a cherub, **toward the palm-tree on the other side; it was made through all the house round about,** from the floor to the roof, wherever the open wall was visible. V. 20. **From the ground unto above the door were cherubim and palm-trees made and on the wall of the Temple.** V. 21. **The posts of the Temple were squared,** in agreement with Egyptian architecture, **and the face of the Sanctuary,** so that the door-posts with the threshold formed a square; **the appearance of the one as the appearance of the other,** "in the signature of the coming universality." V. 22. **The altar of wood,** the altar of incense in the Holy Place, **was three cubits high and the length thereof two cubits,** the plate of the altar being a square of this dimension; **and the corners thereof,** or, "and it had corners," namely, the horns, or projections, which characterized the Jewish altars, **and the length thereof and the walls thereof were of wood. And He said unto me, This is the table that is before the Lord,** the altar of the presence of Jehovah, immediately before the Ark of the Covenant which was just beyond the veil. V. 23. **And the Temple and the sanctuary had two doors.** V. 24. **And the doors had two leaves apiece, two turning leaves,** so that each leaf had two parts which could be opened and shut, **two leaves for the one door and two leaves for the other door.** V. 25. **And there were made on them, on the doors of the Temple, cherubim and palm-trees, like as were made upon the walls; and there were thick planks,** or "a wooden pediment," **upon the face of the porch without.** V. 26. **And there were narrow windows,** closed and latticed, **and palm-trees on the one side and on the other side, on the sides of the porch, and upon the side-chambers of the house, and thick planks,** heavy projecting portions of wood, probably like the open gables of old houses. Even insignificant details are not omitted in order to make the description of the Temple as complete as possible.

CHAPTER 42.

The Sacred Cells and the Outside Dimensions.

THE CELLS OF THE PRIESTS. — V. 1. **Then He brought me forth into the utter court,** the outer court of the Temple, **the way toward the north; and He brought me into the chamber,** a structure containing cells, **that was over against the separate place,** thus at least partly hiding this place, where refuse was stored, **and which was before the building toward the north.** V. 2. **Before the length,** that is, in front of the long side of this cell-building, **of an hundred cubits was the north door, and the breadth was fifty cubits,** v. 3. **over against the twenty cubits which were for the inner court,** this passage separating this cell-building from the main structure of the Temple; **and over against the pavement which was for the utter court,** which extended on the other side of this building, **was gallery against gallery in three stories,** or, "gallery ran before gallery in the third," so that the galleries of the two buildings were just opposite each other. V. 4. **And before the chambers was a walk of ten cubits' breadth inward,** extending from west to east, the long side, **a way of one cubit,** this denoting the narrow approach to the inner court, **and their doors toward the north.** V. 5. **Now, the upper chambers were shorter,** since the building became narrower as it rose in height, **for the galleries were higher than these,** they took away from the breadth, **than the lower and than the middlemost of the building.** V. 6. **For they were in three stories, but had not pillars as the pillars of the courts,** the third story and the second story did not rest upon pillars, **therefore the building was straitened more than the lowest and the middlemost from the ground,** by the width of the gallery in either story. V. 7. **And the wall that was without,** the enclosure, **over against the chambers,** serving as a dividing-wall or boundary-fence, **toward the utter court on the forepart of the chambers, the length thereof was fifty cubits.** This wall concealed, in a measure, the things that were carried on in certain parts of this building. V. 8. **For the length of the chambers that were in the utter court was fifty cubits; and, lo, before the Temple were an hundred cubits.** V. 9. **And from under these chambers was the entry on the east side,** rather, "and from under it," that is, the dividing-wall, "were these chambers," for, since their lower part was hidden by the boundary-wall, it might seem to one coming from the east that they arose out of this wall, **as one goeth into them from the utter court,** literally, "the entrance was from the east in coming to them from the outer court." The purpose of the wall on this side was probably to hide the priests from the gaze of the curious, especially when they changed their garments. V. 10. **The chambers were in the thickness of the wall of the court toward the east,** resting on the wall which separated the outer court from the inner, **over against the sepa-**

rate place and over against the building, the meaning being the same as in front of the length of a hundred cubits in verse 2. V. 11. **And the way before them was like the appearance of the chambers which were toward the north, as long as they and as broad as they,** they agreed exactly in architecture and arrangement with this section of the Temple-buildings on the north; **and all their goings out,** their various entrances, **were both according to their fashions and according to their doors.** The meaning is that the cells on the south side of the building agreed in appearance with those on the north side, in length, in width, in the location of the portals, and in the arrangement, both outward and inward. V. 12. **And according to the doors of the chambers that were toward the south was a door in the head of the way,** literally, "And like their doors," namely, those of the cells toward the north, "so were also the doors of the cells toward the south: an opening was at the head of the way," where the passages connecting the cell-buildings came together, **even the way directly before the wall toward the east, as one entereth into them,** as one approached the cells. V. 13. **Then said He unto me, The north chambers and the south chambers,** the cells as just described, **which are before the separate place,** since they ran along in front of the long side, **they be holy chambers,** set apart for a most exclusive use, **where the priests that approach unto the Lord shall eat the most holy things,** the so-called priests' portions; **there shall they lay the most holy things,** setting them aside for later use, **and the meat-offering and the sin-offering and the trespass-offering; for the place is holy.** Cp. Lev. 2, 3. 10; 6, 9—20; 7, 6; 10, 12. "Because neither the meal, mingled with oil, of the meat-offering nor the flesh of the sin- and guilt-offerings could be eaten by the priests immediately after the presentation of the offering, but first the one had to be baked and the other cooked; they were, until this preparation, allowed to be set aside, but not in any place one pleased." V. 14. **When the priests enter therein,** after performing the functions of their office, **then shall they not go out of the Holy Place into the utter court,** where they might come into contact with some unclean thing; **but there they shall lay their garments wherein they minister, for they are holy,** the cells thus serving also as vestries; **and shall put on other garments and shall approach to those things which are for the people.** Just as the priests were here instructed to keep themselves strictly uncontaminated in the performance of their duties, so Christians will ever keep themselves unspotted from the world and from the deeds of the flesh.

THE OUTSIDE MEASUREMENTS.—V. 15. **Now, when He had made an end of measuring the inner house,** the Temple-buildings proper, **He brought me forth toward the gate whose prospect is toward the east and measured it round about,** the outer circumference of all that was comprised within the Sanctuary area. V. 16. **He measured the east side with the measuring-reed, five hundred reeds, with the measuring-reed round about.** V. 17. **He measured the north side, five hundred reeds, with the measuring-reed round about.** V. 18. **He measured the south side, five hundred reeds, with the measuring-reed.** V. 19. **He turned about to the west side and measured five hundred reeds with the measuring-reed.** The dimensions of the Temple proper were thus five hundred cubits square, but the entire area in which the Temple was situated was five hundred rods square. V. 20. **He measured it by the four sides; it had a wall round about, five hundred reeds long and five hundred broad, to make a separation between the Sanctuary and the profane place,** so that the separation would be clearly observed, not between Jew and Gentile, but between sacred and profane. The vast extent of the area of this singular Temple is a feature which clearly marks its ideal character. "It symbolizes the great enlargement of the kingdom of God, when Jehovah-Messiah shall reign to the ends of the earth."

CHAPTER 43.

The Lord in His New Temple.

THE ENTRANCE OF JEHOVAH'S GLORY.—V. 1. **Afterward He brought me to the gate, even the gate that looketh toward the east,** the main entrance of the Temple, v. 2. **and, behold, the glory of the God of Israel came from the way of the east,** to make the Temple of the New Testament, the glorious structure of His Church, the dwelling of His merciful presence; **and His voice was like a noise of many waters,** that associated also with other manifestations of the Lord's glory, cp. chap. 1, 24; Rev. 1, 15; 14, 2; **and the earth shined with His glory,** with the reflection of the Shechinah, the wonderful cloud of the presence of Jehovah in the Old Testament, that which was also seen at the transfiguration of the Lord, Matt. 17, 5. V. 3. **And it was according to the appearance of the vision which I saw,** chap. 1, 4. 28, **even according to the vision that I saw when I came to destroy the city,** at the time when he was given the prophecy concerning the fall of the city, in the first chapters of his book; **and the visions were like the vision that I saw by the river Chebar,** chap. 3, 23. **And I fell upon my face,** overcome by the glory of a manifestation which sinful men cannot behold without quaking. V. 4. **And the glory of the Lord came into the house by the way of the gate whose prospect is toward the east,** the majesty of God appearing in the fulness of His grace, to enter into the portal of His everlasting Temple. Cp. Ps. 24, 7—10. V. 5. **So the Spirit,** cp. chap. 3, 12. 23; 10, 15, **took me up and brought me into the inner court,** while the prophet was in this state of ecstasy; **and, behold, the glory of the Lord filled the house,** as it did at the dedication of Solomon's Temple, 1 Kings 8, 10. 11. V. 6. **And I heard Him speaking unto me out of the house,** out of the Sanctuary, where Jehovah at once established His throne; **and the Man stood by me.** Note that a distinction is made between the person of Him speaking on the inside of the Temple and Him who stood beside Ezekiel; and yet their identity is clear from the following. V. 7. **And He said unto me, Son of man, the place of My throne and the place of the soles of My feet,** their permanent resting-place, **where I will dwell in the midst of the children of Israel forever,** as the King of His people, **and My holy name shall the house of Israel no more defile, neither they nor their kings, by their whoredom,** by the spiritual adultery of their idolatry, **nor by the carcasses of their kings in their high places,** the latter referring to their idols as having had lordship over Israel in past times. What the Man says identifies Him entirely with Jehovah; His speech legitimates itself as the Word of Jehovah; He is the Word of God which was with God from the beginning. Cp. John 1. V. 8. **In their setting of their threshold by My thresholds and their post by My posts,** as when Manasseh built altars in the courts of the Temple to the host of heaven, 2 Kings 21, 5, **and the wall between Me and them,** or, "with only the wall between Me and them," **they have even defiled My holy name by their abominations that they have committed,** as was so abundantly set forth by the various prophets before the Exile; **wherefore I have consumed them in Mine anger.** V. 9. **Now let them,** all those who wish to be members of the spiritual Israel, **put away their whoredom,** their idolatry in every form, **and the carcasses of their kings,** of their dead idols, **far from Me, and I will dwell in the midst of them forever,** in the everlasting manifestation of His grace and mercy in Christ Jesus, the Redeemer. V. 10. **Thou son of man, show the house,** this new wonderful structure of the Messianic Temple, **to the house of Israel that they may be ashamed of their iniquities,** for the realization of the unmerited greatness of God's goodness and mercy awakens a feeling of shame and repentance; **and let them measure the pattern,** the harmony of proportion shown in this marvelous edifice, so that they would understand what the Lord is offering through His Church. With the picture of its perfection before their eyes always, Eph. 5, 26. 27, they would have the strongest incentive to keep themselves in the way of holiness. V. 11. **And if they be ashamed of all that they have done, show them the form of the house,** as it appeared to the beholder in its entirety, **and the fashion thereof,** its arrangement, **and the goings out thereof, and the comings in thereof,** the various ascents and stairways, **and all the forms thereof,** the individual sections, **and all the ordinances thereof, and all the forms thereof, and all the laws thereof,** everything pertaining to all its parts; **and write it in their sight that they may keep the whole form thereof and all the ordinances thereof and do them.** V. 12. **This is the law of the house: Upon the top of the mountain,** on which this wonderful structure is supposed to have been built, **the whole limit thereof round about shall be most holy,** preserved from all acts of idolatry and every profaning influence. **Behold, this is the law of the house.** In the New Testament the entire edifice of God's Church is altogether holy, not having a spot, or wrinkle, or any such thing, but altogether holy and without blemish. Cp. Eph. 5, 27.

DESCRIPTION AND DEDICATION OF THE ALTAR OF BURNT OFFERING. — V. 13. **And these are the measures of the altar after the cubits (the cubit is a cubit and an hand-breadth,** the so-called sacred cubit); **even the bottom,** literally, "the bosom," probably a paneled recess in the side of the altar, **shall be a cubit and the breadth a cubit, and the border thereof by the edge thereof round about shall be a span,** that is, the molding, or ornamental border, enclosing such a panel; **and this shall be the higher place of the altar,** or its elevation. V. 14. **And from the bottom,** literally, "the bosom," **upon the ground even to the lower settle,** the rest, or projection, running round about the altar, **shall be two cubits and the breadth one cubit; and from the lesser settle,** near the bottom, **even to the greater settle,** the second projection, or ornamental rest, **shall be four cubits and the breadth one cubit.** The altar was thus built in successive units, or cubes, each one set off with a molding. V. 15. **So the altar,** according to the Hebrew, the mountain of God, the altar proper, with its plate, as it were the sanctuary upon a high mountain, **shall be four cubits, and from the altar and upward,** on the four corners of its plate, as on the altars of Solomon's Temple, **shall be four horns.** V. 16. **And the altar shall be twelve cubits long, twelve broad, square in the four squares** thereof, so that its plate had an area of 144 square cubits. V. 17. **And the settle,** the lower ledge, **shall be fourteen cubits long and fourteen broad in the four squares thereof,** the extra cubits being added on account of the depth of the panel; **and the border about it shall be half a cubit,** the span spoken of in verse 13; **and the bottom thereof shall be a cubit about; and his stairs shall look toward the east,** that is, the ascent for the officiating priests faced the east. The altar of burnt offering is so minutely described because under the Old Dispensation it was the place where the ordinary worship centered, where the believing Israelites drew near to God, where their relation to Him, disturbed by the fact of their trespasses, was once more restored. V. 18. **And He said unto me, Son of man, Thus saith the Lord God,** the sovereign Ruler of the universe, **These are the ordinances of the altar,** the regulations concerning its service, **in the day when they shall make it, to offer burnt offerings thereon and to sprinkle blood thereon,** in the act of atonement combined with that of consecration to Jehovah. V. 19. **And thou shalt give to the priests, the Levites,** the descendants of Levi, **that be of the seed of Zadok,** of this line of the family, the other line having been discontinued since the time of Solomon, 1 Kings 2, 26. 27, **which approach unto Me to minister unto Me, saith the Lord God, a young bullock for a sin-offering.** Cp. Lev. 4, 3 ff. V. 20. **And thou shalt take of the blood thereof and put it on the four horns of it,** according to the ancient ritual, **and on the four corners of the settle,** of the ledge below, **and upon the border round about; thus shalt thou cleanse and purge it,** this purification and expiation of the altar being symbolical of the complete sanctification of the people. V. 21. **Thou shalt take the bullock also of the sin-offering,** Ex. 29, 10; Lev. 8, 14, **and he shall burn it,** rather, impersonal, "one shall burn it," **in the appointed place of the house, without the Sanctuary.** Cp. Ex. 29, 14. V. 22. **And on the second day thou shalt offer a kid of the goats without blemish,** this being a prime requisite in all sacrificial animals, **for a sin-offering; and they shall cleanse the altar,** namely, the priests engaged in this work, **as they did cleanse it with the bullock,** the offering of expiation thus being a daily occurrence. V. 23. **When thou hast made an end of cleansing it,** of purifying the altar by these rites, **thou shalt offer a young bullock without blemish and a ram out of the flock without blemish,** for atonement and consecration. V. 24. **And thou shalt offer them before the Lord,** in whose worship they were brought, **and the priests shall cast salt upon them,** as required by the ordinance, Lev. 2, 13, **and they shall offer them up for a burnt offering unto the Lord,** again to make propitiation for the sins of the people. V. 25. **Seven days shalt thou prepare every day a goat for a sin-offering,** Ex. 29, 35; Lev. 8, 33; **they shall also prepare a young bullock and a ram out of the flock without blemish.** V. 26. **Seven days shall they purge the altar and purify it,** by means of these sacrifices; **and they shall consecrate themselves,** literally, "fill their hands," namely, with offerings to the Lord, as when the priests of old were inducted into office. Cp. Ex. 29, 24. 35. V. 27. **And when these days are expired, it shall be that upon the eighth day, and so forward, the priests shall make your burnt offerings upon the altar and your peace-offerings,** or thank-offerings, in the regular work of their calling; **and I will accept you, saith the Lord God.** While this passage is clearly retrospective, that is, looking backward to the Levitical sacrifices, it is also prophetical, looking forward to the great sacrifice of propitiation whereby Christ, by one offering, forever atoned for the sin of mankind. Cp. Heb. 10, 1—18.

CHAPTER 44.

The Relations of Various Classes of the People to the New Sanctuary.

THE STATUS OF THE PRINCE, THE LEVITES, AND THE PRIESTS. — V. 1. **Then He brought me back the way of the gate of the outward Sanctuary which looketh toward the east,** so that Ezekiel could observe it closely from the court; **and it was shut,** locked against all those who might desire to enter. V. 2. **Then said the Lord unto me,** in explaining this unusual condition of affairs, **This gate shall be shut, it shall not be opened, and no man shall enter in by it; because the Lord, the God of Israel, hath entered in by it,** chap. 43, 4, **therefore it shall be shut,** so that the glory of the God of the covenant would everlastingly dwell in the midst of His Church. V. 3. **It is for the prince,** the ruler of the Lord's people; **the prince, he shall sit in it to eat bread before the Lord; he shall enter by the way of the porch of that gate and shall go out by the way of the same.** It is evident that the prophecy here has Messianic conditions in mind, that we have here "an ideal description of coming realities under the form and aspect of the old relations." The leaders of the Church of the New Testament were to refrain from all corruptions which brought destruction upon the Old Testament Israel. V. 4. **Then brought He me the**

way of the north gate before the house, that is, the inner north gate; **and I looked, and, behold, the glory of the Lord filled the house of the Lord,** as the prophet could see from his position near the Sanctuary; **and I fell upon my face,** once more overcome by the majesty of the divine glory. V. 5. **And the Lord said unto me, Son of man, mark well,** literally, "direct thy heart," **and behold with thine eyes and hear with thine ears all that I say unto thee concerning all the ordinances of the house of the Lord and all the laws thereof,** cp. chap. 43, 11. 12; **and mark well the entering in of the house, with every going forth of the Sanctuary,** the approach of the house of God by the priests as well as the way by which they left the place of their service. V. 6. **And thou shalt say to the rebellious, even to the house of Israel, Thus saith the Lord God,** He who has unlimited power and authority, **O ye house of Israel,** they who bore the name of the faithful patriarch, **let it suffice you of all your abominations,** of which they surely had performed their fill and might now abstain, cp. 1 Pet. 4, 3, v. 7. **in that ye have brought into My Sanctuary strangers,** literally, "children of a stranger," **uncircumcised in heart,** knowing nothing of repentance and faith, **and uncircumcised in flesh,** not having even the outward badge of the covenant people, **to be in My Sanctuary,** for non-Israelites were not permitted to perform the functions of the priesthood, **to pollute it, even My house, when ye offer My bread,** the sacrificial food placed on the Temple altars, **the fat and the blood; and they have broken My covenant because of all your abominations;** for since the children of Israel permitted this infraction of the rules of the Lord, it was their act that brought about the desecration of the Sanctuary, and the abomination was laid to their charge. V. 8. **And ye have not kept the charge of Mine holy things,** in treating the appointments of the Temple without the reverence which He demands; **but ye have set keepers of My charge in My Sanctuary for yourselves,** literally, "but ye appoint for keepers of My charge in My Sanctuary those," that is, such people, such men, as their representatives in performing the functions of their religious cult. Their worship, therefore, was not a service of God, but a service of their own inclination and thus altogether sinful. In condemnation of such practises the Lord now gives some definite rules concerning the service in His new Temple. V. 9. **Thus saith the Lord God, No stranger, uncircumcised in heart nor uncircumcised in flesh, shall enter into My Sanctuary, of any stranger that is among the children of Israel.** Only such as have, by repentance and faith, become fellow-citizens with the saints and of the household of God, are acceptable in His sight. Cp. Eph. 2, 19—22. V. 10. **And the Levites that are gone away far from Me, when Israel went astray,** joining the people in their apostasy, in spite of better knowledge, **which went astray away from Me after their idols,** in the idolatry which was Israel's chief transgression; **they shall even bear their iniquity.** V. 11. **Yet they shall be ministers in My Sanctuary,** in charge of some minor services, **having charge at the gates of the house,** as porters and guards, **and ministering to the house,** thereby demoted from the rank and functions of priests to those of ordinary Levites; **they shall slay the burnt offering and the sacrifice for the people, and they shall stand before them to minister unto them,** no longer in positions of authority and influence, but in the station of porters. V. 12. **Because they ministered unto them before their idols and caused the house of Israel to fall into iniquity,** instead of hindering their idolatrous endeavors; **therefore have I lifted up Mine hand against them, saith the Lord God, and they shall bear their iniquity,** by having their rank and position taken away from them. When men who are supposed to be leaders and guides of the people of the Lord promote idolatry and other acts of transgression, as in many recent instances, this fact aggravates their offense in a very decided manner. V. 13. **And they shall not come near unto Me to do the office of a priest unto Me, nor to come near to any of My holy things,** the appointments used in the service of the Sanctuary, **in the Most Holy Place, but they shall bear their shame and their abominations which they have committed.** V. 14. **But I will make them keepers of the charge of the house,** of a decidedly secondary rank, **for all the service thereof and for all that shall be done therein.** There is only one comforting thought in this section, namely, that one may be a believer, and that in a distinguished place, and yet lose some special honor, be acknowledged as pious, yet be excluded from some dignity. The sin is forgiven, but the consequences of the sin must often be borne throughout life. V. 15. **But the priests, the Levites, the sons of Zadok, that kept the charge of My Sanctuary when the children of Israel went astray from Me,** remaining faithful in the midst of the general apostasy and therefore types of the true priestly character, **they shall come near to Me to minister unto Me,** in performing all the functions of the priesthood, **and they shall stand before Me to offer unto Me the fat and the blood, saith the Lord God.** V. 16. **They shall enter into My Sanctuary,** being accorded this privilege with all those who are children of God in truth, **and they shall come near to My table,** namely, the altar of incense, **to minister unto Me; and they shall**

keep My charge. The priests of the line of Ithamar were discharged from the office as priests of the Temple because of the corrupt manner in which they followed in the footsteps of the sons of Eli, against whom the same denunciation was uttered. Cp. 1 Sam. 2, 32. 35. Zadok is the son of Ahitub of the line of Eleazar, 1 Chron. 5, 34; 6, 37. 38, who at the time of Absalom's rebellion was faithful to David, 2 Sam. 15, 24, and also anointed Solomon to be king over Israel, 1 Kings 1, 32 ff., while the high priest Abiathar of the line of Ithamar took the part of the pretender Adonijah. Cp. 1 Kings 1, 7. 25. In consequence of this defection the office of the high priest was given to Zadok and his descendants. Cp. 1 Kings 2, 26—35. When the Lord's patience is exhausted, His punishment strikes the offenders with terrible force and lasting effect.

ORDINANCES FOR THE PRIESTS IN THE PERFORMANCE OF THEIR DUTIES. — V. 17. **And it shall come to pass that, when they enter in at the gates of the inner court,** for the performance of the special functions pertaining to their office, **they shall be clothed with linen garments,** as were the priests of old, Ex. 28, 39; **and no wool shall come upon them whiles they minister in the gates of the inner court and within,** namely, in the Sanctuary proper. "Wool soon induces perspiration in the sultry East and so becomes uncleanly." V. 18. **They shall have linen bonnets upon their heads,** a special kind of turban, **and shall have linen breeches upon their loins; they shall not gird themselves with anything that causeth sweat,** literally, "in sweat," so that their garments would carry the odor of perspiration. V. 19. **And when they go forth into the utter court, even into the utter court to the people, they shall put off their garments wherein they ministered and lay them in the holy chambers,** in the vestry-cells provided for that purpose, **and they shall put on other garments; and they shall not sanctify the people with their garments,** by having on the peculiar priestly vestments in which they performed the service of the Sanctuary. V. 20. **Neither shall they shave their heads,** which was a heathenish custom and therefore forbidden to priests of old, Lev. 21, 5, **nor suffer their locks to grow long,** Lev. 10, 6; **they shall only poll their heads,** keep their hair properly trimmed. V. 21. **Neither shall any priest drink wine when they enter into the inner court,** as being typical of the sobriety of the soul, which could be expected from one who devoted his life to the Lord. V. 22. **Neither shall they take for their wives a widow,** the ordinance of Lev. 21, 14. 13 thus being extended to include not only the high priest, but all the ordinary priests as well, **nor her that is put away,** namely, with the stain of guilt upon her, Lev. 21, 7; **but they shall take maidens of the seed of the house of Israel, or a widow that had a priest before,** this being the one exception to the prohibition in the first part of the verse. V. 23. **And they shall teach My people the difference between the holy and profane and cause them to discern between the unclean and the clean.** Cp. Lev. 10, 10; Deut. 33, 10. V. 24. **And in controversy they shall stand in judgment,** perform the office of judge in deciding controversies pertaining to the Law of God, thus extending the duties enjoined Deut. 17, 8 ff.; 19, 17; 21, 5; **and they shall judge it according to My judgments,** in all matters of difference between people of the nation; **and they shall keep My laws and My statutes in all Mine assemblies,** in all the festivals of the Lord, namely, by performing the duties of their office with strict regard to every detail; **and they shall hallow My Sabbaths,** particularly by observing the injunctions concerning the Sabbath rest. V. 25. **And they shall come at no dead person to defile themselves,** namely, by touching or handling a corpse; **but for father, or for mother, or for son, or for daughter, for brother, or for sister that hath had no husband, they may defile themselves.** Cp. Lev. 21, 1—3. V. 26. **And after he is cleansed,** namely, after coming into contact with the body of a dead person, **they shall reckon unto him seven days,** this period being demanded in addition to the time of cleansing, Num. 19. V. 27. **And in the day that he goeth into the Sanctuary,** to resume the functions of his office, **unto the inner court, to minister in the Sanctuary, he shall offer his sin-offering, saith the Lord God.** Cp. Lev. 4, 3. V. 28. **And it shall be unto them for an inheritance: I am their Inheritance; and ye shall give them no possession in Israel: I am their Possession.** Cp. Num. 18, 20; Deut. 18, 1; 10, 9. They were not to concern themselves with the cares of life, but be devoted entirely to the service of the Lord, as all His servants at all times will be. V. 29. **They shall eat the meat-offering and the sin-offering and the trespass-offering,** in agreement with the ancient provisions of the Law, Lev. 2, 3; 6, 9—19; 7, 6. 7; **and every dedicated thing in Israel shall be theirs.** Cp. Lev. 27, 21. V. 30. **And the first of all the first-fruits of all things,** which had to be dedicated to the Lord, Ex. 23, 19; 34, 26; Num. 18, 13; Deut. 28, 4, **and every oblation of all,** gifts offered to the Lord by heaving and waving, **of every sort of your oblations, shall be the priest's,** as part of his emoluments; **ye shall also give unto the priests the first of your dough,** of the grain-corn, **that he may cause the blessing to rest in thine house,** for the blessing of God rests upon him who, in simple faith, performs the duties laid upon him. V. 31. **The priest shall not eat of anything that is dead of itself,** as a result of disease, or **torn, whether it be fowl or beast,** for to do so defiled every man, all the more therefore the priests of Jehovah. "Only what Jehovah gives to them and His Sanctuary in offerings and dues, which, however, must never be unclean, shall accrue to them; and this, at the same time, forms the best transition to the awards which follow." (Ewald.)

CHAPTER 45.

The Portion for the Sanctuary.

THE PORTION OF THE LAND. — V. 1. **Moreover, when ye shall divide by lot the land for inheritance,** the division of the land being thought of as in the time of Joshua, **ye shall offer an oblation unto the Lord,** as consecrated to His service, **an holy portion of the land,** literally, "holiness from the land," as of something separated for sacred purposes; **the length,** namely, of this strip of land set apart for the Lord, **shall be the length of five and twenty thousand reeds, and the breadth shall be ten thousand. This shall be holy in all the borders thereof round about.** V. 2. **Of this there shall be for the Sanctuary,** as shown in chap. 42, 20, **five hundred in length, with five hundred in breadth, square round about, and fifty cubits round about for the suburbs thereof,** as its environs, a space to be kept free of buildings, lest they come too close to the sacred square of the Temple compound. V. 3. **And of this measure,** that is, according to this measure, **shalt thou measure the length of five and twenty thousand and the breadth of ten thousand; and in it shall be the Sanctuary and the Most Holy Place,** or, "therein shall the Sanctuary be the Most Holy Place." V. 4. **The holy portion of the land shall be for the priests, the ministers of the Sanctuary, which shall come near to minister unto the Lord; and it shall be a place for their houses,** so that they would have sufficient room for their dwellings on this sacred strip, **and an holy place for the Sanctuary.** V. 5. **And the five and twenty thousand of length and the ten thousand of breadth,** that is, another strip of the same size, **shall also the Levites, the ministers of the house,** as performing the minor services of the Temple, **have for themselves, for a possession for twenty chambers,** an expression which may mean that the Levites occupied barracklike cells with smaller portions of pasturage. V. 6. **And ye shall appoint the possession of the city,** as the capital of the new nation, **five thousand broad and five and twenty thousand long,** this being the total area or region under its immediate control, **over against the oblation of the holy portion,** that is, running next to the strip reserved for the Sanctuary; **it shall be for the whole house of Israel,** all the tribes having an equal interest in it. V. 7. **And a portion shall be for the prince on the one side and on the other side of the oblation of the holy portion and of the possession of the city before the oblation of the holy portion and before the possession of the city, from the west side westward and from the east side eastward,** extending outside of the boundaries of these strips as far as the country extended toward the east and west; **and the length shall be over against one of the portions, from the west border unto the east border,** so that the strips belonging to the prince run parallel to the strips assigned to the several tribes. V. 8. **In the land shall be his possession in Israel,** or, "it shall be land to him for a possession in Israel"; **and My princes shall no more oppress My people,** as had been the case with many of the former rulers; **and the rest of the land shall they give to the house of Israel according to their tribes,** assigning the several parts as described in chapter 47. The context once more clearly indicates that an ideal country and nation is meant, which we cannot understand but of the spiritual Israel, of the Church of God.

THE PORTION OF THE PEOPLE. — V. 9. **Thus saith the Lord God,** in connecting up this paragraph with the last statement of the previous section, **Let it suffice you, O princes of Israel: remove violence and spoil,** so that they would no more be guilty of the oppression formerly practised, **and execute judgment and justice,** so as to make righteousness the guiding principle in all their actions; **take away your exactions from My people saith the Lord God,** for this had been done by expelling lawful possessors from their property, as in the case of Naboth. V. 10. **Ye shall have just balances,** for weighing, **and a just ephah,** for dry measure, **and a just bath,** a correct measure also for liquids. V. 11. **The ephah and the bath shall be of one measure,** of the same cubic content, **that the bath may contain the tenth part of an homer and the ephah the tenth part of an homer,** the homer thus being the larger standard; **the measure thereof shall be after the homer.** V. 12. **And the shekel shall be twenty gerahs; twenty shekels, five and twenty shekels, fifteen shekels, shall be your maneh.** "The threefold enumeration of shekels, twenty, twenty-five, fifteen, probably refers to coins of different value, representing, respectively, so many shekels, the three collectively making up a maneh." V. 13. **This is the oblation that ye shall offer,** made to the ruler as a gift consecrated to the Lord for purposes of worship: **the sixth part of an ephah of an homer of wheat,** about ten pints; **and ye shall give the sixth part of an ephah of an homer of barley,** the same amount of grain in either case. V. 14. **Concerning the ordinance of oil,** the regulation concerning the gift of oil, **the bath of oil: ye shall offer the tenth part of a bath out of the cor,** a homer being equal to about sixty pints, **which is an homer of ten baths, for ten baths are an homer;** v. 15. **and one lamb out of the flock, out of two hundred, out of the fat pastures of Israel,** of the rich blessings given by the Lord, **for a meat-offering, and for a burnt offering, and for peace-offerings,** also known as thank-offerings, **to make reconciliation for them, saith the Lord God,** for the making of an atonement for the sins of the people was the chief purpose of the sacrifices. Cp. Lev. 1, 4. V. 16. **All the people of the land shall give this oblation,** making it a special point to render it, **for the prince in Israel,** who would thereby be enabled to provide for the service of worship and also to give evidence of his representation of the people. V. 17. **And it shall be the prince's part to give burnt offerings,** the special duty of his office, **and meat-offerings, and drink-offerings, in the feasts, and in the new moons, and in the Sabbaths, in all solemnities,** upon all the great festal occasions, **of the house of Israel,** he furnishing the material for the sacrifices; **he shall prepare the sin-offering, and the meat-offering, and the burnt offering, and the peace-offerings to make reconciliation for the house of Israel.** In the Church of the New Testament all offerings are gifts of free love to acknowledge the reconciliation made by Jesus Christ.

SPECIAL ORDINANCES CONCERNING SOME OFFERINGS. — V. 18. **Thus saith the Lord God, In the first month, in the first day of the month, thou shalt take a young bullock without blemish,** instead of the goat prescribed by Moses for similar occasions, Num. 28, 15, **and cleanse the Sanctuary,** by a sacrifice of purification according to the ancient rite; v. 19. **and the priest shall take of the blood of the sin-offering,** as described in chap. 43, 20, **and put it upon the posts of the house,** the gate-posts of the Sanctuary, **and upon the four corners of the settle of the altar,** its lower part and ledges, **and upon the posts of the gate of the inner court.** V. 20. **And so thou shalt do the seventh day of the month for every one that erreth,** transgressing by reason of human frailty, **and for him that is simple,** foolish, easily led astray. **So shall ye reconcile the house.** "Thus shall the year, newly consecrated by such a beginning, most truly represent the appearance of a holy year." (Haevernick.) V. 21. **In the first month, in the fourteenth day of the month, ye shall have the Passover,** according to the ancient rule commanding its celebration, **a feast of seven days; unleavened bread shall be eaten,** the festival of Unleavened Bread and that of the Passover being spoken of as one as early as this. V. 22. **And upon that day shall the prince prepare for himself and for all the people of the land a bullock for a sin-offering,** the idea of the Feast of Atonement thus being transferred also to the Passover. V. 23. **And seven days of the feast he shall prepare a burnt offering to the Lord, seven bullocks and seven rams without blemish daily the seven days,** these sacrifices thus being much more numerous than those commanded in the Old Dispensation, cp. Num. 28, **and a kid of the goats daily for a sin-offering.** V. 24. **And he shall prepare a meat-offering of an ephah for a bullock,** this also being much more than that required by the Mosaic Law, **and an ephah for a ram and an hin of oil for an ephah.** V. 25. **In the seventh month, in the fifteenth day of the month,** at the former time of the Feast of Tabernacles, **shall he do the like in the feast of the seven days, according to the sin-offering, according to the burnt offering, and according to the meat-offering, and according to the oil.** The entire description of the festivals is such as to remind one of the words of Luther: "In the New Testament all days are feast-days." We are no longer under the Mosaic Law, but bring the sacrifices of our worship in a measure unhampered by the restrictions of a legalistic system.

CHAPTER 46.

Ordinances Concerning the Worship of the Prince.

VARIOUS SACRIFICES. — V. 1. **Thus saith the Lord God, The gate of the inner court that looketh toward the east shall be shut the six working days,** just like the outer portal, chap. 44, 1; **but on the Sabbath it shall be opened, and in the day of the new moon,** another day of peculiar sanctity, **it shall be opened.** V. 2. **And the prince shall enter by the way of the porch of that gate without,** from the outer court, **and shall stand by the post of the gate,** by a pillar of the gate leading to the Court of the Priests, **and the priests shall prepare his burnt offering and his peace-**

offerings, and he shall worship at the threshold of the gate, offering his prayers from that point; **then he shall go forth,** returning the same way in which he had come; **but the gate shall not be shut until the evening.** "As, on the one hand, the prince is unreservedly acknowledged in his special exaltation, so, on the other, his rights appear in due limitation, in reference to encroachment of any kind on the priestly prerogatives." (Haevernick.) V. 3. **Likewise the people of the land shall worship at the door of this gate before the Lord,** through which they could get a glimpse of the altar of burnt offering and of the priests engaged in the work of their ministry, **in the Sabbaths and in the new moons,** thus partaking in all the privileges granted the prince, but at a greater distance. V. 4. **And the burnt offering that the prince shall offer unto the Lord in the Sabbath-day shall be six lambs without blemish, and a ram without blemish.** "The offerings on the Sabbaths are larger than those of the Mosaic Law, to imply that the worship of God is to be conducted by prince and people in a more munificent spirit of self-sacrificing liberality than formerly." V. 5. **And the meat-offering,** usually in the form of flour, **shall be an ephah for a ram,** also an increase of that of the Mosaic dispensation, **and the meat-offering for the lambs as he shall be able to give,** with correspondingly increased faithfulness and devotion, **and an hin of oil to an ephah,** this again representing an advance over the ancient rites. V. 6. **And in the day of the new moon it shall be a young bullock without blemish and six lambs and a ram,** this sacrifice presenting a decrease over that formerly required, Num. 28, 11. 12; **they shall be without blemish.** V. 7. **And he shall prepare a meat-offering, an ephah for a bullock and an ephah for a ram, and for the lambs according as his hand shall attain unto,** the factor of voluntary sacrifices standing out prominently throughout the passage, **and an hin of oil to an ephah.** V. 8. **And when the prince shall enter, he shall go in by the way of the porch of that gate, and he shall go forth by the way thereof,** this repetition of verse 2 serving to connect the next ordinances with those pertaining to the Sabbaths and new moons. V. 9. **But when the people of the land shall come before the Lord in the solemn feasts,** at the set time and assembling of the congregation, **he that entereth in by the way of the north gate to worship shall go out by the way of the south gate,** to prevent disorder and tumult; **and he that entereth by the way of the south gate shall go forth by the way of the north gate; he shall not return by the way of the gate whereby he came in, but shall go forth over against it,** so that all confusion might be avoided at the time of divine worship, for our God is a God of order. V. 10. **And the prince in the midst of them,** joining the great throng of worshipers as one of them, **when they go in, shall go in,** Ps. 42, 4; **and when they go forth, shall go forth.** We have here a "beautiful picture of a religious people: the highest in rank freely mingling with the mass of worshipers and inspiriting their devotions by the elevating influence of his presence and example." V. 11. **And in the feasts and in the solemnities,** when there are two festival days in succession, **the meat-offering shall be an ephah to a bullock and an ephah to a ram and to the lambs as he is able to give, and an hin of oil to an ephah,** the factor of voluntary offerings once more appearing at this point. V. 12. **Now, when the prince shall prepare a voluntary burnt offering or peace-offerings voluntarily unto the Lord,** by reason of special inward impulse, a joyful readiness to serve the Lord, **one shall then open him the gate that looketh toward the east, and he shall prepare his burnt offering and his peace-offerings, as he did on the Sabbath-day,** this rule therefore applying to all festivals; **then he shall go forth, and after his going forth one shall shut the gate,** so that the rule concerning its being closed would always be observed. The passage rightly sets forth the fine rivalry which may exist between the various ranks and classes of people in their acts of homage and adoration to God. V. 13. **Thou shalt daily prepare a burnt offering unto the Lord,** as by the Mosaic ordinances, Ex. 29, 38; Num. 28, 3, **of a lamb of the first year without blemish; thou shalt prepare it every morning,** literally, "morning for morning." V. 14. **And thou shalt prepare a meat-offering for it every morning,** cp. Lev. 2; 6, 14—23, **the sixth part of an ephah and the third part of an hin of oil, to temper with the fine flour,** for the sacrificial cakes; **a meat-offering continually by a perpetual ordinance unto the Lord.** If the evening sacrifice was thus to be discontinued, the increase of the meat-offering in the morning was probably intended to compensate for it. V. 15. **Thus shall they prepare the lamb and the meat-offering and the oil every morning for a continual burnt offering.** The considerable, in part radical, departures from the Mosaic ordinances almost throughout again indicate that the entire description is symbolical of the Messianic era, when the essence of worship would be voluntary homage to the Lord.

THE SACRIFICIAL KITCHENS. — V. 16. **Thus saith the Lord God,** in making provisions for the future, lest conditions arise which would result in acts of violence on the part of the ruler, **If the prince give a gift unto any of his sons, the inheritance thereof shall be his sons'; it shall be their possession by inheritance,** to remain permanently under their dominion. V. 17. **But if he give a gift of his inheritance,** of the special land set aside for his use and enjoyment, **to one of his servants,** as a reward of service or loyalty, **then it shall be his to the year of liberty,** the so-called year of the jubilee, Lev. 25, 10; **after, it shall return to the prince,** revert to him as his property; **but his inheritance shall be his sons' for them,** that is, only what the prince has presented to his sons shall remain in their property at that time. V. 18. **Moreover, the prince shall not take of the people's inheritance by oppression,** a feature against which these ordinances guarded, **to thrust them out of their possession,** as when Ahab took Naboth's vineyard; **but he shall give his sons inheritance out of his own possession,** cp. 1 Sam. 8, 14; 22, 7, **that My people be not scattered every man from his possession.** V. 19. **After,** that is, afterward, **He brought me through the entry which was at the side of the gate,** the entry mentioned chap. 42, 9, **into the holy chambers of the priests,** those nearest to the inner north gate, **which looked toward the north; and, behold, there was a place on the two sides westward,** a section of the Temple area which had not yet been described. V. 20. **Then said He unto me, This is the place where the priests shall boil the trespass-offering and the sin-offering, where they shall bake the meat-offering,** the food of the priests thus being prepared in immediate proximity to their chambers lest its sanctity be in any way polluted, **that they bear them not out into the utter court to sanctify the people,** to bring them into contact with this consecrated food and thus to defeat the object of the ordinance. V. 21. **Then He brought me forth into the utter court and caused me to pass by the four corners of the court; and, behold, in every corner of the court there was a court,** a smaller tributary of the larger court. V. 22. **In the four corners of the court there were courts joined,** closed, shut off from the rest of the court, **of forty cubits long and thirty broad; these four corners were of one measure,** of the same size. V. 23. **And there was a row of building round about in them,** along their walls, **round about them four, and it was made with boiling-places under the rows round about,** roofed cooking apartments or kitchenettes, with a fireplace in each, next to the walls. V. 24. **Then said He unto me, These are the places of them that boil, where the ministers of the house,** the ordinary Levites as servants of the Sanctuary, **shall boil the sacrifice of the people,** that part which belonged to the priests. By the sacrificial meals eaten by the people, then, was the communion and fellowship of all believers brought out symbolically.

CHAPTER 47.

The Blessings of the New Canaan.

THE STREAM OF LIVING WATERS. — V. 1. **Afterward He brought me again unto the door of the house,** from the outer court to the main portal of the Temple; **and, behold, waters issued out from under the threshold of the house eastward,** symbolical of the divine blessings which flow from His Church; **for the forefront of the house stood toward the east,** the Temple facing in the same direction as had the Tabernacle and the Temple of Solomon, **and the waters came down from under from the right side of the house, at the south side of the altar,** welling up from below the center of the Sanctuary as its fountainhead. V. 2. **Then brought He me out of the way of the gate northward,** for the portal on the east was locked, **and led me about the way without unto the utter gate by the way that looketh eastward,** so that Ezekiel might follow the course of the wonderful stream; **and, behold, there ran out waters on the right side,** before the southern half of the front. V. 3. **And when the Man that had the line in His hand went forth eastward, He measured a thousand cubits,** namely, at this distance from the walls; **and He brought me through the waters: the waters were to the ankles.** V. 4. **Again He measured a thousand,** namely, from the first place of crossing, **and brought me through the waters: the waters were to the knees,** being supplied and increased in this marvelous manner from the sacred miraculous source in the Temple. **Again He measured a thousand and brought me through: the waters were to the loins,** ever growing deeper. V. 5. **Afterward He measured a thousand, and it was a river,** it had grown to the dimensions of a great stream, **that I could not pass over, for the waters were risen, waters to swim in, a river that could not be passed over,** like an impetuous mountain torrent, swollen by the spring rains, making swimming necessary if a person wanted to cross at all. V. 6. **And He said unto me,** in order to impress upon the prophet every detail of the picture, **Son of man, hast thou seen this? Then He brought me, and caused me to return, to the brink of the river,** back to the bank of the stream which he had apparently attempted to wade. V. 7. **Now, when I had returned,** his attention now being directed to the bank rather than to the stream, **behold, at the bank of the river,** lining it on either side, **were very many trees on the one side and** on the other. V. 8. **Then said He unto me, These waters issue out toward the east country,** the term used designating the entire valley of the Jordan, **and go down into the desert,** a word used of the steppes of Southeastern Judea, **and go into the sea,** here the Dead Sea; **which being brought forth into the sea, the waters shall be healed,** its deadly saltness being relieved so that it could again be inhabited by fishes. V. 9. **And it shall come to pass that everything that liveth, which moveth,** literally, "every living soul that creepeth," which had the breath of life in itself, **whithersoever the rivers shall come, shall live,** on account of the fulness of life borne by them; **and there shall be a very great multitude of fish, because these waters shall come thither,** their freshness enabling the fishes to live and to multiply most abundantly, **for they,** the waters of the Dead Sea, **shall be healed; and everything shall live whither the river cometh,** being endowed with a miraculous vitality by coming into contact with it. V. 10. **And it shall come to pass that the fishers shall stand upon it from En-gedi,** on its western shore, where David had once found refuge, **even unto Eneglaim,** on the eastern shore, in the confines of Moab; **they shall be a place to spread forth nets; their fish shall be according to their kinds as the fish of the Great Sea, exceeding many.** V. 11. **But the miry places thereof,** the swamps formed by the natural recession of the waters, **and the marshes thereof shall not be healed; they shall be given to salt,** unfit for cultivation and for every living thing. V. 12. **And by the river upon the bank thereof, on this side and on that side, shall grow all trees for meat,** springing up and bearing the richest kind of food, **whose leaf shall not fade, neither shall the fruit thereof be consumed; it shall bring forth new fruit according to his months,** fruit maturing every month, **because their waters they issued out of the Sanctuary,** and were thus filled with marvelous life; **and the fruit thereof shall be for meat and the leaf thereof for medicine,** its foliage for healing. Without attempting to give an interpretation of every detail of this picture, its general meaning is clear. The miraculous river pictures the spread of the Gospel, the gaining of new members for the Church, the increase of divine blessings in the Messianic era. The trees represent the wonderful blessings given through the ministry of the Word. The fishermen of the Lord are busily engaged in bringing in the base-born and the noble, the rich and the poor, out of the sea of the world to the salvation earned by Jesus Christ. "Searching into the deep things of God, we find some easy to understand, others more difficult, others beyond our reach, of which we can only adore the depths." Where the stream of the Gospel flows, the putrid and poisonous waters of this world are cleansed, but the swamps and morasses of men's hatred and enmity toward God are shut off, by their own fault, from His mercy. All this, and more, is indicated in Rev. 22, 1—6, where we also have a description of the final perfection of the Church of Christ.

THE BOUNDARIES OF THE NEW CANAAN. — V. 13. **Thus saith the Lord God, This shall be the border,** the boundary of Canaan proper, **whereby ye shall inherit the land according to the twelve tribes of Israel: Joseph shall have two portions,** as in the first division of the land. Cp. Gen. 48, 5; 1 Chron. 5, 1. V. 14. **And ye shall inherit it, one as well as another,** every one an equal portion, **concerning the which I lifted up Mine hand,** in a solemn oath accompanying His promise, Gen. 12, 7; 13, 15; 15, 7; 17, 8; 26, 3, **to give it unto your fathers; and this land shall fall unto you for inheritance.** V. 15. **And this shall be the border of the land toward the north side, from the Great Sea,** the Mediterranean Sea, **the way of Hethlon, as men go to Zedad,** these two towns being on the northwestern border: v. 16. **Hamath,** the ancient northernmost point, **Berothah,** a city in Syria conquered by David, 2 Sam. 8, 8, **Sibraim, which is between the border of Damascus and the border of Hamath,** on the caravan road toward Palmyra; **Hazar-hatticon, which is by the coast of Hauran,** a province on the east side of Jordan, south of Syria. V. 17. **And the border from the sea,** as one draws the northern border from the Mediterranean Sea to the beginning of its eastern boundary, **shall be Hazar-enan,** in the extreme northeastern corner, **the border of Damascus, and the north northward, and the border of Hamath,** the description indicating that this entire northeastern section was included. **And this is the north side.** V. 18. **And the east side ye shall measure from Hauran,** from the extreme northeastern boundary of this section, **and from Damascus,** as indicating the limit of extent in that direction, **and from Gilead,** in the center east of Jordan, **and from the land of Israel by Jordan,** extending to the river along its whole length, **from the border unto the East Sea,** that is, the Dead Sea. **And this is the east side,** which therefore included Canaan proper only. V. 19. **And the south side southward,** along the southern boundary, **from Tamar,** probably south of the Dead Sea, **even to the waters of strife in Kadesh,** cp. Num. 20, near Kadesh-barnea, **the river to the Great Sea,** the Wady el Arish, whose brook flows into the Mediterranean Sea, the boundary toward the southwest being clearly defined. **And this is the south side southward.** V. 20. **The west side also shall be the Great Sea from the**

border, all along from the river of Egypt, **till a man come over against Hamath,** the Philistine coast thus being included in the Holy Land and the whole description being held along ideal lines. **This is the west side.** V. 21. **So shall ye divide this land unto you according to the tribes of Israel,** this statement summarizing what has been said concerning the boundaries of Canaan. V. 22. **And it shall come to pass that ye shall divide it by lot for an inheritance unto you and to the strangers that sojourn among you, which shall beget children among you;** for he who connects himself with the true Church may enjoy the privileges and blessings of the true Church; **and they shall be unto you as born in the country among the children of Israel,** as Hobab and his tribe did at the time of Moses; **they shall have inheritance with you among the tribes of Israel.** V. 23. **And it shall come to pass that in what tribe the stranger sojourneth, there shall ye give him his inheritance, saith the Lord God.** In the New Testament the middle wall of partition between Jews and Gentiles has been fully removed, so that through Him they both have access by one Spirit unto the Father. Cp. Eph. 2, 14—18.

CHAPTER 48.

The Allotment of the Land to the Several Tribes.

THE DIVISION OF THE NEW CANAAN. — V. 1. **Now, these are the names of the tribes,** as they followed in the order of their allotment, the land being divided into portions of ideal exactness. **From the north end,** along the extreme northern boundary, **to the coast of the way of Hethlon,** on the northwest, **as one goeth to Hamath,** this being the northernmost point, **Hazar-enan,** on the northeast, **the border of Damascus northward, to the coast of Hamath; for these are his sides east and west,** his possession with the boundaries fixed toward the east and toward the west: **a portion for Dan,** that is, so much should belong to Dan. V. 2. **And by the border of Dan,** immediately south of his portion, **from the east side unto the west side,** as all the sections are described, **a portion for Asher.** V. 3. **And by the border of Asher,** along its southern boundary, **from the east side even unto the west side, a portion for Naphtali.** V. 4. **And by the border of Naphtali, from the east side unto the west side, a portion for Manasseh.** V. 5. **And by the border of Manasseh, from the east side unto the west side, a portion for Ephraim.** V. 6. **And by the border of Ephraim, from the east side even unto the west side, a portion for Reuben.** The northern tribes thus retained their relative position in the distribution of the land, the portion of Reuben being added at this point because he had formerly had his allotment east of Jordan. V. 7. **And by the border of Reuben, from the east side unto the west side, a portion for Judah,** the tribe which had had the leadership in ancient Israel. V. 8. **And by the border of Judah,** adjoining it on the south, **from the east side unto the west side, shall be the offering which ye shall offer,** the section set apart for the Sanctuary and its surroundings, **of five and twenty thousand reeds in breadth, and in length as one of the other parts, from the east side unto the west side,** between the Jordan and the Mediterranean; **and the Sanctuary shall be in the midst of it.** Cp. chap. 45, 1—6. V. 9. **The oblation that ye shall offer unto the Lord shall be of five and twenty thousand in length and of ten thousand in breadth.** The priest's portion, in whose midst the Temple was to be situated, was in the center of this consecrated portion. V. 10. **And for them, even for the priests, shall be this holy oblation,** to yield dwelling-places for them, **toward the north five and twenty thousand in length and toward the west ten thousand in breadth and toward the east ten thousand in breadth and toward the south five and twenty thousand in length,** these being the measurements toward the four points of the compass; **and the Sanctuary of the Lord shall be in the midst thereof.** V. 11. **It shall be for the priests that are sanctified of the sons of Zadok,** chap. 44, 15, **which have kept My charge,** being loyal to the ordinances and commands of the Lord when others became guilty of faithlessness, **which went not astray when the children of Israel went astray, as the Levites,** the tribe of Levi in general, **went astray.** Cp. chap. 44, 10. V. 12. **And this oblation of the land that is offered shall be unto them a thing most holy,** a heave-portion from the oblation of the land, **by the border of the Levites.** V. 13. **And over against the border of the priests,** apparently along their southern boundary, **the Levites shall have five and twenty thousand in length and ten thousand in breadth; all the length,** or "the whole length," **shall be five and twenty thousand and the breadth ten thousand,** the two lengths and the two breadths thus being clearly defined. V. 14. **And they shall not sell of it, neither exchange,** since God is the real Landowner, **nor alienate the first-fruits of the land,** which likewise belonged to the Lord, Ex. 22, 29; **for it is holy unto the Lord.** V. 15. **And the five thousand that are left in the breadth over against the five and twenty thousand,** after deducting the breadth of the priests' and of the Levites' portions, **shall be a profane place for the city,** common land, not used for sacred purposes, **for dwelling,** that is, for the erection of dwelling-houses, **and for suburbs,** for free use, for pasture and garden land; **and the city shall be in the midst thereof.** V. 16. **And these shall be the measures thereof,** of the city district: **the north side four thousand and five hundred and the south side four thousand and five hundred and on the east side four thousand and five hundred and the west side four thousand and five hundred,** thus forming a perfect square of four thousand five hundred on each side. V. 17. **And the suburbs of the city shall be toward the north two hundred and fifty and toward the south two hundred and fifty and toward the east two hundred and fifty and toward the west two hundred and fifty.** The entire city district, with its suburbs, thus occupied a square with sides five thousand rods long, or one-fifth of the entire portion from east to west. V. 18. **And the residue in length over against the oblation of the holy portion shall be ten thousand eastward and ten thousand westward; and it shall be over against the oblation of the holy portion,** that is, as a part of it, although assigned neither to the priests nor to the levites nor to the city; **and the increase thereof shall be for food unto them that serve the city,** so that the workmen or laborers employed in the Temple city would derive their support from this land in the immediate vicinity. V. 19. **And they that serve the city,** the laboring classes, **shall serve it out of all the tribes of Israel,** that is, people from the various tribes would form this class and derive their support in the manner indicated. V. 20. **All the oblation shall be five and twenty thousand by five and twenty thousand,** inclusive of the possession of the city; **ye shall offer the holy oblation four-square, with the possession of the city,** which was one-fourth the portions of the priests and Levites. V. 21. **And the residue shall be for the prince, on the one side and on the other of the holy oblation, and of the possession of the city,** that is, bounding it and parallel to it, **over against the five and twenty thousand of the oblation toward the east border, and westward over against the five and twenty thousand toward the west border, over against the portions for the prince,** whose portion would thus extend from north to south along the border of the holy territory; **and it shall be the holy oblation; and the sanctuary of the house shall be in the midst thereof,** equally distant from the eastern and the western border. V. 22. **Moreover, from the possession of the Levites,** beginning at their boundary, **and from the possession of the city, being in the midst of that which is the prince's,** which was located on either side, **between the border of Judah and the border of Benjamin,** whose portions would be, respectively, north and south of the holy territory, **shall be for the prince.** V. 23. **As for the rest of the tribes,** those whose portion would be in the southern part of the New Canaan, **from the east side unto the west side,** extending through the breadth of the country, **Benjamin shall have a portion.** V. 24. **And by the border of Benjamin,** along its southern boundary, **from the east side unto the west side, Simeon shall have a portion,** designated here as a separate tribe, although formerly receiving his portion within the boundaries of Judah's territory, Deut. 33. V. 25. **And by the border of Simeon, from the east side unto the west side, Issachar a portion.** V. 26. **And by the border of Issachar, from the east side unto the west side, Zebulun a portion.** V. 27. **And by the border of Zebulun, from the east side unto the west side, Gad a portion,** whose territory in ancient times had been east of Jordan. V. 28. **And by the border of Gad, at the south side southward,** this being the boundary of the New Canaan, chap. 47, 19, **the border shall be even from Tamar unto the Waters of Strife in Kadesh and to the river toward the Great Sea,** the "river" being the so-called brook or river of Egypt, which flowed into the Mediterranean Sea. V. 29. **This is the land which ye shall divide by lot unto the tribes of Israel for inheritance, and these are their portions, saith the Lord God.** The immense areas indicated show that the Lord intended to have a large covenant people in Messianic times, who would be united in the communion of saints.

CONCERNING THE CAPITAL CITY. — V. 30. **And these are the goings out of the city,** the extreme ends, or the gates, of the city, **on the north side, four thousand and five hundred measures,** this being the extent of the wall with reference to its portals, inclusive of its gates, cp. v. 16. V. 31. **And the gates of the city shall be after the names of the tribes of Israel,** bearing the names of the individual tribes: **three gates northward, one gate of Reuben,** as the first-born in point of time, **one gate of Judah,** as the first-born by virtue of the patriarchal blessing, **one gate of Levi,** as the one chosen to be the representative of all the first-born in Israel in the service of the Lord. V. 32. **And at the east side four thousand and five hundred; and three gates: and one gate of Joseph,** whose two tribes are here taken together, **one gate of Benjamin, one gate of Dan.** V. 33. **And at the south side four thousand and five hundred measures; and three gates: one gate of Simeon, one gate of Issachar, one gate of Zebulun.** V. 34. **At the west side four thousand and five hundred, with their three gates: one gate**

of Gad, one gate of Asher, one gate of Naphtali. The gates had a general relation to the location of every tribe's portion in the New Canaan. V. 35. **It was round about eighteen thousand measures; and the name of the city from that day shall be "The Lord Is There,"** which is not a mere name, but expresses the fact that Jehovah, the God of the covenant, truly lives in the midst of His Church. The entire wonderful vision, as stated at the beginning, is Messianic in character. Every attempt at interpreting the individual points of this great painting are both futile and foolish; but this one great fact stands out, namely, that the Lord, speaking in terms of Old Testament worship, intended to give the believers some idea of His great Temple of the New Testament, of the communion of saints, bound together by the true faith in Jesus, the Messiah.

THE BOOK OF THE PROPHET DANIEL.

INTRODUCTION.

Daniel, according to the testimony of this book and of various historical references, cp. Matt. 24, 15. 21; Mark 13, 19; 1 Pet. 1, 10. 11; 2 Thess. 2, 3. 4, its author, was a member of one of the foremost Jewish families, possibly even of kingly descent. Having been led away into captivity at one of the conquests of Jerusalem, about in the year 606 B. C., he was taken to Babylon and there, under the name Belteshazzar, trained for special service at the court of Nebuchadnezzar. Although surrounded by temptations of every kind, Daniel remained true to the religion of his fathers. God endowed him with an extraordinary measure of wisdom, particularly with reference to the interpretation of dreams. Owing to the fact that he gave the correct explanation of a strange dream of the king, he was elevated to a high position in the kingdom, in which he was continued by some of Nebuchadnezzar's successors, such as Evil-merodach, Belshazzar, and later Darius. He was still living when Cyrus became the head of the empire, but did not return to Jerusalem with the other exiles. Cp. Ezra 1, 2. The fame of his wisdom and of his justice extended far beyond his immediate neighborhood and beyond the circle of his own people. Apparently Daniel reached an age of more than ninety years, but there is no authentic account of the time and manner of his death, although there is some apocryphal material concerning various incidents in his life.

The Book of Daniel may readily be divided into two fairly equal parts, the first of which is chiefly historical, telling of various outstanding experiences in the life of Daniel, while the second gives an account of various visions which he had concerning the kingdoms of the world and Messiah, the King, the interpretation of the strange matters being given him by angels. There is a close inner connection between the two parts, a fact which emphasizes the unity of the book, which is further substantiated by the linguistic agreement. A feature of the book is the fact that all the sections intended specifically for the Jewish people are written in Hebrew, while those pertaining to the whole world are written in Aramaic, which at that time was the language of the world.

The purpose of the book, which, with respect to its prophecies, is apocalyptic in character, is to show the Lord's people, who were at that time in the power of their enemies, that God is able to protect His children, who fear Him, even against the greatest and mightiest men of the earth, and to give them the comforting reassurance that all the machinations of the enemies of God must come to an end at His command, while the kingdom of the Lord remains forever.

As far as the character of Daniel's work is concerned, we may say: "Daniel and Ezekiel were contemporaries and lived in the same country, the kingdom of Babylon. But while Ezekiel labored among his captive countrymen on the banks of the Chebar, Daniel preached the name of God in the court of the king who had conquered the Jews. His preaching produced a profound impression. Nebuchadnezzar declared at different times that he was greatly moved by the words of Daniel (chap. 2, 47; 3, 29; 4, 33. 34). King Darius spoke in a similar vein (chap. 6, 26. 27). This does not imply, however, that these great kings became true believers of the Gospel; history shows that they did not experience a real change of heart; they continued to worship their heathen idols and died as idolaters. Due to the peculiar circumstances under which Daniel spoke, his style is also peculiar. He does not use the common prophetic expression, 'Thus saith the Lord,' nor does he, as the prophets usually do, address the people of his time. His predictions are highly symbolical. Regarding the final revelation he writes: 'And I heard, but I understood not' (chap. 12, 8. 9)." [1]

---

1) *Concordia Bible Class*, May, 1919, 76—78; Fuerbringer, *Einleitung in das Alte Testament*, 74—78.

CHAPTER 1.

The Early History of Daniel.

DANIEL AND HIS FRIENDS BROUGHT TO BABYLON. — V. 1. **In the third year of the reign of Jehoiakim, king of Judah,** cp. 2 Kings 24, 1; 2 Chron. 36, 6. 7, **came Nebuchadnezzar, king of Babylon, unto Jerusalem, and besieged it.** This account, which has been declared to be untrue by unbelieving Bible critics, is abundantly supported and verified by secular accounts, as recent investigations have shown; for even if Nabopolassar was king of Babylon at the beginning of this year, his death took place while Nebuchadnezzar was in the midst of his expedition against Jerusalem, and so the latter was king in fact before the city was taken.[2] V. 2. **And the Lord gave Jehoiakim, king of Judah, into his hand, with part of the vessels of the house of God,** the rest being taken in later expeditions, 2 Kings 25, **which he carried into the land of Shinar,** the ancient name for Babylonia, **to the house of his god,** the temple of Bel, one of the chief deities of Babylon; **and he brought the vessels into the treasure-house of his god,** the usual storage-place of vessels made of precious metals. The object of this expedition was merely to make Jerusalem and Judah tributary to the king of Babylon. Later expeditions increased the power of the world empire over Jerusalem, until it was finally subjugated and destroyed, some twenty years later. V. 3. **And the king spake unto Ashpenaz, the master of his eunuchs,** the chief of all the officers of the court, **that he should bring certain of the children of Israel,** of those who had been taken captive to Babylon, **and of the king's seed and of the princes,** 2 Kings 20, 17. 18, v. 4. **children,** young men of the middle adolescent period, between the ages of sixteen and twenty, **in whom was no blemish,** that is, no physical defect, so that they would be faultlessly handsome, **but well favored,** this being considered essential among Oriental nations in the case of those destined for court service, **and skilful in all wisdom,** with the evident talent to acquire knowledge and ability rapidly, **and cunning in knowledge and understanding science,** that is, with good, sound judgment and common sense in applying the knowledge which they possessed and gained, **and such as had ability in them to stand in the king's palace,** to become accustomed to the ways and manners of a king's court, **and whom they might teach the learning and the tongue of the Chaldeans,** that of the learned classes of the Babylonian people. Their course of study would thus comprise all that was taught in the highest schools of the empire, and their training would be that of the noblest youths of the empire. V. 5. **And the king appointed them,** namely, for those who were to be selected, **a daily provision of the king's meat,** of the food which was served on his own tables, **and of the wine which he drank,** literally, "of the wine of his drinking," or "banqueting," **so nourishing them three years,** their education and their physical development going hand in hand, **that at the end thereof they might stand before the king,** fully equipped for his service as courtiers and advisers, or in whatever capacity he might choose to use them. V. 6. **Now, among these,** among the youths selected in accordance with this royal order, **were of the children of Judah,** of the most prominent tribe of the Jewish people, **Daniel, Hananiah, Mishael, and Azariah,** v. 7. **unto whom the prince of the eunuchs,** as being in charge of this entire experiment, **gave names; for he gave unto Daniel the name of Belteshazzar, and to Hananiah of Shadrach, and to Mishael of Meshach, and to Azariah of Abed-nego.** "The changing of names as a sign of entrance into the condition of subjection to a ruler is a frequently attested custom of Oriental and classical antiquity." It is significant that all these names had definite meanings, a fact which it might be well for Christian parents to remember as they bring their children to Christ, their merciful King, in Holy Baptism. The giving of meaningless and heathen names ought certainly to be discouraged in all Christian congregations.

DANIEL FAITHFUL TO HIS RELIGIOUS CONVICTIONS. — V. 8. **But Daniel purposed in his heart,** definitely made up his mind, **that he would not defile himself with the portion of the king's meat nor with the wine which he drank,** chiefly because the heathen had the custom of consecrating their food and, in fact, their entire meals by offering a portion to their gods, cp. 1 Cor. 10, 18—20; **therefore he requested of the prince of the eunuchs that he might not defile himself.** Daniel's resolution to refrain from the king's food thus was due to the fact that he had the proper spiritual understanding of the Law, that he desired to be obedient to its spirit as well as to its letter. V. 9. **Now, God,** whose kind providence is brought out throughout the narrative, **had brought Daniel into favor and tender love with the prince of the eunuchs,** so that the latter was favorably disposed toward Daniel, was ready to grant him any reasonable request from the outset. V. 10. **And the prince of the eunuchs,** to whom Daniel promptly presented his petition, **said unto Daniel,** as he gave evidence of the favorable mental attitude which he had toward the Jewish youth, **I fear my lord, the king, who hath appointed your meat and your drink,** by a definite command; **for why should he**

2) Cp. Wilson, *Studies in the Book of Daniel,* 58.

see **your faces worse liking**, of a meager and emaciated appearance, in a worse condition, **than the children which are of your sort?** The question has the meaning of a most emphatic denial: He must not see you in that condition. **Then shall ye make me endanger my head to the king**, that is, the king held his life as a pledge for the faithful fulfilment of his commandment concerning the training of the Jewish youths. V. 11. **Then said Daniel to Melzar, whom the prince of the eunuchs had set over Daniel, Hananiah, Mishael, and Azariah**, the official who was their immediate superior during the course of their training, v. 12. **Prove thy servants, I beseech thee, ten days**, making an experiment in their case; **and let them give us pulse to eat and water to drink**, the simplest kind of vegetable food with water, all luxuries in the line of food being omitted in their diet. V. 13. **Then let our countenances be looked upon before thee**, in a careful examination of their physical condition, **and the countenance of the children that eat of the portion of the king's meat**, making a comparison between these four and the youths who complied with the king's order concerning their diet; **and as thou seest**, according to the result of the observations made after the period, **deal with thy servants**, the test determining the matter once for all. V. 14. **So he consented to them in this matter and proved them ten days**, making the experiment in accordance with their petition. V. 15. **And at the end of ten days their countenances appeared fairer and fatter in flesh**, they were clearer-eyed and in better condition in every way, **than all the children**, or youths, **which did eat the portion of the king's meat.** V. 16. **Thus Melzar**, who evidently was in charge of the king's kitchen, **took away the portion of their meat and the wine that they should drink**, he no longer set it aside for their diet; **and gave them pulse**, vegetables, especially legumes. V. 17. **As for these four children, God**, who thus rewarded their faithfulness, **gave them knowledge and skill in all learning and wisdom**, so that they mastered the Chaldean literature and scientific knowledge; **and Daniel**, in addition to these accomplishments, **had understanding in all visions and dreams**, this being clearly a miraculous gift granted by God for a special purpose and not identical with the gift of prophecy. V. 18. **Now, at the end of the days that the king had said he should bring them in**, that is, at the end of the three-year period originally fixed, **then the prince of the eunuchs brought them in before Nebuchadnezzar**, so that all the Jewish youths were presented for inspection and examination. V. 19. **And the king communed with them**, examining them in all the branches which they had studied; **and among them all was found none like Daniel, Hananiah, Mishael, and Azariah**, none of the others equaled them either in physical beauty or in mental excellencies; **therefore stood they before the king**, they entered the royal service, they were given a position of importance at the royal court. V. 20. **And in all matters of wisdom and understanding that the king enquired of them**, namely, at the general examination, **he found them ten times better than all the magicians and astrologers**, the most learned men and those who practised occult arts, **that were in all his realm.** V. 21. **And Daniel continued**, he held positions at court, he lived in Babylonian court circles, **even unto the first year of King Cyrus.** If God's children are faithful in their adherence to His Word and commandments, He often rewards them even in this life by giving them positions of wealth and influence in the world.

CHAPTER 2.

The Vision of the Monarchies.

THE DREAM OF NEBUCHADNEZZAR. — V. 1. **And in the second year of the reign of Nebuchadnezzar**, when he had advanced from the position of coregent to that of sole regent of the Babylonian Empire, which must have been shortly after he had examined the Jewish youths brought before him, **Nebuchadnezzar dreamed dreams**, he was, by the interposition of God, vouchsafed a vision of the future in the form of symbols, **wherewith his spirit was troubled**, very strongly agitated, **and his sleep brake from him**, so that he was unable to regain the tranquillity of mind necessary for quiet sleep. V. 2. **Then the king commanded to call the magicians**, the men who were learned in the Chaldean language and literature, **and the astrologers**, those who were masters of incantation, **and the sorcerers**, the men who employed witchcraft, **and the Chaldeans**, the noblest and most exalted among the highest class of influential men in the kingdom, **for to show the king his dreams**, to tell him the contents of his dream which he could not remember. **So they came**, in obedience to his summons, **and stood before the king.** V. 3. **And the king said unto them, I have dreamed a dream, and my spirit was troubled to know the dream**, for he had only a vague impression of the importance of his dream, whence he was all the more anxious to have it presented to him in all its details, together with its explanation. V. 4. **Then spake the Chaldeans**, as the foremost representatives of the wise men of the realm, **to the king in Syriac**, in the East-Aramaic dialect in which this section of the book is also written, **O king, live forever!** This was the usual form of salutation at the courts of the Chaldean and the Persian monarchs. **Tell thy servants the dream, and we will show the interpretation.** It was necessary for them to know the contents of the dream before they would even venture an interpretation. V. 5. **The king answered and said to the Chaldeans, The thing is gone from me**, that is, the statement of what he required from them had gone forth from him, he had stated his purpose of having called them; **if ye will not make known unto me the dream**, giving its contents, **with the interpretation thereof**, both of which he now clearly demanded, **ye shall be cut in pieces**, such hewing to pieces being a punishment in vogue among the Chaldeans, **and your houses shall be made a dunghill**, that is, razed to the ground and covered with refuse and dung. V. 6. **But if ye show the dream and the interpretation thereof**, what it consisted in and what it meant, **ye shall receive of me gifts and rewards and great honor**, both in money and in advancement. **Therefore show me the dream and the interpretation thereof.** The insistence of the king was that of a true Oriental despot, who demanded without a reason, simply because it suited his fancy. V. 7. **They answered again and said**, in an effort to bring home to the king the unreasonableness of his request, **Let the king tell his servants the dream, and we will show the interpretation of it.** V. 8. **The king answered and said, I know of certainty**, most assuredly, **that ye would gain the time, because ye see that the thing is gone from me**, because he insisted upon a speedy answer to his demand. He declared that they were merely trying to put off the matter, to postpone it indefinitely, in the hope that he would sufficiently relent to tell them the contents of his dream. V. 9. **But if ye will not make known unto me the dream, there is but one decree for you**, one and the same sentence of condemnation would strike them all: **for ye have prepared lying and corrupt words to speak before me**, base misrepresentations, by which they kept him for a fool, **till the time be changed**, until by some lucky chance they might get into possession of the secret, or until the king would withdraw his demand. **Therefore tell me the dream**, which he would immediately recognize, **and I shall know that ye can show me the interpretation thereof.** It was clear to Nebuchadnezzar that the wise men were unable to reveal hidden things, and therefore he concluded that the interpretation which they would offer in case they would find out the contents of the dream would, at best, be mere guesswork. V. 10. **The Chaldeans answered before the king**, in an attempt to establish the impossibility for mere human beings to satisfy the king's demand, **and said, There is not a man upon the earth that can show the king's matter**, revealing this secret thing; **therefore there is no king, lord, nor ruler that asked such things at any magician or astrologer or Chaldean.** The fact that no ruler on earth, no matter how great and mighty he was, had ever made such a demand, was to them a proof that the fulfilment of his command transcended the highest human wisdom. V. 11. **And it is a rare thing that the king requireth**, most singular and unusual, the like of which was not known in history, **and there is none other that can show it before the king except the gods, whose dwelling is not with flesh.** "God makes the heathen, out of their own mouth, condemn their impotent pretensions to supernatural knowledge in order to bring out in brighter contrast His power to reveal secrets to His servants." V. 12. **For this cause the king was angry and very furious and commanded to destroy all the wise men of Babylon**, either of this city or of the province. V. 13. **And the decree went forth that the wise men should be slain**, the slaughter being apparently begun; **and they sought Daniel and his fellows**, who had not been summoned with the older members of the Chaldeans, but belonged to their class, **to be slain.** The enemies of the believers often seem to be on the verge of triumphing over them and of taking their life, but God holds His sheltering hand over His children so that without His consent no harm may come near them.

DANIEL PREPARES TO INTERPRET THE KING'S DREAM. — V. 14. **Then Daniel answered with counsel and wisdom**, with sound and prudent advice, **to Arioch, the captain of the king's guard**, who was also in charge of the sentence of execution, **which was gone forth to slay the wise men of Babylon;** v. 15. **he answered and said to Arioch, the king's captain**, thereby displaying the wisdom for which he afterward became so famous, **Why is the decree so hasty from the king?** Why the furious and sharp command, which came upon the people concerned like a bolt out of the blue sky? **Then Arioch made the thing known to Daniel**, giving him the information which he sought. V. 16. **Then Daniel went in**, naturally after being properly announced, **and desired of the king that he would give him time**, postponing the execution of the cruel decree for some days, **and that he would show the king the interpretation**, thereby giving the king a definite promise. V. 17. **Then Daniel went to his house and made the thing known to Hananiah, Mishael, and Azariah, his companions**, who were of one mind with him in their observation of the religion of their fathers, v. 18. **that they would desire mercies of the God of heaven,** the fulfilment of their united prayers being represented as a taking of gifts from before the throne of God, **concerning this secret, that Daniel and his fellows,** his Jewish companions, **should not perish with the rest of the wise men of Babylon,** whose death, according to the king's decree, seemed inevitable. V. 19. **Then was the secret revealed unto Daniel in a night vision,** the Lord Himself granting the knowledge needed in this urgent case. **Then Daniel,** properly giving all glory and honor to God alone, **blessed the God of heaven,** the one and only Lord. V. 20. **Daniel answered and said,** responding, as it were, to the goodness of God with his hymn of praise, **Blessed be the name of God forever and ever,** this name including His entire essence and attributes; **for wisdom and might are His,** the two qualities coming into consideration here; v. 21. **and He changeth the times and the seasons,** as would appear in the carrying out of the king's prophetic vision; **He removeth kings and setteth up kings,** all the events in the history of nations being determined by Him; **He giveth wisdom unto the wise and knowledge to them that know understanding,** Daniel thus tracing his own accomplishments entirely to the gift of God; v. 22. **He revealeth the deep and secret things,** which are hidden before the eyes of such as are mere human beings; **He knoweth what is in the darkness,** what is covered before human eyes, **and the light dwelleth with Him,** abiding with Him as His possession, so that He is the Source of all light, physical and spiritual. V. 23. **I thank Thee and praise Thee, O Thou God of my fathers,** of the patriarchs of the Jewish nation, **who hast given me wisdom and might and hast made known unto me now what we desired of Thee,** that for which they had so eagerly implored Him; **for Thou hast now made known unto us the king's matter,** the very thing which the Chaldeans had declared to be an impossibility. V. 24. **Therefore Daniel went in unto Arioch, whom the king had ordained to destroy the wise men of Babylon; he went and said thus unto him, Destroy not the wise men of Babylon,** their execution thus being summarily stayed; **bring me in before the king, and I will show unto the king the interpretation.** V. 25. **Then Arioch brought in Daniel before the king in haste and said thus unto him, I have found a man of the captives of Judah that will make known unto the king the interpretation.** V. 26. **The king,** having duly received Daniel in audience, **answered and said to Daniel, whose name was Belteshazzar, Art thou able to make known unto me the dream which I have seen and the interpretation thereof?** V. 27. **Daniel answered in the presence of the king,** whose amazement at his assertion concerning his ability to undertake what the wisest of the realm had found beyond their wisdom had just appeared in his question, **and said, The secret which the king hath demanded cannot the wise men, the astrologers, the magicians, the soothsayers, show unto the king,** it was clearly impossible for any mere man, no matter what degree of wisdom was his, to solve the king's difficulty; v. 28. **but there is a God in heaven that revealeth secrets,** possessing the attribute of omniscience of which the heathen gods and their servants knew nothing, **and maketh known to the King Nebuchadnezzar what shall be in the latter days,** at the period to which the believers of the Old Testament were looking forward with such intense eagerness. **Thy dream and the visions of thy head,** those which he saw in his mind, **upon thy bed are these:** v. 29. **As for thee, O king, thy thoughts came into thy mind upon thy bed,** he was engaged with these problems, **what should come to pass hereafter; and He that revealeth secrets,** the one true God, whom the Jews worshiped, **maketh known to thee what shall come to pass.** V. 30. **But as for me, this secret is not revealed to me for any wisdom that I have more than any living,** because he possessed such an extraordinary measure of wisdom by virtue of his own efforts or natural abilities, **but for their sakes that shall make known the interpretation to the king, and that thou mightest know the thoughts of thy heart.** The indefinite expression was used purposely, so that the person of Daniel might be as little conspicuous as possible. When God endows a person with unusual understanding and wisdom in the interest of His Word and work, it behooves such a person to be properly humble, giving the glory to God alone and working in His service with cheerful energy.

THE DREAM INTERPRETED; DANIEL ADVANCED. — V. 31. **Thou, O king, sawest,** that is, he beheld before his eyes, he had his gaze fixed upon the vision, **and behold a great image,** a statute in human form. **This great image, whose brightness was excellent, stood before thee,** over against him, in full view; **and the form thereof was terrible,** on account of its colossal proportions and its terrifying aspect. V. 32. **This image's head was of fine gold,** or, "as far as the image was concerned, its head was of pure gold," **his breast and his arms of silver, his belly and his thighs,** or, "his hips with the upper thighs," **of brass,** v. 33. **his legs of iron, his feet part of iron and part of clay.** "Only the first part, the head, constitutes a unity; the second, in the arms, shows evidence of division; the third has the same feature in the thighs; the fourth, while proceeding from a common source, is entirely divided, although it also possesses ability of motion; the fifth is divided from the start and is finally subdivided still further in the ten toes. The material becomes less precious as we proceed, until it reaches common clay." V. 34. **Thou sawest,** that is, the king's gaze was still directed toward this image, **till that a stone was cut out,** being torn loose from a mountain above, **without hands,** without human agency, by a special act of God, **which,** in rolling down from the mountainside, **smote the image upon his feet that were of iron and clay and brake them to pieces.** V. 35. **Then,** as a result of this smashing blow, **was the iron, the clay, the brass, the silver, and the gold,** all the perishable materials of the image named in reverse order, **broken to pieces together and became like the chaff of the summer threshing-floors,** reduced to the finest dust to be carried away by the wind, totally demolished; **and the wind carried them away that no place was found for them,** that not a vestige remained; **and the stone that smote the image became a great mountain and filled the whole earth,** the image and all it represented sinking into insignificance beside it. V. 36. **This is the dream,** all the details of which must now have come back to the king's recollection, so that he recognized them; **and we will tell the interpretation thereof before the king,** Daniel here classing himself with his companions, the believing worshipers of Jehovah, with whom together he had access to the mysteries of the divine revelation. V. 37. **Thou, O king, art a king of kings,** a great sovereign, ruler of a world-power; **for the God of heaven hath given thee a kingdom,** or dominion, **power and strength and glory,** the attention of the king being here directed to the one Lord, the Dispenser of all good gifts. V. 38. **And wheresoever the children of men dwell,** even in the most remote parts of the habitable world, **the beasts of the field and the fowls of the heaven hath He given into thine hand,** in an absolute dominion such as man possessed at the beginning, **and hath made thee ruler over them all,** his power extended over practically the entire world then known, at least to all parts which might be termed civilized. **Thou art this head of gold,** this being all the more appropriate since Babylon possessed an immense wealth, also in precious metals. V. 39. **And after thee shall arise another kingdom inferior to thee,** with a lower standard of political morals, lacking in internal strength, although still possessing a world sovereignty, **and another third kingdom of brass, which shall bear rule over all the earth,** by virtue of its unyielding hardness, though also inferior in quality. V. 40. **And the fourth kingdom shall be strong as iron, forasmuch as,** or, "just as," **iron breaketh in pieces and subdueth all things,** crushing them and utterly destroying them; **and as iron that breaketh all these, shall it break in pieces and bruise,** its destructive power being the point of comparison. V. 41. **And whereas thou sawest the feet and toes, part of potters' clay and part of iron,** total weakness and lack of power being implied in the terms, **the kingdom shall be divided; but there shall be in it of the strength of the iron,** this being retained in spite of the internal division, **forasmuch as thou sawest the iron mixed with miry clay,** in its sticky form, just as it came from the pits. V. 42. **And as the toes of the feet were part of iron and part of clay,** indicating the weakness of the feet supporting the great colossus, **so the kingdom shall be partly strong and partly broken,** that is, chiefly brittle, and therefore always on the verge of disintegration. V. 43. **And whereas thou sawest iron mixed with miry clay, they,** the rulers and the various ruling elements making up the fourth kingdom, **shall mingle themselves with the seed of men,** making an effort to establish harmony; **but they shall not cleave one to another,** in a firmly coherent mass, **even as iron is not mixed with clay,** namely, in a solid and permanent union. The meaning is clear. The world-power in its totality appears as a colossal human form: Babylon, the head of gold; Medo-Persia, the breast and the two arms of silver; the Greco-Macedonian Empire, as the belly and the two thighs of brass; and Rome, with its various branches and dependent kingdoms, as the legs of iron and the feet of iron and clay. "Those kingdoms only are mentioned which stand in some relation to the Lord's people." V. 44. **And in the days of these kings,** while the various minor rulers were in power under the general sovereignty of Rome, **shall the God of heaven set up a kingdom which shall never be destroyed,** its divine and eternal character being evident throughout; **and the kingdom shall not be left to other people,** its dominion taken over by a new power which might arise, **but it shall break in pieces and consume all these kingdoms,** bringing all world powers to an end, **and it shall stand forever.** The kingdom of Christ is not of this world, and yet its power is such as to overcome all human might and authority and to establish instead the glorious reign of the Gospel of peace; for Christ is the King of kings and the Lord of lords. V. 45. **Forasmuch as thou sawest that the stone was cut out of the mountain without hands,** without human agency and influence, **and that it brake in pieces the iron, the brass, the clay, the silver, and the gold,** all these materials being equally powerless to stand before its impetuous rush:

the great God hath made known to the king what shall come to pass hereafter, the one and only true God having might not only to make such wonderful revelations, but also to bring His promises to pass. **And the dream is certain and the interpretation thereof sure,** a fact which Daniel's emphatic statement properly brought to the foreground in conclusion. V. 46. **Then the King Nebuchadnezzar fell upon his face,** overcome by the wisdom contained in this straightforward declaration, **and worshiped Daniel,** giving him adoration as a prophet of the true God, worshiping the Lord in the person of Daniel, **and commanded that they should offer an oblation and sweet odors unto him.** Cp. Acts 10, 25; 14, 13. V. 47. **The king answered unto Daniel and said, Of a truth it is that your God is a God of gods,** in the eyes of Nebuchadnezzar the mightiest of all gods, **and a Lord of kings, and a Revealer of secrets, seeing thou couldest reveal this secret,** which was so obviously beyond mere human ability. V. 48. **Then the king made Daniel a great man,** exalting him to a position of great dignity and power, **and gave him many great gifts,** rewarding him after the manner of Oriental rulers, **and made him ruler over the whole province of Babylon,** a civil appointment which gave him the administration in the most important province of the empire, **and chief of the governors over all the wise men of Babylon,** a position of influence as well as of honor. V. 49. **Then Daniel requested of the King, and he set Shadrach, Meshach, and Abed-nego over the affairs of the province of Babylon,** as those immediately in charge of the business of administration; **but Daniel sat in the gate of the king,** as his chief counselor and president over the various orders into which the wise men of Babylon were divided. Christians may well occupy even the highest positions in the state, for then they may perform the work of their office to the honor of God and for the true welfare of the state.

CHAPTER 3.

The Test of the Faith of Daniel's Three Friends.

THE THREE MEN LOYAL TO JEHOVAH. — V. 1. **Nebuchadnezzar, the king,** at some later period of his reign, **made an image of gold,** an immense idol figure, probably in the form of a human being, **whose height was threescore cubits and the breadth thereof six cubits,** that is, its height with its pedestal was about ninety feet and its width nine feet; **he set it up in the Plain of Dura,** very likely in the level country east of the Tigris, or in a smaller valley near the capital, **in the province of Babylon.** V. 2. **Then Nebuchadnezzar, the king, sent to gather together the princes, the governors, and the captains,** executive officers of superior rank with both civil and military duties, **the judges,** or chief officers of administration, **the treasurers,** the financial directors or managers of the public treasury, **the counselors,** those learned in the law, **the sheriffs,** the inferior judges, **and all the rulers of the provinces, to come to the dedication of the image which Nebuchadnezzar, the king, had set up,** to have a great celebration in honor of the occasion, all the officials of the empire being the king's guests during the festival. V. 3. **Then the princes, the governors, and captains, the judges, the treasurers, the counselors, the sheriffs, and all the rulers of the provinces were gathered together unto the dedication of the image that Nebuchadnezzar, the king, had set up,** proudly obedient to the king's summons; **and they stood before,** over against, **the image that Nebuchadnezzar had set up,** ready to take part in all the ceremonies of the dedication, since the picture was a symbol of Babylon's world power and of the king's divine majesty, as they believed. V. 4. **Then an herald cried aloud,** literally, "with might," raising his voice to reach all the members of the assembled multitude, **To you it is commanded, O people, nations, and languages,** this evidently being a formula used in the official edicts of the Chaldean Empire, by which the sovereign addressed himself to all the subjects of his great empire, v. 5. **that at what time ye hear the sound of the cornet,** the horn or tuba of the ancients, **flute,** the reed-flute, or shepherd's pipe, **harp,** a small four-stringed harp like a zither, **sackbut,** a triangular stringed instrument, **psaltery,** another kind of harp, **dulcimer,** a bappipe consisting of two pipes thrust through a leathern bag, **and all kinds of music,** the enumeration being characteristic of the pompous language used by a world ruler, **ye fall down and worship the golden image that Nebuchadnezzar, the king, hath set up;** v. 6. **and whoso falleth not down and worshipeth shall the same hour be cast into the midst of a burning fiery furnace.** This mode of punishment was in use among the Babylonians, and since all men were required to fall on their faces in the act of adoration, it would be all the easier to pick out all such as might refuse to obey the king's decree. V. 7. **Therefore at that time,** in accordance with the announcement of the herald, **when all the people heard the sound of the cornet, flute, harp, sackbut, psaltery, and all kinds of music, all the people,** represented here by their respective rulers, **the nations, and the languages,** as many as had appeared for the great celebration, **fell down and worshiped the golden image that Nebuchadnezzar, the king, had set up.** It is to be noted here that, whereas most of the heathen nations tolerated the gods of the countries conquered by them, they at the same time required of the subdued people a greater veneration for their own gods, whose superiority they considered fully established by the fact of their being victors. V. 8. **Wherefore at that time certain Chaldeans,** who were filled with jealousy on account of the promotion of the strangers, while they were obliged to be satisfied with inferior positions, **came near and accused the Jews,** literally, "they ate their pieces of flesh," a term used in the Aramaic for slandering, for casting hateful suspicions. V. 9. **They spake and said to the King Nebuchadnezzar, O king, live forever!** this being the ordinary form of address in Babylonia. V. 10. **Thou, O king, hast made a decree,** issued an unmistakable order, **that every man that shall hear the sound of the cornet, flute, harp, sackbut, psaltery, and dulcimer, and all kinds of music, shall fall down and worship the golden image;** v. 11. **and whoso falleth not down and worshipeth, that he should be cast into the midst of a burning fiery furnace.** V. 12. **There are certain Jews whom thou hast set over the affairs of the province of Babylon,** who, therefore, as the accusers intimate, were under special obligations toward the king as their benefactor, **Shadrach, Meshach, and Abed-nego; these men, O king,** whose influence and example were of such great importance, **have not regarded thee,** paying no attention to his commands; **they serve not thy gods nor worship the golden image which thou hast set up.** What made the behavior of these Chaldeans so particularly odious at this time was the fact that they used this one instance of disobedience to the king's command on the part of the Jewish officials as an occasion for removing them from their offices, that, in other words, envy was the one motive which caused them to take such steps at this time. "The mention of their exalted official rank was designed to emphasize the dangerous feature connected with the disobedience of such men to the royal command and also to direct attention to the blackness of their ingratitude toward their royal benefactor." V. 13. **Then Nebuchadnezzar, in his rage and fury,** in the extreme violence of his anger, **commanded to bring Shadrach, Meshach, and Abed-nego,** to have them delivered into his presence at once. **Then they brought these men before the king.** V. 14. **Nebuchadnezzar spake and said unto them, Is it true, O Shadrach, Meshach, and Abed-nego, do not ye serve my gods,** literally, "With deliberate, evil intent are ye not serving my god?" **nor worship the golden image which I have set up?** His gods were here taken together and represented under the golden image, and Nebuchadnezzar construed the absence of the three men from the festive assembly as an endeavor purposely to avoid any participation in the ceremonies. V. 15. **Now, if ye be ready that at what time ye hear the sound of the cornet, flute, harp, sackbut, psaltery, and dulcimer, and all kinds of music, ye fall down and worship the image which I have made, well,** the completion of the conditional clause being omitted in the Aramaic, as in Ex. 32, 32; Luke 13, 9; **but if ye worship not, ye shall be cast the same hour into the midst of a burning fiery furnace; and who is that God that shall deliver you out of my hands?** This was not a direct blasphemy of the true God, but it was a very presumptive statement, since the king thereby declared the deliverance from the fiery furnace to be a work which no god was able to perform. V. 16. **Shadrach, Meshach, and Abed-nego answered and said to the king, O Nebuchadnezzar,** the directness of their address giving added emphasis to their statement, **we are not careful to answer thee in this matter,** that is, they did not consider it necessary to search for a reasonable excuse or explanation. V. 17. **If it be so, our God, whom we serve, is able to deliver us from the burning fiery furnace,** rather, "If our God is able to deliver us," **and He will deliver us out of thine hand, O king.** This was not casting doubt upon the strength and ability of the Lord to help them; it only left the matter under the disposition of the gracious and good will of Him whose actions are always right and good. V. 18. **But if not,** that is, if a deliverance is not in agreement with His counsel and will, **be it known unto thee, O king, that we will not serve thy gods, nor worship the golden image which thou hast set up.** We have here a fine example of the loyalty of faith and of meek submission to the will of God. Christians in a similar situation may also find it impossible to produce an understanding of the issues involved in the minds of their adversaries. They will, therefore, not attempt to justify their attitude, but leave the matter entirely in the hands of God, whose ways are always good.

THE MIRACULOUS PRESERVATION OF GOD'S SERVANTS. — V. 19. **Then was Nebuchadnezzar full of fury,** of extreme and unreasonable anger, **and the form of his visage was changed against Shadrach, Meshach, and Abed-nego,** his expression showing the extremity of the fury which possessed him; **therefore he spake and commanded that they should heat the furnace one seven times more than it was wont to be heated.** He did not realize in the heat of his passion that he was really defeating his own ends; for the hotter the fire, the sooner his victims were liable to be put out of misery. V. 20. **And he commanded the most mighty men that were in his army,** upon whom he could depend for absolute obedience and trustworthiness, **to bind Shadrach, Meshach, and Abednego and to cast them into the burning fiery furnace,** a task which was here connected with considerable danger because it involved a close approach to the intense heat of the furnace. V. 21. **Then these men were bound in their coats, their hosen, and their hats,** rather, "in their undergarments, their tunics, and their mantles," **and their other garments,** part of which at least were of delicate, easily inflammable material, **and were cast into the midst of the burning fiery furnace,** the repetition of this phrase tending to make the element of danger stand out more prominently. V. 22. **Therefore, because the king's commandment was urgent,** because he spoke in fury, **and the furnace exceeding hot,** far in excess of its usual degree of heat, **the flame of the fire,** a blast sweeping out from the opening, **slew those men that took up Shadrach, Meshach, and Abed-nego,** after the king's servants had cast them through the opening above. V. 23. **And these three men, Shadrach, Meshach, and Abed-nego, fell down bound,** as they had been trussed up by the executioners, **into the midst of the burning fiery furnace.** V. 24. **Then Nebuchadnezzar, the king, was astonied,** greatly astounded, **and rose up in haste,** due to his great agitation, **and spake and said unto his counselors,** the ministers, or governors, who formed his council, **Did not we cast three men bound into the midst of the fire?** The king's chair seems to have been placed opposite the side door of the furnace, which was open to permit a strong draught to fan the fire, and it was from here that he witnessed the execution. **They answered and said unto the king, True, O king.** V. 25. **He answered and said, Lo, I see four men loose,** no longer bound as they had been cast in, **walking in the midst of the fire,** not leaving it, but waiting for God's time to leave them out, **and they have no hurt,** as one might have expected by reason of the rough treatment accorded them; **and the form of the fourth,** on account of the compelling dignity of his appearance, **is like the son of God,** rather, "like a son of the gods," one pertaining to a divine family and generation. The fourth man was an angel of God, sent for the protection of His pious servants, so that the flame could not harm them. God protects those who place their trust in Him in the midst of death and destruction, so that not a hair may fall from their heads without His will. V. 26. **Then Nebuchadnezzar came near to the mouth of the burning fiery furnace,** which was now opened at his command, **and spake and said, Shadrach, Meshach, and Abed-nego, ye servants of the most high God,** of whose superior greatness he had just received an overpowering impression, and whom he was therefore willing to designate in this manner, **come forth and come hither. Then Shadrach, Meshach, and Abed-nego came forth of the midst of the fire.** V. 27. **And the princes, governors, and captains,** the representative rulers of his entire empire, **and the king's counselors,** the members of his own privy council, **being gathered together, saw these men, upon whose bodies the fire had no power,** having had not the slightest effect upon them, **nor was an hair of their head singed,** this being ordinarily the first result of fire, **neither were their coats changed,** their undergarments touched by fire, **nor the smell of fire had passed on them,** in other words, one could not even notice that they had been anywhere near fire. V. 28. **Then Nebuchadnezzar spake and said, Blessed be the God of Shadrach, Meshach, and Abed-nego,** whose superiority to his own gods the king thus recognized, **who hath sent His angel and delivered His servants, that trusted in Him and have changed the king's word,** boldly transgressing his commands, **and yielded their bodies,** offering them without flinching in the interest of their loyalty to their God, **that they might not serve nor worship any god except their own God.** V. 29. **Therefore I make a decree,** literally, "And from me is set forth a decree," **That every people, nation, and language which speak anything amiss against the God of Shadrach, Meshach, and Abed-nego shall be cut in pieces, and their houses shall be made a dunghill,** cp. chap. 2, 5, **because there is no other god that can deliver after this sort.** While this confession does not imply faith in the one true God, it decreed toleration to the worshipers of Jehovah throughout the empire of Babylon. V. 30. **Then the king,** having once more restored the three men to his full favor, **promoted Shadrach, Meshach, and Abed-nego in the province of Babylon.** So the firmness of these men in confessing their God, far from bringing misfortune upon them, resulted in further blessings upon them. Note also that the miracles which the Lord performs in the interest of His Church result in benefits for the state as well, so that men are obliged to acknowledge the hand of God in the affairs of men, even if they do not accept Him as the God of their salvation.

CHAPTER 4.

Nebuchadnezzar's Dream and Its Appalling Consequences.

THE KING TELLS DANIEL HIS DREAM.—V. 1. **Nebuchadnezzar, the king, unto all people, nations, and languages,** this term, in a public proclamation or royal edict, including all the subjects of the empire, **that dwell in all the earth,** for the Babylonian Empire embraced practically the entire world then explored: **Peace be multiplied unto you,** literally, "Peace be imparted to you in rich measure," a greeting which was in use in the Orient for many centuries and was later taken over by the Christians. Cp. 1 Pet. 1, 2; 2 Pet. 1, 2. V. 2. **I thought it good,** it pleased the king, he regarded it as the right and seemly thing, **to show the signs and wonders that the high God hath wrought toward me,** the reference here being to the true God, of whose omnipotent power Nebuchadnezzar had received further unmistakable evidence, as he relates in this edict. V. 3. **How great are His signs, and how mighty are His wonders!** exceeding those of any so-called gods of the heathen. **His kingdom is an everlasting kingdom, and His dominion is from generation to generation.** It is a doxology which gives due honor to the true God, even though it does not confess faith in Jehovah. Now follows the account of the happenings which caused this outburst of praise. V. 4. **I, Nebuchadnezzar, was at rest in mine house,** his wars victoriously concluded, his kingdom at peace, **and flourishing in my palace,** enjoying wonderful prosperity. V. 5. **I saw a dream which made me afraid,** the suddenness of whose coming filled him with alarm, **and the thoughts upon my bed,** which exercised him in connection with his dream, **and the visions of my head,** those which were presented to the eyes of his mind, **troubled me,** their fancies and images filling him with apprehension of approaching evil. V. 6. **Therefore made I a decree,** he issued the command, **to bring in all the wise men of Babylon before me that they might make known unto me the interpretation of the dream,** the dream itself with all its details, in this instance, being very clear in the recollection of the king, so that he desired an explanation only. V. 7. **Then came in the magicians, the astrologers, the Chaldeans, and the soothsayers,** cp. chap. 2, 2, **and I told the dream before them; but they did not make known unto me the interpretation thereof,** their merely human wisdom was unable to penetrate into the depths of the mysteries which God wanted to make known in this instance. V. 8. **But at the last Daniel came in before me, whose name,** given him when he entered the king's service, **was Belteshazzar, according to the name of my god,** "the foremost of Bel," the chief god of Babylon, **and in whom is the spirit of the holy gods,** of whose eminent prophetic gifts the king had been given evidence on previous occasions, although he was in this case, for some unexplained reason, reserved to the last; **and before him I told the dream, saying,** v. 9. **O Belteshazzar, master of the magicians,** whose comparatively independent position as the chief of all the wise men at Babylon made it possible for him to be absent from a large assembly of the officials of the royal court on this occasion, **because I know that the spirit of the holy gods is in thee, and no secret troubleth thee,** no secret being too difficult for him to explain, **tell me the visions of my dream that I have seen and the interpretation thereof.** V. 10. **Thus were the visions of mine head in my bed,** literally, "And regarding the visions of my head upon my bed," **I saw, and behold a tree in the midst of the earth,** therefore evidently possessing great importance for the whole earth, **and the height thereof was great,** it was of conspicuous size to begin with. V. 11. **The tree grew and was strong,** became great and mighty, **and the height thereof reached unto heaven and the sight thereof to the end of all the earth,** so that it extended far enough to be seen from the very ends of the world; v. 12. **the leaves thereof were fair,** its branching, forming the crown, was very beautiful, **and the fruit thereof much,** growing in large quantities, **and in it was meat for all,** food for all who lived under its shelter being found on it; **the beasts of the field had shadow under it, and the fowls of the heaven dwelt in the boughs thereof, and all flesh was fed of it,** the image being that of the entire human race united under the scepter of Nebuchadnezzar and enjoying prosperity under his beneficent government. V. 13. **I saw in the visions of my head upon my bed, and, behold, a watcher and an holy one,** that is, a holy watchman, an angel delegated by God to watch over the affairs of men, **came down from heaven;** v. 14. **he cried aloud and said thus,** making announcement with a mighty voice, as the herald of almighty God, **Hew down the tree and cut off his branches, shake off his leaves,** causing them to fall quickly, **and scatter his fruit,** in a contemptuous manner, as though possessing no value; **let the beasts get away from under it,** as no longer safe within his shelter, **and the fowls from his branches,** which no longer offered them a safe retreat; v. 15. **nevertheless, leave the stump of his roots in the earth, even with a band of iron and brass, in the tender grass of the field,** this description already indicating that the application must be made to an animate being, whose fetters were those of the mental and spiritual darkness brought on as the result of the loss of reason; **and let it be wet with the dew of heaven,** there being no shelter to keep the weather away from him, **and let his portion be with the beasts in the grass of the earth,** so that he would partake of their food; v. 16. **let his heart be changed from man's,** so that this center of intellectual life would lose its human aspect, **and let a beast's heart be given unto him,** so that he would fully descend to the level of a brute; **and let seven times pass over him,** the exact length of these periods not being given. V. 17. **This matter is by the decree of the watchers,** according to their uniform judgment, **and the demand by the word of the holy ones,** the angels of God having reminded Him, as it were, of the requirements of His holiness and justice upon so flagrant a transgressor, **to the intent that the living,** all human beings on earth, **may know that the Most High ruleth in the kingdom of men,** dispensing authority and power according to His will, **and giveth it to whomsoever He will, and setteth up over it the basest of men,** a man from the humblest rank of life, if God so chose, assuming the reins of government according to His disposition. V. 18. **This dream I, King Nebuchadnezzar, have seen,** all its details being clear before his eyes and set forth in the same manner. **Now, thou, O Belteshazzar, declare the interpretation thereof,** setting forth its meaning, **forasmuch as all the wise men of my kingdom are not able to make known unto me the interpretation;** v. 7. **but thou art able, for the spirit of the holy gods is in thee.** The affairs of the whole world and of every nation on earth are in the hands of God, who directs them according to His good pleasure, in the interest of His Church.

The Interpretation and the Fulfilment of the Dream. — V. 19. **Then Daniel, whose name was Belteshazzar, was astonied,** he stood aghast at the dream and its meaning, **for one hour,** for a long period of time, **and his thoughts troubled him,** for he was overwhelmed with awe. **The king,** concluding from the appearance of his face that he had found the interpretation, **spake and said, Belteshazzar, let not the dream or the interpretation thereof trouble thee,** fill him with apprehension for his safety if he revealed its meaning. **Belteshazzar answered and said,** speaking as a loyal subject of the king in whose empire he now lived, **My lord, the dream be to them that hate thee and the interpretation thereof to thine enemies!** that is, Would that the dream concerned the enemies of the king, and that its meaning related to his foes rather than to him! After this introductory remark Daniel immediately plunged into his explanation. V. 20. **The tree that thou sawest,** rather, "of which thou sawest," **which grew and was strong,** or, "that it was great and strong," **whose height reached unto the heaven and the sight thereof to all the earth,** the power of the empire reaching to the uttermost boundaries of the known world, v. 21. **whose leaves were fair and the fruit thereof much, and in it was meat for all, under which the beasts of the field dwelt, and upon whose branches the fowls of the heaven had their habitation,** just as the king had described it in his account of his dream: v. 22. **it is thou, O king, that art grown and become strong; for thy greatness is grown and reacheth unto heaven,** since his power exceeded that of any living monarch, **and thy dominion to the end of the earth,** a real world-power. Note that Daniel, while filled with pity for the king, yet speaks with uncompromising straightforwardness. The same calm and dispassionate condemnation of sin should be found in pastors of to-day. V. 23. **And whereas the king saw a watcher and an holy one coming down from heaven,** one of God's holy angels delegated for this purpose, **and saying, Hew the tree down and destroy it, yet leave the stump of the roots thereof,** the root-stock, **in the earth, even with a band of iron and brass, in the tender grass of the field, and let it be wet with the dew of heaven, and let his portion be with the beasts of the field till seven times pass over him,** cp. vv. 15. 16: v. 24. **this is the interpretation, O king, and this is the decree of the Most High which is come upon my lord, the king,** being fully decided in God's counsel, v. 25. **that they,** the subject being purposely indefinite, **shall drive thee from men,** casting him out from the society of human beings, **and thy dwelling shall be with the beasts of the field,** entirely on a level with unreasonable brutes, **and they shall make thee to eat grass as oxen, and they shall wet thee with the dew of heaven; and seven times,** definite periods of time, **shall pass over thee, till thou know,** recognizing and acknowledging openly and freely, **that the Most High ruleth in the kingdom of men,** as the real Sovereign of the several nations of the earth, **and giveth it to whomsoever He will.** Nebuchadnezzar would, in other words, be seized with madness, which would exclude him from human society for some time, the purpose of the Lord in thus punishing him being to bring him to a realization of his utter helplessness before the true Ruler of the universe. V. 26. **And whereas they commanded,** namely, the council of watchers speaking in the name of God, **to leave the stump of the tree-roots: thy kingdom shall be sure unto thee,** it would be preserved for him, so that he could reassume his rule after the interval, **after that thou shalt have known that the heavens do rule,** after he would gladly make this confession, thereby yielding all honor and glory to God alone. V. 27. **Wherefore, O king, let my counsel be acceptable unto thee,** for Daniel honestly had the welfare of his sovereign in mind, **and break off thy sins by righteousness,** repudiating all the transgressions for which Oriental monarchs were noted in favor of the exercise of true righteousness and justice, **and thine iniquities by showing mercy to the poor,** to those in any kind of tribulation, **if it may be a lengthening of thy tranquillity,** or, "if thy present good fortune is to endure." A complete change of heart was necessary on the part of the king, together with a consistent practise of the highest virtues as a proof of his regeneration, in order to avert the threatened punishment on the part of the Lord. V. 28. **All this,** exactly as it had been foretold by the prophet, **came upon the King Nebuchadnezzar.** V. 29. **At the end of twelve months,** so soon after he had received his warning, **he walked in the palace of the kingdom of Babylon,** upon its flat roof, from which he could look over the entire city and get a fitting impression of its splendor. V. 30. **The king spake and said, Is not this great Babylon that I have built for the house of the kingdom,** to be the seat or capital of his entire empire, **by the might of my power and for the honor of my majesty?** It was a statement of inordinate pride, by which Nebuchadnezzar made himself the creator of the size and glory of his kingdom, thereby robbing God of the honor which fitly should be given to Him alone. V. 31. **While the word was in the king's mouth,** before he had finished his blasphemous utterance, **there fell a voice from heaven,** with great suddenness, which made the consequences stand out all the more by way of contrast, **saying, O King Nebuchadnezzar, to thee it is spoken,** the emphasis being upon the pronoun: **Thy kingdom is departed from thee,** that is, he was to be deprived of his position and office as ruler. V. 32. **And they shall drive thee from man,** away from the society of human beings, **and thy dwelling shall be with the beasts of the field,** with the irrational brutes; **they,** the subject again impersonal, **shall make thee to eat grass as oxen, and seven times shall pass over thee, until thou know,** being fully aware of, and accepting, the fact, **that the Most High ruleth in the kingdom of men and giveth it to whomsoever He will.** V. 33. **The same hour was the thing fulfilled upon Nebuchadnezzar,** so that there could be no doubt as to cause and effect; **and he was driven from men and did eat grass as oxen, and his body was wet with the dew of heaven, till his hairs were grown like eagles' feathers and his nails like birds' claws.** This form of insanity is well known to medical science, a few cases having been found from time to time which exactly agree with the description of the symptoms here given, even to the eating of grass and the living outdoors without clothing; since people in this condition often believe themselves to be wolves, it is known as lycanthropy. V. 34. **And at the end of the days,** the time appointed for this punishment, **I, Nebuchadnezzar, lifted up mine eyes unto heaven,** in the gesture of one seeking help from there alone, **and mine understanding returned unto me,** so that he once more had the full use of his reason, **and I blessed the Most High,** thereby acknowledging Him as the one true God, **and I praised and honored Him that liveth forever, whose dominion is an everlasting dominion, and His kingdom is from generation to generation,** as the king had said in the introduction of this edict, v. 3; v. 35. **and all the inhabitants of the earth are reputed as nothing,** they are helpless in comparison with His almighty majesty, **and He doeth according to His will in the army of heaven,** so that the companies of even the highest angels bow to His will, **and among the inhabitants of the earth; and none can stay His hand or say unto Him, What doest Thou?** God is the supreme, the absolute Sovereign of all created things. V. 36. **At the same time,** namely, when Nebuchadnezzar thus gave all honor and glory to God alone, **my reason returned unto me; and for the glory of my kingdom, mine honor and brightness returned unto me,** so that his former dignity and power were restored to him; **and my counselors and my lords,** who had repudiated and deserted him when madness seized upon him, **sought unto me,** so that he was officially requested to resume his position at the head of the nation; **and I was established in my kingdom, and excellent majesty was added unto me,** so that the authority of his position was even greater than before the strange madness seized upon him. V. 37. **Now I, Nebuchadnezzar,** in issuing this decree with its frank confession, **praise and extol and honor the King of heaven,** the heaping of synonyms showing the intensity of the king's convictions, **all whose works are truth, and His ways judgment,** so that Nebuchadnezzar freely acknowledged his punishment to have been well deserved; **and those that walk in pride,** exalting themselves at the expense of God's honor, **He is able to abase.** While Nebuchadnezzar recognized the humiliation which he had suffered as a just punishment of his pride, yet he did not realize the greatness of God's grace and mercy which was striving to gain him for true repentance. It is safe to assume, however, that this experience was a step in the right direction, and that this great heathen king finally died in the true faith.

CHAPTER 5.

Belshazzar's Feast and End.

THE FEAST AND THE HANDWRITING. — V. 1. **Belshazzar, the king,** the son of Nabonidus, either natural or adopted, and coregent with him, apparently the grandson of Nebuchadnezzar, **made a great feast to a thousand of his lords and drank wine before the thousand,** the banquet becoming a drunken orgy. He was in command of the capital at that time and excelled in most of the vices for which Oriental rulers were known. V. 2. **Belshazzar, whiles he tasted the wine,** sitting before them on a platform or dais, when he had just gotten under the influence of the wine's intoxicating power, **commanded to bring the golden and silver vessels which his father,** or grandfather, **Nebuchadnezzar had taken out of the Temple which was in Jerusalem,** cp. Jer. 52, 19; 2 Kings 25, 14—17, **that the king and his princes,** the foremost nobles of the realm, **his wives and his concubines,** whose presence at the royal banquets is mentioned also by secular historians, **might drink therein,** using them to parade their drunken mockery. V. 3. **Then they brought the golden vessels that were taken out of the Temple of the house of God,** out of the Sanctuary proper, **which was at Jerusalem; and the king and his princes, his wives and his concubines, drank in them.** This act can in no wise be excused or condoned, not even as an act of religion, as a libation to the God of the Jews: it was a deed of reckless profanity. V. 4. **They drank wine and,** in their intoxicated condition, **praised the gods of gold and of silver, of brass, of iron, of wood, and of stone.** It was thus essentially an exaltation of their idols above Jehovah, of whom they thought that they had conquered Him in battle; but the prophet indicates the vanity of their idols by enumerating the materials of which they were made. V. 5. **In the same hour,** suddenly, while they were still in the midst of their drunken revelry, **came forth fingers of a man's hand and wrote,** or were writing, **over against the candlestick upon the plaster of the wall of the king's palace,** which had no paneling or tapestry; **and the king saw the part of the hand,** the extremity of the moving fingers, **that wrote.** "Upon a spot of the wall which was particularly exposed to the light from the lamp above the king, he suddenly beheld the mysterious and terrifying phenomenon of the hand engaged in writing." V. 6. **Then the king's countenance was changed,** literally, "Then the king, his color was changed unto him," **and his thoughts troubled him,** as his guilty conscience filled him with terror, **so that the joints of his loins were loosed,** they no longer possessed the strength to hold the body together firmly, **and his knees smote one against another,** his terror causing him to lose control of them entirely. "How changed the scene from the glee of his blasphemous revelry to this paleness of cheek, convulsion of frame, remorse of conscience, and dread foreboding of doom! Many a sinner has had a like experience, and other thousands must have it!" (Cowles.) V. 7. **The king cried aloud,** his terror causing him to raise his voice with might, **to bring in the astrologers, the Chaldeans, and the soothsayers,** that is, all the wisest men of the realm. **And the king spake and said to the wise men of Babylon,** as many as followed his summons at once, **Whosoever shall read this writing and show me the interpretation thereof,** explaining its meaning and applying its significance, **shall be clothed with scarlet,** with the costly purple garments worn by Oriental rulers, **and have a chain of gold about his neck,** this golden necklace serving as the mark of special favor from the king, **and shall be the third ruler in the kingdom,** occupying the highest position in the realm, next to its emperor and coregent. V. 8. **Then came in all the king's wise men,** one after the other appearing in agreement with his summons; **but they could not read the writing nor make known to the king the interpretation thereof.** In other words, they had to confess their complete failure. V. 9. **Then,** on account of the utter inability of the wise men to give him the desired information, **was King Belshazzar greatly troubled,** he was filled with deepest apprehension and trepidation, **and his countenance was changed in him, and his lords were astonied,** not only being filled with alarm, but also with confusion, which showed itself in excited movements. "None retained their places; a general uproar ensued; groups were formed; and the people talked and ran hither and thither to no purpose." V. 10. **Now the queen,** the queen-mother, or dowager, very likely the wife of Nebuchadnezzar, **by reason of the words of the king and his lords,** the sound of which, as they raised their voices in their excitement, penetrated to her apartments, **came into the banquet house; and the queen spake and said, O king, live forever!** the customary address in her mouth detracting in no way from the quiet dignity of her coming. **Let not thy thoughts trouble thee, nor let thy countenance be changed,** by the worry and terror inspired by the mysterious writing on the wall. V. 11. **There is a man in thy kingdom in whom is the spirit of the holy gods,** the queen-mother thus repeating the very language of Nebuchadnezzar, chap. 4, 8. 9. 18; **and in the days of thy father,** or grandfather, **light and understanding and wisdom, like the wisdom of the gods, was found in him; whom the King Nebuchad-**

nezzar, thy father, the king, I say, thy father, the repetition serving to give her words greater emphasis, made master of the magicians, astrologers, Chaldeans, and soothsayers, chap. 4, 9, v. 12. forasmuch as an excellent spirit, a most extraordinary talent, and knowledge and understanding, interpreting of dreams and showing of hard sentences, giving the explanation of riddles and conundrums, and dissolving of doubts, literally, "untying knots," that is, finding the solutions of the most intricate problems, were found in the same Daniel, whom the king named Belteshazzar. Now, let Daniel be called, and he will show the interpretation. "As Daniel was probably, according to Oriental custom, deprived of the office to which Nebuchadnezzar had promoted him, as master of the magicians, at the king's death, although he may still have remained in the service of the state, Belshazzar might easily have been ignorant of his services." V. 13. Then was Daniel brought in before the king, summoned to appear without delay. And the king spake and said unto Daniel, Art thou that Daniel which art of the children of the captivity of Judah, whom the king, my father, or grandfather, brought out of Jewry? The question was intended merely to fix the identity of Daniel beyond the slightest doubt and as such required no answer. V. 14. I have even heard of thee that the spirit of the gods is in thee, the king omitting the adjective "holy" which the queen-mother had used, and that light and understanding and excellent wisdom is found in thee. V. 15. And, now, the wise men, the astrologers, the soothsayers only being mentioned as representing the entire class of wise men of the kingdom, have been brought in before me that they should read this writing and make known unto me the interpretation thereof; but they could not show the interpretation of the thing, they could not give the explanation of the words on the wall; v. 16. and I have heard of thee that thou canst make interpretations and dissolve doubts, untie the hardest knots. Now, if thou canst read the writing and make known to me the interpretation thereof, thou shalt be clothed with scarlet and have a chain of gold about thy neck and shalt be the third ruler in the kingdom, the promise made earlier in the evening in a more general way thus being applied to Daniel alone. Like Belshazzar, the unbelievers are often troubled by the terrors of an evil conscience and readily have recourse to almost any solution which offers in order to know their fate or to gain peace of mind.

THE INTERPRETATION AND THE FULFILMENT. V. 17. Then Daniel answered and said before the king, Let thy gifts be to thyself, and give thy rewards, the presents which he intended as a fee to Daniel, to another, the prophet of Jehovah rejecting everything which might afterwards be construed as having influenced him in his message; yet I will read the writing unto the king and make known to him the interpretation, as an act of loyalty to both the earthly ruler and the heavenly Sovereign; for he intended to speak without reservation, no matter whether the result would please or displease the king. V. 18. O thou king, the formal and solemn address bringing out the importance of the message from the outset and placing its entire import into direct relation to the king, the most high God gave Nebuchadnezzar, thy father, a kingdom, and majesty, and glory, and honor, far above that enjoyed by Belshazzar; v. 19. and for the majesty that He gave him, the imperial authority and supremacy which he enjoyed, all people, nations, and languages trembled and feared before him, were in a constant state of fear and trepidation lest they incur his displeasure; whom he would he slew, and whom he would he kept alive, being the absolute master of life and death; and whom he would he set up, and whom he would he put down, for both the advancement and the demotion of the subjects of his realm were matters of his whim. V. 20. But, that is, in spite of this unexampled position of power, when his heart was lifted up and his mind hardened in pride, so that he thought he could deal proudly, with an utter disregard of the will of the Lord, he was deposed from his kingly throne, and they took his glory from him, as related in chapter 4; v. 21. and he was driven from the sons of men, excluded from their society, and his heart was made like the beasts, and his dwelling was with the wild asses, this picturesque item being added for the sake of further embellishment of the narrative; they fed him with grass like oxen, and his body was wet with the dew of heaven, till he knew that the most high God ruled in the kingdom of men, and that He appointeth over it whomsoever He will, that is, until he gave all honor and glory to the true God alone. The lesson of this story is now driven home. V. 22. And thou, his son, or grandson, O Belshazzar, hast not humbled thine heart, not having profited by the example of his relative, though thou knewest all this, v. 23. but hast lifted up thyself against the Lord of heaven, in blasphemous pride; and they have brought the vessels of His house, of the Temple of Jehovah, the one true God, before thee, and thou and thy lords, thy wives and thy concubines, have drunk wine in them; and thou hast praised the gods of silver and gold, of brass, iron, wood, and stone, which see not, nor hear, nor know, cp. Deut. 4, 28; Ps. 115, 5 ff.; Ps. 135, 15 ff.; and the God in whose hand thy breath is, and whose are all thy ways, the one Creator and Ruler of the universe, hast thou not glorified, as was the solemn duty resting upon him. V. 24. **Then was the part of the hand,** the outstretched fingers of the writing hand, **sent from Him, and this writing was written,** to announce the doom which was now inevitable. V. 25. **And this is the writing that was written, MENE, MENE, TEKEL, UPHARSIN,** literally, "numbered, numbered, weighed, and divided." V. 26. **This is the interpretation of the thing,** of the writing on the wall: **MENE, God hath numbered thy kingdom and finished it,** that is, the duration of Belshazzar's kingship, of his reign, was now determined, brought to the end assigned to it. V. 27. **TEKEL: Thou art weighed in the balances,** namely, in those of God's righteousness and justice, his character analyzed according to the demands of God's holiness, **and art found wanting,** below weight in moral worth and capacity. V. 28. **PERES: Thy kingdom is divided,** severed, cut into two pieces, **and given to the Medes and Persians,** the Lord Himself making the division. V. 29. **Then commanded Belshazzar,** in accordance with his promise, **and they clothed Daniel with scarlet, with royal purple, and put a chain of gold about his neck and made a proclamation concerning him that he should be the third ruler in the kingdom,** next in power to Nabonidus and Belshazzar. Even if this proclamation was made in the banquet-hall only, it reached the representatives of the entire kingdom who were there assembled. V. 30. **In that night was Belshazzar, king of the Chaldeans, slain,** namely, when his city was taken by the victorious armies of the enemy, who took the city as the result of a ruse. V. 31. **And Darius, the Median, took the kingdom, being about threescore and two years old.** We have evidence from secular sources also that Darius, the Mede, whose other name was Gobryas, received from Cyrus, his overlord, the kingdom of Belshazzar, the Chaldean, which constituted a small part of the empire of the Persians at that time.3) As is indicated in this story, the hand of God has often interfered with the blasphemous works of the unbelievers, so that all their laughter was turned to the bitterest sorrow. And all God's judgments here in time are but faint preambles introducing the last great Day of Judgment with its condemnation of the godless.

3) Wilson, *Studies in the Book of Daniel,* 144. 145.

CHAPTER 6.

Daniel in the Lions' Den.

DANIEL A VICTIM OF JEALOUSY. — V. 1. **It pleased Darius,** when he had fully taken over the government of the kingdom, **to set over the kingdom an hundred and twenty princes,** called satraps in secular history, **which should be over the whole kingdom,** as governors of the smaller sections, or provinces, into which the empire was divided, v. 2. **and over these three presidents,** chief prefects, or ministers, **of whom Daniel was first,** not higher in rank, but first in dignity, **that the princes might give accounts unto them,** the satraps thus being responsible to their superiors chiefly in financial matters, **and the king should have no damage,** his interests being taken care of by virtue of this statesmanlike arrangement. V. 3. **Then this Daniel was preferred above the presidents and princes,** that is, he showed himself superior to them, **because an excellent spirit was in him,** chap. 5, 12; **and the king thought to set him over the whole realm.** This intention the king very likely made known, with the result that it stirred up the jealousy of the other presidents. V. 4. **Then the presidents and princes,** actuated by an envy which caused them to disregard the best interests of the kingdom, **sought to find occasion against Daniel concerning the kingdom,** that is, they tried to find some delinquency in the work of his official position; **but they could find none occasion nor fault,** no reason for impeachment, no ground for an accusation, **forasmuch as he was faithful, neither was there any error or fault found in him,** he was beyond reproach in his entire administration. "Fidelity is the leading political virtue of the servant or officer of a government, in like manner as justice and mercy should be the ornament of rulers." (Lange.) V. 5. **Then said these men,** in conferring with one another concerning ways and means of removing the hated rival, **We shall not find any occasion against this Daniel except we find it against him concerning the Law of his God,** regarding the practise of his religion. This is the course which is often followed by the enemies of the believers: if they cannot discredit the Christians in any matter pertaining to their duties, they try to show that the observance of their religious worship is dangerous to the state. V. 6. **Then these presidents and princes assembled together to the king,** running to him in stormy haste, with fierce impetuousness, **and said thus unto him, King Darius, live forever!** V. 7. **All the presidents of the kingdom,** a statement which stretched the truth rather dangerously, **the governors, and the princes,** or satraps, **the counselors and the captains,** the lower prefects, **have consulted together to establish a royal statute and to make a firm decree,** rather, "that the king ought to establish a statute and issue an interdict," **that whosoever shall ask a petition of any God or man for thirty days,** within the next thirty days, **save of thee, O king, he shall be cast into the den of lions.** The request was cleverly worded to flatter the king, particularly since it seemed to be the desire of all the officials of the realm. V. 8. **Now, O king, establish the decree and sign the writing,** recording the proclamation by stamping it with his official seal, **that it be not changed, according to the law of the Medes and Persians, which altereth not,** it could not be repealed in the Medo-Persian Empire. V. 9. **Wherefore King Darius,** carried away by the suddenness and the fervor of the request, which hardly gave him time for reflection, **signed the writing and the decree,** placing his royal seal upon the interdict and thus establishing it for his entire realm. V. 10. **Now, when Daniel knew that the writing was signed,** when he found out that the edict was established by the affixing of the king's seal, **he went into his house, and, his windows being open in his chamber,** in the upper story of his house, **toward Jerusalem,** where he could be undisturbed in his devotions, **he kneeled upon his knees three times a day,** according to ancient Jewish custom, Ps. 55, 17, **and prayed and gave thanks before his God, as he did aforetime,** the royal decree changing his custom of daily worship not one whit. He did not indulge in stormy protests, but quietly ignored a law which virtually, if not actually, demanded from him a denial of the true God. Such passive resistance is often the most effective protest against laws interfering with the service of the true God. V. 11. **Then these men assembled,** they came together frequently for hasty and tumultuous meetings, **and found Daniel praying and making supplication before his God,** the open windows of Daniel's chapel enabling them to spy upon him without trouble. V. 12. **Then they came near,** they arranged for an audience immediately, **and spake before the king concerning the king's decree,** reminding him of it, insisting on calling it to his remembrance, **Hast thou not signed a decree that every man that shall ask a petition of any God or man within thirty days, save of thee, O king, shall be cast into the den of lions? The king answered,** without hesitancy and guile, for he was not aware of their hidden intention, **and said, The thing is true, according to the law of the Medes and Persians, which altereth not,** thereby indicating the certain punishment of any one who might transgress the royal edict. V. 13. **Then answered they and said before the king,** full of joyful satisfaction over the fact that the king's answer suited their design so well, **That Daniel,** to whom they refer with sneering contempt, **which is of the children of the captivity of Judah,** whom one might always reasonably suspect of an act of rebellion against the king's authority, **regardeth not thee, O king, nor the decree that thou hast signed,** the intimation being that Daniel maliciously spurned the edict and thereby openly challenged the king's authority, **but maketh his petition three times a day.** V. 14. **Then the king, when he heard these words, was sore displeased with himself,** literally, "sorrow came on him," he was deeply grieved and troubled by this turn of events, **and set his heart on Daniel to deliver him,** for he prized Daniel's ability and faithfulness very highly; **and he labored till the going down of the sun to deliver him,** he pondered over the matter and held the conspirators off in the hope that some way of escape might be found before morning. V. 15. **Then these men assembled unto the king,** they pressed upon him in a most importunate and tumultuous manner, **and said unto the king, Know, O king, that the law of the Medes and Persians is, That no decree nor statute which the king establisheth may be changed.** The success of their entire infamous plan, in fact, was based upon this tradition. V. 16. **Then the king,** unable to find an excuse or to hold out against the conspirators, **commanded, and they brought Daniel and cast him into the den of lions,** the execution following the sentence at once, as custom required. **Now the king spake and said unto Daniel,** since he was powerless to help him in this extremity, **Thy God, whom thou servest continually, He will deliver thee.** This did not amount to a confession of the true God, but was merely a pious wish that the God of the Jews might prove equal to this emergency. V. 17. **And a stone was brought,** probably one used for similar executions, **and laid upon the mouth of the den,** over the opening through which the condemned were cast down; **and the king sealed it with his own signet and with the signet of his lords,** of the highest officers in his realm, **that the purpose might not be changed concerning Daniel,** that is, that no one might interfere, either by attempting to liberate him or by working his evil will upon him. It is significant that Daniel made no effort to have his execution delayed or suspended, but calmly placed the outcome in God's hands. True faith in God rests upon His will, no matter what may come, knowing God's ways are always good and right, and all things work together for good to them that love God.

Daniel's Remarkable Deliverance.—V. 18. **Then the king went to his palace and passed the night fasting,** unable to sleep or eat for worry about the fate of Daniel; **neither were instruments of music brought before him,** rather, "neither were concubines brought to him"; **and his sleep went from him,** he was in genuine distress, decidedly ill at ease on account of the course into which he had been drawn. V. 19. **Then the king arose very early in the morning,** with the dawn, as soon as it became light, **and went in haste unto the den of lions,** the royal zoological gardens being located conveniently near. V. 20. **And when he came to the den, he cried with a lamentable voice,** which testified to the sorrow possessing his heart, **unto Daniel; and the king spake and said to Daniel, O Daniel, servant of the living God,** whom he was ready to acknowledge as such in accordance with Daniel's confession, **is thy God, whom thou servest continually,** with constant, unflagging devotion, **able to deliver thee from the lions?** V. 21. **Then said Daniel unto the king,** calmly answering the king from his position down in the pit, **O king, live forever!** V. 22. **My God hath sent His angel,** who may even have been visible to the eye of Daniel, **and hath shut the lions' mouths that they have not hurt me, forasmuch as before Him innocency was found in me,** God had declared him not guilty by preserving him so wonderfully; **and also before thee, O king, have I done no hurt,** that is, by transgressing the edict of the king he had not become guilty of rebellion against the person of the king, as the king's personal interest in his case also demonstrated. V. 23. **Then was the king exceeding glad for him,** on account of the miraculous deliverance which Daniel had experienced, **and commanded that they should take Daniel up out of the den,** through an opening which made it convenient for him to be removed. **So Daniel was taken up out of the den, and no manner of hurt was found upon him,** not so much as a scratch from the paw of one of the ravening beasts, **because he believed in his God,** and this firm confidence was rewarded by the Lord in this manner. V. 24. **And the king,** who now realized that the enemies of Daniel had used him as their instrument in trying to vent their jealous spite, **commanded, and they brought those men which had accused Daniel, and they cast them into the den of lions, them, their children, and their wives,** according to the custom of the country, and since they were guilty of the same wickedness as the men; **and the lions had the mastery of them,** fell upon them and overwhelmed them, **and brake all their bones in pieces or ever they came at the bottom of the den,** they were reduced to a pulp before their bodies reached the bottom of the pit. V. 25. **Then King Darius,** still under the influence of the miraculous deliverance which he had witnessed, **wrote unto all people, nations, and languages that dwell in all the earth,** in issuing a solemn proclamation, **Peace be multiplied unto you.** V. 26. **I make a decree, That in every dominion of my kingdom,** as far as his kingly power extended, **men tremble and fear,** in reverent awe, **before the God of Daniel; for He is the living God and steadfast forever,** eternal and unchanging, **and His kingdom that which shall not be destroyed, and His dominion shall be even unto the end,** outlasting all earthly kingdoms. V. 27. **He delivereth and rescueth,** literally, "He is a Deliverer and Rescuer," **and He worketh signs and wonders in heaven and in earth,** such as are outside the laws of nature, **who hath delivered Daniel from the power of the lions,** who would ordinarily have torn him to pieces in the twinkling of an eye. V. 28. **So this Daniel,** the same one of whom the princes had spoken so contemptuously, **prospered in the reign of Darius and in the reign of Cyrus, the Persian,** for the Persian monarchy followed shortly after the Median. The miracles which the Lord performs in the interest of His children are intended to serve, among other things, for the unbelievers, so that they also may realize that the God of Israel, the God of the Christians, is the true, living God, the only Savior and Redeemer.

CHAPTER 7.

Vision of the Four World Kingdoms and the Messianic Kingdom.

THE VISION OF THE FOUR BEASTS. — V. 1. **In the first year of Belshazzar, king of Babylon,** who was coregent with his father Nabonidus and the grandson and adopted son of Nebuchadnezzar, according to the most reliable secular accounts, **Daniel had a dream and visions of his head,** distinct images of his mind, quite distinct from confused pictures, **upon his bed,** that is, during the night; **then,** immediately or soon after it transpired, **he wrote the dream and told the sum of the matters,** setting forth the main facts in due order and omitting matters of secondary importance, such as details pertaining to the appearance of the beasts. V. 2. **Daniel spake and said,** in introducing his narration of the strange experience which befell him, **I saw in my vision by night, and, behold, the four winds of the heaven,** from the four main points of the compass, **strove upon the great sea,** storming along against one another upon the face of the ocean. V. 3. **And four great beasts,** monstrous beings, **came up from the sea,** world-powers rising out of the agitation of the political sea of the heathen world, **diverse one from another,** one after the other issuing from the great deep. V. 4. **The first was like a lion and had eagle's wings,** emblem of kingly power and authority; **I beheld till the wings thereof were plucked,** taking from the beast the ability to fly. **And it was lifted up from the earth,** to which it was confined after having been deprived of its unrestrained motion, **and made stand upon the feet as a man,** standing upon its hind feet in an upright position, **and a man's heart was given to it,** so that it partook of the mind and the feelings of a human being. V. 5. **And behold another beast, a second, like to a bear,** appearing later in point of time, **and it raised up itself on one side,** so that it leaned over sideways, as it lifted the shoulder on that side to move forward; **and it had three ribs in the mouth of it between the teeth of it,** a part of a prey which had been seized by it, of animals which it had overcome; **and they said thus unto it, Arise, devour much flesh,** being given to conquest and plunder. V. 6. **After this I beheld, and, lo, another,** a third animal coming on the scene somewhat later in history, **like a leopard, which had upon the back of it four wings of a fowl,** enabling it to move with great rapidity; **the beast had also four heads,** indicating that its authority would be divided among four sovereigns; **and dominion was given to it,** great authority and power in the world. V. 7. **After this I saw in the night visions, and behold a fourth beast,** coming on the scene as the last world-power, **dreadful and terrible,** of awe-inspiring fierceness, **and strong exceedingly; and it had great iron teeth,** symbolizing the lust of conquest and destruction; **it devoured and brake in pieces,** greedily feeding on whatever it could get into its power, **and stamped the residue,** whatever it could not devour, **with the feet of it,** bent upon annihilating all that stood in its way. **And it was diverse from all the beasts that were before it,** so that the entire animal kingdom could furnish no beast to which it was similar; **and it had ten horns,** giving further impression of power and ferocity. V. 8. **I considered the horns,** observing them very closely, **and, behold, there came up among them another little horn,** springing up as the eleventh and, at first, insignificant in size, **before whom there were three of the first horns plucked up by the roots,** to make room for the newcomer; **and, behold, in this horn were eyes like the eyes of man,** symbols of understanding, although not possessing the characteristics of divinity, **and a mouth speaking great things,** full of proud and blasphemous boasting. V. 9. **I beheld,** still engaged in close observation, **till the thrones were cast down,** by a great act of judgment, **and the Ancient of Days,** symbol of the eternal and majestic God, **did sit, whose garment was white as snow and the hair of His head like the pure wool,** both symbols of unsullied purity and holiness; **His throne was like the fiery flame,** flashing as though composed of a fiery mass, **and His wheels as burning fire,** symbolical of the fiery zeal with which the Lord punishes the transgressors, but also purifies His people and prepares them for the future glorification. V. 10. **A fiery stream issued and came forth from before Him,** to devour the sinful and hostile forces of the world and to purify the children of the Kingdom. **Thousand thousands ministered unto Him, and ten thousand times ten thousand stood before Him,** an uncounted number of holy angels ready to do His bidding. **The Judgment was set,** everything was made ready for the trial, **and the books were opened,** namely, the books of record, in which the deeds of men were entered, to serve as the basis of the sentence to be pronounced upon men by the heavenly Judge. V. 11. **I beheld them because of the voice of the great words which the horn spake,** for it was due to the boasting of the ruler represented by the last horn that the judgment and destruction came upon the world; **I beheld even till the beast was slain,** namely, the fourth, the fierce and destructive beast, **and his body destroyed and given to the burning flame,** whose devouring fiery streams issued from the throne of the eternal Judge. V. 12. **As concerning the rest of the beasts,** the three which were first described, **they had their dominion taken away,** their power was also taken away in the general judgment; **yet their lives were prolonged for a season and time,** rather, "for the duration of their life was fixed," as to the season and time; God had determined beforehand how long their power should last. V. 13. **I saw in the night visions, and, behold, one like the Son of Man came with the clouds of heaven,** riding upon them as on a celestial chariot, **and came to the Ancient of Days, and they brought Him near before Him.** It is on the basis of this passage, which describes the formal inauguration of the Messiah as King of His eternal kingdom, that Jesus applied the name "Son of Man" to Himself so frequently in the gospels. V. 14. **And there was given Him dominion and glory and a kingdom,** divine authority over the domain of the earth, **that all people, nations, and languages should serve Him. His dominion is an everlasting dominion which shall not pass away, and His kingdom that which shall not be destroyed.** The description clearly shows that the Son of Man is a person distinct from the Father, and that the fact of His eternal dominion and power is a direct argument for His deity. Cp. Rev. 11, 15; 19, 16.

THE INTERPRETATION OF THE VISION. — V. 15. **I, Daniel, was grieved in my spirit in the midst of my body,** for the body contains the spirit as the scabbard contains the sword, **and the visions of my head troubled me,** he felt apprehensive concerning them.

V. 16. **I came near unto one of them that stood by,** one of those engaged in the service of God, **and asked him the truth of all this,** the true explanation of the judgment scene which was here enacted. **So he told me and made me know the interpretation of the things,** so that Daniel understood the vision in all its parts. V. 17. **These great beasts, which are four, are four kings,** the heads of mighty empires, each one the founder of a dynasty, **which shall arise out of the earth,** from the surface of the earth, of the earth, earthy. V. 18. **But the saints of the Most High shall take the kingdom,** receiving it as a gift from above, **and possess the kingdom forever, even forever and ever.** The true members of the covenant nation, the believers of the New Testament, the congregation of the Lord, gathered from the elect of all nations, are, by virtue of their faith in the Messiah, possessors of the kingdom of God, they enjoy all the blessings of the Lord in this relationship to the Messiah and to their heavenly Father here in time and hereafter in eternity. V. 19. **Then I would know the truth of the fourth beast,** that is, Daniel was anxious to know, he desired to be informed, about this beast also, **which was diverse from all the others,** so utterly different from them, **exceeding dreadful, whose teeth were of iron and his nails of brass,** the feature of the brazen claws being added in this description; **which devoured, brake in pieces, and stamped the residue with his feet;** v. 20. **and of the ten horns that were in his head and of the other which came up, and before whom three fell, even of that horn that had eyes and a mouth that spake very great things,** in boastful blasphemy, **whose look was more stout than his fellows,** that is, his appearance was such as to inspire terror. V. 21. **I beheld, and the same horn made war with the saints and prevailed against them,** this being a part of its campaign of destruction, it involved a temporary defeat of the forces of the Lord, v. 22. **until the Ancient of Days came,** the true and only God coming to judgment upon His enemies, **and judgment was given to the saints of the Most High,** for the Lord took their part and effected their deliverance from the oppression of the beast; **and the time came that the saints possessed the kingdom,** the Church holding the blessings of the Lord even here in time, in spite of all hostility of Satan and his evil forces, and entering into undisturbed possession of them in the Kingdom of Glory. V. 23. **Thus he said, The fourth beast shall be the fourth kingdom upon earth,** following the Babylonian, the Medo-Persian, and the Greek empire, respectively, **which shall be diverse from all kingdoms, and shall devour the whole earth, and shall tread it down, and break it in pieces,** the general effect of its rule being decidedly destructive. V. 24. **And the ten horns out of this kingdom are ten kings that shall arise,** that is, the Roman Empire, upon its disintegration, would be resolved into a number of smaller states, all of which would, however, carry on the traditions of the mother state and still be one in spirit with her; **and another shall rise after them,** a ruler wielding a great deal of power, **and he shall be diverse from the first,** differing from his predecessors, **and he shall subdue three kings,** causing them completely to lose their identity. V. 25. **And he shall speak great words against the Most High,** in blasphemies of an unusually vicious character, **and shall wear out the saints of the Most High and think to change times and laws,** setting aside human and divine laws at will; **and they shall be given into his hand,** for him practically to work his will as he chose, **until a time and times and the dividing of time,** the entire length of time, divided into three distinct periods, being figured in terms of God's time. V. 26. **But the judgment shall sit,** the sentence will be carried out, **and they shall take away his dominion, to consume and to destroy it unto the end,** so that its final destruction is not to be expected before the end of the world. V. 27. **And the kingdom and dominion and the greatness of the kingdom under the whole heaven,** throughout the world, **shall be given to the people of the saints of the Most High,** so that the Church of the Lord would finally be victorious, **whose kingdom is an everlasting kingdom, and all dominions shall serve and obey Him.** Cp. Eph. 1, 21. 22; Col. 1, 16. V. 28. **Hitherto is the end of the matter,** this is the gist of the vision. **As for me, Daniel, my cogitations much troubled me,** namely, after he awoke from his dream, **and my countenance changed in me,** his face showed the effect of his worry over the matter; **but I kept the matter in my heart,** he did not make it known, did not discuss it with others.

The interpretation of this vision may briefly be given as follows. The lion with the eagle's wings was the Babylonian Empire, whose victorious progress was halted about the time that Nebuchadnezzar was stricken with the peculiar madness, which caused him to seek the fellowship of beasts, which, however, later received at least some understanding of the true God. The bear which raised himself up on one side is the Medo-Persian Empire, whose warlike nature is testified to in secular accounts. The leopard upon whose back wings appeared is the Grecian Empire, which, under Alexander the Great, spread over the world with great rapidity. The fourth beast is the Roman Empire with its insatiable fierceness and love of conquest, whose spiritual descendant and successor is the kingdom of Antichrist, of the Pope at Rome, just as delineated in the Book of Revelation. The ancient empire indeed came to an end, but it was revived in the empire of Charles the Great, and the political power of the Pope is felt in practically every nation of the earth to-day. Practically every feature of the description fits the rule of the Roman Antichrist from the very start. The kingdom of the Pope grew up like a horn, exerting its political power very gradually, but none the less surely. From small beginnings it developed until it reached a station in which it practically controlled the fate of nations. The Popes have, in many cases, made use of the highest wisdom, together with an almost diabolical cunning, to further their cause. By dint of their cunning they made their authority felt in the counsels of nations; they have impressed people with their power far above the real status of affairs. The kingdom of the Pope is unlike every other kingdom, since he exerts political power under the guise of spreading the kingdom of God. Time and again the Pope of Rome has spoken blasphemous words against the one true God. History records numerous instances of persecutions carried on by Popes and their minions, as during the terrible inquisitions. Popes have altered the Word of God to suit their own convenience and to serve their selfish interests. In spite of the reverses which the kingdom of Antichrist has suffered in the past, as when Emperor Otto I deposed Pope John XII, when the councils of the fifteenth century tried to effect at least an outward reformation, and, above all, when Martin Luther carried the fight into the enemy's ranks, the kingdom of Antichrist will remain till the end of time. Cp. 2 Thess. 2; Rev. 17. The prophecy of Daniel was fulfilled and is being fulfilled in a most remarkable manner, a fact which tends to strengthen our faith in every word of the Bible.[4)]

4) Cp. *Lehre und Wehre,* Vol. 59 (1913), 49 ff.

CHAPTER 8.

Vision of the Ram and the He-Goat.

THE VISION ITSELF. — V. 1. **In the third year of the reign of King Belshazzar,** two years after Daniel had had the vision of the four monarchies, **a vision appeared unto me, even unto me, Daniel, after that which appeared unto me at the first,** that is, in addition to that other important prophetic vision which he had recorded in the previous chapter. It is evident that this vision did not come to Daniel in a dream, but that he was awake and conscious while this information came to him. V. 2. **And I saw in a vision,** in a state of ecstasy; **and it came to pass, when I saw, that I was at Shushan,** or Susa, **in the palace, which is in the province of Elam,** for Susa was the capital of this province during the Babylonian supremacy, while under Persian reign it was located in the satrapy of Susiana; **and I saw in a vision, and I was by the river of Ulai,** or Eulaeus, on which Susa was situated. Daniel evidently, in his capacity as one of the foremost officials of the empire, visited the various provinces from time to time, or he may even have had a winter-home in this city. V. 3. **Then I lifted up mine eyes and saw, and, behold, there stood before the river,** probably to the east of it, **a ram,** not in a flock, but alone, **which had two horns; and the two horns were high,** both of them expressive of royalty and power, **but one was higher than the other, and the higher,** the one possessing the greater power, **came up last,** it was later in point of time. V. 4. **I saw the ram pushing westward and northward and southward,** to subdue all the countries located in these directions, **so that no beasts might stand before him, neither was there any that could deliver out of his hand,** his power, for the time being, was absolute; **but he did according to his will and became great,** so that the empire which he represented became a world-power. V. 5. **And as I was considering,** observing very closely everything that transpired, **behold, an he-goat came from the west,** from Europe, across Asia Minor, **on the face of the whole earth,** sweeping along over all the intervening countries, **and touched not the ground,** that is, his advance was so rapid that it was like a flight; **and the goat had a notable horn between his eyes,** in the midst of his forehead, so that his whole force was behind it. V. 6. **And he came to the ram that had two horns,** not stopping for any consideration, **which I had seen standing before the river, and ran unto him in the fury of his power,** in irresistible, mighty rage. V. 7. **And I saw him come close unto the ram, and he was moved with choler against him,** with sudden, explosive anger, **and smote the ram,** in a fierce overthrow, **and brake his two horns; and there was no power in the ram to stand before him, but he cast him down to the ground and stamped upon him,** so that the complete overthrow of the ram was speedily accomplished; **and there was none that could deliver the ram out of his hand,** all the resources that he commanded availing him nothing. V. 8. **Therefore the he-goat waxed very great,** his power developed mightily; **and when he was strong,** just as he reached the highest point of his might, **the great horn was broken,** the unity of the attacking power was disrupted with the death of its leader; **and for it came** up four notable ones, four leaders, who divided the power among themselves, toward the four winds of heaven. V. 9. And out of one of them came forth a little horn, sprouting in a diminutive manner, like the branches in the prongs of an antelope, which waxed exceeding great toward the south and toward the east and toward the pleasant land, Judea, the glorious land, the land of God's chosen people. V. 10. And it waxed great, even to the host of heaven, to the congregation of the Lord's people, for the Jews were at that time representatives of the Lord's Church on earth; and it cast down some of the host and of the stars to the ground and stamped upon them, presuming, in its pride, to wage warfare even against the kingdom of the Lord. V. 11. Yea, he magnified himself even to the prince of the host, placing himself on a level with the most high God, with the King of kings and the Lord of lords, and by him the daily sacrifice was taken away, that is, he interfered with the worship of the true God as then carried on in the Temple, and the place of His Sanctuary was cast down, profaned with blasphemous behavior. V. 12. And an host was given him against the daily sacrifice by reason of transgression, that is, "warfare was inaugurated against the daily sacrifice with outrage," with idolatrous worship by the heathen ruler represented by the last horn, and it cast down the truth to the ground; and it practised and prospered, it accomplished this much, it was successful by divine permission: God permitted the profaning to go on for some time. V. 13. Then I heard one saint, one of the Lord's angels, speaking, and another saint said unto that certain saint which spake, as they were conversing, the interruption being made in the interest of Daniel, How long shall be the vision concerning the daily sacrifice, that is, how long would the subject of this vision, the destruction of the Lord's worship, continue, and the transgression of desolation, the horrible transgression which had just been described, to give both the Sanctuary and the host to be trodden under foot? so that the Church of God, then represented by the nation of the Jews returned from Babylon, would be made desolate and be hindered from spreading. V. 14. And he said unto me, Unto two thousand and three hundred days, literally, "evening-mornings"; then shall the Sanctuary be cleansed, or "justified," which may mean reconsecrated. The figures in the vision are strangely interwoven with direct statements, which anticipate, in a measure, the interpretation given in the second part of the chapter.

THE EXPLANATION OF THE VISION. — V. 15. And it came to pass when I, even I, Daniel, had seen the vision and sought for the meaning, pondering over it, viewing it from every angle, then, behold, there stood before me as the appearance of a man, the apparition coming with startling suddenness. V. 16. And I heard a man's voice, the speaker being invisible to Daniel, between the banks of Ulai, coming from between the two branches of the Eulaeus River, which called and said, Gabriel, make this man to understand the vision. So the being who appeared to Daniel in the aspect of a man, was one of the Lord's angel princes. Cp. Luke 1, 19. V. 17. So he came near where I stood; and when he came, I was afraid, the close proximity of a holy being filled him with fear, and fell upon my face; but he said unto me, Understand, O son of man, the address reminding Daniel of his human weakness, without, however, humiliating him; for at the time of the end shall be the vision, that is, it gives information concerning occurrences at the end of time, the final period of the earth's history. V. 18. Now, as he was speaking with me, I was in a deep sleep on my face toward the ground, in a state of numbness or ecstasy, which shut off his senses from earthly things; but he touched me and set me upright, strengthening him for the time being, that he might witness the rest of the vision. V. 19. And he said, Behold, I will make thee know what shall be in the last end of the indignation, when the wrath of God would be poured out upon the godless world; for at the time appointed the end shall be, or, "it [the vision] pertains to the period of time of the end." It is indicated, even at this point, that the tribulation suffered by the Jews at the time of the Maccabees, especially by the tyranny of Antiochus Epiphanes, is symbolical of the afflictions to be expected at the end of the Messianic era. V. 20. The ram which thou sawest having two horns are the kings of Media and Persia, the Medo-Persian monarchy in its entire historical development. This empire subdued, under Persian leadership: toward the west, Babylon, Mesopotamia, Syria, and the countries of Asia Minor; toward the north, Colchis, Armenia, Iberia, and the states along the Caspian Sea; toward the south, Judea, Egypt, Ethiopia, and India. V. 21. And the rough goat, moving eastward across Asia Minor in victorious advance, is the king of Grecia, literally, "of Javan," Macedonia, Greece, and the Ionian colonies being included in the term; and the great horn that is between his eyes is the first king, Alexander the Great, the founder of this world-power. V. 22. Now, that being broken, whereas four stood up for it, or, "concerning the horn, that it was broken, and that four then took its place," this is the meaning: four kingdoms shall stand up out of the nation, out of the world of nations united under the rule of the first king, but not in his power, not equal to the founder, neither singly nor all taken together. These four are the dynasties of the Diadochi, of whom indeed five, Antigonus, Antipater, Ptolemeus, Cassander, and Lysimachus, adopted the title of king; but Antigonus was soon defeated in battle, so that there were really four monarchies, Lysimachus taking Thrace and Bithynia, Cassander Macedonia and Greece, Seleucus Syria, Babylonia, and the eastern countries, and Ptolemeus Egypt, Palestine, and Arabia Petraea. Antipater had meanwhile died. V. 23. **And in the latter time of their kingdom,** that is, after these dynasties had been in existence for some time, **when the transgressors are come to the full,** when the apostate Jews would once more have fulfilled the measure of their wickedness, **a king of fierce countenance,** shameless, without the slightest regard for God and men, **and understanding dark sentences,** hiding his true purposes behind ambiguous statements, **shall stand up,** coming into power as the ruler of that section of the Greek Empire. V. 24. **And his power shall be mighty, but not by his own power,** rather on account of his cunning dissimulation, with the permission of God; **and he shall destroy wonderfully,** so that men would be astonished at his activities in this respect, **and shall prosper and practise and shall destroy the mighty and the holy people,** venting his spite both upon the warlike enemies opposing him and upon the congregation of the Lord's saints. V. 25. **And through his policy also he shall cause craft to prosper in his hand,** that is, in accordance with his cunning he would succeed in his deception, in various hypocritical plans which he had decided upon; **and he shall magnify himself in his heart,** becoming proud by reason of these successful maneuvers, **and by peace shall destroy many,** while they were living in care-free security, the suddenness of the attack causing them to yield without a struggle; **he shall also stand up against the Prince of princes,** presuming to set himself even against God. **But he shall be broken without hand,** God Himself taking his punishment in hand. V. 26. **And the vision of the evening and the morning which was told,** concerning the length of the time of the affliction, **is true; wherefore shut thou up the vision,** to preserve it for such later day, **for it shall be for many days,** the vision, being concerned with things of the distant future, would retain its prophetic value and should therefore not be revealed generally at this time. V. 27. **And I, Daniel,** overcome by the startling and overwhelming character of the revelation, **fainted and was sick certain days. Afterward I rose up and did the king's business,** attending to the duties of his office as before; **and I was astonished at the vision,** he kept his counsel concerning it, **but none understood it,** for the full significance of the revelation he received would be possible only with its fulfilment. Antiochus Epiphanes is rightly regarded in history as a type of Antichrist, the papacy of Rome, for he made every effort to drive out the worship of the true God in the Holy Land and to substitute instead a veneration of himself.

CHAPTER 9.

The Seventy Weeks.

DANIEL'S CONFESSION AND PRAYER. — V. 1. **In the first year of Darius, the son of Ahasuerus,** known in secular history as Gobryas and mentioned as a viceroy of the empire after the fall of Babylon,[5]) **of the seed of the Medes,** who were joined with the Persians in the conquest of Babylon, **which was made king over the realm of the Chaldeans,** not by accession, but through the agency of the victorious army and by the hand of Cyrus, v. 2. **in the first year of his reign I, Daniel, understood by books,** he observed, he got his information, and then drew his conclusions, **the number of the years whereof the word of the Lord came to Jeremiah, the prophet,** cp. Jer. 25, 11, **that he would accomplish seventy years in the desolations of Jerusalem,** or, "that seventy years would be completed in the desolate condition of Jerusalem." Note that Daniel was in possession of a book of Jeremiah's prophecies, which, therefore, must have been in existence in a number of copies even then, that he considered the words of this book as the Word of Jehovah, and that he definitely believed the words of the prophecy, as the words of the Lord, would be fulfilled. V. 3. **And I set my face unto the Lord God,** the one sovereign God of the universe, **to seek by prayer and supplications,** to plead for the restoration of the city of his fathers, **with fasting and sackcloth and ashes.** It was thus an importunate, moving prayer which Daniel sought by the operation of the Holy Spirit, by which he made known his requests before God. V. 4. **And I prayed unto the Lord, my God, and made my confession,** a frank acknowledgment of one's sinfulness preparing the way for the proper worship of the Lord, and said, **O Lord, the great and dreadful God,** He whose fear and terror is upon all those who are His enemies, **keeping the covenant and mercy to them that love Him and to them that keep His commandments,** cp. Deut. 7, 9: v. 5. **we have sinned and have committed iniquity,** by leaving the path of God's commandments, **and have done wickedly and have rebelled,** shown rebellious be-

5) Cp. Wilson, *Studies in the Book of Daniel,* chaps. VII, X, XI, XII.

havior, **even by departing from Thy precepts and from Thy judgments,** the introduction of the confession being modeled after the words of Solomon's prayer, 1 Kings 8, 47; v. 6. **neither have we hearkened unto Thy servants, the prophets,** his confession now being made in the name of his entire people with their open disregard of the admonition of the prophets, **which spake in Thy name to our kings, our princes, and our fathers, and to all the people of the land.** Cp. 2 Kings 17; Jer. 44, 17. V. 7. **O Lord, righteousness belongeth unto Thee,** He is the possessor of absolute righteousness, who alone can dispense righteousness, **but unto us confusion of faces,** namely, the confusion which shows itself in the guilty blush on account of the consciousness of sin and the consequent disgrace and tribulation, **as at this day: to the men of Judah and to the inhabitants of Jerusalem,** these being concerned first of all, as the leaders of the Lord's people, **and unto all Israel,** for many members of the other tribes had joined the southern kingdom when the downfall of the northern kingdom was imminent, all those who professed their belief in the true God thus casting their lot together, **that are near and that are far off, through all the countries whither Thou hast driven them,** as they were deported into shameful exile, **because of their trespass that they have trespassed against Thee,** the guilt of the people thus being brought out time and again. V. 8. **O Lord, to us belongeth confusion of face, to our kings, to our princes, and to our fathers, because we have sinned against Thee,** this statement being repeated for the sake of emphasis, just as the synonymous expressions were heaped at the beginning of Daniel's confession, in order that the full scope of the people's guilt might be brought out. Over against this confusion and guilt stands the one hope of sinful mortals, the mercy of God showing itself in the forgiveness of sins. V. 9. **To the Lord, our God, belong mercies and forgivenesses,** of which the repentant sinners feel the great need, **though we have rebelled against Him,** rather, "for we have rebelled," and the need of His forgiveness as their one hope has become apparent to them; v. 10. **neither have we obeyed the voice of the Lord, our God, to walk in His laws,** following them exactly, **which He set before us by His servants, the prophets,** His ministers, in making known His will to men. V. 11. **Yea, all Israel have transgressed Thy Law, even by departing, that they might not obey Thy voice,** their turning away from Him being done with this deliberate purpose; **therefore the curse is poured upon us,** like a rainstorm with hail, **and the oath that is written in the Law of Moses, the servant of God,** cp. Lev. 26; Deut. 28, **because we have sinned against Him.** V. 12. **And He hath confirmed His words which He spake against us,** maintaining them, confirming them in deed, as they now had the proof before them, **and against our judges that judged us,** the term including all those in authority in the entire nation, **by bringing upon us a great evil; for under the whole heaven hath not been done as hath been done upon Jerusalem,** the severity of the Lord's punishment was without equal. V. 13. **As it is written in the Law of Moses,** in the two chapters which contain the dreadful statements of the Lord concerning His punishment upon the transgressors of His Law, **all this evil is come upon us; yet made we not our prayer before the Lord, our God,** by entreating or conciliating His face, by attempting to propitiate His anger, as suggested in King Solomon's great prayer, **that we might turn from our iniquities and understand Thy truth.** The truth of God is His plan of salvation as revealed in His Word, according to which He wants the sinner to turn from his evil ways, accept the salvation offered him in the Gospel, and lead a life in accordance with the will of the Lord. V. 14. **Therefore hath the Lord watched upon the evil,** He was concerned about its coming upon the transgressors, **and brought it upon us; for the Lord, our God, is righteous in all His works which He doeth,** all His actions being essentially just; **for we obeyed not His voice,** wherefore the punishment meted out to them had to be admitted to be just and righteous. V. 15. **And now, O Lord, our God, that hast brought Thy people forth out of the land of Egypt with a mighty hand,** Ex. 32, 11, **and hast gotten Thee renown, as at this day,** His acts of mercy being acknowledged wherever they became known among the nations: **we have sinned, we have done wickedly,** this confession now also introducing the final petition of Daniel's prayer. V. 16. **O Lord, according to all Thy righteousness, I beseech Thee,** in agreement with the righteousness which demanded the fulfilment of His promises, **let Thine anger and Thy fury be turned away from Thy city Jerusalem, Thy holy mountain,** designated thus because His Sanctuary had been situated there for so many centuries, **because for our sins and for the iniquities of our fathers Jerusalem and Thy people are become a reproach to all that are about us,** so that the heathen looked upon them with scorn and mockery. V. 17. **Now, therefore, O our God, hear the prayer of Thy servant and his supplications and cause Thy face to shine,** in merciful love, **upon Thy Sanctuary that is desolate,** for the fact that the Temple was lying in ruins was the chief ground for Daniel's prayer, **for the Lord's sake,** for the glory of the restoration would then be the Lord's. V. 18. **O my God, incline Thine ear,** in the attitude of willing attention, **and hear; open Thine eyes and behold our desolations,** both the cities and their ruins being included in this term, **and the city which is called by Thy name,** literally, "upon which Thy name is called," where God had so gloriously revealed Himself, which He had, by choosing it for His Sanctuary, elevated so highly among the cities of the world; **for we do not present our supplications before Thee,** casting them down before Him, as it were, **for our righteousnesses,** in dependence upon any state or act of righteousness on the part of the petitioners, **but for Thy great mercies,** since the unmerited grace of God, His free favor, is the only hope of sinners. V. 19. **O Lord, hear; O Lord, forgive; O Lord, hearken and do!** the prophet here rising to the very climax of an importunate and fervent prayer. **Defer not, for Thine own sake, O my God; for Thy city and Thy people are called by Thy name,** and therefore His zeal for His own glory should be the motive urging Him to heed the prophet's prayer. The prayer of faith is always certain, meekly importunate, and, when supported by promises on the part of the Lord, may rise to a clamor for mercy which is sure to find a hearing.

GABRIEL COMFORTS DANIEL BY THE PROPHECY OF THE SEVENTY WEEKS. — V. 20. **And whiles I was speaking and praying and confessing my sin and the sin of my people Israel and presenting my supplication before the Lord, my God,** piling up his petitions in seeking the mercy of God, **for the holy mountain of my God,** in the interest of the Lord's Sanctuary and the true worship; v. 21. **yea, whiles I was speaking in prayer,** making the concluding remarks of his prayer, **even the man Gabriel,** one of the angel-princes, **whom I had seen in the vision at the beginning,** chap. 8, 15. 16, **being caused to fly swiftly, touched me about the time of the evening oblation,** rather, "the man Gabriel, whom I had formerly in a vision seen while in a state of great exhaustion, . . . came to me about the time of the evening oblation," about three o'clock in the afternoon, for this was one of the hours of prayer observed by the Jews. V. 22. **And he informed me and talked with me and said, O Daniel, I am now come forth to give thee skill and understanding,** a skilful and correct insight into the problem perplexing him and an assurance for the future. V. 23. **At the beginning of thy supplications the commandment came forth,** namely, the decree, or oracle, which is presently stated, **and I am come to show thee,** to make it known, **for thou art greatly beloved,** this being the reason why the Lord was so ready to make known to him the solution of the problem of the seventy weeks; **therefore understand the matter and consider the vision,** observing the oracle as now to be set forth and explained. V. 24. **Seventy weeks are determined upon thy people and upon thy Holy City,** the capital which was so dear to the heart of Daniel, the determination of the time being purposely indefinite, **to finish the transgression and to make an end of sins,** to restrain the rebellion and to seal up the sins, so that they would no longer find expression, **and to make reconciliation for iniquity,** to effect an expiation for guilt, **and to bring in everlasting righteousness,** the result of the expiation of sin, **and to seal up the vision and prophecy,** rather, "and the prophet," for there would be no further need of prophets when the chief and greatest prophecies would be fulfilled, **and to anoint the Most Holy,** the new, spiritual Temple spoken of by Ezekiel being meant, the establishment of the Church of the New Testament on earth, and especially its consummation in heaven, at the end of time. V. 25. **Know therefore and understand that from the going forth of the commandment to restore and to build Jerusalem,** from the time that the decree of Cyrus concerning the rebuilding of Jerusalem went forth, Ezra 1, 1; Is. 44, 28, **unto the Messiah,** the Anointed One, **the Prince, shall be seven weeks,** that is, until the coming of Christ, the Savior, **and threescore and two weeks,** during which the great spiritual Temple of the Lord would be constructed. **The street shall be built again and the wall, even in troublous times,** while the Church of Christ would still properly be a Church Militant. V. 26. **And after threescore and two weeks shall Messiah be cut off,** namely, at the time of the great denial, one of the signs preceding the end of the world, **but not for Himself,** literally, "and not is to Him any one," that is, for the time being there seems to be no helper; **and the people of the prince that shall come,** a mighty opponent, Antichrist, **shall destroy the city and the Sanctuary,** so that everything, apparently, would be lost before his attack; **and the end thereof shall be with a flood,** so that the attacking prince himself would perish in the end, by a divine judgment, **and unto the end of the war desolations are determined,** or, "until the end there will be warfare," until the end of this world. V. 27. **And he,** the hostile prince, **shall confirm the covenant with many for one week,** so that the great mass of people would be forced to accept this covenant, to acknowledge him as being in the place of God; **and in the midst of the week he shall cause the sacrifice and the oblation to cease,** so that there would be a serious interference with the true worship of God, **and for the overspreading of abominations he shall make it desolate,** literally, "on wings of abominations he comes destroying," namely, with his idolatrous customs, **even until the consummation, and that determined shall be poured upon the desolate,** literally, "until the perfected and fully determined" extirpation and judicial punishment, "shall be poured out upon the desolator," God Himself bringing destruction upon him. The prophecy thus sets forth the vicissitudes of the Church of God, which would be relieved by the coming of the promised Messiah. But even after His coming the congregation of saints would be in fact a Church Militant, the great Roman Antichrist making the first attack upon the Lord's forces and being supported in the last days of the world by other antichristian elements following his leadership, until the Lord will definitely and finally bring destruction upon him and them at the time of the Great Judgment.

CHAPTER 10.

Daniel's Last Great Vision.

THE BEGINNING OF THE VISION. — V. 1. **In the third year of Cyrus, king of Persia,** two years after his decree concerning the restoration of Jerusalem and the Temple had gone forth, **a thing was revealed unto Daniel, whose name was called Belteshazzar,** both his names being given here, one as a member of the people of God, the other as an official of the Persian court, who could render his nation a better service by remaining at court than by joining them in the restoration of their city, especially since he was now of advanced age; **and the thing,** the word of God revealed to the prophet in this vision, **was true, but the time appointed was long,** literally, "and great tribulation," that is, the revelation was concerned with misery, wretchedness, and trouble on earth; **and he understood the thing and had understanding of the vision,** he observed the word which the Lord made known to him and gave close attention to the vision. V. 2. **In those days I, Daniel, was mourning three full weeks,** very likely on account of the conditions in the land of his fathers, where the small handful of Jews were trying, under peculiar difficulties, to rebuild the Temple and restore the city, a fact which caused Daniel, at the beginning of a new year, to give himself to fasting and prayer. V. 3. **I ate no pleasant bread,** partaking only of the unleavened bread of affliction, Deut. 16, 3, **neither came flesh nor wine in my mouth,** thus discarding all food otherwise used on festival days, **neither did I anoint myself at all,** he abstained from all expressions of joy and happiness, **till three whole weeks were fulfilled.** Daniel thus observed a complete fast, with all the expressions of sorrow and mourning assumed by men at such a time. V. 4. **And in the four and twentieth day of the first month,** of the month Nisan, apparently at the end of his fast, **as I was by the side of the great river, which is Hiddekel,** the Tigris River, v. 5. **then I lifted up mine eyes and looked,** as in the vision on the banks of the Eulaeus, chap. 8, 3, **and behold a certain Man clothed in linen,** the color symbolizing holiness, **whose loins were girded with fine gold of Uphaz,** the gold indicating His princely rank. V. 6. **His body also was like the beryl,** or chrysolite, so that it shone with the golden luster of topaz or amber, **and His face as the appearance of lightning,** blindingly bright, **and His eyes as lamps of fire,** cp. Rev. 1, 14, **and His arms and His feet like in color to polished brass,** gleaming like glowing brass, **and the voice of His words like the voice of a multitude,** the voice of roaring like that of the ocean or of a great concourse of people. V. 7. **And I, Daniel, alone saw the vision,** so that all its details were clear to him; **for the men that were with me saw not the vision,** as was the case also with the companions of Saul on the way to Damascus, Acts 9, 7; 22, 11; **but a great quaking fell upon them, so that they fled to hide themselves,** literally, "they fled by hiding themselves," an expression showing the greatness of their fear. V. 8. **Therefore I was left alone and saw this great vision,** cp. Ex. 3, 3, **and there remained no strength in me,** on account of the overwhelming terror of the vision; **for my comeliness was turned in me into corruption,** literally, "the healthy appearance of my face changed to me for disfigurement," **and I retained no strength.** It is evident from the entire description that Daniel here had a vision of the Angel of the Presence, the Angel of the Countenance, the Messiah Himself, as He revealed Himself to the believers of the Old Testament. Cp. Rev. 1, 13—15. V. 9. **Yet heard I the voice of His words; and when I heard the voice of His words, then was I in a deep sleep on my face, and my face toward the ground.**

THE FIRST PART OF THE ANGEL'S MESSAGE. V. 10. **And, behold, an hand touched me,** the stunned prophet not being able to say whose hand it was, although the text indicates that it was that same Angel in white, **which set me upon my knees and upon the palms of my hands,** gently shaking him into a half-waking state, so that he assumed at least a crouching position, although his stupor was not yet entirely gone. V. 11. **And He said unto me, O Daniel, a man greatly beloved,** cp. chap. 9, 23, **understand the words that I speak unto thee,** marking them very closely, **and stand upright,** shaking off the last effects of the numbness besetting him; **for unto thee am I now sent,** as the bearer of a message of comfort and blessing. **And when He had spoken this word unto me, I stood trembling,** still in fearful expectation of the matters which would be revealed to him. V. 12.

Then said He unto me, Fear not, Daniel; for from the first day that thou didst set thine heart to understand, applying himself most earnestly to the solution of the problems, **and to chasten thyself before thy God,** in the proper humiliation of mind, **thy words were heard, and I am come for thy words,** in consequence of the prayer which had come to the attention of God. The Lord always hears all prayers of those who believe in Him, though He may sometimes delay His answer or give it in a manner different from that which His children expect. V. 13. **But the prince of the kingdom of Persia,** the angel of darkness representing the Persian world-power in its idols and therefore identical with some evil spirit, **withstood Me one and twenty days,** trying to hinder the Angel of the Presence in carrying out His mission of comfort; **but, lo, Michael one of the chief princes,** the first in rank in possessing the strength of the Almighty, **came to help Me; and I remained there with the kings of Persia,** using His influence in the interest of the Lord's people. There is a world of angels and spirits, and these spirits often have a very decided influence upon the happenings of history. V. 14. **Now I am come to make thee understand what shall befall thy people in the latter days,** during the Messianic era; **for yet the vision is for many days,** it extends far into the future. V. 15. **And when He had spoken such words unto me, I set my face toward the ground,** in awe and consternation over the revelations to be expected, **and I became dumb,** remaining speechless for the time being. V. 16. **And, behold, one like the similitude of the sons of men,** an angel having the appearance of a human being, probably again the Angel of the Lord in the special sense of the word, **touched my lips,** to heal his dumbness. **Then I opened my mouth and spake and said unto Him that stood before me, O my Lord, by the vision,** as a result of his seeing the vision, **my sorrows are turned upon me,** with acute and overwhelming power, **and I have retained no strength.** V. 17. **For how can the servant of this my Lord talk with this my Lord?** whose majesty was of a nature to terrify a poor, sinful mortal. **For as for me, straightway there remained no strength in me, neither is there breath left in me,** he could neither stand nor breathe properly for agitation and consternation. V. 18. **Then there came again and touched me one like the appearance of a man, and he strengthened me,** v. 19. **and said, O man greatly beloved, fear not,** for his terror was the real cause of his weakness. **Peace be unto thee; be strong!** the repetition of the comforting words serving to give emphasis to them. **And when he had spoken unto me, I was strengthened and said, Let my lord speak,** he now felt able to hear and receive the message; **for thou hast strengthened me.** V. 20. **Then said he, Knowest thou wherefore I come unto thee?** The serious and highly important character of the message must be borne in mind by the prophet. **And now will I return to fight with the prince of Persia,** in order to hinder him from performing his evil designs against the children of God; **and when I am gone forth,** prepared to wage war, **lo, the prince of Grecia shall come,** another hostile spirit, representing Greece, destined to be the next world-power. V. 21. **But I will show thee that which is noted in the scripture of truth,** in the sacred document of God's divine decrees; **and there is none that holdeth with me in these things,** standing fully on his side, **but Michael, your prince,** the particular champion of the people of God. The prince of this world, with all his hosts of evil spirits, is continually engaged in attempts to break and hinder the gracious and good will of the Lord over against His children; but the Lord is more powerful than all His enemies and keeps those who believe in Him from all harm and danger. Chap. 11, 1. **Also I, in the first year of Darius, the Mede, even I, stood to confirm and to strengthen him,** or, "even as I stood by to strengthen him," the inference being that the various angelic spirits come to the support of one another when special efforts in behalf of the people or nations in their care are required. The gist of the verse is evidently this, that Michael had been active in overthrowing the power of Babylonia by the armies of Medo-Persia, and that the Angel of the Lord had given him mighty assistance in this labor. In the great crises of history, in the change of monarchies, and in the midst of every tribulation we may rely upon the faithfulness and mercy of our God.

CHAPTER 11.

A General Prophecy Concerning the Future.

HAPPENINGS OF THE NEAR FUTURE. — V. 2. **And now I will show thee the truth.** Cp. chap. 10, 21. **Behold, there shall stand up yet,** namely, after Cyrus, who was then king, **three kings in Persia,** whose names are commonly given as Cambyses, Pseudo-Smerdis, and Darius Hystaspes; **and the fourth shall be far richer than they all,** literally, "shall acquire far greater riches than they all"; and **by his strength through his riches,** as he applied his immense wealth in order to fit out a mighty army, **he shall stir up all against** the realm of **Grecia**, Xerxes staking his all on the invasion of the rival kingdom beyond the Dardanelles. V. 3. **And a mighty king shall stand up**, a heroic, warlike king, namely, Alexander of Macedonia and Greece, **that shall rule with great dominion and do according to his will**, with tyrannical authority. V. 4. **And when he shall stand up**, just as soon as his power is fairly established, **his kingdom shall be broken**, the brief duration of Alexander's rule being here indicated, **and shall be divided toward the four winds of heaven**, in a fourfold division of his kingdom after the battle of Ipsus, 301 B. C.; **and not to his posterity, nor according to his dominion which he ruled; for his kingdom shall be plucked up, even for others beside those**, so that the natural heirs and rightful successors of Alexander were eliminated. Both of Alexander's sons were put to death, and after the generals of Alexander had first broken up his empire into small divisions, the result finally was a fourfold monarchy, but still Greek in character. V. 5. **And the king of the South shall be strong**, the ruler of Egypt, **and one of his princes; and he shall be strong above him**, the reference most likely being to Seleucus Nicator, **and have dominion; his dominion shall be a great dominion**, which, as a matter of fact, extended from Phrygia on the west to the Indus on the east. V. 6. **And in the end of years**, that is, after several years have elapsed, **they shall join themselves together**, the king of the South and the king of the North forming a confederacy, when Antiochus II Theos, the second successor of Seleucus Nicator, married Berenice, the daughter of Ptolemeus Philadelphus; **for the king's daughter of the South shall come to the king of the North to make an agreement**, to establish just and peaceful relations by virtue of this marriage; **but she shall not retain the power of the arm, neither shall he stand nor his arm**, neither of them retaining the power acquired through their marriage and the joining of their forces; **but she shall be given up, and they that brought her, and he that begat her, and he that strengthened her in these times**, when the critical position in which he found himself suggested the marriage to him. Secular accounts set forth the situation as follows: "As soon as Ptolemy Philadelphus died in B. C. 247, Antiochus Theos expelled Berenice, and recalled the formerly rejected Laodice. The latter, however, aimed at further revenge, and to achieve it, she poisoned the king, had her son by him, Seleucus II Callinicus, declared his successor, and sent assassins against Berenice, who had fled to the sanctuary of Daphne. The latter queen was slain, together with her little son, and the hope of the Ptolemies to behold one of their lineage on the throne of the Seleucidae was thus wholly destroyed." V. 7. **But out of a branch of her roots**, a shoot out of the apparently dead stock, **shall one stand up in his estate**, to take her place in this controversy, her own brother, Ptolemy III Euergetes, **which shall come with an army and shall enter into the fortress of the king of the North**, against all the strongholds of the Northern power, **and shall deal against them and shall prevail**, this being done to the extent that the entire Syrian country from Cilicia to beyond the Tigris was conquered, numerous fortresses taken, and Laodice, the rival and murderess of Berenice, slain; v. 8. **and shall also carry captives into Egypt their gods with their princes**, their molten or cast images, **and with their precious vessels of silver and of gold**, all this being welcome booty; **and he shall continue more years than the king of the North**, holding out against him with his superior strength. V. 9. **So the king of the South shall come into his kingdom**, rather, "and he," the last-named king of the North, "shall come into the kingdom of the king of the South," **and shall return into his own land**, to Syria. This was fulfilled in the expedition of Seleucus Callinicus, in which he sent a fleet against Egypt, which, however, was destroyed in a storm, while his army was defeated and overthrown. V. 10. **But his sons**, again those of the Northern king, **shall be stirred up**, preparing for war, **and shall assemble a multitude of great forces**, in waging war upon the Southern kingdom; **and one shall certainly come and overflow and pass through**, the activities of Antiochus the Great in his victorious advance upon Egypt being described here; **then shall he return and be stirred up**, renewing his campaign against the Egyptians in the following spring, **even to his fortress**, very likely the fortified city of Gaza. V. 11. **And the king of the South shall be moved with choler**, with a fierce and sudden anger, **and shall come forth and fight with him, even with the king of the North; and he shall set forth a great multitude; but the multitude shall be given into his hand.** This undoubtedly describes the attack made by Ptolemy Philopator by which he tried to break the power of Antiochus. V. 12. **And when he hath taken away the multitude, his heart shall be lifted up**, literally, "and shall rise up the multitude and shall lift up his heart," as he took up the campaign with great courage; **and he shall cast down many ten thousands**, killing myriads in the battle of Raphia, near Gaza; **but he shall not be strengthened by it**, because he did not follow up his victory with any degree of energy. V. 13. **For the king of the North shall return and shall set forth a multitude greater than the former and shall certainly come after certain years with a great army and with much riches.** This was approximately thirteen years later when Antiochus the Great had strengthened himself by successful campaigns against the kingdoms toward the east, so that his army was composed of veterans and his equipment of the very best. V. 14. **And in those times there shall many stand up against the king of the South,** particularly in insurrections which were caused by bad administration of affairs at home; **also the robbers of thy people shall exalt themselves to establish the vision,** literally, "violent persons of thy [Daniel's] people will revolt against him," namely, when a number of Jews entered into a league with Antiochus the Great against Egypt; **but they shall fall,** the Lord sending tribulations and afflictions upon them for their rebellion against the authorized government, the reference probably being to the oppression of Antiochus Epiphanes. V. 15. **So the king of the North shall come,** advancing to the attack once more, **and cast up a mount and take the most fenced cities,** literally, "city of fortifications," a term used of the fortresses of the South in general; **and the arms of the South shall not withstand, neither his chosen people,** their armies being unable to ward off the threatened blow, **neither shall there be any strength to withstand,** all the resources of the Southern kingdom availing them nothing in this emergency. V. 16. **But he that cometh against him shall do according to his own will,** for Antiochus, the victor of Paneas, near the sources of the Jordan, now overran the entire country, **and none shall stand before him; and he shall stand in the glorious land,** literally, "in the land of ornament," the Holy Land, especially when considered from the standpoint of its spiritual blessings, **which by his hand shall be consumed,** literally, "and annihilation is in his hand." V. 17. **He shall also set his face to enter with the strength of his whole kingdom,** intending to follow up his successes with a further attack on the country now almost subjugated, **and upright ones with him,** rather, with the purpose of restoring a proper political relationship, the agreement consisting in this, that the marriage of Cleopatra, the daughter of Antiochus, with Ptolemy Epiphanes was agreed upon, Antiochus receiving Coelesyria in return; **thus shall he do, and he shall give him the daughter of women,** namely, Cleopatra, who was then but a girl and in the care of her mother and others, who educated her, **corrupting her,** rather, "bringing destruction upon her"; for the marriage, which took place five years later, resulted in the ruin of the land which she represented; **but she shall not stand on his side, neither be for him,** that is, she was unable to carry out the plans of her father. V. 18. **After this shall he,** the king of the North, **turn his face unto the isles,** including the coast-lands of the Mediterranean, **and shall take many; but a prince for his own behalf shall cause the reproach offered by him to cease,** or, "yet his scorn which he heaped upon the generals they will revenge upon him," that is, the men in command of the islands and coast-lands promptly repulsed his attacks, so that he was obliged to retire to the fortresses formerly in his power; **without his own reproach he shall cause it to turn upon him.** V. 19. **Then he shall turn his face toward the fort of his own land,** withdrawing to them on account of the force of the attack against him; **but he shall stumble and fall and not be found,** for this reversal was the beginning of his end, for history records that he was slain in an insurrection of the inhabitants of Elymais. V. 20. **Then shall stand up in his estate a raiser of taxes in the glory of the kingdom,** literally, "then shall arise in his stead one who causes exactors (or oppressors) to pass through the ornament of the kingdom," so that his subjects were oppressed with various afflictions and burdens; **but within few days he shall be destroyed, neither in anger nor in battle,** this being the end of Seleucus Philopator, who was poisoned by Heliodorus, his former favorite, who sought the crown for himself. Thus the Lord directs the fortunes of individuals and nations and punishes such as oppose His plans for the benefit of His people.

FURTHER REVELATIONS CONCERNING THE FUTURE. — V. 21. **And in his estate shall stand up a vile person,** a despicable and morally contemptible character, **to whom they shall not give the honor of the kingdom,** who seized the royal power and authority against the will of the nation; **but he shall come in peaceably and obtain the kingdom by flatteries,** that is, come in unexpectedly; while men thought that the rightful heir would succeed to the throne, Antiochus Epiphanes obtained the kingdom by dissimulations and deceitful behavior, so that he was in possession of the throne before men really realized it. V. 22. **And with the arms of a flood shall they be overflown from before him and shall be broken; yea, also the prince of the covenant,** literally, "and the overflowing armies will be submerged from before him and broken, and princes of the covenant as well"; that is, even if men would come against him with great armies, his own forces, still stronger, would overthrow them, so that not only his enemies, but his confederates as well would feel his heavy hand; for his idea was to be the sole and only ruler of the entire realm. V. 23. **And after the league made with him,** after he had caused a conquered enemy to accept his terms, **he shall work deceitfully,** make use of further clever ruses; **for he shall come up and shall become strong with a small people,** his smaller force being sufficient for his purposes, because he used it so cleverly. V. 24. **He shall enter peaceably,** while no one was expecting him to act with such quick decision, **even upon the fattest places of the province,** where the greatest wealth was to be found; **and he shall do that which his fathers have not done nor his fathers' fathers,** deviating from the more humane practises of his predecessors; **he shall scatter among them the prey and spoil and riches,** by squandering the plunder which he had made and causing the provinces to become impoverished; **yea, and he shall forecast his devices against the strongholds, even for a time,** namely, until the time fixed in the counsels of God would be reached. V. 25. **And he shall stir up his power and his courage against the king of the South with a great army,** summoning all his energy and making use of his great wealth in staging a successful campaign; **and the king of the South shall be stirred up to battle with a very great and mighty army,** in trying to repel the invasion; **but he shall not stand, for they shall forecast devices against him,** his own associates making use of treachery in aiding the invader. This was fulfilled when Antiochus Epiphanes overthrew Philometor of Egypt, some of whose most trusted advisers espoused the cause of the enemy. V. 26. **Yea, they that feed of the portion of his meat shall destroy him,** the very members of the Egyptian royal household, the king's ministers, becoming guilty of such treachery, **and his army shall overflow,** but without accomplishing anything for him, **and many shall fall down slain.** V. 27. **And both these kings' hearts shall be to do mischief,** in feigning friendship and thus trying to harm one another, **and they shall speak lies at one table,** all their protestations of high regard to each other being invented for the sake of playing politics; **but it shall not prosper,** neither one succeeding in carrying out the particular designs which he had in mind at this meeting, of which no accounts are found in secular history; **for yet the end shall be at the time appointed.** The prophecy looks forward to the time in which the oppression exerted by these kings in wronging the children of God's people would reach its climax, but incidentally, with the overthrow of these enemies, their oppression would be brought to an end. V. 28. **Then shall he,** the king of the North, **return into his land with great riches,** with much booty, chiefly secured in Egypt; **and his heart shall be against the holy covenant,** against the divine institution of the Jewish theocracy, the Jewish people in their country, as representing the visible Church of God at that time; **and he shall do exploits and return to his own land,** accomplishing his wicked intentions by committing atrocities of various kinds while marching through Judea, as the books of the Maccabees relate. V. 29. **At the time appointed he shall return and come toward the South,** in another campaign against Egypt and the countries tributary to it; **but it shall not be as the former or as the latter,** that is, the triumphs of the other expeditions were not repeated. V. 30. **For the ships of Chittim shall come against him,** a fleet coming from the direction of Cyprus, that is, from the west, in this case a Roman embassy with a number of ships, the Roman emissaries landing in Alexandria in order to prevent the Syrian king from conquering Egypt; **therefore he shall be grieved and return,** retracing his steps in discouragement and anger on account of being foiled in his design, **and have indignation against the holy covenant. So shall he do,** venting his spite on Judea, accomplishing his displeasure in acts of rapine and plunder; **he shall even return and have intelligence with them that forsake the holy covenant,** that is, he observed such apostates from the Jewish religion, he fixed his attention upon them, he made them his favorites and established an idolatrous religion with their assistance. V. 31. **And arms shall stand on his part,** armed forces sent by him, **and they shall pollute the Sanctuary of strength,** the Temple, as the fortress of Jehovah, **and shall take away the daily sacrifice, and they shall place the abomination that maketh desolate,** the reference being to an altar of idolatry erected on Jehovah's altar of burnt offering. "Antiochus, on his way home from Egypt, sent Apollonius with 20,000 men to destroy Jerusalem, two years after its capture by himself. Apollonius slew multitudes, dismantled and pillaged the city. The soldiers then, from a fortress which they built commanding the Temple, fell on and slew the worshipers, so that the Temple-service was discontinued. Also, Antiochus decreed that all, on pain of death, should conform to the Greek religion, and the Temple was consecrated to Jupiter Olympus. Identifying himself with this god, Antiochus with fanatical haughtiness wished to make his own worship universal." V. 32. **And such as do wickedly against the covenant,** namely, the apostate Jews, **shall he corrupt by flatteries,** inducing them to return to heathenism by flattering promises of earthly gain, of worldly advantages; **but the people that do know their God shall be strong and do exploits,** that is, they would resist all his blandishments and adhere to the covenant. V. 33. **And they that understand among the people,** those who know the Lord and walk in His fear, **shall instruct many,** making every effort to keep them in the right way; **yet they shall fall by the sword and by flame, by captivity and by spoil, many days,** these words evidently prophesying the uprising which took place at the time of the Maccabees, when the faithful among the Jews, although with great losses to themselves, overcame their oppressors. V. 34. **Now, when they shall fall,** in sacrificing themselves for the sake of their religious principles, **they shall be holpen with a little help,** for the theocratic kingdom was retained as a result of their efforts; **but many shall cleave to**

them with flatteries, hypocritically casting their lot with the victorious party of the Jews in order to save themselves. V. 35. **And some of them of understanding shall fall,** death and various attendant tribulations taking their toll, **to try them and to purge and to make them white, even to the time of the end,** for all these afflictions would serve as trials in separating the dross from the pure metal, **because it is yet for a time appointed,** that is, the period of tribulation would extend until then. Thus the enemies, in trying to harm the believers, succeed only in contributing to the purifying of God's people, in the great process of winnowing out the real from the false, the hypocritical from the true. It will readily be seen that the entire description of the career of Antiochus Epiphanes shows him to have been a bitter opponent of the true God. By an ignoring of the factor of time, now, which is peculiar to prophetic utterances, the following section is devoted to a description of Antichrist, of whom Antiochus was a type. V. 36. **And the king,** the Roman Antichrist as foreshadowed by Antiochus Epiphanes, **shall do according to his will,** arbitrarily asserting his power and authority; **and he shall exalt himself,** in the pride of his heart, **and magnify himself above every god,** arrogantly and blasphemously setting aside gods of every kind and description, **and shall speak marvelous things against the God of gods,** making statements beyond reasonable comprehension, which would be unexplainable in the case of a normal human being, **and shall prosper till the indignation be accomplished,** until the wrath of God upon His people would be fully carried out, until His punishment would accomplish its purpose; **for that that is determined shall be done,** it cannot be recalled, it must be executed. V. 37. **Neither shall he regard the God of his fathers,** thereby breaking with the true worship of his nation, the proper service of God as it had existed in the Christian Church, **nor the desire of women,** denying and rejecting the natural inclination of man toward woman, as implanted in the sexes by the Creator, **nor regard any god,** it being characteristic of him that he will set aside all reverence and all natural feeling, including that of the natural knowledge of God; **for he shall magnify himself above all,** both divine and human, in a challenging supercilious arrogance. V. 38. **But in his estate shall he honor the god of forces,** literally, "and the god of fortresses in his place shall he honor," that is, he would make war, the application of force, his god, would extend his power by means of force; **and a god whom his fathers knew not shall he honor with gold, and silver, and with precious stones, and pleasant things,** the most costly jewelry, sacrificing all his wealth for the attainment of his ends, for the spreading of his power. V. 39. **Thus shall he do in the most strongholds with a strange god,** literally, "he will do toward the fortified places with the aid of the strange god," that is, he will pursue a definite course against them; **whom he shall acknowledge and increase with glory,** rather, "to them who will acknowledge him, he shall make the honor great"; **and he shall cause them to rule over many and shall divide the land for gain,** as a reward to those who accept his claims. This has ever been the policy of the men who sat on the throne of Antichrist, to reward their henchmen with the spoils gained by their political intrigues. V. 40. **And at the time of the end,** namely, that of the present age of the world, during the Messianic era, **shall the king of the South push at him, and the king of the North shall come against him like a whirlwind with chariots and with horsemen and with many ships,** with the aid of powerful forces; **and he shall enter into the countries,** the king of the South carrying forward his campaign with all energy, **and shall overflow and pass over.** V. 41. **He,** namely, Antichrist, **shall enter also into the glorious land,** the land of Palestine, **and many countries shall be overthrown; but these shall escape out of his hand, even Edom and Moab and the chief of the children of Ammon,** these ancient enemies of the people of God being representative of all the forces opposing the Lord, and therefore, from the beginning, allies of Antichrist, whom he would not need to overthrow. V. 42. **He shall stretch forth his hand also upon the countries,** namely, in order to take possession of them; **and the land of Egypt shall not escape.** V. 43. **But he shall have power over the treasures of gold and of silver,** the possession of which was ever one of the chief objects of Antichrist, **and over all the precious things of Egypt; and the Libyans and the Ethiopians,** representative of the southernmost people of the world, **shall be at his steps.** We have here, in a few bold strokes, and in terms taken from the campaigns of the antichristian forces in the third and second centuries before Christ, a picture of Antichrist in the development of his power. Although he suffered temporary reverses on account of the secession of the Greek Orthodox Church and the rise of Mohammedanism, he still managed to subjugate one country after the other, so that his strongholds were found throughout the world. V. 44. **But tidings out of the East,** setting forth the extent of the Oriental secession, **and out of the North,** when the era of the Reformation began, **shall trouble him,** for what he had at first considered an empty quarrel of idle monks soon assumed alarming proportions; **therefore he shall go forth with great fury to destroy and utterly to make away many,** in the Counter-reformation, by means of the inquisition and through the efforts of the Jesuits. V. 45. **And he shall plant the tabernacle of his palace between the seas, in the glorious holy mountain,** literally, "between seas, over against the mountain of the glory [or ornament] of holiness," so that his palace was intended to be a rival of the ancient seat of Jehovah's power in the midst of His holy people; **yet he shall come to his end,** his true nature being exposed and realized by at least some of those who read the signs of the times, **and none shall help him.** The Reformation dealt the Roman Antichrist a blow from which he has never fully recovered, although he will continue his campaign of deceit until the end of time.

CHAPTER 12.

The End of the Revelation Vouchsafed Daniel.

THE DELIVERANCE OF THE LORD'S PEOPLE. — V. 1. **And at that time,** at the end of the present world age, **shall Michael stand up, the great prince which standeth for the children of thy people,** as the heavenly protector of Israel, chap. 10, 13. 21; **and there shall be a time of trouble,** of tribulation and affliction for the believers, **such as never was since there was a nation, even to that same time,** the climax of the oppression brought upon the spiritual Israel by all antichristian forces; **and at that time thy people,** the true believers, **shall be delivered, every one that shall be found written in the book,** whose name had been entered in the book of life. Cp. Rev. 13, 8. V. 2. **And many of them that sleep in the dust of the earth shall awake,** literally, "many, a great multitude of those who sleep in the dust-land, shall awake," shall return to life in the final resurrection, **some to everlasting life and some to shame and everlasting contempt,** this being the division at the Last Judgment, the believers destined for heaven, the unbelievers to hell with its torments. V. 3. **And they that be wise,** the true teachers of the people, **shall shine as the brightness of the firmament,** in a wonderful glorification, **and they that turn many to righteousness,** by instructing them in loyalty and faithfulness in the midst of the tribulations of the latter days, **as the stars forever and ever,** this statement being rightly applied to the work of faithful preachers of the Gospel in these latter days of corruption and apostasy. V. 4. **But thou, O Daniel, shut up the words and seal the book,** so that its contents, for the present, would not be revealed to men, **even to the time of the end,** the present Messianic era; **many shall run to and fro, and knowledge shall be increased,** literally, "many shall search it through, and thus understanding will become great." It is true in general that the knowledge and interpretation of the prophecies of old comes to those who search the Scriptures most carefully, diligently comparing prophecy and fulfilment as indicated in the directions of the Lord. Cp. John 5, 39.

A FINAL WORD OF CHEER. — V. 5. **Then I, Daniel, looked,** after the angel had finished his message, **and, behold, there stood other two,** two more angels besides the one who had spoken to him, **the one on this side of the bank of the river and the other on that side of the bank of the river,** on either side of the Tigris. V. 6. **And one,** only one of these angels being introduced as speaking, **said to the man clothed in linen, which was upon the waters of the river,** occupying a position above the water, **How long shall it be to the end of these wonders?** literally, "Till when the end of these marvelous things?" the end being the period, or era, of the Messiah with all that happened in it. V. 7. **And I heard the man clothed in linen, which was upon the waters of the river,** as though enthroned there or floating on the waters, **when he held up his right hand and his left hand unto heaven,** in the gesture of a most solemn oath, **and sware by Him that liveth forever,** by the one everlasting true God, **that it,** the period of these wonderful things, **shall be for a time, times, and a half,** the duration of the period being the same as that of Antichrist's reign, cp. chap. 7, 25; **and when he shall have accomplished to scatter the power of the holy people,** when the Christian Church would have reached a point apparently near annihilation on account of the oppression of Antichrist, **all these things shall be finished,** including also the deliverance of the people of the Lord by the angel Michael and everything else that had been included in the great prophecy of the angel. V. 8. **And I heard, but I understood not,** he did not grasp the meaning of the angel's announcement; **then said I, O my Lord, what shall be the end of these things?** He wanted a more exact explanation and interpretation of the period to which reference was made and to the sequence of events in that era, for he was still in the dark concerning them. V. 9. **And he said, Go thy way, Daniel,** the words being encouraging although in the nature of a refusal; **for the words are closed up,** altogether concealed, **and sealed till the time of the end,** so that it would not be lost or mutilated throughout the times then coming and until the Messianic era. V. 10. **Many shall be purified and made white and tried,** the time of tribulation bringing out their faithfulness to their Lord; **but the wicked shall do wickedly,** deliberately closing their eyes and minds to the lessons intended also for them; **and none of the wicked shall understand,** the eyes of their understanding being blinded by their own fault; **but the wise shall understand,** for they would read and interpret the signs of the times aright. V. 11. **And from the time that the daily sacrifice shall be taken away,** cp. chap. 11, 31, **and the abomination that maketh desolate set up,** in the idolatry introduced by Antiochus Epiphanes, the antitype of Antichrist, **there shall be a thousand two hundred and ninety days,** a period of time whose duration in human days and years cannot be exactly determined. V. 12. **Blessed is he that waiteth and cometh to the thousand three hundred and five and thirty days,** evidently the end of the great trial intended to test the loyalty of the Lord's children. V. 13. **But go thou thy way till the end be,** calmly awaiting death as a deliverance from all present affliction; **for thou shalt rest,** in the peace of the grave, **and stand in thy lot at the end of the days,** in the possession of the inheritance of the saints in light, Col. 1, 12, whose enjoyment he will share with all those who, like him, are faithful to the Lord until the end. Blessed are all who await their death in this spirit of calm hopefulness and certain trust in the promise of God!

THE BOOK OF THE PROPHET HOSEA.

INTRODUCTION.

Hosea ("Jehovah has redeemed,") was the son of Beeri, a citizen of the kingdom of Israel. He was an early contemporary of Isaiah and Micah. But while these two prophets preached in the southern kingdom, Hosea prophesied in the midst of the northern kingdom, which he regularly called Ephraim, which was then, in the eighth century before Christ, at the zenith of its power. Jeroboam II had greatly enlarged the borders of the land, so that the material prosperity of the country became proverbial. But to this outward glory of the kingdom its moral corruption corresponded, for shameless idolatry went hand in hand with an open transgression of all the commandments of the Second Table. The people of the land forgot and forsook the true God and followed after false gods. Chaps. 1, 2; 2, 5. 13; 3, 1; 4, 17.

The prophecies of Hosea fully take these conditions into account, for the two sections of his book, clearly as they are distinguished (chaps. 1—3 and 4—14) both treat of the faithlessness of Israel and of the divine love which calls His people to repentance. In the first part of the book, which seems to have been written toward the end of Jeroboam's reign, the prophet sternly reproves the people for their spiritual adultery and admonishes them to repent. In the second part, which seems to presuppose the unsettled conditions following the death of Jeroboam, the prophet announces to the godless and self-hardened people of his nation the inevitable judgment of the Lord. The entire section may be subdivided into three parts: chaps. 4, 1—6, 3; 6, 4—11, 12; 12, 1—14, 9, each concluding with a thought opening up a brighter future to such as will heed the Lord's admonition.

The style of the book is unique, with a strong character of individuality and an equally strong subjective trend. It is rich in bold and strong figures, often with passages of marked beauty, sometimes rather abrupt, particularly in passing rapidly from one picture to another. The vocabulary is sometimes strange and the language involved, with peculiar grammatical constructions.

Hosea has some Messianic passages of singular power and beauty; for while he declares that the Lord must and will disown His reprobate children, he says, at the same time, that Jehovah will gather for Himself a numerous people. He predicts that in the days of the Messiah the true Israel, including men from all nations of the world, shall return and seek the Lord and shall fear Him and His goodness.1)

1) Cp. Fuerbringer, *Einleitung in das Alte Testament*, 78—80; *Concordia Bible Class*, June, 1919, 79—81.

CHAPTER 1.

The Spiritual Whoredom of Israel.

ISRAEL TO BE REJECTED ON ACCOUNT OF ITS IDOLATRY. — V. 1. **The word of the Lord that came unto Hosea, the son of Beeri, in the days of Uzziah, Jotham, Ahaz, and Hezekiah, kings of Judah,** who are probably mentioned in the sequence of their reign on account of the stability of their rule, **and in the days of Jeroboam, the son of Joash, king of Israel,** this statement being added to bring out the fact of Hosea's having prophesied in the earlier part of the century, before there was any indication of decay in Israel from which one might reasonably have deduced the probability of the nation's downfall, a fact which would have weakened the idea of a prophecy. V. 2. **The beginning of the word of the Lord by Hosea,** literally, "In the beginning when Jehovah spoke with Hosea," **and the Lord said to Hosea, Go, take unto thee a wife of whoredoms,** most commentators believing this to have been done internally and in a vision, since the force of the symbolical act would otherwise be lost, **and children of whoredoms.** The figure represents the northern kingdom in its relation to Jehovah at the time of the prophet, when the nation as such had become unfaithful and in its individual members could well be compared to children of adultery, as the prophet says; **for the land hath committed great whoredom, departing from the Lord,** its idolatry was of a kind to call forth the righteous anger of the Lord. V. 3. **So he,** the prophet, **went and took Gomer, the daughter of Diblaim,** whose very name was descriptive of the life in which she delighted; **which conceived and bare him a son.** V. 4. **And the Lord said unto him, Call his name Jezreel,** the name of a very fruitful valley in the northern part of the land; **for yet a little while, and I will avenge the blood of Jezreel,** namely, the blood that had been spilled by Ahab and other wicked kings in this garden spot, **upon the house of Jehu,** who had loaded blood-guiltiness upon himself by acts of murder for which he had no command of God, cp. 2 Kings 9 and 10, **and will cause to cease the kingdom of the house of Israel,** the end of the kingdom thus being predicted while it still seemed to be at the height of its power. V. 5. **And it shall come to pass at that day that I will break the bow of Israel,** the military force on which the strength of the kingdom rested, on which its existence depended, **in the Valley of Jezreel,** for the Assyrians, within four decades, overthrew the power of Israel completely. V. 6. **And she conceived again and bare a daughter,** a female child being named in order to represent the entire nation, both men and women, in the sons and daughters of the people. **And God said unto him, Call her name Lo-ruhamah** ("not having obtained mercy"); **for I will no more have mercy upon the house of Israel, but I will utterly take them away,** literally, "for not will I add any more to have compassion on the house of Israel that I should keep on forgiving them," that is, His patience was now exhausted, and His judgment upon them would soon be carried out. V. 7. **But I will have mercy upon the house of Judah,** the southern kingdom, in which His worship was still being observed by the few who represented His kingdom on earth, **and will save them by the Lord, their God,** by an almighty deliverance, **and will not save them by bow nor by sword nor by battle, by horses nor by horsemen,** the heaping of the synonyms showing the futility of all human power over against the Lord's decrees. V 8. **Now, when she had weaned Lo-ruhamah, she conceived and bare a son,** there being no interruption in the announcement of evil. V. 9. **Then said God, Call his name Lo-ammi** ("not My people"); **for ye are not My people,** namely, on account of their rejection of Him, **and I will not be your God,** they could not claim Him as their highest good, they could not call upon Him as their Helper. When people deliberately reject the true God, they cut themselves off from all the manifestations of His grace and mercy; they bring misfortune upon themselves and can blame no one but themselves for their unhappy state.

THE ACCEPTANCE OF THE TRUE ISRAEL. — V. 10. **Yet the number of the children of Israel,** the spiritual Israel in Messianic times, **shall be as the sand of the sea, which cannot be measured nor numbered,** cp. Gen. 22, 17; 32, 13; **and it shall come to pass that in the place where it was said unto them, Ye are not My people,** namely, in the center of the Lord's worship in the midst of His visible Church, wherever He would establish His congregations in the Messianic era, **there it shall be said unto them, Ye are the sons of the living God,** this being the message which is proclaimed wherever the Gospel is preached. V. 11. **Then shall the children of Judah and the children of Israel,** all the true members of the Church of the Lord, all those who have acknowledged Him in faith as their Father, **be gathered together,** in the communion of saints, **and appoint themselves one Head,** accepting the Messiah as the one Master in the Church, **and they shall come up out of the land,** being removed from the unbelievers in whose midst they live; **for great shall be the day of Jezreel,** the day of Israel's overthrow being at the same time the day of its deliverance; for only such as are conquered by the forces of the Messiah may become partakers of His grace and mercy. Cp. Luke 2, 34. Chap. 2, 1. **Say ye unto your brethren, Ammi** ("My people"); **and to your sisters, Ruhamah** ("having obtained mercy"). The original names of the children were thus changed to indicate their changed relationship toward God and their Savior. No matter how far a person has fallen away from the truth of God's Word, there is always mercy for Him through the redemption of Christ, if he but returns in true sorrow over his sins and accepts the offered deliverance.

CHAPTER 2.

The Idolatrous People Punished and Converted.

A THREAT OF PUNISHMENT. — V. 2. **Plead with your mother,** the members of Israel, as the children of an adulterous wife, being addressed, plead; **for she is not My wife,** she was no longer Jehovah's bride, **neither am I her Husband,** for He had been obliged to reject her on account of her adultery; **let her therefore put away her whoredoms out of her sight,** namely, the shameless idolatry which was practised throughout Israel at the time, **and her adulteries from between her breasts,** for Israel, in her shamelessness, was like a public harlot, who displays her profession in her bared breasts, v. 3. **lest I strip her naked,** as a punishment for her shameless exposure of herself in the practise of her spiritual wantonness, **and set her as in the day that she was born,** cp. Ex. 16, 4, when she was without covering, **and make her as a wilderness and set her like a dry land,** altogether desert in every way, **and slay her with thirst,** thus depriving her of all the wonderful blessings which He had given her in the past, for the Lord had had mercy on His people in Egypt, He had led them out of the house of bondage, and He had made a covenant with them. The desert is a picture of the various tribulations and sufferings of the exile. V. 4. **And I will not have mercy upon her children,** all the members of the nation being included in His punishment; **for they be the children of whoredoms,** all of them being guilty of the same shameless idolatry. V. 5. **For their mother hath played the harlot,** the whole nation, as the various prophets show, being guilty of the same idolatrous behavior; **she that conceived them hath done shamefully,** openly committing her shameless acts, making no attempt to hide her bold practises; **for she said, I will go after my lovers, that give me my bread and my water, my wool and my flax, mine oil and my drink,** food, clothing, and the enjoyments of life; for Israel's commercial enterprise was stimulated by the riches and power of the nations round about, and it was with the idea of getting and holding their friendship that the Israelites began to practise idolatry. V. 6. **Therefore, behold, I will hedge up thy way with thorns,** setting insurmountable obstacles to keep Israel away from the heathen nations with their allurements and temptations, **and make a wall that she shall not find her paths,** namely, to the temples and altars of the idols. The Lord undoubtedly refers to the oppression and affliction of the exile, which opened the eyes of the children of Israel to the vanity and helplessness of the idols. V. 7. **And she shall follow after her lovers,** determined, at first, to cling to the false gods whom she had accepted, **but she shall not overtake them; and she shall seek them, but shall not find them,** for she would be reduced to such straits as would show her how vain was her hope in these idols and their assistance. **Then shall she say, I will go and return to my first Husband,** having learned, by bitter experience, that He is the only true God, **for then,** at the time when Israel followed Him alone, **was it better with me than now.** V. 8. **For she did not know,** she did not realize at that time, **that I gave her corn and wine and oil and multiplied her silver and gold,** giving her all these temporal blessings in rich measure, **which they prepared for Baal,** using it for his cult and worship, in open idolatry. Many a person serves a false god, not knowing that the very gifts which he brings are the blessings of God's goodness upon him. V. 9. **Therefore will I return and take away My corn in the time thereof,** namely, at the very time of the harvest, when men would expect a full supply, **and My wine in the season thereof and will recover My wool and My flax,** all these being gifts of His bounty, and therefore rightly belonging to Him, **given to cover her nakedness.** If God takes the gifts suddenly and at the very time of the harvest, the punishment would be more severe than if He had taken them after the outlook already was poor. V. 10. **And now will I discover her lewdness,** uncover her nakedness and shame to her disgrace, **in the sight of her lovers,** cp. Ezek. 16, 37, **and none shall deliver her out of Mine hand.** Cp. Jer. 13, 26; Nah. 3, 5. While the nations round about were looking on, partly in helpless idleness and partly in malicious joy, Israel was delivered to her punishment. V. 11. **I will also cause all her mirth to cease,** the hypocritical evidence of a joy which was no longer real among the people, **her feast-days,** especially the three highest festivals, Passover, Pentecost, and the Feast of Tabernacles, **her new moons, and her Sabbaths, and all her solemn feasts,** whatever days were observed in the course of the year. V. 12. **And I will destroy her vines and her fig-trees,** representative of the wealth of the country in farm products. **whereof she hath said, These are my rewards that my lovers have given me,** thus blasphemously taking the honor from the Lord; **and I will make them,** the fine orchards and vineyards, **a forest, and the beasts of the field shall eat them.** Cp. Is. 7, 23 ff.; Micah 3, 12. V. 13. **And I will visit upon her the days of Baalim,** punishing her for devoting the great festival days of the Jewish church-year to the service of heathen idols, **wherein she burned incense to them, and she decked herself with her earrings and her jewels,** decorating herself for the purpose of making an impression upon those whom she had permitted to seduce her, **and**

she went after her lovers and forgat Me, saith the Lord. That is the outstanding reprehensible feature of unbelief and idolatry: the rejection of the true God, for He wants no other gods beside Himself.

THE RENEWAL OF THE LORD'S MARRIAGE CONTRACT. — V. 14. **Therefore, behold, I will allure her,** deliberately leading the idolatrous Israel astray and visiting His punishment upon her, but with a wonderful object in mind, **and bring her into the wilderness,** where there was nothing to detract her attention any more, **and speak comfortably unto her,** in a friendly, heart-to-heart talk, with the intention of once more manifesting His love, now that Israel was ready to acknowledge her transgression. V. 15. **And I will give her her vineyards from thence,** the very wilderness again blossoming as the rose, that is, the Gospel-teaching once more bringing forth glorious fruits, **and the Valley of Achor,** southwest of Jericho, here used only in a figurative way, **for a door of hope,** so that the crime of Achan would not be repeated, Josh. 7, 26; **and she shall sing there,** once more with the true happiness of a believing people, **as in the days of her youth,** when the Lord first led His people into the Land of Promise, **and as in the day when she came up out of the land of Egypt,** when the Lord first made His covenant with His people. V. 16. **And it shall be at that day,** at the time of this wonderful deliverance of the Messianic period, **saith the Lord, that thou shalt call Me Ishi,** that is, "My Husband," **and shalt call Me no more Baali,** in the form of idolatry by which Israel had transferred the worship of the one true God to the Phenician idol. V. 17. **For I will take away the names of Baalim out of her mouth,** so that the people would no longer mention them in prayer, **and they shall no more be remembered by their name,** so that idolatry would completely be forgotten in the midst of the Lord's people. V. 18. **And in that day will I make a covenant for them with the beasts of the field and with the fowls of heaven and with the creeping things of the ground,** with all those things which might prove harmful and dangerous to them, under the picture of ravenous beasts, birds of prey, and poisonous reptiles, **and I will break the bow and the sword and the battle out of the earth,** so that the instruments of war would be destroyed and war itself cease, **and will make them to lie down safely.** All this, of course, is figurative description of the time when there would be peace on earth through Him who is our Peace. V. 19. **And I will betroth thee,** so the Lord says to His bride, the Church of the New Testament, **unto Me forever; yea, I will betroth thee unto Me in righteousness,** namely, that earned by Christ when He cleansed His Church from all unrighteousness through the blood of His cross, **and in judgment,** by which He interferes in behalf of His people on the basis of Christ's perfect atonement, **and in lovingkindness,** in His free and merciful favor, **and in mercies.** Every idea of merit on the part of man is thus entirely excluded; God accepts every member of the Church on the basis of His own mercy in Christ Jesus alone. V. 20. **I will even betroth thee unto Me in faithfulness,** with a pledge of the eternal duration of the covenant on His side; **and thou shalt know the Lord,** the saving knowledge of Jehovah being imparted through this Gospel-message. V. 21. **And it shall come to pass in that day, I will hear, saith the Lord,** His ears, as it were, being attuned to the slightest stirring on the part of those who know Him as their Savior, **I will hear the heavens,** who here appear as interceding in behalf of the believers, **and they shall hear the earth,** which likewise is represented as pleading for mercy; v. 22. **and the earth shall hear the corn and the wine and the oil,** so that its blessings would once more richly be given; **and they shall hear Jezreel,** the people of the true Israel, of the Church of God, becoming partakers of the rich blessings of the Lord in the Messianic era. V. 23. **And I will sow her unto Me in the earth,** planting His Church anew by the operation of His divine grace; **and I will have mercy upon her that had not obtained mercy,** the congregation of Israel; **and I will say to them which were not My people,** men and women from every part of the world, chosen by the Lord to be included in His communion of saints, **Thou art My people; and they shall say,** accepting their salvation at the hand of the Father through the redemption of Christ, **Thou art my God.** That is the confession of the Church and of all its members. Wherever the Gospel of Christ is preached, members are won for the Church, and the sum total of these believers are the bride of Christ and partake of all the blessings which He has gained for all men by His redemption.

CHAPTER 3.

The New Marriage of the Adulteress.

In a second symbolical marriage the faithful love of God, which for that very reason is also jealous and intends to lead to repentance, is pictured. V. 1. **Then said the Lord unto me, Go yet,** that is, once more, again, in a second venture, **love a woman beloved of her friend,** the word being used often for husband, **yet an adulteress,** one still regarded and surrounded with conjugal love by her lawful husband, though estranged from him on account of her adulterous acts, **according to the love of the Lord toward the children of Israel, who look to other gods and love flagons of wine,** rather, raisin-cakes, such as were used in idol-worship. Cp. Jer. 7, 18. Just as Jehovah loves the children of Israel, although they turn to other gods, so the prophet should love this woman, who would become guilty of adultery. V. 2. **So I bought her to me for fifteen pieces of silver,** a shekel being worth about 62 cents, **and for an homer of barley and an half homer of barley,** a total of some twelve bushels of grain. This was dowry-money, but the amount was that paid for a slave, cp. Ex. 21, 32; Zech. 11, 12. The transaction undoubtedly pointed to the fact that the Lord had chosen Israel as His people while they were still in bondage in the land of Egypt, and the fact that half of the amount was paid in common grain indicated the lowly condition of the bride at this time. V. 3. **And I said unto her, Thou shalt abide for me many days,** in a faithful union with him alone; **thou shalt not play the harlot, and thou shalt not be for another man,** in an adulterous union; **so will I also be for thee,** not taking any other consort, loyal in wedded love. The reference is undoubtedly to the time of the exile, when Israel was estranged from the public worship of Jehovah and yet was to remain faithful to Him until the time of the restoration. V. 4. **For the children of Israel shall abide many days without a king and without a prince,** without a government of their own, **and without a sacrifice,** namely, those of public worship in the Temple, **and without an image,** pillars as used in connection with their worship, **and without an ephod,** the beautiful vest of the high priest which was used in determining the will of God and uncovering the future, Ex. 28, 6—12, **and without teraphim,** household gods which had been retained from the earliest days of Israel's history. The exile brought to an end not only the public worship of Jehovah, but also the remnants of idol-worship as practised as a matter of tradition. During the captivity the children of God realized the vanity of all idol-worship and were ready to accept the true God. V. 5. **Afterward shall the children of Israel return and seek the Lord, their God,** the Jewish Church after the exile being the organization in which the belief in the true God was still taught, **and David, their King,** namely, the Son of David, the Messiah, who is called so also in other Messianic prophecies, cp. Jer. 30, 9; Ezek. 34, 23. 24; **and shall fear the Lord and His goodness,** as shown in His manifold blessings, **in the latter days,** in the Messianic period, which is always designated in this manner. In the midst of the sternest reproofs the light of God's mercy shines forth like a beacon directing the believers to heaven.

CHAPTER 4.

The Sins of Israel and the Divine Visitation.

THE FIRST PART OF THE ACCUSATION. — V. 1. **Hear the word of the Lord, ye children of Israel,** Jehovah here both raising the accusation and pronouncing the sentence of punishment; **for the Lord hath a controversy with the inhabitants of the land,** just cause for complaint, a matter which ought to be decided in a court of justice and the punishment dictated, **because there is no truth,** which makes intercourse between human beings dependable, **nor mercy,** neighborly compassion, **nor knowledge of God in the land,** these three virtues being mentioned together in many other passages of the Bible. V. 2. **(By) swearing,** a forbidden use of the name of God, **and lying,** against the Eighth Commandment, **and killing, and stealing, and committing adultery,** these vices being general, these transgressions common, **they break out,** bursting through the restraint of the Law of God, eager to be engaged in crimes of the worst kind, **and blood toucheth blood,** one act of bloodshed following another. V. 3. **Therefore shall the land mourn,** the moral corruption of its inhabitants resulting in the physical destruction of the land and its products, **and every one that dwelleth therein shall languish,** as though wilting in a universal drought, **with the beasts of the field and with the fowls of heaven,** all of whom would be affected by the punishment descending upon the land; **yea, the fishes of the sea also shall be taken away,** so that they would disappear and perish. In spite of the approaching punishment, however, the people persisted in their wickedness. V. 4. **Yet let no man strive nor reprove another,** that is, conditions being as they are, all attempts to change the corruption would be vain; **for thy people are as they that strive with the priest,** that is, they are rebellious against the decisions which the priests were authorized to make in minor controversies, Deut. 17, 12, they no longer regarded the authority established by God. V. 5. **Therefore shalt thou,** Israel, **fall in the day,** stumbling and falling in broad daylight, **and the prophet also shall fall with thee in the night,** for neither day nor night would be free from some form of slaughter, **and I will destroy thy mother,** the entire nation being cut off on account of its transgressions. V. 6. **My people are destroyed for lack of knowl-**

edge, because they refused to acknowledge Jehovah. **Because thou hast rejected knowledge**, so freely offered in the preaching of the prophets of God, **I will also reject thee that thou shalt be no priest to Me**, no longer a priestly people, as set forth Ex. 19, 6; **seeing thou hast forgotten the Law of thy God**, His holy will, as revealed so abundantly, **I will also forget thy children**, the entire congregation of Israel. V. 7. **As they were increased**, namely, in population, wealth, and power, **so they sinned against Me**, their transgression increasing in the same proportion; **therefore will I change their glory into shame**, so that their greatness and prosperity would become a mockery in the eyes of the heathen. V. 8. **They eat up the sin of My people**, namely, when the priests consumed the sin-offering, as a part of an act of worship intended to remove the guilt of the worshipers, Lev. 6, 19; 10, 17, **and they set their heart on their iniquity**, lusting after the transgressions of the people, instead of doing all in their power to suppress them. Since the priests lived upon the sins of the people, they wished for nothing more earnestly than that the people would keep on sinning more and more, namely, in idolatry. V. 9. **And there shall be**, in consequence of this situation, **like people, like priest**, the people following their spiritual leaders in their hypocrisy and therefore both of them together sharing the punishment of the Lord following upon such wickedness; **and I will punish them for their ways and reward them their doings**, for the position and wealth of the priests would not prevent their being compelled to share the same fate with the rest of the nation. V. 10. **For they shall eat**, in unsatiable greediness, **and not have enough; they shall commit whoredom**, the entire nation being involved in immoral practises, **and shall not increase**, namely, in number, by growth in population, **because they have left off to take heed to the Lord**, they no longer pay any attention to His holy will. They who forsake the Lord must sooner or later pay the penalty of their sin.

THE SECOND PART OF THE ACCUSATION. — V. 11. **Whoredom**, the general immorality just referred to, **and wine and new wine**, drunken debauchery in every form, as practised in those days in connection with the Syrian idol-worship, **take away the heart**, the understanding, making men perverse and stupid in every respect. V. 12. **My people ask counsel at their stocks**, from their wooden idols, **and their staff declareth unto them**, the reference being to the practise of setting up two rods, with proper incantations, the oracle depending upon the direction in which the rods fell; **for the spirit of whoredoms**, which has made them so stupid, **hath caused them to err**, to become addicted to such foolishness as they would despise under normal conditions of mind, **and they have gone a-whoring from under their God**, their idolatry causing them to forsake the subjection which was their natural relation to the true God. V. 13. **They sacrifice upon the tops of the mountains**, after the manner which they had taken over from the heathen Canaanites, **and burn incense upon the hills**, in a form of worship which should have been reserved for the true God alone, **under oaks and poplars and elms**, or terebinths, **because the shadow thereof is good**, green and pleasant, a fact which made this nature worship appeal to them; **therefore your daughters shall commit whoredom, and your spouses**, young brides, or daughters-in-law, **shall commit adultery**, for such lewdness was connected with the cult of the gods of nature, with the worship of Baal and Astarte. V. 14. **I will not punish your daughters when they commit whoredom, nor your spouses when they commit adultery**, as just set forth; **for themselves**, the fathers and husbands, **are separated with whores**, going aside to be alone with them in their lewd practises, **and they sacrifice with harlots**, with the temple-girls, who freely sold themselves to the worshipers; **therefore the people, that doth not understand**, being dense with impudence and shamelessness, **shall fall**, being destroyed as a consequence of such conditions. The Lord therefore adds a warning lest Judah join Israel in this idolatry and shameless conduct. V. 15. **Though thou, Israel, play the harlot**, in such blasphemous adultery and idolatry, **yet let not Judah offend**, for the members of this nation were still trying to maintain the Lord's worship; **and come not ye unto Gilgal**, a place southwest of Shiloh, **neither go ye up to Beth-aven**, or Bethel, on the southern boundary of Israel, the shrines at these two places being devoted to idol-worship, **nor swear, The Lord liveth**, for an oath by the life of Jehovah in idolatrous service was a further insult to His majesty. V. 16. **For Israel slideth back as a backsliding heifer**, stubborn and unbroken; **now the Lord will feed them as a lamb in a large place**, by removing them to a distant and large country, where they would be far removed from those with whom they associated in their idolatry. V. 17. **Ephraim**, the northern kingdom, **is joined to idols**, so linked with idolatrous worship as to make it impossible for them to leave it alone at this time; **let him alone**, for it would be useless to try to take him from his idolatry; he is utterly stubborn. V. 18. **Their drink is sour**, or, "they are abandoned to their carousing"; **they have committed whoredom continually**, in an excess of lewdness; **her rulers with shame do love, Give ye**, literally, "loving have loved their shields' shame," that is, the rulers of the nation, by loving sin, loved also shame, the result of their transgression; in other words, the whole nation, from the highest to the lowest, was corrupt. V. 19. **The wind hath bound her up in her wings**, or, "the tempest seizes them with its wings," **and they shall be ashamed because of their sacrifices**, for their trust in their idolatrous sacrifices would prove to be a vain hope. Thus the hopes of unbelievers and idolaters will ever be found to be vain and foolish, for there is no salvation outside of the deliverance announced by the one true God.

CHAPTER 5.

The Judgment Announced.

THE ACCUSATION AGAINST THE PRIESTS. — V. 1. **Hear ye this, O priests**, the spiritual leaders of the people; **and hearken, ye house of Israel**, the family of the ten tribes as such; **and give ye ear**, in paying most careful attention, **O house of the king**, as the temporal rulers of the nation; **for judgment is toward you**, it is intended for them, to strike them down in due time, **because ye have been a snare on Mizpah**, this being the town in the northern part of their country or beyond Jordan, **and a net spread upon Tabor**, a mountain in what was later known as Galilee. The leaders are charged with being snares and nets on account of their leading the people entrusted to them into sins. V. 2. **And the revolters are profound to make slaughter**, literally, "and into the corrupt doings of excesses they have sunken deeply," so that the leaders, in their open rebellion against the Lord have carried their transgressions to extremes and beyond; **though I have been a rebuker of them all**, earnestly trying, by His admonitions, to bring them back to the right way. V. 3. **I know Ephraim, and Israel is not hid from Me**, He was well acquainted with the spirit which possessed them both; **for now, O Ephraim, thou committest whoredom**, that is, idolatry, **and Israel is defiled**, by likewise taking part in the spiritual adultery. V. 4. **They will not frame their doings to turn unto their God**, for as long as they are guilty of such transgressions, their evil works will not permit their return to the Lord; **for the spirit of whoredoms is in the midst of them**, so that the service of idolatry occupies all their thoughts, **and they have not known the Lord**, for under the circumstances the knowledge of the true God is impossible for them. V. 5. **And the pride of Israel**, as they boast of their glory, **doth testify to his face**, namely, when the punishment of such pride is suffered; **therefore shall Israel and Ephraim fall in their iniquity**, stumbling and being brought to destruction because of it; **Judah also shall fall with them**, tottering and stumbling with Israel, since both are guilty of idolatry. V. 6. **They shall go with their flocks and with their herds to seek the Lord**, as though eager to bring their sacrifices; **but they shall not find Him; He hath withdrawn Himself from them**, since He has no delight in sacrifices brought in a spirit of hypocrisy, without true repentance. V. 7. **They have dealt treacherously against the Lord**, in blasphemous faithlessness; **for they have begotten strange children**, as though by illicit intercourse with idols; **now shall an month devour them with their portions**, or, "the new moon will devour them." Their hypocritical festal offerings were so little appreciated and acceptable in the sight of God that, instead of bringing them deliverance, they were rather a cause of their ruin. Many a person will find out that his self-appointed worship of God will bring down upon him the wrath of the Lord instead of His mercy.

THE THREAT OF PUNISHMENT. — V. 8. **Blow ye the cornet in Gibeah**, the ancient city of Saul, **and the trumpet in Ramah**, another city located on an eminence, both of them most suitable for giving signals on account of their lofty situation; **cry aloud at Beth-aven**, or Bethel, on the border of the northern kingdom, **After thee, O Benjamin!** that is, the danger is coming, the enemy is close behind. V. 9. **Ephraim**, the entire country of the ten tribes, **shall be desolate in the day of rebuke**, namely, when the Lord's punishment would strike them; **among the tribes of Israel have I made known that which shall surely be**, continuous plagues, a lasting punishment. Cp. Deut. 28, 59. V. 10. **The princes of Judah were like them that remove the bound**, cp. Deut. 19, 14, namely, by removing the boundary between the worship of the true God and idolatry, which should have been kept apart forever; **therefore I will pour out My wrath upon them like water**, in an overwhelming degree, in proportion to the greatness of their offense. V. 11. **Ephraim is oppressed and broken in judgment**, cut to pieces by the punishment of the Lord, **because he willingly walked after the commandment**, it thought good to follow idol-images, it clung to the calf-worship of Jeroboam throughout its existence. V. 12. **Therefore will I be unto Ephraim as a moth and to the house of Judah as rottenness**, both of these being figurative of destructive powers, which steadily eat into the very marrow of things. V. 13. **When Ephraim saw his sickness**, becoming aware of the illness of the body politic, **and Judah saw his wound**, realizing that something was rotten in the nation, **then went Ephraim to the Assyrian**, looking for assistance from the heathen instead of consulting the Lord, **and sent to King Jareb**, to the warlike monarch through whose intervention the kingdom hoped to recover; **yet could he not heal you nor cure you of your wound,** for the help of men is vain in such cases. V. 14. **For I will be unto Ephraim as a lion and as a young lion to the house of Judah,** who takes hold of his prey and tears it to pieces; **I, even I, will tear and go away,** as a lion withdrawing to his den; **I will take away, and none shall rescue him,** for with the Lord's merciful presence removed, there is no hope of deliverance. V. 15. **I will go and return to My place,** as though shutting Himself up in heaven and withdrawing His favor entirely, **till they acknowledge their offense and seek My face,** this being the hope which is held before them. **In their affliction they will seek Me early.** This is a truth which is found also in other passages of the Bible, namely, that men seek out the Lord when they are in trouble, they pour out a prayer when His chastening is upon them. Cp. Is. 26, 16.

CHAPTER 6.

An Earnest Invitation and a Further Admonition.

Having stated his threat in a most uncompromising form, the prophet adds a powerful appeal to the people of his nation to heed the warning of the Lord and to accept His mercy. V. 1. **Come and let us return unto the Lord,** the appeal being to seek the Lord in agreement with the last statement of the preceding chapter; **for He hath torn,** by the punishments for sin which He sent upon them, **and He will heal us; He hath smitten,** so that they were suffering with wounds, **and He will bind us up.** Even if the Lord does not always send punishments in the same degree as those which He visited upon Israel, He has a most impressive way of administering correction. The hammer of the Law must smite and soften the hard hearts before the gentle message of the Gospel may find entrance. V. 2. **After two days will He revive us,** the early and certain return of His love being promised to a repentant people; **in the third day He will raise us up, and we shall live in His sight.** Cp. Deut. 32, 39. V. 3. **Then shall we know, if we follow on to know the Lord,** or, "Therefore let us understand, follow after the knowledge of Jehovah!" for such pursuit, on the basis of true faith, was bound to have results. **His going forth is prepared as the morning,** as sure as the dawn comes, the Lord will return, bringing salvation; **and He shall come unto us as the rain, as the latter and former rain unto the earth,** as welcome and as fruitful as these two rainy seasons were for the harvest of Palestine. But from this pleasing picture, promising the mercy of Jehovah to all those who repent, the prophet must once more abruptly turn to his doleful cry. V. 4. **O Ephraim, what shall I do unto thee? O Judah, what shall I do unto thee?** Cp. Is. 5, 4. What more was to be done in a case of this kind? **For your goodness is as a morning cloud,** their godliness and brotherly love passing away just as quickly, **and as the early dew it goeth away,** there was nothing durable and stable about it; it vanished away upon close inspection. V. 5. **Therefore have I hewed them by the prophets,** endeavoring to give them the right shape; **I have slain them by the words of My mouth,** in most emphatic rebukes; **and thy judgments are as the light that goeth forth,** that is, the Lord's judgment upon the apostate people was so obvious that every one had to admit its source and object. V. 6. **For I desired mercy and not sacrifice,** the true piety of the heart rather than a mere outward form of worship, **and the knowledge of God more than burnt offerings.** Cp. Matt. 9, 13; 12, 7. To have a form and shell of godliness, but to deny its substance, is the essence of hypocrisy. V. 7. **But they,** the people whom the prophet is rebuking, **like men,** rather, like Adam, **have transgressed the covenant,** this statement being a testimony to the historical character of the first man and his transgression of God's command; **there have they dealt treacherously against Me,** in a faithless rejection of the one God of their salvation. V. 8. **Gilead is a city of them that work iniquity,** the entire province being a gathering-place of wicked people, **and is polluted with blood,** so that the entire district east of Jordan was guilty in the sight of God. V. 9. **And as troops of robbers wait for a man,** lying in ambush in order to fall upon the unsuspecting traveler unawares, **so the company of priests murder in the way by consent, for they commit lewdness,** or, "they murder on the way to Shechem," surprising the travelers and cutting them down in cold blood, probably as they sought refuge there, or as they were on their way to Bethel with rich sacrificial gifts. V. 10. **I have seen an horrible thing in the house of Israel,** abominable things happening in the northern kingdom; **there is the whoredom of Ephraim,** its shameful idolatry; **Israel is defiled,** namely, as the result of such unparalleled transgressions. V. 11. **Also, O Judah, He hath set an harvest for thee,** the harvest of the judgment of the Lord being prepared, **when I returned the captivity of My people.** The great misery of the entire nation of the Jews could be changed only by means of God's judgments of punishment, through which the godless would be destroyed and those who repented would be saved. To this day the only way for any person to be acceptable in the sight of God is by repentance and faith.

CHAPTER 7.

The Rebuke of the Lord Continued.

THE MORAL CORRUPTION OF ISRAEL. — V. 1. **When I would have healed Israel,** when the Lord attempted to remove their corruption, **then the iniquity of Ephraim was discovered,** it became known openly, **and the wickedness of Samaria; for they commit falsehood,** so that intercourse became impossible because no man could trust the other; **and the thief cometh in, and the troop of robbers spoileth without,** so that no traveler was sure of his life. V. 2. **And they consider not in their hearts that I remember all their wickedness,** that it is known and recorded in the book of God's remembrances; **now their own doings have beset them about,** like mountains hedging them in on every hand; **they are before My face,** making it impossible to ignore them. V. 3. **They,** the criminals of every type, **make the king glad with their wickedness and the princes with their lies,** a fact which shows that the highest ranks of the people were infested with the corruption. V. 4. **They are all adulterers,** the spiritual and moral condition of the entire people being the very lowest, **as an oven heated by the baker, who ceaseth from raising,** that is, from heating the oven further, **after he hath kneaded the dough, until it be leavened.** The adulterous and idolatrous lust of the people was inflamed to such an extent that it was like a baker's oven which was already at such an extreme heat that he could omit adding more fuel while the fermentation of his bread was finished. V. 5. **In the day of our king,** his birthday or the day of his inauguration, **the princes have made him sick with bottles of wine,** or, "the princes became ill with the heat of the wine"; **he stretched out his hand with scorners,** accepting their company with a ready spirit, making them his boon companions, so that everything which men hold sacred was dragged in the dust. V. 6. **For they have made ready their heart like an oven whiles they lie in wait,** that is, as men bring fuel for an oven, so they have brought their hearts into their cunning; **their baker sleepeth all the night; in the morning it burneth as a flaming fire.** The baker is the ringleader, who inspires passion, who starts the conspiracy; the night provides a time of rest, so that the passion of idolatry, which burns throughout, may break forth with new strength and fierceness after the interval. When the evil thoughts of their hearts have fully matured, when they find time and opportunity for the execution of their plans, then they carry them out with eagerness. V. 7. **They are all hot as an oven,** aflame with the various passions to which they have yielded themselves, **and have devoured their judges,** their magistrates; **all their kings are fallen,** the references probably being to the time when the last kings of Israel, Zechariah, Shallum, Menahem, Pekahiah, and Pekah, followed one another in quick succession. **There is none among them that calleth unto Me;** for even the great calamities in which they found themselves did not cause them to repent. V. 8. **Ephraim, he hath mixed himself among the people,** by entering into friendships with heathen nations, adopting their ways and serving their idols. **Ephraim is a cake not turned,** like a pancake burned on the lower side, while the upper side is not yet done. The entire cake is then not fit for eating. V. 9. **Strangers have devoured his strength,** partly on account of the wars waged against Israel, partly as a consequence of the heathen ways which had been adopted in the northern kingdom, **and he knoweth it not,** he was not even aware of his unfortunate condition; **yea, gray hairs are here and there upon him,** signs of the approaching national dissolution; **yet he knoweth not,** being blind to all evidences of the inevitable end. V. 10. **And the pride of Israel testifieth to his face,** cp. chap. 5, 5, **and they do not return to the Lord, their God, nor seek Him for all this.** The situation was like that of which also other prophets complain when they state that the people have become hardened to the chastising hand of the Lord. Cp. Is. 9, 13; Jer. 5, 3.

HYPOCRISY REBUKED. — V. 11. **Ephraim also is like a silly dove without heart,** one which is too simple to notice the snare of the fowler. **They call to Egypt, they go to Assyria,** not realizing that the very nations whose help they invoked would prove their undoing. V. 12. **When they shall go,** when their embassies are dispatched to seek the aid of the great foreign nations, **I will spread My net upon them,** using the foreigners as His instruments to carry out His punishment upon them; **I will bring them down as the fowls of the heaven,** dragging them down into the net of the exile; **I will chastise them, as their congregation hath heard,** in accordance with His repeated proclamations concerning their doom. V. 13. **Woe unto them! For they have fled from Me,** forsaking the one Rock of their salvation. **Destruction unto them! because they have transgressed against Me,** they have rebelled and thereby forsaken Him, who is the only One who could and would help them. **Though I have redeemed them,** from the bondage of Egypt and from all other enemies, **yet they have spoken lies against Me,** by both words and actions, in seeking help elsewhere. V. 14. **And they have not cried unto Me with their heart,** for whatever praying they did was performed in hypocrisy, **when they howled upon their beds,** with cries of sleepless anguish, after the usual manner of their kind, resorting to extremes in order to make an impression; **they assemble themselves for corn and wine,** their one thought and object being to fill their stomachs with the best products of the land, **and they rebel against Me,** they have forsaken Him and, at the same time, turn against Him with open hostility. V. 15. **Though I have bound and strengthened their arms,** teaching them where to get and how to use their strength, **yet do they imagine mischief against Me,** by their idolatry and rebellion. V. 16. **They return, but not to the Most High,** or, "upwards," with their faces turned to His power alone; **they are like a deceitful bow,** whose string has lost its tenseness and cannot carry the arrow to its mark. **Their princes shall fall by the sword for the rage of their tongue,** on account of their proud boasting concerning the aid of Egypt; **this shall be their derision in the land of Egypt,** for the Egyptians themselves ridiculed them on account of the weakness revealed in their overthrow. That is ever the result of man's turning to men for help, for the very ones upon whom he depended for assistance will jeer at his fall. God is the only One in whom we may safely place all our trust.

CHAPTER 8.

The Judgment upon the Apostates.

THE JUDGMENT ANNOUNCED. — V. 1. **Set the trumpet to thy mouth,** so the Lord calls out to the prophet in bidding him give a warning concerning the approach of the judgment. **He shall come as an eagle against the house of the Lord,** the enemy, especially the Assyrian, invading the country with the swiftness of an eagle pouncing upon his prey, Deut. 28, 49, **because they have transgressed My covenant and trespassed against My Law.** While God, according to His mercy, would like to live in the midst of His people, they make His presence impossible by their rebellious behavior. V. 2. **Israel shall cry unto Me,** literally, "To Me will they cry," presuming upon the relation which had formerly obtained between Jehovah and them, **My God, we know Thee** (we, Israel). But it is a dead knowledge of the head only, faith no longer being found in their midst. The Lord wants to have the entire trust of the heart, as expressed in a person's whole life, He is not satisfied with a mere external worship. V. 3. **Israel hath cast off the thing that is good,** they are filled with aversion and loathing for the covenant of Jehovah. **The enemy shall pursue him,** as a punishment for such rebellious behavior, which is now more fully explained. V. 4. **They have set up kings, but not by Me,** not by His direction nor with His consent; **they have made princes, and I knew it not,** for even in the case of Jeroboam and Jehu the manner of their accession did not meet with the Lord's approval, and in the case of most of the other rulers, murder and violence were the determining factors. **Of their silver and their gold have they made them idols,** thus cutting themselves off entirely from the covenant of the Lord, **that they might be cut off,** for on account of their idolatry they rushed into their own destruction with open eyes. V. 5. **Thy calf, O Samaria, hath cast thee off,** or, "Is rejected thy calf," one of the idols made with their gold, "O Samaria?" the reference being to the calf of Bethel and Samaria, which is being addressed for the whole nation. **Mine anger is kindled against them; how long will it be ere they attain to innocency?** How long would they be incapable of purity? How long would it be before they would cease from polluting themselves with their idol-worship? V. 6. **For from Israel was it also,** that is, this calf originated from men; **the workman made it, therefore it is not god. But the calf of Samaria shall be broken in pieces,** smashed into tiny fragments. This is the result of Israel's idolatry. V. 7. **For they have sown the wind,** by all their transgressions, **and they shall reap the whirlwind,** a fitting harvest for such a sowing; **it hath no stalk,** their sowing produces no stalk, **the bud,** the kernels of the ear, **shall yield no meal; if so be it yield, the strangers,** the invading enemies, **shall swallow it up.** Such is the result of seeking the friendship of the enemies of God; in the end they turn upon those who depended upon them and bring destruction upon them.

A FURTHER THREAT OF JUDGMENT. — V. 8. **Israel is swallowed up,** its judgment being practically accomplished even now, the statement being made as though the prophecy were already fulfilled; **now shall they be among the Gentiles as a vessel wherein is no pleasure,** which is discarded as useless. Cp. Jer. 22, 28; 48, 38. V. 9. **For they are gone up to Assyria,** their object being to gain the friendship of the powerful nation, **a wild ass alone by himself; Ephraim hath hired lovers.** While the wild ass, an irrational brute, shuns the company of men, in order to maintain his independence, Ephraim seeks unnatural affiliations, such as are not in agreement with his high destiny. V. 10. **Yea, though they have hired among the nations,** in the unnatural attempt of buying friendships, **now will I gather them,** bringing them together among the nations, but in the capacity of captives, **and they shall sorrow a little for the burden of the king of princes,** they will be diminished in number by reason of the oppression which they must suffer in exile. Thus all their great plans and hopes turned out in just the opposite way, to their own detriment. V. 11. **Because Ephraim hath made many altars to sin,** in practising idolatry to such an exceptional degree, **altars shall be unto him to sin,** the idolatry practised has made him guilty in the sight of God. V. 12. **I have written to him the great things of My Law,** literally, I presented to him a myriad of My Law, the many precepts by which the Israelites might fulfil His will; **but they were counted as a strange thing,** they simply ignored the commandments of the Lord, as though they did not concern them. V. 13. **They sacrifice flesh for the sacrifices of Mine offerings and eat it,** intending it as a burnt offering; the Lord, however, looks upon it as a slaughtered animal, not as a sacrifice in His honor, because the right condition of the heart is missing; **but the Lord accepteth them not; now will He remember their iniquity and visit their sins,** with the punishment which they so richly deserved. **They shall return to Egypt,** once more be delivered into bondage. V. 14. **For Israel hath forgotten his Maker,** cp. Deut. 32, 18, **and buildeth temples,** either palaces or idol-temples; **and Judah hath multiplied fenced cities,** in a false reliance upon his own strength. **But I will send a fire upon his cities,** by bringing the invading enemies into the country, **and it shall devour the palaces thereof.** When men forsake and deny the Lord, relying upon their own ability and power instead, the Lord destroys the fortresses of such a false confidence; for He is a jealous God and will not tolerate any one but Himself to be acknowledged as the supreme Being in heaven and earth.

CHAPTER 9.

The Distress and Captivity of Israel.

WARNING AGAINST FALSE SECURITY. — V. 1. **Rejoice not, O Israel, for joy, as other people,** rather, "unto exultation," like the heathen, with a joy which, after the fashion of the heathen, attributed a bountiful harvest to the idols; **for thou hast gone a-whoring from thy God,** in the idolatry which the Lord had so earnestly rebuked; **thou hast loved a reward upon every corn-floor,** namely, the lover's reward which Israel expected from the idols for the homage shown them, which they hoped to get on the threshing-floor in the form of an abundant yield. Over against this the Lord says, v. 2. **The floor,** the corn-floor or threshing-floor, **and the wine-press,** these two representatives of the products of the country, **shall not feed them, and the new wine,** the must as pressed out of the grapes, **shall fail in her,** so that they would be sorely disappointed in their hopes of a rich harvest. V. 3. **They shall not dwell in the Lord's land; but Ephraim shall return to Egypt,** which is here once more representative of the land of bondage, the name standing for any kind of captivity, **and they shall eat unclean things in Assyria,** which to them was the real land of the exile. Their food in the land of their captivity would be unclean because it would no longer be sanctified by the sacrifice of the first-fruits during the Feast of the Unleavened Bread. V. 4. **They shall not offer wine-offerings to the Lord,** in the drink-offerings, as representative of all unbloody sacrifices, **neither shall (they) be pleasing unto Him their sacrifices,** for the bloody offerings which they might consider bringing to Him would not be pleasing in His sight; **(the food which they eat) shall be unto them as the bread of mourners,** cp. Deut. 26, 14, because the food eaten upon such an occasion was regarded as unclean, since all objects in a house where there was a dead person were unclean, Num. 19, 14; **all that eat thereof shall be polluted,** being Levitically defiled by their meal, **for their bread for their soul shall not come into the house of the Lord,** that is, the food which they needed to support their life could not come into the house of God to be consecrated. V. 5. **What will ye do in the solemn day and in the day of the feast of the Lord?** Since the Temple and its cult would be missing in the land of their exile, festal days with their solemn joy would not be possible. V. 6. **For, lo, they are gone because of destruction,** the prophet already seeing them in banishment. **Egypt,** the land of bondage, **shall gather them up,** chap. 8, 13; **Memphis,** the capital of the land of their captivity, **shall bury them; the pleasant places for their silver,** their houses and palaces filled and decked with silver, **nettles shall possess them,** the place where they stood being overgrown with weeds; **thorns shall be in their tabernacles,** the places of their habitation. V. 7. **The days of visitation are come,** with the Lord's punishment descending upon the apostate people, **the days of recompense are come,** with the Lord repaying the sins of Israel in His holy vengeance; **Israel shall know it,** at last be fully aware of it; **the prophet is a fool,** will become foolish with the immensity of the tragedy coming upon the people, **the spiritual man,** he who is inspired by the Spirit of the Lord, **is mad,** will almost be driven to insanity by the conditions then obtaining, **for the multitude of thine iniquity and the great hatred.** Hosea here pictures the terrible condition which would drive him and other prophets almost mad, since they saw the inevitable destruction coming nearer and yet were unable to prevent it, because Israel would not listen to the admonitions intended to bring about their repentance. V. 8. **The watchman of Ephraim was with my God,** literally, "A seer (or searcher) is Ephraim with my God," beside the true God; that is, instead of relying upon the revelations received by Hosea, the children of Israel were on the lookout for other revelations, from sources more acceptable to them. **But the prophet is a snare of a fowler in all his ways,** he is surrounded by snares wherever he turns, **and hatred in the house of his God,** while he is performing the duties of his office. V. 9. **They have deeply corrupted themselves,** becoming guilty of the most horrible abominations, **as in the days of Gibeah,** when the moral sense of the Israelites was very low, Judg. 19; **therefore He will remember their iniquity, He will visit their sins.** By such powerful appeals the Lord tried to work repentance in the hearts of His people, so that they would acknowledge their wickedness and return to Him with a godly sorrow.

THE CORRUPTION OF ISRAEL AND ITS CONSEQUENCES. — V. 10. **I found Israel like grapes in the wilderness,** at the time when Jehovah chose them as His people and led them forth from the land of bondage; **I saw your fathers as the first-ripe in the fig-tree at her first time,** the description being expressive of the high regard in which the Lord held them at that time; **but they went to Baal-peor,** as related in Num. 25, **and separated themselves unto that shame,** being led astray with the greatest ease by the women of the Moabites; **and their abominations,** both in bodily and spiritual adultery, **were according as they loved.** V. 11. **As for Ephraim, their glory,** that of which they boast, of which they are proud, **shall fly away like a bird,** swiftly taken from them, **from the birth and from the womb and from the conception,** the population being decreased even by the prevention of births, by the Lord's withholding His blessing of fruitfulness from them. V. 12. **Though they bring up their children,** those whom the Lord would still permit them to have, **yet will I bereave them,** depriving them of their children by death, **that there shall not be a man left,** cp. Deut. 32, 25; **yea, woe also to them when I depart from them!** It is a terrible thing when the Lord departs from a people with the blessings of His goodness and grace. V. 13. **Ephraim, as I saw Tyrus (is) planted in a pleasant place,** that is, the Lord had intended for it the growth, wealth, and power of the mighty Phenician city; **but Ephraim shall bring forth his children to the murderer,** that is, its citizens would be destined for violent deaths. V. 14. **Give them, O Lord; what wilt Thou give?** the question interrupting the flow of thought showing the deep indignation of the prophet over the wilful corruption of His people. **Give them a miscarrying womb and dry breasts,** sterility being considered a disgrace and a reproach, one of the sternest punishments of the Lord. V. 15. **All their wickedness is in Gilgal,** which seems to have been one of the chief places of idolatrous worship, so that the wickedness of the nation was there concentrated; **for there I hated them. For the wickedness of their doings I will drive them out of Mine house,** expelling them out of His congregation, **I will love them no more; all their princes,** the leading men of the nation, **are revolters,** rebellious and faithless with regard to the Lord's covenant. V. 16. **Ephraim is smitten,** like a plant struck by the too direct rays of the sun, **their root is dried up, they shall bear no fruit; yea, though they bring forth, yet will I slay even the beloved fruit of their womb,** by permitting their children to be killed. V. 17. **My God will cast them away,** rejecting them as His people, **because they did not hearken unto Him,** their disobedience to His revealed Word being their chief transgression; **and they shall be wanderers among the nations,** exiles, fugitives, and vagabonds. Cp. Deut. 28, 65.

CHAPTER 10.

Another Reproof of Israel.

THE SEATS OF WORSHIP DESTROYED. — V. 1. **Israel is an empty vine,** a thriving, climbing vine; **he bringeth forth fruit unto himself,** growing up with every indication of strength and fruitfulness, but utterly selfish and godless in aim; **according to the multitude of his fruit he hath increased the altars,** that is, the more Israel grew in prosperity, the more the members of the nation rejected the Lord and became addicted to idolatry; **according to the goodness of his land,** in proportion to the riches obtained, **they have made goodly images,** statues of idols. V. 2. **Their heart is divided,** rather, "smooth, false, insincere"; **now shall they be found faulty,** they will have to make expiation, they will have to suffer for their duplicity; **He shall break down their altars,** destroying them by demolishing their horns, **He shall spoil their images,** the true God thereby proving Himself to be the Master of the idols. V. 3. **For now,** when the punishment of the Lord would strike them, **they shall say, We have no king because we feared not the Lord,** for the man whom they selected for the position against the Lord's will was unable to help them in their emergency; **what, then, should a king do to us?** that is, of what benefit could he be, what possibility was there of his helping them in their difficulty? V. 4. **They have spoken words,** empty, vain statements, **swearing falsely in making a covenant;** for they were not fair and honest in their treaties with other nations, keeping them only as long as they hoped to have some benefit or advantage from them; **thus judgment,** what they wanted to consider right and good, **springeth up as hemlock,** a poisonous plant, **in the furrows of the field.** Cp. Amos 6, 12. Since they themselves were not clear on what was right, their hazy notions reacted in a most unfavorable manner on themselves, like a poisonous weed overgrowing a field. V. 5. **The inhabitants of Samaria,** the capital of the northern kingdom, **shall fear because of the calves of Beth-aven,** trembling for the fate of their idol at Bethel; **for the people thereof shall mourn over it,** at its loss or destruction, **and the priests thereof that rejoiced on it,** its idol-priests shall tremble for it, **for the glory thereof, because it is departed from it,** being taken away into captivity. V. 6. **It shall be also carried unto Assyria for a present to King Jareb,** to the warlike monarch; **Ephraim shall receive shame,** be completely overcome with shame, **and Israel shall be ashamed of his own counsel,** of all its planning with regard to its idolatrous cult. V. 7. **As for Samaria, her king is cut off as the foam upon the water,** for its kingdom had just as little solidity and stability, it was as speedily dissolved as the foam which rides on the breakers. V. 8. **The high places also of Aven,** of Bethel, **the sin of Israel,** where idolatry was practised to such a shocking extent, **shall be destroyed; the thorn and the thistle shall come up on their altars,** so that they would be overgrown with weeds; **and they,** the inhabitants of the country, **shall say to the mountains, Cover us! and to the hills, Fall on us!** That is the cry of the unbelievers, of the enemies of God, when they see the judgment approaching them, when it is too late for salvation. Cp. Is. 2, 19; Luke 23, 30.

THE KINGDOM DEVASTATED. — V. 9. **O Israel, thou hast sinned from the days of Gibeah,** when such an abominable atrocity happened in the midst of the people of God, cp. chap. 9, 9; Judg. 19, 22; **there they stood,** continuing in the same immorality which was committed by the inhabitants of Gibeah. **The battle in Gibeah against the children of iniquity did not overtake them,** that is, while they were guilty of the same immorality, they were mercifully not punished in the same manner as the criminals of those early days. V. 10. **It is in My desire that I should chastise them,** the Lord had firmly made up His mind to that effect; **and the people,** various heathen nations, **shall be gathered against them when they shall bind themselves in their two furrows,** the purpose of the invasion being to place the fetters of captivity on Israel for their twofold transgression, namely, that they left Jehovah, the one true God, and that they rejected the rule of the house of David. V. 11. **And Ephraim is as an heifer that is taught,** trained for some particular work, **and loveth to tread out the corn,** which was a pleasant task because the animals were permitted to eat as much as they liked during the process, Deut. 25, 4; **but I passed over upon her fair neck,** coming down upon it with the object of making a decided change. **I will make Ephraim to ride,** placing the yoke for drawing heavy loads upon her neck; **Judah shall plow,** being likewise guilty of transgressing the Lord's will, **and Jacob,** here standing for the northern tribes, **shall break his clods,** by laboriously drawing the harrow over the plowed surface. V. 12. **Sow to yourselves in righteousness,** so that fairness and justice would be practised toward all; **reap in mercy,** in showing the true love toward all men and thereby being assured also of a benignant acceptance on the part of God; **break up your fallow ground,** plowing new soil, turning a new leaf; **for it is time to seek the Lord, till He come and rain righteousness upon you,** rewarding those who are sincere in the evidence of their faith with the richest spiritual blessings, those of His salvation. V. 13. **Ye have plowed wickedness, ye have reaped iniquity,** that being the harvest which one must naturally expect under the circumstances; **ye have eaten the fruit of lies,** of idolatrous worship, **because thou didst trust in thy way,** upon their own false manner of doing things, **in the multitude of thy mighty men,** in proud self-confidence, all this instead of relying upon Jehovah, the God of the covenant, and His Word. V. 14. **Therefore shall a tumult arise among thy people,** namely, the noise of war against her armies, **and all thy fortresses shall be spoiled,** taken and devastated, **as Shalman,** very likely Shalmaneser, **spoiled Beth-arbel,** in Northern Galilee, **in the day of battle; the mother was dashed in pieces upon her children,** in an excess of unnatural cruelty. V. 15. **So shall Bethel do unto you because of your great wickedness,** Bethel, as the main center of idolatry, being the cause of the punishment which descended upon them; **in a morning,** while the dawn rises, while it seems that the fortunes are turning toward the better, **shall the king of Israel utterly be cut off,** so that the kingdom would no longer be in existence. Such is the end of hypocrisy and unrighteousness when the patience of the Lord with the wicked is exhausted.

CHAPTER 11.

Evidences of God's Unchanging Mercy.

THE PROOF OF JEHOVAH'S LOVE. — V. 1. **When Israel was a child,** at the time of the youth of the nation, **then I loved him and called My son out of Egypt,** in choosing the nation for His own peculiar people. The inspired writer of the first gospel applies this statement to the return of the Christ-child from Egypt after the abrupt flight of His parents from Bethlehem. Matt. 2, 15. V. 2. **As they,** the prophets, **called them,** with the Lord's tender invitation to follow the way of salvation, **so they,** the children of Israel, **went from them,** turning away from the path of deliverance which was offered them; **they sacrificed unto Baalim,** the idols of the Canaanites, **and burned incense to graven images,** in the open practise of idolatry which the Lord had ever so severely censured. V. 3. **I taught Ephraim also to go, taking them by their arms,** that is, the Lord Himself took His people in His arms to lead them safely through the dangers of the desert, Deut. 1, 31; **but they knew not that I healed them.** Cp. Ex. 15, 26. V. 4. **I drew them with cords of a man,** as with bands which support the first weak steps of a child, **with bands of love,** not with chains to hold them captive against their will; **and I was to them as they that take off the yoke on their jaws,** as when a man slips back the yoke on the neck of a draft animal in order to give it the liberty to eat freely, **and I laid meat unto them,** gently offering them food for their souls. The entire passage refers to the many evidences of love which the Lord showed His people on the way through the wilderness and in the Promised Land. V. 5. **He shall not return into the land of Egypt,** Egypt here being used in its literal sense, **but the Assyrian shall be his king,** Assyria being the new land of bondage, **because they refused to return,** because they rejected the Lord's offers of love. V. 6. **And the sword shall abide on his cities,** making the rounds in a campaign of destruction, **and shall consume his branches,** destroying their bars or defenses, **and devour them because of their own counsels,** because they were determined to leave the Lord and His ways. V. 7. **And My people are bent to backsliding from Me,** they were ever inclined to fall away and to reject the Lord; though they, the prophets, **called them to the Most High,** pointing them upwards to the one Rock of their Salvation, **none at all would exalt Him,** rather, "all together they refuse to arise." If men are lost, it is not due to a lack of love on the part of the Lord, but altogether to their own stubbornness in refusing His invitation.

ASSURANCES OF GOD'S MERCY. — V. 8. **How shall I give thee up, Ephraim?** What would be the proper measure of punishment to mete out to such a stubborn people? **How shall I deliver thee, Israel?** namely, to a proper measure of chastisement. **How shall I make thee as Admah? How shall I set thee as Zeboim?** the two cities of the vale of Siddim which were destroyed together with Sodom and Gomorrah, cp. Deut. 29, 22. **Mine heart is turned within Me,** namely, with a feeling of mercy in spite of Israel's transgressions; **My repentings are kindled together,** being most violently stirred at the contemplation of Israel's condition. God is ever more ready to show mercy than to let His stern justice punish men. V. 9. **I will not execute the fierceness of Mine anger,** although He had every reason to be deeply incensed over the behavior of Ephraim; **I will not return to destroy Ephraim,** He still holds out a hope of deliverance to a repentant people; **for I am God and not man,** not filled with the vindictiveness which men might exhibit upon similar occasions, **the Holy One in the midst of thee,** the pure and perfect God, whose counsel is ever unchanged; **and I will not enter into the city.** V. 10. **They,** the people of the Lord, **shall walk after the Lord,** turning back to Him with a converted heart. **He shall roar like a lion,** by His judgments upon His foes; **when He shall roar, then the children shall tremble from the West,** literally, "from the sea," along the shores of the Mediterranean, that is, throughout the Western world. V. 11. **They shall tremble as a bird out of Egypt,** from the lands of the South, **and as a dove out of the land of Assyria,** from the mighty country on the East, so that all the quarters of the earth would be affected by His call, **and I will place them in their houses, saith the Lord,** so that they would enjoy His inheritance. The reference is clearly to the blessings of the Messianic period.

CHAPTER 12.

(Chapter 11, 12—12, 14.)

Israel's Depravity.

THE LORD'S ACCUSATION. — Chap. 11, 12. **Ephraim compasseth Me about with lies,** on account of the hypocrisy with which its members still tried to create the impression that they clung to the true God, **and the house of Israel with deceit,** this being their general practise and not an individual instance of a temporary transgression; **but Judah yet ruleth with God and is faithful with the saints,** rather, "and Judah still wanders unrestrained over against God, against the faithful Holy One," so that both kingdoms were guilty before the Lord. Chap. 12, 1. **Ephraim** feedeth on wind, striving after vain and empty things, and followeth after the east wind, a hot wind coming up from the Arabian Desert, scorching everything with which it comes into contact; he daily increaseth lies and desolation, faithlessness and violence, whereby the nation was undermined in morals and stability; and they do make a covenant with the Assyrians, one of the world-powers against whom the prophets had warned, and oil is carried into Egypt, olive-oil being a gift with which they hoped to buy the alliance of the southern neighbor. V. 2. The Lord hath also a controversy with Judah, a contest to be decided in a court of law, by a formal suit, and will punish Jacob, the ten northern tribes, according to his ways; according to his doings, as he has deserved by his transgressions, will He recompense him. The name Jacob calls to mind the original bearer of the name. V. 3. He took his brother by the heel in the womb, showing subtlety even before he was born, Gen. 25, 26, and by his strength he had power with God, Gen. 32, 25—29; v. 4. yea, he had power over the Angel, who is thus identified with God, and the ancient conception of Him as the Angel of the Lord, the revelation of the Son of God in the Old Testament, is correct, and prevailed, as the Angel Himself stated; he wept and made supplication unto Him, by stating that he would not let Him go without having received a blessing; he found Him, the God of the covenant, in Bethel, on his way to Mesopotamia and after his return, Gen. 28, 11; 35, 9 ff., and there He spake with us, for what was said to Jacob at that time, has validity for the believers of all times, v. 5. even the Lord God of hosts, the most exalted Ruler of the universe. The Lord is his memorial, who had revealed Himself to the patriarchs as the God of salvation. V. 6. Therefore, because the God of Israel, who had revealed Himself in the words of the prophets, was the God of the covenant known to the patriarchs, turn thou to thy God, for Jehovah was still ready to stand in this relation to Israel; keep mercy and judgment, observing the demands of brotherly love and justice over against their brethren, and wait on thy God continually, in fearing Him, trusting Him, and loving Him above all things; for the summary of both tables of the Law is here understood.

ANOTHER SERIOUS REPROACH. — V. 7. He is a merchant, rather, "Canaan," the name here applied to the northern kingdom, since, like a dishonest merchant, he sought greatness by deceit and oppression, the balances of deceit are in his hand; he loveth to oppress, so that the inhabitants practised the very opposite of what was enjoined in the preceding verse. V. 8. And Ephraim said, in refusing to heed the Lord's admonitions through His prophets, Yet I am become rich, thus trying to excuse his dishonest ways, I have found me out substance, becoming prosperous as a result of doubtful cleverness; in all my labors they shall find none iniquity in me that were sin, or, "all my gains shall find no transgression in me which would be sin." This blindness toward their own guilt and the culpability of their sin was the big misfortune of the Israelites, for it hindered them from feeling sorry for their transgressions. V. 9. And I that am the Lord, thy God, from the land of Egypt, where He first revealed the greatness of His mercy toward Israel, will yet make thee to dwell in tabernacles as in the days of the solemn feast, the allusion doubtless being to the Feast of Tabernacles, which not only commemorated the privations of the wilderness journey, but also brought to the attention of the Israelites the blessings with which the Lord so richly supplied them in the Land of Promise. V. 10. I have also spoken by the prophets, so that He had always been in close touch with His chosen people, and I have multiplied visions and used similitudes, making known His will by parables, by the ministry of the prophets. All this surely showed the interest which the Lord had in His people and should be an inducement to them to return to Him with a repentant heart. V. 11. Is there iniquity in Gilead? Surely they are vanity, or, "If Gilead," representing the eastern half of the northern kingdom, "is worthlessness and iniquity," if it has reached the depths of moral ruin, then physical annihilation will certainly follow. They sacrifice bullocks in Gilgal, which represents the western part of the kingdom, with its idolatrous practises; yea, their altars are as heaps in the furrows of the fields, the altars being demolished and their stones scattered over the fields. V. 12. And Jacob fled into the country of Syria, and Israel served for a wife, and for a wife he kept sheep, the purpose of this reference being to remind Israel of the labor and misery which their forefather endured in comparison with the blessings which the Lord was pouring out over his descendants. V. 13. And, this being noted by way of contrast, by a prophet the Lord brought Israel out of Egypt, Num. 12, 6—8; Deut. 18, 15, and by a prophet was he preserved, for it was the intercession of Moses which saved Israel from being destroyed by the Lord. V. 14. Ephraim provoked Him to anger most bitterly, in spite of all the blessings which God had showered upon His people; therefore shall He, the Lord, leave his blood upon him, leave Israel in his blood-guiltiness, and his reproach shall his Lord return unto him, so that it would be charged to his account and kept there. When men refuse to repent and scorn all the efforts of the Lord aiming at their deliverance from sin and guilt, the Lord leaves them to their fate and to the punishment which they invited upon themselves.

CHAPTER 13.

Israel's Base Ingratitude.

GOD'S BENEFITS SCORNED BY ISRAEL. — V. 1. **When Ephraim spake trembling, he exalted himself in Israel,** rather, "When Ephraim," as the mightiest of the northern tribes, "spoke, there was trembling"; for the other tribes were so much weaker that they could not hold out against the leading tribe; he exalted himself in Israel, assuming the leadership and enforcing his will; **but when he offended in Baal,** when he transgressed through his idolatry in serving Baal, **he died,** his destruction was determined upon. V. 2. **And now,** after idolatry had thus been introduced, **they sin more and more,** multiplying their transgressions, **and have made them molten images of their silver and idols according to their own understanding,** making use of their ideas of art in constructing these statues, **all of it the work of the craftsmen; they say of them, Let the men that sacrifice kiss the calves,** literally, "to them they are speaking, men who sacrifice: they kiss the calves"; that is, the foolish idolaters speak with the very work of their hands and pray to them; they even kiss these pictures of calves, as though they were on a level with human beings. The reproof is purposely couched in words of cutting irony. V. 3. **Therefore they shall be as the morning cloud,** the vapor which arises at dawn, **and as the early dew that passeth away,** cp. chap. 6, 4, **as the chaff that is driven with the whirlwind out of the floor,** being carried away from the threshing-floor by every passing breeze, **and as the smoke out of the chimney,** rather, like smoke from a window; for chimneys were not in general use in the Orient. V. 4. **Yet,** over against the faithlessness of an apostate people, **I am the Lord, thy God, from the land of Egypt,** since the days when He delivered His people from the house of bondage, **and thou shalt know no god but Me,** there being no deliverer like the true God; **for there is no savior beside Me.** V. 5. **I did know thee,** with true love and compassion, **in the wilderness,** even during the desert journey, **in the land of great drought,** where the land and its inhabitants languished with thirst. V. 6. **According to their pasture, so were they filled,** their enjoyment of the goodness of God causing them to become proud in their own conceit; **they were filled, and their heart was exalted,** at the very time when they should have bowed down before the Lord with the greatest feeling of humility; **therefore have they forgotten Me.** Cp. Deut. 6, 11. 12. V. 7. **Therefore I will be unto them as a lion; as a leopard by the way will I observe them,** lurking by the path ready to pounce upon his victims; v. 8. **I will meet them as a bear that is bereaved of her whelps,** which is known for her fierceness, **and will rend the caul of their heart,** the pericardium or membrane enclosing the heart, **and there will I devour them like a lion; the wild beast shall tear them.** The punishment of the apostate people is represented as a rending and devouring of a herd, which has grown fat with a rich pasture, by wild beasts. In the midst of His most serious rebukes the Lord still inserts a pleading cry admonishing men to turn to their only Savior with a repentant heart.

THE RETRIBUTION COMING. — V. 9. **O Israel, thou hast destroyed thyself; but in Me is thine help,** literally, "It has destroyed thee, Israel, because [thou art] against Me, against thy Help." That is the great contrast: on the one side, certain help and deliverance, on the other, destruction which Israel brings upon himself by opposing the true God and His way of redemption. There is no way of bringing about an agreement and of reconciling God and man but by accepting God's way of salvation. V. 10. **I will be thy King,** so the Lord's offer still holds good; **where is any other that may save thee in all thy cities?** Who else could really deliver them from the power of the Assyrians? **And thy judges, of whom thou saidst, Give me a king and princes?** Because the people continued in their rebellious attitude, the Lord gave them kings as they desired them, and through these kings He punished them. V. 11. **I gave thee a king in Mine anger,** the expression referring, in general, to the kings of Israel, **and took him away in My wrath,** the constant change of kings being a decided misfortune to the country, while the end of the kingdom was now in sight. V. 12. **The iniquity of Ephraim is bound up,** one does not need to seek the evidence, it is all collected and preserved; **his sin is hid,** sealed in a package, for ready reference. This being true, the punishment was bound to follow. V. 13. **The sorrows of a travailing woman shall come upon him,** in the most violent pains accompanying the Lord's punishment. **He is an unwise son,** foolish as a baby detained; **for he should not stay long in the place of the breaking forth of children,** that is, if the birth does not take place at the proper time, the lives of both mother and child are endangered. Thus Ephraim is a foolish son, because now, when the time for repentance is come, he delays his new birth, refuses to be converted. But lest the true children of God be led to despair, the Lord announces a deliverance from death and destruction through His almighty power. V. 14. **I will ransom them from the power of the grave,** from the hand of the world of death, of hell; **I will redeem them from death. O death, I will be thy plagues,** a series of pestilences bringing about the death of death; **O grave, I will be thy destruction. Repentance shall be hid from Mine eyes,** that is, His plan of salvation would most certainly be carried out. In the very midst of a proclamation of wrath and punishment, then, we have a most glorious promise of the victory gained through the redemption planned in God's counsel of love, and the Apostle Paul was right in using this passage as his song of triumph on account of Christ's victory over death and hell. Cp. 1 Cor. 15, 55—57. V. 15. **Though he be fruitful among his brethren,** the Hebrew text here containing a play upon the name Ephraim, which means fruitfulness, **an east wind shall come,** with its parching heat, **the wind of the Lord,** sent by Him in punishment, **shall come up from the wilderness, and his spring shall become dry, and his fountain shall be dried up,** so that he would no longer be known as a fertile land; **he,** namely, Assyria, **shall spoil the treasure of all pleasant vessels,** of all the wealthy and proud cities of the northern kingdom. V. 16. **Samaria shall become desolate,** suffering its punishment by being made desolate; **for she hath rebelled against her God; they,** the inhabitants of the capital and of the country, **shall fall by the sword,** as the invader proceeds on his campaign of conquest; **their infants shall be dashed in pieces, and their women with child shall be ripped up,** according to the unspeakably cruel methods of warfare then in use. The call of the Gospel, as we see here once more, sounded even in the midst of degenerate Israel; for it is not the desire of the Lord that any man should perish, but that all should be led to repentance.

CHAPTER 14.

A Final Exhortation to Return, with a Promise of Redemption.

After having shown the apostate Israelites in various ways in what their guilt consisted, the Lord here once more appeals to them to return to Him in true repentance, since He desires to show them His mercy in full measure. V. 1. **O Israel, return unto the Lord, thy God,** to the God of the Messianic covenant; **for thou hast fallen by thine iniquity,** but there is still a possibility of returning. V. 2. **Take with you words,** expressed in prayers of forgiveness, **and turn to the Lord; say unto Him,** in a full and frank confession of sins, **Take away all iniquity,** forgiving the transgression with its guilt, **and receive us graciously,** receiving the one good thing which they have to offer; **so will we render the calves of our lips,** literally, "and we will render as bullocks our lips," namely, the confession of guilt and the promise to amend their ways. V. 3. **Asshur,** the world-power upon which they had relied till then, **shall not save us; we will not ride upon horses,** depending upon their cavalry, their army; **neither will we say any more to the work of our hands,** the idols which they had molded and fashioned, **Ye are our gods,** this being an open confession of the vanity of their idolatrous practises; **for in Thee,** in the true God alone, **the fatherless findeth mercy.** Cp. Ex. 22, 22; Deut. 10, 18. In the entire prayer of repentance the trust in the mercy of the Lord is evident. The Lord's answer, therefore, is a wonderful promise of mercy. V. 4. **I will heal their backsliding,** all the calamities brought upon them by their unfaithfulness to the Lord; **I will love them freely,** with the fulness of His abundant love and mercy; **for Mine anger is turned away from him,** having readily been withdrawn at the evidence of real sorrow which their prayer showed. V. 5. **I will be as the dew unto Israel,** refreshing and strengthening; **he shall grow as the lily,** known for its fruitfulness, **and cast forth his roots as Lebanon,** the mountains having their foundations in the innermost recesses of the earth. V. 6. **His branches shall spread,** as he flourishes and develops with vigorous life, **and his beauty shall be as the olive-tree,** with its evergreen leaves and rich-gleaming fruit, **and his smell as Lebanon,** with its cedars and aromatic shrubs. So the attributes of firmness, of fruitfulness, of beauty and glory, and of amiability and loveliness are ascribed to the repentant people once more received into the grace of God. V. 7. **They that dwell under His shadow,** the members of Israel as they have turned to the Lord in repentance, **shall return, they shall revive as the corn,** rather, shall produce grain once more, be a soil fruitful in good works, **and grow as the vine, the scent thereof shall be as the vine of Lebanon,** which was known of old for its excellent flavor. V. 8. **Ephraim shall say,** in addressing the Lord, **What have I to do any more with idols?** Or the sentence may be considered as an appeal to Ephraim to renounce all idolatry. **I have heard him and observed him,** Jehovah regarding His people with favor; **I am like a green fir-tree,** a cypress, symbol of everlasting life; **from Me is thy fruit found,** it is the Lord's strength which nourishes the bodily and spiritual strength of His people. V. 9. **Who is wise, and he shall understand these things?** namely, all that the prophet has written by way of warning, rebuke, admonition, and correction; **prudent, and he shall know them? For the ways of the Lord,** particularly in the manner in which He deals with His children on earth, **are right, and the just shall walk in them,** finding their delight in doing the Lord's will; **but the transgressors shall fall therein.** Cp. Deut. 32, 4. The preaching of truth is to some a savor of life unto life, to others a savor of death unto death. Cp. Deut. 30, 19. 20; 1 Cor. 1, 18.

THE BOOK OF THE PROPHET JOEL.

INTRODUCTION.

The prophet Joel ("Jehovah is God") is distinguished from other men bearing this rather common name by the statement that he was the son of Bethuel. Nothing definite is known concerning the circumstances of his life. Nor can we tell with certainty where he lived, although it seems most probable that he labored in Judea and proclaimed his prophecies in Jerusalem. Joel belongs to the earliest of the so-called minor prophets, for there are evident references to his book in the writings of Amos and even of Isaiah. The fact that he names the Phenicians, Philistines, Egyptians, and Edomites as the enemies of Judah, but neglects to mention the Syrians, indicates that this world-power and others were not yet a factor when he lived. Altogether, it seems best to assume that Joel lived in the earlier half of the ninth century before Christ.

The Book of Joel was occasioned by a terrible visitation of grasshoppers and drouth, which he explains as the precursors and signs of the last Great Judgment of Jehovah, which may be averted only by a sincere repentance. The book is clearly divisible into two parts. The first part is a heartrending lament over the affliction of the people on account of the plague of locusts, together with an urgent call to repentance, chap. 1, 1—2, 17. The second part is a promise of divine mercy for all those who repent, first concerning temporal blessings in the near future, then also regarding spiritual, Messianic benefits, particularly the outpouring of the Spirit, as the last great deed of God before the coming of the terrible Day of the Lord.

The language of the prophet excels in classical beauty and purity, and some of his passages are without a parallel for force of expression. The blessings of the Messianic age are brought out in periods of surpassing splendor and power. The salient points of the book are named by Peter in his great sermon on Pentecost, Acts 2, 16—21, and by Paul, Rom. 10, 13.

CHAPTER 1.

Lament over the Desolation of Judah.

A DESCRIPTION OF THE CALAMITY. — V. 1. **The word of the Lord that came to Joel, the son of Pethuel,** the superscription assuring us that we are not getting Joel's own ideas, but the inspired words of Jehovah. V. 2. **Hear this, ye old men,** whose memory reached back through generations of men, **and give ear,** in yielding a most willing and careful attention, **all ye inhabitants of the land.** It is a spirited challenge to all the people of Judah to mark the lesson of the great calamity which has befallen them. **Hath this been in your days or even in the days of your fathers?** A visitation of this kind, and grievous to this extent, had never yet been seen in Palestine. V. 3. **Tell ye your children of it and let your children tell their children and their children another generation,** passing it on from father to son, all of them accepting this tradition with awe, fear, and trembling, as being an unparalleled manifestation of God's anger against men on account of their sins. V. 4. **That which the palmer-worm,** literally, "the gnawer-off," **hath left hath the locust eaten,** the swarming or multiplying locust of the Orient; **and that which the locust hath left hath the canker-worm,** the devouring grasshopper, **eaten; and that which the canker-worm hath left hath the caterpillar eaten,** that is, the consuming locust. All four names describe the devastation wrought by the great Oriental locust, which apparently came into the land in successive swarms at that time, gnawing off first the tender shoots of the orchards and vineyards, then the vegetables and field fruits, and finally the foliage of the trees and every spear of green that was in sight. The desolation wrought by the plague of the locusts is described in the most graphic manner, one feature after another being depicted in a way to arouse the people to a realization of the seriousness of the situation. V. 5. **Awake, ye drunkards, and weep; and howl, all ye drinkers of wine, because of the new wine,** since the supply of grapes and therefore of the liquor made from them was not available; **for it is cut off from your mouth.** This appeal is introduced to describe, with poetical power, the complete devastation of the country. V. 6. **For a nation is come up upon My land,** a great and mighty army of fierce warriors, **strong and without number,** in swarms of countless myriads, **whose teeth are the teeth of a lion, and he hath the cheek-teeth of a great lion,** the jaw-teeth of a lioness protecting or avenging her young, grinding to pieces everything that came in their path. V. 7. **He hath laid My vine waste,** by consuming its foliage, **and barked My fig-tree,** gnawing off the bark and laying bare stem and branches, so that they were ruined; **he hath made it clean bare and cast it away; the branches thereof are made white,** by the complete removal of the bark. This being the condition in which the land was left after the visit of the locusts, the prophet now urges his countrymen to mourn.

V. 8. **Lament like a virgin, girded with sackcloth,** the dress of mourning, **for the husband of her youth,** whom, after their betrothal, death took away. The grief of a bereaved virgin and bride is represented also in other passages as deep and overwhelming. Cp. Is. 54, 6. V. 9. **The meat-offering and the drink-offering,** the sacrifices in the worship of Jehovah, **is cut off from the house of the Lord,** because it was impossible to procure the necessary materials, since everything was destroyed; **the priests, the Lord's ministers, mourn,** on account of the decay resulting from the devastation, which was followed also by a dearth of the animals used for sacrificial purposes. V. 10. **The field is wasted,** made desolate; **the land mourneth,** both the uncultivated and the cultivated sections of the land suffering in the same measure; **for the corn is wasted,** the grain completely consumed; **the new wine is dried up,** the grapes being spoiled for want of foliage on the vines; **the oil languisheth,** because the olive-trees produced no fruit. V. 11. **Be ye ashamed, O ye husbandmen,** bearing the shame of disappointed hopes after working hard for a crop; **howl, O ye vine-dressers,** these two representing the agricultural classes of the land, **for the wheat and for the barley, because the harvest of the field is perished,** this being the cause of the farmers' lament. V. 12. **The vine is dried up, and the fig-tree languisheth,** so that gardener and horticulturist likewise had reasons for mourning; **the pomegranate-tree, the palm-tree also,** the date-palm, which ordinarily escaped the onslaughts of the locust, **and the apple-tree,** or the quince, **even all the trees of the field, are withered; because joy is withered away from the sons of men,** so that there could be no rejoicing over a bountiful harvest, as usual. Cp. Ps. 4, 7; Is. 9, 3. The description of the swarming grasshoppers and the desolation following in their wake is one of the most powerful in all literature, and the picture is rightly regarded as one which ought to call all men to repentance.

PRESCRIBING FASTING AND PENITENCE. — V. 13. **Gird yourselves,** namely, with garments of mourning, **and lament, ye priests; howl, ye ministers of the altar,** whose chief duties were concerned with the sacrifices brought on the two altars of the Temple. **Come, lie all night in sackcloth, ye ministers of my God,** extending their exercises of mourning even through the night season; **for the meat-offering and the drink-offering is withholden from the house of your God,** cp. v. 9, so that all the usual sacrifices had to be discontinued. V. 14. **Sanctify ye a fast,** appointing a day or a number of days for a special religious service, during which the depth of the people's grief should be indicated by their abstaining from food; **call a solemn assembly,** such as were held in connection with the great festivals; **gather the elders and all the inhabitants of the land into the house of the Lord, your God, and cry unto the Lord,** with impetuous and importunate praying. V. 15. **Alas for the day!** so the prophet himself laments, **for the day of the Lord,** the time of His stern visitation, **is at hand, and as a destruction from the Almighty shall it come,** bringing its desolating scourge upon the land. V. 16. **Is not the meat cut off before our eyes?** as their food supply was destroyed by the invading hordes of locusts, **yea, joy and gladness from the house of our God?** since the various sacrifices and meals of thanksgiving were no longer possible. V. 17. **The seed is rotten under their clods,** withering in the soil on account of the terrible drouth; **the garners are laid desolate,** the granaries being empty because there could be no harvest; **the barns,** which otherwise harbored such rich crops, **are broken down,** falling to pieces for want of money to repair them; **for the corn is withered.** V. 18. **How do the beasts groan!** since the meadows also were dried up. **The herds of cattle are perplexed,** the word being chosen to denote the restless hunting of hungry cattle, **because they have no pasture; yea, the flocks of sheep are made desolate,** bearing their sufferings as a consequence of the transgressions of the people of the land. All this causes the prophet to lift up his voice to the Lord in a cry for help. V. 19. **O Lord, to Thee will I cry; for the fire,** the parching heat, **hath devoured the pastures of the wilderness,** of the great Judean steppes, **and the flame,** the fierce heat of the drouth, **hath burned all the trees of the field.** V. 20. **The beasts of the field,** both domestic and wild animals, **cry also unto Thee,** their dumb misery being a powerful appeal for help; **for the rivers of waters are dried up, and the fire hath devoured the pastures of the wilderness.** Cp. Job 38, 41; Ps. 104, 21; 145, 15; 147, 9; Jer. 14, 5. 6. All creation groans and travails in pain together until now on account of the burden of man's guilt. Rom. 8, 19—22.

CHAPTER 2.

An Admonition to Repentance. A Promise of Blessings.

THE PROPHET URGES REPENTANCE. — V. 1. **Blow ye the trumpet in Zion,** this signal of the priests announcing the coming calamity, **and sound an alarm in My holy mountain,** from the Temple mountain, as the center of Jehovah's worship and the place of His presence in the midst of His people. **Let all the inhabitants of the land tremble,** shaken up out of their care-free condition; **for the day of the Lord cometh, for it is nigh at hand,** the visitation is no longer in the dim and distant future, but is an event to be expected very soon, v. 2. **a day of darkness and of gloominess,** as when the light of the sun is shut out by immense swarms of locusts, **a day of clouds and of thick darkness,** of heavy, dense, and obscuring cloudiness, **as the morning spread upon the mountains, a great people and a strong,** the wings of the locusts reflecting the rays of the sun in a murky light before their immense numbers shut out the sun altogether. **There hath not been ever the like, neither shall be any more after it, even to the years of many generations,** cp. chap. 1, 2. V. 3. **A fire,** a most intense and parching heat, **devoureth before them,** in preparing for the desolation to follow, and **behind them a flame burneth,** the terrible, withering heat continuing even after the swarms of grasshoppers had passed. **The land is as the Garden of Eden before them,** like the beautiful park of paradise described in Gen. 2, **and behind them a desolate wilderness; yea, and nothing shall escape them,** the devastation would be so thorough. V. 4. **The appearance of them,** of the locusts, **is as the appearance of horses,** whom they resemble as to the shape of their heads; **and as horsemen, so shall they run,** with uncanny swiftness. V. 5. **Like the noise of chariots on the tops of mountains,** as they clatter along over rough mountain roads, **shall they leap,** such would be the noise of their crackling movements in a great mass, **like the noise of a flame of fire that devoureth the stubble, as a strong people set in battle array,** for there is a strong similarity to all these rushing, pounding sounds in the movements of vast swarms of locusts. V. 6. **Before their face,** as they proceed on their path of devastation, **the people,** all those so visited, **shall be much pained,** trembling and helpless with terror; **all faces shall gather blackness,** losing the glowing color of health, growing pale with conscious helplessness. V. 7. **They shall run like mighty men,** straightforward to the attack; **they shall climb the wall like men of war,** in an advance that cannot be stopped; **and they shall march every one on his ways, and they shall not break their ranks,** this peculiarity being noted by all observers. It was and is vain to resist them by the means ordinarily used to stop the progress of an invading army. V. 8. **Neither shall one thrust another,** not pressing ahead upon those going before; **they shall walk every one in his path,** like a well-drilled army; **and when they fall upon the sword, they shall not be wounded,** for they are represented as an invincible army of the Lord. V. 9. **They shall run to and fro in the city,** being altogether unhindered in their advance; **they shall run upon the wall, they shall climb up upon the houses; they shall enter in at the windows like a thief.** Jerome writes concerning this phenomenon: "When the locusts come and fill the whole space between earth and sky, they fly in perfect order, as if obedient to a divine command, so that they look like the squares of a pavement. Each one holds its own place, not diverging from it even so much as by a finger's breadth. To these locusts nothing is impenetrable, fields, meadows, trees, cities, houses, even their most secret chambers." V. 10. **The earth shall quake before them,** terrified by their dreadful host, **the heavens shall tremble,** resounding with the rushing of their flight; **the sun and the moon shall be dark, and the stars shall withdraw their shining,** their light shut out by the immense hosts of locusts; v. 11. **and the Lord shall utter His voice before His army,** which the grasshoppers here represent; **for His camp is very great,** the host under His command exceedingly large; **for He is strong that executeth His word,** carrying out the will of the Lord; **for the day of the Lord,** His coming visitation, **is great and very terrible; and who can abide it?** It is evident that the entire description is incidentally symbolical of the great and mighty Judgment of the Lord, which, in its preliminary features, is seen in the Deluge, in the two destructions of Jerusalem, and in various other calamities and cataclysms, but which is destined to be immeasurably greater than man can conceive of when it actually comes to pass. Cp. Mal. 3, 2. This being true, the admonition of the prophet comes with particular force. V. 12. **Therefore also now, saith the Lord, turn ye even to Me with all your heart,** in a true repentance, **and with fasting and with weeping and with mourning,** as outward indications of the change of heart, v. 13. **and rend your heart,** in a true and unfeigned sorrow, **and not your garments,** for the latter may be done also by hypocrites, **and turn unto the Lord, your God; for He is gracious and merciful, slow to anger, and of great kindness, and repenteth Him of the evil,** that is, He is persuaded not to let stern justice alone rule. Cp. Ex. 34, 6. V. 14. **Who knoweth if He will return,** not carry out the threatened punishment, **and repent, and leave a blessing behind Him,** namely, when He, as men pictured Him, returns to His throne in heaven, **even a meat-offering and a drink-offering unto the Lord, your God?** for by an abundant harvest, which He may be persuaded to give, the people would again be enabled to bring their usual sacrifices in the Temple. In order to accomplish this, however, it was necessary that the people unite in a great service of prayer and supplication. V. 15. **Blow the trumpet in Zion,** the call once more going forth; **sanctify a fast; call a solemn assembly,** v. 16. **gather the people,** for a great meeting of worship and supplication; **sanctify the congregation,** so that no one would be Levitically unclean; **assemble the elders,** the aged people of the congregation; **gather the children and those that suck the breast,** for no one is to be omitted in this great appeal for mercy, since all of them, from the smallest to the greatest, were guilty; **let the bridegroom go forth of his chamber and the bride out of her closet,** where they were preparing for the coming wedding. The fact that even infants in arms and bride and groom were included in the appeal of the prophet shows that the guilt was universal and beyond excuse. V. 17. **Let the priests, the ministers of the Lord,** who occupied the position of mediators between God and His people, **weep between the porch and the altar and let them say,** in a solemn litany chanted at the very door of the Holy Place, **Spare Thy people, O Lord, and give not Thine heritage,** the people of His own possession, **to reproach,** cp. Ex. 32, 11. 12, **that the heathen should rule over them,** or, "make mockery of them." **Wherefore should they say among the people,** among the heathen nations everywhere, **Where is their God?** thus bringing disgrace upon the holy name of the Lord. This is one of the strongest arguments which believers may advance in presenting their supplication before the Lord, namely, that the glory of His own name requires His looking upon His children in mercy, so that they may not be abandoned to the wiles of the enemy.

God's Promise of Temporal and Spiritual Blessings. — V. 18. **Then,** when the Lord saw that His people were truly penitent, **will the Lord be jealous for His land,** be filled with the zeal of His love, rather, He was so filled and acted accordingly, **and pity His people.** V. 19. **Yea, the Lord will answer and say unto His people,** actuated with the zeal of His love for them, **Behold, I will send you corn and wine and oil,** the richest temporal blessings made possible by the renewed fertility of the land, **and ye shall be satisfied therewith; and I will no more make you a reproach among the heathen,** of which their prayer had complained, v. 20. **but I will remove far off from you the northern army,** the swarms of locusts which came from that direction, **and will drive him into a land barren and desolate,** into the desert of Arabia, **with his face toward the East Sea,** that is, the Dead Sea, **and his hinder part,** his rearguard, **toward the utmost sea,** that is, the Mediterranean; **and his stink shall come up,** the terrible stench of the decaying insects, **and his ill savor shall come up, because he hath done great things,** the entire description picturing the rapid and total destruction of the great plague. V. 21. **Fear not, O land,** the entire country being included in this new admonition, as before; **be glad and rejoice,** namely, over the hosts that laid waste the country; **for the Lord will do great things,** Jehovah is able to perform marvelous works in delivering His people. V. 22. **Be not afraid, ye beasts of the field,** which had been so sorely in need of food supplies; **for the pastures of the wilderness,** of the great prairies of the South, **do spring,** once more verdant with an abundance of grass; **for the tree beareth her fruit,** as before the terrible visitation, **the fig-tree and the vine do yield their strength,** so as to bring forth fruit as of old. V. 23. **Be glad, then, ye children of Zion,** the inhabitants of Judah, the children of the Lord, **and rejoice in the Lord, your God,** the God of the covenant, the Lord of mercy; **for He hath given you the former rain moderately,** literally, "a teacher for righteousness," or "rain in just measure," the meaning of the Hebrew word being in dispute to some extent; **and He will cause to come down for you the rain, the former rain, and the latter rain in the first month,** the former rain being due right after seeding-time, in the fall, and the latter rain coming just before harvest, in the spring. V. 24. **And the floors,** the threshing-floors, **shall be full of wheat,** the result of a new, rich harvest, **and the fats shall overflow with wine and oil,** the receptacles of the vineyards being unable to hold the rich measure of blessings. V. 25. **And I will restore to you,** make up, **the years that the locust hath eaten, the canker-worm and the caterpillar and the palmer-worm, My great army which I sent among you,** the insects of chap. 1, 4 being named in the reverse order. V. 26. **And ye shall eat in plenty,** having an abundance of the best food, **and be satisfied and praise the name of the Lord, your God, that hath dealt wondrously with you,** making His wonders known through the manner in which He dealt with them; **and My people shall never be ashamed,** never be justly heaped with mockery and disgrace, since it would be so evident that the Lord was on their side. This would, moreover, be substantiated more than ever by the fulness of spiritual blessings which He intended to pour out upon His children after their restoration to His sonship. V. 27. **And ye shall know that I am in the midst of Israel,** as His chosen people, **and that I am the Lord, your God,** the God of the covenant, **and none else; and My people,** the true spiritual Israel, **shall never be ashamed.** V. 28. **And it shall come to pass afterward,** in the Messianic period, toward which this prophecy converged, **that I will pour out My Spirit upon all flesh,** upon men of every race and nation; **and your sons and your daughters shall prophesy,** openly proclaiming the great deeds of God, **your old men shall dream dreams, your young men shall see visions,** the great possibilities of the Lord's work and the energy for carrying out the plans of the Lord coming to them and urging them forward with irresistible power, the barriers of both sex and age being removed, except as limited in other parts of the Scripture; v. 29. **and also upon the servants and upon the handmaids,** upon the lowliest of the land, **in those days will I pour out My Spirit,** all social distinction being abandoned in the New Testament era as far as the work of the Church is concerned. This prophecy was fulfilled, so far as its beginning is concerned, on the great Day of Pentecost, as Peter also states in the introduction to his powerful sermon held before the astonished inhabitants of the city of Jerusalem, Acts 2, 17—21. But this event by no means exhausted its wonderful promises; for the Spirit of the Lord is being poured out on the members of the Church of the New Testament to-day and will continue to be given to all true believers until the end of time. But this great and wonderful deed of the Lord is placed side by side with His judgment upon the nations. V. 30. **And I will show wonders in the heavens and in the earth,** strange and terrifying portents, **blood and fire and pillars of smoke,** miracles in the sky above and signs of His majesty on the earth beneath, blood and fire and smoky vapor. V. 31. **The sun shall be turned into darkness,** being changed into a dark and cold mass, **and the moon into blood,** as bloody wars and devastations would occur on the earth, **before the great and the terrible Day of the Lord come,** namely, the day of the final Judgment. Cp. 1 Thess. 5, 2; 1 Cor. 1, 8; 2 Cor. 1, 14; 2 Thess. 2, 8. V. 32. **And it shall come to pass,** throughout this great period of the Lord's preparation for the final Judgment, during the entire Messianic period, **that whosoever shall call on the name of the Lord,** confessing Jehovah and accepting Him as the one Savior of mankind, **shall be delivered,** saved from the wrath to come; **for in Mount Zion and in Jerusalem shall be deliverance,** the Gospel-message proclaimed in and by the Church of God bringing redemption and the assurance of eternal life to all believers, **as the Lord hath said, and in the remnant whom the Lord shall call,** namely, the remainder according to the election of grace, the people whom the Lord has chosen from all nations of the earth. This glorious promise is held out to this day to all who turn to the Lord in repentance and faith, confessing His name as the only Savior and fervently calling upon Him for deliverance from all evil, especially that of the body of sin.

CHAPTER 3.

The Salvation of Israel and the Destruction of His Enemies.

GOD'S JUDGMENT UPON HIS ENEMIES. — V. 1. **For, behold, in those days and in that time,** in the Messianic period which had just been described according to its outstanding features, with the Day of Judgment very prominent in the description, **when I shall bring again the captivity of Judah and Jerusalem,** of the spiritual Israel, by the deliverance through Christ, of which the return of Judah from exile was but a type, v. 2. **I will also gather all nations,** with the great and mighty heathen nations, **and will bring them down into the Valley of Jehoshaphat,** which is here made the scene of the last great Judgment upon men, **and will plead with them there,** conducting a formal trial with them, **for My people and for My heritage Israel,** in the interest of the Lord's people, **whom they have scattered among the nations,** in the various oppressions and captivities which have struck the Lord's people from the earliest days, **and parted My land,** appropriating it or dividing it as they saw fit. V. 3. **And they have cast lots for My people,** after they had taken them captive, **and have given a boy for an harlot,** namely, as the price for which they secured the services of a prostitute, **and sold a girl for wine,** for the sake of a drunken debauch, **that they might drink.** The description is typical of the manner with which the Lord's enemies have ever dealt with the believers. V. 4. **Yea, and what have ye to do with Me, O Tyre and Zidon and all the coasts of Palestine?** that is, what object did they have in acting as they did, when not only the capitals of Phenicia, but also the city-states of Philistia were showing such enmity against Him? **Will ye render Me a recompense?** seeking revenge for what they consider a wrong done them. They had neither cause to seek revenge nor occasion to carry it out. **And if ye recompense Me, swiftly and speedily will I return your recompense upon your own head,** cp. Ps. 7, 17, v. 5. **because ye have taken My silver and My gold,** in the Temple-treasures and throughout the city of Jerusalem, **and have carried into your temples,** including also the palaces of their rulers, **My goodly, pleasant things,** His most costly possessions; v. 6. **the children also of Judah and the children of Jerusalem have ye sold unto the Grecians,** the Philistines being those who reduced the captives to slavery, the Phenicians those who acted as agents in selling the Hebrew slaves, **that ye might remove them far from their border,** to be slaves in distant countries. V. 7. **Behold, I will raise them out of the place whither ye have sold them,** delivering them from the masters to whom they had been sold, **and will return your recompense upon your own head,** so that their revenge would react upon themselves; v. 8. **and I will sell your sons and your daughters into the hand of the children of Judah,** when Tyre and Sidon were captured and their inhabitants either killed or reduced to slavery, **and they shall sell them to the Sabeans,** who are mentioned as being the remotest nation toward the east, in the Arabian Desert, **to a people far off; for the Lord hath spoken it.** The imagery of this paragraph is based, at least in part, upon happenings of those days; but the application includes far more than this, for the Lord makes those incidents typical of the punishments which He intended for all His enemies.

JEHOVAH THE HOPE OF THE PEOPLE. — V. 9. **Proclaim ye this among the Gentiles,** as they made ready to wage war against the Lord's people, **Prepare war,** consecrate the undertaking by means of sacrifices, **wake up the mighty men,** let them arouse themselves from their inactivity, **let all the men of war draw near, let them come up,** assembling for the campaign. V. 10. **Beat your plowshares into swords and your pruning-hooks into spears,** bending every effort toward the winning of their unholy war. **Let the weak say, I am strong,** as when warlike excitement takes hold of a whole nation. V. 11. **Assemble yourselves and come, all ye heathen, and gather yourselves together round about,** for the Lord's people are ever regarded as occupying a central position in the earth; **thither cause Thy mighty ones to come down, O Lord,** to meet the invasion of the enemies with a fearless countercharge. V. 12. **Let the heathen be wakened,** stirred up for warfare, **and come up to the Valley of Jehoshaphat; for there will I sit to judge all the heathen round about,** all the heathen nations of the world, since they all, by the time of the final Judgment, would have come into contact with the Gospel-message. V. 13. **Put ye in the sickle,** so the Lord shouts to His mighty champions, **for the harvest is ripe,** the crop of the world having reached its maturity. **Come, get you down,** stamping the vats of gathered grapes, **for the press is full, the fats overflow,** the earth being more than ripe for the Lord's Judgment; **for their wickedness is great.** Cp. Rev. 14, 15—18. V. 14. **Multitudes, multitudes in the Valley of Decision,** for with the preaching of the Gospel among all nations the hour of decision for them all is come, cp. John 3, 18—21; **for the Day of the Lord,** the final Judgment, **is near in the Valley of Decision,** bound to be revealed as soon as all men would have had an opportunity to learn the Gospel-message. V. 15. **The sun and the moon shall be darkened, and the stars shall withdraw their shining.** Cp. chap. 2, 31. V. 16. **The Lord also shall roar out of Zion,** with a voice of thunder terrifying His enemies, **and utter His voice from Jerusalem,** in the Word which was proclaimed there for so many centuries; **and the heavens and the earth shall shake. But the Lord will be the Hope of His people and the Strength of the children of Israel.** "Zion, or Jerusalem, is naturally not the earthly, Palestinian Jerusalem, but the Holy City of the living God, in which the Lord will be forever united with His saved and glorified congregation." V. 17. **So shall ye know that I am the Lord, your God, dwelling in Zion, My holy mountain,** in the midst of the congregation of believers. **Then shall Jerusalem be holy,** a true communion of saints; **and there shall no strangers pass through her any more,** only those who have been brought nigh by the blood of Christ. V. 18. **And it shall come to pass in that day,** when the blessings of the Messianic period would be dispensed, **that the mountains shall drop down new wine, and the hills shall flow with milk, and all the rivers of Judah,** most of which were dry except during the rainy season, **shall flow with waters, and a fountain shall come forth of the house of the Lord,** cp. Ex. 47, 1—12, **and shall water the Valley of Shittim,** otherwise an arid desert. The description aptly shows the power of the Gospel-message going forth from the Church of Christ and bringing fertility even to the unfruitful places of the earth, to the hearts of unbelievers and godless people everywhere. V. 19. **Egypt shall be a desolation, and Edom shall be a desolate wilderness,** these two being representative of the Lord's enemies, **for the violence against the children of Judah,** the representatives of the Lord's Church, **because they have shed innocent blood in their land.** V. 20. **But Judah shall dwell forever and Jerusalem from generation to generation,** for the Church Militant will merge into the Church Triumphant. V. 21. **For I will cleanse their blood that I have not cleansed,** namely, through the atonement wrought by the Messiah; **for the Lord dwelleth in Zion.** The entire description clearly does not speak of a mere earthly, temporal glorification of Jerusalem and a corresponding desolation of Egypt and Edom, but the latter are types of the powers opposing the Church of God, and Jehovah is setting forth the blessings which the work of the Church is bringing to men, on the basis of the redemption brought about by Jesus Christ. Cp. Rev. 22, 2. The Lord is dwelling in the midst of His Church and revealing Himself as the King of His people, partly by the destruction of His enemies, partly by the perfection of His kingdom in glory.

THE BOOK OF THE PROPHET AMOS.

INTRODUCTION.

Amos ("burden, burden-bearer") was a herdsman and a dresser of fig-trees, an inhabitant of Tekoah, a small fortified town in Judea, lying on the borders of the Wilderness of Judea, about nine miles south of Jerusalem, when the Lord called him to be a prophet in the midst of the northern kingdom. He went to Bethel, the chief center of idolatrous calf-worship in the ten tribes, and there testified to the truth. His fearlessness in reproving the manifold transgression of Israel was bitterly resented by the chief priests of Bethel, who made every effort to have Amos driven out of their land.

Amos prophesied during the reign of Uzziah of Judah and Jeroboam of Israel, some time in the first half of the eighth century before Christ. His book reflects the conditions of his day and age. The kingdom outwardly showed a great extent and a corresponding prosperity, but there was also a corresponding corruption on the moral side, with the pride of the wealthy aiming at the oppression of the poor, with luxury and dissipation, with idolatry and shameless profligacy on all sides. Amos therefore became a preacher of repentance and punishment, the fundamental thought of his book being that of the coming judgment.

The book of Amos is most readily divided into two parts, chapters 1—6 and 7—9. In the first part, chapters 1 and 2 are in the nature of a general introduction with a prophecy concerning the judgment upon neighboring nations; then follow three prophetic announcements, which, with a steadily mounting indignation, picture the impending destruction of the kingdom and the captivity of its inhabitants. The second part of the book contains visions which picture the threatened punishment in vivid flights of oratory, until the end comes with a beautiful Messianic prophecy.[1]

1) Cp. Fuerbringer, *Einleitung in das Alte Testament*, 82. 83; *Concordia Bible Class*, June, 1919, 82. 83.

CHAPTER 1.

The Divine Judgment Announced.

Against Damascus and Gaza. — V. 1. **The words of Amos, who was among the herdmen,** a man who owned and tended sheep, **of Tekoa, which he saw concerning Israel,** chiefly with regard to the northern kingdom, **in the days of Uzziah, king of Judah, and in the days of Jeroboam,** the second of that name, **the son of Joash, king of Israel, two years before the earthquake,** an event of some importance in the history of that century. Cp. Zech. 14, 5. V. 2. **And He said,** speaking to Amos in a vision, by a special revelation of the Lord, **The Lord will roar from Zion and utter His voice from Jerusalem,** cp. Joel 3, 16; **and the habitations of the shepherds,** the pastures where they fed their flocks, **shall mourn, and the top of Carmel,** the mountain by the sea, with its forested summit, **shall wither,** so that the whole land, from north to south, would be included in the punishment. From the outset the purpose of the message of Amos was to call the sinners to repentance and to oppose the foolish notion as though the judgment of God would strike the heathen world only, although the various nations in the neighborhood are enumerated first, in an introductory series of prophecies. V. 3. **Thus saith the Lord, For three transgressions of Damascus,** the capital of Syria, with its country, **and for four,** the number being by no means restricted, **I will not turn away the punishment thereof,** literally, by way of parenthesis, "not will I reverse it," both threat and punishment being irrevocable, **because they have threshed Gilead,** the territory of Israel east of Jordan, **with threshing instruments of iron,** in a most cruel treatment of the conquered inhabitants, 2 Kings 10, 32. 33; 13, 7, v. 4. **but I will send a fire into the house of Hazael,** the cruel king of Syria, **which shall devour the palaces of Benhadad,** the son of Hazael, 2 Kings 13, 8, so that both would suffer the Lord's punishment. V. 5. **I will break also the bar of Damascus,** shattering the bolt of its gate at the conquest of the city, **and cut off the inhabitant from the Plain of Aven,** possibly a place near Damascus, or the valley between Lebanon and Anti-Lebanon, **and him that holdeth the scepter from the house of Eden,** in the district of Laodicea; **and the people of Syria shall go into captivity unto Kir,** very likely a district of Assyria, **saith the Lord.** This prophecy was fulfilled when the Assyrian king Tiglath-pileser took the city of Damascus and dissolved the Syrian kingdom. Cp. 2 Kings 16, 9. V. 6. **Thus saith the Lord, For three transgressions of Gaza,** the leading city-state of Philistia, **and for four, I will not turn away the punishment thereof,** rather, He would not reverse His intention of punishing this city, **because they carried away captive the whole captivity,** all the prisoners who had been taken in a certain campaign, very likely that mentioned 2 Chron. 21, 16, to **deliver them up to Edom,** the arch-enemy of Israel, who would be sure to treat the captive Israelites with the highest degree of cruelty; v. 7. **but I will send a fire on the wall of Gaza, which shall devour the palaces thereof,** Gaza being a proud and rich city; v. 8. **and I will cut off the inhabitant from Ashdod,** to make the city desolate, **and him that holdeth the scepter from Ashkelon,** the ruler of this city-state with his people, **and I will turn Mine hand against Ekron,** so that four of the five city-states are expressly mentioned, the fifth, which bore the name **Gath,** being omitted because it was not essential to name them all; **and the remnant of the Philistines shall perish, saith the Lord God,** the prophecy finding its fulfilment in the repeated conquest of Philistia by the great world-powers, so that it did not retain its existence for any length of time.

AGAINST TYRE, EDOM, AND AMMON. — V. 9. **Thus saith the Lord,** the individual announcements coming with a special reference to the inspired nature of their contents, **For three transgressions of Tyre,** the great metropolis and seaport of Phenicia, cp. Is. 23, **and for four, I will not turn away the punishment thereof,** refusing to change the punishment which He had decided upon, **because they delivered up the whole captivity,** all the captives obtained from the Philistines or the Syrians as the result of one of their campaigns, **to Edom and remembered not the brotherly covenant,** both David and Solomon having been allied with Phenicia by a special treaty; v. 10. **but I will send a fire on the wall of Tyrus, which shall devour the palaces thereof,** the prophecy being fulfilled during the Babylonian and Grecian conquests. V. 11. **Thus saith the Lord, For three transgressions of Edom, and for four, I will not turn away the punishment thereof,** refusing, also in this instance, to give them any consideration after once their doom was decided upon, **because he did pursue his brother with the sword,** in the ineradicable hatred which always marked the attitude of the Edomites against Israel and Judah, **and did cast off all pity,** deliberately smothering every feeling of compassion, **and his anger did tear perpetually,** being bent upon murder, **and he kept his wrath forever;** v. 12. **but I will send a fire upon Teman,** which was probably a northern province of Idumea, **which shall devour the palaces of Bozrah,** the capital of the country, south of the Dead Sea. V. 13. **Thus saith the Lord, For three transgressions of the children of Ammon,** the ancient enemies of Israel, who lived northeast of the Dead Sea, on the edge of the Arabian Desert, **and for four, I will not turn away the punishment thereof,** not reverse His intention of punishing them severely, **because they have ripped up the women with child of Gilead,** in the unspeakably cruel manner employed in many instances in those days, **that they might enlarge their border,** taking possession once more of the territory gained by the tribes of Israel east of Jordan, Reuben, Gad, and half of Manasseh; v. 14. **but I will kindle a fire in the wall of Rabbah,** the capital of their country, **and it shall devour the palaces thereof, with shouting in the day of battle,** as soon as the enemies would enter the city, **with a tempest in the day of the whirlwind,** for the enemies would come in a tumultuous assault and carry all before them; v. 15. **and their king shall go into captivity,** cp. Jer. 49, 3, **he and his princes together, saith the Lord.** A nation may indulge in heinous crimes for some time, but when the Lord so decides, its career will come to an abrupt end.

CHAPTER 2.

Further Announcements of God's Judgments.

AGAINST MOAB AND JUDAH. — V. 1. **Thus saith the Lord, For three transgressions of Moab,** the nation occupying the country east of the Dead Sea, **and for four, I will not turn away the punishment thereof,** being fully determined upon His way of punishing the Moabites, **because he burned the bones of the king of Edom into lime,** taking vengeance upon the dead by burning his body to powder, a crime showing an almost unbelievable vindictiveness; v. 2. **but I will send a fire upon Moab, and it shall devour the palaces of Kirioth,** the capital in the valley of the Arnon; **and Moab shall die,** be overthrown in battle, **with tumult, with shouting, and with the sound of the trumpet,** in a victorious attack on the part of the enemies; v. 3. **and I will cut off the judge,** all the magistrates, **from the midst thereof and will slay all the princes thereof with him, saith the Lord,** so that Moab would cease to exist as a nation. This came to pass at the time of the Babylonian and Chaldean conquests. V. 4. **Thus saith the Lord, For three transgressions of Judah, and for four,** the southern kingdom being named here in order to have a full list of the countries adjoining Israel, **I will not turn away the punishment thereof,** refusing also here to change His decision, **because they have despised the Law of the Lord and have not kept His commandments,** the complaint which is voiced by practically all prophets, **and their lies caused** them to err, their idols leading them into every kind of foolishness and sin, **after the which their fathers have walked,** for idolatry had been practised in the country almost continually, secretly, if not openly; v. 5. **but I will send a fire upon Judah, and it shall devour the palaces of Jerusalem.** Here it was true, as the maxim has it, that a person is rightly judged by the company he keeps and may be obliged to share the lot of his friends.

AGAINST ISRAEL. — V. 6. **Thus saith the Lord,** now turning at last to the people of the northern kingdom among whom Amos was laboring, **For three transgressions of Israel, and for four, I will not turn away the punishment thereof,** literally, "not will I reverse it," **because they sold the righteous for silver and the poor for a pair of shoes,** namely, by the unjust condemnation of innocent people when they were brought into court, the judges being guilty of shameless bribery to the detriment of justice; v. 7. **that pant after the dust of the earth on the head of the poor,** by oppressing the poor so severely that the latter, in their misery, show their grief by placing dust on their heads, Job 2, 12, **and turn aside the way of the meek,** by placing obstacles in their way, thereby causing them to stumble and fall; **and a man and his father will go in unto the same maid,** in an excess of shameless lechery, which was regarded as being on a level with incest, **to profane My holy name,** for such sins brought disgrace upon the name of the God who had chosen Israel as His people; v. 8. **and they lay themselves down upon clothes,** the upper garment of the poor, **laid to pledge by every altar,** although the Law required that such pledges be returned in the evening, because the garments also served as covers by night, cp. Ex. 22, 25; Deut. 24, 12. 13, **and they drink the wine of the condemned,** such as was purchased with money gotten from the poor by oppression, **in the house of their god,** being brazen enough to do this in the very Sanctuary, in places which, after all, were originally intended as altars consecrated to Jehovah. V. 9. **Yet destroyed I the Amorite before them,** when Joshua overthrew them in battle, Num. 21, 24; Deut. 2, 31, **whose height was like the height of the cedars, and he was strong as the oaks,** a powerful people; **yet I destroyed his fruit from above and his roots from beneath,** the picture of a mighty tree being retained to make the fact of his annihilation more vivid. V. 10. **Also I brought you up from the land of Egypt,** by the deliverance to which the prophets point time and again, Ex. 12, 51, **and led you forty years through the wilderness to possess the land of the Amorite,** for so the entire land of Canaan might fitly be called, as having been in the possession of this nation before the Hittite invasion. V. 11. **And I raised up of your sons for prophets,** a distinction which they had evidently not appreciated, **and of your young men for Nazarites,** this also being a special favor which the Israelites had despised. **Is it not even thus, O ye children of Israel? saith the Lord.** They themselves, thus challenged, would have to admit the truth of the Lord's accusations. V. 12. **But ye gave the Nazarites wine to drink,** contrary to the command of the Lord, cp. Num. 6, 2—12, **and commanded the prophets, saying, Prophesy not;** they refused to hear the words which the Lord told them through His servants. V. 13. **Behold, I am pressed under you,** rather, "Behold, I will press you down," **as a cart is pressed that is full of sheaves,** as a cart loaded with sheaves presses down the ground beneath. V. 14. **Therefore the flight shall perish from the swift,** literally, "is lost to the swift," he will not have time to escape, **and the strong shall not strengthen his force, neither shall the mighty deliver himself,** all his strength and skill would avail him nothing; v. 15. **neither shall he stand that handleth the bow, and he that is swift of foot shall not deliver himself,** all his fleetness would not avail to carry him to safety; **neither shall he that rideth the horse deliver himself,** even so he would not escape. V. 16. **And he that is courageous among the mighty,** among the champions of the army, **shall flee away naked in that day,** leaving behind the very garment by which the enemy seizes him, **saith the Lord.** This threat, which implies the destruction of the kingdom, is further elaborated in the next chapter.

CHAPTER 3.

The Announcement of the Divine Judgment.

THE LORD READY TO PUNISH. — V. 1. **Hear this word that the Lord hath spoken against you, O children of Israel,** all the descendants of Jacob being here addressed, **against the whole family which I brought up from the land of Egypt,** by the mighty deliverance which resulted in their becoming His covenant people, **saying,** v. 2. **You only have I known of all the families of the earth,** acknowledging them and choosing them on the basis of His peculiar favor toward them; **therefore I will punish you for all your iniquities;** for the greater the privileges granted, the heavier is the punishment for the abuse of them, as the transgression is made worse by ingratitude. V. 3. **Can two walk together except they be agreed?** This and the following propositions, bringing out illustrations from daily life, are intended to substantiate the prophet's right to speak to the people in this manner, even if they were inclined to resent his sharp words. Jehovah and His prophet are in perfect agreement, as the sequel was bound to show. V. 4. **Will a lion roar in the forest when he hath no prey?** Jehovah is the lion, and His roaring is that of satisfaction over the certainty that His prey cannot escape, that is, that Israel, in its present state of mind, will surely be punished. **Will a young lion cry out of his den,** with a satisfied roaring, **if he have taken nothing?** In the same way Jehovah already has the guilty people in His power and is ready to carry out His judgment upon them. V. 5. **Can a bird fall in a snare upon the earth,** a trap placed on the ground, **where no gin is for him?** That is: Could destruction come upon Israel if his own sinfulness did not draw him into it? **Shall one take up a snare from the earth and have taken nothing at all?** literally, "Does the trap rise from the ground if a snared bird does not cause it to do so?" that is, Did Israel, knowing his own corruptness, hope to escape destruction, which was bound to take hold of him? V. 6. **Shall a trumpet be blown in the city and the people not be afraid?** As the signal of the trumpet was intended to arouse the people out of their security, so the message of the prophet was intended to awaken the people of Israel to the peril of their position. **Shall there be evil in a city and the Lord hath not done it?** The destruction which would strike Israel on account of the iniquities of the people was indeed planned by Jehovah, who in this sense is the Author of the calamities which come upon men on account of their sins. V. 7. **Surely the Lord God will do nothing but He revealeth His secret unto His servants, the prophets,** that is, Jehovah does not send His judgments without warning, but gives the people knowledge of His counsel and opportunity to turn from their evil ways. V. 8. **The lion hath roared,** in sounding the warning of his approach, **who will not fear? The Lord God hath spoken, who can but prophesy?** Amos was simply carrying out the work of his calling in announcing to his people the impending judgment of Jehovah. Even so the servants of God are bound to make known His holy will, regardless of the manner in which their hearers react to the truth.

THE LORD DECLARING HIS PURPOSE. — V. 9. **Publish in the palaces of Ashdod, in the land of the Philistines, and in the palaces in the land of Egypt,** two of the neighboring heathen countries being summoned as witnesses, **and say, Assemble yourselves upon the mountains of Samaria,** those near the city, **and behold the great tumults in the midst thereof,** caused by the fact that the mighty ones of the nations were oppressing the poor, **and the oppressed in the midst thereof,** right and order being overthrown by open violence on the part of those in authority. V. 10. **For they know not to do right, saith the Lord,** having so thoroughly become accustomed to unrighteousness, **who store up violence and robbery in their palaces,** like evil treasures stored up for purposes of destruction. V. 11. **Therefore, thus saith the Lord God, An adversary there shall be even round about the land,** literally, "and that, too, from every side of the land," attacking Israel, and particularly Samaria, from all sides; **and he shall bring down thy strength from thee,** dashing it down to the ground, **and thy palaces,** heaped with the treasures of unrighteousness, **shall be spoiled.** V. 12. **Thus saith the Lord, As the shepherd taketh out of the mouth of the lion two legs or a piece of an ear,** insignificant, useless remnants, **so shall the children of Israel be taken out that dwell in Samaria in the corner of a bed,** occupying the most comfortable part of the divan, sitting in carefree idleness, **and in Damascus in a couch,** rather, "on the damask of the bed." The powerful men of Samaria, living a life of luxury and ease, would save their lives only with the greatest difficulty. V. 13. **Hear ye and testify in the house of Jacob,** the heathen bearing witness against the iniquities of Israel, **saith the Lord God, the God of hosts,** v. 14. **that in the day that I shall visit the transgressions of Israel upon him,** with an adequate punishment, **I will also visit the altars of Bethel,** the center of idolatrous worship in Israel; **and the horns of the altar shall be cut off and fall to the ground,** thus demolishing the altars themselves. Cp. Ex. 27, 2. V. 15. **And I will smite their winter-house with the summer-house,** for not only the kings, but the noble and the rich as well had at least two establishments; **and the houses of ivory,** whose walls were decorated with inlaid ivory, cp. 1 Kings 22, 39, **shall perish, and the great houses shall have an end, saith the Lord.** All extravagance of luxury is displeasing to the Lord, especially if it is connected in any manner with denial of the Lord's truth.

CHAPTER 4.

A Further Reproof of Various Sins.

DENUNCIATION OF THE OUTSTANDING VICES. V. 1. **Hear this word, ye kine of Bashan,** this name being taken from the strong, well-fed cattle of the pasture country east of Jordan, **that are in the mountain of Samaria,** the description agreeing with the extortions and the luxurious life of the rulers of Samaria, **which oppress the poor, which crush the needy, which say to their masters** (the picture of the cattle of Bashan being retained), **Bring and let us drink.** V. 2. **The Lord God hath sworn by His holiness,** by a most solemn oath, **that, lo, the days shall come upon you that He will take you away with hooks,** or, "when men will drag you away with hooks," **and your posterity,** or the remnant of you, that which is left after the first punishment, **with fish-hooks,** as fish are drawn from the water. V. 3. **And ye shall go out at the breaches,** through the breaches which had been torn in the walls by the attacking enemies, **every cow at that which is before her,** literally, "every one before her," anxious to get away, looking neither to the right nor to the left; **and ye shall cast them into the palace, saith the Lord,** or, "be cast forth to Harmon," apparently the place where they were led away captive. So much having been said of the rulers of Samaria and of Israel, the Lord now, in bitter irony, turns to the entire nation, bidding the people just continue in their idolatry and transgression; the divine punishment would not be kept away by their tactics. V. 4. **Come to Bethel and transgress,** in their idolatrous worship; **at Gilgal,** another seat of idol-worship, **multiply transgression; and bring your sacrifices every morning,** in a wonderful zeal for worship, **and your tithes after three years,** rather, "after three days," for Amos purposely speaks hyperbolically: Even if you should offer burnt offerings every morning and tithes every three days, it would only increase your guilt before Jehovah; v. 5. **and offer a sacrifice of thanksgiving with leaven,** cp. Lev. 7, 12—14, **and proclaim and publish the free offerings,** making a great show of their religious fervor; **for this liketh you,** this they delighted in doing, **O ye children of Israel, saith the Lord God.** The more zeal the hypocrites show in imitating the outward worship of the true believers, the more guilt they heap upon themselves in the sight of God, whose all-seeing eye penetrates their flimsy pretexts and causes Him to emphasize His threats of punishment.

VARIOUS PUNISHMENTS LEADING UP TO THE LAST JUDGMENT. — V. 6. **And I also have given you cleanness of teeth in all your cities,** namely, because they had nothing to eat, **and want of bread in all your places,** by famines sent at various times; **yet have ye not returned unto Me, saith the Lord,** His punishment had not had the desired effect. V. 7. **And also I have withholden the rain from you,** the latter rain, which was necessary to insure a crop, **when there were yet three months to the harvest,** which occurred in the latter part of May or in early June; **and I caused it to rain upon one city and caused it not to rain upon another city,** both granting and withholding this great blessing according to His will; **one piece was rained upon, and the piece whereupon it rained not withered.** To this day this is, in spite of spurious claims of scientists concerning reasonable causes for everything, the only explanation which suffices for the fact that moisture in a given locality is often found in definite strips only. V. 8. **So two or three cities,** impelled by necessity, **wandered unto one city to drink water,** to get enough at least to sustain life; **but they were not satisfied,** they could not drink their fill, and their trip, made with unsteady feet as it was, brought them nothing. **Yet have ye not returned unto Me, saith the Lord.** V. 9. **I have smitten you,** as a third chastisement, **with blasting and mildew,** with a blight upon the cereal grains; **when your gardens and your vineyards and your fig-trees and your olive-trees increased,** the enumeration of the individual cases tending to emphasize the visitation, **the palmer-worm,** the Oriental locust, **devoured them. Yet have ye not returned unto Me, saith the Lord.** V. 10. **I have sent among you the pestilence after the manner of Egypt,** so called because it was prevalent in that country; **your young men have I slain with the sword,** especially when the Israelites suffered defeats at the hand of the Syrians, **and have taken away your horses,** these also being slaughtered in battle; **and I have made the stink of your camps to come up unto your nostrils,** namely, that of the dead bodies of men and beasts. **Yet have ye not returned unto Me, saith the Lord,** even this chastisement having no effect upon them. V. 11. **I have overthrown some of you,** some of Israel's cities, **as God overthrew Sodom and Gomorrah, and ye,** those who escaped such utter extinction, **were as a firebrand plucked out of the burning,** the escape being very narrow. **Yet have ye not returned unto Me, saith the Lord.** V. 12. **Therefore, thus will I do unto thee, O Israel,** namely, what He now says in conclusion; **and because I will do this unto thee, prepare to meet thy God, O Israel,** namely, to stand before the Lord's judgment-seat, and therefore to make due preparation to avert the final destruction by true repentance. V. 13. **For, lo, He that formeth the mountains,** calling them into existence by His almighty power, **and createth the wind, and declareth unto man what is his thought,** His omniscience readily penetrating into the mind of man, **that maketh the morning darkness,** turning back the dawn into night, **and treadeth upon the high places of the earth,** ruling the whole earth with unlimited power, **The Lord, the God of hosts, is His name,** the Ruler of all the heavenly armies. The entire creation proclaims the one true God, and it is a matter of wisdom for man to stand before Him in a relation which will cause Him to show mercy rather than stern justice.

CHAPTER 5.

An Elegy over Israel's Fall.

ISRAEL'S ONLY SAFETY IN SEEKING THE LORD. V. 1. **Hear ye this word which I take up against you, even a lamentation, O house of Israel,** an elegy, dirge, or mournful song sung over the downfall of Israel. V. 2. **The virgin of Israel,** the people called thus because they were to be the Lord's congregation, His chaste bride, **is fallen; she shall no more rise,** not return to her former powerful and prosperous state; **she is forsaken upon her land,** stretched out upon her soil, by a violent overthrow; **there is none to raise her up.** V. 3. **For thus saith the Lord God, The city that went out by a thousand,** sending so many soldiers into war, **shall leave an hundred,** the rest being destroyed by war and pestilence, **and that which went forth by an hundred shall leave ten, to the house of Israel,** all the rest being devoured by the punishment of the Lord. V. 4. **For thus saith the Lord unto the house of Israel,** in a last attempt to save its people from themselves, **Seek ye Me,** in sincere worship of the one true God, **and ye shall live;** v. 5. **but seek not Bethel,** where idolatry was so openly and blasphemously practised, **nor enter into Gilgal,** another center of idol-worship, **and pass not to Beersheba,** in the extreme southern part of Canaan, where evidently another altar had been erected to idols; **for Gilgal shall surely go into captivity,** its idols unable to save it, **and Bethel shall come to naught,** its heathenish worship unable to save it. V. 6. **Seek the Lord,** to serve and worship the God of the covenant only, **and ye shall live, lest He break out like fire in the house of Joseph,** a name for Ephraim, the son of Joseph and the ancestor of the mightiest tribe of the northern kingdom, **and devour it, and there be none to quench it in Bethel,** even their mightiest idols being powerless before the might of Jehovah. V. 7. **Ye who turn judgment to wormwood,** by perverting justice into a bitter wrong, **and leave off righteousness in the earth,** casting it down, trampling it under foot, v. 8. **(seek Him) that maketh the seven stars,** one of the constellation of the sky, **and Orion,** cp. Job 9, **and turneth the shadow of death into the morning,** the darkest hour being just before dawn, **and maketh the day dark with night; that calleth for the waters of the sea and poureth them out upon the face of the earth,** in fearful tidal waves and floods: **the Lord is His name,** the one true God; v. 9. **that strengtheneth the spoiled against the strong,** literally, "who makes desolation to flash upon the strong," as the catastrophes caused by Him suddenly take hold of men, **so that the spoiled shall come against the fortress,** rather, "and desolation comes upon the fortress," for none can withstand the power of the Almighty. V. 10. **They hate him that rebuketh in the gate,** him who raises his voice against the universal unrighteousness, **and they abhor him that speaketh uprightly,** for the very fact that some one is honest and true is a rebuke to the hypocrisy of the wicked. V. 11. **Forasmuch, therefore, as your treading is upon the poor,** in the oppression which was then so generally practised, **and ye take from him burdens of wheat,** exacting such gifts by methods of violence: **ye have built houses of hewn stone,** costly dwellings, **but ye shall not dwell in them; ye have planted pleasant vineyards,** with their unlawful gains, **but ye shall not drink wine of them.** V. 12. **For I know your manifold transgressions and your mighty sins,** outstanding even in the midst of a nation steeped in wickedness; **they afflict the just,** making life a burden for him, **they take a bribe,** causing such bribe money to be paid, in order that men might buy their freedom from the oppression of these same rulers, **and they turn aside the poor in the gate,** where the courts of justice were held, **from their right.** Thus the poor were without champions of their right and were obliged to bow to the mighty, a condition which still prevails almost universally.

WOE UPON FOOLS AND HYPOCRITES. — V. 13. **Therefore the prudent shall keep silence in that time, for it is an evil time,** and when things have reached such extremities as here pictured, all admonitions are futile. Still the love of the prophet for his people and his desire to further their welfare in every possible way causes him to address them once more. V. 14. **Seek good, and not evil, that ye may live,** for there lies the way to true life; **and so the Lord, the God of hosts, shall be with you as ye have spoken,** that is, by following His will and not by a mere external membership in the Church of Israel.

V. 15. **Hate the evil and love the good,** cp. Rom. 12, 9, **and establish judgment in the gate,** so that justice would truly be administered in all cases brought to trial; **it may be that the Lord God of hosts,** in that event, **will be gracious unto the remnant of Joseph,** to the few of the northern nation who would be left after the punishment now impending. V. 16. **Therefore the Lord, the God of hosts, the Lord,** the one and only true God, **saith thus, Wailing shall be in all streets,** mourning on account of the chastisement which has come upon them for ignoring the appeal of the prophet; **and they shall say in all the highways,** expressing their grief in open lamentations, **Alas! Alas! And they shall call the husbandman to mourning,** to join in the death-wail over some relative, **and such as are skilful of lamentation,** the professional wailing women, **to wailing,** so that the entire country would resound with cries of grief. V. 17. **And in all vineyards shall be wailing,** instead of the shouts of joy formerly heard there; **for I will pass through thee, saith the Lord,** with His visitation of wrath. V. 18. **Woe unto you that desire the day of the Lord!** believing that their external communion with the Lord's people would save them from the judgment which was to strike the heathen. **To what end is it for you?** What result would it have for them? What good would it bring them? **The day of the Lord is darkness and not light;** it would bring to wilful sinners destruction and not deliverance. V. 19. **As if a man did flee from a lion, and a bear met him,** so it would be with those who desired the day of the Lord's judgment, **or went into the house and leaned his hand on the wall, and a serpent bit him.** Hoping to escape the one calamity, the wicked Israelites would be overtaken by another. V. 20. **Shall not the day of the Lord be darkness and not light?** full of tribulation and misery; the day of the Lord is darkness and not light; it would bring no deliverance to those who trample justice and right beneath their feet; **even very dark, and no brightness in it?** not a ray for the wilful transgressors. Therefore even the feasts of the people would avail them nothing under the circumstances as here presented. V. 21. **I hate, I despise, your feast-days,** so the Lord calls out to them, **and I will not smell in your solemn assemblies,** by taking pleasure in the odor of the offerings brought by them. V. 22. **Though ye offer Me burnt offerings and your meat-offerings,** as they still continued to do in their effort to have the Lord accept their outward worship, **I will not accept them; neither will I accept the peace-offerings,** or thank-offerings, **of your fat beasts,** since their entire service was hypocrisy. V. 23. **Take thou away from Me the noise of thy songs,** as He contemptuously calls their congregational singing; **for I will not hear the melody of thy viols,** of the harps and other instrumental music used in public services. V. 24. **But let judgment,** the just punishment of the Lord, **run down as waters,** in a great and consuming flood, **and righteousness,** namely, that of the divine justice, **as a mighty stream.** V. 25. **Have ye offered unto Me sacrifices and offerings in the wilderness,** during the journey from Egypt to the Promised Land, **forty years, O house of Israel?** Even at that time the people were guilty of idolatry, and since then they added to their guilt. V. 26. **But ye have borne the tabernacle of your Moloch,** the war-god of the Moabites and Ammonites, **and Chiun,** a star-divinity, **your images, the star of your god, which ye made to yourselves.** Even in the wilderness the children of Israel, as Ezekiel also shows, did not quite discard their idolatry, but carried their idol-pictures along with them and thus provoked the Lord. V. 27. **Therefore will I cause you to go into captivity beyond Damascus,** in the power of a mighty Eastern nation, **saith the Lord, whose name is The God of hosts.** The last words were employed by Stephen in his powerful rebuke of the Jews after his arrest, Acts 7, 43, in order to show that idolatry had ever been in vogue among the people in spite of all the efforts of the Lord to stamp it out. The modern idolatry in high places is just as persistent and apparently cares as little for the admonitions and rebukes of the Bible.

CHAPTER 6.

Woe upon the Secure Rulers of the People.

THE PEOPLE GUILTY OF SECURITY AND LUXURY. — V. 1. **Woe to them that are at ease in Zion,** given to a false security, **and trust in the mountain of Samaria,** those who are apparently without a care as they occupy their mountain dwellings where they consider themselves safe, **which are named chief of the nations,** the most excellent heads of the chosen people in both Judah and Israel, **to whom the house of Israel came,** namely, for counsel and direction, for the decision of their controversies. V. 2. **Pass ye unto Calneh,** a city in Babylonia, on the river Tigris, **and see, and from thence go ye to Hamath, the great,** a district and city of Syria beyond the extreme northern boundary of Canaan; **then go down to Gath of the Philistines,** so that they would visit some of the most powerful of the neighboring nations. **Be they better than**

these kingdoms? that is, these two kingdoms were in no better condition than Judah and Israel, **or their border greater than your border?** Israel thus ranking at that time with the first of the nations, unexcelled by any of their heathen neighbors. But for this very fact, on account of their reliance upon their prosperity and power, the Lord pronounces a woe upon them. V. 3. **Ye that put far away the evil day,** refusing to believe that a day of reckoning is near, **and cause the seat of violence to come near,** so that violence and oppression come ever nearer to them, that they become guilty of these transgressions with ever-increasing frequency. This ignoring of the Lord and His holy will was apparent particularly in their luxurious feasting; v. 4. **that lie upon beds of ivory,** on costly couches, inlaid with ivory, **and stretch themselves upon their couches,** reclining, in luxurious self-indulgence, on the sofas of their dining-rooms, **and eat the lambs out of the flock and the calves out of the midst of the stall,** in either case the choicest animals, v. 5. **that chant to the sound of the viol,** in quavering and silly songs, **and invent to themselves instruments of music, like David,** but only for the gratification of their own vanity and sensuality, instead of for the glory of God, as did David; v. 6. **that drink wine in bowls,** out of sacrificial vessels, such as were used in worship, **and anoint themselves with the chief ointments,** using only the finest grades for their purpose; **but they are not grieved for the affliction of Joseph,** literally, "the breach of Joseph," that is, the impending calamity, the destruction of the northern kingdom. This same fact stands out time and again in the history of nations, namely, that they indulge in wanton luxury even while their country is hastening to its ruin.

THE DESTRUCTION OF THE KINGDOM FORETOLD.—V. 7. **Therefore now shall they,** those who indulged themselves in this manner while their country was getting ready for dissolution, **go captive with the first that go captive,** this being said in bitter irony concerning the position of the rulers in the procession of captives, **and the banquet of them that stretched themselves,** reclining in careless ease, **shall be removed,** so that they could no more indulge in feasts and drinking-bouts. V. 8. **The Lord God hath sworn by Himself, saith the Lord God of hosts,** a most solemn oath, **I abhor the excellency of Jacob,** the pride which they exhibited regarding their prosperity and power, **and hate his palaces,** as one evidence of such pride; **therefore will I deliver up the city with all that is therein,** both houses and men being delivered into the hands of the enemy to be destroyed. V. 9. **And it shall come to pass, if there remain ten men in one house, that they shall die,** that is, no matter how large the number, not one would escape. V. 10. **And a man's uncle shall take him up, and he that burneth him,** literally, "his cousin and his burier," that is, a near relative who had the duty of providing for his burial, **to bring out the bones out of the house, and shall say unto him that is by the sides of the house,** a last survivor hiding in the innermost recesses of the house, **Is there yet any with thee? And he shall say, No. Then shall he say, Hold thy tongue,** quickly cautioning him not to say any more; **for we may not make mention of the name of the Lord,** he should not utter Jehovah's name, lest, by doing so, he call the Lord's attention and bring down judgment upon himself. V. 11. **For, behold, the Lord commandeth, and He will smite the great house with breaches,** so that it would become a total ruin, **and the little house with clefts,** so that it would be reduced to splinters. Such would be the punishment which would strike the people, which they would not be able to avert by any reliance upon their own might. V. 12. **Shall horses run upon the rock? Will one plow there with oxen?** As little as either feat is possible, so little is it possible that one, by perverting right and justice into the opposite, can bring deliverance to himself and his country. **For ye have turned judgment into gall,** justice into poison, **and the fruit of righteousness into hemlock,** the tree which ought to prosper in their midst into wormwood; v. 13. **ye which rejoice in a thing of naught,** depending upon something which does not exist, except in their own imagination, **which say, Have we not taken to us horns by our own strength?** trusting in the strength of their armies by which they hoped to overcome all enemies. V. 14. **But, behold, I will raise up against you a nation, O house of Israel, saith the Lord, the God of hosts, and they shall afflict you,** by overthrowing and oppressing them, **from the entering in of Hemath,** the northernmost boundary, where the invading army of the Assyrians would enter, **unto the river of the wilderness,** literally, "the brook of the desert," here most likely that which formed the boundary between Moab and Edom, on the southeastern corner of the Dead Sea. Warfare is one means in the hands of the Lord by which He punishes the pride of nations.

CHAPTER 7.

Three Visions of National Calamities.

THE VISIONS OF THE GRASSHOPPERS, OF THE FIRE, AND OF THE PLUMB-LINE. — V. 1. **Thus hath the Lord God showed unto me,** in visions and pictures shown by the Spirit of God, **and, behold, He formed grasshoppers in the beginning of the shooting up of the latter growth,** of the second crop of the season; **and, lo, it was the latter growth after the king's mowings,** the first crop, apparently, belonging to the king as a part of the nation's revenue. The time of the grasshoppers' coming, therefore, was very unfortunate, since the first crop had been delivered as the law required, and the second crop was bound to be ruined. V. 2. **And it came to pass that, when they had made an end of eating the grass of the land,** all the plants which came up at that time, in the rest of the season, **then I said, O Lord God, forgive, I beseech Thee; by whom shall Jacob,** the northern kingdom, **arise?** maintain his ground, not be annihilated altogether. **For he is small,** even now reduced in numbers and strength. V. 3. **The Lord repented for this. It shall not be, saith the Lord,** He was willing to spare the people and the land upon the intercession of the prophet. V. 4. **Thus hath the Lord God showed unto me,** in a second vision; **and, behold, the Lord God called to contend by fire,** that is, He directed that the punishment was to be made by fire, **and it devoured the great deep,** the great ocean itself, **and did eat up a part,** the heritage of Jehovah, which is Israel. It was a picture of the Lord's devouring anger directed against His own people. V. 5. **Then said I, O Lord God, cease, I beseech Thee; by whom shall Jacob arise? For he is small,** the prophet thus once more interceding in behalf of his sinful nation. V. 6. **The Lord repented for this. This also shall not be, saith the Lord God,** as little as the punishment of the first vision. V. 7. **Thus He showed me,** in a third vision; **and, behold, the Lord stood upon a wall made by a plumb-line,** one which was built upright and according to all the rules of the craft, **with a plumb-line in His hand.** V. 8. **And the Lord said unto me, Amos, what seest thou?** the purpose of the question being to impress the importance of the vision upon the prophet's mind. **And I said, A plumb-line. Then said the Lord, Behold, I will set a plumb-line in the midst of My people Israel,** the object, in this case, like in 2 Kings 21, 13; Is. 34, 11, being to tear down a building. **I will not again pass by them any more,** He was determined not to show lenience any longer; v. 9. **and the high places of Isaac,** in this case used of the northern kingdom, **shall be desolate, and the sanctuaries of Israel,** the various places devoted to idolatrous purposes, **shall be laid waste; and I will rise against the house of Jeroboam,** in this instance representing the entire kingdom and royal family, **with the sword.** Thus the destruction of the kingdom, the dissolution of the nation, was definitely foretold, and the prophet did not dare to intercede any more in behalf of his people.

THE PROPHET AT BETHEL. — V. 10. **Then Amaziah, the priest of Bethel,** the high priest in charge of the sanctuary of idolatry at Bethel, **sent to Jeroboam, king of Israel, saying, Amos hath conspired against thee in the midst of the house of Israel,** in its religious center, namely, by announcing the coming punishment of the Lord without fear or favor; **the land is not able to bear all his words.** This is a common charge against the teachers of truth to this day, that their preaching creates a disturbance in the land. V. 11. **For thus Amos saith, Jeroboam shall die by the sword,** for this was actually included in the statement of verse 9, **and Israel shall surely be led away captive out of their own land.** Amaziah purposely stated the threat of the Lord in its severer form in order to provoke the king's wrath. V. 12. **Also Amaziah said unto Amos, O thou seer, go, flee thee away into the land of Judah and there eat bread,** earning some sort of a livelihood, **and prophesy there,** v. 13. **but prophesy not again any more at Bethel,** where his words naturally made it very uncomfortable for Amaziah; **for it is the king's chapel,** a sanctuary established by the king, **and it is the king's court,** the chief place for the cult ordained by the king for his entire kingdom. His argument was that for this reason it was altogether improper for Amos to continue his threatening sayings. V. 14. **Then answered Amos and said to Amaziah,** in defending himself against the high priest's insinuations, **I was no prophet, neither was I a prophet's son,** that is, he was not born to that honor nor did he attend any school of the prophets, **but I was an herdman,** a shepherd of humble position, **and a gatherer of sycomore fruit,** that is, of the sycomore-fig-tree; v. 15. **and the Lord took me as I followed the flock,** giving him a direct call, **and the Lord said unto me, Go, prophesy unto My people Israel.** V. 16. **Now, therefore, hear thou the word of the Lord, Thou sayest, Prophesy not against Israel and drop not thy word,** cp. Ezek. 21, 2. 7; Micah 2, 6. 11, **against the house of Isaac.** V. 17. **Therefore, thus saith the Lord, Thy wife shall be an harlot in the city,** dishonored by the enemies at the storming of the city, **and thy sons and thy daughters shall fall by the sword, in the** slaughter of the same attack, **and thy land,** his own landed possession, **shall be divided by line,** allotted to the invaders, **and thou shalt die in a polluted land,** as a prisoner among the heathen; **and Israel shall surely go into captivity forth of his land.** With people who are unwittingly caught in the meshes of a false religion one may have patience, but the leaders of false religions must be rebuked with all severity, for it is their leadership which results in the loss of souls, and the leaders are rightly held responsbile.

CHAPTER 8.

Israel Ripe for the Judgment.

THE VISION OF THE BASKET OF SUMMER-FRUIT. — V. 1. **Thus hath the Lord God showed unto me,** in another vision revealing the fate of Israel, **and behold a basket of summer-fruit,** dead ripe, ready to be consumed. V. 2. **And he said,** again anxious to impress the meaning of the vision upon the prophet, **Amos, what seest thou? And I said, A basket of summer-fruit. Then said the Lord unto me, The end is come upon My people of Israel,** for they were ripe for the punishment which would end their national existence; **I will not again pass by them any more,** namely, to spare them, that they would not be punished. V. 3. **And the songs of the Temple,** originally intended to convey the spirit of the highest rejoicing, **shall be howlings in that day,** cries of the deepest grief and mourning over the large number of the slain, **saith the Lord God. There shall be many dead bodies in every place; they shall cast them forth with silence,** with an admonition to hush, to bow in silence under the terrible severity of the divine judgment. If a sinner acknowledges his sin, he will also be ready to bow in silence and humility under the hand of God when some punishment comes upon him.

A LAST ADMONITION OF THE LORD. — V. 4. **Hear this, O ye that swallow up the needy,** panting after the poor in their anxiety to destroy them and to grasp their property, **even to make the poor of the land to fail,** in order to take their property by a show of right, v. 5. **saying, When will the new moon,** the day which they considered a time of enforced idleness, **be gone that we may sell corn?** speculating at the expense of the poorer in the land, **and the Sabbath, that we may set forth wheat,** opening their storehouses in order to make unjust gains, **making the ephah small,** giving the people short measure, **and the shekel great,** by raising the price which they charged those in need, **and falsifying the balances by deceit?** so that they sold below weight, their scales having been arranged to cheat, v. 6. **that we may buy the poor for silver and the needy for a pair of shoes,** compelling him to sell himself either for a certain amount of money which he owed or for a pair of shoes which he had gotten and was unable to pay for; **yea, and sell the refuse of the wheat?** only the poor grain, for which they charged just as much as for the best grade. History repeats itself also in this respect, for the same tactics are used in our days by such as speculate in foodstuffs and in the necessaries of life, the manipulators always fixing the prices in their favor or else selling inferior goods for the price of that which is really high-grade. V. 7. **The Lord hath sworn by the excellency of Jacob,** He Himself being Israel's Pride and Glory, **Surely I will never forget any of their works;** for by leaving such sins unpunished, He would deny His glory in Israel. V. 8. **Shall not the land tremble for this,** for the deeds of such conscienceless scoundrels, **and every one mourn that dwelleth therein?** namely, on account of the force of the Lord's punishment. **And it shall rise up wholly as a flood,** be changed into a mighty, billowing ocean; **and it shall be cast out and drowned, as by the flood of Egypt,** the reference being to the regular overflow of the Nile. V. 9. **And it shall come to pass in that day,** the day of the Lord's punishment upon Israel, **saith the Lord God, that I will cause the sun to go down at noon, and I will darken the earth in the clear day,** by a terrible catastrophe, the picture being well applicable to the fate of a nation or of the earth when it is destroyed while in the very midst of its earthly fortune and power; v. 10. **and I will turn your feasts into mourning,** taking away all joy, **and all your songs into lamentation,** cp. Hos. 2, 13; **and I will bring up sackcloth upon all loins,** the usual garment of deepest grief, **and baldness upon every head,** for shaving the head was a sign of the deepest mourning; **and I will make it as the mourning of an only son,** a most intense sorrow, which cannot be appeased, **and the end thereof as a bitter day,** one whose objectionable taste would not soon be forgotten. V. 11. **Behold, the days come, saith the Lord God, that I will send a famine in the land, not a famine of bread nor a thirst for water, but of hearing the words of the Lord,** causing men anxiously to search for the divine counsel, which they had so consistently rejected; v. 12. **and they shall wander from sea to sea,** from the Dead Sea to the Mediterranean, **and from the North even to the East,** to the limitless extent of the Arabian Desert, **they shall run to and fro to seek the Word of the Lord,** the pressure of punishment causing them to make this outward show of zeal, **and shall not find it.** V. 13. **In that day shall the fair virgins and young men**

faint for thirst, this in spite of their natural strength and stamina, which was lacking in those who had been overcome before them. V. 14. **They that swear by the sin of Samaria,** namely, the golden calf of Bethel, **and say, Thy god, O Dan,** the other golden calf in the extreme northern city of Canaan, **liveth; and, The manner of Beersheba liveth,** literally, "By the life of the way to Beersheba," this being a third city of an idolatrous cult, **even they shall fall and never rise up again.** In those days they made pilgrimages to the cities where the altars of idolatry were erected and refused to heed the words of the true God; therefore the time would come when they would be only too glad to heed the Word of God, but would find no one who would proclaim it to them. History shows that this judgment of the Lord has repeatedly gone into effect upon such as first rejected His message, His Gospel. The word of Luther that the Word of God is like a rainstorm which quickly passes over may well be heeded also in our day.

CHAPTER 9.

A Final Rebuke and a Wonderful Promise.

THE WICKED KINGDOM OVERTHROWN. — V. 1. **I saw,** in a fifth vision, **the Lord standing upon the altar,** most likely that of the idolatrous sanctuary at Bethel, to which reference has just been made; **and He said, Smite the lintel of the door,** the prophet himself striking the blow against the supporting pillars, **that the posts may shake, and cut them in the head, all of them,** dashing down the pieces, as the building collapses, upon the heads of the whole people assembled about the national sanctuary; **and I will slay the last of them with the sword,** namely, the remnant which would succeed in escaping the downfall of the building. **He that fleeth of them shall not flee away,** though he may fancy himself safe, **and he that escapeth of them shall not be delivered,** not succeed in saving his life. V. 2. **Though they dig into hell,** in the uttermost depths of the universe, **thence shall Mine hand take them; though they climb up to heaven, thence will I bring them down,** cp. Ps. 139, 7. 8; v. 3. **and though they hide themselves in the top of Carmel,** whose wooded heights were at the extreme western boundary of their kingdom, **I will search and take them out thence; and though they be hid from My sight in the bottom of the sea,** in the nethermost caves of the ocean, **thence will I command the serpent, and he shall bite them;** v. 4. **and though they go into captivity before their enemies,** hoping to save their lives by surrendering to the foe, **thence will I command the sword,** wielded by those who hated them, **and it shall slay them; and I will set Mine eyes upon them for evil and not for good,** keeping them under observation without ceasing, so that escape would be an utter impossibility. The omnipresence and the almighty power of the Lord is further brought out. V. 5. **And the Lord God of hosts is He that toucheth the land, and it shall melt,** cp. Ps. 46, 7; 75, 4, **and all that dwell therein shall mourn,** for the melting is done by the judgments of the Lord, who makes the invaders and conquerors of the land His instruments; **and it shall rise up wholly like a flood,** rather, "the whole of it riseth like the Nile," **and shall be drowned as by the flood of Egypt,** the annual overflow of the Nile being once more made a picture of the overwhelming judgments of the Lord. V. 6. **It is He that buildeth His stories in the heaven,** literally, "His upper chambers," to which one would have to ascend by steps, **and hath founded His troop in the earth,** firmly fixing the vault of His sky above; **He that calleth for the waters of the sea and poureth them out upon the face of the earth,** either in tidal waves or in another deluge: **The Lord is His name.** After this emphatic declaration of His almighty power and sovereignty the Lord shows the children of Israel that they may not rely upon the fact of their being His chosen people. V. 7. **Are ye not as children of the Ethiopians unto Me, O children of Israel? saith the Lord.** Since they had broken the covenant, they stood no nearer to Him than the heathen. **Have not I brought up Israel out of the land of Egypt,** this being a deed for which He alone should receive credit, **and the Philistines from Caphtor,** from the island of Crete, **and the Syrians from Kir?** very likely a province of Assyria. V. 8. **Behold, the eyes of the Lord God are upon the sinful kingdom,** directed against it to work His punishment, **and I will destroy it from off the face of the earth,** namely, the sinful people as such, **saving that I will not utterly destroy the house of Jacob, saith the Lord,** namely, the spiritual Israel, the true descendants of the patriarchs. V. 9. **For, lo, I will command, and I will sift the house of Israel,** shaking them as in a colander, or sieve, **among all nations, like as corn is sifted in a sieve, yet shall not the least grain fall upon the earth.** The nations of the world are the sieve by which Israel is cleaned of the chaff found in its midst, of the godless people that claimed membership in the congregation of the Lord. V. 10. **All the sinners of My people,** namely, those who persist in their godlessness and false security, **shall die by the sword, which say, The evil shall not overtake nor prevent us,** that is, precede or reach us. When God is once determined to punish the wicked, there is no power which may stop Him, and all the efforts of the godless to escape His wrath are futile.

The Kingdom of Messiah Established. — V. 11. **In that day,** in the great Messianic period to which the entire Old Testament looks forward, **will I raise up the tabernacle of David that is fallen,** the monarchy and family of David, **and close up the breaches thereof; and I will raise up his ruins, and I will build it as in the days of old,** so that the kingdom of the true Son of David, of the Messiah, would once more be secure, established forever, v. 12. **that they may possess the remnant of Edom, and of all the heathen which are called by My name,** rather, "upon whom My name is called," that is, all those whom He had chosen from all the people of the earth, **saith the Lord that doeth this.** V. 13. **Behold, the days come, saith the Lord, that the plowman shall overtake the reaper, and the treader of grapes him that soweth seed,** by spreading it broadcast. So fruitful would the land be that the ripe grain would be cut while the plowman was still preparing the soil for the seed, and the harvest of grapes would be so plentiful that it would take till seeding-time to tread out the grapes. **And the mountains shall drop sweet wine,** so that new wine would be continually dripping from them, **and all the hills shall melt,** dissolving themselves in blessings. V. 14. **And I will bring again the captivity of My people of Israel,** all those who accept the deliverance from the powers of evil being assembled in the congregation of the Lord's people, **and they shall build the waste cities,** being secure in their citizenship, **and inhabit them; and they shall plant vineyards and drink the wine thereof; they shall also make gardens and eat the fruit of them.** V. 15. **And I will plant them upon their land, and they shall no more be pulled up out of their land which I have given them, saith the Lord, thy God.** Thus the prophet, in the conclusion of his book, under the type of Israel restored to its land, pictures the peace and prosperity of the true spiritual Israel, of the Church of the New Testament, in which every congregation is a garden of His mercy, and the streams of His love come down in the preaching of the Gospel, in order to bring peace to the hearts of poor sinners throughout the world.

THE BOOK OF THE PROPHET OBADIAH.

Of the author of this book, the shortest in the Old Testament, very little is known. It appears from his book that Obadiah ("servant of Jehovah") was a member of the southern kingdom, and it may be right to identify him with the man of the same name who lived under Jehoram, the son of Jehoshaphat. This would place him in the first half of the ninth century before Christ, an assumption which receives some further support by the fact that both Joel (chap. 2, 32; 3, 2. 3. 7. 14. 17) and Jeremiah (chap. 49, 7—16) evidently refer to the prophecy of Obadiah.

The vision of Obadiah contains a severe arraignment of the Edomites for their traditional enmity against the people of God, on account of which he announces the divine judgment upon Idumea. After a further paragraph, in which the justice of this punishment upon Edom is established, the book closes with a promise of the restoration of Judah, a prediction which finds its complete fulfilment in the victories of the Church of Christ in the Messianic period. It is clear that the judgment upon Edom is intended as a type of the punishment upon all the enemies of the Lord, and that the fulfilment of the kingdom of the Messiah are the basic thoughts of the vision.[1)]

1) Cp. Fuerbringer, ***Einleitung in das Alte Testament***, 83. 84; ***Concordia Bible Class***, June, 1919, 83. 84.

Edom's Destruction Foretold. — V. 1. **The vision of Obadiah: Thus saith the Lord God,** the supreme Ruler and Sovereign of the universe, **concerning Edom: We have heard a rumor from the Lord,** tidings from Jehovah, the God of the covenant, the Protector of His people, **and an ambassador is sent among the heathen,** with a powerful and comforting message, as far as the Lord's people are concerned, **Arise ye and let us,** the various nations of the world acting with, and in behalf of, Jehovah, **rise up against her in battle,** the struggle between the powers of light and of darkness thus being brought out. V. 2. **Behold, I have made thee small among the heathen,** the humiliation of Idumea being represented as having already been accomplished; **thou art greatly despised,** humiliated exceedingly. V. 3. **The pride of thine heart hath deceived thee,** the Hebrew text making this very emphatic: "Betrayed hath thee the pride of thine heart," upon which Idumea depended, **thou that dwellest in the clefts of the rock,** in the mountain fastnesses of its rugged country, **whose habitation is high,** for the territory of Edom was a rocky mountain mass, full of caverns, **that saith in his heart, Who shall bring me down to the ground?** The Edomites considered themselves so secure in their rock dwellings, which, in their opinion, were practically inaccessible, that they were filled with overweening pride. The Lord now shows the vanity of this confidence. V. 4. **Though thou exalt thyself as the eagle,** with his home placed on inaccessible crags, **and though thou set thy nest among the stars,** on the summit of the highest mountains, **thence will I bring thee down, saith the Lord,** for no one can escape His avenging justice. V. 5. **If thieves came to thee, if robbers by night,** this being said for the sake of comparison, **(how art thou cut off!) would they not have stolen till they had enough?** They take whatever they find, what is lying there to be taken readily. **If the grape-gatherers came to thee, would they not leave some grapes?** the usual remnants left for gleaning. Ordinarily, if enemies come against a country, they will satisfy their immediate desire for vengeance; but in this case the ruin would be too complete to be ascribed to ordinary causes; it would clearly be God's pitiless punishment. V. 6. **How are the things of Esau searched out!** the spoiling of the country being complete in every respect. **How are his hidden things sought up!** so that not one of its hiding-places would be unexplored by the foe. V. 7. **All the men of thy confederacy have brought thee even to the border,** or, "To the border have they escorted thee, all thy confederates," that is, the allies, to whom Idumea sent for assistance, sent these ambassadors back, not wishing to be involved in the downfall of that nation; **the men that were at peace with thee,** the neighboring nations, who had formerly professed friendship, **have deceived thee and prevailed against thee,** by withdrawing their assistance at the critical moment; **they that eat thy bread have laid a wound under thee,** literally, "Thy bread have they placed as a snare," or "wound," under thee, that is, they broke their pledge of alliance to hospitality, treacherously leaving them in the lurch when they needed help most. **There is none understanding in him,** for Edom, overcome by the misfortunes which struck it, lost its usual cleverness in finding a way of escape from his perilous position. V. 8. **Shall I not in that day, saith the Lord, even destroy the wise men out of Edom,** who formerly had given such excellent counsel in every emergency, **and understanding out of the mount of Esau?** so that the people of Idumea would be hopeless in the face of the calamity which would strike them. V. 9. **And thy mighty men, O Teman,** the inhabitants of the southern district of Idumea, **shall be dismayed, to the end that every one of the mount of Esau,** of their entire mountainous country, **may be cut off by slaughter,** for that was the object of the Lord in taking away from them their wisdom and the use of their former power. When God decides to punish a nation, then all the cleverness of its most learned men, all the strength of its mightiest men, will be of no avail.

THE PUNISHMENT A CONSEQUENCE OF IDUMEA'S HOSTILITY. — V. 10. **For thy violence against thy brother Jacob,** the two nations being so closely related through their common ancestor, but the Edomites having continued the family feud practically from the time of Esau, **shame shall cover thee,** so that Idumea would be disgraced before the eyes of the world, **and thou shalt be cut off forever,** in an extermination demanded by God's will and Law. V. 11. **In the day that thou stoodest on the other side,** opposed to his brother Jacob, to the children of Israel, **in the day that the strangers carried away captive his forces,** probably when the Philistines and Arabians made a raid against Jerusalem, 2 Kings 8, 20—22, **and foreigners entered into his gates and cast lots upon Jerusalem,** upon its inhabitants, whom they distributed among them by lot, to sell into slavery, Joel 3, 3, **even thou wast as one of them,** taking the part of the enemies of the Lord's people. V. 12. **But thou shouldest not have looked on the day of thy brother in the day that he became a stranger,** namely, when Edom feasted his eyes upon the misfortunes which befell Judah; **neither shouldest thou have rejoiced over the children of Judah in the day of their destruction,** when calamity came upon the Lord's people as a result of their estrangement from the Lord; **neither shouldest thou have spoken proudly,** literally, "made great thy mouth," in utter mockeries, **in the day of distress.** V. 13. **Thou shouldest not have entered into the gate of My people in the day of their calamity,** with a feeling of satisfaction over their misfortune; **yea, thou shouldest not have looked on their affliction in the day of their calamity,** with a malicious delight, **nor have laid hands on their substance in the day of their calamity,** when the enemies plundered the city; v. 14. **neither shouldest thou have stood in the crossway,** at the crossroads, where everybody was obliged to pass, **to cut off those of his that did escape,** either to slay them or to deliver them to the enemies; **neither shouldest thou have delivered up those of his that did remain in the day of distress.** As a brother of Israel, Edom had the duty of standing by him, and this duty he had not performed. V. 15. **For the day of the Lord,** when His punishment would descend upon all His enemies, **is near upon all the heathen; as thou hast done, it shall be done unto thee; thy reward,** what he had earned by his wicked behavior, **shall return upon thine own head.** V. 16. **For as ye have drunk upon My holy mountain,** in the desecration of a drunken orgy, **so shall all the heathen,** of whom Edom was a type, **drink continually,** being obliged to drink the cup of the Lord's wrath; **yea, they shall drink, and they shall swallow down,** compelled to bear His punishment; **and they shall be as though they had not been,** exterminated by the Lord's judgment. All enemies of the Lord and of His holy Church will eventually feel the heavy hand of His wrath on account of their hostility against that which He has ordained.

THE DELIVERANCE OF GOD'S PEOPLE. — V. 17. **But upon Mount Zion,** in the midst of the Lord's Church, **shall be deliverance,** the congregation of such as are saved from the judgment of destruction; **and there shall be holiness,** that is, Mount Zion would be a sanctuary, no longer to be desecrated by the enemies; **and the house of Jacob shall possess their possessions,** people from all the nations of the world being added to the Lord's congregation. V. 18. **And the house of Jacob,** Judah, as representative of the Church of God in the Old Testament, **shall be a fire,** through the burning zeal of God which lives in His believers, **and the house of Joseph,** the northern tribes in their believing representatives, **a flame, and the house of Esau,** the nation of Edom as type of all enemies of the Lord, **for stubble, and they shall kindle in them and devour them,** for all the enemies of the Lord's Church will eventually be destroyed; **and there shall not be any remaining of the house of Esau; for the Lord hath spoken it,** and His Word is certain to be fulfilled in every instance. V. 19. **And they of the South,** the members of the tribe of Judah, **shall possess the mount of Esau,** according to the prophecy which states that the Messiah would dwell in the midst of His enemies, **and they of the plain,** the Lord's people of the southwestern plains, **the Philistines,** another tribe and country hostile to the Lord; **and they shall possess the fields of Ephraim,** the territory of the northern kingdom, **and the fields of Samaria; and Benjamin shall possess Gilead,** the country east of Jordan. V. 20. **And the captivity of this host of the children of Israel,** the very ones who had suffered on account of the hostility of the enemies, **shall possess that of the Canaanites, even unto Zarephath,** or Sarepta, a city in the extreme northern portion of the country, **within the** boundaries of Phenicia; **and the captivity of Jerusalem,** the captives from the capital, **which is in Sepharad,** either Sardis or Sparta, **shall possess the cities of the South,** the names being given only as representative of nations near by. V. 21. **And saviors,** men who would bring the deliverance of the Lord, **shall come up on Mount Zion,** appearing in the Church of the Lord as His messengers, **to judge the mount of Esau,** as typical of the entire heathen world; **and the kingdom shall be the Lord's;** for Jehovah's Kingdom of Grace will be established throughout the world. The entire paragraph evidently sets forth the marvelous deliverance of the people of the Lord from the oppression of all their enemies and their preservation in the Church of the Messiah, which, from being the Church Militant here in time, will merge into the Church Triumphant in eternity.

THE BOOK OF THE PROPHET JONAH.

INTRODUCTION.

The prophet Jonah ("dove"), the son of Amittai, was undoubtedly identical with the man who is called a prophet in 2 Kings 14, 25. The village of Gath-hepher in Galilee, in the tribe of Zebulun, was his home town, which makes it probable that he lived under Jeroboam II of Israel and prophesied at about the end of the ninth century or at the beginning of the eighth century before Christ. The period in which he lived was approximately that of the prophets Amos and Hosea in the northern kingdom and of Isaiah and Micah in the southern kingdom. As he had announced to King Jeroboam the restoration of the ancient boundaries of the kingdom, whereby the glory and majesty of Israel were once more established, so he was here sent to Nineveh as a special messenger of the Lord in order to preach the need of repentance to this wicked Assyrian metropolis.

The Book of Jonah, obviously a historical account of the chief events connected with the sending of Jonah to Nineveh, restricts itself to this one narrative. It abounds in miraculous circumstances, such as that of the great fish in whose stomach the life of the prophet was preserved, of the terrible storm sent by God, which died down as soon as the prophet had been delivered to the waves, of the remarkable growth of the gourd planted by Jonah, and other extraordinary features. Unbelievers and scoffers have tried, for this reason, to make the book the target of their mockery. But all their attacks are found to be idle talk if we remember that our Lord Jesus Christ Himself referred to the Book of Jonah as a record of facts, even using the experience of Jonah as a type and prophecy of His own burial and resurrection.

The purpose of the book is to show that the true God is not the God of the Jews only, but of the Gentiles as well, that God will have all men, including the Gentiles, to be saved and to come to the knowledge of the truth. The book treats, in chronological order, the call of Jonah, his flight, his being preserved in the stomach of the sea-monster and his deliverance, his preaching to the Ninevites and its effect, the prophet's consequent great displeasure and complaint, the Lord's loving correction.[1]

1) Cp. Fuerbringer, *Einleitung*, 85. 86; *Concordia Bible Class*, June, 1919, 85. 86.

CHAPTER 1.

Jonah's Attempt to Evade the Call of the Lord.

JONAH'S COMMISSION AND FLIGHT. — V. 1. **Now the word of the Lord came unto Jonah, the son of Amittai,** in a vision or by a direct revelation, **saying,** v. 2. **Arise, go to Nineveh, that great city, and cry against it,** by preaching a call to repentance; **for their wickedness is come up before Me,** as had that of Sodom and Gomorrah hundreds of years before. Cp. Gen. 18, 20. The name Nineveh was applied to a complex of four ancient cities, including Nineveh proper, which lay between the Tigris River and a low range of hills, about 500 miles northeast of Jerusalem. The entire length of the compound city was about twenty-five miles, while its breadth was fifteen. At that time it had more than half a million inhabitants and was the capital and metropolis of the entire heathen world. V. 3. **But Jonah,** instead of showing the proper obedience to the Lord, **rose up to flee unto Tarshish,** Tartessus in Spain, one of the westernmost cities of the ancient world and always considered as lying on the very boundary of the earth's inhabited area, **from the presence of the Lord,** from before the face of the Lord, who was thought of as having His habitation in the Temple at Jerusalem, **and went down to Joppa,** the harbor of Jerusalem on the Mediterranean Sea. **And he found a ship going to Tarshish,** for there was a lively commercial intercourse with the western metropolis even at that time on account of its trade in metals and fine products of the soil; **so he paid the fare thereof,** he engaged passage, **and went down into it to go with them unto Tarshish from the presence of the Lord,** thus deliberately denying his services to Jehovah, the King of Israel, chiefly because the idea of preaching repentance to a heathen nation was repugnant to him, since he feared that the Lord might show the Gentiles mercy. V. 4. **But the Lord,** whose presence was by no means confined to the Land of Promise, **sent out a great wind into the sea,** a very severe storm, which caused the billows to rise in dangerous mountains; **and there was a mighty tempest in the sea, so that the ship was like to be broken,** it was on the point of foundering. V. 5. **Then the mariners,** the sailors on the boat, **were afraid and cried every man unto his god,** for the seamen were from various countries and worshiped various gods, **and cast forth the wares that were in the ship,** the freight which she was carrying, **into the sea to lighten it of them,** so that she would ride higher in the water and no longer be in danger of foundering. **But Jonah was gone down into the sides of the ship,** into its cabin, or hold; **and he lay and was fast asleep,** thinking himself secure from all danger. V. 6. **So the shipmaster came to him and said unto him, What meanest thou, O sleeper?** Why should he withdraw at the time of this great peril? **Arise, call upon thy God, if so be that God will think upon us that we perish not,** by lending them His assistance and rescuing them from the impending destruction. V. 7. **And they said every one to his fellow,** after Jonah had obeyed the call of the captain, **Come and let us cast lots,** a common method of determining the guilt of men at that time, **that we may know for whose cause this evil is upon us,** who was to blame for the present condition of affairs. **So they cast lots, and the lot fell upon Jonah,** the Lord Himself directing this method of determining the guilty one. V. 8. **Then said they unto him, Tell us, we pray thee, for whose cause this evil is upon us,** who and what was responsible for this condition of affairs. **What is thine occupation?** his business, which might have been of a nature to arouse the wrath of God. **And whence comest thou,** from what nation and people? **What is thy country? And of what people art thou?** The questions are shouted in a confused mass, as always under the stress of a great emotion. V. 9. **And he said unto them,** in an open confession of his guilt, **I am an Hebrew,** the usual name applied to the people of Israel by the surrounding nations; **and I fear the Lord, the God of heaven,** worshiping Him alone, **which hath made the sea and the dry land,** the one Creator of the world and all it contained. V. 10. **Then were the men exceedingly afraid,** filled with terror at the scope of this confession, which showed them that they were, although unwittingly, assisting Jonah in his effort to escape the Lord, **and said unto him, Why hast thou done this?** a cry of horror and fear more than a question, for the God of the Hebrews was known as a powerful Deity. **For the men knew that he fled from the presence of the Lord, because he had told them,** this statement having been included in the confession which he made before them. Even unbelievers quake at any evidence of the wrath of God, much as they otherwise scoff at those who worship Him.

JONAH AND THE SEA-MONSTER. — V. 11. **Then said they unto him, What shall we do unto thee that the sea may be calm unto us?** What would Jonah himself suggest or advise in order to turn away the wrath of God from those who were not implicated in his guilt? **For the sea wrought,** continued to rage, **and was tempestuous,** still rising in angry billows. V. 12. **And he said unto them,** showing the right spirit in offering himself up as a sacrifice in their behalf, **Take me up and cast me forth into the sea; so shall the sea be calm unto you,** be quieted down; **for I know that for my sake this great tempest is upon you.** V. 13. **Nevertheless the men,** not desiring to carry out the prophet's suggestion, **rowed hard to bring it to the land,** that is, they tried everything they knew in the line of seamanship in order to break through the billows which hemmed in the ship; **but they could not, for the sea wrought and was tempestuous against them,** so that they could make no headway against the surging waves. V. 14. **Wherefore they cried unto the Lord,** in this case addressing Jehovah, the true God, **and said, We beseech Thee, O Lord, we beseech Thee, let us not perish for this man's life,** be held accountable for the fact that they would now deliver him to what appeared to them a certain death, **and lay not upon us innocent blood,** by imputing it to them, since Jonah had not harmed them in any manner; **for Thou, O Lord, hast done as it pleased Thee,** He had determined it, the lot, as directed by Him, made the execution necessary. V. 15. **So they took up Jonah and cast him forth into the sea; and the sea ceased from her raging,** it stood still and no longer rose in such tremendous billows. V. 16. **Then the men,** seeing in this sudden change of the weather the almighty hand of God, **feared the Lord exceedingly and offered a sacrifice unto the Lord and made vows,** as men will under the stress of such a sudden fear and emotion, although there is no real change of heart in them. V. 17. **Now, the Lord had prepared a great fish,** not a whale, but a special sea-monster, **to swallow up Jonah. And Jonah was in the belly of the fish three days and three nights,** being alive and conscious through the power of the Lord, whose plans called for a further use of this prophet. In the entire story there are many elements of the miraculous, but not a line which makes the narrative appear unreasonable. It is for us to believe what the Lord has here recorded.

CHAPTER 2.

Jonah's Prayer of Thanksgiving and Praise.

The words, as here recorded, are not a prayer for deliverance, but a thanksgiving to the Lord for the deliverance already effected. From this we see, as Luther also remarks, that the thoughts which Jonah had during his confinement in the belly of the sea-monster were afterwards edited by him to form the powerful hymn of worship which we here have before us. V. 1. **Then Jonah prayed unto the Lord, his God, out of the fish's belly,** these thoughts occurring to him again and again during his awful experience, v. 2. **and said, I cried by reason of mine affliction,** out of the midst of the distress which he was suffering, **unto the Lord, and He heard me; out of the belly of hell,** literally, "out of the womb of sheol," the realm of death, **cried I, and Thou heardest my voice,** delivering him from what seemed to be certain destruction, cp. Ps. 18, 6; 30, 4. V. 3. **For Thou hadst cast me into the deep,** the sailors on the ship being but the executors of the punishment placed upon him by the Lord, **in the midst of the seas,** literally, "into the heart of the oceans"; **and the floods compassed me about,** namely, as he sank to the bottom; **all Thy billows and Thy waves passed over me.** Cp. Ps. 42, 8. V. 4. **Then I said, I am cast out of Thy sight,** cut off from the gracious experience of God's favor; **yet I will look again toward Thy holy Temple,** certain that he would again be permitted to worship with the Lord's people. V. 5. **The waters compassed me about, even to the soul,** so that he was ready to despair of his life, cp. Ps. 18, 5; 69, 2; **the depth closed me round about, the weeds were wrapped about my head,** apparently enclosing him so that he could not escape. V. 6. **I went down to the bottoms of the mountains,** the very depths of the ocean abyss, where the mountains have their foundations; **the earth with her bars,** the walls of the sea-basin, **was about me forever; yet hast Thou brought up my life from corruption,** from the pit which threatened to be his grave, **O Lord, my God.** V. 7. **When my soul fainted within me,** when he was at the point of yielding to the night of death, **I remembered the Lord; and my prayer came in unto Thee,** like a petitioner presenting his appeal in person, **into Thine holy Temple,** where the Lord had promised to hear those who put their trust in Him. V. 8. **They that**

observe lying vanities, placing their trust in idols and in false worship, **forsake their own mercy,** deliberately abandon their one hope of deliverance, namely, through the loving-kindness and tender mercies of Jehovah. V. 9. **But I will sacrifice unto Thee with the voice of thanksgiving,** loudly proclaiming his gratitude for mercies received, Ps. 42, 5; **I will pay that that I have vowed.** Cp. Ps. 50, 14. 23. **Salvation is of the Lord,** it belongs to Jehovah, it is in His power, He alone can grant deliverance from all evil. V. 10. **And the Lord,** who heard the repentant prayer of His servant, **spake unto the fish,** giving it a definite command, **and it vomited out Jonah upon the dry land,** very likely on the coast of Palestine. As far as the subject-matter of the story is concerned, it will be well to remember that one of the ancient teachers of the Church rightly calls all subtle inquiries concerning these things a foolish officiousness.

CHAPTER 3.

Jonah's Message to the Ninevites and Its Results.

The disobedient prophet had received a severe lesson at the hand of God, but he now profited by this lesson and was ready to undertake the commission which had originally been issued to him. V. 1. **And the word of the Lord came unto Jonah the second time, saying,** v. 2. **Arise, go unto Nineveh, that great city,** the Assyrian capital and metropolis, **and preach unto it the preaching that I bid thee,** loudly proclaiming the message which the Lord would reveal to him in due time, yielding himself in ready obedience to whatever the Lord may see fit to have him speak. V. 3. **So Jonah arose and went unto Nineveh, according to the word of the Lord,** in unquestioning obedience. **Now, Nineveh was an exceeding great city,** literally, "a great city to God," regarded by Him as such, **of three days' journey,** that is, it took three days to make the round of its main sections, if a person passed through all the chief market-places. V. 4. **And Jonah began to enter into the city a day's journey,** he commenced his trip through the various centers comprising the larger city, preaching wherever he found a suitable place and a fitting opportunity; **and he cried and said, Yet forty days and Nineveh shall be overthrown,** this threat being the climax of his proclamation, of his call to repentance. V. 5. **So the people of Nineveh believed God,** they accepted His word, they were filled with a wholesome fear, **and proclaimed a fast,** as an outward evidence of their sorrow, **and put on sackcloth,** the garment of mourning, **from the greatest of them even to the least of them,** old and young, all without exception. V. 6. **For word came unto the king of Nineveh,** into the neighborhood of whose palace the prophet had very likely progressed in his first day's journey, **and he arose from his throne,** symbol of his earthly power, **and he laid his robe from him,** his royal mantle, **and covered him with sackcloth,** also adopting the mourning-dress, **and sat in ashes,** all signs of sorrow and repentance. Cp. Job 2, 8; Ezek. 27, 30. V. 7. **And he caused it to be proclaimed and published through Nineveh by the decree of the king and his nobles,** the royal heralds being dispatched in accordance with the custom of making edicts of this kind known, **saying, Let neither man nor beast, herd nor flock, taste anything,** the domestic animals being included in this order, as sufferers with the people; **let them not feed nor drink water,** v. 8. **but let man and beast be covered with sackcloth,** clothed in mourning, **and cry mightily unto God,** the very lowing of the cattle and the bleating of the sheep in their distress being considered appeals for mercy; **yea, let them turn every one from his evil way,** from his sinful habits, **and from the violence that is in their hands.** Cp. Is. 59, 6. V. 9. **Who can tell if God will turn and repent,** the possibility of His doing so being suggested by His interest in sending a prophet to warn them, **and turn away from His fierce anger that we perish not?** It was a true repentance on the part of the Ninevites and is so cited by Christ in reproof of those who, with much greater light and privileges, did not repent, Matt. 12, 41; Luke 11, 32, even if its effects were not lasting. V. 10. **And God saw their works, that they turned from their evil way,** from the security of their open transgressions of the Lord's will; **and God repented of the evil that He had said that he would do unto them; and He did it not,** letting His mercy guide His actions rather than a stern and immutable justice. As God spared Nineveh when its inhabitants turned to Him in repentance, so He is ready to show mercy to all those who lay aside their obstinate impenitence and plead with Him for forgiveness.

CHAPTER 4.

Jonah's Displeasure and the Lord's Reproof.

That Jonah was easily swayed by his emotions is evident from the entire story of his book, but appears particularly from the last chapter. At the same time, the Lord's patience in dealing with His erring children is brought out in a most remarkable manner. V. 1. **But it displeased Jonah exceedingly**, namely, that the Lord did not carry out His threat of punishment upon the people of Nineveh, **and he was very angry**, provoked, filled with grief and vexation. V. 2. **And he prayed unto the Lord and said, I pray Thee, O Lord, was not this my saying**, the argument which he had used within himself, **when I was yet in my country?** when he first received the commission to go to Nineveh. **Therefore I fled before unto Tarshish**, that is, he anticipated the fruitlessness of his errand, the fact that his prediction against Nineveh was not fulfilled; **for I knew that Thou art a gracious God and merciful, slow to anger and of great kindness, and repentest Thee of the evil.** Cp. Ex. 34, 6. The words were spoken out of a very decided ill humor, because Jonah, as he thought, had been sent to deliver a message which the Lord intended to revoke, and which so readily produced repentance. It was a sad contradiction between a peevish mood and the better knowledge of his head and heart. V. 3. **Therefore now, O Lord, take, I beseech Thee, my life from me; for it is better for me to die than to live.** "Jonah's impatience of life under disappointed hopes of Israel's reformation through the destruction of Nineveh is like that of Elijah at his plan for reforming Israel, 1 Kings 18, failing through Jezebel. Cp. 1 Kings 19, 4." V. 4. **Then said the Lord**, in a preliminary, gentle reproof, **Doest thou well to be angry?** Was there any justification for Jonah's attitude? V. 5. **So Jonah**, still smarting under the displeasure which he felt, **went out of the city and sat on the east side of the city**, choosing a place in its immediate neighborhood, **and there made him a booth**, a temporary hut of branches and leaves, **and sat under it in the shadow, till he might see what would become of the city**, whether the original judgment would not, after all, be carried out upon it; for the forty days named in his message had not yet elapsed. V. 6. **And the Lord God prepared a gourd**, the castor-oil plant, commonly called palm-crist, **and made it to come up over Jonah**, the plant growing up very rapidly, with its large leaves quickly casting a pleasant coolness, **that it might be a shadow over his head, to deliver him from his grief**, to cause his peevishness to disappear and thus to afford him some relief. **So Jonah was exceeding glad of the gourd**, he enjoyed the shadow offered by the green plant. V. 7. **But God**, intending to teach Jonah a further lesson, **prepared a worm**, appointing it to that end, **when the morning rose the next day**, at the breaking of the dawn, **and it smote the gourd that it withered**, for it is a peculiarity of the castor-oil plant that it fades readily when injured. V. 8. **And it came to pass, when the sun did arise, that God prepared a vehement east wind**, blowing with a sultry heat; **and the sun beat upon the head of Jonah that he fainted**, overcome with the heat, **and wished in himself to die**, the reaction once more being rapid and furious, **and said, It is better for me to die than to live**, namely, in such circumstances, with everything combining to make life unpleasant. V. 9. **And God**, taking this opportunity to drive home His lesson, **said to Jonah, Doest thou well to be angry for the gourd? And he said**, with a sudden flare of bitterness, **I do well to be angry, even unto death.** V. 10. **Then said the Lord, Thou hast had pity on the gourd, for the which thou hast not labored**, which had cost him no toil to rear, **neither madest it grow**, Jonah not being obliged so much as to water it; **which came up in a night and perished in a night**, being, as the Hebrew has it, the son of a night, of only a night's duration; v. 11. **and should not I spare Nineveh, that great city, wherein there are more than sixscore thousand persons that cannot discern between their right hand and their left hand**, that is, 120,000 infants, who could not be accused of any particular wrong-doing, **and also much cattle?** This argument of Jehovah, in exposing the selfishness of the prophet, was at the same time sufficient to silence him, as he stood rebuked before this exhibit of God's mercy. Moreover, the tidings which Jonah was able to bring back to his countrymen was a most emphatic call to repentance, as Jesus brings out in His reference to the repentance of the Ninevites. Israel failed to learn the lesson and therefore was cast out of its land. All the more is it necessary for us to consider the sign of the prophet Jonah and to cling to the confession of Him who could say of Himself, "Behold, here is more than Jonah!"

THE BOOK OF THE PROPHET MICAH.

INTRODUCTION.

The prophet Micah ("Who is like Jehovah?") was a native of Moresheth, near Gath, a small town about twenty miles southwest of Jerusalem, and therefore was known as the Morasthite. His prophetic activity extended through all or parts of the reigns of Jotham, Ahaz, and Hezekiah, kings of Judah, during the second half of the eighth century before Christ. He was therefore a contemporary of Isaiah and Hosea. Like the former prophet, he prophesied chiefly in Jerusalem, against the southern kingdom, but the northern kingdom is also included.

The prophecy of Micah agrees with the conditions under which he labored. He witnessed a gradual falling away from the worship of the one true God, especially under Ahaz, and even Hezekiah experienced great difficulty in introducing the reforms which he knew to be necessary. The conditions in the northern kingdom were even worse. At the same time, Assyria was developing as a world-power, and both kingdoms made the bad mistake of calling upon the foreign power for assistance. Thus the history of Micah's time is a history of a gradual decay, and it was one of the prophet's objects to stem the tide of destruction. For that reason his message abounds in rebukes of the idolatrous people, of the greed of those in power, of the unrighteousness of the judges, and of the lying spirit of the false prophets. However, after the judgment has been executed, the Lord's people are to be rescued, their full deliverance being accomplished through the coming of Messiah, to whose coming the true believers ever looked forward.

The Book of Micah is readily divisible into three parts, the first, chaps. 1 and 2, containing a call to repentance addressed to Israel and to Judah, the second, chapters 3 to 5, a rebuke of the cruel heads and princes of the people and of the false prophets, together with promises of the Messiah and of the spiritual glory of His Church, and the third, chapters 6 and 7, a recital of the Lord's controversy with His people, of the nation's moral corruption, and of the renewal of God's former mercies. "A summary of the contents of Micah's prophecies clearly indicates that this prophet, in the certainty and clearness of his Messianic prophecy, as well as in the power and energy exhibited by him in combating the sins and vices of his people, does not rank beneath his contemporary Isaiah, while the main point of difference consists in this, that Micah raises his voice against the religious and moral corruption of the people's rulers only and is not concerned with the political side of their machinations." [1]

1) Cp. Fuerbringer, *Einleitung in das Alte Testament*, 87. 88; *Concordia Bible Class*, June, 1919, 86. 87.

CHAPTER 1.

The Judgment upon Samaria and Judah.

EPHRAIM'S DESTRUCTION THREATENED. — V. 1. **The word of the Lord that came to Micah, the Morasthite, in the days of Jotham, Ahaz, and Hezekiah, kings of Judah, which he saw concerning Samaria and Jerusalem,** the two capitals being named as representative of the respective nations. V. 2. **Hear, all ye people,** cp. 1 Kings 22, 28; **hearken, O earth, and all that therein is,** cp. Is. 1, 2; **and let the Lord God be witness against you,** in testifying to their transgressions, **the Lord from His holy temple,** that is, from heaven; cp. Ps. 11, 4. V. 3. **For, behold, the Lord cometh forth out of His place,** as one getting ready to execute His vengeance, **and will come down and tread upon the high places of the earth,** on the mountains, as the places where He has revealed Himself to His people in more than one instance. V. 4. **And the mountains shall be molten under Him,** dissolving before His almighty power, **and the valleys shall be cleft,** cleaving asunder before His majesty, **as wax before the fire and as the waters that are poured down a steep place,** tearing down the abysses and causing a general dissolution of the entire surface of the earth. V. 5. **For the transgression of Jacob is all this,** as a due recompense for the wickedness of the covenant people, **and for the sins of the house of Israel. What is the transgression of Jacob? Is it not Samaria?** The sin of idolatry had reached such a climax in Samaria that it was part and parcel of the life of the people. **And what are the high places of Judah? Are they not Jerusalem?** The inhabitants of Jerusalem had also become so guilty of idolatry that its hills were entirely devoted to the worship of idols. V. 6. **Therefore I will make Samaria as an heap of the field,** as ruins that fall into dust and finally become a part of the soil, **and as plantings of a vineyard,** that is, places where vineyards may be planted; **and I will pour down the stones thereof,** those which King Omri had used in building the city, **into the valley, and I will discover,** lay bare, **the foun-**

dations thereof, destroying it to the very ground. V. 7. **And all the graven images thereof shall be beaten to pieces and all the hires thereof,** namely, those of spiritual harlotry, the consecrated offerings placed on the idol altars, **shall be burned with the fire, and all the idols thereof will I lay desolate,** making them a wilderness; **for she gathered it of the hire of an harlot,** by her spiritual adultery, **and they shall return to the hire of an harlot,** for the rich treasures were taken away by the enemies and devoted to their own idols. The vanity of false worship, also in this respect, seems rarely to strike the consciousness of idolaters.

LAMENTATION OVER JUDAH'S CHASTISEMENT. V. 8. **Therefore,** on account of the calamity which would strike Samaria and Judah, **I will wail and howl,** in a most bitter and mournful cry, **I will go stripped and naked,** robbed by the enemies and deprived of his upper garment, that is, in the condition of a captive; **I will make a wailing like the dragons,** like the jackals of the desert, **and mourning as the owls,** like ostriches crying in pain. Cp. Job 30, 29. V. 9. **For her wound is incurable,** deadly her strokes, **for it is come unto Judah,** the territory which harbored the Sanctuary of the Lord being included in the general ruin; **he is come unto the gate of My people,** to the place where the solemn assemblies of Jehovah were held, **even to Jerusalem.** V. 10. **Declare ye it not in Gath,** one of the chief cities of the Philistines, **weep ye not at all,** lest the message cause these enemies to rejoice; **in the house of Aphrah roll thyself in the dust,** literally, "in Beth-leaphra I wallow in the dust," for such scattering of dust was a sign of deep grief. Throughout this paragraph the prophet, in the Hebrew, uses puns, for Gath means "announcement" and Ophra "dust-house." V. 11. **Pass ye away, thou inhabitant of Saphir** (fair-view), **having thy shame naked,** in shameful nakedness, also robbed by the enemy; **the inhabitant of Zaanan** (outlet) **came not forth in the mourning of Beth-ezel; he shall receive of you his standing,** rather, "not has gone out the inhabitant of Zaanan," since she did not have the courage to face the enemy in the open field, "the mourning of Beth-haezel [house of separation] takes you away from its standing-place"; for its inhabitants would not permit the Jews to seek shelter behind its walls. V. 12. **For the inhabitants of Maroth** (bitterness) **waited carefully for good,** being anxiously and bitterly concerned about it, writhing in grief and pain on account of her lost prosperity; **but evil came down from the Lord unto the gate of Jerusalem.** But while all these towns were in the neighborhood of Jerusalem, the prophet next shows that the punishment would not be confined to the immediate neighborhood of the capital. V. 13. **O thou inhabitant of Lachish,** a fortified city in the plain toward the southwest, **bind the chariot to the swift beast,** to the fastest horses, namely, to escape the impending punishment; **she is the beginning of the sin to the daughter of Zion, for the transgressions of Israel were found in thee,** she was the first city of Judah to introduce the idol-worship of the northern kingdom. V. 14. **Therefore shalt thou give presents to Moresheth-gath** (the betrothed of Gath), the daughter of Zion being obliged to dismiss or release this city to the enemy, like the gift of a marriage portion; **the houses of Achzib** (deception) **shall be a lie to the kings of Israel,** a deceitful brook, which offers no refreshment to the thirsty wanderer; just so the city would slip from the grasp of the kings of Judah (the southern kingdom being meant in this instance), so that it would no longer be in their possession. V. 15. **Yet will I bring an heir unto thee, O inhabitant of Mareshah** (town of inheritance), for Israel had been the heir obtaining it from the Canaanites, and the enemy would now be the heir receiving it from the people of Judah; **he shall come unto Adullam, the glory of Israel,** rather, "even unto Adullam will the nobility of Israel come," to hide themselves in the cave in which David once sought refuge from Saul. Cp. 1 Sam. 22, 1. V. 16. **Make thee bald,** Zion as the mother of the nation being addressed, **and poll thee,** shearing her head, **for thy delicate children,** in deep grief and sorrowful lamentation; **enlarge thy baldness as the eagle,** the griffin vulture of the Orient, the entire forepart of whose head is without feathers; **for they are gone into captivity from thee.** The entire paragraph is a powerful and vivid description of the overthrow of the land by the armies of the invaders, which would be sent to punish the transgression of Judah.

CHAPTER 2.

The Wickedness, the Punishment, and the Restoration of Israel.

DENUNCIATION OF THE PREVALENT EVILS. — V. 1. **Woe to them that devise iniquity,** not on a sudden impulse, but with deliberate planning, **and work evil upon their beds!** using even the night-time to hatch out further schemes of wickedness. **When the morning is light,** as soon as the day dawns, **they practise it, because it is in the power of their hand,** or, "their hand is as a god"; they know no higher authority, they recognize no other power but that of their arm; they think they have a right to do what they please.

V. 2. **And they covet fields,** the property and inheritance of others, **and take them by violence,** seizing them as it suits their fancy, **and houses, and take them away,** oppressing the poor with a show of right. **So they oppress,** overwhelm and put to their own use, **a man and his house, even a man and his heritage,** which by the Law of God was to remain in the possession of his family. Cp. Ex. 20, 14. 17; Deut. 5, 18. V. 3. **Therefore, thus saith the Lord, Behold, against this family,** upon this generation of evil-doers, **do I devise an evil,** He, in turn, planning how He may punish them adequately with a severe judgment, **from which ye shall not remove your necks,** like a yoke which may not be shaken off no matter how heavy it presses; **neither shall ye go haughtily,** walking and behaving themselves in lofty pride; **for this time is evil,** in which depression of spirits and gloomy silence would come upon the members of the nation on account of the yoke of oppression laid upon them by the conquest of their country and the distress of the exile. V. 4. **In that day shall one take up a parable against you,** the enemies inventing bywords and mocking jingles, **and lament with a doleful lamentation,** for the mocking song of the enemies would be a mournful dirge in the mouths of the children of Israel, **and say, We be utterly spoiled,** completely destroyed! **He hath changed the portion of my people,** Jehovah Himself permitting the heathen to take possession of it; **how hath He removed it from me!** so that it was no longer in Israel's possession. **Turning away, He hath divided our fields,** dealing out the portions to the invaders. V. 5. **Therefore thou shalt have none that shall cast a cord by lot in the congregation of the Lord,** to cast a measuring-line on a lot of ground in the assembly of Jehovah, for the possessions of the children of Israel belonged to them only as long as they remained faithful to the God of the covenant and would be taken away when they became unfaithful. V. 6. **Prophesy not, say they to them that prophesy,** literally, "Drop not," or, "drivel not, they drivel," almost like the American slang, "Dry up! they drivel," in speaking to the true prophets in a silly fashion. **They shall not prophesy to them that they shall not take shame,** that is: If the prophecy, which the apostate Jews regarded as drivel, would not continue, then there would be no chance for them to escape the shame which would come upon the entire nation by the conquest of the enemies. The unbelievers to this day refuse to realize that the very preaching which they consider drivel and rot is the one means of saving them from the impending Judgment.

EXPULSION OF THE LEADERS AND RESTORATION OF THE LORD'S PEOPLE. — V. 7. **O thou that art named the house of Jacob,** the people who still considered themselves the covenant nation, **is the Spirit of the Lord straitened,** impatient? Did He not exercise patience and long-suffering? **Are these His doings?** Are the impending punishments coming because He delights in them, because He is vindictive? **Do not My words do good to him that walketh uprightly?** Is He not always ready to show goodness to those who conduct themselves in accordance with His righteous and holy will? The guilt, therefore, is entirely on the part of the people. V. 8. **Even of late,** in fact, yesterday, **My people is risen up as an enemy,** taking an open stand against Jehovah. And this hostility is openly shown. **Ye pull off the robe with the garment,** stripping off the mantle or upper garment, **from them that pass by securely,** considering themselves safe from robbery and violence, **as men averse from war,** that is, from peaceable people, such as seek no quarrel with any one. V. 9. **The women of My people,** the unprotected widows, **have ye cast out from their pleasant houses,** the houses of their delight, to which they were attached by the memory of their wedded love; **from their children have ye taken away My glory,** the ornament or gift which He has given them, **forever,** namely, by depriving them of their dress and of their rightful property. Cp. Ex. 22, 25. V. 10. **Arise ye and depart!** into the exile which the enemies would force upon them; **for this is not your rest,** they would not be permitted to remain in Canaan; **because it is polluted, it shall destroy you, even with a sore destruction,** or, "on account of the corruption which brings destruction, and that a most powerful destruction." Such prophecies, setting forth the depth of the nation's corruption, are, of course, very unwelcome to the wicked leaders. V. 11. **If a man walking in the spirit and falsehood,** in vanity and falsehood, namely, in preaching his own ideas, **do lie, saying, I will prophesy unto thee of wine and of strong drink,** that is, of the enjoyment of this present life, **he shall even be the prophet of this people,** he would meet with the approval of their leaders and those who desired a cover for their lives of luxury and dissipation. But in the very midst of this denunciation the prophet places a wonderful promise of the restoration of the Lord's people in the Messianic era. V. 12. **I will surely assemble, O Jacob, all of thee,** all those whom He intended as members of His congregation; **I will surely gather the remnant of Israel,** collecting the believers from all the nations of the earth; **I will put them together,** in one fold, John 10, 16, **as the sheep of Bozrah,** the rich meadowland east of Jordan, **as the flock in the midst of the fold,** secure from the attack of the enemies. **They shall make great noise by reason of the multitude of men,** surging with their great numbers. V. 13. **The breaker is come up before them,** rather, "There will go up before them He that breaketh through," their powerful Champion; **they have broken up**, rather, "they break up," **and have passed through the gate**, passing into the gate of the Lord's Church, **and are gone out by it**, having free access to the throne of grace; **and their King**, Messiah Himself, **shall pass before them and the Lord on the head of them**, leading them through all the vicissitudes of this life to the promised life of eternity. While men are clamoring for a gospel which will suit their fleshly lusts and desires, all true preachers will continue to proclaim sin and grace, especially the salvation and the victory of the Messiah, Jesus Christ.

CHAPTER 3.

The Sins of the Rulers and the Desolation of Zion.

Also in this chapter the discourse is directed to the nobility of the people, who abused the authority of their high official station by oppressing the poor and abandoning the way of justice. V. 1. **And I said, Hear, I pray you, O heads of Jacob**, the leading men of the nation, **and ye princes of the house of Israel**, in whose hands was the administration of justice: **Is it not for you to know judgment?** to give heed to that which is right and just. V. 2. **Who hate the good and love the evil**, doing just the opposite of that which their station required of them; **who pluck off their skin from off them**, as though flaying the children of their people, **and their flesh from off their bones**, robbing them of their most precious possessions, v. 3. **who also eat the flesh of My people**, the address here turning to the third person, since the princes, as it were, turned away from the message intended to call them to repentance, **and flay their skin from off them; and they break their bones and chop them in pieces, as for the pot, and as flesh within the caldron.** The prophet thus, with the emphasis of detail, pictures the excess of cruelty which the rulers of the people were practising. V. 4. **Then shall they**, the guilty ones, **cry unto the Lord, but He will not hear them**, namely, at the time of the revelation of His wrath; **He will even hide His face from them at that time**, refusing to pay the slightest attention to their distress, **as they have behaved themselves ill in their doings**, and were thus fully ripe for the judgment. V. 5. **Thus saith the Lord concerning the prophets**, namely, the false prophets, who presumed to speak in the name of the Lord without being sent, **that make My people err**, leading them astray, **that bite with their teeth and cry, Peace!** that is, who, if they have anything to bite with their teeth, when they receive a sufficient amount of bribe money, proclaim peace, prophesying as it pleases the heart of men; **and he that putteth not into their mouths**, who refuses to pay them bribe money, **they even prepare war against him**, solemnly declaring warfare as for the honor of God. V. 6. **Therefore night shall be unto you that ye shall not have a vision**, being excluded from the light granted by the Spirit of God; **and it shall be dark unto you that ye shall not divine**, be granted no revelation of the future; **and the sun shall go down over the prophets**, namely, the sun of salvation and good fortune, **and the day shall be dark over them**, with the darkness of the Day of Judgment. V. 7. **Then shall the seers be ashamed**, be disgraced on account of the fact that their predictions are not fulfilled, **and the diviners confounded**, blushing with shame on account of their miserable failures in trying to uncover the future; **yea, they shall all cover their lips**, literally, "their beard," their face up to the nostrils, as a sign of shame; **for there is no answer of God**, He refuses to vouchsafe them any kind of information that might establish their false claims. V. 8. **But, truly, I am full of power by the Spirit of the Lord**, Micah here placing his own person in opposition to the false prophets, **and of judgment**, the divine right which he was sent to proclaim, **and of might**, of a virile and unflinching power, **to declare unto Jacob his transgression and to Israel his sin**, uttering the cry to repentance without fear and favor. He immediately acts in accordance with this statement. V. 9. **Hear this, I pray you, ye heads of the house of Jacob and princes of the house of Israel**, the very leaders whose wickedness had been described in the first part of the chapter, **that abhor judgment**, everything that was right and good, **and pervert all equity**, making crooked that which should have been kept straight. V. 10. **They build up Zion with blood**, with blood-guiltiness, **and Jerusalem with iniquity**, caring only for gain and bloodshed in building their stately mansions, their wealth being obtained by the condemnation and murder of the innocent. V. 11. **The heads thereof judge for reward**, being influenced in their decisions by bribe money, **and the priests thereof teach for hire**, for additional fees, although the Law required that they decide controversies without pay, **and the prophets thereof divine for money**, their oracles being fashioned according to the presents which men gave them; **yet will they lean upon the Lord**, insisting that they were performing the work of their office by authority of Jehovah, as of the God living in the midst of His people, **and say, Is not the Lord among us?** namely, with His power and protection. **None evil can come upon**

us, all this being said with a great show of piety. V. 12. **Therefore shall Zion for your sake,** on account of their wickedness in making the Lord's Temple a den of murderers, **be plowed as a field,** the king's quarter turned into tillable soil, **and Jerusalem,** the rest of the city, **shall become heaps,** piles of broken stones, **and the mountain of the house,** that is, of the Temple, **as the high places of the forest,** being overgrown with brush and trees. It is a vivid description of the ruin which comes upon the enemies of the Lord.

CHAPTER 4.

The Glory, Peace, and Victory of the Church.

THE GLORY OF THE HOUSE OF THE LORD. — V. 1. **But in the last days,** in the great Messianic period, **it shall come to pass that the mountain of the house of the Lord,** of old typical of the Church of the true God, **shall be established in the top of the mountains,** the ideal Zion being elevated above all else in the world, cp. Is. 2, 17; 2 Cor. 10, 5, **and it shall be exalted above the hills,** visible before the eyes of all men; **and people shall flow unto it,** members of all the nations of the world being added to the communion of saints. V. 2. **And many nations shall come,** namely, in the representatives whom the Lord would choose and call, **and say, Come and let us go up to the mountain of the Lord,** the place where salvation is proclaimed, **and to the house of the God of Jacob,** the Church of the Messiah; **and He will teach us of His ways,** the one way of deliverance and sanctification, **and we will walk in His paths,** in agreement with the revealed truth concerning the sanctification of the Lord's people; **for the Law,** as the revelation of the holy and righteous will of God, **shall go forth of Zion and the Word of the Lord,** particularly in the revelation of the way of salvation, **from Jerusalem,** the proclamation of the Word, in speaking of sin and grace, being in the hands of the Church. V. 3. **And He,** the God of the covenant, **shall judge among many people,** teaching them true justice in accordance with His will, **and rebuke strong nations afar off,** to make them cease their enmity against Him; **and they shall beat their swords into plowshares and their spears into pruning-hooks,** not in an earthly, temporal, millennial peace of which men are dreaming from time to time, but in the spiritual peace in Him who is our Peace, Eph. 2, 14, in whom there is truly peace on earth; **nation shall not lift up a sword against nation, neither shall they learn war any more,** this being said of the inner peace and harmony of the Church of Christ. Cp. John 17, 21. V. 4. **But they shall sit every man under his vine and under his fig-tree,** in the enjoyment of the rich blessings of the New Testment; **and none shall make them afraid,** all the enemies of mankind having been overcome by the power of the Messiah; **for the mouth of the Lord of hosts hath spoken it,** His solemn declaration being the consolation of all believers until the end of time. V. 5. **For all people,** all those concerned in this prophecy, **will walk every one in the name of his God,** in the power of the one true God in whom he believes, whose essence is thus made known, **and we will walk in the name of the Lord, our God, forever and ever,** with a full trust in His supporting strength and powerful protection, which turns aside all the efforts of the enemies to disturb the inner peace of the Church. V. 6. **In that day,** in the great Messianic period, **saith the Lord, will I assemble her that halteth,** all those who are in distress, suffering with the misery of this world, **and I will gather her that is driven out,** those who are dispersed among the nations, **and her that I have afflicted,** whom He has punished for their sins; v. 7. **and I will make her that halted a remnant,** the nucleus of His Church, **and her that was cast far off a strong nation,** those gathered from spiritual exile; **and the Lord shall reign over them in Mount Zion,** in His Church, **from henceforth even forever,** throughout all eternity. Thus this sketch, composed of bold figures taken from the general aspects of Judah's history, sets forth the glory of the Church of the New Testament, beginning here in time, and continuing through all eternity, as the Church Triumphant.

ZION ESTABLISHED THROUGHOUT THE EARTH. V. 8. **And thou, O tower of the flock,** the term being applied to a tower of refuge for flocks in time of danger, here as a fort from which the great King and Shepherd, the Messiah Himself, observes and guards His flock, **the stronghold of the daughter of Zion,** the impregnable palace of the Church of Christ, **unto thee shall it come, even the first dominion,** the glory of the New Testament Church being compared with that of the kingdom of Israel under its mightiest king; **the kingdom shall come to the daughter of Jerusalem.** Since the earthly Jerusalem is always at the foundation of the type, the vicissitudes and afflictions of the Jewish capital are made typical of the experiences of the Lord's people. V. 9. **Now, why dost thou cry out aloud?** at the approach of the Chaldean invasion. **Is there no king in thee?** no visible representative of the Messianic promises? **Is thy counselor perished?** this name also being applied to the reigning member of the house of David? **For pangs have taken thee as a woman in travail,** the true believers in Israel feeling the deepest grief and sorrow over the desolation of the kingdom. V. 10. **Be in pain and labor to bring forth, O daughter of Zion, like a woman in travail,** the catastrophe of the destruction of Jerusalem and of the exile of the people being imminent; **for now shalt thou go forth out of the city,** after it had been taken by the enemies, **and thou shalt dwell in the field, and thou shalt go even to Babylon,** being dragged into captivity; **there shalt thou be delivered,** namely, when Cyrus issued the decree setting the Jews free and thus laid the foundation upon which later arose the New Testament Church; **there the Lord shall redeem thee from the hand of thine enemies,** so that the people of the covenant would be restored to the Land of Promise, the land where the Messiah was to appear. V. 11. **Now also,** namely, at the time of Judah's deepest humiliation before and at the time of her exile, **many nations are gathered against thee,** in bold hostility, **that say, Let her be defiled, and let our eye look upon Zion,** namely, in malicious joy over her downfall. V. 12. **But they know not the thoughts of the Lord,** the object which He has in mind in thus dealing with His people, **neither understand they His counsel,** which intended to lead His people to repentance and to lay the foundation for a renewed Church in which the believing Jews were to be the nucleus; **for He shall gather them as the sheaves into the floor,** the enemies being heaped up for destruction in the Lord's judgment. V. 13. **Arise and thresh, O daughter of Zion,** according to the Oriental custom of having the sheaves threshed out on the open threshing-floor with the aid of oxen; **for I will make thine horn iron and I will make thy hoofs brass,** giving to His people a new and unconquerable strength; **and thou shalt beat in pieces many people,** not by victories of the flesh, but by those of the spirit; **and I will consecrate their gain,** what the enemies had gotten by robbery and plunder, **unto the Lord,** as devoted to Him, **and their substance,** all their possessions, **unto the Lord of the whole earth,** whom the heathen would eventually have to acknowledge as the one Ruler, even if they consistently refused to accept Him as the God of their salvation. Cp. Phil. 2, 11.

CHAPTER 5.

The Person and the Rule of Messiah.

Having described the conditions and circumstances under which the period of Messianic glory would be established, the prophet now turns to the direct prediction concerning the person and the work of the coming Redeemer. V. 1. **Now gather thyself in troops,** namely, in order to resist the enemy, **O daughter of troops,** Jerusalem herself being so designated as the type of the Church Militant; **he hath laid siege against us,** rather, impersonal, "siege is laid against us," by the enemies which never rest; **they shall smite the judge of Israel,** the ruler of the people, **with a rod upon the cheek,** for the Messianic period was preceded by Judah's deepest humiliation, when all the former glory was taken away from the nation. But at this time of the deepest humiliation of the Lord's people the greatest glory of all would come upon it. V. 2. **But thou, Bethlehem Ephratah,** the little city of Judah south of Jerusalem being addressed with impressive solemnity, **though thou be little among the thousands of Judah,** among the districts of the country containing a thousand families, the town being of little importance over against the mighty Jerusalem so near by, **yet out of thee shall He come forth unto Me that is to be Ruler in Israel,** the selection of the Messiah as the true King of Israel serving the Lord's plan of salvation, **whose goings forth have been from of old, from everlasting.** Thus the Father's will and purpose from eternity was made manifest in the coming of the Prince of Peace. And even as His outgoings were from eternity, since He is the everlasting Son of the Father, so His generation as man is from Bethlehem, for as a true human being He became subject to time and permitted Himself, as a rule, to be governed by the limitations of space as well. V. 3. **Therefore,** because Israel, the people of the Lord, is to be redeemed not by his own power, but by the gracious gift of the Messiah, **will He give them up,** the Lord giving the covenant nation into the hands of the enemy, **until the time that she which travaileth hath brought forth,** until the Messiah would have been born; **then the remnant of His brethren shall return unto the children of Israel,** for at that time the Lord would bring together from the various nations of the world those whom He intended to add to His true Israel, to His spiritual nation. The humiliation of the house of David and of Israel had been included in the plan of God, but the final result would be that the Messiah, like His ancestor David, would go forth from the humble city of Bethlehem. To this end it was necessary for the people to remain under the rule of the enemies. V. 4. **And He shall stand and feed,** both ruling and nourishing, as the Governor and Shepherd of His people, **in the strength of the Lord,** He Himself being the mighty God, Is. 9, 6, **in the majesty of the name of the Lord, His God,** which was com-

is the Lord, thy God? in the scornful question usually asked by the enemies of the Church. **Mine eyes shall behold her,** with quiet satisfaction; **now shall she be trodden down as the mire of the streets.** V. 11. **In the day that thy walls are to be built,** rather, "a day of building thy walls" (is coming), so the prophet assures the believing members of His people, those who were truly awaiting the Messiah's coming, **in that day shall the decree be far removed,** namely, the decree which fixed a sharp line of division between Israel and the heathen nations. V. 12. **In that day also He shall come even to thee,** the restored Zion, **from Assyria and from the fortified cities,** from the cities of Egypt, **and from the fortress,** namely, Egypt, **even to the river,** the Euphrates, to indicate all the countries lying between, **and from sea to sea, and from mountain to mountain,** from all the regions and countries of the earth, all those whom the Lord had chosen from the various countries of the world. Cp. Is. 19, 18—25. V. 13. **Notwithstanding the land shall be desolate,** the reference very likely being to the earthly Palestine, **because of them that dwell therein, for the fruit of their doings.** While the Land of Promise, which formerly flowed with milk and honey, has largely lost its fertility, the spiritual Zion, the Church of God, is built up by members added from all the nations of the earth.

THE PROPHET'S LAST SUPPLICATION. — V. 14. **Feed Thy people with Thy rod,** with a true shepherd's care, the staff being the mark of the shepherd, Zech. 11, 4 ff.; Ps. 23, 4, **the flock of Thine heritage,** the possession of Jehovah, **which dwell solitarily in the wood, in the midst of Carmel,** rather, "in the forest in the midst of Carmel let them feed," surrounded by the richest blessings; **let them feed in Bashan and Gilead,** whose rich meadows were proverbial in Israel, **as in the days of old,** when, under David, the kingdom enjoyed the fulness of material and spiritual prosperity. The Lord answers this plea with an assurance of His mercy, to be given in a larger measure than His people asked for. V. 15. **According to the days of thy coming out of the land of Egypt** when He overthrew the enemies with a mighty hand and revealed His goodness to Israel, **will I show unto him marvelous things,** His Church being given the wonders of His grace. V. 16. **The nations shall see and be confounded at all their might,** because all their vaunted power would be as nothing in the sight of the almighty God; **they shall lay their hands upon their mouth,** in reverent silence, in extreme astonishment, **their ears shall be deaf,** before the thunder of Jehovah's mighty deeds. V. 17. **They shall lick the dust like a serpent,** in deepest humiliation; **they shall move out of their holes like worms of the earth,** literally, "as those things that creep on the earth"; they shall tremble forth out of their hiding-places; **they shall be afraid of the Lord, our God,** approaching to Him with terror, **and shall fear because of thee.** With these words the prophet once more turns directly to Jehovah, addressing Him in words of praise. V. 18. **Who is a God like unto Thee, that pardoneth iniquity,** in the act of justification which is the basis of the work in His Church, **and passeth by the transgression of the remnant of His heritage?** in granting forgiveness to those who are His people in truth. Cp. Ex. 34, 6. 7. **He retaineth not His anger forever, because He delighteth in mercy,** His great acts of mercy being the outstanding feature of His work in His Church. V. 19. **He will turn again,** so the prophet assures the believers; **He will have compassion upon us, He will subdue our iniquities,** treading them down like enemies that rise up against the believers; **and Thou wilt cast all their sins into the depths of the sea,** so that they are covered over and can no more rise to condemn the Lord's people. V. 20. **Thou wilt perform the truth to Jacob and the mercy to Abraham,** as contained in the wonderful Messianic promises, **which Thou hast sworn unto our fathers from the days of old.** With this exalted hymn of praise Micah closes his book, speaking in a strain similar to that of Paul in Rom. 11, 33—36. We have here true Gospel-preaching, such as sustained the believers of the Old Testament in their eager watching for the time of the Messiah, to which we also may turn for comfort in the midst of the corruption of these last days of the world, knowing, however, that our salvation is nigh.

THE BOOK OF THE PROPHET NAHUM.

INTRODUCTION.

Concerning Nahum ("consolation," or "the consoler") we have only so much authentic information that we know he was a native of Elkosh, probably a village of Galilee. The period in which he prophesied may only approximately be fixed by the fact that he was active before the destruction of Nineveh in the year 606 B. C., but after the dissolution of the northern kingdom through the Assyrian hosts and after some serious visitation which struck the southern kingdom. The time of his activity may thus be placed either at the very end of the eighth century or in the first half of the seventh century before Christ. He seems to have been at that time a citizen of Judah, residing in Jerusalem. The object of Nahum's book was to bring his nation, representative of the spiritual Israel, comfort and strength over against the Assyrian world-power, which at that time had subdued Israel and assumed the sovereignty over Judah. The gist of the book is the Lord's announcement of Nineveh's total destruction, in accordance with which its conquest took place in the year 606 B. C.

The Book of Nahum evidently forms a well-ordered unit, which may be divided in agreement with its chapters. It sets forth the vengeance decided upon by the mighty and jealous God, the conquest and destruction of Nineveh as determined upon by the Lord, and the reason for the Lord's judgment, namely, the guilt and wickedness of the city and its inhabitants. The form of presentation is vivid and powerful, the style rhythmical, the language of classic beauty, with passages breathing a true fire of divine enthusiasm and power. The Messianic element is not entirely wanting, and the entire book supports the plan of God of preserving His people over against the oppression of the world-power.[1]

[1] Cp. Fuerbringer, *Einleitung in das Alte Testament*, 89.

CHAPTER 1.

The Divine Counsel Concerning the Judgment upon Nineveh.

God, who is at the same time the God of the covenant and the almighty Sovereign of the universe, states that He has fully decided to bring about the overthrow and destruction of Nineveh, as the enemy of His people. V. 1. **The burden of Nineveh,** the sentence bringing the threat of Jehovah against the wicked city. **The book of the vision of Nahum, the Elkoshite,** the term probably indicating that Nahum did not deliver his prophecy in person, but reduced it to writing at once. V. 2. **God is jealous, and the Lord revengeth,** or, "A God jealous and taking vengeance is Jehovah," as He had stated of old, Ex. 20, 5. **The Lord revengeth and is furious,** literally, "An Avenger is Jehovah and a Master of fury," terrible in His wrath. **The Lord will take vengeance on His adversaries,** His punishment sometimes being delayed, but always inevitable in coming, and **He reserveth wrath for His enemies,** for it is not weak indulgence that causes His delay in punishing, but an exhibition of His love and mercy, which would have all men to be saved and to come to the knowledge of the truth. V. 3. **The Lord is slow to anger,** long-suffering and patient over against wickedness of long standing, **and great in power,** His almighty strength becoming evident when He does strike, **and will not at all acquit the wicked,** those who have shown that they are guilty. **The Lord hath His way in the whirlwind and in the storm,** which are but instruments and exhibitions of His power, **and the clouds are the dust of His feet,** they are insignificant before Him, and He uses them as He pleases. V. 4. **He rebuketh the sea and maketh it dry,** as when He caused the Red Sea to part before the children of Israel, Ex. 14, 15, **and drieth up all the rivers,** since they all are subject to His directions; **Bashan,** the rich pasture-land east of Jordan, **languisheth, and Carmel,** the wooded slopes of the mountain overlooking the Mediterranean, **and the flower of Lebanon,** otherwise a symbol of rich fertility, **languisheth,** namely, when He withholds the moisture or bids the river go dry. V. 5. **The mountains quake at Him,** cp. Amos 8, 8, **and the hills melt,** as at the time of terrible earthquakes, **and the earth is burned at His presence, yea, the world, and all that dwell therein,** both men and the irrational brutes. V. 6. **Who can stand before His indignation?** before His wrath when it burns freely. **And who can abide in the fierceness of His anger?** Cp. Jer. 10, 10. **His fury is poured out like fire,** in a torrent consuming everything before it, Deut. 4, 24, **and the rocks are thrown down by Him.** Cp. Jer. 23, 29. But this wrath of God does not strike those who put their trust in Him. V. 7. **The Lord is good,** even in the midst of His judgments, **a stronghold in the day of trouble,** a refuge when distress and misery come upon the believers; **and He knoweth them that trust in Him,** He has that intimate knowledge of them, that peculiar insight into their needs which guarantees them His help. V. 8. **But with an overrunning flood,** a deluge which carries everything before it, **He will make an utter end of the place thereof,** so that Nineveh would cease to be a city and its very site be used for altogether different purposes, **and darkness shall pursue His enemies,** a figure of a complete desolation. V. 9. **What do ye imagine against the Lord?** Did the people of Judah think that Jehovah was not able to carry out His threat against Nineveh? **He will make an utter end; affliction shall not rise up the second time,** for the one blow on the part of the Lord would be quite sufficient, so that the affliction which Judah suffered on the part of Assyria would not arise twice. V. 10. **For while,** or though, **they be folden together as thorns,** braided together or entangled, **and while they are drunken as drunkards,** though they are drowned in their carousing, in their wine, so that it might seem that fire would not be able to reach them or to affect them seriously, **they shall be devoured as stubble fully dry.** The comparison shows the pride and the boldness which the Assyrians possessed, also in their idea that they were invincible. V. 11. **There is one come out of thee,** namely, Sennacherib or one of the other rulers who invaded Judah, **that imagineth evil against the Lord,** meditating and speaking in this sense, **a wicked counselor,** one who advised worthlessness, things that were foolish and brought no results. Cp. Is. 36, 14—20. V. 12. **Thus saith the Lord, Though they be quiet and likewise many,** no matter how tranquilly secure and how numerous they are, **yet thus shall they be cut down,** suddenly disappearing as though mowed down, **when he shall pass through,** rather, and he passes away, namely, the daring invader who had meditated evil against Jehovah. **Though I have afflicted thee,** bending Judah down to the ground, **I will afflict thee no more,** this being a source of consolation to the Lord's people. V. 13. **For now will I break his yoke from off thee and will burst thy bonds,** which the proud invader had laid upon Judah, **in sunder.** V. 14. **And the Lord hath given a commandment concerning thee that no more of thy name be sown,** that the dynasty of the Assyrian kings should become extinct; **out of the house of thy gods will I cut off the graven image and the molten image,** in whom the Assyrians placed their trust; **I will make thy grave, for thou art vile,** morally unworthy, no longer fit to live and to be in power. Thus the destruction of the power of Assyria was clearly set forth, in outlines that could not be misunderstood.

CHAPTER 2.

(Chapter 1, 15—2, 13.)

The Conquest, Plundering, and Destruction of Nineveh.

The conquerors of Nineveh would be Jehovah's instruments, who would effect the destruction of the city with all its vaunted glory. V. 15. **Behold upon the mountains the feet of him that bringeth good tidings,** of the messenger of joy hastening forward to bring the good news, **that publisheth peace,** announcing to Judah the overthrow of the enemies. **O Judah, keep thy solemn feasts,** resuming their celebration especially at this time, when the deliverance of the Lord's people from violence and oppression constituted a further incentive for joy and thanksgiving, **perform thy vows,** those made in anticipation of this deliverance; **for the wicked shall no more pass through thee, he is utterly cut off.** The use of Is. 52, 7 in this connection is very clear, and Luther is undoubtedly right in finding here a Messianic allusion, especially since Assyria, as the great world-power, was the type of the antichristian forces which try to overthrow the Church of God. Chapter 2, 1. **He that dasheth in pieces,** the Babylonian invader, **is come up before thy face,** appearing before the walls of Nineveh. **Keep the munition,** rather, "Guard the fortress!" in an effort to withstand the foe; **watch the way,** having spies out on all the roads leading to the city; **make thy loins strong,** as a warrior preparing for battle; **fortify thy power mightily.** All this detailed description is given to emphasize the futility of these preparations. V. 2. **For the Lord hath turned away the excellency of Jacob,** Jehovah being on the side of the invading army, and He intends to restore the glory of His people, **as the excellency of Israel,** when the covenant nation was at the height of its glory; **for the emptiers have emptied them out,** or, "plunderers have plundered them," **and marred their vine-branches,** outrageously destroying the land and outraging its inhabitants, so that the Lord felt obliged to avenge this indignity. V. 3. **The shield of His mighty men,** of the heroes commissioned by the Lord to execute His punishment, **is made red,** all shining for the battle, **the valiant men are in scarlet,** their war-clothes being made of this color; **the chariots shall be with flaming torches in the day of his preparation,** blazing with their iron equipments, **and the fir-trees shall be terribly shaken,** the spears made of cypresses are brandished. V. 4. **The chariots shall rage in**

the streets, as they are driven furiously in the attack, **they shall jostle one against another in the broad ways,** running to and fro in the market-places or squares of Nineveh, all confused by the attack of the enemy; **they shall seem like torches,** as the light struck the steel ornaments of the chariots, **they shall run like the lightnings,** namely, as lightning plays in blinding flashes. V. 5. **He shall recount his worthies,** the Assyrian king remembering, and counting on, his heroes; **they shall stumble in their walk,** all confused and uncertain in their effort to reach the point where the attack is launched against the city; **they shall make haste to the wall thereof, and the defense shall be prepared.** The entire paragraph pictures the haste and confusion which takes hold upon the citizens and the soldiers of a city which has been too secure and now finds itself surrounded by a host of enemies. V. 6. **The gates of the rivers shall be opened,** the reference being to some natural or artificial inundation of the city which helped in its destruction, **and the palace shall be dissolved,** its inmates being overcome with terror and losing all semblance of careful thinking and planning. V. 7. **And Huzzab shall be led away captive,** literally, "It is determined," by God; "she is made bare," namely, Nineveh, "like a ravished woman, and carried away." **She shall be brought up, and her maids shall lead her,** the inhabitants of the city being so regarded, **as with the voice of doves,** with mournful cries, **taboring upon their breasts,** beating upon them as though they were tabrets. V. 8. **But Nineveh is of old like a pool of water,** a term expressing her great population and prosperity; **yet they shall flee away,** her great population leaving her to her fate. **Stand, stand! shall they cry,** in an attempt to stop the heedless rush; **but none shall look back,** refusing to return to the ravished city. V. 9. **Take ye the spoil of silver,** so the victors are admonished, **take the spoil of gold! For there is none end of the store and glory out of all the pleasant furniture,** of the various rich treasures with which the palaces of the city were filled. V. 10. **She is empty and void and waste,** literally, "emptiness and being emptied out and desolation!" **and the heart melteth,** in utter discouragement, **and the knees smite together,** in the terror which cannot control itself, **and much pain is in all loins,** Is. 21, 3, **and the faces of them all gather blackness,** all of them pale with fear. Thus the mighty city would be destroyed with all its rich treasures. V. 11. **Where is the dwelling of the lions and the feeding-place of the young lions,** for the Assyrians liked to compare themselves with the king of beasts, **where the lion, even the old lion, walked and the lion's whelp, and none made them afraid?** none of the nations, in the early days, daring to disturb the Assyrians in their possession of the land. V. 12. **The lion did tear in pieces enough for his whelps,** as much as his young ones desired, **and strangled for his lionesses and filled his holes,** the dens occupied by him, **with prey and his dens with ravin,** his lurking-places with spoil. Even so the kings of Assyria heaped up treasures taken from every part of the world for the use of the inhabitants of Nineveh. V. 13. **Behold, I am against thee, saith the Lord of hosts,** the ruler of the heavenly armies, **and I will burn her chariots in the smoke,** so that all her war material goes up in smoke, **and the sword shall devour thy young lions,** the mighty men of the city; **and I will cut off thy prey from the earth, and the voice of thy messengers shall no more be heard,** as they boasted of the might and prowess of Assyria and Nineveh. God has ways of subduing even the mightiest enemies, no matter how mightily they rise up in their own conceit.

CHAPTER 3.

The Miserable Ruin of Nineveh.

Jehovah now shows that the cause of Nineveh's destruction is its wickedness, and that for this reason the city is bound to submit to the sentence which has been pronounced upon her. V. 1. **Woe to the bloody city,** or, "O city of blood, of blood-guiltiness!" **It is all full of lies and robbery,** so that deceit, violence, and extortion were the order of the day; **the prey departeth not,** robbery goes on without ceasing; v. 2. **the noise of a whip,** its sharp crack heard as the horses are urged forward in battle, **and the noise of the rattling of the wheels and of the prancing horses and of the jumping chariots,** bounding along over the ground, as the horses broke into a gallop. V. 3. **The horseman lifteth up,** rather, "horsemen rearing," as they directed their mounts to charge, **both the bright sword and the glittering spear,** or, "the flame of the sword and the lightning of the lance"; **and there is a multitude of slain,** or of wounded, **and a great number of carcasses,** a wall of corpses heaped up; **and there is none end of their corpses; they,** the invading enemies, **stumble upon their corpses,** unable to pick their way forward because the entire battle-field is strewn with dead; v. 4. **because of the multitude of the whoredoms,** the acts of idolatry and wickedness, **of the well-favored harlot, the mistress of witchcrafts,** idolatry and witchcraft being the special marks of the heathen character, **that selleth nations through her**

whoredoms, with her hypocritical friendship and feigned interest, **and families,** smaller tribes, **through her witchcrafts,** namely, by her political schemes and intrigues. For this reason the Lord will plunge Nineveh into a shameful destruction. V. 5. **Behold, I am against thee, saith the Lord of hosts, and I will discover thy skirts upon thy face,** uncover them and throw them up so high that they would reach over her face, **and I will show the nations thy nakedness,** as that of a lewd woman, **and the kingdoms thy shame,** in bringing the utmost disgrace upon Nineveh. V. 6. **And I will cast abominable filth upon thee,** as an expression of the utmost disgust and loathing, **and make thee vile,** an object of disgrace, **and will set thee as a gazing-stock,** upon which men would look with contempt and derision. V. 7. **And it shall come to pass that all they that look upon thee shall flee from thee,** with a feeling of deepest revulsion, **and say, Nineveh is laid waste; who will bemoan her? Whence shall I seek comforters for thee?** so the prophet interjects his question. No one would have the slightest sympathy with the stricken city, because she had so thoroughly deserved her punishment. V. 8. **Art thou better than populous No,** that is, No-Amon, Thebes, the capital of Upper Egypt, **that was situate among the rivers, that had the waters round about it,** namely, in the great irrigation canals, **whose rampart was the sea, and her wall was from the sea?** the great expanse of the Nile. V. 9. **Ethiopia and Egypt,** the countries along the Nile, **were her strength, and it was infinite; Put and Lubim,** the countries to the west, along the Mediterranean Sea, **were thy helpers,** Thebes itself being addressed in the excitement of the orator. V. 10. **Yet,** in spite of all her own power and the strength of her allies, **was she carried away, she went into captivity,** after a conquest by Sargon, Esarhaddon, or Tir-haqua; **her young children also were dashed in pieces at the top,** that is, at the corners, **of all the streets; and they cast lots for her honorable men,** the conquerors dividing them among themselves by lot, as slaves, **and all her great men were bound in chains.** V. 11. **Thou also,** namely, Nineveh, **shalt be drunken,** upon receiving the cup of God's fury in judgment; **thou shalt be hid,** covered over, as though she had never existed; **thou also shalt seek strength because of the enemy,** protection or refuge before the advancing enemy, without being able to find it. V. 12. **All thy strongholds,** the fortresses and castles of the Assyrian country, **shall be like fig-trees with the first-ripe figs,** considered a special delicacy; **if they be shaken, they shall even fall into the mouth of the eater,** they would readily be taken by the invading enemy. V. 13. **Behold, thy people in the midst of thee are women,** without strength and courage for the battle; **the gates of thy land shall be set wide open,** the Lord making the land easy of access to the invaders, **unto thine enemies; the fire shall devour thy bars,** those which held the great gates of the city shut. V. 14. **Draw thee waters for the siege,** that needed for a long period of siege of the enemies; **fortify thy strongholds,** strengthening the forts; **go into clay,** for making bricks, **and tread the mortar,** in order to fashion bricks for the bulwarks; **make strong the brick-kiln,** in order to burn the bricks. V. 15. **There shall the fire devour thee,** in the very midst of these preparations; **the sword shall cut thee off, it shall eat thee up like the canker-worm,** as locusts destroy; **make thyself many as the canker-worm,** like devouring insects; **make thyself many as the locusts.** The thought is this: The fire and the sword, like locusts devouring everything before them, would consume Nineveh, even though the city with its masses of houses and inhabitants would resemble a swarm of locusts. V. 16. **Thou hast multiplied thy merchants above the stars of heaven,** the number of its people engaged in commercial pursuits of every kind being very great; **the canker-worm spoileth,** literally, "the licking locusts enter to plunder," **and fleeth away,** the military might of Assyria being powerless before the armies of the invaders. V. 17. **Thy crowned,** the vassal princes, **are as the locusts, and thy captains,** the commanders of her armies, **as the great grasshoppers, which camp in the hedges in the cold day,** too chilled to use their wings; **but when the sun ariseth, they flee away, and their place is not known where they are.** In a similar way the Assyrian army would vanish from sight; it would not be in evidence to withstand the invaders. V. 18. **Thy shepherds slumber, O king of Assyria,** that is, the mighty ones, the leaders of the people, were resting in a false security; **thy nobles shall dwell in the dust,** rather, "thy powerful ones are lying still," not making a move to defend their country; **thy people is scattered upon the mountains, and no man gathereth them,** no one assumes the leadership over them, and so their identity as an Assyrian nation is lost. V. 19. **There is no healing of thy bruise,** of the fracture which the Lord had inflicted; **thy wound is grievous,** the stroke or ruin being deadly; **all that hear the bruit,** the report, **of thee shall clap the hands over thee,** in a gesture of joy over the downfall of the oppressor; **for upon whom hath not thy wickedness passed continually?** The Lord indeed used Assyria as His scourge, but He, at the same time, wanted Assyria to acknowledge His sovereignty. When Nineveh and the entire country, therefore, persisted in its wickedness, His punishment came upon the land with crushing force.

THE BOOK OF THE PROPHET HABAKKUK.

INTRODUCTION.

The prophet Habakkuk ("embrace," "one who loves most dearly and sincerely") was a member of the tribe of Judah and apparently a Levite, who was thoroughly familiar with the ancient psalms and the liturgy of the Jewish Church, who was called by God to be His prophet. Otherwise nothing is known concerning his person, although some scholars have made various statements regarding his family and occupation. The period of his activity may be determined quite definitely by the contents of his prophecy, for he predicted the invasion of Judah by the Chaldeans, which took place in the year 606 B. C. At the same time, his apparent references to the reformation of the Temple cultus under Josiah make it probable that he prophesied some years before the first subjugation of Judah by the Babylonians, and it seems safe, therefore, to say that his chief activity falls in the third decade of the seventh century before Christ. He was contemporary of Zephaniah and of Jeremiah, both of whom use expressions similar to those found in his book.

The object of Habakkuk was to show Judah that the newly arisen power, the Chaldean monarchy, which even then was threatening the authority of the Assyrian supremacy, was destined to be a scourge of the southern kingdom. For in spite of the outward reformation under Josiah the inner corruption of the nation was becoming increasingly apparent, so that violence and oppression were the order of the day. Yet the trend of Habakkuk's prophecy was to bring comfort to the believers by a reference to the eventual redemption of the true Israel. In agreement with this general outline the book may be divided into three parts, the first part picturing the imminent, terrible punishment by the Chaldeans, the second containing the fivefold cry of woe upon the proud and idolatrous world-power, and the third offering the hymn of the prophet addressed to the majestic God.

The presentation and the language of Habakkuk show the classical beauty of Hebrew prophecy. The style is poetical and sublime, the parallelisms generally regular. Many sections are notable for original expressions and for powerful periods. The prayer with which the book closes touches the summit of the sublime.[1]

1) Cp. Fuerbringer, *Einleitung in das Alte Testament*, 90. 91; *Concordia Bible Class*, June, 1919, 88—90.

CHAPTER 1.

The Chastisement of the Lord Set Forth.

THE ANNOUNCEMENT OF JEHOVAH'S JUDGMENT. — V. 1. **The burden,** the prophetic sentence with its threat of punishment, **which Habakkuk, the prophet, did see,** his first statements being in the nature of a complaint on the part of righteousness, accusing the people of sin. V. 2. **O Lord, how long shall I cry,** until when would he have to raise his voice, **and Thou wilt not hear?** Jehovah, the God of the covenant, refused to heed any appeal in the interest of the people while they persisted in their wickedness. **Even cry out unto Thee of violence,** of the criminal acts of the people of the land, **and Thou wilt not save?** The fact that the Lord apparently remained indifferent to conditions in Judah and did nothing to stop the criminal activity, seemed to the prophet incompatible with the holiness of God. V. 3. **Why dost Thou show me iniquity,** permitting him to see it on every hand, **and cause me to behold grievance?** rather, "and Thou observest distress inactively," seemingly paying no attention to perverseness. **For spoiling and violence are before me,** so that he could not help but be a witness of them daily; **and there are that raise up strife and contention,** literally, "there is strife, and contention arises." V. 4. **Therefore the Law is slacked,** the leaders not being interested in its enforcement, since God remained indifferent, **and judgment doth never go forth,** there is never a righteous sentence delivered; **for the wicked doth compass about the righteous,** a whole circle of such wicked people surrounding one righteous person, so that he is often forced to bow to superior power; **therefore wrong judgment proceedeth,** righteousness and truth are perverted. Jehovah answers this complaint by saying that He intends to perform a marvelous work, namely, by pronouncing a sentence in agreement with the greatness of the transgression. V. 5. **Behold ye among the heathen,** out of whose midst the storm of judgment would proceed, **and regard and wonder marvelously,** literally, "be astonished! astonished!" **For I will work a work in your days which ye will not believe though it be told you,** one which in ordinary circumstances is unbelievable. V. 6. **For, lo, I raise up the Chaldeans, that bitter and hasty nation,** a fierce and impetuous nation, **which shall march through the breadth of the** land, whose campaigns would extend throughout the earth, **to possess the dwelling-places that are not theirs,** to take possession of strange countries, to wage wars of conquest. V. 7. **They are terrible and dreadful,** arousing terror, causing fear; **their judgment and their dignity,** what they consider their right and their eminence, **shall proceed of themselves,** they take this much upon themselves, they themselves decide the norm and the right of their actions. V. 8. **Their horses also are swifter than the leopards,** so that their attacks could be made with the greatest speed, **and are more fierce than the evening wolves,** when hunger makes them ravenous; **and their horsemen shall spread themselves,** rushing along with a fearful sound, **and their horsemen shall come from far,** from the remote country of Babylonia; **they shall fly as the eagle that hasteth to eat,** pouncing upon his food to devour it. V. 9. **They shall come all for violence,** or, "all its multitude," the entire hostile nation, "comes for deeds of violence," so that none can withstand the impact of its attack; **their faces shall sup up as the east wind,** panting to go forward to the attack, **and they shall gather the captivity as the sand,** their captives being innumerable. V. 10. **And they shall scoff at the kings,** rulers that attempt to stop their victorious onslaught, **and the princes shall be a scorn unto them; they shall deride every stronghold; for they shall heap dust,** any kind of little earth-mound, **and take it.** The enemy would simply mock at every show of resistance to their advance as a ridiculous and futile effort. V. 11. **Then shall his mind change,** then the spirit of the enemy revives, **and he shall pass over,** passing on in his whirlwind campaign, **and offend, imputing this his power unto his god,** or, "he becomes guilty, for this his power is his god," he deifies himself. With these words the Lord points out that the climax of Babylonia's power would thereby be reached, for He cannot permit such idolatrous ideas to gain the upper hand in a nation.

THE PROPHET'S PRAYER. — V. 12. **Art Thou not from everlasting, O Lord, my God, mine Holy One?** To this certainty the prophet clings; from it he derives consoling confidence. **We shall not die,** the people of the Lord would not be wholly exterminated. **O Lord, Thou hast ordained them,** the children of Israel, the Lord's people, **for judgment,** to carry out His judgment of punishment upon them; **and, O mighty God,** literally, "Thou Rock," **Thou hast established them for correction,** to be chastised and thus brought to the realization of their sins. V. 13. **Thou art of purer eyes than to behold evil,** too pure to endure to behold it, **and canst not look on iniquity,** the wickedness and distress which men inflict upon others; **wherefore lookest Thou upon them that deal treacherously,** the violent Babylonian conquerors, **and holdest Thy tongue when the wicked devoureth the man that is more righteous than he,** for the children of God in the midst of Israel gave them a higher moral standing than that which the Chaldeans possessed, v. 14. **and makest men as the fishes of the sea,** helpless in the face of the fisherman's net, as **the creeping things that have no ruler over them,** one who might act as their protector and defender in times of peril? V. 15. **They take up all of them with the angle, they catch them in their net, and gather them in their drag,** in the largest kind of fish-net; **therefore they rejoice and are glad,** the enemies being pleased with the ease with which they overcame the Lord's people. V. 16. **Therefore they sacrifice unto their net and burn incense unto their drag,** a custom which was actually found among some heathen nations; **because by them their portion is fat and their meat plenteous,** present in rich and great quantities. V. 17. **Shall they therefore empty their net,** namely, with the intention of casting it out again for a new draught, **and not spare continually to slay the nations?** or, "and always strangle nations without sparing?" The enemies' angles, or hooks, nets, and drags are clearly his great and powerful armies, with which he has conquered nations and brought the treasures of the world to Babylon. Mark: He who puts his trust in anything on earth and glories in it to the exclusion of God makes this creature his idol.

CHAPTER 2.

The Overthrow of the Wicked World-Power.

THE INTRODUCTION AND THE FIRST WOE. — V. 1. **I will stand upon my watch,** as an observer on a solitary height, **and set me upon the tower,** on the pinnacle of a fortress, where he would have an unobstructed view and could prepare his soul to receive the word and testimony of God, **and will watch to see what He will say unto me,** in an inner revelation, **and what I shall answer when I am reproved,** literally, "to my complaint," how he would satisfy himself and others by the answer of Jehovah. V. 2. **And the Lord answered me and said, Write the vision,** what would be shown him in this revelation, **and make it plain upon tables,** the writing-tablets on which he should engrave its contents, **that he may run that readeth it,** so that every one passing by, even hastily, would be able to read it quickly. V. 3. **For the vision is yet for an appointed time,** it awaits its fulfilment in the future, but nevertheless in a fixed period, **but at the end it shall speak and not lie,** like the predictions of the false prophets. **Though it tarry, wait for it,** not becoming foolishly impatient, **because it will surely come, it will not tarry,** not be postponed beyond the time fixed for its fulfilment. V. 4. **Behold, his soul which is lifted up is not upright in him,** that is, the conqueror is puffed up, he is not sincere in his attitude over against God; **but the just shall live by his faith,** that is, he who relies on God's merciful promises in the Gospel would, and does, by this confidence, receive eternal life as a gift of God. Cp. Rom. 1, 17; Gal. 3, 11. V. 5. **Yea, also, because he transgresseth by wine,** rather, "and, moreover, wine is treacherous," not bringing those who are addicted to it life and power, as it seems to promise, but unhappiness and destruction; **he is a proud man, neither keepeth at home,** the tendency of the Chaldeans in this respect being known, **who enlargeth his desire as hell,** in an insatiable greed, **and is as death and cannot be satisfied, but gathereth unto him all nations,** as vassals and captives and slaves, **and heapeth unto him all people,** collecting them under his scepter; v. 6. **shall not all these take up a parable against him,** a proverbial saying, **and a taunting proverb,** a satirical speech or sententious poem, **against him and say, Woe to him that increaseth that which is not his!** as the Babylonian conqueror did in this instance. **How long?** that is, How long could this still last? **and to him that ladeth himself with thick clay!** rather, "and loads upon himself a burden of pledges gained by usury." "The Chaldean is compared to a harsh usurer and his ill-gotten treasures to heaps of pledges in the hands of a usurer." V. 7. **Shall they not rise up suddenly that shall bite thee,** the Hebrew having a play upon words between the bite of a snake and the interest which the usurer demands, **and awake that shall vex thee?** rather, "and those who shake thee violently," as a creditor might shake a debtor in driving him out of his possession, "wake up," **and thou shalt be for booties unto them?** so that they would, in turn, plunder. V. 8. **Because thou hast spoiled many nations, all the remnant of the people,** either those who were left after being spoiled, or those who had not yet been subjugated, **shall spoil thee; because of men's blood,** as shed by the Chaldeans, **and for the violence of the land, of the city, and of all that dwell therein,** the entire nation being guilty of such wickedness upon the various countries conquered by the Chaldeans, especially Judea and Jerusalem.

THE FOUR REMAINING WOES. — V. 9. **Woe to him that coveteth an evil covetousness to his house,** who accumulates the gain of wickedness for his house, seeking to establish his house by unrighteous, wicked methods, **that he may set his nest on high,** secure against every form of attack, as the Chaldean did, **that he may be delivered from the power of evil,** considering himself safe against every form of misfortune. V. 10. **Thou hast consulted shame to thy house,** for the Chaldean's counsel, as outlined in the preceding verse, was bound to bring disgrace upon him, **by cutting off many people,** the plan to bring about the destruction of many nations being the reason for the Lord's judgment upon Babylonia, **and hast sinned against thy soul,** transgressing in such a way as to forfeit his life. V. 11. **For the stone shall cry out of the wall and the beam out of the timber,** the spar out of the woodwork, **shall answer it,** agreeing with the stone in its charge against the builder on account of the crimes committed in building the city. V. 12. **Woe to him that buildeth a town with blood!** with blood-bought spoils, as Babylon was built, **and stablisheth a city by iniquity,** by violence and oppression. V. 13. **Behold, is it not of the Lord of hosts that the people shall labor in the very fire,** for it was due to His dispensation that men strained themselves to the utmost, only, however, to have their buildings consumed by fire in the burning of their cities, **and the people shall weary themselves for very vanity?** For all the proud buildings erected by them would eventually be destroyed. V. 14. **For the earth shall be filled with the knowledge of the glory of the Lord,** the destruction of the world-power being a necessary condition to this end, in order that the honor of Jehovah, the almighty Ruler of the heavenly armies, might be known throughout the world, **as the waters cover the sea.** Cp. Is. 11, 9. The enemies who refuse to accept the Lord in the beauty of His mercy will be obliged to acknowledge Him in the majesty of His almighty power. V. 15. **Woe unto him that giveth his neighbor drink,** as the Babylonians did, figuratively speaking, **that puttest thy bottle to him,** or, "while thou addest thy wrath," **and makest him drunken also that thou mayest look on their nakedness!** The picture of one lying in a drunken, shameful stupor well emphasizes the entire subjection of a conquered people. V. 16. **Thou art filled with shame for glory,** or, "so, then, shalt thou be satisfied with shame instead of glory," satiated with disgracefulness; **drink thou also,** draining the cup of the Lord's wrath, **and let thy foreskin be uncovered,** showing Chaldea to be uncircumcised, heathenish. **The cup of the Lord's right hand,** offered in a manner that it could not be refused, **shall be turned unto thee,** so that it would eventually be Chaldea's turn to empty it to the last dregs, **and shameful spewing,** the vomiting of drunkenness and shame, shall be on thy glory. V. 17. **For the violence of Lebanon,** the outrage committed in ruining its cedar forests, **shall cover thee and the spoil of beasts,** the dispersion of the animals of Lebanon, **which made them afraid because of men's blood,** shed by the conquerors, **and for the violence of the land, of the city, and of all that dwell therein.** Cp. v. 8. V. 18. **What profiteth the graven image that the maker thereof hath graven it,** such trust is utterly useless, **the molten image and a teacher of lies,** the idol itself, **that the maker of his work trusteth therein, to make dumb idols?** All this is vain and foolish. It follows, therefore, v. 19. **Woe unto him that saith to the wood, Awake!** expecting help from a carved idol; **to the dumb stone,** the hewn idol, **Arise, it shall teach!** rather, "Can it teach?" **Behold, it is laid over with gold and silver, and there is no breath at all in the midst of it,** whence it follows that idolatry is a most foolish undertaking. V. 20. **But the Lord,** the contrast being sharply emphasized, **is in His holy temple,** the Ruler in His mighty kingdom; **let all the earth keep silence before Him,** awaiting His judgment in silent and humble submission. If the whole earth is obliged to acknowledge His majesty and authority, then the glory and power of the Chaldean state cannot maintain itself in His sight.

CHAPTER 3.

The Prophet's Prayer for Mercy in the Lord's Judgment.

JEHOVAH'S MAJESTIC COMING TO JUDGMENT. V. 1. **A prayer of Habakkuk, the prophet,** in the form of the Davidic psalms, **upon Shigionoth,** after the manner of a dithyramb, in reeling, exciting time, with triumphal music. V. 2. **O Lord, I have heard Thy speech,** the announcement of the judgment of punishment through the Chaldeans, **and was afraid. O Lord, revive Thy work,** call into existence once more the former way of dealing with Thy people, as well as the double judgment of which the prophecy had spoken till now, **in the midst of the years, in the midst of the years make known,** so that the delay in bringing eventual redemption to His people may not be too great; **in wrath,** namely, while He expressed His indignation through the punishment carried out by the Chaldeans, **remember mercy,** so that the severity of the punishment might be tempered at least to some extent. The prophet having thus announced the theme of his psalm, he immediately launches forth in his prayer. V. 3. **God came from Teman,** cp. Deut. 33, 2, the eastern division of Edom, **and the Holy One from Mount Paran,** the mountainous country between Idumea and Egypt. **Selah.** The description shows the Lord approaching from this region with all the glory of His majesty. **His glory covered the heavens,** extending as far as the eye could see, **and the earth was full of His praise,** so that His splendor covered its whole expanse. "The flaming glory of Jehovah filling everything is a vision of such excessive sublimity that one scarcely dares to follow the prophet in spirit to meditate upon it." (Lange.) V. 4. **And His brightness was as the light,** bursting forth as the sunlight when the ball of the sun rises above the horizon; **He had horns,** the rays of the sun as it first appears, **coming out of His hand,** on either side, the appearance of God being attended with brilliant light; **and there was the hiding of His power,** His almighty power, as it were, being veiled by the splendor of His appearance. V. 5. **Before Him went the pestilence,** or, the plague goes before Him, **and burning coals went forth at His feet,** the excessive heat of the fever of various pestilences, these angels of death being His attendants on His triumphal march. V. 6. **He stood and measured the earth,** calmly standing, amidst the general commotion, as the Judge of the world, measuring the countries and their doings, or causing them to shake in terror, in order to execute judgment; **He beheld and drove asunder the nations,** making the heathen tremble; **and the everlasting mountains were scattered,** or, "the primeval mountains burst asunder," dissolving in dust, **the perpetual hills did bow,** the hills of the early world sink down. **His ways are everlasting,** or, "the paths of olden time, He follows them." As He once came in earthquakes and terrible manifestations of His majesty in order to make Israel His covenant nation, so He may once more be expected to come to Judgment. V. 7. **I saw the tents of Cushan,** of the Ethiopian armies, **in affliction,** in the distress of terror; **and the curtains,** the tent-cloths, **of the land of Midian did tremble,** that is, all the inhabitants of the heathen countries round about were filled with terror. V. 8. **Was the Lord displeased against the rivers? Was Thine anger against the rivers?** literally, "Was it against the rivers that was kindled, Jehovah, was it against the rivers that Thy wrath was kindled?" **Was Thy wrath against the sea that Thou didst ride upon Thine horses and Thy chariots of salvation?** the winds and clouds being considered the vehicles bearing the Lord as He goes forth to redeem His people. The cause of His dividing the Red Sea and the Jordan was not His displeasure against these waters, but His intention of interposing for His people's salvation. V. 9. **Thy bow was made quite naked,** drawn forth from the quiver and made ready to send forth its arrow, **according to the oaths of the tribes, even Thy word,** literally, "sworn are the scourges by the word, rods of chastisement are sworn by the word," that is, the chastisements of Jehovah are definitely decided upon and even supported by oaths. **Selah. Thou didst cleave the earth with rivers,** as when masses of water rush from the mountains, or when tidal waves cut deep gullies into the earth. V. 10. **The mountains saw Thee, and they trembled,** shaken by storms and earthquakes; **the overflowing of the water passed by,** a torrent of water, from subterranean sources or as the result of a cloudburst, rushes along; **the deep,** the abyss of the ocean, **uttered His voice and lifted up His hands on high,** in a mighty noise accompanying their breaking forth. V. 11. **The sun and moon stood still in their habitation,** or have entered their dwelling, so that a terrifying darkness ensues; **at the light of Thine arrows they went and at the shining of Thy glittering spear,** as God manifested Himself as the judge of the world, executing justice and righteousness upon all men. V. 12. **Thou didst march through the land in indignation,** through all the countries of the earth; **Thou didst thresh the heathen in anger,** stamping them under foot. V. 13. **Thou wentest forth for the salvation of Thy people,** Israel, as representative of all true children of God, **even for salvation with Thine Anointed,** all the leaders of the people being types of the Messiah, by whom the Lord's kingdom would be permanently established. **Thou woundedst the head out of the house of the wicked,** crushing the Chaldean nation with its ruler, typical of the antichristian forces, **by discovering the foundation unto the neck,** laying bare the foundations being the same as razing the entire building to the ground. **Selah.** V. 14. **Thou didst strike through with his staves,** piercing with the spear or weapons of the wicked one, **the head of his villages,** the ruler of his hordes, or the chief of his princes, so that the soldiers of the hostile armies would turn one against the other; **they came out as a whirlwind to scatter me,** rushing in to disperse the people of Israel; **their rejoicing was as to devour the poor secretly,** that is, the enemies are like assassins, who delight in pouncing upon the unsuspecting wayfarer and in taking his life. V. 15. **Thou didst walk through the sea with Thine horses,** as when Jehovah destroyed the army of Pharaoh and delivered His people, **through the heap of great waters,** upon the billows of great waters, the expression serving to bring out the almighty power of Jehovah in the deliverance of His people. Thus the majesty of the Lord in overcoming all His enemies is set forth in a word-painting of singular beauty and power, with the Messianic background clearly in evidence.

A PLEA FOR MERCY. — V. 16. **When I heard, my belly trembled,** namely, with terror at the revelation of the mighty judgment of Jehovah, **my lips quivered at the voice,** so that he was unable to steady them; **rottenness entered into my bones,** a feeling of overpowering weakness, **and I trembled in myself that I might rest in the day of trouble,** quietly, in silent submission, awaiting the day of distress. **When he cometh up unto the people, he will invade them with his troops,** or, "when he comes up against the people who will attack it," when the conquest on the part of the invader may be expected. V. 17. **Although the fig-tree shall not blossom, neither shall fruit be in the vines; the labor of the olive,** as it brings forth its blossoms and yields its fruit, **shall fail,** shriveling up, **and the fields shall yield no meat,** no grain for food; **the flock shall be cut off from the fold, and there shall be no herd in the stalls,** orchards and cultivated fields are barren, granaries and barns are empty in consequence of the desolation of the land caused by the enemy; v. 18. **yet I will rejoice in the Lord,** in spite of all these afflictions, **I will joy in the God of my salvation,** exulting in Him on whom the salvation of all mankind rests. V. 19. **The Lord God is my Strength,** Ps. 27, 1, **and He will make my feet like hinds' feet,** strong and sure-footed, **and He will make me to walk upon mine high places,** on the heights of salvation to which one climbs from the valley of affliction on the basis of the confidence of faith. **To the chief singer on my stringed instruments,** this being a note to the leader of the Temple-music, directing him to have the psalm accompanied by music on stringed instruments. The God of salvation is on the side of His children, so that they are safe in the midst of all their enemies and will eventually enjoy the fulness of the redemption earned and prepared by the Messiah.

THE BOOK OF THE PROPHET ZEPHANIAH.

INTRODUCTION.

The prophet Zephaniah ("Jehovah hides") himself traces his family back to Hizkiah, or Hezekiah, and there seems to be little doubt that this is the king of that name and that Zephaniah was of royal descent. He prophesied under King Josiah, and was therefore a contemporary of Jeremiah, of Habakkuk, and of the prophetess Huldah, in the last half of the seventh century before Christ. The date of his book may safely be placed at about the year 625 B. C. His preaching, of which a summary is offered in his book, strongly supported the king in his work of reforming the Jewish Church.

The Book of Zephaniah offers his prophecies in a condensed form and in a continuous discourse. Its theme is the great day of Jehovah's judgment upon Judah and Jerusalem, as well as upon the entire sinful world. But his powerful, at times overwhelmingly impressive call to repentance concludes with a most cheering promise of salvation through the Messiah.

The style of the book, though not uniformly sublime, is graphic and vivid in the presentation of details. There are passages which agree to a remarkable extent with the sayings of former prophets, a factor which supports the brotherhood existing between the inspired men of that day. The comforting promises of the third chapter are the outstanding feature of the entire book.1)

1) Cp. Fuerbringer, *Einleitung in das Alte Testament*, 92. 93.

CHAPTER 1.

The Universality of the Judgment.

THE NATURE OF THE JUDGMENT. — V. 1. **The word of the Lord which came unto Zephaniah,** being communicated to him by special revelation of the Lord, the prophet tracing his genealogy as follows: **the son of Cushi, the son of Gedaliah, the son of Amariah, the son of Hizkiah,** four representative members from his ancestry being given, **in the days of Josiah, the son of Amon, king of Judah,** who made the last consistent effort to bring about a reformation of the people. V. 2. **I will utterly consume all things from off the land, saith the Lord,** sweeping it off the face of the earth in an utter devastation. V. 3. **I will consume man and beast,** even the creatures being affected by the universality of the judgment; **I will consume the fowls of the heaven and the fishes of the sea, and the stumbling-blocks with the wicked,** that is, whatever men have offended and transgressed with together with the objects of their idolatry; **and I will cut off man from off the land, saith the Lord,** certainly destroying them off the face of the earth, in a last great destruction. V. 4. **I will also stretch out mine hand upon Judah,** the particular object of His wrath, **and upon all the inhabitants of Jerusalem,** for the people of the land followed the inhabitants of the capital in their transgressions; **and I will cut off the remnant of Baal from this place,** for there were still such as adhered to his idolatrous worship, **and the name of the Chemarim,** the idol-priests, those engaged in the worship of Baal, **with the priests,** for these also had polluted themselves and were therefore destined for destruction, v. 5. **and them that worship the host of heaven upon the housetops,** regarding sun, moon, and stars as their gods; **and them that worship and that swear by the Lord and that swear by Malcham,** by their king, so that they tried to combine the service of the true God and that of Baal, solemnly pledging themselves to the latter's service, v. 6. **and them that are turned back from the Lord,** drawing back from Jehovah, **and those that have not sought the Lord nor enquired for Him,** both the openly wicked and the irreligious being included in the list of Jehovah's enemies. V. 7. **Hold thy peace at the presence of the Lord God!** ready to submit to His judgment as outlined above; **for the day of the Lord is at hand,** when His punishment must strike the transgressors; **for the Lord hath prepared a sacrifice,** the Jewish nation itself, **He hath bid His guests,** namely, the world-powers and their allies, all ready to devour Judah. V. 8. **And it shall come to pass in the day of the Lord's sacrifice,** when His punishment is put into effect, **that I will punish the princes,** the mighty ones, the dignitaries of state, **and the king's children,** all those belonging to the royal family, **and all such as are clothed with strange apparel,** their dress showing that they were estranged from the national spirit and customs. V. 9. **In the same day also will I punish all those that leap on the threshold,** namely, that of the temple of Dagon, the idol of the Philistines, 1 Sam. 5, 5, **which fill their masters' houses with violence and deceit,** bringing their money and their treasures, unjustly acquired as they are, into the houses of their idols. V. 10. **And it shall come to pass in that day, saith the Lord, that there shall be the noise of a**

cry, of a woeful shout, **from the fish-gate,** that through which the road to Joppa passed, **and an howling from the second,** from the lower city, where the attack of the enemy would be launched, **and a great crashing from the hills,** those extending upward from the lower city. The Lord set out to punish, and His judgment was thorough, as it always is in the case of such as refuse to heed His words of warning.

THE EXTENT OF THE JUDGMENT. — V. 11. **Howl, ye inhabitants of Maktesh,** meaning the mortar, a small section of Jerusalem, so called because it presented a depression or hollow, **for all the merchant people are cut down,** entirely destroyed; **all they that bear silver,** the traders laden with silver, who occupied that part of the lower city, **are cut off.** V. 12. **And it shall come to pass at that time that I will search Jerusalem with candles,** investigating even the dark and hidden corners, so that not one of the wrongdoers is overlooked, **and punish the men that are settled on their lees,** like old wine which is not drawn off, a fit picture of moral and religious indifference, Jer. 48, 11, **that say in their heart, The Lord will not do good, neither will He do evil,** that is, there is no need of worry, matters will go on as they always have been. V. 13. **Therefore their goods shall become a booty,** to be robbed by the enemies, **and their houses a desolation,** in the overthrow of the city; **they shall also build houses, but not inhabit them,** the destruction taking place before they can move into them, **and they shall plant vineyards, but not drink the wine thereof.** Cp. Amos 5, 11; Micah 6, 15. V. 14. **The great day of the Lord,** the day of His mighty judgment, **is near, it is near, and hasteth greatly,** there will be no further delay, **even the voice of the day of the Lord,** or, "Hark! the day of Jehovah"; **the mighty man shall cry there bitterly,** the hero crying in bitter lamentation, because he cannot save himself, and must yield to the power of the foe. V. 15. **That day is a day of wrath,** cp. Is. 19, 18, **a day of trouble and distress,** of anguish and pressure, Job 15, 24, **a day of wasteness and desolation,** of the greatest devastation, **a day of darkness and gloominess,** Joel 2, 2, **a day of clouds and thick darkness,** Deut. 4, 11, v. 16. **a day of the trumpet and alarm against the fenced cities,** in proclaiming God's power upon a sinful people, in the war-signal of desolation, **and against the high towers,** the battlements of the forts. V. 17. **And I will bring distress upon men, that they shall walk like blind men,** groping about in a futile effort to escape from existing evils, **because they have sinned against the Lord; and their blood shall be poured out as dust,** in endless quantities, **and their flesh as the dung,** which is not regarded. V. 18. **Neither their silver nor their gold shall be able to deliver them in the day of the Lord's wrath,** they would not be able to buy themselves off when His fury is once set in motion; **but the whole land shall be devoured by the fire of His jealousy,** His indignation jealous for His honor; **for He shall make even a speedy riddance of all them that dwell in the land,** consuming them with a suddenness which they had not anticipated. Even so will the Day of Judgment come upon a world which, as a whole, is not prepared for the Lord's last advent. Cp. Matt. 24, 44.

CHAPTER 2.

The Lord's Call to Repentance.

THE EXHORTATION AND THE DOOM OF THE PHILISTINES. — V. 1. **Gather yourselves together, yea, gather together,** as for a penitential assembly with earnest self-examination, **O nation not desired,** literally, "that does not grow pale," which till now has felt no sense of shame, v. 2. **before the decree bring forth,** when, according to God's plan, the day of judgment upon Judah would suddenly come, **before the day pass as the chaff,** coming on quickly as when the wind carries the chaff along, **before the fierce anger of the Lord come upon you, before the day of the Lord's anger come upon you,** as it surely would if they would not show the proper repentance. V. 3. **Seek ye the Lord,** in proper repentance, **all ye meek of the earth,** the humble of the land, those who were still disposed to be guided by His will, **which have wrought His judgment,** observed His right, trying to fulfil the decrees of His holy Word; **seek righteousness,** with ever greater truth and sincerity, **seek meekness,** with all humility, with a constant sense of their own unworthiness; **it may be ye shall be hid in the day of the Lord's anger,** so that the Lord would make use of mercy rather than a strict accounting and save them in the general overthrow. This exhortation is now supported by a reference to the doom of three heathen nations. V. 4. **For Gaza shall be forsaken,** overthrown and forgotten, **and Ashkelon a desolation; they shall drive out Ashdod,** the chief seat of the worship of Dagon, **at the noon day,** since she would be helpless even at midday, so that there would be no need of resorting to a night attack, **and Ekron shall be rooted up.** The four Philistine city-states here mentioned are clearly representative of the entire country, as the next statements show. V. 5. **Woe unto the inhabitants of the seacoast,** of the plains along the Mediterranean sea, **the nation of**

the Cherethites, for a part of the Philistines, at least, traced their descent to the ancient people of Crete; **the word of the Lord is against you, O Canaan, the land of the Philistines**, the word Canaan here applied chiefly to the lowlands of Palestine to the west; **I will even destroy thee that there shall be no inhabitant**, the nation as such to be destroyed. V. 6. **And the seacoast**, then teeming with the life of rich commercial cities, **shall be dwellings and cottages for shepherds**, dugouts and shanties, or places for pastures where they would carry on the work of their calling, **and folds for flocks**, the land reverting to the use of nomads. V. 7. **And the coast shall be for the remnant of the house of Judah**, those whom the Lord would lead back to their own country; **they shall feed thereupon**, making the country a pasture-ground; **in the houses of Ashkelon**, which would no longer be inhabited, **shall they lie down in the evening; for the Lord, their God, shall visit them**, the remnant of Judah, whom He intended to make the nucleus of a renewed people, **and turn away their captivity**. The members of the Jewish nation that returned from Babylonia were those in whose midst the Lord preserved His Church and among whom He established the Church of the New Testament. So the Messianic idea is brought out even in this connection.

THE DOOM OF MOAB, ETHIOPIA, AND ASSYRIA. — V. 8. **I have heard the reproach of Moab**, cp. Jer. 48, 27, **and the revilings of the children of Ammon**, the two nations east of Jordan and of the Dead Sea, which were related to the children of Israel, but later became the enemies of God's people and made known their hostility in bitter blasphemies, **whereby they have reproached my people**, in proud mockery and scorn, **and magnified themselves against their border**, acted violently against the boundary of the Lord's people, constantly attempting to get into possession of some of Israel's territory. V. 9. **Therefore as I live, saith the Lord of hosts, the God of Israel**, the supreme Ruler of the world, **Surely Moab shall be as Sodom, and the children of Ammon as Gomorrah**, being overwhelmed by the destruction which was the fate of their ancestor's cities, **even the breeding of nettles**, a weed growing only in desolate places, **and salt-pits**, on the shore of the Dead Sea, **and a perpetual desolation**, a desert until the end of time; **the residue of My people shall spoil them**, take possession of their land, **and the remnant of My people shall possess them**, these events being typical of the destruction of the sinners and the redemption of the Lord's people. V. 10. **This shall they have for their pride**, in proper retaliation for the manner in which they had dealt with Jehovah's people, **because they have reproached and magnified themselves against the people of the Lord of hosts**. V. 11. **The Lord will be terrible unto them**, dealing with them in a manner which is bound to strike terror to their hearts; **for He will famish**, or destroy, **all the gods of the earth**, all the idols in which men placed their trust; **and men shall worship Him**, acknowledging His supremacy, **every one from his place, even all the isles of the heathen**, namely, when men from every nation of the earth would be gained for the Gospel-truth, this being a further Messianic feature in this chapter. V. 12. **Ye Ethiopians also**, representatives of the heathen nations of the South, **ye shall be slain by My sword**, the statement in the third person dismissing them as of no further importance. V. 13. **And He will stretch out His hand against the North, and destroy Assyria**, powerful though it was at that time, **and will make Nineveh**, the capital of Assyria, Jonah 1, 2, **a desolation**, although it was then surrounded by a network of irrigation canals, **and dry like a wilderness**. The prophet purposely devotes more time to Assyria, because it was at that time the greatest world-power and particularly hostile to the Lord's people. V. 14. **And flocks shall lie down in the midst of her**, the former great city having been leveled to the ground and reverted back to a pasture-ground, **all the beasts of the nations**, beasts of all kinds in droves or great masses; **both the cormorant**, the pelican, **and the bittern**, or hedge-hog, **shall lodge in the upper lintels of it**, on the capitals of pillars standing in the midst of the ruins; **their voice shall sing in the windows**, or, "hark how the singer sings in the window," where he has built his nest; **desolation**, or dirt, **shall be in the thresholds; for He shall uncover the cedar work**, all the beautiful cedar paneling of their palaces the Lord has torn away, and it has fallen into decay. V. 15. **This is the rejoicing city**, where shouts of gayety were heard without ceasing, **that dwelt carelessly**, in perfect security, **that said in her heart**, in proud self-confidence, **I am, and there is none beside me. How is she become a desolation**, a deserted place, **a place for beasts to lie down in!** a lair for the animals of the desert. **Every one that passeth by her shall hiss and wag his hand**, both astonished and gratified at the overthrow of the proud city. It is a graphic description of the manner in which the Lord carried out His judgments upon His enemies.

CHAPTER 3.

The Doom of Jerusalem and the Messianic Promise.

THE OBDURACY OF THE CAPITAL CITY. — V. 1. **Woe to her that is filthy and polluted,** stubborn and full of uncleanness, **to the oppressing city!** where violence against the weak and downtrodden was the order of the day. V. 2. **She obeyed not the voice,** paying no attention to the Lord's admonitions; **she received not correction,** the instruction or discipline which was intended to be of benefit to her; **she trusted not in the Lord,** placing no confidence in His exhortations and promises; **she drew not near to her God,** she has become indifferent to Jehovah. V. 3. **Her princes within her are roaring lions,** bent upon rapine and murder; **her judges are evening wolves,** driven forth by hunger in the evening, their greed being insatiable; **they gnaw not the bones till the morrow,** their voracious appetite causing them instantly to devour their victims, laying nothing aside for the next day. V. 4. **Her prophets are light and treacherous persons,** boastful and faithless knaves; **her priests have polluted the Sanctuary,** desecrating the Temple by their neglect of the prescribed sacrifices or by their blasphemous manner in offering them; **they have done violence to the Law,** simply setting aside the precepts of God whose guardians they were supposed to be. V. 5. **The just Lord is in the midst thereof,** He, the righteous One, having left nothing untried; **He will not do iniquity,** He commits no wrong; **every morning doth He bring His judgment to light,** giving evidence of the justice of all His dealings; **He faileth not,** no blame, therefore, rests on Him. **But the unjust knoweth no shame,** the wicked people of Jerusalem are not influenced either by the example of God or by His threat of punishment. V. 6. **I have cut off the nations,** also as an act of warning for Israel; **their towers are desolate,** their walls and fortresses leveled to the ground; **I made their streets waste,** the roads obliterated, **that none passeth by; their cities are destroyed, so that there is no man, that there is none inhabitant,** all this being done, in part at least, to serve as an example of warning to the people of Jerusalem and Judah. V. 7. **I said, Surely thou wilt fear Me,** the kindness and tenderness of the warning being emphasized; **thou wilt receive instruction,** if only thou wouldst suffer thyself to be taught! **So their dwelling should not be cut off, howsoever I punished them,** or, "in accordance with all that I had appointed concerning them"; that is, Jehovah hoped still to have mercy on them, so that He would not have to send the threatened punishment; **but they rose early,** zealous for their wicked works, **and corrupted all their doings,** they were eager to speed their perverted actions, their infamous deeds. Thus many a godless person refuses to heed the Lord's call to repentance and deliberately plunges all the more deeply into transgressions of every kind.

THE SALVATION OF THE DAUGHTER OF ZION. V. 8. **Therefore wait ye upon Me, saith the Lord,** this merciful invitation being extended to all who will still listen to His words, **until the day that I rise up to the prey,** when He pours out His wrath upon the nations; **for My determination is to gather the nations,** to carry out His punishment upon them, **that I may assemble the kingdoms, to pour upon them Mine indignation, even all My fierce anger,** all the burning wrath which He has stored up against them; **for all the earth shall be devoured with the fire of My jealousy,** by the zeal which He would show on His great Day of Judgment. That is the promise of the Messianic period, the elimination of the enemies as a factor in interfering with the progress of the Lord's kingdom. V. 9. **For then will I turn to the people a pure language,** by purifying their sinful lips and thereby enabling them to call upon Him with pure lips, **that they may all call upon the name of the Lord,** in the true unity of a common faith which is described in John 17 and Eph. 4, **to serve Him with one consent,** literally, "with one shoulder," all bearing together the pleasant yoke of Jehovah. V. 10. **From beyond the rivers of Ethiopia,** from the remotest corners of the earth, **My suppliants,** those who would worship Jehovah in spirit and in truth, **even the daughter of My dispersed,** gained for the Lord from the midst of a strange nation, **shall bring Mine offering,** turning to Him with true worship. V. 11. **In that day shalt thou,** the restored Israel, the Church of the New Testament, **not be ashamed for all thy doings wherein thou hast transgressed against Me,** there being no more occasion for such a feeling; **for then I will take away out of the midst of thee them that rejoice in thy pride,** the wicked and blasphemous whom the prophet had described at the beginning of the chapter, **and thou shalt no more be haughty because of My holy mountain,** all boastfulness and pride being eliminated in favor of a meek and humble submission to Jehovah's reign of mercy. V. 12. **I will also leave in the midst of thee an afflicted and poor people,** one fully conscious of its absolute dependence upon the grace and mercy of the covenant God, **and they shall trust in the name of the Lord,** placing all their confidence in Him alone. V. 13. **The remnant of Israel,** the nucleus of the Jewish Church, which would become the stock of the Church of the New Testament, **shall not do**

iniquity, not wilfully serve wickedness, **nor speak lies,** becoming guilty of deliberate falsehood, **neither shall a deceitful tongue be found in their mouth,** particularly so far as false doctrine is concerned; **for they shall feed,** of the rich pasture offered by the Good Shepherd, **and lie down,** in calm satisfaction, **and none shall make them afraid.** Cp. Micah 7, 14; Ps. 23. V. 14. **Sing, O daughter of Zion,** the Church of the New Testament; **shout, O Israel,** namely, the spiritual Israel; **be glad and rejoice with all the heart, O daughter of Jerusalem,** for the communion of the saints is established in the Jerusalem which is above. Cp. Gal. 4, 26. V. 15. **The Lord hath taken away thy judgments,** the sentences of condemnation which had rightly been spoken upon her on account of her sins; **He hath cast out thine enemy,** sweeping away the world-power which personified all the hostile forces of the world. **The King of Israel, even the Lord, is in the midst of thee,** namely, in the person of Messiah; **thou shalt not see evil any more,** His blessings removing everything that might bring evil. V. 16. **In that day,** in the great Messianic period, **it shall be said to Jerusalem, Fear thou not,** this being the fundamental note of the Gospel-message, as both the Christmas- and the Easter-stories show; **and to Zion, Let not thine hands be slack,** namely, in terror at the prospect of danger and affliction from without. V. 17. **The Lord, thy God, in the midst of thee is mighty,** not at a dim distance, but in the closest proximity, and powerful to help; **He will save,** He is the Savior; **He will rejoice over thee with joy,** in His delight over the renewal of the marriage covenant between Himself and His Church; **He will rest in His love,** in quiet satisfaction; **He will joy over thee,** after His meditation has proved so satisfactory, **with singing.** Moreover, the Lord will let all humble and afflicted partake of His joy. V. 18. **I will gather them that are sorrowful for the solemn assembly,** mourning far from the festive gathering when the Lord would make His salvation known, **who are of thee,** they were of the same family and descent, but were now far removed from the visible congregation of the Lord, **to whom the reproach of it was a burden,** who felt the weight of their captivity among the heathen nations. V. 19. **Behold, at that time,** in the Messianic period, **I will undo all that afflict thee,** dealing with the oppressors according to His justice; **and I will save her that halteth,** heal the limping, **and gather her that was driven out,** those who were dispersed; **and I will get them praise and fame in every land where they have been put to shame,** so that the name of the Lord's people would be celebrated everywhere. V. 20. **At that time will I bring you again,** the calling of the Lord to join His Church being an act of His mercy, **even in the time that I gather you,** in His Church; **for I will make you a name and a praise among all people of the earth, when I turn back your captivity before your eyes, saith the Lord.** The fulfilment of this prophecy is clearly found in the gathering of the Christian Church, its members being called from the various nations of the earth, and the consummation and climax will be reached in the eventual complete deliverance from this present evil world as the Kingdom of Glory opens its portals.

THE BOOK OF THE PROPHET HAGGAI.

INTRODUCTION.

Concerning the prophet Haggai ("festive") we have no more definite information than that given in the superscription of his book and supported by Ezra 5, 1, namely, that his activity is to be placed in the second year of Darius Hystaspes, which means that he prophesied from September to December of the year 520 B. C. To him, together with Zechariah, was entrusted the task of encouraging the returned exiles to continue the construction of the Temple, which, on account of the enmity of the Samaritans and the subsequent indolence of the people, had not progressed beyond the foundation and the erection of the altar of burnt offering. The activity of Haggai was successful. A new zeal took hold of the people, and they applied themselves to the task entrusted to them by the Lord with all diligence, so that the Temple was completed some four years later. Beyond these facts we know nothing about the person and the history of the prophet.

The Book of Haggai consists of four messages, each one of which is headed by a notice giving the date of the particular revelation of the Lord. After rebuking the Jews on account of their indifference in the building of the Temple, the prophet adds a message of encouragement on account of the inferiority, as to outward splendor, of the second Temple. In the next paragraph the fact that building operations had once more commenced leads the prophet to sound a warning regarding a mere outward observance of the forms of religion, and the fourth message is addressed to Zerubbabel, as the representative of the people. The four messages thus concern the building of the Temple and the worship in the Temple and were apparently written down soon after their first proclamation.

The style of Haggai is in agreement with his messages: pathetic in exhortation, vehement in reproach, elevated in contemplation of the glorious future, particularly that of the Messianic period. Parts of the book are purely prose history; the rest is somewhat rhythmical, showing a fine poetic parallelism.[1])

1) Cp. Fuerbringer, *Einleitung in das Alte Testament*, 92. 93; *Concordia Bible Class*, June, 1919, 91. 92.

CHAPTER 1.

The Indifference of the People Rebuked.

When the exiles, under the leadership of Zerubbabel and Joshua, had returned to Jerusalem, they had begun the work of rebuilding the Temple with great eagerness. But when the Samaritans and others had placed various obstacles in their way, they had discontinued their efforts, making no determined effort to remove the difficulties. A few years after, when a certain measure of prosperity was found in Judea, they grew indifferent to the project, and so the situation continued for some sixteen years. It was then that the Lord selected Haggai as His messenger to rebuke the people. V. 1. **In the second year of Darius, the king,** the year 520 B. C., **in the sixth month,** that is, of the Jewish year, corresponding roughly to our September, **in the first day of the month, came the word of the Lord by Haggai, the prophet,** who was therefore simply the medium through which the Lord communicated His message and in no way presented his own ideas, **unto Zerubbabel, the son of Shealtiel, governor of Judah, and to Joshua, the son of Josedech, the high priest,** cp. Ezra 3, 2, **saying,** v. 2. **Thus speaketh the Lord of hosts,** the prophet employing this formula in order to bring out the importance of his message, **saying, This people say, The time is not come, the time that the Lord's house should be built,** that being the lame excuse with which the people tried to cover their indifference, for they had reached a stage in which they were ready to let matters take their course, allow them to drift along. V. 3. **Then came the word of the Lord by Haggai, the prophet,** saying, v. 4. **Is it time for you, O ye, to dwell in your ceiled houses,** for yourselves to dwell in wainscoted houses, paneled in the most expensive manner, showing that they lived not only in comfort, but in luxury, **and this house lie waste?** since it had never gotten beyond the foundations, only the altar of burnt offerings standing on the top of Moriah. V. 5. **Now, therefore, thus saith the Lord of hosts, Consider your ways,** literally, "Set your hearts upon your ways," contemplating the consequences of their late behavior and upon the manner in which the Lord had regarded it, as His treatment of them showed. V. 6. **Ye have sown much,** or have been sowing much, in the expectation of big crops, **and bring in little,** the harvest being small in spite of all their efforts; **ye eat, but ye have not enough,** they were not really satisfied in spite of the apparent abundance; **ye drink, but ye are not filled with drink; ye clothe you,** seemingly having enough clothes, **but there is none warm; and he that earneth wages earneth wages to put it into a bag with holes,** that is, they found themselves unable to save anything. All this indicated that there could be no real prosperity without the blessing of the Lord, and that was evidently lacking, as it always is when people think only of themselves and not of Him. V. 7. **Thus saith the Lord of hosts, Consider your ways,** think them over very carefully, for the matter was urgent, v. 8. **Go up to the mountain,** to the great forests of the country, **and bring wood,** timber for building, **and build the house; and I will take pleasure in it,** glad to regard it as the house where He might be worshiped, **and I will be glorified, saith the Lord,** receiving the honor which was due to Him, which had been withheld on account of their indifference to the state of His house. V. 9. **Ye looked for much,** expecting still greater crops and a corresponding prosperity, **and, lo, it came to little; and when ye brought it home,** believing that at least the little which they had gotten was safe, **I did blow upon it,** thus dissipating and scattering it. **Why? saith the Lord of hosts.** He Himself undertakes to explain this condition to the people in order to explain it to them more impressively. **Because of Mine house that is waste,** still unfinished and desolate, **and ye run every man unto his own house,** in a base selfishness, which regarded only their own interests. V. 10. **Therefore the heaven over you is stayed from dew,** withholding the moisture necessary to insure full crops, **and the earth is stayed from her fruit,** it does not yield even its ordinary harvest. V. 11. **And I called for a drought upon the land,** upon the cultivated fields, **and upon the mountains,** with their rich meadows, **and upon the corn,** the grain products, **and upon the new wine, and upon the oil,** all the chief products of the country, and upon that which the ground bringeth forth, and upon men, and upon cattle, and upon all the labor of the hands, His blessing being withheld from all animate and inanimate beings. — This earnest rebuke was heeded by the people. V. 12. **Then Zerubbabel, the son of Shealtiel, and Joshua, the son of Josedech, the high priest, with all the remnant of the people,** all the rest of the returned exiles, **obeyed the voice of the Lord, their God, and the words of Haggai, the prophet, as the Lord, their God, had sent him,** probably an additional discourse or a further explanation which was not recorded, **and the people did fear before the Lord,** with reverence and awe. V. 13. **Then,** when the people showed such obvious signs of repentance, **spake Haggai, the Lord's messenger, in the Lord's message unto the people,** the fact that his mission was that of Jehovah being brought out time and again, **saying, I am with you, saith the Lord,** He accepted their repentance as genuine and acted accordingly. V. 14. **And the Lord stirred up the spirit of Zerubbabel, the son of Shealtiel, governor of Judah, and the spirit of Joshua, the son of Josedech, the high priest, and the spirit of all the remnant of the people, and they came and did work,** they took steps to continue building operations, **in the house of the Lord of hosts, their God,** v. 15. **in the four and twentieth day of the sixth month,** twenty-three days after the first message of Haggai, **in the second year of Darius, the king.** When people are filled with the spirit of repentance and of the fear of the Lord, it is an easy matter for them to take up any part of the work which the Lord has entrusted to them, and to bring it to a successful issue, with His blessing.

CHAPTER 2.

Further Addresses Concerning the Temple and Its Meaning.

A COMFORTING ASSURANCE. — V. 1. **In the seventh month, in the one and twentieth day of the month,** not even a full month after the construction of the Temple had been resumed, **came the word of the Lord by the prophet Haggai, saying,** v. 2. **Speak now to Zerubbabel, the son of Shealtiel, governor of Judah, and to Joshua, the son of Josedech, the high priest, and to the residue of the people,** the rest of those who had now returned from Babylon, **saying,** v. 3. **Who is left among you that saw this house in her first glory?** the Temple of Solomon with its almost unequaled rich ornamentation. **And how do ye see it now?** What impression did this second Temple make upon them as they observed it? **Is it not in your eyes, in comparison of it, as nothing?** Any kind of comparison was so much to the disadvantage of this second Temple that the older men had fallen to weeping even when they saw the foundation finished and the altar of burnt offering placed, Ezra 3, 10 ff. V. 4. **Yet now be strong, O Zerubbabel, saith the Lord,** filled with reassuring comfort; **and be strong, O Joshua, son of Josedech, the high priest; and be strong, all ye people of the land, saith the Lord,** all filled with the same reassurance, **and work,** to complete the erection of the Temple; **for I am with you, saith the Lord of hosts;** v. 5. **according to the word that I covenanted with you when ye came out of Egypt,** when Israel was formally accepted as Jehovah's people in the great assembly at Mount Sinai, **so My Spirit remaineth among you,** to strengthen them for the successful conclusion of their work. **Fear ye not!** V. 6. **For thus saith the Lord of hosts,** the same powerful God of the covenant who had entered into fellowship with them at Horeb, **Yet once, it is a little while,** but a short time as men reckon time, **and I will shake the heavens and the earth and the sea and the dry land,** in a mighty commotion involving practically the entire known world, such as took place when the Roman emperors ordered their periodical censuses of the empire, v. 7. **and I will shake all nations,** all of them being drawn into this agitation, **and the Desire of all nations,** the long-expected Messiah, **shall come; and I will fill this house,** now so lowly and unpretentious, **with glory, saith the Lord of hosts.** V. 8. **The silver is Mine, and the gold is Mine, saith the Lord of hosts,** for which reason it would be a small matter for Him to fill any mere earthly house with ornamentation and treasures beyond the dreams of avarice. But that is not the Lord's chief concern. V. 9. **The glory of this latter house,** of the New Testament Church, of which this second Temple was but a feeble type and shadow, **shall be greater than of the former,** of the Jewish Church of the Old Testament, of which the Temple of Solomon was a type, **saith the Lord of hosts; and in this place will I give peace,** namely, the peace of the redemption gained by the promised Messiah, **saith the Lord of hosts.** In this way the content of the New Testament Gospel-message was proclaimed even in the Old Testament, and the believers in both instances rest their faith on the same hope. Cp. Luke 2, 14; Eph. 2, 14.

A WARNING ADMONITION CONCERNING FALSE RIGHTEOUSNESS. — V. 10. **In the four and twentieth day of the ninth month,** a little more than two months later, in the second year of Darius, came the word of the Lord by Haggai, the prophet, again by direct inspiration, saying, v. 11. **Thus saith the Lord of hosts, Ask now the priests concerning the Law, saying,** v. 12. **If one bear holy flesh in the skirt of his garment,** namely, the meat of sacrifices which had been offered, **and with his skirt do touch bread or pottage,** any of the holy food that was sodden, **or wine or oil or any meat,** such as was used in offering sacrifices or in connection with sacrificial meals, **shall it be holy? And the priests answered and said, No.** This was in agreement with the Law, Lev. 6, 20. 27; for though the garment itself was sanctified by such consecrated food, it could impart no holiness to one who, by neglecting the will of the Lord, had become unholy. V. 13. **Then said Haggai, If one that is unclean by a dead body,** by touching a corpse, **touch any of these, shall it be unclean? And the priests answered and said, It shall be unclean,** again in perfect agreement with the Ceremonial Law of the Jews, Lev. 22, 4; Num. 5, 2. 9. 10. V. 14. **Then answered Haggai and said, So is this people, and so is this nation before Me, saith the Lord,** in His presence as Ruler and Judge; **and so is every work of their hands,** everything that they might undertake; **and that which they offer there is unclean.** The children of Israel were in disgrace because of their neglect to finish the house of the Lord, and though their land was holy land, consecrated to the Lord, yet its fruits found no favor in His eyes and could not serve to make the people clean by a mere outward service, as long as their hearts were not in the right relation to Him, so that they were constrained to give Him the worship which He desired. V. 15. **And now, I pray you, consider from this day and upward,** by applying their hearts to this problem, **from before a stone was laid upon a stone in the Temple of the Lord,** before its reconstruction was resumed; v. 16. **since those days were, when one came to an heap of twenty measures,** a stack of sheaves which promised a yield of twenty bushels or pecks, **there were but ten; when one came to the press-fat for to draw out fifty vessels out of the press,** thinking that the harvest should have brought that much, **there were but twenty.** V. 17. **I smote you with blasting,** with blight of the fruits and grains, **and with mildew,** from excessive moisture, **and with hail in all the labors of your hands,** the harvests over which they had worked so hard; **yet ye turned not to Me, saith the Lord,** all His punishments did not have the desired effect. V. 18. **Consider now from this day and upward,** applying their hearts to the consideration of that which pertained to their best interests, **from the four and twentieth day of the ninth month, even from the day that the foundation of the Lord's Temple was laid, consider it,** for the entire period of time since the Jews, in accordance with the decree of Cyrus, had first laid the foundation till the day of the assembly at which these words were spoken, was a time during which the blessing of the Lord was not poured out in its fullest measure, because all their labor for the new Temple had been fitful. V. 19. **Is the seed yet in the barn?** They were still suffering as a consequence of the shortage. **Yea, as yet the vine and the fig-tree and the pomegranate and the olive-tree hath not brought forth,** the results of their former lack of zeal were still in evidence; **from this day will I bless you.** Times would now change, since they were showing evidence of the change which had come over their hearts. If men turn to the Lord in true repentance, He may turn to them in mercy and give them blessings of this life in rich measure.

A SPECIAL PROMISE TO ZERUBBABEL. — V. 20. **And again the word of the Lord came unto Haggai in the four and twentieth day of the month,** this being a second revelation on the same day, **saying,** v. 21. **Speak to Zerubbabel, governor of Judah, saying,** in a message of encouragement which was nevertheless intended for the entire assembly of returned exiles, **I will shake the heavens and the earth,** setting their machinery in motion in the interest of His plans for His people; v. 22. **and I will overthrow the throne of kingdoms,** all the world-powers opposed to His reign, **and I will destroy the strength of the kingdoms of the heathen,** all the forces of evil that are opposed to the Church of the Lord; **and I will overthrow the chariots and those that ride in them,** the leaders of the hostile forces; **and the horses and their riders shall come down,** being overthrown and destroyed, **every one by the sword of his brother;** for that, in the end, is a condition which favors the Lord's kingdom, the fact that the enemies are often not at peace among themselves, but turn their weapons against one another. V. 23. **In that day, saith the Lord of hosts, will I take thee, O Zerubbabel, My servant, the son of Shealtiel, saith the Lord,** Zerubbabel as a member of the family of David being a type of the coming Messiah, **and will make thee as a signet,** a very precious possession in the eyes of its Oriental possessor; **for I have chosen thee, saith the Lord of hosts.** The fulfilment of this prophecy is found in Jesus Christ, the son of David and descendant of Zerubbabel, for He established the kingdom of His father David in a most unique manner, as a spiritual rule and reign, which is to last throughout eternity. Cp. Luke 1, 32. 33.

THE BOOK OF THE PROPHET ZECHARIAH.

INTRODUCTION.

The prophet Zechariah ("Jehovah remembers," "he whom Jehovah remembers") was a son of Berechiah and a grandson of Iddo, a member of a priestly family. Cp. Neh. 12, 4. As late as the time of the high priest Joiakim, Neh. 12, 12. 16, he was the chief of his generation or order. His prophetic activity followed immediately upon that of Haggai, as far as his writing is concerned, for he received his first recorded revelation in November of the year 520 B. C. Both Haggai and Zechariah were active in furthering the construction of the second Temple. Cp. Ezra 5, 1; 6, 14. He was still a comparatively young man when he began his work as prophet, and there is no record of the length of his activity. We may conclude from certain references in the Book of Nehemiah that he reached a ripe old age.

The Book of Zechariah may be divided into four or, more exactly, into three parts. After an exhortation admonishing the Jews to be obedient to the words of the Lord we have eight visions, in the manner of the prophet Ezekiel, all of which were vouchsafed the prophet in one night in February of the year 519. The second part of the book, dated December, 518, contains a message with both admonition and promise. The third part contains a prophetic description of the future of God's people, which, again, is divided into two parts, both highly Messianic in character.1)

"The style of the prophet varies with his subject: at one time conversational, at another, poetical. His symbols are enigmatical and therefore accompanied by explanations. His prose is like that of Ezekiel, diffuse, uniform, and full of repetitions. The rhythm of his poetry is somewhat unequal, and the parallelisms are not altogether symmetrical. Still there is often found much of the elevation met with in the earlier prophets and a general congruity between the style and the subject. Graphic vividness is his peculiar merit. Chaldaisms occur occasionally. Another special characteristic of Zechariah is his introduction of spiritual beings into his prophetic scenes." (Fausset.)

1) Cp. Fuerbringer, *Einleitung in das Alte Testament*, 92—96.

CHAPTER 1.

The Introduction and the First Visions.

A CALL TO REPENTANCE. — V. 1. **In the eighth month, in the second year of Darius,** that is, in the year 520 B. C., **came the word of the Lord unto Zechariah, the son of Berechiah, the son of Iddo, the prophet, saying,** v. 2. **The Lord hath been sore displeased,** with a vehement anger, **with your fathers,** as shown in the overthrow of Jerusalem, the destruction of the Temple, and the exile in Babylon. V. 3. **Therefore say thou unto them, Thus saith the Lord of hosts,** the almighty Sovereign of the universe, **Turn ye unto Me, saith the Lord of hosts,** a most impressive call to the children of the former trespassers to repent, **and I will turn unto you, saith the Lord of hosts.** V. 4. **Be ye not as your fathers,** those before the exile, **unto whom the former prophets have cried, saying, Thus saith the Lord of hosts, Turn ye now from your evil ways and from your evil doings,** this being the gist of many admonitions in the earlier prophets, cp. Is. 31, 6; Jer. 3, 12; 18, 11; Ezek. 18, 30; Hos. 14, 1; **but they did not hear nor hearken unto Me, saith the Lord.** Cp. 2 Kings 17. V. 5. **Your fathers, where are they? And the prophets, do they live forever?** The former members of Israel and Judah had perished, as God had threatened; and if the people should say that the prophets also were dead, the Lord would remind them of the fact that His words, as spoken through these prophets, are not dead, but had been abundantly fulfilled. V. 6. **But My words and My statutes, which I commanded My servants, the prophets,** namely, that they should proclaim them, threatening the Lord's punishment in case of disobedience, **did they not take hold of your fathers?** the threatened punishments having overtaken them like swift messengers. **And they,** the fathers before the exile, **returned and said,** in acknowledging their afflictions as the result of their wickedness, **Like as the Lord of hosts thought to do unto us, according to our ways and according to our doings,** just as they had deserved it, **so hath He dealt with us.** This was the state of mind which the Lord wanted to find in the midst of His people in making known to them the wonderful facts contained in the visions of Zechariah. The proper attitude for hearing and learning the Word of God is that of a humble acknowledgment of one's sinfulness.

THE VISION OF THE HORSES AMONG THE MYRTLE-TREES. — V. 7. **Upon the four and twentieth day of the eleventh month, which is the month Sebat,** five months after the building of the Temple had been resumed, **in the second year of Darius, came the word of the Lord unto Zechariah, the son**

of Berechiah, the son of Iddo, the prophet, saying, v. 8. **I saw by night,** in a night vision, some time between six o'clock in the evening and six o'clock in the morning, **and behold a man riding upon a red horse,** the color of war and bloodshed, **and he stood among the myrtle-trees that were in the bottom,** most likely a valley in the neighborhood of Jerusalem; **and behind him were there red horses, speckled,** or bay, the color of fire and flames and burning, **and white,** in this connection the color of victory. V. 9. **Then said I,** anxious to know what the Lord intended to make known through this vision, **O my Lord, what are these? And the angel that talked with me said unto me, I will show thee what these be,** for the Lord wanted Zechariah to know the meaning of the vision in order that he might reveal it to others. V. 10. **And the man that stood among the myrtle-trees,** the first angel, **answered and said, These are they whom the Lord hath sent to walk to and fro through the earth,** to find out how matters stood everywhere. V. 11. **And they answered the Angel of the Lord,** that peculiar uncreated Angel, the Son of God as He revealed Himself to the believers of the Old Testament, **that stood among the myrtle-trees, and said, We have walked to and fro through the earth, and, behold, all the earth sitteth still and is at rest,** the great commotion among the nations, of which the prophet Haggai had spoken, chap. 2, 7. 8, had not yet begun, that is, the time for the Messiah to appear in the flesh had not yet come, a statement which naturally had a most depressing effect upon the Jews. But the Lord has a word of comfort ready for them. V. 12. **Then the Angel of the Lord answered and said,** the second person of the Godhead Himself giving them a reassuring word of comfort, **O Lord of hosts, how long wilt Thou not have mercy on Jerusalem and on the cities of Judah, against which Thou hast had indignation these threescore and ten years?** so that the seventy years of the exile seemed extended, as though the affliction of the captivity would never end. V. 13. **And the Lord answered the angel that talked with me with good words and comfortable words,** words of salvation and blessing, which he, of course, was immediately to pass on to the congregation of the Lord. V. 14. **So the angel that communed with me,** he who had first given an interpretation of the Lord's intentions as expressed in the vision, **said unto me, Cry thou, saying, Thus saith the Lord of hosts,** He whose exact message the prophet brought to Judah, **I am jealous for Jerusalem and for Zion,** He was agitated with the zeal of His love for His congregation, **with a great jealousy.** V. 15. **And I am very sore displeased with the heathen that are at ease,** believing that they had been permanently victorious over the Lord's people; **for I was but a little displeased,** as His punishment went out upon His people for seventy years, **and they helped forward the affliction,** they rioted in the sufferings of helpless Israel and were anxious to prolong them. V. 16. **Therefore, thus saith the Lord, I am returned to Jerusalem with mercies,** for He had withheld them from His people for a time in order to punish them, but now He was once more ready to accept His repentant children; **My house shall be built in it,** namely, the Temple as the seat of the Lord's merciful presence in the midst of His congregation, **saith the Lord of hosts, and a line shall be stretched forth upon Jerusalem,** in this case the builder's line signifying the rebuilding of the city. V. 17. **Cry yet, saying, Thus saith the Lord of hosts, My cities through prosperity shall yet be spread abroad,** overflowing with the outward pressure of abundant growth as a stream overflows its banks; **and the Lord shall yet comfort Zion,** the Church of His love, **and shall yet choose Jerusalem,** the communion of His saints. Thus the Lord, who occasionally has punished His Church with heavy stripes, ever again has turned to His children with the wealth of His blessings in the Gospel.

THE VISION OF THE FOUR HORNS AND THE FOUR SMITHS. — V. 18. **Then,** after the first vision had fully come to an end, **lifted I up mine eyes and saw,** in a second distinct vision, **and behold four horns,** the common Scriptural symbol of strength. V. 19. **And I said unto the angel that talked with me, What be these?** the prophet again desirous of knowing their significance. **And he answered me, These are the horns which have scattered Judah, Israel, and Jerusalem,** the heathen nations that had destroyed the twelve tribes as a people. V. 20. **And the Lord showed me four carpenters,** rather, four craftsmen in iron, four smiths. V. 21. **Then said I, What come these to do?** What was the object in introducing them into the picture? **And He spake, saying, These are the horns which have scattered Judah, so that no man did lift up his head,** being altogether discouraged; **but these are come to fray them,** to terrify the great powers of evil, **to cast out the horns of the Gentiles,** to break them off, **which lifted up their horn over the land of Judah to scatter it.** It has ever been a characteristic of the enemies of the Lord that they rejoice over the misfortune of His people; but in the end the Church will triumph.

CHAPTER 2.

Vision of the Man with the Measuring-Line.

The second vision had pictured the overthrow of the enemies of the people of the Lord. But this defeat being administered, the growth of the Lord's Church was assured. V. 1. **I lifted up mine eyes again,** once more being in a state of ecstasy, **and looked, and, behold, a man with a measuring-line in his hand,** evidently an angel sent for a special purpose. V. 2. **Then said I,** addressing the angel himself, **Whither goest thou? And he said unto me, To measure Jerusalem,** the city of Jehovah, **to see what is the breadth thereof, and what is the length thereof,** to get the dimensions of the city even then in existence. V. 3. **And, behold, the angel that talked with me went forth,** he was removed from the scene. **And another angel went out to meet him,** a third angel thus meeting him who acted as interpreter, v. 4. **and said unto him, Run, speak to this young man,** namely, to the prophet, **saying, Jerusalem shall be inhabited as towns without walls for the multitude of men and cattle therein.** It is clearly not the earthly city to which the angel refers, but a wonderful spiritual city without local dimensions, the Jerusalem of the New Testament, the one holy Christian Church. V. 5. **For I, saith the Lord, will be unto her a wall of fire round about,** so that the city of God would be secure under the sheltering wings of His power, **and will be the glory in the midst of her,** so that His blessings would rest upon her and His name be praised within her. So much being established, the prophet is given a summary of what he should proclaim to this Church of the Lord. V. 6. **Ho, ho, come forth!** so the Lord addresses His people through the Angel of the Covenant, **and flee from the land of the North,** out of Babylon, as typical of all powers of evil banded together against His Church, **saith the Lord; for I have spread you abroad as the four winds of the heaven, saith the Lord,** namely, in the New Testament Church which extends to the most remote ends of the world. V. 7. **Deliver thyself, O Zion, that dwellest with the daughter of Babylon,** or, "Ho, Zion, save thyself!" the separation between the children of God and the children of the world being absolute, even if not local. Cp. 2 Cor. 6, 17. V. 8. **For thus saith the Lord of hosts, After the glory hath He sent Me unto the nations which spoiled you,** the Angel of the Lord being sent to the heathen to get back the glory which they, by their hostile treatment of His people, had taken from Him; **for he that toucheth you toucheth the apple of His eye,** so dear are the believers, the members of the Church, in the eyes of the Lord. Every adversary who dares to touch the kingdom of God and its members thereby becomes guilty of a blasphemous act, which grieves the Lord most deeply. This insult Jehovah will not accept without the most emphatic resentment; He will punish the people, He will visit their sins upon them. V. 9. **For, behold, I will shake Mine hand upon them,** swinging it back and forth over them in order to deliver a heavy blow, **and they shall be a spoil to their servants,** so that the latter become the lords of their former masters; **and ye shall know that the Lord of hosts hath sent Me,** that through Him the great Sovereign of the earth was carrying out His punishment upon the enemies of His Church. For this reason the people of the Lord are exhorted to sing praises to Him. V. 10. **Sing and rejoice, O daughter of Zion,** the Church of Jehovah, especially in the New Testament; **for, lo, I come,** the Messiah Himself addressing those who were longing for His coming, **and I will dwell in the midst of thee, saith the Lord.** This was so wonderfully fulfilled when the Word was made flesh and dwelt among us. Cp. John 1, 14; Gal. 4, 4. V. 11. **And many nations,** representatives of the various races and countries of the world, **shall be joined to the Lord in that day,** to be added to His people, **and shall be My people,** Eph. 2, 19; **and I will dwell in the midst of thee,** in the city of God of the New Testament, **and thou shalt know that the Lord of hosts hath sent Me unto thee,** the great God of heaven sending His only-begotten Son for the salvation of His people. V. 12. **And the Lord shall inherit Judah his portion in the Holy Land,** so that He would possess His Church, **and shall choose Jerusalem again,** as the place of His dwelling and of His blessing. V. 13. **Be silent, O all flesh,** in a spirit of awe and reverence, **before the Lord; for He is raised up out of His holy habitation,** He is preparing to rise from His throne in heaven to visit the enemies with His righteous punishment and to lead His children to glory. Cp. Ps. 76, 8. 9; Zeph. 1, 7.

CHAPTER 3.

The Vision of the High Priest.

The Lord had just referred to the glorification of His people. He now proceeds to show how this would take place. V. 1. **And He showed me Joshua, the high priest,** the man who, with Zerubbabel, had been the leader of the people when they returned from exile, **standing before the Angel of the Lord,** here pictured as the Judge in a court of law, **and Satan standing at his right hand to resist**

him, to accuse the high priest, to have him condemned, if possible, Satan here appearing as the true adversary of the Church. V. 2. **And the Lord,** Jehovah, for it is He who is the Angel of the Lord, **said unto Satan, The Lord rebuke thee, O Satan,** the adversary and accuser being condemned instead of him whom he wanted to condemn, **even the Lord that hath chosen Jerusalem rebuke thee,** He has accepted the believers in Him as His people and will not permit Satan to interfere with His choice. **Is not this a brand plucked out of the fire?** The Lord's people had been at the very brink of destruction, but the Lord had interfered before it was too late; therefore Joshua also, standing before the Lord as the representative of the sinful people, is shielded from condemnation. The scene is now further elaborated in order to bring out its full meaning. V. 3. **Now, Joshua was clothed with filthy garments,** typical of the sinfulness which was still found in the Lord's people, Is. 64, 5, **and stood before the Angel,** it was thus that he had presented himself in the Lord's court. V. 4. **And He,** the presiding Angel of Jehovah, **answered and spake unto those that stood before Him,** some of His ministering angels, **saying, Take away the filthy garments from him,** this signifying the removal of the people's guilt. **And unto him He said, Behold, I have caused thine iniquity to pass from thee,** by an act of complete forgiveness, **and I will clothe thee with change of raiment,** with the festival garments of a perfect righteousness. V. 5. **And I said,** the prophet here suddenly interposing in his eagerness to have the work of cleansing completed, **Let them set a fair miter upon his head,** to give him the crowning assurance that the priesthood was restored, that the name of Jehovah was once more borne on the turban of the high priest. **So they set a fair miter upon his head and clothed him with garments. And the Angel of the Lord stood by,** having arisen from His judge's chair to see that the prayer of Zechariah was executed in every detail. Thus Joshua, the representative of the people, particularly of its priestly character, was restored to the full dignity of the olden days, and thereby the people were likewise restored to their position as the Lord's people. But all this was significant also for the future. V. 6. **And the Angel of the Lord protested unto Joshua,** testifying with impressive solemnity, **saying,** v. 7. **Thus saith the Lord of hosts, If thou wilt walk in My ways,** as a true child of God, **and if thou wilt keep My charge,** performing every part of his office with due faithfulness, **then thou shalt also judge My house,** have charge of the Lord's Temple, **and shalt also keep My courts,** in observing every provision of the Ceremonial Law concerning Jehovah's worship, **and I will give thee places to walk among these that stand by,** that is, he would have open and unhindered access between the holy angels to the very throne of Jehovah; for in the New Testament all human mediators have been discarded, so that every believer may draw nigh to the Throne of Grace without hesitation. V. 8. **Hear now, O Joshua the high priest, thou and thy fellows that sit before thee,** his fellow-priests; **for they are men wondered at,** literally, "men of wonder are they," that is, men about whom one might marvel; **for, behold, I will bring forth My Servant, the BRANCH.** Cp. Jer. 23, 5. 6; Is. 11, 1. This Zemach, or Branch, of whom the priests of the Old Testament were but types, is the Servant of Jehovah in a most singular sense, who was to carry out the will of Jehovah concerning the redemption of the world. Cp. Is. 53. V. 9. **For behold the stone that I have laid before Joshua; upon one stone shall be seven eyes,** that is, seven eyes, the number of perfection, would be directed upon him, the loving care of Jehovah being indicated, as He observes His people, the believers in Him. **Behold, I will engrave the graving thereof,** with beautiful ornamental sculpture, **saith the Lord of hosts, and I will remove the iniquity of that land in one day,** both the transgressions and their punishment. This great day is the day of Calvary, for it was then that God, in one day, took away the sins of the whole world. V. 10. **In that day, saith the Lord of hosts, shall ye call every man his neighbor under the vine and under the fig-tree,** inviting him in the communion of Christian fellowship, doing mission-work in calling others to enjoy the blessings of the Gospel. We thus have the entire period of the New Testament in outline in this one vision, a Gospel-message which might well be heeded by all men in our days.

CHAPTER 4.

The Vision of the Candlestick and of the Two Olive-Trees.

After the prophet had been a witness of the first four visions, he was so overwhelmed by the revelations vouchsafed him that he fell into a trancelike condition, somewhat like Peter and his companions on the Mount of Transfiguration. Cp. Luke 9, 32; Matt. 17, 5. 6. V. 1. **And the angel that talked with me,** he who acted as the interpreter of the Lord in making known the message concerning the future, **came again and waked me, as a man that is wakened out of his sleep,** out of his state of exhaustion. The angel had evidently left the prophet for a short while and now returned for the purpose of interpreting further visions. V. 2. **And said unto me, What seest thou?** thus calling the prophet's attention to a new vision, whereas in the other instances Zechariah had asked for information. **And I said, I have looked,** he was even then observing very closely, **and behold a candlestick all of gold, with a bowl upon the top of it,** a round vessel, or reservoir, for oil, **and his seven lamps thereon and seven pipes to the seven lamps,** or seven feed-pipes to each of the seven lamps, to insure a plentiful supply of fuel, **which are upon the top thereof,** the candlestick in general being formed after that in the Tabernacle, Ex. 25, 31—37; v. 3. **and two olive-trees by it, one upon the right side of the bowl and the other upon the left side thereof,** this being a new feature, indicating the source of the oil for the lamps. V. 4. **So I answered,** the prophet having meanwhile recovered to some extent from his dazed condition, **and spake to the angel that talked with me, saying, What are these, my lord?** He could not quite grasp the significance of it all. V. 5. **Then the angel that talked with me answered and said unto me, Knowest thou not what these be?** He was surprised that a man of Judah, and he of priestly descent, should not find some meaning in the vision of such a candlestick. **And I said, No, my lord.** V. 6. **Then he answered and spake unto me, saying, This is the word of the Lord unto Zerubbabel, saying, Not by might,** that is, the force of armies, **nor by power,** namely, that of any earthly agency, **but by My Spirit, saith the Lord of hosts.** The candlestick of the Tabernacle was a type of the congregation of the Old Testament, which was supposed to be a light shining in the darkness of the world. Its oil was a type of the Holy Ghost, and the high priests of the Old Covenant received the strength for the performance of the duties of their office from the Spirit symbolized in the light of the great candlestick. Thus the candlestick of the vision was a type of the Church of God to be established anew in the midst of Judah. Moreover, Zerubbabel, the governor of the people, was to be informed that the great work which he was to perform could be carried on only through the Spirit of the Lord. V. 7. **Who art thou, O great mountain?** the building of the Temple being thus represented. **Before Zerubbabel thou shalt become a plain,** he would easily overcome all the difficulties connected with the completion of this momentous work; **and he shall bring forth the headstone thereof,** the uppermost stone of its walls, **with shoutings, crying, Grace, grace unto it!** that is, May God grant grace to this stone and to the building which it represents, so that it may stand forever! But the Temple of Zerubbabel was only a type of the true Temple of Jehovah, the Church of the New Testament. V. 8. **Moreover, the word of the Lord came unto me, saying,** v. 9. **The hands of Zerubbabel have laid the foundation of this house,** this having been done some sixteen years before; **his hands shall also finish it,** as they did some four years later; **and thou shalt know that the Lord of hosts hath sent me unto you,** whence it follows that the entire situation has a deeper significance than that of a mere earthly temple, namely, that the Lord Jehovah, in the Word that was made flesh, was coming to the temple of His Church. V. 10. **For who hath despised the day of small things?** It seemed indeed that the days in which Judah was then living were days of insignificant things, when the entire nation was living in deepest poverty and contempt; yet these days were the forerunners of the most momentous period in the history of the world. **For they,** the people concerned, **shall rejoice and shall see the plummet in the hand of Zerubbabel,** as the chief builder of the Temple, **with those seven, they are the eyes of the Lord, which run to and fro through the whole earth,** cp. chap. 3, 9. But if the eyes of God's majesty rest upon this building with such evident joy and satisfaction, it surely must be a Temple of the greatest importance, and the days in which it is being built must not be despised. V. 11. **Then answered I and said unto him,** anxious to get some further information on this most interesting point, **What are these two olive-trees upon the right side of the candlestick and upon the left side thereof?** The candlestick was in the center with its arms extended on either side, and next to these arms stood the two olive-trees which were puzzling the prophet. V. 12. **And I answered again and said unto him, What be these two olive-branches,** literally, "ears," because they were bunched to resemble ears of grain, **which through the two golden pipes,** special spouts, or funnels, placed under them, **empty the golden oil out of themselves?** so that the oil was fed directly from the trees into the pipes connecting with the reservoir of the candlestick. V. 13. **And he answered me and said, Knowest thou not what these be? And I said, No, my lord.** V. 14. **Then said he, These are the two anointed ones,** literally, "the two sons of oil," **that stand by the Lord of the whole earth,** as His servants. They were symbols of Zerubbabel and of Joshua, the temporal and the spiritual leader of the people, respectively, anointed by God for the performance of the work of their office. The meaning for our day and age is clear. The Church is the Lord's candlestick, Matt. 5, 14, and therefore has a great and important duty to fulfil in this world. This duty may not be performed by the power and might of men, but solely and alone through the Spirit of the Lord given to His Church and to its ministers in and through the Gospel.

CHAPTER 5.

The Flying Roll and the Woman in the Ephah.

THE VISION OF THE FLYING ROLL. — V. 1. **Then I turned,** after an interval of some time, **and lifted up mine eyes and looked, and behold a flying roll,** a book-scroll, or parchment, of great size, or consisting of many large leaves fastened together. V. 2. **And he said unto me, What seest thou? And I answered, I see a flying roll,** a parchment loose or unrolled moving through the air; **the length thereof is twenty cubits and the breadth thereof ten cubits,** the dimensions approximately ten yards by five yards. V. 3. **Then said he unto me,** without waiting for a question on the part of the prophet, **This is the curse that goeth forth over the face of the whole earth,** as written on the roll; **for every one that stealeth shall be cut off as on this side according to it, and every one that sweareth shall be cut off as on that side according to it,** that is, the sinners who refuse to repent, who persist in their wickedness, must be cut off and removed; the holiness of God cannot rule in any other way. V 4. **I will bring it forth,** namely, the curse and the judgment in agreement with it, **saith the Lord of hosts, and it shall enter into the house of the thief and into the house of him that sweareth falsely by My name,** these two classes of sinners being named as representatives of all unrepentant transgressors; **and it shall remain in the midst of his house,** lodging there, dwelling there permanently, **and shall consume it with the timber thereof and the stones thereof,** not leaving a vestige of it. These words are properly expressive of the curse and of the punishment of God upon every form of deliberate transgression. The Lord is like a consuming fire upon everything that is called sin.

THE VISION OF THE WOMAN IN THE EPHAH. V. 5. **Then the angel that talked with me,** who acted as the interpreter of all these visions, **went forth,** so that there was a pause in the revelations of the Lord, **and said unto me, Lift up now thine eyes and see what is this that goeth forth,** appearing before his eyes, something that he should observe very closely. V. 6. **And I said, What is it?** for Zechariah evidently did not recognize the object at once. **And he said, This is an ephah that goeth forth,** the ephah being a dry measure corresponding roughly to our peck. The object in the vision was evidently a receptacle having the shape of an ephah, and the ephah was chosen because it was often called the measure of unrighteousness and of deceit. **He said moreover, This is their resemblance through all the earth,** literally, "This their eye in all the land," that is, this is the object of their gaze, all eyes are centered upon it. V. 7. **And, behold, there was lifted up a talent of lead,** a great round piece, weighing about a hundred pounds; **and this is a woman that sitteth in the midst of the ephah,** the female personification of wickedness held within the ephah by the great weight. V. 8. **And he said, This is wickedness,** false doctrine, godlessness personified. **And he cast it into the midst of the ephah,** thus preventing her escape; **and he cast the weight of lead upon the mouth thereof,** this acting as a cover keeping her shut up within the measure. V. 9. **Then lifted I up mine eyes and looked,** fascinated by a further wonderful thing that happened, **and, behold, there came out two women, and the wind was in their wings,** aiding them in their movement forward as they carried the ephah; **for they had wings like the wings of a stork; and they lifted up the ephah between the earth and the heaven,** carrying it along very quickly, away from the Holy Land. V. 10. **Then said I to the angel that talked with me, Whither do these bear the ephah?** V. 11. **And he said unto me, To build it an house in the land of Shinar,** typical from olden times as the land of rebellion against the Lord, Gen. 11, 1—9; **and it shall be established and set there upon her own base.** In the land of Babylon, representative of the ungodly world, wickedness was to have its place, to be forever excluded from the kingdom of the Lord. The congregation of the Lord is the holy Christian Church, and for that reason the Lord will brook no open wickedness in its midst. Wilful and unrepentant sinners must be excluded from the communion of saints. Note: There may be a special reason for comparing the essence of all wickedness with a woman; for so also the great harlot of the Book of Revelation is described, the kingdom of Antichrist being the climax and summary of all godless doctrine.

CHAPTER 6.

The Four Chariots and the Crown upon Joshua's Head.

THE VISION OF THE FOUR CHARIOTS. — V. 1. **And I turned and lifted up mine eyes,** or, "And again I lifted up my eyes," **and looked, and, behold, there came four chariots out from between two mountains,** the location of the vision being somewhere in the mountainous country near Jerusalem, very likely between Mount Zion and the Mount of Olives; **and the mountains were mountains of brass,** firm and immovable. V. 2. **In the first**

chariot, harnessed to it, **were red horses,** signifying war and bloodshed; **and in the second chariot black horses,** the color of misfortune, of mourning, and of death; v. 3. **and in the third chariot white horses,** implying joy and victory; **and in the fourth chariot grizzled and bay horses** Cp. Rev. 6, 8. V. 4. **Then I answered and said unto the angel that talked with me,** the one who had acted as interpreter in all the visions, **What are these, my lord?** V. 5. **And the angel answered and said unto me, These are the four spirits of the heavens,** the four winds as the instruments of the Lord's will, **which go forth from standing before the Lord of all the earth.** Cp. Ps. 104, 4; 148, 8. The agency of the winds in the work of destructive judgment is mentioned also elsewhere in the Bible Cp. Rev. 7, 1. V. 6. **The black horses which are therein,** that is, the chariot drawn by these horses, **go forth into the North country,** where the great world-powers, Assyria and Babylon, were situated; **and the white go forth after them,** victory following death and destruction; **and the grizzled go forth toward the South country,** where Idumea and Egypt were situated. V. 7. **And the bay went forth and sought to go that they might walk to and fro through the earth,** visiting all the countries of the world with a terrible, universal judgment, with war and bloodshed, with death and destruction; **and he said, Get you hence, walk to and fro through the earth. So they walked to and fro through the earth,** carrying out the Lord's command upon the various nations. V. 8. **Then cried he,** the angel, **upon me and spake unto me,** in great excitement, **saying,** in the name of the Lord, **Behold, these that go toward the North country have quieted My Spirit in the North country,** have caused the Spirit of Jehovah to rest there, to be satisfied with the extent of the punishment inflicted upon the world-powers. It is clear that the angel is speaking of a last great Judgment, by which all the enemies of the Lord would be overthrown, in order that His Church may be safely established.

THE CROWNING OF THE HIGH PRIEST. — V. 9. **And the word of the Lord came unto me, saying,** v. 10. **Take of them of the captivity,** exiled Jews living in Babylon, who had come up to Jerusalem at that time, **even of Heldai, of Tobijah, and of Jedaiah, which are come from Babylon,** as a committee of the Jews residing at Babylon, **and come thou the same day and go into the house of Josiah, the son of Zephaniah,** who was showing these emissaries the hospitality of his house; v. 11. **then take silver and gold,** evidently of the precious metals sent by the Jews of Babylon, **and make crowns,** a double crown or one of several bands, **and set them upon the head of Joshua, the son of Josedech, the high priest,** as a type of the combined priesthood and kingdom which shall be conferred upon the Messiah; v. 12. **and speak unto him, saying, Thus speaketh the Lord of hosts, saying, Behold, the man whose name is The BRANCH,** the Zemach spoken of in chap. 3, 8; **and He shall grow up out of His place,** Jer. 33, 15, as a root out of a dry ground, Is. 53, 2, **and He shall build the Temple of the Lord,** the real Sanctuary of Jehovah, the Church of the New Testament; v. 13. **even He shall build the Temple of the Lord,** accomplishing His great work in spite of the lowliness of His origin; **and He shall bear the glory,** being adorned with kingly glory and honor, **and shall sit and rule upon His throne,** as the true King of His Church; **and He shall be a Priest upon His throne,** uniting in His person the offices of king and of priest; **and the counsel of peace shall be between them both,** the two offices being united in one person. Cp. Ps. 110. V. 14. **And the crowns shall be to Helem,** or Heldai, **and to Tobijah, and to Jedaiah, and to Hen, the son of Zephaniah,** to the hospitable kindness of the son of Zephaniah, **for a memorial in the Temple of the Lord,** so that future generations would be reminded of the example of these two men. Moreover, the example of the messengers from Babylon was not to be forgotten. V. 15. **And they that are far off,** like the men who had in this case brought their offerings, **shall come and build in the Temple of the Lord,** representatives of various heathen nations joining in the upbuilding of the Lord's great spiritual Temple, His holy Church, **and ye shall know that the Lord of hosts hath sent me unto you,** as the Messiah Himself says, John 3, 16. **And this shall come to pass, if ye will diligently obey the voice of the Lord, your God,** this being added by way of admonition lest any one deliberately lose the blessings which are offered in and by the coming of the Messiah. Thus the establishment and growth of the Church of the New Testament is definitely sketched, also for the strengthening of our faith.[2]

---

2) On the night visions, cp. *Syn. Ber.*, North Wisconsin, 1918.

CHAPTER 7.

A Double Admonition.

THE QUESTION PROPOSED. — V. 1. **And it came to pass in the fourth year of King Darius,** in the year 518 B. C., **that the word of the Lord,** by special inspiration, **came unto Zechariah in the fourth day of the ninth month, even in Chisleu,** corresponding roughly to our December, v. 2. **when they had sent unto the house of God Sherezer and Regem-melech and their men to pray before the Lord,** rather, Bethel, that is, the citizens of this city, sent Sherezer and Regem-melech, the first one evidently having been born in exile and bearing a Chaldean name, with their men, to entreat Jehovah, literally, "to conciliate by caresses," v. 3. **and to speak unto the priests which were in the house of the Lord of hosts,** who were on duty, although the Temple was not yet finished, **and to the prophets,** also servants of the true God in the more specific sense, **saying, Should I weep in the fifth month,** observing a special fast in commemoration of the taking of the city of Jerusalem by Nebuchadnezzar, **separating myself,** abstaining from food, **as I have done these so many years?** for this fast had become a custom during the captivity, and now that the Jews were once more living in Palestine, was being observed throughout the country. For this reason the question was of practical importance for all the Jews, both at home and abroad. V. 4. **Then came the word of the Lord of hosts unto me, saying,** v. 5. **Speak unto all the people of the land and to the priests,** His message concerning them all, **saying, When ye fasted and mourned in the fifth and seventh month,** the latter observation being in memory of the murder of Gedaliah, cp. Jer. 41, **even those seventy years,** during the entire captivity, **did ye at all fast unto Me, even to Me?** Had it really been done in His honor, for the purpose of serving Him, or was it a work performed in a sense of selfishness, to foster the spirit of resentment and revenge? V. 6. **And when ye did eat, and when ye did drink, did not ye eat for yourselves and drink for yourselves?** Both their fasting and their feasting, so the Lord reminds them, was conducted without regard to Him, simply for the gratification of their own ideas. V. 7. **Should ye not hear the words which the Lord hath cried by the former prophets, when Jerusalem was inhabited and in prosperity and the cities thereof round about her,** the suburbs dependent upon the capital, **when men inhabited the south,** the semiarid section of Judah toward the southeast, **and the plain,** the lowlands toward the southwest? They should have been familiar with the messages of the prophets before the exile, which time and again emphasized the need of a true worship of the heart, of sincere repentance and faith. The fasting in itself is a matter of indifference to the Lord. The fasting which is well-pleasing to God does not primarily consist in abstaining from food, but in one's observing the Word of the Lord and living in accordance with it at all times, as the prophets have ever preached.

AN APPEAL TO THE PAST. — V. 8. **And the word of the Lord came unto Zechariah, saying,** v. 9. **Thus speaketh the Lord of hosts,** rather, "Thus spake Jehovah," in addressing the children of Judah in former days, before the exile, **saying, Execute true judgment,** literally, "judge the judgment of truth," **and show mercy and compassions every man to his brother,** so that kindness and pity should be practised at all times, Is. 58, 6. 7; Jer. 7, 23; v. 10. **and oppress not the widow nor the fatherless,** the orphans, **the stranger nor the poor,** these four classes ever being in the care of the Lord, Is. 1, 17; Jer. 5, 28; **and let none of you imagine evil against his brother in your heart,** this being a summary of a number of admonitions with which the earlier prophets had tried to influence the people for their own good. V. 11. **But they refused to hearken,** they were consistently rebellious, **and pulled away the shoulder,** like an ox who refuses to accept the yoke on his neck, **and stopped their ears,** cp. Is. 6, 10, **that they should not hear.** V. 12. **Yea, they made their hearts as an adamant stone,** like the hardest stone, impervious to every impression from without, **lest they should hear the Law,** the books of Moses, **and the words which the Lord of hosts hath sent in His Spirit,** inspired by His Spirit, **by the former prophets,** who were the instruments of God in making known His will; **therefore came a great wrath from the Lord of hosts,** as shown in the captivity of Judah. V. 13. **Therefore it is come to pass, that as He cried,** in the exhortations of His prophets, **and they would not hear, so they cried,** they called when in trouble, so Jehovah says, **and I would not hear, saith the Lord of hosts;** v. 14. **but I scattered them with a whirlwind,** in a terrible storm of His wrath, **among all the nations whom they knew not,** strange to them in language, customs, and religion. **Thus the land was desolate after them, that no man passed through nor returned,** all of Judea practically being a wilderness; **for they laid the pleasant land desolate,** the children of Judah themselves being to blame for the desolation which came upon the land. When sinners receive the just punishment of their sins, they have but themselves to blame for their afflictions, though their pride would attempt to deny it.

CHAPTER 8.

The Renewal of the Covenant.

THE RESTORATION DESCRIBED.—**V. 1. Again the word of the Lord of hosts came to me, saying,** v. 2. **Thus saith the Lord of hosts, I was jealous for Zion,** rather, I am jealous, for His zeal is that of a husband for the wife of his youth, **with great jealousy, and I was jealous for her with great fury,** in a most vehement affection directed toward His congregation and a corresponding anger against her oppressors. V. 3. **Thus saith the Lord, I am returned unto Zion and will dwell in the midst of Jerusalem,** once more occupying the dwelling-place of His honor in the midst of His people, which He had forsaken because of the wickedness of the idolatrous nation; **and Jerusalem shall be called a city of truth,** where the Lord's truth, the truth of His eternal Word, would once more be found; **and the mountain of the Lord of hosts,** where His Temple arose, **the holy mountain,** because it was the center of the true worship on the earth. V. 4. **Thus saith the Lord of hosts,** the name used throughout these prophecies to denote His majesty and power, **There shall yet old men and old women dwell in the streets of Jerusalem,** since they would not be torn away in the fulness of their strength by war and pestilence, **and every man with his staff in his hand for very age,** literally, "because of the multitude of his days." V. 5. **And the streets of the city shall be full of boys and girls playing in the streets thereof,** without any fear of an enemy. It is a beautiful picture representing the extremes of life dwelling in all security and happiness in the midst of the Lord's Holy City, the blessings of the Messianic period. V. 6. **Thus saith the Lord of hosts, If it be marvelous in the eyes of the remnant of this people in these days,** in the opinion of those who had returned from the Babylonian captivity, **should it also be marvelous in Mine eyes? saith the Lord of hosts.** In spite of the miraculous character of the restoration, if looked at from the standpoint of men, it would yet certainly take place, for it was not too hard for Jehovah, His promise affecting both the greatness and the certainty of the coming salvation. V. 7. **Thus saith the Lord of hosts, Behold, I will save My people from the East country,** from the rising of the sun, **and from the West country,** from the setting of the sun, so that Jehovah would rescue His people from all lands, as far as the sun shines; v. 8. **and I will bring them, and they shall dwell in the midst of Jerusalem,** be members of the congregation of the Lord; **and they shall be My people, and I will be their God, in truth and in righteousness.** This is truly the glory of the Christian era, when, as St. John writes, we saw His glory, the glory as of the Only-begotten of the Father, full of grace and truth. Cp. John 1, 14. V. 9. **Thus saith the Lord of hosts, Let your hands be strong,** full of good courage for doing the work of the Lord, **ye that hear in these days these words by the mouth of the prophets,** namely, Haggai and Zechariah, **which were in the day that the foundation of the house of the Lord of hosts was laid, that the Temple might be built.** These prophets had begun their activity at the time when the foundation of the second Temple had already been built, and the good effects of their preaching were now apparent in the nation. V. 10. **For before these days there was no hire for man nor any hire for beast,** for the yield of the land at that time was so small as hardly to be called fair wages, cp. Hagg. 1, 6—11; **neither was there any peace to him that went out or came in because of the affliction,** there was so much envy and hostility among the people themselves, and on account of jealousy stirred up by the Samaritans, that the ordinary occupations of life were continually being interfered with; **for I set all men every one against his neighbor,** as the account of Nehemiah shows. V. 11. **But now,** since the old covenant relation was restored, **I will not be unto the residue of this people,** to the small congregation which had returned from Babylon, **as in the former days, saith the Lord of hosts,** He was now ready once more to gladden them with the rich blessings of His goodness and mercy. V. 12. **For the seed shall be prosperous,** or, "there shall be a seed of peace"; **the vine shall give her fruit, and the ground shall give her increase,** all crops showing great productiveness, **and the heavens shall give their dew,** affording the necessary moisture to secure growth; **and I will cause the remnant of this people to possess all these things,** these being evidences of His goodness. V. 13. **And it shall come to pass that, as ye were a curse among the heathen, O house of Judah and house of Israel,** cp. Jer. 42, 18, **so will I save you, and ye shall be a blessing,** an example of God's blessings of mercy. **Fear not, but let your hands be strong.** V. 14. **For thus saith the Lord of hosts, As I thought to punish you when your fathers provoked Me to wrath, saith the Lord of hosts,** Jer. 31, 28, **and I repented not,** He could not, in point of fact, without denying His own holiness, fail to execute His threat of punishment, v. 15. **so, again, have I thought in these days,** now that the covenant relation was once more established, **to do well unto Jerusalem and to the house of Judah. Fear ye not!** this being the content of every true Gospel-message. Since God is gracious for the sake of the Messiah, therefore men have no reason to fear as long as they put their trust in Him alone. V. 16. **These are the things that ye shall do,** as an evidence of the new relation which obtained between them and Jehovah, the God of the covenant, **Speak ye every man the truth to his neighbor,** this being the basis of a proper brotherly relationship among men, **execute the judgment of truth and peace in your gates,** so that all their dealings, particularly those pertaining to their courts of law, would be in agreement with these principles, v. 17. **and let none of you imagine evil in your hearts against his neighbor,** deliberately planning harm, **and love no false oath,** for perjury makes the administration of justice impossible; **for all these are things that I hate, saith the Lord.** It is a most emphatic declaration, spoken with great solemnity, and it holds true for all time. God hates and despises wickedness in every form, and He wants those who are His children to wage continual warfare against every transgression of His holy Law.

THE EXTENT OF THE MESSIANIC INFLUENCE. V. 18. **And the word of the Lord of hosts came unto me, saying,** v. 19. **Thus saith the Lord of hosts, The fast of the fourth month and the fast of the fifth and the fast of the seventh and the fast of the tenth,** special days of fasting and affliction which the Jews had observed during their captivity in memory of certain dark days in the history of their nation, cp. chap. 7, 3, **shall be to the house of Judah joy and gladness and cheerful feasts,** festivals of highest happiness, since the Lord intended to pour out upon them such a multitude of blessings as to make them forget all the disagreeable facts in their past history and to rejoice in the goodness and mercy of their God; **therefore love the truth and peace,** this reaction on the part of the Jews being a necessary consequence of their appreciation of the Lord's goodness and mercy. V. 20. **Thus saith the Lord of hosts, It shall yet come to pass that there shall come people,** representatives of many nations, **and the inhabitants of many cities,** of the foremost centers of the world; v. 21. **and the inhabitants of one city shall go to another,** in mutually encouraging and admonishing one another, **saying, Let us go speedily,** literally, "Going let us go, with speed and earnestness," **to pray before the Lord and to seek the Lord of hosts,** in an invitation and exhortation to worship the one true God; **I will go also,** the vivid form of speech showing the alacrity with which men would respond. V. 22. **Yea, many people and strong nations,** the foremost countries of the world, **shall come to seek the Lord of hosts in Jerusalem,** to become members of His holy congregation, **and to pray before the Lord,** to worship Jehovah. V. 23. **Thus saith the Lord of hosts, In those days it shall come to pass that ten men shall take hold out of all languages of the nations,** that is, men of so many different nations, speaking so many different tongues, **even shall take hold of the skirt of him that is a Jew,** in great eagerness, **saying, We will go with you,** casting their lot with the people of the Lord in every way, **for we have heard that God is with you.** This has been fulfilled time and again during the New Testament era, when people from various nations have actually come and begged Christian missionaries to come to them and preach the Gospel. The glorious conversion of Gentile nations in the age of the Gospel dispensation is here clearly foretold, and in a most graphic manner.

CHAPTER 9.

The First Burden.

JUDGMENT UPON THE LAND OF HADRACH. — V. 1. **The burden of the word,** the sentence of judgment, **of the Lord in the land of Hadrach,** a term which seems to apply to the entire Medo-Persian empire, as the world-power opposed to the people of God, **and Damascus shall be the rest thereof,** the Syrian capital being the place on which the burden of the Lord's wrath rests; **when the eyes of man, as of all the tribes of Israel, shall be toward the Lord,** both the people outside of Israel, and Israel itself, being directed to the Lord at this evidence of His anger, when He goes about to establish a more equitable proportion between His people and the heathen. V. 2. **And Hamath also shall border thereby,** or, "Hamath," the district bounding Palestine on the north, "which borders thereon," this, together with Damascus, representing Syria; **Tyrus and Zidon,** the cities of Phenicia, **though it be very wise,** or, "because their inhabitants were wise in their own conceit," multiplying wealth and power and trusting in them. V. 3. **And Tyrus did build herself a stronghold,** the city proper being on an island surrounded by a double sea-wall, which made it practically impregnable in those days, **and heaped up silver as the dust and fine gold as the mire of the streets,** for the commerce of Tyre had made her immensely wealthy. V. 4. **Behold, the Lord will cast her out,** seizing her through the agency of some earthly conqueror, in this case Alexander, **and He will smite her power in the sea,** as represented by her army and her navy; **and she shall be devoured with fire,** so that everything on which her inhabitants depended was consumed and exterminated. V. 5. **Ashkelon shall see it,** namely, the punishment descending upon Tyrus, **and fear; Gaza also shall see it and be very sorrowful,** be exceedingly troubled, **and Ekron, for her expectation shall be ashamed,** her hope, that in which she trusted, being taken from her; **and the king shall perish from Gaza,** the ruler being removed entirely, **and Ashkelon shall not be inhabited,** its citizens being killed or dragged into captivity. V. 6. **And a bastard,** or mongrel, one of blemished birth, **shall dwell in Ashdod, and I will cut off the pride of the Philistines,** four of whose city-states are mentioned here, as representative of the entire country. V. 7. **And I will take away his blood out of his mouth,** the term describing an idolater who is engaged in eating the flesh of his sacrifice, **and his abominations from between his teeth,** striking him down while he is engaged in his idolatrous behavior; **but he that remaineth, even he, shall be for our God,** a few of the heathen being gained for the true religion, **and he shall be as a governor in Judah,** like the prince of one of the tribes, **and Ekron as a Jebusite,** for as the Jebusites were amalgamated with the children of Judah, so these heathen, and others, would be joined to the true Church. V. 8. **And I will encamp about Mine house,** not merely the Temple, but the renewed people, as representative of the Church which was to be established, **because of the army, because of him that passeth by, and because of him that returneth,** enemies marching to and fro, looking for an opportunity to attack; **and no oppressor shall pass through them any more,** no enemy daring to disturb the Lord's people, His holy Church; **for now have I seen with Mine eyes,** He was exercising His providential control and the power of His mercy. Thus the Lord reigns in the midst of His enemies, overthrowing those who refuse to submit, but always gaining some also for His adherents.

ZION'S KING OF PEACE AND HIS SALVATION. V. 9. **Rejoice greatly, O daughter of Zion!** the members of the Lord's people; **shout, O daughter of Jerusalem!** with a shout of gladness. **Behold, thy King cometh unto thee,** the Messiah Himself appearing in her midst; **He is just,** possessing righteousness as the first requisite of a true ruler, **and having salvation,** bearing the salvation which the Lord had planned, **lowly, and riding upon an ass and upon a colt, the foal of an ass.** This passage is rightly quoted by Matthew, chap. 21, 4, and John, chap. 12, 15, as having been fulfilled when the Lord entered Jerusalem on the Sunday before His death. The King Messiah was to rise through lowliness and suffering to the might and glory which was hidden in Him even in the state of His humiliation, but which He is now using to full extent in His state of exaltation. V. 10. **And I will cut off the chariot from Ephraim and the horse from Jerusalem,** as the means by which the kingdoms of this world establish and extend their power; **and the battle-bow shall be cut off,** for the Lord does not build His kingdom with might of arms, since His kingdom is not of this world; **and He shall speak peace unto the heathen,** this being the gist of His Gospel-message; **and His dominion shall be from sea even to sea,** as far as the earth extends, **and from the river,** the Euphrates, as the extreme eastern boundary of the then known world, **even to the ends of the earth,** that is, Messiah's kingdom would be established throughout the earth, it would be a universal kingdom. V. 11. **As for thee also,** so the Lord addresses the entire nation of His people, which afterward, in the ideal sense, merged into His Church, **by the blood of thy covenant,** on account of the blood of the covenant, Ex. 24, 8, by which Israel was separated from the rest of the nations and accepted into the most intimate fellowship with the Lord, **I have sent forth thy prisoners out of the pit wherein is no water,** delivering them from the oppression of the world-power, from all the hostile forces of the earth. V. 12. **Turn you,** or, "return," **to the stronghold,** the fortified city, in opposition to the pit which had just been mentioned, **ye prisoners of hope,** who in spite of the present afflictions maintained their hope in the covenant-keeping God. **Even to-day do I declare that I will render double unto thee,** namely, a double measure of glory instead of the tribulations endured, v. 13. **when I have bent Judah for Me,** as a bow in the hand of Jehovah, **filled the bow with Ephraim,** as the arrows in His hand, **and raised up thy sons, O Zion,** stirring them up for war, **against thy sons, O Greece,** for here was another world-power with its hostility against the people of the Lord, **and made thee as the sword of a mighty man,** so that the Lord's people are able to wage the Lord's wars. V. 14. **And the Lord shall be seen over them,** appearing above them or at their head, as He who fights from heaven in their behalf, **and His arrow shall go forth as the lightning,** bringing instantaneous destruction to His foes; **and the Lord God shall blow the trumpet,** summoning His people to the attack, **and shall go with whirlwinds of the south,** which were always the most violent of all. V. 15. **The Lord of hosts shall defend them,** acting as their Shield against the weapons of the enemy; **and they shall devour and subdue with sling-stones,** treading down the enemy like pebbles of the brook, cp. Num. 23, 24; **and they shall drink,** consuming the blood of the enemies, **and make a noise as through wine,** noisy as though under the influence of wine; **and they shall be filled like bowls,** the vessels in which the priests caught the blood of the sacrifices, **and as the corners of the altar.** The entire passage speaks of a holy war and victory, although in pictures taken from a battle of warriors on earth. V. 16. **And the Lord, their God, shall save them in that day as the flock of His people,** with the deliverance of the Messiah's redemption; **for they shall be as the stones of a crown, lifted up as an ensign upon His land,** Zion's sons and daughters being like jewels of a crown which sparkles over Jehovah's land as He proudly marches through the territory belonging to Him. V. 17. **For how great is His goodness,** so the prophet exultantly exclaims, **and how great is His beauty!** Cp. Ps. 45, 3. **Corn shall make the young men cheerful and new wine the maids,** the reference being to the blessings of the grace of God as bestowed upon His people through the Word of His mercy. We have here another summary concerning the gifts of God given to His people in the Messianic era.

CHAPTER 10.

Further Blessings of Jehovah upon His People.

The subject discussed in the last chapter was so great and wonderful that the Lord has not begun to exhaust it, but takes the opportunity of giving a fuller description of its beauties. V. 1. **Ask ye of the Lord rain in the time of the latter rain,** making their appeal to Him in all confidence, as they were in need of His blessings; **so the Lord shall make bright clouds,** create lightnings, **and give them showers of rain,** in a refreshing thunder-shower, **to every one grass in the field,** all the crops of the field. V. 2. **For the idols,** to whom the children of Israel had formerly applied for help, **have spoken vanity,** their household oracles not being dependable, **and the diviners have seen a lie,** they have announced deceitful oracles, **and have told false dreams,** proclaiming their own inventions as revelations from above; **they comfort in vain,** because their words are a hollow mockery; **therefore they,** the people who relied upon their words, **went their way as a flock,** wandering astray, **they were troubled, because there was no shepherd,** no reliable leader and guide. V. 3. **Mine anger was kindled against the shepherds,** the rulers of Israel to whom He had entrusted the leadership, **and I punished the goats,** visiting them with a severe punishment; **for the Lord of hosts hath visited His flock, the house of Judah,** looking after them with tender care, **and hath made them as His goodly horse in the battle,** like the glorious charger on which the general leads his troops to battle. V. 4. **Out of Him,** namely, Jehovah, **came forth the corner,** that is, He furnished the corner-stone on which the entire building of the new Judah rests; **out of Him the nail,** the pegs of the wall, from which the household utensils were suspended, types of the dependable men in a state; **out of Him the battle-bow,** the means for carrying on the Lord's wars; **out of Him every oppressor together,** every mighty ruler whom Judah would need in its wars against the enemies. V. 5. **And they,** the Lord's people, **shall be as mighty ones, which tread down their enemies in the mire of the streets,** cp. chap. 9, 15, **in the battle; and they shall fight because the Lord is with them,** always in the majority because of His help, **and the riders on horses shall be confounded,** cavalry being mentioned as the chief part of the enemy's army. V. 6. **And I will strengthen the house of Judah, and I will save the house of Joseph,** the southern and the northern kingdom together being typical of the Church of God, **and I will bring them again to place them,** letting them dwell in safety, **for I have mercy upon them,** His mercy is the one reason for His kindness toward them; **and they shall be as though I had not cast them off,** as in the time before the captivity; **for I am the Lord, their God, and will hear them,** they could be sure of His gracious attention to all their needs. V. 7. **And they of Ephraim,** the true descendants of Joseph, the spiritual children of him who was given the right of the first-born in the house of Jacob, **shall be like a mighty man,** like a hero, **and their heart shall rejoice as through wine,** with a fierce exultation; **yea, their children shall see it and be glad,** a fact which indicates that the joy would be lasting; **their heart shall rejoice in the Lord,** giving all honor to Him who granted them such a glorious victory. V. 8. **I will hiss for them,** as a signal for them to assemble, **and gather them, for I have redeemed them,** both by entering into a covenant with them and by promising them the Redeemer; **and they shall increase as they have increased,** that is, the growth of the people of God in the Messianic era would be like that of Israel when it first came to the Promised Land. V. 9. **And I will sow them among the people,** as a token of their quick increase; **and they shall remember Me in far countries,** wherever the spiritual children of Israel would be found; **and they shall live with their children,** enjoying the blessing of the Lord in a permanent flow of mercy, **and turn again,** returning to the fellowship of the Lord in His Church. V. 10. **I will bring them again also out of the land of Egypt and gather**

them out of Assyria, the two world-powers being named as representative of the enemies of the Lord and the oppressors of His people; **and I will bring them into the land of Gilead and Lebanon,** to occupy the land on both sides of Jordan once more; **and place shall not be found for them,** there will not be sufficient room for them to expand, the number of the spiritual children of Israel being so great. V. 11. **And he shall pass through the sea with affliction,** rather, "of distress," in allusion to the affliction felt by the children of Israel when they passed through the Red Sea, **and shall smite the waves in the sea,** keeping them under control by His powerful word; **and all the deeps of the river shall dry up,** the river Nile being referred to as the stream of the country of bondage; **and the pride of Assyria shall be brought down, and the scepter of Egypt shall depart away,** so that none of the former oppressors would remain. V. 12. **And I will strengthen them in the Lord,** in Jehovah, the covenant God, **and they shall walk up and down in His name, saith the Lord,** so that they would live under His protection and in accordance with His will. The entire connection brings out the characteristics of the New Testament Church, whose members form a royal priesthood and find their delight in walking in the ways of the Lord.

CHAPTER 11.

Israel's Rejection of the Good Shepherd.

THE DESOLATION OF THE HOLY LAND. — V. 1. **Open thy doors, O Lebanon,** the district on the northernmost border of the Holy Land, **that the fire may devour thy cedars.** Instead of describing the destruction of the land outright, the prophet calls upon its border to open its doors for the consuming fire. V. 2. **Howl, fir-tree,** the cypresses which occupied second place among the trees of the Lebanon forests, **for the cedar is fallen, because the mighty are spoiled. Howl, O ye oaks of Bashan,** the northernmost district of the Holy Land east of Jordan, **for the forest of the vintage is come down,** the high, the inaccessible forest is laid low. V. 3. **There is a voice of the howling of the shepherds,** those occupying the rich meadow-lands of Bashan, **for their glory,** the fine pasture on which they depended, **is spoiled; a voice of the roaring of young lions, for the pride of Jordan,** the thickets along the river, which offered excellent opportunties for dens, **is spoiled.** The description is short and bold, but comprehensive enough to indicate that the Lord is speaking of another desolation of the Holy Land, by which everything that was great and mighty in the country would be overthrown and the Holy Land once more become a wilderness. It is an evident reference to the conquest of Palestine by the Romans.

THE GOOD SHEPHERDS. — V. 4. **Thus saith the Lord, my God,** in formally engaging the prophet as His pastor with regard to the congregation of Israel, **Feed the flock of the slaughter,** those suffering with oppression at the present time, v. 5. **whose possessors slay them and hold themselves not guilty,** the buyers and masters of the covenant people dealing with them as they pleased, without incurring blame; **and they that sell them say, Blessed be the Lord, for I am rich,** the expression fitly describing the self-satisfaction felt by the hard-hearted masters in enriching themselves at the expense of the flock; **and their own shepherds pity them not.** One is compelled to think of the attitude of the rulers of the people at the time of Jesus and before the destruction of Jerusalem by the Romans. V. 6. **For I will no more pity the inhabitants of the land, saith the Lord,** no longer spare them after a last effort to save them; **but, lo, I will deliver the men every one into his neighbor's hand,** so that internal strife and dissension would ruin the country, **and into the hand of his king,** the foreign emperor or governor; **and they shall smite the land,** oppressing it in various ways; **and out of their hand,** out of the power of such oppressors, **I will not deliver them.** V. 7. **And I will feed the flock of the slaughter,** rather, "I fed the flock," for the prophet here describes how he undertook the commission which the Lord gave him, **even you, O poor of the flock,** those in his charge being in a very sad condition, lacking in spiritual knowledge. **And I took unto me two staves,** such as shepherds used in their work; **the one I called Beauty,** or "loveliness, favor," such as the Lord intended to show His people through the work of His servant, **and the other I called Bands,** to indicate that the Lord wanted to have His people feel the blessings of true unity over against the oppression of all their enemies; **and I fed the flock,** performing his work as pastor according to the names of the two staves. V. 8. **Three shepherds also I cut off in one month,** the wicked civil authorities, the priests, and the scribes of the Jewish nation being probably meant, who were removed from power in a very short time; **and my soul loathed them,** since he, the type of the one Good Shepherd and Ruler of His Church, became impatient with their perverse impenitence, **and their soul also abhorred me,** the sheep foolishly refusing to follow the kind leadership of their shepherd. V. 9. **Then said I, I will not feed you,** he declared that he would no longer be their shepherd; **that that dieth, let it die,** he would let them rush to their own ruin since they refused to be guided by him; **and that that is to be cut off, let it be cut off,** destroyed by the power of the oppressor; **and let the rest eat every one the flesh of another,** in the civil war, such as preceded the final destruction of Jerusalem. V. 10. **And I took my staff, even Beauty, and cut it asunder,** to indicate the withdrawal of God's favor from His people, **that I might break my covenant which I had made with all the people.** The person of the prophet here merges into that of his antitype, of the Good Shepherd Himself, for it is He who finally withdrew the blessings of His solemn promise from His former chosen people. V. 11. **And it was broken in that day,** the covenant being annulled by Israel's disobedience; **and so the poor of the flock that waited upon me,** the lowly among the people, those who were Israelites in truth, **knew that it was the word of the Lord.** It was from among the poor and lowly that the Lord, even in those days, recruited His Church, even as St. Paul speaks of it, 1 Cor. 1. V. 12. **And I said unto them,** to the flock that did not recognize the things of its peace, **If ye think good,** if they desired to recognize and acknowledge the services rendered them, **give me my price; and if not, forbear. So they weighed for my price thirty pieces of silver,** the value of a slave that had been killed, Ex. 21, 32, the ordinary price of a female slave, Hos. 3, 2. Cp. Matt. 26, 15. V. 13. **And the Lord said unto me, Cast it unto the potter,** thereby rejecting the insult which they offered. **A goodly price that I was prized at of them!** this being said in impressive irony. **And I took the thirty pieces of silver and cast them to the potter in the house of the Lord.** This statement has no meaning in this connection, but it receives a meaning through its fulfilment, for the thirty pieces of silver which the rulers of the Jews weighed to Judas for his betrayal of the Lord were by him cast into the Temple, the money later being used for the purchase of a potter's field. Cp. Matt. 27, 1—10 and Jer. 32, 6—15. V. 14. **Then I cut asunder mine other staff, even Bands, that I might break the brotherhood between Judah and Israel,** so that, by the punishment of God, there might be lasting dissension in the Jewish camp, a peculiarity which, in the later history of the people, contributed much toward the rapid overthrow of the nation. Sin is a reproach to any people, but the height of folly is the denial and rejection of the Messiah, the one Good Shepherd.

THE FOOLISH SHEPHERD. — V. 15. **And the Lord said unto me, Take unto thee yet the instruments of a foolish shepherd,** of a wicked hireling, who bears the insignia of a true shepherd, but cares nothing for the sheep. V. 16. **For, lo, I will raise up a shepherd in the land,** one assuming the functions of a true shepherd, **which shall not visit those that be cut off,** paying no attention to those who perish, **neither shall seek the young one,** those that have gone astray, **nor heal that that is broken,** suffering with broken limbs, **nor feed that that standeth still,** those who are strong, but in need of food; **but he shall eat the flesh of the fat and tear their claws in pieces,** in order to get even the last vestige of meat from the bones. V. 17. **Woe to the idol shepherd,** the worthless shepherd, **that leaveth the flock,** neglecting his chief duty toward its members. **The sword shall be upon his arm,** causing him to lose this important member of his body, **and upon his right eye,** also a most precious possession; **his arm shall be clean dried up, and his right eye shall be utterly darkened.** It will hardly do to limit this prophecy to an earthly, temporal power. It seems rather that the Spirit of the Lord, looking forward in the history of the Church, outlined in a few strokes the kingdom of Antichrist erected in the midst of those who rejected the Redeemer in the fulness of His grace and mercy, indicating at the same time that his power would be broken by the power of the Lord, as it was in the Reformation.

CHAPTER 12.

Israel's Conflict and Victory.

JEHOVAH'S SOLICITUDE FOR ISRAEL. — V. 1. **The burden of the word of the Lord for Israel,** His almighty, creative power being in evidence at this point, **saith the Lord, which stretcheth forth the heavens,** a favorite picture to show the unlimited power of Jehovah, Is. 42, 5; 44, 24, **and layeth the foundation of the earth,** which, if it were not upheld by His power, would wander from its orbit and fall into ruins, **and formeth the spirit of man within him,** controlling the thoughts and purposes of men so as to accomplish His own plans through them. V. 2. **Behold, I will make Jerusalem a cup of trembling,** a vessel filled with the intoxicating beverage of His wrath, **unto all the people round about,** the neighboring nations reeling and falling in hopeless weakness and misery, **when they shall be in the siege both against Judah and against Jerusalem,** literally, "and also upon Judah shall it be in the siege of Jerusalem," the entire country and its capital being involved in the severe trial which would come upon its neighbors. V. 3. **And in that day will I make Jerusalem a burdensome stone for all people,** for those who attempt to lift and remove it; **all that burden themselves with it shall be cut in pieces,** suffering sprains and dislocations, **though all the people of the earth be gathered together against it,** all the powers of evil being united in an effort to overthrow the city of the Lord. V. 4. **In that day, saith the Lord, I will smite every horse with astonishment,** so that it would shy in terror, **and his rider with madness,** all the warlike forces finding themselves at a loss to effect their evil purposes; **and I will open Mine eyes upon the house of Judah,** with His protecting care, **and will smite every horse of the people with blindness,** so that the hostile forces would not be able to find their way. V. 5. **And the governors of Judah shall say in their heart,** in the firm conviction which upholds them, **The inhabitants of Jerusalem shall be my strength,** a reliable source of confidence, **in the Lord of hosts, their God,** because the Lord has chosen this city, His Church, and by virtue of this choice is bound to redeem His people. V. 6. **In that day will I make the governors of Judah,** the leaders of the people by the Lord's choice, **like an hearth of fire among the wood,** so that they would consume their enemies like a basin of fire devouring fagots, **and like a torch of fire in a sheaf,** burning up the dry straw; **and they shall devour all the people round about, on the right hand and on the left,** so that none of the adversaries can hold out against them; **and Jerusalem shall be inhabited again in her own place, even in Jerusalem,** so that the renewed people could fitly become the nucleus of the New Testament Jerusalem, the Church of Christ. V. 7. **The Lord also shall save the tents of Judah first,** the dwellings of the country outside of the capital with its stone palaces, **that the glory of the house of David and the glory of the inhabitants of Jerusalem do not magnify themselves against Judah,** the house of David being the royal family as continued in the descendants of Zerubbabel. The meaning evidently is this, that Jerusalem would have no preference before the rest of the country at the approach of the enemies, but the entire covenant people would in the same degree enjoy the protection of the Lord. V. 8. **In that day shall the Lord defend the inhabitants of Jerusalem,** by a special strengthening against the foe; **and he that is feeble among them,** literally, "the stumbler," one who can hardly hold himself up, **at that day shall be as David,** to the Jew the highest type of strength and courage; **and the house of David shall be as God,** like a supernatural being, **as the Angel of the Lord before them,** like the Son of God in His Old Testament form, whose power lived in His believers. V. 9. **And it shall come to pass in that day,** even while Jerusalem was exalted to a degree of strength and glory far transcending anything in its past experience, **that I will seek to destroy all the nations that come against Jerusalem,** this being the definite, energetic purpose of the Lord with regard to His people. It is a remarkable fact, one full of glorious comfort, that the Church of God has emerged from all its conflicts with renewed strength and power, that even in the worst persecutions, the blood of the Christians was the seed of the Church.

Repentance and Conversion. — V. 10. **And I will pour upon the house of David,** the entire royal family, the royal priesthood of the Church of the New Testament, **and upon the inhabitants of Jerusalem,** the members of His congregation in general, **the Spirit of grace and of supplications,** Him who works in the heart of man the certainty of the divine grace and urges him to seek forgiveness of sins by daily prayer; **and they shall look upon Me whom they have pierced,** as they nailed their Redeemer to the cross, John 19, 34; Rev. 1, 7, **and they shall mourn for Him as one mourneth for his only son,** acknowledging their transgression in killing the Prince of Life, Acts 3, 15, **and shall be in bitterness for Him as one that is in bitterness for his first-born,** almost the greatest grief and sorrow known to the Jews. V. 11. **In that day,** when the greatness of their crime in putting their own Messiah to death, would be brought home to some of the people, **shall there be a great mourning in Jerusalem,** as is ever the case when men realize that their sins were the cause of Christ's death, **as the mourning of Hadad-rimmon,** when the men of Judah mourned so bitterly over the death of their King Josiah, who was mortally wounded near that place in the Plain of Esdraelon, 2 Chron. 35, 22 ff., **in the Valley of Megiddon,** this being the name of the battle-field. V. 12. **And the land shall mourn, every family apart,** every section of the nation taking part in this expression of sorrow: **the family of the house of David,** those of royal descent, **apart and their wives apart; the family of the house of Nathan,** probably those belonging to the prophetic order, **apart and their wives apart;** v. 13. **the family of the house of Levi,** those belonging to the priestly family, **apart and their wives apart; the family of Shimei,** the teachers of the people, **apart and their wives apart,** so that two were of royal line and two of priestly descent; v. 14. **all the families that remain, every family apart and their wives apart.** Nor would this sorrow of true repentance be in vain. Chap. 13, 1. **In that day there shall be a fountain opened to the house of David and to the inhabitants**

of Jerusalem, to the entire nation, as representative of the Church of the New Testament, in whose members the fruit of Christ's redemption is realized, **for sin and for uncleanness.** The blood of Christ, shed for the sins of the whole world, has prepared a water of sprinkling which thoroughly cleanses sinners from their uncleanness. Cp. 1 John 1, 7. It is the washing of regeneration and renewing of the Holy Ghost which is shed on us abundantly through Jesus Christ, our Savior, also in Holy Baptism. Titus 3, 5. 6.

CHAPTER 13.

Further Results and Revelations.

THE FRUITS OF PENITENCE. — V. 2. **And it shall come to pass in that day, saith the Lord of hosts,** in the great Messianic period, **that I will cut off the names of the idols out of the land,** so that the very names which had formerly been in the mouths of men everywhere were no longer mentioned, **and they shall no more be remembered,** the loathing of every form of superstition being so great that men would put aside every thought of the former idolatry and superstition; **and also I will cause the prophets and the unclean spirit,** who speaks through the false prophets, **to pass out of the land.** This is one of the results of the preaching of the Gospel, as we see also in the case of the people of Ephesus when Paul proclaimed the true God to them. Cp. Acts 19, 19. V. 3. **And it shall come to pass that when any shall yet prophesy,** continuing his wicked profession in spite of the changed attitude of men, **then his father and his mother that begat him shall say unto him, Thou shalt not live, for thou speakest lies in the name of the Lord; and his father and his mother that begat him shall thrust him through when he prophesieth.** This is in line with the command of the Lord in the Old Testament. Cp. Deut. 18, 20. Translated into terms of our day, it means that the mere fact of prophesying is a proof that a man is a deceiver. V. 4. **And it shall come to pass in that day that the prophets,** those who still assert that they possess the power to prophesy, **shall be ashamed every one of his vision when he hath prophesied; neither shall they wear a rough garment,** after the manner of Elijah and of John the Baptist, **to deceive,** to impress men with their status as prophets, just as men nowadays affect the dress, speech, and manners of certain professions in order to make an impression; v. 5. **but he shall say, I am no prophet, I am an husbandman,** vehemently disclaiming any connection with the prophetic profession; **for man taught me to keep cattle from my youth,** rather, "a man has purchased me from my youth." V. 6. **And one shall say unto him, What are these wounds in thine hands?** the scars which he bore as a result of his wounding himself in the service of idols, 1 Kings 18, 28. **Then he shall answer,** in trying to evade the issue and to place the blame elsewhere, **Those with which I was wounded in the house of my friends,** possibly when he was chastised in his capacity as slave. The entire paragraph shows with what utter loathing idolatry and superstition is to be regarded in the Church of the Lord and may be taken as a warning in our days when men are turning to deceivers for counsel and guidance.

THE SHEPHERD SMITTEN. — With great abruptness the prophecy here takes a different turn, as the prophet sets forth the manner in which redemption was secured. V. 7. **Awake, O sword, against My Shepherd,** the same one who addressed the people in chap. 11, 12, **and against the Man that is My Fellow,** Him who is true God, together with the Father and the Holy Spirit, for the Messiah is the eternal Son of God, who was in the bosom of the Father from eternity and by Him begotten in the great eternal to-day, **saith the Lord of hosts,** who here summons the sword for the Messiah's great Passion, to carry out the infliction of suffering by which the redemption of mankind was to be gained. **Smite the Shepherd, and the sheep shall be scattered,** a word which Jesus applied to Himself on the evening before His death, Matt. 26, 31; **and I will turn Mine hand upon the little ones,** literally, "I will bring back My hand upon the little ones"; for He intended to redeem the wretched, the poor and lowly, for of these was made up His Church. V. 8. **And it shall come to pass that in all the land, saith the Lord, two parts therein,** the great majority of the people, **shall be cut off and die,** being offended in Him and therefore rejected from His herd; **but the third,** only a small part, **shall be left therein.** V. 9. **And I will bring the third part through the fire,** the test of affliction and persecution as it soon came to the first congregation, **and will refine them as silver is refined and will try them as gold is tried,** cp. 1 Pet. 1, 6. 7. **They shall call on My name, and I will hear them,** graciously giving them the attention which assured them of His certain assistance; **I will say, It is My people, and they shall say, The Lord is my God.** This has ever been the relationship obtaining between the God of the covenant and His Church on earth, and this intimate communion is one of the miracles of the Church till the end of time. Cp. John 14, 23.

CHAPTER 14.

The Final Conflict and Triumph of God's Kingdom.

THE JUDGMENT AND THE REDEMPTION.—V. 1. **Behold, the day of the Lord cometh,** a great Day of Judgment, **and thy spoil,** that gained by the enemies in overcoming Jerusalem, **shall be divided in the midst of thee,** the enemies being at leisure and secure in the conquered city. V. 2. **For I will gather all nations against Jerusalem to battle,** the enemies being recruited from all countries of the world; **and the city shall be taken and the houses rifled and the women ravished,** a picture of an apparent complete overthrow of the Church such as she experienced during the dark ages; **and half of the city shall go forth into captivity,** yielding to the power of Antichrist, **and the residue of the people shall not be cut off from the city,** some at least would remain faithful to the true God in the Church of the Reformation. V. 3. **Then shall the Lord go forth and fight against those nations, as when He fought in the day of battle,** on the many occasions when He went forth to battle with them and for them. V. 4. **And His feet shall stand in that day upon the Mount of Olives,** this location being considered the center of the earth and the throne of the Lord, as He makes ready for judgment, **which is before Jerusalem on the east, and the Mount of Olives shall cleave in the midst thereof toward the east and toward the west,** an earthquake having this effect as the earth trembled under the footsteps of Jehovah, **and there shall be a very great valley; and half of the mountain shall remove toward the north and half of it toward the south,** thus opening a road from Jerusalem straight toward the east. V. 5. **And ye shall flee to the valley of the mountains,** since it would offer safe hiding-places; **for the valley of the mountains shall reach unto Azal,** a small town east of Mount Olivet; **yea, ye shall flee, like as ye fled from before the earthquake in the days of Uzziah, king of Judah; and the Lord, my God, shall come,** His advent being looked for by His children with joyful expectation, **and all the saints,** the holy angels, **with thee.** The picture sketched by the prophet shows Jehovah preparing to judge the nations, while the believers flee to Him for refuge, knowing that their salvation is near. V. 6. **And it shall come to pass in that day that the light shall not be clear,** that is, there would not be full daylight, **nor dark,** literally, "the glorious things will withdraw themselves," evidently said of the lights of heaven, the sun, moon, and stars; v. 7. **but it shall be one day,** a most singular day in every way, **which shall be known to the Lord,** He alone being acquainted with its true nature, **not day nor night,** because the lights of heaven will have lost their power to shine; **but it shall come to pass that at evening time it shall be light.** This picture represents the Church of the Middle Ages gradually sinking into darkness as the light of the Word of God was obscured by its leaders. Fortunately, however, the Lord, through the Reformation, caused the glorious light of His Gospel to shine forth once more. V. 8. **And it shall be in that day,** after the restoration of the light of the Word in its original position, **that living waters shall go out from Jerusalem,** from the Church of the Lord in its renewed state, cp. Ezek. 47, 1; **half of them toward the former sea,** toward the east, **and half of them toward the hinder sea,** toward the west, so that the blessings of the Gospel would be distributed throughout the world; **in summer and in winter shall it be,** without intermission. V. 9. **And the Lord shall be King over all the earth,** as the Ruler of His Kingdom of Grace; **in that day shall there be one Lord,** the Triune God once more accepted by the Church as He had revealed Himself in Christ, **and His name one,** to be glorified wherever His Word is proclaimed. V. 10. **All the land shall be turned as a plain,** with no more mountains to obstruct the work of the Church, **from Geba,** some twelve miles north of Jerusalem, **to Rimmon, south of Jerusalem,** at the southern border of Judah; **and it shall be lifted up,** Jerusalem alone being placed up on high, **and inhabited in her place,** or, "shall dwell in her place," **from Benjamin's gate,** in the wall of the north side of the city, **unto the place of the first gate,** on the east or northeast, **unto the corner gate,** that on the west, **and from the tower of Hananeel,** on the northeast corner of the city, Neh. 3, 1, **unto the king's wine-presses,** in the royal gardens on the south side of the city. V. 11. **And men shall dwell in it, and there shall be no more utter destruction,** such as came upon the Church through the wickedness of Antichrist; **but Jerusalem shall be safely inhabited.** The Church, as renewed by the Reformation, will, on the whole, remain in possession of the truth and its blessings.

THE REMNANT OF THE NATIONS SAVED.—V. 12. **And this shall be the plague,** the special infliction, **wherewith the Lord will smite all the people that have fought against Jerusalem,** those who oppose the Church and its work: **Their flesh shall consume away while they stand upon their feet,** so that they would rot away in a living death, **and their eyes shall consume away in their holes, and their tongue shall consume away in their mouth,** all these punishments making them unfit for further attacks upon the city of God. V. 13. **And it shall come to pass in that day that a great tumult,** a confusion and panic, **from the Lord**

shall be among them; and they shall lay hold every one on the hand of his neighbor, and his hand shall rise up against the hand of his neighbor. It has always been a matter of good fortune, so far as the Church is concerned, that its enemies disagree among themselves and thus often frustrate their own evil intentions. V. 14. **And Judah also shall fight at Jerusalem,** the Church itself taking part in the warfare against the enemies threatening her life; **and the wealth of all the heathen round about shall be gathered together,** the treasures of the enemy, their most precious possessions, being taken by the Church, **gold and silver and apparel, in great abundance.** V. 15. **And so shall be the plague of the horse, of the mule, of the camel, and of the ass, and of all the beasts that shall be in these tents, as this plague,** so that the defeat of the enemy would be complete in every way. All the enemies of the Church of God who persist in their enmity will finally, inevitably, be destroyed. V. 16. **And it shall come to pass that every one that is left of all the nations which came against Jerusalem,** after the destruction of the enemies that would not repent, **shall even go up from year to year to worship the King, the Lord of hosts, and to keep the Feast of Tabernacles,** to join with the Church in its adoration of the one true God. V. 17. **And it shall be that whoso will not come up of all the families of the earth unto Jerusalem to worship the King, the Lord of hosts, even upon them shall be no rain,** the spiritual blessings of the Lord being withheld from them. V. 18. **And if the family of Egypt,** representative of all the world-powers and enemies that have tried to oppress the Church of God throughout history, **go not up and come not that have no rain,** or, the lack of rain would be its plague or infliction; **there shall be the plague wherewith the Lord will smite the heathen that come not up to keep the Feast of Tabernacles,** refuse to be received into the Church and take part in its worship. V. 19. **This shall be the punishment of Egypt and the punishment of all nations that come not up to keep the Feast of Tabernacles.** It is a fact borne out by history and experience that the enemies of the Lord, in opposing His Church and refusing to accept His Word, entrench themselves behind a wall of their own foolishness and shut themselves out from the highest spiritual blessings. Meanwhile the Lord is building up His Church to a state of glorious perfection. V. 20. **In that day shall there be upon the bells of the horses,** those suspended from their harness, which tinkled as they marched forward in a triumphal procession, **HOLINESS UNTO THE LORD; and the pots in the Lord's house,** used for the seething of the sacrificial meat, **shall be like the bowls before the altar,** in which the blood of the sacrifices was kept. In other words, the difference between the sacred and profane would be entirely eliminated, everything used in the service of the Lord being equally sacred in His eyes. Cp. 1 Tim. 4, 4. 5. V. 21. **Yea, every pot in Jerusalem and in Judah shall be holiness unto the Lord of hosts,** all the distinctions of the Ceremonial Law being eliminated; **and all they that sacrifice shall come and take of them and seethe therein,** preparing for the sacrificial feasts without fear of contamination; **and in that day there shall be no more the Canaanite in the house of the Lord of hosts,** no openly godless people being permitted as members of the Church of God. The nearer the Church approaches its perfection, the clearer is shown the cleavage between those who are in truth the servants of the Lord and those who merely bear the name of His ministers; and the final revelation of those who in the accepted time, in the day of salvation, were for and against the Lord Jehovah will come on the Last Day.

THE BOOK OF THE PROPHET MALACHI.

INTRODUCTION.

Concerning the person of Malachi, the last prophet of the Old Testament, so little is known that some people have even insisted that it was not the name of a person at all, but only a title, for Malachi means messenger of Jehovah. However, all the reasons advanced for this supposition are so weak that it seems best to hold, with the majority of orthodox teachers, that there was actually a prophet who bore that name, and that he wrote under his own name. The period of Malachi's activity must be placed in the days of Nehemiah, very likely before the second visit of Nehemiah in Jerusalem. Cp. Neh. 13. His rebukes and admonitions evidently concern the same deplorable conditions which the leaders of the people found it necessary to correct with such emphasis, among these being sacrifices of a poor quality, neglect in paying tithes, marriages with heathen women. All this is further substantiated by the fact that Malachi refers to himself as the last prophet of the Old Covenant, chiefly in prophesying of the forerunner of the Messiah and in stating that the New Dispensation was to be expected very soon.

The Book of Malachi may readily be divided

into two parts, chapters 1 and 2 dealing of the love of God to the children of Israel and reproving the sins of the priests and of the people, and chapters 3 and 4 comforting the God-fearing Jews with promises of the twofold coming of Christ. The style of the book is animated, but less grand and the rhythm less marked than in some of the older prophets.[1])

1) Cp. Fuerbringer, *Einleitung in das Alte Testament*, 96. 97.

CHAPTER 1.

The Love of God and the Contempt of His Name.

GOD'S PECULIAR LOVE FOR ISRAEL. — V. 1. **The burden of the word of the Lord,** the sentence which He found Himself compelled to pronounce, **to Israel by Malachi.** V. 2. **I have loved you, saith the Lord,** Jehovah placing this at the head of His message as a fundamental, absolute fact. **Yet ye say,** in expressing their doubts of His sincerity, **Wherein hast Thou loved us?** What proofs could He adduce to show the greatness of His love? The form of presentation throughout is nervous, vivid. **Was not Esau Jacob's brother? saith the Lord,** his full brother at that; **yet I loved Jacob** v. 3. **and I hated Esau,** in the sense of not loving him, without any idea of vindictiveness, **and laid his mountains and his heritage,** the land which he inhabited south of the Dead Sea, **waste for the dragons of the wilderness,** so that it was a fitting home for jackals. V. 4. **Whereas Edom saith,** or, "Although Edom should say," in an attempt to set aside the ruling of the Lord, **We are impoverished,** ruined, **but we will return and build the desolate places,** rebuild the ruins, **thus saith the Lord of hosts, They shall build,** make an attempt to restore their original power, **but I will throw down,** destroying their country a second time; **and they shall call them "The border of wickedness,"** that is, men would designate them as the region of wickedness, punished by God, **and "The people against whom the Lord hath indignation forever,"** a monument of God's wrath. V. 5. **And your eyes shall see,** the facts before their eyes convincing them, **and ye shall say, The Lord will be magnified from the border of Israel,** rather, "over the border of Israel." The children of Israel would be compelled to acknowledge the particular favor and love which the Lord showed them by so many manifestations.

A REBUKE OF THE PRIESTS. — V. 6. **A son honoreth his father and a servant his master,** in agreement with the commandment of God; **if, then, I be a Father, where is Mine honor?** Why were they persisting in their unnatural behavior and denying Him the obedience which He had a right to expect? **And if I be a Master, where is My fear?** Why did they not give Him the reverence and respect which were His due? **saith the Lord of hosts unto you, O priests, that despise My name,** the very ones who should have been leaders of the people in keeping the Law being their leaders in transgressing the Law. **And ye say,** as if honestly resenting the charge against them, **Wherein have we despised Thy name?** But the Lord has His answer ready, v. 7. **Ye offer polluted bread upon Mine altar,** in connection with some of the offerings brought to the Lord; **and ye say, Wherein have we polluted Thee? In that ye say, The table of the Lord is contemptible,** their practise of offering sacrifices which were expressly forbidden by God and their manner in the entire administration of their work being an insult to the holiness of Jehovah. Cp. Lev. 22, 22. V. 8. **And if ye offer the blind for sacrifice, is it not evil?** or, "there is no evil," that is, in their opinion. **And if ye offer the lame and the sick, is it not evil?** The Lord had expressly forbidden the members of His people to bring animals as sacrifices that had any kind of blemish. **Offer it now unto thy governor,** so the Lord ironically bids them do; **will he be pleased with thee or accept thy person? saith the Lord of hosts.** The Jewish priests were offering the Lord an insult which they would not have dared to offer an earthly ruler. V. 9. **And now, I pray you, beseech God that He will be gracious unto us,** they should just make an attempt to serve Him with such worship,—**this hath been by your means,** — that is, this their hand had done: **will He regard your persons? saith the Lord of hosts.** If not even an earthly ruler would accept imperfect gifts at their hands, how much more was this true of Jehovah, the God of the covenant! V. 10. **Who is there even among you that would shut the doors for naught?** rather, "Oh, that there were one among you that would even shut the doors of the Temple!" **neither do ye kindle fire on Mine altar for naught.** If one would but lock the doors leading to the altar of burnt offering, in order to keep the priests from bringing such vain oblations! **I have no pleasure in you, saith the Lord of hosts,** being thoroughly disgusted with their behavior, **neither will I accept an offering at your hand,** no matter of what kind it was. V. 11. **For from the rising of the sun even unto the going down of the same,** as far as the world extends, **My name shall be great among the Gentiles,** among the recruits gained for the Church of the New Testament from the heathen world; **and in every place incense,** namely, that of the prayers of the faithful, **shall be offered unto My name and a pure offering**, on the part of those who had accepted the God of the covenant as their God; **for My name shall be great among the heathen, saith the Lord of hosts**, for the kingdom of God was taken from the Jews, since they openly rejected the Messiah and His grace, and was given to the Gentiles. V. 12. **But ye have profaned it**, have brought disgrace upon the name and the glory of the one true God, **in that ye say, The table of the Lord is polluted**, cp. v. 7, **and the fruit thereof, even His meat, is contemptible**, for the priests themselves did not regard the sacrifices brought on the altar as in any way efficacious. V. 13. **Ye said also, Behold, what a weariness is it!** They regarded their service at the altar as an offensive drudgery. **And ye have snuffed at it, saith the Lord of hosts**, publicly showing their contempt for the work of their ministry; **and ye brought that which was torn and the lame and the sick**, in a contemptuous disregard for the Law of the Lord; **thus ye brought an offering: should I accept this at your hand? saith the Lord.** He expresses in a most emphatic manner that He would not permit His glory thus to be despised. V. 14. **But cursed be the deceiver**, the hypocrite, **which hath in his flock a male**, a sound and normal animal for sacrifice, **and voweth**, as if preparing to bring the good animal as a sacrifice, **and sacrificeth unto the Lord a corrupt thing!** one with a blemish; **for I am a great King, saith the Lord of hosts, and My name is dreadful among the heathen**, mentioned only with fear and trembling. God will not permit any one to heap disgrace upon His majesty by hypocritical worship.

CHAPTER 2.

Further Stern Reproofs.

CONCLUSION OF THE REBUKE TO THE PRIESTS. V. 1. **And now, O ye priests, this commandment is for you**, they must be aware of the seriousness of the situation and accept the Lord's rebuke and threat accordingly. V. 2. **If ye will not hear, and if ye will not lay it to heart**, if they persisted in their callousness over against His commands, **to give glory unto My name, saith the Lord of hosts**, by a worship in agreement with His commands, **I will even send a curse upon you, and I will curse your blessings**, His own gifts to them turning into the opposite and bringing harm upon them; **yea, I have cursed them already because ye do not lay it to heart**, presenting an indifferent front to the Lord's admonitions. V. 3. **Behold, I will corrupt your seed**, rebuking that which had been sowed in the fields, thus reducing also the amounts which the priests received as tithes, **and spread dung upon your faces**, as an expression of His extreme contempt, **even the dung of your solemn feasts**, that of the sacrificial animals, which was ordinarily dumped outside of the city; **and one shall take you away with it**, treating them as though they were themselves dung, to be thrown out in disgraceful heaps. V. 4. **And ye shall know**, by the token of this punishment, **that I have sent this commandment unto you**, this decree of punishment, which they thought they might so calmly disregard, **that My covenant might be with Levi**, all the priests, **saith the Lord of hosts.** The Lord's sentence of punishment upon all those who despised His worship was included in the original covenant with the members of the tribe of Levi. V. 5. **My covenant was with him of life and peace**, with the promise of life and peace attached; **and I gave them**, namely, life, deliverance, and salvation, **to him for the fear wherewith he feared Me**, as a reward for this attitude, **and was afraid before My name**, cp. Num. 25, 12. V. 6. **The Law of Truth was in his mouth**, so that everything which he did and taught was in agreement with the divine truth, **and iniquity was not found in his lips**, he was in no way guilty of perverseness in his ministry; **he walked with Me in peace and equity**, in a communion of peace, integrity, and righteousness, **and did turn many away from iniquity**, this being the praise which the Lord bestowed upon the members of the tribe of Levi. V. 7. **For the priest's lips should keep knowledge**, preserving the right understanding of Jehovah among the people as a precious treasure, **and they**, the people, **should seek the Law at his mouth**, to be instructed in it; **for he is the messenger of the Lord of hosts.** That is what the Lord found praiseworthy in the members of the tribe of Levi in the early days; that is as it should be. V. 8. **But ye**, the present members of the tribe, **are departed out of the way**, leaving the path shown them by the Law of the Lord; **ye have caused many to stumble at the Law**, so that they became guilty of transgressing the Law; **ye have corrupted the covenant of Levi**, that which their fathers had kept so faithfully, **saith the Lord of hosts.** V. 9. **Therefore have I also made you contemptible and base**, an object of contempt and loathing, **before all the people, according as ye have not kept My ways**, in the same degree as they had transgressed, **but have been partial in the Law**, in applying the Law to the conduct of the people. The conduct of the spiritual leaders of people is particularly reprehensible if it misleads others and plunges them into sin and guilt.

AGAINST DIVORCES AND MARRIAGES WITH

HEATHEN WIVES. — V. 10. **Have we not all one Father? Hath not one God created us?** These questions, with the statement they contain, the prophet places at the head of his discussion, to remind the Jews that they were still, in a peculiar sense, the Lord's people and should keep themselves unspotted from the Gentiles. **Why do we deal treacherously,** faithlessly, **every man against his brother, by profaning the covenant of our fathers?** The action on the part of the people which the prophet found it necessary to censure was a violation of the relation sustained to Jehovah as a common Father and as the Author of the covenant which governed all their lives. V. 11. **Judah hath dealt treacherously,** with a calm disregard of the covenant faithfulness, **and an abomination is committed in Israel,** throughout the nation, **and in Jerusalem,** the capital, which should have led in the observance of the Law; **for Judah hath profaned the holiness of the Lord which He loved,** namely, the people as a body, whom the Lord had chosen as His holy people, **and hath married the daughter of a strange god,** by the fact that numerous members of the nation had entered into the marriage relationship with women addicted to idolatry, an act which was distinctly prohibited in the Law of God, Ex. 34, 11; Deut. 7, 1—4. V. 12. **The Lord will cut off the man that doeth this,** since it was a profanation of the sacred position of the people, **the master and the scholar,** or "the watcher and the answerer," **out of the tabernacles of Jacob, and him that offereth an offering unto the Lord of hosts,** so that there would be a complete extermination of all those who had transgressed. V. 13. **And this have ye done again,** as the second transgression which the Lord found it necessary to rebuke, **covering the altar of the Lord with tears, with weeping, and with crying out,** namely, by causing their divorced wives to come to the Sanctuary and there register their lament over the injustice received, **insomuch that He,** the God of the covenant, **regardeth not the offering any more or receiveth it with good will at your hand,** He wanted nothing of their worship while the conditions were such. "Their divorced wives repair to the altar of Jehovah, there to pour out their hearts before Him, to complain of the cruel treatment accorded them, and to seek His help." (Lange.) V. 14. **Yet ye say,** apparently surprised that the Lord should repudiate their prayers, **Wherefore? Because the Lord hath been witness between thee and the wife of thy youth,** every true marriage being entered into with His sanction and the Lord therefore being the witness for the rights of the wife, **against whom thou hast dealt treacherously,** in breaking the promised faith, the troth which had been plighted; **yet is she thy companion,** the partner of her husband's joys and sorrows, **and the wife of thy covenant,** she with whom the husband had entered into the relation controlled by a mutual promise. V. 15. **And did not he make one? Yet had he the residue of the spirit,** literally, "And not one acted so who still had a particle of reason," that is, this manner of acting was unknown among men of reason. Of course, the people might raise the objection, **And wherefore one?** What did Abraham do when he repudiated Hagar? But the prophet cuts off the objection short, **That he might seek a godly seed.** The object of Abraham in going in to Hagar was not to gratify the lust of the flesh, but he honestly thought that he might thus get the son whom God had promised him. **Therefore,** so the prophet concludes, **take heed to your spirit,** watching over themselves with the greatest care, **and let none deal treacherously against the wife of his youth,** namely, by lightly dismissing her. V. 16. **For the Lord, the God of Israel, saith that He hateth putting away,** cp. Deut. 24, 1; **for one covereth violence with his garment,** or, "iniquity covers his garment," **saith the Lord of hosts,** so that it would cling to him forever; **therefore take heed to your spirit that ye deal not treacherously.** The same thought is found in the New Testament, not only in various sayings of Jesus concerning the sanctity of the marriage covenant, but also in the words of Peter regarding the living together of a man with his wife according to reason. Cp. 1 Pet. 3, 7.

CHAPTER 3.

The Great Day of the Lord.

JEHOVAH'S MESSENGER AND THE ANGEL OF THE COVENANT. — Chap. 2, 17. **Ye have wearied the Lord with your words,** with their dissatisfied grumbling over recent events. **Yet ye say, Wherein have we wearied Him?** the same disobedient people again standing out in opposition to God, in resenting the rebuke of His prophet. **When ye say, Every one that doeth evil is good in the sight of the Lord, and He delighteth in them,** this being the statement of godless insolence in direct opposition to the rebuke of the prophet, **or, Where is the God of judgment?** The great mass of the people boldly declared that there was no foundation for the prophet's threat, that the talk of the coming Judgment was unfounded. Cp. 2 Pet. 3, 4. Over against this question of doubt and unbelief the Lord places a very definite statement. V. 1. **Behold, I will send My messenger,** the special prophet spoken of Is. 40, 3, the passage upon which the present statement is evidently founded, **and he shall prepare the way be-**

fore Me, Mark 1, 3; **and the Lord whom ye seek**, for whose coming they were so anxiously waiting, **shall suddenly come to His Temple**, to dwell in the midst of His people, of His Church, **even the Messenger of the Covenant**, the great Angel of the Lord, the Son of God Himself, **whom ye delight in**, namely, all those who still desire the covenant of the Lord with His people to be fulfilled. **Behold**, so the announcement is once more made with impressive solemnity, **He shall come, saith the Lord of hosts.** This is the preaching of repentance in order to prepare the hearts for the great advent of Jehovah. V. 2. **But who may abide the day of His coming?** be able to endure that Day of Judgment upon the disobedient and secure? Cp. Matt. 3, 8—12; Luke 3, 9. **And who shall stand when He appeareth?** Cp. Joel 2, 11. **For He is like a refiner's fire**, which separates the dross from the pure metal, **and like fullers' soap**, thoroughly to cleanse the garment of His Church from all impurities; v. 3. **and He shall sit as a refiner and purifier of silver**, the entire Messianic period being a time of testing and of judgment, John 9, 39, culminating in the day of the final Judgment; **and He shall purify the sons of Levi**, for the judgment begins at the house of God, **and purge them as gold and silver that they may offer unto the Lord an offering in righteousness**, so that all the members of the New Testament priesthood, in fact, might serve Him in holiness and righteousness. V. 4. **Then shall the offering of Judah and Jerusalem be pleasant unto the Lord**, the entire Church worshiping Him in spirit and in truth, **as in the days of old**, when the children of Israel were still in truth His Church, **and as in former years.** Cp. Titus 2, 14; 1 Pet. 2, 5. V. 5. **And I will come near to you to judgment**, namely, the judgment of wrath upon the wicked; **and I will be a swift witness against the sorcerers**, the transgressors of the First and Second Commandments, **and against the adulterers**, those disregarding the Sixth Commandment, **and against false swearers**, with reference both to the Second and the Eighth Commandments, **and against those that oppress the hireling in his wages**, by withholding them altogether or by underpaying him, **the widow, and the fatherless**, as being without a natural protector, **and that turn aside the stranger from his right**, cp. Deut. 27, 19, **and fear not Me, saith the Lord of hosts**, this last point indicating the source of all iniquity — lack of the fear of the Lord. V. 6. **For I am the Lord, I change not**, the name Jehovah itself indicating that He is the same from everlasting to everlasting; **therefore ye sons of Jacob are not consumed**, literally, "and ye, the sons of Jacob, ye are not yet consumed," that is, the Lord will keep the true spiritual Israel safe while He sends His judgment upon the wicked in their midst. Even so the Church of Christ in the New Testament is preserved in the midst of hypocrisy and deceit, and the wicked will finally be destroyed.

THE PEOPLE REBUKED. — V. 7. **Even from the days of your fathers ye are gone away from Mine ordinances and have not kept them**, this being the reason why He has withheld the fulness of His blessing and salvation from them. **Return unto Me, and I will return unto you, saith the Lord of hosts**, His appeal being made in all sincerity, since He wants all men to be saved and to come to the knowledge of the truth. **But ye said**, still blind toward their transgressions, **Wherein shall we return?** They did not realize that the real service of Jehovah must be a growth from within, from a heart which lives in His fear. Therefore the prophet asks, in turn, in order to arouse them to a consciousness of the true meaning of worship, v. 8. **Will a man rob God**, defraud Him? Is not the very idea preposterous and revolting? **Yet ye have robbed Me**, actually trying to defraud Jehovah of the service which He rightly expected. **But ye say, Wherein have we robbed Thee?** And the answer is, **In tithes and offerings**, for these the people had deliberately withheld, thus making a mockery of their worship of Jehovah. V. 9. **Ye are cursed with a curse**, as a consequence of such behavior; **for ye have robbed Me, even this whole nation**, for the practise rebuked was general among the people. Therefore He admonishes them with great solemnity: v. 10. **Bring ye all the tithes**, the entire tithes, not only a part, **into the storehouse**, not keeping back a part, as heretofore, **that there may be meat in Mine house**, as food for His servants, Num. 18, 24; **and prove Me now herewith**, to find out whether He is not still the same righteous and holy God as of old, **saith the Lord of hosts, if I will not open you the windows of heaven and pour you out a blessing**, in plentiful harvests, **that there shall not be room enough to receive it**, their prosperity being practically limitless. V. 11. **And I will rebuke the devourer for your sakes**, not permitting the locusts to devour the crops, to ravage the land, **and he shall not destroy the fruits of your ground**, all the ordinary field-crops; **neither shall your vine cast her fruit before the time in the field, saith the Lord of hosts**, that is, the grapes would not fall before they had matured. V. 12. **And all nations shall call you blessed**, praising them for the obvious blessings which they enjoyed as a gift of Jehovah; **for ye shall be a delightsome land**, an object of pleasure, **saith the Lord of hosts.** Even to-day the Lord often rewards a life sincerely led in agreement with His Word with outward gifts of His goodness.

THE WAYS OF GOD VINDICATED. — V. 13. **Your words have been stout against Me, saith the Lord**, namely, in the murmuring which He has rebuked above. **Yet ye say,**

What have we spoken so much against Thee? The Lord's answer through His prophet is, v. 14. **Ye have said, It is vain to serve God,** it does not pay, just as scoffers in our days say; **and what profit is it that we have kept His ordinance, and that we have walked mournfully before the Lord of hosts?** with all indications of deep sorrow and mourning over their sins. Their complaint was that it was poor business, that it did not pay. V. 15. **And now we call the proud happy,** they had actually reached the stage when they praised the wicked, with their apparent happiness in matters of this world; **yea, they that work wickedness are set up,** they are the lucky ones, in their opinion; **yea, they that tempt God are even delivered,** they have no misfortune, they have everything that their heart desires. This is ever the accusation which the backsliders try to bring against the Lord. V. 16. **Then,** namely, when the scoffers were making these blasphemous remarks, **they that feared the Lord spake often one to another,** they made it a practise to encourage one another over against such blasphemous talk; **and the Lord hearkened and heard it,** He paid attention to their remarks, **and a book of remembrance was written before Him for them that feared the Lord and that thought upon His name,** the subject of their conversations being things which pertained to His glory. V. 17. **And they shall be Mine, saith the Lord of hosts,** the precious people of His inheritance, 1 Pet. 2, 9, **in that day when I make up My jewels,** when He would impart to them the fulness of His glory; **and I will spare them,** in manifesting His tender mercies upon them, **as a man spareth his own son that serveth him,** ready to show his love and goodness in such an instance. V. 18. **Then shall ye,** those who were now grumbling, **return and discern between the righteous and the wicked,** noting the difference between the two classes, also in the manner in which God dealt with them, **between him that serveth God and him that serveth Him not.** The time of grace is still at hand, but infidels and scoffers will do well not to delay repentance.

CHAPTER 4.

The Sun of Righteousness and His Forerunner.

The prophet, having addressed the scoffers in words of warning, in conclusion describes the results of the Lord's appointing that day of which He had spoken. V. 1. **For, behold, the day cometh,** the entire New Testament period being considered a day of sifting and of judgment, because it culminates in the Day of Judgment, **that shall burn as an oven,** one which holds the refiner's fire; **and all the proud, yea, and all that do wickedly, shall be stubble,** under the fire of His wrath, cp. Matt. 3, 10—12; **and the day that cometh shall burn them up, saith the Lord of hosts,** cp. Is. 5, 24; Zeph. 1, 18, **that it shall leave them neither root nor branch,** the final, eternal destruction of the wicked being coincidental with the last Judgment. Such is the terrible fate of those who do not avail themselves of the Lord's mercy. V. 2. **But unto you that fear My name,** those who believe in Jehovah, the God of the covenant, and His redemption, **shall the Sun of Righteousness,** the Messiah, with the fulness of His salvation, **arise with healing in His wings,** in the rays of His mercy sent out through His Word; **and ye shall go forth,** with joyfully uplifted heads, **and grow up as calves of the stall,** nourished by the Word of Truth and Grace. Cp. John 1, 14. V. 3. **And ye shall tread down the wicked,** whose final overthrow is consistently prophesied in Scripture; **for they shall be ashes under the soles of your feet,** powerless and worthless, **in the day that I shall do this, saith the Lord of hosts.** All believers are happy in their faith, in the enjoyment of Jehovah's mercy; they enjoy true liberty and will finally celebrate an eternal victory over all their enemies. The prophet therefore, in concluding his message, adds an admonition: V. 4. **Remember ye the Law of Moses, My servant, which I commanded unto him in Horeb for all Israel, with the statutes and judgments,** the Word which contained His solemn covenant. V. 5. **Behold, I will send you Elijah, the prophet,** a prophet like him, namely, John the Baptist, the forerunner of the Messiah, Matt. 11, 10. 14; 17, 10—13; Luke 1, 17, **before the coming of the great and dreadful day of the Lord,** Joel 2, 31, namely, before the Lord Himself would begin His ministry, which ushered in the period of the New Testament, culminating in the Last Judgment; v. 6. **and he shall turn the heart of the fathers to the children and the heart of the children to their fathers,** in having them both realize the love of Jehovah in sending the Messiah and in the subsequent salvation wrought for all men, Luke 1, 17, **lest I come and smite the earth with a curse,** namely, in the event that men will not heed the preaching of repentence unto the forgiveness of sins. The Jews as a nation rejected the Messiah and have come under the curse. But this did not result in the overthrow of the kingdom of God and Christ. The spiritual Israel, rather, has heeded, and is heeding, the Word of Grace and is enjoying the fulness of the blessings promised throughout the Old Testament and so gloriously fulfilled in the New Dispensation.

SUBJECT-INDEX OF VOLS. I AND II.

(NOTE. — This is not a topical index, — for that will be supplied by any concordance, such as Cruden and Walker, — but a subject-index for cursory reading and to aid the average Bible-student in quick orientation. It is a working index and makes no claim to being exhaustive.)